Management An Evidence-Based Approach

Doede Keuning
Bart Bossink
Brian Tjemkes

Third edition

Noordhoff Uitgevers Groningen / Houten

Cover design: G2K Designers, Groningen
Cover illustration: Getty Images

If you have any comments or queries about this or any other publication, please contact: Noordhoff Uitgevers bv, Afdeling Hoger Onderwijs, Antwoordnummer 13, 9700 VB Groningen, e-mail: info@noordhoff.nl

0 1 2 3 4 5 / 14 13 12 11 10

ISBN 978-90-01-70382-0
NUR 801

Preface

Every type of organization – whether profit-making or non-profit-making – requires some form of management if it is to operate effectively. As such, management is of importance to everyone who comes into contact with organizations, whether this be as employees, managers, suppliers or clients.

This book is intended as a comprehensive introduction to management. It acquaints the reader with all aspects of the subject, and by using examples and case studies from the world of business, enables the reader to relate the theory of management to everyday situations.

Every chapter starts with a *Management in action* case study and ends with a *Research-based exercise* and a *Management case study*. These extended case studies and exercises give the reader the opportunity to look at the evidence and practical application of the concepts discussed in the chapter.

Positioning this book

As an introduction to the discipline of management and the organization, this book takes the reader on a 'guided tour' through the various aspects of management, as depicted in the step-by-step process model in Fig A. It is important to stress two points with regard to this approach. Firstly, organizations and management are always concerned with people and their motivation (that is why we have positioned motivation at the top of Fig A). In every aspect of management (and in every step of the model) the motivation of the people concerned must be taken into account. Secondly, the person who acts as manager must not lose sight of what a manager actually is and does. In both a symbolic sense and in Fig A, the reader has to start the tour at the beginning.

Students in management and organization courses and programs of study at universities, colleges and MBA schools will find this book useful. It can also be used in higher level management courses.

The organization is examined in the context of its environment – that is, the outside world in which the organization operates and which influences the organization's performance. The challenges currently facing managers are discussed, as are those confronting the managers of the twenty-first century.

Structure of 'Management: an Evidence-Based Approach'

This book consists of five parts of two chapters each. It is arranged according to the process approach to management.

Part One 'Management and Society' deals with the role of managers and organizations in society, the history of management theory and the stages of development of individual organizations. In addition, the interrelationship between society and organizations is discussed.

Part Two 'Strategic Management and the Learning Organization' looks at the questions that every organization needs to address: what is our direction? Do we have to change? These are questions relating to mission and strategy formulation, decision making, creativity and learning.

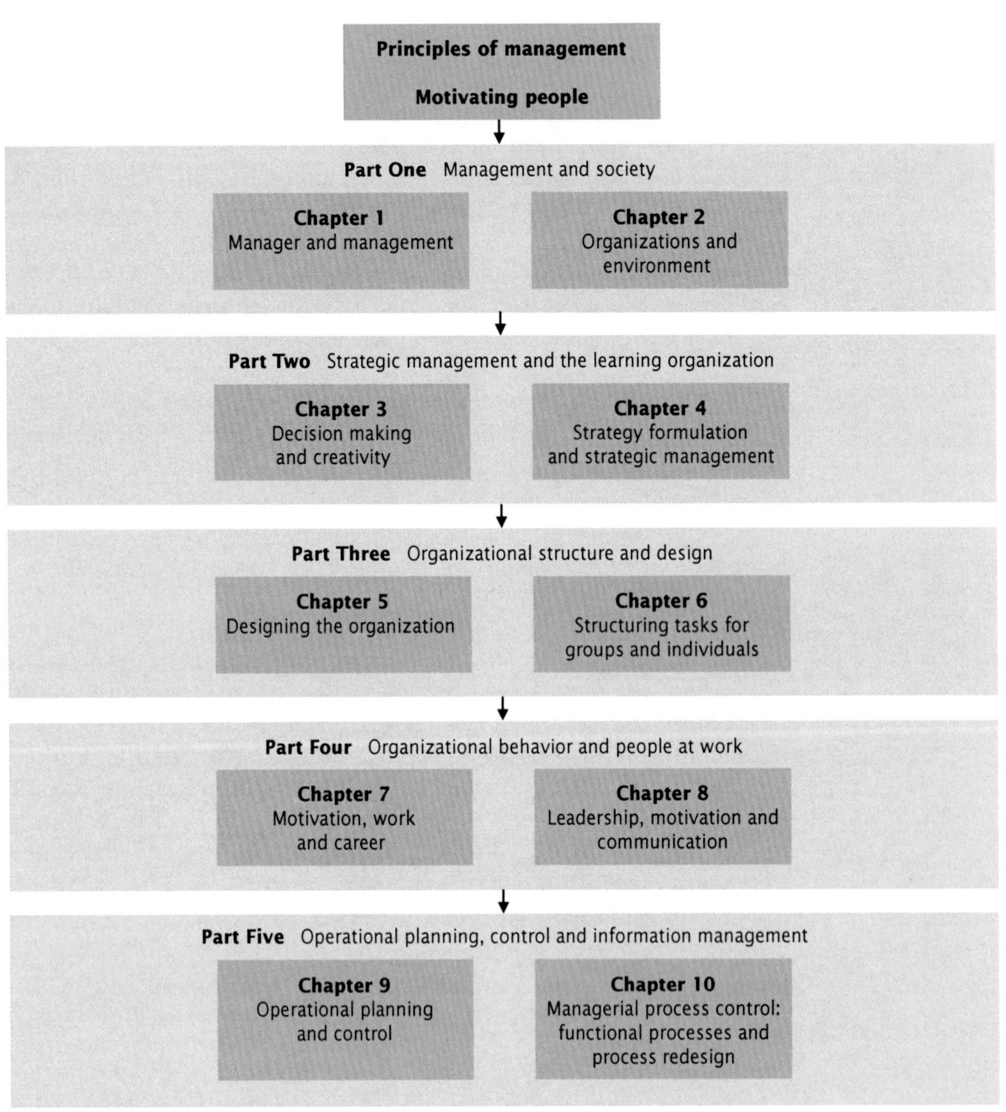

Figure A
The 'step-by-step' process model

In *Part Three*, 'Organizational Structure and Design', the structuring of organizations and the ways in which work can be divided are covered. The organizational structure that is chosen needs to fit the organization's strategic positioning. The formulation of tasks, departmentalization, organizing around processes and the ways in which employees work – for example, in group structures or autonomous teams – are all described.

Part Four 'Organizational Behavior and People at Work' deals with issues regarding people in the organization – employee motivation, manager motivation and manager leadership styles. Human resources management, fostering of talent, and the distribution and execution of power are described, as are the shared expectations of the members of the organization concerning work behavior – that is, the organizational culture.

Part Five 'Operational Planning, Control and Information management' explores the control of organizational processes. Planning and corrective action are discussed, and special attention is given to quality management, performance measurement and the possibilities and pitfalls of information technology in relation to management and organization. The management aspects of several functional processes, including logistics and human resources are covered. This part concludes with a look at the organization in relation to business process re-engineering (BPR) and e-business utilizing web 2.0 technologies in its daily operations.

Website www.management-evidencebasedapproach.noordhoff.nl

This edition is supported by a periodically updated website **www.management-evidencebasedapproach.noordhoff.nl**, which reinforces the book's practical orientation. The site demonstrates once more the practical implications of management theory and concepts in class discussions on case studies and topical issues in managerial practice.
An Instructor's Manual accompanies this book. It contains additional assistance for lecturers using this book with students and is directed at enhancing the learning process.

New in this edition

The text has been integrally reviewed and adapted to recent developments in management practice and theory. Some new sections concerning new insights and trends which are relevant for the leaders of tomorrow have been added. Current topics of management are described in new case studies and recently published research-based exercises.

Chapter 1
In this chapter an introduction is given to the nature of to-day's management (1.1.3) and the importance of expressive and inspiring leadership is underlined (in 1.4.2 and 1.5.3) in the context of high-performance organizations (1.8). In describing the essentials of today's management topics (in 1.1.3) attention is given to the 'hot' issue of branding, as well as to spending on R&D, the role of science and technology, globalization and the relationship between business and a sustainable society.

In 1.1.5 attention is given to the earliest management theories and recent developments in the modern school of management and organizational theory as an interdisciplinary field of study and practice.

Chapter 2
Relevant societal trends and developments are updated (in 2.3). These include transformation of the EU, eurozone aspirations and scepticism, technological innovations and scarce new resources, sustainability and responsible entrepreneurship. Worldwide geo-political shifts, increasing competition, strategic alliancies, mergers and reorganizations, outsourcing, nearshoring and off-shoring and changing consumer behavior are described in 2.4. This chapter also deals with risk management, corporate integrity, governance, ethical dilemmas and crisis and reputation management.

Chapter 3
ICT-driven multitasking and its effects on workefficiency is dealt with in section 3.4.4. The utilisation of virtual teams in the context of timeshifting and day-extension is illustrated (in 3.5.3).

Chapter 4
This edition deals more extensively (in 4.2.2) with rivalry and competition. As shown in Porter's model, revised in 2008, economic and technological developments are exerting pressure on prices and scarce new resources are influencing bargaining positions in markets and the innovation and development of substitute products. In 4.2.6 the concept of synergy is further illustrated and in 4.4.3 the success or failure of strategic alliances is discussed at the hand of evidence.

Chapter 5
5.2.2 deals in greater depth with the position of middle managers. Problems in project management are explained in 5.3.2.

Chapter 6
In the context of management's scope of control (in 6.8) and designing high-performance jobs, attention is given to the relevance of such concepts as the 'span of influence' and the 'span of support'. In 6.9.9 attention is given to work engagement and recent ideas on involving employees in change through direct voice systems and voicing new ideas. 6.9.10 incorporates a paragraph on recent ideas relating to the irrational aspects of change management.

Chapter 7
Chapter 7 has been brought up to date and includes a new section on work satisfaction in practice (in 7.4.5) and coaching and talent development (in 7.6.3). In 7.2. extra information is given on demotion and sustainable employability as practised in Scandinavian countries: the so-called Nordic model.

Chapter 8
8.1.4 enumerates the characteristics of inspiring leaders. 8.3.1 describes the shortcomings of ineffective leaders and identifies those behavioral aspects that employees associate with 'good' and 'bad' bosses.

Chapter 9
Recent insights in relation to the pitfalls of performance management are described in 9.9.2.

Chapter 10
Recent developments in relation to ICT are described in this chapter. They include (in 10.4.1) 'software as a service' and new topics for CIOs. Webshops and Web 2.0 technology is discussed in 10.4.7. The business advantages associated with Web 2.0 and its various applications is elaborated (in 10.5.7 and 10.7) in the context of the networked organization, social networks, co-creation and crowd-sourcing.

Glossary, bibliography and index have been updated with new terms and relevant recent books and articles.

A new book is always open to improvement; comments and suggestions are very welcome.

Amsterdam, June/July 2010

Doede Keuning
Bart Bossink
Brian Tjemkes

Contents

Part 1 Management and society 3

Chapter 1 ***Manager and management*** 5

Management-in-action 6
1.1 Organization and management 7
1.2 The company: its governance structure and management 26
1.3 Levels of management within an organization 30
1.4 Core activities of managers 34
1.5 Managers: born or made? 39
1.6 The management process and core activities 44
1.7 Process model of an organization 46
1.8 Characteristics of an effective organization and successful management 51
1.9 The manager and the organizational culture 53
Summary 55
Discussion questions 55
Research-based exercise 56
Management case study 57

Chapter 2 ***Organizations and the environment*** 61

Management-in-action 62
2.1 An organization in its environment 64
2.2 External stakeholders 68
2.3 Environmental factors 71
2.4 Relevant trends in the environment 82
2.5 Social responsibility, external reporting, risk management and corporate governance 110
2.6 Industrial and organizational democracy in a European context 122
2.7 Management and ethics 128
2.8 Communication with external groups 132
Summary 140
Discussion questions 141
Research-based exercise 142
Management case study 143

Part 2 **Strategic management and the learning organization** 147

Chapter 3 *Decision making and creativity* 149
Management-in-action 150
3.1 The nature of decision making 152
3.2 The decision-making process 153
3.3 Factors influencing decision making 159
3.4 Decision making: techniques and approaches 163
3.5 The creative and learning organization 173
3.6 The role of work groups in participation and decision making 181
3.7 The use of external consultants 183
Summary 185
Discussion questions 185
Research-based exercise 186
Management case study 187

Chapter 4 *Strategy formulation and strategic management* 191
Management-in-action 192
4.1 Conditions for success 194
4.2 The strategy formulation process 200
4.3 The organization of strategic planning 231
4.4 Strategic collaboration 235
4.5 Implementation of strategic plans 242
4.6 Managing organizational resistance 246
4.7 The emerging strategy 247
Summary 249
Discussion questions 250
Research-based exercise 251
Management case study 252

Part 3 **Organizational structure and design** 255

Chapter 5 *Designing the organization* 257
Management-in-action 258
5.1 Structure of the organization: division of work and coordination 260
5.2 Vertical and horizontal organization designs 264
5.3 The choice of organizational structure 271
5.4 Organizational and management considerations for growth and development 288
5.5 Organizational structure in development 292
5.6 Towards flatter organizations 300
5.7 Towards intelligent organizations in networks of organizations 303
Summary 310
Discussion questions 311
Research-based exercise 312
Management case study 313

Chapter 6 *Structuring tasks for groups and individuals* 317

Management-in-action 318
6.1 Structuring tasks and design of functions: criteria 319
6.2 P-grouping and F-grouping: advantages and disadvantages 321
6.3 Organization and group design 326
6.4 Delegation: task, authority, responsibility and accountability 329
6.5 Organizational principles: relationships and authorities 329
6.6 Centralization and decentralization 342
6.7 Coordination and internal adaptation 344
6.8 Scope of management control 346
6.9 Organization in development: reorganization and planning for change 348
Summary 362
Discussion questions 363
Research-based exercise 364
Management case study 365

Part 4 Organizational behavior and people at work 367

Chapter 7 *Motivation, work and career* 369

Management-in-action 370
7.1 The employee of the future and changing work behavior 371
7.2 Groups and the organization 374
7.3 The power of teams 378
7.4 Motivation: a closer view 382
7.5 Empowerment 390
7.6 The new context for human talent development and human resource management 394
7.7 Human resource development: an integral concept and a set of instruments 403
7.8 Payment systems and salary structures 418
7.9 Careers and management development 424
Summary 427
Discussion questions 427
Research-based exercise 428
Management case study 429

Chapter 8 *Leadership, motivation and communication* 433

Management-in-action 434
8.1 Leadership, management and entrepreneurship 435
8.2 Inspiring leadership: the seven habits and the eighth one (from Covey) 438
8.3 Managers and their motivation 444
8.4 Leadership and styles of leadership 448
8.5 Influencing human behavior 457
8.6 Styles of leadership and conflict resolution 469
8.7 Organization, styles of leadership and organizational culture 474
Summary 481
Discussion questions 481
Research-based exercise 482
Management case study 483

Part 5 **Operational planning, control and information management** 487

Chapter 9 *Operational planning and control* 489
Management-in-action 490
9.1 Planning 491
9.2 From planning to budgeting 496
9.3 Management of operations 502
9.4 Production planning: methods and techniques 507
9.5 Time management: project and network planning 510
9.6 Improving quality: quality management 512
9.7 Benchmarking: learning through comparison 523
9.8 Ratios: a method of self-regulation 527
9.9 Performance measurement: financial and non-financial indicators 531
9.10 Operational control: adaptation and corrective actions 543
Summary 544
Discussion and review questions 544
Research-based exercise 545
Management case study 546

Chapter 10 *Managerial process control: functional processes and process redesign* 549
Management-in-action 550
10.1 Information and control 551
10.2 Management and operational information systems 557
10.3 Information planning and planning of automation 562
10.4 Information and communication technology (ICT) 564
10.5 Functional processes and process control 574
10.6 Process redesign 602
10.7 ICT entrepreneurship 606
Summary 613
Discussion and review questions 613
Research-based exercise 614
Management case study 615

Bibliography 616

Glossary 623

Index 639

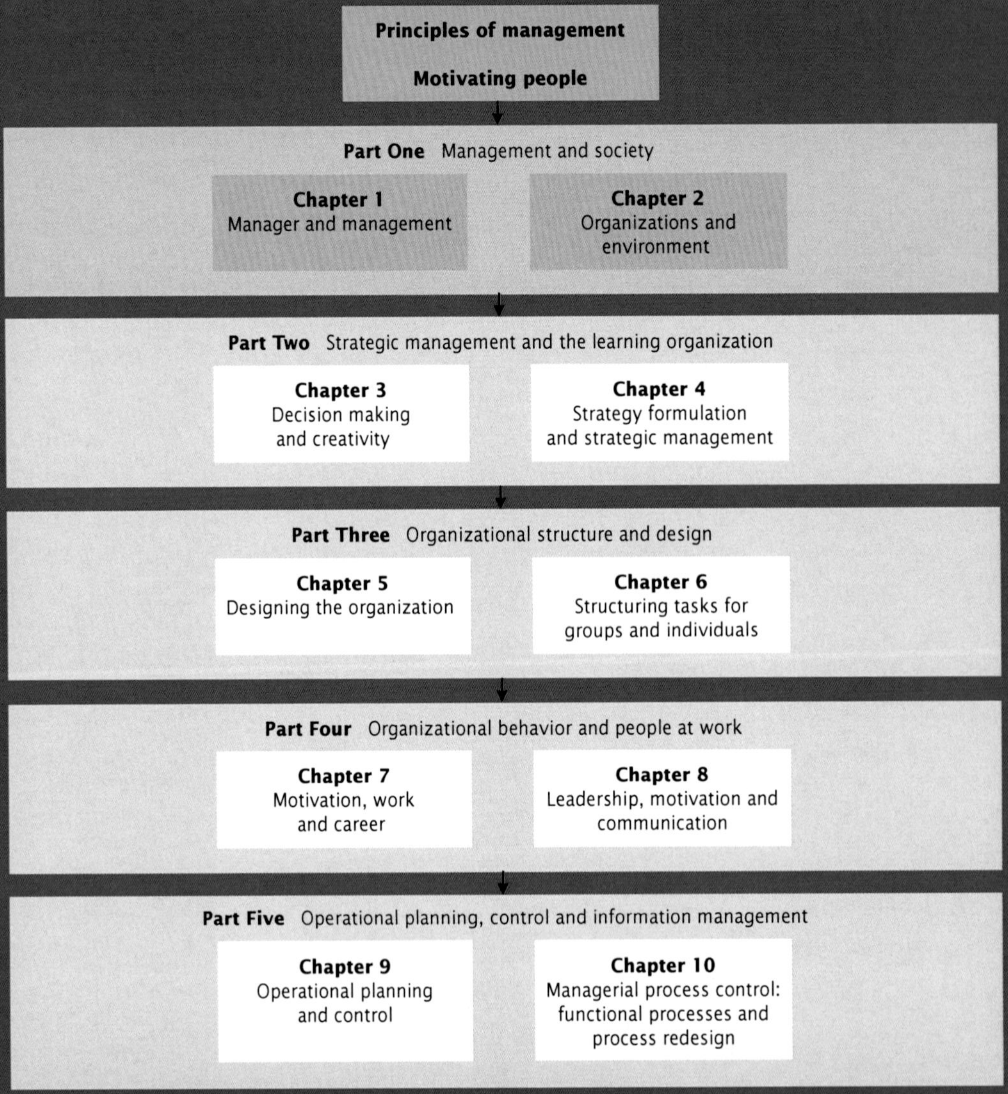

Principles of management

Motivating people

Part One Management and society

Chapter 1
Manager and management

Chapter 2
Organizations and environment

Part Two Strategic management and the learning organization

Chapter 3
Decision making and creativity

Chapter 4
Strategy formulation and strategic management

Part Three Organizational structure and design

Chapter 5
Designing the organization

Chapter 6
Structuring tasks for groups and individuals

Part Four Organizational behavior and people at work

Chapter 7
Motivation, work and career

Chapter 8
Leadership, motivation and communication

Part Five Operational planning, control and information management

Chapter 9
Operational planning and control

Chapter 10
Managerial process control: functional processes and process redesign

Management and society

Part 1

CHAPTER 1 Manager and management

CHAPTER 2 Organizations and the environment

We begin with a general introduction and examination of some of the basic concepts of management and the organization. In later chapters we deal with particular aspects of the managerial process itself. In today's world 'management' is an important social phenomenon. In chapters 1 and 2 we look at management and its place in society, and ask the following questions:

- What are managers and organizations, and what is management all about? (Chapter 1)
- How does the organization relate to the environment in which it operates? (Chapter 2)

CONTENTS

1.1 Organization and management
1.2 The company: its governance structure and management
1.3 Levels of management within an organization
1.4 Core activities of managers
1.5 Managers: born or made?
1.6 The management process and core activities
1.7 Process model of an organization
1.8 Characteristics of an effective organization and successful management
1.9 The manager and the organizational culture

Management, a dynamic world

Manager and management

Chapter 1

LEARNING OUTCOMES

After studying this chapter, you should be able to do the following:

- Describe the concepts of management and organization and explain why these are important
- Identify the levels of management within the organization and explain why each level requires different types of knowledge and skills
- List the core activities of the managerial process and show how they relate to each other
- Identify the characteristics of the modern manager
- Indicate the criteria, requirements and standards that are or should be met by effective and healthy organizations
- Distinguish between the concepts of effectiveness and efficiency and explain why these are important for reviewing an organization
- Give examples of instruments for assessing or evaluating management performance

CASE

Management-in-action

2009 Global Champions: Seeing through the Haze

The world's best companies of 2009 were those with the savviest strategic planning, sharpest peripheral vision, and consistent flexibility

A.T. Kearney's 2009 Global Champions report proves the conventional wisdom wrong: with the right strategic planning, peripheral vision, and flexible execution, companies were able to generate positive returns even in the most challenging climate.

Looking over this year's Global Champions, it's tempting to see only the differences between the finalists. From Nintendo (consumer electronics) to Komatsu (KMTUF.PK) (heavy equipment) to MTN (MTNOF.PK) (telecommunications) to BHP Billiton (BHP) (mining), a broad range of industries and geographies are represented. However, beneath the surface lie two common threads. First, the companies on this list are emblematic of underlying trends in the global economy. Second, they have each demonstrated the ability to look through the kaleidoscope of changing global business conditions, *identify meaningful trends*, and *implement strategies* to capitalize on them.

The global financial crisis, to paraphrase General Electric's (GE) Jeff Immelt, has caused a fundamental 'reset' of the global economy. At A.T. Kearney, we believe the result is a faster pace of change in the underlying 'drivers' of global business conditions: globalization, demographics, consumer preferences, government regulation and activism, natural resource availability, and the environment. And all of this is turbocharged by the leveraging of technology.

Governments vs. Consumers

In the 'reset' world, demand is also polarized between two divergent consumers: governments focused on job creation through investments in infrastructure and consumers who have cut back on spending but are still willing to come out of their foxholes and buy products that appeal to their desire for a simpler, sustainable, more fulfilled lifestyle.

The Global Champions list contains companies involved in both the 'hard' infrastructure of roads, ports, and buildings (Komatsu, Hyundai (HYHZF), Fluor (FLR)) and 'soft' infrastructure such as telecommunications (America Movil (AMX) and MTN). On the consumer side, Global Champions Nintendo and Apple (AAPL) each sell products that are not necessities and might be expected to wither in a recession, but both companies have continued to thrive by offering lifestyle-enhancing products that consumers feel compelled to buy.

These companies understand the world around them and implement appropriate business plans. They also have the peripheral vision and agility to respond to changes in business conditions. That is, they understand that strategy is a sense of direction that we continuously fine-tune, to paraphrase the great management scientist Peter Drucker.

The success of this year's winner, Nintendo, also suggests that it helps to have a leader who articulates the strategy in a way that is easy to understand. At Nintendo, CEO Satoru Iwata advocates 'increasing the gaming population' and that's precisely what the company has done with its Nintendo DS and Wii products.

Broadening the Footprint

Sometimes *serendipity* sets the stage for foresight. Sasol (SSL), for example, was originally established to develop technologies to turn coal into synthetic oil to promote energy independence in apartheid-era South Africa. South Africa's reintegration into the global economy – a fundamental change in business conditions if ever there was one – offered Sasol new opportunities. Sasol responded by broadening its footprint to create a global company with operations in 30 countries. It also expanded its portfolio to include gas-to-liquid technologies to help meet rising energy demand. Today, Sasol is well-positioned in a world of continued resource scarcity. It is also ahead of the curve in terms of sustainability, voluntarily participating in the Carbon Disclosure Project and publishing sustainability reports since 2000.

Doosan Heavy Industries (DOHIF.PK) has shown both foresight and *agility* as it has bought new technologies and businesses, while maintaining a consistent corporate culture that emphasizes high performance. Doosan expanded from its traditional focus on power plants to include nuclear and desalinization facilities, successfully anticipating the growth potential of both industries. At the same time, Doosan integrated vertically through raw-materials investments, providing insurance from commodity price swings, and consulting and services offerings.

Proving that success comes in many ways, Inditex (IDEXY.PK) pioneered a highly flexible business system that allows it to rapidly deliver high-fashion merchandise at a reasonable price. The company conducts continuous trend analysis and keeps new styles moving into its Zara chain and other stores. At the production level, Inditex offers best-in-class time to market, guaranteeing that its stores will carry cutting-edge styles. Local store managers also are given significant flexibility in ordering to ensure that the unique needs of each location are met.

Of course, corporate success is the result of a variety of factors, both internal and external, and the strategies that work for one organization may not be appropriate for others. However, this year's rankings show that value-building companies have the foresight to identify significant trends that affect their businesses and the ability to capitalize on them.

Source: *BusinessWeek*, October 1, 2009 (Paul Laudicina and Norbert Jorek)

When people work together to achieve something, management of some kind is always *management* involved. Until the middle of the nineteenth century management was never seen as a specific or defined task, let alone as a profession or discipline. In the past the possession of almost *managers* absolute power over people and other resources meant that 'managers' worked towards their own personal objectives and goals and could realize these as they wished. Major and frequent failures were allowed; experience was the only way to learn. Changing power structures, especially after the Industrial Revolution, set limits on the manager's power. It was no longer acceptable for capital and labor to be used at will or wasted. This was a new concept and it created a style of management in which the first societal goal was, and still is, the effective and efficient use of people and other resources.

Social change and scientific development have launched us into a new era in which management is, so to speak, at the service of the community. Rational use of people and resources involves more than simple administration, direction and control. The main *profession of management* characteristic of the 'new' profession of management is the making of decisions that enable many diverse and externally oriented objectives to be reached while taking continuity and societal interest into account. Furthermore, management remains a people-oriented activity. To a large extent, it is based on the personality of the manager and the capabilities of employees. The diverse nature of modern management provides many people with the opportunity to participate in the process of management, each according to their own abilities, skills and knowledge.

1.1 Organization and management

In everyday life, we all come into contact with organizations in the form of companies and institutions. We use the products and services which are made available to us through organizations such as factories, schools, hospitals and travel companies – bread, dairy products, clothes, education, health care, public transport, and so on.

Organizations ... an integral part of our daily lives

society of organizations We all work and live in a society of organizations. When we go to work, we are dealing with an organization – it might be an industrial firm or an institution in the service sector. Even our spare time and vacations are based around organizations: think of travel agencies, camp sites, hotels and restaurants, sports clubs and so on. In fact, we take organizations so much for granted in our daily lives that we rarely consider what organizations are, how they are designed or how they are managed or governed.

Organizations ... a challenge

This all changes when we have to accomplish something with the cooperation of other people, when we want to start up a company, when something goes wrong in the company we work for, or when the daily supply of goods and services is disrupted. Then we start to notice how important good management and organization really are. Then we appreciate the issues that the manager and the organization need to address – namely the design, the functioning of processes and the management of the company or institution.

management and organization

Although we frequently conclude that 'they' should have done things differently or better, what happens if we are directly involved ourselves? We realize then that things are not as self-evident and straightforward as we considered them to be, and it becomes clear how important it is to have insights into the problems of management and organizations. We also realize how useful it is to be able to draw on techniques, tools and instruments that help us to set up and design an organization and to manage resources and people effectively.

CASE *Mini case study 1.1*

Nokia tries to reinvent itself ... can the world's largest handset-maker regain the initiative?

Ask Finns about their national character and chances are the word *sisu* will come up. It is an amalgam of steadfastness and diligence, but also courage, recklessness and fierce tenacity. 'It takes *sisu* to stand at the door when the bear is on the other side,' a folk saying goes.

There are plenty of bears these days at the doors of Nokia, the Finnish firm that is the world's biggest maker of mobile handsets. Although it is still the global leader in the fast-growing market for smartphones, its devices are losing ground to Apple's iPhone and to the BlackBerry, made by Research in Motion (RIM). On January 5th Google took a further step into the market with the launch of the Nexus One, a handset made by HTC of Taiwan that the Internet giant will sell directly to consumers, and which runs Android, Google's operating system for smartphones.

Especially in America, where Apple and RIM reign supreme in the smart-phone market, many already see Nokia as a has-been. Developers are rushing to write programs for the iPhone and for Android, but shun Symbian, Nokia's rival software platform. And Nokia's efforts in mobile services, mostly under its Ovi brand, have yet to make much headway.

Nokia has overcome many crises in the past. In 1995 poor logistics caused it to stumble. It responded by developing one of the world's most efficient supply chains, capable of churning out some 1.2m handsets a day. A decade later it failed to anticipate the demand for 'clamshell'-type handsets, but bounced back quickly to restore its market share in handsets to 40% and thus its industry dominance.

But this time the problems go deeper. In more than one way, Nokia has to become a different company, says Jay Galbraith, a management expert. Until now, it has excelled in making and distributing hardware. This has trained the organisation to focus on planning and logistics. Deadlines are often set 18 months in advance. Teams developing a new device also work in relative isolation and even competitively, to make each product more original. And although Nokia has always done a lot of market research and built phones for every conceivable type of customer, it sells most of its wares to telecom operators and designs its products to meet their demands.

With the rise of the smart-phone, however, software and services are becoming much more important. They require different skills. Development cycles are not counted in quarters and years, but in months or even weeks. New services do not have to be perfect, since they can be improved after their launch if consumers like them. Teams have to collaborate more closely, so that the same services and software can run on different handsets. Nokia also has to establish a direct relationship with its users like Apple's or Google's.

Last February Nokia's management kicked off what is internally known as a 'transformation project' to address all these concerns. 'We needed to move faster. We needed to improve our execution. And we needed a tighter coupling of devices and services,' explains Mary McDowell, Nokia's chief strategist. The firm has since introduced a simpler internal structure, cut its smart-phone portfolio by half, ditched weaker services and begun to increase Ovi's appeal to developers by allowing them to integrate Nokia's services into their own applications. While giving Symbian a makeover it is also pushing a new operating system, called Maemo, for the grandest, computer-like smartphones.

All this will no doubt help Nokia come up with better, if not magic, products. The firm may even reach its goal of 300m users by the end of 2011 because its efforts are not aimed just at rich countries, but at fast-growing emerging economies where Nokia is still king of the hill, such as India. There, services such as Nokia Money, a mobile-payment system, and Life Tools, which supplies farmers with prices and other information, fulfil real needs, says John Delaney of IDC, another market-research firm.

Yet it is an entirely different question whether Nokia will manage to dominate the mobile industry once more – not just by handset volumes, but by innovation and profits. The example of the computer industry, in which the centre of gravity began shifting from hardware firms to providers of software and services over two decades ago, is not terribly encouraging: of the industry's former giants, only IBM really made the shift successfully. Then again, Nokia has reinvented itself many times since its origin in 1865 as a paper mill. That, points out Dan Steinbock, the author of two books on the firm, is thanks not only to sisu, but also to a remarkable willingness to embrace change and diversity. Nokia will need those traits in the years ahead.

Source: *The Economist*, January 7, 2010

1.1.1 Managers: what kind of people are they?

manager

Is the word 'manager' simply a new word for a supervisor or a boss? Is 'management' simply a group of people who tell others what to do? The word 'manager' is certainly a relatively new addition to the English language. It comes from the Latin words manus, which means 'hand' and agere which means 'to set in motion, to carry along, to act.'

Defining management

A manager is someone who directs processes, someone who gets work done through other people by initiating and directing actions. As an executive, a manager makes ongoing decisions about what work has to be done, how it has to be done, and who has to do it. As a result, the manager has to be prepared to give explanations at any time. All levels of management – whether the managing director, supervisor, foreman or boss – are at the cross-roads between work group, team, department, company, parent group and the societal environment.

management meanings

In common usage the word 'management' can have three different meanings. In this book, which is intended as a review and discussion of practice as well as a means of preparing for that practice, all three meanings are used, so it is important to be familiar with them.

employees

1 The word 'management' refers to all the employees in an organization whose job it is to set in motion, prepare and control the actions of other people and resources, given the objectives – implicit or explicit – of the organization. This meaning is expressed in sentences such as: 'management had a meeting at 10 am.'

activities

2 The word 'management' refers to the process or activities (thinking as well as acting) which have to be performed in order to get something done. This meaning is expressed in sentences such as: 'Management of a world tour involves a vast amount of work.'

field of knowledge and discipline

3 'Management' is a specific field of knowledge and discipline in which the everyday work and practices of 'managers' and 'organizations' are studied. This meaning can be found in sentences such as: 'I am doing an exam in management next week.'

This book is intended as a basic introduction to the study of management (definition 3) in which management is considered both as a group of employees in an organization (definition 1) and as a process made up of discrete but interrelated activities (definition 2).

Characteristics of managers

It is the responsibility of managers to accomplish tasks and goals through other people, often without being able to exert a direct or substantial influence over what those people do and how they do it.

Dependency on others

In principle, a manager is dependent on the dedication and contributions of other people. This applies as much to top managers as it does to all other managers within the organization. Often this dependency relates to colleagues with whom lines of authority have been clearly established. However, it can also involve reliance on employees from other parts of the company or with departments or divisions with which there are no clear lines of authority. Managers then need to develop work methods through which they can gain the cooperation of all those from whom a contribution is required in order to reach the specified goals and objectives.

clear/no clear lines of authority

Responsibility for the working climate

As the leader of a company, department or division, a manager is responsible for creating a good working climate. The manager has to stimulate cooperation. There has to be a certain degree of harmony between the work that has to be done and the needs of individuals and groups. A manager also has joint responsibility for the staffing of his or her department, division or working unit, for education and training, for assessment and promotion and for motivating employees.

harmony
needs of individuals

Receiving and transmitting information

A manager has to be well informed at all times about what is going on both outside and within the organizational unit. If problems are to be spotted and dealt with in time, information is required. The organizational unit must receive sufficient and timely information in order to be able to react to events effectively.

sufficient and timely information

Decision making

All managers will face unexpected situations even though they may strive for and prefer planned action. Problems are sometimes ignored for a long time and this may eventually result in an acute crisis – for example, a conflict between departments or divisions, or between employees in work groups, or a sudden disruption to the supply of essential resources. Managers have to find solutions and make decisions regarding these problems. The first priority is to implement immediate short-term measures so that work can be resumed as soon as possible. They then have to search for more fundamental adjustments or changes in aspects of the organization such as structure and policies in order to prevent the same problems from happening again.

decisions

Time management

Managers need to possess good time-management skills. The need for joint consultation and participation in various work situations makes it important for the manager to learn the art and skills of effective meetings and communication. Setting priorities and delegating to others whenever possible are very important. Prioritizing is a key skill for everyone who wants to work effectively.

meetings
delegating

Field knowledge and focus on results

Managers need to have knowledge of the specific field in which they work and should be result-oriented, for themselves as well as for the company as a whole.

CASE

Mini case study 1.2

Kidnapped ... bosses are taken hostage in France

SERGE FOUCHER, the head of Sony in France, was taken hostage on March 12th by factory workers seeking better severance terms. They shut him in a meeting room and barricaded the plant with huge tree trunks. Released the next day, Mr Foucher seemed to take things in his stride. 'I am happy to be free and to see the light of day again,' he said.

Business people in France are not amused. They note that the authorities did not ask the police to free Mr Foucher. Instead, the local deputy prefect accompanied him into further talks with the workers, who got what they wanted: a better redundancy deal. It all confirms France's general lack of sympathy for business, complains one executive.

Taking executives hostage is a well-established tactic in France, which has a history of confrontational labour relations. But it seems to be becoming more common. In January 2008 the British boss of an ice-cream factory was held hostage overnight after announcing plans to fire over half of its workers (on that occasion, the police did intervene). In February 2008 the head of a car-parts factory was seized after workers realised that he was planning to move the operation to Slovakia. Ten days later, workers at a tyre factory owned by Michelin locked in two senior executives in protest at plans to shut the plant.

Workers in other countries take bosses captive on occasion, but France is the only nation where it happens often. Might the practice spread? 'Because of the state of the world economy, it would not surprise me if bosses were held hostage by workers more frequently,' says David Partner, a kidnap and ransom expert at Miller Insurance, an insurance broker affiliated with Lloyd's of London.

Sit-ins are already becoming more common. In America, says Gary Chaison, professor of industrial relations at Clark University in Massachusetts, workers are likely to become more militant, because of a sense of injustice over pay.

Source: *The Economist*, March 21, 2009

1.1.2 Organizations and organizing

People work together in companies or institutions, with technical, information and financial resources all being used in order to reach specific goals.

goal-realizing unit

An organization is a cooperative goal-realizing unit in which participants consciously enter into a mutual relationship and work together in order to attain common goals. These goals can often be best realized by means of a joint effort rather than by individuals acting alone. Thus, an organization is the 'instrument' used to make products or provide services which meet the needs of society and individual people.

An organization does not come into being by chance. Organizations are always the result of conscious decision making and actions. This is what we call organizing. Organizing as an activity is the creating of effective relationships between available people, resources and actions in order to attain certain goals.

A good organization ... effective and efficient

A good organization is one in which people work purposefully, are goal-oriented and try to make efficient use of available resources. In organizations where people work at cross-purposes, strive for different goals, or use up more resources and time than is really necessary, actions and behavior are described as ineffective (that is, failing to attain multiple goals) and inefficient (that is, wasting skills and resources). Specified goals are not reached, or, when they are reached, more resources have been used and more time taken than would have been necessary in an organization where work is carried out effectively and efficiently.

In the latter type of organization goals are reached according to plan, on time, and at the lowest possible cost, and the people who work in such an organization experience high levels of job satisfaction. They like their work and derive intrinsic satisfaction from it. In this sense, good organizing and a good organization constitute the most important conditions for success.

Organizations ... in all shapes and sizes

Organizations come in all sorts of shapes and sizes: profit and non-profit organizations and institutions; industrial companies and service industries; private and government-controlled firms; large, medium-sized and small companies; national and multinational companies; charities and voluntary organizations; unions, political organizations and so on. Whatever grouping we choose, all organizations have certain common features:

- people who
- work together and cooperate
- in order to reach a specific set of goals.

Why do they do this? For the simple reason that an organization is a powerful instrument which performs actions that can never be matched by an individual working alone and through which it is possible to accomplish goals which could not be reached otherwise.

definition

As with the word 'management', the word 'organization' can be defined in three different ways:

institutional

1 It can be used in the institutional sense – for example, when we want to identify a company or association, such as Philips, IKEA, Marks & Spencer, Volvo, The Red Cross.

instrumental

2 It can have an instrumental meaning, referring to the internal arrangements, especially the structure, of a company or institution. An example of this use is: 'We are going to improve the organization of the company as it does not currently contribute to the realization of our goals.' 'Organization' in this sense refers to elements such task division, coordination, decision-making processes and planning and policy procedures.

functional

3 It can be used in a functional sense, by which we mean the process of carrying out a set of activities. For example: 'The organization of the party was very poor.'

1.1.3 The nature of today's management

History demonstrates that management was involved whenever people wanted to accomplish something by means of joint effort. Think, for example, of the building of the pyramids in Egypt, the Coliseum in Rome or the Great Wall of China. When we consider how the stones were cut and transported over great distances in order for them to be used in such impressive construction projects, it is clear that leading and masterminding these projects must have demanded excellent management skills. No wonder that in the ancient documents of philosophers like Plato and Xenophon, we find passages which are devoted to management. For example, in one of his debates on management, Socrates says:

> *... if a man knows what he wants and can get it, he will be a good controller, whether he controls a chorus, an estate, a city or an army. Don't look down on businessmen ... for the management of private concerns differs only in point of number from that of public affairs ... neither can be carried on without men ... and the men employed in private and public transactions are the same ... and those who understand how to employ them are successful directors ... and those who do not, fail in both ...*
>
> *Taken from Socrates' debates as recorded by Xenophon in* Memorabilia *(III.IV. 6-12) and* Oeconomicus*.*

Based as they are on experience, these statements are still valid today. The same applies to a number of management principles which were already in use in ancient Rome and which will be covered later in this book – for example, *unity of direction, hierarchy, chain of command and unity of command, centralization/decentralization, line relationships and staff relationships* (see chapters 5 and 6).

elements of modern management

Developments over the last 200 years have given us the following important elements of modern management:

- the interrelationship between business and society
- business growth and internationalization: globalization
- changes in power/authority relationships

- the role of science and technology
- marketing philosophy

The interrelationship between business and society

The time when a business enjoyed an almost totally autonomous position in society is long gone. Never before has there been so much influence exerted by society on what happens within a business and other forms of labor organization. The extent of this influence is apparent from contemporary ideas about the objectives and goals of a company and the way in which people think these should be realized. In their roles as societal stakeholders, people now make demands with regard to:

- optimal satisfaction of the needs, wishes and requirements of the consumer
- the spending of profits
- the provision of appropriate employment, that is, employment which suits the qualitative and quantitative supply and demand in a particular region
- the promotion of the well-being of every employee through the creation of a favorable working environment, as well as a contribution to a sustainable society and to the upkeep of that environment
- the guarantee of reasonable compensation to suppliers of capital and employees for their contributions to the company

Other demands on organizations include governmental policies on health, safety and welfare, regulations concerning the environment, regulations with regard to minimum wages and the social security system, not to mention the efforts of consumer associations and trade unions. In addition, there are government policies relating to the realization of economic markets like the European Union (EU) and regulations concerning wages, pricing policy and so on.

shareholder value

In recent times, which have seen the creation and highlighting of shareholder value, every action undertaken by the management of companies quoted on the stock market has been undertaken with shareholder interests in mind. Other stakeholders have felt that shareholder interests have been too strongly represented. Since 2000, there has been talk of 'the end of shareholder value' (Kennedy, 2000) as well as a strong demand for responsible and sustainable societal entrepreneurship (see Section 2.4.3).

Business growth and internationalization: globalization

In recent times many organizations have transformed themselves by increasing the size of their business (either through internal growth or through acquisitions and mergers) and by arranging their operations on an increasingly international basis.
After the Second World War, a large number of countries and continents became increasingly interdependent in the economic, social and strategic sphere. Within Europe, supranational collaboration was created (the EU) and, after the disappearance of the so-called Iron Curtain in the late 1980s, all kinds of relationships became possible between the former Eastern bloc countries and the West. Growth is increasing in many countries in Eastern Europe, as it is in Turkey too. Japan and South-East Asia have become new economic superpowers with China also undergoing very strong growth. ICT-driven India is emerging strongly. Because of their relative poverty, Africa, parts of Asia and South America (with the exception of Brazil) have played a lesser role in international trade.
Enormous technological developments have encouraged international cooperation. Many small, national companies have not been able to afford the enormous investments that these developments involve and so they have merged. Internationalization and increase in business size mean that new problems have arisen in the cultural-technical sphere, and these have had a big influence on present-day entrepreneurs and managers.

mega-mergers

In the meantime, in another world-wide wave of mergers, we are experiencing the occurrence of mega-mergers. At the same time, a fundamental reorganization of organizations that operate world-wide is occurring. (See Section 2.4.)
It would not be surprising if in the years to come, large-scale mergers were announced in the

fields of pharmacy, bio-pharmacy, chemistry, aviation, telecommunications and the banking and insurance businesses. These could well take the form of so-called hostile takeovers. As demonstrated by the takeover struggle between Vodaphone and Mannesmann, accelerating globalization is even affecting the German 'Rhineland model,' a model which has aimed to prevent foreign takeovers of business. Only five GSM companies are predicted to survive in Europe. In the automobile branch, the wave of mergers and/or takeovers continues, while on the other hand, there have also been some remarkable split-ups: for example, Ford and Volvo, General Motors and Saab (see also 2.4). Chemical giant Hoechst has amalgamated with the French Rhône-Poulanc. Pfizer bought Pharmacia for US $60 billion and is now the biggest pharmaceutical concern. Analysts have seen this takeover as the start of a new merger and acquisition era.

hostile takeovers

globalization

While an EU directive on cross-border takeovers has aimed to provide guidelines for improving entrepreneurial efficiency and thus prevent protective directives from blocking hostile takeovers, there have been a number of cases in which proposed mergers have faced being thwarted (by the European Commission, for example). In what has been seen as a government protectionist measure, China rejected Coco-Cola's bid to take over the juice producer Huiyuan (for $2.3 billion) in 2009, arguing that Coca-Cola, already a market leader in China, would become too powerful and negatively affect the market for soft drinks and juices. Had it gone ahead it would have been the biggest takeover of a Chinese business by a foreign company.

EU directive on cross-border takeovers

It would appear that most of the mergers end in a fiasco for the shareholders. Another price that has had to be paid is loss of jobs and high unemployment. The main focus of global restructuring has been the streamlining of organizations and the reduction of costs (see also Section 2.4). Reorganizations have led to the cutting of millions of jobs worldwide since 2000. In the US alone, from the beginning of 2000 until the summer of 2003, 3.2 million jobs were cut in order to increase profits (Donald Kalff, 2006).

The results of this cutting back of jobs have, however, been somewhat disappointing (partly because of reorganization fatigue resulting from subsequent restructuring and rationalization rounds) and it is becoming increasingly difficult to indicate what the savings are. Mass dismissal still remains one of the main tools that managers (especially the more American-orientated ones) have.

reorganization fatigue

Mass dismissal

In 2009, large multinationals in the industrialized countries again announced the imminent cutting of many thousands of direct jobs as a result of reorganizations and turnarounds. The major job cutters were at that time General Motors (13,000), Philips (12,000), Arcelor Mittal (10,000), Nissan (20,000), Japan Airlines (15,700), British Telecom (15,000), Opel (in Europe, 8,300), 'Alcatel'-Lucent (7,000), but also such companies as Nike (1,750), Dell (in the Netherlands, 500) and Campina (about 600). The reorganization that Shell announced in 2009 is expected to affect nearly a quarter of its 102,000 employees. Dutch industries are expected to lose an estimated 100,000 jobs, and in the UK, 60,000 jobs will go in the financial services sector alone. However, recent reports would suggest that companies are expecting to shed jobs less dramatically in the post-2010 period. Asian businesses are most optimistic in this regard.

reorganization

turnaround

The cuts are partly due to the financial crisis. Recent job cuts in Europe were also caused by outsourcing and/or offshoring of corporate activities, as the cases of IBM and Siemens illustrate. IBM cut 10,000 to 13,000 jobs in Europe and the US and took on 14,000 IT employees in India. Siemens shifted 10,000 jobs worldwide to low-wage countries, including some eastern European EU countries Accenture's main business centre is in India (with nearly 50,000 employees), as is that of Cap Gemini (20,000). The French and Dutch-owned company Atos has 13% of its employees in low-wage countries and Logica intends to shift more of its work to India. Up to now, Ordina has operated solely via partnerships in India. Companies such as Unilever, Philips, ING and many others are making their own contributions and usually for the same reasons, and it is predicted that the end is not yet in sight.

These events gave rise in 2000 to the term the 'terror of globalization' (Viviane Forrester, 2000).

terror of globalization

Changes in power/authority relationships

authority and power

It is important to make a distinction between authority and power. Authority is the legal or official right to exert a certain influence. Power is the capacity to influence the behavior of others and to get others to act in a certain manner, possibly even forcibly. The number of people who exert influence or authority over others without having the legal authority to do so has greatly increased in recent times. Within a company, the formal authority is still with the shareholders, but in reality a number of people can pull the strings.

acceptance of authority

Prestige is paramount. Acceptance of authority through personal prestige is crucial to effective implementation. Having prestige means that employees are spontaneously willing to cooperate and accept the exerted authority without objection (and without the necessity to invoke legitimate means of punishment anchored in the formal entitlement).

To clarify this, it might be better to speak of 'positional authority' (formal competence) and 'personal prestige' as the basis of power instead of authority. People have power when they possess or have at their disposal the resources and characteristics with which they can motivate others to do things that they otherwise would not do, or with which they can at least influence the behavior of others. The exercise of power means someone using his or her authority and prestige, and thereby influencing (for example, by means of communication) the behavior and ideas of others.

willingness of others to listen

All this means that the influence which managers can exert partly depends on the willingness of others to listen. When managers have little or no prestige at their disposal, then the simple fact that they have a degree of authority will not be enough to determine the way work is carried out within the organization. The relatively high level of education and development of the average employee means that the exercise of power is increasing less likely to be based simply on the possession of resources of production and formal authority.

PRIVATE EQUITY FIRMS EYE STAKE IN SPRINGER

Leading private equity groups are competing to inject about €400 ($530m) of equity into Springer Science and Business Media, the German academic publisher, which is looking to sell a stake of as much as 49 per cent.
Blackstone, CVC Capital Partners and TPG are all considering submitting first-rounds bids, due by next month.
Other groups mulling over a bid are Kohlberg Kravis Roberts, Hellman & Friedman, Carlyle, EQT and Providence Equity Partners.

Springer, owned by UK private equity groups Candover and Cinven with Derk Haank as chief executive, is the world's second-largest publisher of scientific and medical books. The attraction for the many private equity groups is the potential, eventually, to merge Springer with Informa, the London-listed business-to-business publishing group.

Informa last year rejected a £1.9bn ($2.8bn) takeover bid from a private equity consortium made up of Providence, Carlyle and Blackstone. One private equity executive considering a bid for the company said the deal was expected to value Springer at about nine-times last year's EBITDA of €275m. 'It's a good company, very well run, but with too much debt,' said the executive.

Springer was created in 2003 by Cinven and Candover through a merger of BertelsmannSpringer and KAP, a Dutch publishing group that was formerly owned by Wolters Kluwer.

Source: *Financial Times*, April 27, 2009

Real influence has to be supported by ability and competence, and has to be experienced as being useful and fair in relation to the task.
Closing down a company is often a contentious matter since employers are likely to prioritize the social security needs of their employees as least as much as the rate of return. Nevertheless, the position of shareholders seems to have been reinforced, with 'shareholder value' being increasingly prioritized. In this era of corporate governance, the question has to be raised of whether too much influence by shareholders, particularly speculative ones such as private equity and hedge funds, is leading to premature and short-sighted company decisions.

shareholder value
corporate governance
short-sighted company decisions

Although European leaders do not value the shareholders' approach very highly, Dutch managers and directors, along with those in other European countries, act in very much the same way where reorganizations and their own remuneration are concerned, and sometimes even display irresponsible behavior through vanity or greed at the top.

greed at the top

The role of science and technology

operations research
cybernetics
information technology
management tools

Areas of management science such as operations research, cybernetics and information technology have gradually developed into management tools. These areas of study are so sophisticated and powerful that some believe that one day making decisions will be one of the jobs of a computer. Others refute this on the basis that the human brain is too complex to be completely simulated with the aid of digital technology. After all, it will be people who pose the problems, interpret the information and set priorities. In future management the emphasis will be on the accurate timing of decisions crucial to the survival of the organization. Central to this will be the creativity which makes this possible and which stimulates new developments.
The so-called millennium problem (the prediction that at the turn of the century, computers would undergo disruptions to their data and programs) again showed the extent to which we are becoming (and feel ourselves to be becoming) dependent on technology and science in our lives and our work.
However, after we have overcome the serious problems posed by our technologies, the accent in management will revert to the making of decisions crucial to the continuity of the organization and to making these decisions at the right time. Creativity is the crux of management, since it enables or even provokes new developments.

fracture lines
unbundling
rebundling
call centers
Internet

Under pressure exerted by laws aimed at deregulation, worldwide competition and technological development, it is expected that traditional industries, and within them, their various branches, will be subdivided along the fracture lines of customer relations management, product innovation and the management of infrastructure. The role of ICT in this is unequivocal. We have taken over from the US the terms 'unbundling' and 'rebundling'. (See Section 2.4.7.) ICT-related technologies such as call centers and the Internet are causing changes to traditional distribution channels. (See Section 10.4.7.)

genetics
life science industry

During the coming decades, progression in genetics, DNA research, neuro-sciences and other bio-related sciences will have far-reaching effects. In the so-called life science industry, these influences are already being felt. Farmers, the medical profession, computer companies, pharmaceutical companies, the chemical industry and organic food companies are noticing the effects.

EUROPE PUTS STRESS ON R&D SPENDING

While the growth in R&D investment slowed across the world in 2008, European companies continued to plough money into research at a significantly higher rate than their US and Japanese counterparts, and at a rate that exceeded the lacklustre pace of underlying economic growth.
R&D spending in Europe has been weaker than in competing economies such as the US and Japan for much of the past decade, and the relative progress in 2008 will not have reversed this. The non-EU spend is dominated by trends in the US, Japan and, to a much lesser extent, countries such as Switzerland and South Korea.

In some emerging economies it has been growing quite strongly. In China, for example, privately financed R&D rose from about 0.7 per cent of GDP in 2003 to about 1 per cent in 2006 and 2007. In individual companies the EU's showing was also weaker. It managed only two places in the world's top 10 R&D spenders – Volkswagen, which shelled out €5.93bn ($8.87bn, £5.27bn) and Nokia with €5.32bn.

By contrast, the US held five places – namely, Microsoft (€6.48bn), General Motors (€5.76bn), Pfizer (€5.72bn), Johnson & Johnson (€5.45bn) and Ford (€5.25bn). The top spot went to Toyota Motor, which spent €7.61bn. Also in the top 10 were Swiss pharmaceutical groups Roche with €5.88bn and Novartis with €5.19bn.

The EU scoreboard is based on the top 2,000 corporate spenders on R&D, which in turn account for about four-fifths of worldwide business enterprise expenditure on research.

Source: *Financial Times*, November 17, 2009

sustainable business
genetic manipulation

The expectations are that biogenetics, agronomics and nanotechnology will create a revolution and bring about an industrial transformation. The possibilities (as well as the challenges) are endless. In an era of green and sustainable business, the genetic manipulation of organisms, seeds, animals, and even human beings has naturally raised opposition, and not only from farmers (see Bove & Dufour, 2002).

The development of a marketing philosophy

The development of a marketing philosophy has helped management to realize that the actual goal of the organization lies outside the organization itself, namely in the market. The customers or clients who buy products or services will eventually decide if an organization is to reach its goals and survive.

customer-focused marketing
B2C
B2B
brand values

Since 2000, which marked the start of the most recent marketing era, there has been a sharper focus on the individual customer. Customer-focused marketing, made feasible with e-markets and online ordering systems, is directed both to the individual customer (B2C) and to business-to-business relationships (B2B). The approach being taken is similar: brand and customer orientation is reinforced by the groups that target them. The most recent marketing and advertising approaches direct attention mainly to brands and the creation of so-called brand values, so much so that it has been argued that annual company reports should give a financial value to the brand in question.

The assumption is that at a time when the world is striving to achieve a free market and there is increasing competition for cross-border market share, only the strongest and best-managed brands will survive. Coca-Cola, for example is more capable of creating brand value than Pepsi and consequently has for years been the stronger brand. The same holds for McDonald's as compared to Burger King. The marketing philosophies and strategies of Unilever, Shell, Philips, Heineken, Wal-Mart, H&M, Zara, Nike, Calvin Klein, IKEA and many other companies are now guided by brand and brand value. Well-known brands obviously exert an attraction that can be felt by consumers from Tokyo to Oxford and Heidelberg and now mean that these consumers – transformed into world citizens – eat and drink in the same way, listen to the same music and dress uniformly.

THE WORLD'S MOST VALUABLE BRANDS 2010: THE TOP 20

Rank	Brand	Brand value	% Brand value change 2010 vs 2009
1	Google	114,260	+14
2	IBM	86,383	+30
3	Apple	83,153	+32
4	Microsoft	76,344	0
5	Coca-Cola	67,983	+1
6	McDonald's	66,005	–1
7	Marlboro	57,047	+15
8	China Mobile	52,616	–14
9	GE	45,054	–25
10	Vodafone	44,404	–17
11	ICBC	43,927	+15
12	HP	39,717	+48
13	Walmart	39,421	–4
14	BlackBerry	30,708	+12
15	Amazon	27,459	+29
16	UPS	26,492	–5
17	Tesco	25,741	+12
18	Visa	24,883	+52
19	Oracle	24,817	+16
20	Verizon Wireless	24,675	+39

Source: *Financial Times*, april 28, 2010 (Millward Brown Optimor/BrandZ)

Americanization
demarketing
culture jammers
anti-advertisements

Counter forces have been aroused, however. Marketing has been equated with globalization and Americanization, and 'culture jammers,' demarketing campaigns and anti-advertisements have been the result. Culture jammers resist the top-down dictates of advertising and television, and have even held mocking anti-campaigns (the 'buy nothing today!' campaign of 20 November 2002) and placed anti-advertisements (look at adbusters.org).

Definition

What is a brand?
'A brand is a name, term, sign, symbol or design, or a combination of them which is intended to identify the goods or services of one seller or group of sellers and to differentiate them from those of competitors.'

Philip Kotler

branding

Designing and branding makes the difference. Older people buy a Nokia, youngsters choose a Samsung. The 'age-groups' are differentiated at about the age of 20, it is said. Nokia is 'not cool', and Samsung has no business-exposure. Positioning, profile, core value, key messages and identity are the notions associated with a 'brand'.

WHAT IS BRANDING?

Branding is the foundation of marketing and is inseparable from business strategy. It is therefore more than putting a label on a fancy product. Nowadays, a corporation, law firm, country, university, museum, hospital, celebrity, and even you in your career can be considered as a brand.

As such, a brand is a combination of attributes, communicated through a name, or a symbol, that influences a thought-process in the mind of an audience and creates value. As branding is deeply anchored in psycho-sociology, it takes into account both tangible and intangible attributes, e.g., functional and emotional benefits. Therefore, those attributes compose the beliefs that the brand's audience recalls when they think about the brand in its context.

Coca-Cola, for example, has become a cliché of brand management. Before branding or even management emerged as disciplines, the Atlanta-based company was already spending over US$11,000 on a mass advertising campaign as early as 1892. Its trademark was officially filed in the US that year and has consistently been displayed with the same script to this day. Over time, it also associated its brand with a bright red color, the hour-glass shaped bottle (1915) and the ribbon logo (1970). Together these aspects contribute to differentiating Coke from rivals such as Pepsi-Cola, which has applied competitive pressure since 1898.

Source: www.brandchannel.com

world-wide brands
local brands
private labels

Branding is a 'hot' issue, though even the biggest companies such as Proctor & Gamble and Unilever make mistakes in this respect. Unilever reduced its brands from 1,400 to 400 'world-wide brands', this aiming at market leadership, but the move was resisted by their consumers ... (and) local brands were reintroduced. Proctor & Gamble made a wrong bet by launching high-end products and price rises during a recession, while at the same time doing battle with private labels. A sharp drop in P & Gs market share was the result ... Unilever dropped prices (in 2009) to resist the competition of cheaper private labels. Private labels are doing well in the meantime.

While Albert Heijn is the trendsetter in the Netherlands, the brand names are fighting back: Unilever, for example, is making organic soup, Verkade 'fair trade' chocolate and so on. Genuine top brands are expected to be different to the generic brands and to that end the major manufacturers are lifting their innovation budgets. However, real success stories are increasingly rare. Even when generic brands create 'fighter brands' aimed at regaining lost ground, experience has shown that such a strategy rarely works. *Cannibalism* is often the result: the new brand takes over some of the generic brand's own territory instead of that of the competing brand. Fighter brands can also lead to loss of reputation and financial loss. Marketing, brand and the globalization of companies are clearly interrelated: critics of international business have been pointing this out for years. For Coca-Cola, the slogan 'think globally, think regionally, but act locally' is a call to decentralize and give greater autonomy to national branches in order to better predict the local needs of customers and consequently a better match between Coca-Cola and the local culture of the country in which the product is bought.

THINK REGIONALLY, ACT LOCALLY ...

McKinsey's experience suggests that even the most sophisticated multinationals must change significantly to realize Asia's growth potential. The region is as diverse as it is vast. Its markets come in a bewildering assortment of sizes and development stages, and its customers hail from a multitude of ethnic and cultural backgrounds. Their tastes and preferences evolve constantly. The speed and scale of change in Asian consumer markets can surprise even experienced executives. To meet the challenge, global companies will have to organize themselves regionally to coordinate strategy and use resources in the most efficient way while at the same time targeting the tastes of consumers on a very local level.

Adapting quickly to capture growth from direct-to-consumer channels will also probably become more important in Asia, as it already is elsewhere. In some urban clusters, for categories such as consumer electronics and apparel, online sales growth is beginning to overtake traditional channels. In Japan, sales in direct channels have exceeded those in department stores so far this year. Sales at TaoBao, China's largest online retailer, have soared to more than $14 billion annually since it was launched, in 2003. Lancôme reports that its partnership with Baidu, China's largest search engine, helped lift online sales in China by 30 percent. And AmWay has become one of China's largest consumer packaged-goods companies by selling its products door-to-door through a network of 300,000 sales representatives. As Asia's economies evolve and mature, today's frenetic, hypercompetitive, fragmented marketplace will inevitably give way to a more settled one, with fewer players enjoying larger market shares and better margins. The penetration of modern retail formats will increase. But the journey will be long and filled with twists and turns.

As the winners learn to make decisions quickly to meet the demand for speed, scale, localization, and low costs, they will test and adopt new and more entrepreneurial management practices. These companies will probably share four characteristics. Their fast, adaptive business models will leverage scale and innovation throughout Asia, and regional organizational structures and operating practices will reflect this shift. But resources will be focused locally, on the development of category, format, and brand strategies targeting the explosive growth opportunities of sharply defined urban clusters, not countries. Products tailored and priced to meet cluster-level tastes and needs will be supported by faster, lower-cost supply chains.

'In China, consumer technology and infrastructure are blending together to create a once-in-a-lifetime opportunity for companies that understand the market.'

Ed Chan, *President and CEO, Wal-Mart China*

Finally, brand marketing skills will be used to market and sell across a variety of channels. For global consumer businesses, the struggle for Asia has now been joined - cluster by cluster, city by city.

Source: *McKinsey Quarterly* 2009, Number 4

1.1.4 *The first management theories*

The first management theories formulated were about scientific management, human relations theory and management as a process theory. They will be dealt with individually in this section.

The rise of 'scientific management'

During the Industrial Revolution in the USA, management started to be based on scientific principles and experimentation – so-called scientific management, as developed by F.W. Taylor. The problems addressed included the following:

- Raising productivity
- Organizational problems in production
- Production management, cost analyses, payment systems (e.g. Taylor's 'differential piecework' plan)
- Time studies, motion studies, method studies.

efficiency

With the development of industry, efficiency became a central issue. Opportunities to raise productivity levels were being sought. Inefficient working methods (those which took up too many resources and too much time) were being replaced by objective and scientifically based norms which indicated the level of performance expected of the laborer. In this period, it was mostly engineers who laid the foundations of scientific management. Names like Taylor, the Gilbreths, Emerson and Gantt are inextricably linked with this area. F.W. Taylor (1856-1915), the 'father of scientific management', was determined to find an answer to the question of how productivity could be raised. He focused his first research on what constituted a 'fair day's work' – that is, a 'feasible, normal labor performance' for a first-class worker. He did this by using new techniques such as time, motion and method studies.

Taylor
father of scientific management

For example ...

... one of Taylor's later and best known experiments – the so-called Bethlehem experiment – concerned the loading of pig iron into train wagons. His first observations showed that about 47 tons of pig iron could be loaded instead of the 12.5 tons that had previously been the average daily capacity of a worker. To prove this, Taylor experimented with working times, rest times, weight per unit of time, working methods, tools, and so on. To establish what a 'fair day's work' was, Taylor selected a so-called Pennsylvania Dutchman (i.e. 'Deutchman'), a very strong, diligent and thrifty man who had to carry out in detail what he was told to do. As compensation he was promised a higher wage per unit of performance. The man was able to perform to suit the requirements, and many other laborers then followed suit and appeared to achieve the same level of performance.

In applying his methods, Taylor met a degree of hostility which can be explained to a great extent by the belief at that time that higher productivity would lead to unemployment. By a 'systematic soldiering' and a reduction in performance, the employees tried to protect themselves against 'arbitrary management' in the form of 'cutting the rates'.

systematic soldiering
cutting the rates

To improve the organization's production function, Taylor proposed a division of work between management and the workmen – the establishment of the concept of management. In addition, the processes of planning and work preparation were separated and an operations function was introduced for the first time. Finally, Taylor introduced the manager who had a specialized task as part of a more complicated, wider set of tasks – that is, a 'narrow' task specialization and 'functional foremanship'.

task specialization
functional foremanship

With the introduction of the differential piecework wage plan, Taylor appealed to the human need for higher wages. He supported this view by paying extra to those with enhanced performance levels, with percentages increasing the nearer workers got to top performance. As such, he made it clear that the worker, as well as the entrepreneur, could profit from higher productivity.

In terms of a 'motivational theory', Taylor considered only one stimulus to be dominant and relevant – namely, the money stimulus (via a form of piecework wage). According to the workings of this stimulus, a maximum performance would be reached. This solution to the motivational problem, as advocated by Taylor and his followers, was to prove too simplistic.

money stimulus
motivational problem

The rise of human relations theory

human relations theory
Mayo

The founder of human relations theory was the psychologist Mayo (1880-1949). This theory was based on research in the Hawthorne factories of the Western Electric Company during the years from 1924 to 1932. (Mayo was in charge from 1927 onwards.)

working conditions

In the research at the Western Electric Company, studies were made of the effects of changes in working conditions on productivity. Without exception, production appeared to rise after a change in the working conditions, regardless of the nature of that change. In the last phase of the study, when employees returned to the original working conditions – that is, shorter rest breaks, no refreshment and longer working times – the highest performance to that date was registered. It became clear that the rise in productivity could only be explained by a changed attitude to the working situation, including the following factors:

- The workers were consulted on the nature and the design of the experiments.
- A new style of management was introduced.
- A higher degree of personal freedom was experienced.
- There was personal recognition of the performances delivered.
- Workers had control over their own work.
- Workers got the feeling of being an elite, as they were considered interesting enough to warrant study.
- Loyalty developed, workers helped each other and there was an element of social contact.

style of management
informal social group

From the experiments at Western Electric Company, Mayo concluded that the morale of the workers could be affected by the style of management. Furthermore, Mayo was convinced that satisfaction in the workplace was strictly dependent on the informal social group pattern. In other words, Mayo came to the conclusion that a great number of socio-psychological factors influence the functioning of an organization and as a result managers needed to acquire social skills in order to be able to make positive use of human relationships in production groups. Technological knowledge and technical skills alone, considered the major factors by Taylor and others, were insufficient if the process of management was to attain optimal production results. As a result, the importance of a socially oriented style of leadership and management was placed at the forefront of management theory.

Later theories of motivation

Theories of management and motivation based on the notions of scientific management and the human relations theory, were further developed in the years after 1950. This will be covered in more detail in chapters 7 and 8.

The rise of management process theory

Fayol
founder of management theory

Henri Fayol (1841-1925) was described in Chapter 1 as the founder of management theory. Fayol was of the opinion that management skills could be learned. The problem was that in his time, there was no theoretical model available that could be seen as the basis for management education. The contribution of Fayol from 1916 onwards filled the gap and can be seen as the first systematic analysis of the elements of management behavior in governing a business. As indicated in section 1.5 Fayol broke down the managerial function into five essential parts:

1. Policy making and planning (prévoir)
2. Organizing (organiser)
3. Giving instructions and support during implementation (commander)
4. Coordinating (coordonner)
5. Control and if necessary adjustment (contrôler)

Characteristics of the first management theories

The first management theories had the following features in common:

- They were derived from what happened in practice on a day-to-day basis. Current daily activities were scientifically analyzed and then systematized; normative actions were not subject to the same level of discussion.

- They arose out of a situation in which it was assumed that the employer enjoyed a great deal of autonomy, being rarely affected by the world outside the organization. (In those days the employer pretty well ran the show.)
- They were directed at finding the best solution and a method which could be applied to every situation and which seemed to lead to a preferred and uniform way of management.

1.1.5 The modern schools of management and organizational theory

In addition to the first three founding schools of management theory, described in Section 1.1.4, a further nine areas of development in management and organizational theory can be identified. These are:
- Structure theory
- Revisionism
- Decision-making theory
- Communication and information theory
- Systems theory
- Strategy theory
- Environment theory
- Theory of the growth and development of organizations
- Contingency theory.

The contributions of these schools of thought are described in the course of this book, as we follow the development of management and organizational theory (without necessarily making direct and repeated reference to each of them). A brief description of each of the nine schools follows, with an indication of where a more detailed discussion can be found.

Structure theory

organizational structure
organization as an 'instrument'

Structure theorists focus attention on the rules and principles of designing – that is, building up and extending – the organizational structure. In addition, they often provide further insights, by way of empirical research, into the internal functioning of the organization as an 'instrument'. Obviously, sociological considerations will play an important role in this approach. Although organizational structure was covered in the preceding schools of thought, the subject was given far greater emphasis from 1945 onwards. (See chapters 5 and 6 on effective organization structure for more detail.)

Revisionism

Bennis
revisionism
Argyris
democracy
humanization

Bennis (1961) once characterized the scientific management movement as a way of thinking through the theme of 'organizations without people,' while the human relations movement concerned the theme of 'people without organization'. Similarly, revisionism can be described as an approach whereby the theme of 'people and the organization' becomes the focus of problem formulation. In the 1950s, earlier elements of organizational theory were being reviewed, expanded and enriched. For example, Argyris (1964) referred to an 'individual integrated into the organization.' This integration can be given a concrete form by means of task enlargement, task enrichment and task rotation (see Section 6.2), as well as by developing a new, more appropriate style of leadership (see Chapter 8). In the contributions of the Revisionism school, internal democracy and the humanization of work are placed at the forefront. This direction of thought is especially relevant to the handling of problems of organizational design and leadership style.

Decision-making theory

Decision making becomes a problem if the view is held that the individuals concerned have limited cognitive abilities and are also affected by subjective or emotional (i.e. irrational) factors. Individual decision makers cannot know all the possible alternatives for action, while subjective and irrational influences play a role in the consideration of alternatives. Since the late 1940s, the postulate of complete objective rationality that characterized the homo economicus as a decision maker has been changed by Simon (1947) into bounded rationality or subjective rationality. The notion of 'one omniscient decision maker' at the top of the hierarchy in an organization is also no longer considered valid. The focus is now on the total process of decision making instead of decision making as a decision imposed from above. The decision-making process has now been broken down into its constituent parts in a complex organization and is conceived of as a process that consists of a series of steps (see Chapter 3).

objective rationality
Simon
subjective rationality

Communication and information theory

This area of management theory concentrates on the key role of communication and information systems. Such systems have many similarities with cybernetics. Communication is a process of which feedback is considered to be an integral part. A system of 'two-way traffic' is emphasized. The feedback principle is also an essential ingredient in the managing of other processes, including the setting of targets and operational norms, regulation, adjustments and corrective actions – in short, planning and control. Communication can take various forms – oral, written, electronic, horizontal, vertical, and lateral – within each particular structure or system. (Communication structures and the effectiveness of communication and decision making are covered in chapters 3, 7, 8, 9 and 10.)

feedback principle

Systems theory

The influence of systems theory on management and organizations is said to have developed around 1950 (although systems theory was applied to biology as far back as 1932). The theory is based on the general concept of a system which can be applied in all sorts of scientific fields. In organization and management theory, the system model views organizations as 'open' systems – that is, systems which are in interaction with their surrounding environment (for example, the acquisition of energy, information and other resources and the provision of goods and services). This approach calls for renewed attention to be focused on the relationships between the organization's constituent parts and for the control of processes in the context of the whole organization. Business process redesign (BPR) – sometimes referred to as process re-engineering or business network redesign (see Chapter 10) – can be seen as a 1990s revival of these concepts from the 1950s in the era of information technology.

open systems
business process

Strategy theory

The central issue in strategy theory is striving for the survival, self-preservation or continuity of the organization in an ever-changing and complex environment. This school focuses further attention on the relationship between the organization and the surrounding environment with which it is interacting on a continuous basis. This relationship was first given prominence in the early 1960s during a period of dramatic change in the nature of the technological, societal and market environment. The relationship between organization and environment has been investigated further in the intervening years (see Chapter 4).

survival
organization and environment

Environment theory

From 1965 onwards, the external environment of the organization was seen as an independent entity, laying down the rules of engagement for the organization, in stark contrast to earlier views which had seen the organization as autonomous and setting its own rules. Environment theorists try to develop models whereby events in the environment can be observed and can become manageable. In organization and management theory, it is important not only to study the features of the environment, to which the structure and behavior of the organization can be related, but also to study the links and dependencies that exist in a network of organizations. The concepts of 'the organization as a network' and 'organizational webs' relate to inter-organizational cooperation between intelligent organizations (see chapters 2 and 4 for further detail).

network of organizations

Theory of the growth and development of organizations

phases of growth

This school of thought, which has emerged since 1970, is concerned with both the various phases of growth and development in the economic and technological sense, as well as the problems of growth in the socio-psychological sense. (For economic and technological aspects of management, see Chapter 5; for socio-psychological aspects, see chapters 1 and 8.)

Contingency theory

situationally dependent

The starting point for organizational contingency theory can be summarized in the phrase 'situationally dependent'. In other words, there is no predetermined best way of carrying out such activities as structural design or best leadership style. Recommendations, 'laws' or principles of planning, organizing and leadership have to be adapted to fit specific situations. These contingency contributions to theory, contributions which emerged after 1960, were intended as a means of reviewing and enhancing earlier insights and theories, and they were mostly based on empirical research results. Contributions to the development of theory from this school of thought appear in every chapter of this book.
Figure 1.1 relates the various schools of management and organizational theory to the core tasks of management.

Management and organizational theory: an interdisciplinary field

interdisciplinary

The theory of organization and management is by definition interdisciplinary in nature. In theory, human behavior can be divided into areas of study which can be researched as single disciplines (for example, economics, psychology, sociology). In reality, however, human behavior can only be viewed as a unity and a whole.
Those seeking practical solutions to specific problem situations will find only limited support in those single disciplines or subject-specific theories. Managers and specialists in the field need to realize that the direct application of insights from just one of the single disciplines carries risks.

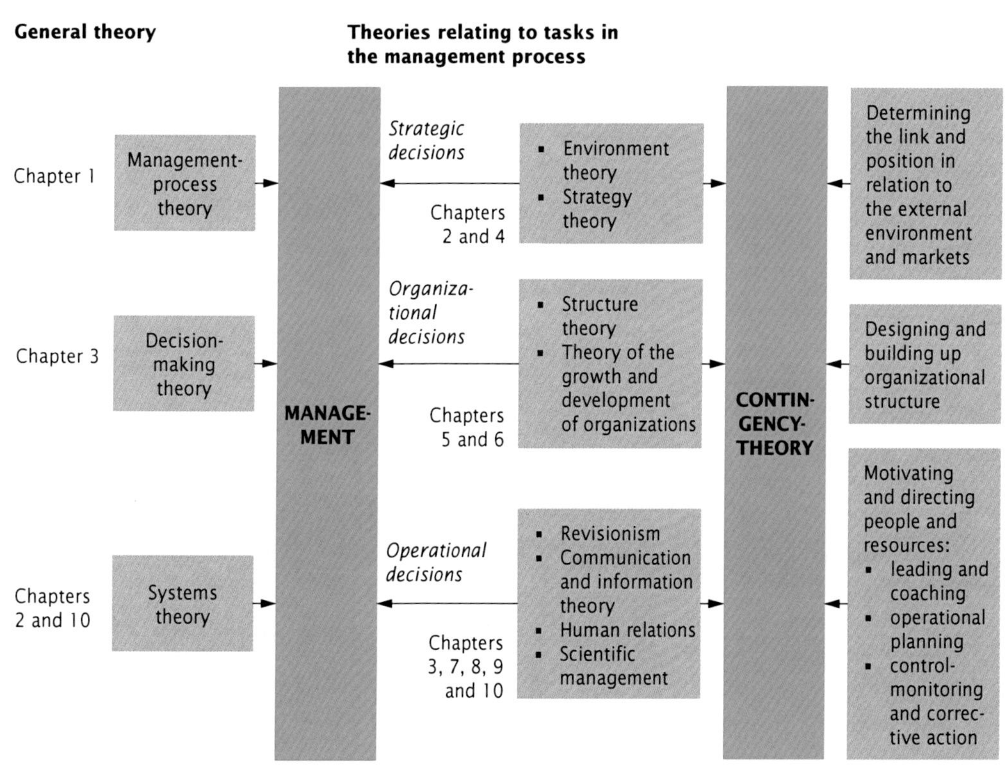

Figure 1.1
Schools of thought in relation to core tasks in management

It means that only one aspect of a problem is put under the microscope, while other aspects receive little or no attention. This does not reflect reality; it gives an unbalanced and biased view. An example would be a head of a department who has spent too little time acting as a leader during the evaluation of results, and too much time as a psychologist or lawyer. The various aspects of the problem need to be related to each other – that is, the demands that are made by the various factors first have to be integrated into the thoughts and actions of the manager. Only then can we do justice to reality.

1.2 The company: its governance structure and management

distinct entity in society

A company or corporation is a distinct entity in society with its own personality and identity formally distinguished from those of its owners. The owners are not personally liable for the company's debts; it can hold property and can do business in its own right. A company continues to exist as an entity even though the individuals who own it may constantly change. In contrast, a partnership is automatically dissolved on the death or departure of one of the owners, unless special arrangements have been made in the agreement.

control

The holders of common stock (that is, the shareholders) are the true owners of the company and have the power to control it. Directors are elected by shareholders; they select and nominate the president and other executive officers of the company, who together make up the top management team or board of management. The precise structure and the terms used to identify the levels of the organizational structure vary according to whether the system adopted is a 'one-tier' or 'two-tier' system (see sections 2.5.8 and 2.5.9).

one-tier
two-tier system
board of directors

The governance structure of a large company whose shares are widely held by the public is sometimes pictured as an hour-glass (see Fig 1.2). At the top are many thousands of shareholders. The structure then narrows down to the board of directors. (In a two-tier system (see Section 2.5.9) this would consist of non-executives only and there would be a second tier of top management in the form of a board of management or executive committee headed by the Chief Executive Officer (CEO) as president.) Below the president is a relatively small group of executive managers, a larger group of middle managers, an even larger group of front-line managers or supervisors, and, last but not least, all the other employees at the operational core of the organization.

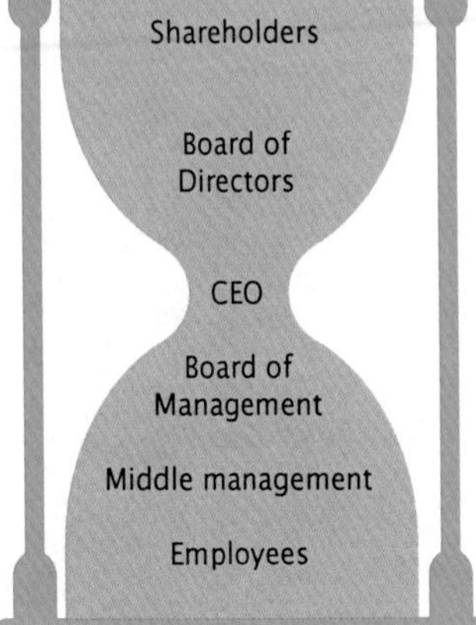

Figure 1.2
Hour-glass model of the company, indicating governance structure and management levels within the organization

The board of directors constitutes a bridge between the shareholders and society on the one hand and the managers of the corporate organization on the other. They are supposed to exercise broad supervision in terms of setting objectives, establishing policy and appraising the results of actions. As representatives of shareholders and other societal stakeholders – such as employees and unions, consumer organizations and banks – the directors must pay sufficient attention to the business, show interest in the company – from a certain distance in the case of non-executive directors – and exercise prudent control in the management of the company's affairs.

non-executive directors

In a publicly quoted company, the board of directors usually consists of three to twelve members, although it could be even larger. Small companies tend to have relatively small boards; some companies, such as banks and public government organizations, have larger boards – sometimes 20 or more members.

chief executive

Directors select and nominate (and may even dismiss) the chief executive and other executive officers, determine their remuneration and act as a court of the last resort when managers disagree. They can issue new stock to the market, they are required to authorize capital spending over a certain amount and they are involved with formulating corporate objectives and strategies such as the type of business the company should be in, should develop, should enter or should leave. They determine what proportion of the company's profits will be paid out in dividends and what proportion will be retained by the company. Under a system of co-optation they would normally nominate their own successors, with the formal nomination subject to election by shareholders.

shareholders

CEOS EARN ANNUAL BLUE COLLAR SALARY IN A DAY

According to the American Association of Labor Unions (AFL-CIO), an average chief executive officer (CEO) of a large company in the US earns 476 times more than the average production employee (blue collar worker). His Dutch colleague earns about 17 times the salary of the average man on the work floor. Elsewhere, top managers are content with less. According to AFL-CIO, the highest manager in Japan only earns 13 times the salary of a production worker. In Germany, the figure is 13 times that salary.

A new analysis by the left-leaning Canadian Centre for Policy Alternatives concludes the country's richest corporate executives pocketed an average of $40,237 by 9:04 a. m. yesterday. 'By the time your computer has finished booting up on your first day back after the New Year's holiday, the average CEO would have already banked what took the average Canadian worker an entire year's worth of work to earn,' the report states.

Source: *The Canadian Press*, January 3, 2009 (Colin Perkel)

CEO

The CEO, generally the company president in European-based companies, is likely to be the chief policy maker in the company although others are expected to make recommendations and will influence decisions. The CEO probably has the final word on most of the important questions that arise. Even in companies where organization charts show a group of apparent equals at the top, there is often one man or woman who is first among the equals – the primus inter pares.

primus inter pares

In the case of group control and group decision making at the top, some executives may be freed from day-to-day operational duties (or at least a proportion of them) in order to devote themselves entirely to overall policy issues. Such a top management structure can address issues relating to strategy, planning, organization and control and may also deal with specific functional issues which need overall coordination, thus bringing more than one mind to bear on the company's most serious problems. It is easier to consider problems with an open mind when not operationally involved and committed to previous decisions, and since members of

the top management group are more or less equals this stimulates free discussion.
This group structure may work well in some companies; in others it will be less successful. Success depends largely on the personalities of group members. While some will work well together, supplementing each other's knowledge and experience and stimulating ideas, for others, the group structure might dilute the sense of responsibility and perhaps give rise to a tendency to postpone necessary action.
Against this background, three important functions of a board of directors can be identified:
- The board provides advice and counsel.
- The board serves as a source of discipline.
- The board acts in crisis situations.

A typical meeting of a board of directors might have some of the following items on the agenda:
- Consideration of a refinancing plan
- Liquidation of obsolete or surplus plant
- Dividend action
- Consideration of an acquisition proposed by top management
- Company's position and risk of devaluation abroad
- A report on research and development programs and products

In a one-tier system, such as that common in UK companies, few if any questions are usually asked during the meeting by external non-executive directors, and questions are only rarely asked by internal executive directors. It is generally accepted that it is the role of the board of directors to do the following:
1 To establish the basic objectives, corporate strategies and broad policies of the company
2 To ask discerning questions
3 To select the president

Assessing management

Assessing management – that is, fulfilling the key function of deciding whether management is doing a good job – and making difficult decisions such as whether management has to be changed are difficult tasks for an external director.

For example ...

... in a company with 15 board members, eight of whom were insiders, earnings had declined steadily for 18 months. Concerned about the company's leadership, the seven external directors met to discuss what, if anything, should be done. Most of the directors reluctantly concluded that the president had to be replaced, but two directors put forward alternative solutions. They suggested that the president be promoted to a post created for the occasion – vice-chairman of the board; that the president be appointed head of the finance committee; or that the president be retained and the vice-president be asked to take over as chief executive officer. These suggested compromises were rejected by the other five external directors and the president was forced to resign.

For example ...

... according to one president: 'The board of directors serves as a sounding board, a wall to bounce the ball against. It is a kind of screen on major moves, whether they be acquisitions or major shifts of policy or product line – the broad decisions of the business. Board members serve as sources of information ... The decision is not made by the board, but the directors are a checkpoint for management in adding their experience and knowledge to the program.'
According to another president: 'Let's be honest: my board is a group of advisors and they know it. I select and throw up ideas, opportunities and problems to them and they respond. The board is not a decision-making body. Although there may be times when it could rise up and say no, this would be foolhardy. But I hope that we in management are never stupid enough to come up with such a proposal.'
A third president had this to say: 'One of my outside directors is a real "pro" on acquisitions and he has been most helpful to me. He does not know much about our operations or our problems, but he does know a lot about the process of identifying and acquiring other companies. Also he knows the people involved, and this is useful. There is a lot of stuff on acquisitions that is common to all acquisitions. He has been through a bundle of them and has helped me out of some tight spots – in negotiating, for example.'

owner-managers

Owner-managers of small corporations possess and exercise de jure powers of control, because for them ownership is the same as management. Owner-managers, therefore, determine what directors do or do not do. This is also often the case in family-owned companies.
In large and medium-sized companies where ownership is spread and dissipated among thousands of shareholders, the powers of ownership, while theoretically equivalent to those of the small company owner-managers, are actually minimal and almost non-existent.

presidents

Presidents of these companies have assumed and do exercise de facto powers of control over the companies for which they are responsible. To them the shareholders constitute what is in effect an anonymous mass of paper faces. Thus, presidents in these situations determine what directors do or do not do. As was found by Myles L. Mace (1986), most presidents choose to exercise their powers of control in a moderate and acceptable manner with regard to their relationships with boards of directors. However, they do make it clear, either explicitly or implicitly, that they, as presidents, control the enterprise they are heading and this is generally

non-executive directors

understood and accepted by the directors. Many non-executive directors are presidents of companies themselves and they thoroughly understand the nature and location of powers of control.

AT AMAZON, MARKETING IS FOR DUMMIES

The world's best-known companies typically spend hundreds of millions of dollars a year on advertising and marketing to build their brands. Not Amazon.com (AMZN). The giant online retailer has created one of the world's strongest brands by eschewing conventional tactics. Instead of shelling out big bucks for lavish trade shows and TV and magazine ads, Amazon pours money into technology for its Web site, distribution capability, and good deals on shipping. The result: a smooth shopping experience that burnishes the company name. 'It is pretty unprecedented that their brand has ascended so quickly without a large marketing budget,' says Hayes Roth, chief marketing officer at brand consultant Landor Associates. 'It's not about splaying their logo everywhere. They are all about ease of use.'

Amazon declined to participate in this story, in part because executives say they don't spend much time on branding. Still, the company had the biggest jump in this year's ranking of the Best Global Brands, rising 13 spots, to No. 43. One reason is that Amazon has thrived during the recession, even as other retailers have been battered and pushed into bankruptcy. The company's reputation for offering low prices, broad selection, and quality service has resonated with strapped consumers. In the past six months, Amazon reported 16% revenue growth, while most retailers saw sales fall. 'By investing back in the user experience, you get high loyalty and repeat usage,' says Sebastian Thomas, head of U.S. technology research for RCM Capital Management, an investment firm with a stake in the company.

The performance is something of a vindication for Chief Executive and founder Jeffrey Bezos. After the dot-com bubble burst, critics hammered him for investing so much in technology and physical distribution centers. Some investors called for Bezos to pull back and produce more short-term profits. Now those heavy investments are paying off big time, helping the company sell an ever-widening range of products to more than 94 million customers. Amazon's stock has more than doubled over the past three years, while the Standard & Poor's 500-stock index is up about 20%. 'Amazon has taken the long-term perspective,' says Thomas. 'Things they were criticized for have become essential assets.'

There are limits to the Amazon brand. The company hasn't had much luck selling luxury items, and some expansions, such as its shoe site Endless.com, have failed to gain much traction, prompting Amazon's bid for rival Zappos in July. 'They have not been successful in all categories,' says Citigroup (C) analyst Mark Mahaney.

Such disappointments won't stop Amazon from new experiments, though. The company plans to dabble in conventional marketing this fall, with a national TV ad campaign. But instead of hiring a hotshot ad agency, Amazon started a contest in which anyone could create their own commercial. The company picked five finalists and then asked customers to vote for their favorite. The filmmaker with the highest average customer rating, to be announced on Sept. 21, will get a $10,000 Amazon.com gift card. 'I am sure they will get a great deal of press,' says Landor's Roth. 'They won't have to spend a lot of money on media because they will get everyone else to do it for them.'

Source: *BusinessWeek*, September 17, 2009 (Spencer E. Ante)

1.3 Levels of management within an organization

levels of management

Having considered what managers and organizations are and how they are built up in layers in the governance structure, we will now examine the various levels of management within the

organization in greater detail. The levels that can usually be distinguished within companies and institutions are as follows:
- Top management
- Middle management
- Front-line management and operational employees

In the hierarchy of a company, each of these layers has its own job specification with corresponding responsibilities.
If a large number of management layers with limited scope of control and little delegation are discernible, we speak of a 'tall' or 'steep' organization. If, on the other hand, only a few management layers are present, with extensive scope of control and a high degree of delegation, we speak of a 'flat' organization (see Fig 1.3).

tall or steep organization
'flat' organization

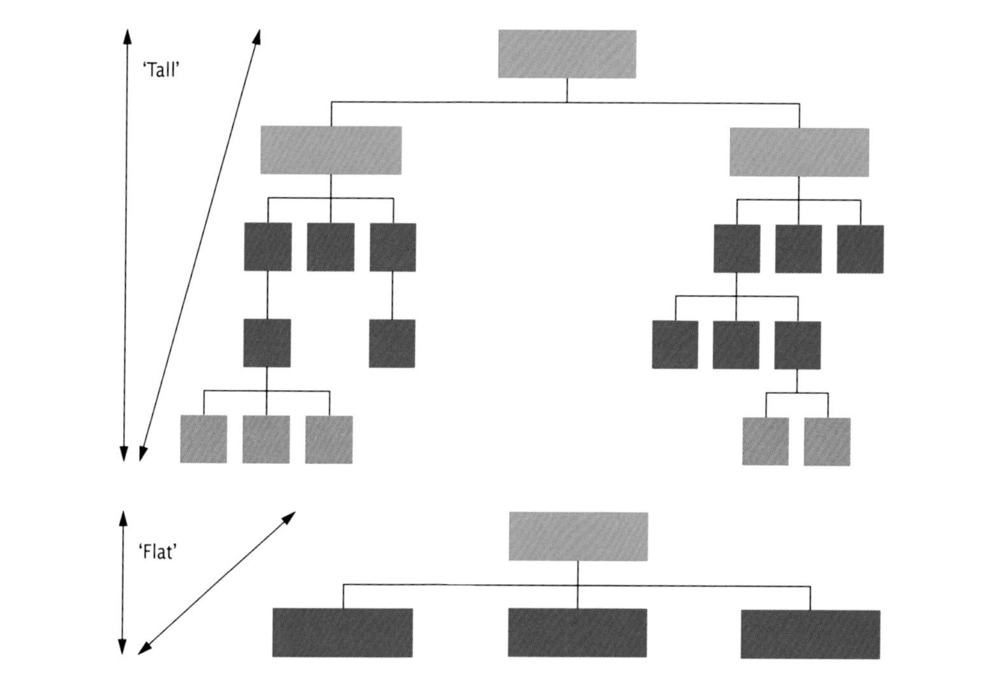

Figure 1.3 *Tall and flat organizational structures*

1.3.1 Top management tasks

top management

Top management refers to managers such as the owner-leader-manager of the company, the chief executive, the board of directors or the board of management of a hospital or a union. Figure 1.4 shows the position of top management in relation to the wider external environment and the other levels of management in the internal organization of the company.
The task of top management within the organization is to give content to the relationships between the organization and the market and the wider societal environment in such a way that the continued existence of the organization is secured. To do this, strategic decisions are needed. These decisions concern the organization's long-term mission and the route to be followed by the organization in its external positioning. Furthermore, top management needs to ensure that decisions relating to products and services target the right markets and consumer groups. Organizational and administrative arrangements must be made. Middle management can then make the required detailed organizational and operational decisions. In a company, the assignment of responsibility, tasks and authority to managers further down the line and to specialists in staff and support services takes place by means of delegation. Nevertheless, top management retains its own responsibility for the management of the entire operation of the company.

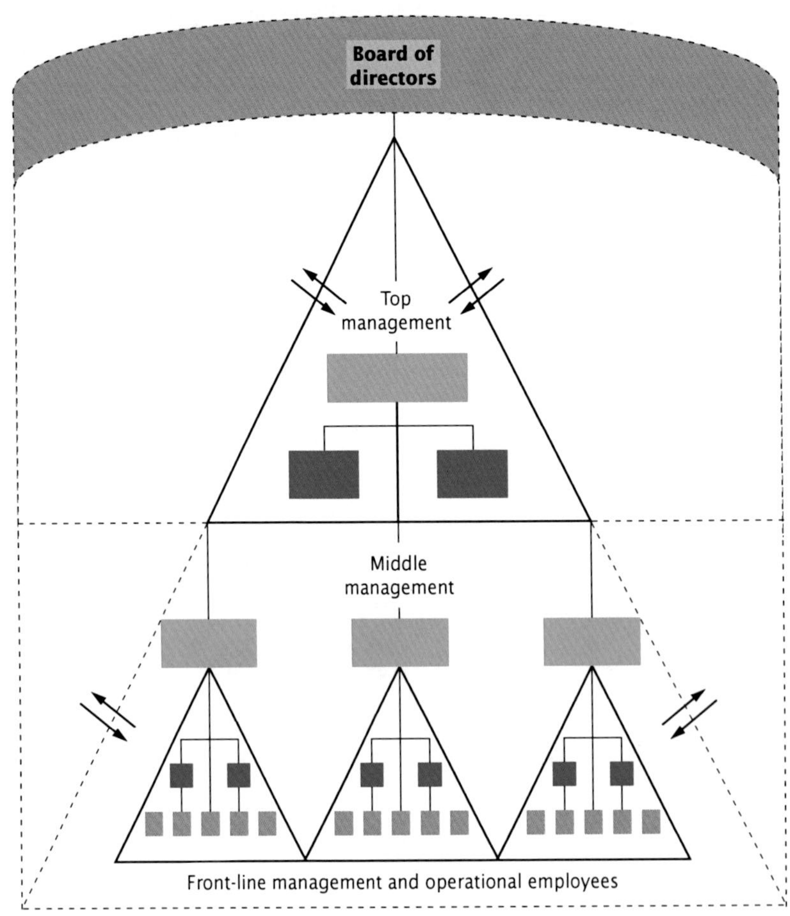

Figure 1.4 *Position of top management in relation to the board of directors, lower levels and the societal environment*

The management of a Public Limited Company (PLC) in the United Kingdom – Societé Anonyme (SA) in France, Naamloze Vennootschap (NV) in the Netherlands, and Aktiengesellschaft (AG) in Germany – has to periodically render account with regard to the fulfillment of tasks and the results reached. After audit and approval, discharge is granted. This means that after a review of policy and auditing of results and procedures, management is discharged from further obligations in relation to the period in question. In other words, it has been established that top management has done everything possible to attain a satisfactory result. Owners (shareholders) are then expected to be satisfied. On behalf of the shareholders, the board of directors exercises the ultimate supervision over management as specified in Section 1.2.

discharge

1.3.2 Middle management tasks

As top management cannot concern itself with all the activities of the organization, middle management has responsibility for the timely and accurate execution of operational activities. Within the organization, middle management has both an executive function in relation to the 'top' and a managerial function in relation to the 'bottom'. This means that middle management is positioned at the point where the interests of the various layers of the organization cross. In theory, the term 'middle management' refers to the managers positioned below the top management level – that is, assistant directors, production managers, marketing managers and sales managers – and above the front-line managers – for example, the heads of department, team leaders and supervisors.

middle management

In an organization which is built up on a divisional basis, the divisional managers are also considered to be middle management. In large organizations, therefore, a number of layers of middle management can be found. These can be referred to as 'higher middle management' and 'lower middle management'.

higher middle management
lower middle management

Higher middle management directs the activities of lower management and sometimes those of executives. The most important responsibilities of these higher middle managers are translating the strategic decisions and policy of top management and assisting in directing the operational activities. In this respect, it is particularly important for them to strike a balance between the demands from the top and the capacity of the front-line management to satisfy these demands. They perform a kind of buffer function.

buffer function

Middle management has increasingly come under fire in recent years. For that matter, expectations with regard to the position and role of middle management in organizations seem to be in a state of flux. In the one breath, middle management is being described as indispensable, in the next it is under attack and its added value is being questioned in the light of the increasing discretionary power of front line managers and even of operational employees. Its function varies according to the manager's position relative to top management and operations. As the managers move higher up the hierarchical ladder, they have more planning and organizing to do, while at the lower levels they are more concerned with instructing, motivation and operational control. As a result the position of managers in the middle is particularly difficult; they are, so to speak, pinned between the top level and the lowest levels, and are under pressure from both. From a leadership perspective (that is, from the point of view of maintaining and developing good, motivating and stimulating relationships) these middle managers seem to have a considerably tougher task than the managing director at the very top of the ladder.

front line managers

Middle management has to translate the plans of top management into the daily execution of tasks. It has the authority, to a greater or lesser degree, to direct operational activities. Operational execution is directly supervised and operational problems are identified on the spot. If these involve several departments, higher management needs to be called in.
Middle managers spend a great deal of their time on managerial activities (motivating and operational execution) and on organizing the activities of other people.
The responsibilities of middle management include formulating departmental policies, making departmental plans, maintaining network contacts for the company (both internally and externally), the timely gathering of information to help assess and amend operational results, and reporting to higher management on the execution of operations.

1.3.3 Front-line management and operational employees

Front-line managers at the operations level are directly responsible for the work carried out by other operational employees.

For example ...

... Harry Jones is responsible for a machine in a door factory. At his machine, two panels are glued together to form a door. The panels pass through a stretch of 12 meters. Three employees who have to be directed and coached by Harry work along the stretch of this machine. Harry is responsible not only for the quantity and quality of the doors, but also for the correct supply of materials, the correct supply and mix of glues and the maintenance of the machine.

Front-line managers coach and have management authority over the operational staff. The front-line manager is the immediate supervisor or 'boss' in the factory, office or research department. To the operational staff, the front-line manager is their 'real' and most direct boss. Other 'higher' bosses are indirect and often hardly visible, leading to doubts with regard to their contribution. The front-line positions are the key players in keeping the company in action and production. For this reason it is important that front-line managers know the problems of managing and organizing, are able to analyze the situations that can arise, talk about these with higher management, and translate solutions into terms of operational assignments and tasks.

self-steering autonomous process-oriented teams *management levels*

'Self-steering' or autonomous process-oriented teams are increasingly taking frontline management tasks into their own hands. In operations, resources (raw materials, components, information, etc.) are transformed into products and services. The management levels discussed earlier can be seen in this context as formulators of policy and facilitators of conditions with respect to the operational execution of tasks. They have a regulative and supportive relationship to the operational processes of production or to the rendering of services by which, for example, cars are assembled, machines are manufactured, reports are drawn up or patients are treated or cared for.

operational staff

Operational staff have to concentrate on achieving the specified level of production or demanded level of service. The required output level and the way in which the work is to be done can be decided through consultation with operational staff. The allocation of tasks and the style of leadership are major determining factors in the commitment and motivation of operational staff. (In chapters 6 and 7 we will cover this subject in more detail.)

Having examined the levels of management in an organization, for the remainder of this chapter we will consider the demands that are made of managers. Among other issues, attention will be given to decision making, time management, the workload of managers, and the culture of the organization.

1.4 Core activities of managers

top management *middle management* *front-line management*

So far we have considered management as a group of managers in an organization who are placed above the operational staff, and have separated them into top management, middle management and front-line management. In principle, these levels apply to all forms of organization – to both profit-oriented and non-profit-making organizations.

1.4.1 Similarities between management levels

The most important task common to all managers is the direction of people and resources in an organization. According to Mintzberg (1973), managers divide their time between the following:

- Interpersonal activities
- Information-related activities
- Decision-making activities

Interpersonal activities

network of relationships

Managers manage people. They are responsible for progress and for the results from processes which are under their authority. By maintaining network relationships, they are able to control the processes as well as promote the interests of the group, both inside the organization at a higher level as well as to the outside world. The building up of a formal and informal network of relationships inside as well as outside the organization is an integral part of this activity.

Information-related activities

To control an organization, managers need to have information at their disposal. This is why managers need to be kept informed of changes within the organization and the performance of each department. In turn, managers communicate with other members of the organization, stakeholders and other interested parties. Information is essential to enable managers to act and intervene appropriately in an ever-changing environment.

Decision-making activities

As head of a department, group or unit of the organization, the manager has to give direction to the policies that are to be implemented. Based on information gathered and by maintaining personal contacts, the manager will consider the opportunities and threats in the environment and, with due consideration of the strengths and weaknesses of the organization, will translate these into management decisions. The manager has to be constantly prepared to make decisions about the optimal use of people and resources in order to realize the goals. Managers cannot oversee everything, however: managers need their employees.

1.4.2 Differences between management levels

From the activities described above, it will be obvious that the manager spends a significant amount of time communicating with organization members and people and institutions outside the organization. However, this varies at each management level.

Top management

The demands made of top managers vary. The following are likely to rank highly as managerial qualities in the years to come:

- leadership qualities
- ability to manage strategy and change
- negotiating and influencing skills
- a focus on both the employee and productivity

While strategy, marketing and sales were important aspects of the traditional approach – a functional one – and were the main company departments, the future is likely to see the emphasis change towards attracting employees, creating employee loyalty and engaging the interest of the employees. Furthermore, researchers indicate that in the twenty-first century, hostile takeovers, protectionism and company espionage will make the life of a top manager more difficult. This explains in part the relevance of negotiating and conflict resolution.

excellent communicator
clean past
politician

The top manager will have to be an excellent communicator who can inspire employees. Furthermore, he or she will have to display creativity, enthusiasm, and an open mind. The top person will also have to have a 'clean past' in the ethical sense, and last but not least, the top manager will have to know how to be a politician, both inside and outside the company.

Since the start of the financial crisis in 2008, the following six managerial aspects have become crucial to top management and can be expected to dominate it even beyond 2010:

1. cutting of costs
2. a focus on growth
3. firmer governance
4. the demise of the Anglo-Saxon model
5. moral leadership
6. reflection

Source: *Management Scope*, February 2009

While cutting costs is a reflex that comes naturally to organizations, its challenge is to operate more intelligently and innovatively and to create growth by calling on the creativity and talents of their employees. Tighter control and more particularly, greater involvement on the part of the board of directors in directing the top management level, should lead to a better understanding of how to run a business. The ability to look critically at one's own performance is a much-needed aspect of this. Shareholder value and a short-term focus based on the financial denominators will disappear as the primary goals, being replaced by a broader and long-term perspective which includes value adding on the basis of reputation and a

customer orientation. Past financial scandals (those involving Enron, Ahold and others) have increased the need for credibility, moral leadership and authentic leadership. If we take stock of things and learn from the past we will be able to clean up our organizations and hopefully make them healthier and improve the way they operate. If not, the cynical cry of 'on to the next crisis!' will be self-fulfilling. We must learn from the 'leadership lessons for hard times' and realize the necessity of rebuilding corporate reputations.
Most particularly, what is required of future leadership is that it be *inspiring leadership*. (See also Section 8.2.)

Middle and front-line management

middle management

The largest group of managers is the level under the top management level of the organization – middle management. Middle management is important since it has to implement general policies and give direct *leadership* to the implementation of operations. The most important tasks of middle management are as follows:

- Leading and controlling activities
- Taking operational decisions
- Passing on information from the top down and from the bottom up
- Planning
- Organizing activities
- Motivating employees
- Maintaining internal and external contacts
- Reporting
- Generating new activities

With the tendency of top management to delegate authority, an increasing number of policy formulating tasks are being placed within the higher middle-management ranks. In organizations where change is taking place, middle management has a key position. After all, while top management may devise ambitious plans, middle management will have to take these plans to the employees and motivate them to put them into action.

1.4.3 Managers and types of decisions

We have already stated that managers spend a certain amount of their time in decision-making activities. We shall now consider the link between the position of a manager within the organization and the nature of the decisions to be taken and the amount of time spent on decision-making activities. (Decision making is discussed fully in Chapter 3.)

types of managerial decisions

The decisions that need to be made in organizations vary widely in nature. In theory, three types of managerial decisions can be identified:

- Strategic decisions
- Organizational (or administrative and tactical) decisions
- Operational decisions

Strategic decisions

Strategic decisions concern selection of the objectives or goals of an organization, the choice and positioning of product-market activities, the choice of resources and the route by which the goals are attained. (See Chapter 3 for more detail.)
Since these decisions concern the entire organization, they need to be made at the highest level. This does not mean, however, that employees at the lower managerial levels can be excluded from decision making. On the contrary, they are a necessary source of information. The final decisions are nevertheless made by the board of directors (or board of management in some companies). These decisions are characterized by a large degree of uncertainty and a lack of available information. They are mostly one-off decisions with far-reaching implications, such as a major investment in a new production process, a merger, the closure of a subsidiary or the development of a new product.

Organizational decisions

Sometimes referred to as administrative or tactical decisions, organizational decisions concern choices relating to the design of an organizational structure and the allocation of the firm's resources – that is, structuring the flow of information and tasks and responsibilities in relation to the members of the organization. (See chapters 5 and 6 for more detail.) The structure of an organization may need to be changed as a result of changes in strategy, or due to problems which arise during implementation of operational tasks. In searching for the most appropriate organizational structure design, choices have to be made from various forms of division of work and coordination. Tasks and authority may have to be allocated under changing conditions – for example, due to technological developments. It may be necessary to set up a new information system or to develop new procedures and guidelines.

Operational decisions

These decisions concern the daily arrangements relating to the operational execution of tasks and optimization of potential resources within the organization. Operational decisions can be made at lower levels of the organization. Were this not the case, overloading would result at the top and delays would occur in the decision-making process. These decisions include those which relate to repetitive operational problems, possibly of a routine nature. Operational targets and levels have to be determined and operational (day-to-day) plans made. Finally, there are the daily regulation and control elements of recording and reporting – for example, in terms of inventory levels, sales figures and cost budgets. (These aspects will be discussed in more detail in Chapter 9.)
In Fig 1.5, the types of decisions and the time and attention devoted to them are related to the levels of management.

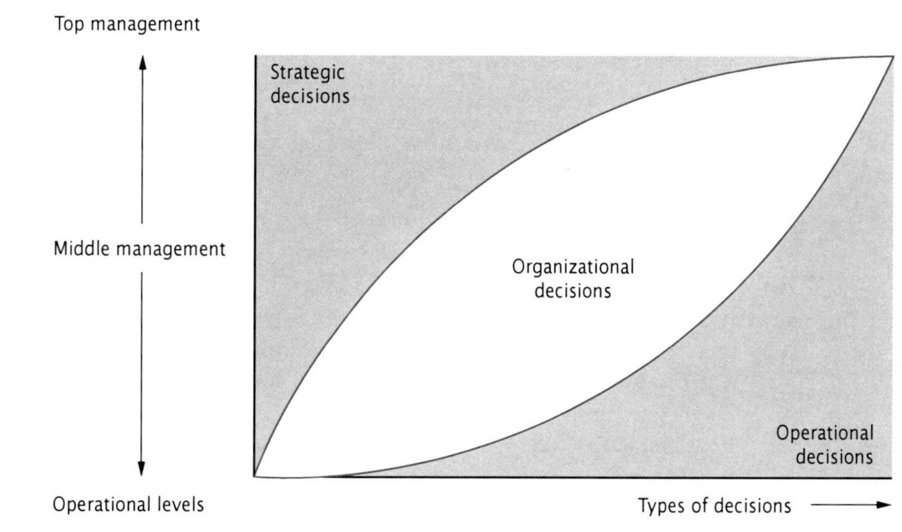

Figure 1.5 *Types of decisions in relation to managerial levels*

Preparation for, the eventual making of, and the ability to implement decisions usually call for deliberation, consultation and participation. Whether the decision results in its intended goal depends on the quality of the decision as well as on the degree of its acceptance by the members of the organization. This can be expressed in the following way:

E(ffect) = Q(uality) × A(cceptance)

In chapters 3, 6 and 8 aspects of the acceptance of decision making and management will be discussed in more detail.

1.4.4 Policy decisions and business goals

The owner-manager or the appointed managing director has to make policy decisions with regard to product range, direction of growth, location, legal company form, company size (including personnel and financial considerations), investment in and the acquisition of production resources, spatial planning in terms of technical layout and possible collaboration with other companies. A mature company will have staff specialists available within the company to assist it in the making of these decisions, though it may be necessary to consult external professionals in specialized areas. The aim of consultation is to find answers to questions like the following:

- Should we strive for growth? To what extent and in which direction do we want to grow?
- Should we devote ourselves to a specific product, to a specific market segment/niche, or to a specific geographical market area?
- Should we focus on low prices, low costs or superior quality?
- Should we stay small and independent, or seek some form of collaboration?

strategic plan

The answers that are found to such questions form the basis of the business policy which is to be implemented. In mature companies such policies are often made explicit, are written into the mission statement and company objectives, and are worked out in a strategic plan (see Chapter 4). In small companies, goals such as the proposed direction and size of the business are often implicit; they are in the head of the owner-entrepreneur-manager and take shape in actions rather than being established in formally worded company documents. However, in small and medium-sized companies, a plan needs to be drawn up for the purposes of getting company credit or financing expansion activities. Furthermore, external directors in small companies may 'force' management to make company policy explicit in its plans and budgets for the medium and long term by posing explicit questions.

It is the ongoing task of management to see to it that relationships with the organization's external environment as well as with forces inside the organization are such that the survival of the company is assured as much as possible. This means that the organization's management has to take continuous account of what is happening in and around the organization and has to react to matters such as conflicts between departments, a slowdown in decision making, a rise in staff turnover, increases in the prices of resources, a scarcity of labor, the supply of new materials and substitutes or technological breakthroughs.

societal and market environment

In this, management has to realize that these kinds of changes and forces are occurring in an existing organizational framework and within a societal and market environment in which departments, a works council, unions, suppliers, banks, and local and national governments or action groups may exercise their influence. An owner-manager of a small company or the professional management of a large company has to take all of these factors into account in drawing up the company's mission statement, in determining goals and setting out a course of action, choosing the design of the organization and obtaining and employing resources required for the task.

1.4.5 Objectives, goals, policies and planning

policies
planning
plan

To ensure effective and efficient functioning of an organization, all relevant commercial, technological, financial and personnel considerations must be taken into account. Policies have to be formulated and planning has to take place at the various levels of the organization.

The drawing up of a business policy involves the formulation and implementation of ways and means by which management intends to realize its goals. Once the goals are set, a plan has to be formulated which sets out the methods, time scale and resources with which the goals are to be attained.

The difference between a company's success and failure is often its ability or inability to appreciate the demands of its markets and its own limitations with regard to what it wishes to company strategy

achieve. This appreciation of the demands of the market (external appraisal) and the organization's own capabilities and will (internal appraisal) is the essence of company strategy (see Chapter 4). A strategy includes statements about the goals a company wants to attain, the ways in which this will be achieved, and the resources that will be required. During the process of strategic decision making and policy making in companies, goals are determined and policies are drawn up which relate to, among other things:

- Market position – ranges of products or services, nature of customers and clients and geographical markets
- Productivity and added value
- Profitability or the relationship between costs and revenues
- Societal responsibility – employment, the environment, etc.
- Growth and continuity
- Income, working conditions, prestige, status and authority of the managerial and operational staff of the organization.

objectives
methods and resources
organizational structure

In a strategy and business plan, management stipulates the objectives, goals and the guidelines for the activities which will have to take place. A policy stipulates the methods and resources which will be needed if the company goals are to be attained. It is also necessary to determine which organizational structure will be best for the attainment of the company's goals. In this respect, planning precedes commercial, technological, financial and personnel considerations. Planning is the systematic preparation and adjustment of decisions which are directed at realizing future goals. Plans have the following functions:

- They describe the goals which need to be attained by a company and company departments.
- They establish the measurements for attaining these goals.
- They pass down the personnel and financial resources which are necessary for attaining these goals.
- They state the time span during which the set goals will have to be attained.

When drawing up a plan, decisions have to be made regarding *what* has to be produced, *where* this will happen, *how* this will happen, *when* this has to happen, *how much* has to be made, *who* will do this and *with what resources* (see also Chapter 9).
If an organization does not have all the necessary resources itself, it has to look externally, perhaps through measures such as collaboration with another company. Decisions will have to be made relating to the way in which the resources can effectively and economically be spent. Plans need to be based on adequate and reliable data with regard to the future. During the operational implementation, plans need to be monitored and adjusted. Unexpected developments and sudden changes naturally give rise to reviews and adjustments.

1.5 Managers: born or made?

It is often said that 'leaders are born, not made'. There is certainly an element of truth in this statement as some leadership qualities are, of course, part of our genetic make-up. However, leadership always takes place within a socio-cultural context. As a result, in the area of policy development and the daily operational control of the organization, a great deal can be learned. An important managerial responsibility is helping the organization to realize its goals. At the same time, the manager has to see to it that the personal ambitions of fellow workers are utilized to optimum advantage and that the expectations of team members are met. However, while staff can be satisfied and contented, this does not say anything about results. The manager always has to strike the right balance between the interests of employees and the attained results.

management effectiveness

In assessing a manager, the issue is always management effectiveness – that is, the ability to use and handle resources and instruments which contribute to the attainment of organizational goals. This requirement holds true for all managers at the various levels of management. At each organizational level, the relative differences in the capabilities of managers are then of further importance.

1.5.1 Manager or leader?

At the various organizational levels, various managerial skills are required in varying degrees. As far back as 1916, Fayol explained how the relative importance of the manager's various skills was related to the manager's position in the company hierarchy and the size of the company itself. Fayol stated that for lower company managers, their technical capability was of prime importance, while for the higher managers it was their management capability that was significant. In a small company the technical capability will dominate; as the company becomes larger, the managing capabilities become relatively more important.

technical capability
management capability

The differences between managers and leaders – the subject of many studies – will be covered in detail in Chapter 8. For now, we will simply make a few comments. According to some studies, leaders work actively and generate ideas. They are emotionally involved, create tension, are focused on ideas, are visionary and evoke feelings of appreciation and hatred. Managers, on the other hand, concentrate on the careful administration of work to be done. If necessary, they consciously manipulate. They are focused on people and are settled in their working environment. Managers are compromising when directing their efforts towards the objectives of the organization, whereas leaders may want to break up and transform that same organization. The manager keeps things going and controls the operations of the company; the leader strives for change.

HAPPY COMPANIES

The best managers are those who listen to their employees. Strangely, though, there are still managers who don't do this. We need friendly, modest people at the top.

Why don't all companies coddle their employees the way Google does? Just about everybody has heard about the yoga and sports areas in the offices of the Internet company, not to mention the table-top football, the canteens that serve food that's good for you and the employees who are allowed to spend some of their time (or as some would even say, 'have to spend') doing 'things that they like doing'.

Zappos, the American Internet-based shoe shop has a similar philosophy. As chairman of the board Tony Hsieh (pronounced 'shey') said in *The New Yorker*, he is aiming to create such a fantastic company culture that everyone will love going to work. He wants to spread *zappiness*: happiness Zappo-style. 'We are more than a team: we are family', as zappos.com puts it. And that family feeling extends to its customers. Employees are prepared to talk for hours to people who ring the free customer service line.

Like Google, Zappos is highly successful. Founded in 1999, the company has now become the world's biggest Internet-based shoe shop – the Amazon.com of footwear, you could say. Amazon noticed this too. In July, this bookseller giant bought the footwear giant for 850 million dollars, promising to keep Zappo's business structure intact.

At Semco, a successful Brazilian manufacturer, the employees are allowed to determine their own jobs and the time that they do their work. Not only that: they also have a say in what they earn.

Source: Science section, *NRC Handelsblad*, 7/8 November 2009

charismatic leader

When managers appear to show shortcomings or even fail, the demand for a charismatic leader becomes louder. In other words, a leader inspires and provides such a lively and appealing image of the future that employees are motivated by it in such a way that they are prepared to accept change. In his book on leadership, Kotter (1988) considers that even the leader will have to have knowledge of the field and will have to have demonstrated past success. In this respect perhaps the differences between the leader and the manager are fading.

1.5.2 Management capabilities: knowledge, skills and attitude

directing and control
communication
interpersonal effectiveness

In the execution of the various management tasks, the main issues are directing and control, communication and interpersonal effectiveness.

- In order to be effective in directing and control, we need to make time for 'managing from behind the desk': reading notes and extracting key points from them, making choices in the drawing up of the annual budget, putting on to paper the headlines for a business plan, drawing up and reading letters, sorting and prioritizing, and so on.
- *communication* In order to be effective in communication, mastery of all forms of oral and written language skills is required: attending meetings effectively or leading them efficiently, giving presentations, writing speeches, conducting a follow-up conversation, drafting notes and many other forms of non-verbal communication.
- *interpersonal effectiveness* Interpersonal effectiveness has to do with leadership, persuasive power, influence and assertiveness.

What competencies does a good manager need?

It will already have become clear that in order to be able to do their job successfully, managers need to have many, and sometimes extremely diverse qualities. Some people still believe that these qualities can only be developed by trial and error. Although this statement is partly true, it is important to realize that such a way of learning is more difficult, time consuming and costly than it need be. It is far better if, at an early stage, the manager can draw on existing knowledge and experience based on the best practices of others. The areas of knowledge which managers need to cover can be divided up as follows:

areas of knowledge

- *knowledge of planning, organizing and governing* Knowledge of planning, organizing and governing an organization. Managers need to have knowledge of the areas of *planning*, *organizing* and *governing* an organization or part of it, otherwise their management will be of little use. They may be able to hide their weaknesses in these areas for a long time and with considerable effort, but in the end they will always fail.
- *knowledge of people organizational behavior* Knowledge of people and organizational behavior. Managers work among and with people and are to a great extent influenced by the behavior of other people. In turn the behavior of managers influences those with whom they work. They should therefore at least be able to recognize normal behavior patterns of people in the work environment and know how people are likely to react to their actions. Only then can managers expect their actions in the areas of coordinating and motivating to be generally effective.
- *knowledge of technology and the field* Knowledge of technology and the field. Managers cannot completely do without knowledge of the specific field in which they work. The head of accounts will need to have some knowledge of bookkeeping. It is impossible to imagine a successful marketing manager with no knowledge whatsoever in the areas of sales, distribution and advertising. Managers need to have, as is often mentioned in recruitment advertisements, some demonstrable technical knowledge of the department which they will be managing and of the sector in which they will work. As the manager climbs further up the hierarchical ladder, the work becomes less operational and the importance of specific technical knowledge diminishes.
- *knowledge of the organization* Knowledge of the organization in which they work. It speaks for itself that managers without knowledge of their own organization, its goals, and its way of operating, can hardly operate successfully. They have to be fully informed about the history of the organization and also of

its policies, philosophy and culture, strengths and weaknesses, problems, place in the sector, image, etc. It is clear that the only source of this kind of information is the organization itself. If the initiative for gathering this information does not come from the institution, the wise manager will acquire it through his or her own initiative.

BOX CLEVER AND KEEP YOUR STAR PERFORMERS HAPPY

Something else to worry about. When business is bad, your best people get twitchy. They struggle. They start looking around for something better to do. 'Clever, creative people want to go to work and have fun,' says Gareth Jones, a fellow of the centre for management development at London Business School (LBS). 'They don't like gloomy workplaces.'

We have heard enough for one lifetime about the 'war for talent'. But this doesn't mean that leaders can ignore who is on their team. Last week I went to a seminar hosted by the Corporate Research Forum which, thankfully, injected new life into that increasingly tired debate over talent, knowledge workers and the rest of it. It is time to reframe this debate. What we should be thinking about, you see, are clever people.

Who are these clever people? What are they like, and why are clever people difficult to lead and manage? Having researched the subject, Prof Jones (and Goffee) has come up with a 10-point check list for managers.

1. Cleverness is central to their identity. They take negative feedback badly.
2. Their skills are not easily replicated. Not many people can do what they do.
3. They know their worth.
4. They ask difficult questions.
5. They are organizationally savvy. Their projects will get funded.
6. They are not impressed by corporate hierarchy. Job titles don't mean much to them, but status does.
7. They expect instant access to the chief executive. If they don't get it they may lose interest, slipping rapidly from obsession in their work to indifference.
8. They are well connected both inside and outside the organization.
9. They have a low boredom threshold.
10. They won't thank you. They do not feel they need to be led.

But there is also good (and slightly less daunting) news for business leaders. Clever people need organizations. Their work usually involves complex tasks that are performed in a team setting. They want 'a high degree of organizational protection', Goffee and Jones say. And they are more effective when they are well led.

Source: *Financial Times*, May 26, 2009 (Stefan Stern)

Other characteristics of good managers

The manager has to be incorruptible – to have a certain measure of self-knowledge and sincerity. Employees will expect promises and expectations to be met. Managers have to set an example. Employees will not so much do as managers *say*, but rather they will do as they *do*.

creativity *innovative*

Creativity and the ability to be innovative are necessary, especially in a changing environment where the manager will always be expected to solve new and unfamiliar problems. Creativity will help to generate new ideas, solutions and approaches.

expert knowledge

As we have mentioned more than once already, thorough expert knowledge is of importance. In this respect, of course, a great deal can be learned: managers have to intervene, make proposals, come up with solutions and give instructions. When employees recognize a manager's expertise, he or she will be accepted as leader more quickly and his or her motivational influence on employees will be greater.

social abilities

The social abilities of a manager are also important. It is necessary to be able to manage relationships (especially in teams in which employees work closely together) as conflicts, disappointments, tensions and rivalry will occur. The manager needs to have social skills in order to resolve these situations tactically or find ways of avoiding or reducing them.

social skills

Managers need to be driven by and totally devoted to the task of managing. Their active acceptance of the organization's goals should be seen as an example to employees. The steps which they take to serve the organizational goals – even if not popular – have to be accepted by employees without regard for their own interests.

degree of self-confidence

The manager needs to have a certain degree of self-confidence. He or she needs to support organizational policies and exude an aura of calm and confidence. The courage to take risks, the ability to delegate and readiness for action are all important skills. No one best solution exists; there are always other possible solutions. Once a manager has decided on a solution, he or she will have to take the risks associated with that choice.

MEN AND WOMEN AT WORK: CAN WE TALK?

Do men resent powerful women? One of the most intriguing statistics in 'A Woman's Nation,' the recently released survey by Maria Shriver and the Center for American Progress, is this: 69% of women think men resent women who have more power than they do. Only 49% of men agree. Who knows who's right? What we know for sure is that men and women can't agree about power–and aren't very comfortable talking candidly about it.

To research *Getting to 50/50*, the book I wrote with Joanna Strober, we found that fear of candid talk is the biggest logjam blocking the progress of women in the workplace. For one thing, men shy away from giving women honest feedback. One male CEO of a tech start-up told us: 'Every senior male executive I know has been threatened with discrimination charges regardless of the goodness of their track record.' He added, 'I've seen it make cynics out of a lot of men who started out very differently.'

All of us–men and women alike–contribute to this problem. In our politically correct workplaces, discussing male/female differences has become so taboo that the topic is broached only in heated moments, when colleagues let loose their true opinions about gender and power.

Source: *Fortune Magazine*, November 16, 2009 (Sharon Meers)

1.5.3 Expressive and inspiring: developing leadership in high performance organizations

behavioral traits

Future leaders are assessed particularly with regard to the following behavioral traits: their ability to develop a vision and map out a strategy, whether they are geared towards getting results, whether they can create high performance teams and develop entrepreneurial skills, whether they are geared towards change and whether they have a customer orientation. The things that should be looked for when scouting for and selecting future talent are whether they are visionary, can take the initiative, can cope with complex problems and are flexible. To be able to unite business culture and people and get results and bring innovation requires team skills and leadership skills: preconditions for inspiration and motivation. In combination, these skills will achieve results in which innovation and change are the recurring factors. It is important to consider both the business and the human aspects. In production terms, what this means in particular is that managers should have trust in people and should give others the opportunity to expand in a business sense.

inspirational leadership

Passion and generating energy are key factors in this age of inspiration and inspirational leadership. It is of the utmost importance that a top manager should inspire others and energize them to grow and to develop into people with whom customers would like to do business, to turn them into team players who are involved within the company but who are at the same time right in the middle of society, and into leaders who work hard alongside their staff, are focused on results, have their employees at heart, but do not shy away from making hard decisions. This is the picture that comes to mind in a time when everybody is talking about high performance organization and high performance jobs throughout all levels of the organization. The new top people must be 'energized' (in other words, be bouncing with energy) and they must endorse the motto 'to change the company, start with the leader'. It is a challenge for companies to find such people. Instead of the aloof top manager who manages on the basis of figures, there is at the moment a strong need for a new type of leadership, of collaboration and making people enthusiastic.

high performance organization
high performance jobs

This emphasizes once more the fact that the essence of managing lies in creating an inspirational vision and encouraging internal and external collaboration. This is particularly relevant if the aim is to turn a company into a network organization, in which alliances and other forms of collaboration are crucial. The important things are integrity, involvement, authenticity, consistent behavior and adherence to the set priorities and the course that has been mapped out. These characteristics are constantly referred to in recent publications on the 'fundamental state of leadership' and how to reach it, and previously on 'level 5 leadership' (Jim Collins, 2001) as well as on managing one's own 'human sigma' or 'your own human habits' (Covey, 1989 and 2004) and other challenging essays on intrinsic and exceptional leadership. Leaders need to exceed themselves, as it were, and while taking account of others, perform at an exceptional level. At a time of 'performance management' and the creation of a 'high performance organization' leadership is a basic requirement (see also 8.1.4 and 8.2).

inspirational vision
internal and external collaboration

1.6 The management process and core activities

In this introductory chapter we have explained the concepts 'organization', 'leader', 'manager' and 'management' in that we have shown what organizations are and what managers can experience at the various levels of the organization. We have been considering management as a group of people. We now move on to consider management as a process and to draw up a picture of the various management tasks. (These will be discussed in greater detail in chapters 4 to 10.)

1.6.1 Management as a process

Fayol

Henri Fayol (1841-1925) is considered to be the founder of modern management-process theory. Fayol stated that management could be learned. However, the problem was that in his time no theory existed on which management education could be based. With the first systematic analysis of the elements of the managerial function, Fayol met this need himself in 1916. Fayol broke down management (as an activity) into five essential parts:

activity

- Policy making and planning (prévoir)
- Organizing/designing organizational structure (organiser)
- Giving instructions and assistance during the execution of tasks (commander)
- Coordinating (coordonner)
- Controlling and making adjustments, if necessary (contrôler)

Taking Fayol's idea as a starting point, management can be said to always contain the elements depicted in Fig 1.6.

The figure shows that management in its broad sense is a logical series of activities. The concept of 'leading' refers especially to giving orders, motivating people and checking activities which have been performed by other people – that is, managing in the 'narrow' sense (as it is only one of the managerial functions). Managing in the 'broad' sense also includes other management functions, such as determination of the organization's mission

managing in the narrow sense
managing in the broad sense

and course, positioning and the maintenance of external contacts. By seeing management as a process, we are better able to study the activities of 'management' as a group of people and gain insight into the function of management and the role and position of the manager within the organization.

Management is concerned with the process of planning, organizing, governing and controlling – a process in which the skills and talents of the managerial team play an important role.

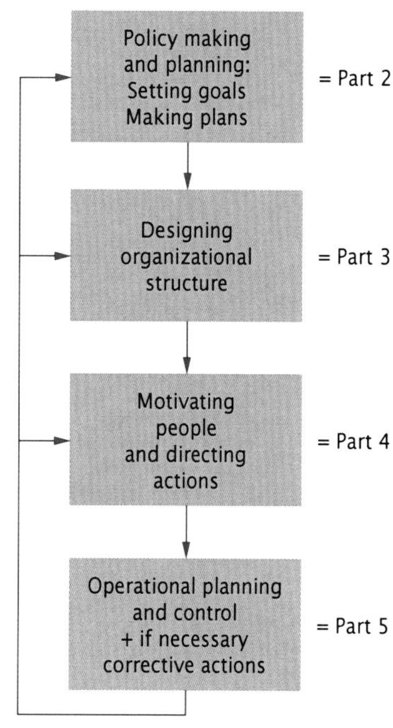

Figure 1.6
A logical series of steps

1.6.2 The management cycle and core activities

communication

Good communication is demanded for the execution of all management tasks. All managers have to be able to explain their reasons, intentions and decisions to others in such a way that they will be understood. To achieve this in practice, managers need to have an insight into communication as a process. In the future, communication will become increasingly important to managers as they perform their job. Managers will have to understand others as well as they understand themselves.

The management cycle: areas of knowledge for managers

effective performance
planning

We should never consider the core tasks of the managerial process as independent activities, even though they are described separately. Effective performance of each of these functions depends on the way in which the others are being performed. Effective coordination, for example, is impossible without good planning, while good communication is strongly dependent on good organization. However, the sequence of planning, organizing, giving orders, controlling and adjustment does take place within a sequential time frame.

control cycle
decision making
coordinating
communicating

A business plan is the basis for organizing, while task implementation and output are, in their turn, the basis for daily adjustment of the control cycle. The results of the adjustment and corrective process provide in turn information on the necessity to revise plans. Decision making, coordinating and communicating are functions which are used in planning and organizing as well as managing. The interrelationship between the functions is depicted in Fig 1.7.

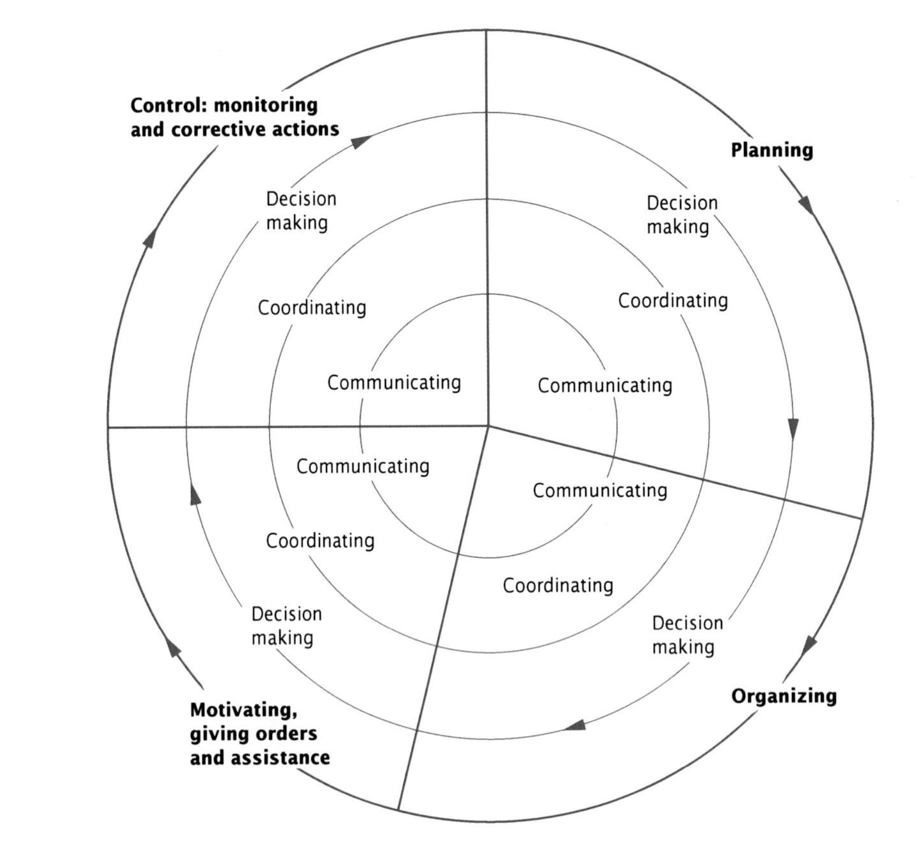

Figure 1.7
Management cycle showing communication with other people at the core

1.7 Process model of an organization

management and organizational processes

Management and organizational processes direct the operational functions in an organization, and where manufacturing processes are concerned, effect an actual transformation of resources derived from the environment. In other words, manufacturing processes (and particularly service-provision processes) bring about a technical transformation which adds value, after which products or services are made available to the environment. This process is depicted in Fig 1.8.

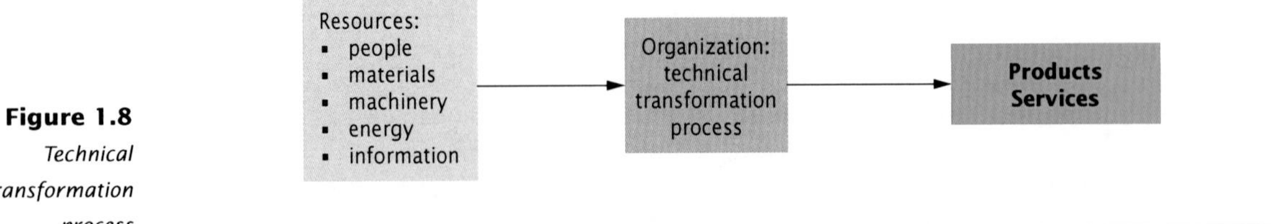

Figure 1.8
Technical transformation process

The technical transformation process can, for example, produce screws or cars, and various service-provision processes can result in credit being granted, patients cared for or reports written.

These operations are managed by a managerial process in which decisions are made about what products will be supplied, what services rendered, and how, by whom and where the necessary activities will be undertaken. This flow of management information is illustrated in Fig 1.9.

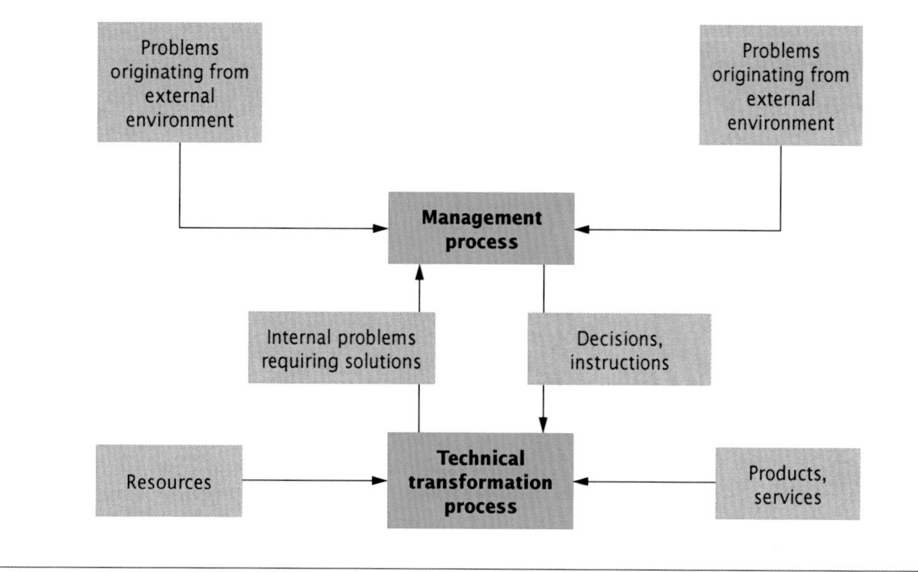

Figure 1.9
Simple process model of an organization

1.7.1 A more detailed process model

Management processes can be defined as the direction given to the primary operational processes or main organizational processes. These processes are illustrated in greater detail in Fig 1.10.

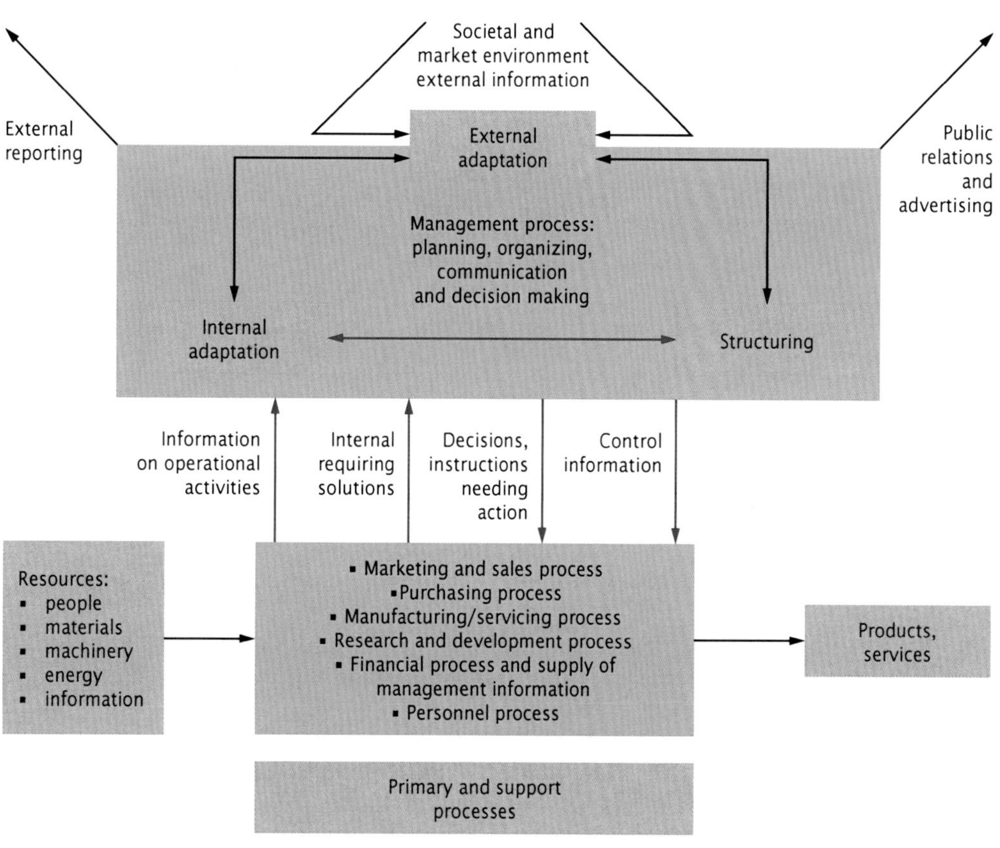

Figure 1.10
More detailed process model of an organization

The following processes have already been identified above:
- Primary or main processes
- Secondary or supporting processes
- Managerial or regulatory and condition-setting processes

Primary processes or main processes are comprised of the activities that make a direct contribution to the manufacturing of a product or the provision of a service (for example purchasing, production and sales). In other words, the primary processes are those processes from which an organization derives its existence.

Secondary processes or supporting processes consist of those activities required to maintain the primary processes or to facilitate production. These tasks are not performed for their own sake but to maintain the effectiveness and continuity of the primary processes.

Managerial or regulatory and condition-setting processes involve all those activities that determine goals for and give direction to the primary and secondary processes. Managerial processes set the conditions according to which value is added, and they ensure that the organization is directed towards the attainment of the organizational goals.
Consequently, the activities with which an organization creates value can be divided into primary, supporting and managerial categories, which together constitute the so-called value chain (Porter, 1985) (see Fig 1.11).
Primary activities can be divided into incoming flow of goods, production or servicing in the widest sense of the words, marketing, sales and servicing. The supporting activities are the purchasing of products and services on behalf of the primary activities and other supporting functions, such as the development of technology (organized, for example into a research and development program), human resource management and the infrastructure which comprises matters such as financing, legal activities and so on.

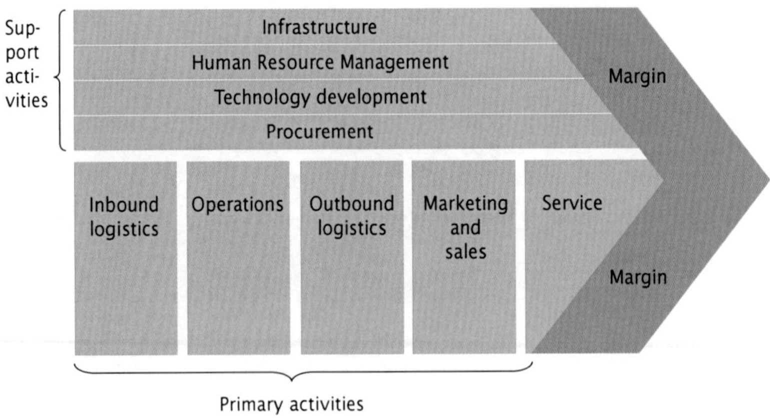

Figure 1.11
The value chain

Source: *Porter*, 1985

Management or managerial activities are concerned with the optimization of relationships, the reduction of cost levels and the enlargement of revenue potential. By giving direction, form and content to operational processes and by performing a steering function, management, even at a general level, adds value to the value chain. These general management activities which form the content of the managerial task are:
- Strategic policy making and positioning
- Design of a suitable organizational structure
- Provision of content and means of performing the organizational processes, including the imposition of controls

As we have seen in Section 1.1.4, the founder of modern management theory, Henri Fayol, represented management (or rather the governance of an organization) as a process. Fayol (1916) broke organizational government up into five essential management functions: prévoir, organiser, commander, coordonner and contrôler. Fayol's five categories can be clumped into three core areas of managerial activity:

external tuning and adaptation
structuring
internal tuning and adaptation

- External tuning and adaptation
- Structuring
- Internal tuning and adaptation

These three management functions are closely related (Fig 1.12). While they are separate functions they are inextricably linked. Thus, in the managerial process they interrelate as shown in Fig 1.12.

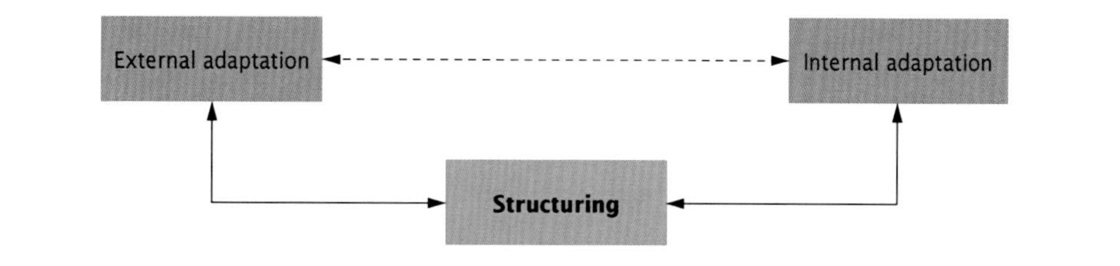

Figure 1.12
Coherence between key managerial problems

Fig 1.10 identifies the following primary and secondary company processes:
- Marketing and sales process
- Purchasing process
- Manufacturing process or servicing process
- Research and development process
- Financial and information supply process
- Personnel process

Other processes often need to be included. They may include the quality process, the environmental care process, and logistic processes (both in and outgoing).
These processes are connected via the activities of managing and organizing them (= management process). The organization's information and communication systems interconnect them further. Via decision making, information is then transmitted into action, after which execution can take place in the various parts of the organization.

1.7.2 Process and process control

Processes constitute the ongoing function of a company or institution. In other words, an organization can no longer function if there are no more processes to be performed. Structuring, performing and controlling the organizational processes is therefore crucial. In general, the following is demanded for process control:
- Mapping out the various functional or partial processes
- Fine tuning of the processes through the regulating or steering activities of management

The fine tuning includes:
- Formulating overall organizational objectives and goals
- Deriving partial goals, norms and standards from the above in order to attain the goals
- Formulating and transmitting policy
- Determining guidelines, procedures, instructions and assignments
- Distributing tasks and assigning the authority to take the necessary actions

1.7.3 A process control model

In order to be able to control the process of goal attainment it needs to be monitored and assessed both during the process and after it has been completed. If there is any deviation from the plans, adjustments will have to be made. This can be done by taking corrective action during the process, but can also take place afterwards by adjusting the standards set for the process.

cybernetic cycle

In Fig 1.13, the control process is shown diagrammatically. A cybernetic cycle (comparable to the functioning of a thermostat in a central heating system, see also Section 9.3) always involves the following processes:

- Setting operational standards
- Giving an assignment or signal for execution
- Giving information to a steering organ. The managerial or operational employee is always informed about the actual situation
- Checking, i.e. testing received information according to established standards
- Acting to adjust or correct. Whenever the actual situation deviates from the operational standard an authorized party adjusts or corrects the information relating to the detected deviation from the standard. The correction which follows is also called feedback or feedforward

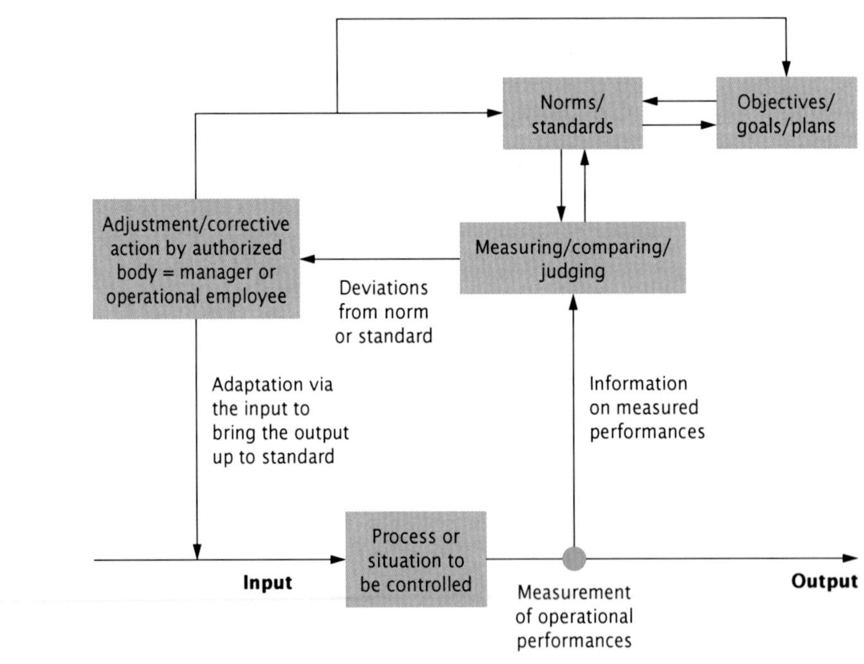

Figure 1.13
Model of the control process (the cybernetic cycle)

In the practice of management, we encounter such cybernetic cycles in budgetary practices for example. Deviations between the allowed and the actual costs are signaled. Possible corrections or adjustments are then investigated and implemented. Car manufacturing processes are another example. Numerically managed production equipment is used to assemble the coachwork of a car. The feedback mechanisms built into the highly automated production system detect deviations that exceed a certain margin of tolerance. Once they are detected, action needs to be taken to adjust the process. If no deviations are found, the process can simply continue within acceptable tolerance levels (see also Section 9.2).

1.8 Characteristics of an effective organization and successful management

In their book *In Search of Excellence*, Peters and Waterman (1982) have described eight characteristics of successful management:

- A bias towards action – preferring to undertake something actively instead of endlessly studying and analyzing a concept
- A customer-directed attitude – knowing the customer's preference and serving that preference
- Autonomy and entrepreneurship – dividing the company up into smaller units and encouraging an independent and competitive working attitude
- Productivity through people – making employees aware of the fact that effort is essential and that they profit from the company's success
- Hands-on and value-driven – showing personal commitment and keeping in touch with the essence of the company, stimulating a strong company culture
- 'Stick to the knitting' – stick to the activities that the company performs best
- 'Simple form and lean staff' – few administrative and managerial layers and few people at the top
- Simultaneous loose-tight properties – freedom from constraints, which means taking care of the central values of the company, combined with respect for all employees who accept these values

These eight characteristics were observed in very well functioning ('excellent') organizations, although the degree to which these characteristics were present differed. However, it is known that some years after the research, not all of these 'excellent' companies were still functioning as well. Explanations of successful management are sometimes very complex. Meeting these eight characteristics is no guarantee of continuous success. Such success requires hard work and commitment to attaining and improving the company's performance in changing times and market conditions.

In *Built to Last: Successful Habits of Visionary Companies* (1949), a much-discussed book that has been compared to *In Search of Excellence*, the authors, Collins and Porras investigate what makes a company a 'visionary company': i.e., a company whose vision takes on a concrete form. This book puts a number of persistent management myths under the microscope. As Collins and Porras see it, successful companies have a core ideology.

Jim Collins' bestseller *Good to Great* (2001) also has an inspiring message for companies, describing how good ones can become great ones. The metamorphosis of 11 selected companies is described from the perspective of each of these companies. However, research dating back to 2008 has shown that of these 11 companies, only one is still performing excellently. Success thus obtained turned out to be only temporary, therefore, and could make no easy claim to permanency.

In a later book entitled *How the Mighty Fall* (2009), Collins describes the reasons for successful companies eventually failing, setting out the five stages which end in failure. They are as follows: (1) overconfidence as a consequence of success, (2) striving for more but in an undisciplined way, (3) denial of the risks and ignoring or making light of the warning signals, (4) a 'quick fix' to save the company (a more daring but less familiar strategy, for example, or a substantial change to the company's culture, or a major takeover), and (5) becoming dependent on quick fixes rather than returning to those elements that made the company great in the first place, thus weakening the company financially and causing it to lose ground or even cease to exist.

In short, the managerial rules that Collins describes earlier have turned out not to apply forever or to be universally applicable or transferrable. We can, however, now conclude that to be successful always seems to require a unique combination of situation-determined factors that cannot easily be copied.

THE WORLD'S MOST INNOVATIVE COMPANIES

Each year, the Boston Consulting Group asks thousands of senior executives worldwide what, in their eyes, are the most innovative companies. Traditionally, there are few truly spectacular changes – if a company is already highly innovative it is apparently never suddenly much less innovative the following year. Just as in the previous year, Apple is still in first place, followed by Google and Toyota. Wal-Mart Stores has risen from 23rd place to 10th place, mainly as a result of its pioneering work in the area of systems for digital 'health registration', energy-efficient shops and the social-networking site 'Elevenmoms'. General Electric, whose financial divisions have been hard hit, has fallen from 4th place to 17th. A newcomer – VW – is at 18th place. Its position is partly due to its advanced car options at affordable prices, such as electronic parking aids. MacDonald's has risen from 30 to 19, reflecting its radical innovations, ranging from its interiors to its menus.

The top 20

1.	(1)	Apple	11.	(11)	Amazon.com
2.	(2)	Google	12.	(8)	Procter & Gamble
3.	(3)	Toyota	13.	(6)	Tata
4.	(5)	Microsoft	14.	(9)	Sony
5.	(7)	Nintendo	15.	(19)	Reliance Industries (oil and gas)
6.	(12)	IBM	16.	(26)	Samsung Electronics
7.	(15)	Hewlett-Packard	17.	(4)	General Electric
8.	(13)	Research In Motion (=BlackBerry)	18.	(-)	Volkswagen
9.	(10)	Nokia	19.	(30)	McDonald's
10.	(23)	Wal-Mart Stores	20.	(14)	BMW

Source: *BusinessWeek* April 20, 2009 / Management trends, July-August, 2009

1.8.1 *High performance organizations: some characteristics*

From around 2004 onwards, the 'high performance organization' has been overtaking the 'excellent' or 'visionary organization' of the preceding period as the preferred choice. The characteristics of a high performance organization are still somewhat intangible. There are not many organizations that fit the bill, but when they do they are immediately recognizable as such. They include Toyota, General Electric, Cisco and Dell. But while we can identify such companies, as yet we cannot identify these new characteristics. The questions that are being asked are as follows: under what conditions does 'high performance' take place? How do we experience it? Can we imitate it elsewhere? As things stand at the moment, we have to admit that we have little knowledge about how to manage 'high performance', although we recognize it when we see it. However, consensus on what constitutes high performance is growing (Kirby, 2005). At least some of the aspects involved are the management of innovation and creativity, the creation of masterly high performance teams and high performance jobs, the efficient conversion of strategies into action, fundamental and excellent leadership, rules for effective collaboration and discipline, quality improvement in the relationship between staff and customers (via an improvement in the 'human sigma') and organizational management that makes use of the indicators that influence behavior and that are incentives for excellent performance. Prahalad has recently (in 2009) added a new business competency, namely 'agility'. In times of change it is crucial that businesses have a flexible production capacity and multi-deployable employees. (For interactive methods of leadership in times of change, see boxing.hbr.org.) These topics will be dealt with in chapters 3 to 10.

1.8.2 Criteria for measuring the effectiveness of an organization

organizational effectiveness

Organizational effectiveness is a characteristic which is difficult to identify because it concerns the degree to which and the means through which goals are attained.
The measuring of effectiveness is only possible if an instrument exists for this purpose. The organization can be seen as a 'lasting complex of people and resources for realization of specific, but in time shifting, goals.' Criteria for effectiveness can be derived from this. Keuning and Eppink (1979, 9th edition, 2008) drew up four main criteria:

efficiency
- Efficiency is the degree to which a set of goals is achieved while using up a minimum of resources, leading to technical and economic efficiency.

satisfaction
- Satisfaction is the degree to which the needs of the members of the organization are satisfied by means of labor-intrinsic and labor-extrinsic factors, leading to psychosocial efficiency.

fulfillment
- Fulfillment of stakeholders' needs is the degree to which the demands and needs of the stakeholders from the external environment are met, leading to societal efficiency.

self-preservation
- Self-preservation through flexibility and responsiveness is the degree to which an organization can speedily adjust its short-term strategies, structure and operational goals in reaction to changing external circumstances, leading to managerial efficiency.

In an evaluation of an organization, all these aspects of an effective and healthy organization can be observed and scored. The organization has to show positive scores in relation to these criteria if it wants to be considered effective.

1.9 The manager and the organizational culture

When a newly appointed employee is getting to know an organization, or a recently recruited manager wants to make changes to the organization, it is important to realize that an organization is more than just a structure and a system of behavior that follows guidelines and procedures. Upon further acquaintance, we usually experience 'something' within the organization which is, to a certain degree, elusive. This 'something' seems to pervade all aspects of the organization, including statements, ways of thinking and the actions of the people within the organization. In recent years, we have started calling this 'something' *organizational culture*.
In the first place, an organizational culture is formed by the prevailing ideas which are disseminated by a large proportion of the members of the organization, members who carry those ideas with them in terms of operative values, norms and convictions.

values
behavior

Values are the things that people consider to be important and which consciously – but often unconsciously – determine human behavior. In organizations, values are expressed in the way in which the organization is managed and the way in which people associate with each other, in things that the members of the organization do or do not do, and in choices that are made. Underlying this behavior are the most influential values and norms, expectations, convictions and attitudes. This is the existing organizational culture. For example, 'loyalty to the company' (a value) results in 'wanting to be on time' (a norm) and finding this to be important.

convictions

Convictions are expressed by members of the organization, whether asked for or not. Convictions are the notions and views of reality which are shared by the members of the organization. These convictions cause them to show certain types of behavior, disseminate information in a certain way, and so on. From one perspective, a conviction brings order to experiences; however, it can also lead to distortions or discord – for example, in statements such as ' … those staff members, they are far too theoretical' or ' … research managers, they are always late.'

Organizational culture is important because it makes organizational life predictable and structures it in certain ways, it creates a relationship between the members of the various parts of the organization, and it means that it is not always necessary to adapt or make new decisions to fit individual circumstances. Organizational culture can be considered as the mutual understanding between the members and the stakeholders of the organization.

mutual understanding

In those positions within the organization where examples are being set, it is important to be aware of the organizational culture. At first sight, this may seem vague and elusive, but it shows itself in all forms of organizational practice, including various forms of sanctions and rewards, traditions and habits, and norms and rules which are in force at various levels or within various parts of the organization. For example, the culture of an organization expresses itself, in the use or otherwise of first names, in the physical environment and corporate image, in the communication between employees, in the way in which customers are treated, in the work effort and the degree of commitment shown by employees, in the dress code and in the language and attitude to time keeping. It is therefore important to 'know' an organization and the existing relationships and interrelationships within it.

Summary

- In this chapter we have introduced the basic concepts of management.
- Management is both a very old and very modern field of study. This is because management has to do with people in collaborative relationships.
- An organization is defined as a 'goal-realizing collaborative unit of people.'
- In this book we cover the management of labor organizations in which paid work is carried out.
- Every person in a labor organization who is in control of others and has to make decisions is a manager. This is what distinguishes a manager from other employees. In every organization, various levels of management can be identified. Each level has its own tasks and responsibilities.
- Elements in today's management are highly influenced by the interrelationship between business and a sustainable society, globalization, changes in power relations and the role of science, technology and marketing philosophy.
- A manager has to make decisions and coordinate activities, and for these tasks good communication within the organization is essential. Management can be described as a process of planning, organizing, giving orders and controlling and adjusting.
- The management cycle depicts the managerial process as being set in motion and maintained by the manager by means of decision making, coordination and communication. From this we can derive the demands that are made of modern managers, which include the following:
  - reacting to internal and external developments
  - achieving acceptance, quality and effectiveness in decision making
  - efficient use of own time
  - working according to the organizational culture
- The criteria for judging the effectiveness of the organization include the following:
  - efficiency
  - satisfaction
  - fulfillment of stakeholders' needs
  - self-preservation through flexibility and responsiveness

Discussion questions

1 With reference to *Management in Action* at the beginning of this chapter:
a) Explain why some industries are more thriving than others
b) Explain the decline in commodities
c) Explain why firm size is not necessarily pivotal to superior performance

2 Does a manager have power or is she/he dependent on others?

3 Is a group of university students waiting at a bus stop an organization?

4 'When we refer to companies or hospitals we describe them as organizations, though we do not use this term when we refer to forms of co-existence such as families or people who live together.' Discuss this comment.

5 What is your opinion of the following contention: 'Why should organizational culture be important to management? Isn't management only concerned with time and money?'

6 'Managers are men in three-piece suits.'
'Managers sit behind desks.'
'Managers are driven around in big cars by chauffeurs.'
Give your opinion on each of the above contentions. In particular, consider the following:
- whether the image presented matches the way managers are described in this chapter
- where the image probably originated
- whether the image relates to the increasing number of women in management

7 'The various management theories mirror the time in which they arose.' What is your opinion of this contention? Which of the theories do you find most convincing?

Research-based exercise

Leadership skill requirements across organizational levels

Introduction
This research-based exercise is based on a research article by Mumford, Campion and Morgeson (2007), published in *The Leadership Quarterly*. The research question, data collection, method, and some of the results of the research project are presented. The exercise consists of three questions based on the research article and the theory in this chapter. The answers should be based on both the theory in Chapter 1 and your own insights into the practical implications of your answer.

Research Question
What are management leadership skill requirements and how do those requirements vary according to organizational level?

Data Collection
The sample consisted of 1023 professional employees working in an international agency of the U.S. government. These employees were generalists working in five different career specialties in 156 different countries, including the United States: administration, public relations, economic analysis, political analysis, and multi-functional positions. The employees were sampled from three levels of the organization that will be referred to as junior (1–5 years experience), mid level (6–20 years), and senior (21+ years).

Outcomes
The researchers demonstrate that heterogeneity of the leadership requirements exists at different organizational levels. That is:

- In terms of leadership skill requirements, the following ranking was found: Cognitive > Interpersonal > Business > Strategic
- Cognitive, Interpersonal, Business, and Strategic leadership skills requirements increase at higher levels within the organization
- Strategic and Business skill leadership requirements have, however, a stronger relationship with organizational level compared to Cognitive and Interpersonal leadership requirements

(Based on Mumford, T., Campion, M., and Morgeson, P. (2007) 'The leadership skills strataplex: Leadership skill requirements across organizational levels.' *The Leadership Quarterly, (18), 154-166.*)

Questions

1 Explain why Cognitive leadership skill requirements are more important relative to other types of skill requirements for each level within the organization.
2 Which types of leadership skill requirements can be taught and learned or represent a personal characteristic a manager or leader is born with?
3 Given the study's results, provide a list of practical implications in terms of hiring, training, and promoting employees.

CASE

Management case study

How to innovate ... 'everything-as-a-service'

In early 2007, Shane Robison, Hewlett-Packard's (HPQ) executive vice-president and chief strategy and technology officer, gathered the seven chief technology officers from HP's business units together. Robison, as a Compaq vice-president, had played a major role in the two companies' controversial 2002 merger and the integration that followed. But when he summoned his division technology chiefs, he was focused on the future: What technologies were emerging, how would they shape the market, and what were the implications for HP?

After months of debate, the group came up with a strategy dubbed 'everything as a service', based in part on the then-emerging trend of cloud computing – the idea that the computing and storage needs of a person or a company could be handled off-site. Companies including HP had already begun offering 'software as a service' rather than on a shrink-wrapped CD, and HP wanted to build on the service model by developing the supporting hardware and software, as well as its own services. Less than three years later, HP has introduced at least six completely new service offerings, along with several cloud-related software and hardware products and consulting services. More are in development.

How HP implemented its new strategy relatively quickly across its many divisions is worth some attention. As Harvard Business School professors Robert Kaplan and David Norton showed in their 1996 book, *The Balanced Scorecard: Translating Strategy into Action*, and in subsequent research and books, it's common for companies to develop strategies and then fail to implement them. Following through on innovative strategies is even more difficult. Here's a look at how HP made 'everything as a service' more than an empty buzz-phrase.

New V-P for cloud services & strategy

Faced with executing a new idea, Robison had a head start because he had already involved the company's divisional CTOs in the process. In other words, the executives who would be key to realizing the strategy within the business groups – as well as the director of HP Labs responsible for developing new technologies to support the strategy – were already invested in the plan.

While each individual CTO was developing an 'everything as a service' strategy for his unit, Robison created a temporary position – vice-president of cloud services and strategy – to take a broader approach. For 18 months, Russ Daniels, who had previously served as CTO in HP's software services group, took on that role. 'I was able to approach the cloud computing opportunity from a pan-HP perspective,' he says. That included looking for possible opportunities outside of the existing business units, as well as helping ensure that the units' individual efforts worked in unison. For instance, was the group that was charged with developing next-generation servers considering the needs of potential users of the company's planned services? Meanwhile, Prith Banerjee, vice-president of research, was reorganizing HP Labs. Under Banerjee, a rough total of 150 projects then at the labs was cut to 21, all of which supported the new strategy in some way.

For instance, one research project that came out of the reorganization was a technology enabling people to print from a mobile device. Patrick Scaglia, the CTO of HP's Imaging and Printing Group (IPG), then stepped forward to have his group take the project on and conduct a market test. 'If our strategy makes sense, then we should be able to deliver a proof point,' he says. And he did. After diverting some of his incubation funds – venture capital-like money that HP gives each CTO to market-test high-risk and potentially high-payoff technologies that don't fit naturally into the existing road map – to create a prototype, Scaglia got Blackberry-maker RIM (RIM) interested in the product. In May 2009, HP announced CloudPrint, a service allowing RIM users to print documents on the nearest available printer.

The new partners are now testing the program, with plans to launch it early next year.

Translating strategy into action is 'a messy process,' says Scaglia. 'You can't just send everyone a memo saying: "Now we're going to do this".' But money talks. This year, more than half of Scaglia's budget went to support services – CloudPrint, MagCloud (a printing, mailing, and subscription-management service that allows anyone to publish a magazine), and BookCloud (a similar service for book publishers – as did 100% of his incubation funds. HP won't disclose revenues related to the new strategy and many of its new services are too young to have made a significant top-line impact. But the company says it expects 'everything as a service' to remain a key part of its future.

What can executives learn from HP's approach to implementing its innovative strategy?

Appreciate the Difficulty

You can't just send a memo. For tips on executing a strategy successfully, read *The Balanced Scorecard: Translating Strategy into Action*.

Engage Key Leaders in the Process

Robison involved all of the company's group CTOs to help develop the new strategy. When the time came to implement that strategy in their divisions, they never felt it had been imposed on them.

Make Sure You Have the Right People in Place

Sometimes a new strategy requires fresh blood, but if you have people who can adapt to it, keep them. HP asked Russ Daniels to take on a temporary CTO role to help realize the strategy.

Buy or Partner

A new strategy often requires new skills, some of which can come through partnerships. Bigger companies should consider acquisitions, as HP did when it bought Mercury, a company with experience in the technology behind software as a service.

Be Flexible

Your standard procedure for rolling out a new strategy might not work when you enter unknown waters. In HP's case, Robison formed a novel strategy-development team of CTOs and then created a temporary CTO position to flesh out the new approach.

Source: *BusinessWeek*, September 23, 2009, (Jessie Scanlon)

Case study questions

1 Companies commonly develop strategies and then fail to implement them. Describe why companies are likely to fail at strategy implementation and why, in contrast, HP was successful.
2 In the HP case, strategy implementation focuses on technology. Describe whether strategy implementations pertaining to production, marketing, or internalization are likely to be equally successful when a similar implementation strategy is adopted.
3 What would be the next step for HP to further capitalize on their new 'everything-as-a-service' strategy?

CONTENTS

2.1 An organization in its environment
2.2 External stakeholders
2.3 Environmental factors
2.4 Relevant trends in the environment
2.5 Social responsibility, external reporting, risk management and corporate governance
2.6 Industrial and organizational democracy in a European context
2.7 Management and ethics
2.8 Communication with external groups

Chapter 2

Organizations and the environment

LEARNING OUTCOMES

After studying this chapter, you should be able to do the following:

- Identify the various stakeholders who both influence and make a specific contribution to the organization
- Describe the contribution of each of the stakeholders to the organization and what induces them to make their contribution
- Identify the various environmental factors and external developments to which the organization is exposed and to which the organization has to react
- Understand the concepts of 'external environment' and 'external adaptation,' 'internal environment' and 'internal adaptation'
- Explain what is meant by organizational equilibrium as a basis for the survival of an organization
- Describe an organization's place in the societal system
- Identify the consequences for the organization of the relevant trends in the environment
- Examine the interrelationships between developments in moral and organizational behavior
- Discuss the links between societal responsibility, external reporting and corporate governance
- Be aware of the effects of national cultures on organizations

CASE

Management-in-action

Toyota Losing its shine

It is not unusual in Japan for corporate leaders to make semi-ritualised displays of humility. But when Akio Toyoda, president of Toyota Motor Corporation since June and grandson of the firm's founder, addressed an audience of Japanese journalists in October his words shocked the world's car industry.

Mr Toyoda had been reading *How the Mighty Fall*, a book by Jim Collins, an American management guru. In it, Mr Collins (best known for an earlier, more upbeat work, *Good to Great*) describes the five stages through which a proud and thriving company passes on its way to becoming a basket-case. First comes hubris born of success; second, the undisciplined pursuit of more; third, denial of risk and peril; fourth, grasping for salvation; and last, capitulation to irrelevance or death.

President en CEO Akio Toyoda (links) en Yoshiumi Inaba (CEO Noord-Amerika) van Toyota tijdens een hoorzitting in Washington over de problemen met het gaspedaal in sommige Toyota's.

Only 18 months ago Toyota displaced General Motors (GM), a fallen icon if ever there was one, as the world's biggest carmaker. But Mr Toyoda claimed that the book described his own company's position. Toyota, he reckoned, had already passed through the first three stages of corporate decline and had reached the critical fourth. According to Mr Collins, fourth-stage companies that react frantically to their plight in the belief that salvation lies in revolutionary change usually only hasten their demise. Instead they need calmness, focus and deliberate action.

Is Toyota really in such dire straits? And if it is, can a company that for decades has been the yardstick for manufacturing excellence turn itself around in time?

Toyoda's to-do list

There is plenty here to concern Mr Toyoda. The first is that for a global carmaker, Toyota has been slow off the mark in several emerging markets that are likely to provide nearly all the growth in sales when the mature markets of America, Western Europe and Japan have recovered to something like normality. VW is far ahead of Toyota in China and out of sight in Brazil. GM, for all its difficulties, is still doing better than Toyota in China and sells nearly ten times as many vehicles in Brazil. Hyundai almost overtook Toyota in China this year and is the biggest foreign car brand in India. Toyota's first low-cost car designed especially for the price-sensitive Indian market is still a year away.

The second thing that Mr Toyoda should reflect upon is that Toyota is sluggish for different reasons in different markets. This may make answers harder to find. In China, it took longer than rivals to respond to tax breaks for vehicles with smaller engines and it has made less effort to develop cars specifically for the Chinese market. In Europe, the solid but ageing Yaris and the dull Auris left it poorly placed to exploit the scrappage schemes that boosted sales, and its lack of a full range of competitive diesels continues to hinder it.

In America, Toyota is still hugely powerful. It sells more cars there than anyone (the Detroit Three remain highly dependent on big pickups and sport-utility vehicles), it leads in small trucks and it has the bestselling luxury brand in Lexus. But it has also been clobbered by an avalanche of bad publicity, after the recall of 3.8m Toyota and Lexus vehicles. The recall was prompted by the crash of a Lexus saloon in which a California Highway Patrol officer and his family were killed. The apparent cause was 'unintended acceleration'.

At first the National Highway Traffic Safety Administration (NHTSA) and Toyota thought that a badly fitting floor mat could have jammed the accelerator open. Both still think that probable. But the NHTSA is continuing its investigation, having received more than 400 complaints about acceleration problems that appear to have been responsible for several fatal accidents. It is now focusing on possible problems with the design of the throttle pedal and the vehicles' electronics. On November 25th Toyota announced that it would reshape the suspect pedals or fit redesigned ones in 4.26m vehicles. Some will also get reshaped floor-pans and a brake-override system.

Almost every carmaker has had to contend with recalls and ambulance-chasing lawyers, but in a place as litigious as America the reputational damage can be severe. Audi (part of the VW Group) has taken more than 20 years to recover from reports of unintended-acceleration allegations that ultimately proved to be groundless.

The danger in all of this for Toyota is that its loyal (and mostly satisfied) customers in America have long believed that the firm was different from others and thus hold it to a higher standard. The moment that Toyota is seen as just another big carmaker, a vital part of the mystique that has surrounded the brand will have been rubbed away. People within the company believe these quality problems were caused by the strain put on the fabled Toyota Production System by the headlong pursuit of growth. Toyota now looks as though it has been largely successful in solving them. In the latest annual reliability study published by *Consumer Reports*, Toyota boasted 18 of the 48 leading vehicles. Honda, the next best, had only eight.

If Toyota can no longer rely on its superior quality to give it an edge, its vehicles will inevitably be judged increasingly on more emotional criteria, such as styling, ride, handling and cabin design. In America, Toyota is likely to face much more consistent competition from at least two of Detroit's Big Three, while both Hyundai and VW are starting to snap at its heels. The South Korean company has put on an astonishing spurt this year, adding about two points of market share to take it to 7.2%. Its Lexus-rivalling Genesis saloon was named North American car of the year. In 2010 it will start selling the new Sonata, which looks like being a great improvement over the old model, aiming it squarely at the Camry.

Pizzazz, please

How will Toyota respond? Publicity-shy Toyota executives hate announcing detailed strategies to the outside world. Nor have many of them yet come to terms with Mr Toyoda's urgency and appalling frankness. Uniformly they spout that his words about the firm 'grasping for salvation' were widely misunderstood. But for all that, there is plenty going on behind the scenes beyond ferocious cost-cutting. Upon seizing the reins in June, Mr Toyoda immediately ordered a back-to-basics overhaul of product development across the firm's global operations.

One conclusion was that Toyota should be more ruthless in exploiting its early leadership in commercialising hybrid systems and electric-vehicle technology. Although every other big carmaker is launching new hybrids (including plug-ins) and purely battery-powered vehicles, or is preparing to, Toyota is convinced that it is still ahead of the pack. Within a few years there will be a hybrid version of every car Toyota makes and there are plans to extend the Prius brand to cover a range of innovative low- and zero-emission vehicles.

Another conclusion – and possibly a more radical notion – was that Toyota must stop making so many dull cars with all the appeal of household appliances. Importantly, Mr Toyoda is what is known as a 'car guy', a part-time racer and an enthusiast for cars that are designed with passion to engage the right-side as much as the left-side of the customer's brain. At the Tokyo motor show in October he said pointedly: 'I want to see Toyota build cars that are fun and exciting to drive.'

As Morizo, the alter ego under which he blogs, Mr Toyoda went further. He said of the cars at the show: 'It was all green. But I wonder how many inspired people to get excited. Eco-friendly cars are a prerequisite for the future, but there must be more than that.' After trying VW's hot Scirocco coupé in July, he blogged: 'I'm jealous! Morizo cannot afford to lose. I will tackle the challenge of creating a car with even more splendid flavour than the Scirocco.' His favourite metaphor is that Toyota's engineers should be like chefs, seasoning their cars with tantalising flavours.

There is also only so much that one man can do to shift the culture of a vast organisation. But there is nothing engineers like more than to be challenged, and Toyota employs many of the world's finest. The latest, third-generation Prius and the brilliant little iQ city car show what they are capable of. So, in a very different way, does the 202mph (325kph) Lexus LFA. *Kaizen*, the pursuit of continuous improvement, is, after all, embedded deep in Toyota's DNA and only needs prodding.

The test will be to keep the ingredients that have made Toyota great – the dependability and affordability – while adding the spice and the flavours that customers now demand. It will not be easy, and the competition has never looked more formidable. But by recognising the scale of Toyota's problems, by proclaiming their urgency and then by drawing on the firm's strengths to fix them, Mr Toyoda has already taken the first, vitally important, step towards salvation.

Source: *The Economist*, December 10, 2009

environmental factors

relevant trends

In this chapter we examine the environmental factors which influence organizations and their operations. Organizations are always subject to influences from external groups and stakeholders, situations and events in the markets and society as a whole. Organizations, in turn, influence others in their business environment. Organizations have to consider the environmental factors which influence the way in which they operate and have to react to changing demands and needs. Relevant trends in the environment have to be recognized and the consequences for future operations have to be explored.

2.1 An organization in its environment

Companies and institutions are organizations which derive the reason for their existence from the function which they fulfill in society as a whole. As such, organizations are part of our society; society can be seen as the environment in which organizations operate. As a result the functioning of organizations is always subject to influences from the societal and market environment and the organization influences in turn the environment in which it operates. This applies not only to industrial and agricultural companies and financial institutions, such as banks and insurance companies, but also to institutions such as schools, hospitals and nursing homes.

2.1.1 The organization and its external influences

stakeholders

situations

An organization's environment consists of stakeholders or interest groups and of situations – events and circumstances which are determined by environmental factors. The main stakeholders/groups and environmental factors that influence the functioning of an organization are shown in Fig 2.1.

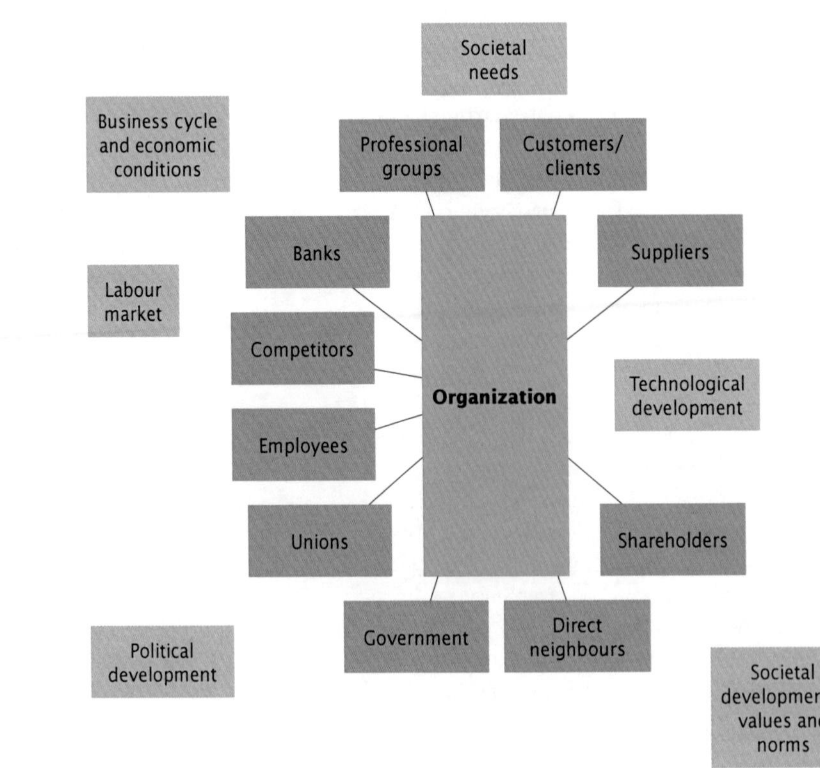

Figure 2.1
The organization and its environment

stakeholders
interest groups

Stakeholders or interest groups are tangible, visible and approachable groups or institutions that can exercise a direct influence on the functioning of an organization – for example, customers, investors, suppliers, competitors, government institutions, interest groups such as consumer associations, and unions. These groups exercise a direct influence on the individual organization, for example, by buying products and services, providing labor, creativity and knowledge, supplying resources and components or by providing financial resources. Furthermore, an influence is exercised by societal demands, since they set constraints and impose responsibilities and other limitations on the products and services which are to be supplied and the processes by which these arise – for example, environmental regulations, health and safety legislation, price constraints, and quality demands.

An organization exercises an influence in turn on potential interest groups and stakeholders in the business environment by advertising, by information supplied with products and services or by maintaining contact with these groups by means of direct negotiations and by making deals. Furthermore, organizations supply the external environment with information and account for their business operations – for example, annual reports to shareholders, government and banks on environmental issues.

situations
events
circumstances

Situations, events or circumstances arise from all sorts of developments in the environment which affect the organization – for example, inflation and interest rates, unemployment levels and scarcity of supply in some parts of the labor market and technological developments. Organizations respond to environmental influences, but in many cases cannot really influence the actual macro-environment factors themselves. Other important environmental factors that organizations have to take into account include demographic, ecological and political factors.

2.1.2 *Organizations and their environments as a cycle of events*

In order to survive, an organization must be constantly interacting with its environment. On the input side, for example, the organization must interact with the markets for labor, capital, information, components, energy, raw materials and other resources. An individual organization's relationship with its environment is shown in Fig 2.2.

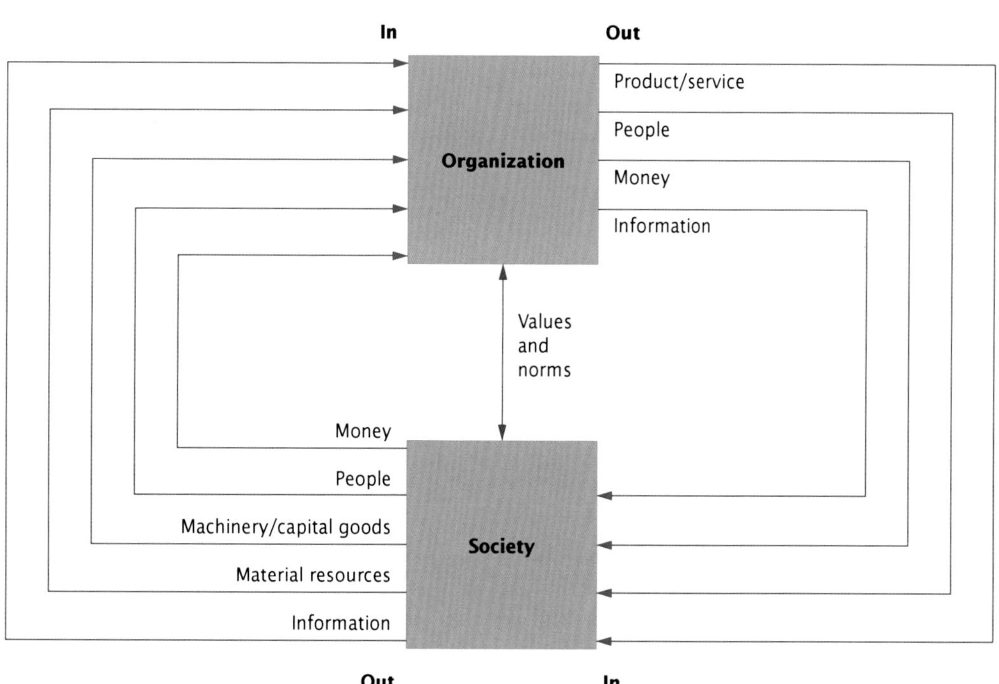

Figure 2.2
Organizations and the societal macro-cycle of events

The diagram illustrates how an organization influences its environment and its markets and how the organization in turn is influenced by society and market developments. Society as a whole exercises an influence on the organization by, for example, laws, values and norms. This has consequences for factors such as the way in which the production function is organized and working conditions. Unemployment levels in the community also have an effect on the functioning of an organization because of their effect on wage levels, while societal pressure can influence the company in the case of a reorganization. In some cases, this can lead management to postpone a reorganization or have it take place in another subsidiary in a different country or region.

Societal forces are always interrelated, but can be grouped as follows:
- Economic influences: state of the economy, employment situations, price and wage relationships, situation in the capital markets, specific markets in the sector or industry in which the company is active (oligopoly, monopoly, etc.).
- Technological influences: new tools, new production methods, innovative changes, new or improved products, degree of automation, substitutes, and so on.
- Cultural/societal influences: population developments, changes in power structures and power relationships, external and internal influences through unions and works councils.
- Political influences: wages and pricing policy, legislation relating to labor conditions and working conditions, industry and investment policy, tax policy, subsidies, and so on.

Over time, environmental forces can differ in the degree of their influence. New situations which bring new forces into play can also arise. For example, higher wages as a result of new governmental policy can make the costs of labor rise. This can in turn lead to an increased demand for automation which in turn can influence political ideas.

Taking in materials, energy and information from society

labor force
thinking
being creative

Just as the human body takes in oxygen, food and information from its environment, the organization – on the input side – takes in resources such as machines, money, energy and raw materials from its environment (see Fig 2.2). In addition, people are recruited to the labor force on the basis of certain skills, such as thinking and being creative. At the same time, an organization needs to take in a steady supply of external information relating to societal developments in general and purchasing resources and sales markets in particular. The organization also needs a good supply of accurate and timely internal information. This is necessary to plan activities, to control progress and where necessary for adjustment of norms and/or corrective measures in respect of current activities (see Section 1.7).

Processing resources, energy and information

specific products
services
resources

The organization transforms resources into specific products or services. The organization and management are required to set such a transformation process in motion and to maintain it. The activities which have to be conducted demand a rational approach within a consciously chosen organizational design. Raw materials are used up during production processes. Other resources, such as people and machines are subject to ageing and wear and tear. The flow of people and resources is directly connected to the continuous flow of information. By combining human abilities with other resources and with internal and external information, the transformation process delivers products and services which can be sold to external markets.

Giving back a range of products and services

external societal needs

Organizations provide for external societal needs by producing a range of goods and services. On the output side, there are people who retire at the usual age, who take early retirement, resign or are fired, and worn out and obsolete machines that are cast aside. The incoming energy and materials are either completely or partially used up or may end up in the form of smoke or refuse. Furthermore, by means of instruments such as advertising and public relations, information is given out about the company and its products and services. Some organizations are obliged to render accounts of their operations and results to the outside world – for example, in the form of external annual reports to shareholders, the government and banks.

cycle of activities

The output of the products or services maintains this cycle of activities. The revenues generated allow the organization, in by then changed circumstances, to purchase the same or other raw materials, labor and machines depending on the needs of society and specific markets.

2.1.3 External adaptation and matching

A company or institution always has to be fully aware of what goes on in the outside world. It has to react to changes in the market such as the demands for new products or services, fluctuating prices of raw materials, reduction of labor supply, availability of substitute components or raw materials and new technological findings. In this outside world, stakeholders also play a part. They invariably make additional demands and set new conditions and attempt to exercise an influence from their position and changing interests. Unions, the government, shareholders and environmental interest groups are some of these stakeholders. If an organization wants maintain its raison d'être, a match with its external environment is the first step. To take into account interest groups/stakeholders and circumstances/events in the external environment is referred to as external adaptation. Sections 2.2 and 2.3 cover in more detail the groups and situations which exercise an influence over an organization, and as a result, determine its position and actions.

2.1.4 Internal adaptation and matching

An organization has been described as a cooperative, goal-realizing unit. In a company or institution, people and resources are consciously and purposefully brought together and co-operate to achieve an efficient and effective realization of those goals. In doing so, resources are used up. The organizational goals are expected to justify the right of the organization to exist in society.

internal stakeholders

Within the organization we have to pay special attention to the internal stakeholders, who include the managers and the operational staff. In addition to the external environment, therefore, we have to take into account the internal environment – that is, the organization as an economic, social and technical system consisting of social components.

The main internal environment components are the managers and other members of the organization, the company culture, the machines, buildings and the financial resources. An organization can thus be seen as a subsystem or a relatively broad societal system.

Internal adaptation and the matching of components is a function of the match between the organization, the individual members of the organization and the various components (people and financial resources, organizational systems and culture).

2.1.5 Organizations and 'organizational equilibrium'

If an organization wants to survive, it has to see to it that both the external and internal stakeholders are and remain satisfied, for it is their requirements, needs and demands or wishes and their efforts, ambition and expectations that will determine the basis for survival of an organization.

Each of these groups has its own stake in the survival of the organization. Consequently every stakeholder is prepared to make a certain contribution to the organization. Of course, in exchange for their contribution a certain form of incentive, inducement or reward is expected, and as long as the inducement is in reasonable proportion to the contribution, the stakeholder will be prepared to continue his or her participation.

organizational equilibrium

One can speak of an 'organizational equilibrium' when an organization succeeds in rewarding its external and internal stakeholders in such as way that they remain motivated to play a part within the organization in exchange for their contribution. Despite all possible sorts of contradictory interests, stakeholders have one common interest – namely, the survival of the organization. The organization allows them to realize at least some of their own goals (needs and wishes) directly or indirectly, in exchange for their contribution. The organization's management needs to see to it that the contributions that are made and the inducements or rewards received are and remain in balance.

static dynamic

Organizational equilibrium is certainly not a static concept; it is more a matter of a shifting and dynamic equilibrium which has to be constantly regained on a day-to-day basis and under changing circumstances and the shifting needs and demands of external and internal stakeholders.

Table 2.1 describes the contributions stakeholders make and the associated rewards.

Stakeholders	Contribution	Inducement/Reward
Owners, funders of equity, interest, and debt capital, fee payers	Money, equity capital	Ownership, interest, dividend
Members of the organization: manager and other employees	Labor, knowledge and expertise	Wages, prestige, status, social contacts, markets, self-realization
Suppliers	Raw materials, services, energy, information, other resources of production	Market prices, clientele
Customers/clients	Market prices, clientele	Products, services
Unions	Work and working environment, labor satisfaction and labor conditions	Employment, industrial democracy, participation and control
Government	Social, economic and legislative framework, infrastructure	Taxes, impositions and refunds

Table 2.1
Contributions and rewards of stakeholders

2.2 External stakeholders

external stakeholders

External stakeholders dependent on how well the business is managed and who are concerned as a group with the continued existence and survival of an organization include the following:

- Customers/clients
- Suppliers
- Suppliers of equity and debt capital such as shareholders, banks, fee and contribution payers
- Government
- Competitors
- Societal stakeholders and interest groups, including unions, consumer organizations, action groups, and sector organizations

These groups of stakeholders are capable of directly influencing the organization by their purchasing decisions or, for example, by decisions to put their resources at the disposal of the organization. The groups themselves will frequently have obtained a certain degree of organization, will be visible and will represent a particular interest. In any event, these groups will show a certain organizational behavior, and be representative and approachable for the purposes of negotiating, lobbying, and so on.

shareholder value

Shareholder value has become a dominant (some would say too dominant) criterion by now, and has led to the functioning of companies being constantly under assessment: the rating on the stock exchange changes daily and the quarterly figures of companies are under constant scrutiny. A lower performance level than a rival and a disappointing profit growth can provoke cutbacks even if developments are otherwise positive. Cutbacks have become the rule rather than the exception. Share prices will invariably rise when a reorganization with cutbacks is announced, but in the medium term no positive effects are usually to be seen, either in the form of more profits or a rise in sales or productivity. There is not even any (or hardly any) convincing proof that costs will go down in the long run.

In fact, what it boils down to is that the stock exchange is encouraging cutbacks more than investments in research and development, training and age-related human resource policy. The priority given to shareholder value is particularly at the expense of stakeholders with a slower tempo of development. Investments in product innovation and in the training and education of employees, for example, are not reflected in the stock market quotation. Employees need more time to develop into creative and productive members of the organizational culture than merely the interval between the quarterly figures. There is, in other words, an ongoing need for the financiers and the top management level of the company to take a long-term view.

financiers
long-term view
stakeholders
customer value

The various interests need to be considered. Stakeholders of all types need to be rewarded, including customers (through 'customer value'), the employees themselves and all kinds of interest groups with their various perspectives on sustainable entrepreneurship and business management (see also Section 2.4.3).

2.2.1 Customers/clients

customers
clients

Customers or clients buy the products of a manufacturing company or make use of the services offered (by, for example, a hospital, a bank or a consultancy agency). If the customers are to stay loyal and to continue to demand the product or service, the company or institution has to continue to provide quality supplies for fair and acceptable prices and rates. It is also important to deliver products or services on time. All of these considerations will help to ensure that an organization earns its revenues. If an organization does not apply itself to the changing needs of the buyers or its products or services, or does not do so to a satisfactory standard, the existing products will no longer be bought and the organization will lose the basis of its existence.

2.2.2 Suppliers

external suppliers

Every organization uses products or services produced by other organizations and consequently conducts relationships with external suppliers. As their contribution, suppliers deliver the raw materials, services, energy, information, machinery or components which the company orders. In return, they expect to receive the invoiced market prices on the agreed terms of payment. In the event of non-payment by the client, future supplies may be stopped. Usually, both parties are likely to be keen to continue the relationship. To an increasing degree, especially in cases of co-makership, outsourcing and/or offshoring, demands are made with respect to quality, delivery times, flexibility and fair price-setting.

2.2.3 Suppliers of equity and debt capital: shareholders, banks, contribution payers

Owner-shareholders, banks and other suppliers of equity or debt capital, and fee or contribution payers will have all put money at the disposal of the organization in order to finance its operations. Their contributions consist of the provision of equity or debt capital in the form of shares, loans or mortgages. In return, they expect to have a certain degree of control of the organization and receive interest of a financial nature, a dividend or a rise in the value of the shares. If the organization underperforms, then the capital suppliers can shut off the flow of money, demand a reorganization or intervene in the management of the board.

2.2.4 Government

The government provides the socio-economic and legislative framework within which organizations fulfill their functions. Furthermore, the government is responsible for the provision of infrastructure elements such as roads, shipping routes and the railway network. The government also provides legislation in all sorts of fields (labor, wages, working conditions, opening and closing times of shops, etc.). Both national and regional government exercises an influence in macro-economic terms by means of national and regional budgets, subsidies, and wage and price conditions. In return for its contribution, the national, regional or local government receives a reward in the form of taxes at various rates on, for example, the profit, income or property. At the international level, the decisions of organizations are influenced by decisions made by bodies such as the European Union (EU), the Organization for Economic Cooperation and Development (OECD) and the Organization of Petroleum Exporting Countries (OPEC).

infrastructure
macro-economic terms
European Union decisions

2.2.5 Competitors

Some important factors relating to competition are the number of competitors, their positioning and their market share. In order to compete with other organizations, advertisements are published, offers of products and services are made, prices and quality levels are determined, and use is made of distribution channels. Organizations sometimes make certain deals with each other, such as wage and price deals, or activities are undertaken together in alliances or through collective advertising or joint research and development.
To protect the interests of the general public, government often introduces restrictions on, for example, price agreements, unfair competition and monopoly situations. In other circumstances, government may even promote collaboration, for example, in health care and in small businesses.

market share
offers of products

2.2.6 Societal interest groups

In recent years, a growing number of interest groups have arisen whose aim is to promote certain points of view or to defend interests during negotiating processes – for example, unions, employers' organizations and so on.
'Action groups' sometimes hold very strong views in relation to the decision making of companies and institutions and consequently cannot be ignored (think of Greenpeace and the World Wildlife Fund, and recently also anti-globalists and so-called culture jammers). Each group will try to bring attention to and present its own position and interests with arguments and, if necessary, by means of specific action. Sometimes legal action is taken or strikes organized. Sometimes an influence can be exercised on other organizations that have a societal stake.

action groups
anti-globalists
culture jammers

degree of organization

To counterbalance this influence effectively (= 'countervailing power'), a certain degree of organization and representation is almost always required. This enables the interests of individuals, be they employees, employers or consumers, to be joined together and become an effective force that can bring about shifts in power positions. In certain cases, these representative organizations can, for example, restore a disrupted equilibrium and 'neutralize' discrepancies between powerless individuals and over-powerful organizations. In principle, consultative bodies and sector-based cooperative arrangements between competitors can do the same.

2.3 Environmental factors

environmental factors
marco forces

Every organization may be influenced by environmental factors and developments. When an organization experiences the force of environmental factors we call these macro forces; the organization has little influence over them. Sometimes some influence can be exerted by cooperation between organizations but technological and societal developments are not easily influenced by single organizations. The organization cannot escape these macro forces entirely, however. These 'DESTEMP' forces can be categorized as follows:

- Demographic factors
- Economic factors
- Societal factors
- Technological factors
- Ecological factors
- Market and industry factors
- Political factors

2.3.1 Demographic factors

growth rate of the population

Demographic factors include factors such as the growth, size, structure and composition of the population. These factors often determine how large a sales market will be. For example, changes to these factors will have consequences for companies in the building industry. Changes to the growth rate of the population will have implications for the sales of bread, detergents and so on. If the number of children between the ages of five and ten decreases, this will have consequences for the toy industry.

living on their own
ageing population

An important recent demographic development is the overall population growth. The number of households is on the increase in most countries. This has been caused for a large part by an increase in the number of two-member households and an explosive growth in the number of people living on their own, and include a large number of women. The average age of the total population is continuing to rise. Within the EU, the proportion of people 60 years of age and over will have grown to 23 per cent of the total population by 2010. Alongside the so-called ageing population is a remarkable decrease in the number of young people, both in relative and absolute terms.

world's population

By the year 2070, the world's population will probably have reached 9.0 billion, after which it is expected that it will drop to 8.4 billion by the end of this century. At the present moment, the world's population is 6.0 billion. By the year 2100, those older than sixty years of age are estimated to account for 34 percent of the world's population.

In comparison with 30 years ago, the European population is better educated. Compared to the same period, a large number of jobs have disappeared from agriculture and industry and reappeared in other sectors. Job-directed education has had to make way for general education. If we relate the theme of education to the trends described above, the proportion of elderly people participating in education in the future may possibly increase spectacularly.

ethnic composition

Another demographic factor which is of importance in this regard is the change in the ethnic composition of the population of some countries in Europe, for example, Germany, France, Belgium and the Netherlands.

2.3.2 *Economic factors*

Economic factors such as the size of a person's disposable income exert a powerful influence on organizations which are directed at the consumer/user. Trends in national income, the state of the economy, interest rate fluctuations, costs of labor, exchange rates and so on, are all matters that organizations need to take into account. Together, these factors determine the competitive position and the investment climate – that is, the attractiveness of an investment. This is important for companies if they want to expand further in their own country or for companies that want to start up or expand in other countries.

competitive position
investment climate

LEGACY OF PAST FAILS TO SHAKE FAITH IN MARKET

Since the fall of the Berlin Wall, the countries that broke free of totalitarian rule in 1989-1990 – Poland, Hungary, Czechoslovakia, Romania and Bulgaria – have achieved more than the first post-communist leaders thought possible.
Soviet troops are gone, democracy has taken root, membership of the European Union and NATO has guaranteed security, and the economy has been transformed through a surge in trade and investment. Meanwhile, living standards have risen 50 per cent and life expectancy has grown four years to an average of nearly 75. Foreign travel, once a rare privilege, is commonplace. For most central Europeans, life has, literally, never been so good.

But all is not well. Despite the achievements of the past 20 years, societies face serious challenges – income inequalities, a lack of trust in public institutions and, above all, a failure to deal fully with the legacy of communism.
Meanwhile, despite many administrative reforms, the region still struggles with corruption. Transparency International, the corruption watchdog, says central European countries have recently dropped down the list of states ranked by perceived transparency levels. The Czech Republic, for example, has fallen from 39th place in 1999 to 45th last year. Poland is down from 44 to 58 and Bulgaria from 63 to 72.

The EU's east European new members were growing until recently at an annually – about 3 percentage points faster than western Europe. Without this margin, the east cannot hope to reach west European living standards. And if it does not, frustration will grow. Laszlo Csaba, a politics professor at the Central European University, says: 'The main problem is not the recession but the slow pace of future growth. The years we lose now will never come again.'

But the crisis has also revealed the region's resilience. Beside states such as Hungary whose economies are performing badly, there is Poland, which is forecast to see 1 per cent growth this year – the only EU economy with a likely positive result. Erik Berglof, chief economist at the European Bank for Reconstruction and Development, the multilateral bank, says that while governments have fallen over the crisis, no country has abandoned liberal economic policies. Far-right nationalists have done well in Hungary this year, but have failed to capitalize on the crisis elsewhere. There have been sporadic strikes and demonstrations, for example in Bulgaria, but, despite rising unemployment, nothing resembling mass protests against economic orthodoxy.

If the biggest economic crisis since the 1930s cannot shake eastern Europe's faith in western values it is difficult to imagine what will. There are troubles ahead but the record of the past 20 years suggests the EU's eastern citizens will cope. Jan Krzysztof Bielecki, a former Solidarity activist in Gdansk and a former prime minister who now heads Bank Pekao, says: 'We did not give up in the 1980s. Today, we are confident people. We will not give up now.'

Source: *Financial Times*, Special Report Review of Central and Eastern Europe, December 14, 2009

A steady growth in the Gross National Product (GNP) normally leads to more spending by customers, and, in theory, this offers chances for new companies and supports the growth of existing companies. In addition to national economic factors, international economic developments are also important. The rise of the Japanese economy, which started in the 1960s, has had major consequences, in the first place for the shipbuilding industry and then for companies producing cameras, watches, computers and cars. Just as remarkable is the rapid rise of other Asian economies: those of South Korea, Taiwan, Hong Kong and Singapore. The relative costs of labor and the relative rise in labor productivity are equally significant.

national and international developments

It has also been noted that the economies of Eastern bloc countries such as Poland, Hungary, the Czech Republic and also Turkey are booming. It even looks likely that Turkey will be admitted to the EU (as well as to NATO).
Strong growth can also be expected in countries such as China (which joined the WTO in 2001), India, Russia, Brazil and Indonesia and smaller countries such as Vietnam, Thailand, Indonesia and Malaysia. The 1997 crisis in this region had major consequences for a large number of Western companies: not only did part of the market disappear, but the companies in that region also started to focus on the markets of the West.

The euro: currency without governance

Under the terms of the Economic and Monetary Union (EMU), the exchange rates of eleven participating countries have been permanently linked since the first of January 1999. The other four EU members may join the EMU within a few years. But the new EU member states in Central Europe are not in any hurry to introduce the euro. The fact that countries like Poland, Hungary and the Czech Republic will not be able to get their budgets ready in time and will be ready for the euro in 2010 at the earliest also plays a part. Euro skepticism plays a role too, just as it does in Britain, where it is still a factor to be reckoned with. In conservative circles in Britain the euro is regarded as a failure because the European currency has still not succeeded in providing a new stimulus to the economies of the participating countries and thus creating new prosperity. Quite the contrary: those countries that have stayed outside of the euro zone are growing the fastest. Romania and Bulgaria are not ready for the euro and the EU member states are quite divided over the admission of Turkey.
Optimists believe that the EMU will keep inflation low, decrease the high rate of unemployment in Europe, decrease prices and stimulate wealth. One of the tasks of the recently reorganized ECB (European Central Bank) is to encourage strong anti-inflationary measures. A common European currency – the euro – was one such measure. Bank notes and coins in euros were first issued on the first of January 2002.

ECB

Pessimists predict that the euro will not have a long lifetime and see this as the biggest strategic failure in Europe since 1914 and the Versailles treaty. Prior to this were the failures of the Latin Monetary Union (1865) and the Scandinavian Monetary Union (1873). According to some European experts, there has never been a monetary union that was not preceded by political unification. In the United States of America, it took more than one hundred years for monetary policies to become unified. Monetary union took place as recently as 1914, when the Federal Reserve System was introduced. The famous American economist and winner of the Nobel Prize for economics, Milton Friedman, indicated as recently as 2004 that he regards the collapse of the euro zone within a few years as being 'very probable'.

collapse of the euro zone

European constitution

The no-vote against the European constitution, the putting on ice of the constitution until 2009, the constant bickering about the budget and the annually recurring disagreements about reduction in the budgetary deficits (with Italy, Germany and France) in order to bring them within the terms of the Stability and Growth Pact, are not making the euro any stronger either. In the meantime, euro-cynics are speaking in terms of an 'ex-pact'. There is 'euro skepticism' all around and in Italy, Germany and even the Netherlands the constantly recurring call to return to the lire, mark or guilder. In the long run, this will give rise to instability and a withdrawal from the euro zone, even though this is officially considered impossible.

Stability and Growth Pact

euro skepticism

Time will tell which prediction will come true: the EMU will collapse or it will ultimately be viewed as a unique and successful experiment. Even if it is successful, the risks will have been

enormous, though they do not seem to have deterred companies both large and small, which were prepared to switch to the euro even at considerable expense.
However, it is naive to assume that the eurozone will not evolve. The question is whether the weaker countries will take the initiative and leave the monetary union or whether the stronger euro member states will chose to re-amalgamate into a smaller and/or better union. The deficits of Spain, Portugal, Italy and Greece are primarily financed by Germany, the Netherlands and Finland, forming a strong argument (stronger even than previous ones) for a revolt within the ranks. The recent financial crisis has shown that there can be no question of a genuine economic and monetary union. Greece constitutes a threat to the euro and Italy, Spain, Portugal and Ireland are in dire straits. A currency devaluation in these countries is no longer an option: there is, however, speculation about the return of the drachma in Greece, as there has been (much earlier, even) about a return of the lire to Italy.

EUROZONE DREAMS OF UNITY STILL UNFULFILLED

The eurozone has failed to develop into the harmonised economic unit that was intended when the euro was introduced a decade ago, putting the future of the single currency at risk, a recent study has found.

A survey of households found a 'striking disparity' in the strength of household balance sheets. It identified Italians and Spanish as the least prudent financial planners, with high debt and low saving levels, while the Dutch were the most prudent.

One of the hopes for the first decade was that you would see much more convergence, but the dominant feature was the scale of national differences. The euro could be destabilised in the future if more uniformity is not achieved.

Source: *The Daily Telegraph*, October 8, 2009

SHRINK THE EUROZONE, OR CREATE A FISCAL UNION

Source: FT, March 16, 2010

BAD EURO COUNTRIES DRIVE OUT GOOD EURO COUNTRIES

Source: Het Financieele Dagblad, April 24, 2010

SPECULATING OVER THE END OF THE EURO IS NO LONGER TABOO

Source: NRC Handelsblad, February 13, 2010

Europe: a market without state

currency without governance

Stability Pact

The euro is a 'currency without governance.' The necessary political integration seems unlikely to eventuate. As soon as it comes to imposing fines and sanctions, Europe demonstrates how weak is really is. The refusal to conform to Stability Pact demands made this particularly clear, especially when Germany was the culprit at the beginning of 2002. There is no real belief in

any further political integration within the ever expanding and increasingly heterogeneous European Union. What actually seems to be happening is that inflation differences are increasing, there are large price differences, and market integration has hardly been accompanied by European unionism. A new slogan has arisen in this context: 'Europe is a market without a state'.
Twenty years after the fall of the Wall, the Eastern European countries are becoming aware of the hard side of the free market economy (look at what is happening in Poland, Latvia, Hungary and the Ukraine, for example). Europe's sense of solidarity is being put to the test, also in relation to those EU countries that do not belong to the eurozone. While the EU consists by now of 27 autonomous member states, it is far from being a 'United States of Europe'. Further extension of the EU to include the Balkan countries (such as Slovenia, Croatia, Macedonia and Montenegro) as well as Turkey eventually will certainly not make the process any simpler. Quite the contrary: there is no communal policy in the fields of taxes and social politics at all. The basic conditions for a real integration into a communal market are lacking and at the same time there is a complete mistrust of the ever-increasing bureaucracy in Brussels.
The possibility that some countries will even leave the EMU, whether compulsorily or voluntarily, should not be dismissed either. The survival of the euro – the 'unity coin' – will depend on whether its assumed advantages – convenience, expansive trade, more investments and a greater sense of European identity – outweigh the restrictions on and interference in national freedom of trade. The answer to this question will gradually become evident during the course of the present decade.
Fluctuations in the exchange rates have a major influence on the competitive position and profit of companies operating internationally, so strong fluctuations in the dollar rate have enormous consequences for companies which export to or import from the United States. With an increase in the dollar rate, exports from European countries are stimulated and imports slowed down; in the case of a decrease, the reverse is true.

JAPAN DRUG GROUP OPENS CENTRE

Eisai, the Japanese pharmaceutical group, yesterday demonstrated its confidence in the UK's scientific strength by opening a £100m European centre in Hatfield.

Mr Haruo Naito, chief executive, inaugurated the European Knowledge Centre, which will employ 500 staff.
The move consolidates Eisai's international expansion in Europe and the US, following which he said it planned to intensify its presence in middle-income countries.

Source: *Financial Times*, June 27, 2009

2.3.3 *Societal factors*

consumerism

Consumerism is a key feature of the business world of the early twenty-first century. An increasing number of consumers are actively demanding that their personal needs and requirements be met. Sometimes these demands are expressed via action groups, or more usually via consumers' organizations. Adjustments to the working environment are also demanded as a response to changing human and societal needs – for example, the striving for more participation and joint responsibility.

action groups

Consumerism has also yielded views and demands relating to products (about safety and environmental impact, for example). Action groups expressing societal wishes and demands have sprung up; the media play their part in making these known. No organization can afford to ignore these factors. On the contrary, if after evaluation and review these demands appear to be justified, it is important to react positively to them.

individualization

The increasing complexity of society can be partly explained by a trend towards individualization – the desire of people to live their lives in their own way – and this demands a more personal approach to servicing and tailoring needs.

nationalism
terrorism
migration streams
globalization

Research into safety risks has shown that organizations operating at the international level are having to take into account factors such as considerable labor unrest, the rise of nationalism and possibly terrorism, as well as the considerable negative effects of a crisis in Asia or in South America. As predicted, foreign companies are being greeted with less enthusiasm in various countries, including some of the Asian countries. Differences in wealth, nationalism, natural disasters such as those caused by the El Niño effect, migration streams and globalization are problems that are having a world-wide effect on society and are making business life risky.

It is predicted that changes during the 21st century will largely be determined by the further development, manufacture and marketing of genetic technology. Growing insight into the genetic coding of all life forms through research into the molecular structure of DNA is bringing about a revolution in the life sciences. Many companies from once separate fields are now working together. They include companies in the areas of agriculture and nutrition, chemicals and pharmaceutical products, and in the computer and communications industry: BASF, Dow Chemical, Novertis, Genzyme, Transgenics, IBM, Compugen, Ciba, Gerber and so on. For example, protein protecting against cancer can be produced by goats. Biogenetics and food engineering can have favorable effects on, for example, heart and vascular disease.

This is also the case with applications of nanotechnology in medicine and cosmetics. These new technologies, however, are also meeting resistance from such groups as Friends of the Earth, who are urging a boycott of cosmetics produced by L'Oreal, Nivea, Lancôme, Dove and others. In the case of food production, 'agriceutica' (a contraction of agriculture and pharmaceutics) is already part of our lives, as evidenced by the production of fruit and vegetables for protection against cholera, tetanus and hepatitis B. New applications in gen tech-products are having tremendous consequences for human beings, society and organizations. The resistance this is meeting (especially in Europe) is only to be expected. Some organizations are focusing their marketing policy on their products not being genetically manipulated. They include Nestlé, Unilever and Danone. Action groups and consumer organizations have also become forces to reckon with in this regard.

2.3.4 Technological factors

technological developments
hybrid car

Technological developments have important consequences for the modernization and renewal of production processes and the arrival on the market of new products, such as the transistor, electronic calculators and quartz watches. Such products quickly became a serious threat to more traditional products; in some cases they replaced them completely. The rise of substitutes – for example, synthetics like plastics – made major inroads into the market shares of producers of more natural products. The development of the hybrid car technology is also revolutionary.

Technological developments have accelerated in the past decade. The development of the electronic chip has made possible an increasing number of new products which, in turn, form a basis for the development of more new products and services.

teleworking

Technological developments have had a major effect on labor as a factor of production. Countless jobs have disappeared. New functions – such as systems developers and engineers, programmers and a new generation of electronic maintenance engineers – have appeared (and sometimes disappeared). The individual functions or parts of a company can now operate at a physical distance from each other while still remaining in direct contact through a web of information systems. These developments have allowed teleworking and similar innovative work arrangements to come to the fore (which in turn have made a contribution to reducing traffic congestion and the resulting impact on the environment).

THE CHINESE CONTROL THE SCARCE EARTH METALS

Hybrid cars, flat-screen televisions and solar energy panels all contain scarce metals which are primarily found in China and countries that lack stability. The West is vulnerable.

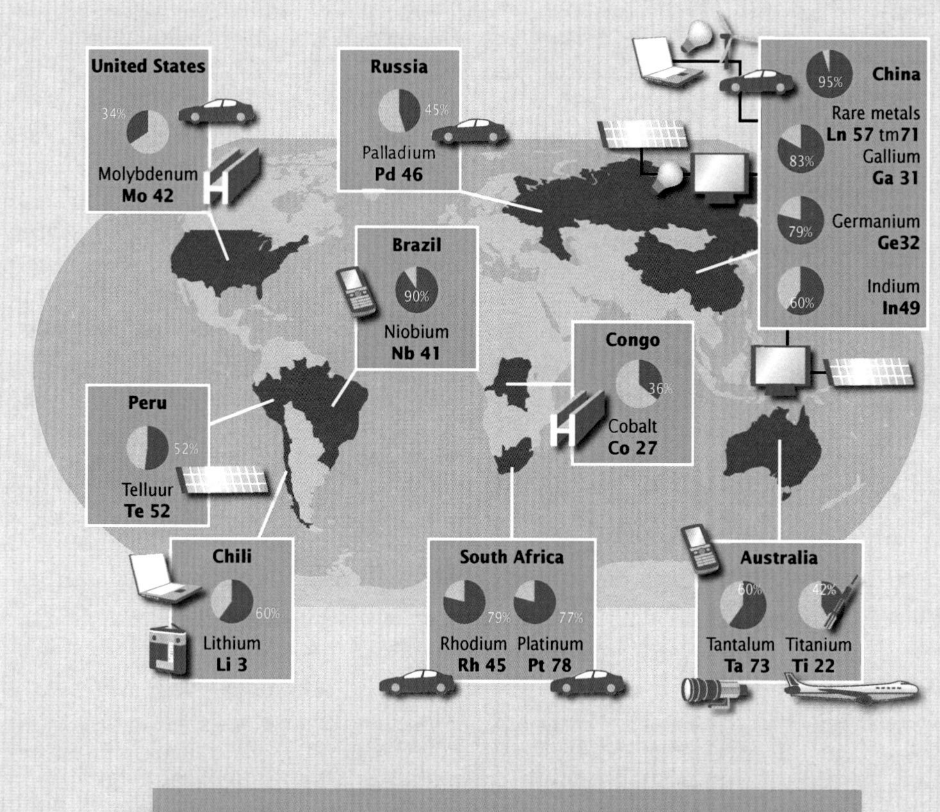

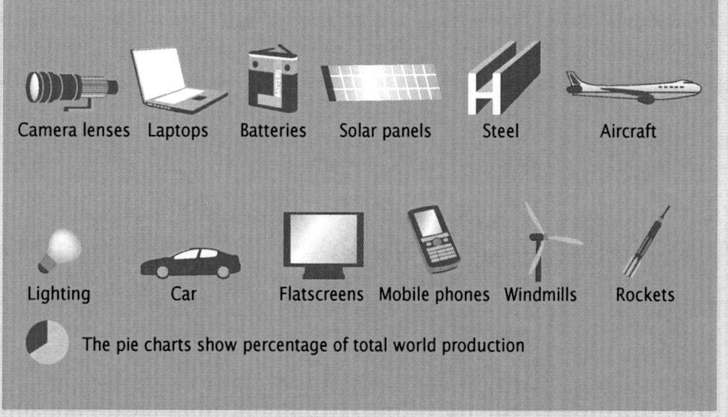

Source: *NRC Handelsblad*, 16 january 2010

Europe is dependent on the rest of the world for crucial metals

ICT

The application of ICT sometimes leads to a reduction of operational links in the chain between the producer and the consumer. European automobile manufacturers are increasingly making automobiles to order: color, accessories and the like can all be changed right up until the start of production. This has the advantage that the customer can get exactly the car he had in mind. The manufacturer does not need to keep large amounts of stock, meaning that his interest costs are reduced and he runs less of a risk of ending up with unmarketable automobiles. In the field of food production and sales, ICT is making it possible to decrease stock throughout the entire producer-to-consumer chain. Research has shown that stock can be reduced by electronic coordination of the various parts of the chain, leading to a possible reduction in costs by six percent.

producer-to-consumer chain

telecommunication revolution

The telecommunication revolution is changing production processes in many companies. Research, product development and manufacturing are being done in an increasing number of countries, as are sales, advertising, customer service, financing, personnel recruitment and outsourcing. For every 10,000 dollars an American spends on a car made by General Motors, 30 percent goes on assembly in South Korea, 17.5 percent on high-quality components (engines and electronics) from Japan, 7.5 percent on German design, 4 percent on smaller components from Taiwan, Singapore and Japan and 2.5 percent on advertisements and promotional activities in the UK. Less than 40 percent is left for internal staff operations, external advisors and for the headquarters in Detroit (USA), and even these areas are becoming increasingly international. In short, information technology is having the effect of globalizing supply and outsourcing (see also Section 2.4.2).

manufacturing technology

As far as efficient car manufacturing technology is concerned, there is still much to be learned. Volkswagen, for example, needs 35 working hours to manufacture a car while Nissan can do it in half the time: 14 hours. Opel is more efficient than VW, its competitor: it can manufacture a car in 21 working hours.
The first 'flying car' – the Transition – will come onto the market in 2011 (for $194,000). This flying car – an American invention – recently made its first test flight. In the Netherlands too, a flying car is in the process of development, with its first flight planned for the start of 2010.

technological innovation

New scarce metals such as tellurium, selenium, palladium, gallium, indium, niobium and tantalite are now being used in the production of innovative products such as hybrid cars, LCD screens, LED lights, solar energy panels, mobile phones, iPods and so on and will partly form the basis of further technological innovation.

2.3.5 Ecological factors

Care of the environment has become increasingly important in recent years. Increasing levels of water, soil and air pollution are likely to lead to the tightening of regulations – for example, those governing the dumping of toxic materials. Stricter environmental protection has consequences for production processes. For certain products, such as CFCs, it can even lead to production being prohibited. Such demands can also create opportunities, however. For companies in the field of environmental technology and in the fight against 'noise pollution,' more severe regulations can result in more sales opportunities.
Government and industries have joint responsibility for the environment. The sacrifice of natural beauty to economic necessity is becoming less and less acceptable. Government is confronted with this in the form of public outcry and legal action, as evidenced by the outcry whenever plans for the construction of roads and railways are published.

environmental policies

At a time when environmental measures finally seem to be having some effect, environmental policies are increasingly taking on an international character. There is growing interest in sustainability and responsible entrepreneurship. The focus has come to lie on air quality (CO_2 and ozone pollution) and on the international provision of energy, on climate control, water and waste management and on the production of food. National figures are showing that pollution and the amounts of fertilizer being applied are both decreasing. As production increases, consumer trash and that derived from industrial packaging is leveling out. Half of all once-only industrial packaging is already being recycled. To be globally sustainable, energy systems need to be based on solar energy: the use of fossil fuels must become the exception rather than the rule. Water power and geothermal warmth (warmth from the earth) are currently also under development. Recent research suggests that in many ways, the current development of alternative energy sources (including wind and solar energy) can be compared to the introduction of steam power. Politics will have to focus on international environmental agreements, and it can be expected that these will ultimately become compulsory.

sustainable energy systems

In the meantime, plans are being developed to limit greenhouse effects on a massive scale via so-called geo-engineering (by, for example, cloud seeding, sulphur dioxide spraying or the creation of enormous sun screens). However, anything that involves tampering with the climate is likely to arouse a great deal of resistance.

geo-engineering

Because oil is becoming scarcer and much more expensive, nuclear energy and keeping nuclear power stations running are once again debated issues.

With oil reserves being depleted partly because of demands on the expensive reserves by

RENAULT DRIVES DOWN A NEW AVENUE WITH ELECTRIC CARS

Like its peers, Renault is betting heavily on the development of electric cars and other low-emission vehicles. But perhaps even more than its competitors, it has made the production of a new generation of clean, compact cars the cornerstone of its longer-term recovery strategy. Indeed, while it has been cutting back research and development and other spending in the face of the industry crisis, it has continued to invest in next generation green and, especially, electric cars.

This is forcing it to revise its approach and shift the emphasis on services. Electric cars will require an altogether different business model. In short, their fixed costs are considerably higher than those of traditional vehicles while their running costs are significantly lower.

Then there is the additional problem of the batteries necessary to power these cars. They are expensive and will be leased by car companies from battery manufacturers. Electric cars are thus expected to accelerate the trend in car sharing and other related services. With such a high initial fixed cost it makes sense for individuals to pay an annual fee for use of an electric vehicle in a car-sharing scheme.

The development of electric cars is also expanding the range of partnerships and co-operation with companies that Mr Pelata admits Renault would never have entertained in the past. For example, the French group has been forging links with EDF, the French state-owned electricity utility, as part of its efforts to become the world's leading manufacturer of zero-emission vehicles.

Daimler is doing the same. It is already working with Italy's Enel state electricity group to provide electric car services in four Italian cities. Mr Pelata yesterday confirmed that Renault was in discussions with Daimler without disclosing precisely what projects. But it would not be a bad guess if it related to low emission cars or the German group's plans to launch a four-door version of its Smart city vehicle.

Sustainable mobility has become the car industry's latest buzz word. For the Renault executive this will provide the sector, and especially Renault, with the necessary 'oxygen' to emerge from the current crisis. That said, it still looks like a bold gamble.

Source: *Financial Times*, December 18, 2009

BRIC countries

fast-growing newcomers to the world market (the BRIC countries: Brazil, Russia, India and China), oil and gas are increasingly becoming the stakes in political showdowns. This will greatly increase calls for an alternative in the form of sustainable hydrogen-based energy. The increasing pollution of our environment and the changing of ecosystems will make this call even more urgent.

hydrogen technology

Hydrogen technology along with bio-fuels and the like are certain to be the new sources of sustainable energy in the future.

2.3.6 Market and industry factors

Market factors are influenced by the size and composition of the market. Measuring the size of the market is not always easy, however. It is important to have an idea of the market which will be targeted, and a useful starting point is the function of the product. The technological aspects of the product are of less importance.

For example ...

... a car fulfills the function of transportation. This means that an automobile manufacturer's competitors are not only cars, but also products like trains, trams, planes and ships. However, as a description of the market this is too wide. Even the car market as a whole is too wide a definition – a Rolls-Royce is not in competition with a standard saloon car. After all certain segments of the market are determined by price, income of the buyer and optional extras, among other factors.

In determining the size of the market, demographic and economic factors are highly relevant. Competition between existing companies within an industrial sector is influenced by four factors:

- The bargaining power of the supplier
- The bargaining power of buyers/clients
- The threat of substitute products
- The threat of new entrants

demand-driven communication and economy

As demonstrated by the Internet, which provides consumers with ever increasing possibilities to determine for themselves what to get and when to get it, technical innovations can cause changes in the balance of power. New users are almost literally creating a world of their own and are using search machines, communities and on-line networks to determine what product they want to buy, where they want to buy it and sometimes even what they want to pay for it. A new Internet generation is giving rise to an 'empowered consumer' via a variety of sites that are part of what has become known as Web 2.0. At least up until 2020, changes in the balance of power will largely determine marketing strategies, demand-driven communication and the demand-driving economy.

These factors together determine how much rivalry there is among existing firms in an industry (Porter, 1980/2008). The intensity of competition within an industry depends on factors, such as:

- The number and size of the competitors (in relative market share)
- The costs the client has to incur if switching suppliers
- The costs of withdrawal from an industry

Are there, for example, a few large giants or are there a large number of small organizations active in a specific market? What costs would be incurred if the organization ceased trading (redundancy payments, extra depreciation)? Does the leader-owner actually want this?

2.3.7 Political factors

Societal factors sometimes lead to legislative processes and new laws which usually involve a limitation of the freedom of the organization to implement plans in an unrevised form – for example, the location of a certain industry in a densely populated area. Governments also directly intervene in economic life – for example, by setting maximum and minimum prices, establishing working conditions or fixing minimum or maximum wage levels. In a number of countries, government influences economic life through forms of transfer payment/minimum wage support or by the commissioning of large infrastructure works via the public expenditure budget.

government influences

Besides fiscal legislation, dividend and interest policy is important for trade and industry. The government may also design special tax arrangements such as stock options which make saving for example more attractive.

Jurisdictional developments also have an effect on organization. They may lead to substantial compensation claims being awarded.

There are also certain international bodies whose work influences the decisions within organizations – for example, the EU, the OECD, OPEC, the World Bank and the International Monetary Fund (IMF).

In recent years, there has been a noticeable decrease in the influence of national or local governments in a number of fields. One has only to look at the liberalization of telecommunications, public transport and public utilities such as electricity, gas and water. This has led to rapid and extensive changes in the mutual relationships between companies. The pressure exerted by Brussels to make competition more transparent is a contributing factor whose importance should not be underestimated.

liberalization

Switzerland has the best climate for entrepreneurs. The US has been relegated to second place, while Singapore occupies third place. The Netherlands do not score poorly by any means. According to this research, government bodies operate effectively and use of technology (particularly the Internet) is high. Dutch harbours rate amongst the best in the world.

However, Dutch roads rate poorly both in terms of quality and serviceability. The Netherlands also score lower in terms of innovation, with company investment in research and development – necessary for maintaining a knowledge economy, according to the researchers – being rated as only fair to average (1.7% GNP). Finland is investing the most in research and development – 2.4%. Belgium and Germany – countries which border on the Netherlands – score higher in terms of investment in R&D than the Netherlands.

Country	2009	2008
Switzerland	1	2
U.S.	2	1
Singapore	3	5
Sweden	4	4
Denmark	5	3
Finland	6	6
Germany	7	7
Japan	8	9
Canada	9	10
Netherlands	10	8
Hong Kong	11	11
Taiwan	12	17
Britain	13	12
Norway	14	15
Australia	15	18
France	16	16
Austria	17	14
Belgium	18	19
South Korea	19	13
New Zealand	20	24

Table 2.2 *Most Competitive Countries in 2009*

Source: *Business Week*, 2009

OECD

competitive strength

criminality

At the international level, the OECD (Organization for Economic Cooperation and Development) is likely to call on the Netherlands to either increase its productivity or increase its hourly production rate. While the Netherlands is still scoring highly as far as competitive strength is concerned (as measured by the International Institute for Management Development in Lausanne) a recent tendency towards decreased labor productivity has even been observed. The Netherlands is not benefiting sufficiently from information and communication technologies. Entrepreneurs have recently started listing safety and the suppression of criminality as being among the factors likely to influence their choice of location and how long they stay there.

2.4 Relevant trends in the environment

The main underlying trends in an organization's environment which can lead to operational problems are outlined in Fig 2.3. These trends will make it necessary for adjustments to be made to an organization's procedures.

Increasing competition, internationalization of markets and geo-political shifts

In a number of markets there is evidence of increasing competition.
Christopher Columbus said that 'the world is smaller than the average human being assumes' even before he discovered America, and this statement is still applicable today. The single European market, the GATT agreements, the increasing sophistication of communication technology and improvements in the transportation of people and products mean that companies can now operate and indeed compete on a truly international basis.

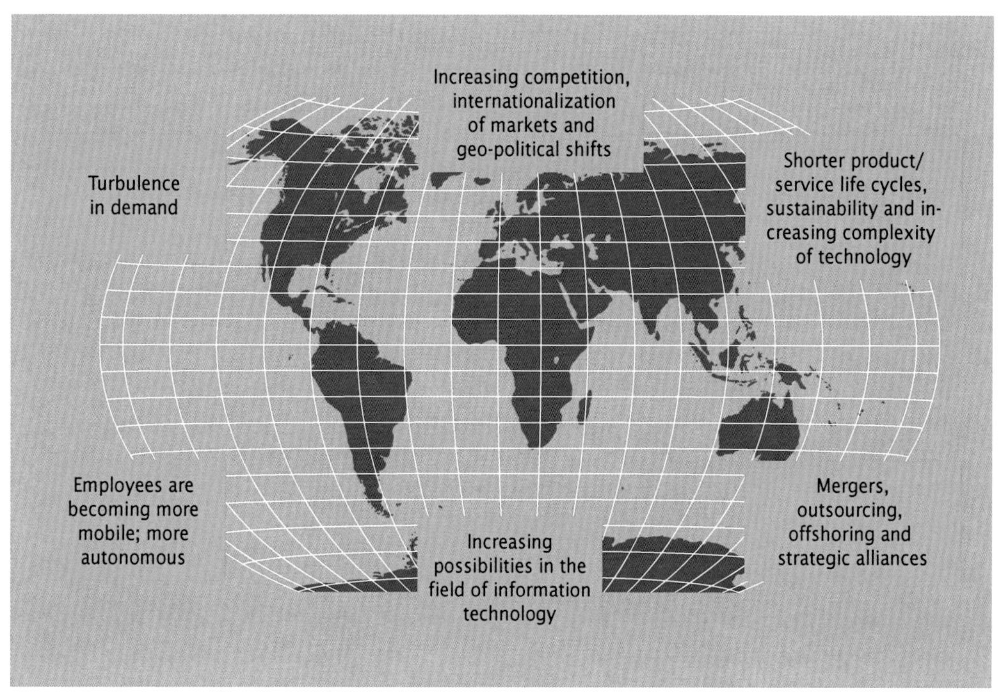

Figure 2.3 *Trends and developments in an organization's environment*

physical, psychological and cultural borders

internationalization of markets

The creation of a single European market has been an ongoing process that started with the Treaty of Rome in 1956 and has involved the breaking down of physical, psychological and cultural borders. While the removal of trade barriers has intensified competition and put margins under pressure, societies are getting to know each other better and are being influenced by the other's customs and habits. Similar patterns of consumption and methods of production have arisen, and these are enabling companies to sell their products all over the world. The internationalization of markets can be expected to accelerate and will be intensified when Japan, China and the Eastern European countries open up their markets to a greater extent and become more involved with Western economies.

Conversely, multinationals based in some of the so-called emerging markets are rapidly making their their presence felt: take Wuxi Pharma tech, for example, or Mahindra & Mahindra. New companies in countries such as India and China may soon become powerful competitors, with Lenovo (that took over IBM's PC business) and Tata Motors (now the owner of such companies as Jaguar and Range Rover) already setting the pace.

Exhibit 2.1

Shortage of essential raw materials is causing friction within global relationships

Large companies that receive government support are going to have to compete more intensively with each for access to these raw materials, perhaps by investing directly in areas that are rich in raw materials. Chinese companies are doing this already in African countries and in Australia. Unlike issues relating to the scarcity of water and energy, those relating to raw materials are only now starting to be discussed.

rare earth metals

The availability of raw materials, including new types, will, of course, have a major effect on global *geo-political relationships*. The need for the 'new' *rare earth metals* is making economies such as the European economy dependent on imports from other parts of the world (see 2.3.4).

China produces more than 95% of the world's supply of these crucial metals. The many applications of these raw materials in ICT, consumer electronics, 'green' technologies including environmentally friendly cars and sustainable energy provision has meant that the demand for these raw materials is growing exponentially.

In the longer term, Africa will also form an important source of supply and demand as well as becoming an investment destination.

Companies operating on a global basis do still encounter trade barriers and have to become efficient at coping with them. The following areas can expect to exhibit differences:

- Culture and language
- Tax and legislative procedures
- Banking systems
- Stock exchange regulations
- Exchange rate risks and foreign bill restrictions
- Social climate and regulations concerning industrial democracy and participation
- Environmental regulations
- Subsidy and government regulations which provide incentives

Notwithstanding this, national rules and sentiment remain important.

Shorter life cycles of products/services, sustainability and increasing complexity of technology

new products

New technologies are being developed at an ever-increasing pace, and as a result products are becoming obsolete more quickly. Organizations are being forced to develop their products further or to introduce new products at more regular intervals. This reduction in the product life cycle means that there is hardly time to earn back the often high production and development costs. Companies have to be alert and flexible in response to new technologies and market developments in order to stay ahead of their competitors.

reduction in the product life cycle

A reduction in the product life cycle forces organizations to remove any remaining internal barriers between research and development as well as those between manufacturing and marketing, and to make the contributions and responsibilities of each as clear as possible to facilitate direct communication between these functions. Sometimes the formation of business units is a solution, since it can bring a functional specialist closer to the market (see also chapters 6 and 7).

environmental responsibility

Concern for the environment and for sustainable production has meant that companies are increasingly becoming aware of their environmental responsibility and this should aid in preventing pollution of the environment. Developing products that can contribute towards a more sustainable world will be of particular importance in the future. Entrepreneurial activities must be socially responsible. While sustainable growth may sound paradoxical, 'green' growth does actually provide many new opportunities (see also 2.4.3).
At the same time, the strong growth of so-called life-science economies means that we will spend increasingly on health and care. A bio-economy underlines the importance of linking the supply of products and services to health advances and to make this profitable.

Mergers, strategic alliances, outsourcing, offshoring and worldwide reorganizations

co-operate
merge

In order to finance the high costs of product development and worldwide operations, many organizations are tending to co-operate in alliances or even merge, outsource business activities, or offshore activities to lower (wage) cost countries. In the resultant large organizations there is then a movement towards decentralization as autonomous units encourage more appropriate decision making.

Companies have a number of 'shoring' and 'sourcing' options open to them. It is important to have a broad-based and mixed shoring and sourcing (or outsourcing) model. It could include nearshoring (relocating activities to countries in close geographical proximity), inshoring (working with shared services), homeshoring (teleworking), backsourcing (bringing back activities that have been outsourced).

For example ...

... automobile manufacturer Peugeot/Citroën and India based steel producer Corus IJmuiden (part of Tata Steel) have worked together to develop new materials – in particular a substitute for steel – for the bodies of future cars. Suppliers and clients are working together in research and development activities without giving up their autonomy and independence.

strategic alliance

An organization large enough to produce efficiently and to overcome any barriers to trade it encounters – for example by forming a strategic alliance or joint venture with a local entrepreneur – will occupy the most competitive position in an international market.

READY, STEADY, SPEND ... BIG FIRMS ARE READYING TO SPLASH OUT ON TAKEOVERS AND EXPANSION

What a difference a year makes. At the start of 2009 many companies were obsessed with scraping together enough cash to survive, and even the blue-chips were cutting costs where they could, having had a nasty shock when the capital markets seized up the previous autumn. Depressed prices in the junk-bond market seemed to foretell an unprecedented Armageddon of bankruptcy as record numbers of firms defaulted on their debt. Gloom was the order of the day.

Twelve months later the mood in many boardrooms has been transformed. Fear and trepidation have given way to cautious optimism. Admittedly, this is mostly a reflection of the improvements firms have made to their own operations, and of the remarkable revival of the capital markets, rather than any firm signs of a return to strong growth in the rich world. But, while the chill wind of recession may continue to whistle through the streets, there will be a cosy warmth up in the executive suites as bosses contemplate the opportunities that the improving outlook, and their strengthening finances, will bring.

Companies' improving financial health will lead to a sharp increase in both capital spending and mergers and acquisitions. Firms that do have cash will not be allowed to sit on it.

Source: *The Economist*, January 10, 2010

research and development programs

The increasing complexity of technology makes it very unlikely for a single company to have the necessary knowledge and skills for all its research and development programs. Even the largest companies are likely to find that they have a lack of knowledge and skills in specific fields. Furthermore, the costs and risks associated with research and development are so high that a very large market share is required if the investments are to be earned back in time. The combining of complementary knowledge and the sharing of risks are important reasons for engaging in a strategic joint venture or alliance. Such ventures are also engaged in for the purpose of maintaining or intensifying market share – as Lufthansa-Delta Airlines, British Airways-American Airlines and Northwest-KLM have demonstrated. (See further in 4.4.) There were four European clusters: the Star Alliance, Lufthansa and United Airlines group; the

One World, British Airways and American group; the Wing, KLM and Northwest group, and the Sky Team, Air France and Delta group. The takeover of KLM by Air France (connected to Delta via an alliance) caused the basis of the collaboration to change and they all became members of the Sky Team. Partnering gives Northwest and Delta a substantial market advantage (within the US) compared to other alliances such as One World (American Airlines) and Star (United Airlines) that only have one major US airline company each (see also 2.4.8). In the meantime (May 2010) United Airlines and Continental Airlines announced a merger, and British Airways reached a mergerdeal with Iberia.

Daimler pulled out of Hyundai in 2004. It sold its share in the South Korean company and at the same time started joint ventures in China for the assembly of luxury cars of the C and E class (in collaboration with BAIC – Chinese Beijing Automotive Industry Holding company) and for the construction of trucks and motors (together with Beiqi Foton Motor Corporation). Volkswagen also signed an agreement in 2004 for the building of a factory in Shanghai to produce 800,000 to 1,600,000 cars in 2007.

COULD SUZUKI PROVIDE VOLKSWAGEN'S MAGIC NUMBER?

Ferdinand Piëch, VW's veteran chairman and consummate empire builder, has always said he would like to see the German group controlling 12 brands. It currently has 10 if you include Porsche and Scania. It is now seeking to secure truckmaker MAN and with Suzuki and this would give Mr Piëch his magic number of 12 brands. VW is already Europe's biggest and is challenging Toyota for the top spot in the world car league.

The deal with the Japanese company would help resolve VW's Achilles heel. Despite its success, VW has in recent years struggled to manufacture profitably low-cost small vehicles. Sure, the German group started out life as a low-cost manufacturer producing the so-called people's car. But no longer is the VW Beetle the flagship of small cars. If anything, the latest models are mid-range and quite expensive.

Suzuki, by contrast, has long had an impressive record of making small cars profitably and an enviable emerging markets exposure in countries such as India or Indonesia that can make a partnership even more attractive for VW.

In return, the Germans would offer larger car, diesel and electronics expertise and better access to European and US markets to Suzuki. For the Japanese company has struggled to build a strong position in Europe and has had trouble hanging on to the North American market.

Mr Piëch would presumably also enjoy undermining some of his biggest rivals by striking a deal with Suzuki.
Renault-Nissan, too, is believed to have considered investing in Suzuki and bringing it into its international alliance. But talks between the two parties apparently collapsed because of differences of opinion and personality.
Suzuki also has some production links with Fiat and GM, its original 20 per cent partner before the US group was forced to sell its stake to raise desperately needed cash.

If, as many increasingly expect, VW clinches a deal with Suzuki early next year, you can expect Mr Piëch to demand that his new Japanese partner breaks its links with Nissan, Fiat and GM.

Source: *Financial Times*, December 4, 2009

At the same time Peugeot is negotiating to buy a further stake in Mitsubishi and General Motors is joining forces with China's SAIC to gain a stronger foothold in India. In 2009, Tata Motors, India's biggest carmaker, reported an 81% increase in commercial vehicle sales and a 48% rise in domestic car sales. India's automotive market, while growing rapidly, is also one of the world's most competitive of producers, jostling to release the lower cost cars and light trucks.

'Almost everyone on the stock market can be bought,' or so the saying goes. The 'buyout' market is growing faster in Europe than in the US. Asia plays a minor role in this regard. In the meantime, the managers of large companies have come to fear the venture capitalists and the raiders more than ever before. Managers who regarded themselves as unassailable have by now become acquainted with the purchasing power of the big buyers. It has been said that the only company that is still too big to take over is Shell – but is it?

takeover fever

As of 2004/2005, Europe has been caught up in takeover fever. Takeovers have once again been put on the management agenda and the cash boxes and safes have apparently filled to capacity. In 2004, there were 5,100 major mergers and takeovers recorded in Europe alone, with a total value of $1,100 billion, 50% more than in the previous year. Large firms are all pressing for expansion again: Telefonica (Spain) took over OZ (GB) for €25.8 billion, P&O Nedlloyd (Netherlands) passed to Maersk (Denmark) for €2.3 billion, and so the list continues.

In the first nine months of 2005 alone there were there were worldwide takeovers to the value of $1,980 billion, 39% more than in the previous year. Takeover activity is the highest it has been for five years.

Chinese companies

Since 2004/2005 there have also been reports of large takeovers by Chinese companies, not only in the US (the energy concern Unocal by CNOOC and IBM by Lenovo), but also in Australia, South Korea, France and Britain (Rover came into the hands of Nanjing Automotive). In the US there is considerable fear of what is perceived as the Chinese threat: they do not quite know how to deal with the new rival on the world market.

investment companies

Investment companies are also becoming increasingly active in the takeover field. They include KKR (which has made a bid of 7.2 billion for VNU, but is also interested in KPN amongst others), Apax (which has bought Tommy Hilfiger, Gouden Gids, and others), Alpinvest, Carlyle and Weather Investments. More than one fifth of all takeovers in Europe have been made by investment companies. In the Netherlands, NIB Capital, Petroplus, HEMA, Wehkamp, Wavin and the sweets division of CSM have been taken over by such companies.

SO WHICH BRIGHT SPARK MADE THE WORST DEAL OF THE CENTURY; THE INSIDER

Jerry Levin, who sold Time Warner to AOL, has recently described the $124 billion (GBP 77 billion) deal as the 'worst of the century'. The title could also go to Vodafone's hostile acquisition of Mannesmann in 2000 (debatably last century) when the UK mobile giant used overvalued shares to buy even more over-priced German equity. However, the carve-up of ABN AMRO in 2007, which nearly sank both the Royal Bank of Scotland and Fortis, is also a contender.

Levin said many banks need to apologise. 'Let's hear publicly from Lehman Brothers, Bear Stearns, Merrill Lynch and on and on,' he said.

Source: *Sunday Express*, January 10, 2010

The same thing is happening at the international level. Google has bought YouTube, J. P. Morgan has incorporated Cazenove, Cyrte Investment has bought Bol.com, Unilever has bought Sanes and Zwitsal, Kraft (the owner/producer of Philadelphia Cream Cheese and Milka and Toblerone chocolate) has bought up Cadbury (known for its chewing gum brands Stimorol and Trident) for €13.6 billion after first having made a hostile bid, and following the takeover of XTO Energy (one of the biggest natural gas producers in the US) by Exxon Mobil in a megadeal involving $41 billion, more takeovers can be expected in the energy sector. Recently (in 2009) Cisco lifted the offer for Tandberg (Norway) to $3.4 billion, Canon made a bid for Océ, the Dutch printer and photocopier company, and BA and Iberia reached a preliminary agreement on a merger that would create Europe's third largest airline in terms of revenue. Xerox, Dell and Friesland Campina are looking out for takeovers and the pharmaceutical giants are hoping to grow by scaling-up: for example, Roche, the Swiss pharmaceutical concern, has taken a 'bio-farm' approach and bought up the American company Genentech, the world's biggest biotech company.

While the profits will often only be evident in the long term, the costs will often be immediately apparent. 80% of the mergers and takeovers that have occurred during recent years will turn out not to have created any value or barely so. These companies will often have thrown away many of their resources. That magic *synergy* will often turn out to be illusory. Despite this, the wave of merger and takeovers continues unabated, as it has been doing since 2009/2010. Analyses have shown this pattern to repeat itself every five years.

The top managers of our biggest organizations are now claiming that they spend half of their time on merger and acquisition cases. With new mergers and acquisitions being reported daily, the terms 'merger-euphoria,' 'merger mania' and 'macho-acquisitions' have been coined. The 'mega-merger,' aimed particularly at getting additional market leverage, has come into existence. According to research, this extra market leverage is not being translated into higher profit levels: generally speaking, production is not being done more efficiently and the 'post merger' period is not characterized by better scores in the area of research and development. Mergers are primarily defensive moves, though other considerations also play a role. The large organization collapses less frequently than the small organization and the top managers of large companies have more status (and income via salary, bonuses, stock options etc.) than those of smaller companies.

mammoth mergers
conglomerates breaking up

Simultaneously with the increase in 'mammoth mergers,' conglomerates seem to be breaking up (in the USA, this is a process that has been underway since the end of the 80s), as evidenced by the splitting up of AT&T and TT (in the USA), ICI (in the UK), and Akzo Nobel and Philips (in the Netherlands). Throughout the world, organizations like these are continually reorganizing their operations, with cost reduction the main goal. Such reorganizations often involve many jobs being cut.

reorganizations

Philips has been considering splitting up the concern for a long time; ABN Amro has not excluded the possibility of splitting up, and for Akzo Nobel, splitting up its operations into independent pharmaceutical and chemical activities had been under consideration as a serious strategic option since 2000. The splitting up took place in 2007.

Since 2009, there has been open speculation that General Electric will also be split up in order to avoid having its industrial and its financial activities both housed under the same roof. Unilever has also been mentioned as a candidate for being split up, and at the end of 2009, a hedge fund was putting pressure on TNT to split itself up.

Developments in information technology

e-commerce
multi-channel marketing
intermediation
disintermediation

Developments in the field of information technology provide opportunities for improved efficiency and effectiveness. More sophisticated telecommunication networks and management information systems have improved the possibilities for decentralized decision making, while at the same time allowing management to maintain an overview at the center. If organizations are to exploit these opportunities, change will be inevitable. This change may take the form of an increase in e-commerce and multi-channel marketing and sales, or in traditional industries, ICT-related changes through 'unbundling' and 'rebundling' through the processes of intermediation and disintermediation respectively (see also sections 2.4.7 and 10.6).

In this connection, *social networking* – for example, the creation of communities, and not only those in the area of supply chain analysis, sales and marketing, but also in the area of R&D, recruitment and selection and so on (see also 10.4.6.) – could certainly prove to be an important business tool. Technologies such as blog and wiki software are symptoms of an increasing and omnipresent *desire for information*.

Greater employee mobility and autonomy

autonomy There is a trend in organizations towards increasing the involvement and autonomy of employees who wish to have a say in the allocation of work and are also prepared to change jobs. Consequently, employee mobility and skill levels have become important issues for management.

WOULD YOU LIKE A McPhD WITH THAT?

McDonald's hopes to offer its own PhD, throwing down the ultimate challenge to the popular wisdom that the high-street fast-food chain creates nothing but low-paid, low-quality 'McJobs' to replace high-skilled work in old manufacturing industries.

The company's ambition is not as bizarre as it might sound to the average visitor to a McDonald's restaurant. The company has developed a reputation over recent years for its training. It took a further step towards educational respectability last year when it became one of Britain's first employers to win the power to award its own nationally recognised qualifications. McDonald's has taken advantage of this to start offering courses in basic shift management that are equivalent to A-levels.

These teach 'the whole dynamics about customer interactions', stretching even to the hardships of 'dealing with aggressive customers' and 'safety during the night-time shift'. They also deal with less dangerous but equally sensitive matters, such as how to approach and aid unserved customers wandering around at the front of the restaurant.

The CPO said McDonald's had become an attractive employer both to graduates and other workers, in large part because of its training, with its status as an awarding body adding to the prestige of its qualifications. The company also offers a 'flexibility' that suited young people studying at university, including 'McTime' – a system that allows workers to change their shifts via their mobile phones.

Aside from McDonald's, eight employers and employer groups have won the right to award their own qualifications since last year. The government has encouraged them because it wants more workers to have nationally recognised certificates that increase their employability across the economy.

Source: *Financial Times*, May 11, 2009

As a result of rapid demographic changes, a lot of employees will retire in the coming years, potentially leading to a loss of essential knowledge and skills. A focus on expanding the productivity of every employee would thus seem advisable. If, as predicted, more than 60% of the world's population is living in cities by 2030 a focus on products and services that mainly take advantage of the effects of *urban concentration* would seem advisable in the long term.

Turbulence in demand

Consumer behavior is constantly changing and consumer needs are becoming increasingly varied. Organizations are thus forced to provide the various customer groups with a variety of products. They also need to react increasingly quickly to changes in taste and preferences. The Internet via Web 2.0-technology is expected to change demand patterns dramatically.

There is clear evidence of this in the 'fast fashion' area, with its extremely short product cycles for fashion with mass appeal (fashion as sold by such fashion chains as Zara, H & M, Benetton and Topshop). 'Fast' may sometimes have to be very fast indeed: fashion items to meet new trends must sometimes be made available within a matter of weeks. To this end, designers, market specialists and buyers analyze almost real-time marketing data. If the news items prove popular, local production networks must be able to manufacture and supply to order. Decisions are being made faster than ever and to short decision-making processes; the required information needs to be made available very quickly, which demands real-time achievement-oriented management. Innovative ('first-move') products are dominating the market for increasingly shorter period of time, with new products following in quick succession, making it even more difficult to turn a profit. The rapid expansion of free services (including Internet services and search engines such as Google) are complicating things even more (see also Section 10.4.6).

Bottom of the Pyramid (BOP)

C.K. Prahalad, a management guru from India, has drawn attention to the change in demand volume in relation to the dramatic change in demand patterns. Briefly, his theory is as follows: the greatest purchasing power lies with the millions of poor people and the 'Bottom of the Pyramid' (BOP) (his term) is the driving force behind demand changes, innovation and prosperity, and even revolutionary change. The bottom of the economic pyramid is formed by the 4 billion people who live on less than $2 a day. The World Bank, several donor nations, several aid organizations, national governments and civilians have done their utmost for more than 50 years, but have not been able to eradicate poverty. Prahalad contends that thinking about the poor as victims or as a burden should stop. Instead, we should start seeing them as resilient and creative entrepreneurs and as quality-conscious consumers. In the 18 largest developing countries, some 680 million families with an income lower than $6,000 are involved. A whole new world of opportunities will arise here and they will be a new source of world trade, prosperity and innovation. In other words, the four billion people at the bottom of the economic pyramid – at the BOP – are rearing to become a part of the globalization process.

globalization

To ignore this market means missing out on great commercial possibilities. BOP consumers also want brand products, not cheap rubbish. For them too – the billions of consumers in China, India, Brazil, Mexico, Russia, Indonesia, Thailand and South Africa – innovation is the key to change and growth. This will eventually cause a complete turnabout in the economic structure. Companies (multinationals included) will find themselves forced to take a closer look at the poorest people in the world and at their needs and possibilities. (See Prahalad, *The Fortune at the Bottom of the Pyramid: Eradicating Poverty through Profits*).

Some of these developments – namely, internationalization, repositioning, sustainable business, industrial transformation, outsourcing, off-shoring and shared services, unbundling and rebundling, cultural differences, strategic alliances, and network organizations – will now be examined in some detail. The influence of IT, changes in employee attitudes and corporate behavior are covered in chapters 7 and 10.

2.4.1 Repositioning and industrial transformation

production industries

Globalization and increasing competition are the driving forces behind industrial transformation and the repositioning of many industrial companies. The production industries are searching for higher margins and are increasingly focused on providing service activities, though they are going about the 'revolution' silently. Océ, the producer of photocopying machines and printers, has created a new organization, one based not on the devices themselves but on these devices being used by the customer. The consumer does not only want to buy a product, but also wants to be relieved of the responsibility of looking after it. If the producer takes this problem off their hands, they can concentrate on their core activities. In response to this need, DAF is now not only delivering the truck, but also seeing to it that it is always ready to operate: that is, that it fulfills the function of providing transport. In addition to providing maintenance and repair, leasing may also be part of the terms, and those who operate the devices may be included too. In the United States, where companies like General Electric, IBM and Boeing are leading the way in transforming traditional industrial companies into industrial service providers, Océ has been attracting attention for the last two years by providing a broader service package than its competitors. Several thousand employees of this Dutch-based company are concentrating on providing so-called 'document services'. These services encompass the organization's entire paperwork flow: providing and maintaining the entire printer and photo copying machine network as well as the staff that carry out the activities involved.

providing functional services

Providing functional services as a differentiation tactic and to strengthen brand loyalty demands a different kind of business approach by the company. The accent comes to lie on providing full service and 'total care' instead of sales. In other words, there is a trend within industry towards a service approach (it has been described as the 'servicization' of industry). Even though the trend seems to be unmistakable, not all companies are taking the approach of providing activities to placate customer desires and thereby obtain higher margins. For industrial organizations, it may even make sense to oppose this trend and focus solely on the manufacturing side. The search for higher margins by such concerns as Océ or DAF represents, in fact, real opportunities for quintessentially manufacturing companies, because device and machine builders are outsourcing the production of components and parts to an increasing degree. However, in the 'put it together' industry, with its high percentage of electronics, software engineering, electro technology and mechanical engineering (in other words, 'mechatronics'), cooperation between end producers of systems and modulus is unavoidable if a company wants to stay in the business at a global level.

mechatronics
cooperation

Being in a regional chain of business clusters is profitable when times are good, but when they are not (as in the recent crisis), the mutual interdependency of companies can be a disadvantage and there will not be enough work for everybody. Expenditure cutbacks, retrenchments and shorter working hours have an immediate flow-on effect within such chains. 'Clustering' has also helped the aviation industry in its battle for existence. The aviation industry came under great pressure during 2008, and this has had consequences for suppliers and maintenance companies.

2.4.2 Outsourcing, nearshoring, offshoring and shared services

product life cycles
flexibility

Present developments are encouraging companies to concentrate on their core activities (the activities that play the key role in their business), meaning that the business chain is undergoing a change. An increasing part of the production process is being outsourced, because product life cycles are becoming increasingly shorter and investments in research and development and in fixed assets are having to be depreciated within an increasingly short time span. Outsourcing brings the added advantage of greater flexibility during periods of rapid changes in market demand and of being able to transfer a part of the business management, with its ever increasing complexity (a consequence of the broader range of products) to the supplier.

outsourcing of production

Outsourcing of production often results in the outsourcer economizing on capital expenditure and on the budgets for product development and research. During the course of time a situation of dependency could arise because the partner has control of both product development and production initiative. The partner will have learnt a lot about the desires of the end consumer in the meantime, and will have obtained a great deal of experience in product development.

strategic risk

The introduction by the partner of a competing product on the market will only be a matter of time. This constitutes an important strategic risk. In the reverse direction along the chain, the supplier will not want to be too dependent on a major client. A new and successful supplier is frequently required not only to have the knowledge and the skills to participate in the design and development of his client's new target systems, but also to carry some of the development costs, risks and investments. This is the case with many industrial firms: for instance, firms in Brabant and Limburg that work for big clients such as Philips, Medical, ASML, DAF, Stork and Océ. A striking number of the hundreds of industrial suppliers in that region are considering forming close collaborative ties or even merging to increase capacity and so keep up with the internationalizing of their clients, thus exercising greater market power and reaching a certain equality with them.

Outsourcing and offshoring

outsourcing
offshoring
nearshoring

The terms 'outsourcing' and 'offshoring' are very often used as synonyms. Offshoring and nearshoring always implies that the activities are transferred to a supplying unit in another country, which is at the same time a low-wage country nearby or far away, such as India, China, South Africa, the Philippines, Poland or Turkey. In other words, offshoring is a global process, a way of transferring activities to a low-wage country, often ICT-based and often involving long physical distances. Océ, who has transferred machines and/or software production to Malaysia, China, India and the Czech Republic, forms a good example of this.

However, offshoring does not necessarily involve the transfer of activities to another business: this is outsourcing. Offshoring of activities to the company's own branch in a low-wage country will, of course, only occur if activities can be carried out far more cheaply there. The activities could theoretically be farmed out to an independently operating supplier, but offshored processes are normally carried out in-house and under the company in question's own supervision.

Offshoring is particularly popular for the service activities of companies (a Wehkamp call center in South Africa, for example), in telecommunication and in financial services – processing and administration – (ABN Amro in Chennai, Madras), or for the purposes of software development, IT services and contract support (Oracle, Deloitte research, IBM and Siemens), and the like. Reduction of expenses, quality improvement, flexibility, retraining advantages and resilience are usually regarded as the main advantages.

Experiences in outsourcing, nearshoring and offshoring

The envisaged advantages of outsourcing and offshoring are often overestimated.

dissatisfied with the results

Investigations show that many businesses are dissatisfied with the results. The *Financial Times* (2003 and 2004) repeatedly referred to the fact that 66% of businesses were either disappointed about the results of outsourcing, or were of the opinion that there had been no advantage at all. Reports from India, to name just one country, have shown the other perspective: that Western businesses had spent too little effort on maintaining the relationship. Apparently it was thought that once a certain activity was contractually organized, no further effort was required. In fact the opposite is the case.

INDIA: OUTSOURCING HIT BY FRAUD

For many years, the combination of highly educated personnel and low costs has lead to a massive flow of work to rapid expanders such as Tata and Wipro in India. At the start of this year, it was discovered that the IT giant Satyam had been overvaluing its income and assets for years. It had managed to acquire the custom of about one third of the world's biggest companies by reducing its profit margins to an absolute minimum.
Although it seemed as though Satyam's massive loss of customers would cause it to go under, it was sold, 20,000 workers were made redundant, its top management was replaced and it underwent a transformation. By the end of 2009, it was slowly regaining lost ground.

As a result of a fall in demand, Western IT companies still have little need for additional capacity, especially since nearshoring to countries such as Eastern Europe is virtually as cost-effective an alternative as it is a transparent one.

Source: *Het Financieele Dagblad*, 20 April 2009 and the *Financial Times*, December 29, 2009

backsourcing

The same holds for producers of concrete products (as opposed to ICT service provision at a distance). Recent reports that businesses are bringing back physical production to the Netherlands ('backsourcing'), or that companies are deciding after all to start up new production plants in the Netherlands (for example, Scania trucks in Zwolle) are highly indicative. There certainly is a place for production activities here: fear that industry will move away is not always justified. As long as trained personnel is required for such things as

OUTSOURCING BLURS INTO SERVICES

As recently even as 2009, experts were still warning that that outsourcing was unlikely to deliver rapid savings (*Financial Times*, 2009). While cost savings can be considerable, they will only be made in the medium to longer term. It is not the fastest way to eliminate costs. Instead, companies looking to cut costs quickly are more likely to adapt different strategies, such as shedding staff.

But it is not only the economic environment that is at stake. According to industry observers, IT outsourcing could be entering a new phase, with vendors such as Microsoft, Google and Amazon offering straightforward easy to-buy services on a per person per month, or even per transaction, basis. This represent a radical departure from the conventional view of IT outsourcing. Nowadays, providers are becoming aware of potential competition from cloud computing and software-as-a-service providers, and are adjusting their products in response. In particular, outsourcing companies are becoming more flexible in areas where they face direct or emerging competition from the cloud – an umbrella term used in this context to describe web-based delivery of services – or from other remote providers that will 'host' a company's technology, such as e-mail, customer relations management and sales force automation or via hosted networks and security. Some providers are also going in the direction of flexible pricing, especially some of the bigger Indian companies. The technology can be delivered in a variety of ways. We have seen an evolution from building up your data centre to bringing someone in to run it to a change to global delivery from remote locations. The technology is improving access to alternative acquisition and delivery models.

Source: *Financial Times*, May 14, 2009

(See also 'Outsourcing risks' www.ft.com/digital business)

developing a production line, sorting out teething problems and reducing production costs further, or where high wages do not play an important role, the Netherlands will remain a relatively attractive proposition. The strong position of Dutch suppliers in 'high-tech mechatronics' in the south-eastern part of the Netherlands is no fiction and they are also major suppliers to production chains in Germany and Belgium.

Shared services

shared services

concentrating back office activities

As well as outsourcing and offshoring there has been a renewed interest during the last few years in organizing 'shared services' in a central unit within a company (often situated in one location) to provide supporting services so as to cut down on costs. This is, in fact, just another way of concentrating activities, usually back office activities, and centralizing the relevant powers of decision. A new element in this old organizational concept is that it is integrated in a service concept in which a customer-supplier relationship is created between the supplier (the shared service center) and the customer (a division, business unit, a unit in another country or department).

2.4.3 Eco-efficiency and sustainable and societal entrepreneurship

eco-efficiency

sustainable entrepreneurship

The increasing attention to eco-efficiency is another important trend within the business world. Prompted by the concept of sustainable entrepreneurship, ambitious environmental goals are starting to be seen as market opportunities. Shell is a good example. Together with Daimler-Benz, Shell is working on an automobile driven by a fuel cell. The new motor for this automobile operates on the principle of hydrogen-based catalytic partial oxidation. Hydrogen is already emerging as the solution to environmental problems. Solar energy has not really come into its own yet. However, it has been reported that Shell has signed a contract with Greenpeace whereby the company undertakes to be an advocate for solar energy in the Netherlands in return for lower prices.

chain-focused approach

To bring about eco-efficiency, a chain-focused approach makes considerable strategic sense. Such an approach demands communication and cooperation with production chain partners such as suppliers. One way of obtaining an overall improvement in the intensive pig breeding industry, for example, is better cooperation between all links of the chain, from the pig breeder (primary producer) to the abattoir, the meat packaging industry, mash producers and health organizations.

Recent research (by Prahalad, 2009, amongst others) has shown that *sustainability* is an important cause of organizational and technological innovation. Eco-friendliness allows companies to lower their costs and increase their income since it brings new opportunities for creating profitable businesses. To take an example, DSM's new synthetic material Stanyl Fortii, which does not break down at 300 degrees and is not flammable, is allowing car manufacturers to replace metal parts in cars, making them lighter and more economical with fuel and consequently they emit less carbon dioxide. DSM has with justifiable pride reported that it is now high on the list of the Dow Jones Sustainability World Index. In the 4-year period from 2003 to 2007, Hewlett Packard saved about $100 million in recycling costs, FedEx halved the fuel consumption of its planes and cars by taking part in a Fuel Sense program, IBM encouraged working from home among a quarter of its 320,000 employees, saving $700 million in property expenses and raising productivity by between 10% to 20%.

As such, sustainability as an overall concept has many aspects to it:

- Economical sustainability: for organizational continuity, there must be stable economic growth, synergy and a sense of unity.
- Organizational sustainability: sustainable organizational solutions involve taking an integral approach to problems, one that is not ad hoc, the hype of the week or based on what every new management guru that comes onto the scene preaches.

- Social sustainability: this must be based on good labor relations, on the development of talent, on opportunities for self-development for everyone: in other words on both 'empowerment' but also the maintenance of cultural values.
- Ecological sustainability: this must not only be based on the protection of nature and the building of environmental awareness, but also on cultural values.
- Societal sustainability: for stable societal development, there must be a sensible division of roles between private and public partners, and justice and a well-functioning constitutional state, one in which the majority complies with rules for the common good.

To sum this up: sustainability involves resolving our current problems and searching consistently for sustainable solutions for the future.

sustainability

Multinationals in particular have been more reluctant to endorse a policy of sustainability, as evidenced by Shell and the Brent Spar affair. It is often activists or other stakeholders that pressure companies to do so, regardless of the potential risks (financial and otherwise) involved (see Porter & Kramer, 2006). Companies often try to create the impression that their sustainability strategy is more extensive and brings more benefits than it actually does. Too many businesses are using sustainability as a means for gaining publicity (*The Economist*, 2008), applying symbolic measures that at the most only have a short-term effect. It is only serious initiatives that will have a permanent effect and will provide opportunities for a strategic advantage (Berrone et al., 2009). In this regard, KLM seems to be setting an example to the aviation industry.

SOCIALLY RESPONSIBLE ENTREPRENEURSHIP AT KLM

In the aviation sector, KLM is striving to become what is known as a 'smart leader' in socially responsible entrepreneurship and a model for others to follow. KLM's dedication to this ideal is set out in a Corporate Social Responsibility Statement (Air France-KLM, 2006). The commitment as laid down in this statement is to 1) creating trust among all stakeholders, 2) safety and security as undeniable obligations, 3) developing as a socially responsible group on a national and on an international scale, and 4) investing in environmental protection that extends beyond a mere adherence to the rules. KLM accounts for its actions in a specific CRS report (Air France-KLM, 2009) and in sections of its annual report (KLM 2007/2008 and 2008/2009), which is made public.

Towards eco-effectiveness with 'Cradle-to-Cradle'

downcycling

cradle- to-cradle (C2C)

The Cradle-to-Cradle (C2C) concept is about a sustainable natural environment that can be perpetrated forever. It can only be achieved by paying heed to the principles of bio and technical recycling right from the conceptual and design stage of product creation and by banning 'design for reincarnation' environmental damage. Eco-efficiency will be replaced by eco-effectiveness, with recycling or 'downcycling' (less damaging ways of doing things) replaced by 'upcycling'. Waste products will be transformed into food to the extent that material after having been used in one product is usefully put into the production of another product (as described by McDonough and Braungart, 2002). The following are some examples of cradle- to-cradle (C2C) products: recyclable synthetics, soluble ink, biodegradable car materials, integrated chain management (including such things as environment technical recycling analyses).

2.4.4 Internationalization of industrial life

A decision by an organization to target international markets and/or operate on a global basis may be made for a variety of reasons. Sometimes growth in the home market is no longer possible and so further growth is dependent on the organization operating beyond its own national borders. In other cases, profits may be increased and the costs of production lowered by embarking on a large-scale investment program. The spreading of activities over a greater number of countries or regions makes a company less vulnerable to the effects of specific developments and risks in one particular region or country.

The internationalization of company activities may be prompted by the unplanned ending up of an order abroad, leading on to the formation of an export/import section within the sales department and later perhaps even to licensing or franchising. Sometimes internationalization may be prompted by a 'daughter' company or a strategic alliance.

Growth in the importance of international activities means an increase in the complexity of business considerations as well as the need for a greater level of management involvement. International operations may take many various forms:

- The export of products/services
- The export of technology, patents and licenses
- Franchising of the export formula
- Investments in foreign subsidiaries or manufacturing facilities
- Acquisitions, joint venture and alliances
- Worldwide operations in a so-called global company

global company

In the case of the global company, considerable emphasis must be placed on the coordination of activities in the various countries (see Fig 2.4). For example, the designs may be made in Country A, produced in Countries B, C and D and eventually sold in a number of different countries. The activities of individual countries have to be coordinated and the flow of goods and information between the countries has to be controlled.

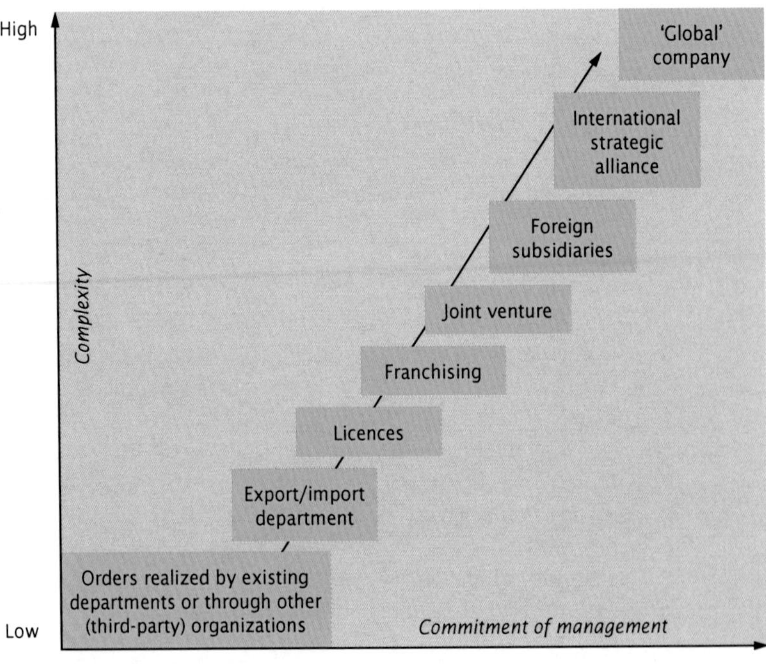

Figure 2.4 *Stages of development in the internationalization of an organization's operations*

Source: *Stoner and Freeman*, 1992

In the case of a multinational company operating on an international basis, the company will have autonomous subsidiaries in various countries, each with its own products, brands and markets.

think globally, act locally

The slogan 'think globally, act locally' refers to the necessity for an organization working on a global scale to balance the specific needs of the local market with the overall need for a high degree of efficiency and impeccable coordination. Local knowledge is the key: it would be a serious mistake to simply transfer what is known to work at home to a new market. This poses a great challenge for management. Operating on an international basis means that managers must appreciate the significance of differences in culture and their role in determining the relative success or failure of projects worldwide.

CASE Mini case study 2.1

Multinationals eat into the Russian market

Multinational food companies are moving into Russia to snap up local businesses, but Russian group Wimm-Bill-Dann Foods says it is determined to make acquisitions of its own and remain independent. International food groups believe Russia will become one of the strongest consumer markets in Europe over the next few years as its expanding economy makes people wealthier.

International food companies that have made big acquisitions in Russia over the past year to take advantage of the country's growth include Unilever, PepsiCo, Kellogg, Kraft, Nestlé, Coca-Cola and Carlsberg. Wimm-Bill-Dann has also attracted the interest of foreign buyers, such as French dairy group Danone. It has remained independent, although Danone has quietly built up a stake, today owning some 18 per cent. The company's Russian founders, a group of about half a dozen individuals, control the company with a 47 per cent share, allowing it to defend itself from unwelcome predators.

Wimm-Bill-Dann, which was established in the early 1990s and specialises in selling mid-priced dairy foods such as milk, cheese and yoghurts, as well as baby food and juices, has been one of Russia's most successful consumer goods companies, with its market capitalisation tripling over the past two years to about $5.5bn. It is the leader in the Russian dairy market, with some two-thirds of the market, although it has lost the top spot in beverages to Lebedyanksy, the juice company recently bought by PepsiCo.

Wimm-Bill-Dann has grown by acquiring dairy producers and processors throughout Russia, giving it the scale to compete successfully, and it has also benefited from expansion in the Russian dairy market. But the company also plans to focus on developing its national dairy brands, which have folksy names including 'Little House in the Village', 'Happy Milkman' and 'Kuban Cow'.

Source: *Financial Times* (Asia Edition), June 18, 2008

A thorough examination of investment opportunities is equally important when preparing to do business with other regions of the world such as the Far East, South and Central America. Organizations operating on a global basis can provide a local dimension to their operations in a number of ways. For example, the involvement of local representatives seems to be a prerequisite for successful market entry in Central and Eastern Europe. This local dimension may take the form of a complete takeover of an existing local business, joint venture, the opening of a wholly owned local subsidiary or simply the contracting of a local representative. Each solution has its own problems.

The following options should be given serious consideration.

- Local management may need to be supplemented by Western management at the top of the local enterprise, giving a better basis for quality, financial control and technical expertise and ensuring the standard of day-to-day management activities.
- A business plan and the implementation of tools and techniques to measure the results of quality improvement are essential.

- Gaining the full commitment of the partners is also of great importance. If this is not achieved, the only basis for cooperation is the signed contract or the formal takeover agreements.
- A thorough understanding of the cultural differences and the attitudes prevailing in the country and among the local people is crucial to success. This is often the cause of persistent problems.

A long-term vision is a basic condition of investing in certain countries or parts of the world, whether this be Central or Eastern Europe, China or Mexico. The desire for short-term gains results time and time again in costly misadventures. A solid, well thought out, long-term perspective might prevent this type of business mistake. It would give a sound basis for developing a network of contacts essential for keeping abreast of business developments and information in the informal business environment which often exists in countries like these.

2.4.5 *Effects of national cultures on organizations*

Cultural differences are reflected in national variations in consumer behavior and consumption patterns, including the way people dress or the food they prefer.

For example ...

Tea is served in different ways in various parts of the world. The British like to drink their tea as a light brew diluted with milk; the Americans prefer iced tea and regard it primarily as a summer drink to be served over ice; the Saudi Arabians drink theirs as a thick, hot brew, heavily sweetened.

To succeed in a world of such diversity companies often have to modify their plans for global efficiency through worldwide standardization so that they can respond to the needs and opportunities created and demanded by cultural differences.
Research by Hofstede (1980), Trompenaars (1995) and others shows that there is a relationship between the culture of a nation and the specific organizational models which prevail in that country. Hofstede's study also demonstrates how distinct cultural differences across countries result in wide variations in social norms and individual behavior in areas such as respect for elders or response to the pressure of time which are also reflected in the effectiveness of the various organizational forms and management systems.
Figure 2.5 indicates how organizations are characterized in countries around the world. The countries' position within the diagram is determined by the level of power distance and uncertainty avoidance within the organizational environment. Power distance is the difference in the extent to which one person can determine someone else's behavior. A variety of factors can lead to countries having different attitudes towards power distance within all types of social relationship (parent and child, teacher and pupil, boss and employee, etc.). Different societies also deal differently with the uncertainties of life, with some cultures attempting to minimize or avoid uncertainties as far as possible. In countries where people tend to avoid uncertainties there is a greater need for clear organizational structures with clear procedures and a clear hierarchy.

Power distance

		Power distance	
		Small	Large
Uncertainty avoidance	Small	**Village model** Denmark Sweden UK US Holland	**Family model** Singapore Hong Kong India Indonesia Philippines East Africa West Africa
	Large	Switzerland Finland Germany Austria Israel **Well-oiled machine**	Iran Thailand Arabic countries Italy Mexico Turkey Spain Japan France Greece Belgium **Pyramid**

Figure 2.5
Characterization of countries and organizations

Source: *Hofstede*, 1980, p319

1 Organizations in Scandinavia, Anglo-American countries and the Netherlands (small power distance and a low degree of uncertainty avoidance) are generally quite informal and the degree of labor division and formalization is comparatively low. There is relatively little hierarchy, reflected in a limited number of levels. This form of organization is sometimes referred to as the village model (implicit structure).

village model
implicit structure
pyramid
full bureaucracy

2 At the other cultural extreme, we find Japan and Latin America, the Islamic and some Asian countries. Organizations in these countries are often characterized by a 'pyramid' with one person at the top and many layers of employees supporting the leader from below (full bureaucracy). The interrelationships between individual employees on the one hand, and between employees and the work process on the other are strictly prescribed according to formal rules and laws or by tradition. Great emphasis is placed on the hierarchy of the organization.

3 In countries like South-East Asia (low degree of uncertainty avoidance behavior and relatively large power distances) the relationships between people are strongly determined by rules, hierarchy and tradition, but the work process is not as strictly structured. The most common organizational form can be compared to the family (personal bureaucracy).

family
personal bureaucracy

4 In German-speaking countries, Finland and Israel, the work processes are strictly structured, but there is little power distance and formulation of relationships between people (in Germany the group or team often has central authority). Such an organizational structure is often referred to as a well-oiled machine (workflow bureaucracy).

well-oiled machine
workflow bureaucracy

According to Hofstede, it is particularly interesting to compare the relative positions of Germany and France in this respect. In contrast with Anglo-American, the Scandinavian countries and the Netherlands, power distances in French organizations appear to be very large. This is reflected in the large number of layers within the organization and an extensive and powerful 'cadre'. The power distance in German organizations is similar to that in the Anglo-American and Scandinavian countries. Indeed, in Germany there is a stronger need for rules and procedures in order to avoid uncertainty (the 'well oiled machine').
In a comparison of industrial companies, French companies had an average of five organizational levels and the German companies an average of three. The ratio of management and specialists in relation to total personnel in the French companies was 26 per cent compared with 16 per cent in German companies.
The wage differential between the highest and lowest paid employees in the French companies was also many times larger than that of the German companies. Employees on the lowest level were paid more in the German companies and were better trained.
Research by Lincoln and others (1985) showed that Japanese companies tended to have one and a half more organizational levels than their American counterparts (average number of levels was five). The number of managers per level was smaller in the Japanese companies and the Japanese companies had more sub-groups. In one respect the Japanese companies seemed more centralized because of the larger hierarchy and yet at the same time more sub-groups were involved in the decision-making process.

managers per level

QUALITY OF LIFE WORLDWIDE

As far as ranking is concerned, it is important to realize that the UK has overtaken the USA to take top place among the world's leading financial centers. The World Economic Forum (WEF) places the UK at the top of 55 of the world's largest financially focused countries, with the US slipping to third, behind Australia, ranked second. From the point of view of financial stability, Norway takes the top spot, which is also the case where quality of life is concerned, measured through three criteria: population health, average life expectancy, level of education and per capita income.

Quality of life worldwide

Ranking 2009	Ranking 2008
1 Norway	(2)
2 Australia	(4)
3 Iceland	(1)
4 Canada	(3)
5 Ireland	(5)
6 The Netherlands	(6)
7 Sweden	(7)
8 France	(11)
9 Switzerland	(10)
10 Japan	(8)
22 Germany	(23)

Source: UN, Human Development Report, 2009

The Nordic model as example

The Nordic model (i.e., the model of capitalism practiced in Norway, Sweden, Denmark and Finland) is currently being regarded as one of the few winners to emerge from the current economic and financial situation. From its response to an earlier banking crisis to its promotion of women in the boardroom, the Nordic model is attracting interest around the world in the same way as the Japanese style of capitalism did in the 1980s or the Germans in the 1960s. While an economy that is open to the world and offers considerable worker involvement is attracting attention, the benefits are hard to replicate elsewhere. Openness to globalization combined with strong social protection and egalitarianism, especially in the education system, defines this region's form of capitalism. Thanks to legislation, Norway has the highest level of female directorships in the world, with Sweden, Finland and Denmark all scoring well too.

egalitarianism

Executive pay also reflects egalitarianism, with many companies paying senior executives well below the international average out of a concern to limit the wage gap between the highest and lowest earners.
In the Netherlands, the Nordic model is being used as an example in the debate surrounding demotion within the ageing worker population in business and governmental institutions (see 7.7.2).

NORDIC MANAGEMENT STYLE

Swedish managers – the best paid in the region – earn just one-third of what their German counterparts receive while Norwegian executives, who receive the lowest salaries, typically earn just NKr3m ($480,000, £290,000, €340,000) to NKr4m.

The lack of hierarchy in companies extends right to the top. Workers 'just pop up and knock on the door': ... they feel responsible for the company.

Worker participation in the strategy of companies is an important factor. Employees sit on the boards of many Nordic companies thanks to a heavy trade union presence. Executives say the relationship has matured in recent years, allowing companies to make big restructurings with the cooperation of workers. There's a better understanding on both sides today: it's less about conflict. It's quite easy to add people in good times but also to adjust downwards in tougher times.

If demand were down 30 per cent at a company, executives and employees would discuss whether to cut the same percentage of jobs or make 60 per cent work half-time ... there are really grown-up discussions between management and workers. They solve the problem together.

Pontus Braunerhjelm, economics professor at Sweden's Royal Institute of Technology, says the success of Nordic companies suggests their informal management style provides a competitive advantage. But as groups such as Nokia and Ericsson have expanded across the globe, not everyone has found the Nordic way to their liking. People from other cultures sometimes find it a little imprecise in terms of who is taking responsibility, what is the order, what is the objective.

Source: *Financial Times*, July 30, 2009

Cultural differences in international firms

In organizations with subsidiaries in several countries or with significant numbers of immigrant employees in their workforce, it is important that managers (and of course also researchers and consultants) take into account the effect of differing value patterns. Some examples will illustrate this further.

Sweden and the United Kingdom

One analysis showed that the Swedish management of a Swedish subsidiary of a British company was strongly characterized by competitive values – a more common feature of British culture than of Swedish culture. The Swedish subsidiary had been founded by someone from the UK and although top management within the organization had recently changed from British to Swedish, a process of selection and succession had meant that those Swedish managers who had best adapted to the British style of work were the ones who had reached the top.
The average Swedish employee, however, was not happy with this style of leadership, though this had not affected the effectiveness of the company to a significant degree until recently. A large number of skilled workers and respected middle managers left the company. Those who stayed showed a low degree of motivation and loyalty. This was due to the fact that the

company culture was perceived as closed and because workers felt treated as a technical factor of production instead of human beings of flesh and blood. In this case, national cultural difference had an indirect and negative effect on the organizational culture of the Swedish subsidiary.

France and the Netherlands
A worldwide investigation relating to the organizational culture of a multinational company asked employees whether they expressed their disagreement to their bosses when they disagreed with them. In France and the Netherlands many employees gave a negative response – not surprising given French culture, but definitely so given Dutch culture. In France, decisions made by a superior will not be questioned as a rule. Although employees may be critical of superiors, they would not make a habit of frequently opposing them. In the Netherlands, on the other hand, employees do not generally hesitate to disagree openly with their boss.

Germany
In another investigation it was asked whether a sense of humor was appreciated by the organization. In the case of a German company, the answer was a whole-hearted 'yes'. However, when employees were asked whether this was desirable, their response was negative.

Schadenfreude

It seems that in Germany pleasure at the misfortune of others (Schadenfreude) is more prevalent than in other European countries. While elsewhere a joke at the expense of the organization does not immediately have a negative connotation, this was definitely felt to be the case in the German company. If an organization operating on an international basis were unaware of this aspect of German culture, misunderstandings might easily occur.

USA
In the United States it is seen as important that a person be assertive in a way which in Europe would be regarded as exaggerated or excessive behavior. In the US it is also very important that every person be able to show how much he or she is contributing to the success of the organization. A typical American employee is a conformist extremely dedicated to his or her career and to serving the public. There is a subconscious fear that non-conformist behavior could result in missing out on career opportunities, a promotion, a salary increase or public recognition and acknowledgement. This seems somewhat inconsistent with the perceived individualistic value patterns of Americans.

International mergers and cultural differences

When mergers or acquisitions are being considered, companies should take into account not only financial and market-oriented considerations, but also the culture of the organizations. It is widely known that one of the main reasons for unsuccessful mergers is the failure to bridge

cultural differences

the existing cultural differences. Although cultural differences can even play a role in mergers of two companies within the same country, they are particularly problematic with companies originating from different countries. It is often the case that even many years after a merger has taken place, people in the merged organization still regard themselves as members of a specific 'blood group,' with all the negative connotations that such an attitude brings with it. It is not always the case that groups of people originating from the same cultural region will necessarily have fewer problems relating to each other than groups of people from totally different cultural regions. Think, for example, of the people of the various republics of the former Yugoslavia, the Roman Catholic and Protestant peoples of Northern Ireland or the Flemish and Walloon communities of Belgium.

THE FUTURE OF ISLAMIC FINANCE … AND SHARIA COMPLIANCE

Uncertainty over payments to bondholders of the world's biggest *sukuk*, or Islamic bond, the $3.5bn deal from Nakheel, the emirate's property developer, could pose grave problems for the standing of Islamic finance. Yet most investors think the fall-out will hit the Middle East region rather than sharia-compliant financing, which avoids the use of interest, or *riba*, in line with religious rules.

For a start, Islamic finance has seen strong growth this year as more sharia banks have been launched and more markets open up to products that are structured to pay investors profits or rent. China, the world's most populous nation, with 80m Muslims, has started to wake up to the opportunities of Islamic finance. It recently awarded its first licence for Islamic banking to Bank of Ningxia, which could pave the way for sharia-compliant financing in the vast Chinese retail and wholesale sectors.

The potential for growth is huge. Of the 1.6bn Muslims in the world, only 14 per cent use banks. By comparison, 92 per cent of US households use banks: in the UK it is 95 per cent.
As the emerging Muslim nations grow and become more sophisticated, more of their citizens will start using banks and financial institutions, and many will want to do so in line with their religion. Growth among the 57 Muslim nations is much higher than in the rest of the world.

The crisis, however, has helped encourage bankers to become more realistic about what products can be adapted from the conventional world. For example, excitable pre-credit-crunch talk of Islamic hedge funds has faded as it has become increasingly clear that developing products, involving speculative bets on the direction of the market, is extremely difficult as they are so far removed from the principles of Islam, which forbids *gharar*, or gambling.
There is a tension in the interpretation of *sharia* between the more liberal scholars in Malaysia and the more conservative ones in the Middle East. In Malaysia, they are inclined to say: 'We can allow a little bit of interest', whereas in the Middle East all interest is bad.

In spite of the hurdles, however, Islamic finance has come a long way since it was launched in its modern form in the 1970s. It is now attracting many non-Muslim investors in the west, as well as more Middle Eastern and Asian funds. London is also establishing itself as a financial centre for Islamic finance.

A growing band of western insurers – from Allianz and Aviva to Munich Re and Swiss Re – have been establishing *sharia-compliant* operations in recent years as they look to compete with established Islamic insurers in the Middle East and Asia. Sharia-compliant insurance, or *takaful*, is seen as one of the areas of Islamic finance with the best potential growth because it is a product that should appeal to all market areas from individual Muslims to businesses and large corporations. *Takaful*, which is conceived as a form of *mutual assistance* and *risk-sharing*, came second after Islamic retail loans as the products offering most potential revenues. Only 5 per cent of the total insurance market in Saudi Arabia is family *takaful*. Islamic medical insurance dominates the market, accounting for 57 per cent of Saudi premiums. It is mostly bought by large corporations on behalf of their expatriate employees. The insurance is compulsory and companies must buy it from a Saudi *takaful* company, such as HSBC's separately constituted and Saudi-listed HSBC Amanah.

More recently, Islamic equity funds have proliferated thanks to the development of 'sharia screening'. Islamic funds and indices filter out excessively indebted companies, and those that are involved in conventional finance, gambling, pornography and alcohol.

However, the industry continues to be plagued by differences of opinion on the finer points of interpretation – hamstringing its growth, bankers say. Malaysian scholars are often seen as more liberal than their Gulf peers, and the Iranian Islamic sector, one of the largest in the world, is completely separate from the rest of the global Islamic finance sector. Debates on religious compliance may be a permanent fixture of the industry, experts say. After all, Islamic finance is an attempt to reconcile modern finance and economics with centuries-old religious principles that are interpreted differently across a diverse Muslim world.

Source: *Financial Times* Special Report, December 8, 2009

When the cultural differences are well known, it has been shown that people are less able to get along together when these differences are deeply rooted in the past. This, of course, does not necessarily mean that people from different cultural regions are unable to cooperate effectively. For example, despite negative impressions and political problems between the

Flemish and the Walloons, people from both sections of the community seem to be able to work together very well.
Hofstede's research results make it possible to predict to a certain extent whether an international merger will cause problems related to national cultural differences. Mergers between British and French companies are fraught with difficulties due to major cultural differences. Mergers between German and Dutch companies and between Belgian and Dutch companies seem to experience similar difficulties. Mergers between Dutch and British companies are relatively straightforward in comparison.
In the light of the possible consequences of cultural differences, it is important for an organization to devote a great deal of time and effort to the development of its own company culture and to the selection and training of employees who will fit into this.

CASE

Mini case study 2.2

Don't lose your way in the rush for foreign markets

When overseas customers come knocking, most UK entrepreneurs embrace them with open arms. After all, who wouldn't want to boast that they have clients 'or offices' in New York, Milan and Delhi, as well as Huddersfield and Derby?

However, business experts say it is common for companies to overreach themselves when expanding internationally, putting pressure on finances and staff. Maureen Berry, founder and managing director ofThe Strategy Business, a company offering entrepreneurs advice on how to enter foreign markets, says companies must be clear on their strategy: 'This means identifying markets where further investment is worthwhile because there is actually a real demand for the company's skills or products.' Berry has 23 years' experience in international marketing and says owners should gather extensive local information on their particular sector. 'Who are the competitors, what is the size of the industry and what are the routes to market?'

Entrepreneurs nervous about opening offices overseas could go down the franchising route instead, so long as their service is straightforward to learn and duplicate, and provides sufficient returns for all parties ... One of the biggest barriers to UK companies going global is language. According to a recent study, web users are four times more likely to purchase from a site in their own language, but businesses are warned to beware of translation blunders. Colgate, for example, introduced a toothpaste in France called Cue - also the name of a French adult magazine.

Taking a business beyond the UK's shores can seem exciting and risky, but with a well-planned strategy in place, globalisation is a realistic possibility for any entrepreneur.

Source: *The Sunday Times*, March 16, 2008

2.4.6 Network organizations

dynamic network model

At the beginning of the twenty-first century it is possible to see the beginnings of a new type of organization with new roles and assignments for managers and employees (and also, for example, for unions). This new organization form is called the dynamic network model (sometimes referred to as inter-organizational networks or organizational webs).

What is a dynamic network?

The best way of understanding a dynamic network is to consider a practical example of one.

For example ...

Consider the following situation. A piece of ice hockey equipment is designed in Scandinavia, made ready for production in the United States, adapted according to the demands of the entire North American market, manufactured in Korea and distributed by a multinational sales network, with first deliveries originating from Japan. Where and what is 'the organization' in this case? Product design, process development, production, sales and the distribution functions each take place in a different location and in a number of different organizations (which may only be linked for this particular project).

network organization

This sequence of events is said to be taking place in a network organization (see Fig 2.6) made up of discrete but interrelated parts consisting of a number of collaborating organizations. The role of the center as an intermediary does not have to be an independent function; it can be taken over by any of the other participants. The coordination of the entire network of important components is the main issue.

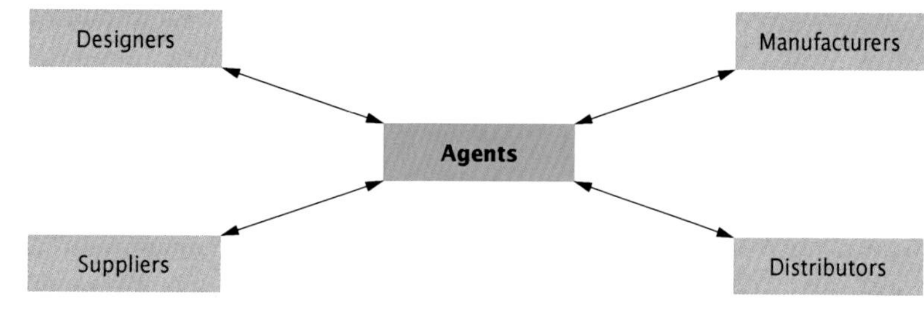

Figure 2.6
The dynamic network organization

Source: *After Miles*, 1989

Networking

'Networking' – the building up of contacts and connections – becomes increasingly important in fast-developing economies. Whether this concerns the tracking down of the right materials, the bringing together of the designers and an appropriate location for manufacturing or the hiring of temporary personnel, the ability to bring together people and components fast and efficiently (often with the help of a computer) is the key factor behind the organization's flexibility.

The more networks are used, the more refined and efficient they become. They can thus be used more often as a useful tool for expansion, supply and outsourcing. With a network approach, organizations can be more flexible and can adapt more quickly to innovations and shifts in the demand for products or services.

The network is not a new concept. In many lines of business relatively stable networks of suppliers, manufacturers and distributors already exist. What is new is the speed with which the network can now be built up.

2.4.7 The new business model: ICT, unbundling and rebundling

value adding chains

The changes that have recently been taking place in the 'traditional' industries – or value adding chains – are epitomized in the developments that have taken place within the automobile industry.

outsourcing *co-sourcing* *chain producers* *product development*

As a traditional producer of automobiles, Ford has always been product oriented and has carried out all of its activities itself, from steel manufacturing right up to sales. Until recently, mass manufacturing has enabled optimization of these processes. The last decades, however, have seen an increase in the number of specialized production chain processes. Departments specializing in certain processes (for example, cabling and lighting) have grown up, sometimes becoming autonomous units. There has been an increasing amount of outsourcing and price-conscious purchasing. Apart from such factors as price and quality, upstream suppliers are increasingly being selected on the basis of their flexibility in adapting to product specifications (= 'co-sourcing'), a trend which can be expected to continue. Similar developments are taking place downstream. Distribution, marketing and sales are being taken over by specialized companies according to a formula agreed upon beforehand. Importers and dealers are selected with an eye to value and do not have much room to negotiate. Automobile producers like Ford, General Motors and others are becoming 'chain producers' who derive their market leverage from product development (together with carefully selected partners) and usually their financing power. In recent years, outsourcing the original core task, namely production (= assemblage) has even been under consideration. The process can be described as ongoing and extensive leveling out of the organization.

From 'push' to 'pull' and multi-channel distribution

push driven *supply guided* *demand guided* *pull model* *downstream*

Traditional ways of doing business are usually 'push' driven. In other words, a product or service is supply guided from the supplier to the customers, with each of the consecutive links in the chain adding more value. However, processes have become more and more demand guided: the 'pull' model. In this model, the customer exerts the main influence, driving the chain from downstream until the so-called customer decoupling point is reached.

multi channel distribution *upstream*

The picture is also becoming more complex, with companies downstream using more than one distribution channel to sell products or services to various target groups or market segments, generally in different versions and/or different brands: so-called multi channel distribution. Often this is done in collaboration with other parties such as franchise partners or independent intermediaries. Collaboration upstream also takes place via outsourcing of parts through partnerships with upstream suppliers.

segmentation of business functions

The traditional chain model is no longer representative of the complex relationships that have arisen between all kinds of old and new market parties. Collaboration is the hallmark of the new business model: everybody connected through network relationships is in a collaborative relationship. This new model (see Figure 2.7) is characterized by far-reaching segmentation of business functions, both on the supply side as well as on the demand side. New roles have arisen and existing roles have changed. Sometimes various roles will be filled by the one party, as has always been the case.

intermediaries *disintermediation* *reintermediation* *unbundling* *rebundling*

An analysis of current business models will show they have changed in three main ways. These new ways have been largely brought about by ICT. The relationship with the customer has changed, the relationship with suppliers and other business partners has changed, and the relationship with intermediaries (distribution channels), both on the supply side as well as on the demand side, has changed. New developments such as the Internet which have made information more accessible have brought new parties into the equation. The traditional intermediaries have also regrouped (via disintermediation and reintermediation; see Section 10.4.7). 'Unbundling' – outsourcing of core processes until recently part of the chain – is another recent development, though the opposite process is also occurring in the form of mergers ('rebundling') or via vertical integration of companies which carry out consecutive parts of the operational management chain.

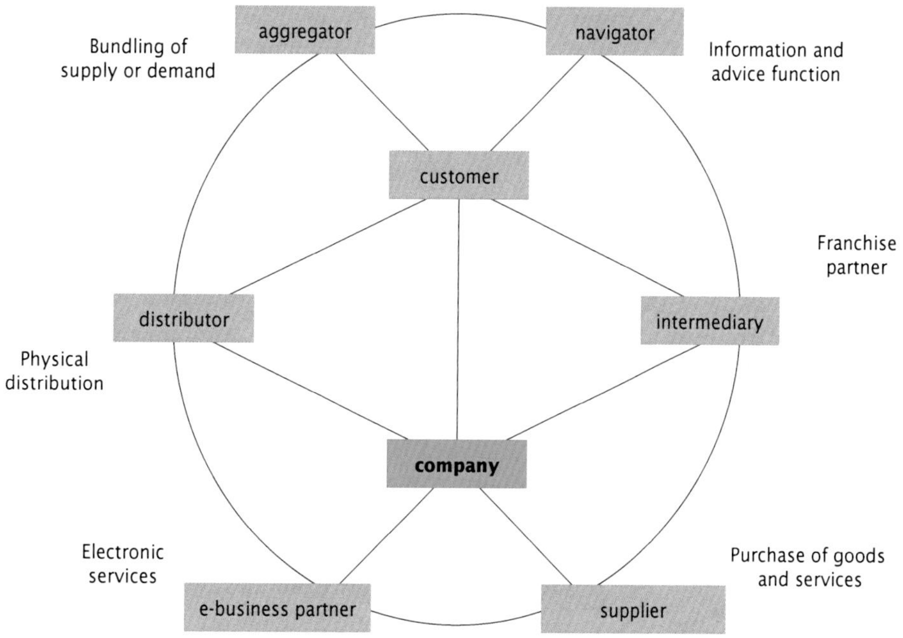

Figure 2.7
The new business model

New roles and old patterns of separation and joining

The newspaper industry constitutes a good example, since until recently its core processes were part of an integrated chain which included customers (readership and advertisers), production and product development (news, opinion pages etc) and the extensive infrastructure (print facilities and distribution via the company's own transport). In the United States, unbundling (differentiation) has led to the outsourcing of an increasing number of individual stages of the process and to a growth in entrepreneurial activity. Related to specialization is the removal of units which perform a distinct phase of the process (product innovation, for example) from the main company processes. The units become independent, specialized companies that focus on specific techniques: in the field of bio technology, for example, the mapping of gene patterns. The companies from which they originally came then link up financially or enter into alliances with these new niche players. One of the tendencies of our present times is for large composite companies to redefine their traditional roles, and if needs be, rearranging their business activities into core and non-core activities. These will be both business-to-business (B2B) directed and customer-directed business activities (B2C). Many organizations are reviewing their positions and roles within the vertical industrial column and asking themselves whether they want to remain (or become) a supplier, a coordinator, a niche player or a dominant market party. On both the sale and purchase side, horizontal collaborative relationships are being explored and other sectors that offer some potential for collaborative relationship are investigated (look at the examples of Unilever and Ford, for example). Partners for performing the whole or parts of the primary process are also being looked for. The main issue is whether the company should do it itself or whether it should be outsourced, even if it involves a core activity. This is essentially an issue of value adding.

unbundling (differentiation)

niche players

redefine traditional roles

B2B

B2C

dominant market party

2.4.8 *Strategic partnering*

In recent years, an increasing number of strategic partnerships have been set up between American, Japanese and European-based companies. This rise in the incidence of partnerships can be explained by the need for increased flexibility in organizational structures due to developments such as the following:

- The increased internationalization of markets which introduces new competitors to existing geographical markets
- The ever increasing complexity of technology which increases the amounts of money needed for investment in research and development
- The increase in the speed with which successive innovations are launched, shortening the pay-back period of these investments

The funding of research and development thus requires a strong market position. Companies with large market shares should be able to raise the required funding quite easily. Small companies have to find ways to resist such competition.

Star Alliance

1 Air Canada (CAN)
2 Air New Zealand (NWZ)
3 All Nippon airways (JAP)
4 Asiana Airlines (KR)
5 Austrian Airlines (AUS)
6 BMI (UK)
7 LOT Polish Airlines (POL)
8 Lufthansa (DE)
9 SAS (SCAN)
10 Singapore Airlines (CHN)
11 South African Airways (ZA)
12 Spanair (SPA)
13 Swiss Inter. Air Lines (CH)
14 TAP Portugal (POR)
15 Thai Airways (THA)
16 United airlines (US)
17 US Airways (US)
18 Varig (BRA)

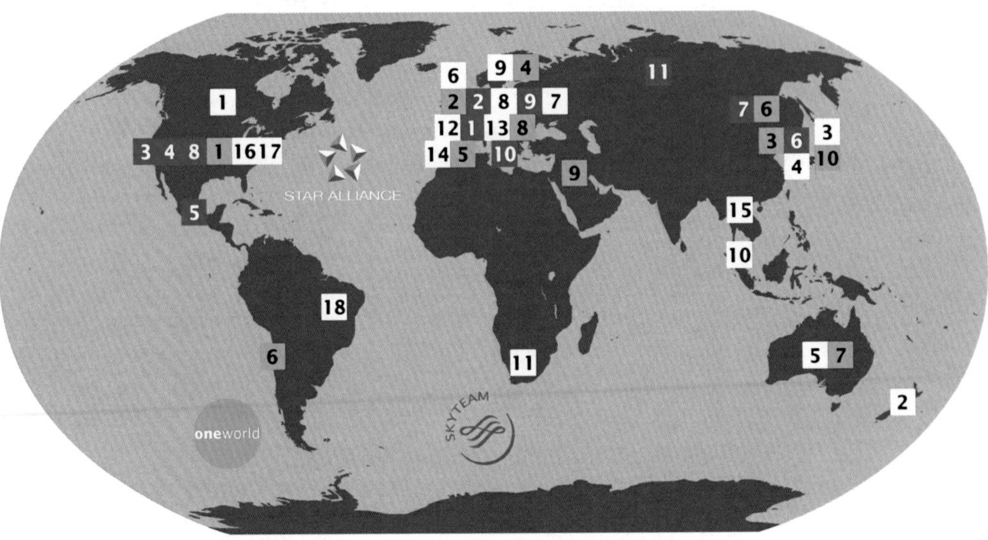

Oneworld

1 American Airlines (US)
2 British Airways (UK)
3 Cathay Pacific (CHN)
4 Finnair (FIN)
5 Iberia (SPA)
6 LAN (CHI)
7 Qantas (AUS)
8 Malév (HON)
9 Royal Jordanian (JOR)
10 Japan Airlines (JAP)

Skyteam

1 Air France (FRA)1) 2)
2 KLM (NL)1) 3)
3 Delta Air Lines (US)2)
4 Northwest Airlines (US)3)
5 Aeroméxico (MEX)
6 Korean Air (KOR)
7 China Southern Airlines (CHN)
8 Continental Airlines (US)
9 CSA Czech Airlines (CZ)
10 Alitalia (FRA)
11 Aeroflot (RUS)

1) Air France and KLM have merged
2) Air France collaborates with Delta
3) KLM collaborates with Northwest

Figure 2.8
Three aviation alliances dominate global air traffic

Source: *NRC Handelsblad*, 15 february 2008

This is sometimes possible by adopting a strategy of specialization by collaborating with other companies in a strategic partnership arrangement. In other cases, a company has to become an international competitor itself.
Strategic partnering is the only way in which a company can ensure that it is able to react in a flexible way to fast changing circumstances within the organizational environment or even to survive. With strategic partnering the partners who have entered the collaboration maintain their independence and their own identity and the effect on the competitive position of the partners will be noticeable in the long term. Strategic partnering and mutual cooperation can take many forms (see Section 4.4).
Many forms of strategic collaboration are possible. We have already looked at the strategic alliance of Corus (IJmuiden) and Peugeot/Citroën. Strategic alliances are common in the airline industry. Every large airline company has found partners or is searching for some to extend their coverage (see also Section 2.4).

alliance

Even the small European 'flag carriers' are subject to airline consolidation, with such companies as Alitalia, Austrian Airlines, Brussels Airlines (the successor to Sabena), SAS all changing hands at an international level.

The high fuel costs and weakening economies of recent times have made a lot of companies as well as politicians realize that expansion is necessary. While the major European aviation powers Air France/KLM and Lufthansa have taken the necessary steps, the Chinese and Russian players have also become aware of the opportunities open to them.

The automobile industry is also a rich source of mutual alliances. Volvo and Renault are working to establish a truck alliance. Volvo has joint truck manufacturing ventures with Mitsubishi in Asia and Renault has a monitoring interest in Nissan. In September 2002, Daimler Chrysler gained a 43% interest in the truck division of Mitsubishi as well as a 50% interest in the truck division of the South Korean company of Hyundai that was sold in 2004, while at the same time starting alliances in China. In 2002, GM took over Daewoo for 1.2 billion dollars. With this takeover, GM acquired production facilities in Asia, the world's fastest growing automobile market.

joint ventures

In 2009, Volkswagen acquired an interest in Porsche and Volkswagen – whose goal is to become the world's biggest company – is attempting to overtake Toyota by acquiring an interest in Suzuki. General Motors has divested itself of Saab. Fiat is going to collaborate with Chrysler. The Swedish company Volvo, until 2009 part of the Ford company, may end up in Chinese hands, while Jaguar and Land Rover have been sold by Ford to Tata, the Indian company.

Exhibit 2.2

Worldwide alliances

At the global level, about 37,000 alliances are formed per year. About 35% of the value of companies on the stock exchange is produced by alliances. The average success rate of alliances is 52%. The main failure factor (accounting for 55% of failures) is a mismatch between one company's strategies and those of its partner. Operational problems account for 52%. As contributing factors, about the same percentage (52%) mention mismatch of cultures, with 45% mentioning mistrust between partners.

Strategic partnering can be the key to new technologies, skills and competencies. At the same time there is a danger that knowledge and skills will be 'borrowed' by a better organized partner. Partnering with a competitor can bring significant advantages, but at the same time caution is vital. In the long term, there is a real danger that one of the partners will lose out (see Section 4.5).

Each partnership, in whatever form this is realized, has both advantages and disadvantages. It is important to investigate these thoroughly before taking the first step on the road to partnering. (Joint production, licensing and outsourcing are covered in greater detail in Section 4.4.3.)

2.5 Social responsibility, external reporting, risk management and corporate governance

An organization is a goal-realizing unit through which people and resources come together to survive in a socio-economic and technological market environment. A condition of this is that the rewards of the stakeholders – employees, consumers, shareholders and others – be such that they are willing to continue their contribution to the organization. Consequently, an organization has to justify its societal function and 'raison d'être' over and over again. Nowadays, this involves society as a whole and the actions of organizations are followed with close critical interest.

2.5.1 External information and reporting

Companies and other organizations are more or less separate and distinct entities in society, each with its own personality and identity and an ability to grow, survive or die. To function effectively, organizations have to communicate with persons or groups of stakeholders who have no direct access to the internal organizational information system. They must apply the information they have available to questions that may arise from external interested parties. If this is not carried out properly, problems will arise – for example, societal criticism, negative reports in the press – and there will be reactions from specific interest groups such as unfavorable stock market performance, a fall in stock prices, problems with raising external finance, labor unrest, and so on.

communicate
apply information

New IFRS (International Financial Reporting Standard) regulations

From 2005 onwards all stock exchange securities – including Dutch ones – have to present their figures according to IFRS (International Financial Reporting Standard) regulations. Until that time companies had drawn up their financial reports according to local regulations. The purpose of IFRS is to make companies more transparent and their figures easier to compare. IFRS deals first and foremost with changes in bookkeeping. This affects things like valuation and depreciation regulations: for instance, when one company takes over another. The assets and liabilities of the party taken over have to be included at their real value under 'purchase accounting' rules. Compared to the old regulations, more immaterial assets have to be specified (these were formerly included under the heading 'goodwill'). As well as this the IFRS affects pension arrangements and pension valuations and the pension valuation of other assets and liabilities.

IFRS regulations
bookkeeping
purchase accounting

The chief financial officers (CFOs) of the listed companies that had to apply IFRS in 2005 do not have much confidence in it. Only one in every three CFOs is of the opinion that IFRS leads to a more accurate impression of the financial position of their company, half of them think that applying IFRS makes no difference when compared to the national standards that were used before and eighteen percent think that IFRS gives a less accurate picture of the financial position of the company. The latter group mentioned the fair value principle as the main source of misleading results.
Companies have cleaned up their balance sheets well under the new regulations. More depreciation might cause price fluctuations in the future, but for the time being the effect on stock exchange prices has been minimal.

REASONS TO MOVE TO A GLOBAL IFRS

The US Securities and Exchange Commission (SEC) has proposed rules ultimately requiring US issuers to use International Financial Reporting Standards (IFRS) rather than the US Generally Accepted Accounting Principles (GAAP).

Does a global accounting standard benefit investors? As markets become increasingly global, it is important to be able to rely on financial reporting and make international comparisons, both of which require a uniform set of high quality accounting standards. Investors also stand to benefit from a single financial 'language' with which to interpret corporate activities.

The IFRS are developed by the International Accounting Standards Board (IASB) in London in collaboration with the Financial Accounting Standards Board (FASB) and other global accounting standard-setters. As a principles- based system, IFRS can allow issuers to reflect more fully the economic substance of transactions that may be unique to their industry, compared with a prescriptive, rules-based system such as GAAP.

Learning a new 'language' for accounting and reporting certainly requires time and effort for education. Investors, issuers, auditors and regulators will all need to learn and understand IFRS, which will require training across the board.

Requiring adoption by 2014 is reasonable. It allows time for reporting standards to converge and for the necessary training and education. An interim period of allowing a dual system now rushes matters. Given the vital role financial statements play in the world's capital markets, it is advisable to adopt a more deliberate, less experimental pace that ensures everyone is well-prepared.

Source: *Financial Times*, January 12, 2009 / CFA Institute

2.5.2 *Target groups*

external and internal stakeholders provide information insight

Most organizations are legally required to account for their actions and performance to their stakeholders – that is, external stakeholders such as shareholders, banks, unions, government and internal stakeholders in the form of its employees – and provide information to these parties which will give them an insight into the workings of the organization.
An employee is not only a supplier of labor, but is also willing and able to participate in organizational problems and to take joint responsibility. Just because a person has a specific role and occupies a subordinate position, this does not mean that he or she does not want to be informed about the organization's affairs as a whole.
To a certain degree the employee as a participant is often prepared to subject his or her personal goals to the goals of the organization as a whole. The employee also wants to have an influence over the way in which the organization is run. Internal stakeholders, therefore, not only wish to receive information, but also want to participate in decisions about important organizational affairs.

solvency liquidity annual reports

Insight into the internal affairs of an organization is necessary for the shareholders as financial stakeholders if they are to form an opinion about the equity capital and the solvency, liquidity, and profitability of the company. At the very least, shareholders have to approve the annual reports that reflect such opinions; it is for this reason that the needs of financial stakeholders are given such priority.

governmental agencies creditors

Other stakeholders such as governmental agencies and creditors also have to be able to form an opinion about the organization's affairs. Based on this, they have to decide whether they want to continue their support and contributions.
All participants, agencies or groups that are directly involved with an organization have to know how things are going, therefore.

- Entrepreneurs have to be able to determine whether there has been a profit or a loss. In the case of non-profit-making organizations, it has to be determined whether there is a budget or credit balance.
- When considering an application for debt funding, a bank will want to know what the financial position of the organization is like.
- Unions which negotiate employee labor conditions have to determine their constraints and basis for deliberation on the basis of the company results in a particular line of business.
- Members of a works council have to be able to determine their point of view in respect of organizational policies which are partially based on the annual figures.

It is important, therefore, that manageable financial information be available about the organization. It is for this reason that ordering of financial data is governed by legislation and by regulations set by the accountancy profession. There are also rules which prescribe that certain types of information be included and made available to parties other than direct stakeholders.
For companies and other organizations to balance the demand and supply of information (both internal and external) is thus a somewhat complicated affair. While there is no market mechanism to establish a form of equilibrium, there are opposing interests. The supply side of information gathering consists of more or less autonomous organizations and as a result they will display some reluctance to the giving of information and a desire for privacy. The board of directors of a company requires a certain degree of autonomy and will therefore be unhappy about communicating too much about its area of responsibility. This seems to be particularly the case with organizations operating in the free market, where the provision of information could lead to a competitive disadvantage.

board of directors

On the demand side there is also a need for limitation of the flow of free information: too much information can create confusion and make it difficult for outsiders to discriminate between what is important and what is not. Furthermore, the demand side is in general of a rather heterogeneous nature. It can include many different groups with individual interests varying according to their relationship with the specific organization. The demand side may include the following:
- Stockholders
- Suppliers/creditors
- Suppliers of capital, bankers
- Employees and their unions
- Competitors
- Fiscal authorities
- Governmental institutions responsible for economic policy, environmental protection, and so on
- Financial press and analysts
- Scientific research
- Pressure groups

diversity of interests

The very diversity of interests means that it is almost impossible to tailor the scope and contents of the information to satisfy every external stakeholder, given their specific demands. So that the parties concerned know what they can expect, the process is governed by legislation and complemented by generic rules, agreements and conventions. Besides financial information, there is a need for information of a broader type in order to be able to assess the position of a company in terms of social policy, safety and well-being as well as the overall risks (an area which at present is covered by the concept of risk management and is the ultimate responsibility of top management).

risk management

There is a small but perceptible trend towards sustainable business practices, though at the moment only a handful of large Dutch companies (both those quoted on the stock exchange and otherwise) clearly and verifiably indicate in their annual reports what exactly is being done. Most of the organizations say that they take sustainable practices into consideration, but omit to mention what exactly the activities are and whether they are successful or not.

sustainable business practices

Sustainable business practices are those that at the operational management level take into account issues such as the environment, human rights, security, and personnel well-being. A prominent group of six large companies provide detailed information about their activities: Unilever, Shell, ING, Schiphol, Philips and ABN Amro. They report their results and whether they have complied with statutory obligations and international norms and have had their reporting audited independently.

2.5.3 National and international directives

There are several bodies which set standards for the provision of business information on behalf of national governments and supranational associations such as the European Union. At first these bodies were mainly concerned with the provision of periodic external information to shareholders, but their tasks now include the provision of information to all stakeholders.

EU directives

In the EU member states, legislation is strongly influenced by directives which harmonize the prescribed external information throughout the EU (with special directives for banks, insurance companies and investors). In some countries there are special national directives relating to information to works councils.

In EU countries, external reporting has to be based on the 4th and 7th Directives. However, the form this external reporting takes depends on the country.

- In *Germany* reporting is included in the *Aktiengesetz* (for public limited companies (*Aktiengesellschaften*, AG)) and in the *Handelsgesetzbuch* (for private companies (*Kapitalgesellschaften*, KG)). The EU legislation is closely linked with the traditional German practice of external reporting.
- Since the Second World War, *France* has had legislation requiring both external reporting and a system of company accounting. Through the so-called *plan comptable* the French government tries to promote a uniform accounting system which facilitates the compiling of figures from annual reports.
- In *the Netherlands* the compiling of figures from companies and other organizations is an activity for which the Central Bureau of Statistics has the overall responsibility.
- Legislation relating to external reporting in *Belgium* is quite similar to the French regulations. The compiling of figures from officially published annual reports is one of the objectives since this data is put into a central databank.
- In the *United Kingdom*, legislation concerning the external reporting of companies is included in several Companies Acts.
- In contrast, there is hardly any legislation in the *USA*. The US government uses a form of self-regulation. It is mainly the concern of stock exchange authorities (SEC) and private organizations to organize their own regulations (within certain limits set by federal laws).

Both in the US and European countries it is quite common for legislation and directives concerning external reporting to be drawn up by representatives of relevant societal interest groups, such as users of information (associations of financial analysts, consumers and employee organizations), suppliers of information (employers' associations) and auditors (associations of certified public accountants).

international harmonization of external reporting

For international companies quoted on the stock exchange and for readers/users of their annual reports, it is especially important that the international harmonization of external reporting continue. This will not only facilitate cross-border comparability of annual reports, but will also reduce costs for these companies. Further harmonization of external reporting seems to be less important to small businesses. There is a generic obligation of publication of annual figures for this type of company in the EU, but this does not necessarily mean that these companies will be included in the ongoing process of harmonization.

2.5.4 International organizations

The increasing internationalization of business operations and the movement of capital have made the harmonization of standards of external reporting at both regional and global levels a priority.
Within the EU, harmonization is implemented through directives (as mentioned in Section 2.5.3). At the global level, harmonization is being worked on by the International Accounting Standards Committee (IASC), an association of national organizations of certified public accountants. The IASC is striving to come to an agreement with the international umbrella organization of stock exchange supervisors (IOSCO) to acknowledge the International Accounting Standards (IAS) as the basis for the requirements which have to be met by all corporations in their financial reporting systems.

IASC

The United Nations (UN) and the Organization for Economic Cooperation and Development (OECD) are also working on international regulations, especially as part of an ethical code for multinational companies.

2.5.5 Corporate governance

In its broadest sense, corporate governance concerns the way in which firms are managed and control is exerted. The phenomenon of corporate governance exists because of the separate identities in law of the professional managers of an organization on the one hand and shareholders with their financial interests in the organization on the other. It is a phenomenon which manifests itself as soon as one person does business with someone else's money.
Today, corporate governance is a keenly debated issue all over the world, especially in relation to big corporations owned by a large number of shareholders. Wider society also has an interest in the effective management and control of such organizations and so the quality of management and both internal and external control are coming under closer scrutiny. Internal control concerns the entire process by which the company's board of directors, management and other personnel provide reasonable assurance regarding the achievement of objectives in the following categories:

- Effectiveness and efficiency of operations
- Reliability of financial reporting
- Compliance with applicable laws and regulations

This process not only involves the role of management, but also the role of the board, especially the role and the duties of executive and non-executive directors. Some form of independent control has to be in place.

monistic or one-tier system

dualistic or two-tier system

Two types of board system have developed during the course of time: the monistic or one-tier system and the dualistic or two-tier system. On the European continent, the dualistic system is the most common form, while the monistic system is the most prevalent one in Anglo-Saxon countries.
In the dualistic system, the tasks of objectively monitoring the activities of the company are assigned by the board of directors to a separate independent body, such as a supervisory council. In the monistic system there is no separate supervisory body; the supervisory tasks are carried out by certain members of the main board, referred to as 'non-executive directors' in the United Kingdom and 'outside directors' in the United States. There is no US or UK legislation which obliges boards to nominate supervisory board members; this has simply developed from business practice. In the recent debate on corporate governance, criticism was especially directed at those companies with no non-executive directors or in which non-executive directors formed a minority and could not therefore stand up to executive directors.

2.5.6 Corporate governance: an international perspective

The governance systems in mainland Europe (and those in Japan) differ from those in the United Kingdom and the United States not only with regard to their structure, but also in relation to the importance of capital markets and the effects of market-oriented mechanisms (such as raider threats, takeovers, buyouts, etc.), stock market reactions and so-called Wall Street Talk.
The various legal requirements currently in force in EU countries stem from two basic models of corporate structure: the Anglo-Saxon model and the Continental model. The Continental model can be further divided into two models: one for the so-called Rhineland countries (Germany, Austria, Switzerland and the Netherlands) and another for countries which include Italy, Spain, France and Belgium (which can be grouped together under the heading of Latin European countries). The Japanese corporate structure differs in many important respects from those listed above.
These models of corporate structure will now be described.

The Anglo-Saxon model (UK and USA)

The financial markets of the United Kingdom and the United States are long established and well developed. The 'open' corporation has assumed enormous proportions and share ownership is widespread. Legislation has resulted in banks not developing into shareholders with substantial packages of shares in non-financial companies, in contrast to the systems in countries such as Germany and Japan.
In the Anglo-Saxon model, the enterprise is seen as an extension of the shareholder. The objective is first and foremost profit maximization. Companies often raise finance via the stock exchange. The internal organization and the external environment of the corporation are characterized by competition and there is a wariness of corporatism. Management is considered to be somewhat short-term oriented; the results for the next financial quarter are the main focus of interest. External financial reporting is in accordance with the highest international standards. Widespread share ownership may result in potential conflicts of interest between corporate governors and shareholders which are often difficult to control and can create high drama during takeover negotiations.

corporatism

The Rhineland model (Germany, Austria, Switzerland, the Netherlands)

In these countries substantially fewer companies are listed on the stock exchange. There are also conceptual differences in the nature of the enterprise and/or corporation. Instead of 'corporate enterprise' as an extension of the shareholders, there is a more institutional form of corporation. The organization shows characteristics of corporatism and is more concerned with consensus than with competition. Goals and time scales are oriented more towards the long term. The main objective is continuity.
Corporate interests have to be balanced and integrated with the interests of the other participants in the corporation – for example, the managers, employees, suppliers of capital and suppliers of resources, customers/clients. The stock exchange is of secondary importance. Internal funding and financing through banks are the preferred source of finance.
Traditionally, banks have played an important role in financing the expansion of companies. In Germany in particular, the rise of the big industrial banks (Universalbanken) has been instrumental in industrial development. Nowadays, big banks such as the Deutsche Bank, Commerzbank and Dresdner Bank still play an important role in financing and in the corporate governance of big German corporations, not only as suppliers of debt but also as financiers of equity capital and as shareholders. If, as is often the case, there are various types of shares, this will facilitate the concentration of control. External financial reports are of limited use in that they are not always published at regular intervals and the information contained in them is often out of date and superficial.

corporate interests

Universalbanken

For example ...

... in Germany the *Aufsichtsrat* (or supervisory council) was created shortly after the Second World War. *Mitbestimmung* (the right of both labor and capital to participate in joint decision making) was introduced by the Allied forces not only to ensure equal representation by the providers of labor and the providers of capital, but also to ensure that the unions shared responsibility.
All companies are required to have a 20-member supervisory council in which employees and shareholders are equally represented in terms of seats. As a result the labor representatives in the German supervisory councils are very well informed and representatives of management and the providers of capital cannot openly and critically discuss crucial company problems without reference to them. Banks are strongly represented on supervisory councils in Germany. The role of the managerial team in the German system is also given considerable prominence.

The Latin-European model (Italy, Spain, France, Belgium)

financial holding
interlocking directorships

Ownership in Latin-European countries is largely characterized by family ownership, financial holding companies, cross-financial participation, and state ownership. Pre-eminent families (such as the Agnelli family in Italy) and multinational industrial groups control ownership and management in almost every corporation quoted on the stock exchange. In Spain cross-participation and bank participation play an important role. The state also exercises an influence over corporate structure. France has several forms of financial holding (competing financial groups with cross-participation and 'interlocking directorships'; that is, companies interlinked at board level by virtue of the fact that one of their directors also holds directorships in other companies), bank participation (banques d'affaires) and state ownership. In recent years there has been a marked tendency towards privatization.
Ownership in Belgium is largely in the hands of families and financial holding companies. The Generale controls a large number of Belgium's top companies and as a result some important industrial sectors.

Japan

keiretsu

Industrial life in Japan is characterized by the presence of a number of major industrial groups, the keiretsu. Each group may comprise hundreds of companies interconnected through cross-participation, with one bank functioning as the primary source of finance, especially with regard to the supply of debt capital. This bank is also active in corporate governance as a consultant, supervisory body and supplier of management expertise in areas such as career development, crisis management and corporate turnarounds.

The Japanese structure is comparable to the German structure as far as the role of the industrial banks is concerned and to the Latin-European structure with regard to the industrial corporate groups.
Separation of the interests of management (and employees) from the interests of shareholders in all these models has led to problems of communication and control. As a result effective independent supervision and external control have become crucial. The differences between the models are due not only to their respective structures, but also to the patterns and level of industrial democracy in the various countries (see Section 2.6.4).

industrial democracy

2.5.7 *The Code of Best Practice*

All forms of governance structure are currently under close scrutiny. The Anglo-Saxon model sees the company as an extension of its shareholders and having the objective of serving shareholder needs. However, this approach also means that in the long run the creation of economic value is only possible when the interests of all stakeholders are adequately taken

societal responsibilities

into account and that the company must heed its wider societal responsibilities in terms of the 'common good of the community.'

At the same time the Rhineland model is beginning to lose its sparkle. This system of ownership has shown serious weaknesses. For example, in Germany, the Metallgesellschaft has suffered from major governance problems, despite the presence of long-term shareholders. The equal representation of employee directors and other types of directors (for example, bank or shareholder directors) on the supervisory councils seems to hinder effective monitoring and discussion of the real issues at stake.

Furthermore, the position of the banks with regard to proxy voting – a mechanism which allows banks to vote on behalf of clients who deposit their stock with them – is under discussion, as it is an important way of influencing corporate decision making.

Cadbury Committee

In the United Kingdom, the Cadbury Committee was set up to make recommendations relating to better guidance and control of directors. The committee's report, *Cadbury: The Code of Best Practice*, was published in December 1992 and contained three essential recommendations:

- The board of directors should meet regularly and no decisions should be made by a single person alone. In view of the monistic system in the United Kingdom there should be a strong countervailing power within the board in the form of independent, non-executive directors with objective opinions and views of the corporation's strategy, results realized and nominations for key management posts.
- It is preferable for the functions of chief executive and chairman of the corporation to be kept separate.
- From 1995 on, corporations must report in their annual reports on their systems of 'internal control' and the continuity of the corporation.

More recently, statements of directors' responsibilities have also been included in the annual reports of large corporations.

2.5.8 The advantages and disadvantages of the one-tier system

audit committee
nomination committee
remuneration committee
executive committee

The Anglo-Saxon model of a publicly quoted company features a single top management level. Top managers are chosen by the owners of the company, the shareholders. An important characteristic of this model is that there are a number of committees – for example, an audit committee, a nomination committee (for the selection of top managers) and a remuneration committee (for salaries, bonuses, etc.). Major decisions are made by the executive committee (the top management team) and are later ratified by the board as a whole.

Advantages

- There is widespread ownership of shares in these countries. Shareholders have a number of powers.
- The Anglo-Saxon system is fair. Everything is out in the open and board members play an overt role within the firm. Board members, whether executive or non-executive, share joint responsibility. Although the role of the non-executive directors is supervisory, these directors are still regarded as colleagues.
- The executive and non-executive directors occupy the same legal position. They provide joint leadership of the organization.

Disadvantages

- When it comes to the selection of new directors, the board and/or chairman/CEO can issue a 'proxy statement' to propose a shortlist of candidates to the shareholders' meeting. The choice is confined to this list. In practice, this means that the board has the power to dictate who is selected.
- When earnings per share, price/earnings ratios, stock exchange quotations and other indicators change, Anglo-Saxon boards intervene much more quickly than their European

counterparts. As a rule, when the need for short-term profits per share is weighed against the desire for long-term continuity, short-term profits will generally win the day. In the United States, this is mainly due to the formidable and ever-present risk of hostile takeovers.

2.5.9 The advantages and disadvantages of the two-tier system

Advantages

- The Rhineland model puts less power in the hands of individuals. Responsibilities are shared by the managerial team and the advisory supervisory board, resulting in a more balanced approach. In this model, it is possible for the same person to have both an operational and a supervisory function.
- Discussions within the supervisory board tend to be more in-depth and direct than those in the one-tier system. Formal discussions about strategy are rarely on the agenda of board meetings in the US. This system also seems to provide a more satisfactory system of feedback and approval.
- Decision making is more efficient and effective with the combination of management team and supervisory board.

Disadvantages

- The power of the shareholders has waned. In the large publicly quoted companies, shareholders have almost no power at all. The question of ownership has become somewhat obscure. Institutional investors rarely appear at shareholders' meetings.
- It is unclear who 'controls the controllers.' When problems arise, the supervisory council cannot take over operations. The result is a potential power vacuum and this can be very dangerous. The members of the supervisory councils have fewer options than those directors with supervisory roles on one-tier boards.
- The role of the supervisory council can be unclear. Its dual function as a source both of advice and control can sometimes lead to conflicts of interest.
- Supervisory council members choose who will be admitted as new members of the council – a system of co-option – and this has several disadvantages:
  1. The supervisory council is not under the control of any part of the corporation.
  2. The stimulus for maximizing economic and market value of share equity is removed.
  3. The supervisory council sets its own salary level, which inevitably results in substantial remuneration packages.
  4. There is a risk that inappropriate members will be selected.
  5. Supervisory councils tend to favor maintaining the independence of the corporation even in situations where a merger or takeover would be economically advantageous.

2.5.10 Recent developments in the one-tier and two-tier models

Despite the considerable cultural differences, the two systems are coming closer together. The EU is encouraging this trend by, for example, enabling the Netherlands to change its laws to allow the establishment of one-tier systems. This will mean that financial vulnerability alone will determine the way in which the corporation functions.

two-tier system
one-tier system

In practice, there is no longer any significant difference between the decision-making function of the managerial team/supervisory council in the two-tier system and that of the board of directors in the one-tier system. The managerial team is still clearly dominant in the two-tier system due to the fact that it has the opportunity for more thorough preparation, quicker access to information and operational responsibility.

Two ways of overcoming the disadvantages of the co-option system in the supervisory councils are available: the supervisory council could be made more open and more accountable with regard to its supervisory role, or the supervisory council could be reorganized so that the claim that it is nothing more than an 'old boys' club' is no longer valid.

The simple 'one-tier system' was unable to prevent the fall of companies like Enron and WorldCom. In fact, it could even be claimed that the Anglo-Saxon model has proven to be a blatant failure. Successful supervisory control depends ultimately on how effective and how involved those people who take on supervisory responsibilities are. With ABN-AMRO, one of the problems was that its commissioners were without exception people who had little understanding of banking and who kept themselves at too much of a reserve (see *The Perfect Prey*, 2009).

Moreover, recent research (Schenk, 2009) has shown that European companies with a two-tier system were just as successful during the 1990s as companies with a one-tier organizational management system. As such, one can question whether having even more rules is likely to lead to more effective supervision.

Female Board Index

Women are still very much in the minority within the echelons of top management: according to the *Female Board* Index (2009), a mere 7% of commissioners are women. In this regard, the Netherlands rates poorly on the international scene: at the current rate of change, it will take until 2090 before 30% of the country's top management is female.

2.5.11 Risk management, the tasks of top management and the governance code

integrated risk management

Code on Corporate Governance

risk profile

Integrated risk management has become an important aspect of business policy. The affairs of recent times – the Enron affair (and the involvement of Arthur Andersen in it), and the WorldCom, Adelphia Communications, Asea Brown Bovery and Allied Irish Bank affairs, but also the fire disaster in Enschede (May 2000), various environmental disasters and product recalls (Firestone/Ford) – have meant that top management is becoming increasingly conscious of the risks they run. There is a noticeable movement away from a narrow concern with financial risks to concern about risks in a broad and everyday sense and the internal control and auditing that such risks involve. The Code on Corporate Governance, which has been operative in Great Britain since 2001, has fueled this concern. Much has recently been made of so-called integrated risk management: drawing up a risk profile and taking a strategic approach to organizational risk.

Any sort of risk that a company might run has to be taken into account, whether it be strategic, operational or financial risk, but also risks relating to legal issues, safety, corruption or bribes, political risks (terrorism, kidnapping etc. included) and the risk of loss of reputation. This last has taken on new dimensions with the development of world markets and world-wide brands and the growing role of international pressure groups (as the examples of Coca-Cola and Heineken demonstrate). Environmental risks are another source of concern (as the examples of Shell, Exxon and General Electric demonstrate).

organizational risks

strategies

Reporting of the procedures for determining, evaluating and managing significant organizational risks is now expected in annual reports. Moreover, the procedures need to be reassessed regularly and tested against the guidelines. There may be various strategies for managing a certain risk, including accepting it or transferring it to another party (for example, by taking out insurance or engaging in a joint venture), eliminating it by devising a solution, managing it by building precautionary measures into the operations or ensuring that the employees can deal with it.

organizational risk Organizational risk is, simply speaking, the risk that organizations knowingly take in order to attain a competitive advantage and add value for the shareholders. Such a risk may relate to the product-market combinations the company has focused upon and include the area of product technology, product design and sales. Taking an organizational risk can be profitable or precisely the opposite. In theory, organizations exist in order to take risks of this type.

financial risks *operational risk* *events* Financial risks are those that relate to the effects of financial variables. Operational risk is the risk of direct and indirect losses due to failures or shortcomings in processes, systems and human beings. Risks associated with events are those risks an organization does not have any control over. They are likely to lead only to losses, some of which can be covered by traditional insurances.

risk profile When an organization's risk profile is drawn up, only information obtained directly from the organization can determine what risks the organization faces. The top management level has to decide which risks can be regarded as acceptable and how big the chance is that these risks will actually eventuate.

formulate proactive guidelines As such, it is particularly important to formulate proactive guidelines that the organization can use in the event of a crisis or a product recall, or help it deal effectively with a disaster (see also Section 2.8), including how to communicate with the parties involved.

Product market risks	**Legal risks**	**Financial risks**
▪ Loss of customer capital ▪ Product ageing ▪ Increased competition ▪ Decreased demand for the product	▪ Product liability ▪ Changes in trade restrictions ▪ Shareholders initiating proceedings against the company ▪ Proceedings relating to unfair treatment of employees	▪ Change in the cost of capital ▪ Fluctuations in the exchange rate ▪ Inflation ▪ Breach of contract ▪ Doubtful debts
	Risks relating to regulations	**Risks on the production side**
	▪ Changes in environmental legislation ▪ Stricter antitrust regulations ▪ Termination of price-supporting regulations ▪ Termination of import regulations	▪ Increase in raw material processes ▪ Strikes by personnel ▪ Departure of key personnel ▪ Default by key personnel ▪ Default by suppliers
	Tax risks	**Operational risks**
	▪ Increase in income taxes ▪ Termination of industrial income agreements ▪ Increase in VAT	▪ Failure of machinery ▪ Increase in production errors ▪ Devastation of factory following a disaster ▪ Ageing of capital equipment

Table 2.3 *Risks ...*

external regulators
board of directors

In theory, external regulators, whether called in by the parties in question themselves, on behalf of the stockholders or board of directors, or by government (regulators such as the SEC, National Bank and Insurance Authorities, Safety and Environmental inspectors, etc.) are able to ensure that regulations are observed and the company's or institution's public performance conforms to valid rules and financial criteria. However, integrity and moral awareness on the part of the organization itself are crucial aspects of performance monitoring.

By now, most organizations, whether big or small, have *risk managers* and *compliance officers*. These employees accept no responsibility for any risks that are taken: at the most they are responsible for the supervision and management of the process of risk management within an organization. The question is whether there should there be a CRO (Chief Risk Officer) on the Board of Management. In the banking sector, for example, would having a CRO on the board have helped prevent some of the problems that have arisen recently? While this may be so, those at the top managerial level of a company should be fully aware of the key risks faced by their own company and by the sector itself: a CRO can be no substitute for such awareness.

risk management

Despite this, research has shown that risk management does not always rank high on the board's agenda. Here, too, having more rules is not likely to improve the situation much. The application of rules depends primarily on the *integrity* of directors and managers as well as their sense of morality and the urgency with which they view the need for a suitable company or organization risk profile.

Accounting rules, reform bills, signing of financial reports by CEOs and/or CFOs and legal authorities are never sufficient guarantee of fair business practices. Following a number of instances of 'white collar balance sheet criminality,' corporate integrity is being questioned seriously. The collapse of Enron and the scandals surrounding WorldCom, AOL, Adelphia Communications, KPN Quest and so on contain important lessons for managers and boards. Running a business ethically and responsibly has become a major issue, whether the area of concern is law and ethics, conflicts of interest, the limits of delegation, heeding early signs of dissention (or later on whistle-blowers), or the need for new regulations and the creation of a transparent and responsible government system (both at the local and at the global level) that will protect the interests of corporate and societal stakeholders.

Sarbanes Oxley (USA 2002)

Sarbanes-Oxley Act (SOX)

risk management

managing reporting risks

The Sarbanes-Oxley Act (SOX) of 2002 in the US and the Tabaksblat (Frijns/Streppel) Code in the Netherlands (2003/2006/2010) are primarily intended to protect investors against a repeat of corporate scandals like those of Enron, WorldCom, Ahold, Parmalat, and others. However, there are hardly any recommendations regarding risk management in the Tabaksblat Code. At best the board of directors will state that internal control regulations are adequate and effective and provide evidence to that effect. Sarbanes-Oxley goes one step further and includes requirements about managing reporting risks and in fact requires a company to show that it is in control at any one time. A manager who signs the act and is shown not to have his business under control faces a long prison sentence. Ebbers, the former top executive of WorldCom, was jailed for fraud for 25 years.
Under the Sarbanes-Oxley Act, businesses will have to spend many millions more on their reporting obligations and the work of auditing committees. The question arises as to whether this is not over-reacting on the basis of a few incidents and would give rise to bureaucracy and 'paper tigers'. The essence of good corporate governance is, after all, a mental attitude and is wholly dependent on the integrity and trustworthiness of managers and supervisors.

US-style ... or UK's? ...

The debate over the best system of corporate governance is also in progress in the USA and UK. Whether US-style or UK-style is the best ... is the question. In the meantime UK stakeholders have agreed on governance topics such as shareholders' right to vote on executive remuneration, required separation of the role of chief executive and chairman and the point at which directors are 'overboarded' or sit on too many boards to be effective.

Sox, as it is called, was mainly created to ensure accuracy in financial reporting rather than to change the governance structure as such. UK's new company rules incorporate elements of the Rhineland's two-tier model, especially where this concerns the vote to split the roles of chairman and chief executive. In the USA, the debate on separation of these functions is by no means decided. But the European-style separation of positions is gaining ground in North America. Shareholder activists have certainly been making their opinions known since 2009.

2.6 Industrial and organizational democracy in a European context

Flatter organizations

Flatter organizations with less of a hierarchy, participative decision making and increased self-determination by workers seem to be inevitable steps in the organizational development of firms. Sweden, Norway, Germany, the Netherlands and Denmark have lead the way with such developments; Finland, Ireland, United Kingdom, France, Belgium and the Latin-European countries such as Italy, Greece, Spain and Portugal are some distance behind these north-west European countries. Increasing industrial democracy enables firms to better realize their societal responsibilities and to act in a more ethical way. Participative arrangements are often implemented in the belief that participation will improve productivity and performance. A movement towards various forms of organizational democracy (which began after the Second World War) is still underway, though the changes are now slower and taking different forms. They are also occurring in a different and somewhat piecemeal fashion. Students and worker uprisings in France, Germany and the Netherlands in the late 1960s and early 1970s gave new momentum to legislative processes in several European countries. Industrial democracy might again become an issue and could be somewhat accelerated by European Union (EU) legislation which permits and promotes different styles of participation and democratic processes. Respecting existing differences in national cultures and value patterns and acknowledging pluralistic national regulations seem likely to be important in future EU legislation.

industrial democracy

EU legislation

At the Maastricht Summit (December 1991) the EU member countries – with the exception of the UK – agreed to strengthen employee participation rights in the states of the European Union and to further harmonize employment practices and laws. British firms, operating in other EU countries or doing business with clients in EU member countries, will of course be affected by these socio-political decisions of the EU.

The notion of joint decision making is already accepted and established as a feature of corporate life in the majority of countries in Western Europe (see Table 2.4 for a Europe-wide overview). Managers in Germany, Sweden and the Netherlands, for example, are already working within the institutional and legal framework of joint consultation with works councils on the one hand, and boards of directors which include worker representatives on the other.

Exhibit 2.3

The European works council

The European directive of 1994 in respect of the establishment of a European works council led to the implementation of the Act on European Works Councils in the Netherlands on 5 February of that year. The guidelines and the law aim to improve the right of information and consultation of employees about cross-border cases involving multinational companies.
To make it clear what organizations this affects, in simple terms, a multinational company is an organization with at least a thousand employees spread across the EU member states, with in a minimum of two member states at least one hundred and fifty employees. By 'consultation' is meant the exchange of ideas and the establishment of a dialogue between employee representatives and the main board of directors.

the European works council

The European works council has gained ground gradually. European works councils (including Dutch works councils) have already been established in a few international operating companies. The corporate seat of most of these companies is located in Germany or France. England also has a few European works councils in operation; these have been established on a voluntary basis.
Research (2000) has shown that one hundred and five Dutch companies have been obliged to have European works councils (though this number includes thirty-five companies which already had a European WC, including Philips, Shell, Unilever, Hoogovens and Canon).
The European works councils have a right to information concerning cross-border developments and activities such as mergers or company foreclosures which have effects on establishments in the various European countries. Every state member has the freedom to adjust the law to his own view. The multinationals have to act in conformity with the law of the country in which their corporate seat is located.

Of the approximately 820 European work councils, a handful of them are doing a good job as managerial sparring partners. Too many of them are pining away. A necessary revision of the guidelines, expected in 1999, has still not been completed, despite the fact that experience has long since shown what measures are necessary to improve effectiveness: information and advisory rights that conform to those that appear in other European documents, the obligation to be timely in providing information, more meetings with management, the right to attend preparatory sessions and post-meeting discussions, to training and expert advice and the right to extraordinary sessions in the event of a crisis.

Ideally, European work councils make arrangements with top management in respect of themes such as internal job mobility within the company, the creation of a system of financial participation by employees and harmonization of personnel policy. But responding in a timely way to major reorganizations constitutes one of the tasks of a European works council: the campaign aimed at keeping the Enci cement works in Maastricht open for longer – at this stage until 2011 – is one example. This campaign took place in close consultation with the Dutch and European works councils of Heidelberger Cement.

2.6.1 Organizational democracy

Organizational democracy in its broadest sense encompasses a considerable variety of interpersonal and/or structural arrangements which link organizational decision making to the interests and influence of employees at all levels of the organization. It determines the degree to which employees can influence the decision making of the firm or institution in which they work.

decision making
work consultation

Examples of relatively weak forms of organizational democracy, where employees have only a small measure of influence over decision making, include quality circles and informal work consultation during meetings on certain aspects of work. However, many people only use the word 'democracy' to describe circumstances involving substantial influence on important decisions – not only consultation with workers at the operational core or via a works council, but also decision making at top management or board level. Supervisory boards – with members elected by employees or nominated by a union to represent the views of employees – as a form of decentralized decision making from the top of the organization, as well as a vehicle for initiatives relating to safety, health care and working conditions at the bottom of the organization can indeed be seen as forms of organizational democracy.

supervisory boards

decentralized decision making

Research among British managers and shop stewards has shown almost unanimous (95 per cent) support for work group meetings and job design, with a large majority considering these to be of interest to employees as well as management in organizations. These findings are consistent with further research which showed that employees welcomed direct participation – as well as indirect participation – in every respect, and at the same time recognized that such participation was of advantage not only to themselves but also to the company for which they work.

It is significant that the great majority of workers do not expect participation (either direct or indirect) to affect power differences between management and workers. These findings therefore indicate that it is functional democracy that is beneficial from the workers' perspective.

Various studies have produced circumstantial evidence to support the fact that participation not only influences the atmosphere of an organization in a positive way, but ultimately also has a positive influence on efficiency and effectiveness. Research studies into US experiences (Crouch & Heller 1983, Wilpert & Sorge 1988) with the Scanlon plan and the Quality of Working Life (QWL) programs, the long-term effects of socio-technical reorganization in Indian textile mills, Swedish organization development (OD) programs and Norwegian industrial democracy experiments all point to the successful implementation of functional democracy, and an accompanying increase in performance and improvement in the working climate of the organization.

Scanlon plan

Quality of Working Life (QWL) programs

CASE

Mini case study 2.3

Trade union official: Opel Antwerp will close

A German trade union official says General Motors Corp. plans to close Opel's Belgian plant, with the loss of more than 2,300 jobs.

Franco Biagiotti, the head of the Bochum work council, told the DAPD press agency that Opel's head Nick Reilly had said this week that the plant would close.

Opel had no comment on speculation that it would announce the plant's closure later Thursday.

Workers at Antwerp have blockaded the factory's parking lot in protest at the job losses.

Source: *The Associated Press State & Local Wire*, January 21, 2010

2.6.2 Future EU legislation and directives on industrial democracy

On 22 September 1994, the EU member states implemented a directive (Directive 94/95 Concerning the Institution of the Euro Works Council) that could lead to fully fledged employee participation across Europe. The directive states that employees in companies and institutions which meet certain criteria have to be informed and/or consulted on cross-border affairs. This EU directive was to be included in national legislation no later than 22 September 1996. Negotiations to establish a European Works Council (EWC) are continuing. It must be said, however, that in this respect EU harmonization, not to mention unification, is still a long way off.

European Works Council

No further directives have been published since 1999. The somewhat unrealistic belief within *employee participation*

EU political circles is that the four models of employee participation which can be identified in the EU at this point in time and which reflect the degree of workers' influence in the diverse corporate governance structures are equivalent to each other. These models are:

1 A minimum of one-third and a maximum of one half of the members of the supervisory board are nominated by the employees (the German Mitbestimmungs variant).
2 The members of the supervisory board are all nominated according to the system of controlled co-optation (the Dutch variant).
3 An employee representative body is installed at the highest level of the organization and has to be kept informed and consulted on all matters which are on the agenda of the supervisory board (the French-Italian variant).
4 There is compulsory regulation of employee participation through collective labor agreements (the so-called Swedish collective bargaining variant).

These official models can be seen as more or less a reflection of three dominant patterns of thought, patterns which are recognizable in the various structures of industrial relations at corporate levels in the EU member states – negotiation, opposition and integration – currently applied most unambiguously and coherently in the United Kingdom, France and Germany respectively. In other countries we often see combinations of these three approaches (see Table 2.4).

2.6.3 The German and Dutch system

The German and Dutch system of industrial democracy is regarded as the most comprehensive in Europe. The system comprises a works council (Betriebsrat/ Ondernemingsraad), representative from the board of directors or supervisory board (Aufsichtsrat/ Raad van Commissarissen) and the executive board or board of management (Vorstand/Raad van Bestuur).

works councils

Works councils exist in organizations in all areas of both the private and public sectors. Representatives on works councils are elected by their fellow workers. The works council has three basic rights:

1 The right to receive information concerning the financial position, performance, future prospects and strategic position of the organization
2 The right to be consulted by top management on decisions of strategic importance such as major investments, reorganization, changing of location, acquisitions or closing down of subsidiaries, and so on

co-determination

3 The right of co-determination with regard to essential aspects of the management of personnel. By law the works council has discretionary power in relation to policies relating to work regulations, regulations concerning pensions, profit sharing or savings, working day and holiday arrangements, regulations concerning safety, health care and the welfare of personnel, regulations on appointment, dismissal or promotion, salary policy, position of junior workers within the organization, and so on.

The works council also has the right to be consulted about any decision to appoint or dismiss an executive manager at board level and to veto board appointments.
The formal authority to appoint members of the board of management is vested in the supervisory board (or board of directors). If necessary, the supervisory board can veto policy decisions made by the board of management – for example, in the case of a merger or an excessively risky acquisition – or can urge the board of management to abandon a policy. Representatives on the supervisory board – whether nominated by shareholders, workers or unions – are always required to act and make decisions on behalf of the company or the institution as a whole. Supervisory board members should not simply represent the interest of a specific group.

The board of management in German organizations (Vorstand) includes a so-called Arbeitsdirektor – a personnel director. This Arbeitsdirektor cannot be appointed without the consent of a majority of worker representatives on the Aufsichtsrat (the supervisory board), according to the Mitbestimmungsgesetz 1976. The chosen Arbeitsdirektor has the same rights and legal status as the other members of the board of management. Naturally, the works council is an important point of reference for the execution of the duties of the Arbeitsdirektor.

2.6.4 Industrial democracy in Europe: a comparative survey

A range of attitudes to work councils across the European Union is shown in Fig 2.9, with the individual approaches to industrial democracy described in greater detail in Table 2.4. Germany and the Netherlands are influenced by a different view of the organization (it is considered as a cooperative working organization rather than as an arena) and a different concept of the works council (as a meeting point between the entrepreneur/owner and the unions – the works council is seen as a representative body for the employees).

works council

	Works council as meeting point of entrepreneur and unions	Works council as representative of employees
The firm as a co-operative working organization; not as an arena	Belgium Denmark	Germany The Netherlands
The firm as an arena	France	Spain

Figure 2.9
Position of works councils in relation to different views of the organization in some EU countries

The countries in the upper boxes of the diagram in Fig 2.9 – Belgium and Denmark, Germany and the Netherlands – have in common the notion of joint decision making through cooperation with the works council; they are different with regard to the position of the works council vis-à-vis the unions and vis-à-vis the owner/entrepreneur. In the lower boxes, this notion is less developed; the firm is organized as an arena in which the entrepreneur meets with the unions. The works council is still regarded as a 'strange intruder,' although in several ways regulations are similar to those in the countries in the upper boxes.
The left-hand column indicates the dominance of unions in the works council. The works council is not the most important instrument for democracy and participation; that remains union representation. In the right-hand column the works council is relatively removed from union influence. It enjoys greater autonomy with respect to the unions compared to those in the left-hand column, but not complete autonomy (as regulations concerning the nomination of candidates for the works council might show).
In the right-hand column, the formal authority of the works councils is more extensive, but this is balanced out as a rule by the weaker presence of unions in the firm's organization – something that applies more to Germany and the Netherlands than it does to Spain.

Austria, Germany, Luxembourg and the Netherlands (North-West European model)	▪ Legislation exists concerning participation and joint decision making in enterprises and public institutions. ▪ The instrument for joint decision making is the works council *(Betriebsrat/comité mixte d'enterprise/Ondernemingsraad)* with a varying level of influence (more in Austria, Luxembourg and Germany; less in the Netherlands) through the supervisory council and/or board of management. ▪ The influence of employees is enhanced through representation on the supervisory council and board of management. ▪ There is a right of co-determination in personnel affairs and a right of consultation and information in economic and organizational affairs.
Ireland and the United Kingdom (the Anglo-Irish model)	▪ No legislation exists concerning participation and joint decision making in enterprises and public institutions (voluntarism). ▪ The instrument for employee participation is the union through the shop steward. No participation or representation of employees on the board of directors (the two-tier system of supervisory board/ board of management is rare), with the exception of Ireland where in public institutions employee representatives have been nominated to the board of management since the end of the 1970s. ▪ There is no right of co-determination; negotiations are the way to influence social policy and the economic affairs of an organization (including conditions of employment).
Denmark, Finland, Norway and Sweden (North-West European/ Anglo-Irish mixed model)	▪ Legislation exists concerning participation and joint decision making in enterprises and public institutions in Sweden and Norway; in Denmark the existence of works councils (*Samarbejdsudvalg* (SU)) goes back to a gentlemen's agreement between employers' organizations and unions (*DanskArbejdgiverforening* (DA)) and the *Landsorganisationen* (LO) in Denmark in 1947, renewed in 1986). The degree of statutory participation is a step behind that of the other Scandinavian countries. ▪ Instruments for employee participation are the unions through the shop stewards, in Denmark the representation of employees on the supervisory council (the *Bestyrelse),* in Sweden the appointment of two workers' directors on the board of directors and in Norway the election of one third of members of the board of directors and supervisory board by employees, after nomination by local unions. ▪ There is a right of co-determination in social policies, conditions of employment, pension fund administration and the organization of the production function. Only rights of information and consultation apply in economic affairs.

Table 2.4
Diversity in patterns of industrial democracy in EU countries

Belgium, France, Greece, Italy, Portugal and Spain (Latin-European model)	▪ Legislation exists concerning participation in enterprises and public institutions. Instruments for employee participation in two- or three-way structures include: *a* union representation through syndical delegation (Belgium, Greece, Italy, Portugal and Spain); *b* works councils in all countries (in Belgium Ondernemingsraad; in France comite d'enterprise (CE); in Spain comite de empresa (CE); in Italy consiglio difarica dei delegatr, in Portugal comissoes de trabalhadores (CT). *c* personnel council (in France *delegues du personnel* and in Spain the *delegados de personal*) ▪ No worker representatives on supervisory councils in Belgium; in France a CE member has the right to attend a meeting of the board of management or supervisory council (*conseil d'administration);* in Italy, there are no legal obligations to have employee representatives on the boards. In 1984, on the basis of so-called protocol, some major industrial groups including IRI, ENI, EFIM created bilateral committees to be consulted on the economic affairs and social strategies of the firms. In Greece, Portugal and Spain employees are represented on the board of management of government enterprises and public institutions. ▪ No prescribed rights of co-determination, with the exception of the conditions of employment; rights of information and consultation exists concerning social and economic policies, pension funds and production organization. ▪ In all these countries (with the exception of Portugal) there are health and safety committees prescribed by legislation. In Portugal, existing health and safety committees in the bigger firms are installed on the basis of collective bargaining.

Table 2.4
Diversity in patterns of industrial democracy in EU countries

In Fig 2.9, Germany and the Netherlands are placed in the same box because of the common logic behind the formal works council regulations and legislation. However, there are substantial differences between these two countries, the most important of which is representation by the employees and the unions on the supervisory council, which is not particularly strongly or explicitly regulated in the Netherlands.

2.7 Management and ethics

There is a whole range of unwritten rules and habits which society uses to judge whether something is decent or fair: its ethics.
The current trend towards the development of such codes of conduct reflects society's concern in recent years regarding business practices and crime. In 1992 a report was published by the US Committee of Sponsoring Organizations of the Treadway Commission (COSO) on the possibility and the desirability of a common frame of reference with regard to monitoring internal controls. To be effective, such a system would have to be efficient and reliable and the company would have to abide by the laws and regulations. The COSO Report identified five individual elements:

- A control environment
- An evaluation of risks
- Internal control measurements
- Information and communication
- A focus on proper functioning

CASE

Mini case study 2.4

Corporate crime is on the rise

The recession has taken its toll on morals as well as profits. PricewaterhouseCoopers (PwC), a consulting and accounting firm, has conducted a biennial survey of economic crime for the past ten years. The most recent, published on November 19th, is not only the most thorough, based on over 3,000 responses from firms in 54 countries. In many ways it is also the most worrying.

A third of those responding reported that they had suffered at least one economic crime in the past year. The incidence was particularly high in developing countries, notably Russia: in financial services and communications, in big companies and in state-owned enterprises.

The three most common forms of crime are theft, accounting fraud and corruption. Of these, fraud has shown a particularly sharp rise (see chart): 43% of all corporate victims of crime and 56% of those in financial services reported an increase. The rise in fraud stems from a mixture of increased opportunities and growing incentives. Companies have been reducing the number of people employed to monitor workers at a time when employees are more tempted to break the rules because their living standards are eroding and their jobs are looking shakier. The proportion of frauds committed by middle managers has shown a particularly sharp rise, from 26% in 2007 to 42% today.

Source: *The Economist*, November 19, 2009

Cadbury Report

At just about the same time, the Cadbury Report on which the stock exchange and the accountancy organizations worked together was published in the UK. The significance of the Committee's findings was increased by two business scandals which gained a great deal of international publicity in the early 1990s: the Maxwell Affair and the BCCI Affair. The Committee addressed the question of whether it was possible to draw up a code of conduct which could be monitored by accountants and that would commit a company's management to operating a system of internal control which would prevent abuse. The Committee published a preliminary Code of Best Practice which contained the following recommendations:

- There has to be a clear division of tasks at the top of the organization for an effective distribution of authority.
- There should be no ambiguity with regard to the authority of management.
- The board of directors should be independent and impartial. It should meet regularly, should participate in the audit committee and should participate in decisions relating to appointments and their duration.
- The remuneration of board members should be published, and the extent to which this is performance-related should be made clear.

The London Stock Exchange urged all quoted companies to endorse and publish such a code of conduct. The head of a central anti-fraud unit of one of the big accountancy firms could see both advantages in such a code as well as limitations:

> *To start with, you will never be able to cover every business with a statement like that. There will always be room for different interpretations of norms and deviations. There is no way that an auditor can cover everything.*

crime prevention

management audit

fraud

However, it is essential that crime prevention be taken seriously. This is only possible if there has been a thorough analysis of the risks involved – perhaps as a joint responsibility of government, employers' organization and accountants. The notion of the management audit which was first mooted in the 1970s but failed to materialize, is now being given more serious consideration now that the auditor is expected to uncover fraud and report it to the authorities. Once again questions are being asked regarding how strictly these internal rules are applied, what the procedures are for auditing the application of the rules and who is responsible for overseeing this.

justice Ethics needs to be distinguished from justice. The law can enforce certain types of behavior, while ethics tries to convince with arguments. Ethics involves thinking about the unwritten rules which regulate human society. Ethics encompasses a voluntary rather than a formal set of rules which are required if a good society or a good organization is to survive. A society or organization can be maintained because the members keep more or less to the universal rules of behavior, written or unwritten.

New moral stances arise out of major events that are considered to be of importance (for example, Live Aid in the 1980s) and risks both personal (for example, the HIV infection risk) and collective (for example, environmental pollution). *moral development* Moral development is both fueled by public debate and proceeds at its own pace. 'Safe sex' and recycling are part of the group moral of our society at the end of the twentieth century.

rules and norms Individual morals deviate from the universal and may cause it to change. Setting rules and norms and living according to them are, in practice, two completely different things. Deviation from the norms is perhaps simply human: the difference between the ideal and reality.

2.7.1 Ethical dilemmas

Many organizational and managerial problems have an ethical dimension – for example, the implementation of social policy, the relocation of manufacturing abroad, the handling of chemical waste and so on. An interesting issue in this regard is how far *business or corporate intelligence* business or corporate intelligence activities should extend. Should they include investigating what its competitors are up to and incorporating its findings into its strategies, or finding out whether competitors have developed new technologies? The borders between these and contravening business security or committing business or economic *espionage* espionage may be very fine, as the Volkswagen/GM and Airbus/Boeing cases illustrate.

At present, corporate intelligence activities also involve the gathering of information not accessible by standard channels of communication relating to non-governmental organizations (NGOs) and action groups. Sometimes journalists with leftist views are hired to gather such information, but it is also known that action groups are infiltrated by undercover agents. Hakluyt and Company Ltd, the London-based corporate intelligence firm, claims to be supplying information relating to 25% of the FTSE-index companies.

corporate values codes While many companies now have their attractively bound 'corporate values' on display, such codes rarely provide guidelines for use in genuinely difficult situations. The American firm of Nike forms an exception in this regard. Suppliers to the firm have to sign the concern's code of behavior. While Shell does not demand this of its business partners, Shell did report that in the last fiscal year, 106 contracts with partners and two joint ventures were ended because their activities did not conform to Shell's code of ethics.

But do morality and money really have to be at odds with one another? Since Shell's Brent Spar affair, companies have become increasingly aware that it is in their own best interests to be seen to be conforming to ethical standards. Nowadays, corporations such as Shell, BP and Akzo-Nobel require their managers to sign a code of conduct.

Research has shown, however, that to have any real effect, there has to be more than mere lip service paid to such codes. *ethical programs* Ethical programs have more effect when they are integrated within the company's structures and rules (for example, within the company's reward systems, or by requiring people in certain positions to account for their actions). At the time, Enron did have 'corporate values' that had been formulated: it owes its ruin to the fact that executive managers did not put them into practice. The power of the public is increasing in recent times, as a top executive at Boeing found out. His relationship with a female staff member, forbidden according to ethical conduct rules at Boeing, became his downfall, especially since he had been brought in not long before the incident to improve the relationship between the aircraft building industry with the government after there had been some conflicts of business ethics. The driving force behind fraud seems to be the very high variable remuneration and the extremely high bonuses accompanying high profits. They have made some CEOs greedy, and greed – even at the top – makes one blind.

establish reputation

As well as this, potentially fraudulent people tend to have a great need to establish their reputation, requiring and receiving *three* times as much attention from the financial press as their honest colleagues. CEOs apparently like to have their egos gratified (Cools, Boston Consulting Group, 2005).

whistle blowers

Where there is a code of ethics, it may even discourage the so-called whistle blowers: those who feel called upon to draw attention to companies that do not comply with the regulations, particularly when they do so deliberately but even when it is indirect, by breaking security regulations systematically, showing favoritism, giving bribes, manipulating figures, breaking contracting rules, acting in high-handed ways or being guilty of mismanagement.

whistleblowing regulation

More than half of the listed companies in the Netherlands do not have a whistleblowing regulation as required by both the Tabaksblat Code and the Sarbanes-Oxley Act. This enables employees to report (anonymously or otherwise) breaches of rules and regulations and fraud (such as tax fraud via UBS in the USA) as well as any suspicion that this is happening. More than 90% do have a behavioral code which contains the norms and values that are valid within the company (also required by Tabaksblat). More than 80% of these monitor observance of the code, especially by registering and analyzing incidents that occur. This has been shown in an investigation carried out by KPMG (KPMG Integrity Services, 2005).

corporate culture

fraud line

An increasing number of companies are opening a fraud line via which fraud can be reported. The aim is to create a healthier corporate culture. For example, Ahold has been operating a 24-hour line for unethical matters since 2004, after it suffered much damage from bookkeeping scandals. DSM, ABN Amro and ING have also opened lines in keeping with the Tabaksblat Code, but these have apparently not produced many reactions. Perhaps a 'fraud line' does not belong in the Dutch corporate culture. Open dialogue is, admittedly, preferable, but that requires a fair amount of trust.

Corporate ethics also requires that the environment, product and service quality, and financial and social policy issues not be overlooked.

The green problem: the environment

To what degree do environmental problems influence actual organizational behavior? Have we accepted that there is a problem? If so, do we expect government to supply the solution? Should we, as an organization, continue to dispose of waste materials which are generally accepted to be harmful?

sustainable business

One of the main ethical issues that business is faced with is the 'green' issue: the formidable number of environmental issues relating to the consideration and setting of limits on the processing, disposal or dumping of waste, the use of energy, the choice of materials, and so on. Sustainable business seems to provide a way out.

Product and service quality

Is decent building, construction and manufacturing a matter for the legislator – as the 'social problem' was in the nineteenth century – or should industrial companies address issues of quality and the environment?

morality

ethical considerations

Some will say that with new developments, the first step is for new rights and rules to be drawn up by government. Company scandals should be held up as examples of where regulations have fallen short, though lack of a proper morality or ineffective management is usually the real reason. Raising the profile of ethical considerations by appealing to the ability of people, business firms and all sorts of organizations to regulate themselves is another way of approaching the issue.

ETHICS AND VALUES ARE VITAL TO FINANCIAL RETHINK

The economic crisis is also a crisis of ethics and values and must lead to a 'rethink' of the moral framework around finance, according to a report to be released in Davos.

The forum has responded to the crisis by expanding its dialogue with faith communities beyond its focus on Islam and the West to look at education, health, climate change and business ethics. In a series of essays by religious leaders for the report, Dr Rowan Williams, the Archbishop of Canterbury, said: 'Politics left up to managers and economics left up to brokers add up to a recipe for social and environmental chaos.'

Ecumenical Patriarch Bartholomew, of the Orthodox Church, said: 'No economic system – no matter how technologically or socially advanced – can survive the collapse of the environmental systems that support it.'

The Muslim cleric Professor Mustafa Cagrici, Grand Mufti of Istanbul, said: 'We cannot possibly manage a political and economic arena expanded to this extent by globalisation by using a model of humankind that is so exaggeratedly individualistic, hedonist, materialistic and, in the last analysis, destructive.'

The Most Rev Katharine Jefferts Schori, Primate of The Episcopal Church in the US, said: 'If the wealthy of this world continue to reap outsized profits in the face of mounting poverty, we can expect only that violence and bloodshed and growing global insecurity will be the result.'

Source: *The Times*, January 23, 2010

Financial policy

How do we handle mass dismissals when the long-term outlooks are gloomy, though the present financial situation not too bad? Should we be prepared to make less of a profit if the environment benefits? Financial criteria in the narrow sense do not provide solutions to these problems. The eventual decision will be affected by both moral and in some cases even idealistic considerations. Decent financial policy needs to be viewed alongside other production factors. It is not only a matter of having a business 'conscience'. The Enron affair raises serious questions about morally responsible behavior.

Social policy

A good social policy from an ethical point of view is one in which the rights of individuals are not secondary to the rights of the organization. This raises issues relating to autonomy, the relative degree of dependency of individual employees, loyalty and organizational norms. Organizations should not promise more than they can deliver. Even in large companies, school-leavers in their first jobs cannot be promised 'jobs for life'. Nevertheless, loyalty based on trust between the employer and the employee is an important consideration. This has to be reflected in the way in which the organization conducts itself in good times as well as bad. For example, a wage decrease in bad times puts obligations on the organization to increase wages in good times, although this need not apply in a situation in which the employees are more or less temporary.

loyalty
trust

2.8 Communication with external groups

How does an organization get what it wants? How does an organization – whether in the private, public or voluntary sector – make the customer, client or citizen behave the way the organization wants? How does the organization handle pressure groups? In both trade and business, public relations is an area of activity that is especially directed at the handling of problems relating to the organization's external environment. It is especially concerned with the image and the identity of an organization and has to do with an organization's mission and its strengths and weaknesses. Many organizations are alarmed to find that there is quite a difference between how employees judge their organization (identity) and how the organization is valued by others (image). Certain incidents can have negative long-term effects and do great damage to the reputation of the organization. It is crucial that such incidents be handled properly. Consistent information is essential, both that directed internally (to employees) and externally (to customers/clients, government, suppliers, etc.) but is often very difficult to achieve.

identity
image

Expressive organization: the topics

The expressive organization is an organization that consciously and actively plays its part in relation to the internal and external stakeholders of the company and in doing so communicates on the subject of the desired image and aims at an interaction on the basis of factual images. The following issues are both explicitly and proactively relevant in this regard: transparency that derives from a keen sense of self-interest, attractive corporate values, internal and external involvement, consistency and the conviction that organizing is communicating. A recent publication on the 'expressive organization' (SMO 2005) used the expression 'from claiming to proving': communication that conveys the corporate identity, identity management and HRM consequences and a corporate design that stimulates functionality in this regard. In all this, ethics play a central role (see Section 2.7) and for at least the next ten years 'good governance' (in other words, corporate behavior and corporate responsibility) will largely depend on the marketing and communication factor.

transparency
corporate responsibility

In principle, image and identity need to be in harmony. Many organizations are unaware of the fact that they can play an active role in influencing their image; it is simply a matter of communication. Ideally, the desired and experienced reality (identity) within an organization should be consistent with the reality which is observed from the outside of the organization (image). In practice, this is not always the case, or so it would seem.
A new phenomenon in this regard is the emergence of 'corporate philanthropy'. In the US this has taken on massive proportions: think, for example, of Bill Gates (Microsoft) with his gift of billions of dollars to combat AIDS in Africa. Companies, institutions and extremely rich individuals in Europe (including the Netherlands) have not elected to boost their images via philanthropy and gifts to the same extent.

corporate philanthropy

CASE Mini case study 2.5

Being trustworthy is the top driver of corporate reputation in the UK

Seventy-two per cent of those surveyed in the UK said being able to trust a company was the most important criterion for corporate reputation. Trust came third in the global data. In the US and much of Western Europe, trust and transparency ranked higher than product quality. This is the first time these two attributes have been considered as important to corporate reputation as the quality of products and services themselves. Financial return is now one of the least important considerations, dropping from its third place spot in 2006. 'We are seeing a vastly different set of factors driving reputation than we did ten years ago,' said Edelman president and CEO Richard Edelman. 'Trust is now an essential line of business.' Globally, expertise still drives credibility of information sources. Stock or industry analyst reports and articles in business magazines were by far the most credible sources of information. Traditional media were also more highly trusted than social networking sites, blogs or websites. Academics or experts, financial or industry analysts or NGO representatives were also viewed as the most credible spokespeople. CEOs saw a rise in credibility, by 13 points in the UK, but they still remained in the bottom two. Overall, global trust in business had increased. In the US, it jumped 18 points to 54 per cent. But nearly 70 per cent suspected business and financial companies would revert to 'business as usual' after the recession. Trust in banks declined from 68 to 29 per cent in the UK from 2007 to 2010.

The 2010 Edelman Trust Barometer is the firm's tenth annual trust and credibility survey. It surveyed 4,875 'informed publics' in two age groups (25-34 and 35-64) in 22 countries.

Source: *PR Week*, January 29, 2010

2.8.1 Active management of image, identity and reputation

identity
image

Identity (how we see ourselves) and image (how we are seen by others) can often be quite contradictory. Many organizations are disappointed to learn that there is a difference between the self-image of the employees and how they are seen and valued by others. Unless this mismatch is addressed, personnel and management problems may arise. Management needs to strive for the following:

- A better match of activities and image for specific target groups
- A better match of activities and identity for specific employees

A company's reputation is highly dependent on moral behavior on the part of management and the employees as well as by the supervisory board. Acting honestly, sticking to arrangements, preventing misuse of power and fraud and not accepting bribes and kickbacks are at the heart of integrity. Sticking to the law and to the rules is part of the broader category of trustworthiness and meeting societal expectations. A company that people are talking about will usually land itself a bad name instantly (as Lockheed, Siemens end others have shown). In the worst-case scenario, this can lead to the demise of the company (think back to Lehman Bother's investment bank, DSB Bank and Icesave).

communication
research into image

The communication function has an important role to play. Research into image and the setting up of a program to improve an organization's image are well-known tools. Identity can also be managed and structured. An organization can develop more than one image or identity, each connected to a particular target group or a group of employees. This is more common in business life than it is in bureaucratic circles. A common house style can also support a desired overall identity.

Wal-Mart's image: 'bad and greedy' and the counteroffensive

Wal-Mart is a case in point. The last few years has even seen criticism of Wal-Mart increasing globally. New Wal-Mart branches and supercenters – a combination of a supermarket and a department store – are often not welcomed in the US. The same also applies to Germany, Switzerland and elsewhere in the world. The objections to this retail giant originate in the threatened ruin of local retailers and deserted main streets with empty shops in the places where Wal-Mart establishes itself, the squeezing out of suppliers in the US (but also in low-wage countries), the very low wages of their own staff and illegal workers, the exclusion of trade unions, the taking on of employees without protective terms of employment and in such a way that the employees either cannot or can hardly afford the basic necessities of life and cannot afford health insurance, low overtime rates, discrimination and so on. In order to halt the arrival of a particular new Wal-Mart branch – the world's largest chain store – a film with the title *Wal-Mart – The high cost of low price!* was even made. In America, this film has been shown in community centers, in private homes and in churches. It was first shown in November 2005.

CASE

Mini case study 2.6

How big is Wal-Mart?

1 At Wal-Mart, Americans spend $36 million every hour of every day.
2 This works out to $29,928 profit EVERY minute!
3 Wal-Mart will sell more from Jan. 1 to St. Patrick's Day (March 27) than Target sells all year.
4 Wal-Mart is bigger than Home Depot, Kroger, Target, Sears, Costco and Kmart combined.
5 Wal-Mart employs 1.6 million people and is the largest private employer.
6 Wal-Mart is the largest company in the history of the world.
7 Wal-Mart now sells more food than Kroger and Safeway combined ... and keep in mind they did this in only 15 years.
8 During this same period, 31 supermarket chains sought bankruptcy (including Winn-Dixie).
9 Wal-Mart now sells more food than any other store in the world.
10 Wal-Mart has approximately 3,900 stores in the U.S.A. of which 1,906 are SuperCenters. This is 1,000 more than it had five years ago.
11 This year, 7.2 billion different purchasing experiences will occur at a Wal-Mart store. (Earth's population is approximately 6.5 billion.)
12 Ninety per cent of all Americans live within 15 miles of a Wal-Mart.
13 Let Wal-Mart bail out Wall Street and the auto industry!

Source: *Stratford Beacon Herald* (Ontario), January 2, 2009

Wal-Mart

Since the autumn of 2005, Wal-Mart has stopped its past habit of ignoring criticism of its way of conducting business. The company has started a counteroffensive because its bad image is starting to have an effect on results. For the first time, Wal-Mart is hiring in a renowned PR consultancy firm.

There have been talks with environmentalists and a non-profit organization has been contacted to make contact with the lawyers that represent workers in low-wage countries, where a lot of the products of Wal-Mart are made. Wal-Mart has become hypersensitive to negative publicity because it wants to entice better-earning Americans to their shops and it is less prepared to accept a bad name in exchange for low prices.

The darling of the stock exchange of the nineties has seen the price of its shares drop by about a quarter since the turn of the century. The growth in turnover in the existing shops has dropped during recent years. Cities where a new branch of Wal-Mart is not welcome are increasing in number. During the last few months, Wal-Mart was rebuffed in Chicago, Los Angeles and New York, among other places. At the end of 2005 this was also happening in other countries.

Wal-Mart is taking the documentary seriously and has immediately made a film to counter it. As well as that, the company has announced that it has installed a 'war room' where spin doctors who had been involved in presidential campaigns are coordinating the counteroffensive. The counter website – walmartfacts.com – is part of the campaign. Wal-Mart claims that the counter film gives a 'more balanced' view and that the spin doctors are the only remedy against the 'trade union supported propaganda'. The present anti Wal-Mart campaign has cost the firm 25 million dollars. The title of the counter film is Why Wal-Mart works and why that drives some people c-r-a-z-y. As well as this, Wal-Mart has announced a number of remarkable measures: it is going to invest in businesses run by women and it has called on Congress to raise the minimum wage. If everybody has to raise their wages, Wal-Mart can do the same without any loss of competitive power.

It also invited a number of economists to do research into the company. The outcome of these investigations was varied: whenever Wal-Mart opens a branch somewhere, households save 2,300 dollars a year, but there is also loss of jobs.

Russell Branca, who made showing the film possible, concluded after viewing that it does not deal with the criticism in depth, but that 'it is certainly a powerful medium for carrying the message. Now let the viewers decide'.

Since then Wal-Mart's profits have risen to above $400 billion (= €318 billion) in 2009 and they continue to grow, with a sharp focus on Asia and new markets in Vietnam, Indonesia and Thailand. As of 2008, Wal-Mart's international operations include Mexico (1201 branches since 1991), Puerto Rico (56 branches since 1992), Canada (310 branches since 1994), Brazil (349 branches since 1995), Argentina (28 branches since 1995), China (225 branches since 1996), UK (358 branches since 1999), Japan (387 branches since 2002), Costa Rica (164 branches since 2005), El Salvador (77 branches since 2005), Guatemala (160 branches since 2005), Honduras (50 branches since 2005) and Nicaragua (51 branches since 2005). Wal-Mart has withdrawn from Germany (where it had 85 branches in 2006) and South Korea (where it had 16 branches in 2006. There are prospects for expanding into the Eastern European and Russian markets rather than the 'mature' European markets, though acquisitions in the form of takeovers or collaborative enterprises have not been ruled out.

This US-based price-fighter's image and reputation as a bad employer that pays low wages and provides other poor terms of employment continues to arouse controversy. It is hoped that it will endorse sustainability (i.e. to deal with employees and suppliers in socially acceptable ways) as well as favoring green policies and eco-friendly products.

2.8.2 Lobbying or problem management

Problem management or lobbying – an everyday feature of business life in the US – is gaining a desired outcome by using certain means. The following instruments can be used:

- Written documents (letters, memos)
- Oral contacts (personal conversations, telephone calls)
- Company visits, work visits
- Internships or work experience with Members of Parliament
- Receptions
- Informal lunch meetings with Members of Parliament (exchanging points of view, exploring political ideas)
- Speeches at congresses and symposia
- Hearings
- Calling in of specialists
- Exploiting possible contradictions between ministries or sectors within a ministry
- Publicity (public reactions, giving opinions in newspapers and magazines)
- Own media (annual report, personnel news)

The following would seem to be the golden rules of the lobbying industry:

- Always know your business (with regard to both content and procedures). Define the problem in terms that are clear and brief. Keep letters short and to the point. Leave behind one or two sheets of paper stating your position or other relevant information after a meeting.
- Always intervene in time and approach the right person. Adopt an open attitude. Acknowledge self-interest, but explain why the problem is so important. Government officials and politicians are often grateful for information.
- It is top management's task to be involved in what is going on, and to be prepared to negotiate. Widen the lobby as far as possible by approaching allied organizations at industry/sector level or employers' organizations.
- Always consider the arguments of opponents. Never underestimate them.
- Always ensure a coordinated approach (not more than one contact from the same company). Make discrete use of publicity.
- Always make sure you have room to maneuver. Be flexible.
- Never give incorrect information. Never provide expensive or unnecessary dinners or display any behavior which could be misinterpreted as corrupt. Never whine. Never aim too high. Never hire a lobbyist when it comes to negotiating. Never have nothing to offer.

2.8.3 Crisis management

A crisis can overwhelm the best companies with the most skilled managers. It can have technical, natural or human causes and have minor, considerable or fatal consequences. Crises can arise from bad investments, acid rain, toxic waste, a hostile takeover, inferior products, accidents or strikes, legislation which has a negative effect on the interests of the company, a smear campaign in the media, or hostile action such as threats, kidnapping or sabotage by third parties.

withholding information

If an organization is perceived to be withholding information, this can become a crisis in itself, one in which the right of the public to 'know the facts' will become the most important issue.

CASE

Mini case study 2.7

Toyota's troubles

Safety recalls are a common enough occurrence in the car industry. If handled correctly, few have long-term consequences for the manufacturer involved. However, the disaster now engulfing Toyota is of a different order. Not only is Toyota's brief reign as the world's largest carmaker threatened but, more importantly, so too is its reputation for matchless quality and management. Rivals that had grown used to living in the Japanese firm's shadow are quietly celebrating.

Toyota's decision last month to recall 2.3m vehicles in America and then to suspend sales and production of eight models with potential faulty accelerator pedals (it later took similar steps around the world, involving 8m vehicles) has sent shock waves through the industry. The good news was that Toyota announced on February 1st that it had come up with a cure for the sticking pedals which, along with badly fitting floor mats (the subject of another massive recall late last year), have been blamed for at least 19 deaths and more than 2,000 incidents of 'unintended acceleration'.

Whether Toyota will speedily recover from this setback or suffer permanent harm is uncertain, but the betting must be on the latter. As the recriminations continue and the company's public relations machine stumbles, the aura that surrounded the firm and allowed it to grow rapidly in recent years, even while charging premium prices, is being dispelled. Other carmakers, notably Ford and the ambitious Volkswagen Group, have closed the quality gap and are offering more interesting cars. Korea's Hyundai is unapologetic about seeing Toyota's (and corporate Japan's) loss as its gain. Toyota still has great strengths, not least financial, but it has lost something precious and may never get it back.

Source: *The Economist*, February 4, 2010

While crises may vary in nature, size and intensity, the consequences of a crisis are almost always far-reaching and never pleasant. Crises often strike at the very heart of a company and organization, affecting credibility and putting reputations at stake. The business may be rocked to its very foundations.

Most crises have the following characteristics:

- Decisions having to be taken quickly
- Doing nothing having undesirable consequences
- A limited number of options
- Wrong decisions having far-reaching consequences
- Groups involved having conflicting interests
- Top management having to become directly involved

The electronic media have become the most important source of information in the industrialized world. News is sometimes compared to an avalanche. A small report – perhaps one on a company closure, merger, stock exchange flotation, demonstration, accident, inferior product or product recall – can lead to a reaction from the unions, which in turn can provoke a reaction from an employers' organization. This can, in turn, lead to reactions from other groups wishing to make a socio-economic contribution. A small snowball can very quickly become an avalanche: a crisis, in short.

Simulations have demonstrated that few managers have good crisis plans. They are inclined to stick their heads in the sand. The maxims should be 'never lie' and 'keep a cool head', and in the event of a crisis, try to create a good relationship with the media, the police and the authorities. It is important that all communication be credible.

2.8.4 *The crisis action plan*

Communication and planning is the key to good crisis management.
Having an action plan which it has worked out in advance for the type of crisis that can occur in a particular line of business can make all the difference for a company. Teams which can take on the strategic and tactical aspects of the issue at stake will be at the ready. An emergency plan that is tailor-made to suit an organization's needs and the specific problems that can occur will usually stop the problems from taking on outrageous proportions.
A threatening crisis can be averted by someone looking out for signs of trouble. Mass resignation of employees, a suspicious pattern in customer order cancellations, the arrival of a group of activists who set up camp in the neighborhood are all unmistakable signs that trouble is at hand. The real problem is that people do not usually pay attention to these early warning signs because they do not wish to see them. It is important to keep in contact with external groups, to actively search out sources of information and to remain alert at all times.
In her book, Ten Berge (1989) comments: 'The interesting thing about crises, which occur in a wide variety of circumstances, is that they are awfully similar.'
The external pattern of events will usually include the following:
- Damage sustained in some form
- A series of escalating events
- Time not being on the company's side
- Unwonted attention by the press
- Rumors and speculation threatening to take the upper hand

Common psychological reactions to these factors are:
- Disbelief
- The drawing in of horns
- A narrow-minded reaction
- Panic-based kamikaze action
- The attribution of blame
- Hurt feelings

crisis plan Having a crisis plan worked out and ready for implementation can save valuable time when a crisis hits. The situation can deteriorate if the names and phone numbers of important people have to be looked up or logistical problems have to be solved. An organization should estimate the probability of a particular crisis occurring and use these calculations to draw up a program of advance crisis management.

2.8.5 Crisis management procedures

The following recommendations for good crisis management were suggested by Ten Berge in her book (1989).

The handling of a crisis

- When a crisis occurs, take immediate action in order to gain control over the situation as fast as possible and limit the harmful consequences. You have 24 hours at most to set the tone.
- Contact the members of the board, union leaders, the appropriate authorities or other stakeholders.
- Ensure that you are well informed about the various communication techniques beforehand.
- If appropriate, make sure that the organization has the necessary resources to communicate immediately and effectively with interest groups and the general public.
- Bring all stakeholders – employees and their family members, shareholders, suppliers, distributors, local or regional governments and neighbors – up to date with developments as quickly and as fully as possible.
- See to it that the content of the message is exactly in tune with the needs of the target group. For example, television needs pictures which require little explanation; the financial world needs figures and forecasts.
- Be open and fair when you present the news.
- Publish an official statement as quickly as possible. Rumors and speculation thrive in an information vacuum.
- Seek the support of independent third parties and make use of this when conveying your message to the public.
- The best solicitor is one who does not have any interest in the case.
- It might be necessary to immediately cancel any planned advertising campaigns and abandon any plans for forthcoming campaigns because people might otherwise unconsciously relate the bad news of the crisis to the contents of the ad.

Handling the press

- Be human.
- Announce the bad news promptly and fully.
- Explain how you are going to resolve the problem.
- Tell the truth.
- Realize that he who is silent admits his guilt.
- 'No comment' is probably the worst comment to make. Always give a reason for not being able to answer a question. For example, it could be that you have not yet informed your own staff, or that you yourself do not yet know the facts.
- When you do not know the answer, admit it and commit yourself to finding out.
- See to it that there is an information kit ready for the press containing information and pictures.
- Centralization of information is important. Appoint one spokesperson. If there is more than one spokesperson, make sure that the statements that are made tally with each other. Everyone should be speaking the same language.
- Give clear instructions to your personnel that all questions should be passed on to the appointed spokesperson.
- Allocate a central point which can serve as a press center and where journalists can work and gather information.

Summary

- Organizations and managers operate in a societal environment, never in a vacuum. An organization can only survive if it supplies the products and services the environment wants.
- All kinds of environmental factors have an influence on organizations. These environmental factors include situations and events as well as groups and interested parties such as stakeholders who contribute to the survival of the organization in return for a particular reward or incentive.
- There are some environmental factors over which the individual organization has no influence: the forces and developments in the macro-environment which can be observed in an analysis of demographic, economic, technological, societal, political, ecological, market sector or business factors.
- The organization is also affected by trends in the environment such as the internationalization of markets (with the knock-on effects of differing national cultures), the shortening of life cycles, strategic joint ventures and network organizations.
- An organization always has to account for its operations to its internal and external stakeholders.
- Based on the information provided – which can take the form of an annual report and a social report on personnel matters and health and safety – the stakeholders have to judge whether they want to continue to make a contribution to the organization in the future.
- Societies can only continue to function when the members of each individual society live by written and unwritten rules – that is, by laws and regulations as well as rules of the generally accepted group moral.
- New technologies such as the digital storage of personally sensitive data and significant global changes such as environmental pollution, can lead to changes in the generally accepted group morality. Individual notions of morality can deviate from those of the ruling group.
- Variations and developments in the generally accepted morality mean that managers and internal and external stakeholders of the organization must ask themselves what decent management within that particular organization should consist of. This area of study is referred to as organizational or company ethics.
- It is possible for an organization to be perceived differently by its external environment (image) than by its own members (identity). In principle, image and identity should be similar. If these differ too much, communication will play an important role in resolving the differences.
- A crisis is a sudden and undesirable change in the relationship between an organization and its environment. The nature and intensity of a crisis is unpredictable.
- Sound crisis management is based on the existence of a crisis action plan and good communication between internal and external interest groups.
- A manager should keep abreast of both macro-environmental changes and the developments discussed above.
- It is important for an organization to determine the contribution it is to make to the societal environment. In other words, it must have goals and a strategy. This is covered in more depth in Chapter 4.

Discussion questions

1 With reference to *Management in Action* at the beginning of this chapter:
   a) Explain how Toyota's management (or rather, non-management) of its environment(s) has contributed to Toyota's rise and possibly even fall.
   b) What path would you suggest Toyota take in the short and the long term in order to overcome the dangers that threaten it?

2 Why should an organization be studied in the context of its stakeholders (e.g., competitors, government, and societal interest groups) and the environmental factors (e.g., economic, demographic, and technological factors)?

3 To what extent can an organization be regarded as a 'spider in a web'?

4 It would seem that one particular environmental development is that products are increasingly being replaced by new ones. Customers needs have become more diverse and customers are making greater demands. What are the consequences for business management? List some of them.

5 How can innovation, specialization, and exporting increase a firm's competitive advantage?

6 It is sometimes suggested that development and manufacturing problems can be passed on from individual manufacturers to the so-called network organizations. In what way?

7 Is it acceptable for a company to use a hazardous production process prohibited in the company's home country, a so-called low-wage country where environmental legislation is not enforced?

8 Comment on the following statement: 'Because the nature and magnitude of a crisis cannot be known in advance, firms should abstain from developing preemptive crisis action plans and instead manage crises as they emerge.'

Research-based exercise

Responses to economic recession

Introduction
This research-based exercise is based on a research article by Latham (2009), published in the *Journal of Small Business Management*. The research question, data collection, method and some of the results of the research project are presented. The exercise consists of three questions based on the research article and the theory in this chapter. The answers should be based on both the theory in Chapter 2 and your own insights into the practical implications of your answer.

Research Question
What is the likely effect of company size in a situation in which the company is faced with an environmental threat in the form of an economic recession?

Data Collection
The study focuses on the last economic downturn (2001-2003) in the software industry (classification code 7372). The software industry offers an appropriate sampling frame for the context of this study since extant research demonstrates that the industry is influenced by economies of scale, economies of scope, and learning effects, suggesting significant variation in the nature and manner of response between large and small firms. 137 software executives at both large established software organizations and smaller start-ups were surveyed to determine the strategies they adopted during the economic downturn.

Outcomes
Acting on a hypothesis that firms experiencing decline due to internal and/or external causes may adopt three distinct strategic responses – asset reduction, cost reductions, and revenue generation – the researcher found the following: Larger firms that derive competitive advantage from economies of scale, economies of scope and learning effects, are more likely to adopt strategies designed to capitalize on efficiency through cost reductions, whereas smaller firms will rely on their more flexible organizational structure and proximity to the market to find niches that might offer a moderate level of revenue generation.

(Based on Latham, S. (2009). 'Contrasting strategic response to economic recession in start-up versus established software firms.' *Journal of Small Business Management*, (47)2, 180-201.)

Questions

1 Describe the relationship between strategic responses (i.e., cost reduction, asset reduction, and revenue generation) and an organization's environment.
2 Explain why smaller firms operating in the software industry adopt revenue generation strategies while in contrast, larger firms adopt cost reduction strategies.
3 Consider other industries (e.g., financial services, manufacturing) and discuss why you would (or would not) expect similar findings.

CASE

Management case study

Cadbury takeover raises doubts over Kraft's business ethics

Kraft's proposed takeover of Cadbury has raised widespread fears that the US food group will abandon a landmark deal by the British confectioner to buy only Fairtrade cocoa beans for its Dairy Milk brand. The Fairtrade Foundation has begun urgent talks with Cadbury's executives to see if the company's agreement to buy all its cocoa beans for Dairy Milk direct from the foundation's farmer-led co-operatives will continue after the takeover.

Jack McConnell, the former first minister of Scotland, tabled a motion in the Scottish parliament urging Kraft to honour the deal, while at Westminster, the Labour MP Mark Lazarowicz put down a similar motion in the Commons.

Kraft is widely seen amongst development campaigners as being hostile to the Fairtrade Foundation, in particular after it criticised the movement for only dealing with 'an extremely small number' of companies, claiming it was too small-scale for its needs.

Todd Stitzer, Cadbury's chief executive, appeared to bitterly criticise Kraft's business ethics at a fair trade retail conference last September when takeover hostilities were in their infancy. Without naming Kraft directly, he attacked the 'unbridled' capitalism of large, heavily indebted firms, and urged shareholders to keep Cadbury independent. He said 'principled capitalism (was) woven into the very fabric' of his company. Without it 'you risk destroying what makes Cadbury a great company,' he said.

Lazarowicz, a long-standing fair trade campaigner and MP for Edinburgh North and Leith, said: 'It was a major breakthrough when Cadbury agreed to work with Fairtrade, and it would be a tragedy if that breakthrough was now to be set at nought.'

McConnell, who has close links with the development movement in Africa and was proposed in 2008 as high commissioner to Malawi, is to contact campaigners in the US to pressurise Kraft to honour the Cadbury deal and extend it to the US.
'There have been concerns expressed for many years that Kraft has never shown any enthusiasm for fair trade and therefore this must be under threat as a result of the takeover,' he said. 'I've seen with my own eyes the very positive impact that fair trade has on individuals and communities across Africa.'

Cadbury's decision to rebrand all its Dairy Milk bars with the Fairtrade logo last year was seen at the time as the movement's biggest coup: it was the first mass market chocolate in the world to use Fairtrade cocoa, and brought the product into 30,000 UK stores. The foundation has since brokered major deals to supply Starbucks with coffee and cocoa beans for Nestlé's Kit-Kat bars, and believed Cadbury was ready to expand its range of Fairtrade-branded sweets. Cadbury planned to expand the sale of Fairtrade Dairy Milk to Canada, Australia and New Zealand.

Kraft insists it supports the principle of sustainability after signing up with the Rainforest Alliance, which promotes conservation and fair business dealings with small growers, to supply some coffee beans for its Kenco and other brands. But Oxfam has accused Kraft of undermining attempts to treat small farmers fairly, defending the Fairtrade scheme as 'the only system that guarantees farmers a price that allows them a good return (whilst) at the same time working towards a sustainable future.'

A Fairtrade spokeswoman confirmed that the London-based foundation had made contact with Cadbury soon after Kraft's offer was accepted, to ensure that their contract would be honoured. 'We've had a very productive relationship and this landmark switch has come about as a result of it; of course we would like it to continue, and at some point see further switches,' she said.

Cadbury's deal tripled the amount of fairly traded, higher value cocoa sold by Ghana to 15,000 tonnes. The foundation said after Kraft's offer was accepted by Cadbury's board that it believed the success of the deal 'presents a unique and compelling case for continuing to pursue the Cadbury commitment to their Cocoa Partnership and to Fairtrade, and taking it further in coming months and years.'

Case study questions

1 In contrast to Kraft's narrow view on stakeholder management, Cadbury has a broader conception of who the stakeholders are and how they should be dealt with. Explain how this distinction may affect each firm's strategic decision making.

2 Todd Stitzer, Cadbury's CEO, states that 'principled capitalism [was] woven into the very fabric' of Cadbury. Explain what he means by this. Can you provide examples of other organizations?

3 Do you think that acquiring Cadbury, Kraft should maintain the contract between Cadbury and the Fairtrade Foundation to buy fair trade cocoa beans?

Principles of management

Motivating people

Part One Management and society

Chapter 1
Manager and management

Chapter 2
Organizations and environment

Part Two Strategic management and the learning organization

Chapter 3
Decision making and creativity

Chapter 4
Strategy formulation and strategic management

Part Three Organizational structure and design

Chapter 5
Designing the organization

Chapter 6
Structuring tasks for groups and individuals

Part Four Organizational behavior and people at work

Chapter 7
Motivation, work and career

Chapter 8
Leadership, motivation and communication

Part Five Operational planning, control and information management

Chapter 9
Operational planning and control

Chapter 10
Managerial process control: functional processes and process redesign

Part 2

Strategic management and the learning organization

CHAPTER 3 Decision making and creativity

CHAPTER 4 Strategy formulation and strategic management

In Part One we were introduced to the subject of organization and management, to the history of this discipline and to the societal environment within which organizations function. In Part Two we will be looking at the strategic management process within an organization. Every organization needs to address the question of what our actual contribution to society is. An organization's response to this question will determine its mission, goals and strategy.

The strategy process is both a creative and a decision-making process and this is discussed in Chapter 3. In the search for new opportunities to ensure the continued survival of the organization, management has to ask itself whether current policies should be retained or whether change is necessary. When an organization conducts a systematic review of its members' experiences and adapts its operations to match these it is said to be a 'learning organization'.

Chapter 4 deals with the actual formulation of strategy and management of the strategy process.

CONTENTS

3.1 The nature of decision making
3.2 The decision-making process
3.3 Factors influencing decision making
3.4 Decision making: techniques and approaches
3.5 The creative and learning organization
3.6 The role of work groups in participation and decision making
3.7 The use of external consultants

Decision making and creativity

Chapter 3

LEARNING OUTCOMES

After studying this chapter, you should be able to do the following:

- Identify the various kinds of decisions
- Describe the phases of the decision-making process
- Discuss the problems which can arise in the various phases of the decision-making process
- Recognize the pitfalls which make decision-making difficult
- Specify the various levels of learning
- Explain the concept of the 'learning organization'
- Evaluate the contribution of consultative groups in decision making
- Explain why managers call in management consultants

CASE

Management-in-action

Hyundai smokes the competition

On the second floor of the 21-story Hyundai Motor headquarters to the south of Seoul is a 24-hour operations hub, the Global Command and Control Center (GCCC). Modeled after the CNN newsroom in Atlanta with dozens of computer screens relaying video and data, it keeps watch on Hyundai operations around the world. Parts shipments are tracked from the time they leave the supplier until they reach a plant. Cameras peer into assembly lines from Beijing to Montgomery and keep a close watch on Hyundai's giant Ulsan, Korea, plant, the world's largest integrated auto factory and the scene of frequent labor unrest.

Are competitors' spies lurking? The GCCC watches over Hyundai R&D activities in Europe, Japan, and North America, as well as its sprawling, 4,300-acre test facility in California's Mojave Desert, with its 6.4-mile oval track. Almost no outsiders, and certainly no visitors from Fortune, are allowed inside the GCCC to view the operation firsthand. Hyundai employees aren't even supposed to talk about it. But its existence says volumes about how Hyundai views itself and the rest of the world. Hyundai is a confident, hyper aggressive company that not only wants to win, it expects to win. By monitoring operations in real time, Hyundai can identify problems in an instant and react quickly. It is a different philosophy for an auto company. Whereas Toyota (TM) thrives on consistency and Honda (HMC) on innovation, Hyundai is all about aggressiveness and speed.

These days Hyundai (rhymes with 'Sunday') could get ticketed for exceeding the limit. Powered by a weak Korean won and a revitalized product line, it is ramping up volumes in major markets around the world. Along with sister company Kia, of which it owns 39%, Hyundai has a hammerlock on Korea, with 80% of sales this year. In the U.S. generous incentives for retail customers and fleet purchases have pushed sales up a strong 7% in a market down 24%. November was a spectacular month: Hyundai brand sales jumped 46% from the previous year, and Kia rose 18%.

In China, where auto sales have skyrocketed this year thanks to government stimulus, Hyundai leaped 150% in September, leaving the company in second place, behind Volkswagen, among international automakers.

Behind the scenes at Hyundai

To take advantage of its momentum, Hyundai is pushing new models out of its factories faster and faster. American customers got to see the slick new 2011 Sonata in December, two months ahead of schedule, because, in an unusual move, Hyundai sped up the start of production. Automakers hate to interfere with factory schedules because it is expensive, disrupts the flow of parts, and invites assembly problems. But Hyundai decided to move ahead. It was receiving good reads on early quality checks, suppliers showed ample stocks of parts, and engineers had prepped its Alabama plant. Speed became a competitive advantage.

Moving quickly and boldly has made Hyundai Motor Co. the fastest-growing major automaker in the world. Amid the global sales slump, it made a record $832 million in the third quarter ended Sept. 30. Analysts expect its net profits to rise almost 40% this year. Despite its relative youth – it is only 43 years old – Hyundai already ranks fifth in volume among the world's auto producers, according to IHS Global Insight, and passed 107-year-old Ford Motor (F, Fortune 500) in 2009 to move into fourth place. Years ago, Toyota used to say that Hyundai was the company it feared most. Today those fears have grown into a nightmare.

New leadership, new focus

Hyundai's success reflects a shift in attitude that occurred nearly a decade ago. In the 1990s the company was more interested in how many cars it could build than in how good it could make them. That changed in 1999 when founder Ju-Yung Chung passed corporate leadership to his son, Mong-Koo Chung. According to company lore, the younger Chung decreed that Hyundai would henceforth concentrate on quality, not volume. With the chairman behind the push, and with its characteristic intensity, Hyundai went after quality improvements with a vengeance.

Hyundai benchmarked Toyota, then the industry's quality leader, to understand its processes. It installed Six Sigma at its engineering center to measure its improvement. It made quality a cross-functional responsibility, with involvement from procurement, finance, and sales and marketing. It enlisted outside suppliers and put them together with designers and engineers to work out problems before they occurred. Quality oversight meetings, which had been poorly attended, became must-go events after chairman Chung began to show up for twice-monthly gatherings.

At 71, Chung still takes an active role in the company. He typically arrives in the office by 6:30 a.m. and gets frequent briefings from the CEOs of Hyundai and Kia, as well as their subsidiaries. He has taken a particular interest in a new $5 billion mill being built by Hyundai Steel to make lightweight, high-tensile steel for automobiles, and travels to the construction site by helicopter as often as four times a week.

Chung, who rarely gives interviews to English-language publications, spoke with Fortune through an interpreter from his penthouse office in the Hyundai tower. Chung attributes his company's success to the investment it has made in improving its products. He believes that Hyundai's quality, as well as its technology, 'are head to head with Toyota at this moment,' a statement he makes with some confidence since 'we are monitoring what is going on with Toyota all the time.' Asked what scares Hyundai the most, he replied, 'The thing we fear is uncertainty. There are many announcements about demand shrinking, and all the numbers are different.'

Whatever the attraction, customers seem to be getting a new message about Hyundai. Five years ago Hyundai was known for its low prices, so-so quality, and a 100,000-mile powertrain warranty. Today, Ewanick says, Hyundai stands for softer, more positive qualities like smart, fresh, and high-tech. 'Consumers,' he says, 'want brands that feel the same way they do about society and the environment. But they don't want to pay for it.'

Labor union disputes to Genesis' success

Hyundai's growth was accompanied by a decade of labor union disputes that produced paralyzing strikes. Labor rights in South Korea had been long suppressed, and a series of healthy pay increases kept its militant labor unions at bay until the mid-1990s.

The two trends – better quality, sharper designs – came vividly together in 2008 with the launch of the Genesis sedan. A step up from the midsize Sonata, Hyundai's best U.S. seller, the Genesis is powered by a V-6 engine (with an optional V-8) and is designed to compete in the so-called entry luxe segment with cars like the Lexus ES 350.

Speedy in most matters, Hyundai has been a laggard when it comes to developing alternative-fuel vehicles. It didn't introduce its first fuel-saving hybrid until last summer, a decade after Toyota started selling the Prius. Typically, Hyundai's ambitions remain huge. Despite its late start, it has stated its intention to sell 500,000 hybrids a year by 2018. Hyundai has developed a lithium-polymer battery that is 40% smaller and weighs 35% less than conventional nickel-metal-hydride ones used in the Toyota Prius.

A wave of new models should keep both Hyundai and Kia hustling over the next few years. The two companies are due to turn over their entire U.S. product line in the course of the next four years, the highest replacement rate in the industry, according to a forecast by Merrill Lynch/Bank of America's John Lynch. He sees Hyundai and Kia gaining 3 1/2 points of market share over the span. That would be enough to vault the Koreans past Chrysler and Nissan into fifth place in the U.S., with a share of 10.8% by 2013.

The old bumper sticker used to preach that speed kills, but Hyundai shows no signs of slowing down – and so far has no need to report any casualties.

Source: *Fortune Magazine*, January 5, 2010, Alex Taylor

Before addressing the issue of formulation of strategy in Chapter 4, it is important to first examine the decision-making process within the organization. The choice of a strategy is one of the most important decisions an organization will take.

In this chapter we will describe the various stages of the decision-making process (referred to as the phase model of decision making). We will then identify the factors that influence decision making and suggest how decision making can be improved.

Decision making and the resulting planning and, if necessary, adjusting of business activities are key elements of managerial and operational functions. A good supply of information is of crucial importance for these functions, for without it, decisions cannot be made and potential problems will not be spotted. Information needs to be gathered in time and has to be presented in a clearly structured way. Transmitting information, receiving signals in return from the organization and relaying decisions are all communication processes. Decision making, planning, the supply of information and communication are all elements which are directly linked to each other in the management and control of business processes.

All of these elements are examined in detail in this book. In this chapter, we will consider the decision-making process itself and, in so doing, describe influencing factors such as communication, information and motivation.

Communication is discussed in greater detail in Chapter 8, and information management and information technology are covered in more depth in Chapter 10.

3.1 The nature of decision making

Problems will always arise in the working environment and every manager will have to make decisions in order to resolve them. The analysis of problems and the search for solutions are an integral part of the managerial function.

When an organization increases its output by, for example, offering more products or delivering more services, resulting in a higher level of product-market activities, or when the production process becomes more sophisticated, this often means that more complex problems will arise within the organization. The preparation for decision making, the decision making itself and the enforcement of these decisions usually involve three procedures: consultation, deliberation and participation.

It is important that decision making involve not only specialists from the staff departments, but also line managers from the various levels and departments within the organization, as they will later have to deal with the repercussions the decisions will have. In this respect, line managers also possess operational know-how and expertise, the importance of which should not be underestimated. The successful enforcement of the decision depends as much on its degree of acceptance by the employees involved as it does on the quality of the decision itself. It is therefore paramount that all those involved be included in the preparation and the making of the decision.

Many decisions are often preceded internally by a consideration of the legal obligations of the organization with regard to consultation with employees (in particular through the works council). This will involve much advance deliberation in, for example, staff meetings, consultative groups, task forces, project groups (temporary) or committees (permanent). In an organization, consultation and deliberation in groups in order to solve problems, give advice and propose decision alternatives can take place at various levels. These groups can be established on either a permanent or temporary basis, depending on the nature and size of the problems. It is important to always take into account the consultative and communication structure in relation to the decision-making process.

3.1.1 Types of decisions

As we stated in Section 1.4.3, the process of management involves the making of three types of decisions:

- Strategic decisions
- Organizational or administrative decisions
- Operational decisions

In Fig 3.1, these three types of decisions are related to the job duties and the input of the various levels of management and operations within the organization.

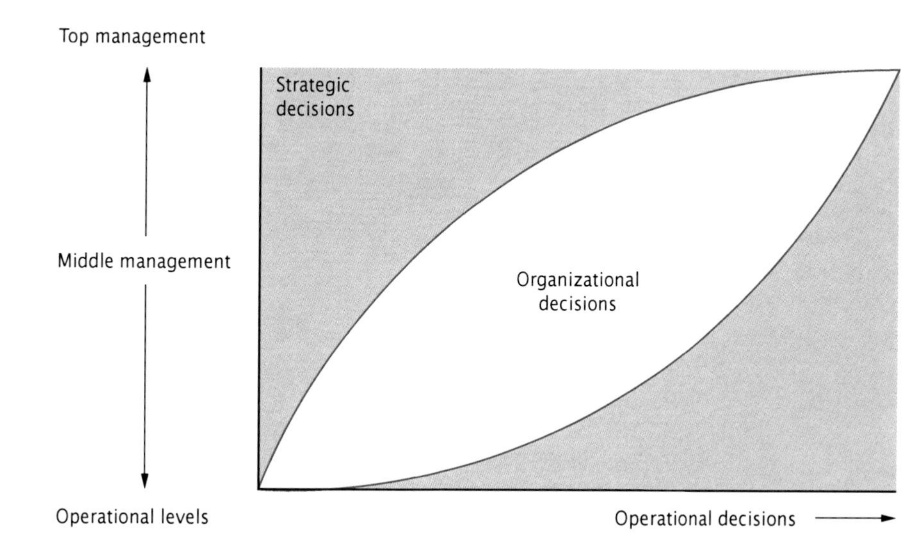

Figure 3.1
Types of decisions in relation to managerial levels

Organizations have to make a large number of decisions on a daily basis. The nature of these decisions will be affected by the following factors:

- How much money is involved (a decision to purchase 100 ball-point pens, for example, being very different from a decision to purchase a highly automated production line)
- The number of people affected by the decision
- The degree of responsibility
- The time span within which the effects of the decision become noticeable
- The level of risk or uncertainty involved
- Emotional reactions likely to be provoked by the decision.

As the decisions become increasingly complex and their importance increases, a greater number of specialists (from the organization's staff departments) are likely to be consulted in the preparatory phases of the decision-making process. A decision about the introduction of flexible working hours in a bank or about early retirement in an industrial company has technical as well as economic and socio-psychological aspects. Of course, all these considerations have to be taken into account before the actual decision can be made.

3.1.2 Consultation and participation

consultation
deliberation
participation

In organizations, consultation, deliberation and participation is done regularly (see Section 6.5) by consultative groups such as work groups, project groups and/or committees. In many countries there is also a legal requirement that consultation and participation take place in works councils (see Section 2.6).

3.2 The decision-making process

Decision-making can be described as a process which is made up of successive phases which begin the moment it becomes known that there is a problem and lasts until the chosen solution is implemented. The four phases of the decision-making process are shown in Fig 3.2.

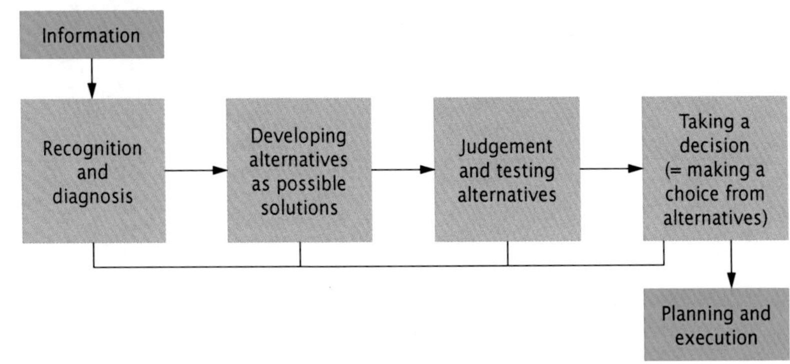

Figure 3.2
The four phases of the decision-making process

This model applies to all types of decision, though the content and the availability of information at each stage may vary. The order in which the decision-making process should take place is important if the organization is to make as effective a decision as possible. Adequate attention should therefore be paid to the various phases of this process. It is not uncommon for participants in meetings where decisions are being made to be at different phases of the decision-making model. This often leads to confusion and certainly does not result in optimal decision making.

There are three golden rules for good decision making:
- Never skip a phase.
- Go through each phase in depth.
- In joint decision making, proceed from one phase to the next in groups.

feedback

This phase model of the decision-making process is also characterized by a 'feedback' element. Indeed, the possibility that a manager will have to return from Phase 2 or 3 to Phase 1 cannot be ruled out if it is thought that in earlier phases the problem was not tackled correctly or completely. The Phase 1 analysis of the problem will have to be repeated before the manager can proceed. As such, decision making may be an iterative process – that is, a process which is repeated over and over again.

iterative process

3.2.1 *Phase 1: recognition and diagnosis*

main problem

The first step should be to gain a clear impression of the problem that needs to be solved. The problem should be described in as much detail as possible and the individual issues which come together to make up the main problem identified. This can be done by, for example, asking questions, by studying a problem in depth in small work groups or by means of a joint discussion.
It is always tempting to suppose for the sake of convenience that the problem is clear to everybody involved. Starting off with an inaccurate definition of a problem only leads to far greater problems at a later stage. If a problem is not properly or completely identified, there is little chance that a good solution can be found in the further course of the decision-making process. On the contrary, a well-defined problem is already well on the way to being solved.

For example ...

... suppose that in a certain company the stock of finished products of a specific item has been seen to rise by a substantial margin. Management will spot this from weekly or monthly reports and needs to find out what is going on. Is this a temporary decrease in demand, or is it of a more structural nature? What is the cause? Too high a price? Too little direct advertising?
Before these questions can be answered, the problem has to be defined clearly, since the various corrective measures which management has at its disposal – for example, a temporary price decrease, an improvement in services, the intensifying of direct advertising, doing nothing as the sales are expected to recover eventually, the dismissal of some representatives who are selling too little in the region – will depend on the nature of the problem.

Some investigation will therefore have to precede a decision. The following aspects must be kept in mind:

symptoms
causes

1 The root cause of the problem has to be determined. Symptoms have to be distinguished from causes.

company blind

2 It is important to reach mutual agreement regarding definition of the problem. This is not always easy. Sometimes this process is hindered because a manager has gone 'company blind' and as a result is not open to new developments. For example, he might still believe in the success of a product because he was the one who originally developed it.
3 There is often a tendency to keep seeing problems in terms of past experience. A new problem is handled in the same way as all past problems.

identification phase
recognition
diagnosis

4 This phase, which is also called the identification phase, involves both recognition and diagnosis of the problem. Recognition of a problem is an admission that something is wrong and that something has to be done about it. Diagnosis is directed at describing the precise nature of the problem in practical terms.

At the end of this phase, it is important that the problem be described in such a way that in the next phases, solutions may be sought with relative ease.

The first phase of the decision-making process is of enormous importance for the successful completion of later phases. An incorrect or incomplete diagnosis can mean that later in the process there is no longer a clear image of what the problem actually is. This will involve a loss of time (as it will be necessary to return to Phase 1 for further investigations), or even the choice of inappropriate solutions. It is therefore crucial that all the involved parties are in agreement with regard to the formulation of the problem.

CASE

Mini case study 3.1

Managers do the daftest things ... but how can they be stopped?

In the film '12 Angry Men', released in 1957, Henry Fonda turns in a remarkable performance as a juror convinced of the innocence of a teenager accused of killing his own father. His 11 fellow jurors are equally convinced of the defendant's guilt. Mr Fonda's character battles to prevent the others from leaping to a hasty verdict – and wins them round, one by one.

Business needs more people like 'juror number eight'. Mr Fonda's character has the courage to question the rationale for important decisions – even if that means swimming against the tide. Poor decisions in risk management and a host of other areas have helped plunge many of the world's largest banks and other financial outfits into a seemingly bottomless abyss.

Financial firms are not the only ones that have made mistakes. So, too, have business giants such as Yahoo!, which rejected a $40 billion takeover offer from Microsoft in February 2008, only to see its share price plunge. The woes of GM and Chrysler, which have been forced to grovel for government handouts, are evidence not just of the scale of the downturn but of the decisions in the upper echelons of the two American car giants.

All of this will come as no surprise to the authors of a new book called *Think Again*, which argues that even the cleverest business leaders slip up in crucial choices. Its authors – Sydney Finkelstein of the Tuck School of Business, and Jo Whitehead and Andrew Campbell of Ashridge Business School – point out that decision-making in business is often far from the rational, data-driven exercise that companies pretend it is. In fact, a decision is susceptible to a whole range of psychological biases that can trip up even experienced executives.

One of these biases is to assume that past experience is relevant today, even when the circumstances are different. Another psychological bias is 'pre-judgment'. This happens when managers let a strongly held belief blind them to arguments against it. Managers can make daft decisions for a host of other reasons too – including close friendships with colleagues and pure self-interest in hoped-for bonuses and other rewards. So how can companies try to stop these biases from causing calamities?

Messrs Finkelstein, Whitehead and Campbell suggest several safeguards. One is to seek out as much data from different sources as possible to ensure that managers weigh all sides of an argument. BP, a British oil giant, sometimes hires two law firms to get contrasting views on important decisions such as a potential acquisition.
Another safeguard is to encourage internal debate before a decision, perhaps by formally asking an individual or a team to play devil's advocate. GE, an American conglomerate with a financial arm that has been battered by the credit crisis, recently announced that it would encourage more 'naysayers' to take part in its planning and operating meetings, in order to stimulate debate. A third safeguard is to monitor the progress of decisions so that errors can be spotted fast – though this does nothing to prevent a bad decision in the first place.

Even with such safeguards, an imperial chief executive surrounded by yes men might neuter the checks – perhaps by undermining devil's advocates. So boards of directors need a further line of defence. Hence, using their own resources and outside consultants if necessary, they should conduct their own reviews of important decisions.
The book's authors say that an independent chairman is essential if such oversight is to work. They warn that firms are asking for trouble if they have a single person as chairman and chief executive. Better to have a handful of angry executives than an army of angry shareholders.

Source: *The Economist*, March 24, 2009

3.2.2 Phase 2: developing alternatives as possible solutions

solution possibilities

Only when the first phase of the decision-making process has produced as clear and as complete a definition of the problem as possible can potential solutions to the problem be considered. Solution possibilities or alternatives have to be developed. In this phase, the employees of the organization with the problem can, for example, be asked to offer as many solution proposals as possible – a process known as brainstorming. The problem may not be a new one and a previous solution can be suggested. However, decision makers are frequently confronted with new problems and new solutions will have to be developed, taking full advantage of the creative abilities of the organization.

creative abilities

A number of factors could stifle such creativity, however – for example, traditional ways of working or an authoritarian manager who always knows best. If creativity is to be encouraged, conditions must allow the free exchange of thoughts (see also Section 3.5). It is also important that consideration not be restricted to only one possible solution – for example, one the boss has chosen earlier or one for which someone has a particular preference, conscious or otherwise. It is advisable at this stage to put all alternatives down on paper, to gather extra information to support these alternatives, and perhaps to examine these further in smaller work groups.

development phase

In Phase 2 – the development phase – a direct search should therefore be carried out for solutions to problems which were clearly defined in Phase 1. Phase 2 can consist of two discrete activities:

1 The search for an existing solution. This can involve research into alternatives which have been used successfully in the past with a similar or related problem. An existing solution can be adjusted to suit the problem in question.
2 The development of a new solution. If there is no ready solution available, it will be necessary to develop a new solution.

These processes take time. This phase cannot be rushed as haste may lead to an inappropriate solution. In practice, new solutions seem to work well. Only one alternative will usually be tried out. However, it is advisable to at least have several alternatives at this phase, as this will enable the working party to weigh up the pros and cons of each alternative in the next phase of the process, and thus make the best possible choice.

3.2.3 Phase 3: judgement and testing of alternatives

Once alternative solutions to the problem have been suggested, it is then necessary to consider the consequences of each of the alternatives. This will form the basis of the eventual choice.

critical approach

In contrast with Phase 2, at this stage a critical approach is what is required – playing 'the devil's advocate.' The decision maker must check that the consequences have been mapped out as fully as possible, and that the analyses are all correct. When considering the consequences of the alternatives, it is important to map out the anticipated changes if a specific alternative is followed. Not only should the desired and possible consequences be taken into account, but also the undesired consequences of each possible solution.

In Phase 3, therefore, the decision maker considers which of the proposed alternatives will solve the problem best. A probable solution should be tried out on the basis not only of the available information but also on experience, feasibility and so on. It is important not to succumb to pressure from individual team members and omit testing. A proposal may sometimes not be critically tested because of pressure of time, bad management or because of power differences existing in a work group or committee. This may be related to inadequate explanations of the proposals or by the overwhelming pressure of work group members unwilling to consider anything other than their own proposals. Sometimes proposals are discounted unjustifiably because of a personal dislike of the employee putting forward the proposal.

selection phase

Once again this selection phase can be divided into two separate activities:

screening

1 Screening. This involves the comparison of alternative solutions resulting in the less satisfactory alternatives being rejected. This can often be carried out on the basis of relatively superficial criteria.

judgement and selection

2 Judgement and selection. The remaining alternatives are subjected to even closer scrutiny and those with the best results are then selected as the preferred alternatives.

In this phase, it is important to create a good and open conversational climate and to call in specialists to look over proposals in order to judge the relative quality and effectiveness of each alternative.

3.2.4 Phase 4: making a decision

choice criteria

The final choice will depend upon whether the consequences of the solution shortlist have been measured against certain choice criteria.

One possible first criterion is the degree to which each of the alternatives results in the desired solution of the original problem, as specified in Phase 1. It is possible that two alternatives will lead to the same end result, be it in different ways. For example, a company wishing to enter a foreign market could either establish its own sales office in the area or could enter into an agreement with a foreign sales agent. In both cases the same end result can be expected. At this point, the decision maker must take into account other factors affecting his choice – for example, the relative costs, the time scales within which the goals must be reached, the risks involved or the resources the organization wants to commit.

The choice is made more difficult if more than one goal needs to be attained at the same time. In such a situation, it is unlikely that all the alternatives will be realized to the same degree.

list of priorities

There has to be a list of priorities. For example, there could be two possible ways of addressing a problem: one in which efficiency is raised but at the expense of relatively low labor satisfaction; another possibility is increasing job satisfaction but at the likely expense of a decrease in productivity. Each of the alternatives will have its merits. Dilemmas can often be overcome by consultation with members of the organization with a view to finding a compromise.

decision making

Decision making usually takes place under less than perfect conditions. The decision maker will be unsure of many details and the data on which decisions are based may be incomplete or unclear. There may be a lack of information relating to future developments. Further information could be gathered with a view to limiting the degree of uncertainty, although this

extra time and expense

will involve extra time and expense and no guarantee of success. It may be that the decision cannot be postponed because otherwise a market-opportunity will be lost or an expected result not attained at all. All these factors must be taken into account at this stage.

Endless hesitation and prolonged investigation of the 'ifs and buts' should be avoided. The final choice is often made by a single person.

For example ...

... when considering decision making in a business context, it is worth taking a look at decision-making theory as part of the discipline of psychology. The following examples from a research project provide some interesting insights.

When asked to choose between a certain profit of 800 Swiss francs or an 85 per cent chance of a profit of 1000 Swiss francs, most people chose the first option, in spite of the fact that the second option involved an expected profit of no less than 850 francs. The opposite happened when a loss was involved. Given a choice between a certain loss of 800 Swiss francs or an 85 per cent chance of a loss of 1000 Swiss francs, the second option was taken. In the first situation, there is an aversion to risk; in the latter case risk is welcomed.

Consider the following scenario. You buy a cinema ticket in advance for £5. You lose the ticket. Would you buy a new ticket? In the majority of cases, the answer is 'no'. Now consider a slightly different case. You arrive at the cinema to buy a ticket and discover that you have lost a £5 note. In such circumstances, almost everyone will go ahead and buy the ticket regardless.

Where alternative solutions have quite different consequences for those involved, procedures such as negotiations can be implemented. After a solution to the problem has been decided

authorization

on, the next step is the authorization or formalization of the decision.

formalization

In this phase, good judgment, as clear as possible an image of the consequences of the solution alternatives, and a desire to reach an agreement or solution are all of importance if a justified decision is to be made. Careful comparisons, a review of the available information and a final check that all phases of the process of decision making have been completed all contribute to this.

3.2.5 Planning and implementing the decision

When all the steps in the process of decision making have been worked through and a

implementation plan

solution has been chosen, an implementation plan has to be made.

At this point, responsibility for the implementation of the decision should be assigned.

Responsibility should not lie with just one individual. It is extremely important that there be commitment to the decision at all levels of the organization and that the decisions be supported by those members of the organization who now have to live with the consequences of the decisions that have been made. In this respect, it is useful to examine the degree to which individual goals are consistent with the goals of the company as a whole. If these are in conflict, an employee may try to give his or her own goals priority by failing to implement aspects of the decision. Consideration of the willingness of the employees to accept the decision is therefore crucial to its successful enforcement.

consideration

Once the effects of the measures are known, a decision may be made to carry out a part of the decision-making procedure again in order to see whether the set goals are being attained. There are sometimes advantages in repeating one of the preceding steps. However if a number of practical operational problems or undesired effects remain during the enforcement phase, it is wise to question the desirability of continuing along the chosen path. Perhaps there will need to be a change of direction after all.

3.2.6 The phase model of the decision-making process

As we have seen, the phase model covers the whole decision-making process from the initial signaling of the problem to the searching for alternative solutions and finally the actual choice of solution and ratification of a decision.

Each of the four phases – identification, development, selection and decision making (plus ratification) – involves a certain number of specific and structured activities.

phase model

The phase model of Fig 3.2 can now be extended to include all aspects of the decision-making process (see Fig 3.3).

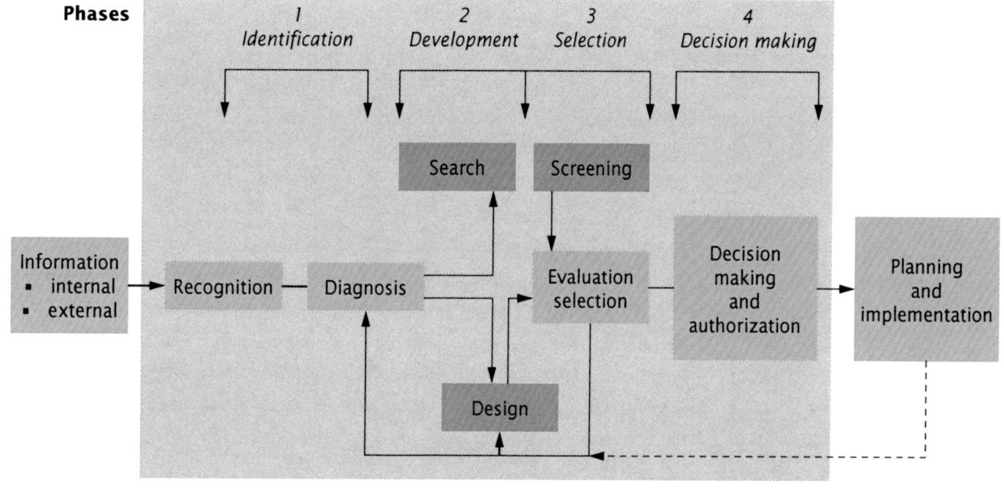

Figure 3.3
The extended phase model of the decision-making process (combining the models of Staerkle, Keuning–Eppink and Mintzberg)

3.3 Factors influencing decision making

The phase model in Fig 3.3 depicts the process of decision making as a succession of discrete steps arranged in a logical order, and can therefore be used as a practical aid to structuring the process. However, the model does not take into account factors which can influence the course of such a process in practice. For example, the interests of the individual stakeholders will affect the decision-making process. Conflicts of interest may arise. In practice, progress in the decision-making process may be subject to complications or delays. Even with these limitations, however, the phase model continues to fulfill the important function of

conflicts of interest

highlighting the stage in the process that the decision makers have reached in the resolution of their own particular problems.

However, it is important to realize that processes of decision making are enacted in a complex organizational environment. To understand these decision making processes fully, we need to examine them in the context of the three factors which have an important influence over them:

structure of the organization
centralization
decentralization
communication
behavioral factors
irrational factors

- The structure of the organization. The degree of division of the organization into departments, the degree of centralization or decentralization and the degree to which, for example, individual employees are involved will affect the outcome of the process.
- The quality of communication. In decision making, communication takes place between people in their roles as members of the organization. As such, the decision-making process will be influenced by a number of behavioral factors, including bias, fear, frustration, ambition, cognitive dissonance, forgetfulness, and so on. Decision making is therefore subject to a number of non-rational or irrational factors. The absence of good and open communication channels and the censoring or disruption of messages can mean that decisions are based on misconceptions or a distortion of reality. It is also important that communication take place at the right time. Premature notice of certain plans can be problematic. On the other hand, late or inadequate involvement of certain managers in the decision-making process can have serious consequences, especially if they are involved in the operational implementation of the decision.

motivation

- The motivation of the members of the organization. The role of employee motivation in the decision-making process cannot be underestimated. Singling out behavior desired by the organization and rewarding that behavior (positive sanction) will make it possible to lead the behavior of individuals in the desired direction, to a certain degree. Undesirable behavior can be simultaneously 'punished' (negative sanction).

(The problems of communication, motivation and conflict handling are covered in more detail in chapters 7 and 8. Problems concerning organizational structure are discussed further in chapters 5 and 6.)

It is therefore important to take into account the factors which influence and complicate the decision-making process if we are to understand how the process works in practice. This includes the irrational aspects of organizational behavior and political factors applicable to the company, such as the division of power, reasons for conflict and use/misuse and absence of information.

information

Information sharing is not a neutral matter in this context; it is an important source of power in the realization of goals. Information sharing is often done to serve the interests of the decision maker (O'Reilly, 1983). Information sharing usually has the following characteristics:

- The information derives from a powerful source.
- There is no other source and verification is therefore impossible.
- The decision maker needs the information to be made available.
- The information is accessible.
- The source is credible.
- Desired visions are supported.
- Use of the information does not lead to conflict.
- The information is supplied directly (not via third parties).

SONY DELAYS RIVAL TO NINTENDO'S WII

Japanese electronics firm puts back launch of motion-sensitive controller by six months to enable software developers to produce more games for it

Sony has delayed the launch of its motion-sensitive rival to Nintendo's highly successful Wii games console by six months and it will not now hit the shops until the autumn. The delay means that the Japanese gaming giant now has only a slim timing advantage over Microsoft, which is due to launch its revolutionary hands-free gaming interface – codenamed Project Natal – for the Xbox 360 in time for Christmas. But it does mean that by the festive season, video gamers will have the choice of three different devices, all of which will use motion-sensitive control, giving players a far more interactive experience.

The news is an obvious setback for Sony, which was plagued by delays when it launched the PlayStation 3 three years ago. It also comes after the company last week admitted that the launch of hotly anticipated racing game Gran Turismo 5 had had to be delayed yet again. It has been more than five years since the last instalment of the very popular franchise. But the company stressed that the decision to delay the launch of its new controller was not linked to any particular hardware or design fault. Instead the company wants to ensure that there are enough games available that can use the new controller before launching it on the market.

The success of the Nintendo Wii, launched in 2006, has revolutionised the games market. Allowing players to ditch their joysticks and traditional button-heavy controllers in favour of a wand they can wave at their TV screens has helped widen the appeal of video games, taking consoles out of teenage bedrooms and back into the living room.
Sony unveiled its answer to the Wii, a controller for the Playstation 3, at the E3 electronics show in Los Angeles last summer. It uses a television-top camera to track a wireless controller held by the player. Sony claims it can track actions with 'sub-millimeter accuracy'.

Microsoft's Project Natal, however, is more ambitious and does not require players to hold a controller at all. Microsoft maintains it can track a player's movements in three dimensions. It can also recognise faces and react to voice prompts, greatly expanding the range of actions which software developers can use in their games.

Source: *The Guardian Unlimited*, January 20, 2010

3.3.1 The organization as a political arena

power and conflict

Power and conflict need to be given special attention when it comes to decision making. An organization is a kind of coalition of participants to which each person brings his or her own specific demands. In this respect decision making is a political process.
Companies are usually split into departments or divisions and complex interdependencies often develop between these units. This often gives rise to conflict, especially when there is a scarcity of resources. Whether these potential conflicts lead to actual 'control problems' will depend on the importance of the issue and the degree to which power is spread throughout the organization.

consensus

In the 'arena' model of decision making, there is often so little agreement among the main players of the organization and such preoccupation with power and politics, that consensus on the main issues facing the organization may be very difficult to achieve.

For decision-making processes to be truly dynamic, the following four characteristics of organizational processes should be kept in mind:

1 Organizational conflicts due to the diversity of interests and preferences of the coalition partners are usually not totally resolved, but are instead reduced to acceptable proportions by means of a variety of procedures. To reconcile the various partial or quasi solutions, the organization can use the mechanism of optimizing rather than maximizing results, and paying attention to the attaining of goals which are actually in conflict with each other at any one time, using the intervening time as a buffer.
2 Organizations try to control the environment as far as possible by means of agreements, contracts and traditions. Furthermore, they constantly adjust their decision-making procedures in response to reactions from the environment.
3 Organizations keep searching for solutions to specific problems and only when a problem has been solved or seems to have been solved does the searching stop. The search proceeds according to three patterns: looking for a direct solution to the problem, looking for indirect solutions in the form of known alternatives, and trying to pass the problem to organizationally weak sectors of the organization.
4 Organizations seem to learn. They appear to be able to adapt to changed circumstances during the course of time. Though they may occasionally do irrational things, organizations almost always work along traditional lines. The organization operates according to an obvious hierarchy of preferences and a number of choice rules: avoid uncertainty, maintain rules and keep rules simple. An organization makes decisions in such a way that the results are satisfactory for the decision makers in that they attain a desired or target level (optimizing, rather than maximizing behavior).

3.3.2 The organization as a garbage can

garbage can

According to the 'garbage can' model of decision making, organizations are seen as 'organized anarchies' characterized by unclear and inconsistent goals, complex and little understood technology, as well as a varying degree of participation by the members of the organization. Universities and colleges are considered to be prototypes of such a model.

selection opportunities

The 'garbage can' model views organizations as consisting of four elements: problems, solutions, participants and selection opportunities. Selection opportunities are situations in which participants are expected to match a particular problem and a particular solution and in so doing, make a decision. These four elements exist in many different and totally unpredictable combinations. Solutions can precede problems, or problems and solutions can await the right occasion for a decision. This decision-making model turns the phase model described in Section 3.2 – identification, development, selection and decision making – completely on its head.

apparent anarchy

In the 'garbage can' model the organization is seen as a collection of relatively autonomous departments and interest groups whose only link is the overall budget to which each must adhere. This does not mean, however, that there is no system at all to the decision making in this type of organization. On the contrary, from the decision-making point of view, the apparent anarchy has a structure which can enable a relatively good, if not optimal, response to be made to any insecurities emanating from the environment that decision makers and departments have to deal with.

Decision making can only progress if the organization's stakeholders appreciate the problems involved. The stakeholders usually have more to worry about and decisions may be put off or are made without due consideration of the problem by the stakeholders. However, it is the task of the board of directors or the divisional or departmental management to involve the stakeholders in the decision-making process and to direct decision making along the path desired by the organization.

3.3.3 Recommendations for better decision making

The degree to which decision making in an organization is rational, ordered and logical depends on all sorts of factors. Koopman et al. (1988) compiled a list of the main limiting factors.

- Lack of information. Decision makers seldom have all the relevant information at their disposal. They will often not have the time, tools, techniques or resources to gather all the relevant information.
- Lack of courage and internal stability. Information of a negative nature often leads decision makers to close their eyes to important aspects of reality. Stress can result in decision makers avoiding problems and risks as a defensive action. Both will lead to bad decision making. Group thinking can reinforce this further. The perception of the environment is false; deviating views are not taken into account.
- *'arena' model* Lack of consensus. In the 'arena' model of organization the opposite of group thinking occurs – that is, a total lack of agreement on the main issues tears the organization apart. Power processes and conflicts between the important players or coalitions threaten the lucidity of the decision making.
- Lack of policy and insight into organizational processes. According to the 'garbage can' model of organizations, decision makers often have to work with unclear and inconsistent goals and an insufficiently understood technology, resulting in a wide range of decision-making problems. Insufficient vision and a lack of policy can reinforce this.
- Lack of guidance and control. Highly complex decision-making processes demand well-considered phasing and process handling. This involves good management skills, both in diagnosing the problem and handling the politics of the organization. Logical and political aspects must be carefully integrated.
- Lack of attunement to the strategic situational factors. Some situations will demand an approach that is directed towards participation and negotiation; others will require a one-sided policy direction, formulated at the top. A flexible, step-by-step approach is sometimes necessary; in other cases, detailed planning and supervision of time and cost constraints will be the most important factors.

recommendations With these limitations on decision making in mind, we can draw up a list of recommendations for improving decision making within the organization.

1. Define the problem and plan the decision-making process carefully.
2. Consider all the alternatives.
3. Use your intuition when necessary (a high level of uncertainty, little experience, no objective data).
4. Adopt group decision making when appropriate (complex problems requiring specialist knowledge, need to build up trust and acceptance).
5. Avoid group thinking otherwise; use the 'devil's advocate' technique.
6. Delegate wherever possible.
7. Strive for consensus as far as possible.
8. The diagnostic and political skills of decision makers should be respected.
9. Adapt the decision-making strategy to the demands of the situation.
10. Ensure that the choice of decision-making process gives equal weight to both technical content on the one hand and socio-political aspects on the other.

3.4 Decision making: techniques and approaches

In the individual phases of the decision-making process, various techniques can be used to help solve the problems at hand. Some techniques promote creativity and so can be of help in Phase 2. Others can be used in Phase 4 to ensure a responsible choice will be made from the available alternatives.

3.4.1 Techniques for improving creativity

brainstorming
lateral thinking

When there is an open organizational culture, several techniques can be used to stimulate creative ability and to make optimal use of it. We will cover two of these techniques: brainstorming and lateral thinking. These techniques are based on the premise that human beings are more creative the less they feel pressured by others.

Brainstorming

The purpose of brainstorming is to generate as many solutions to a problem as possible in as short a period of time as possible. The aim is not to think through the ideas or to make a choice from them. During a brainstorming session, suggestions should not be criticized at all. This interferes with the development of new, daring and unconventional ideas. Spontaneity should not be impeded; participants need to stimulate each other.
To be effective, a group needs to consist of 10 to 15 people. Attention should be given to ensuring an appropriate spread of knowledge, experience and background, as this will encourage contributions from different points of view. Experience shows that brainstorming is especially suitable for clearly defined problems – for example, problems in the field of product development or the improvement of production methods – and is less appropriate for problems which are difficult to describe or very complex, or for problems which require in-depth specialist knowledge to be resolved.

BRAINSTORMING MISERY

Many experiments have shown that brainstorming does not produce the hoped-for improvements. Obstacles preventing the exchange of information often make brainstorming a pointless exercise. The obstacles to sharing of information can take a number of forms. For example, there is little point in bringing people together who do not know each other or have little respect for each other. If the group members do not know each other, they are likely to hold back in presenting ideas that others may find strange.

Whether a person who has a good idea is prepared to air it during a brainstorming session will depend on the reaction that that person expects to get: somebody in the group may make fun of you either during or after the session. One way of resolving this problem is having those participating in the session write down their answers anonymously. It is not enough that the participants know each other; there must also be trust. Group participants must be certain of the others paying serious attention for them to air their ideas.

This condition explains another finding, namely, that the bigger the group, the less information the group's members will pass on. After all, the bigger the group, the less chance there will be of everybody knowing each other sufficiently well and having mutual respect for each other.

As such, brainstorming sessions are only likely to be profitable under very strict conditions. The groups should not be large and the participants must show full respect to each other. If these conditions cannot be met, we would be better off deriving the information needed from those within the organization itself.

Source: *Het Financieele Dagblad*, 1 September 2008

Lateral thinking

vertical thinking

Lateral thinking is a technique applied to change existing ideas and procedures. Vertical or logical thinking follows ready-made paths and obvious patterns and for this reason will not generate new insights or ideas. Vertical thinking is based on common sense and logical reasoning and involves proceeding one step at a time. Each step has to be justified. Mistakes

are not allowed. At the end of the thinking process, the best solution is chosen or a conclusion drawn.
Lateral thinking is not a replacement for 'vertical' thinking. Its function is complementary. Lateral thinking is the searching for side entrances rather than using a front-door approach to resolving a problem. De Bono, one of lateral thinking's main advocates, states that 10 to 15 minutes of lateral thinking a day can make an important contribution to the development of creativity.
It is important to first map out existing ideas concerning a particular problem before we start searching for new points of view. Several methods of lateral thinking have been developed. These advocate following illogical paths and prompting new ideas by trying to look at things differently – for example, turning the reasoning around, reversing procedures, or choosing a random word and seeing whether it provides a new starting point.

For example ...

... consider the problem of shoplifting. A challenging lateral idea is to give all the articles away – that will definitely solve the shoplifting problem. Seen as an interim solution, this may generate, in turn, the idea of charging an entrance fee or getting people to pay a contribution according to turnover. With some adjustments these ideas might lead to a practical suggestion at a later stage. An idea that sounds strange at first can often lead to useful approaches.

Lateral thinking can be used to develop new ideas or points of view. It is not appropriate for systematically working out and evaluating ideas. This involves the field of logical, vertical thinking.

3.4.2 Decision-making techniques

Various decision-making methods can be employed in Phase 4 to ensure that a responsible choice is made from the available alternatives. Two of these methods will be covered here – the decision tree and the decision matrix.

The decision tree

The decision tree allows us to visualize a series of choice possibilities and their respective consequences under externally determined circumstances. We will clarify the principles of this technique by means of an example.
Fig 3.4 shows an example of a decision tree organized according to the parameters of choice, externally determined circumstances, and results. This can be applied to relatively complex situations. Suppose that a company has to make the choice between investing £3.5 million in order to bring a new product on to the market, and placing this sum in the bank at an interest rate of 10 per cent. If it chooses the first option, there is always a chance that a competitor will bring a similar product on to the market. The company can react to this by means of high, medium or low price setting. However, the competitor also has these possible choices.
The decision tree shows that each combination of choice possibilities and externally determined circumstances results in a certain profit or loss. The next step could consist of calculating the probability of each external circumstance arising (competition and the price setting of the competition). The probability value of each branch of the decision tree can be calculated and this can be used as the basis of determining whether the money should be invested in the launching of a new product or put in the bank.

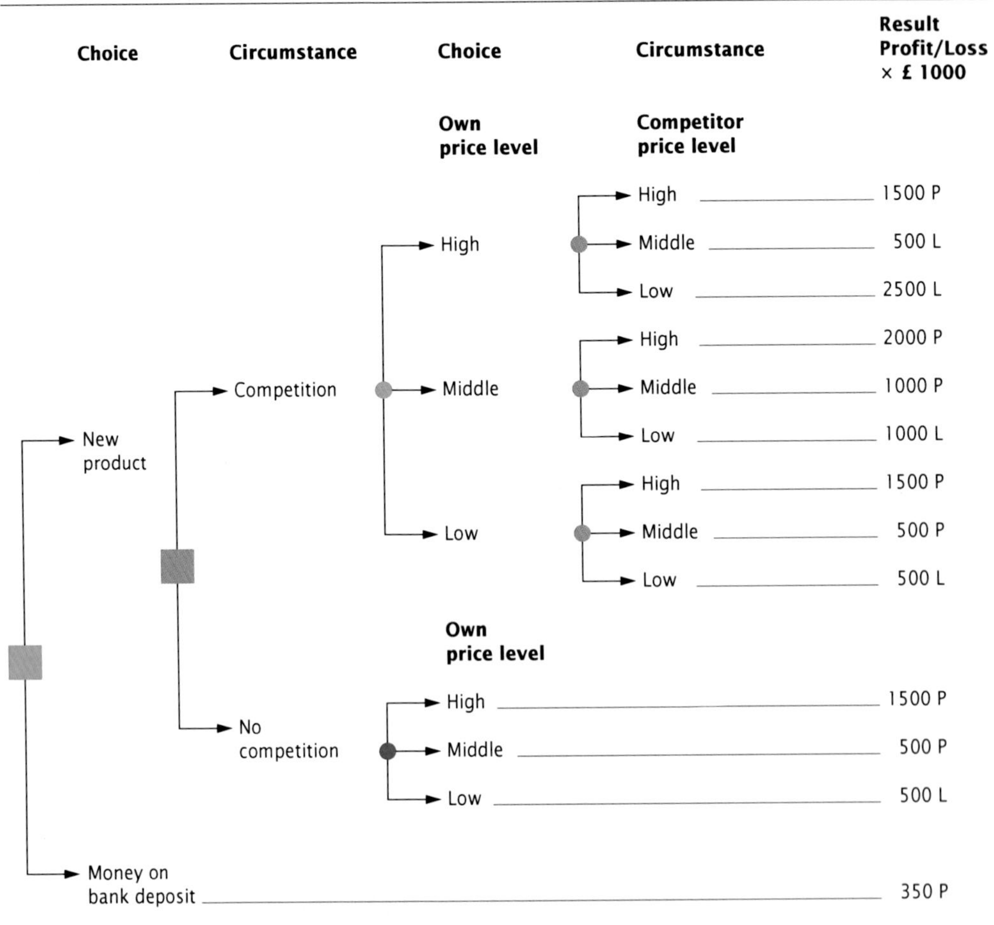

Figure 3.4 *Example of a decision tree*

The decision matrix

Choice options usually have consequences in various other fields. Sometimes these consequences will be in conflict with one another and may make a necessary decision even more difficult to make. The decision matrix allows us to map out the consequences and compare the alternatives. For example, suppose that a company's management has to make a decision about the location of a factory it wants to build. For each alternative, a calculation is made of the expected return on investment (ROI). In addition to this key measure, however, a number of qualitative factors have to be taken into account. They include the following:

- The accessibility of potential clients
- The accessibility of the main suppliers
- The availability of enough qualified personnel
- Subsidies and taxes

Each factor is then assigned a weighting (1 to 5) according to its perceived importance relative to the other factors. In addition, each of the alternative locations is given a score (also 1 to 5) according to how appropriate each is in relation to the four factors. Multiplication of the score and the weighting gives the total score for each of the factors. Addition of the total scores gives an overall score for each of the locations. This calculation is summarized in the decision matrix in Fig 3.5.

	Customers	Suppliers	Personnel	Subsidies	Total score	ROI(%)
Weighting	*5*	*3*	*4*	*5*		
Location						
1	4 × 5 = 20	4 × 3 = 12	5 × 4 = 20	4 × 5 = 20	72	14.5
2	3 × 5 = 15	2 × 3 = 6	2 × 4 = 8	4 × 5 = 20	49	17.5
3	5 × 5 = 25	3 × 3 = 9	3 × 4 = 12	4 × 5 = 20	66	19.5
4	4 × 5 = 20	4 × 3 = 12	2 × 4 = 8	4 × 5 = 20	60	12.5

Figure 3.5
Example of a decision matrix

With the help of such a decision matrix, management can gain a clear insight into the consequences of the various alternatives. The alternatives can now be compared with each other. The eventual choice will depend on the relative importance given to the quantitative consequences of each alternative.

Effectiveness of decision-making methods

There are some methods that can be used to calculate the best alternative. They have a very important side effect in a necessary systematic analysis of the problem: the application of decision-making methods forces those involved to ask crucial questions about key factors relating to the decision-making process.

3.4.3 *Types of decisions and procedures/techniques*

It is important to distinguish the various types of decisions (as mentioned in Section 3.1.1) because general statements and guidelines about one type of decision do not necessarily apply to another type. This is also true for the use of decision-making process techniques. The relative importance of a decision depends on factors such as the following:

- The amount of money involved
- The number of persons the decision affects
- The time span within which results will have to be reported and within which the effects of the decision should be noticeable

Decisions can be categorized into strategic, organizational and operational decisions (see Section 3.1.1). Simon (1965) makes a distinction between programmed and non-programmed decisions (see Fig 3.6).

Programmed decisions

Programmed decisions are decisions of a routine-like nature. Once a problem has been tackled, experience is gained and any future recurrence of such a problem will result in the appropriate solution being immediately implemented without any need for further consideration.

		Decision-making techniques	
		Traditional	*Modern*
Types of decisions	*Programmed:* Routine, repetitive decisions Organization develops specific processes for handling them	1 Habit 2 Clerical routine: ▪ standard operating procedures 3 Organization structure: ▪ common expectations ▪ a system of subgoals ▪ well-defined information channels	1 Operations research: ▪ mathematical analysis ▪ models ▪ computer simulation 2 Electronic data processing
	Non-programmed: One-shot, ill-structured novel, policy decisions Handled by general problem-solving processes	1 Judgement, intuition, and creativity 2 Rules of thumb 3 Selection and training of executives	Heuristic problem-solving technique applied to: ▪ training human decision makers ▪ constructing heuristic computer programs

Figure 3.6
Matrix of decision-making techniques and types of decisions

Source: *Simon*. 1965

Non-programmed decisions

Problems in this category are new and have no precedent. They usually have major consequences for the organization. Given these characteristics, the approach cannot be dictated by standard procedures with advance solutions/routines. There is no cut-and-dried method set for handling such problems. Tailor-made solutions are required in this context. In relation to this decision category, Simon also makes a distinction between traditional and modern methods (see Fig 3.6). Simon suggests the use of heuristic methods as a modern approach to making non-programmed decisions. Heuristics is the theory of solving problems methodically. Simon states that heuristic methods can be used in two different ways:

heuristic methods

1 People can learn to solve problems better or to handle them differently. In order to achieve this it is important to gain a better insight into human thinking processes. Decision makers can learn alternative and better ways of working by means of education and training.
2 Computer programs can be developed to help us solve complex problems in much the same way as computers play games of chess. Such programs should not only be able to process quantitative information, but also qualitative information. The development of such programs and artificial intelligence is in its early stages.

3.4.4 *Information technology, computers and decision making*

Uncertainty and the reduction of uncertainty to acceptable and workable levels are recurring themes in decision making. Computer technologies can reduce uncertainty to a certain degree because a large number of variables can be taken into consideration, consequences can be calculated and information can be gathered more quickly and more accurately. Computer technologies can aid in addressing the practical problems of decision making in a number of management areas. They include the following:

- Office automation
- Decision support systems (DSS)
- Artificial intelligence (AI)

office automation

Office automation influences the productivity and efficiency of management in particular. DSS and AI go further: they contribute to problem identification, the generation of alternatives and the setting of priorities. The value of these last techniques lies in their being able to help improve the whole decision-making process, not only the processing of information.

decision support systems

Decision support systems were first developed at the end of the 1960s and were made possible by the opportunities the computer offered in the form of databases and direct access to information for manipulation purposes. The goal of DSS is contributing to the effectiveness of semi-structured decision-making processes, such as production and inventory planning, strategic planning, financial planning and investment decisions.

If current approaches to decision making are unable to remove barriers to the generation of alternatives, the designing of solutions and the selection of these, DS systems can provide support. Artificial intelligence goes one step further than DSS in that the application possibilities of DSS are limited to situations in which the decision-making process can be represented by a formal model. AI can cope with conflicting or missing data. It is concerned with the processes that produce intelligent action – that is, involving decisions which are goal-oriented, attained by means of a logical reasoning process and which are underpinned by rule of thumb.

artificial intelligence

Artificial intelligence consists of three discrete fields: sense systems, natural language systems and expert systems. The sense system could be used for such purposes as the interpreting, and retrieving of as much information as possible from two-dimensional pictures. Language systems are directed at the interpretation of, for example, English as it is spoken. Expert systems or knowledge systems are defined as programs which solve the most difficult problems: those which demand specialist knowledge. This area will without doubt have the greatest impact on management. Applications exist in diagnosis, medical information systems, process control, planning and industrial processes.

sense system
language systems
expert systems

Groupware, ICT and decision making

Application of 'groupware' can influence the various phases of the decision-making process in several ways. The collection of information will be faster and easier through the electronic consulting of internal and external sources of information (the Internet), making it easier to do such things as defining the problem.

Groupware usually has the following applications: sending and receiving electronic messages, keeping up diaries and making appointments for meetings, access to documents used by other users, access to the Internet, and the possibility of holding electronic discussions. With the right use of groupware, the entire organization can take advantage of the knowledge that is present, in whatever distant corner. In this sense, groupware makes certain forms of knowledge management technically possible (see Section 3.5.3).

groupware

Applications of groupware (automatic support of collaborative work, irrespective of place or time) assume that the relevant information is available for everyone. Among these are group decision-making systems, video conferencing, e-mail, bulletin boards etc. Using this kind of technology, experts can work on resolving the same problem world-wide. When the working day ends in the USA, intermediary products can be sent on, including directions and questions, to a team in Europe working on the same task. As such, 'time-shifting' and 'day-extension' enables experts to work world-wide 24 hours a day on the development of a new type of Boeing aeroplane.

time-shifting
day-extension

MULTITASKING, MULTISTRESSING

It sounds dynamic: e-mailing all day long, sending text messages, ringing mobile phones, communicating via Skype or MSN. But what does it all achieve? As research shows, not much.

Multitasking sounds dynamic. But it is not productive. Researchers from Stanford University had at least expected to find that multitasking had a few advantages. But no. All of these new streams of information – coming at us criss-cross and never-endingly – are distracting us and making us less productive. All these notifications of new e-mails and chat screens that shoot up in our faces all the time are having a disastrous effect on our concentration. We get less done and when we do finally finish off a big job, it turns out to be of a disappointing quality.

One hundred people took part in the Stanford research. Half of the group consisted of hardcore multitaskers, the other half of people who were not accustomed to constantly communicating in multiple ways. Those who were exposed on an on-going basis to five or six streams of information simultaneously (e-mail, telephone, voicemail, SMS, Skype and so on) considered that they performed their work well and were quite capable of processing information at a rapid pace. Before they participated in the research they had assumed that they would score better in terms of processing of information than the other test group, which was exposed to only one or two streams of information during their work days.

It took a couple of tests only to demonstrate that the dedicated multitaskers were completely wrong. All that multitasking had reduced their ability to concentrate and they were unable to divide their attention evenly over the various sources of information. (*In extreme cases, 'infobesitas' can even result.*) In fact, the better they thought themselves able to multitask, the poorer the performance.

This is the paradox of multitasking: those who do it least do it best.

Kicking the multitasking habit

- Set aside part of each working day for working undisturbed: switch off your e-mail, your telephone and Skype, and close the door.
- When you arrive in the morning, do not put your computer on immediately. First take a piece of paper and make a to-do list.
- Do the most difficult or most boring jobs first. This will create a sense of satisfaction that will last for the rest of the day. Deal calmly with those e-mails, voicemails and text messages later in the day instead of constantly interspersed throughout the day.

In view of the above, it is strange that companies want their employees to be constantly available via Skype and e-mail, according to professor of communication Clifford Nass. 'It has an adverse effect on their productivity and that of the entire company.' Despite this, banishing multitasking from office life would seem unthinkable.

Life hackers

Fortunately, some people seem to have found a solution to the problem of multitasking. They specialize in 'life hacking' whereby new techniques are employed to enable people to work more effectively. For example, many life hackers avail themselves of ingenious programs for keeping track of the things that need to be done and they use special filters for getting through vast quantities of e-mail.

Author Jim Stolze confirms in his book *How to survive your inbox* (2009) that multitasking can take a toll on people. He refers to research done by David Meyer, a lecturer in psychology at the University of Michigan, which shows that employees who constantly switch between e-mailing, telephoning and on-line reading exhibit the same symptoms of burn-out as traffic controllers at busy airports. Companies that require their employees to react constantly and immediately to more than one stream of information simultaneously risk losing many of them to burn-out.

So it can be good to work in the old-fashioned way now and then. In a quiet space. Without dozens of electronic notifications. Concentrating. And as soon as you have finished those big jobs, multitask to your heart's content. Or just relax.

Source: *NRC Weekblad*, 24 October 2009

To a certain degree, ICT makes the physical workplace unimportant. Personal computers, linked to an electronic mail system, a central database or the office automation network of the organization, make it possible for employees to work at home or while travelling. The advantages of telecommunications are obvious: flexible working hours, less office space, and opportunities for disabled people and employees with domestic commitments.

3.4.5 *Problem solving and decision making: situational or contingent approaches*

Situations sometimes arise where the nature of the problem is all too clear, but those involved have differing or even contradictory views on what should be done to resolve it (see also sections 3.3.1 and 3.3.2). The only way in which a solution can be found is for all concerned to make compromises. While this is of course not the ideal approach, at least an attempt is being made to improve the existing situation. Experience shows that the best solution is often a solution which is acceptable to all those involved and which seems to be practicable in the given situation. Thompson (1967) states that decision making demands an approach that is appropriate to the situation. Two basic situational factors influence the choice of decision strategy:

- Insight into the structure of the problem (cause-effect relationships)
- Preferences in respect of possible outcomes.

Shown diagrammatically, this produces four different approaches or strategies (see Fig 3.7).

computational strategy

judgmental strategy

1 Good insight into the problem and certainty in respect of causation and outcome preferences mean we are dealing with a calculation problem and should adopt a computational strategy for decision making. Such a problem can be converted into a formula or arithmetical terms.
2 Where outcome preferences are clear but cause-effect relationships are uncertain, a judgmental strategy for decision making is required. The decision makers will have to judge the problem and relevant factors. With such problems, and given their lack of insight into the problem, decision makers usually fall back on their judgmental abilities.

		Clear preferences regarding possible outcomes	
		Yes	*No*
Certainty in beliefs about cause–effect relations	*Yes*	Computational	Compromise
	No	Judgemental	Inspirational

Figure 3.7
Four types of decision strategy

Source: *After Thompson*, 1967

compromise strategy

inspirational strategy

charisma

3 If those involved have a clear insight into the problem but have differing goals, then a compromise will be required. This compromise strategy will involve negotiations during which all the parties, depending on their negotiating abilities, will have to shift their positions to a certain extent.
4 When there is no insight into the problem and no agreement on the preferences or goals, a solution can only be attained by inspiration. First and foremost, the inspirational strategy assumes that there is a belief and trust in someone's vision. This way of approach assumes that each of the decision makers involved has confidence in a particular approach and believes it can be successful. In such a situation, management charisma is of decisive importance.

CREATIVE TENSION; GOOGLE'S CORPORATE CULTURE

FEW companies are as creative as Google, which serves up innovations almost as fast as its popular search-engine serves up results. This week the firm unveiled a new version of its Chrome web browser and launched Fast Flip, which lets users scroll through the contents of an online newspaper in much the same way that they leaf through its pages in print. On September 30th the company will roll out another fledgling product, Google Wave, for a test involving some 100,000 people. Billed as a revolutionary way to collaborate online, Wave is also the product of a new, more structured approach to innovation within the company.

For years Google has had a fairly informal product-development system. Ideas percolated upwards from Googlers without any formal process for top managers to review them. Teams working on innovative stuff were generally kept small. Such a system worked fairly well while Google was in its infancy. But now that it is a giant with 20,000 employees, the firm risks stifling potential money-spinners with a burgeoning bureaucracy.

To stop that happening, Google has begun to hold regular meetings at which employees are encouraged to present new ideas to Eric Schmidt, the firm's chief executive, and Larry Page and Sergey Brin, its co-founders. It has also given some projects more resources and independence than in the past. Both moves are designed to ward off the conservatism that can set in as companies mature. 'We are actively trying to prevent middle-agedom,' explains Mr Schmidt.

Google Wave has benefited from this anti-ageing treatment. The new software allows people to create shared content that is hosted on Google's servers online, or 'in the cloud'. When they open Google Wave, users see three columns on their screens. The left-hand one contains folders and address books, while the middle column is a list of 'waves'– online conversations users have initiated or signed up to. Clicking on a wave displays its contents in the right-hand column. People can post text, photos, web feeds and other things into a wave and exchange comments with one another instantly.

The software excites tech folk, some of whom reckon it poses a threat to Microsoft's SharePoint collaboration package. Inside Google the project has generated much enthusiasm too, plus some controversy. The Wave team deliberately distanced itself from Google's headquarters, choosing to be based in the company's Sydney office. And it insisted that its work be kept secret for a long time so its nascent idea was not subject to nit-picking criticism. Some Googlers felt this was a betrayal of the firm's open culture. 'Not everyone inside the company thought that this was super cool,' admits Lars Rasmussen, one of the two brothers leading the project, which was allowed to recruit dozens of software engineers to its ranks.

That has not dented Google's enthusiasm for creating more such teams. Mr Schmidt wants the number to grow from a dozen or so today to perhaps 50. The challenge, he says, is to find leaders with the calibre of Mr Rasmussen, who previously worked on an initiative that evolved into the successful Google Maps.

Some Google-watchers see a much bigger challenge. 'Google has been masterful at coming up with a lot of ideas, but none of them has matured to become something that moves the revenue needle,' says Gene Munster of Piper Jaffray, an investment bank. In fairness to the company, that is partly because many of its popular innovations, such as Gmail, have been given away to boost search-related advertising, which accounts for almost all of Google's revenues. But search has been suffering in the downturn: in the second quarter of 2009 Google's revenues were $5.5 billion, barely 3% higher than the same period in 2008. Time, then, for the company to find new ideas that can make a big splash.

Source: *The Economist*, September 19, 2009, vol. 392, Iss, 8649

It is not only the interests and goals of the decision makers' department or organization of the decision maker that are of importance in the decision-making process but also those of other decision makers in other departments and/or organizations. The most appropriate approach will depend on the relative importance attached to personal preferences or goals. These approaches will be covered in Chapter 8 when we discuss negotiations and the resolution of conflict.

3.5 The creative and learning organization

An organization which is not capable of tapping creative resources will slowly be eliminated from the market by competitors who either manufacture better products at lower costs or who employ managers with more imaginative power and more of an eye for alternative solutions. When creativity results in new inventions, an organization needs to devote time and resources to processing and coordinating their introduction. While products may have been improved or changed in some way, it is rare for new goals to be formulated. However, an organization that wants to stay healthy and productive and continuously adapt itself to the changing needs of society will have to use all its creative powers and be prepared to learn from experience, in particular from its past mistakes. This involves the creativity and learning abilities of employees, managers and the organization as a whole. It is important for managers to set a good example by being creative themselves while they are encouraging creativity, learning behavior and learning abilities in all areas of the organization. Only in this way can the organization make the most of its employees.

processing
coordinating
creativity
learning abilities

Training in techniques which stimulate creativity is very important (see Section 3.4.1). However, very few organizations have permanent programs that aim to expand the creative abilities and the learning behavior of all employees. Employees often think up valuable ideas, but these are rarely acted upon. Many employees who have good ideas lack the authority needed to implement them. In many cases such ideas are not even made known.

stimulate creativity

It is important to set up systems so that valuable ideas can be picked up and put into practice – not an easy task. Creative thinking is relatively unstructured, undisciplined and often does not seem logical. However, it is the basis for the generation of the new ideas the organization needs. It is often the case, however, that creative ideas upset the status quo, creating resistance from those who do not endorse or appreciate the importance of such ideas. The ultimate goal of creative thinking and of learning is to discover and put into practice something which the organization does not currently possess and which will enable the organization to function better.

creative thinking
status quo

3.5.1 The creative organization: some characteristics

creative organization

What is the difference between a creative organization and an organization which works under creative management? An organization can be an effective instrument for the implementation of ideas and yet not be creative itself – for example, an orchestra which is conducted by a creative conductor, or a firm managed by a creative director.

At this point, it is important to identify the specific characteristics which contribute to the creativity of an organization. We can start by considering the overall image of an organization. When the organization has an outstanding name in the field of growth, product development, renewal and problem solution, it can create the image of a very creative institution. Whether this overall image is the product of the influence of a few individuals or, alternatively, is the result of the creative contribution of all or most of the members of the organization, does not seem to be relevant: the organization is generally seen to be creative. The characteristics of creativity, as they apply both to individuals and to the organization are described below.

Exhibit 3.1

Characteristics of creativity

The creative individual:

- Can quickly produce a large number of ideas
- Is original
- Has unusual ideas
- Looks at ideas based on their merits, not on their origin
- Is motivated by the problem itself (follows it, wherever it may lead)
- Postpones personal judgment, avoids premature acceptance of a solution
- Spends a lot of time on analysis and explanation
- Is not high-handed/authoritarian
- Is flexible
- Accepts his or her own impulses
- Is often undisciplined in his or her investigations
- Makes independent personal judgments
- Is a non-conformist
- Often deviates from established ideas
- Sees him- or herself as being different
- Has a rich and fanciful fantasy and a clear insight into reality

The creative organization:

- Has ideas that are relevant to society
- Has open communication channels
- Encourages contacts with resources outside the environment
- Employs various types of persons
- Lets non-specialists help in the solving of problems
- Allows eccentricity
- Has an objective, factually based approach
- Evaluates ideas on their merits, not on the status of their creator
- Selects ideas on their merits
- Does not show short-term satisfaction with the financial and material aspects of the present products and policy
- Invests in basic research
- Has flexible long-term planning
- Experiments with new ideas and does not dismiss them before they have been thoroughly tried out
- Gives everything a chance
- Is relatively decentralized
- Allows time and resources for mistakes
- Tolerates and expects the taking of risks
- Has employees who have high job satisfaction and the freedom to discuss ideas and tackle problems
- Is autonomous and independent
- Has original goals
- Does not encourage the belief that the leader should always be followed, no matter what
- Finds enough certainty in fixed rules
- Provides groups with the opportunity to generate and evaluate ideas

From this comparison, we can conclude that creativity within the organization is not necessarily dependent on having very creative employees. In principle, creativity is spread out among all company personnel. That is why it is not important to recruit a large number of very creative people. It is important, however, for the organization to be structured in such a way that everybody's input is shown to full advantage. This can only be done when there is a climate which does not suppress or smother originality. Creative management is essential. Even the most creative individuals become helpless in an environment which is indifferent or hostile to new ideas.

creative employees

There are a number of features which can negatively affect creative thinking in an organization:

- Extreme structuring and formal planning result in barriers being raised between the functional units of an organization.
- Individual responsibilities in the work situation are seldom based on the particular talents of the personnel working there. The tasks will have been structured already; the employee has to adjust to them. Work units will have been formalized into fixed positions.
- The work is controlled by a hierarchical authority structure. Even with appropriate coordination such an authority structure can result in a number of negative consequences.
- The communication pattern is determined according to the characteristics of the formal organization and not according to the demands of the task. A good communication process plays a key role in stimulating initiative.

If these situations apply, a clearer separation of fields of authority is required. However, the disadvantage of this is that the barriers between the functions will become even more difficult to overcome, especially with regard to initiative taking and coordination.

Promotion of creativity in organizations

All members of the organization should be encouraged to use their creative abilities, regardless of function or status. Not everyone will determine the goals of the organization, but they do have to think about how these are reached. Managers should be called upon to participate creatively in any decisions regarding the organization's function, especially with regard to instigating innovations.

instigating innovations

The creation of an 'open atmosphere' is dependent on conditions such as the following:

- The centralization of activities directed at innovation. For example, this could involve the formation of a core group whose function is to actively encourage creativity.
- Appointment of sufficient staff with non-specialized knowledge. Specialists will be hindered by their tendency to relate their own abilities and experiences to problems in other fields.
- Access to support services. The availability of all necessary information is crucial.
- The breaking down of barriers. The effects of authority, status and specialties and other forms of behavior which erect barriers should be minimized.
- Minimization of interlinks. Interlinks in terms of interlinking positions/functions often function as buffers between groups.
- The encouragement of innovation. Organizations which are not innovation-oriented are often resistant to change.

CREATIVE IDEAS COME FROM INDIVIDUALS, NOT THE GROUP

Managers persistently fail to understand how they can best promote creativity within their teams. Brainstorming within the group is what they associate creativity with. However, research results fail to confirm this idea. Groups hinder creativity instead of promoting it.

Creative ideas tend to derive from individuals rather than groups. However, it's the group that selects the ideas and implements them. There are a number of conditions attached to the game: you are not allowed to be critical and the only questions allowed are those to elucidate things. Random associations are also permitted.

To be creative, you first need to ensure that you are in an active mood. It doesn't really matter whether you are happy or angry. However there does need to be a certain amount of pressure: too much relaxation is not good for creativity. 'Without some pressure, people tend not to be creative. As pressure mounts, so too will creativity, though if the pressure becomes too great, it will have a negative effect on creativity. Everybody is different in this regard: some people can take more pressure than others.

Persistence and refusing to give up can also produce creative results. People who are irritated or angry can be creative: they will refuse to give ground, making progress step-by-step and not giving up until they have reached their goal.

Source: *Het Financieele Dagblad*, 1 September 2008

These conditions relate to the structure of an organization. Creativity can also be encouraged by taking into account the following considerations:

1 All employees should be encouraged to think creatively, and to train themselves in the skills involved. They include the following:
   - Being wary of conditions which inhibit creative thinking
   - Being flexible
   - Holding back before criticizing
   - Avoiding nipping ideas in the bud
2 Managers should strive to create a climate in which creativity can thrive. Some ways of encouraging creativity are as follows:
   - Showing respect for unusual questions
   - Showing respect for unusual ideas
   - Showing employees that their ideas are valued

3.5.2 Learning and the learning organization

learning organization

The essence of an organization lies in its people, not in its systems and procedures. Organizations make mistakes; whether they learn from them is the crucial thing. This obviously depends on the attitudes of the people who work there. The learning organization is much more than just a collection of learning individuals, however. It involves both individual learning and the learning of the organization – that is, the transfer and integration of knowledge between individuals, groups and the organization resulting in a structure of individual and collective learning.

The experimental learning model

According to Lewin (1957) (and later Kolb 1984, and Kim 1993) a human being follows a particular cycle of learning (see Figure 3.8).

This basic cycle is repeated in various contexts, both in the private and in the work environment. It can be expressed as:

observing – judging – designing – applying

and as such resembles the activities performed by an organization. In the OJDA cycle (see Fig 3.9), specific experiences and active observation of events in relation to them then lead to evaluation of the experiences, either consciously or unconsciously. Next, a concept which supports this evaluation is designed and tested in the actual situation. This then leads to a new specific experience and the cycle starts all over again.

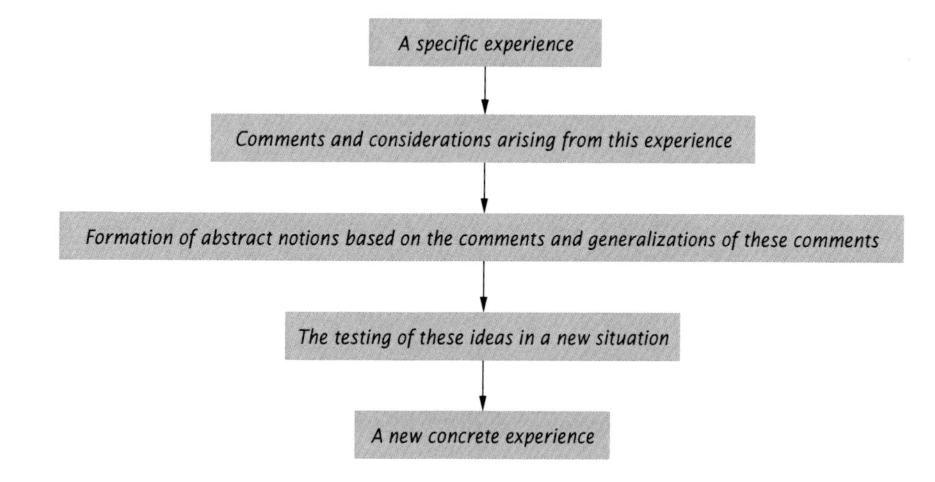

Figure 3.8
Lewin's learning cycle

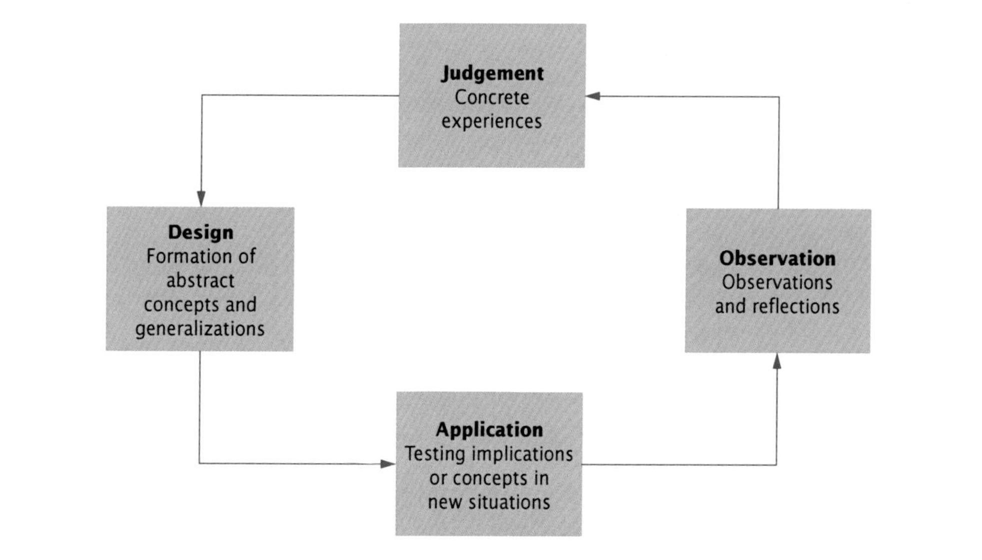

Figure 3.9
The experimental learning model

Source: *Kolb*, 1984, *adapted by Kim*, 1993

The operational and conceptual levels of learning

ability to act effectively

Learning can be described as the enhancing of the ability to act effectively. It consists of two components:

- The acquiring of abilities or directly applicable knowledge – that is, a physical ability to act
- The acquiring of rational knowledge – that is, the ability to understand the reasons for an experience

operational and conceptual learning

Learning involves both thinking and doing. Both are of importance: acquiring the knowledge of how something needs to be done on the one hand, and understanding and applying this knowledge on the other. These two components of learning can be described as operational and conceptual learning.

The learning done by the organization cannot simply be seen as individual learning on a more extended scale. When we move from the learning done by one person to the learning done by a large collection of individuals, there is a disproportionate increase in the complexity and dynamics of the process involving elements such as motivation and rewarding. Learning is still learning, of course, but the process is fundamentally different at the level of the organization. There is no doubt, however, that a non-human unit – that is, the organization – has intellectual capacities and can learn.

A learning organization is one that operates systematically on its own, learning routines and new behavior. If such procedures are not in place, then the organization only learns in an ad hoc, dissipated or opportunistic manner.

ad hoc learning

- Ad hoc learning. A good example of this is crisis management. Each problem is solved when it arises, but what is learned from the experience is not transferred to the next problem. The opposite of this is quality improvement in which situational learning is kept to a minimum by the systematic collecting of data, analysis and standardization.

dissipated learning

- Dissipated learning. Universities are classic examples of dissipated learning. Professors may be the world's leading experts in the fields of management, finance, operations and marketing, but universities do not employ that knowledge to manage their own organization. Organizations with highly decentralized management structures which do not provide the opportunity to build up internal networks suffer from the same problem.

opportunistic learning

- Opportunistic learning. Organizations sometimes try to deliberately bypass their own standard procedures because the normal working procedures are becoming obstructive. Such an organization needs to break the link between common mental models and action – for example, to be able to take advantage of a once-in-a-lifetime opportunity. Waiting for the organization to undergo the necessary changes would take much too long.

When the learning that takes place within an organization is a consequence of the actions of one person or a small group of persons, and not as a result of a common experience of the organization – that is, its values, culture, myths or standard procedures – this can be described as opportunistic learning. A good example of opportunistic learning is the use of separate work units in the development of the IBM PC. IBM bypassed the overall bureaucratic structure and formed a completely separate, very dedicated team to develop the PC. Indeed, this was accomplished in a relatively short period of time.

3.5.3 Knowledge management: more than just a hype?

knowledge management

Recent research shows that approximately 40% of the available mental capacity of the Dutch workforce is not used. In the USA the figure is even worse: 60%. In the Netherlands, the government/non-profit sector scores worst on all points. Since the Dutch economy is usually characterized as a knowledge economy and brainwork seems to be gradually becoming more important than manual labor, these are remarkable facts. It means that the potential brainpower as identified by thorough selection and recruiting procedures is not being adequately utilized by the management of organizations and institutions (Van Aken & Camps, 1997). It is therefore no wonder that knowledge management has received so much attention in recent years. Knowledge management is, however, now being seen within a broader framework: as an element of the process of making the organization dynamic and organizing its brainpower, and as a basis for strategic innovation. To make the most of opportunities, to avert threats and to continue on a healthy and profitable basis, knowledge and insight not only has to be available, it also has to be embedded within the organization. Knowledge management can be seen as both a method for managing the gathering of knowledge as well as of using that knowledge, spreading it and especially applying it.
Research into the utilization of knowledge and brainpower shows that there are formidable obstacles. The five most frequently mentioned obstacles are as follows:

USA
1 Bad organizational policies
2 Time pressure
3 Lack of support by top management
4 Insufficient involvement in decision making
5 Lack of peer support

The Netherlands
1 Time pressure
2 Lack of skills
3 Insufficient involvement in decision making
4 Lack of support by top management
5 Fear of failure

The following five aspects have been mentioned as requiring particular attention:
- The quality of management (49%)
- Setting priorities (44%)
- Following up arrangements (44%)
- Motivating people (42%)
- Ability to plan (42%)

Organizing brainwork

knowledge management

There are more dull organizations than learning organizations. Knowledge management in the narrow sense runs the risk of a lot of knowledge being applied to resolving problems that have already been resolved. Especially with the ready availability of information technology (IT), there is a tendency to pay insufficient attention to the thinking techniques that are used for finding solutions and to new tactics. Learning should result in an improvement in brainpower and brain skills (the ability to reflect). A logistical approach to knowledge management only leads to good descriptions and identification of things (an approach reinforced by the availability of IT). Such an approach does not really get at the essence of learning.
In the broader approach to organizing brainwork, the view that knowledge is merely reproduction of prior learning (and thus can be accessed via information technology) is rejected. Organizational theory explicitly describes knowledge and information as being embedded in the factor of labor, particularly the knowledge and information in the head of the employee. As such, there can be no knowledge or information without people: at the most there can only be facts or data. One could even classify 'people-less' knowledge as a type of raw material, though this is possibly too cynical a view.

brainwork

organizing brainpower

Working will, to an increasing degree, be thinking work: brainwork of a 'higher' kind. As such, the tasks performed by leaders and managers will increasingly involve more than mere knowledge management: they will require organizing brainpower. If this is not recognized or if the obstacles and areas that demand improvement are underestimated or ignored, knowledge management will be futile. It will remain one of the reasons that knowledge management to this point has amounted to virtually nothing and thus is merely a fad or hype. Value in organizations accrues via the knowledge and expertise that people possess. In the traditional hierarchical organizational structure in particular, social codes and promotional and appraisal systems hinder the exchange and sharing of knowledge. Knowledge management must be embedded in a more embracing framework of 'organization of brainwork' and have more to do with the development of talent, the development of competencies and the development of core competencies and human resources than with IT-driven systems focused on information and data.

Examples of types of knowledge

- Human knowledge derives from one's upbringing, education, observations and intuition. While part of this knowledge will always be inaccessible by others, at least some of it can be put in a form that others can access.
- Documented knowledge is that in archives, documents, accounts, drawings, and so on. This can be made accessible in paper or electronic form.
- Mechanized knowledge is knowledge that is embedded in software.
- Automated knowledge is knowledge which is embedded in computers, and is mainly of a specialized knowledge system type.

Knowledge and knowledge management in the narrow sense

tacit knowledge

In their work, Nonaka and Takeuchi (1991/1994, 1995) refer to explicit knowledge in knowledge-creating organizations as well as implicit (or silent) knowledge, so-called tacit knowledge. This last form of knowledge is highly personal in nature and largely consists of habits, intuition and insights of various kinds. Their view is that knowledge is created via the linking and exchanging of explicit and implicit knowledge.

It is to be hoped that the knowledge management hype of the late 90s will be replaced by knowledge management that is fed by these and similar insights. If not, the obstacles will remain and the improvements will be inadequate.

content management

By now (early into the 2000s) it has become clear that knowledge management is only being applied to a very limited extent and is also scoring low in terms of the value attributed to it. In a survey by Bain and Company (2001), only one user was really satisfied with it. A proposal to change this state of affairs by changing the term to 'content management' (Financial Times, July 2002) would seem to stand little chance of success.

Knowledge management as process

Knowledge management consists of two main processes:

new knowledge
existing knowledge

- The acquisition of new knowledge
- The utilization of existing knowledge

Current models of knowledge management involve the following steps:

- Drawing up an inventory of the existing knowledge
- Determining what needs to be known
- Developing, spreading and applying that knowledge.
- Disposing of any knowledge that has lost meaning for the organization.

The acquiring of new knowledge can only occur through the collection and acquiring (importing in, buying etc.) of externally available sources of knowledge and the internal development of new knowledge (best practices, 'lessons learned,' R&D, etc.). In order to use or reuse existing knowledge, it has to be made accessible.

stock approach

Knowledge management in the narrow sense involves the so-called stock approach, which focuses on storing information in systems and databases. IT plays a dominant role in this.

flow approach

In the so-called flow approach, knowledge is not viewed as being objectively transferable. Subjective values are conscious or unconsciously always added during the transfer of the knowledge to other 'actors'. IT is mainly viewed as a facilitator of the process of knowledge exchange. Knowledge transfer methods such as information markets, open days during which multidisciplinary professional information can be obtained, presentations on current projects, and so on all fall under the flow approach. As such, the approach fits the 'organizing of brainwork' approach and goes further than knowledge management in the narrow sense. The already emphasized obstacles and improvement aspects apply to the success or failure of both approaches.

VIRTUAL TEAMS ARE HIGHLY EFFICIENT

'Good morning!' Three IT specialists enter a meeting room in the Utrecht offices of Capgemini. Their four discussion partners are already waiting at the other end of the table. Or at least, as projections on a screen. In reality, the four are seated seven thousand kilometers away, in the Indian city of Mumbai.

The meeting room is one of Capgemini's so-called cPorts: spaces where employees in various offices throughout the world have meetings with each other. Sure, they're virtual spaces, but they come as close as possible to real-life meeting spaces.

We do everything on the 'right shore': the things that we do better here we do here, and the things that they do better in India are done in India. In the past, communication with India was inclined to be somewhat awkward. 'To our ears, Indians sound pretty much the same when they speak English. For them, the same applies to us. During telephonic meetings it was virtually impossible to tell who was speaking at the other end.

By now, Capgemini has fifteen cPorts throughout the world, from Oslo and London to Atlanta and Mumbai. And these contribute immensely to the international teamwork ... 'Of course, we still do fly backwards and forwards, but for routine discussions the cPorts are excellent. To the extent even that they are somewhat overused: each international team wants to meet at least once a week.'

Virtual teams which collaborate with each other from various places in the world function just as well as traditional teams. 'Initially, the virtual team's functioning was noticeably worse. In the course of time, the differences in performance will disappear.'

The advantages of virtual collaboration only really emerge when the technical problems have been surmounted and the team members have grown used to each other. 'Take "time shifting" and the daily shuffling of work across the world. When Dutch employees are going to sleep, America picks up the project where it was left off.'
The time difference between Mumbai and Utrecht – four hours – is too small for any real time shifting to take place. With 'day extension' work is sent off to India at the end of the working day. The first results will be already be coming in by the next day.

Virtual – but at eye level

- Capgemini has cPorts throughout the entire world ... and they are in high demand.
- They are partly replacing physical meetings and collaborative work.
- Research done by TNO has shown that virtual teams can be even more efficient.
- New virtual forms of collaboration have yet to be conceived.

For virtual teams to function effectively, it is important for each team to know what the other is doing. An 'us against them' feeling is highly counterproductive.

In addition to its cPorts, Capgemini uses various other methods for collaborating virtually. Take its 'communities of practice': virtual collaborations between professionals in particular fields, or its theme-based approach, such as socially responsible entrepreneurship. 'Every community has a team room – a sort of virtual office where information is gathered and disseminated. You could, for example, leave documents behind in that team room for others to edit. This way you can avoid the problem of everybody working in different versions.'

'A team room is a good way of demonstrating the advantages of working at a distance.' But there is room for improvement. 'We could be doing digital brainstorming whereby everybody types in his or her ideas into the computer and instantly reacts to the ideas of others.'

Virtual teams are enabling new forms of collaboration. We must take advantage of them.

Source: *Het Financieele Dagblad*, 21 April 2008

3.6 The role of work groups in participation and decision making

Work groups carry out the consultation, deliberation and participation within an organization. They may be project groups (temporary), task forces or committees (permanent) at all levels of the organization. Work and consultation groups are created in order to bring together expertise and information in the analysis of problems and the development of solutions and thus improve the quality of decision making. Furthermore, such groups provide an opportunity for participation in decision making, as a result of which the basis of decisions is extended and their acceptance stimulated.

The tasks of such groups vary, and may include innovation, automation, organizational changes, personnel policy and long-term planning. The problems will involve different types of decisions. The groups may be referred to as 'higher' or 'lower' depending on whether the decisions taken are strategic, organizational or operational. The nature of the assignment will also determine whether the groups have an advisory, coordinating or even executive authority.

It is important to choose the members of consultation and work groups with care. A good result is dependent on the necessary information and expertise being present in sufficient quantities. Attention must therefore be paid to the information and expertise of individual members. In addition, it is important to assign authority within the groups clearly and satisfactorily. When different levels and different departments are represented in a team, the members have to be given a mandate to address the issue in question if a meaningful contribution is to be made. The team has to be able to make decisions or make recommendations.

The will and the capacity to co-operate are key factors in the successful functioning of a group. The interests of individual departments and individual job requirements should be of secondary importance in that joint decisions or recommendations should be directed at a higher common goal. When choosing members of consultation groups or teams it is therefore important to pay attention to the individual's abilities to cooperate with others.

It is also crucial that members of work and consultation groups – whether they are representative or expert – be accepted by the rest of the work force, because only then can they exert an influence on the making of decisions and their eventual acceptance and implementation.

3.6.1 Higher-level teams and participative decision making

Higher consultation groups contribute at the level of strategic and organizational decisions. They are concerned with complex problems which can only be solved on the basis of a large amount of information and investigation. For example, a director can be supported by a permanent 'committee of long-term planning' which is composed of heads of departments, if necessary supplemented by an external consultant. A temporary task force can be set up to consider decisions about product innovation. Such a group would draw up proposals within the framework of the production policy. These proposals would have to be approved by the top management level and the directors.

permanent committee
temporary task force

In the case of organizational change, a team could be formed to deal with the changes. For example, an 'automation steering committee' could be commissioned to set up a new information system or a 'quality team' to address the question of how to make the organization more market-, customer-, and quality-oriented.

steering committee

3.6.2 Lower-level teams and participative decision making

Lower working and consultation groups contribute to operational decisions made at lower levels of the organization. Operational decisions are about the fixing of implementation plans and operational norms – for example, for productivity or sales.

Lower working groups can be set up in order to implement – either partially or fully – the guidelines determined by a higher policy group (for example, in the field of product innovation or automation). Such an operations-directed group may be composed of representatives from the marketing, research and development and production departments.

operations-directed group

3.7 The use of external consultants

external consultant

A manager often seeks the advice of an external consultant either when a specific, clearly defined problem needs to be addressed, or when there is a vague feeling that problems exist but they have not yet been identified. Although it is usually the task of management to solve the problems by themselves, they may conclude that for some reason problems cannot or will not be solved without external help. For example:

- Management may not be able to solve the problem because it is too difficult or too time consuming. Management may wish to take advantage of the consultant's knowledge of the problem and solution possibilities and alternatives based on previous experience. Management may have the ability to solve the problem, but not the time because of other (more important) activities. The consultant's time is used instead.
- *complete and objective* *wider view* *objectivity* Management may want a complete and objective investigation to bring the real cause of the problems to light and explain. A wider view of the problem in question is more likely to be supplied by an external consultant than by the organization itself, because the consultant is not involved in the daily events, which can lead to a certain narrowing of view. Objectivity is also more difficult if an organization carries out its own internal investigations.
- The organization sometimes finds it hard to accept problems resolved internally when there are conflicting ideas within the organization. The hiring of an independent consultant will overcome this difficulty.
- The client may not know the problem, but can detect the symptoms. The issue is not so much the difficulty of the problem as ignorance of or unfamiliarity with the problem.
- The client may require information which it cannot produce itself. This may involve knowledge of the sector and market data which a consultancy firm with specific knowledge of the sector can supply.
- *second opinion* The client may require a second opinion to confirm or reject a point of view. External consultants see things differently from the client as they will not suffer from 'company blindness'. Requesting a second opinion is often done in the case of a very radical plan. Such a study would often be commissioned by the board of directors and/or the works council of an organization.
- *instrument of power* The client may wish to use the consultant as an instrument of power in the solving of problems – that is, the consultant is hired for organizational-political reasons. The power of the consultant is often determined by the influence exercised by the use of his or her skills. Internal resistance to solutions can often only be overcome once an independent person has considered them. The consultant should only be used to deliver a message which certain members of the organization find hard to deliver themselves, or to express a message in different words. Management consultants have justifiable difficulty with such commissions. They usually clearly insist on determining the message (or solution) themselves. In principle, the consultant will not accept an engagement purely on a 'ritual' basis as part of an internal political game.
- The client may wish to use the consultant to bring a problem to the attention of his or her own organization or the supervisory bodies (for example, the board of directors). The consultants are unlikely to object to such assignments as they will be aware that their advice carries more weight in some situations than that of management itself.
- The client may not dare or want to take responsibility. If management abdicates, or at least appears to abdicate, responsibility for a potentially risky solution, it may be difficult to find a consultant who is willing to adopt the manager's ideas. If the solution works, the manager can still take the credit; if the solution fails, then the consultant can be blamed. Such commissions usually involve the functioning of 'important' members of the organization and dismissals may form part of the suggested solutions.

- A financier may seek assurance that a debt or credit extension is a good idea via an independent judgment. The client may use the fact that a consultant has been engaged to impress a financier.
- *win time* The client may want to win time while making a particular decision or may want to lose so much time that he or she does not have to implement the measures after all. In both cases, the client would be merely using the consultant's time rather than skills. No self-respecting consultant would accept such an assignment if he or she were aware of the client's intention.
- The client may only want a general or periodic check, or a general orientation in relation to the future.
- In certain situations – for example, in case of the sudden departure or death of a manager – a management consultant may be asked to support management in the short term or to fill in temporarily. The assignment sometimes involves 'turnaround management' – that is, through the implementation of all sorts of (often unpopular) measures, moving the organization out of the red or curbing negative developments within a relatively short period of time. The roles of an interim manager and turnaround manager are both at the edge of or even outside the usual professional field of consultancy. By becoming part of the organization, they cease to be independent and objective.

interim manager
turnaround manager

Summary

- Decision making is often referred to as the central task of management.
- Decisions are, in fact, the result of a process which begins the moment the information which highlights the problem becomes available, and lasts until a chosen solution is implemented.
- This process involves four steps or phases: identification of the problem; development of alternatives; selection and finally a decision about which of the alternatives is the best or optimal one.
- This process of decision making is influenced by many different factors – for example, the structure of the organization, the quality of the communication processes and the motivation, involvement and commitment of the members of the organization.
- Once the decision has been made, it is important to proceed carefully and to draw up an initial plan. A number of steps are involved, from words or policy decisions to deeds and specific actions. (Planning and various kinds of plans for various parts of an organization are covered in more detail in Chapter 9.)
- Decision making also involves learning, both by individuals and by organizations, via an observing-judging-designing-applying cycle. Learning takes place at two levels: operational and conceptual learning.
- When organizations are striving for continuity and effectiveness, decisions will be based on actual and anticipated experiences.
- Constant change means that on occasions it will be necessary to adjust the 'world picture' of both the individual and of the organization if continuity and effectiveness are to be maintained.

Discussion questions

1 With reference to Management in Action at the beginning of this chapter:
   a) Do you think that decision making changed at Hyundai when founder Ju-Yung passed corporate leadership to his son, Mong-Koo Chung? Give reasons for your answer.
   b) Speed and aggressiveness are part of Hyundai's competitive advantage. How will this affect decision-making across hierarchical levels? Compare Hyundai with its competitors,

2 'If everyone in a department participates in decision making, coordination costs will increase exponentially and the quality of the decisions will decrease. As such, decision-making authority should be designated to the department manager.' Discuss this statement.

3 'Having everyone in a department participate is too time-consuming. It is better if the department manager makes the decisions because that's a lot faster.' Discuss this statement.

4 How do the formula E = f (quality × acceptance) and the statement in Question 3 relate to each other?

5 Is there a relationship between lateral thinking and conceptual learning?

6 Compare Lewin's learning cycle (Figure 3.8) with the experimental learning model (Figure 3.9). What are the key differences and similarities between the two models? Can you think of some examples in the business world?

Research-based exercise

CEOs and single and double-loop learning

Introduction
This research-based exercise is based on a research article by García-Morales, Verdú-Jover and Lloréns (2009), published in the *International Journal of Manpower*. The research question, data collection, method, and some of the results of the research project are presented. The exercise consists of three questions based on the research article and the theory in this chapter. The answers should be based on both the theory in Chapter 3 and your own insights into the practical implications of your answer.

Research Question
What influence do CEO perceptions of personal mastery, shared vision, environment and strategic proactivity exert on organizational innovation and performance, as mediated by the degree of single- and double-loop learning?

Data Collection
As part of this investigation, a structured questionnaire aimed at better understanding of how CEOs face learning issues was devised. The population for this study consisted of the main Spanish firms in the four sectors examined (food-farming/manufacturing/construction/services), according to the Dun and Bradstreet Spain (2000) database. Firms were selected on the basis of possessing characteristics (e.g. billing volume, employees, assets) able to provide them with the resources and means to undertake action to develop the variables analyzed in this research. A total of 900 questionnaires were sent and 408 valid questionnaires returned, giving an approximate response rate of 45 percent.

Outcomes
The researchers found that:

- CEO perceptions of several strategic factors and capabilities (personal mastery, shared vision, environment and strategic proactivity) influence single and double-loop learning, which in turn influence organizational innovation and performance.
- Single-loop learning is influenced by personal mastery, shared vision, stable environment and strategic proactivity.
- Double-loop learning is influenced by personal mastery, shared vision, ambiguous environment, and strategic proactivity.

(Based on García-Morales, V.J., Verdú-Jover, A.J., and Lloréns, F.J. (2009) 'The influence of CEO perceptions on the level of organizational learning: single-loop and double-loop learning.' *International Journal of Manpower*, (30)6, 567-590.)

Questions

1 Explain in your own words the difference between single-loop and double-loop learning.
2 A key difference between single-loop and double-loop learning is that a CEO's perception of the environment (i.e., stable versus ambiguous) has a different impact. Explain this difference.
3 Explain why both single and double-loop learning are necessary and generate an increase in organizational innovation and performance.

CASE

Management case study

How Mars Built a Business

Launching a business selling customized candies was risky and required a series of internal innovation moves by Mars executives.

'There is little reason for an individual to have a computer in their home,' Ken Olsen, the president and founder of the Digital Equipment, famously said in 1977. As Olsen's quote suggests, predicting demand for new, innovative products and services can be difficult, in part because many of the traditional methods of market testing – using historical data to forecast sales, for instance, or asking customers in a focus group to compare a new product with an existing, competing one – aren't well-suited to the innovation process.

This was the dilemma that Dan Michael, then R&D director for Mars' M&Ms brand, faced in 2000. He and his research team at the advanced R&D lab in Hackettstown, N.J., had an idea: to make customizable M&Ms printed with the word or image of a customer's choosing. So they began experimenting with new printing technologies. Initially hacking together prototypes using printers bought from Staples, they had settled by early 2003 on the best printing technologies for the task, applied for patents, and taken their concept to Mars top management.

'Everyone thought the idea of customized M&Ms was phenomenal,' says Jim Cass, now general manager of Mars Direct. But it was just that – an idea. The R&D team didn't have a marketing strategy or even customer research showing that customized candies would be a viable business, so there was some skepticism. Michael and team needed to convince management there could be a market for customized candies. To do that, they had to reinvent the development process – and the role of marketing within it.

Mars had recently launched an innovation initiative called Pioneer Week. Select research teams were given a modest budget and 90 days to build a trial production line, after which the new product would be made available to Mars' 65,000 employees. 'The teams were allowed to bypass some of the testing normally associated with product development,' says Marc Meyer, a professor at Northeastern University's College of Business in Boston, who has studied the company.

'A Real Skunkworks'

Michael's team, still fewer than a dozen people, was selected at Pioneer Week, and in June 2003 – after three hectic months – their product, then called M&M's Colorworks Print Shop Milk Chocolate Candies, went on sale. They received orders for 800 pounds of custom-printed white M&Ms (the only color offered initially) within the first day.

'It was still a real skunkworks operation – we had one small printer, and we hand-bagged everything,' says Cass. 'But the strategy was, 'make a little, learn a little; make some more, learn some more.'

The internal trial provided critical marketing feedback: the four-pound minimum order size was too big, and customers wanted colored candy and 'party favor' packaging options.

Setting the price was another challenge. For the internal launch, the team chose $12 a pound, $4 more than the retail price for standard M&Ms. Since then, according to Cass, the price has changed four or five times. 'We were learning incredible amounts of information on a daily basis and continued to optimize the price/value equation,' he says. Today consumers can buy one seven ounce bag of customized M&Ms for $16.99. Larger orders cost less per bag, with a 10-pound bulk order going for $250.

Customers, who often order the customized candies for weddings or milestone events, have proved willing to pay the premium.

Learning from the Customers

Ready to take it to the next level, the team began selling My M&Ms, as the custom candies are now known, to the public through a small link from the main M&M Web site in March 2004. Without any marketing blitz, sales took off. That's also when the team began to do more serious customer research.

'We reached out to every (my m&ms) customer, and roughly 25% responded, providing detailed demographics as well as information on why they had made the purchase,' says Cass. Because the customer feedback relates to actual purchases, it is more reliable than answers from traditional focus groups, where people talk hypothetically about why they would make a purchase.

In 2006, Mars' My M&Ms experiment became a formal business unit called Mars Direct. Famously secretive, the company won't share sales data, although Meyer, the Northeastern professor, wrote in his 2007 book, *The Fast Path to Corporate Growth*, that soon after the public launch sales had surpassed $10 million and continued to accelerate.' The product was launched in Europe in 2007 and will soon be introduced in Australia.

What can executives learn from Mars' approach to marketing an innovative product?

Think Iteratively, Not Linearly
Give up the idea that you need to have all the answers about product features, packaging, target market, and so on before a product launch. Instead, run a small trial of the actual product or service, learn from it, revise, repeat.

Forget Focus Groups
When it comes to new-to-the-world products or services, don't rely on what customers say they think or want. As Henry Ford is quoted as saying, if he'd asked his customers what they wanted, they would have said a faster horse.

Be Your Own Test Market
Big companies can gain invaluable information, at far less than the cost of hiring a market research firm, if they treat their employees as a test market. Smaller companies can look to friends and family.

Source: *BusinessWeek*, December 28, 2009, Jessie Scanlon

Case Study Questions

1 What sort of decision-making and learning processes are described in the case?
2 Mars decided to actively involve customers in their research and development. The M&M product was improved through trial and error, based on customer feedback. Explain the advantages and disadvantages (i.e., risks) of having customers involved in Mars' research and development trajectory. Can you think of other firms with similar approaches?
3 The Mars case study can teach executives three lessons: 'Think iteratively, not linearly,' 'Forget focus groups,' and 'Be your own test market.' How do these three insights relate to the learning organization concept?

CONTENTS

4.1 Conditions for success
4.2 The strategy formulation process
4.3 The organization of strategic planning
4.4 Strategic collaboration
4.5 Implementation of strategic plans
4.6 Managing organizational resistance
4.7 The emerging strategy

Chapter 4

Strategy formulation and strategic management

LEARNING OUTCOMES

After studying this chapter, you should be able to do the following:

- Explain the concepts of strategy and strategic management
- Identify the various steps of the process of strategy formulation
- Discuss important issues in the field of strategy formulation
- Understand how strategy formulation takes place and the methods and techniques that are used to determine policy
- Indicate the problems that can arise during the implementation of a strategy
- Describe the measures that can enhance the effect of planned action
- Appreciate that strategy can also be 'discovered'

CASE

Management-in-action

Can Nike Do It?

The sneaker maker's new CEO laid out an ambitious plan to boost revenues 50% over the next five years. Some wonder whether he's pushing too hard.

Nike (NKE) never lacks for boldness. The Beaverton (Ore.) sneaker goliath recently offered the German National Soccer Federation $778 million to sponsor its national soccer team for 10 years in an audacious move to rattle its German rival Adidas and longtime sponsor of the German team. Nike's new chief executive, Mark Parker, upped the boldness quotient again on Feb. 6, when he outlined an ambitious plan to grow revenues by $8 billion in five years.

In his first major initiative since inheriting the top spot in January, 2006, Parker explained to investors at Nike's annual analyst conference how the company aims to grow to $23 billion in revenue by 2011. The comprehensive long-term strategy calls for reshaping the management structure; redefining Nike's relationship with its fast-changing, digitally driven consumer; and adding 100 new company stores worldwide in three years. 'We're fundamentally changing the way we organize the company,' Parker said. 'Nike is as hungry and as driven as we've ever been before and becoming more focused and more competitive.'

While analysts and investors applauded much of Nike's new strategy, some questioned whether the company could actually do it. After all, revenues would need to rise 53% over five years, or average about 9% a year, to reach the target of $23 billion. It's going to be challenging to achieve $8 billion in new sales without turning around slumping sales in Europe, Japan, and the U.S. basketball market – a crucial $3 billion to $3.5 billion market segment.

'I think it's going to be tough for them,' said John Shanley, financial analyst for Susquehanna Financial. 'Basketball, for example, is shrinking in terms of sales. They have 96% of the market share in the $100 or more price point. How do you get high single-digit growth when you already have more than 96% of the market?'

Focus on Retail

Nike executives fell short in offering specific details to some of these questions and focused more on painting a broader picture of the new strategy. They stressed a multipronged approach that includes reorganizing the Nike brand into six main athletic divisions – running, basketball, soccer, women's fitness, men's training, and sport culture – that are expected to generate 75% of the brand's growth. The company had previously divided the brand into three segments: footwear, apparel and equipment.

Growth is also expected to come from emerging markets and potential acquisitions. But Nike Brand President Charlie Denson said the company can reach the $23 billion target without new acquisitions. As for new markets, China is expected to become Nike's second biggest market behind the U.S., potentially chalking up $1 billion in sales, and Nike's India business has grown 40% since last year thanks in part to its efforts in cricket. Nike executives also said they plan to invest aggressively in other potential billion-dollar markets – such as Russia, India, and Brazil.

Clearly, Nike's efforts to add new retail stores and 'elevate' its partnership with existing retailers are a big part of its new strategy. This effort comes at a time of sluggish sales from some of its biggest retailers – mall-based chains Foot Locker (FL) and Finish Line (FINL). Nike executives said the company plans to grow its direct-to-retail business to 15% of total sales, or $3.5 billion, from 12% today. The segment includes its own stores, factory outlets, and an e-commerce division, which executives expect to see a significant increase in revenues over the next five years. For the planned retail investment, Nike will increase capital spending to $475 million annually, up from just under $400 million, Nike said. Gary DeStefano, president of Nike's global operations, stressed its retail goal is to make Nike a better retail partner: 'This is not about Nike vs. the retailers,' he said. 'This is a partnership. We believe this could be a growth strategy.'

Meeting Consumers Where They Live

But probably Nike's boldest bet is on the consumer. In the eyes of Parker, this new and evolving digitally driven consumer is reshaping the retailing landscape. The power is now in the consumer's hands, and Parker believes Nike and other consumer brand companies need to adjust to the new market dynamics. 'Consumers have never held as much power as they do today,' Parker said. 'And clearly the power has shifted to consumers.'

Nike's Denson said this fundamental shift can be captured in the way the company studies its consumer profiles. In the past, managers used to consider 18- and 22-year-olds as part of the same demographic target. Now he says they are treated as separate and distinct markets when it comes to age, interests, and tastes. 'We spent the last 30 years trying to bundle things, and now it's almost the reverse and we have to unbundle things,' Denson said, explaining Nike's new efforts to tailor products to individual consumers.

Despite these fundamental changes in how Nike approaches its customers and its reshaped management structure, some things never change. Nike remains its audacious self and competitive juices still run strong. It still has goals to dominate markets where it is not already No. 1, and it is redoubling efforts to unseat rival Adidas as the world's top supplier of soccer shoes and apparel.

Its recent bid to sponsor the German national team is part of its 2010 goal to 'dominant the football brand,' said Nike marketing vice-president Trevor Edwards. 'We believe it's time to create separation. This is not a game of chicken.' Some things never change.

Source: *BusinessWeek*, February 7, 2007, Stanley Holmes

This chapter describes how organizations balance their own internal capabilities with the demands of the external environment. An organization can take either a systematic or intuitive approach. Strategy can develop more or less according to plan, or it can emerge from action that the organization undertakes.

strategic formulation
strategic management

Strategic formulation involves a systematic, step-by-step approach to strategy development. Strategic management also involves a consideration of how skills and capabilities can be maintained and developed as part of that strategy. We will mention some of the reasons for the resistance that some organizations put up against strategic innovations.

Every organization – whether it be a shoe factory or a library – is subject to many kinds of environmental forces. Management needs to recognize the influence of these forces and be aware of what is going on in the external environment. A major rise in the prices of raw materials, the increasing scarcity of labor and the introduction of new technologies are all examples of changes to which management needs to react.

In Chapter 2, we discussed the influence of certain groups and environmental factors on the functioning and the survival of an organization. To survive, an organization's management must nurture the relationships between the organization and the stakeholders and situations in the outside world. The process by which management gives the external adaptation of the organization form and content is referred to as strategy formulation. Strategy formulation is directed solely at the external environment.

strategy formulation

The duties of the organization's management, however, go much further than strategy formulation alone. In addition to tuning into the external environment, management must also maintain and develop the capabilities of the organization that are necessary if strategic change is to take place. Such a process will place certain demands on the organization – for example, the organizational structure may have to be adjusted, new knowledge may have to be developed and/or other management techniques may have to be introduced. This process is called strategic management.

strategic management

Strategic management is directed both at the external environment and the internal environment. It is not only concerned with the preparation and the making of strategic choices (that is, strategy formulation), but also with the question of how those choices can be implemented (that is, planning and execution). The implementation of strategic plans can arouse resistance from those who have to actually implement the strategy. The detecting of any resistance should be a part of the strategic formulation process.

In order to continue to be successful, most organizations will need to make choices, especially those of a strategic nature in relation to external developments. In this respect, organizations can be expected to increasingly choose the weapon of 'higher quality' over that of 'lower costs' in the coming years, though this is an ongoing matter of debate within the company's marketing and sales and product development departments.

higher quality
lower costs

Developments in markets and technology (see Chapter 2) mean that organizations are now concentrating on their core activities (the main organizational activities) and are planning to make changes to the company's value chain. For example, an increasing proportion of the manufacturing and distribution process is being outsourced, partly as a result of the fact that the product life cycle is becoming increasingly shorter and investments must be earned back in an increasingly shorter period. By contracting out more, an organization is more resistant to sudden changes in market demand and can share some of the increasingly complex problems of business activity – caused by the wider product range – with the suppliers.

core activities

In this chapter we examine how these choices arise in relation to future decision making in companies and institutions.

4.1 Conditions for success

The difference between an organization's failure and its success is often its ability (or inability) to react to the wishes of its customers and to achieve this at lower cost or higher quality than other competing organizations.

strategy determination

Strategy determination is the devising of a complex series of actions and goals which can be implemented in order to attain the organization's goals. This is based on the external possibilities (known or assumed) on the one hand, and on what is feasible internally on the other – that is, the organization's capabilities (what it can do) and ambitions (what it wishes to do). This attuning process is depicted in Fig 4.1.

This is obviously not a straightforward, spontaneous or natural process, nor can it be left to take its own course. On the contrary – a decision-making process must be set in motion within the organization: the process of strategy formulation. The first consideration is the creation of a vision, objectives and a set of goals for the organization and working out what its mission is. A clear idea of management intentions is essential to this. Goals will need to develop and change in the light of external developments (which are normally also internally represented in the ideas and goals of the organization members).

strategy formulation

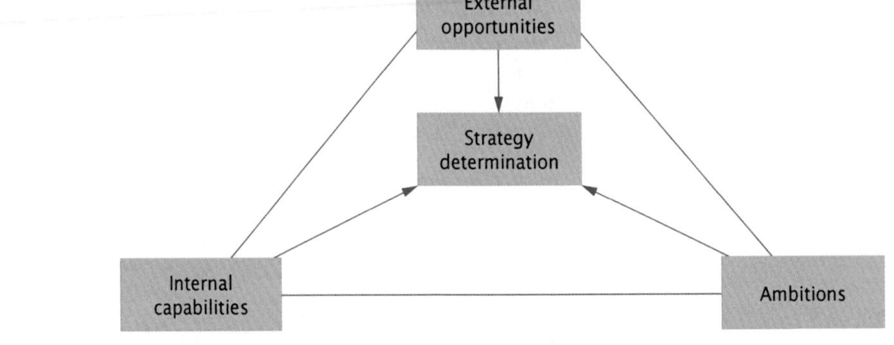

Figure 4.1
Strategy determination, as a function of external opportunities, internal capabilities and ambitions

Ongoing changes to goals also involves making ongoing changes to the organization's vision and objectives. The methods and resources by which the objectives and goals will be realized need to be made explicit, as will the constraints within which the organization will have to operate. Personnel, finance, time and other factors need to be taken into account in working out what is feasible.

CASE

Mini case study 4.1

Companies need flexible approach towards staff management manpower

Forceful enough to change the employment landscape forever, the current economic crisis has taught some hard lessons to employers about the need to transform their talent acquisition strategies in the face of growing global competition. As the business environment begins to improve, employers are poised to respond quickly to a rapidly changing marketplace and growing disconnect between where labour is needed and where it is available.

Manpower Inc, a world player in the employment services industry, forecasts that companies need to adopt a more strategic and flexible approach to workforce management in order to reach their goals and better manage risk in the post-recovery world. Key to this approach will be a growing reliance on the four types of non-permanent or contingent workers, who come under the brackets of temporary employees, outsourced workers, contractors and consultants. These recommendations and findings form part of the 'Rules of engagement: Harnessing the potential of the contingent workforce', a white paper and survey released by Manpower Inc.

Manpower predicts that in order to take full advantage of opportunities in the recovering economy, employers will need to move away from viewing contingent workers as a practical resource to cover maternity leave, meet seasonal demand or keep permanent payrolls in check, and towards viewing them as a valuable strategic asset. According to Manpower's research, the most common reason worldwide for employing contingent workers is to meet peak seasonal demand and nearly one in five employers do this. Only 14% of employers across the globe now turn to contingent employees to derive greater strategic value.

According to the survey, more than 60% of employers worldwide do not view contingent labour as critical to business success. Manpower foresees a new executive mindset in the post-recovery world, with forward-looking companies turning to a dynamic mix of permanent and contingent workers, increasing their flexibility for a competitive advantage. Therefore, the demand for specialist contractors and outsourced workers will rise, especially in knowledge-driven areas where technology allows talented people to work from anywhere in the world. As more and more companies understand how to leverage a contingent workforce to gain strategic value, that percentage will only grow.

Manpower research suggests that contingent workers typically feel more loyal to the host companies where they are working than to the employment agencies that pay them. Thus, keeping contingent workers motivated should be easy, so long as the host organisation integrates them successfully into the workplace, works to keep them committed throughout their assignment, whether it lasts a week or a year and demonstrate to them that they are contributing to the company's overall performance. Organisations should develop customised, flexible strategies to accommodate different segments of the contingent workforce, just as they would with their permanent employees.

Successfully engaging contingent workers rests largely on integrating them fully into the workplace, and keeping them integrated. Loyalty matters and making contingent workers feel like outsiders is no way to promote it. According to Manpower, every company should work to improve induction and orientation processes for contingent workers.

Source: *Financial Express*, November 5, 2009

4.1.1 Strategic management: a luxury or necessity?

dynamic environment

The more dynamic the environment, the more important it becomes to pay explicit attention to strategy formulation. It becomes increasingly difficult to gain an intuitive insight into the changing forces and events that influence the organization. Under such circumstances, an implicit environment and market-oriented strategy will obviously be inadequate, while explicit strategy formulation will yield definite advantages to the organization. A strategy provides direction for the activities of the organization; it makes the pattern visible and more coherent. Coordination of the activities is also made easier.

explicit strategy formulation

On the negative side, formulation of a strategy costs time and money which could be used in a more directly productive manner. Once a direction has been chosen, it may also become difficult to deviate from it.

Intuition

intuition

Intuition is not a conscious or rational way of thinking. An entrepreneur is likely to take an intuitive strategic approach if he or she sees a potentially profitable gap in the market and targets that gap without making an analysis of the viability of the project.

Some entrepreneurs have become very successful with this approach. However, the intuitive approach to business strategy does have some limitations: sometimes entrepreneurs enjoy initial success only to be confronted later on in the project with the consequences of not having given sufficient thought to their actions in its early phases.

intuitive approach

There are two reasons why an intuitive approach will not always work.

1 As the world outside the organization becomes more complex and dynamic, it is becoming increasingly difficult to form an intuitive impression of all relevant developments.
2 The increasing complexity of the activities, applied technologies and other factors within the organization is making it difficult, if not impossible, to manage an organization in an intuitive manner.

Furthermore, an intuitive proposal is hard to discuss with other managers. With increasing complexity, it becomes essential for the organization to gather an increasing amount of information about its external environment and its internal workings.

Planning

Planning for the long term involves a basic assumption that past developments will recur in the future. In an increasingly dynamic environment, however, this basic assumption is often in doubt.

Strategic planning does not assume that the future is just a continuation of the past. On the contrary, the future is more likely to be determined by other forces. Against a background of general change, management must ensure that the product-market combinations it designs and chooses contribute to the realization of the future objectives of the organization.

Plans also need to be implemented: this aspect of the planning process should not be overlooked.

Strategic control

A strategy that is sensitive to the environment and its operations will always have to be supported by changes to the organization's structure and culture and by specified actions. Only then will successful implementation be assured.

strategic control

A strategy is always built on assumptions with regard to future developments. As soon as these assumptions are no longer correct, the plan is of little value. The goal of strategic control is to regularly test whether assumptions/predictions are still in line with actual developments. If the assumptions appear to be incorrect – that is, reality deviates from what was expected – then the plans, the process and the structure will all have to be adjusted. A strategic plan should be able to be adjusted as it is a means to an end, not the end itself.

CASE

Mini case study 4.2

GE Brings a New Strategy to Life

In a rare move, GE took minority stakes in two Hyundai ventures, and their success is reverberating through the conglomerate: two-way learning

GE wasn't expecting such smooth sailing in its voyage with Hyundai, which has a spotty record of corporate governance. So the Americans stationed dozens of managers in key positions in the joint ventures, and both parties had veto power on all critical decisions. But neither side has had to veto anything. 'We haven't encountered any real clash in management,' says Ted Chung, president of both ventures, which operate virtually as one company. 'In fact, we've been asking GE to dispatch more people because we want to learn more from them.'

That learning has gone both ways. Chung says Hyundai originally sought an investor to make up for losses in its credit-card business. But he now calls the capital injection 'the smallest contribution of all the benefits we've enjoyed.' More important, Chung says, was GE's risk-management and financial knowhow, as well as its 'uncompromising implementation of ethics, its interest in talent, and its management philosophy.'

And GE has learned from Hyundai's marketing chops. To give the brand cachet, Chung hired noted designers Karim Rashid and Léon Stolk to develop a distinctive look for the company's cards, worked with design consultant IDEO to revamp and simplify its bills and Web site, and asked Dutch design firm Concrete Architectural Associates to create a more welcoming atmosphere at customer service centers. To nurture exclusivity, Chung set up 'Super Matches' in sports ranging from figure skating and gymnastics to cycling and tennis, where mega-stars such as Rafael Nadal and Roger Federer face off in nationally broadcast competitions.

Hyundai also woos clients with discounts on its vehicles. HyundaiCard lops as much as $380 off the price of a car, which consumers then pay back by accumulating points that equal 2% of purchases with the card. That encourages holders of multiple cards to use HyundaiCard as their primary plastic. It seems to work: Average monthly spending by those customers is 37% higher than that of ordinary card users. HyundaiCard 'has used design and branding to differentiate itself in a very crowded market,' says GE's van Bunnik. That, he says, helps to make the Korean ventures 'a benchmark for GE Money.'

Source: *BusinessWeek*, April 16, 2009, Moon Ihlwan

4.1.2 Strategy at corporate, business and functional levels

Businesses come in all shapes and sizes. Organizations like Philips, ABB, Daimler Benz and General Electric have a highly diversified range of products and serve a vast number of markets. At the other end of the spectrum, some companies have one product, which they sell to only one market. Both kinds of organization require a strategy even though its form and the technical problems to be resolved are likely to differ greatly.

conglomerates

Large conglomerates such as General Electric need to classify their business activities into those which need an injection of funds, those which need to be consolidated, and perhaps other groups of activities which may even have to be phased out, diversified or sold. An organization with only one activity or business needs to focus on how this activity is to be managed in order to achieve the best results. Both cases involve the development of strategy at a business level, in which the problem is the development of an optimal strategy for the existing activity.

strategy at a business level

In the larger companies with a wide range of interests, management not only has to deal with the development of a strategy at a business level, but also has to address problems relating to the long-term course of the organization as a whole as well as of all the individual businesses that make it up. This is referred to as the development of strategy at a corporate level. This often involves a technique called portfolio analysis (see Section 4.2.3).

strategy at a corporate level

portfolio analysis

The relationship between strategy at a corporate or group level and strategy at a business level is depicted in Fig 4.2. The foundation of the organization is always based on the translation of the business strategy into more specific strategic and operational plans at the functional level.

functional level

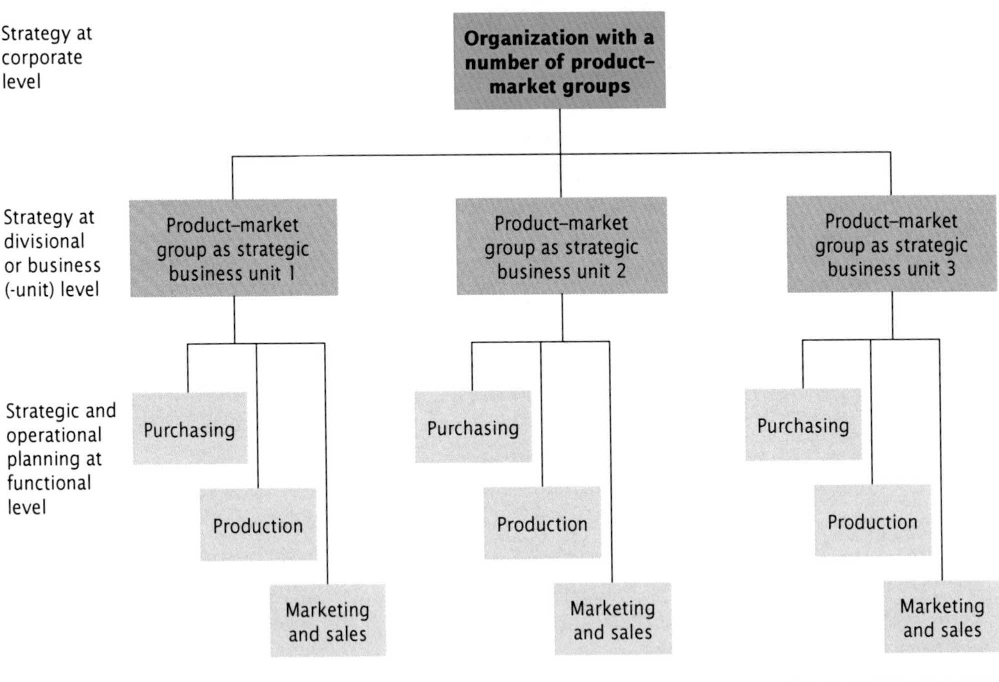

Figure 4.2 *The relationship between strategy at functional, business and corporate or group levels*

diversified enterprise

The term diversified enterprise does not only apply to large enterprises. While these are indeed likely to be diversified, diversification also takes place when an organization (regardless of its size) enters a market which is new to the organization with a product that is also new and not related to its present product-market activities. In small companies, diversification can result in problems in strategy formulation due to the spreading out of activities.

consolidation stage

A balanced package or portfolio of activities is a function of the goals of the organization. The portfolio of a company that wants to grow fast will be different to that of a company which is in the consolidation stage. Portfolio management also involves describing in clear terms the contribution each individual activity needs to make to the whole.

For example ...

... the problem can be compared with the tactics of many team sports, including soccer or hockey. The attackers, the midfield players, the defenders and the goalkeeper all have different roles within the team. If the team wants to play offensively, the attackers have to be reinforced; if the team is hoping for a draw or is trying to limit the scale of a defeat, then the defense will have to be reinforced. Depending on his or her personality, task on the field, age and experience, each player also needs to be managed in a different way.

The performance of an organization – its success or failure – is closely linked to the strategy, structure and the daily functioning of the organization in a changing environment.

Whether an organization is successful, mediocre or fails depends on the strategy, structure and the day-to-day performance of that organization in a changing environment. These elements have been attracting attention since the introduction of strategy theory (1960-1965).

4.1.3 The development of strategy theory

development of processes

During the initial period (from 1960 on) of the development of strategy theory, the emphasis lay on the development of processes to promote the formulation of successful strategies. Igor Ansoff (1965) and others made important contributions to this. From 1970 onwards, fast-growing conglomerates formed the main problem. Activity portfolios, which were frequently relatively unstructured, needed to be put in order.

portfolio approaches

five forces model

generic competitive strategies

The portfolio approaches of the Boston Consulting Group, Arthur D. Little and of other consultants showed how to tackle these problems (see 4.2.3). From about 1980 onwards the strategy concepts were dominated by the ideas of Porter. He developed the five forces model which analyzes the structural profitability of industries (see 4.2.2). After that he investigated the question of how to achieve competitive advantage by using generic competitive strategies). In this connection he described the importance of the value chain for the development of strategies.

resource-based

During the nineties, Hamel and Prahalad drew attention to core competencies as a basis for strategy. Their approach belongs to those theories that take a resource-based approach to entrepreneurship. Strategic alliances and other forms of collaboration also came in for some attention at that time. D'Aveni (1994) and others proposed solutions to retain competitive advantage. The use of strategy at various organizational levels was brought to attention in contributions by Goold and Campbell (1994) and others (see 4.1.2).

Henry Mintzberg et al. take a different approach. In *Strategy Safari* (1998) they classify the various approaches to strategy formulation in ten schools that each concentrate on a different aspect of strategic thought (see Table 4.1).

Table 4.1
Approaches to strategy formulation by Mintzberg

School	Strategy formulated as
design school	a process of conception
planning school	a formal process
positioning school	an analytical process
entrepreneurial school	a visionary process
cognitive school	a mental process
learning school	an emergent process
power school	a process of negotiation
cultural school	a collective process
environmental school	a reactive process
configuration school	a process of transformation

prescriptive schools

descriptive schools

The first three schools are prescriptive schools that lay down how strategy should be formulated. The next six do not give a recipe for strategic behavior, but give a description of strategy. Mintzberg calls them descriptive schools.

The contributions of the last school combine the elements of strategy formulation, strategy contents, organizational structures and environmental situations into configurations or total images.

Prescriptive schools

design school

planning school

positioning school

According to the design school processes are informal and conceptual. Broadly speaking, it is about things such as a strength and weaknesses analysis and a background analysis. According to Mintzberg et al., this school has given rise to two other prescriptive schools. The planning school is concerned with formalizing the process, with occasionally very detailed process descriptions, analyzing methods and diagrams for scores and considerations. Mintzberg et al. mention *Corporate Strategy* (1965) by Igor Ansoff as a publication of this school. The positioning school is not concerned with the process itself, but with analyses to arrive at the best strategy. A well-known exponent of this school is Porter.

Descriptive schools

entrepreneurial school

The entrepreneurial school lays a connection between strategy development and the vision of the leader of the organization. His or her intuition, wisdom and insight are important in reaching a strategy. An exponent of this school is Schumpeter.

cognitive school

The cognitive school looks at strategy from the viewpoint of cognition, based (therefore) on the acquisition and assimilation of knowledge. Strategy development is a collective process, made up of individual thought processes. March and Simon contributed to this school, though they were more concerned with general decision making than with strategy development in particular.

learning school

The learning school regards strategy development as a process that is progressively mastered. The learning takes place at the individual, group and organizational level. Mintzberg et al. regard Hamel & Prahalad, Quinn and Lindblom as belonging to this school.

power school

The power school regards strategy development as a process in which influence, power and politics play an important role. Power can be exercised both within organizations as well as between organizations, and negotiation is at the core of this. Pfeffer & Salancik (1978) contributed to this school.

cultural school

The cultural school emphasizes the importance of the collective interest of all participants for the continuation of the organization. Culture is transferred to newcomers, often implicitly. It affects decision-making, for instance. When it is particularly strong, one effect is that necessary changes may be implemented too slowly. Mintzberg et al. say that this school originated mainly in Scandinavia.

environmental school

The environmental school sees strategy development as a passive process. Power over strategy does not lie with the organization, but with its environment. Attention is paid to power in the environment and its characteristics. Mintzberg et al. mention Hannan and Freeman as authors that have contributed to this school.

Configuration school

According to Mintzberg the configuration school combines all the other schools in one single vision. Strategy development, strategy contents, structures and contents are bundled into one. The transformation that takes place during the development of an organization is even a matter for study. Exponents of this school are Chandler, Mintzberg himself and others.

In this chapter we will deal with the process of strategy formulation in parallel and sequential steps using the insight just mentioned, after which we will discuss implementation of strategic plans. Organizational implications will be discussed in greater detail in chapters 5, 6 and 9.

4.2 The strategy formulation process

strategic formulation process

Definition and resolution of a strategic problem can be a somewhat complicated process for an organization. It is, however, possible to approach the problem in a structured way. A model that may be useful in strategy formulation is shown in Fig 4.3. The strategic formulation process shown in the figure is followed, albeit with some adjustments, by many organizations. Implementing this procedure will enable an organization to gain an insight into important developments. If necessary, adjustments and/or improvements will have to be made to existing business policies.

The process can be divided into the following steps:

strategic profile

1 The present strategic profile is determined. The purpose of this is to have a snapshot of where the firm, products and market are at the present time. The present situation will be used as a starting point from which the new strategy will be mapped out.

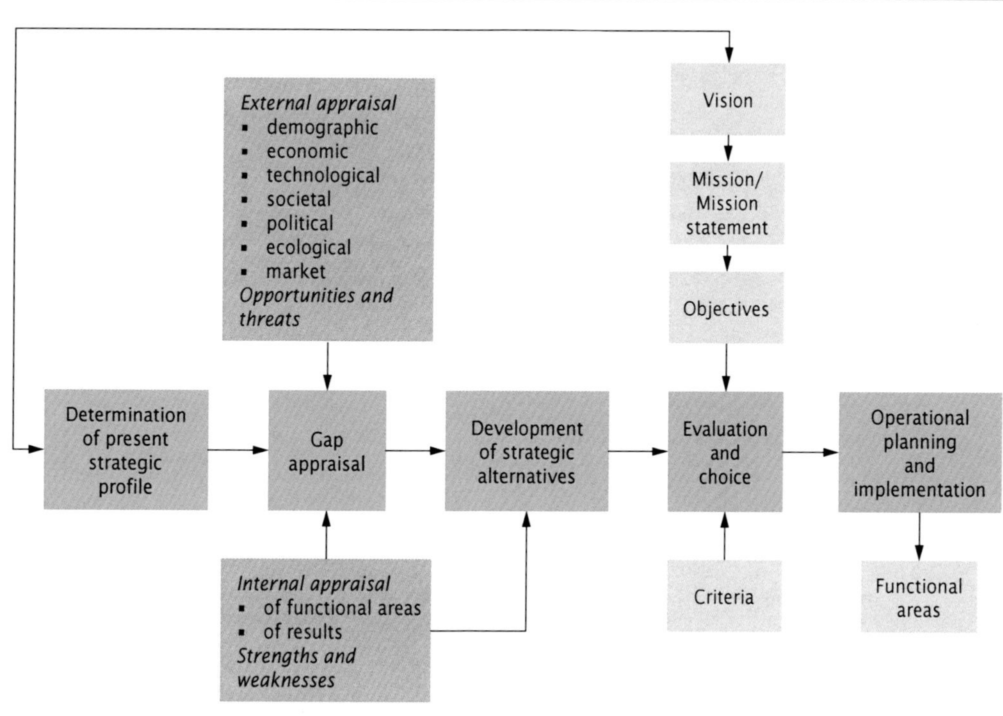

Figure 4.3
Model of the strategy formulation process

The steps that follow can be implemented either in a parallel form or sequentially.

SWOT analysis

2 A SWOT analysis is carried out. This comprises an internal appraisal (strengths and weaknesses) and an external appraisal (opportunities and threats) and highlights the circumstances under which the strategy will be developed.

strategic gap

3 On the basis of Step 2 the question of whether the survival of the organization is likely to be threatened in the near future is addressed. The organization determines whether a strategic gap exists – that is, a discrepancy between what the organization hopes to achieve and what the organization looks like achieving.

alternatives

4 If there is a gap, alternatives have to be sought to close the gap. Useful information in the search for new opportunities can be retrieved from the results of the external appraisal of the environment and the internal appraisal of strengths and weaknesses.

5 Alternatives and their consequences are evaluated. These can be tested against existing objectives on the one hand and a number of specific strategic criteria and constraints on the other.

strategic alternatives

6 The best alternative is chosen and this is followed by the translation of the strategic alternatives into plans for the various functional fields, including purchasing, production, marketing and sales, finance, and personnel fields.

We will now discuss each of these steps in greater detail.

4.2.1 *Present strategic profile*

synergy

The present strategic profile reflects the main characteristics of the present strategy and course as well as the strategic resources and components. In this respect, it plays a useful role in highlighting objectives and goals, areas of current activities and competitive advantages and opportunities for achieving enhanced gains by linking activities (a process referred to as synergy).

Objectives and goals

It is often difficult to identify the objectives and goals targeted by the management of the organization. Sometimes objectives are expressed in relatively general terms that give little direction to the daily events of the organization. It is important to define objectives, goals and targets in economic, technical and social terms.

economic objectives

Economic objectives and goals can be expressed in terms of profit, market share, equity/debt ratios, cost levels, and so on. Management also needs to state how much profit is envisaged and this can then be expressed as a percentage return on equity, for example. If these percentages are not fixed, it is not possible to calculate whether enough profit has been earned. If a profit goal is described as a 'reasonable return for shareholders' it is impossible to determine whether this level has been attained or will be in the future. The consequence is often that action is only undertaken when there is a loss, by which time it is often too late. Successful enterprises have clear operational norms for returns.

non-economic

Objectives can also be non-economic in nature. For example, management or the owner might put the independence of the company above all other considerations; some companies might only want to make aesthetically justifiable or environmentally friendly products. These objectives often exert a major influence on the development and ultimate choice of new strategic possibilities. In this respect, the objectives can be viewed as determining the new course.

Areas of current activities

fields of activity

It is important to determine what fields of activity the organization is familiar with. Total sales can be split up into product groups, markets, distribution channels, countries, and so on. With endless possibilities it is useful to prioritize the most relevant ones as the gathering and compiling of data can take up a great deal of time. It is also worthwhile calculating the profitability of the various areas of activity.

For example ...

... surprising new insights often result from these analyses. A company may calculate the contribution to the profit of the various client categories. One client group may provide 50 per cent more profit per unit of product than the least profitable client group. By selling 10 per cent more to the most profitable clients and less to the low-profit category, the profit can improve spectacularly. The gathering of numerical data may take several days, but the effect on profits can be compared with a sales increase of about 50 per cent.

Competitive advantage

advantage over its competitors

added value

A study of the present strategic profile should include a consideration of how the organization envisages attracting customers in order to gain an advantage over its competitors. There are various ways of winning the competitive battle – for example, by offering the lowest price for the product, or by offering a product (with the services that accompany it) that has a clear 'added value' over what the other suppliers offer in the market. The strategy of companies like Mercedes Benz and BMW, on the one hand, and companies like Skoda and Lada on the other, illustrate this.

Synergy

2 + 2 = 5 effect

Synergy is the advantage (or disadvantage) that arises when two activities are carried out which complement each other – the so-called 2 + 2 = 5 effect. This effect may arise when, for example, a company lets its sales staff sell various different products through the same distribution channel.

For example ...

... in some cases, the advantage lies in product development. For example, a number of electronics companies use a specific technology for a number of product lines (calculators, cash registers, microcomputers and so on). In this way, massive investments in research and development can be spread over a much larger number of end products with resulting cost advantages.
The synergy can also lie in the brand name as it might result in the advertisement cost per product sold being lower than if a manufacturer uses different names.

4.2.2 External appraisal: threats and opportunities

An investigation into the external environment can be carried out from two points of view: total societal environment on the one hand and the specific business sector on the other. Both points of view are entwined with each other.

Developments in the societal environment
In Section 2.3 we discussed some factors which play an important role in determining the future of the organization. We will now deal more fully with them. They can be classified as follows:

Demographic factors
Products and services are ultimately put at the disposal of the population, and as a result demographic factors such as the size, composition and growth rate of the population are of importance to the organization. For example, a decrease in the birth rate will lead to a reduction in the number of consumers of educational products. This has consequences for the demand for products such as school books, classrooms, and teachers. A decreasing birth rate would also have repercussions for companies such as Nestlé.
The increasing ageing of the population or a lowering of the retirement age will eventually have an influence on the social security system. In addition, the multicultural nature of society in many European countries has implications not only for government, but also for private organizations and companies. Education, social and cultural services and the management and realization of participative structures in companies are areas which are particularly affected by multiculturalism.
Companies should also be aware of charges to population concentrations. For example, it is important for the store chains to follow any drift of the population out of larger cities into smaller towns so that market share can be maintained.

multicultural society

Economic factors
Both nationally and internationally economic forces are always an important field of attention for management. It is estimated that within the next 30 years, East Asian countries will increase their share of world production from 15 per cent to 25 per cent. These and other developments mean that international economic negotiations (for example, negotiations relating to EU or GATT regulations) are increasingly important. In recent years, negotiations between Japan and Western countries relating to restrictions on the Japanese export of cars and electronic supplies have been underway. The so-called North-South dialogue between developed and developing countries will have future implications for governments and companies.

North-South dialogue

For example ...

... the fluctuations in the dollar rate during the past years have had a major influence on the market position of a number of companies. The incorrect estimation of the exchange rate influences company's profits dramatically in the short term and in the long term sales expectations have to be adjusted.

Societal factors

Important recent societal developments have included individualization, greater assertiveness and consumerism, greater concern for health and the environment, a decrease in the total number of working years, a desire for greater comfort, the increased importance of paid labor for women, emancipation of second and third-generation ethnic minorities, redistribution of domestic tasks, safe sex and so on.

Societal factors are an important element of any investigation into the environment as they can have a profound impact on the organization. They also affect the working environment – for example, the tendency towards more participation and co-determination. Higher levels of education have also resulted in fewer people being prepared to do unskilled labor.

Technological factors

Technological progress is an essential feature of our time. One could even speak of a new industrial revolution. Few organizations remain unaffected. Two important consequences of technological progress are the modification of production processes and the launching of innovative new products.

The development of the transistor has had a major influence in the past few decennia on the way in which products such as radios, television sets and computers are manufactured. Not only have they changed technically and become more reliable, but they are also a lot cheaper than 10 to 15 years ago. The influence of bio-genetics will become clear during the next 10 to 20 years.

bio-genetics

communication technology

Developments in the field of communication technology – for example, the rise of commercial satellite television – are also important. If these developments continue, they will have consequences for both organizations which currently operate in broadcasting as well as organizations which currently receive advertising revenues (i.e. media companies). Other developments have affected areas such as postal services, telecommunications and computer manufacturing.

For example ...

... until recently, laser technology was only used in laboratories. This technology is now applied worldwide in consumer products such as compact disk players.

Ecological factors

Increasing concern for the environment has led many organizations to instigate a policy of sustainability and environmental friendliness in respect of their products and their packaging. Nowadays packaging that does not cause any pollution during the incineration of refuse is not out of the ordinary.

Political factors

For enterprises operating in international markets, the political situation in countries in which they are active, and/or wish to be active, plays an important role. Becoming attuned to economic and political developments is a complex matter. Volkswagen considered the events in Eastern Europe in the 1980s much more promising than did many other Western enterprises. Volkswagen developed a very ambitious strategy. To achieve an increase in sales of 25 per cent in three years, Volkswagen invested 50 million DM in the Trabant factory in the former East Germany and in the Czech Skoda factories.

Developments in the market and business sectors

Any study of the forces which affect a particular business sector can be divided into an analysis of competitors and an analysis of the forces which affect the entire sector, including all competitors.

Analysis of competition: intensity of rivalry

Knowing your opponents was already a basic strategic principle (albeit military strategy) many centuries ago. Sun Tzu, the Chinese general, wrote about this subject around 300 BC. In management literature, the competitive profile and analysis has only recently become a focus of attention (see Ansoff, 1965, and Porter, 1980/2008). The intensity of rivalry and competition will determine to a great extent the structural opportunities for profit in a particular business sector. The following points relating to rivalry and competition should be taken into account:

competitive analysis

1 It is important for an organization to ascertain whether its competitors are rash or cautious. A cautious competitor will weigh up the effects of individual actions. A cautious competitor will not plunge into a price war with eyes closed. Such a competitor may well engage in a price war, but only after ensuring that it will not damage the organization's current position.
2 In situations of slow economic growth, competition often takes on a more intensive nature. This is especially the case when costs rise and sales grow less quickly, particularly when such a business sector is characterized by a high level of fixed costs, as is the case with the steel and aerospace industries. Any extra sales will always make a contribution toward covering fixed costs.
3 Competition can become more intense when an organization is dealing with many different types of competitor. In the insurance business, for example, regionally based insurance companies compete with both direct underwriters and traditional companies. The various kinds of competitors will each have their own cost patterns, which will make analysis of competition complex.

withdrawal threshold

4 The existence of a withdrawal threshold can also lead to more intensive competition. Withdrawal thresholds can make it more advantageous for a company to keep producing at a loss rather than incurring the costs involved in withdrawing from the market. Withdrawal from a market can also be affected by emotional factors. Leaders of a family company are sometimes not prepared to close down companies founded by their ancestors. The government may prevent retrenchment within a sector by determining minimal redundancy agreements.
5 Knowledge of individual competitors is also important. A competitor's tactics can be determined by its economic and other goals. Some managers are pre-occupied with making high returns, while others feel strongly about maintaining the independence of the organization. A decrease in profits will give rise to highly diversified responses, depending on the organization.

strategy

6 The behavior of competitors is also determined by the kind of strategy that the competitor has pursued in the past. For example, a competitor who has always had a low sales profile will not be able to change to a strategy based on the quality of the product overnight. Consider, for example, the brands of Yoko and Bang and Olufsen (B&O) in the consumer audio market.

strengths and weaknesses

7 The strengths and weaknesses of the organization will also determine the opportunities available to a competitor. A weak financial position will rarely allow large investments in product innovation or process development to take place.

All these factors combine to determine how aggressive or defensive a competitor will be, how and where it is vulnerable, which strategic changes it can carry through and what factors it will react to.

For example ...

... on the basis of an extensive competitive analysis a Swedish company once decided to enter the electronic scales market (as it had decided its competitors in this market were dormant), but not that for electronic cash registers (as it had decided that those competitors could not be beaten).

Analysis of the forces which affect industry competition
Competition in an industry is affected by a number of factors (see Fig 4.4).

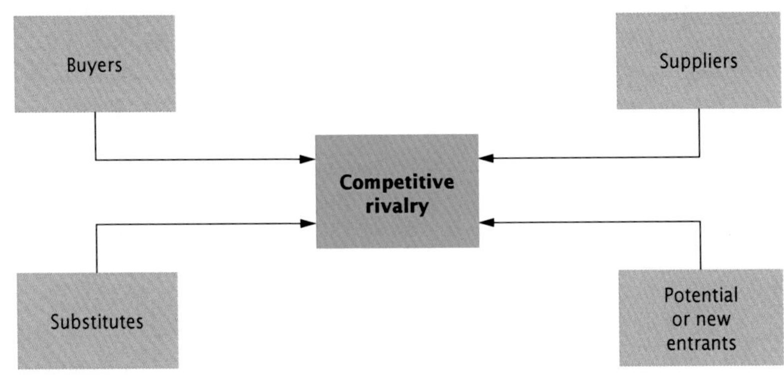

Figure 4.4 *Factors influencing competition in a market*

Source: *Porter*, 1980, revised version 2008

1 Buyers/Clients. Buyers/clients affect the degree of competition in two ways. First of all, the number of final customers will influence product sales levels. Some of the factors relating to the social environment discussed in Section 4.2.2 – for example, a decrease in the birth rate – will affect these numbers.

power position *degree of concentration*

Secondly, the influence exerted by the buyers/clients depends on the power position which they enjoy relative to the suppliers in the market. The power position can be determined by a great many factors, including the degree of concentration compared to that of the suppliers.

For example ...

... the insurance market shows a relatively high degree of concentration in the life insurance section and a relatively low degree of concentration in the accident insurance section. This can be explained by the low profit margins for accident insurers and the high ones for life insurers. The suppliers of a quality product often have a much stronger position than suppliers of a product which anyone can make. Think, for example, of the profit figures of Mercedes Benz compared to those of Peugeot and Renault. The buyers of exclusive brands are impressed by the quality of the products and are prepared to pay a premium for them.

purchase amount

The size of the purchase amount also plays a part. Research has shown that the profitability of producers of articles with a low unit price is often higher and more stable than the profitability of manufacturers of investment goods. It is not usual (or realistic) to negotiate the price of a tube of toothpaste at the checkout. When negotiating does have a chance of success, this can lead to suppliers being prepared to give price concessions. The supplier's fear of losing the client permanently enhances the negotiating power of the client and lowers the sales price and/or leads to a deterioration of the sales conditions from the point of view of the seller. Recognizing the power of clients is less important in existing markets, as not much can be done to change the situation. However it is a major consideration when entering new markets.

TOYOTA PRESSES SUPPLIERS ON PRICE

Toyota Motor is pressing suppliers to deliver unusually steep price cuts over the next few years as the Japanese carmaker seeks to reclaim its position as the industry's profit leader. The world's biggest carmaker told a gathering of suppliers this week that it expects to pay 30 per cent less for many components by the time it rolls out new models for 2013, according to people briefed on the matter.

Squeezing out cost savings has long been a Toyota hallmark but the company has intensified its efforts this year.
Analysts said that the price cuts demanded of suppliers were the largest in the company's recent history. 'Toyota is going to have to do a lot of work itself, by switching more quickly to global platforms and using more common part'.

Toyota is known to work closely with suppliers on the design and manufacturing of key components, a strategy that has led to the development of a tightly integrated procurement network. 'To achieve its cost-saving goals, the company may be forced to look further outside that network. Toyota is going to have to look at what components are commodities that can be bought more cheaply from China, for example.'

Toyota will have to balance cost savings with concerns about quality control, however.

Source: *Financial Times*, December 23, 2009

supplier power

2 Suppliers. The position with regard to supplier power is similar to that of client power. The manufacturer of a product is now in the position of being a client for raw materials, components and so on. Companies have occasionally decided to withdraw from a specific market because the suppliers have had such a strong position that the revenue from the activities would never have exceeded a marginal return.

For example ...

... collaboration on a European scale is common in the retail food area. Ahold (the Netherlands) has entered into a so-called strategic alliance with Argyll (UK) and Casino (France) in the hope of achieving lower purchase prices by joint purchase.

The availability of scarce *new raw materials* is, of course, having a major impact on market supply and consequently on the balance of power within markets (see sections 2.3.4 and 2.4), as demonstrated in recent years by the rapid expansion of economies such as the Chinese and Indian economies. Companies such as Corus and Philips are experiencing the consequences in terms of their bargaining power with their suppliers of raw materials as well as the opportunities for ongoing technological innovation and the development of substitute products.

substitute products

3 Substitute products or services. The appearance on the market of products or services which can take over the function of another product often has a negative influence on results. This often happens as a result of technological developments – for example, the ball-point pen drove the fountain pen off the market. The quartz watch, the diesel locomotive and more recently the compact disk and the video recorder are other products that have replaced existing products. The arrival of this kind of product leads in time to a decrease in the demand for the traditional product, which will result in increased competition between the traditional suppliers.
Studies relating to the introduction of new products show that it can take five to ten years before a new product has a fatal impact on the old products. In part, this can be explained by the slow reactions of clients. The new products often seem to suffer from growing

pains, and this lulls many traditional suppliers into a false sense of security. According to the studies, the blow is only fatal once perfected products have been introduced to the market.

new entrants

barriers to entry

4 Potential or new entrants. New entrants to the market lead to the intensification of competition. A larger number of market suppliers are now fighting for the same amount of sales. When considering whether new entrants to a market are likely, any barriers to entry – for example, the size of the investment required, access to distribution channels, existing government policy or the advantages of existing suppliers (patents, location, etc.) – should be identified.
In addition, an organization can consider which companies would want to enter a certain market. Although not exhaustive, the following groups of organizations are worth thinking about:
- Manufacturers from other regions (for example, Japan, Europe, but also regional chain stores that want to grow)
- Suppliers from other segments of the market who want to upgrade
- Manufacturers in adjacent fields (for example, telecommunication and data processing companies)

Experience shows that many companies underestimate the effects of new entrants to a market.

Concluding remarks

appraisal of an organization's environment

An appraisal of an organization's environment may be divided up into the categories of opportunities and threats. It is often tempting to view any change as a threat. However, if an organization reacts appropriately to changes in its environment, they can become an opportunity. It is important to consider the positive aspects of a signaled development. Experience shows that what is not seen often does harm, and what is seen often has a greater effect than expected.

total picture

The external appraisal should be concerned with drawing up a total picture of the situation the company can be expected to face. Any changes within the organization's environment should be highlighted, as should the ways in which they affect each other and are dependent on each other. The combined effect of a number of separate developments is often larger than the sum of the individual effects. Although such information is more difficult to obtain than other data, the importance of an organization allocating resources to such an analysis cannot be too highly stressed.

costs and revenues

In short, it is necessary to weigh up the costs and revenues involved in making a more in-depth analysis. If, for reasons of cost, it is decided to proceed no further with the investigation, the organization should at least try to form a picture of the possible positive and or/negative consequences of specific developments.

4.2.3 Internal appraisal: strengths and weaknesses

An internal appraisal of strengths and weaknesses can be described as a systematic analysis of the characteristics and functioning of an organization at a given moment in time. Such an analysis can relate to a set of circumstances in the past or in the future of the organization carrying out the research or another similar organization.
This appraisal of strengths and weaknesses can then be used as the starting point for further decision making and planning within the organization. Such an investigation has two objectives:

1 It highlights the shortcomings or weaknesses in skills and competencies which will need to be addressed in the short term if current performance is to be improved.
2 It identifies strengths which can form the basis and give direction to possibilities for further expansion of activities or diversification.

However, in such an appraisal it should be remembered that determination of strengths and weaknesses is always a relative judgment. The assessment of strengths and weaknesses can be carried out in two complementary ways: according to functional areas and according to results.

The functional areas approach

appraising strengths and weaknesses

A common method of appraising strengths and weaknesses is to examine the major functional areas. This involves an assessment of the skills and resources of the organization, complemented, if necessary, by support and specialist functions within other departments. Table 4.2 sets out a useful way of assessing strengths and weaknesses. Each of the functional areas is considered and assigned a score ranging from weak to strong.

Table 4.2 *Rating strengths and weaknesses in functional areas*

Area	Weak	Normal	Strong
Product development			
Purchasing			
Production			
Marketing			
Sales			
Human resources			
Finance			
Management/Organization			

The calculation of scores can be based on a comparison of competitors and/or a study of the demands of the markets. Such a judgment needs to be based on opinions and visions on the one hand and on the other, on hard, quantitative and financial data. Each functional area can be examined from a number of perspectives. In the following sections we will look at each of the functional areas in more detail and will identify measures of performance.

Product development

Performance considerations include the following: number of new products per year, new products as a percentage of sales, development costs as a percentage of sales, clarity of direction, employee know-how and external contacts.

To gain a clear picture, it is useful to gather information not only from the organization itself, but also from customers, suppliers and so on. The organization's own sense that everything is rosy can sometimes be contradicted by information from customers that competitors are developing many new products and are doing so quickly. It is important to remember that strengths in an existing market are not necessarily transferred to new markets. The innovation of products for the consumer market makes different demands on a product development department than the adjustment of a product for an existing commercial client.

Purchasing

Performance considerations include the following: information about suppliers, buying procedures, who decides, spreading of purchases over suppliers, purchase prices and purchase policies.

The relative importance of this department will depend on the extent to which the quality of the purchased raw materials, components or semi-finished goods is crucial to the organization's own product, or the purchase value is a large percentage of total sales revenues. The identification of goods which constitute a strategically important purchase is crucial.

In recent years, large companies have entered into closer cooperative ties with suppliers. Suppliers are more directly involved in the operations of the client organization and in return higher demands are made of them with regard to delivery times and quality. As a result, a close relationship will develop between the manufacturing process of the supplier and that of the client. The purchasing department provides the link between both manufacturing processes, and as a result, is of much greater importance than before. However, in many companies the purchasing function is still considered to be less important than, say, the production or sales functions.

Production

Performance considerations include the following: layout and routing, ageing of machinery, efficiency, quality, working methods, speed of stock turnover, utilization as a percentage of capacity, flexibility of production resources, machinery and so on, process automation and personnel quality. The above list of performance considerations can easily be expanded further. Comparisons of performance over time can be useful management tools. It is not uncommon for management at a certain point in time to base many of its decisions on facts relating to a situation in the recent past, though such data should be used with caution.
Management may sometimes consider purchase of the most modern and expensive machines to be important. However, if the market is such that such an investment cannot be justified, the consequence is often that a substantial depreciation component must be included in a cost price which is too high and which, in the end, reduces profitability.

Marketing

Performance considerations include the following: market knowledge, knowledge of marketing research techniques, sufficient experience, contact with external agencies, degree of external orientation, use of marketing mix components (product, price, place, promotion) and successful product launches.
Marketing is an important function in every business. However, some firms are more marketing oriented than others – for example, those producing branded consumer goods. The relative importance of the marketing function can be determined by comparisons with competitors. For example, the introduction of new products could be compared.

Sales

Performance considerations include the following: sales per salesperson, sales costs as a percentage of sales, composition of range, administration of order processing, distribution costs, number of contacts per salesperson per day and after-sales service.
With many products, sales and distribution costs constitute a significant percentage of the sales price. The amount of effort actually put into sales may also be crucial to the survival of a company. Accurate comparison with competitors is often possible; information can often be obtained from clients.

Personnel

Performance considerations include the following: the existence of a personnel department, personnel education/training policy, turnover/absenteeism/illness and reward systems.
Human resources are a crucial factor in the functioning of a company. Many companies state that their personnel is the most important production factor. Despite this it often turns out that little money is spent on the maintenance of human resources, few or no training courses are made available, and the levels of absenteeism, burn-out and staff turnover are high.

Finance

Performance considerations include the following: cash flow, working capital, equity/debt ratio, loans, liquidity ratios and return ratios.
The financial department can often make an accurate assessment of the actual position of an organization. Many financial publications provide good material for comparative purposes. Business associations in industry sectors and banks gather data which could be useful in such assessments.

Management/Organization

Performance considerations include the following: planning activities (strategic, organizational, operational; mid-term and short-term), accuracy of budgeting, quality of management information, task and function descriptions and goals per department/manager. Management and organization strength are often difficult to assess due to the difficulty of gathering such information. An organization may only be paying lip service to management ideals. Assessing the power, ambition, knowledge and skills of the managers and employees is an important part of an overall appraisal of a company's performance.

VW AND PORSCHE: VOLKSWAGEN AGREES TO BUY 42% OF PORSCHE

Europe's biggest carmaker, Volkswagen, is finally taking over Porsche after agreeing on Thursday to buy a 42% stake in the sports car unit of debt-ridden Porsche, ending months of fractious relations between the two companies.

Volkswagen expects the deal to be completed by 2011 and provide a total of 700 million euros ($999 million) in savings from synergies. The carmaker will launch a capital increase in its preference shares in the first half of 2010 to protect its credit after the merger and to fund the acquisition, it added.

Initially, Porsche's plan had been for the takeover to work the other way around. But in its efforts to raise its 51% stake in Volkswagen to 75%, Porsche built up huge debts as its plans coincided with the global credit crisis and falling demand for cars. Porsche also said on Thursday that its board had appointed Martin Winterkorn as chief executive of the new company with effect from Sept. 15. Winterkorn said the deal marked 'a new era' for both companies. 'Porsche is a real enrichment for our company's portfolio,' he said.

Last month, Porsche Chief Executive Wendelin Wiedeking agreed to step down after the Piech and Porsche families ended a longtime struggle over the future of the debt-laden German sports car maker they are part owners of. The logic was that new management would be better placed to smooth the path to a merger.

The integrated company will have 10 brands, adding the Porsche brand to a portfolio that already includes Audi, Bentley, Bugatti, Skoda, Seat and Lamborghini. VW has pledged it will give Porsche 'independence' and it said it would preserve its 'solid financial base.'

Source: *Forbes*, August 14, 2009, Javier Espinoza

The results approach

The results approach to appraising an organization's strengths and weaknesses concentrates on the financial performance of the various company activities, with particular emphasis on both profit potential and the strategic perspective of each of the activities. Once again, this appraisal has to be seen in the context of the appraisal of the organization's environment. Attention will largely be focused on the following:

1 Trends in the results. The historical pattern of performance may be investigated by studying data on measures such as profitability and sales. For large companies with diverse activities, it is useful to divide a detailed analysis into small units – for example, into business units – although it is important that when these smaller units are brought together, they form a complete whole. The analysis will highlight trends in the results (both positive and negative) and identify those parts of the company activities with performances deviating from the average for the organization.

2 Sources of profits. This analysis can be considered a further development of the analysis of trends. Profitability is analyzed from various perspectives, including the company's example, products, product groups, geographical areas, sales channels, distribution methods or client groups. The accuracy of this analysis obviously is highly dependent on the quality of the information that the organization's information system provides. A useful tool for such analysis is the portfolio analysis developed by the Boston Consulting Group, a US-based consultancy firm.

Several tools and techniques can be employed in any analysis of an organization's results. We will consider the following:
- Portfolio analysis and the product life cycle
- The experience curve
- The product portfolio matrix
- The policy matrix
- Competitor portfolio analysis

Portfolio analysis and the product life cycle
In portfolio analysis, the central financial measure is not profit as such, but cash flow (that is, net profit plus depreciation). The analysis is also based on each product having a commercial life cycle. If an organization wishes to survive, it must ensure that there are always adequate resources to fund new activities which will eventually replace older, no longer profitable activities.

product life cycle
cash flow

Every product goes through various stages of development – the product life cycle – from its launch on to the market to its withdrawal from that market. Each of these stages will have cash flow and sales patterns of their own, whether measured in units or revenue. The life cycle of some products – for example, iron and steel – is very long, while that of products such as fashion articles and CD singles is very short. The stages of the product life cycle are as follows:

introduction
- Introduction. The launch of a new product involves an investment in product development and marketing. At this stage it is not clear whether these costs will bear fruit. There is as yet no revenue, only expenditure.

growth
- Growth. As soon as the product comes on to the market, revenue is received but this is often not sufficient to cover the marketing and other costs. Maintaining quality and reliability is still a priority and will require continued investment.

maturity
- Maturity. The product has gained a substantial proportion of market share by this stage. Revenue should now exceed expenditure and consequently there is a positive cash flow.

decline
- Decline. In the last stage of the life cycle, revenue may be again exceeded by expenditure and the cash flow will again fall to zero or may even become negative. At this point it is advisable to withdraw the product from the market. In extreme cases, the company will have to be closed and redundancies will occur.

A product can only be considered successful when it has a positive total cash flow over the whole life cycle. Figure 4.5 compares the financial life cycle with the commercial life cycle of a product.

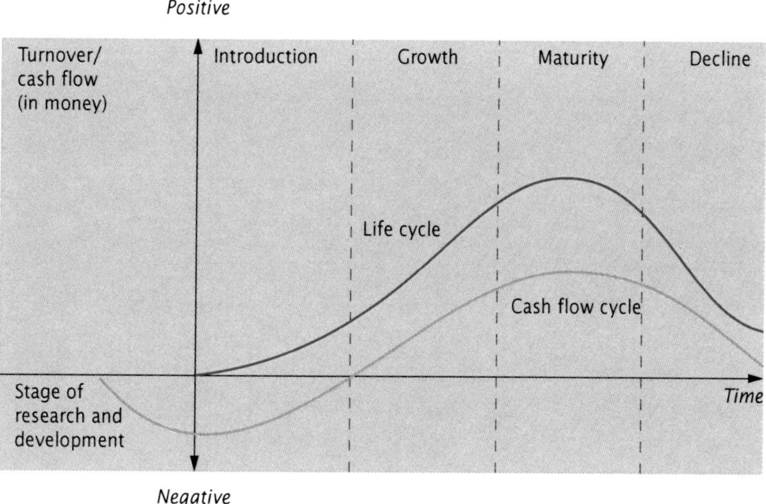

Figure 4.5
The relationship between the commercial and the financial life cycle

The experience curve

cumulated production levels

Research has shown that there is a relationship between cumulated production levels and reduction in costs which cannot simply be put down to economies of scale. This can result in a decrease of between 20 and 30 per cent in the cost of a product as the accumulated production of that product – that is, the total number of that product produced – is doubled. This relationship is explained by the so-called experience curve or learning curve. An increase in cumulated production is accompanied by the following:

- A higher level of productivity due to technological innovation
- A higher level of productivity due to the learning of skills via the routine nature of the process
- Economies of scale and specialization
- Improved product design

To achieve these possible savings, management will have to pay close attention to cost control. There are two important aspects to the 'experience effect'.

1 If an organization cannot match the cost savings of a competitor, this will lead to a less favorable cost position, and in turn to a less favorable competitive position.
2 If an organization grows more slowly than a competitor from a comparable starting position, this will also lead to a less favorable position.

The company with the lowest costs will be able to set the lowest prices in the market. Such a company will, in principle, obtain the highest sales and as a result the highest profits.
The effect of the experience curve in recent years can be seen in the reduction in price of electronic pocket calculators, compact disk players, personal computers, color televisions and airline tickets.

relative market share

An organization's ability to gain market share is also crucial. Its relative market share – that is, its own market share divided by that of its main competitor – will affect its ability to take advantage of the 'experience effect.' The experience effect should result in a better rate of return and cash flow position for the company with the higher market share.

The product portfolio matrix

It is now possible to construct a matrix (see Fig 4.6) in which the various activities of an organization can be plotted according to the growth of the market and the relative market share. The boundary between high and low market growth depends on the growth rate of the gross national product. If the growth expectations of the product are higher than this percentage, then the classification of high growth applies. In the reverse case, the classification of low growth applies.

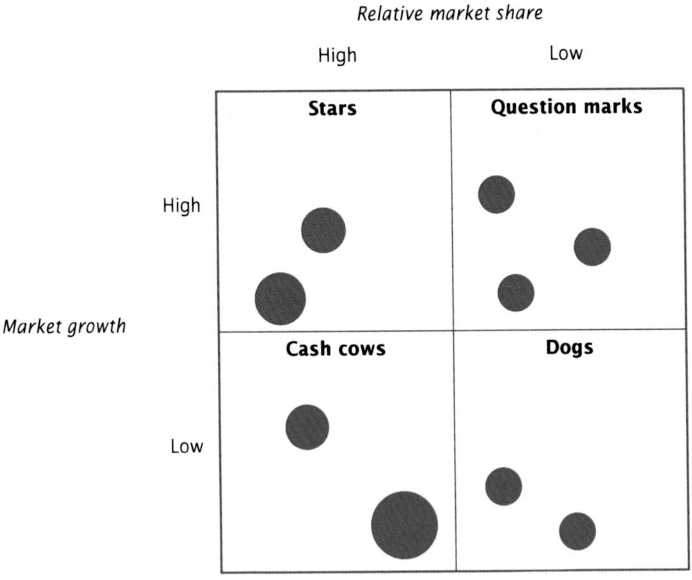

Figure 4.6
The ideal portfolio

As can be seen from Fig 4.6, each of the organization's activities appears in one of four categories – stars, question marks, dogs and cash cows. Each of the activities is depicted as a circle whose size reflects the level of sales. The current spread of activities and the implications for future cash flow are depicted in visual form.

cash cows
stars
question marks

Strategically, the financial resources which are earned from activities with low growth and high relative market share (cash cows) should be redeployed on activities which either follow the growth of the market (stars) or need to acquire a larger relative market share (question marks).

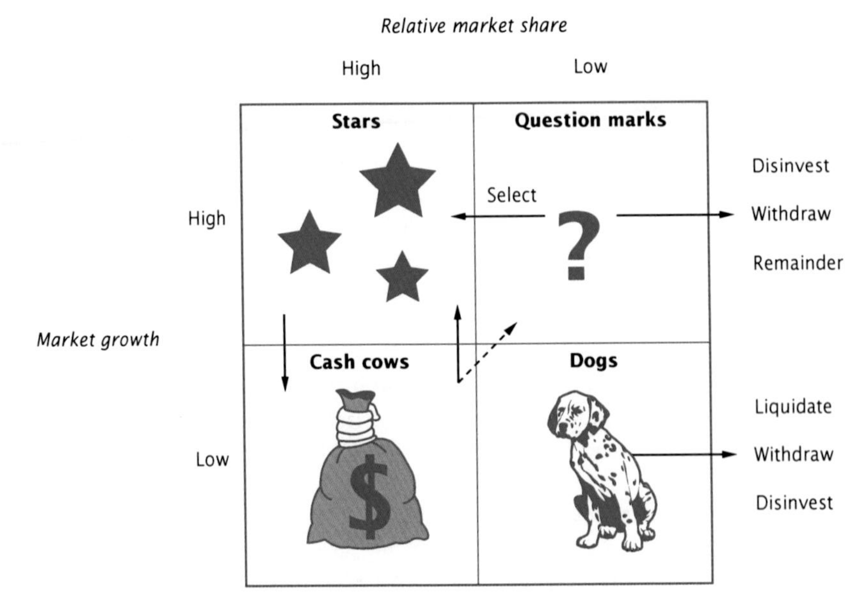

Figure 4.7
Normal pattern of a product–market combination

Since resources are seldom available to finance all new projects, choices will have to be made.

dogs Activities with a low relative market share and low market growth (dogs) will have to be withdrawn.

It is important for an organization that current and future cash flow be maintained. This means that the organization has to have a mix of products and activities which are situated at different stages of their life cycle. Only then can the organization finance its activities on an ongoing basis. A product usually develops from being a 'question mark' via 'star' to 'cash cow' and finally to 'dog'. The 'question marks' and 'stars' can only be developed if the 'cash cows' generate sufficient cash flows (see Fig 4.7). If at a certain point in time an organization only has 'cash cows' and no 'stars' or 'question marks,' future cash flows will rarely be assured.

Policy matrix

policy matrix A policy matrix has been developed (by Shell) from the portfolio concept already discussed. It represents all the available options open to a company when it is considering its future strategies. The horizontal axis of the policy matrix shows the prospects of the sector – that is, attractiveness of the industry – and on the vertical axis we find the 'competitive position' of the organization.

The prospects of the sector are a function of the following:

- Market growth
- Market quality
- Supply of resources
- Environmental influences

An organization's score for each of these factors depends on a number of factors. For example, market quality could be measured on the basis of competitive intensity, the degree of cyclical vulnerability and the threat of new entrants. The factors will vary depending on the particular characteristics of the activities.

To determine the overall prospects of the sector, a weighting needs to be applied according to the relative importance of each of the above mentioned factors (market growth, market quality, supply of resources and environmental influences). For each factor, weighting the score will give the weighted score. The sum of the weighted scores will give the total score for prospects of the sector (see Table 4.3).

Table 4.3 *Factor weighting for policy matrix*

Factor	Weighting	×	Score	=	Weighted score
Market growth		×		=	
Market quality		×		=	
Supply of resources		×		=	
Environmental influences		×		=	
Total score				=	

The competitive position of the organization in a specific sector is assessed based on the following:

- The market share
- Characteristics of the product
- Research and development

The total score is based on a number of different factors, in the same way as that for sector prospects. The position of the various activities is ultimately reflected diagrammatically (see Fig 4.8). Each of the cells gives an indication of which strategy could be followed.

Compared to the product portfolio matrix of the Boston Consulting Group, the policy matrix indicates strategic positions (nine instead of four) and a larger number of strategic options for an activity. The fundamental difference, however, is that in determining the relative positions in the matrix, many more factors must be considered and a high level of judgment is required (analytical, judgmental and strategic) from the managers involved.

Competitive position	*Attractiveness of the industry:* Unattractive	Average	Attractive
Weak	Disinvest	Phased withdrawal	Double or quit
Average	Phased withdrawal	Custodial growth	Try harder
Strong	Cash flow generation	Growth leader	Leader

Figure 4.8
The policy matrix

Interpretation of current portfolio matrices
At this point it may be useful to study some examples of portfolios and draw some conclusions from them.
From Portfolio A in Fig 4.9 (a policy matrix), it can be concluded that:

- There will be little profit
- There will not be adequate internally generated cash flows to finance expansion

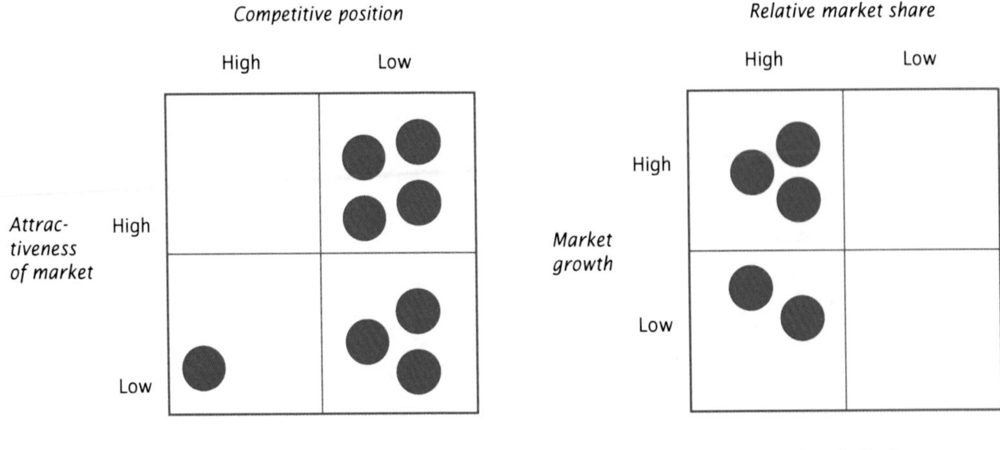

Figure 4.9
Portfolios A and B

A substantial proportion of sales stems from growing and attractive markets which require a high level of investment if the relative market share is to be improved (that is, the competitive position). A further sizeable percentage of sales stems from activities which are unattractive, and in the light of the relative market share, consequently yield little profit and as a result little cash flow.

From Portfolio B in Fig 4.9 (a product portfolio matrix), it can be concluded that:

- Cash flow is urgently needed
- High demands are being made of management
- Growth and profit are not secure

Substantial sales are being realized in growing markets. This makes heavy financial demands with regard to further growth, and yet relatively few financial resources are being made available. Management of the growth requires a high level of attention as these activities tend to develop by leaps and bounds (the personal computer market is an example of this).

Constructing future portfolio matrices

It is important to consider how portfolio matrices will be affected in the future if current policies are not changed. In Fig 4.10, the present position of a portfolio is shown in relation to the predicted position of the various elements in *x* years' time. Compared to earlier grids, picture has become more dynamic.

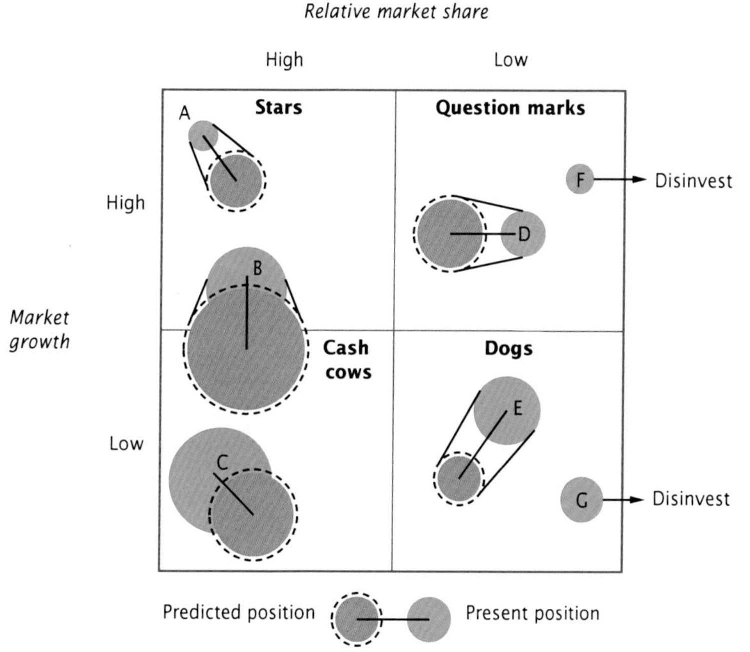

Figure 4.10
The current and projected portfolio

The information required for the building up of this future picture derives from the SWOT analysis (strengths, weaknesses, opportunities and threats). By adding this information to the portfolio analysis, management can make an estimation of the future position. The future picture can then be analyzed in the same manner as the present picture. By overlaying the picture of the present with the picture of the future situation, an insight can be gained into the dynamics of the portfolio.

Analysis of competitors' portfolios

An application of portfolio analysis which is becoming increasingly popular is analysis of the portfolios of competitors. Such a portfolio analysis is naturally likely to be less accurate than that of the organization itself, but that does not mean that useful conclusions cannot be derived from it.

For example ...

... suppose that on the basis of expected growth in the office automation sector, Xerox, the manufacturer of photocopying machines, planned to enter the mainframe computer market in competition with IBM. IBM would get wind of Xerox's plans. What could IBM do to avoid or neutralize the threat?

Using the approach of the Boston Consulting Group, the matrix in the next figure could be drawn up. From this matrix IBM could conclude that Xerox would have to make a very large investment in order to finance the new activity. The financial resources would have to come from the photocopying machines cash flow. IBM could frustrate the plans of Xerox by putting pressure on the cash flows of Xerox by selling the photocopying machines themselves at low prices. The investments required by IBM would be relatively low (the machines could be bought from suppliers) and IBM would not necessarily need to make a profit from this activity, because its only purpose would be to protect another activity (computers). Xerox would be in for a very difficult time.

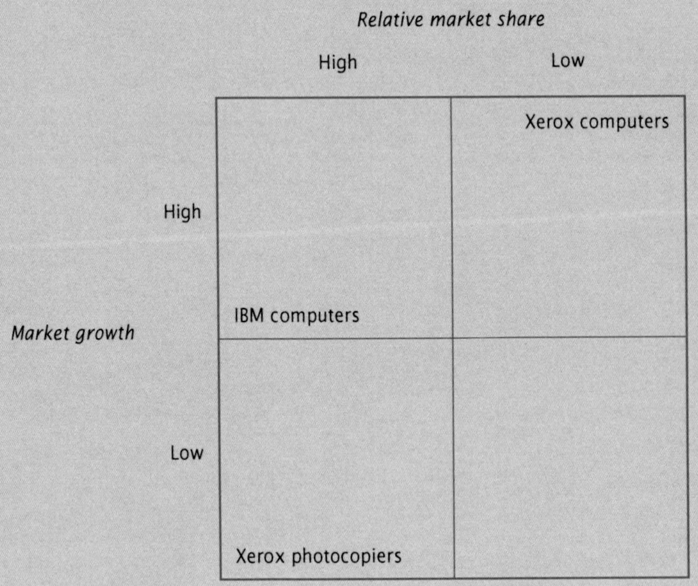

		Relative market share	
		High	Low
Market growth	High	IBM computers	Xerox computers
	Low	Xerox photocopiers	

Hypothetical product portfolio matrix showing relative position of IBM and Xerox products

Forming a complete picture

In this final stage of an analysis of an organization's strengths and weaknesses, all the data gathered in the preceding stages, both quantitative and qualitative, needs to be assimilated. In this respect it is helpful to relate the resources assigned to an activity to the results earned from it. This would eliminate the possibility of an innovative manager being burdened with the responsibility for a product which has entered the last stage of the life cycle. He or she would be better employed on the development of a promising new activity.

Drawing up the internal appraisal

An assessment of the strengths and weaknesses of an organization could best be conducted by a team of managers from inside the organization. This team should consist of managers from all levels. Experience shows that the position of managers in the company hierarchy affects their opinions, visions and the ways in which they search out answers to problems. If a team is made up of members from a variety of backgrounds, this should limit the distortion of information as much as possible.

It is often useful to discuss an appraisal of strengths and weaknesses with a number of external experts (such as non-executive directors, management consultants and accountants) who know the company well and who can see the company from the perspective of the sector. Such a discussion will also increase the objectivity of the total picture. It is, of course, possible to commission a management consultant to carry out the entire assessment of the strengths and weaknesses. This would maximize objectivity but does have the disadvantage that an external consultant does not always have sufficiently in-depth knowledge of the company and the sector, which might lead to a more superficial picture of the strengths and weaknesses.

The assessment could be based on a comparison with competitors and/or the demands of the markets. It needs to be based on both opinions and visions on the one hand, and 'hard,' quantitative and financial information on the other. The rating of each of the functional areas can only be given after an analysis of each area and after considering this from a number of aspects.

reliability of information

As in the whole process of strategy formulation, in the appraisal of internal strengths and weaknesses, problems regarding the reliability of information are sure to arise. Information about the organization itself is often readily available and reliable, although information about the past will sometimes have to be reconstructed. Accuracy and reliability are sometimes compromised due to constraints of time and money. The impact of such inaccuracies on the quality of the final overall picture must be taken into account. The analysis of competitors is fraught with problems of accuracy and reliability. In such an analysis, it is better to consciously work with, for example, both optimistic and pessimistic estimations than to pretend information is completely accurate.

4.2.4 *Gap appraisal*

In the preceding steps of the strategy formulation process, we determined the current (starting) position on the basis of a strategic profile, the expected opportunities and threats, and the organization's strengths and weaknesses. We must now address the question of whether the organization will be able to continue to fulfill its objectives in the coming years. In other words, will there be a strategic gap in the near future between the goals of the organization and the expected reality? This strategic problem is depicted in Fig 4.11.

strategic gap

In considering the possibility of a strategic gap, it is necessary to estimate the results the organization can expect if policies remain unchanged. The projection should determine whether the organization is able to realize its objectives without the strategy being adjusted. Of course, this can only happen against the background of the information gathered in the preceding steps of the strategy formulation process.

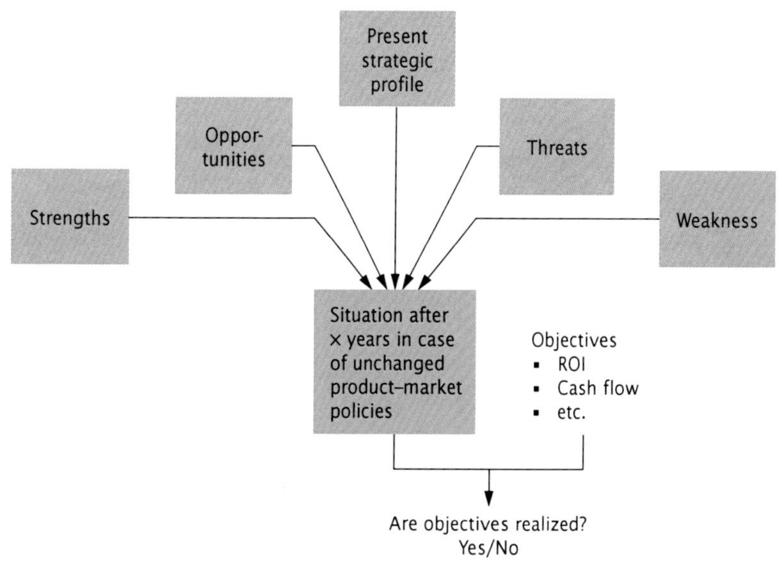

Figure 4.11
The strategic gap

For example ...

... such a projection can identify the effect of the development of a new market (an opportunity) and not having the services of a strong sales force (a weakness). The effect could be that a goal – for example, a projected rise in sales – will not be attained. Alternatively, entry of a new competitor into a market (a threat) where the organization has a cost disadvantage (a weakness) will lead to the conclusion that unless these is a policy change, results will suffer.

unchanged policies

The projected results in the case of unchanged policies can be compared to objectives and goals. From this it will be clear whether a strategic gap exists and whether the company needs to adjust or correct the strategy. In these projections, routine measures such as normal price adjustments are taken into account, but no changes such as the introduction of a completely new pricing policy. If for example it appears that in the future the return on invested capital or the cash flow will drop to an undesirable level, then alternatives need to be developed in order to close the gap between plans and reality.

4.2.5 *The development of strategic survival options*

If the objectives are not being attained, a set of survival options will have to be developed. The basis for their development will be an appraisal of the environment and an internal appraisal of the organization itself.
The first task is to establish what the organization is actually capable of. While it may be clear that a strategy gap exists, working out what the company can do to fill that gap is the important thing.

For example ...

Suppose there is an opening for a new product in the market (an opportunity). To exploit this opportunity, advanced technical knowledge is necessary (a condition). Unfortunately, the company has been spending little on research (a weak point) and as a result the company can probably not take advantage of the opportunity.
To take another example, suppose there is an opportunity to increase sales in a new market area (for example in Germany) which will involve the building up of a dealer network and substantial investment in central distribution facilities (a condition). However, if financial resources are limited (a weak point), the opportunity cannot be utilized in this form. The opportunity could probably be realized in a changed form – for example, by co-operating with another company which has been selling for some time to this market using an existing dealer network. If this company also has some extra financial resources, the sales from this market could be stimulated much more strongly.

product-market matrix

An organization has various growth possibilities. A well-known summary of strategic alternatives is Ansoff's product-market matrix (see Fig 4.12).

		Product	
		Present	New
Market	Present	Market penetration	Product development
	New	Market development	Diversification

Figure 4.12
The product-market matrix showing strategic alternatives

The various growth possibilities available to an organization are plotted on this matrix. These include the following:

market penetration
market development
product development
diversification

- Market penetration – growth from an existing position through an increase in product or market share.
- Market development – new markets are sought for the firm's products.
- Product development – new products are created to replace current ones.
- Diversification – an organization seeks out both new markets and new products.

We shall now consider each of the strategic alternatives in detail, dividing them into three groups:
- Strategies for current product-market activities (market penetration)
- Strategies for new product-market activities (product development, market development and diversification)
- Strategies for phasing out of product-market activities

Strategies for current product-market activities

Strategic alternatives within the framework of the present product-market activities involve competitive forces which are at work in the company's environment. These forces will already have been determined during the external appraisal of the organization's opportunities and threats at the business sector level (see Section 4.2.2). Some possible strategies are:
- Competitive strategies (including reduction of competition and improvement of competitive position)
- Strategies directed at buyers/clients
- Strategies directed at suppliers
- Strategies directed at largely identical products
- Strategies directed at new entrants

Competitive strategies

These strategies can be divided into two groups: those which reduce competition and those which improve the competitive position. In both cases the intended effect is the obtaining of better results.

reduction of competition

1 Reduction of competition. If the level of competition is reduced, the intensity of the rivalry often decreases and as a result economic results improve. Existing competition can be reduced in a number of ways. The number of competitors in a sector may be decreased by means of mergers and takeovers, resulting in a lower intensity of competition. A series of mergers or takeovers can also improve the competitive position of the company carrying out the takeover.

For example ...

... a foreign company operating in the field of welding took over some welding companies in several European countries. This led to both a drop in competition as well as greater opportunities for research made possible by the company's larger size which led to improvements in the company's competitive position. The other companies in the sector could not carry out product development research because of their small size.

In some circumstances, competition can be limited by market agreements. Cartel formation, examples of which can be found in areas such as transport (IATA, conferences) and banking services (minimum payment conditions, interest rates) is one way of doing this. A large number of physical goods are controlled by cartels (for example, bikes).

position improvement

2 Position improvement. Improvement of an organization's competitive position is a much more aggressive option than reduction of competition. There are various ways of going about this. For example:

- A company could strive to become the supplier with the lowest cost price. For example, Akzo-Nobel strives for the position of 'lowest cost producer' in a number of fabric market fields. This is referred to as a lowest cost strategy. *lowest cost strategy*
- A company could improve its position by lowering the break-even point. In this way, the company would become less vulnerable to fluctuations of the production volume.
  A number of the measures used in this area are the same as those used by a supplier with the lowest cost price.
- A company could also achieve a better position by clearly distinguishing the product from that of the competitors (differentiation strategy). This could be done by means of strategies such as changing the characteristics of the product, and/or improving the services that go along with the product. For example, the organization could become more attuned to the specific requirements of the customer than its competitors. When the product is clearly different from that of the competitor, competition will be based less on pricing policy. Akzo follows this strategy for some of its chemical products. The small Fiats and Lancias, which both belong to the same organization and are often also derived from the same technical concept, are another example. *differentiation strategy*

WHO KILLED THE NEW YORK TIMES?

Dan Kennedy: Arthur Sulzberger is being blamed for the newspaper's decline, but it's hard to see what he could have done differently.

The talk of the media world this week is Mark Bowden's exhaustive, 11,000-word *Vanity Fair* profile of Arthur Sulzberger Jr, the no-longer-boy-wonder publisher of the *New York Times* and chairman of its parent company.
Three years ago the New Yorker's mild-mannered media reporter, Ken Auletta, wrote an uncharacteristically harsh profile of Sulzberger, portraying him as immature and unsteady. Auletta found Sulzberger wanting on issues such as the Times' gullible reporting during the run-up to the war in Iraq, and, later, his coddling of the journalist who produced much of that coverage – Judith Miller – after she landed in jail for refusing to reveal that Dick Cheney aide Lewis 'Scooter' Libby had been her source in the Valerie Plame affair.

It was the Auletta piece, Bowden writes, that led to Sulzberger's decision not to be interviewed, which imbues much of his piece with a second-hand sensibility. Still, Bowden is sharp on Sulzberger's business missteps – constructing an expensive and unnecessary new headquarters, buying back shares just before the stock price plummeted, failing to invest in Google and eschewing a partnership with Amazon.com so as not to alienate Barnes & Noble, a major advertiser.

Now, those are some pretty boneheaded decisions. The problem is that Bowden can't tell us how things might have been different with more visionary leadership. No one can. Besides, the *Times* remains an enormous success with readers. In addition to selling a million papers every weekday and 1.4 million or so on Sundays, the *Times*' website draws 19.5 million unique visitors a month – nearly twice that of *USA Today*, its nearest newspaper competitor. For all its endlessly dissected shortcomings, it is still the model for serious public-interest journalism. And what does Bowden have to say about all that?

'Ever the dutiful son, he has made it his life's mission to maintain the excellence he inherited – to duplicate his father's achievement,' Bowden writes. 'He is a careful steward, when what the *Times* needs today is some wild-eyed genius of an entrepreneur.'

Bowden is not wrong. The entire business needs a major infusion of wild-eyed geniuses. But given the disappearance of once-great newspapers companies like Knight Ridder and the decline of Tribune, McClatchy and the like (even Rupert Murdoch is taking a beating, in part because he paid too much for the *Wall Street Journal*), it's hard to see how anyone could have made things better at the *Times* except at the margins.

Bowden correctly observes that disaggregation is breaking newspapers into smaller and smaller parts, with sites cropping up that specialise in politics, sports, the arts and other areas. But he pushes that observation too far in suggesting that Sulzberger should have driven the *Times* to embrace that model. Saving the *Times*, whether online, in print or both, is a worthy goal. If it can't be done, then let someone else preside over its reinvention as something else – or, as Bowden would have it, a collection of something elses.

For all his shortcomings, Sulzberger is doing the best he can. Given the circumstances, it's hard to see how anyone else could have done much better.

Source: *Guardian Unlimited*, March 31, 2009

Strategies directed at customers

Results can sometimes be improved over time by developing customer strategies. The more influential the client, the greater the pressure to achieve results.

market segmentation

- A company may sometimes focus on specific segments of the market which provide better profit opportunities. Careful market segmentation is needed for such tactics – a focus strategy – to succeed. The amount of profit contributed by each segment needs to be calculated. By spreading sales over a greater number of customers the company will become less dependent on individual customers and its negotiation position will improve.
- It is sometimes possible for a system to be set up whereby a client incurs high switching costs if suppliers are changed. This could be done by linking manufacturing processes closely. In the field of order processing, the supplier could provide the customer with a large amount of sales information through EDI (Electronic Data Interchange). This will offer clients the advantages of better information supply, a higher level of service and lower incidence of mistakes. Switching to another supplier would mean that clients no longer receive that information or would have to gather the information themselves and at considerable cost.

forward integration

- A company can improve its negotiation position with regard to the customer if there are realistic prospects of forward integration – that is the opportunity for the organization to become involved in distribution or to open its own stores.

Strategies directed at suppliers

An organization could adopt a number of strategies in an attempt to improve its position with regard to suppliers.

joint purchases

1 Companies or individuals could amalgamate to make joint purchases. With larger purchase contracts, the transaction costs would decrease and the organizations achieve a stronger purchase market position.

different suppliers

2 An organization could use a number of different suppliers in order to avoid becoming too dependent on a single one. This would give the organization a stronger negotiating position.

spreading purchases

3 Spreading purchases over a number of suppliers is also recommended as a way of reducing the risk of dependency. If one of the suppliers gets into difficulty, another supplier could perhaps make up any supply shortfall.

backward integration

4 The realistic possibility of backward integration – that is, the opportunity for the organization to become involved in the production of supplies – could also influence the supplier's negotiation position. Companies could also agree to work jointly towards the establishment of a new supplier.

It is important to have as much information available as possible on a supplier – for example, the supplier's financial position, sales, other clients, and so on. Having background information often makes it easier to understand and predict the actions of suppliers. It sometimes enables an organization and its suppliers to search for mutually satisfying solutions to problems.

Strategies directed at largely identical products produced by competitors

An organization can only hope to limit the success of an identical product. It is almost impossible to stop an identical product coming on to the market.

good value for money

1 To protect itself from the effects of largely identical products coming onto the market, the organization should ensure that in the eyes of the customer, the organization's product is giving good value for money. Such a strategy is also a good way of limiting the impact of competitors.

2 Customers often perceive new products that are largely identical to existing products as having a number of extra attractive features. To counteract this, the intrinsic qualities of the existing product need to be reinforced, possibly by means of advertising campaigns.

product innovation

3 An organization can strive for a greater degree of product innovation, although this will

make heavy demands on the organization with regard to research and development, financial capacity and managerial capabilities.

4 Once a largely identical product has achieved a good market position, it is sometimes possible for the manufacturer of an existing product to enter into manufacturing or marketing agreements with the producers of the other product.

Strategies directed at new market entrants

new market entrants

There is usually nothing an organization can do to prevent new market entrants. It is sometimes possible, however, to make entrance to the market less attractive for newcomers. This can be attained in a number of different ways, including the following:

- If distribution channels are a crucial factor for success within the sector, an organization can attempt to link sellers to its brand exclusively. For example, many official car dealers of well-known car brands are not allowed to sell any other brand. As a result, it is difficult for newcomers to build up a dealer network which covers a whole country, often a condition for business success.
- *avoid giving too much publicity to high profits* It is often advisable to avoid giving too much publicity to high profits as such publicity could make the market more attractive to new entrants. In contrast, when profits are low, publicity will discourage new entrants.
- *patent rights* New suppliers can be excluded from a market through the enforcement of patent rights. In this way, it is possible to legally prevent the number of competitors from increasing. This will not always be an advantage, however.

For example ...

... In the course of 1992, IBM launched a new series of personal computers onto the market in order to decrease the competitive pressure of so-called clones. Experts expected it to be technically possible to use the software developed for the new IBM on the new generation of clones, even though these exhibit technical differences.

- In rare cases, it is possible to influence the process of legislation in such a way that entrance onto a market is made almost impossible – for example, by quotas, tariffs or import restrictions. For example, in the US, the Harley-Davidson factory succeeded in having the import tariff on heavy Japanese motors raised from 4.4 per cent to more than 40 per cent.

Strategies for developing new activities

The Ansoff product-market grid can be used in an organization's search for new activities. New activities may take the form of product development, market development (including internationalization) or diversification.

CASE

Mini case study 4.3

Innovation's Accidental Enemies

Leaders who demand proof that a new idea will work inadvertently stifle innovation. There's a better way to react to brainstorms.

Once upon a time there was a very big bank. Its CEO wanted to better serve its best customers and hired some consultants to tell him what to do.

At the time, the very big bank served its high-net-worth customers at stately private banking offices in downtown branches. The consultants discovered that many of these wealthy customers – lawyers, executives, and partners in big professional services firms – were unattractive customers. They chose plain-vanilla services and were both demanding and price-sensitive.

But the consultants found another high-net-worth segment that was underserved: entrepreneurs and partners from smaller firms. These folks had diverse needs, such as mortgages for their homes and investment properties, and investor agreements for multipartner ventures. But they didn't want to bounce from one banking specialist to another to get a deal done, or drive to a fancy branch filled with high-backed chairs and wood-paneled walls, paid for with their fees. Instead, they wanted integrated, personalized service in their neighborhoods, with no divide between their commercial and personal banking services.

At the final meeting, the consultants presented a strategy built around this new segment. As they wrapped up, the CEO asked: 'Have any other big banks done this?' The lead consultant answered brightly, 'No, you'd be the first,' certain that this would seal the deal.

Not even close. The CEO killed the idea on the spot. And the very big bank's rivals lived happily ever after.
For many companies, innovation is the stuff of fairy tales: fanciful ideas and lurking dangers – all of it unconnected to reality. So it's no surprise that we find it such a struggle. Innovation is killed with the two deadliest words in business: Prove it.

When faced with a new idea, the boardroom impulse is to ask for proof in one of two flavors: deductive and inductive. With deduction, we apply a widely held rule. With induction, we develop a new rule from a wide range of data. In both cases, we use existing information to understand the issue in play. But for breakthroughs, there is no rule or pool of past data to provide certainty. So when a CEO, like our banker friend, demands evidence that an idea will succeed, he is driving innovation away.

Does that mean we are doomed to live in world devoid of proof – that innovation must be consigned to a realm of cross-our-fingers hopefulness? No, it's not so bleak. Instead, when facing an anomalous situation, we can turn to a third form of logic: abductive logic, the logic of what could be. To use abduction, we need to creatively assemble the disparate experiences and bits of data that seem relevant in order to make an inference – a logical leap – to the best possible conclusion.

At Research in Motion, makers of the ubiquitous BlackBerry, abductive logic is embedded in the culture. Mike Lazaridis, RIM's founder and co-CEO, encourages his people to explore big ideas and apparent paradoxes to push beyond what they can prove to be true in order to see what might be true.

In the mid-1990s, RIM was a modestly successful pager company. But Lazaridis saw potential in the idea of a portable e-mail device. He began to consider what it might look like, what it could do. He imagined something much smaller than a laptop but easier to type on than a phone. Laptops were already shrinking and bumping up against limitations on how small a QWERTY keyboard could reasonably get. Lazaridis stepped back to consider how a much tinier keyboard could be feasible – and he achieved a leap of logic: What if we typed using only our thumbs? He soon had a prototype and concrete feedback from it.

Asking what could be true – and jumping into the unknown – is critical to innovation. Nurturing the ideas that result, rather than killing them, can be the tricky part. But once a company clears this hurdle, it can leverage its efforts to produce the proof that leaders depend on to make commitments and turn the future into fact.

Source: *BusinessWeek*, January 25, 2010

Product development
An organization will try to sell other kinds of products to the existing group of clients by focusing on their other needs. For example, a supplier of everyday stationery such as writing paper or cash books and so on may start to supply word processors and cash registers. Product development could also involve a broadening of the existing range.

Market development
Improved results can also be achieved by starting to service other markets: other groups of clients and/or new geographical areas. The latter may involve exporting or setting up foreign subsidiaries, but greater geographical spread is also possible on a national basis – for example by building up a nationwide retail chain rather than restricting operations to the region from which the firm originates.

internationalization

In the light of European integration, internationalization has come to the fore as a strategic option. Organizations must decide whether they want to operate on an international basis, and, if so, by which means of market penetration strategy and in which countries.

Organizations that decide not to 'go international' cannot afford to lose sight of the consequences of this trend toward internationalization, as the nature of competition will change, both internationally and nationally. Strategies directed at increased internationalization may take one of three forms:

internationalization strategy
- Internationalization strategy – in theory, an extension of the export strategy, involving an attempt by the organization to expand abroad by using the same strategy it has used to gain greater national share.

multinational strategy
- Multinational strategy – a strategy aimed at international expansion but using tactics that target individual local markets in various parts of the world.

globalization strategy
- Globalization strategy – with organizations determining their competitive strategy from a global (or, for example, European) perspective and making decisions based on the company's positioning within this global market.

Diversification

Products which are new to the organization can be put on new markets. Some examples of diversified organizations are ITT, Thyssen Bornemisza, Daimler Benz, the Thomson Group and Hanson. Diversification can be very risky, because management may not know the products or the markets sufficiently well to lead the organization through the hard times. Conglomerate diversification is a situation where an organization is created whose constituent parts are in no way dependent on each other and there is no synergy between the parts.

conglomerate diversification

If there is a relationship between the various new activities – for example, in the technological, manufacturing or marketing fields – this is referred to as concentric diversification. Synergy effects can be achieved and the risks are also easier to forecast.

concentric diversification

New activities can be added to a portfolio, either through internal development or through forms of strategic collaboration (mergers, takeovers, alliances). The latter forms can be adopted quite quickly. Companies that have not merged will have to survive on their own by making internal changes. If these prove to be successful, they could be taken over.

Strategies for phasing out activities

A company can withdraw from an activity in two ways: by shutting down operations totally or partially or by selling the activity. A decision to shut down – for example, by closing a factory – is a very radical one, both in terms of its social impact and its economic consequences.
The sale of an activity could involve a third party or the existing management and personnel – referred to as a management buyout. Siemens, Philips and Unilever have all undergone management buyouts in recent years.

management buyout

4.2.6 The mission statement and criteria for evaluation and choice

Formulating a mission statement

During the strategic planning process, management will have to formulate the main objectives of the organization and decide on its main activities – that is, structure the organization's mission.

organization's mission

Vision, mission, goals

vision
mission

Vision is the envisaging of the organization's future by its executive management as well as the bringing to expression of ideals and values. This vision then has to be translated into a mission that the organization itself formulates. An organization's mission is a short description of the business's or institution's product or market activities and shows how the organization adds value and can achieve a durable and sustainable competitive advantage.

goals

The mission then has to be translated into goals: concrete results to be achieved. These are made part of a strategic business plan and then given shape in individual and departmental plans as well as in actual deeds. From words to actions, as it were: making things progressively more concrete and actual.

VISIONS: FROM DREAM TO REALITY

The trouble with visions is that so few are often realized.

Douglas Ready (the London Business School) and Jay Conger (Claremont McKenna College) have signalled a gap between inspiration and implementation. Things usually go as follows: top management develops a vision that everybody is enthusiastic about. However, over time, the excitement and inspiration ebbs away, the vision of the future is snuffed out and it's *business as usual* again.

The causes may be as follows:

- There are either too many major initiatives within the organization, and these threaten to submerge the vision
- or else management fails to provide its employees with the skills needed to put the vision into practice
- or else the vision is undermined by the established order (usually those that relate to the current core processes) within the business.

Source: *MIT Sloan Management Review*, winter 2008, kluwermanagement.nl/managementtrends

Mission statement

mission statement

A 'mission statement' specifies an organization's vision and direction for the following five to ten years. A mission statement is not subjected to ongoing redefinition. It expresses the nature and the range of the organization's market activities (horizontal, vertical and geographical). The following questions are addressed during the formulation of a mission statement:

- What do we want to be?
- What is our business? Where is our business heading?
- Who are our customers? Which customer group do we want to focus on?
- How can we best provide our customers with unique and lasting added value?

While these may seem fairly obvious questions, an organization's answers must be well considered and well thought out, because to a great extent they will determine the results of strategic planning. The mission should not be formulated in terms that are too narrow or too wide: on the one hand, it needs to give clear directions; on the other it should not immediately exclude a whole range of strategic alternatives. The mission is also an organizational directive and as such should be succinct and business-like and, most importantly, should engage, commit and motivate those to whom it is directed.

Criteria for evaluation and choice

In order to make a well considered choice from the alternatives, it is necessary to analyze the expected consequences of each alternative from a number of different perspectives. Both the short-term and long-term consequences can then be identified. A specific alternative could have long-term consequences that are very attractive, but at the same time could cause short-term problems. The reverse could also be the case. An alternative could appear desirable, and yet in practice could have some extremely undesirable consequences. The temptation to ignore or underestimate the undesired consequences and instead stress the positive aspects of an idea must be resisted.

Many of the consequences of a particular strategy can be quantified – for example, market growth, cash flow, etc. Others, such as environmental consequences or image improvement, are not quantifiable and yet are of great importance. Other criteria which should be kept in mind in the choice of strategic alternatives are the following:

consistency

- Consistency in terms of goals
- Consistency in terms of personal values
- Consistency in terms of capabilities
- The possibility of synergy

- The degree of risk and uncertainty
- The degree of flexibility
- The timing
- The implications for change

Consistency in terms of goals

A specific alternative could indeed support the goal of growth in a positive sense, but not a managerial desire to maintain a constant ratio between equity and debts. A new activity could demand more financial resources than could be raised by the organization itself, by shareholders or by other financial stakeholders. In such cases, further consideration of goals relating to growth and financial structures will have to take place, or else new alternatives will have to be sought.

Consistency in terms of personal values

personal values

The personal ambitions and preferences of top management are of great importance to the realization of planned development. Consistency of strategy and personal values is a real condition for success. A strategy of fast growth will demand a great deal of energy and fighting spirit from those at the top. Managers who prefer steady growth will find it hard to keep up.

culture of the organization

Recently, the importance of personal values to an organization has been demonstrated in studies of the so-called culture of the organization – that is, a system of values, norms and behavioral patterns which are shared by all employees. As Peters and Waterman suggest in In search of Excellence, a cohesive value pattern can be highly effective, though not always necessary for the successful implementation of all plans relating to new activities.

Consistency in terms of capabilities

capabilities

The successful execution of a strategy depends for an important part on the capabilities of the organization. An organization which chooses a path of product development as a strategy needs to have a good research and development department at its disposal. If this department is of mediocre quality, then such a strategy is doomed to failure. The same holds true if the financial possibilities are too limiting or the capabilities and skills of the managers are not appropriate.

The possibility of synergy

It is important to consider the extent to which new activities can be supported by and profit from the existing activities and capabilities of the organization. When certain advantages can be obtained from the combining of activities this is referred to as synergy.

synergy effects

Synergy effects are possible in the following areas:

- Sales – when new products can be sold through the existing channels.
- Production – when the same machines can be used for the manufacturing of new products.
- Investment – when the combination of activities demands lower investments in machinery and inventory than when individual activities are performed separately.
- Management – when problems relating to the new activity are similar to problems that have been resolved before.
- Finance – when some cash flow can be allocated to higher yielding activities, whether related or unrelated, which in combination give a higher rate of return.

There may be synergy benefits if, for example, the combining of old and new activities makes it possible to lower costs or shorten deadlines. It is sometimes very important for a company to be first to bring a certain product or service onto the market, because the profit margins will still be high and not yet affected by any competition. Once there is competition, production synergy might start to become of importance in meeting the threat. It is important to establish clearly whether the organization wants to be an innovator – in which case, synergy in the initial phase is of paramount importance – or a follower of new developments, in which case production synergy will be more important.

AKZO CAN SEE SYNERGY ADVANTAGES IN TAKEOVER OF ICI

The Dutch paint and chemical company has raised its estimated pre-tax annual synergy-related savings to an annual amount of €340, a rise of 20% in relation to the previously announced €280 million.

'We remain particularly optimistic about the progress of the integration,' according to Wijers. 'While the initial figures were merely estimations, they are now expectations based on inventories of concrete savings that extend to the very depths of ICI's structure. In addition, we have appointed employees who will be responsible for realizing these benefits.'

Of the €340 million, €180 million will come from Decorative Paints, €85 million from economies at head office and €75 million from economies of scale in purchasing. The company expects 85% of the synergy advantages to be realized within the first three years. It has reconfirmed another synergy-related advantage other than that related to cost saving: to be precise, an ongoing net value of €375 million, of which 75% is in the form of cash assets. It includes synergy-related effects such as the reduction of working capital by €100 million, the consolidation of product locations (€100 million) and costs saved by expansion its position in Asian (€100 million).

As Wijs put it: 'The synergy-related costs will be no higher than the previously mentioned figure of €300 million. In 2008, expenses will outweigh income, in 2009 the reverse will apply, and in 2011 and 2012, profits will predominate.'

Source: *Het Financieele Dagblad*, May 2008

negative synergy effects

Synergy effects can also be negative, i.e. they could fail to materialize. Some combinations of activities may have quite detrimental effects. If, for example, a company which up until now has been active within industrial markets decides to also market consumer goods, there is unlikely to be a positive synergy effect. The characteristics and the demands of these two markets are so different that companies which try to conquer the consumer market using an industrial market approach usually fail dramatically. There will obviously be no synergy between the two markets.

synergy myth

Mergers rarely improve synergy. In 50-70% of cases, mergers lower shareholder value. Synergy effects will come into play only if the constituent parts really fit and if they are individually effective as well. Saving the company via a merger aimed at achieving synergy is a myth. The constituent parties to a merger must be on an equal footing with each other too: if not, the collaboration will deteriorate into a power struggle (as evidenced by the Daimler-Chrysler merger).

SYNERGY AS MAGICAL FORMULA

Shareholders should not let their fears be allayed by the hocus-pocus preached by the advocates of mergers.

At the heart of a merger or a takeover is usually the idea that the sum of the parts is greater than the value of each individual part. This magical increase in value can be achieved by applying a magical formula known as *synergy*. By making cost savings, combining markets and sharing knowledge, one and one will add up to more than two. The greater the amount of that 'two plus' and the faster it can be earned the happier the shareholders and the greater the enthusiasm of the financial world. You do need good information to win them over, of course. In that respect, the advocates are never short of it: Yes, indeed, they *have* already carefully investigated the potential for synergy effects and they are good at presenting the advantages convincingly. But as the many merger scandals and the considerable damage caused by mergers have already shown us, that magic synergy formula rarely achieves what it hoped to achieve.

The reasons for the failure of the hocus-pocus of the advocates of mergers are well known. While the potential advantages of mergers can be set out in hard figures, the disadvantages are made light of. The directors underestimate the willingness and the ability of the merged organizations to jointly reap the greater benefits of the merger. Too little attention is paid to how competitors in the same sector will react, and too little account is made of the departure of top managerial staff and other valued employees, not to mention unexpected and unprovided-for changes within the company's external environment.

$1 \pm 1 = ?$

Source: *Management Scope*, September 2008

Degree of risk and uncertainty

risk and uncertainty

Since strategic decisions often involve the commitment of relatively large amounts of money for long periods of time, it is very important to examine the degree of risk and uncertainty entailed by such decisions. Is management willing and able to live with the increased risks and uncertainty? The dilemma is that projects with high profit expectations are often those that involve a higher degree of uncertainty. On the other hand, a company which only has low risk projects and therefore low profit expectations will rarely enjoy anything other than average economic results.

Degree of flexibility

flexibility

Strategic flexibility is the degree to which adjustments can be made to strategy in the light of changing circumstances, possibly as a means of countering uncertainty. High uncertainty with a low degree of flexibility is less attractive than high uncertainty with a relatively high degree of flexibility. In the case of chemical installations, for example, flexibility will be increased if buildings are erected as modules, because this means that they can be quickly converted to the production of a different or an altered product if a planned product does not perform according to plan.

Timing

timing

This is also an important factor in the choice of strategy. Being able to implement a strategy quickly means being ahead of competitors, with lower costs in the initial phase. A more gradual implementation offers the opportunity to adjust to changing circumstances, although higher costs will be incurred. In many lines of business, once a particular company has obtained a competitive advantage it is very difficult to eliminate it. The attempt by General Electric and European computer manufacturers to attack the position of IBM in the market for mainframe computers is an example of this. These attempts have led to large losses for the aggressors. However, the highly successful late entry of IBM into the market for personal computers is an example of how this can be done – as Apple learned to its cost.

The implications for change

The organization must address the question of to what extent its structure and capabilities will have to be changed to implement the new strategy. Organizations cannot change track overnight. The organizational structure often limits the flexibility and maneuverability of the organization.

maneuverability

For example ...

... IBM recognized that its existing procedures and structure would become a limiting factor in the development of its personal computer business. It resolved this problem by setting up a new division with a totally different internal structure to the rest of the company. An approach which was right for the established products was not appropriate for a new pioneering activity. In the early nineties, IBM's management decided to split up the organization into a number of discrete and independently operated units. The old structure had become too heavy and bureaucratic to cope with the speed of change in the computer market.

Monitoring a strategy

No matter how much thought goes into a strategy, the results are never completely assured. This is why it is always important to compare the results of a strategy with the original plan. If the results are disappointing, the causes need to be traced and the strategy needs to be adjusted or corrective action taken. The cause will sometimes be the strategy itself, especially if it was not sufficiently based on relevant factors. Competitors may counterattack or markets may react differently to expected. Whatever the outcome, the strategy will have to be adjusted to the new circumstances.

Crucial success factors

Before a strategic decision is made, the factors likely to prove crucial to the success of each strategy need to be listed (see Table 4.2). The crucial success factors can be compared to each other and to the SWOT analysis. This will produce a better picture of the following:

- The attainability, potential and risks associated with certain alternatives
- The action required to implement certain alternatives
- The factors which will affect the implementation of the strategy

Making a choice

Due to the dynamic nature of strategic problems making the final choice is never a simple procedure. Neither the organization nor its environment is a constant factor; each is a variable which is constantly changing. Strategic problems are characterized by uncertainty.
The subjective judgment of the managers involved in the strategy formulation process is consequently of crucial importance.

4.3 The organization of strategic planning

A company which wants to introduce strategic planning must decide how to organize the process. This section describes some possible approaches.

4.3.1 Forms of strategic planning organization

specialists

When strategic planning was in its infancy, it was an activity mostly carried out by a small team of specialists who made recommendations (often contentious) or even devised the strategy themselves. However, of the many plans developed by bright staff specialists, few were implemented. The problems were twofold: the plans were often not very realistic and the managers who were responsible for the implementation were not always highly motivated.

committee form of strategic planning

The committee form of strategic planning organization developed out of these growing pains. Line managers at various organizational levels are supported by one or two planning specialists. Such a committee may consist of one or two members from the board of directors, the finance director, the controller, some division managers or a few employees chosen for their knowledge and experience in some specific areas important to strategy formulation. Specialist knowledge of planning techniques and specialist knowledge of the market, production, and so on are thus brought together.

line managers

In recent years, a form of strategy organization with greater involvement by line managers has become increasingly common. The making of plans is viewed as a line activity and not left to staff specialists. In this form, planning specialists only play a supporting and coordinating role.

D BANK AIMS FOR RETAIL AND CORPORATE GROWTH

Deutsche Bank plans a significant expansion in Europe for its core retail and corporate banking business to compensate for an expected downturn in investment banking revenues.

The approach is part of a greater focus on basic consumer banking for Germany's largest bank, which will also set more conservative targets to curb leverage and raise capital ratios in an attempt to reassure nervous investors.

Mr Ackermann told a conference in London that Deutsche would build a European consumer platform, involving online banking, and expand its advisory business and branch network in Italy and Poland as well as at home. Further details, including expansion in Asia, are expected to be given today by Rainer Neske, Deutsche's head of private and corporate banking, at a Frankfurt conference.

'This is part of the new approach and growth strategy,' said a person familiar with the plans.

Mr Ackermann said investment banking remained a 'highly important business' for Deutsche, which had been one of the few European banks to challenge US banks in bulge-bracket investment banking before the onset of the financial crisis.

Deutsche's shares plunged 10.6 per cent to EUR38.94 yesterday.

Source: *Financial Times*, October 9, 2008

4.3.2 The organizational structure

The following organizational structure elements are important to the organization of the strategic planning process:

division of labor

- The division of labor. A functionally structured organization demands a different approach to such things as devising a product-market combination compared to an organization arranged in divisions (see Chapter 5).

degree of centralization/ decentralization

- The degree of centralization/decentralization. Strategy proposals need to be ratified. Those who make the decisions need to be in possession of both accurate information and the strategic plans themselves (see Chapter 6).

4.3.3 The strategic planning cycle

In large organizations with more than one division, the organization of the planning process partly depends on where the main focus of the planning activity lies: in the division (in which case the approach is considered to be 'bottom-up') or with the board of directors (an approach referred to as 'top-down').

bottom-up
top-down

The top-down approach

top-down approach

The planning cycle with a top-down approach is depicted in Fig 4.13.

1 The board of management draws up a planning document in which the expected results from the divisions are set out.
2 The divisional management converts these into relatively general plans and resubmits these to the corporate management.
3/4 The board of management approves these plans and sends them to the divisional management.
5 The individual departments in each division are asked to draw up plans relating to the functional fields.
6 The plans, along with their financial consequences, are assessed by the divisional management and, if judged appropriate, are sent to the corporate management.
7 The board of management approves these plans.
8/9 The plans are sent to the divisions and functional departments as task assignments and budgets.

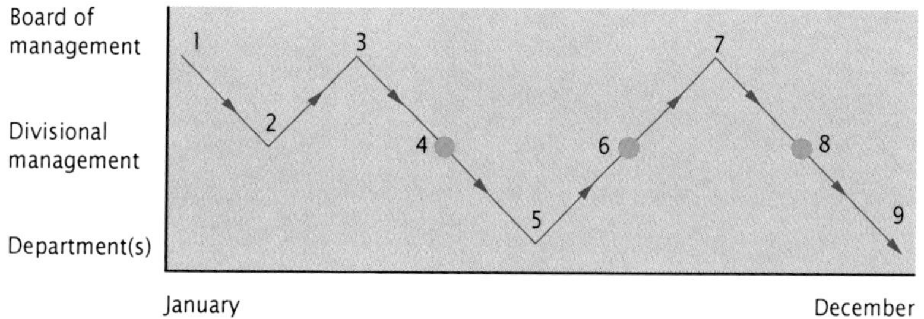

Figure 4.13
The top-down approach

In the case of the top-down approach, top management takes the initiative, though there is also a major contribution from the lower levels.

The bottom-up approach

bottom-up approach

The planning cycle for a bottom-up approach is depicted in Fig 4.14.

1 The various divisions or business units produce plans for the future.
2/3 These are assessed by the corporate management and, perhaps after revision, approved.
4 Divisional management sends the plans to the functional departments for more elaboration and budget preparation.
5/6 These plans and budgets are presented to the divisional management and, after approval, sent to the board of management for approval.
7/8 After approval, the plans and budgets are sent to the divisions and departments in the form of task assignments and budgets.

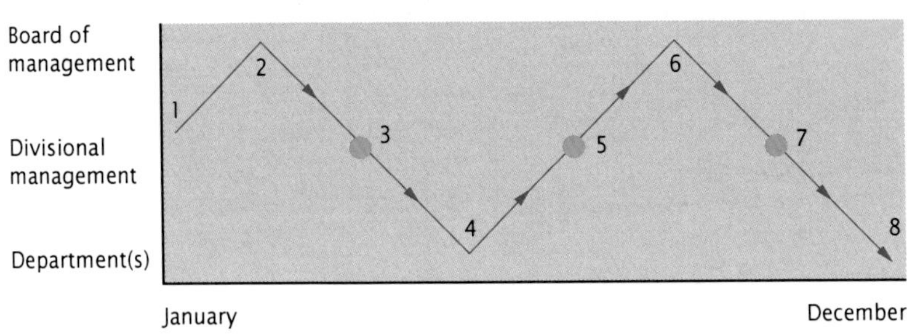

Figure 4.14
The bottom-up approach

Although the bottom-up approach offers advantages with regard to the motivation of those involved, there is always a danger that the planning will simply involve extending existing activities into the future. Innovation will be severely limited by such an approach. In companies where divisional or business unit management is not particularly innovative, very operationally oriented and has a low strategic capability, the top-down approach is the preferred form of strategic planning organization.
In a somewhat adapted form, Fig. 4.15 shows the model of strategy formulation described in Section 4.2.

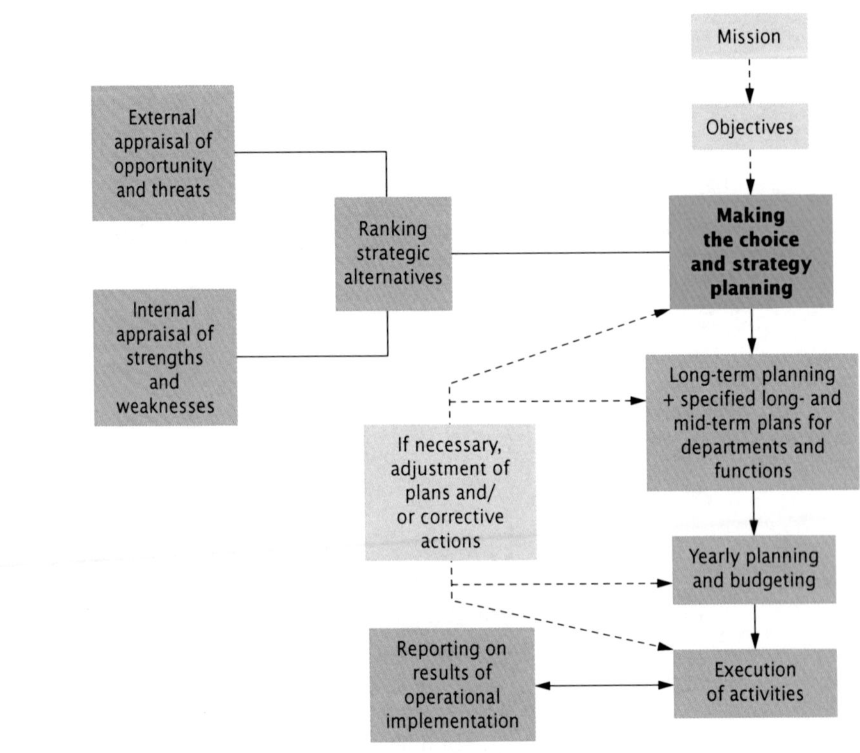

Figure 4.15
Strategy formulation and feedback

The adaptation mainly involves more detailed elaboration of plans for the functional fields. These are further split up into year plans and budgets. The reporting system with regard to implementation and possible feedback is also indicated. Problems associated with the reporting system and how to incorporate feedback will be covered in more detail in Chapter 9.

4.4 Strategic collaboration

In theory, strategic plans of various kinds can be implemented in collaboration with other organizations.

4.4.1 The decision to collaborate strategically

When an organization is considering whether it should enter into a cooperative relationship, it will need to take three factors into consideration:

costs
- The costs. If the costs of a strategic alternative are too high for an individual company, the strategy can still be implemented jointly with another organization. A higher level of financial resources than the organization could have supplied on its own will then be available.

risks
- The risks. If the risk of the strategy failing is great, it may be necessary to adopt other tactics. This would be indicated if, for example, failing to achieve the objectives would lead to the demise of the organization. A way of reducing the risk would be to spread it over other organizations by collaborating with them.

timing
- The timing of the introduction of the strategy. A company may need to implement a strategy quickly in order for it to be successful. If competitors can implement a strategy more quickly, the organization may start to lose ground due to, for example, higher cost levels (on the experience curve) or restricted access to distribution channels.

The relative importance of each of these considerations will vary from case to case.

4.4.2 Choosing a form of strategic collaboration

The choice of one form of strategic collaboration over another will be determined by the following factors:

strategic goals
1. The strategic goals of the organization. These might include the following: identifying and accessing new technologies and skills, acquiring knowledge and skills in relation to existing technologies, reacting quickly and effectively to market opportunities, gaining market share quickly, striving for cost price leadership – to name but a few. It is important to determine the strategic goals of a potential partner and to ensure that they do not conflict with the organization's goals.

market
2. The market in which the organization operates. The form the strategic collaboration takes will often depend on the type of market.

position in the product-market life cycle
3. The position in the product-market life cycle. Certain forms of strategic collaboration will be appropriate for new products and organizations while others will be suitable for mature organizations.

confidentiality
4. The need for confidentiality. Strategic collaboration can provide instant access to new technologies and skills, but also carries risks if the organization's own knowledge and skills are shared with a better organized partner.

The partners need to assess the effect the strategic collaboration will have on their businesses and draw up together a collaboration plan in which both the short- and long-term revenues for all parties are described. During the course of the collaboration, the plan will have to be objectively evaluated on an ongoing basis and adjusted to prevent potential conflict. Terms for the termination of the agreement should also be laid down in advance.

4.4.3 *Types of strategic collaboration*

Figure 4.16 shows some of the many forms strategic collaboration can take.

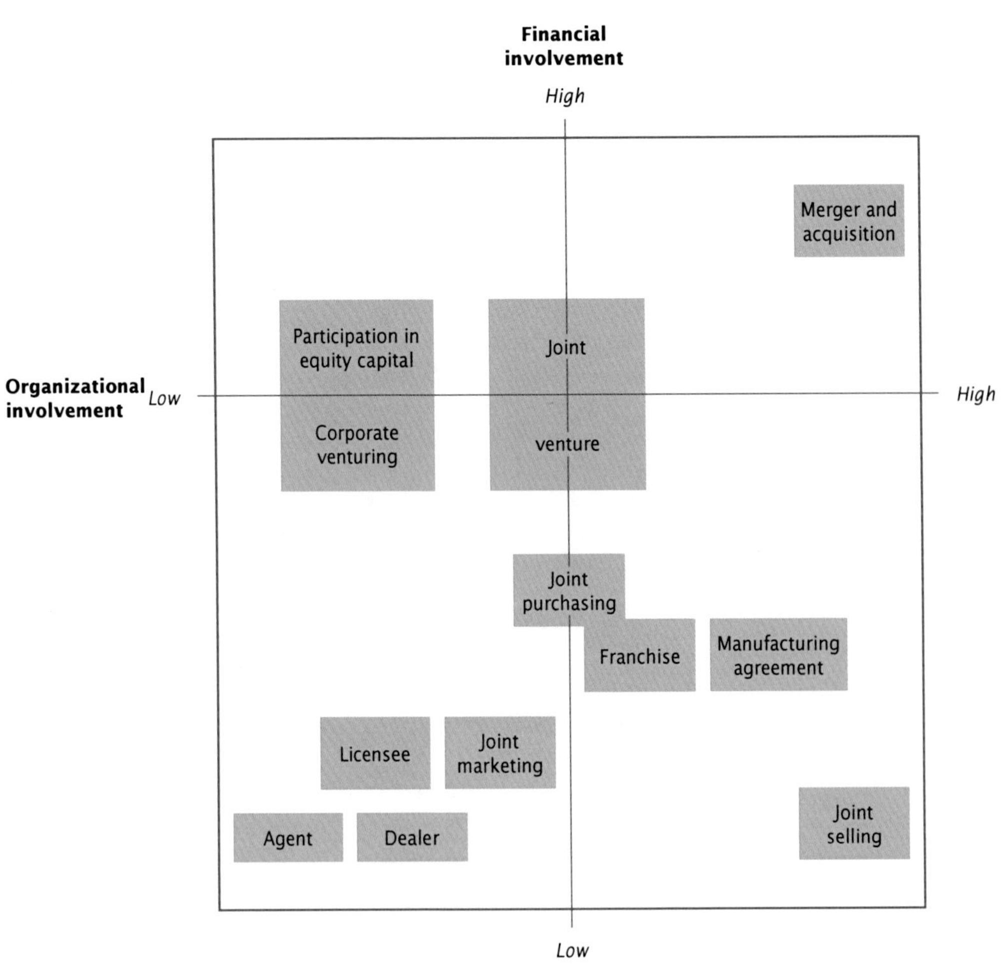

Figure 4.16
Forms of strategic collaboration

Source: *Huyzer*, 1990

The merger

merger A merger involves two companies joining together as equal partners. Mergers usually mean strategic plans can be implemented more quickly due to the sharing of manufacturing resources, distribution channels, brand names and know-how. Mergers also involve relatively minor financial consequences, usually involving a straightforward trading of shares. The disadvantages include the sharing of decision making and the sometimes difficult integration in terms of structure and culture of two companies whose needs are equally important and where responsibility is spread over a group structure.

The takeover

acquisition A takeover or acquisition involves one company buying up another via either a friendly or hostile offer. The advantages of acquisition are that complete control is gained over the activities of the acquired firm, and there can be virtually immediate mutual collaboration as long as a good implementation plan has been drawn up in advance. The disadvantages include the effects of domination by the holding company over the acquired firm in terms of financial policies, management, culture and operational procedures.

GROWTH STRATEGY: WHY MOST CROSS-BORDER DEALS END IN TEARS

Why do a cross-border merger?

1. It can be a quick way to enter a foreign market.
2. International diversification can stabilize cash flows and make the acquiring company appear less risky to financial markets.
3. It widens the opportunities to exploit a company's intangible assets – such as expertise and business processes.

Why not do a cross-border deal?

Acquirers experience lower stock performance when completing a cross-border deal than they do when closing a domestic deal. This is, principally, because of two factors: one, it is difficult to value a foreign target company accurately; and two, it is difficult to realise the synergies that are presumed to exist.

With such a weight of evidence against cross-border M&As, why do companies continue to shop overseas for off-the-peg opportunities? Agency conflicts may be partly to blame. From this view, the hunger of senior executives (agents) for power leads them to make decisions that are not in the best interests of shareholders (principals). Overseas acquisitions offering the glamour of jet-set deal making may be more attractive to self-aggrandising managers than domestic deals.

Source: *Financial Times*, May 30, 2005

The joint venture

joint venture

A joint venture involves two companies deciding to set up a third company together. The company that resulted from the joining of forces by Philips and Whirlpool in the field of household appliances is one such joint venture. One advantage of the joint venture form is that it gives access to the knowledge of another company which would otherwise not be available. Moreover, only limited financial resources are required (relative to acquisitions) and the risk is shared with another. The diffused control structure is sometimes a disadvantage.

NORTHWEST-KLM JOINT VENTURE

'Their model is what we're trying to achieve – they were pioneers.' The 1989 leveraged buy-out of Northwest Airlines, a troubled US carrier, would lay the framework for a new era in international air travel.

Twenty years after the buy-out, the joint venture that the Minnesota-based company eventually formed with one of its investors – the Dutch airline, KLM – remains the 'template' against which all other airline partnerships are measured, says Tom Horton, chief financial officer at rival American Airlines.

'Alliances are about revenues. If you want to rationalize costs, you merge'

'Their model is what we're trying to achieve over the next 18-24 months,' says Glen Hauenstein, an executive vice-president at Delta, now the world's largest airline and a venture partner with Air France-KLM. 'Northwest and KLM were the pioneers.'

Yet the two airlines were not always viewed that way.

By the late 1980s, KLM had grander ambitions than its limited domestic travel market could meet, and it soon sought ways to work in partnership with its newfound American investment.

Northwest was an also-ran airline, too. The carrier's hub cities in Minneapolis and Detroit were less than ideal for international routes, especially when compared to the coastal strongholds of peers such as American and United Airlines.

But in 1993, the US reached a landmark Open Skies accord with the Netherlands, removing restrictions that had limited their airlines' access to each other's airports. KLM and Northwest sought immunity from US antitrust laws, and by 1997 had formalised a joint venture.

The two airlines would soon come as close to operating one transatlantic network as possible without actually merging. They shared revenue on routes, merged sales forces, honoured one another's frequent-flyer miles, co-ordinated fares and standardized business-class seats.

By the time Northwest was sold to Delta last year, the venture had created $4bn in additional revenue and established the carrier's most profitable routes – such as Amsterdam to Minneapolis – according to a former Northwest executive.

Their success has inspired many imitators.

'When you look at something, and say "Hey, this is working", it spurs competition,' says Larry Kellner, Continental's chief executive. 'It says, "Hey, we better get on board." You see everyone else look at the model.'

Source: *Financial Times*, September 10, 2009

Franchising

franchising As a fourth possibility, independent companies can also collaborate in the form of franchising. Franchising provides the right for a sales system that has been developed for a particular branch to be exploited by another in return for a fee. Such a sales system will have been *franchiser* developed and tested for soundness by the so-called franchiser. He/she is prepared to give *franchisee* another party, the franchisee, the right to apply this sales system, to carry stock of a certain type, to use a certain sales formula and to carry the name and the emblem of the franchiser. The franchisee is contractually obliged to adhere to a number of arrangements and has to pay an annual fee. Franchising occurs in such fields as the hotel and catering industry, the car industry, the retail industry and chains such as Hema, Wimpy bars, McDonald's, Holiday Inn and so on. With franchising, decisions about set-up and exploitation are largely made by the franchising organization. The individual organization is subsumed within the larger entity. As a franchisee, one is obliged to stick to policy and execution rules as laid down by the central executive. Non-adherence to the guidelines will result in expulsion.

Exhibit 4.1

Alliance

Studies have shown that between 30% and 70% of alliances fail: they neither meet the goals of their parent companies nor deliver the operational or strategic benefits they promise to provide. In many cases, alliances resulted in shareholder value destruction for the companies that were engaged in these engagements. Strategic alliances are purposive relationships between two or more independent firms that involve the exchange, sharing, or co-development of resources or capabilities to achieve mutual relevant benefits (Gulati, 1995). Alliance success depends highly on the effective use of relevant coordination mechanisms to manage the interdependence between the (two or more) firms, and the successful development of trust between partners as the alliance evolves. This first of all supposes that a firm selected a complimentary, compatible and committed partner at the time of alliance formation and has made a relevant choice with respect to alliance design in terms of equity or contractual or relational governance. Firms, like Philips, improve their overall alliance success if they take systematic action to develop processes and talent in support of alliance management.

Source: Kale and Singh, 2009

The strategic alliance

strategic alliance

The strategic alliance involves two more or less equivalent companies co-operating on the basis of joint agreements. No new legal entities are set up. The risks are spread and the costs are divided among several partners. The agreements often have a precisely described goal and they are limited in time. As a result, control problems are less likely. Sometimes a long-term alliance is set up in the form of share participation by one of the parties concerned (see also Section 2.4.8).

NIKE EXCHANGES PHILIPS FOR APPLE

Runners can now keep track of their achievements on their own mini iPod. As they run, the data are recorded by a small device that Nike can build into its running shoes. The device then passes on the information to the athlete's digital music player. The new system has been made available thanks to a collaborative venture between Nike and the computer manufacturer Apple, which makes the iPod. Apple and Nike announced the venture yesterday. Up until a year ago, Nike and Philips had a similar collaborative agreement. (ANP)

Source: *NRC Handelsblad*, 24 May 2008

Joint manufacturing agreements

In joint manufacturing agreements, an organization works in partnership with a supplier firm to produce a product that meets the desired quality standards and delivery requirements of both companies. This is referred to as co-makership. During this process both partners will wish to keep their stocks of raw materials and components at an acceptable level, improve their competitive positions and reduce their costs as far as possible. In a certain sense this is a form of backward integration, although there is no change in the ownership of either firm. Independence is maintained; interdependence increases. The aim is an intensive, long-lasting relationship based on mutual trust.

co-makership

backward integration

A partner in a joint manufacturing agreement is not just a producer that supplies on the basis of detailed specifications issued by the outsourcing company; the partner is preferably also involved

in the design, development and production of the product concerned. Joint manufacturing agreements are common in some industrial sectors (such as the machinery, metal, synthetic products, electro-technical and rubber industries). It is also found in the services sector – for example in industries such as the cleaning and advertising industries.
It is important that the supplier have particular expertise in the production of a certain component or a specific product. The quality control system of the supplier needs to be of the highest standard.
The outsourcing company is confronted with a make-or-buy decision. As a rule a joint manufacturing agreement will give the outsourcing company a high level of added value and access to new knowledge and skills.

CASE

Mini case study 4.4

Beer M&A to continue – but with smaller deals

Heineken's acquisition of Femsa Cerveza is only the lip of the mug when it comes to mergers and acquisitions in the global beer industry.

The biggest was the 2008 deal that saw InBev take over Anheuser-Busch (BUD) for more than $50 billion, as well as Heineken (HEIA) and Carlsberg's joint acquisition of Scottish & Newcastle for $15 billion.

In 2005, a deal worth $3.3 billion created Molson Coors (TAP) through the merger of Molson and Coors. And Molson Coors got together with SABMiller (SAB) to form MillerCoors, which is a conglomeration of their U.S. interests.

Don't expect the trend to stop, but the complexion of future deals is likely to change. Currently, the four top players control about 50% of the global market. And in his remarks, Heineken CEO Francois van Boxmeer said it is likely they will soon gobble up another 25% between them.

'The trend toward global consolidation is continuing and there is a significant amount more of it that will happen,' said Benj Steinman, editor of Beer Marketer's Insights. Femsa accounts for only a couple of percentage points in the global market, he noted, so there is plenty of room for more acquisitions.

Source: *Market Watch*, January 11, 2010

For the outsourcing company, joint manufacturing agreements include the following advantages:
- The risks of new investments in technology are shared between the outsourcing organization and its supplier partner.
- The outsourcing company gains the full benefits of the supplier partner's expertise.
- It is possible to end the relationship with the supplier partner as soon as the product or component is no longer needed. Since the partnership has a contractual basis, there are no ownership or disinvestment problems.

They also entail some disadvantages:
- The outsourcing organization is dependent on its supplier partner for the supply of important components.
- Due to the fact that supplier partners tend to be relatively small companies, big orders may cause problems.
- There is a potential loss of specific knowledge through the supplier partner to a competitor since such companies often work for a network of outsourcing companies.

For the supplier partner, the joint manufacturing agreement carries the following advantages:
- It is able to focus on specialization.
- It can reduce its business risks by building a network of outsourcing companies to service.
- It limits the likelihood of being replaced by another supplier.

- It benefits from the knowledge of markets and experience of the outsourcing company.
- It optimizes the effects of being relatively small and flexible.

The following are the disadvantages:
- Due to the imbalance in power caused by the difference in size of the two companies, the supplier partner's position will be weaker.
- The supplier company has to meet the specifications of the outsourcing company, in respect of such things as quality or logistical processes.
- It can lose sight of developments in the market at the end of the chain.
- It has to accept the possibility of knowledge and experience being lost to the outsourcing company.

As forms of strategic collaboration, both co-makership and outsourcing often result in the outsourcing organization reducing investment in productive assets and cutting budgets for product design and research and development. After a certain period of time a relationship of dependency will develop due to the fact that the supplier partner is responsible for both product development and the process of manufacturing the product. In the meantime the supplier will have learned a great deal about the wishes, needs and requirements of the final user or consumer and have gained experience in the development of the product(s). The introduction onto the market by the supplier partner of a competing product could be effected quite quickly, with success assured. In the meantime, the competitive advantage of the outsourcing organization will have diminished substantially.

Expansion through mergers/takeover or networks

Theoretically, mergers or takeovers are more or less permanent, or at least they are designed to be so. This being the case, there may be good financial reasons for choosing a different collaborative model: one that can be got out of relatively easily. Such a model may also be more appropriate in the light of the dynamic changes that are taking place in society. Figure 4.17 ranks such collaborative models on a scale ranging from permanent to temporary.

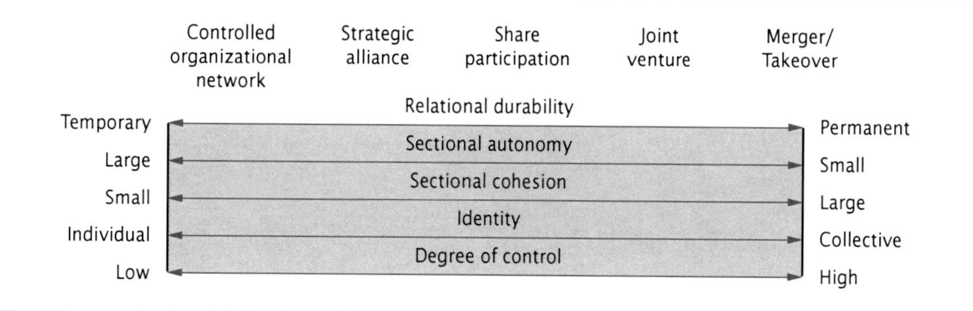

Figure 4.17 *Characterization of cooperative company models*

organizational network

Rapid developments within ICT, in particular those relating to the Internet, are making it possible to build an organizational network rapidly and to exploit and direct it from a strategic center. The benefits derive from network effects and greater profit margins because the partners are equal and financially and legally autonomous. Although mergers are supposed to have scale-related benefits, they often fall short of expectations.

The new entrepreneurial model, namely that of an external and/or internal organizational network (such as is described in Section 2.4.6), assumes that as an economic and legal entity, the huge organization operating on a world-wide scale with a strong central directive management has had its day. There has even been talk of the 'illusion of the global organization' and the end of 'the era of corporate imperialism.'

illusion of the global organization

4.5 Implementation of strategic plans

Implementation of strategic plans involves the drawing up of action plans for the various functional areas and usually also adjustments to the organizational structure and changes to the daily functioning of the organization processes and culture. (Changes in organizational structure are covered in greater detail in chapters 5, 6 and 7. The functioning of the organization, including the influences on the organizational structure is covered in more detail in chapters 8, 9 and 10.)

4.5.1 From overall strategy to functional plans

functional specifications

The translation of strategic plans into functional specifications is depicted in Fig 4.18.

In the light of a multitude of strategic options, it is not possible to lay down a set of simple and unequivocal rules for strategy implementation.

For example ...

... two car manufacturers want to enlarge their share of the market for smaller cars. Manufacturer A strives for sales improvement via a lowest cost strategy, while Manufacturer B strives to attain the same goal via a strategy of product differentiation. The implications for planning in the functional fields are very different. In the case of Manufacturer A, attention will be focused on the lowering of costs per unit of production. This can be attained by, for example, reducing manufacturing, sales and development costs. Manufacturer B will have to pay more attention to product development and marketing in order to bring the differences in performance compared with the other brands to the attention of the buying public.

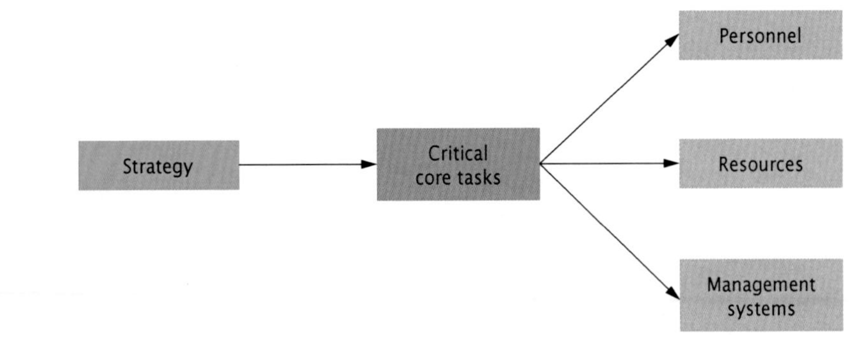

Figure 4.18 *Translation of strategic plan into functional specifications*

These two strategies directed at the same goal – an increase in sales – make completely different demands on the organization.
The translation of a strategic plan into individual tasks for existing functional fields involves determining which crucial core tasks can be derived from the plan. The detailed plans for functional fields and departments are further subdivided into annual plans and budgets. Implementation and feedback reports then have to be drawn up as plans are adjusted and appropriate corrective action is taken. (We return to this in Chapter 9.)
Once the crucial core tasks have been determined, their impact on the following areas needs to be explored:

- Personnel
- Equipment and machinery
- The managerial systems of the units and departments

The wide range of possible strategies will lead in turn to a correspondingly large number of crucial core tasks and an impact on personnel, resources and management systems. The conversion of the strategy into consequences for the functional areas is thus activity which makes very heavy demands on management with regard to creativity and insight into the problem. To take an example: a manufacturer is striving to improve its market position via a low-cost strategy. This strategy will have an impact on the following departments: product development, purchasing, production, marketing and sales.

Product development

For the final products, cost reduction will mean that the product development department has to obtain better results with the same resources or the same results with fewer resources. Some of the ways the department could go about this include the following:

- *Only choosing promising areas*. A consequence of this will be that fewer projects are set up, with lower overall costs as a result.
- *Research into the possibility of manufacturing under license*. This could have several outcomes. Firstly, getting the license would shorten the product development process. Secondly, the fixed-cost component of product development would be lowered and possibly replaced by a royalty agreement – an amount that has to be paid according to the sales of the new products. Thirdly, the level of uncertainty in product development will be much reduced if the organization uses the license to buy an existing and possibly well-tested process.
- *The introduction of application-directed processes*. This would enable basic research to be replaced by the less risky further development of existing products.

These core tasks may have an impact on the following areas:

personnel
1 In the personnel area:
   - a need for more education/training of personnel
   - possible need for new employees
   - possible redundancies among the present employees
   - possible redeployment/transfer of employees.

resources
2 In the resource area:
   - the purchase of new equipment may be required
   - the withdrawal from use or modification of existing equipment

managerial systems
3 In the managerial systems and procedures area:
   - better production control may be required
   - responsibilities and budgets may have to be reassigned
   - procedures with regard to engaging in license contracts may have to be drawn up

Purchasing

An overall reduction in costs could have the following consequences for the purchasing department.

- Better insight into market supply. This could mean that the members of the department are able to purchase on better terms.
- Better negotiating position. Contracts could be closed on better terms than before.
- Inventory control. Good inventory control could result in a corresponding decrease in the costs linked to this (fixed and variable).

These core tasks may have an impact on the following areas:

personnel
1 In the personnel area:
   - training required in negotiating skills
   - training in structuring and storing information
   - redeployment and expansion of personnel

resources
2 In the resource area:
   - better documentation of information may be required

- better availability of good communication equipment required (particularly important for those operating on the world market for raw materials as they need up-to-date information)

managerial systems

3 In the managerial systems and procedures area:
   - better coordination required between production and sales
   - procedures may need to be changed
   - operational norms may need to be set
   - budgeting may be affected
   - inventory control may need to be tightened

Production

In many sectors of business, production department costs account for the largest part of the cost price. This means that this department can probably also make the largest contribution to a reduction in the overall costs. Some of the ways it can reduce costs are as follows:

- *Better utilization of machinery, decreasing inventory levels of materials, using semi-finished components, changing layout and routing and so on.*
- *Cutting of delivery times.* Although this will not reduce costs directly, the speeding up of delivery times can have an indirect effect on costs.
- *Quality improvement.* This too has an indirect influence on costs: improving quality often means improved production processes resulting in less waste and therefore lower costs.
- *The introduction of shift work.* In capital-intensive companies, this would lead to a more intensive occupation of production capacity.

The core tasks may have an impact on the following areas:

personnel

1 In the personnel area:
   - supplementary training/education may be required
   - wider and more flexible availability and employability of personnel
   - changing composition and perhaps size of the workforce
   - changing of working hours

resources

2 In the resources area:
   - replacement or modification of machines
   - improvement of layout and routing
   - increase in flexibility
   - need for working capital

managerial systems

3 In the managerial systems and procedures area:
   - production planning
   - introduction of work consultation/quality circles
   - efficiency measurement: control and norms
   - reward systems

Marketing

The marketing department can make an indirect contribution to keeping costs down by making better analyses. The following are core tasks:

- *Analysis of sales patterns.* A detailed analysis of the sales patterns can sometimes lead to production being scheduled more efficiently. Costs may be high due to inventory levels, but these can be balanced out by a more even use of productive resources, which will result in a reduction in unit costs.
- *Analysis of profitability, product-customer groups and distribution channels.* In many companies, an analysis of this kind has brought to light considerable differences in the profitability of various categories. Tackling this discrepancy can lead both to better margins and to a reduction in manufacturing costs.
- *Analysis of the marketing mix.* Not all of the elements of the marketing mix – product, price, place and promotion – contribute to the same degree to the cost price of the product. Investigating how effective each element of the marketing mix is may show ways of reducing costs.

These core tasks may have an impact on the following areas:

personnel

1 In the personnel area:
  - the acquisition of new knowledge
  - flow and transfer of staff
  - career development

resources

2 In the resource area:
  - documentation
  - data processing equipment

managerial systems

3 In the managerial systems and procedures area:
  - market research
  - budgeting
  - cost/revenue analyses with regard to make-or-buy decisions (outsourcing)
  - role of finance department in analysis

Sales

The sales department (which includes distribution) can contribute to a reduction in overall costs in many ways. The following are core tasks:

- *Increasing sales*. Increased sales with unchanged sales costs will result in sales costs decreasing as a percentage of the cost price. This will also affect advertising costs, which form an important part of the sales costs of some categories of consumer products.
- *Reducing distribution costs*. Some kinds of physical distribution are cheaper than others. A well-considered choice of system can lead to a reduction in distribution costs.

These core tasks may have an impact on the following areas:

personnel

1 In the personnel area:
  - supplementary training
  - transferring or changing staff
  - better instruction

resources

2 In the resource area:
  - distribution systems (for example, type of truck)
  - automation of order processing, EDI

managerial systems

3 In the managerial systems and procedures area:
  - sales planning
  - sales statistics/visit reports per sales representative
  - reward system for sales personnel

4.5.2 From functional plans to budgets

Budgeting is a frequently used management technique. Budgeting is the translation of plans into financial terms. Fig. 4.19 shows how this fits into the overall process.

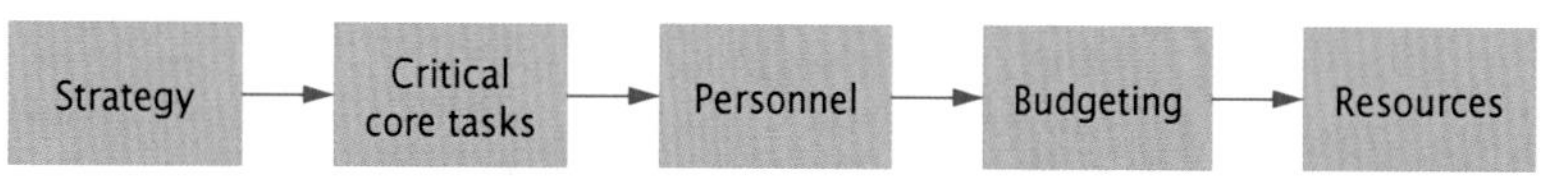

Figure 4.19
Translating a strategic plan into a budget

Action plans can be developed on the basis of the core tasks. The impact these core tasks are likely to have can be used as the basis for the formulation of norms and task assignments. These can be in the form of quality norms (for example, acceptable levels of waste), worked hours per employee, and so on. The budget expresses these task assignments in financial

budget

terms, thereby enabling costing of the policy. The budget will thus fulfill a communication function. The advantage of using budgets is that they enable the success or failure of the plan to be assessed after it has been implemented (see Fig 4.20).

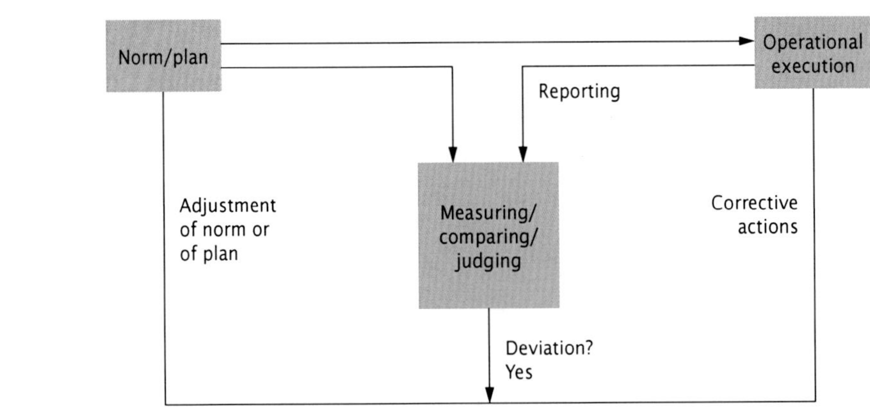

Figure 4.20
A control process model

For a budgeting system to be effective, it has to be clear where responsibility for the execution of tasks or the attainment of results lies. For this, a clear organizational structure is necessary, one in which responsibility and the accompanying duties and authority are clearly set out. (Elaboration of plans and budgets will be covered in Chapter 9.)

Finally, two points need to be made in relation to the use of budgeting in the implementation of strategic plans. Firstly, an organization needs to be careful that norms and goals do not overrule budgets. Budgeting is not only a means of allotting funds to the functional fields, but also a means of verifying the accuracy of strategic decisions and the assumptions on which these are based. Secondly, existing managerial priorities may exert an influence. There may be a certain amount of resistance, both implicit and explicit, to the budgeting process.

assumptions

4.6 Managing organizational resistance

The strategic planning process involves the considered selection of certain courses of action from a range of alternatives. The logical next step in the strategy formulation process is the implementation of the strategy. In practice, this is often delayed and often turns out to be more expensive than budgeted for. This applies as much to product and market development as it does to mergers and takeovers. The reason for this discrepancy is often an inaccurate estimate of the willingness and level of acceptance of the strategy among those involved in its implementation. This resistance will vary in nature depending on whether it is considered from the perspective of the individual or the group.

resistance

individual resistance
uncertainty
personal interests

- Individual resistance is likely to be derived from two factors: uncertainty and personal interests. If managers cannot estimate the importance and the consequences of the changes brought about by the strategy, they are likely to feel uncertain. The strategy may involve risks which the individual has trouble coping with. The manager may fear redundancy or may not be able to fulfill the new task.
- A manager may also resist a proposed strategy for understandable reasons of self interest. This may be the case if the manager sees his or her position, power, income or status threatened. For example, the manager of a well-performing division or business unit who is judged on the level of his or her returns will resist strategies which will result in a decrease in returns.

group resistance
values and norms

- Group resistance is often aroused when the new strategy is perceived to be at odds with the existing organizational culture – its values and norms. The same factors that give rise to individual uncertainty may also be at work. These values and norms may, for example, reinforce the importance of the market approach. The resistance may be based on the quality a group feels it owns. Another possibility is that the group considers that the choice has not been based on relevant criteria. It may, for example, demonstrate resistance to environmental and labor market developments. Groups resist strategic changes which threaten the position, values and norms of the group.

There are three ways in which such resistance can be reduced or eliminated entirely.

reasoned arguments

1 *Overcoming resistance with the aid of reasoned arguments.* The person or group who is resisting may not be sufficiently well informed about the new strategy or aware of the advantages it will bring. Such resistance to implementation can be eliminated by giving sufficient information and showing that these are good reasons for the changes.

training and education

2 *Overcoming resistance via behavioral changes.* Resistance may sometimes be aroused because the strategic plan is in conflict with the values and norms of those involved. This form of resistance can be overcome by organizing training and education aimed at behavioral changes. The widespread participation of stakeholders in the strategic formulation process is crucial. It can be obtained by, for example, using the 'bottom-up' approach to the planning cycle (see Section 4.3.3). In this respect, there is a link between strategy formulation and the 'learning organization' (see Chapter 3).

rewards and punishments

3 *Overcoming resistance with the aid of rewards and punishments, positive encouragement or negative sanctions.* This tactic is often used if resistance can still be detected after trying to remove it using the approaches outlined above.

The attitude of top management with regard to the strategic plans naturally plays a part in all three techniques. Recognizing and management of the resistance should be a part of the strategy formulation process prior to implementation of the plans. This must form part of the process as outlined in Fig. 4.15. The problem of resistance needs to be addressed and investigated during the internal appraisal and via the criteria used in the selection of preferred alternatives – particularly with regard to its impact on the criterion of timing.

4.7 The emerging strategy

Although it is becoming increasingly common for strategic or business plans to be drawn up because parties within the organization's external environment request them – for example, the bank in the case of a request for investment finance or government institutions in the case of a request for a subsidy – many organizations do not have explicit written strategic plans which are the fruit of formal procedures. This does not mean that there is no strategy at all, however. On the contrary, the strategy is situated in, so to speak, the head, heart and hands of the entrepreneur, who often knows what the business should be doing and implements this 'plan' with a considerable degree of consistency.

emerging strategy · *crafting strategy* · *actual strategy*

If such a pattern gradually emerges it is called an emerging strategy (Mintzberg, 1987). With hard work and care, this pattern will be refined and function as a coordinating force behind the business enterprises. Strategy will develop in the traditional way (referred to as 'crafting strategy' by Mintzberg). Behind a recognizable pattern of decisions and action there will be another set of decisions made more or less intuitively. Consequently, it will be the actual strategy the business is pursuing rather than any formalized plans that sets the tone and from which the organization's real intentions can be determined. The good intentions may never be realized.

In organizations with an emerging strategy, there may well be a good picture of the environment in the minds of the staff, a form of accepted leadership (intuitive or charismatic) and a relatively strong informal organization with a lot of 'feelers' in the business world and which creates and implements its own strategies. In this situation, there is usually a good understanding of the forces that have influenced the organization in the past and are likely to continue to exert an influence.

Frequently, however, an intuitive approach to strategy is not enough and the enterprise's measures will be characterized by a lack of consistency. Instead of a detectable pattern there will be a lack of internal cohesion. The business may embark on a certain course of action, but then abruptly terminate it or change course. In other words, the organization will not have a clear sense of direction and its driving forces will, to some extent, be arbitrary. If the organization can be characterized thus, the only way it will be able to survive is by starting out afresh with a new vision of its goals, a new organizational pattern, team building, greater internal and external direction and a new sense of purpose. Under such circumstances, the insights and methods outlined in Section 4.2 would be an appropriate basis for solving the organization's problems.
All this leads us to the conclusion that it is almost impossible for an organization *not* to concern itself with strategy in some shape or form. This applies as much to large companies as it does to small companies, even if limited resources prevent them from engaging in formal strategy formulation processes.

Summary

- The central strategy formulation issue is how an organization can ensure its survival by reacting to developments in its external environment in such a way that optimum use is made of its own capabilities. The gaining of a competitive advantage over other organizations is a key factor in this.
- Explicit strategy formulation gives direction to an organization and coherence to its enterprises and organization. Better results are often the result.
- Strategy formulation procedures can take various forms. Sometimes an intuitive approach is taken and the strategy mapped out retrospectively.
- This chapter's definition of strategy and description of the various approaches to resolving strategy problems apply to both commercial and non-profit organizations.
- A strategy formulation process should involve the following steps:
  - *Determining the strategic profile* – objectives, areas of current activities, competitive advantage and synergy.
  - *External appraisal of the environment in search of opportunities and threats* – with regard to the societal environment (demographic factors, economic factors, societal factors, technological factors, ecological factors, political factors) and with regard to the analysis of the sector (competition/intensity of rivalry, buyers/clients, suppliers, substitute products, new entrants).
  - *Internal appraisal in search of strengths and weaknesses* – an analysis of the functional departments compared to the demands of the market and the performance of the competition. Portfolio analysis is a useful instrument in such an appraisal from the point of view of results. It is not enough simply to gather opinions and visions; they must be supported by 'hard' information. When facts and opinions contradict each other, further analysis is necessary. Not only can an opinion be wrong, but the information and/or interpretation of it can be also incorrect.
  - *Determining a strategic gap* – when the goals which are set and expected future results are not in line with each other. On the basis of the present strategic profile and the SWOT analysis an organization can draw conclusions regarding, for example, the position the organization will be in five years' time.
- *Drawing up strategic options* – with the aim of closing the strategic gap. Alternatives can lie within or outside present activities or can involve the phasing out of activities. For each of these groups of alternatives, many different forms of strategy can be considered.
- *Evaluating and making a choice from various options.* The first step is the determining of the consequences of each alternative and testing them against the criteria of consistency, synergy, uncertainty/risk/ insecurity, flexibility, financial aspects and timing.
- *Translating the choice into plans for functional areas.* Resistance will occur in many cases. Information exchange, education and training are important instruments in the reduction of resistance to strategic change.
- In this way, strategy formulation is seen as a decision-making process in which the decision is taken whether to learn or not to learn new skills and knowledge. This forms the link between this chapter and Chapter 3, which dealt with decision making and creativity.

Discussion questions

1 With reference to *Management in Action* at the beginning of this chapter:
   a) Would you consider Nike's new strategy – focused on reshaping the managerial structure, redefining Nike's relationship with its fast-changing and digitally driven consumer, and adding 100 new company stores worldwide in three years – a well-developed strategy? Explain why.
   b) What would you suggest is the best strategy implementation approach for Nike?

2 'Strategy formulation requires substantial investments in terms of time and (financial) resources, so forget it.' Discuss this statement.

3 'Strategy formulation and competitive analysis are appropriate for profit organizations but inappropriate for non-profit organizations.' Discuss this statement.

4 In a sense, your participation in an educational program (such as a bachelor's degree in business administration) is like being in charge of a one-man organization. Analyze your decision to participate in this specific program using the concepts and tools provided in this chapter. Was it a conscious decision or a more intuitive one?

5 Decision-making and creativity (Chapter 3) and strategy formulation and strategic management (Chapter 4) deal with topics that relate to one another. Discuss several differences and similarities.

Research-based exercise

Successful Strategy Execution

Introduction
This research-based exercise is based on a research article by Neilson, Martin and Powers (2008), published in the *Harvard Business Review*. The research question, data collection, method, and some of the results of the research project are presented. The exercise consists of three questions based on the research article and the theory in this chapter. The answers should be based on both the theory in Chapter 4 and your own insights into the practical implications of your answer.

Research Question
Which organizational traits drive successful strategy execution?

Data Collection
The researchers have over the past five years invited many thousands of employees (about 25% of whom came from executive ranks) to complete an online assessment of their organizations' capabilities, a process that has generated a database of 125,000 profiles representing more than 1,000 companies, government agencies, and not-for profits in over 50 countries. To determine which of the 17 traits in our profiler are most strongly associated with excellence in execution, we looked at 31 companies in our database for which we had responses from at least 150 individual (anonymously completed) profiles, for a total of 26,743 responses.

Outcomes
The researchers found that:

- Employees at three out of every five companies rated their organization weak at strategy execution.
- Actions having to do with decision rights and information are far more important – about twice as effective – as improvements made to the other two building blocks: motivators and structure.
- The top four of most important organizational traits fostering strategy execution are:
  - 'Everyone has a good idea of the decisions and actions for which he or she is responsible';
  - 'Important information about the competitive environment gets to headquarters quickly';
  - 'Once made, decisions are rarely second-guessed';
  - 'Information flows freely across organizational boundaries'.

Questions

1 Explain why the organizational traits decision rights and information are considered more important than motivators and structure.

2 Do you think that the study's findings are consistent, as suggested by the data collection approach, across different industries (e.g., service versus production) and firms (e.g., small versus large)? Give reasons for your answer.

3 Explain how firms can improve the way they implement their strategy.

CASE

Management case study

Danone plans to retain its water brands

French group sticks to health strategy

Danone, the owner of the Evian and Volvic bottled water brands, plans to stick with its water business in developed markets amid calls to sell it as sales recover slowly from an environmental backlash.

A sharp drop in bottled water sales in developed markets in 2008 and early 2009 led some financial analysts to argue that Danone should sell its bottled water brands – which account for about 18 per cent of total company sales – and focus on yoghurts and baby Foods.

But Franck Riboud, Danone's chief executive, is understood to be committed to bottled water in developed markets because it fits with the French group's strategy of owning products with health benefits.

Water will also play an important part in Danone's strategy of switching from sales growth to volume growth – a strategy other consumer goods companies such as Unilever are also pursuing as it becomes harder to push through price rises to retailers.

Danone, along with other big bottled water producers such as Nestlé (owner of the Vittel, Perrier and Poland Spring brands) and PepsiCo (owner of the Aquafina brand), was hit hard by an environmental backlash against water bottled in plastic last year in the US and Europe. Consumers ditched branded bottled water brands for private label brands, soft drinks and tap water.

However, companies have responded to consumers' concerns by using more recycled plastic in their bottles – Nestlé has been trialling a brand in the US called Re-Source made with 25 per cent recycled plastic – leading sales to recover in some markets.

After reporting quarterly declines in underlying water sales in late 2008 and the first half of 2009, Danone's third-quarter underlying water sales rose 4.6 per cent, while volumes jumped 9.8 per cent. Danone is expected to produce underlying water sales growth of about 3 per cent in the fourth quarter.

Although emerging markets such as Indonesia, Argentina and Mexico were the main drivers of growth, Danone's volumes had shown signs of structural recovery in west European markets such as France, Germany and the UK.

But in the US, where Evian competes with the Fiji brand in the premium end of the water category, Evian's sales volumes and sales revenues remain in sharp decline, according to specialist soft drinks newsletter *Beverage Digest*. Evian's volumes have dropped by 29 per cent this year, compared with a 10.5 per cent drop for Fiji and 3 per cent drop for the overall water category.

Just over half of Danone's bottled water sales are in emerging markets.

Source: *Financial Times*, January 11, 2010

Case Study Questions

1 Danone has a portfolio of products, including bottled water, baby food, and yoghurts. Conduct a portfolio analysis and formulate a substantiated recommendation to Danone about what to do with their water brands.

2 Franck Riboud, Danone's CEO, is committed to keeping the water brands as part of the product portfolio because they fit with the strategy of owning products with health benefits. Given Danone's strategy, explain what synergetic effects may exist across Danone's products and brands.

3 Alternatively to selling or maintaining their water brands, Danone could decide to withdraw from specific underperforming markets (e.g. the US), while targeting high performing markets (e.g., Argentina). Could this be considered a viable strategy? Give reasons for your answer.

Principles of management

Motivating people

Part One Management and society

Chapter 1
Manager and management

Chapter 2
Organizations and environment

Part Two Strategic management and the learning organization

Chapter 3
Decision making and creativity

Chapter 4
Strategy formulation and strategic management

Part Three Organizational structure and design

Chapter 5
Designing the organization

Chapter 6
Structuring tasks for groups and individuals

Part Four Organizational behavior and people at work

Chapter 7
Motivation, work and career

Chapter 8
Leadership, motivation and communication

Part Five Operational planning, control and information management

Chapter 9
Operational planning and control

Chapter 10
Managerial process control: functional processes and process redesign

Organizational structure and design

Part 3

CHAPTER 5 Designing the organization

CHAPTER 6 Structuring tasks for groups and individuals

Once the objectives, goals and strategy of an organization have been determined (Part Two), the next step is to design the structure and the activities of the organization in such a way that these aims will be reached.

In this part of the book, we explore the organizational structure – that is, the framework within which various activities take place. At an organizational level, the structure will be affected by two factors: the diversity of the organization's activities and the extent to which the organization's environment is stable or unstable.

Designing an organization's structure involves both the assignment of decision-making authority at the various management levels (Chapter 5) and the more detailed design of individual departments (Chapter 6). Unless tasks and functions are clearly defined at this stage, there is a chance that employees will end up working at cross-purposes and constantly clashing with each other. We explore the possibility of working in groups as self-managing or autonomous teams, within or on behalf of individual departments.

The structure has to be tailor-made for the organization in question, be appropriate for the chosen strategy and enable both the individual employees and the organization itself to work effectively and gain sufficient job satisfaction. When circumstances change, the organization may have to change too. This part concludes with a consideration of the processes of organizational change.

CONTENTS

5.1 Structure of the organization: division of work and coordination
5.2 Vertical and horizontal organization designs
5.3 The choice of organizational structure
5.4 Organizational and management considerations for growth and development
5.5 Organizational structure in development
5.6 Towards flatter organizations
5.7 Towards intelligent organizations in networks of organizations

Designing the organization

Chapter 5

LEARNING OUTCOMES

After studying this chapter, you should be able to do the following:

- Understand the concepts of organizational structure and an organization chart
- Describe how a departmentalized structure matches the organization's activities
- Explain the implications of departmentalization in relation to coordination and the centralized and decentralized assignment of authority
- Identify and explain the different organizational structures and systems
- List the advantages and disadvantages of the various forms of organizational structure with regard to coordination requirements
- Describe the growth of an organization in terms of its structural design
- Consider the effects of tall and flat structures on the functioning of organizations

CASE

Management-in-action

ING hives off Nationale Nederlanden

The banking and insurance company ING is going to split itself up by hiving off its insurance branch Nationale-Nederlanden and part of its banking activities. This puts an end to 18 years of strategic efforts to create synergy advantages by functioning as a combined banking and insurance business.

In order to reduce the complexity even further, between ten and fifteen business units will also be sold off.

According to ING's CEO Jan Hommen, this necessary reorganization results from the need for a revision of its strategy and demands emanating from Brussels.

ING will become more surveyable, and one-third of its total balance will vanish, with the result that ING (and by extension, the Netherlands) will lose much of its importance in the international financial sector.

This simple solution, announced this morning, involves separating bank from insurer. During the 1990s, ING was an international example of how banks and insurers can form strong international conglomerates encompassing the entire financial spectrum. However, the model was rarely emulated in other countries. ING was regularly asked whether it wouldn't be better to split up its activities.

In April, Jan Hommen, the new chairman of the board, made it clear that as far as he was concerned, the model had outlived its time. Since the two branches did not have much affinity with each other, a greater distance between them would be established. He described his reorganization as 'going back to basics'. Until the crisis, the bank and insurance model was regarded as a nice combination since it combined a stable income with advantages of scale. Since then, as Hommen put it today, 'the advantage to us has become less evident'. At the international level, the Netherlands led the field with this banking and insurance model. Despite endorsement by such names as *Bancassurance* and *Allfinanz*, there has not been much interest abroad in this form of financial hypermarket.

Brussels forces the creation of a new Dutch bank

- By 2013, ING intends to have hived off its entire insurance division (Nationale-Nederlanden) as well as its investment management activities via a sale, a stock market flotation or a combination of the two.
- ING is also being forced to sell off some of its banking activities: Westland Utrecht, Interadvies, the Nationale-Nederlanden mortgage portfolio and ING's credit facilities for private individuals. The result will be a new Dutch bank with a total balance of 37 billion euros.
- ING has to sell the American branch of its Internet-based savings bank ING Direct by 2013.
- What remains of ING will be formed into three divisions: commercial banking, retail bank Benelux (for consumers and small business) and retail bank direct & international (Internet banking activities outside the Netherlands).
- The combined measures will shrink ING's balance by about 45 percent compared to its balance as of 30 September 2008.

The rise of the Internet in 1999 made new international advances possible: ING Direct, an Internet-based savings bank modeled loosely on the postal giro bank, the Postbank. It has become a resounding success. In recent years it has expanded rapidly and successfully, firstly in the United States and then in several other countries. However, a year ago, the American savings bank was also the cause of major problems.

ING had become a good example of a financial conglomerate whose size and complexity had made it no longer manageable. Since April, there has been mounting speculation about how long the bank and the insurer could remain under the same roof. Today's announcement makes this clear: the insurer must have been hived off by 2013 at the latest. However, the reorganization goes even further: ING must sell its recent pride and joy, ING Direct, based in the United States.

After the restructuring, ING will be a predominantly European bank with a strong position within the Benelux. In addition to Nationale-Nederlanden, ING is also going to hive off its investment management division and following an explicit injunction from Brussels, the American branch of Internet ING Direct.

All of the hived-off divisions will be sold within the coming four years, floated on the stock exchange, or a combination of these two. Within the Netherlands, ING will continue in a newly created form, as a mortgage market player with a market share of 6 percent. This new company will include Westland Utrecht, Nationale-Nederlanden's mortgage activities and ING Retail Nederland's portfolio of credit facilities to private individuals – all divisions that will also be put up for sale.

The ING organization, showing size as a percentage of the total assets (1.172 billion euro)

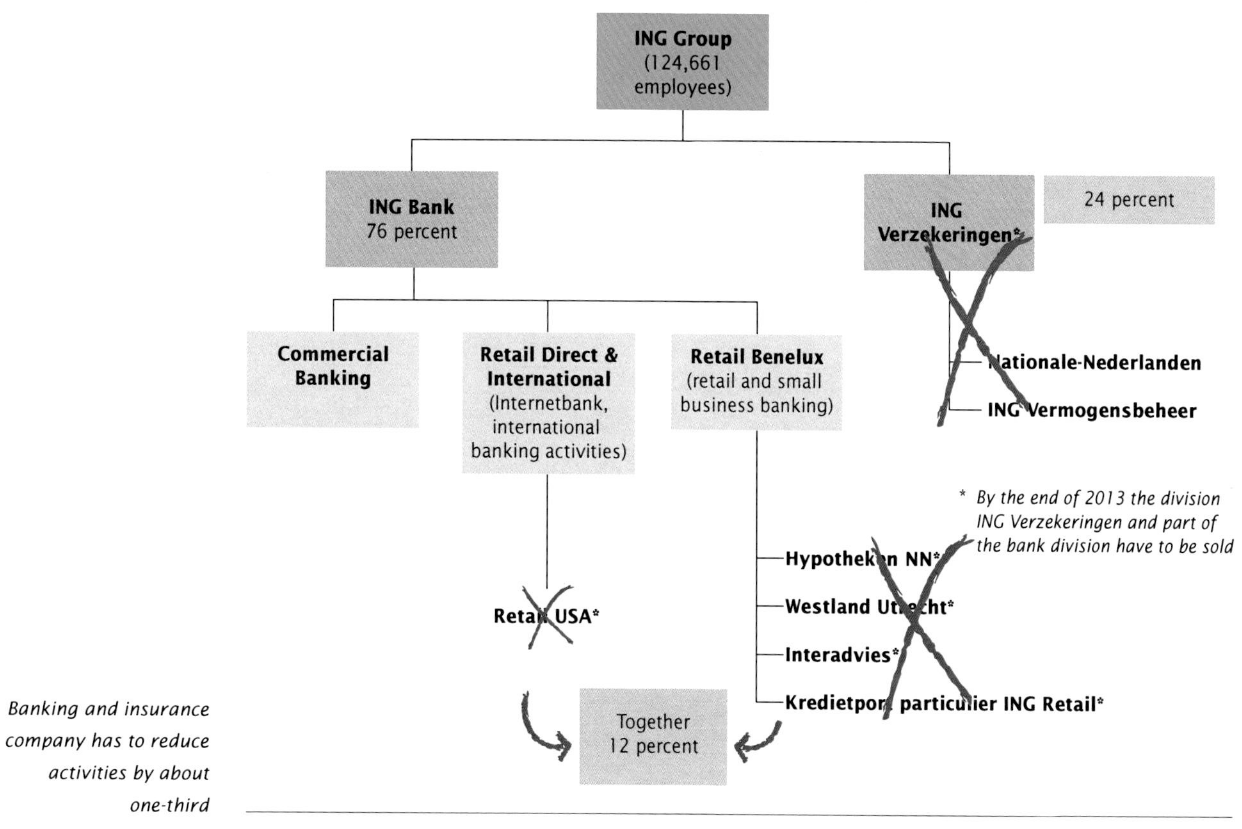

Banking and insurance company has to reduce activities by about one-third

Sources: *Het Financieele Dagblad*, 10 April 2009, 27 and 31 October 2009, and *NRC Handelsblad*, 26 October 2009

In Part Two, we looked at the issue of the organization addressing the needs of its environment and positioning itself accordingly, in order to survive in the long term. The organization then has to consider how it ought to be designed and structured to give it the best chance of attaining its goals. If the organization's structure is inappropriate, the company will not be able to exploit market opportunities to the full. Mistakes will be made and goals will not be attained.
In striving to attain the goals it has set itself, an organization must be both efficient and effective. Organizational structure design has to take into account two factors:

external adaptation

1 The need for external adaptation of the organization to the demands of its environment – its markets, society, and so on. The organization's goals must be kept in mind and ways of achieving these goals determined.

internal adaptation

2 The need for internal adaptation. This involves introducing processes and designing the day-to-day operations of the organization so that they are compatible with the organization's employees, technology and other resources.

structuring of organizations

In this chapter we consider the structuring of organizations – that is, the designing of a structure that best fits the particular circumstances of a firm or institution. Existing organizational systems and 'old,' well tested, organization principles can be used, but the choice of which organizational structure is best will vary from case to case. The key considerations will be:

- Choosing the most suitable division of work
- Introducing the most appropriate coordination mechanisms
- Delegating decision-making authority
- Providing a tailor-made communication and consultative structure.

operational and structural changes

When an organization expands in size and increases in complexity, the organizational structure needs to be adapted. It does not happen automatically. In this chapter we follow the development of an organization through its operational and structural changes: from business start-up via a department-based structure to a fully grown or mature organization.
The activities a firm or institution performs demand a rational and yet flexible approach to the choice of organizational structure. If the organizational design gives rise to operational problems, the organizational structure will have to be modified to avoid this happening.

5.1 Structure of the organization: division of work and coordination

effective and efficient

If an organization wants to be effective and efficient, it is important to give careful thought to the way in which it is structured. A firm's structure should be tailor-made to the particular circumstances in which it finds itself. If activities are to run smoothly, they must be channeled. The structure chosen should ensure that the activities of an organization can proceed without arbitrary or unnecessary interruption.

For example ...

... an organization can be compared to a living organism. We would have little use for a 'loose' organ, operating as a separate entity. Only if the working organs combine with other structures to form systems, each fulfilling its particular function according to a division of labor, and a communication system operates between the organs, can a human function effectively. This also applies to an organization.

5.1.1 A definition of organizational structure

Designing an organizational structure and assessing the existing organizational structure must include the following activities:

- Categorizing to allocate the activities to be performed into the functions, duties and tasks of departments, work groups and individual employees
- Determining where decision-making authority lies and what the relationships between departments, work groups and employees should be for optimal functioning and execution of duties and tasks
- Creating communication channels and designing mechanisms, guidelines and procedures in order to translate will into action.

division of labor
coordination mechanisms

Designing an appropriate structure is therefore a matter both of division of labor and incorporation of the necessary coordination mechanisms. Within an organization there will be various main departments, sub-departments, groups and individual employees, each with their own particular function within the larger whole. The whole is held together, activated and coordinated by links between the individual parts which provide them with appropriate information and conscious management and leadership. If well organized, an organization becomes a well-functioning and effective whole greater than the sum of its constituent parts (see Fig 5.1). The consultative structure and channels of communication which enable the organization to function appropriately by means of frequent exchange of information coordinate this entity.

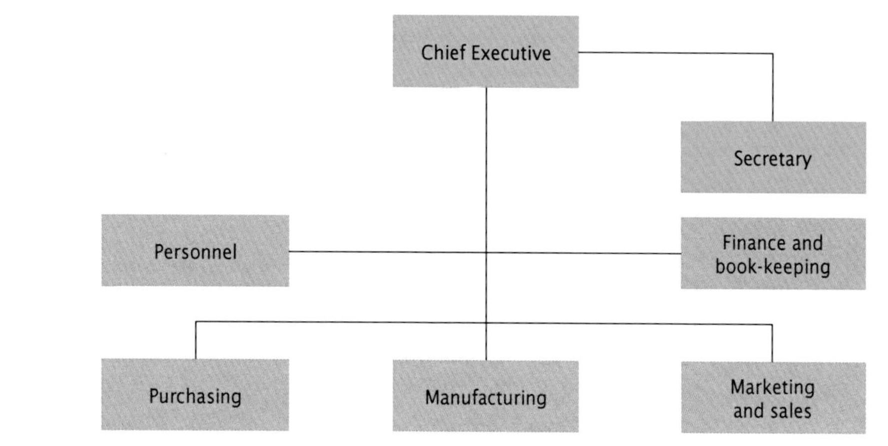

Figure 5.1
A basic organizational structure

As the necessity for mutual cooperation increases, increasingly complex mechanisms will have to be built in order to enable the coordination to be effective.

In the development of an organization from small to large and from simple to complex, problems relating to the division of labor and coordination will have to be addressed on an ongoing basis. Management must continually ask itself:

- Whether the earlier chosen form of labor division is still the right one
- Whether there is any reason for changing the way in which duties and tasks (and their related responsibilities) are delegated or for redefining formal relationships
- Whether different or complementary guidelines and procedures are necessary
- Whether changes need to take place in the consultative structure and coordinating mechanisms (for example, in the frequency of meetings, composition of working groups, etc.)

A clearly designed structure will enable management to encourage effective organizational functioning.

5.1.2 *The organization chart and job description*

An organization chart like the one in Fig 5.1 can provide insight into an organization's formal structure, including the following:

- Its formal division of tasks and duties
- Its formal lines of authority

organization chart
job descriptions

An organization chart is an outline of the way the organizational structure is designed. Precise details of duties, tasks, authority and interrelationships are not included. When detail is required, task or job descriptions are one way of supplying it. Guidelines and procedures to be followed are another way. Job descriptions specify the decisions each holder of authority is empowered to make, and as such, provide an insight into the roles that others are empowered to play.

5.1.3 Organic and personnel structures

An organizational structure has two aspects to it:
- *Its organic structure*: that is, its main departments, work groups and functions, each of which will fulfill a particular role in the larger whole
- *Its personnel structure*: that is, the various functions and who performs them

These organic and personnel structures are interrelated in that a well thought out organizational structure involves a clear divisional structure in which functions are performed by suitably skilled employees. This raises the question of the extent to which the present personnel structure in an organization affects the future building up and expansion of an organizational structure. The design of a desired future organic organizational structure can be reflected in a blueprint or 'target structure'.

5.1.4 Formal and informal organization

formal organization

Formal organization is the division of tasks into an official framework established by management, complemented by job and task descriptions, guidelines and procedures. This often takes the form of charts, procedures, work prescriptions, and so on.
In practice, not everything is able to be anticipated in advance and consequently the formal framework must be supplemented by a set of behavioral rules which will result in more efficient performance of the roles. Sometimes this may even involve deviating from the established rules. This is referred to as informal organization.

informal organization

Informal organization can complement and support the formal organization. It can also work against it: improper use of power or too precise interpretation of guidelines and bureaucratic procedures, perhaps resulting in all kinds of delays, are some of the forms this may take. Informal organization such as when employees join together to further their own aims may also constitute an attack on the organization's formal organizational structure. This may take the form of an individual or group reduction in productivity (that is, systematic soldiering) or resistance to organizational changes or the setting up of an organizational investigation. This usually involves group action.

For example ...

... informal organization can be said to be harming the formal organization if the following situations occur:
- Employees with a long term of service come in half an hour late (and possibly leave early).
- A group of employees makes its own decisions either tacit or stated about what it considers a reasonable day's job performance.

If this happens, informal goals can be said to be more important than formal agreements. In these cases, the formal organization will be harmed.

Informal organization can play a positive, negative or neutral role, depending on the degree to which the informal and formal goals are consistent with each other. If formal organization is harmed by informal organization, corrective action has to be taken. If formal organization fails to address the problem, this can result in serious delays and problems. Some groups may develop ideas and goals which are inconsistent with those of formal organization. Formal

organization sometimes adapts itself to the informal, thus authorizing developments which were not originally intended.
Formal organization maintains itself by means of its lines of authority (see Chapter 1), structure, agreements, procedures and so on. However, there is a large and important area of activity into which the power of formal organization cannot extend. Regardless of a manager's authority, it is difficult to force an employee to carry out a task in a particular way. Little can be achieved without the cooperation of employees.
Informal communication and the creation of informal organization result in people getting to know one another and meeting outside official settings. These contacts can be used for the good of the organization – for example, to arrange matters quickly. However, they can also be used to spread dissatisfaction with the functioning of the organization.

personal relationships and mutual interdependencies

Informal organization arises spontaneously and is essentially based on personal relationships and mutual interdependencies. Where possible, management should try to use informal organization in a positive way. Organization power depends to a great extent on management's recognition of the existence of informal organization and its ability to deal with it.

For example ...

... informal organization could be said to be supporting formal organization in the following cases.

- Employee A intervenes in a work situation involving Employee B – for example, to avoid danger – even though he does not have the authority to do so.
- A manager is passed over by his boss, who gives orders direct to an employee in order to get something done quickly on behalf of a waiting customer.

In times of crisis, situations often occur in which an organization's informal aspects fulfill a more important role than its formal organization. An informal leader may step forward and take control of the situation.
Effective cooperation cannot be extorted from employees; it must take place on a voluntary and agreed basis. Formal organization can ensure that employees live up to certain agreements and procedures. It is an essential feature of every organization and has an influence on every action. It is therefore important that informal organization be constantly and carefully monitored with the needs of the formal organization in mind.

5.1.5 The nature of labor organizations

The organizations featured in this book are all labor organizations in which work in terms of paid labor is being carried out. Such organizations have the following features.

Specific goals

specific goals

Companies and institutions have specific goals such as making a profit, working to a budget and attaining a market share. Small organizations often have a limited (not formally established) but still clearly recognizable goal. In larger organizations, goals are formally established in order to ensure mutual understanding of them.

Deployment of trained labor

Much of the work in organizations is performed by people who have been especially educated and trained for that purpose. In the staffing of the organization, special attention is given to

skills

skills, so selection, education and training are important staffing issues.

Formalized communication

In a company or institution, people need to communicate in order to consult each other and to exchange information for the sake of coordination and the resolution of problems in decision-making processes. When companies become larger, informal communication will eventually not be adequate and the exchange of information will need to be organized by way of consultative and communication structures – for example, regular consultation, committee meetings, interdepartmental consultation, work group meetings, meetings of departmental heads or supervisors, and so on.

consultative and communication structures

Formal rules of behavior, procedures and control

labor behavior

In organizations, a certain standard of labor behavior needs to be observed. Procedures are needed (for the sake of coordination) and results controlled and compared by feeding back or feeding forward information. In the light of the goals or objectives of the organization adjustments may have to be made to the cycle of planning, execution and control.

Layers of authority

authority

In labor organizations, certain people have the authority to issue instructions relating to the execution of activities by other employees. Authority is the right (based on a formally assigned competency) (see Section 1.2) to give orders. This right can be given by the organization's board of directors or by another person who is in turn authorized to do so. As such, authority can be seen as positional power.

Division of labor

In labor organizations, the work that has to be carried out needs to be divided in such a way that each employee (taking into account, among other things, individual competencies and skills) can perform a range of tasks without being overloaded. In other words, a formal system of labor division and structuring of work and tasks needs to be in place.

labor division

5.2 *Vertical and horizontal organization designs*

When a division of tasks is being drawn up, a distinction is often made between management tasks and operational tasks – in other words, between planning and doing.
A *vertical* model of organization design involves the division of the organization into a number of layers, expressed in a hierarchy (as we saw in Chapter 1). The layers are:

- Top management
- Middle management
- Front-line management and operational employees

functionalization

horizontal differentiation

internal specialization

A division of tasks in a *horizontal* direction involves the formal grouping of activities into departments and functions. This is called functionalization or departmentalization and leads to functions being assigned to individual employees, work groups and departments which are in turn grouped into sub-departments, main functions and support functions. With horizontal differentiation (see Section 5.2.5), groups are formed on the basis of similarity of activities; with internal specialization (see Section 5.2.6), groups are formed on the basis of coherent activities.

hierarchy

unity of direction and control

Within the company hierarchy (see Fig 5.2), each of the layers and each of the functions has its own duties, assignment of tasks and related responsibilities (see Chapter 1). Top management has to maintain unity of mission, direction and views and consistency in decision making with regard to the functioning of the departments, in other words, unity of direction and control. Management has to be anchored at all levels of the organization to ensure that there are consistent views and a common direction infusing all action and decision making in relation to operational tasks.

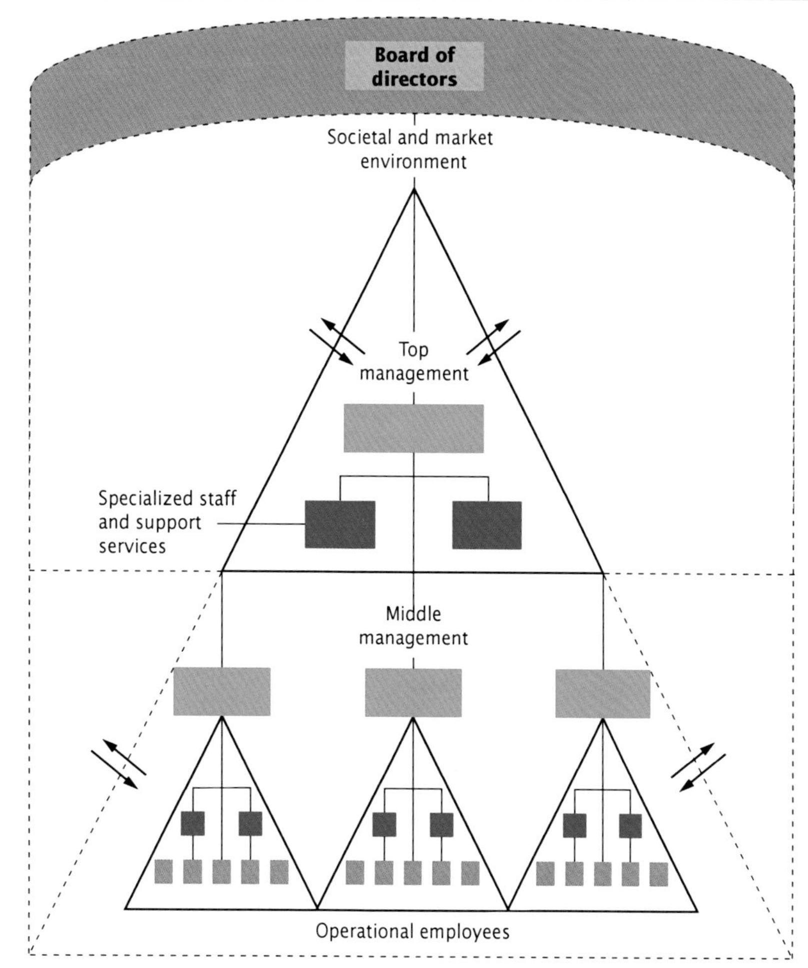

Figure 5.2
An organizational structure incorporating both the vertical and horizontal models of task division

5.2.1 *Top management tasks*

top management

The task of an organization's top management level is to give content to the relationship between the organization and its environment – that is, to take the necessary strategic decisions to guarantee the survival of the organization as far as possible. Top management must carry out investigations necessary for the implementation of decisions regarding products or services in relation to markets or customer groups. This will involve both organizational and administrative measures. Middle management will then be in a position to take any further organizational and operational decisions.

5.2.2 *Middle management tasks*

middle management

When a company grows and becomes complex, a new level of organization will have to be created since a manager can only have a limited number of subordinate employees (see the discussion of span of control in Chapter 6). The middle management level (division managers, business unit managers, heads of department, etc.) will come into being. Middle management is responsible both to the 'top' and to the 'bottom' of the organization. It represents the point at which the various interests meet and in a certain sense serves a buffer function between the various layers of the organization. It exercises supervision over other employees and, of course, reports to the strategic level above.

STUCK IN THE MIDDLE

Research by McKinsey (2009) has shown middle managers to be the biggest victims of the crisis. They have been given greater responsibility and they experience more stress, but are not being given enough support from the top. 'The middle manager is having to do the splits.'

As the McKinsey Global Survey of 1653 managers at both middle and senior levels shows, the crisis has meant that managers are working longer days, doing additional tasks and experiencing greater stress. While most top managers say that they can cope with this, a lot of middle managers are less happy about their current situation. Compared to the top managers in the survey, middle managers are less committed to their company, are less enthusiastic about their work and are more dissatisfied with their bosses.

The crucial word is attention. Top managers focus too much on cost saving measures and increasing productivity and forget to encourage those that they are in charge of. It takes more than to draw the middle manager's attention to the 'big picture': personal attention is needed. And not merely as a cunning maneuver, but to guarantee the survival of the company in the long term.

The cause of the problem lies in the generational differences between the senior echelons and the middle management level. Middle managers are often in their thirties and are building up a career. They often have young children and a partner who also has a career. It takes a lot of energy to maintain the balance between work and private life. Top managers are often insensitive to this since it was rarely an issue in their time.

Middle managers are the first to experience the effects of a crisis. They are much closer to the operational hub than the board. Personal attention is important, particularly in these times of crisis. A good leader understands this and adjust his or her leadership style appropriately. The recent crisis has meant that middle management is having to do the splits. By definition it has to bridge the gap between the top echelons and those below, but being in charge of a department that is being abolished required a double effort. Not only are middle managers obliged to be loyal to their employers (they must act professionally, of course), but they have to be loyal to themselves because they have to go on. And having to deal with employees who know that their time in the company is coming to an end is asking a lot of a middle manager.

The McKinsey research showed that 30 percent of middle managers are dissatisfied with their bosses. The additional tasks they have to do also appear to be having a demotivating effect. Just over one-third believe their role to be less important than it was prior to the crisis and only 36 percent can see themselves still working for the same company two years on.

The research concludes that middle managers have been hard hit by the crisis. Top managers need to focus on more than cost-saving measures and raising productivity: they need to pay more attention to the managers who will be responsible for implementing all these improvements.

Mutual understanding between senior and middle management is crucially important. Top management is busy with spread sheets – the company must expand by 5 percent – and other highly abstract matters. Things are much more concrete at the middle management level – Joe has to work harder. Put yourself in the position of the other: the relationship will improve if you understand what makes the other lie awake at night.

Both sides need to work on improving the relationship. It is too simplistic to blame top management only. Not only are good leaders required: good followers are too. Middle managers need to understand their bosses' position and realize that they determine how successful their bosses are.

Source: 'Leader in the crisis,' *McKinsey Quarterly*, August 2009 and *Management Scope*, no. 10 / 2009, pp 20-23

5.2.3 *Operational and front-line management tasks*

The operational employees and front-line managers have to concentrate on the activities to be performed in order to attain the target production levels and levels of service. The desired levels of production and quality can be determined by mutual consultation and joint decision making with the employees who perform the operational tasks.
These three management layers were discussed in some detail in Chapter 1. They reflect the classical chain of command or hierarchical order – often referred to as 'the line'.

5.2.4 *Auxiliary, specialist and support staff tasks*

As companies and institutions grow, at some stage they need to recruit specialists. When the organization reaches a size at which particular problems are arising constantly, management may decide to bring 'in house' the expertise required to address them. They are usually complex problems relating to aspects of policy and/or execution. When the workload reaches a certain level, it is cheaper for the organization to employ specialists rather than to constantly call in external consultants. When this involves specialized knowledge for the analysis and solution of policy problems, so-called staff functions will be created in such areas as economic research, market research, long-term planning and legislative matters.

specialized knowledge

It is important that specialist knowledge and techniques be exploited during policy formulation and preparation for decision making. By employing specialized knowledge in the form of specialists, problems can be studied in depth and from various perspectives. This ultimately leads to more balanced and better decision making at all levels of the organization. The employment of specialized staff has to result in more efficient and more effective operation on the part of the organization as a whole. Specialist knowledge can be applied to the improvement of working methods, planning and control, and in such areas as the education and training of personnel.

As soon as a company's legal representative or legal department starts to become involved in performing tasks and handling cases, the nature of that function will change. It or they will no longer have a purely consulting or advisory role; there will also be a task performance element to the job. A support service element will have been incorporated into the function.

staff and support services

Staff and support services can be incorporated into various levels of the organization. The difference between specialized staff functions and support services lies in the relative scope of the services' authority and not in the specialist knowledge per se. The character of a department cannot be determined on the basis of its position on an organizational chart.

Staff and support functions have the following identifying features:

- A staff function influences 'the line' only. It, in turn, affects the work of others.
- A staff function provides data or advice on request or at its own initiative.
- A staff function is not directly involved in tasks.
- A support function has a mandate to give advice to the line and must be consulted before action is taken.
- A support function sometimes performs tasks on behalf of the line.

Specialists within the organization who focus on problems of execution in more than one department within the organization are referred to as support staff. They include the personnel, administration and finance and maintenance departments.

For example ...

... a central administration department which provides the purchasing, production and sales departments with guidelines relating to the way in which data has to be processed would be considered a support function. Support staff are authorized to intervene in the functioning of another department, regardless of its area of expertise. A 'pure' staff department does not have this authority (see sections 6.5.2 and 6.5.3).

constituting tasks

directing tasks

In Fig 5.3, these servicing functions are related to management's constituting tasks (that is, developing strategy, designing an organizational structure and coordinating activities: policy-intensive tasks) and directing tasks (that is, giving orders, motivating employees and controlling and adjusting: operationally intensive tasks).

The typing pool, reception, security, cafeteria and so on could be described as support services in the sense that a service is rendered to other departments in a company or institution. However, specialist knowledge plays a minor role. While these departments do indeed perform a number of defined tasks on behalf of other employees within the organization, this does not take the form of specialist advice based on authority and with the aim of improving working methods, planning or education and training. These services can be better described, therefore, as support services rather than support staff.

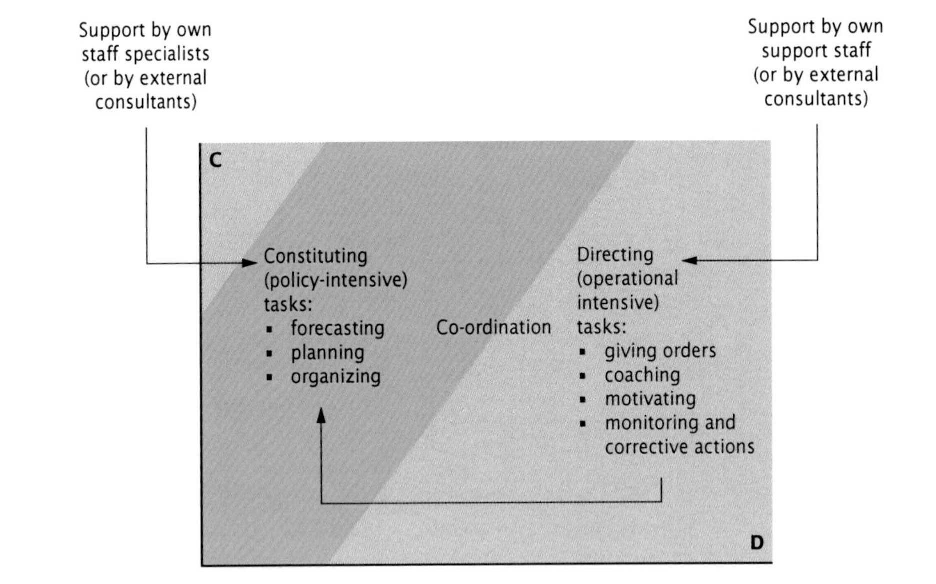

Figure 5.3 *Staff and support services and their role in relation to the constituting and directing tasks of management*

5.2.5 *Internal differentiation*

functional division

The division of work into consecutive phases or steps within a process, based on the nature of the actions which have to be taken is termed internal differentiation. Such a system crosses individual functions or departments and is referred to as a functional division of company activities (the F grouping system). A division of processes or operations may be prompted by certain factors. They include the following:

- A certain level of expertise is needed.
- Employees have appropriate education and training.
- Personal skills and characteristics are similar.

internal differentiation

Internal differentiation can take many forms. For example:

- The designing of departments or main functions directly under top management (see Fig 5.4)
- The designing of sub-departments (for example, within the production department of a furniture factory) (see Fig 5.5)

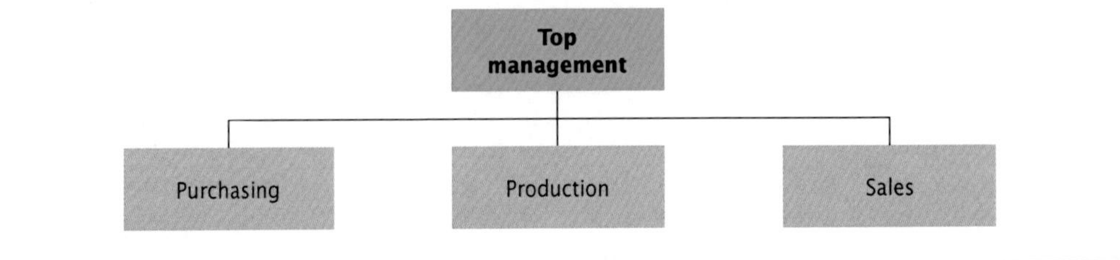

Figure 5.4 *F-grouping of functions directly under top management*

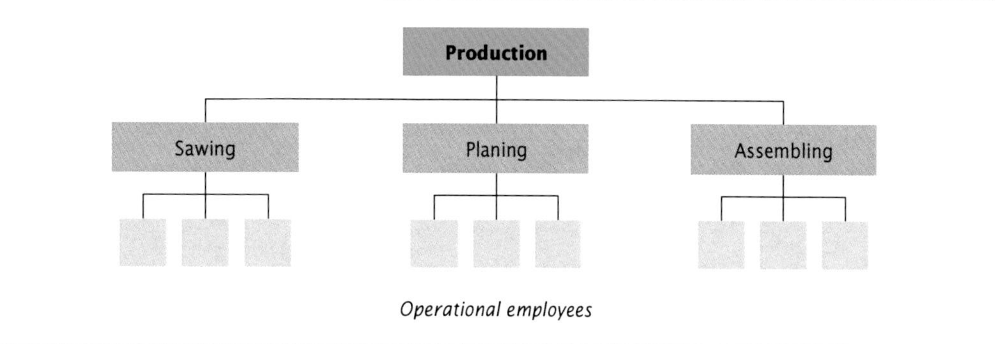

Figure 5.5
F-grouping of production department within a furniture factory, with sub-departments according to phases of the manufacturing process

One of the drawbacks of internal differentiation is that it breaks down the interdependence among employees working on the individual steps of the process of manufacturing a particular product. The natural coherence of a series of actions which result in the final product is lost. Consultation and planning must be introduced to re-establish this coherence and increase communication between functions, departments and individual employees.

5.2.6 Internal specialization

internal specialization Internal specialization is the division of labor according to the common goals of the actions or functions to be performed, according to products, according to a geographical location or according to a market segment. The aim of the division is *primarily* to achieve coherence between *P-grouping* consecutive actions. For example, internal product specialization – that is, a P-grouping – will draw all activities which are directed at production of a single product together. The natural coherence between the various activities will initially be maintained as far as possible. Internal *G-grouping* specialization according to geographical location is referred to as a G-grouping and internal *M-grouping* specialization according to market segment is referred to as an M-grouping. Internal specialization can be seen in different applications. The following are some examples of internal specialization:

- The designing of departments ('divisions') directly under the board of directors or board of management (see figs 5.6, 5.7 and 5.8)
- The designing of sub-departments within departments (see Figs 5.9, 5.10 and 5.11)

Hybrid forms of F-, P- and M-groupings are usual.

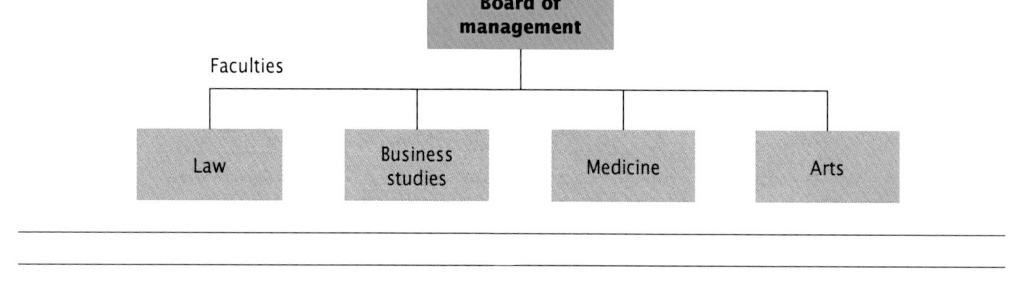

Figure 5.6
P-grouping directly under the board of management (university)

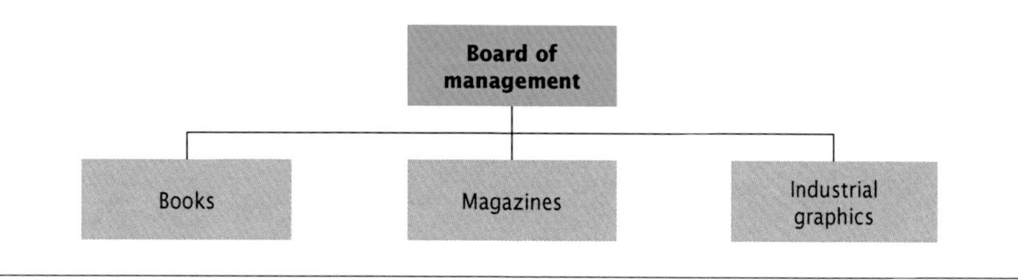

Figure 5.7
P-grouping directly under the board of management (publishing company)

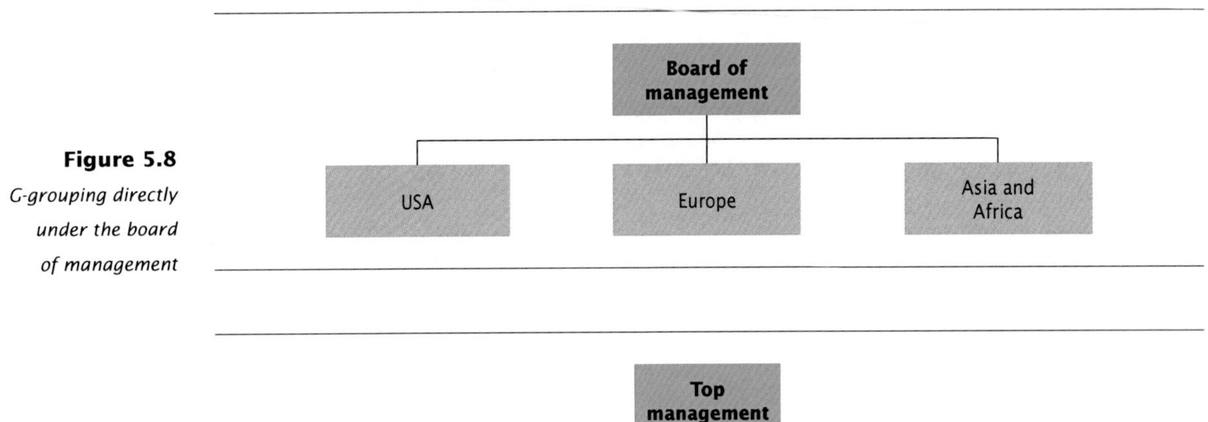

Figure 5.8
G-grouping directly under the board of management

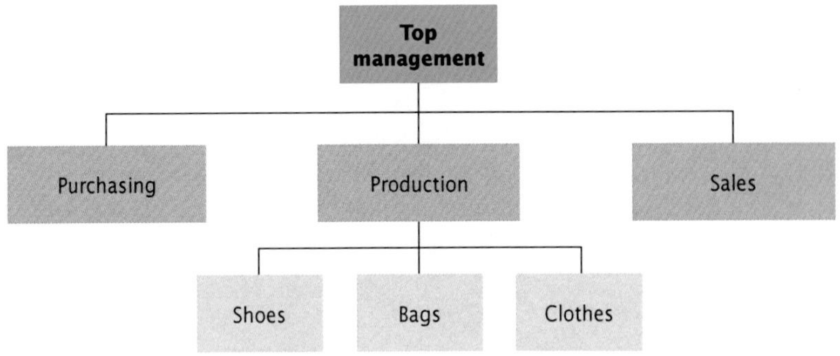

Figure 5.9
P-grouping of the production department

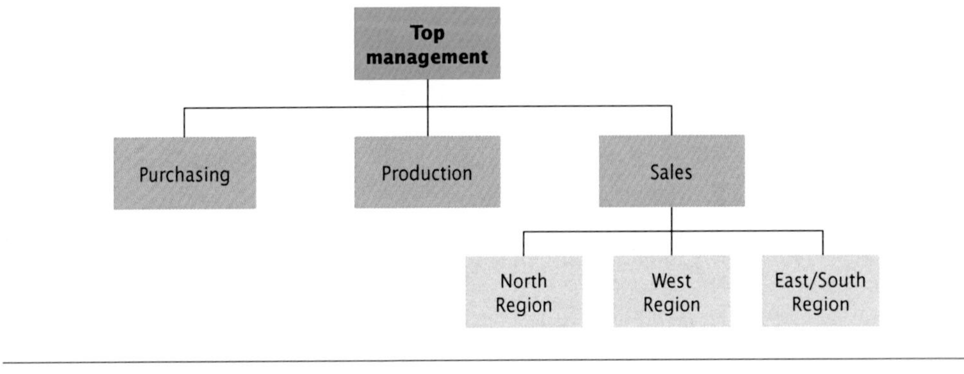

Figure 5.10
G-grouping of the sales department

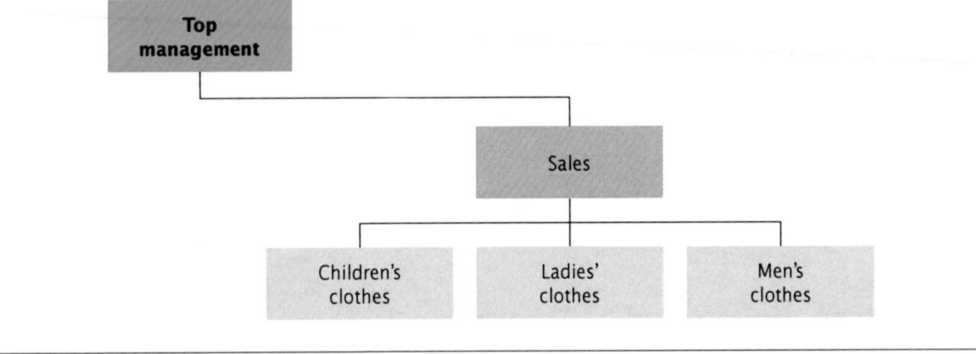

Figure 5.11
M-grouping of the sales department

5.3 The choice of organizational structure

An organizational structure has three distinct elements:

division of work

1 *A form of division of work.* It is possible to divide an organization into the following elements:
   - functions – for example, purchasing, production, sales
   - products – for example, audio products, medical equipment
   - geography – for example, division per region, province or country
   - markets – for example, domestic users, bulk consumers, consumer products, industrial sectors

While organization into functional departmental areas will improve efficiency, it may result in a reduction in flexibility and some interfunctional coordination problems. The advantages of the other three organizational arrangements are a shorter communication line and improved responsiveness to the wishes of the clients. The disadvantages include a higher cost level in some cases and a loss of expertise in the functional aspects of the business and in performing the processes.

degree of centralization or decentralization

2 *A degree of centralization or decentralization.* The decision-making authority will be spread out over the various levels of the organization to a varying degree. A high degree of decentralization often allows the organization to react faster to changes in the environment. A high degree of centralization leads to greater uniformity of decisions, and to top management being better informed about what is going on operationally at the lower levels of the organization.

system of coordination mechanisms

3 *A system of coordination mechanisms.* Coordination mechanisms ensure that the company's constituent parts work together without any major problems. There are a wide range of coordination mechanisms. As the need for cooperation becomes more intense, more complex mechanisms will have to be incorporated. The following list, arranged in order of increasing complexity, is not exhaustive:
   - Task and job descriptions
   - Plans
   - Teams/task forces
   - Coordinators
   - Project groups

If a new company strategy results in a change in organizational structure, this can mean that the division of work will also have to be changed – for example, from a F(unctional)-oriented structure to a P(roduct)-oriented structure. Adjustments will also need to take place as to the degree of centralization or decentralization. Different coordination mechanisms may also be required.
As the required cooperation between the departments becomes more intensive, stronger mechanisms have to be built into the organizational structure. For example, in an organization with a F(unctional) structure, the launching of products is often a very difficult process because everything has to go via top management. Setting up a team consisting of members from all involved departments can considerably speed up such a project.

5.3.1 Factors affecting choice of structure

The choice of an organizational structure will depend on the particular circumstances the company finds itself in. The choice will be affected by two considerations:

variety of activities

1 Variety of activities. If a company makes only one product and sells this to one market, organization according to function (purchasing, production, sales) is preferable. If the number of products or the number of markets were to increase, however, and result in an increase in the variety of the activities, then that change will have to be incorporated in the structure. If size allows, product groups, business units or divisions could be set up.

In other situations, the production function could be split up according to product groups; alternatively, the sales function could be split according to market and customer groups.

nature of the environment

2 The nature of the environment. The greater the amount of change in the environment the greater the amount of information to be processed by the various organizational levels. This information processing capacity is limited – just like a network of roads which can process the flow of traffic well during the day, but not during rush-hours. Allowing decisions to be made at a lower level would mean a reduction in demands on the information processing capacity.

coordination mechanisms

3 Coordination mechanisms. When the collaboration between departments becomes more intensive, more but also stronger mechanisms will have to be incorporated within the organization. For example, in an F-structure, where the introduction of new products to the market is often very difficult to arrange, the process can be accelerated by setting up a team with representatives from all the departments involved (see Galbraith, 1973).

dynamics of the environment

Figure 5.12 brings together two of the elements of an organizational structure – the division of work and the degree of decentralization of decision-making authority. It illustrates the dynamics of the environment in relation to a variety of activities (for example, those relating to products, markets and geographical areas).

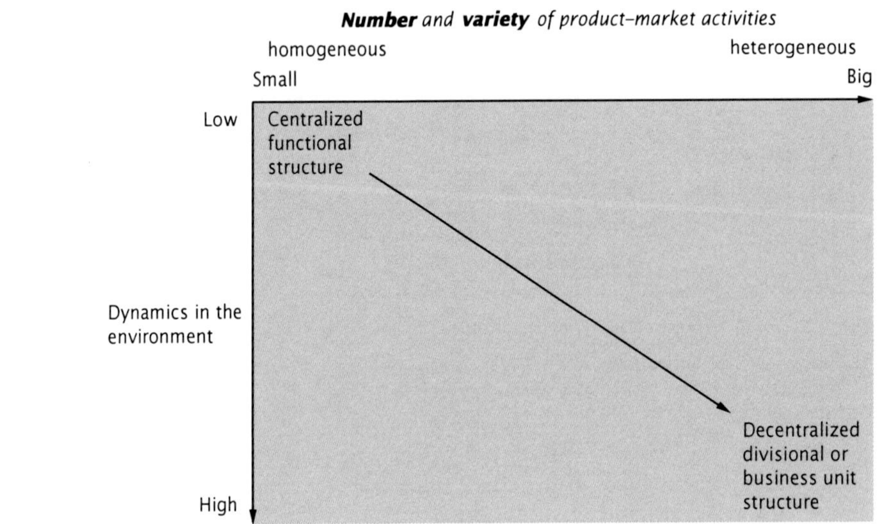

Figure 5.12
Combination of two elements of organizational structure: division of work and centralization/decentralization

It is important for an organization to be structured in a way that reflects the nature of the organization's activities. For example, the organization's activities may be based around the supply of products to certain key geographical areas; alternatively, the organization may revolve around a number of key product or service ranges. In each case, the division of work must reflect the main focus of the organization's activities – a G structure in the former case, a P structure in the latter – if a coherent whole is to be formed from the individual parts of the organization, from the shop floor to the boardroom. This also applies to organizations whose activities are mostly based around serving a particular market segment (M division) or providing a particular functional field of expertise (F division).

Design rules

internal specialization

When the number of activities carried out by an organization increases and they become more varied (and the heterogeneity extends to many of the aspects of the business activities, including purchase, production, marketing and sales), there needs to be an accompanying increase in internal specialization. If there is simultaneously an increase in the amount of change required by both the external task environment and the competitive environment and a need to react faster and more frequently to what is happening in an increasing number of different countries and or market segments, then there must be a discernibly stronger degree of decentralization. If the organizational environment becomes more complex as well as more dynamic, this will increase the capacity of the organization to react, and prompt changes within the organizational structure as well as in the division of labor and the assignment of authority: internal specialization accompanied by an increasing degree of decentralization.

elementary coordination mechanisms

Theoretically, the so-called elementary coordination mechanisms can be applied to the management of the organization as a whole. These include hierarchical structures, task assignment, rules, procedures and budgets. When these are inadequate and the hierarchy becomes top-heavy (as a result of increasingly complex problems and environmental dynamics) the hierarchy can be relieved by building in extra horizontal and/or lateral coordination mechanisms such as direct contact, the introduction of task forces, teams, project groups, product managers, account managers and the like (see Section 5.3.6, also Galbraith, 1973).

extra coordination mechanisms

5.3.2 F-, P-, G- and M-structures

The preferred form of labor division for an organization will depend on the following factors:

- Its size and stage of development
- The nature of its primary activities
- The diversity of its activities

As the company's activities grow, more employees will be recruited for the functions of production, sales, purchasing, and administration. The organization of the production department may, for example, be differentiated on the basis on each individual production phase. Within the marketing and sales department a more detailed organization according to geographical areas or possibly individual countries may be introduced. The role of coordination of the marketing and sales activities in the various areas or countries will then lie with the marketing and the sales managers.

Small and medium-sized companies

F(unctional) form

In small and medium-sized organizations an F(unctional) form of division of work is usually the most appropriate form, with duties assigned directly by top management. When, for example, there are several production locations, these could be arranged as subgroups under one main production function – that is, a G-grouping within the production function.
A division of work according to areas or countries – a G-grouping – has the following advantages:

- It increases the responsiveness of the organization to local circumstances.
- The results of activities per area are directly visible.
- Short communication lines facilitate effective communication.

This means that the specific factors and circumstances relating to a specific area or country will be given greater consideration during the decision-making process.

P(roduct) grouping

However, if the marketing and sales department carries a range of products or articles, a P(roduct) grouping may be preferable. How the tasks and duties are divided up will depend to a great extent on how diverse the technical demands associated with each group are, the degree of expertise needed to manufacture them, and what their markets are. If the articles themselves do not differ too much technically, but are sold to very different client groups (consumers and industrial clients), then possibly a M(arket segment) grouping of the marketing and sales department needs to be considered.

M(arket segment) grouping

Changes in manufacturing, expertise, experience, distribution channels and customer groups may mean that an earlier arrangement may have to be reconsidered.

Medium-sized and large companies

When an organization continues to grow until it is a medium-sized or large company with an increasing number of heterogeneous products, a P grouping (directly under management) may work better than the F grouping used previously. Such a grouping has the major advantage of having the coordination of the various operational activities placed one level lower within the organization. Top management is then free to address policy and strategic interests. Such a P(roduct) grouping is often referred to as the creation of divisions or business units. Each product group then has its own management (that is, division management or business unit management) with its own production department, sales department and so on grouped under that.

G(eographical) grouping

If a company is focusing on operating internationally, then a G(eographical) grouping according to country or continent will sometimes be introduced. It will fall within the area of top management.

We will now look at the main organizational structure options:

- The centralized functional structure (Section 5.3.3)
- The decentralized divisional structure (Section 5.3.4)
- The decentralized business unit structure (Section 5.3.5)
- The project organization (Section 5.3.8)
- The matrix organization (Section 5.3.9).

5.3.3 The centralized functional structure

In the centralized functional structure, processes or actions are grouped into functional areas according to similarity with regard to expertise, knowledge, abilities, attitudes and skills. In principle, these functional areas – purchasing, sales, production, research and development – are assigned, regardless of the final products to which these activities lead, to functional managers who report to top management. This form makes concentration and communal use (synergy) of professional competencies and all other resources possible if there is a high degree of overlap of the phases of processing a range of final products. In this form, the

functional similarities

functional similarities are considered more important than any product, market or geographical links.
Fig 5.13 depicts a functional organizational structure for a manufacturing company.

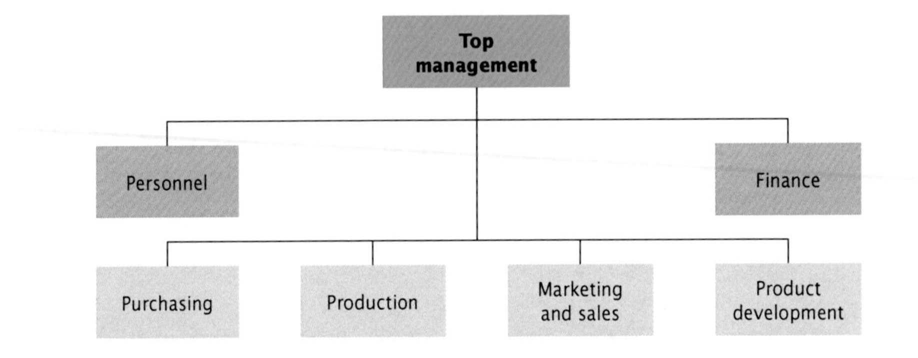

Figure 5.13
An organization with a F(unctional) structure

The functional structure comes into its own when a company wishes to serve one or at most a few relatively homogeneous product-market combinations and do so as efficiently as possible. The emphasis is on the attaining of advantages of scale and synergy through concentration and utilization of resources within departments. In recent years, however, given the increasing importance of flexibility in product supply, long-term thinking, speed of decision making and innovative capabilities, it is rare for an organization to serve only one or a few product-market combinations. The functional structure is usually replaced by a product- or market-oriented, divisionalized or business unit structure.

centralized functional structure

In a centralized functional structure, the role of top management is largely one of coordination and the making of product-market decisions. This takes up a great deal of time and requires a lot of attention. The high costs of such a structure must be earned back by means of a high degree of efficiency.

We can summarize the advantages of the functional structure as follows:
- Suitable for one or a few product-market combinations
- Central control
- Key activities in departments
- Functional expertise and specialization
- Efficiency created by routine jobs
- High degree of capacity utilization

The disadvantages of the functional structure include the following:
- Problems with interfunctional coordination
- Problems with lack of market orientation
- Rivalry between various functions
- Over-specialization
- Limited development of internal management capacity
- Profit responsibility only at the top
- Creation of functional empires
- Limited entrepreneurship and innovation

With the present preference for flat organizations, the functional organization has the disadvantage of providing only a limited possibility for further flattening of the top of the organization, due to the fact that with this structure the top fulfills an important coordinating role. However, within functional organizations, it is usually possible to reduce the number of management layers within the ranks of middle management.

5.3.4 The decentralized divisional structure

strategic business unit (SBU) structure

In the decentralized divisional structure – or strategic business unit (SBU) structure – activities are grouped according to the final performance in terms of product, market, or geographical area. The decentralized divisional structure is appropriate when an organization has an increasing number of different/heterogeneous product-market combinations or geographical areas. The main goal in this type of organizational structure is improving the responsiveness of the organization to the needs of the various product-market combinations or geographical areas.

Each group of activities is assigned to a product group or to a divisional manager. Managers are thus not expected to make decisions about products or areas which are unrelated in terms of product technology and marketing activities. The divisional level addresses issues which are the responsibility of the group under the top management level in the F form (see Fig 5.13). This means that corporate management can concentrate on strategic planning and control, maintaining the performance level and performance capacity of the divisions. Many organizations have a number of central staff or auxiliary services – finance, corporate strategy, legislative matters, and so on. These are not only at the service of top management, however; they can also be consulted by the divisions.

A divisional structure is shown in Fig 5.14. In this structure, an extra management level is situated between the business units and the top. Under this divisional level, the various business units are grouped according to related activities.

The main advantage of the divisional structure is that it facilitates the realization of synergy arising from coherent and related activities. The divisions fulfill either the role of consultant or the role of coordinator. Relatively high costs are involved in such a structure, and the divisions have a tendency to pull power towards themselves by creating their own often fast growing teams of staff. This then leads to an increase in the distance between top management and the shop floor. If this is the case, the advantages of synergy are cancelled out by the higher costs at the divisional level.

We can summarize the advantages of the divisional structure as follows:

- Enhanced business unit synergy and coordination
- Coherence between related activities
- Allocation of capacity based on growth possibilities
- Objective assessment of internal performance by the top
- A good way to structure the business portfolio

The disadvantages of the divisional structure include the following:

- Extra management level between the top and the business unit
- A different course for each division
- Dividing tasks between top, division and business unit can be difficult
- Assessing responsibility for results can be difficult
- Top management may lose touch with the market
- Duplication of staff functions

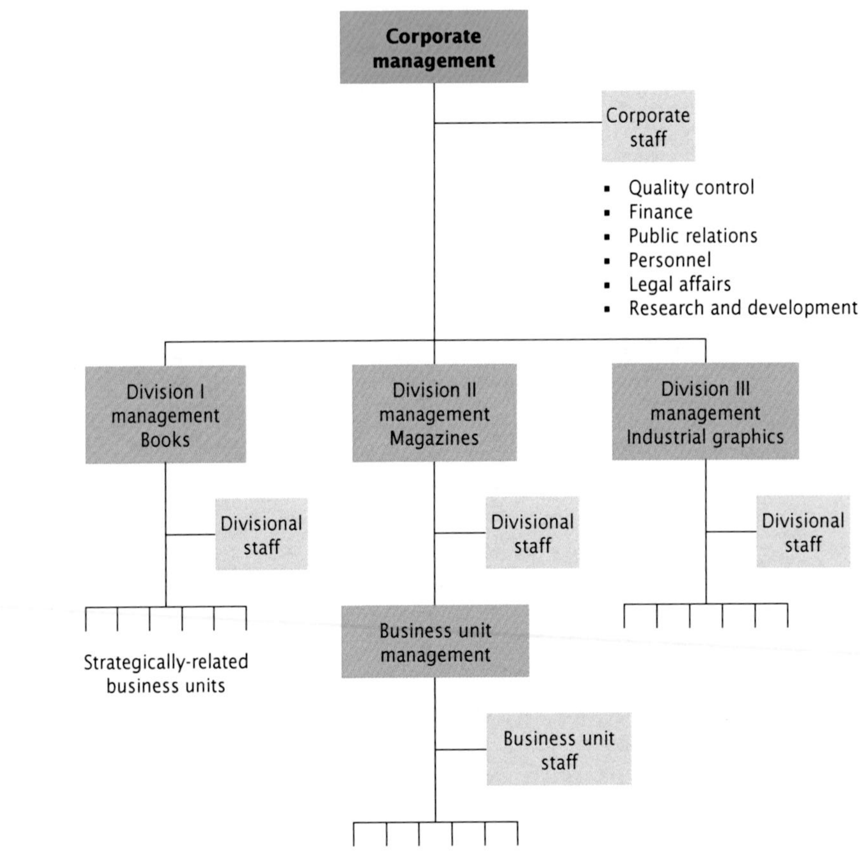

Figure 5.14
A divisional structure

The added value of the divisional level can be reduced in organizations where information technology allows top management to closely monitor the performance of individual business units or where the business unit itself develops a strategic management capacity.

Given the current preference for flat organizational structures, the divisional level has been abandoned in some organizations. One condition for further decentralization to business units is a strong strategic management capacity at the business unit level. These business units then have to be fully equipped to cope with their own strategy development. The top operates at a distance and is responsible for providing an explicit overall vision and determining the path the organization should be taking.

5.3.5 The business unit structure

business unit structure

A business unit structure – or BU structure – is illustrated in Fig 5.15. This structure promotes profit responsibility, decentralization of authority and market orientation. In its purest form, a business unit structure requires business units to be fully equipped with their own service departments.
However, the business unit structure is not without its problems. It keeps top management at a distance from operations and it discourages it from intervening, even though it holds the final responsibility.

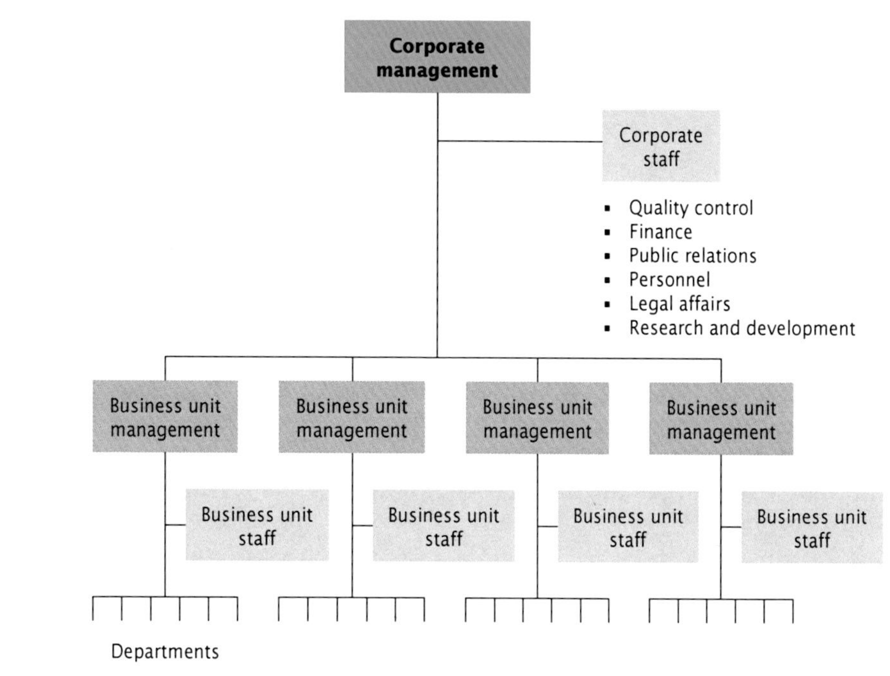

Figure 5.15
A business unit structure

The business unit structure presupposes that the business units have a full strategic management capacity.
The concept of the business unit is currently enjoying a certain degree of popularity, although it rarely appears in its 'purest' form, but instead in a somewhat watered down version which cannot be described as a business unit structure in the real sense. When we refer to a business unit structure here, it is the pure form of structure we have in mind.
The advantages of the business unit structure include:

- It provides a good opportunity for delegation of responsibility for results
- Strategy remains close to the entrepreneurial environment
- Own responsibility for management of processes
- Stimulates entrepreneurship
- Top can concentrate on strategy and portfolio

Disadvantages of the business unit structure include:

- Separation of central and decentralized authority
- Rivalry over services and attention of the top

- Autonomy hampers synergy
- Top now dependent on business unit managers
- Duplication of staff functions

The attraction of synergy did not appeal to all corporate managers: 'Just let the business units compete, as long as they do not pursue a price war. When you wish to attain real synergy, you can merge and integrate the business units.'

CASE

Mini case study 5.1

FUJIFILM Establishes Medical Informatics Organization

New Organization structure strengthens product portfolio while creating a platform for future growth.

Stimulated by the ten years of Synapse® business market leadership, Fujifilm Medical Systems USA announced today, at the Radiological Society of North America (RSNA) annual meeting, the formation of its Medical Informatics Division. Formerly known as Networks Systems, this new group will integrate all functions associated with the company's informatics offering and creates a platform for future growth.

Several organizational changes are part of this restructuring, which integrates the former Empiric and ProSolv Cardiovascular divisions into a single organization. Robert Cooke will have the role of Vice President and General Manager, Medical Informatics USA; Cooke will head all business and customer facing functions of the division. Aaron Waitz, formerly President and CEO of ProSolv Cardiovascular, has assumed the role ofVice President, Product Development, Medical Informatics Global, will manage all aspects of product development for the integrated Medical Informatics portfolio.

'The establishment of the Medical Informatics business unit reflects Fujifilm's vision to integrate medical information into a common platform capable of positively impacting the entire care cycle from prevention to treatment,' says Robert Cooke, Vice President and General Manager, Medical Informatics USA. 'Today, we have been successful with the imaging domains we serve through our integrated Synapse offering across the disciplines of radiology and cardiovascular imaging and in the future our goal is to extend this coverage into additional healthcare domains.'

Under Medical Informatics, the Synapse product portfolio provides a completely integrated solution for PACS, RIS cardiovascular imaging, and women's health imaging. Integrated components of the Synapse family of products are Virtualization, Application Hosting, Database and Mobile application solutions.

Source: *PR Newswire*, November 29, 2009

5.3.6 Interdependencies and their design solutions

Before continuing with our consideration of the main organizational structures, it is worth considering at this point the relationships and interdependencies which result from the structures we have already discussed, and the problems they create for the organization. Once a primary grouping of activities is in place, a certain coordinating effect is automatically exerted on the employees within the organization as it becomes clear who works where and in which department.

For example ...

... Phil Curtis, a maintenance mechanic in the production department at Company A, has no hesitation about reporting directly to the production department every morning. Sharon MacRyan goes straight to the purchasing department every day.
Wondering where you are going to work is a thing of the past with departmentalization. Finding where others are is no problem either: if Phil wants to speak to Sharon or someone in his own department, then he looks up the number in the internal telephone guide. Departmentalization is clearly having the effect of improved coordination.

coordination mechanisms

The relationships between the various departments and employees within each department do, however, have to be spelled out and will require a number of coordination mechanisms. The choice of coordination mechanism is determined by the nature of the mutual interdependence between the departments and the employees concerned.
According to Thompson, 1967, three types of interdependence can be identified:

- Pooled interdependence
- Serial or sequential interdependence
- Reciprocal interdependence

'Pooled' interdependence

In this type of interdependence, an interdependence exists only between 'higher' and 'lower' groups or individuals (that is, vertically). At the horizontal level – between departments – there is no direct dependence: one department cannot influence the daily course of events in another department (although this could be possible indirectly and in the long term).

For example ...

... take the MIGROS retail chain. MIGROS-Switzerland – the organization at national level – and the MIGROS branches are, as higher and lower organizational layers, 'pooled' interdependent. The higher organization (MIGROS-Switzerland) exists thanks to the contributions which are made by the lower organizations (the MIGROS branches).
In turn, the MIGROS branches benefit from the fact that they are part of MIGROS-Switzerland, as the national organization provides all kinds of facilities which a branch would not be able to afford, if it were an independent store. As parts of a larger organization the branches can, for example, borrow money internally at a lower interest rate than the rate set for an external bank.
At the horizontal level, the branches do not tend to affect each other. When light bulbs are sold out in the Basel branch, this does not affect the sales of light bulbs in the Berne or Geneva branches.

pooled interdependence

This type of interdependence is created when an organization opts for internal specialization: a P, G, or M structure. Figure 5.16 illustrates 'pooled' interdependence.

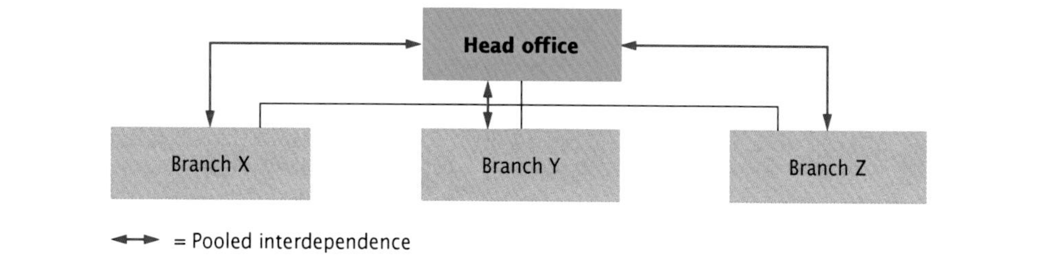

Figure 5.16
'Pooled' interdependence

An appropriate coordination mechanism where there is 'pooled' interdependence is standardization of output per organizational unit. In the case of MIGROS, for example, the national management sets output norms in terms of turnover, profitability and the handling of complaints to be realized by local subsidiaries.

Serial or sequential interdependence

internal differentiation

If an organization opts for internal differentiation (F structure), then serial interdependence arises. This is the case with the purchasing-production-sales grouping. The successive phases in the operational process are now directly dependent on each other and consequently it is essential that the processing order be coherent and fixed. A purchasing activity must take place before production can carry out its activity, and only after that will the sales department be able to start its work.

The possibility of disruption is much greater than with 'pooled' interdependence. If the purchasing activities stop, after a while production will have no components or raw materials and shortly afterwards, sales representatives will have no products to take to clients. In serial or sequential interdependencies, therefore, the activities have to be more closely coordinated than is the case with 'pooled' interdependence and will relate directly to each other. Serial or sequential interdependence is illustrated in Fig 5.17.

serial interdependence

An appropriate coordination mechanism for serial interdependence is planning, because of the absolute necessity for the process to be coherent and predictable.

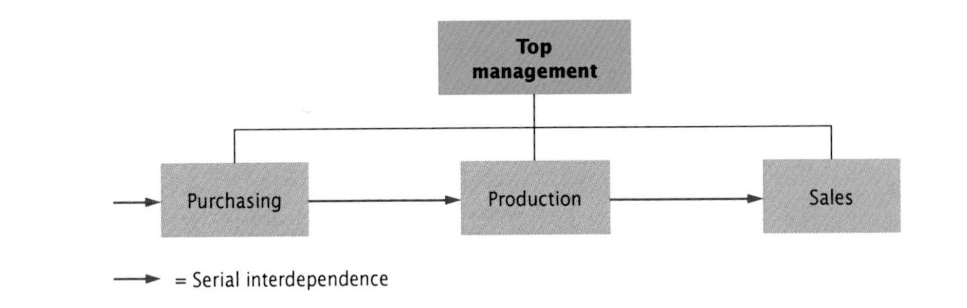

Figure 5.17
Serial interdependence

Reciprocal interdependence

When there is no fixed order between the various phases of processing or between departments, though these phases or departments are directly dependent on each other and can affect each other on a daily basis, this is referred to as reciprocal interdependence. In brief, what this means is that the output of one department can be the input of every other department.

For example ...

... take the design process of a new model of coffee maker in a company which has an F structure. Research and Development put an initial idea for the coffee maker on paper. Before this design can come on to the market, however, the input of other departments is required.

- Marketing and sales has to determine whether this model is what the consumer is waiting for.
- Production has to determine whether this model can be produced on existing machines or whether new machines and new techniques have to be acquired.
- Purchasing has to determine whether the required materials can be obtained in the coming years, and to ensure that these materials are not on any list of prohibited materials.

Research and Development cannot proceed without a reaction from each of these departments. It is directly dependent on them. However, it is impossible to predict when the reaction of each department will be received. Nor can the nature of the reaction be predicted (great idea/technically impossible/attainable with some adjustments/no reaction at all). Moreover, by the time all the departments have reacted to the first idea, four new versions of the new coffee maker may have been produced. The departments' reactions may result in a further proposal – version six of the design – which will have to go the rounds of the departments all over again.
In this kind of situation, there is a high risk of confusion and of mistakes being made – a serious problem in a development process. Throughout such a process, close coordination is crucial.

reciprocal interdependence Reciprocal interdependence is illustrated in Fig 5.18. With this form, an appropriate coordination mechanism is direct communication via a task force or project group.

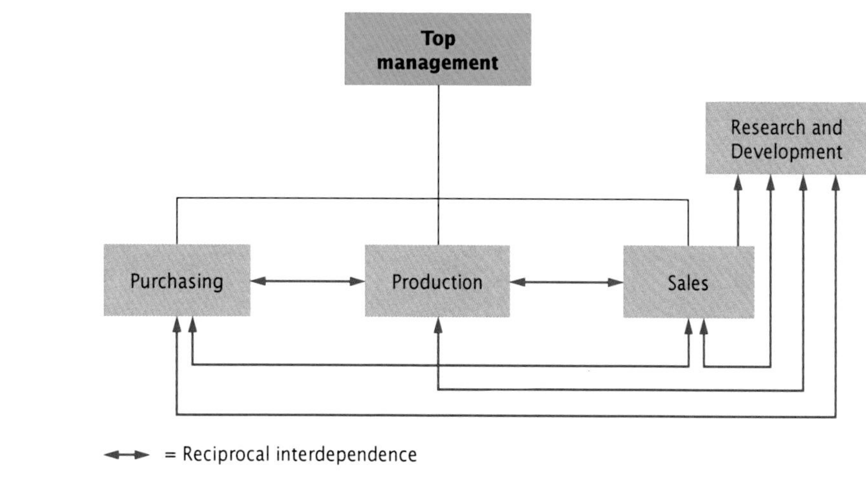

Figure 5.18 *Reciprocal interdependence*

5.3.7 *The three roles of executive authority*

manager's authority Before we can discuss the project organization and the matrix organization, we must first consider the three aspects of a manager's authority as these form an important part of these structures.

A manager has the authority to make decisions. He or she will exercise this authority in one of three ways:

- *administrative boss* *In a hierarchical way* (the administrative boss). The manager with this role is responsible for the general running of the department or team. In addition, such a manager takes care of matters relating to individual employees – for example, evaluation, training or further education, career planning, and so on.
- *work boss* *In an operational way* (the work boss). This type of manager decides how specific work activities need to progress and prioritizes work activities – for example, inserting into the production schedule a rush order which has to be processed quickly.
- *specialist boss* *In a functional way* (the specialist boss). This manager decides how the products and services are to be produced and the professional methods, techniques and instruments to be used in the process. An information and systems control manager who determines that everybody within the organization should use a particular text processing package is exercising a functional form of authority.

unity of command An executive may exercise all three forms of authority; this is referred to as 'unity of command'. However, the roles can also be divided among several persons – referred to as 'breaking the unity of command'. It is unity of direction, not unity of command, that is the main concern within an organization. If there is unity of direction, managers will not make conflicting decisions; rather, they will provide the organization's employees with clear direction.

Having considered the three forms interdependence can take and the three types of executive authority, we can now return to our discussion of the most common forms of organizational structure.

5.3.8 *Project organization*

project organization

Project organization involves the splitting up of an organization into semi-autonomous units or project groups which are focused on a particular project – for example, the automation of a financial administration system.

A project can be defined as:
- a whole set of activities
- to be performed by more than one specialist group
- in a temporary cooperative relationship
- which is directed at a clearly specified result
- which needs to be attained within a limited period of time and with limited resources.

project manager

Employees from the various parts of the organization and various specialist fields are assigned to a project group which then focuses exclusively on completing the project. A project manager is appointed. The project manager and the other members of the project group will return to their former roles as soon as the project or a phase of the project has been completed.
The project manager has operational responsibility for the progress and the prompt completion of the project within the budget limits. The project manager sets priorities, monitors progress, adapts activities and takes corrective action where necessary.
In a firm or institution with a project organization, activities will be arranged in two ways:
- *Within the organization itself*, which can be seen as a reservoir of resources
- *Within the project group*, which can be seen as the executive working unit with a one-off operational task assignment – for example, to develop a new prototype of gasoline engine or to design and build a new hospital

This two-way organizational division is illustrated in Fig 5.19.

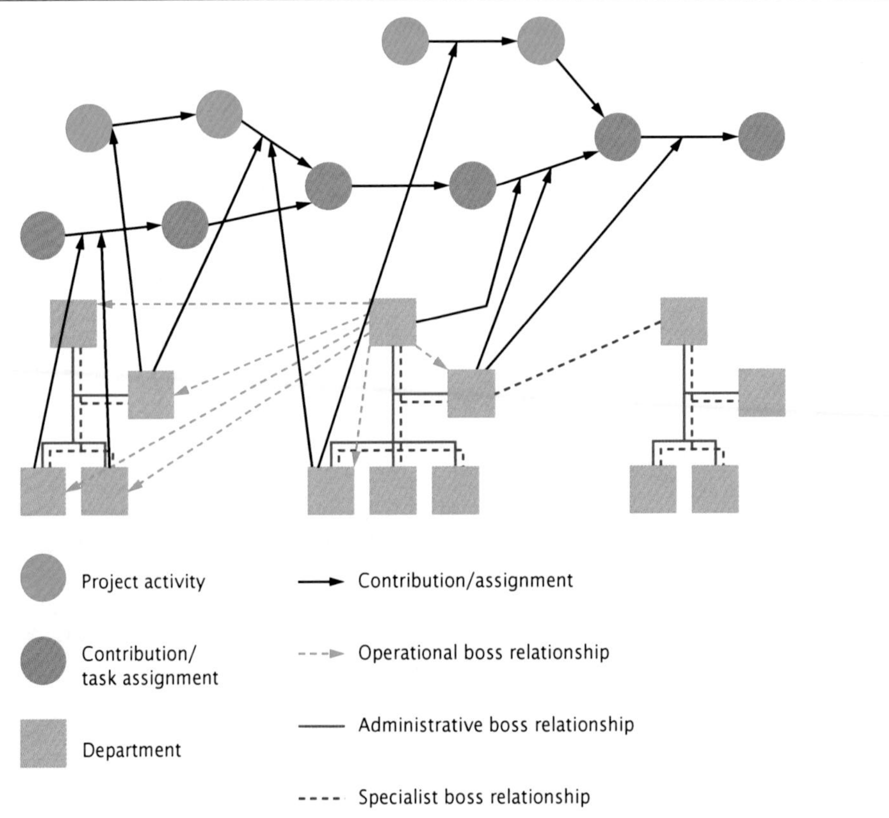

Figure 5.19
The project organization

Problems associated with the management of projects

A project-based approach to organizational structure not only provides solutions for existing problems, but also creates new problems. If there is a lack of effective coordination with the organization itself, it will reject project organization as alien to it. In reaction to this, those responsible for project organization will start to organize their own affairs and distance themselves from the main organization. The appointment of top management to the project group can help to bring it back into the organization and gain the acceptance of the organization itself.
Almost every organization and department encounters development problems caused by the ever increasing pace of change in the fields of technology and marketing. If top management does not address such developments, many official and non-official groups – sometimes working together, sometimes working in competition – will spring up and attempt to resolve the problems.

lack of clarity

If a project-based form of organization is applied to everyday practices and there is a lack of clarity about the philosophy of projects and the project-based approach as well as inadequate cohesion and coordination, this will lead unavoidably to time, budgetary and quality standards being exceeded.

budgetary excesses

Budgetary excesses with infrastructural projects are often caused by decision making that is influenced by political considerations and the machinations of senior bureaucrats, politicians and parliamentary representatives. Rose-colored estimations of the profits and expenses will predictably lead to the budget being exceeded.

problems in the interrelationships

Problems in the interrelationships between those commissioning the project and those commissioned as well as the users and the suppliers will also result in excesses of the above kind. As such, clarity in respect of the internal as well as the external project structure is crucially important. Particularly with large and complex projects, good collaboration between and within the project teams is also a determining factor in the success or otherwise of the project. For the project to remain viable, its leaders will need to have managerial and social skills, not to mention strong personalities.

THE GOVERNMENT FAILS TO LEARN FROM ITS MISTAKES

Lying can be profitable. Or at least, according to Dr Bent Flyvbjerg, a Danish professor who has been attached to the Delft University of Technology for the past year and a half. For many years, Flyvbjerg has been researching the costs associated with major infrastructure projects throughout the world. His conclusion is the project budgetary excesses are universally common.

According to Flyvbjerg, the costs associated with infrastructural projects – which are always extremely expensive – are deliberately underestimated in order for them to be given the thumbs-up. 90% of all projects end up costing more than provided for in the budget. Rail projects are responsible for the biggest blowouts: they end up costing an average of 45% more than estimated.

Lying pays. Project managers will consciously choose to put a politically desirable rail connection up for sale in the expectation of this move speeding up the decision-making process somewhat. By the time that the project is due for completion, they will claim the actual cost. Flyvbjerg's research has shown that this bizarre game has been played for the past 75 years, and throughout the world.
No government seems to have learned from this, and it would seem that Amsterdam is just as stupid as the rest of the world.

Source: *Het Financieele Dagblad*, 23 February 2009 and 16 December 2009

The most frequent problems of a project-based approach, based on the experiences of about 400 project managers from many different organizations, both in the private and public sectors, have been categorized (see Table 5.1).

Table 5.1 *Common problems in project management*

Problem	
Lack of clarity in project philosophy and approach (philosophy)	5%
Lack of cohesion and coordination (phasing)	15%
Exceeding or failing to reach targets in terms of time, money, quality and information (control)	19%
Bottlenecks between the project and its environment (especially customers, users and suppliers) (external structuring))	22%
Lack of clarity in the internal project structure (internal structuring)	6%
Lack of cooperation within the project teams (cooperation)	32%
Lack of managerial and social skills and assertiveness on the part of the project manager (personal quality)	1%
	100%

Source: Wijnen, Renes and Storm (1984)

matrix organization

In the matrix organization (see Section 5.3.9) authority over the operational personnel is shared by the project management and the management of the organizational unit of the organization itself. In this type of organization, project management and departmental management need to be able to work together and coordinate their activities. The project management can assert its authority across the various fields. The project group functions in conjunction with the other departments, not separately.

pure project structure

unity of command

In the pure project structure, project managers have three forms of authority (hierarchical, operational and functional) at their disposal. This is necessary in order to control the activities associated with the projects. In other words, project managers have as much authority over their employees as departmental heads have over theirs – unity of command in a temporary unit. Project managers may even have a complete executive and staff apparatus at their disposal while the managers of more permanent departments may only have a small group of employees. In any case, in this structure the reciprocal interdependence of project management vis-à-vis the permanent department is usually limited to the strategic and sometimes the administrative levels of decision making, and rarely extends to the operational level of decision making.

CASE

Mini case study 5.2

Matrix management ... a structure for running those companies that have both a diversity of products and a diversity of markets

Matrix management is a structure for running those companies that have both a diversity of products and a diversity of markets. In a matrix structure, responsibility for the products goes up and down one dimension and responsibility for the markets goes up and down another. This leaves most managers with a dual reporting line: to the head of their product division on the one hand, and to the head of their geographical market on the other.

Despite the potential confusion that this duality creates, matrix management was enormously popular in the 1970s and 1980s. Leading the fashion was Philips, a Dutch multinational electronics company, which first set up a matrix structure after the Second World War. It had national organisations (NOs) and product divisions (PDs), and for a while they operated successfully as a network. The network was held together by a number of coordinating committees, which resolved any conflict between the two.

The crux came with the profit and loss account. Who was to be held accountable for it? At first, the answer was both the NOs and the PDs. But this was unsatisfactory, and the NOs eventually got the upper hand. Philips's PDs did not like that, and they fought back. In the 1990s, when the company was not doing so well, its organisational structure was completely overhauled. A few powerful PDs were given worldwide responsibility for the profit and loss account, and the NOs became subservient to them.

Dual reporting led to conflict and confusion: the proliferation of channels created informational log-jams as a proliferation of committees and reports bogged down the organization, and overlapping responsibilities produced turf battles and a loss of accountability. Separated by barriers of distance, language, time and culture, managers found it virtually impossible to clarify the confusion and resolve the conflicts.

The authors maintained that matrix management had been part of an attempt by companies to create complicated structures that matched their increasingly complicated strategies. But it focused only on the anatomy of the organisation. It ignored the physiology (the systems that allow information to flow in and around the organisation) and the psychology (the 'shared norms, values and beliefs' of the organisation's managers).

Organisations could implement matrix management successfully ... if they started at the other end. Their first objective should be 'to alter the organisational psychology ... only later do they consolidate and confirm their progress by realigning organisational anatomy through changes in the formal structure'.

Nigel Nicholson of the London Business School says that the matrix structure is 'one of the most difficult and least successful organisational forms'. Evolutionists like him allege that matrix forms are inherently unstable because they have conflicting forces pulling towards too many different centres of gravity.

Source: *The Economist*, October 23, 2009

5.3.9 The matrix organization

matrix structure

An organization may introduce a matrix structure if problems arise which cannot be resolved by one department alone (see Fig 5.20). A matrix structure – so-called because of the existence of both horizontal and vertical lines of authority – can be created to achieve the required level of coordination and cooperation between various departments. It is often a combination of a F(unctional) organizational structure and a project structure and/or business unit or divisional structure.

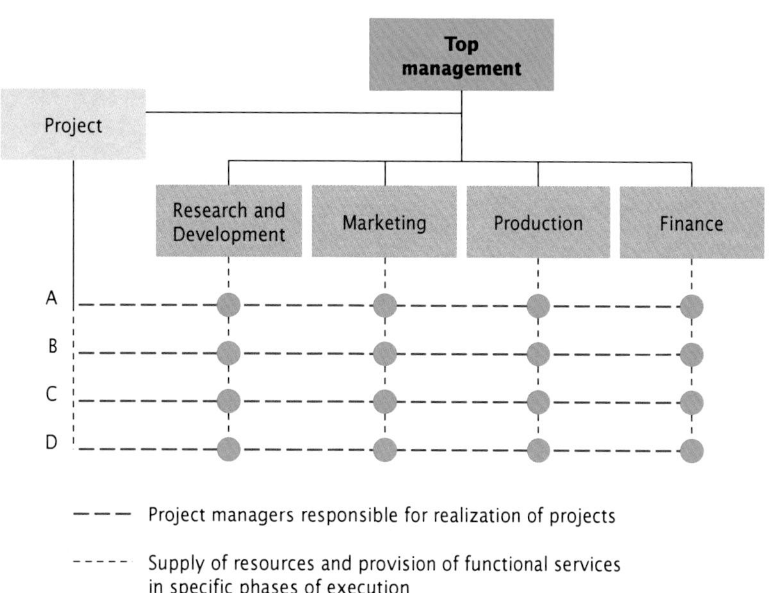

Figure 5.20
Lines of authority in a matrix organization

matrix organization

An employee in a matrix organization is a person who fills two membership roles:

1 He or she is a member of a functional department on the basis of his or her expertise
2 He or she is a member of a project group, operational unit or division in which he or she works on a common development or production task, together with colleagues from other departments, disciplines or units.

The work performed by the employee will be determined by the project group; how the work is carried out is determined by the employee's functional base.

In its temporary form, a matrix organization can be seen as a cross between a departmentalized organizational structure and a project organizational structure. However, if a matrix organization is established on a permanent basis a certain degree of authority is assigned to managers responsible for a particular product range or client, who then have a dual role with regard to the department line managers. A product manager in a manufacturing company and an account manager in a financial services company are examples of such managers. A matrix organization, therefore, has a dual information and reporting function which can often result in problems relating to the balance of power. A balance needs to be struck between the interests of the project, on the one hand, and the interests of the individual department on the other. Tensions and possible areas of conflict will be created if authority is not clearly defined.

During the execution of his or her activities, an employee has to report to two different bosses:

functional boss

- the functional boss of the department from which the employee has been temporarily seconded, and

operational boss

- the operational boss, who as project manager is responsible for the timely, efficient and effective completion of the project.

dual lines of authority

This involves, therefore, dual lines of authority, which break the unity of command, with all the attendant consequences. Overcoming these difficulties and creating a balance between the two dimensions of the matrix requires specific skills on the part of both management and employees. Such a balancing mechanism is illustrated in the model developed by Galbraith (1973) shown in Fig 5.21.

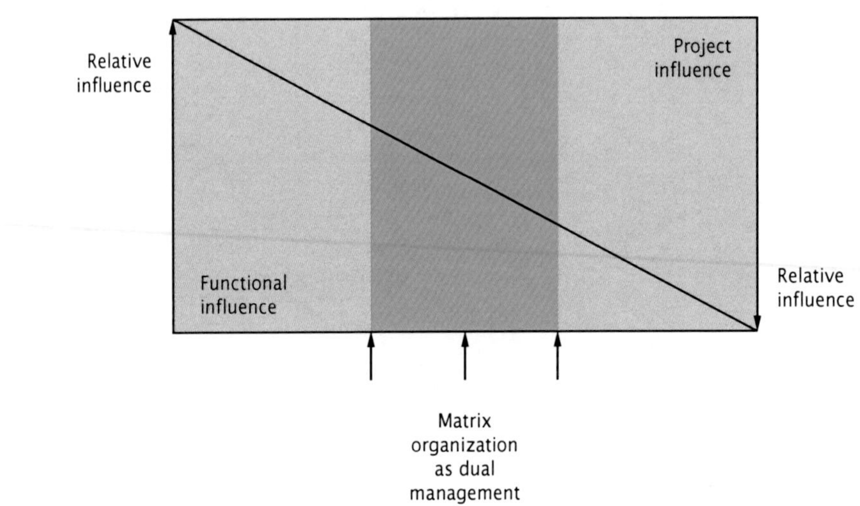

Figure 5.21
Conditions for a matrix organization

Source: *Galbraith*, 1973

A bilateral information and reporting system has to be incorporated so that the project can be monitored and controlled from various areas of responsibility. The quality of coordination will depend among other things on the degree to which project group members have:

- The appropriate expertise,
- Adequate authority, and
- The right information.

If these conditions are not met, this will have a negative effect on the effectiveness of the coordination. The quality and skills of the functional and operational managers will be relatively crucial. The matrix organization has the following advantages:

- There is a focus on both specialist expertise and operational, execution-oriented coordination.
- Consultation and flexibility are directly related to the requirements of the project.
- Teamwork is encouraged.

The disadvantages include the following:

- The structure is complex and often lacks clarity.
- The organizational balance can easily be affected by personal power relationships.
- A high degree of consultation is required.
- Such a structure demands a high level of effective management at all levels.
- Employees must have organizational skills.
- It is difficult to define authority unambiguously.

A matrix organizational structure is most appropriate in the following situations:

- Joint efforts are required from various disciplines or professional fields.
- The project involves the resolution of complex problems.
- High quality standards are expected.
- A large number of cases of intensive reciprocal interdependence are present.

Projects can also be brought to completion via a matrix-like structure when there is a relatively permanent organization as a basic reservoir of resources (see Section 5.3.8). If this is the case, the required functional expertise is brought together on a temporary basis and within the framework of a project organization under the operational authority of a project manager. In cases where value is to be added via projects, the most appropriate organizational form has been described as an 'adhocracy' (Toffler, 1969; Keuning & Eppink, 1978; Mintzberg, 1979).

adhocracy

The enterprise as a structured network: is the matrix back again?

global matrix structure

At the end of the seventies the global matrix structure was adopted by firms that worked worldwide. They expected it to reduce the tensions between product visions and between countries and regions. Most companies, however, soon regarded the system to be unworkable, because decision-making stalled frequently. In the eighties and the middle of the nineties companies such as Dow Chemical and Philips dropped the structure without hesitation.
In the daily practice of the business world, working with a matrix business structure is not an easy task. Philips, Unilever, Procter & Gamble, ABN Amro and others have come back from being directed from two or even more sides: from product (P), geography (G), and/or market (M), and/or fields of expertise (F).
In the nineties, Philips was described by its own top executive as a 'plate of spaghetti' because of its many participation and decision lines, and matrix was outlawed as a subject (see Metze, 1997). In their quest for the ideal organizational form, companies have, in the meantime, again expressed a preference for the unilateral direction, either from P (product), such as Philips, or from G (geographic area).

matrix structure

The term 'matrix structure' has negative associations because of negative experiences. But Goold and Campbell (2003) believe that it should not be completely abandoned. By making some well-thought-out adaptations, the advantages can be utilized and the disadvantages avoided.
It seems preferable to substitute the term 'enterprise as structured network' for 'matrix'.
When designing a structured network, management should concentrate on five issues. Finding

the right balance between self-steering and structure warrants special attention. The five points of special interest are as follows:
- Make sure there are clear responsibilities without too many details.
- Learn from each other, but retain important differences.
- Aim at collaboration without an unnecessary search for synergy.
- Recognize common responsibility, but make sure that the individual segments of the organization bear their own responsibility.
- The higher levels of management in the corporate hierarchy should add value to the individual segments of the organization without unnecessary costs, pointless overheads and misplaced interference.

What this is saying is in fact 'make sure there is enough structure, but not too much', because otherwise you will revert to a cumbersome, unclear matrix structure with unclear reporting requirements, slow decision-making, vague responsibilities, loss of autonomy and so on. The structured network attempts to avoid the typical disadvantages of the old matrix organization. Companies like ABB, IBM, Shell and Siemens are trying out this variant because the emphasis on one competitive aspect is not enough nowadays: customer segments as opposed to product groups and/or geographic regions. It is clear that essentially it is more a matter of a change in behavior in organizations than of a change in the structure. After all, the matrix variant has been around for quite some time.

change in behavior

5.4 Organizational and management considerations for growth and development

Organizations are always in motion and the world within which organizations exist never rests. As a result, various and often new management problems arise. It is often the case that the stage of development of an organization will determine the way in which problems are handled. When an organization becomes larger and more complex, problems are increasingly approached systematically and with reference to policy. Those factors which receive special attention at each stage of growth and development will become clear when we start to examine the relationship between the various management factors and growth.

stage of development

5.4.1 Starting up a business

In theory, there are three ways of starting a business:
- Setting up a new firm
- A company takeover (or management buyout)
- Company succession

Setting up a new firm

For the entrepreneur who is just starting out, the setting up of a new firm has the advantage that many matters can be determined by the entrepreneur him or herself. The founding entrepreneur determines among other things:
- Which products the company will be supplying
- The location where the company activities will be performed
- The legal form which the company will take
- The size of the company
- The scope of the activities, not only in technological terms, but also in the sense of financial and human resources
- The design of production methods, the production line and the organization

founding entrepreneur

On the negative side, starting costs are quite high and it may be some time before revenue starts to be generated.

For example ...

What services do our fellow human beings require? An increasing number of entrepreneurial Europeans are trying to find out. The shoeshiner has made a comeback. For those who can afford to pay someone to do it, even ironing can be done. From the comfort of one's own home, one telephone call is all it takes to send for a Greek meal or a pizza. Kitty litter, videos, breakfast in bed, a new cover for a worn-out chair or merely a filled shopping bag – one telephone call and somebody will bring them to your doorstep.

More and more people are starting up their own businesses. Often these have to be built up from scratch, perhaps by a single individual or a single family. In the past, 'entrepreneur' was a dirty word. An entrepreneur was somebody who got rich on the backs of other people and contributed to the pollution of the environment. Some entrepreneurs were just people who had been looking for work for some time and who wanted to see whether they could work for themselves. Most entrepreneurs also preferred not to have a boss looking over their shoulders all the time or so people thought.

For example ...

Rick Meyer of the dog service company *Paw*, describes himself as 'pig-headed' – which is why being his own boss suits him. 'When you think of something at night, it is more profitable. A boss *appreciates* you thinking after working hours, but that is all.' For the last four years he has run a dog-walking service, together with his partner, Jenny Lane. It started out in a very modest way. 'The starting capital was spent on an answering machine,' Rick comments. They picked up and dropped off the dogs with their own car. The dog service developed out of a hobby of Rick's: dog training. Every now and then he walked other people's dogs. After an advertisement about the dog service in the local newspaper, customers came flocking in. After a while, he resigned from his old job as a distributor of newspapers. Jenny gradually gave up hers too. The couple has now even hired somebody to help them. The customers are usually 'dinkies' – dual-income, no kids – and shift workers or elderly people who want their dogs to receive more exercise.

Entrepreneurs starting out in business for the first time might find the following points useful.

- Be open to advice.
- Let someone from a bank look over plans and make comments on them.
- An ideal entrepreneur can associate well with other people.
- Sales skills are useful, as are strategic thinking and the ability to make deals.
- A new entrepreneur does not need to be superhuman.

Entrepreneurship

entrepreneurs Recent research shows that one out of five starting out entrepreneurs will fail in the first year of existence. Six out of ten companies will end up bankrupt within five years. Some of the factors behind these failures are lacking a proper business plan (56%), too limited starting capital and limited entrepreneurial abilities. The long working hours (an average working week of 66 hours), finding customers, the competition and consumers who fail to pay on time all cause young entrepreneurs quite a lot of headaches.

inventors Other research shows that inventors neglect market opportunities and have difficulty commercializing their inventions in their own company for reasons that include a lack of money (38%), ideas being imitated by others (12%), no market (38%) and not being able to find an appropriate partner (12%). Research shows that only ten per cent of technological inventions appear to be successful on the market. Most of the time the inventors do not have enough insight into market opportunities and lack entrepreneurial ability. If offered a permanent job, one out of five entrepreneurs would take it immediately. One of the recommendations made is that inventors should learn better marketing and planning skills. The creation of special financing facilities (by, for example, starting foundations for technologies) is also recommended, as is a mentor system whereby experienced inventors help inventors just starting out to acquire entrepreneurial skills.

Company takeovers

takeover A takeover of a company often requires a large initial investment. When purchasing an existing company, the entrepreneur will have to thoroughly research the true value of the company involved. Sometimes it is necessary to be mindful of the loss of customers when the company changes owner; sometimes the range of products needs to be revised, or essential company functions such as marketing and sales or production and purchasing are not carried out adequately.

management buyouts In the past few years, management buyouts have become increasingly common. In these cases, the ownership of the company is transferred to its management – often with the help of venture capital from investment companies, private or otherwise. In some cases, the personnel will also be involved in the transaction. It is often the case that after reviewing their current activities, large companies may decide on a strategic reorientation and repositioning of the company which involves a return to core activities. This may involve the liquidation of assets or privatization of peripheral parts of the business in the form of a management buyout or acquisition by another company (for example, ITT, ABB, Philips or Unilever).

intrapreneurship 'Intrapreneurship' is also expected to increase, as are individuals (whether singly or as a group) from an existing company establishing a new company with the help of the existing company. Forty per cent of new companies which start like this have an innovative character.

Company succession

company succession Company succession provides the new starter with the opportunity to acquire knowledge of business matters and make use of the goodwill of the retiring entrepreneur.

When looking to take over a company or take over management of a company by means of gradual succession, where the company is in private hands, it is important to know the true value of the company. In this respect the expertise of an accountant and bank manager are certainly of value. The purchase price can be seen as the sum of the equity of a company and the value of any goodwill. In the case of a takeover, goodwill is an extra amount of money which is paid for the good name of the company that is to be taken over. This good name has arisen from a unique product or service offered.

5.4.2 *Questions of policy after the start*

Once a company has got underway and shows a certain degree of growth, or when a company has gained an established position, policy questions relating to the route to expansion and growth have to be addressed – for example, changes in the legal form, methods of financing (possibly by means of stock exchange flotation), whether or not to cooperate with other companies (partially by alliance and joint venture, or completely by means of takeover or merger).

If a company does not have all the necessary resources at its disposal (for example, finance, new products, distribution channels, etc.), it can perhaps seek external financial resources. It can also seek to collaborate with another company.

5.4.3 Stages in the growth and development of a company

The problems facing a particular company will to a certain extent be a function of the company's position within the cycle of organizational growth and development. Compare, for example, the growth and development problems of a six-month-old company with 20 employees to the growth and development problems of an established company which has existed for 30 years and has 600 employees. In the former case, the planning of cash flow may be vital, while in the latter case, coordination and control of company activities by means of explicit strategic planning and budgeting may be more important.

stages of growth Companies undergo seven stages of growth (see Figure 5.22):

1 Build up
2 Survival
3 Success
4 Take-off and expansion
5 Resource maturity and optimal position
6 Ossification and rigidity
7 New types of growth

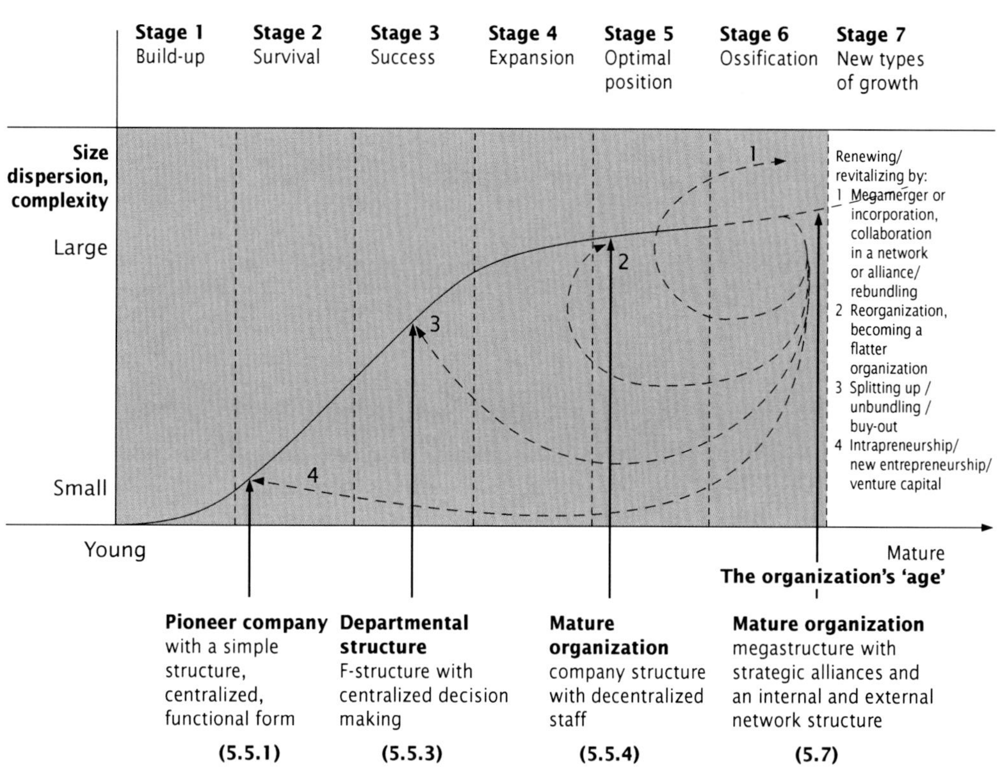

Figure 5.22
Stages of company growth

WHAT ARE SUCCESSFUL ORGANIZATIONS DOING DIFFERENTLY?

Each year, business magazine *Fortune*, in conjunction with the Hay Group, investigates which enterprises are most admired by around 4000 executives, governors and stock market analysts. This year, 689 companies in 28 countries and 64 business sectors were investigated.

The researchers also investigated whether certain forms of organizational structure enhanced (or the opposite: weakened) the effectiveness of large international companies. Is there any one best way of organizing your company? The answer is no: there is no such thing as a best structure. A company can be just as successful with a *highly centralized* structure, for example, as a *highly decentralized* one.

According to research leader Katie Lemaire: 'The structure can work to the company's advantage as long as the structure is aligned with the business model and the company's competitive strategy'.

Nor is there any one operating model that sticks out above the others. Moreover, it doesn't matter if things are done one way in one section of the company and another way in another. In general, the operating models used by the companies that were investigated were highly dynamic, enabling them, for example, to operate differently in growth markets to the way they operate in established markets without needing to make any changes to the organizational design.

For outstanding companies, a good reputation is more important than it has ever been.

A stable strategy
One characteristic shared by the companies in the ranking is that they all have a *strong and stable strategy*. In times of instability, this can be an advantage. Companies that change their strategy usually have to adapt their organizational structure too, and in time of recession, this can be particularly hard to do. Not only does it shift the focus of the employees from the outside to the inside, but structural changes devour time and energy, creating an additional burden during a recession. If your strategy can withstand the bad times, you can simply keep on working without being distracted.

Another characteristic is that these companies all focus on achieving worldwide recognition and developing talented personnel, and they are have CEOs at the helm who have been in the company for some considerable time and who will be replaced in an orderly and predictable manner and without fuss and bother: these companies do not go in for all the antics associated with celebrity replacements.

Source: *Fortune* 2007-2009, www.Kluwer.management.nl

5.5 Organizational structure in development

In Section 5.4, we discussed the growth and development of organizations from the point of view of policy and management factors. We will now explore the development of the organization from the point of view of its structure.
The larger and more complex a company or institution becomes, the more the organization of the various tasks to be fulfilled needs to be adapted to the new demands of the external environment.

5.5.1 Organizational structure in the start-up phase

primary function

When a business has just begun its operations, the organization is usually small and the structure simple. There are likely to be only a few primary functions for which employees are hired to fulfill – for example, the purchasing, production and sales of an industrial company (see Fig 5.23). There is likely to be only one product, aimed at a limited market in a limited geographical area.

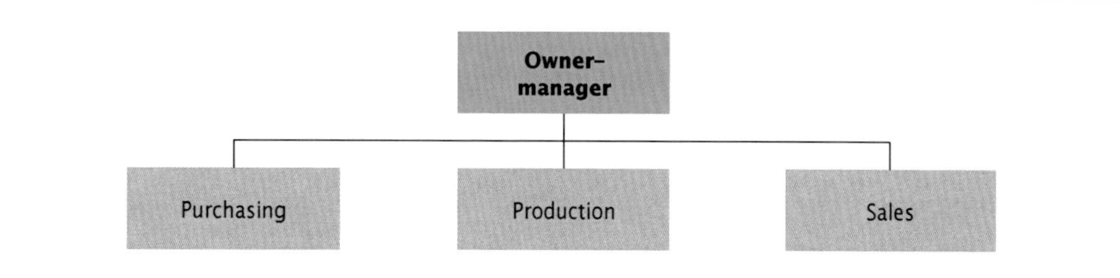

Figure 5.23
Organizational structure in the start-up phase

highly centralized functional organization
simple organization
owner-manager

In this first phase of development, the company is usually still managed by its founder – a person who discovered a market gap and decided to set up a business to fill that gap. An employee may be recruited for the performing of operational activities. In other word, this is a highly centralized functional organization with a single manufacturing and distribution process.
Such companies are characterized by simple organization, the capacity to influence operations directly and direct and informal communication and work practices. There is little long-term planning and few formal prescriptions or procedures. Problems are usually solved on an ad hoc basis, often involving the owner-manager – an approach also applied to the marketing of the business. The owner-manager works closely with his or her employees and market, but at the same time occupies a position of authority. There is rarely a management level directly under the owner-manager. If one exists, it is often a management role fraught with problems. The continuity of such a company is therefore not necessarily guaranteed. Finding a successor to continue the business may be difficult.
A typical business start-up can be characterized as follows:

- *Structure of the organization*: centralized F form, with minimal internal division of work
- *Research and development*: carried out by the owner-manager
- *Performance measurement*: by personal assessment and on the basis of subjective criteria
- *Reward/payment*: often unsystematic and paternalistic.
- *Control system*: strategic control, design of the organizational structure, and control of the operational processes all under personal control
- *Strategic choices*: dependent on the personal aspirations of the owner-manager

5.5.2 Organizational structure in the growth phase

As a company expands, its expansion will probably take the form of a more detailed subdivision of the organization's primary functions. For example, the sales function may be split into areas or client groups, or the production function into production process phases. At the same time some support functions will probably be created alongside the primary functions (see Fig 5.24).

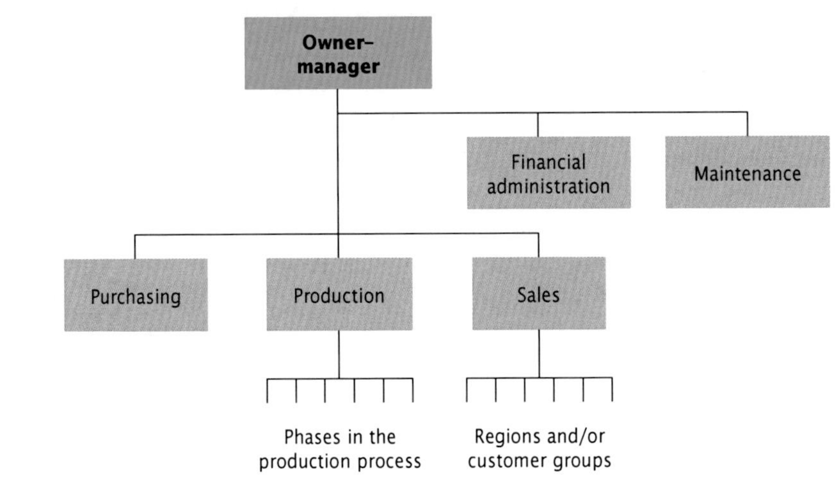

Figure 5.24
Organizational structure in the early stages of the growth phase

specialist departments

If the size of the organization allows it, it is usually necessary at this stage for the managerial functions to be supported by specialist departments in the field of financial administration, maintenance and so on. Further support and advice in particular fields of specialist and professional expertise can be bought in via external consultants – for example, in the areas of market research, organizational efficiency, administration and automation.

As the organization grows, informal communication and commitment are no longer likely to be adequate. The owner-manager must delegate tasks plus the attendant authority to middle managers appointed for the purpose (for example, a production manager or departmental heads) if the organization's market position is to be consolidated. This new level of management needs to be incorporated within the growing organization if it is to survive.

At this point, the company will often convert its legal status into that of a private company. The process of subdivision is then continued. Further growth in sales volume, geographical expansion, market development and vertical integration will result in the need for further subdivision of the primary functions. The organization's size allows the recruitment of in-house specialists – for example, in the areas of marketing, planning, research and personnel – who can provide auxiliary support to the managerial process.

Business growth will lead to a change in orientation and organization; there will probably have to be a more systematic approach to management and the owner-manager will have to adopt a more detached approach to the running of the company. One or more assistant managers may be appointed. A works council and board of directors may be created.

formal organization

Management needs to be based on a clear division of work and coordination. Furthermore, organizational methods and planning techniques need to be introduced. Formal organization will become more important, as will the need for top management to provide a vision and a sense of direction for the organization.

In addition to the creation of new departments, greater demands will be made of existing departments, resulting in increases in staff numbers and the level of expertise. For example, the finance department will probably be headed by a controller rather than a book-keeper. The support functions will also change in character. In addition to supporting the primary functions, these support functions will take on a policy-influencing and governing role by supplying management with information both on request and otherwise. The recently appointed in-house specialists will also make a contribution, although external consultants will still be used when required. The small business will now have grown into a fully departmentalized organization set up with a centralized functional structure under top management (see Fig 5.25).

external consultants
fully departmentalized organization

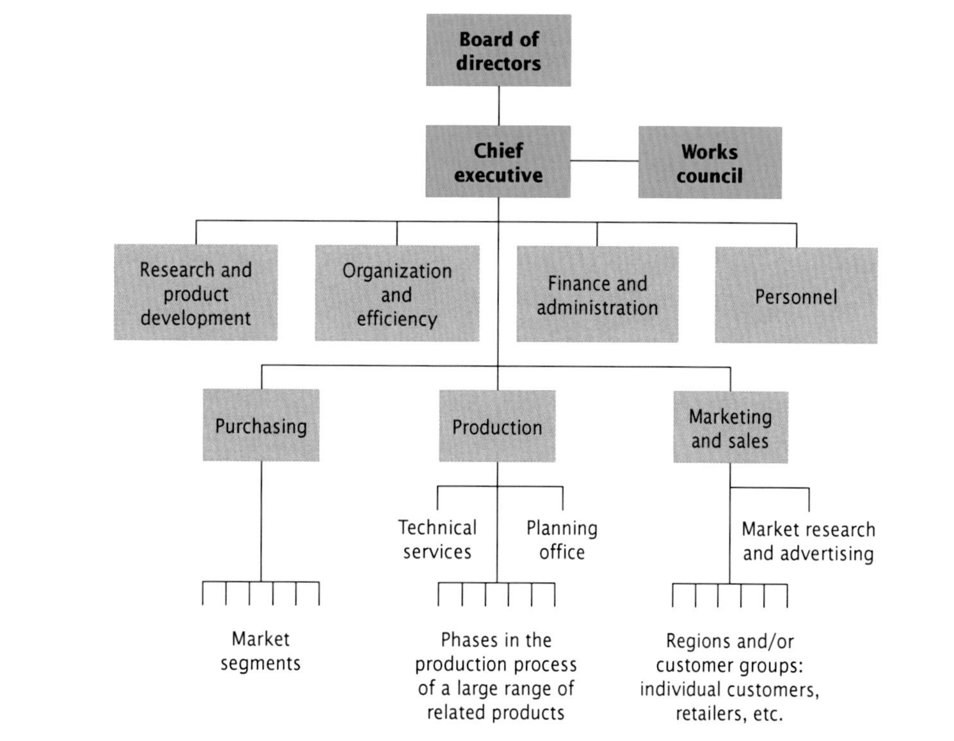

Figure 5.25 *Organizational structure of a company with a fully departmentalized structure in the later stages of growth*

A typical business at the growth stage of development can be characterized as follows:

- *Structure of the organization*: relatively centralized F form, with extensive internal division of work.
- *Research and development*: undertaken by an in-house department which carries out systematic searches for product improvement opportunities, product development and upgrading of processes.
- *Performance measurement*: to an increasing degree impersonal and indirect, involving the setting of technical and/or financial criteria.
- *Reward/Payment*: systematic, objective, focusing on commitment and years of service.
- *Control system*: personal with regard to strategic decision making, but otherwise involving increased delegation of operational decision-making authorities, with control by way of policies, instructions, rulings and procedures.
- *Strategic choice*: including options such as further vertical integration (forward or backward), increase in market share and expansion via development of related product lines or via related markets.

5.5.3 Organizational structure of the full-size and mature company

The departmental structure

P(roduct) grouping
F(unctional) grouping

As the product range increases in medium-sized and large companies, an organizational structure with a P(roduct) grouping (directly under the top) may work better than the existing F(unctional) grouping. Alternatively, if the main focus of such a company is its international operations or a particular market sector, then a G(eographical) grouping into countries, continents or regions, or a M(arket sector) grouping may be preferred. This would mean that the coordination of the various operational activities associated with a certain group of products or a certain geographical area or market sector could be delegated to a lower level within the organization.

This change would involve a large degree of reorganization. The grouping into primary functions would be abandoned in favor of a grouping into product groups, geographical areas

or market sectors; each of these groups would then have its own primary functions.
If a G(eographical) structure is adopted as the basic organizational structure, a more detailed grouping of the primary functions to product groups could take place if felt to be desirable.

F-structure
P- G- or M-structure
centralized departmentalized structure

Support services often remain attached to top management when a business moves from an F-structure to a P- G- or M-structure, and central staff and support services report directly to top management. This is referred to as a relatively centralized departmentalized structure (see Fig 5.26). Top management no longer has to be involved in coordination of the operational tasks and can occupy itself with policies and important strategic issues to a greater extent.

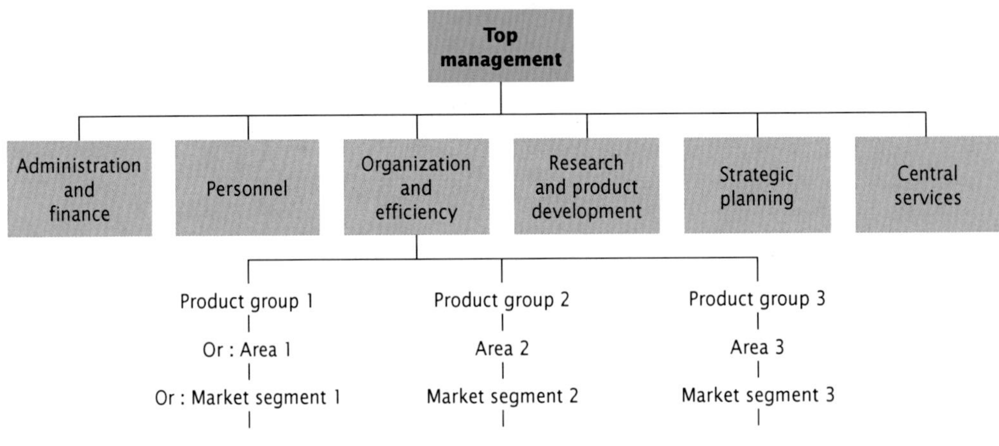

Figure 5.26
Organizational structure of a company with a centralized P-, G- or M-structure

The decentralized multi-divisional structure

The product groups will attempt to develop into relatively autonomous units, each with their own employees in the central staff and support services such as finance and administration, personnel, product development and so on. Within the areas of their semi-autonomous operations and decision making, the individual units will have to delegate their decision-making authority further (that is, decentralize more). The specialized staff and support services which previously reported to top management will also have to do this. Organizational and operational decisions (rather than strategic decisions) will be the area most affected by decentralization. A number of central services will be maintained, but these will take on more of an advisory, coordinating, stimulating and controlling role (see Fig 5.27).

decentralized multi-divisional organization

A company at this stage of development is referred to as a decentralized multi-divisional organization set up directly under the top management level along product-market combinations or geographical areas. Growth is effected via diversification to an even wider and more heterogeneous field of activities. The activities are re-grouped into relatively homogenous units within divisions. These divisions are assisted by their own staff and support services and also by the corporate services which are attached to the top management level.
A typical business at this advanced stage of development can be characterized as follows:

- *Structure of the organization*: decentralized divisional form brought about via internal specialization (or grouping of business units)
- *Research and development*: extended to the search for totally new products as well as products of a different type

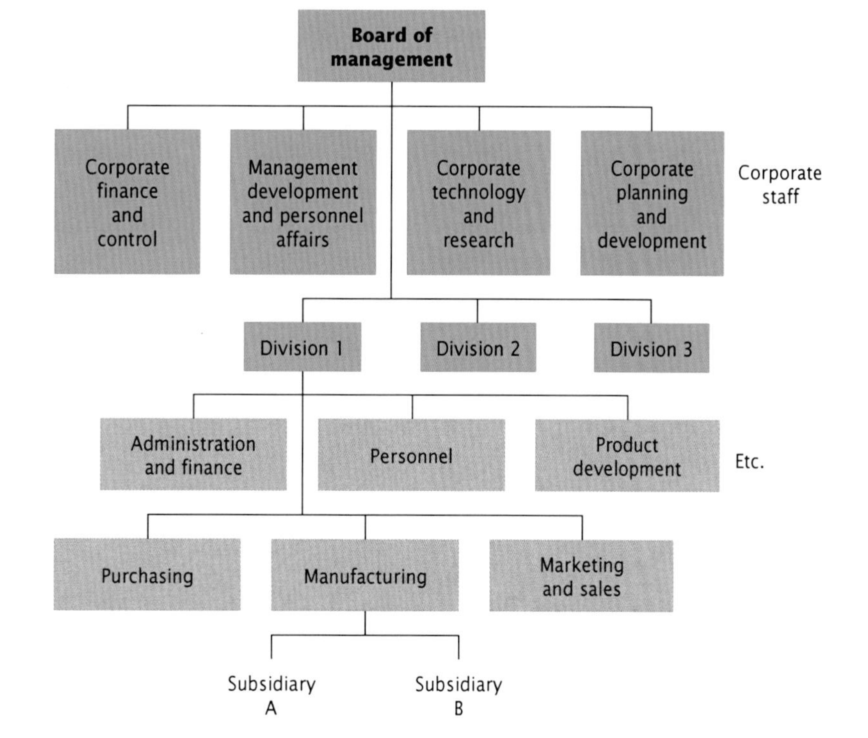

Figure 5.27
Organizational structure of a decentralized multi-divisional company

- *Performance measurement*: impersonal. Because there is now profit decentralization, financial criteria such as return on investment (ROI), or market criteria such as relative market share, can be used
- *Reward/Payment*: systematic, with rewards for top management related to performance
- *Control system*: delegation of product-market decision-making authorities within existing activities
- *Strategic choices*: including options such as entrance into and/or withdrawal from particular sectors, allocation of resources to divisions in identified sectors of industry and setting the speed of growth in each division and within the company as a whole

The holding company variant

financial conglomerate

holding company

At this point, the holding company or financial conglomerate which controls a number of business units should be described. Central services are usually concerned with administrative and financial control, strategy, legal affairs and personnel issues. In the holding company, however, central services play a different role.

Enterprises which have diversified into a wide field of very different company activities will incorporate these company activities into the company by forming a holding company (the mother) to oversee, coordinate and support the activities of the autonomous business units (the daughters). These business units may eventually be regrouped into divisions consisting of business units with a certain degree of internal coherence (for example, an industrial companies division).
A holding company will only have a limited supply of central services at its disposal, and these will be mainly concerned with the financial control of the organization's activities in both the short and the long term.

Changing demands

As a business moves from one stage of development to another (see Section 5.4.3), the relative importance of the individual factors changes. At each stage, the factors can be divided into three categories based on their relative importance:

1. Key factors for the success of the company and to which high priority should be given (referred to as critical success factors)
2. Factors which are clearly necessary for success and which certainly must receive attention
3. Factors which are of little immediate concern to top management

Categorizing each of the factors according to their importance at each stage in the development of the company will enable a clear picture of the demands made on management to be formed (see Fig 5.28). The stage of development of the business will determine what changes in managerial demands are necessary and which factors should be given priority. Figure 5.28 shows the changing nature of managerial challenges.

ability of the owner

In the early stages, the ability of the owner to do the job gives life to the business. Small businesses are built and are dependent on the talents of the owners – for example, their abilities to sell or produce. These factors are therefore of vital importance at Stages 1 and 2.

ability to delegate

The ability to delegate, however, is at the bottom of the scale since there are few, if any, employees to delegate to.

The more a company grows, the more people there are who will specifically devote themselves to sales, production or engineering and technology. At first they will support and then complement the owner, but later they will take over the owner's duties partly, if not completely, thus reducing the relative importance of the owner's capabilities. At the same time, the owner does not have to spend so much time on a diverse range of duties and can spend more time on management.

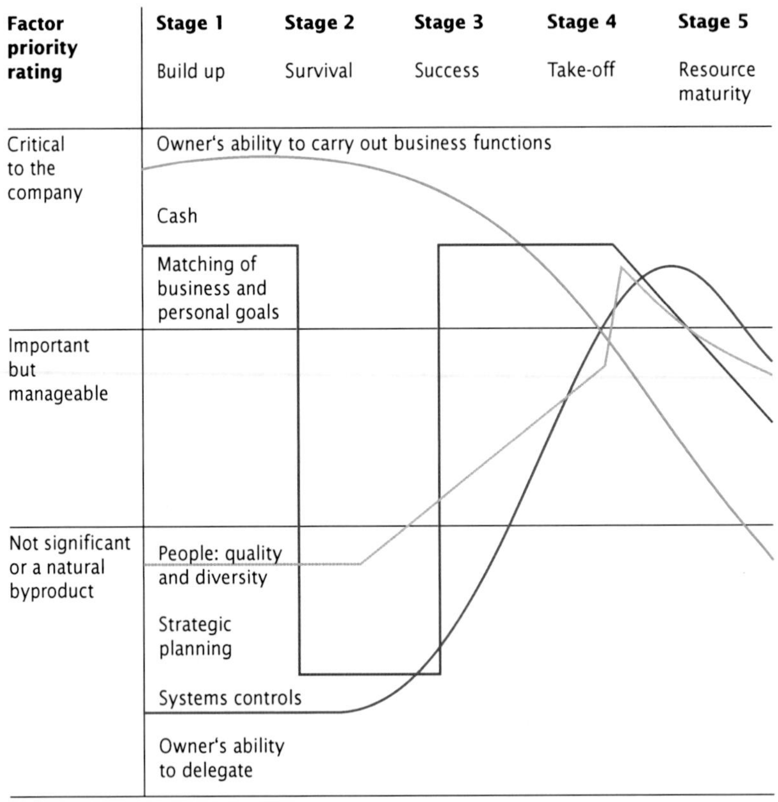

Factor priority rating | **Stage 1** Build up | **Stage 2** Survival | **Stage 3** Success | **Stage 4** Take-off | **Stage 5** Resource maturity

Critical to the company

Owner's ability to carry out business functions

Cash

Matching of business and personal goals

Important but manageable

Not significant or a natural byproduct

People: quality and diversity

Strategic planning

Systems controls

Owner's ability to delegate

Figure 5.28
Factors and their relative importance at various stages of growth and development

Source: *After Churchill and Lewis*, 1983

He or she will have to leave more and more work activities to others, and that means delegating. The inability of founders to stand back from operational activities and to begin managing and delegating is a common cause of company failure at Stages 3 and 4.
An owner who is contemplating a growth strategy must understand that changes in personal activities within the company will become necessary as a result of such a decision and has to consider the managerial demands depicted in Fig 5.28. Similarly, an entrepreneur setting up a new business should appreciate that during the initial stage he or she will have to do all the sales, manufacturing and engineering activities as well as the planning and managing of cash – with a corresponding cost in time, effort, energy and commitment.

cash

The importance of cash also changes depending on the development of the business. At the start, cash is extremely important; this becomes easier to manage in the success stage, but becomes a crucial factor again when the business begins to grow. At the end of Stage 4 or 5, when the pace of growth slows down, cash becomes a manageable factor again. Companies in Stage 3 need to recognize the financial needs and risks entailed in a move to Stage 4.

The issues of people, planning and systems gradually increase in importance when the initial slow growth of the company in Stage 3 converts to the fast growth of Stage 4. The entrepreneur needs to see to it that these resources are already present in the company in advance of the growth stage or are developed so that they are already there when the need for them arises.

personal goals

Matching business goals and the personal goals and ambitions of the owner is especially crucial in the first stage because the owner then has to recognize and accept the high demands which the company makes on his or her financial resources, time and energy. For some, these demands appear to be higher than they can handle. In the survival stage, however, the owner has reconciled these demands and survival is at the top of the list of priorities.

survival stage

success stage

The matching of goals is of little importance at Stage 2, but becomes very important again in the success stage. Owners then have to decide whether to risk the company's accumulated equity built up in order to realize further growth, whether they are prepared to commit all their time to growth, or whether they want to enjoy a few of the advantages which the success already gained has to offer. All too often an owner wants both, but it is very risky to expand a business and at the same time build a new house, for example.
To make a realistic decision with regard to the direction that is to be followed, owners need to consider both the personal as well as the business demands of the various strategies and should try to evaluate their own abilities to meet and live up to these demands and challenges.
Factors affecting business resources – such as market share, customer relations, sources of supply and technological base – are very important in the early stages. In later stages, the loss of, for example, an important customer, supplier or technological source can be borne more easily. As shown in Fig 5.28, the relative importance of this factor declines in line with growth.
The changing priority of the individual factors clearly illustrates the need for owner flexibility. In the first two stages, the company should strive not to pay tax until it is obliged to do so; in the period of growth and success the late payment of tax would seriously distort accounting data and use up too much management time. Furthermore, the conversion from 'doing' to 'delegating' requires flexibility. Holding on to old strategies and methods will not serve a company that is entering the stages of growth and may sometimes prove fatal.

5.5.4 Avoiding future problems

Even a passing glance at Fig 5.28 reveals the demands that the take-off and expansion stage make on the organization. Almost all factors except the owner's 'ability to do' are crucial. This is a stage of action and of potentially high rewards. An owner who wants to realize such growth must pose the following questions (Churchill & Lewis, 1983):

- Do my managers and I have the quality and diversity to fulfill the demands of managing a growing company?

- Do I have or will I shortly have the systems in place to handle the needs of a larger, more diversified company?
- Am I prepared to and do I have the ability to delegate decision making to my managers?
- Do I have enough cash and is my borrowing power big enough to finance fast growth, and am I prepared to risk everything to pursue rapid growth?

entrepreneur

In a similar way, a potential entrepreneur can see that starting a business demands the ability to do something very well (or an idea that is very marketable), a large amount of energy and a favorable cash flow forecast (or a large sum of cash directly to hand). These requirements are less important in Stage 5, when management skills, good information systems and budget controls have the highest priority. Perhaps this is the reason why some experienced people coming from large companies fail to make it as entrepreneurs or managers in a small company; they are used to delegating and are not good enough at carrying out operational tasks themselves.

5.6 Towards flatter organizations

delayering

Introducing changes to existing organizational structures is nothing new. In recent years, however, instead of promoting the development of more complex organizational structures, managers have sought to create 'flatter' organizational structures – that is, to remove some of the managerial levels. This has resulted in organizations being better able to meet the demands of their external environment, be more flexible, improve employee job satisfaction and raise productivity. Delayering is a structural intervention which offers great scope for improving effectiveness.

For example ...

... companies such as McDonnell-Douglas, IBM, SAS, Chrysler, General Electric and Asea Brown Boveri have all implemented extensive delayering programs in recent years. General Motors, a company which has traditionally been strongly hierarchical, has been experimenting with flat organizational units while it has been developing and producing the Saturn.

This phenomenon may be the beginning of a trend towards increasingly flat organizational structures. It is predicted that within the next 20 years, organizations will have less than half the number of management levels compared with today's counterparts, and only a third of the number of managers.

CASE

Mini case study 5.3

Hierarchies flat gives way to six-pack

Over a decade ago, flat hierarchies were the toast of management thinking. Company after company cut layers or grades in the organisational structure to create a flatter and more responsive setup. But by now, the concept has taken a 180-degree turn. The new thinking is that having more rungs will help an organisation address an individual's professional growth aspirations.

An email to FE says: 'We thought a decade ago that flat hierarchies were the key to success, that it made it easier to redeploy workers and made cross-functional work easier. We also thought that workers liked less hierarchy. They probably do when they are not at the top of it. But now US employers are getting worried not only about retention, which is a much bigger problem in India than it is here, but also about worker complaints that they are not being developed, that there is no career advancement,' adding, 'what exactly workers mean by this isn't completely clear – do they mean development in the sense of getting more skills and learning or do they mean development in the sense of just more money or do they have this idea about advancing in a hierarchy?'

'Delayering has been in vogue with the inception of Japanese management in India and it got a boost with the rise in IT industry. The inherent belief is that the less the number of layers of hierarchy the better it is for the organisation. Many organisations have gone ahead and done delayering. But in a country like India, job titles and promotions form an important part of social life and peer comparison.'

'Any process, therefore, is culture-specific and the way people are handled in an organisation depends largely on local culture. Individual expectation is to get promotion and this will have a bearing on a person's social standing. Job titles carry a kind of respect and, hence the craving for promotions and job titles. Only increasing the layers can satisfy this. Many manufacturing organisations that went in for delayering had come back to the relayering process, because in the former they were unable to meet the aspirations of their employees. We did relayering a couple of years ago ... '

'Any management technique blindly applied will not work. Choice of a technique, and the implementation of it, has to be assessed against the context of an organisation. Gimmicks never help in retaining employees – they are both intelligent enough and exposed sufficiently to see what is being done. If we have a rational for relayering, then we will need to explain it to our employees and only then implement it.'

Just by de-layering and making each step painfully high to climb, the organisation cannot provide an employee with an attainable growth path. Employees are savvy enough to realise which positions are genuinely senior and which ones are pseudo-senior. At very junior levels, good title or definition works to some extent but from the middle-level onwards employees are looking for real job content to feel satisfied. The attrition problem can be solved temporarily by such structuring, as re-layering gives opportunities for employees. One can actually give them promotions every year and keep them motivated. However, this population may only be 8%-10% of a company's total strength. In the long run, it's their interaction with team members, care and respect that make employees stick to an organization.

Source: *Financial Express*, July 19, 2008

5.6.1 Delayering in top and middle management

Delayering can take place at two levels:

- Delayering of middle management – as has happened at Douglas Aircraft Company.
- Delayering of top management – as has happened at ABB and General Electric.

Each of the two forms of delayering takes place in response to a different group of organizational problems.

Middle-management problems

delayering of middle management

Delayering of middle management may take place in response to the following organizational problems:

- Weaknesses in market orientation and coordination
- Too great a distance between policy making and execution of operations
- Too little entrepreneurship and accountability
- Few chances to develop integral management skills
- Bureaucratic, role-oriented culture

For many organizations, the hierarchy as a coordination mechanism has become too expensive and too slow. Changes in market conditions cannot be translated into action quickly enough. Product development and delivery times are too long. The gap between policy and execution means that the organization is always one step behind and has difficulty adapting itself to the changing environment. It can also mean that enthusiasm for a project at the top of the organization is not transferred to the shop floor. Top management is often burdened with coordination tasks which could be performed by less senior management.

Top management problems

delayering of top management

Delayering of top management may take place in response to the following organizational problems:

- Lack of commitment to the realization of plans
- Tasks and responsibilities are difficult to allocate
- Duplication of staff and consultative bodies
- Management too busy with ineffectual activities
- An excessive focus on control
- Delays in decision making

DEVELOPED COMPANIES

Retail chains, banks, hotels, restaurants: they are all so-called multi-unit organizations: they fit inside each other just like the well-known Russian dolls.

Retail chains, banks, hotels, restaurants: they are all so-called multi-unit organizations: they fit inside each other just like the well-known Russian dolls. Geographically dispersed units that form part of the overall hierarchy and have their own management do, however, have the same obligation to achieve the financial and operational goals established by the parent organization. This involves specific problems: responsibilities may overlap, the span of control at each level is not always clear, and so on.

Source: *Harvard Business Review*, June 2008, kluwermanagement.nl/managementtrends

The process of decentralization often results in the resultant semi-autonomous units demanding a considerable amount of authority and control over the resources they need to perform their tasks. Management and staff immediately above the decentralized level will however wish to maintain an overview, coordinate the various units and maintain control. Since decentralized units want to operate as independently as possible, they tend to duplicate the management, coordination and control functions at the top level of their units. An increase in management capacity at this level will diminish the added value at the levels directly above. If the organization is top heavy – that is, if there are many levels of top management – the business units will become frustrated by what they see as constant interference in their activities. Business unit managers will spend too much time selling their projects inside the organization instead of selling them outside it. This may even result in business units competing with each other and perhaps missing out on opportunities for working together. In such organizations, distortion and loss of information are common, decision making is slow and over-complicated and top management is inadequately informed about important developments at the business unit level.

5.6.2 *Change in organizational structure as a vehicle for change*

If an organization wishes to be able to adapt better and more quickly to the changes in the external environment, it has several options. For example:

- It could diversify or begin to operate on a more global level.
- It could undertake quality projects.
- It could set up an education and training program.
- It could develop a cost reduction strategy.

Most importantly, however, it could change its own management structure. In most cases, this will lead to changes in the tasks, authority and responsibilities of management – in fact, to changes in the structure of the organization itself.
Delayering involves adapting the structure so that the number of management layers is reduced. This offers new possibilities – a paradox in the eyes of many managers. However, delayering is not just a matter of making cuts. It must be accompanied by a combination of supportive measures if an effective, flat organization is to be achieved. We will return to this point many times during the course of the following chapters.

5.7 Towards intelligent organizations in networks of organizations

outsourcing
benchmarking
empowerment

The organization of the future is an intelligent and learning organization, is flat, slender and maneuverable, performs activities it is really good at, makes use of its own core competencies and of the capabilities of other organizations in strategic collaboration with them, outsources and brings in the best practices of other organizations based on methods such as benchmarking (= systematic assessment of best practices in various organizational processes) in different or comparable companies. Creativity is highly appreciated and there is an ongoing search for improvement, and the organization attempts to put human talent to real use by 'empowerment' (delegation and drawing on the employee's creativity and dedication).
In James Brian Quinn's view, organizations should concentrate on a few selected core competencies which have real customer appeal. *Nike* is a good example. This successful 'running expert' originally created value through an intensive research and development program and effective marketing, distribution and sales of shoes. Nike is to all intents and purposes a research, design and marketing organization. Nike outsources all of its production activities to various production partners. It does not refer to them as suppliers or contractors, but as production partners and co-makers. It is exclusively focused on pre-production activities such as R&D and on post-production activities such as marketing, sales and distribution. Recent developments in ICT clearly play an important role. Data and information exchanges within these networks are essential in monitoring the operational work processes in the chain of adding value and in order to shorten the 'time-to-market' from design to new products and models, all the while maintaining high quality standards.

production partners
co-makers

Benetton and its network is another example. It has more than 200 subcontractors producing its clothes. Almost 95% of Benetton's activities are outsourced, including production, distribution and purchase activities.

intelligent organization

The intelligent organization operates according to the following principles:
- Select and maintain the company's own core competencies by investing in them.
- Only maintain those activities and services which are top class.
- Outsource as much as possible.
- For maximum flexibility, be accepting of and develop unusual organizational forms: minimal hierarchy, network organization, even reversed pyramids and ongoing specialization.
- Develop the skills necessary to establish alliances with other companies at various levels.
- Shift the organization's power to those who maintain contact and do business with the customers.
- Accept that critical, intelligent professionals have to change their workplace if needs be and create a challenging working environment.

Heed early warnings

The intelligent organization has been a popular notion in recent times. The weakest link of this organizational concept is, however, its intensive and large-scale outsourcing. The conscious creation of external dependency to compensate for internal shortcomings also creates a big control problem. Nike's production partners find it hard to match the successes of Nike's R&D

and marketing. The core organization has to manage its web of partners by functioning as a kind of strategic center, has to develop the company's vision and has to ensure the creation of added value by its various partners. Key elements in the role fulfillment of the strategic center are strategic outsourcing, the development of core competencies, controlling and exploiting new technologies and supporting positively focused rivalry and competition in the value chain within the network and outside it with respect to potential newcomers in the network.

strategic center

Exhibit 5.1

The demise of the conventional, hierarchical multinational

Students of organizational design are always on the lookout for the next big thing. Ray Miles, professor emeritus and former dean of the Haas School of Business at the University of California, Berkeley, sees this in the emergence of alliances or networks that link companies in complementary business.
Sometimes these are industry-wide networks to share ideas and drive innovation, such as the broad alliance of chipmakers and manufacturing tool suppliers that is pushing the boundaries of semiconductor technology.
In other cases, a single company sits at the centre of the network. Thus Stan Shih, founder and chairman emeritus of Acer, the Taiwanese computer company, tried to build a network of related companies to drive innovation in the PC business. The trick, says Prof Miles, is to develop enough trust among network participants to encourage a free flow of knowledge and information, while avoiding the power and financial relationships that would turn the network into just another diversified corporation.
This echoes the view of management writers Nitin Nohria of Harvard and the late Sumantra Ghoshal of London Business School, who saw modern multinational companies as evolving towards a network of related affiliates and away from a conventional, hierarchical structure.

Sources: *Managing the Global Network Corporation* by Bruce McKern (ed.), Routledge, 2003 and *Financial Times*, July 4, 2005

It must also be remembered that as the saying goes, the chain (in the network) is as strong as its weakest link. The number of strategic collaboration failures is estimated at seventy percent. Only the future will tell how this organizational form will develop.

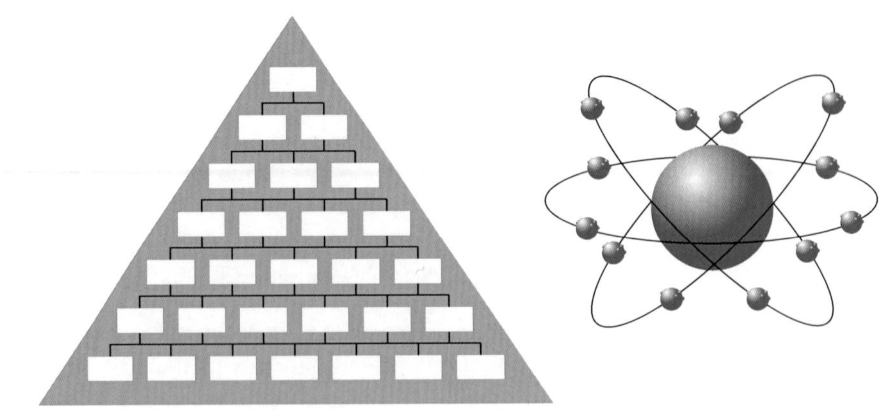

Figure 5.29
From inflexible hierarchical pyramids to flexible rotating collaboration in a satellite or network structure

Externally focused networks have disadvantages, including chain vulnerability and loss of knowledge, reduced quality control, reduced control over input, financial vulnerability and so on. As such, existing integrated companies are only too happy to transform themselves into internal network organizations if the product-market circumstances make this possible (see also Section 2.4.5).

internal network organizations

The disadvantages of networks

supervision and control

The main concern of most managers is that the dynamic network structure will not offer the degree of direct supervision and control that is possible when all activities take place under one roof. The organization whose name appears on the final product may not be involved in its manufacture at all (as in the case of Nike) and thus relies on the other partners in the network adhering to the quality and delivery conditions. If one element of the network falls short in its task, all of the remaining partners in the project will suffer, especially the one directly responsible to the end customer.

staff turnover

There is also a concern that having smaller scale and more flexible structures within the network will lead to higher staff turnover (with more employees crossing over to other functions in other companies) and that the loyalty and devotion of managers and employees will diminish. With higher staff turnover, further uses of supplies and the temporary hiring of specialists, there is also a danger of loss of company secrets and patents.

The advantages of networks

When a dynamic network functions well, however, it has a greater flexibility, a better use of human capital and improved overall efficiency.

For example ...

More products can be produced and produced more quickly when a company is not tied to the limited capacities of its own manufacturing units, designers, technicians and distributors. The provision of contract-based services can expand the range of a small business. The hiring of temporary specialist support can increase the availability of expertise without a substantial rise in overheads.

Often middle managers spend a large part of their time on internal procedural matters at some distance from the company's clients, suppliers and distributors. In the new, flatter and leaner companies there are fewer management functions, but the ones that are there are more demanding, present a greater challenge and often give more satisfaction. The managers in these network organizations have a wider vision. In contrast, most of the middle managers in larger and integrated firms have to fulfill coordinating, controlling and linking functions. They have to maintain the whole and ensure that the numerous bits and pieces come together at the right time. This type of function is less important in a network system, where contracts and agreements take the place of hierarchies.

employees

Furthermore, employees in network organizations expect more of their jobs and derive a higher level of satisfaction from them. In the new, flatter and less complex structures, employees are better able to follow the progress of their products or services on the market and as a result are more directly involved. Most network organizations will probably have fewer managers and as a result more knowledge and skills will be expected of the employees, both with regard to working with ever more complex technology and to building up and maintaining a wider circle of clients.

The notion that employees have to be more responsible for managing themselves and more involved in decision-making processes is not new (see chapters 3, 4 and 7). In many modern factories and offices, almost completely self-controlling and autonomous work groups set their own deadlines, assign work and on an individual basis switch quickly from one task to another. Such groups also have responsibility for quality and internal coordination. The network structure strengthens this approach and introduces even more flexibility with greater opportunities for 'self-management' and autonomy.

self-management autonomy

This trend can be expected to continue. In a flexible world of dynamic networks and webs, future work teams may switch from one company to another on a temporary basis. In such a situation, the training and development of employees will have to be directed at complete systems, not only at the characteristics and special features of one single process within the system. As systems become more flexible and automated, the basis of training must be widened.

Of course, more training makes the employee more mobile. Such mobility will be an asset when employees outgrow their functions and teams, even when these have an extremely wide base. Promotion may involve gaining experience and knowledge in certain technologies and fields of work. This will imply mobility and acceptance of career paths in flat and network organizations where the motto is 'horizontally up' (see Chapter 7) and added value is supplied along these new lines.

EFFECTIVE NETWORKS CAN LEAD TO VALUABLE INNOVATION

Why aren't businesses and organisations more innovative? Are they filled with dull, unimaginative people? Are they lacking crucial 'core competencies'? Or are their people just not working hard enough?

The answer to those last three questions is no, no and no. Something else must explain the inability of companies to display greater innovative flair. What is it?

The problem for top managers is that, as you walk round the business or study the organisational chart, nothing much may seem to be wrong. People are at their desks or in meeting rooms, hard at work. Something that looks like two-way communication appears to be taking place. And then there are all those e-mails, instant messages and texts. You can be confident that good ideas must be flowing freely within the organisation.

The techniques of 'social network analysis' have been known for some time, but businesses have been slow to make the most of them. That is changing.

What stops effective collaborative networks from developing? There are several pitfalls … Of course, there needs to be effective internal communication and a rejection of the silo mentality. But there also has to be management discipline. Big sprawling networks where 'all are welcome' are unlikely to produce practical ideas. They tend to create greater confusion instead. In networks, it is the quality of people involved, rather than the quantity, that counts. Noisy self-promoters do not build useful or interesting networks.

Effective networkers are 'efficient value creators'. You can see them darting round the business, ignoring the org chart, making connections, seeking out useful information and turning it into something valuable.

Leaders should look more critically at their own networks. Are they stuck in a comfort zone, talking only to their type of person and maintaining a bias for the gang they emerged from, be it finance, marketing or research and development? A small, loyal group of people may make for a supportive network, but it probably won't be a very creative one.

Do corporate leaders energise their colleagues or instead drain energy from them? Are people left feeling enthused or depressed after an encounter with the boss? Even in the exciting, leading-edge world of innovation, unglamorous management basics matter. If new employees are not brought on board properly – induction – then no amount of exhortation will get them to create a network. You can kit everybody out with Google's new Wave system, which combines all the latest communication and social networking features, but if the right people are prevented by bad gatekeepers or energy-sapping bosses from working together, nothing will come of it.

You need to understand how informal, unseen networks can be encouraged to work to your benefit. This is where innovation will come from.

On the surface, things at your company may look fine. Dig deeper. Are the right people talking to each other? In the worst cases, as the consultant Jon Katzenbach once put it, everyone is smiling, but the building is on fire.

Source: *Financial Times*, June 23, 2009

Networks within a single organization

In the case of a network of various business units within one organization, each of the individual parts of the organization needs to be in tune with the others, and the abilities of each unit will be exploited in order to improve overall performance. Programs or employees who can contribute to that process are brought together.
At the present time, a 'business unit' can be defined as a unit of a company which is responsible for and operates in a discrete product market. Each unit has guidelines in the form of company procedures, priorities and investment decisions which have been established by central management.
In a network structure within a single company, the work assignments carried out by each individual business unit need to be particularly clearly defined and data relating to the respective performances has to be exchanged. The links and communication between the various business units can be expected to increase. Furthermore, a wider range of process and communication skills will be expected from managers.

network model

In the network model, central management's role involves areas such as taxes, financial administration, collective purchasing (if appropriate), the relationship with the shareholders, the public relations strategy of the company and important group initiatives (new alliances or the taking over or selling off of companies). Top management is concerned with problems which can be better resolved by one central unit rather than by a combination of units. The main role of top management is to function as a kind of 'switch,' an intermediary at the center that delegates responsibility for specific assignments to the individual managers or to a combination of managers because they are closer to the customers, the competitors and the production processes than the staff at the central head office.

local managers

Local managers are given much more responsibility therefore; they are the 'centers of excellence' of the group. They participate in project groups in which all parts of the organization are represented, they have the authority to make decisions which directly influence local results, and they are also responsible for the supply of information needed to review and evaluate the work in progress.

Double challenge

regional and worldwide basis

In the years to come, the greatest challenge by far will be the building up of a closer relationship with customers and competing on both a regional and worldwide basis. To realize these two goals, not only will new organizational procedures be necessary, but also new strategies for the management of the company. Dynamic networks in strategic collaboration or within one larger organization make it possible to develop and implement some of these strategies in an effective way. They also offer new possibilities for personal rewards both for employees and for managers.

Exhibit 5.2

Organizational webs

An *economic web* is a set of companies that use a common architecture to deliver independent elements of an overall value proposition that grows stronger as more companies join the set. Before a web can form, two conditions must be present: a technological standard and increasing returns. The standard reduces risk by allowing companies to make irreversible investment decisions in the face of technological uncertainty. The increasing returns create a mutual dependence that strengthens the web by drawing more and more customers and producers.
Webs are not alliances, however. They operate without any formal relationships between participants. Each company in a web is wholly independent; only the pursuit of economic self-interest drives it into web-like behavior. It prices, markets, and sells its products autonomously.
Within economic webs, *technology webs* are organized around specific technology platforms. One prominent example of a technology web is the desktop computing business. In the desktop computing business of the 1980s, highly specialized participants acted both independently and interdependently to assemble a complex package of technology components and services.

Within technology webs, clusters of players participate in competing *value webs*, which seek to capture a disproportionate share of the value-creation opportunity. Whereas economic activity in technology webs focuses on maximizing value to the customer, value webs add a second objective: to create value for a specific group of companies that have adopted a common technology platform. In the desktop computing technology web, for example, at least two major value webs are in competition. One is organized and shaped by Apple, and promotes the Macintosh as the standard desktop computing platform; the other is controlled by Microsoft and Intel, and champions an alternative standard defined by the use of the Intel microprocessor and the Microsoft operating system.

Market webs represent a third form of web. Unlike customer webs, which focus on the behavior and preferences of an individual customer segment, market webs are organized around a specific type of transaction. The customer web shaper wants to develop the broadest possible relationship with its chosen segment, and to serve these customers across a wide range of needs. The market web shaper tries to build the deepest possible relationship with all the buyers and sellers involved in a particular kind of market transaction.

What strategic roles are created by webs?

Two different strategic roles may be played in webs: adaptation and shaping. Each has the potential to generate considerable value.

In companies that opt for an adapting role, top management deals with uncertainty by trying to stay one step ahead of other players in anticipating and responding to changes in the business environment. Rather than attempting to influence events, these companies endeavor to stay at the edge of them, and to capture value by spotting opportunities earlier and moving more quickly than the competition.

Shapers, on the other hand, focus on the fluidity of events and on opportunities to determine or influence outcomes. They believe it is possible to mold the environment in such a way that it enhances their ability to create value.

Web strategies demand a completely different mindset from that employed in traditional strategic thinking. For one thing, they tend both to narrow and to broaden management focus, the former because they encourage unbundling and the outsourcing of undifferentiated business activities (the extreme form of this is the virtual corporation, where the scope of activities conducted within the enterprise and subject to direct management control is radically reduced), the latter, because the context for defining strategy expands from maximizing value for the enterprise to maximizing value for the web. If the web does not maximize value, neither can the enterprise within it.

Webs represent a whole new way of thinking about industry structure, relationships between companies, and value creation. Though not monopolies, they are just as powerful. For the rest of this decade – perhaps much longer – we shall see industries being shaped by competing webs that relentlessly devour one another.

Source: From *Spider versus Spider* by John Hagel III, 1996

Winning strategies for major web players

	Web formation	Web mobilization	Web evolution
	Get into the flow →	Build momentum →	Encourage lock-in
Shaper	Pick the right technology platform	Manage perceptions actively	Enhance platform technology frequently
	Enter market quickly	Create economic incentives for others	Promote standardization
	Accelerate adoption	Evangelize opportunity	Link and leverage
Adapter	Identify winning web early	Compete aggressively for web share	Exploit customer lock-in
	Focus on near-term profit opportunities	Link up with web shaper's strategy	Undermine supplier/shaper lock-in or diversify into new webs
	Establish dense information links with other web participants		

Summary

- Once the goals and strategy of an organization have been determined, an appropriate organizational structure has to be designed by management – tailor-made to the particular needs of the organization in question.
- When a business is starting up, the work will be undertaken by the owner-manager, perhaps with a couple of helpers. As soon as the workload picks up and more people are employed, decisions have to be made about the division of work (who does what). This almost always involves the separation of management from operations.
- The division of management and operations leads to the creation of a number of layers within the organization. This makes it necessary for authority to be reassigned and the relationships between various employees and groups of employees to be determined.
- The choice of an appropriate form of work division will depend on the particular circumstances of the organization. An organizational structure can be built up both vertically and horizontally. Management can choose from a number of options: F(unctional), P(roduct), G(eographical) and M(arket sector).
- An organizational chart depicts an organizational structure and highlights the division of tasks and the assignment of authorities.
- The functioning of an organization can be clarified by job descriptions. These state the employee's authorities, areas of decision making and responsibilities. They also clarify the authority assigned to other people and the decisions which can be taken by other employees.
- 'Informal organization' – that is, the unofficial allocation of authority based on personal prestige rather than a formal position within the organization needs to be taken into account.
- If the goals of an organization are to be attained, activities at all levels of management and execution need to be coordinated and in tune with each other. This is referred to as 'unity of direction'. Unity of direction can be stimulated by using the correct coordination mechanisms – for example, standardization of output, planning and consultation.
- Organizational structures come in many forms, including the centralized functional organizational structure, the decentralized divisional structure, and the business unit structure. Each has its advantages and disadvantages. Divisional organization involves a different way of managing to centralized functional organization.
- Project organization involves the focusing of management and the organization on a particular set of activities. Project management is concerned with the temporary execution of an entire set of activities directed at achieving a specified goal within a set period of time and with a set supply of resources and people. For effective project management, a number of conditions need to be fulfilled and the relationship between the organization itself and the project organization needs to be clarified.
- A matrix organization combines a project and a departmentalized structure and as such there may be problems associated with dual control.
- As a company or institution grows and develops from a business start-up to a mature organization, its organizational structure – the division of work and the managerial levels – will change.
- Delayering has been a frequent strategy in recent years. It involves reducing the number of management layers in the organizational structure. The aim of this change is to improve the daily functioning of the organization.

Discussion questions

1 With reference to *Management in Action* at the beginning of this chapter:
- **a)** In your opinion, can a company become too big?
- **b)** Would you say that ING has also suffered from 'the illusion of synergy advantages'?
- **c)** **1** In a division-based form of organization, is it difficult for top management to hive off a division?
  2 In what way is the top management dependent on the lower levels?
- **d)** What organizational form is ING deploying within the new ING bank?

2 Comment on this statement: 'When an organization supplies many different products or services, an F grouping is the most appropriate division of work.'

3 'The more management layers in the organization, the more possibilities there are to decentralize.' Comment.

4 'A product manager in a matrix organization always has both hierarchical and functional authority.' Do you agree with this statement?

5 Which of the following statements is the more valid?
- **a)** 'Unity of direction is less important within project structures.'
- **b)** 'Unity of direction is more difficult to realize within project structures.'

6 What possibilities exist for delayering an organizational structure in a turbulent environment?

Research-based exercise

Balanced structures

Introduction
This research-based exercise is based on a research article by Raisch (2008), published in *Long Range Planning*. The research question, data collection, method, and some of the results of the research project are presented. The exercise consists of three questions based on the research article and the theory in this chapter. The answers should be based on both the theory in Chapter 5 and your own insights into the practical implications of your answer.

Research Question
How do organizations create and deploy balanced structures?

Data Collection
The researchers collected data inductively using multiple cases of how balanced organizational structures were created in six multinational companies. The use of multiple cases enabled them to benefit from a replication logic whereby each case was used to test emerging theoretical insights. Six firms agreed to provide access to key decision makers and internal documents. These companies represent various industries, including the automotive industry (BMW Group), the banking industry (Deutsche Bank), the building materials industry (Holcim), electrical engineering (Siemens), the food and nutrition industry (Nestlé) and the insurance industry (Helvetia). Data were collected primarily through semi-structured interviews and questionnaires. A team of researchers conducted 93 semi-structured interviews over a three-year period at different management levels within the six participating firms.

Outcomes
The researchers found that:

- To achieve the dual objective of profitability and innovation, firms can employ three generic types of balanced structures: temporarily cycling through different structures (temporal separation), creating differentiated units (structural separation), and enabling employees to move back and forth between different structures (parallel structures).
- The organizations observed in this study used the three balanced design options as complementary rather than mutually exclusive solutions. The solutions were deployed in different contexts and contributed to different learning outcomes.
- Before selecting a structural solution, firms should conduct a thorough analysis of their specific organizational form and their desired learning outcomes: for example, structural separation is appropriate with entirely new technologies and temporal separation is appropriate when ties exist with existing products.

Questions

1. Explain why balanced structures are becoming increasingly important for firms in the 21st century that want to develop and sustain a competitive advantage.
2. Do you think that successfully designing and implementing balanced structures is a once-off activity or one which is subject to change? Explain your reasons.
3. Explain why the efficiency of an organization design depends on the fit between the design and its context.

CASE

Management case study

The development of Recrea Inc.

At the beginning of 2010, Keith Harding and Jack Nicklas looked back with a certain satisfaction at the fast growth of Recrea Inc., a leisure goods supplier they had set up in 2004.

In that year, Harding and Nicklas had retired from an international consultancy firm and bought their first company, Gereva Inc., a producer of garden sprinklers and other garden supplies. It was exactly what they had been looking for: a producer of consumer products with a good reputation for quality but with weak marketing. They felt their education and consultancy experience and their intention to bring aggressive and young management talent into Gereva Inc. would guarantee growth in Europe and a considerable improvement in profitability.

Recrea developed quickly. The formula applied to Gereva Inc. appeared to be successful. The original plans were quickly adapted, becoming a wider company concept directed at leisure products.

After the purchase of Gereva Inc., the partners acquired a second enterprise – a small family business in Germany which also made sprinklers. Since the two product lines were the same, this takeover could be easily assimilated into the existing Gereva organization. Six other companies from all over Europe in the sector of recreation, garden and sports articles were then purchased.

Between 2004 and 2010, Recrea Inc. grew fast, with sales rising from US$2.5 million to US$20 million and net profits rising from US$160,000 to US$1 million. The 2009 figures showed total sales of US$35 million with a net profit of US$1.8 million. Starting with an equity of US$240,000 (share capital) in 2004, with the issue of new shares in 2009, the equity had been raised to US$16.2 million. By 2010, Recrea Inc. was composed of eight enterprises, brought together via acquisitions and takeovers, and all in the fields of leisure activities and recreation. The number of employees had also grown considerably.

According to Harding and Nicklas, the acquisitions were part of a well-thought-out strategy. They were always drawn to enterprises where there was an opportunity to make savings in the operational processes, to increase sales by streamlining the organization and by strengthening the marketing effort, and to rejuvenate and professionalize the managerial process.

Harding and Nicklas knew growth would create tensions within the organization and were determined not to ignore this even if they themselves were now less involved in the operational control of the business. They consider their success to be founded on having the sales of their product range handled by a single sales organization.

At the present, they can still see large growth opportunities in the markets for leisure products. Changes in distribution and promotion have strengthened their marketing and sales performance. The retail trade has declined in importance and the chain stores and wholesale trade have improved their positions. As a result, the marketing and sales organization consists of not only retail traders in many European countries, but also product managers who are responsible for supplying the various buyer groups with specific product information to back up sales.

Harding and Nicklas are now thinking of expanding into other recreational sectors and activities – namely travel, education and entertainment.

There is no organizational chart as such at Recrea Inc., but the organizational structure is illustrated in the following figure.

There are four key functions: marketing/sales, production (operations), product development and control. All subsidiaries and activities are accommodated within that structure. The sales organization has a geographical grouping (into seven countries/regions within Europe) within which every sales person sells the entire product range. Production takes place under the direct supervision of a production manager with responsibility for production quotas and budgets. Product development is decentralized, with the exception of sprinklers and garden equipment which are developed at the Gereva site. The control function is highly centralized.

Planning is organized within a complex system of combined activities which operate top-down and bottom-up as well as horizontally. The organization has recently noticed some areas of tension which cross functional boundaries. There is some informal communication taking place and employees are in close contact with one another. There is, however, a strong belief in openness in all functions and at all levels.

Recrea Inc. functions according to a number of general guidelines, but the annual plan is the most important point of reference. In the event of recurring problems, employees consult Harding when they are production/operations and control issues and Nicklas when they are marketing issues. Harding and Nicklas plan to continue handling acquisitions themselves and thereby determine the future shape of Recrea Inc. However, in recent years, they have been confronted by a steady stream of operational problems which have required their attention. As a result, planning has been neglected in several production lines and there have been regular disruptions to the production process. Product development continues to perform below expectation and the level of innovation in some sectors of the company is falling below that of competitors.

Following presentation of the interim results for 2010, there has been some concern about their implications and about potential problems in relation to further growth. It has been agreed that these issues will be addressed in the near future.

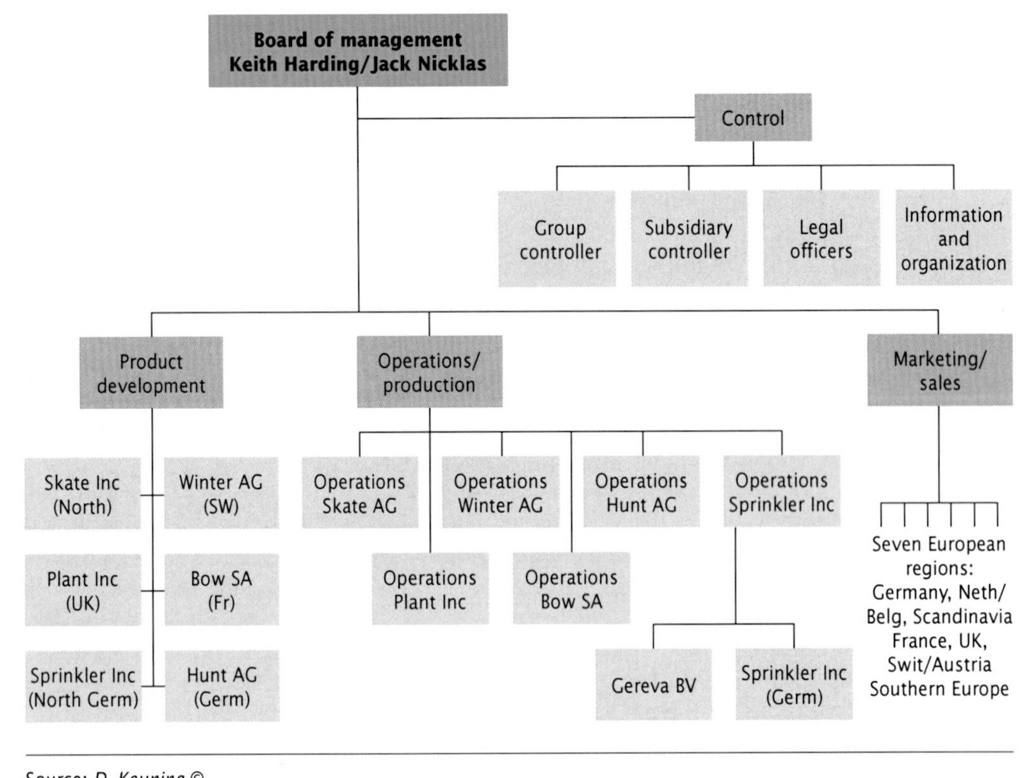

Organization chart for Recrea Inc.

Source: *D. Keuning* ©

Case study questions

1 What are the main organizational areas within Recrea?
2 Given the variety of activities in which Recrea is involved, are these sensible divisions?
3 Do you think Recrea Inc. should have a different departmental structure? What criteria would you base the structure on? Refer to the issues of centralization and decentralization.

CONTENTS

6.1 Structuring tasks and design of functions: criteria
6.2 P-grouping and F-grouping: advantages and disadvantages
6.3 Organization and group design
6.4 Delegation: task, authority, responsibility and accountability
6.5 Organizational principles: relationships and authorities
6.6 Centralization and decentralization
6.7 Coordination and internal adaptation
6.8 Scope of management control
6.9 Organization in development: reorganization and planning for change

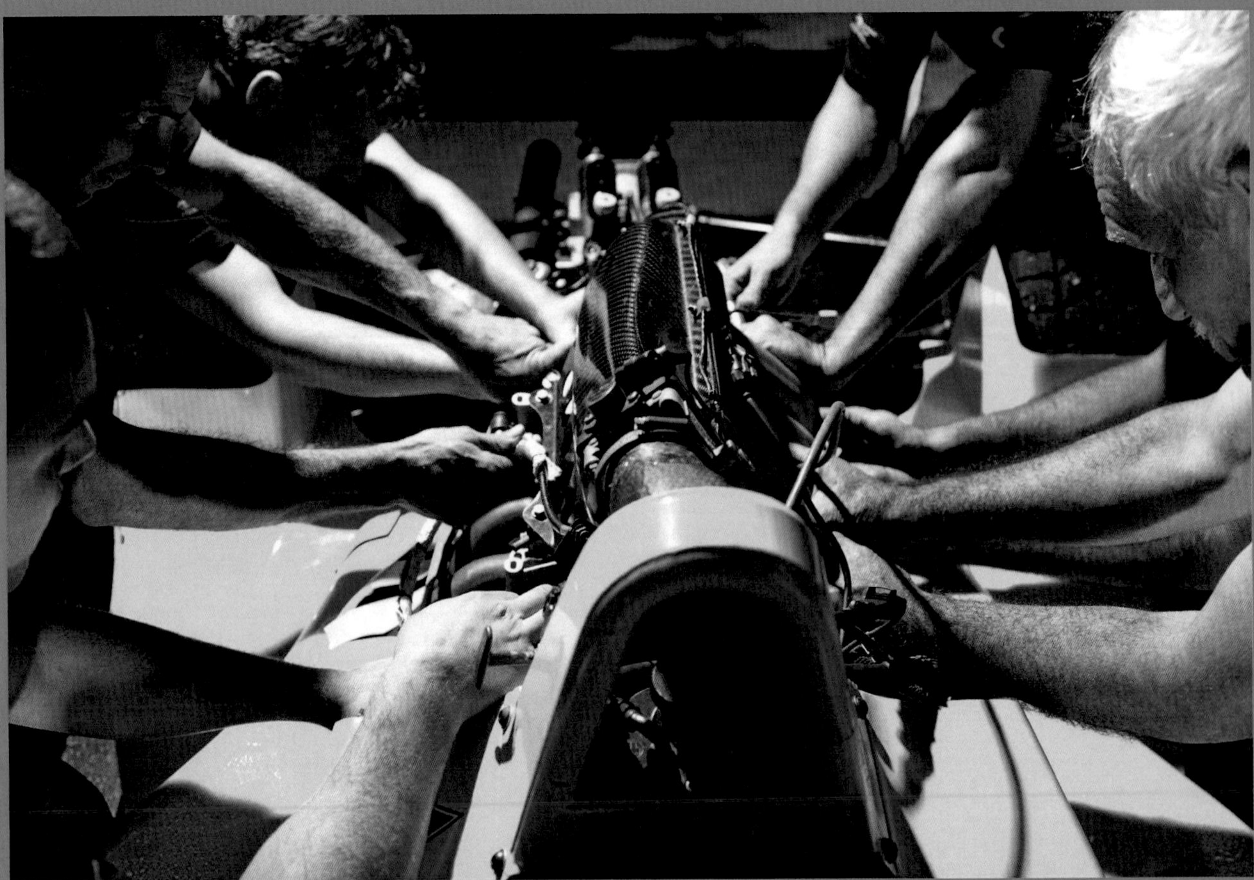

Chapter 6

Structuring tasks for groups and individuals

LEARNING OUTCOMES

After studying this chapter, you should be able to do the following:

- Name and describe the criteria used for the design and grouping of operational tasks and functions
- Identify the advantages and disadvantages of various organizational structures in relation to the grouping of operational tasks and functions
- Describe the consultative and coordination mechanisms needed to establish consultative and communication structures within organizations
- Identify important concepts in the design process of an organizational structure
- Name and describe types of organizational change and the various stages of the processes of change
- Describe some common reactions to organizational change

CASE

Management-in-action

Effective team building

The US military's elite training-programs offer a model for the strategic deployment of human capital and for building effective teams. Five important aspects of the training of Special Operations Forces (SOF) which have proved to be effective are:

1. Winnowing

SOF training is designed to eliminate all but the most determined and suitable individuals. A hundred highly motivated, intelligent, and experienced men might start the eight-week Phase I course, and usually only about 20 or 25 successfully pass that first phase – a ratio that is also typical for the other services' special forces selection programs. If you do 59 pushups instead of 60 during a test, you may get a second chance, but if you fall short again, you're sent back to a conventional unit. This is a vital point: the Navy doesn't stigmatize these men or kick them out, but rather deploys them in other areas and tries to commend them and make them feel good. In corporations, there is often no 'Plan B' when someone drops out of a program or fails to make a promotion, and a disappointment or setback may very well mean the employee leaves the company altogether.

Many trainees are eliminated during the initial selection phase, but others continue to be dropped during later training phases – there's a continual process of culling. This winnowing process can be seen as never-ending. Colonel Wesley Rehorn, a veteran Army Special Forces leader who heads the U.S. Joint Forces Special Operations Command, comments that 'the system is very intolerant of mistakes, even for someone who is 20 years into his career. I may accept an error of commission, but rarely an error of omission.'

2. Deliberate practice

A second characteristic of the training is that it embodies the concept of deliberate practice. Deliberate practice entails isolating the specific elements of performance that will enable you to excel at an activity, repeating them over and over again, and getting objective feedback. A great deal of research supports the notion that intensive, deliberate practice – not innate talent – is the secret of exceptional performance. An Army Special Forces weapons specialist, for example, must master nearly 50 different weapons systems during 65 days of intensive training.

In 1970, Army Special Forces launched a daring commando raid on the Son Tay prisoner of war camp near Hanoi. To prepare for the mission, they conducted 170 full dress rehearsals at a mock-up of the prison camp in Florida. The operation went flawlessly, and although the U.S. prisoners had been moved before the raid, news of the attempt spread throughout camps in North Vietnam; many captured servicemen later said that it gave them the will to survive.

Is doing 170 rehearsals of a major sales presentation to a client a reasonable expectation for a corporation? No, but how about just one rehearsal? That would be above the norm for most managers. Wal-mart Stores Inc. showed how powerful this type of preparedness can be when Hurricane Katrina hit the Gulf Coast of the United States in 2005. The U.S. Federal Emergency Management Agency was woefully unprepared for the disaster: Wal-Mart filled the gap in supplying aid to many Louisiana communities because of the exceptional preparedness of its emergency management department and emergency operations center, which had repeatedly rehearsed for similar contingencies and put in place a series of procedures and protocols for responding to a natural disaster.

3. Realism

Special forces training is characterized by extreme realism. Medics will treat 'injured' soldiers who have pumps squirting 'arterial blood' and sport Hollywood-quality makeup. For a simulated mission, men may be kept awake for two or three nights in a row and subjected to lifelike explosions and bullet fire. The final exercise to earn the Army's Green Beret lasts a full two weeks and involves more than 1,000 personnel. Some corporations use computer-based business simulations or lengthy case study scenarios to teach executives – putting them in charge of a fictitious company for three days, for example – but it is not a widespread practice.

4. Constant feedback

A key feature of SOF training is constant and relentless feedback about performance. Nearly every exercise – from tying knots while holding your breath underwater to building a camouflaged shelter – is graded by experienced instructors, and most exercises have an 'after action' review that bluntly analyzes what went well and what could have been improved. At regular intervals, instructors rank the men in their training units according to performance, and often ask each team member to rank everyone in his unit. They might very well confront a trainee and ask, 'Why do you think your team members ranked you dead last?'

5. Physical and mental stress

Hell Week, or some variation of it, is a feature of most SOF training programs. Navy trainees, for example, are forced to function over a span of 100 hours while being allowed a total of five hours of sleep. These experiences have a purpose: They simulate actual combat conditions, they expand the trainees' comfort zone, and they provide a benchmark experience that makes subsequent hardships more manageable. They also create a powerful (albeit painful) shared experience that is an indelible part of the culture of special operations.

Some companies create such shared experiences early on in their employees' tenure, and it is a very effective technique. General Electric Company's leadership development center at Crotonville, for example, is a legendary hotbed of intense learning experiences that form part of the shared culture of many GE employees. And Japanese companies have traditionally put new recruits through multi-month training and indoctrination programs. These experiences don't approach the brutality of Hell Week, but they often require late nights or weekends spent with colleagues working to solve common problems.

Source: Sobel, A. (2009). Reprinted with permission from the Winter 2009 issue of *Strategy + Business Magazine*, published bij Booz & Company, www.strategy-business.com.

In the preceding chapter, the growth and development of organizations was described in terms of organizational structures and changes to them. Growth entails implementing changes to the organization's structure, even if this plunges the organization into a crisis. Each phase of development of an organization has problems of its own for which solutions have to be found. If an organization wants to survive it is necessary for it to be able to handle the dynamics of crisis and understand the need for organizational changes.
Individual work groups and departments must be involved in the design of organizational structure, especially when it comes to arranging tasks and devising functions for individual employees. The authority to make decisions must be assigned and working relationships organized to make it possible for managerial plans to be implemented and operations coordinated.
The design process of an organizational structure always requires a conscious and systematic grouping of activities into tasks and functions. We will look into these issues in more detail in this chapter.

6.1 Structuring tasks and design of functions: criteria

division of work

The various forms of division of work, grouping of tasks and effective design of functions are based on certain criteria. In the areas of division of work and design of functions at the operational and managerial levels, the organization must systematically examine how and to what degree the various criteria have to be met. In an existing situation, the criteria can also be used to examine whether the way in which tasks are structured and designed is still effective. The division of work is influenced by factors which have either a splitting or a combining effect.
Sometimes it is desirable to split certain activities off from other activities. There is no ideal way of doing this: in practice, the most that can be hoped for is finding a compromise between the various approaches.

6.1.1 The design of operational tasks: criteria

operational level

At the operational level tasks should be structured and job functions designed with the following criteria in mind:

A fair day's work has to be done

The time that someone makes available to a company or institution via a labor contract has to be used as well and as fully as possible in the execution of the activities which have been assigned to him or her. This holds as much for someone who has a full-time job as for someone who works on a part-time labor contract or in a job share arrangement. Here, 'as well and as fully as possible' means taking into account interruptions caused by illness and the ensuing recuperation. Under normal working circumstances, a normal amount of effort and a basic level of performance may be expected of an employee. When insufficient attention is paid to these requirements there will be quantitative underutilization (=idling) or (quantitative) overutilization (=overwork) in relation to the present capacity of people and resources.

underutilization
overutilization

A worthwhile work package

Both the nature and the degree of difficulty of the activities performed by an employee must match that employee's capabilities to a reasonable degree. If an employee's job consists of a number of activities, they should be so similar as to provide all the cost advantages of horizontal differentiation (see Section 5.2.5) but not the disadvantage of being monotonous. This disadvantage can be eliminated or neutralized to a certain degree by introducing some variety to consecutive tasks. This can take place by means of horizontal job enlargement (=lengthening the task cycle through expanding the activities on the same qualitative level): for example, sawing could be extended to planing, drilling, and so on. It can also be done by job rotation.

horizontal differentiation
horizontal job enlargement

The activities should be of approximately the same qualitative level and make demands on about the same level of human capabilities, education, training, abilities and experience. If insufficient attention is paid to this, it will soon be discovered that the all-rounder is a rare thing. Demanding too much and having expectations that are too high can lead to considerable stress among employees. When activities are not challenging enough, the danger of blunting or of qualitative underutilization of human capacities arises. A certain degree of autonomy and freedom in the planning and operational execution of tasks will prevent this happening. This is called job enrichment or vertical task enlargement: the freedom to contact other departments without asking permission to do so, to carry out small repairs and maintenance oneself, and to have enough authority to control and adjust the speed, the quantity and the quality of work oneself.

job enrichment
vertical task enlargement

Coherence between activities

Tasks should not only be sequenced with the capabilities of the employees in mind, they should also be mutually coherent whether they are carried out independently of one another or as consecutively performed interdependent processes. This applies both to the activities themselves as well as to the tools and techniques used. For example, if the fitting and linking of the components in a razor or radio demands successive actions in which different tools are used, the application of these related techniques could be conducted by one operational employee. This would also provide a fair amount of variation with regard to the finished product. As soon as techniques and actions start to become dissimilar and can no longer be conducted by one employee, the processing cycle should become shorter and the production activities split up into phases. The extent to which this can happen will also be dependent on the knowledge, experience, training and education and personal characteristics of the employee in relation to the sort of activities that are to be carried out. The technology available will also affect the extent to which this can happen.

interdependent processes

Work satisfaction

work satisfaction

Experiencing a certain degree of work satisfaction is important for every operational or managerial employee. One has to be able to identify with the job and the organization. Variation, responsibility and a good working environment, being able to exercise control over the quantity and the quality of the tasks oneself, and opportunities for work consultation are also important.

In the designing of functions it is important to define the contribution each employee is expected to make to his working group or department and to make this requirement explicit. How clearly an employee's tasks and authority are spelt out will determine the amount of responsibility he or she carries. A function or job description can serve as an aid.

6.1.2 Additional criteria: the design of managerial tasks

A manager's tasks should also be designed with the scope and extent of his or her authority in mind (see Section 6.4). A manager has to be able to manage the people under his responsibility in a responsible way, and should be able to pay enough attention to consultation and motivation, and to supervising his employees' tasks. The number of people who can be effectively managed directly (=span of control) and indirectly (=depth of control) is limited and when that limit is reached, tasks will need to be delegated to others. Where they are delegated, the necessary authority will also have to be delegated in order to be able to assess the quality of the delegatee's decision making. An optimal degree of delegation can consequently be said to have been reached when responsible decisions are being made at the various levels of management and operation. At such a point, there will be effective use of human capacities and employees will be carrying out their responsibilities fruitfully.

optimal degree of delegation

Unity of managerial direction needs to be guaranteed, and can be stimulated by coordination mechanisms such as procedures, instructions, planning, consultation and so on, all of which are looked at in more detail in Section 6.7.

6.2 P-grouping and F-grouping: advantages and disadvantages

The advantages and disadvantages of the various different forms of division of work on the operational level can be readily seen if the F(unctional) grouping is compared to the P(roduct) grouping (see Figs 6.1 and 6.2). We will see the advantages and disadvantages of these two forms of division of work more closely through comparison of the charts in Figs 6.1 and 6.2.

6.2.1 Horizontal differentiation: advantages and disadvantages

F-group

The nature of the processes performed is the main criterion in the forming of work groups or departments (F-group) according to functional specialization. In theory, operational workers all do the same sort of work and the boss, foreman or department chief is more or less regarded as a specialist in that particular area. In the example, the activities carried out by saw mill A, planing department B and assembly department C are coordinated at X, the point at which the processing phases come together and can be overseen. These departments are gateways through which the components for the products, namely tables, chairs and cupboards, flow (see Fig 6.1).

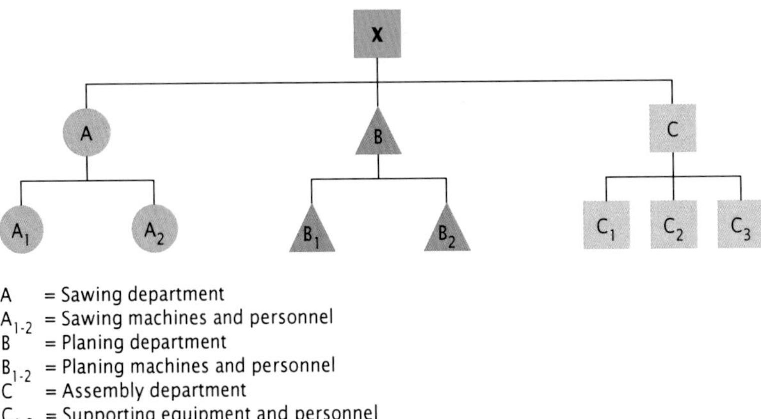

Figure 6.1
F-grouping (horizontal differentiation)

F-grouping advantages

The concentration of similar processes in departments and sub-departments has advantages that derive from following:

- Mechanization and purchase of specialized equipment
- A high degree of utilization of people and machinery
- The attaining of more skills and routines
- The attaining of expertise and process knowledge in part-operations and processes
- Unity of working attitude and language

F-grouping disadvantages

The disadvantages that arise from F-grouping are as follows:

- Monotony, uniformity and one-sidedness
- Lack of flexibility due to concentration on one or a few part-operations or processes
- Coordination problems due to breaking the natural coherence of the processes and operations

6.2.2 Internal specialization

P-group

In the composed work group (P-group) the final product is what determines the organization of tasks and processes. In a P-group production department producing chairs, tables and cupboards, the production of these chairs, tables and cupboards dictates the organizational processes. Operational employees (or project group members) work together to carry out successive processes. The foreman or department chief can be seen as the coordinator-general whose job is ensure that any adjustments are mutual.

Grouping according to the various final products is depicted in Fig 6.2. The overall coordination of the manufacturing activities is located at X, the point from where the various product groups (X1=chairs, X2=tables, X3=cupboards) can be overseen. Per product group, the various pieces of necessary technical equipment and the personnel with their various skills are assigned to the individual manufacturing shops: A. sawing, B. planing, C. assembly.

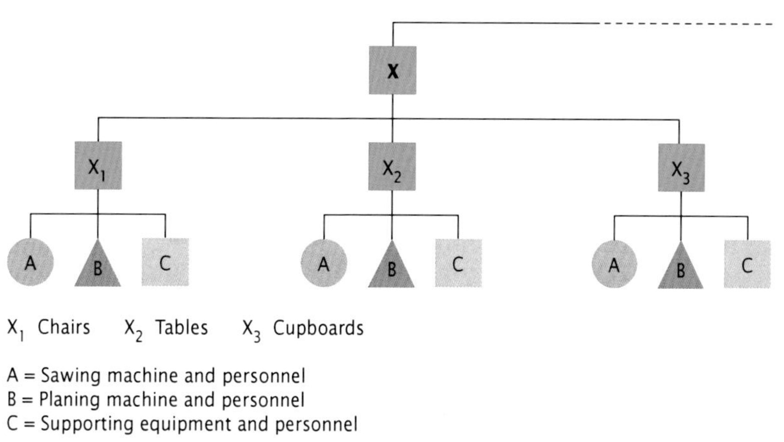

X_1 Chairs X_2 Tables X_3 Cupboards

A = Sawing machine and personnel
B = Planing machine and personnel
C = Supporting equipment and personnel

Figure 6.2
P-grouping as an internal specialization within the manufacturing department

P-grouping advantages

The advantages of a P-grouping arise from the bringing together of dissimilar processes into one product group, especially since this optimizes the coherence between the processes as far as the final product is concerned. The advantages derive from the following:

- Fast flow of products because of the group-like set-up (=product line set-up) of machines and people per product
- Fast problem-solving, because direct product-oriented communication is built into the group
- Short communication channels in the event of a need for feedback of information

P-grouping disadvantages

The disadvantages that arise from P-grouping are as follows:

- Higher costs, because more resources and equipment are needed and less favorable quantitative proportions exist between the various types of resource. For example, each department has its own sawing machine (3 rather than 2 with F-grouping). Consequently, the advantages of scale and the economies of synergy are lost
- A lower degree of functional expertise in part-processes. The employee does not profit to the fullest from knowledge gained during the various phases of the processes.

To summarize the technical and economical advantages derived from shorter delivery times, larger delivery reliability and a higher degree of flexibility are counteracted by the higher costs related to the need for more resources. Quality and motivational issues also have to be taken into account.

6.2.3 *Ingredients of an effective grouping of tasks and design of functions*

A number of conditions that can give rise to improved job satisfaction. Lawler (1988) mentions four which should be built into every function. They are:

- Variety in the tasks to be carried out
- Autonomy in planning and executing the tasks
- Identification with the tasks to be carried out
- Feedback of both quantitative and qualitative data concerning the way in which tasks were/are carried out

Herzberg (1968 and 1974) translates Lawler's four core dimensions into specific recommendations. He proposes some ingredients which have to be built into functions as so-called motivators. These ingredients are discussed by Herzberg within the framework of strategies to humanize labor. He identifies two approaches to job design: 'orthodox task enrichment' and 'socio-technical systems design'. The ingredients for effective job design are relevant to both these approaches, albeit in different ways. The ingredients are as follows:

- Direct task feedback, i.e. not a pre-evaluation, and not via a supervisor, boss or department
- Client-oriented execution of tasks instead of boss-oriented task execution. The main concern is that the external or internal client (e.g. the next working station or department) be satisfied with the performance delivered
- Being able to gather new knowledge and experience in the work situation, either in a horizontal, or vertical direction and with that the possibility to grow in a psychological sense
- Being authorized and being able to plan and dispatch the work, being able to take responsibility for self-imposed norms and for the work to be done, instead of following a set pattern imposed by others
- Freedom to learn from others' experiences, i.e. after finishing his work the worker is free to gather knowledge in and around the organization relating to other aspects of the job, or to transfer knowledge to other employees, and so on.
- Self-control regarding resources, so that the costs incurred by the organization are kept as low as possible. This will enhance cost consciousness
- Opportunities for direct communication, so that if problems arise, the worker can spontaneously discuss them in a horizontal, lateral or vertical direction, whichever may be useful to problem-solving at that moment
- Personal accountability. This ingredient depends on all the other elements mentioned above being available

As designer and builder of the organization a manager has to consider how these recommendations in respect of the grouping of tasks and the design of jobs and functions can be applied in a specific situation. Job enlargement, job enrichment and to a certain degree job rotation are some of the options open to him or her.

6.2.4 *Job enlargement, job enrichment and job rotation*

If a task is experienced as monotonous or if it requires a limited range of physical actions (for example, excessive burdening of certain muscles), there are several ways of making it more attractive. They include work division and different ways of assigning tasks.

Job enlargement

job enlargement

Job enlargement (a horizontal dimension process) is the lengthening of the task cycle via expansion of activities on a qualitively similar level of worker capability. The employees will perform a larger part of the process as a whole, hence the tasks will have a greater unity to them. The traditional structuring principle, where a higher degree of similarity in the sense of narrow task differentiation is regarded as desirable is partially broken down by this action. The contribution of an individual employee to the overall process increases. There will be greater insight into the manufacturing or servicing process and less dependency on the working speed of others. There will also be more freedom of movement and more latitude.

Job enrichment

job enrichment

Job enrichment (the vertical dimension process) is the addition of 'higher' tasks and the integration of direct and indirect productive tasks, including authority and responsibilities that cohere with the task. Tasks previously carried out by support and staff departments will, where possible, be carried out by the employees themselves. The tasks may include dispatching work and work planning, registration, control, small repairs and maintenance. The essential elements of planning, checking and control are consequently now part of the employee's job.

Job rotation

job rotation

Job rotation (a horizontal and, in theory, vertical process) is the interchanging of tasks. Members of a work group may do this from time to time, sometimes by fixed arrangement or mutual agreement. It enables greater insight into the process as a whole. Insight into the mutual interdependencies of tasks stimulates the sense of being an 'all-rounder'. Flexibility increases. Status differences are eliminated and both the unpleasant as well as the nice tasks are carried out by everyone.

6.2.5 Semi-autonomous work groups

Improvement in the working situation (in the sense of being intrinsic to job content though extrinsic to the job environment) can also be brought about by a re-grouping of tasks in autonomous or semi-autonomous groups into which part-tasks can be integrated. Such a P-grouping around a natural and rounded-off group task will also have repercussions for the managerial role.

A semi-autonomous (P-) work group according to the socio-technical approach to work design will be characterized by the following:

- A rounded-off group task
- The opportunity to be able to contact the staff and support services or linked departments independently
- Group members having discretionary powers to regulate the speed, quantity and quality themselves
- A limited size, so that the group members can maintain direct contact with one another and thus can form a 'proper' group.

CASE

Mini case study 6.1

A focus on people's autonomy

The management approach of US presidents changes constantly. Clinton's 'Reinventing Government' initiative led to good ideas but little progress. George W. Bush's top-down approach was aimed at making managers more accountable and outsourcing work to private industry. Some managers felt constrained and outsourcing was no panacea. Today, Barrack Obama is taking a middle path. He has asked agency heads to come up with a handful of high-priority operational goals, with firm deadlines and measurable results – but he leaves it to them to choose the goals. He also encourages letting smart ideas bubble up from the lower ranks.

Source: *BusinessWeek*, December 7, 2009, p. 46, S. Hamm

6.2.6 Quality circles

quality circles

Quality circles is a Japanese method of analyzing and resolving work, employment and organizational issues and improving involvement and motivation amongst employees. This method is also applied in Europe.

Quality circles arose in Japan in the 1950s in Japanese companies that, under the influence of ideas from Deming, Juran and Ishikawa, developed the concept of total quality control. Workgroups ('circles') were created within companies, even on the shop floor. These groups started analyzing and resolving quality problems in their own department, studying techniques of quality control and learning to apply these to their own job. Later, these quality circles started to occupy themselves with manufacturing problems and with analyzing other problems in the workplace, such as safety, cooperation, communication and so on.

goal of quality circles

The goal of quality circles is improving quality in the broadest sense: improving the quality of the product or the service, the work methods and safety on the job. Quality circle methods encourage employees to resolve problems in their own workplace. Training and education in the use of these methods and techniques, and careful planning and guidance in the implementation of quality circles are necessary to fulfill the conditions. Implementation of quality circles not only leads to cost savings but is also generally accompanied by greater involvement and pleasure in the job.

6.3 Organization and group design

line set-up
functional set-up
group set-up
processing station

The layout of manufacturing equipment often follows certain patterns, amongst which the line set-up, the functional set-up, or the group set-up. In the line set-up, the manufacturing equipment and machinery are arranged to match the sequence of processes carried out. When this is mechanized and mutually linked, this production line becomes an assembly line. In the functional set-up, all production equipment performing the same function is arranged together in an order corresponding to the manufacturing processes of most of the products. For example, the sawing, drilling, assembly and packaging departments will be arranged consecutively. In the group set-up, a work group jointly manufactures a final product or an entire component which has to be built into the final product in another department. The group is then a 'mini-factory within the factory.' A group that produces gearboxes for cars which are built into the car somewhere else within the organization is an example of such a mini-factory. In a processing station, the various processes involved in the production of the final product – whether it be a razor or a component of a car – are all performed in the one area.

Group set-up and division of tasks

job rotation
job enlargement

In a group set-up, machinery and people are all located in one 'production cell' in which a specific component or end product is produced. Within a production cell part-processes could be carried out per production employee (F-grouping), with job rotation also an option. After a certain time the various employees would change jobs and thus avoid the possibility of the jobs becoming monotonous.
Another possibility is job enlargement: taking on additional tasks within the one processing station. Combining planning tasks, maintenance tasks and quality control would be a type of task enrichment. It would allow a manufacturing employee to cover all phases of processing up to the final product or part-product (P-grouping). He or she would then start the whole process anew, but now on a new product.

6.3.1 Organizing around processes

Figure 6.3 shows how a product or service is produced within the functional set-up of an organization.
Servicing several product/market combinations often means complex management and coordination, long waiting times and a build-up of stock and inventory. Maximum utilization of both people and production resources requires activities to be matched to one another and the coordination involved requires considerable involvement of management.

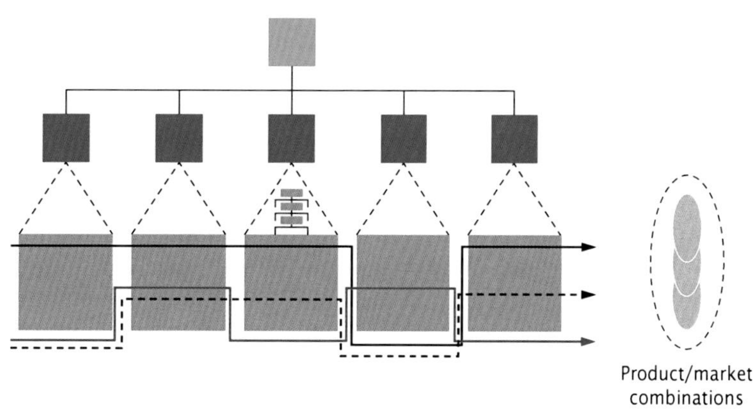

Figure 6.3
Complex process flows in functional organizations

Organizing the work around processes instead of around functions requires fewer managers and decisions can be made more quickly. Because product/market combinations are the center of attention, decentralized responsibility for results increases. While this solution may lead to duplication of expensive and unique capacity, this disadvantage can be avoided by bundling or grouping this capacity into units. Because these smaller units are all relatively mutually interdependent (Chapter 5), they will not disturb one another too readily in their day-to-day functions. The need for coordination will hence be less. The units can be coordinated by standardization of output. Organizing around processes essentially means that the management of processes is decentralized and simplified.

decentralized responsibility for results

standardization of output

An important condition for organizing around processes is that the flow of orders should not fluctuate too much. Should this occur one department may end up underutilized and another temporally overoccupied. Resolving such a situation will require careful analysis of ways in which the company's organization could be changed.

Organizing around processes instead of around functions will reduce managerial complexity. Some advantages will be an increase in responsiveness and speed of translation of market signals into products. There will also be less inventory and stock build-up and shorter waiting lines, which in itself will contribute to an improvement in efficiency.

increase in responsiveness

On the move to more process-oriented structures

work flow

With a focus on processes, attention is directed to the overall work flow and all or as many as possible work steps, including such steps as the order completion process. This process flows, so to speak, from receipt of the customer order through the various processes to the delivery of the order to the customer. In general, a process orientation requires a horizontally focused organizational framework and cross-functional linking and coordination. The latter aspect is crucial. A process focus can be strengthened by giving a team the responsibility for dealing with the overall process and having it report to a process leader or manager. The installment of new information and communication technologies (ICT) makes it possible to maximize the advantages by a reduction of throughput time and 'time to market' of such products as customer-specific new product applications.

cross-functional linking coordination

Process-oriented structures

Process-oriented structures offer a way of breaking the rigidity of the functional organizational structure. They have a greater product, market and/or geographic focus, can accelerate development and throughput times and can improve the delivery of products and services.

6.3.2 Working in broad task groups

task groups

It is also possible to reduce the need for control within a department responsible for part of a process. When the work is split up into different functions within a department, a large amount of planning and coordinating capacity is still required at a decentralized level, a disadvantage that can be counteracted by creating broad task groups as this will reduce the need for control at a decentralized level, and the number of managers providing leadership to the shop floor will be kept to a minimum. Harmonization between these task groups is necessary, and is a matter for management teams. These management teams will have to ensure the following:

- Standardization of the output of task groups which perform similar processes to ensure that the customer receives similar products or services regardless of which task group it is that produces these products or services;
- Mutual adjustment when components are assigned from the one to the other group (in the case of horizontal differentiation).

Introducing broad task groups may lead to an increase in work satisfaction for interested employees. Some ad hoc guidelines for working with broad task groups are as follows:

- Groups should perform their activities as independently as possible. This means that the groups have to have access to regulating capacities and also perform preparing, supporting and controlling tasks.
- The members of the group must be able to handle all activities necessary to the process.
- Groups should consist of a minimum of four and a maximum of twenty members.
- Rewards are largely based on abilities within the group tasks.
- Within the group, the coordinating role can be fulfilled by members of the group (in rotation).

CASE

Mini case study 6.2

Creative tension at Google's

For years Google has had a fairly informal product-development system. Ideas percolated upwards from Googlers without any formal process for top managers to review them. Teams working on innovative stuff were generally kept small. Such a system worked fairly well while Google was in its infancy. But now that it is a giant with 20,000 employees, the firm risks stifling potential money-spinners with a burgeoning bureaucracy. To stop that happening, Google has begun to hold regular meetings at which employees are encouraged to present new ideas to Eric Schmidt, the firm's chief executive, and Larry Page and Sergey Brin, its co-founders. It has also given some projects more resources and independence than in the past. Both moves are designed to ward off the conservatism that can set in as companies mature. 'We are actively trying to prevent middle-agedom,' explains Mr Schmidt.

Source: *The Economist*, September 19, 2009, p. 66

6.3.3 Performance management and team structure

feedback

Recent literature suggests that feedback and goal setting can have a strong motivational effect on individuals and teams. A system for performance management which supplies the necessary feedback for self-controlling teams can be designed according to certain principles. The basic characteristics of such a system for performance management are as follows:

performance management

- Bottom-up development: the team itself decides which areas of results can be improved and how to adjust the performance indicators accordingly. Changes are then made to the managerial structure. Consensus will then have been reached

- Weighting of the various result areas and accompanying performance indicators, thereby creating an index for overall performance in respect of all result areas as well as producing data relating to performances in separate result areas
- Systematic feedback on performance, presented in a clear way. This facilitates discussion relating to improvement in performance and improvement in working methods.

6.4 Delegation: task, authority, responsibility and accountability

When a company or institution expands and more personnel are employed it becomes necessary to address the issue of which tasks can be delegated to other employees. Whether a director or a department chief, an employee can only take on a finite number of tasks.

delegation of tasks

Delegation of tasks is often the only solution to increasing management complexity brought about by growth.

task

A task is a work activity which needs to be done. The content of a task is determined by the activities which have to be carried out. It may be the purchasing of raw material or the keeping of the wage records. To perform the task, many other types of activity may have to be carried out, such as making phone calls, typing, filling in forms and so on.

When tasks are transferred by delegation, the necessary authority to perform these tasks also needs to be assigned so that the responsibility for correct handling of the tasks lies with the right person. Responsibility can be viewed as the moral obligation to perform a task to one's best ability as well as the duty to report on the execution of that task. Task, authority and responsibility should be intrinsically connected. An employee can only be held responsible when he or she has been assigned the authority that goes with the delegated tasks. Responsibility is also a function of the amount of authority that has been assigned. The extent that one can take the initiative also depends having sufficient staff and resources at one's disposal.

Delegation and 'management by exception'

When operational employees and middle management are strongly motivated to achieve company or institutional goals within the boundaries set on their freedom of action, they can be relieved of their responsibility to report on their progress unless that progress falls outside

exception principle

management by exception

certain boundaries: the exception principle. Conscious and systematic application of this principle is termed 'management by exception' (MbE). Management of this type involves the setting of boundaries, constraints and operational norms in consultation and in respect of a certain task. Middle management or operational workers will undertake to achieve results that fall within these boundaries, and if the results fall short, they are authorized to take corrective action. The upshot of such an arrangement is that only exceptional variance is reported to management, leaving it free to spend more time on policy and work creation.

6.5 Organizational principles: relationships and authorities

line organization

There is one basic form that underlies every organizational structure, namely the line organization. Variations on this include the line staff organization and the line organization with specialized support staff services.

6.5.1 Line organization

Line organization: origin
Line organization reflects the managerial and operational functions and employee tasks at the various hierarchical levels. Line organization arises by transferring tasks in a vertical and horizontal direction. Every employee reports to his or her immediate manager.

Advantages of line organization
The major advantages of line organization are clarity and simplicity: the operational employees know exactly what is expected of them, know who their boss is, and consequently to whom they have to report. Assignments, along with the procedures, guidelines and instructions required to be followed, are issued at a certain point along the line. Supervision and assessment of work progress take place from here, as are corrective measures. An advantage is that the processes will have been tried out and tested before the work is assigned. The general manager or supervising manager is expected to have an overview of all of the activities and to have an insight into the various aspects of the work. For example, he or she will have weighed up the costs associated with the production of a short product run in order to prevent sales grinding to a halt due to an unexpected sell out or the ramifications of an interesting rush job for an important customer. In a small and relatively simple company, line organization will work well.

Disadvantages of line organization
If long, intensive consultation between the managerial and operational employees is necessary, or there have to be changes that involve mutual adjustment, the 'pure line pattern' may have to be abandoned. If adaptation problems along the line were passed along vertically to the general manager, communication would soon become extremely complex. It cannot be assumed moreover, that the supervising chiefs hold a monopoly on all aspects of the work as far as knowledge and experience are concerned.

Manufacturing technology, material knowledge, cost calculation, administrative procedures, legal matters, and so on will all involve an expertise that may fall short in some areas. If so, it will be necessary to employ job specialists in these areas. Managers who really are all-rounders are few and far between. Building an organization on the all-rounder principle is dangerous. Management has to delegate both tasks and the relevent authority (see Section 6.4), as well as employ others when this is necessary. If this does not take place to a sufficient degree, management's span of control (see Section 6.8) will be only slight.

CASE

Mini case study 6.3

Here is a test to determine how well you are likely to delegate. You should not study the test first: fill in the answers according to your initial reaction. Tick the box which contains the most correct answer. Only tick one box.

Here is a test which you can use to determine how capable you are of delegation. You should not study the test first: fill in the answers according to your initial reaction. Tick the column which contains the most correct answer. Only one answer is possible each time: you have to choose.

Test: Can you delegate?	**No**	**Not sure**	**Yes**
1 Do you believe that the personnel at your disposal cannot handle the work delegated to them?	☐	☐	☐
2 Within your organization are there detailed job descriptions in which the responsibilities and the authority of each managerial employee are described?	☐	☐	☐
3 Do you prefer to do things yourself rather than delegating, with all the attendant hassle of explaining?	☐	☐	☐
4 Do your employees usually ask for your decision when they have a problem?	☐	☐	☐
5 Are you afraid that subordinates could be a threat to you in your career?	☐	☐	☐
6 Do you know exactly which authority your subordinates should have in order to be able to handle certain assignments?	☐	☐	☐
7 Do you perform a lot of small routine jobs which could be performed just as well by others?	☐	☐	☐
8 Would you be able to handle more work if required?	☐	☐	☐
9 Are you not a little afraid of specialized subordinates who are absolute experts in their field?	☐	☐	☐
10 Is there the possibility for open discussion about certain situations (for example criticism or complaints)?	☐	☐	☐

Line relationships and line authority

The manager exercises his line authority via his line relationships. The authority he exercises is formal and hierarchical, and could be described as 'command and control' authority. Employees are assigned their tasks from above.

The subordinate has to render account to his manager and has to report to him about the execution of the task, orally or in writing. The manager, in turn, has to exercise direct or indirect control over the execution, so that if necessary, he can interfere, adjust or correct in a timely way.

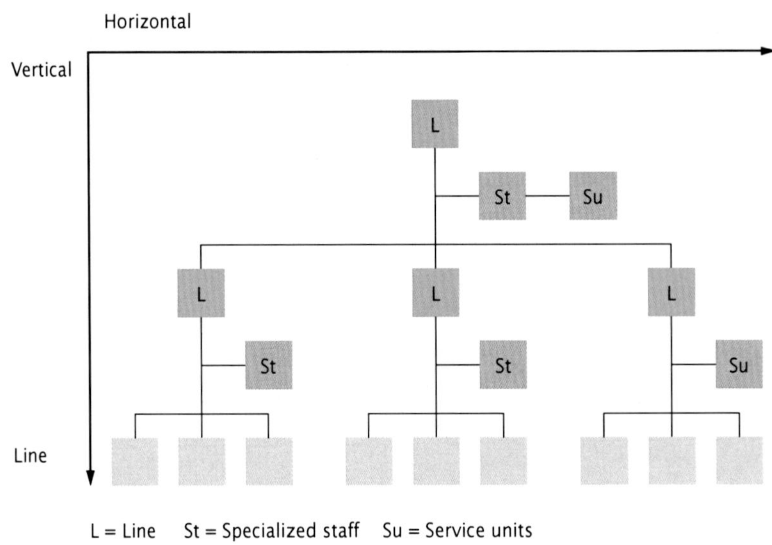

Figure 6.4
Line organization in its basic form with staff and support services

Line organization: functioning

unity of command

Line relationships that form part of line organization are characterized by unity of command of a relatively pure type. A subordinate receives his orders from only one person, the manager who is his immediate superior. As such, managers within such a line form of organization have to be expert in all managerial and operational aspects of their jobs. Their positions have a certain omniscience and they are implicitly assumed to be able to make correct, careful and appropriate decisions without having to consult anyone else. Consequently, their instructions and work orders must be carefully formulated and clearly issued. The necessary unity of points of view and unity of direction is thus readily arrived at.

As soon as problems arise in the execution of the task at hand, they have to be brought to the attention of the manager, who then decides what has to be done. Then, should consultation be necessary with employees from other departments, the overall manager needs to arrange this. By following a vertical organizational line, unity of direction is virtually guaranteed.

If the vertical line relationships are strictly adhered to – the pure form of line organization – this will give rise to clearly hierarchical relationships between director, department managers and operational employees.

This form of organization has, of course, both its advantages and its disadvantages, and these are set out in Table 6.1.

Table 6.1
Line organization: advantages v. disadvantages

Advantages	Disadvantages
1 responsibilities/authority are clear	**1** rapid overloading of managers
2 control is clear	**2** lack of specialization
3 fast decision making	**3** managerial performance impeded because the manager has to become a jack of all trades
4 fast execution of decisions	**4** long lines of communication which can work against desired outcome
5 relationships are clear	

6.5.2 Line and specialized staff organization

Line staff organization: origin

To be an effective and responsible manager, a manager will have to fulfill his policy-oriented tasks well in order to be effective in his operations-directed tasks. If this does not happen, the manager will quickly lose touch with what is going on. The daily problems will probably be solved by 'symptom fighting' or 'fire fighting'. There will be no time for problem-solving by reconstituting or delegating tasks. The problems will thus recur. Delivery times will be exceeded, people over-worked, the quality of products or services fall short, market chances not effectively used and so on.

symptom fighting

The right approach takes a lot of time and attention. The larger the organization and the more complex the problems, the more time and attention will be needed for this task. In relatively small companies some of the activities will be carried out by external experts or consultants. For example, accountants will be responsible for the administration and supply of information, and external consultants for marketing research.

In larger companies or institutions, specialists will be recruited from within the organization itself. The organization will have reached such a size and problems occur with such frequency that management needs the relevant in-house expertise in order to be able to address problems with regard to policy and/or execution of tasks. When there is continuous work of this problem-solving nature, it is cheaper to have people in-house rather than making use of external expertise. Specialist knowledge relating to the analysis and solving of policy problems and specialized staff functions involving economic research, market research, long-term planning and legal matters may be more vitally important to the organization.

specialist knowledge

Line staff organization: functioning

staff organ

A staff organ is a consulting or advisory body which is at the disposal of the board of management or of other managers in a company or institution. Such an organ also serves the function of providing the line manager to whom they are assigned with advice and when necessary, preparing decisions and supplying him with information, tracing problems and analyzing them. A staff organ is a consulting or advisory body which is at the disposal of the board of management or of other managers in a company or institution. It will be at the disposal of the line manager to whom it is assigned, providing him with advice and tracing problems and resolving them when this is required. It will also be at the disposal of the line.

advisory body

A staff organ in its pure form has an advisory role to play. Its position within the organization is illustrated in Fig 6.5. In this figure, the market research section (which may carry out research such as macro-economic research or research relating to organization and efficiency) has a staff relationship to the organization's other sections. Making use of specialized staff departments or of individual specialized staff functionaries enables a line organization to make the most of its advantages as well as counteracting some of its disadvantages (see Section 6.5.1).

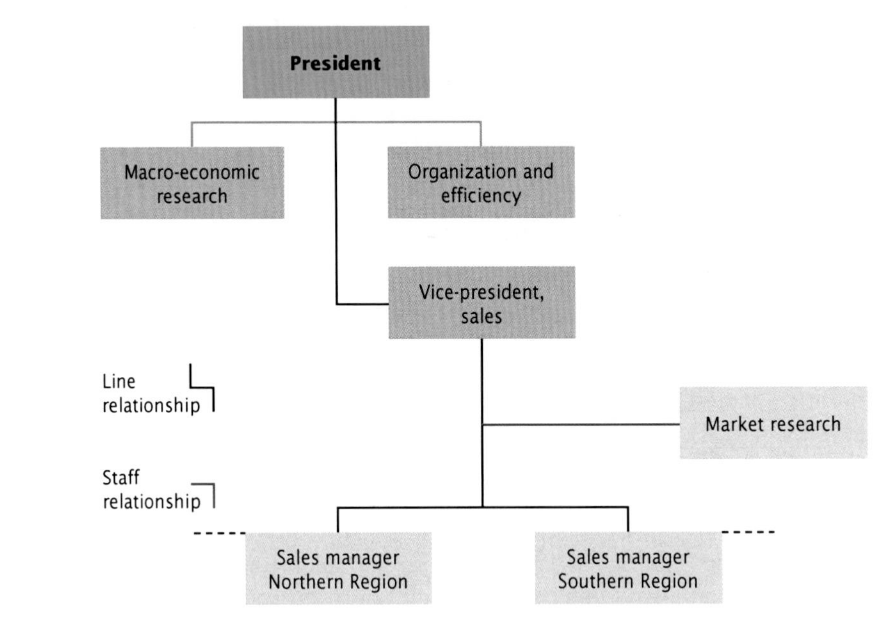

Figure 6.5
Staff relationships within the organizations

line manager

Only a line manager is authorized to convert advice into guidelines, instructions, assignments or orders.

The staff organ is directed mainly at eliminating potentially threatening shortcomings in expertise and skills along the line. However, the line does not need to follow the organ's advice since staff authority is limited to an advisory capacity only. As such, calling in staff specialists does not change the way instructions and assignment reach employees. Rather, specialized staff serve to reinforce line management. The staff has the time, the knowledge and the skills at its disposal to support line management with regard to problems which would otherwise, because of pressure of daily circumstances or by lack of specific know-how or lack of time, receive insufficient attention from the line manager.

Line staff organization: advantages and disadvantages

The advantages of the line staff organization are as follows:
- Better decisions can be made through practical application of specific knowledge and skills
- Delegating line 'headwork' to staff-members saves time
- The scope of control (see Section 6.8) is enlarged
- More efficient use of time makes it possible to focus on other matters.

Line staff organization could have the following disadvantages:
- Too little practical application of specific knowledge and skills is a possibility
- Contact with the line, and through that with the operational core, may be lost (the so-called ivory tower effect)
- The involvement of specialists costs money
- The line's chief may bypassed.

ivory tower worker

A specialized staff worker needs to avoid being an 'ivory tower worker' or 'potentially useful only'. Since decision-making authority is situated along the line, specialist staff have to tailor their advice to meet the requirements of line managers, whose main need is workable solutions to problems. Lack of acceptance may lead to lack of involvement since the line is not obliged to use a given piece of advice. If the advice is too complex or cannot be understood, the line will not be likely to adopt it. As a decision maker, the line manager will not want to be dependent on line staff, and so it is important that line staff give sufficient explanation and provide enough insight, and see to it that the line can foresee the consequences of decisions, because the line ultimately has the responsibility for the execution of the tasks.

6.5.3 Line organization and specialized support staff

Support staff: origin

The services of specialized support staff may be required to perform tasks of a specific nature, whether in the area of personnel, administration and finance, maintenance and so on.

service departments

Specialized support staff units are service departments which perform tasks of a specialized character at the request of a certain department or line employee.

WHEN THE STAFF RULES THE LINE

Does the following sound familiar? Your HR department seems to be exerting an undue influence on the way in which your company is structured: on your finance department, brand management, corporate strategy, chief of staff, credit or risk management and your workers. Do you have a powerful corporate headquarter staffed with managers who are bombarding you for MIS data just to feed their functional heads who are monitoring the performance of the company as they please? Do you need to get past these potentates before you gain an audience with your boss, the CEO? If so, you are definitely working for a CEO in a company in which power is centered around staff functions and money handlers, and managed by people who mistrust a strong line function.
Research shows gross gaps between organisations that have a strong line orientation and are structured into business units with cost management accountability, and organisations that have in their structure people from finance or HR that hold positions of power and are able to influence the fate of the organisation. The latter are likely to form individual power centers whose business heads would need prior CFO approval or an HR head's consent before moving an inch to get things done in their profit centres.

A line orientation is not as simple as making business managers report into the CEO and getting them to deliver results. It is the surrounding space that we offer such business managers to perform their function of planning, organising and delivering results cohesively. The process of establishing an organisational design – a business model that focuses on the powers that are provided to line management to deliver with concurrent curtailed power to staff functions – is a critical aspect of performing organisations. It means that the line decides, the staff implement– not the other way around. Organisational design involves the creation of roles, processes and formal reporting relationships within an organisation. Two phases in the organisational design process can be identified: strategic grouping, which establishes the overall structure of the organisation (its main sub-units and their relationships – in a sense, the functions that generate revenue), and operational design, which defines the more detailed roles and processes. Concurrently, it also makes sure that finance or HR has been provided with a concrete value-adding role that emphatically supports the line function in being closer to the customer, becoming valued employees, appreciating costs consciousness, implementing appropriate technology, educating sustainability priorities, training resources, facilitating research and development processes, and so on.

The HR, accounting, finance, legal and IT departments are staff functions whose job it is to support the performance of the line functions. But an absence of process-based structures, which produce cohesive line and staff and inter-linked activities within a horizontal work stream, tends to have an effect on the performance of the business units. Any absence of alignment at strategic structural levels creates some dissonance between the line and the staff.

Source: *Financial Express*, September 12, 2009 (edited)

Specialized support staff: functioning

support staff

Unlike specialized staff organs, specialized support staff carry out part of the actual job, hence the term 'support staff'. This is illustrated in Fig. 6.6.

In turn, the line is obliged to seek advice from specialized support staff as soon as problems arise that touch on the fields of expertise of the support staff and is obliged to follow that advice, whether it relates to, for example, a discharge problem (via the personnel department), sudden machine stagnation (via the maintenance department), modernization of the manufacturing shop (via the technical services), and so on.

A manager with functional authority in a specific field determines how something could be done, not what should be done. Working assignments are assigned by the line. This holds true for central administration with regard to purchase administration. The functional authority or functional relationship is often built in between central and decentralized staff services in large companies (for example, between the central Administration and Finance department and the Administration department in a subsidiary or business unit).

Unlike staff organs, specialized support staff organs usually conduct only a part of the task, or have a controlling function with regard to the line, and functional authority recommendations relate to the activities of employees who are under the line authority of another manager.

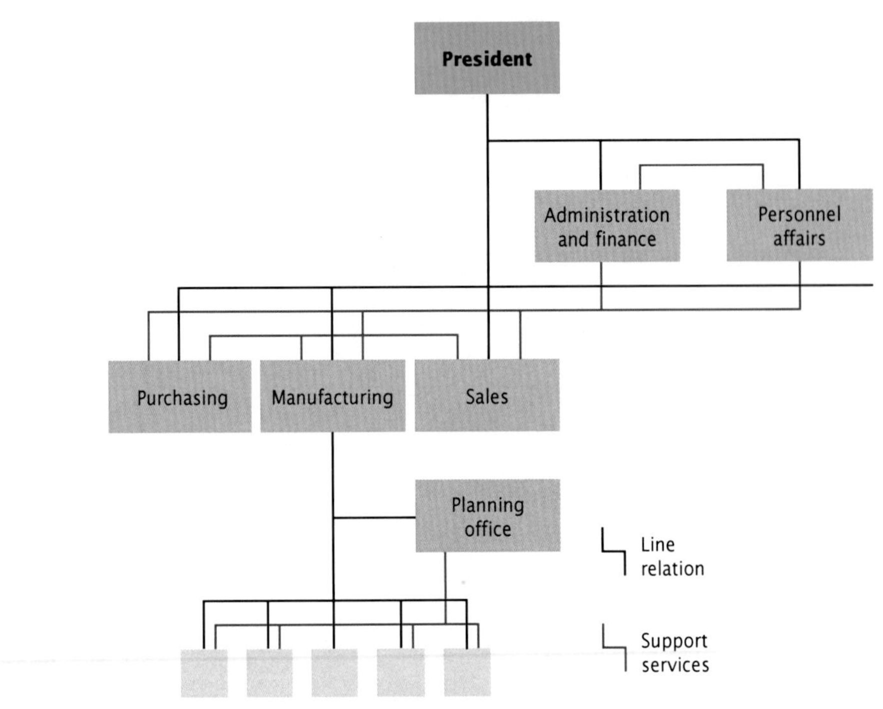

Figure 6.6
Functional relationships within the organization

managers

Operational employees stand in a relationship to several managers, who each contribute their ideas in relation to aspects of operational execution. However, when applied, any lack of clarity in these ideas will cause problems. It is important to issue instructions only after lengthy deliberation or consultation, and in a spirit of cooperation. The problems mentioned earlier can be thereby partially eliminated.

functional authority

In a functional set up, the lines of authority between specialized support services and line are stipulated. Even though a support service is placed outside the line, it can nevertheless issue directives to the line relating to a specific field of expertise, or can require that the directives be made compulsory. So-called functional authority can be exercised; that is, suggestions relating to the activities of employees who are under the authority of another manager in the line may be made. A manager with functional authority can, to a certain extent, state how something could be done, but cannot simply issue an order to do something in a particular way. Work assignments are given by the line. It is more a question of 'when this or that is done, then it has to be done in this way.'

Advantages and disadvantages

The advantages include the following:

- The required expertise, knowledge and skills are brought in.
- A certain degree of coordination, consistency and uniformity can be ensured in, for example, the design of departmental registration systems, the design of forms, the setting up of evaluation systems, the ranking of personnel in wage and salary scales, production planning, maintenance activities and so on. The result will be that in these areas, the same systems and procedures are used throughout the whole organization.

The disadvantages include the following:

- Operational employees are responsible to more than one manager at any one time, each of whom can issue instructions on aspects of execution.
- There will no longer be unity of command.

Essentially, work consultation is a human process. Specialized support service staff need to maintain sufficient communication with the operational manager in respect of 'how to act,' since they ultimately have decision-making authority in respect of the 'what and when'.

Shared services and SLAs

'Shared services' refers to a concentration within a company of activities that previously were carried out at different locations within the organization. For the carrying out of these activities the same know-how, experience and expertise is required as previously. Some examples are the bundling of local administrations into one administrative center (Albert Heijn), and a center for ICT support or personnel. Service to geographically dispersed branches, units or departments is usually provided on the basis of contracts or SLAs (service level agreements). Sometimes this type of activity is farmed out to external service providers, a Randstad for personnel accounting and personnel management, for wages administration or other financial administrative services.

SLAs

Internal and external service takes place on the basis of contracts and SLAs, and this can sometimes also cause a lot of bickering. In the old situation, the unit had an administration of its own, which meant that matters could be taken care of immediately and on the spot. The advantages were immediate availability, usefulness for local coordination, direct communication and greater decisiveness, involvement and loyalty in the carrying out and understanding of local problems within the organizational units. In the case of shared services which operate from a distance, these advantages are traded in for concentration advantages and uniformity and standardization of procedures. Problems will occur when a more intensive or more frequent exchange of information is required and quick and consistent action on the spot is necessary. In situations of mutual dependency (see 5.3.6) a 'shared service center' is liable to fall short if, for instance, the circumstances call for dissimilar or different services or if a great deal of communication is necessary. If no provision is made for this in the SLAs, problems will arise in the internal or external provision of services. There is a lot to be said for not establishing 'shared services' or for abolishing them if necessary, in order to be able to function more efficiently at a local level (see also 2.4.2 on the subject of outsourcing, offshoring and shared services).

immediate availability
local coordination
mutual dependency
shared service center

THE REAL VALUE OF TWEETS

Google and Microsoft are paying Twitter $25 million to crawl the short posts, or tweets, that users send out on the Micro-blogging service. It sounds like big money. Enough for Twitter to turn a small profit in 2009, say two people familiar with the company's finances. Truth is, no one has figured out how to make real money from tweets yet. Google and Microsoft are paying $15 million and $10 million, respectively, as a bet on the future. By laying out what are relatively tiny sums, they get first crack at experimenting with Twitter data. Both are already including tweets in search results. Sean Suchter, general manager of Microsoft's Search Technology Center, predicts the company will end up profiting. 'Many times in history, when you amass the attention of users, that has proven to be a moneymaking endeavor,' he says. For Google and Microsoft, the real payoff may come from tying tweets to local information about products. Twitter is building software that will automatically allow users to add location data to every tweet. Armed with user locations, Microsoft and Google could sell more targeted ads and provide more relevant search results. 'That is potentially very useful,' says Microsoft's Suchter.

Source: *Bloomberg Business Week*, January 18, 2010, p. 31, S.E. Ante

6.5.4 Communication and the design of a consultative structure

direct contact

A manager can give his operational employees the authority to engage in direct contact with another manager's staff in order to solve problems. They can brief him later about what they have done in mutual consultation. A form of horizontal contact is built into the line organization, though the hierarchical principle is maintained. The hierarchy (='the line') can then continue to operate if mutual consultation does not lead to the desired results.

Horizontal relationships

horizontal relationship

A horizontal relationship is one in which (as the term suggests) there is a consultative relationship between employees on the same hierarchical level. They will consult each other directly and thereby coordinate the various activities. For example, consultation between the sales and manufacturing departments is necessary to determine delivery times in the case of acceptance of orders. If these employees at the same hierarchical level do not reach agreement after consultation, then the hierarchy can decide via an exception rule, and the manager they all have in common, in this case the board of management, decides. The horizontal relationship can be built in as a fixed element in the design of the consultative structure; that is, it can be institutionalized; weekly consultation of department heads is an example of horizontal contact.

Lateral (or diagonal) relationships

lateral relationship

In contrast to the definition just given (for horizontal relationships), a lateral (or diagonal relationship is one in which there is a consultative relationship between employees on different hierarchical levels or from different departments, who have to provide suggestions that they mutually agree on relating to a task they have to share. A committee set up either temporarily or permanently in order to give advice to management about the salary policy to be followed, product development and so on would be in such a relationship.

Horizontal and lateral relationships as coordination mechanisms

coordination mechanism

In its pure form, line organization is almost never found. As soon as horizontal contacts are necessary (and horizontal or lateral consultation between managers is necessary in order to achieve coordination of management and execution) the pure line pattern ceases to exist and is replaced by horizontal and lateral relationships as the coordination mechanism. The hierarchy as coordination mechanism would soon become overloaded if all problems occurring along the line had to be resolved by the joint managers. Horizontal and lateral relationships are easy to build into the hierarchy, and pose no threat to it.

Consultative groups

Consultation and participation within a company or institution can take place via consultative or work groups. These can be set up as project groups or as committees at both the higher and the lower organizational levels, in order to initiate innovation, automation and organizational change, or, for example, to draw up personnel policy or perform long-term planning (see Section 3.6). A committee system is part of the normal line structure, though with specialized staff and support services. Problems that temporary project groups or permanent committees occupy themselves with might involve different types of decisions and could be of a policy directed or an operational nature. Depending on the nature of the assignment, the character of the group could range from advising and coordinating to executive tasks. Similarly, higher consultative groups, lower consultative and work groups could be created depending on the decisions which have to be made.

temporary project groups
permanent committees

Consultative groups are created in order to bundle the expertise and information needed to analyze problems and to create solutions to problems. This will improve the quality of the decision-making process. Consultative groups also provide an opportunity for participation in decision making. This makes decision making more broadly based and increases the likelihood that the decisions will be accepted. These elements of decision making were discussed in Chapter 3.

Work consultation

Besides consultation between departments within a company or institution via temporary or permanent consultative groups at any level, managers and operational employees within the departments also have to confer. During periodical work sessions, problems from the most recent work period can be discussed. Information can be transferred from the top to the bottom and vice versa, and work assignments for the coming period made. The consultation will be direct and take place between all members of a work group, sub-department or department. Operational workers are thus involved in decisions which affect their jobs. With this form of consultation and participation an employee will become more willing to accept decisions and there will be greater work involvement.

periodical work sessions

MEETING WITHOUT JETLAG

Video meetings have never really taken off. Not until now, that is. Long-distance work meeting is where we're heading ... according to the advocates. But can it compete with free chatting via the Internet?

Source: *Het Financieele Dagblad*, 20 April 2009

6.5.5 Communication and participation

Work consultation is a form of regulated and structured deliberation between managerial and operational employees about all aspects of the work and the work situation. As a rule, one characteristic of work consultation is that the employees confer directly and not via representatives. Work consultation is structured group deliberation processes. Deliberation between the manager and an individual employee is, therefore, not defined as work consultation. The way in which work consultation is carried out can differ enormously from organization to organization, depending not only on the type of organization (size, nature of the manufacturing process), but also on the organizational culture (style of leadership and history of participation).

structured group deliberation processes

Work consultation processes are usually instigated for the following reasons:
- To improve employee motivation, involvement and development
- To improve the quality of products, services and working methods
- To increase productivity per employee, per department and for the company as a whole.

Conditions

Successful work consultation processes depend on the following conditions:
- The organization needs the maturity to permit the participation of workers in decision-making processes. The operational workers need the maturity to take their new responsibilities seriously.
- The organization has to implement work consultation processes as part of the package. It cannot be introduced in isolation.
- Work consultation has to lead to increased operational worker influence, but not to the undermining of managerial responsibility.
- Work consultation processes have to be directed at the tasks of the department in the context of the actual work situation.
- Work consultation will only work if employees feel responsible for what happens in their department. If not, they will not be able to function properly during the work consultation process.
- The organization has to be able to adopt the internal changes and developments evoked by work consultation (for example, the adjustment of internal relationships, the changing of structures or procedures or changed lines of authority).

6.5.6 *Substitutes for hierarchy*

Middle management fulfills a number of important direction-giving and coordination roles. Once these roles have been identified they can be combined, and/or assigned or can be eliminated as separate functions, making the organization flatter and more efficient. The main roles of middle management are depicted in Fig 6.7.

Figure 6.7 *Roles of middle management*

▪ Motivating	▪ Setting goals
▪ Measuring	▪ Planning
▪ Coordinating	▪ Linking lines of communication
▪ Assigning work	▪ Training/coaching
▪ Looking after personnel matters	▪ Providing leadership
▪ Providing expertise	▪ Record keeping

Source: *After Lawler*, 1988

reducing the roles of middle management

There are various ways of reducing the roles of middle management and replacing it as part of the hierarchy: for example, by organizing around product/market combinations to a greater extent, by working more in teams or by making better use of information systems. If this happens, the time needed for coordinating, planning, measuring and controlling will actually decrease. Although there are a myriad of ways of replacing the old vertical hierarchical forms, it can be said with almost 100 per cent certainty that hierarchical forms of organization will never completely disappear. As such, middle management can indeed be described as indispensible. Old and heavy hierarchical connections can, however, be reduced or made redundant by an increasing capacity for self-regulation by employees. For the coordinating management level, the policy and strategic task assignments for which, after all, it has been employed, will remain.

Fig. 6.8 shows how various organizational instruments, managing methods and techniques can reduce or even replace the need for a hierarchy. The following are some ways in which hierarchies can be replaced and include an explanation of why their replacement is necessary:

Roles of middle management	Grouping of tasks and design of functions	Data processing systems	Financial information	Record systems	Customer contact	Training	Vision/ values	Accepted leadership
Motivating	■	□	■	■	■	■	■	□
Measuring	■	■	□	□	□	□	□	■
Coordinating	■	■	■	■	■	■	■	■
Assigning work	■	□	□	□	□	□	□	■
Looking after personnel matters	■	□	□	□	□	□	■	■
Providing expertise	□	■	□	□	□	■	□	■
Selling goods	■	■	■	■	■	■	■	□
Planning	■	■	■	□	□	□	□	□
Linking lines of communication	■	■	□	■	□	□	■	□
Training/coaching	■	■	□	■	□	□	□	■
Providing leadership	■	□	□	□	□	□	□	■
Record keeping	■	■	□	□	□	□	□	□

Figure 6.8
Substitutes for hierarchy

Source: *Adapted from Lawler*, 1988

- Grouping of tasks and design of functions, P-grouping, self-regulating teams, group set-ups and semi-autonomous groups reduce the need for coordination and direction from above (by supervising middle managers).
- In computer-supported production or data processing systems, operational employees can be in charge of their data and results themselves (instead of staff and controlling line managers).
- Well-trained and educated employees can interpret and draw conclusions from financial feedback information themselves. This also has a motivational effect. Data can even be directed at competitive comparisons in order to stimulate external interest (instead of internal battles and 'passing the buck').
- Reward systems such as profit sharing, performance-based wage systems and rating on merits and productivity also reduce the need for hierarchy. These systems stimulate teamwork and cooperation and improve communication relating to financial and non-financial performance indicators.
- External and internal customer contact: when business units are co-responsible for their own inputs and outputs, they will, to a large degree, be able and willing to structure and plan their work themselves. This is why units often do not need a chief or boss in the old sense.
- Appropriate training (knowledge, skills and problem handling) by employees means that this is to a lesser degree required of a chief/boss or manager. The accent in management tasks is being transferred to facilities, careful use of talents and good communication.
- A clear vision and understandable and transferable values reinforce the organizational culture. This carries the likelihood of security, standardization of problem solving and strong teams.
- Accepted leadership instead of formal boss-related behavior leads to greater task maturity (see Chapter 8) among employees.

All these possible substitutes may cause a traditional hierarchy to be dismantled even further. A flatter organization is one immediate result of this, since these substitutes are a condition for the effective functioning of flatter organizations.

6.6 Centralization and decentralization

When designing an organizational structure, an important issue to address is where the organizational decisions should be made. When this has been decided, the organization will know where to allocate the authority to make decisions. It is also important to know where within the organization actions and tasks are to be performed. With the growth of company activities, the tasks (and the authority that goes with them) that need to be delegated to others also need to be identified (see Section 6.4).

vertical decentralization

horizontal decentralization

When this involves the spreading of formal decision-making authority by means of delegation from top to bottom along the line, one can speak of vertical decentralization. When line authority is placed at the specialist support service level (Section 6.5.3) dealing with areas of coordination, planning and control, one can speak of horizontal decentralization.

The degree of concentration or spreading of decision-making authority, together with the following aspects, need to be addressed:

- What the authority relates to (decision areas such as manufacturing, sales, or finance)
- The directives, guidelines, instructions and procedures that impinge on governing, managing and execution; that is, the degree of freedom and the constraints that apply to each decision-making area
- The phase in the decision-making process during which policy making, planning or problem-solving consultation actually takes place.

The issue of the ideal degree of concentration or spreading cannot be decided in a straightforward way. Far-reaching freedom of decision making may be unrealistic as far as one area is concerned, whereas it may be possible in another area. To ask permission from head office for every local action would cost too much time and money. It would also not be realistic to expect head office to have sufficient local knowledge. All relevant information relating to, for example, local clients, discounts and personnel should be provided to head office without its being allowed to make decisions at the local level, as this would hinder appropriate reactions and influence the motivation at the local level negatively.

discretionary decision-making authority

Several policy aspects, including pricing and range, production planning, manufacturing techniques, standard costs calculation, salary scales and similar areas, can be left with a certain amount of discretionary decision-making authority though the limitations of this authority can be formulated. Areas such as finance, research and development, mergers, acquisitions and major reorganizations may need little or no discretionary decision-making authority.

In order to determine who makes a company's or institution's decisions and what they are, some questions have to be answered, including the following:

- Who has the information at his disposal for making a certain decision, or who can have it at his disposal quickly and easily?
- Who has the capabilities and expertise at his disposal in order to make a correct decision?
- In order to appropriately meet local circumstances, do urgent decisions have to be made at the local level?
- Do activities conducted locally have to be coordinated carefully with other activities, possibly even with activities to be conducted somewhere else?
- How important is the decision?
- How busy and occupied are those employees who are already candidates for the allocation of authority?
- Is decentralization likely to improve the willingness to take the initiative and improve morale to a sufficiently worthwhile degree?

The answers to these questions will give an indication of the place within the organization where the decision can be made. F-decentralization (in functional decision areas), P(roduct)-decentralization, M(arket)-, or G(eographical)-decentralization, according to the chosen form of work division and assignment of authority, are the options available.

F-decentralization

Under some circumstances (for example, urgent or local circumstances), delegation of authority will become imperative. However, the decentralization that this involves may be counteracted by the need for coordination of important decisions, making concentration of decision-making authority at one place necessary; that is, centralization.

centralization

With the help of the questions posed above, one can try to determine the *loci* for optimal decision making in every area of decision making. Decentralization should only take place if control and centralized policy decision can remain in the hands of centralized coordinating authorities. Top management should continue to hold its ultimate authority where expansion and diversification, product policy, research and development projects, extending/raising/changing equity capital from shareholders, finance and budgeting, providing external financial information, investment selection, proposing/selecting/appointing board members, remuneration of top management and similar aspects are concerned.

From this list one might conclude that only operational decision making should be decentralized. The lower organizational levels, however, may also contribute substantially to centralized policy decision making. The 'bottom up' principle then applies. This is the opposite of the 'top down' approach, in which constraints are superimposed and there is no room for personal initiative or contributions from lower level management and operational employees.

economic situation

The economic situation will naturally determine the best way of spreading decision-making authority across the various areas. In an organization which experiences favorable external conditions and positive financial results, the reins will be loosened and organizational slack more than strictly necessary may arise in areas such as stock surpluses, hiring of extra personnel or the purchase of more inventory. When conditions are less favorable, this organizational slack will be cut back. Top management will then limit the discretionary decision-making authority of the lower management levels within the organization.

crisis situations

In crisis situations or in situations in which an organization is confronted with a somewhat hostile environment there will have to be a relative degree of centralization. The more pressure external interest groups or stakeholders put on the organization, the more inclined the organization will be to centralize. The top echelon then is held responsible and needs to be able to act quickly and effectively. The top levels will need to be in greater control than otherwise, will need to be sure that things go as they want them to go and will need to be kept informed. These situations will sometimes lead to a relatively strong temporary centralization, or return to centralization.

'accordion' effect

This phenomenon is sometimes called the 'accordion' effect: a situational or contingent change in the degree of concentration or spread in the decision-making authority. It may occur from time to time while the organization is in a process of growth and development.

6.6.1 *Profit decentralization and divisionalization*

In organizations with product-market grouping or a geographical grouping of activities, the institutionalization of divisions is a possible course of action and it can be combined with profit decentralization.

divisionalization

Divisionalization with profit decentralization can be seen as a specific form of departmentalization. When this takes place, the organization is divided into divisions which may be termed strategic business units. In theory, divisions or strategic business units are self-sufficient and semi-autonomous. A division is likely to contain a number of subsidiaries or 'business units,' though to a certain extent it will retain full profit responsibility for all activities carried out within the division.

An important condition for divisionalization is that self-sufficiency or autarchy be guaranteed. In other words, a division should be able to lead its own life and to have its own base, and thus should be sufficiently independent of other units. This means that all of its supply sources need to be directly accessible. It also means that the activities carried out by each division have to be totally independent (or at least to a very substantial degree) of the activities carried in other divisions. Seen from the perspective of the top managerial level, there will, however, be a 'pooled interdependence' (see Section 5.3.6).

pooled interdependence

Divisions should to a high degree be responsible for their operational business results and for generating profitable business activities. They have only a limited influence on the destination of the profits generated by them. Divisions and subsidiaries or business units render account to the top by means of their own balance sheet and profit and loss accounts. The advantages and disadvantages of the divisionalized organization and business unit management are given in sections 5.3.4 and 5.3.5.

division
semi-autonomous
strategic business unit

A division can be described as a semi-autonomous strategic business unit if its decision-making processes are constrained. These constraints may relate to the following:

- Strategy formulation and the determination of objectives and goals in periodical planning and portfolio decisions (see sections 4.1.2, 4.2.3, 4.3 and 9.1)
- Approval of decisions relating to capital investment when the business is in a process of expansion and/or diversification
- Financial planning and budget procedures
- Standard administrative procedures relating to financial information supply, as well as directives for the supply of information relating to operational tasks
- Selection, remuneration, development and transfer of key personnel in the divisions
- Important reorganizations, mergers and/or acquisitions

These constraints need to be carefully applied. On the one hand, the senior echelons have to retain a sufficient grip on the divisions. Top management is responsible for planning and control and has to be able to pinpoint those divisions and/or business units where problems might occur. On the other hand, top management needs to impose constraints in such a way that the divisional or business unit management can exercise its own responsibility in a situation of optimal independence and full or partial autonomy.

6.7 Coordination and internal adaptation

For an organization to be able to operate effectively, its activities need to be coordinated. Coordinating can be defined as directing the various activities to serve one and the same goal. The activities of employees within the various departments have to be attuned to each other. If the activities are not sufficiently attuned, situations may arise in which employees are working at cross purposes and some jobs are done twice, or even not at all, because the one thought that the other would do it. Despite everyone doing their best, things will still go wrong because of a lack of coordination. This kind of situation must be prevented.

coordination

Coordination may take various forms, but must always be directed at linking the activities at the various levels of operational execution within the organization and within the various departments. This can be encouraged by as wide a coherence as possible between the various activities and functions (see sections 6.1 and 6.2).

assignments and instructions

Business processes must be matched by the means of issuing assignments and instructions, by taking into account the procedures which have been laid down along with the standard methods and the given policy guidelines. Here again, the hierarchy can function as a mechanism of coordination. The line can be called to order if the rules, assignments, instructions or procedures fall short and new decisions made and instructions issued.
The official line is often expressed as 'in cases where the regulations fail, the managers decide.'

Policy guidelines and standard methods and procedures

standing plans

Before we go on to discuss various plans of action in Chapter 9, we need to pay attention to the so-called standing plans. In contrast to action plans, which depend on specific situations, standing plans have to be seen as guidelines with a general validity. They influence plans of action as well as all other decisions. Standing plans are of three kinds:

1 Policy guidelines
2 Standard methods
3 Standard procedures

Policy guidelines

policy guideline

A policy guideline is a general guideline which indicates what in specific cases should or should not be done. Policy guidelines may be applied to many areas. The sales policy 'we only sell our own brand name' is an example of an applied policy guideline. If a potential client wants to purchase a product from the company in order to bring it onto the market under his brand name, the salesman knows that he cannot accept the order. A policy guideline in the personnel sphere might be that employees who have been employed for five years or more will only be fired as a last resort.

Standard methods

standard methods

Standard methods can be seen as a refinement of policy guidelines. They give more information about how one should act in certain situations. These methods are usually applied at a lower level within the organization than the policy guidelines. When a policy guideline states, for example, that the wage level of the company has to be the same as that of other companies in the same line of business, the standard method can determine how this has to be calculated.

Standard procedures

standard procedure

A standard procedure is a set of instructions setting out the steps that must be taken in certain situations. These steps are more detailed and specific than in the standard method. They might stipulate that a warehouse employee must report to the sales department when minimum stock levels are reached. This department then uses a certain formula to calculate the amount that has to be reordered.

Standard procedures can be developed for all aspects of the organization, whether this be personnel, recruiting or the making of investments. A procedure is a series of tasks which together form a more or less complete whole. Coordination of these tasks takes the form of determining which procedure should be followed. Procedures direct activities through the correct channels and guarantee mutual adjustment of decisions. Activities can then proceed 'by the book.'

Standard procedures can be laid down on forms to be filled in by those employees who are responsible for carrying out the tasks associated with a certain procedure. For example, the employees may have to fill out a form that reflects the following data: the making out of the order form, initials for taking delivery of goods, data relating to quality control, the warehouse taking deliveries of goods and so on.

In these 'standing plans' – policy guidelines, standard methods and standard procedures – the question remains of how strictly they should be applied. The advantage of this kind of guideline is that it can create greater uniformity in the ensuing actions. However, they run the risk of not being able to adjust to changing circumstances in time. This should be borne in mind when formulating and applying standing plans.

Not everything proceeds by the book

When deviations from the set rules, procedures and instructions occur, or unexpected situations or delays arise, management has to act to make its operational actions more effective. Alternatively, authority must be allocated to operational employees so that they can act as they see fit. Management must always be able to take action if the desired result is not attained.

6.8 Scope of management control

Managers can only be responsible for managing a certain number of activities to be performed by others. Managing (= planning + organizing + motivating + supervising) costs time and attention: working time is limited and since the managerial capacity itself has limits, the manager's scope of control is also limited.

scope of control

The manager's scope of control can be described as the number of employees the manager can effectively directly manage, coach and lead, and it will usually follow that the more employees, the greater the quality of management is required. The extent and degree of the manager's control is an important factor. 'Span of control' is the number of employees a manager manages directly. A 'flat' organization can be described as one in which the organizational structure reflects the manager being in direct control of as many people as he or she is able to manage effectively (Figure 6.9).

flat organization

When the number of employees to be managed is larger than the number the manager can responsibly manage, his scope of control is exceeded, because he will spend insufficient time and attention on the coordination of activities, and on the quality of activities – he ends up chasing his own tail. Problems will then occur: failure to meet delivery times, quality problems, stress. If a manager does not succeed in keeping a firm grip on the work to be conducted by others, he or she could appoint one or more employees to whom part of the managerial and supervising tasks are delegated. When these extra managers are called in, a 'tall' or 'steep' organizational structure arises, as shown in Fig 6.10.

tall or steep organizational structure

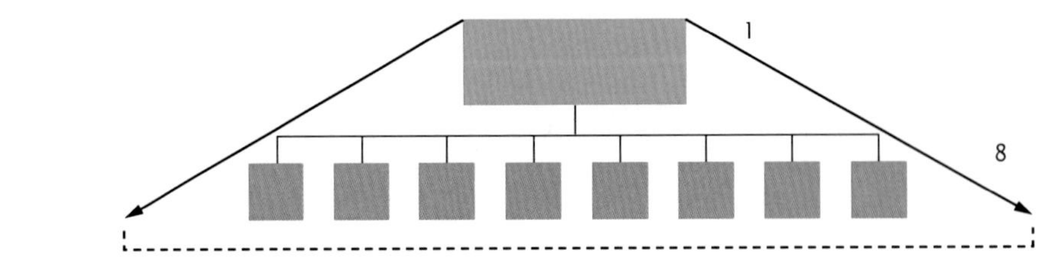

Figure 6.9
Flat structure (wide 'span of control')

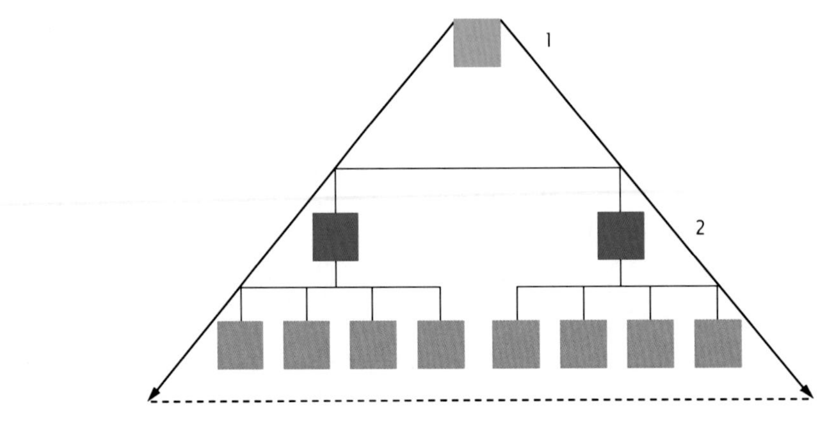

Figure 6.10
Steep structure (narrow 'span of control')

It will be obvious that the scope of management control needs to be viewed from two directions:

- The horizontal direction: the number of employees a manager manages directly: that is, the 'span of control'
- A vertical direction: the number of levels that can be effectively managed directly: that is, the 'depth of control'. How deeply does management's control extend throughout the various levels of the hierarchy?

span of control

depth of control

6.8.1 *Scope of control = span of control + depth of control*

scope of control

The scope of managerial control is limited, but there is unfortunately no formula for working out to what extent. The scope of control will vary according to the situation and depend on the personality of the manager, his willingness to delegate and his ability to have a lot of different things on his plate without losing track of any of them. The expertise and the time available to the manager also play a role, as well as his ability to liaise. Willingness on the part of lower managers and operational employees to take on responsibility is as desirable as their experience and appropriate training.

span of influence

The 'span of influence' – how far the manager's influence needs to extend both within the organizational unit and beyond it in order to be able to manage the necessary manpower, resources and information, including being able to make decisions in respect of these commodities – has a role to play here. It is important to also take account of the so-called

span of support

'span of support' – the amount of support from other members of the organization that a manager can rely on in order to have available the manpower, resources and information needed to work effectively. Whether a manager has to do everything himself or receives support and cooperation on many fronts can make a big difference.

It is also important to examine whether there are further opportunities to employ specialized staff and support services. It also makes a difference whether the work is simple or complex, varied or monotonous, policy intensive or operational.

As such, it is obvious that the structure of the organization, mutual cooperation, the willingness to work together and the type of work are the main determinants of the scope of control.

A PERMA-TEMP WORLD

The trend toward a perma-temp world has been developing for years. Bosses are no longer rewarded based on how many people they supervise, so they have less incentive to hang on to staff. Instead, the increasing use of bonuses tied to short-term profit performance gives managers an incentive to slash labor costs. Temp employment in the U.S. fluctuates wildly, by design. The whole purpose of bringing in workers who are employed by temporary staffing firms such as Manpower, Adecco, and Kelly Services is that they're easy to shuck off when unneeded. Companies that seized on the recession as an opportunity to make drastic organizational changes for greater efficiency and flexibility aren't likely to reverse those changes once the economy begins growing again.

Source: *Bloomberg Business Week*, January 18, 2010, p. 34-35, C. Matlack

6.8.2 *Guidelines*

If the scope of control is too great, various measures can be employed.

- Delegate more tasks and, if possible, more authority to other employees, while still maintaining direct control. However, for this to work, there must be a preparedness to delegate (both the desire as well as the ability to do so) as well as a preparedness to bear more responsibility (with the same conditions).
- Redistribution of tasks within the existing levels of the organization, i.e. redistribute tasks from F- to P-grouping (see figs 6.1 and 6.2), in such a way that the natural coherence of activities is maintained and the necessity to coordinate from the top decreases because of greater overall coordination.

If these measures are not sufficient, other steps can be taken.

- Call in specialized staff services to do some of the 'headwork' or delegate it to others. The manager can use the time which then comes free for his own purposes.
- Call in personal staff as assistants and then delegate the work to relieve the manager. If his or her tasks remain a burden, they can be delegated (for example to an executive secretary); this saves work time and the manager can pay more and better attention to his own necessary activities.
- Call in specialized support services, i.e. make use of the operational expertise of others to bring about better working methods and so on. This will then have a direct effect on some parts of the task being carried out and so the manager will need to spend less time on it.

These measures will encourage the development of a flatter structure (Fig 6.11), in which managers can actually manage more employees along the line effectively.

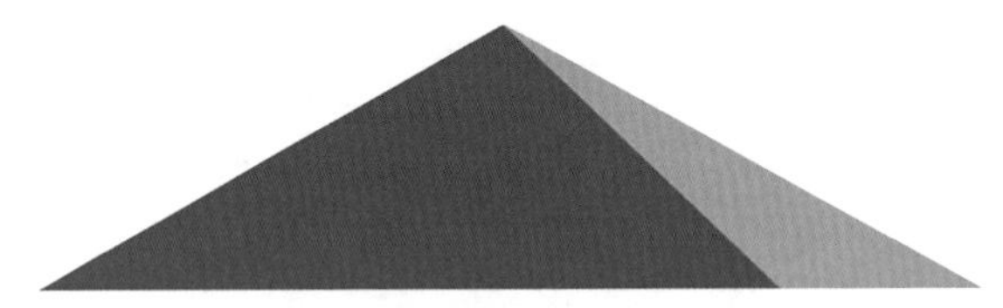

Figure 6.11
Flat structure

If these measures are not effective, there is another possibility: to expand the organization in a vertical direction, thereby creating a relatively tall structure (Fig 6.12).
Such a structure would demonstrate the need for a greater number of managerial layers in order to guarantee sufficient attention to the more operational work aspects.

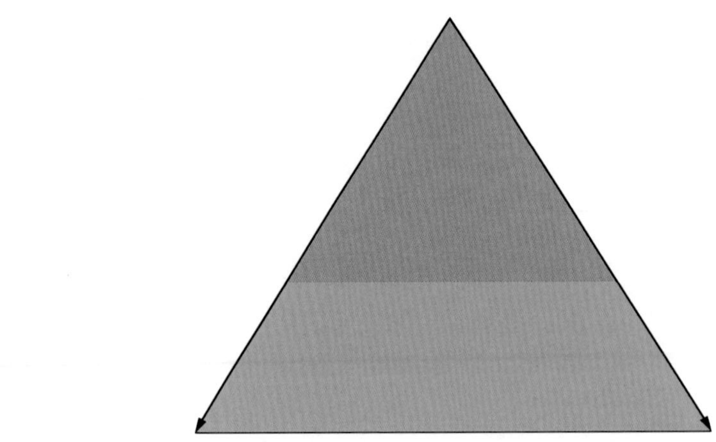

Figure 6.12
Steep (or tall) structure

6.9 Organization in development: reorganization and planning for change

When organizations expand and develop, what in fact happens is that they become larger and more complex (see Section 5.5). Although the strategies described in this section will impose restrictions on the development of new organizational models, growth and change (in particular) are inevitable because of the dynamic nature of organizational processes. As we have already seen in chapters 1 and 2, as part of this dynamic process, information and energy are exchanged with the internal and external environment via relationships with customers,

growth and change

unions, banks, groups of employees and managers. The changes which take place do not usually take place overnight. The speed of change can differ, as can the extent of the change itself.

resistance

Change always brings uncertainty for those involved, whether manager or employee, which means that when change is being considered, any residual resistance to it should be broken down before a new situation can arise and can function effectively.

crisis

However, in the dynamics of organizations, crisis is a more or less necessary condition for a new order and growth and development phase, one which is a better match with the changed internal and external circumstances.

All too often, however, organizations have insufficient energy and vision to renew themselves effectively. In such cases it is probably better that they be dismantled and abolished. If this seems too radical, then the organization will need to play for time by making various emergency decisions. These measures are likely to include the pumping in of a lot of money and energy from outside, and the purchase or import of external visions and people. However, such measures are usually doomed to failure.

6.9.1 Organizational change: flexibility and capability

Before change within the organization is initiated, both its capacity and willingness to undergo the envisaged change needs to be gauged. This will indicate whether an organization has the potential to grow into a new structure or to regress ('backsliding') (see Fig 6.13).

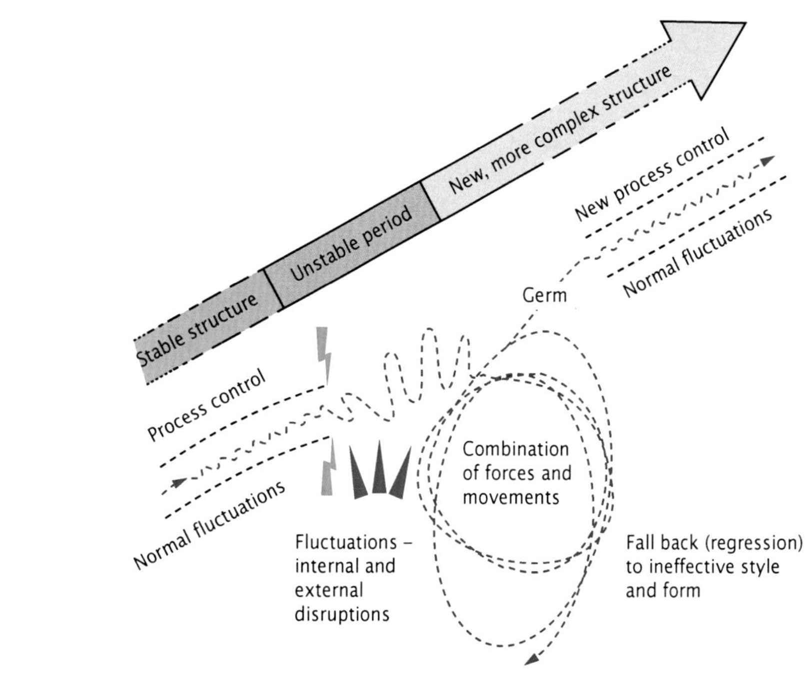

Figure 6.13
The dynamics of organizational crisis

Source: *Adapted from Zuyderhoudt*, 1992

ability to change

The capability and ability to change depends on the qualitative capacities of the members of the organization and on the knowledge and experience of those the organization has at its disposal. To a large extent, the financial and technical possibilities also determine what change is possible and when.

preparedness to change

The willingness/preparedness to change depends a lot on the mentality of the organization at the moment it decides to change. This willingness to change will be influenced by the degree to which management, possibly with the assistance of an external consultant, succeeds in making those involved realize that something has to change.

resistance to change

However, the natural human resistance to change, with the uncertainty it brings to all involved, may also have to be combated. Change is normal and usually inevitable. If not regarded as such, it usually means that external changes in technology, markets and environment are not being sufficiently followed or are being resisted.

Given the ability and the willingness to change, one problem remains: the kind of change envisaged. Change concurrent with growth can be introduced a lot more easily than change directed at downsizing the organization. Changes to organizational structures have far greater consequences than changes within markets or to product/market combinations. The most difficult, and also the longest lasting, are those changes which have to do with organizational culture, for here the style of leadership and the degree of openness will naturally play a role. Sometimes these changes may be accompanied by a change in personnel, which is always a difficult and time-consuming process. However, such a change may well be a condition for bringing about the type of change envisaged (see Section 8.7).

organizational culture

6.9.2 *Organizational change: a process*

Organizational change is the process of moving from an old to a new structural model with new organizational policies and accompanying processes.

CASE *Mini case study 6.4*

In a sense, organizations are like a machine. They take some time to start moving in the direction they have been directed towards since a certain amount of inertia has to be overcome. Heavy bodies take longer to get going than lighter ones. In general, small organizations have an advantage over larger ones: compare the time needed for a larger tanker to change course with that needed by a small yacht.

organizational change

Organizational change is undertaken in order to move from an undesirable situation to a desired one. For this to happen, the organization needs to be jolted into action. This change is depicted diagrammatically in Fig 6.14.

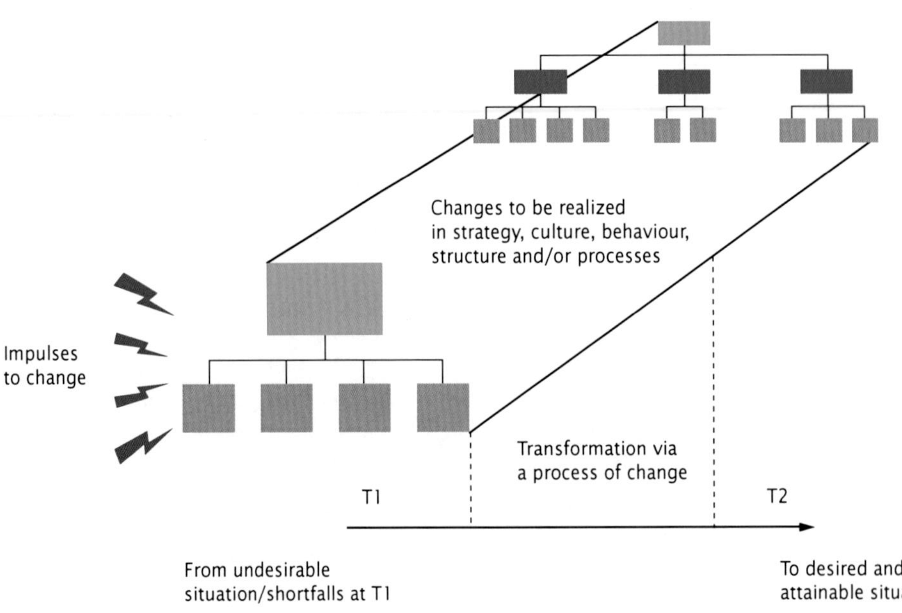

Figure 6.14
Transformation via a process of change

change management In essence, transformation is change management: bringing an organization from passive acceptance of the situation (at T1) to conscious involvement in the new situation (at T2). Change does not happen by itself and the change process cannot be left to itself. The variables *change process* are complex and the change process needs to be managed.

transformation For the transformation to take place, there must be a belief in the positive power of the organization and the people in it. Not only does the organizational model need to change, there usually has to be a cultural and mental change within the organization as well. It is unlikely that this will happen of its own accord: it may well require guidance.

If management feels that the organization has chosen the wrong course of action, it needs to back up its contentions with some relevant data in the form of impressions, conversations, interviews, internal and external documents, and so on. Management may consider the acquisition of this to be its own job, but may eventually have too little time for systematic investigation itself. If this is the case, the investigation should be conducted by internal consultants or external management consultants.

6.9.3 Situational factors and penetration of change

As we saw earlier, cultural change has greater ramifications for the organization than a change in a product/market combination. The ramifications may vary from slight to far reaching, depending on the degree to which the existing structure and/or behavioral patterns need to be changed. The changes may vary in the following ways:

- *superficial change* Superficial change: techno-organizational change that affects staff positions and behavior only moderately. For example, a new form may have to be filled out differently, new ways of working learned and/or a new work process adopted.
- *deep change* Deep change: change which severs existing lines of authority or breaks with existing functional patterns. New roles may need to be learned and new working relationships established.
- *profound change* Profound change: change which affects the behavioral patterns of individuals and/or groups within the organizations to the extent that these individuals or groups need to change their very personalities and ways of operating. In-depth changes are required: adjusting to and learning new behavioral rules until these become self-evident in knowledge, skills and manifested behavior.

6.9.4 The phase model of organizational change

Starting from a situation of apparent stability, organizational change is usually carried out in five phases.

Phase 1: Organization in situation of apparent stability (quasi-equilibrium)
When an organization is in a situation in which there are apparently no processes of change *quasi-equilibrium* underway, it can be said to be in a state of quasi-equilibrium. Since both internal and external circumstances will trigger change, this balance can never be permanent; there will always be a certain amount of change underway at any one time, even though people are not aware of it. Change may not be so clearly visible in an informal organization.

Phase 2: Breaking the quasi-equilibrium – the need for change
The apparent stability will be broken after the need for change has built up to such a degree *change process* that it cannot be ignored. The first phase of a conscious and planned change process then commences: people start to feel the need for change and investigate the options. This will

increase awareness of the need to actually embark on a process of change. At this stage, an external consultant may be sought.

Phase 3: Preparing the change ('unfreezing')

Changes in the techno-economic area then need to be investigated and discussed. There will still be a certain degree of incomprehension and misunderstanding about existing behavioral patterns that may have to be replaced. During this phase, investigations into likely changes will get underway, as will data collection (for example, by interviews and group conversations) and the first proposals will be collated. Those involved will have to get used to the idea of the coming change and be encouraged to accept it, possibly by training or reeducation. During this phase, resistance to change starts to emerge, which means that this phase can last quite a long time. People have to get used to the idea that changes in roles and relationships will occur. This phase is characterized by an 'unfreezing:' that is, unlearning or deroutinizing of accepted and existing behavioral patterns.

unfreezing

Phase 4: Implementation and shifting ('moving')

During this phase, the necessary changes are carried through and the proposed plan is implemented. This is a phase of discovering and learning new organizational behavior, the so-called moving phase. Any resistance will have become apparent. The individuals involved will now experience the repercussions of the change at first hand and new roles must be learnt. If there is a crisis, the changes will be accepted more readily (or at least, apparently accepted) and implemented. It is important that change be managed, if necessary by a manager appointed for that purpose by the organization (possibly by an externally hired interim manager) in conjunction with the personnel department.

moving phase

Phase 5: Consolidation ('refreezing')

refreezing

The last phase in the process is the consolidation phase, a phase that is sometimes called integration. Peace and quiet returns; the new is not so new anymore and may even have started to become routine. By this stage there will be an emotional acceptance by staff of the new situation, and the perception that the new situation has advantages over and/or works better than the old situation. There is an adjustment to the new situation. Those involved are not only technically able to work in the changed situation, they will have become comfortable with it. New behavioral programs and rules will have been adopted. However, the peace and quiet will only be apparent, since further change in the future will have been built into the organization. The organization is in a situation of quasi-equilibrium and is now back at phase 1 (see Fig 6.15).

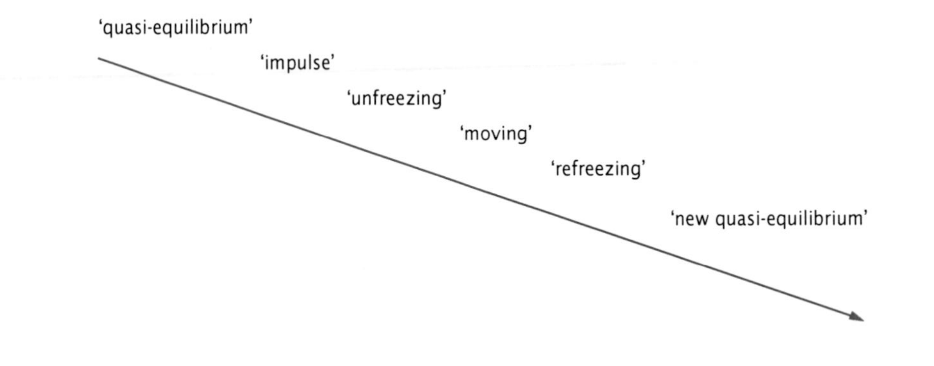

Figure 6.15
Phases in the process of change

continuous process

Organizing and managing is thus a continuous process. It is the task of top management to carry out an assessment of both the organization as a whole and its various components (teams, departments, business units, divisions) and adjust it where necessary. If this task is performed, the organization will undergo gradual change, though the changes will probably only be evident in retrospect.

6.9.5 *Methods for realizing change*

There are ways of bringing about change: by imposing change through power, by letting the changes take place through a learning process, or by allowing the need for change to be discovered by the members of the organization themselves.

speed of change

In the event of reorganization triggered by a crisis, the managerial team or the board of management will often impose change (whether by degree, by replacement or by a structural change). The speed of change will be rapid, the period between phase 1 and phase 3 will be short.

In the learning process approach to organizational development, the top organizational level will assume that people are capable of solving their own problems and/or are able to adjust their roles and behavioral patterns. Change in a participative form is brought about via delegated power, for example via a group directed approach and/or by training and education. This approach assumes that sufficient time and resources are available and that the problems are of a role and/or behavioral type. The leadership style is democratic or participative and preparedness to change and a strong desire to learn is deemed present in the people involved.

6.9.6 *Coping with resistance to change*

Coping with resistance

Whatever the approach to change there must be discussion of how to handle resistance to it. It is, therefore, not surprising that some managers manage change from the resistance perspective. If it is known where the resistance is located, the agent of change can adopt his strategy, and, as Fig 6.16 demonstrates, opponents can possibly even become advocates.

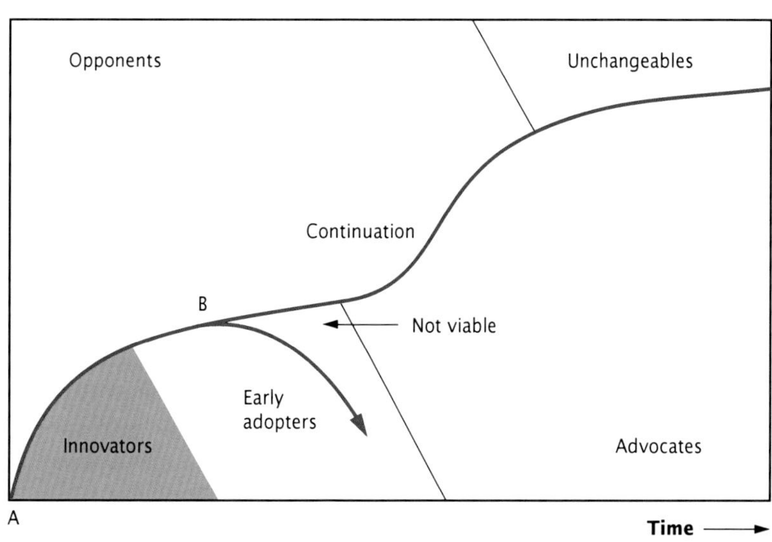

Figure 6.16
From opponents to advocates

With this approach, one assumes that every change starts with people who want something (sometimes merely for the sake of change). When their ideas are accepted by the early adopters, a critical mass of advocates arises that ensures that the renewing activities are continued. Eventually a number of conservatives will be persuaded to accept the inevitability of change.

This approach also assumes that there will always be a number of unchangeable people. In turn they may, however, be the initiators of the next renewal. Sometimes the changes themselves may be blocked by knockdown arguments that block every form of movement. Knockdown arguments are fallacies people refer to when they want to block the implementation of something they are opposed to.

Resistance to change is, to some extent, also valuable. It would appear to be one of those mechanisms that human beings resort to in order to reduce their vulnerability in the face of chaotic changes. Resistance to change can be seen as a mental activity which is directed at maintaining the status quo because a certain value is attached to it. However, holding onto the status quo does, of course, impose restrictions on the development of the individual.
The following are ways of overcoming resistance to change:

unfreezing

- Disengaging (unfreezing)
  - recognizing the need to change
  - investigating what obstacles to change there are
  - imagining where change might lead to

moving

- Changing (moving)
  - deciding on the solutions/changes that should occur throughout the organization simultaneously and at all levels

freezing

- Stabilizing (freezing)
  - making sure that the change is permanent
  - making it possible for the new situation to be maintained
  - maintaining the new situation

6.9.7 *Practical recommendations*

resistance to change

Recent research on change within organizations has suggested that employee resistance to change need not constitute an insurmountable obstacle to the implementation of change. Resistance to change derives from a lack of understanding of what the agents of change want, and why and how they want it, rather than from deep-seated personal factors. On the basis of this research, the following strategies have been devised:

- Prepare employees well in advance; do not implement changes out of the blue.
- Explain what the actual goals are; do not assume the employees will buy anything.
- Show how employees can adapt to the changes and provide practical help.
- Carry through the changes completely and provide feedback on how effective the changes have been.
- Give employees the freedom to suggest some ideas themselves.

6.9.8 *Trying out something new*

New techniques can help set the organization in motion or to give form and direction to that motion. They may be used as a goal in themselves: 'We have never done anything new, let us try something now.' Another reason for applying a new technique may be that a lot of new things have been tried already, but without much effect. In such a situation, a fashionable hype or a new leadership method can be exactly what one has been looking for for so long. Some old and forgotten techniques suddenly come to the fore again, sometimes in a new form. Other techniques may be new to some managers because they tend only to notice a technique when they need it. Some of these techniques may have a scientific foundation, others may be little more than a slogan – not a plausible solution, but still very appealing.

6.9.9 *Organizational change and employee voice*

A key theme in change management is involving employees in change. Although involving people in change is mentioned often enough as the key to the success of a change program, the degree, extent and ways in which this involvement is set up and organized often leaves a lot to be desired. In a McKinsey study (2008) on organizational transformations, executives indicate that they had most difficulty in ensuring ownership of the change among employees.

organizational readiness

To create organizational readiness, organizations need to deploy influence strategies. The need for change has to be communicated clearly by means of persuasive communication (both written and oral), management of external sources such as studies or legislative changes, and active participation: i.e. involvement of employees.

However, in practice, most organizations only use one, or at the most, two, of these influence strategies. More often than not, employee involvement in change is taken up as an internal communication issue: 'Communicating [the change] "at" people after the decisions have been taken and plans are made.'

employee voice

Boxall and Purcell (2003) devote some attention to the employee voice, or the various ways in which employees can participate in the organization through membership of unions, works councils or more direct forms of participation. They discuss the impacts of employee voice systems on organizational interests such as commitment, retention engagement, commitment and involvement in change process. Apart from important social legitimacy issues, well implemented, and well embedded voice practices also have an economic value, both in the short run through reducing problems in the workplace, and in the long run, through helping to facilitate the management of change.

work engagement

Work Engagement is a positive and fulfilling work-related state of mind that is characterized by vigor, dedication and absorption. Commitment refers to the employee's desire to remain in an organization and willingness to exert effort on its behalf as well as acceptance of the values and goals of the organization.

voice

Voice is defined as the process in which individual employees challenge the status quo in a constructive way, with the intent to improve the situation. Voice is a key element in innovation and change (LePine & Van Dyne). Challenging the status quo and standard operating procedures begins with voicing new ideas and different approaches to known or new problems.

voice systems

Voice systems can take the form of any organizational structure, including work groups, steering groups, specific teams, or especially composed cross-functional groups. The composition of the group in the voice system needs to be determined by the current process of change process.

direct voice systems

Direct voice systems offer the possibility of directly involving key staff members and employees in a process of change without the mediation of a representative body such as a union or a works council. In many professional organizations, unions hardly play a role, and if unions or works councils are present, they naturally incline towards adopting conflicting positions with management. Direct voice systems are not so much focused at shifting decision-making power to employees but rather at tapping into available knowledge and skills to address challenges in the internal or external environment of the organization and to use that input to strive for organizational success. Mutual investment on the part of both employer and employee can make the difference between an intelligent enterprise and an average player. As such, involvement in processes of change should form part of the organization's standard operating procedures.

CASE Mini case study 6.5

New management techniques and types – have you made your choice yet?
- flexibilization
- 'just in time' management
- quality circles
- self-control
- delayering
- business process redesign
- unit management
- management by exception
- virtual organization

6.9.10 *The irrational side of change management*

Many programs aimed at bringing about change fail. However, their chances of success can be increased by taking into account nine counterintuitive insights relating to how employees interpret their environment and choose a particular approach. Rationally inclined managers who take a common sense approach often put their time and energy into the wrong things, formulate messages that miss the mark and find that their managerial efforts have frustrating and unintended outcomes.

Recent research by Aiken and Keller (McKinsey, 2009) has identified nine pitfalls to avoid when creating the conditions needed for behavioral change. They have to do with storytelling (1, 2 and 3), example setting (4 and 5), support mechanisms (6 and 7) and developing ability (8 and 9).

Insight is required to bring about behavioral change

1 The things that motivate you will not motivate most of the other employees.
2 It is better to let employees write their own stories.
3 To create real energy, you need as many plusses as minuses.
4 Leaders mistakenly believe that they embody change.
5 Having people with influence does not necessarily guarantee successful change
6 Money is the most expensive way of motivating people.
7 The process and the outcome must be fair.
8 Employees are what they think and feel and what they believe in.
9 Good intentions are not enough.

Real change depends crucially on managers personally overcoming these counterintuitive behaviors and managing to use the process to create the conditions for change in their employees.

From their research, Aiken and Keller derived a number of insights that may help managers enhance their chances of implementing processes leading to change. One of them is that managers need to appeal to every element of human motivation.

human motivation

They identify five elements:
- the impact of their work on society,
- on customers,
- on the company and its shareholders,
- on the work team, and
- on themselves (personal and professional development, salary and bonus).

stories about change

In addition, employees need to be given the opportunity to write their own stories about change and thereby claim ownership of the change. When people are responsible for their own contribution and opt for that contribution they are much more likely to commit themselves to achieving the result.

Another aspect is that most managers fail to include themselves among those who have to change. They fail to realize that in order to become convincing role models, *they themselves* need to change at the individual level.

symbolic gestures and rewards

Managers also need to realize that money rarely motivates people to change. Small, unexpected *symbolic gestures* and *rewards* are much more effective – ranging from a spontaneous check made out to a small amount to a bottle of champagne accompanied by a personal thank-you. It is also very important that the process and the outcomes be seen as fair by their employees, fair to themselves and their colleagues, and also fair to the customers. If fellow workers perceive that their colleagues or customers have been put at a disadvantage by a process of change, the chance is great that they will undermine the change.

6.9.11 Change never ends

Managers, directors and employees will usually be more or less aware of the fact that change is a continuous process in which the emphasis is always different. This process is depicted diagrammatically in Fig 6.17.

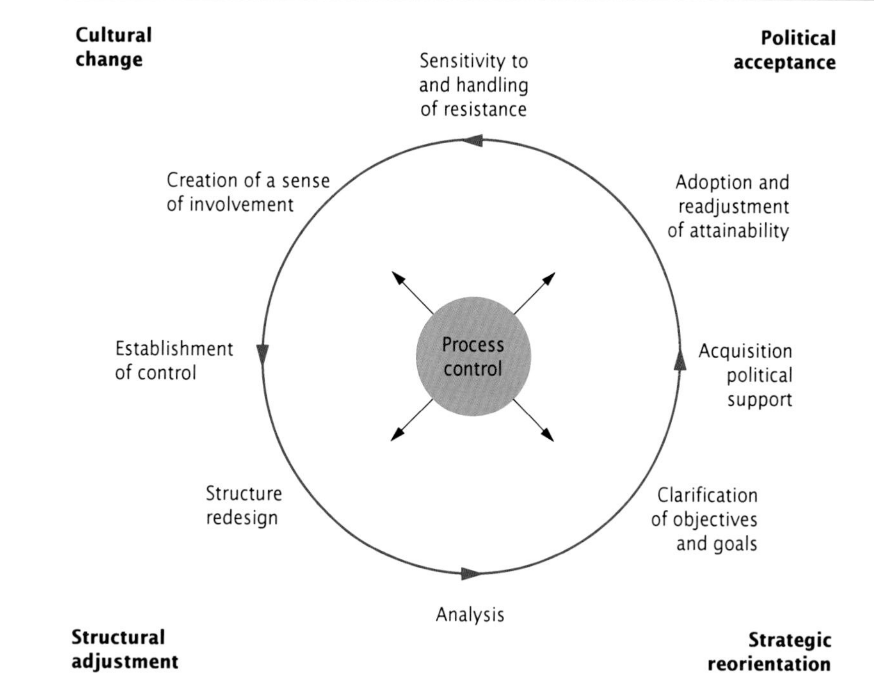

Figuur 6.17 *The ongoing nature of change*

Source: *Adapted from Kimberly and Quinn*, 1986

When change is being undertaken, particular attention should be paid to the following:

- Strategic reorientation
- Political acceptance
- Cultural change
- Structural adjustment

Strategic reorientation

crucial choices

Organizations that are bent on survival have to constantly be on the lookout for what is going on within the market. Sometimes a branch of business undergoes such radical changes that crucial choices have to be made. If the organization is no longer in tune with the business environment, an analysis of the company's financial and organizational affairs may be required. An analysis of this kind often focuses on the company's strengths and weaknesses couched in terms of the business environment's threats and opportunities. Part of such an analysis may consist of posing a number of questions relating to the organization's actual mode of operation and management as well as the added value of its products.

CASE

Mini case study 6.6

Some businesses are constantly engaged in a process of strategic reorientation. Although they may not have a specific plan in mind, the board of directors may decide that it is time for a 'quantum leap' when it meets during one of its regular sessions. If the time is ripe and a suitable opportunity presents itself, a decision to acquire or even merge may be made without the need for much deliberation.
Other companies, however, may seek the help of a consultancy firm to adjust their strategic decisions.

Political acceptance

Making sharp analyses is one thing; implementing the outcomes and setting new goals is at least as important. Since there is a tendency for the opponents and advocates of proposed changes to form two camps it is vital to convince those involved of the necessity for the changes. Not all will be persuaded, however. How should one go about trying to persuade them to change their mind? Power and persuasive force may play an important part. Change often appears only possible where there is an external threat, internal dissatisfaction and a challenging perspective. 'Under pressure, it all looks different,' say managers and consultants. There is no formula for essential changes. In order to attain a basis for acceptance, there must be a mutual exchange of opinions and an examination of common interests, even if there seems little point to this.

mutual exchange of opinions

Changes which aim to scrap functions and which will lead to changes to the structure of power have to be ratified. After this happens, there will be an immediate shift towards the new situation. Nevertheless, it is important that tolerance of the situation be created beforehand, both at the grassroots level and by the board of directors or supervisory council.

Cultural change

Starting something new implies leaving behind the old. This is an important point to consider when rethinking existing working methods and contemplating new ways of acting. It must be clear why the existing behavioral norms do not fit with the newly developed goal. New approaches have to be inculcated, and a new image developed. Descriptions such as 'open,' 'honest,' 'customer-directed,' 'clear' and 'result-directed' are all well and good, but they need to be embodied in some way, otherwise they are merely empty words. Nor should the past be rejected out of hand: essential values have to be maintained. An apparent rejection of past cultural values is a sure recipe for arousing antagonism. Accomplishing new things together is the best way of implementing changes. Cooperating is the means, but not the goal in itself. Change has a greater chance of success if there is mutual cooperation.

cultural change

When insufficient attention is paid to this process of cultural change, the risk is high that changes in the structure will be frustrated 'via the back door': old ways of acting are resumed within the new structure.

Structural adjustment

adaptation of the structure

This and the preceding chapter have dealt with the design and adaptation of the structure. Processes such as delayering or delegation are more than just the designing of a new structure; they are also the implementing of this structure and making it work, in itself a process that requires explanation, education, close monitoring, adjustment where necessary and the provision of assistance.
Fig 6.17 would suggest that adjustment of the structure is never a goal in itself, but rather a consequence of other factors. The model would indicate that these areas of attention have to

be looked at successively: this does not always happen. The manager who manages the process has to divide his attention between these areas and may find he is occupied with more than one area at any one time. This is why the crucial aspects of this model are involvement, direction and control. In order to implement change successfully, attention must be paid to all four processes mentioned above.

involvement, direction and control

6.9.12 *Situational differences in five colors*

According to De Caluwé (1997/2002), the ways in which people or objects change can be seen in terms of ways of typifying the individual. He identifies five different types, and derived from them, five different ways of viewing organizational change in terms of the amount of planning involved and the role of the agent of change. These five ways of thinking about change are typified by De Caluwé by means of color types. The various assumptions about how human beings or things change are shown in Table 6.2.

yellow print thinking

The assumption behind yellow print thinking is that human beings will change only if you take their own interests into account or if you can encourage or force them to adopt certain views. Combining ideas or points of view and the forming of coalitions or power blocks are favored methods in this type of change process. Such an approach fits smoothly into change processes where complex goals or effects must be achieved and in which a number of people or parties are involved.

blue print thinking

In blue print thinking it is assumed that people or things will change if a clearly specified goal is laid down beforehand, if all steps are planned down to the last detail and if there is sufficient control over how the result is to be achieved. The project approach is an expression of this way of thinking. This is a favorite approach when there is a clearly defined objective and it is possible to forecast both the result and the means of obtaining it reasonably well.

Table 6.2 *Assumptions behind the five ways of thinking*

	Things/ people will change if you …
Yellow print	Can unite interests
	Can compel them to accept certain points of view
	Can create win-win situations/can form coalitions
	Demonstrate the advantages of certain ideas (power, status, influence)
	Get everyone on the same wave length
Blue print	Formulate a clear result/goal beforehand
	Make a plan with clear steps from A to B
	Monitor the steps well and adjust accordingly
	Keep everything as stable and under control as possible
	Can reduce complexity as much as possible
Red print	Stimulate people in the right way, for example, by punishments or inducements
	Employ advanced HRM tolls for rewards, motivation, promotions
	Give people something in return for what they give you
Green print	Make them aware of new outlooks/own shortcomings (conscious, incapable)
	Are able to motivate them to see new things/to learn
	Are able to create suitable collective learning situations
White print	Start from the drives, strengths and the 'natural inclinations' of people
	Release the energy of people
	Are willing to diagnose complexity and dynamics
	Remove possible blockades
	Make use of symbols and rituals

red print thinking

Red print thinking assumes that people and organizations will change if you use the right HRM instruments and use them in the right way. In other words, people change if they are rewarded (by means of salary, promotions, a bonus, a good evaluation) or penalized (demotion, negative evaluation).

green print thinking

In green print thinking, the terms 'change' and 'learning' are seen as being similar. People change if they are brought into learning situations and if effective routes for learning other ways of doing things are available.

white print thinking

In white print thinking, the dominant image is that everything changes of its own accord – 'panta rhei': everything is in motion. Where there is energy, things change. Complexity is regarded not as a threat but as an opportunity for enrichment. Influencing the dynamics of the situation is a favorite approach, though more in terms of creating room for change and investigating what potential there is for change and creativity. Creating meaning is a way of going about this.

Ideals and pitfalls

Every color has its own ideal long-term aims. According to De Caluwé, every color has its own pitfalls too: situations or circumstances in which the approach is not effective or no longer effective.

The ideal of yellow print thinking is for people to realize their common interests and be willing to pursue collective goals. The pitfalls are too much wishful thinking and not enough concerted effort: the aims and means/efforts are not connected.

The ideal of blue print thinking is to make everything tangible and controllable via rational planning. One of the pitfalls is ignoring any irrational aspects, potentially creating more resistance than commitment. Others are impatience, haste and giving the other insufficient time.

The ideal of red print thinking is finding the right fit between people and instruments, between organizational and individual goals, and searching for the right way to stimulate people. The pitfall lies in a lack of 'hard' results and a lack of room for individual motives and tailor-made work. It also undervalues power in organizations, both top-down as well as bottom-up.

The ideal of green print thinking is the learning organization and conscious application of learning. The pitfall is that in certain cases (involving conflict or power), people may not want to learn or cannot do so (lack of skills). Lack of 'hard' results is another pitfall.

The ideal of white print thinking is spontaneous evolution: incidental changing and learning. A positive attitude to conflict and crisis is one of this method's strengths. The pitfalls lie in the method's very ideology: too much laissez faire or insufficient understanding of the nature of 'real' chaos, and thus insufficient recognition of its patterns.

color thinking

Color thinking has the following possible applications:

- It can be used to typify people and situations.
- Diagnoses as well as approaches and methods can be designed.
- People can typify themselves (in terms of reflective mindsets, preferred approaches, 'blind spots' and competencies).

intervention color

As the agents of change, managers and consultants can use this theory to investigate what needs to be done in a particular situation, to chose the intervention color that represents the best approach, and even to decide whether to handle things themselves or not. The answer will depend on the color, and on one's strengths and beliefs. For reliability and effectiveness, there will need to be a four-way fit between problems, situational demands, people and approaches and the approach and capabilities of the individual him or herself.

Summary

- This chapter has discussed the various ways of assigning tasks, authority and the consequences of this. The criteria which play a role in the division of work and the grouping of tasks and functions have been extensively covered. New forms which could outweigh the advantages of old methods have been described.
- Structural design needs to include an appraisal of whether the people who can be recruited will in fact fit into the designed functions. Attention must be paid to how functions should be designed and to the consultative structure for employees, since the structure has to be effective and satisfying for the organization as well as for the employees.
- Some examples have been given of organizational systems which can be applied to most of the organization, thereby creating a new structure. Depending on the tasks which have been assigned to the various employees, there may need to be a reallocation of authority. Whether an employee has a managerial position in the line, or a specialized staff or support service position will affect the way authority is allocated. The type of authority assigned must be laid down. This is a necessary condition for being able to influence the actions of others and for the amount of responsibility that the person in question can be expected to bear. The functioning of the line organization, the line staff organization and the line organization with specialized support services have all been examined in some depth in this chapter.
- Along with the three basic forms of relationship within the organization – the line relationship, the staff relationship and the functional relationship – horizontal and diagonal (or lateral) relationships have also been described and demonstrated to be the intrinsic coordinating mechanisms within the hierarchy.
- Some classical organizational principles have been expounded. Old principles are still having their effect on the organization of modern companies and institutions as far as the design of functions, delegation, coordination, assigning of authority, and so on, are concerned. These old principles are, however, being applied differently and in a more modern way: different leadership styles, work restructuring, and, at the customer-directed, organizational levels, a strong customer focus and management by management teams. Substitutes for hierarchy were also investigated.
- If he wants to delegate, a manager must do it properly. There are a number of factors that can hinder optimal delegation. These lie in the personality of the manager, in the personality of the employee, in the structure of the organization and in the nature of the job. The problem of the scope of managerial control, an associated issue, has been covered. The manager himself has to ascertain whether the employees placed below him can be managed in a responsible way, both in the horizontal as well as in the vertical direction. When the scope of control is exceeded or threatens to be exceeded, measures need to be taken. Measures to be taken need to be thought through in terms of their effects.
- Departmentalization and the designing of divisions, the allocation of tasks and functions and the assignment of authority, as well as the building-in of coordination mechanisms are all part of organizational structure design. The structure is the framework within which an organization functions, and changing circumstances within the organization can lead to changes in structure as well as in behavior. Organizational change can take many forms and occur in distinct phases. The various possibilities for change need to be thought through carefully, and during the process of change, managerial drive and the irrational aspects of change management will play a crucial role.

Discussion questions

1 **a)** With reference to *Management in action* at the beginning of this chapter, describe how the navy practices can be applied by organizations to improve their teamwork.
b) Is this simply a matter of copying the navy's program?
c) Which additional elements would you propose for a commercial organization?

2 What are the disadvantages of the 'pure' form of line organization?

3 Is production likely to be faster and more flexible with an F or a P arrangement of tasks?

4 What are the conditions for effective functioning of a flat organization?

5 What do you think of the following statement: 'Resistance to change is a healthy phenomenon, so keep it that way!'

6 Do you agree with the following statement: work consultation is a form of horizontal consultation between departments.

7 Is there a correlation between resistance to organizational change (Chapter 6), learning (Chapter 3) and strategy determination (Chapter 4)?

Research-based exercise

Switching between work tasks

Introduction
This exercise is based on a research article by Sophie Leroy, published in *Organizational Behavior and Human Decision Processes.* The research question, data collection method, and some of the results of her research project are shown. The exercise, which relates to this research article, consists of two questions. Your answers should be based on the theory in this chapter.

Research question
How does work and task design affect individual performance?

Data collection
162 individuals participated in experiments which tested how well they were able to switch from one task to another.

Outcomes
The experiments showed that people need to stop thinking about one task and shift their entire attention away from it in order to perform well on the next task. If that task is unfinished, people find it hard to shift their attention away from it, and their subsequent task performance suffers. However, effective task performance depends on more than an ability to switch from one completed task to the next: the crucial thing is an ability to cope with time pressures while finishing a prior task. This contributes to higher performance on the task that follows.

(Based on Leroy, S. (2009). 'Why is it so hard to do my work? The challenge of attention residue when switching between work tasks.' *Organizational Behavior and Human Decision Processes*, 109, p. 168-181.)

Questions

1 What implications do these outcomes have for the design of tasks for employees in a call center whose employees have to deal with customer complaints?
2 Should the work that these employees do be designed to put low, medium or extreme pressure on them? Give reasons for your answer.

CASE

Management case study

Reinventing Nokia

Nokia has overcome many crises in the past. In 1995, poor logistics caused it to stumble. It responded by developing one of the world's most efficient supply chains, capable of churning out some 1.2m handsets a day. A decade later it failed to anticipate the demand for 'clamshell'-type handsets, but bounced back quickly to restore its market share in handsets to 40% and thus its industry dominance.

But this time the problems go deeper. In more than one way, Nokia has to become a different company, says Jay Galbraith, a management expert. Until now, it has excelled in making and distributing hardware. This has trained the organization to focus on planning and logistics. Deadlines are often set 18 months in advance. Teams developing a new device also work in relative isolation and even competitively, to make each product more original. And although Nokia has always done a lot of market research and built phones for every conceivable type of customer, it sells most of its wares to telecoms operators and designs its products to meet their demands.

With the rise of the smart-phone, however, software and services are becoming much more important. They require different skills. Development cycles are not counted in quarters and years, but in months or even weeks. New services do not have to be perfect, since they can be improved after their launch if consumers like them. Teams have to collaborate more closely, so that the same services and software can run on different handsets. Nokia also has to establish a direct relationship with users like Apple or Google.

Last February Nokia's management kicked off what is internally known as a 'transformation project' to address all these concerns. 'We needed to move faster. We needed to improve our execution. And we needed a tighter coupling of devices and services,' explains Mary McDowell, Nokia's chief strategist. The firm has since introduced a simpler internal structure, cut its smart-phone portfolio by half, ditched weaker services and begun to increase its appeal to developers by allowing them to integrate Nokia's services into their own applications. While giving Symbian a makeover, it is also pushing a new operating system, called Maemo, for the grandest, computer-like smartphones.

All this will no doubt help Nokia come up with better, if not magic, products. The firm may even reach its goal of 300m users by the end of 2011 because its efforts are not aimed just at rich countries, but at fast-growing emerging economies where Nokia is still king of the hill, such as India. There, services such as Nokia Money, a mobile-payment system, and Life Tools, which supplies farmers with prices and other information, fulfil real needs, says John Delaney of IDC, another market-research firm.

Yet it is an entirely different question whether Nokia will manage to dominate the mobile industry once more – not just by handset volumes, but by innovation and profits. The example of the computer industry, in which the centre of gravity began shifting from hardware firms to providers of software and services over two decades ago, is not terribly encouraging: of the industry's former giants, only IBM really made the shift successfully. Then again, Nokia has reinvented itself many times since its origin in 1865 as a paper mill. That, points out Dan Steinbock, the author of two books on the firm, is thanks to a remarkable willingness to embrace change and diversity. Nokia will need those traits in the years ahead.

Source: *The Economist*, January 9, 2010, p. 56-57

Case study questions

1 How would you characterize Nokia's restructuring operation?
2 Would you define Nokia's reinvention as a structural issue? Give reasons for your opinion.
3 What, in your opinion, is the best way of structuring a collaboration with Apple or Google?

Principles of management

Motivating people

Part One Management and society

Chapter 1
Manager and management

Chapter 2
Organizations and environment

Part Two Strategic management and the learning organization

Chapter 3
Decision making and creativity

Chapter 4
Strategy formulation and strategic management

Part Three Organizational structure and design

Chapter 5
Designing the organization

Chapter 6
Structuring tasks for groups and individuals

Part Four Organizational behavior and people at work

Chapter 7
Motivation, work and career

Chapter 8
Leadership, motivation and communication

Part Five Operational planning, control and information management

Chapter 9
Operational planning and control

Chapter 10
Managerial process control: functional processes and process redesign

Organizational behavior and people at work

Part 4

CHAPTER 7 Motivation, work and career

CHAPTER 8 Leadership, motivation and communication

Once the strategic position (Part Two) of the organization has been determined and the organizational structure designed (Part Three), the organization's staff can set to work. Part Four will deal with the 'people' aspect of the organization: people working together to achieve their goals cooperatively.

In Chapter 7, the motivation of the individual, behavior in groups and the reward of organization members will be discussed in relation to the organization's goals. The possibility for individual development will be examined, as well as the notion of a career. The employment and development of human capabilities as reflected in an organization's policy is known as human resources management.

In Chapter 8 managing other people will be discussed first. The personal function of the manager will be discussed and differences in managerial style described. Managing sometimes means having to resolve problems relating to cooperation or lack of it between organization members – conflict handling and resolution. A manager always operates within an established organizational culture, but can try to change that culture so that it contributes more to the implementation of the chosen strategy.

CONTENTS

7.1 The employee of the future and changing work behavior
7.2 Groups and the organization
7.3 The power of teams
7.4 Motivation: a closer view
7.5 Empowerment
7.6 The new context for human talent development and human resource management
7.7 Human resource development: an integral concept and a set of instruments
7.8 Payment systems and salary structures
7.9 Careers and management development

Motivation, work and career

Chapter
7

LEARNING OUTCOMES

After studying this chapter, you should be able to do the following:

- Describe the key variables of individual behavior
- Identify the various aspects of team forming
- Identify some motivation theories
- Explain the relationship between motivation, productivity and design of functions
- Describe the notion of 'empowerment'
- Explain the notion of 'human resources management,' both in the context of daily activities as well as in relation to personnel instruments
- Relate the terms input, throughput and output in relation to the personnel process, including the personnel instruments at management's disposal
- Describe different reward systems
- Identify the various concepts of 'management development'

CASE

Management-in-action

The Art of Motivation

What you can learn from a company that treats workers like owners. A look inside the surprising performance culture of steelmaker Nucor.

In an industry as Rust Belt as they come, Nucor has nurtured one of the most dynamic and engaged workforces around. The 11,300 nonunion employees at the Charlotte (N.C.) company don't see themselves as worker bees waiting for instructions from above. Nucor's flattened hierarchy and emphasis on pushing power to the front line lead its employees to adopt the mindset of owner-operators. It's a profitable formula: Nucor's 387% return to shareholders over the past five years handily beats almost all other companies in the Standard & Poor's 500-stock index, including New Economy icons Amazon.com, Starbucks, and eBay. And the company has become more profitable as it has grown: margins, which were 7% in 2000, reached 10% last year.

Nucor gained renown in the late 1980s for its radical pay practices, which base the vast majority of most workers' income on their performance. An upstart nipping at the heels of the integrated steel giants, Nucor had a close-knit culture that was the natural outgrowth of its underdog identity. Legendary leader F. Kenneth Iverson's radical insight: that employees, even hourly clock-punchers, will make an extraordinary effort if you reward them richly, treat them with respect, and give them real power.

At Nucor, the art of motivation is about an unblinking focus on the people on the front line of the business. It's about talking to them, listening to them, taking a risk on their ideas, and accepting the occasional failure. It's a culture built in part with symbolic gestures. Every year, for example, every single employee's name goes on the cover of the annual report. And, like Iverson before him, DiMicco flies commercial, manages without an executive parking space, and really does make the coffee in the office when he takes the last cup. Although he has an Ivy League pedigree, including degrees from Brown University and the University of Pennsylvania, DiMicco retains the plain-talking style of a guy raised in a middle-class family in Mt. Kisco, N.Y. Only 65 people – yes, 65 – work alongside him at headquarters.

At times, workers and managers exhibit a level of passion for the company that can border on the bizarre. Executive Vice-President Joseph A. Rutkowski, an engineer who came up through the mills, speaks of Nucor as a 'magic' place, representing the best of American rebelliousness. He says: 'we epitomize how people should think, should be.' EVP Ferriola goes even further: 'I consider myself an apostle' for the gospel of Ken Iverson. 'After Christ died, people still spread the word. Our culture is a living thing. It will not die because we will not let it die, ever.'

Source: *BusinessWeek*, May 1, 2006

In organizations oriented towards the market and society, both customers and the organization's own employees are constantly formulating new wishes and making greater demands on the organization. To be effective, an organization must be flexible, motivated, involved, creative and innovative. Employees value interesting work, more responsibility, more participation, discretionary decision making and a tailor-made reward. Modern human resources management requires that all these elements be included in a consistent common policy (see sections 7.6 and 7.7). An awareness that the human factor in organizations has become *the* important factor, is, however, an insufficient basis for operating effectively. For success, one also needs to understand the behavior of the individual organization members and influence and direct that behavior in such a way that the organizational goals can be attained more readily. Since insight into individual behavior is the basis for this, some psychological notions will be examined. We then turn our attention to the behavior of groups in an organization (sections 7.2 and 7.3), and motivation (sections 7.4 and 7.5). We will closely examine the relationship between the design of functions, productivity and motivation, since the content and structure of a function can affect the amount of effort an employee puts into his job.

7.1 The employee of the future and changing work behavior

Making work and getting people to cooperate within an organization in the realization of organizational goals will remain a management task of prime importance in the future. Organizational goals will be formulated in terms of interaction with the employees and with the environment. This requires other patterns and other leadership styles within the organization than were expected in the past. Possibilities will have to be created for development, initiative and entrepreneurship on all levels. This is in line with the higher educational level of employees, and is consistent with their wish to bear more personal responsibility.

A TO Z OF GENERATION Y ATTITUDES

Two studies show that young people's attitudes towards work are not as different from previous generations as had been thought.

Alex and Carrie are both members of 'Generation Y', the population cohort commonly defined as being born between the late 1970s and the year 2000. Also known as 'Millennials' or the 'iPod Generation', they are a group that is keenly debated and dissected by managers and marketers as workers and consumers of the future. Natives of the digital world, they are frequently portrayed as demanding, selfish, text-addicted and job-hoppers with little loyalty to their employers.

Yet two studies into the attitudes of those Generation Ys that are in the workplace suggest that Carrie, Alex and their young professional peers are not as different from other generations as supposed – and not just because the recession has upset their expectations. While craving excitement and challenge, nearly 90 per cent of Generation Ys describe themselves as loyal to their employer. In addition, nearly half of this tech-savvy and 'connected' generation prefers face-to-face communication at work to e-mails, text or phone calls.

Loyalty is also a key finding in European research to be published. Young professionals interviewed for The Reflexive Generation, a report by London Business School's Centre for Women in Business, surprised even themselves by their commitment. However, they are also highly adaptable and realistic about the need to move on if they are not promoted or not gaining new experiences.

New generation in tune with an older one
The Bookends Generation study is based on two large national surveys of US college-educated professionals, focus groups and surveys in two companies. Among the similarities it identified between 20-something and 50-something professionals:

- More than 90 per cent of Gen Ys and 85 per cent of boomers seek new experiences at work
- Flexible work is important to 89 per cent of Gen Ys and 87 per cent of boomers

- Almost as many boomers as Gen Ys want to work remotely some of the time (63 per cent and 69 per cent respectively)
- Only 14 per cent of boomers and Gen Y are work-centric
- Over 60 per cent of Gen Ys and boomers see a parent-child dynamic in work relationships between their generations
- Some 58 per cent of Gen Ys look to boomers for advice and 58 per cent of boomers like helping them 'navigate' work

'Both Gem Y and boomers are looking for what we call a "remixed" set of rewards,' says the study. Both generations place at least as much importance on having high-quality colleagues, flexible work, recognition and access to new challenges as they do on financial compensation. For companies wanting to motivate employees and drive growth as economies recover, a big challenge will be to redesign incentives for the two 'bookend' generations, she adds. The good news is that this will be 'far less costly than raises and bonuses'.

Some companies are already building on the common generational ground. Cisco Systems, the US maker of communications equipment maker, has connected its 'legacy leaders network' for preretirement boomers with its 'new hire network' to encourage a transfer of knowledge. It reports widespread interest in the initiative and says it has been useful for recruiting Generation Ys.

Young professionals' desire for mentoring also emerges from the London Business School study. It finds that they want to shape their careers and have autonomy over their work lives but they seek a work-life balance but also challenges; and that they want to improve themselves, learn fast and dislike rigid rules.

They are at ease with the notion of a diverse workforce and regard gender barriers as a thing of the past – yet they note a lack of diversity around them and identify business as 'a man's world'. A flexible approach is the core strength of this generation. They adapt incredibly quickly to a changing environment.

Source: *Financial Times*, June 18, 2009

7.1.1 *Organizational context and the changing organization*

increased work pressure
educational demands
individualization

Recent research into changes in what employees want and the consequences of this for management has signaled the arrival of a new type of employee. The areas in which changes were detected relate particularly to increased work pressure, higher educational demands and individualization. The demands made on employees have increased, the number of jobs in the office has decreased and because of individual performance planning, the sense of compulsion to perform has increased. Work is taken home, study is done at home and there are meetings outside work hours. The importance of going on courses and gaining certificates has increased. New employees are better educated. Performing well is no longer sufficient guarantee for a higher position on the ladder. Respect for older employees with long service time and experience has decreased. Higher functions are becoming more difficult to attain for home-grown workers; these are going to trainees and more educated people from outside. The focus has also shifted from the team to the individual, loyalty is under pressure, internal entrepreneurship has become the main thing and the attaining of personal targets has taken on undue importance. This is another consequence of horizontal differentiation (F-grouping).

acceptance and resistance

The reaction of most people involved will be a mix of acceptance and resistance. One individual may become convinced of the appropriateness of the strategy that has to be followed and is prepared to devote him or herself to this. Another may think, however, that the changes have gone too fast and that too little attention has been paid to the interests of the individual employee. The ambitious employee will experience the new demands as a challenge and see possibilities for career improvement.

CASE

Mini case study 7.1

Hollywood goes online

Hollywood came late to the Internet. Protected for years from digital piracy by huge file sizes, it was not forced to develop an online retail model, as the music business was. Nor, having watched newspapers struggle on the Internet, did it much want to try. This week it finally stepped forward, touting two systems for selling films and television shows online. The initiatives are well thought out, reflecting the lessons learned from watching others' mistakes. But they may also be too late.

Recently, the Digital Entertainment Content Ecosystem (DECE), a consortium that includes five of the six big studios as well as technology firms and retailers, agreed to a format for digital films and named a single outfit to keep track of purchases. Consumers will be able to buy a film once and then play it on different gadgets. As it will be held on a remote server, they will not have to transfer it from device to device.

DECE's initiative aims to stop a company doing to film what Apple has done to music and Amazon threatens to do to electronic books. By taking a huge lead in the market, and by tying content to their own devices, the iPod and the Kindle, these firms have been able to dictate terms to media firms. Instead of a closed system, Mitch Singer, the head of DECE and a Sony employee, wants to create something more like the CD or the DVD: an open format that will encourage competition and innovation.

Source: *The Economist*, January 9, 2010, p. 57

7.1.2 Good middle management

There is consensus about what constitutes good management. The manager has to pay attention to his staff, must value the employee as a human being and be able to listen well. He has to keep them informed, involve them in policy, give them responsibility and increase their enthusiasm for their work. He has to complement his staff and appraise their performance, back his employees, be clear and honest, divide tasks well and be able to chip in when necessary.
A bad manager devotes his attention to production, does not keep his staff informed, likes to have them at his beck and call, and does not welcome new work. Favoring newcomers and bad education and coaching are also common flaws.
Current theory strongly advocates that managers adopt a coaching role. Research shows that in practice, people management is currently the most neglected of the tasks of middle managers. Top management often fails to give the right example. Only 27% of managers actually use coaching as a managerial method. 75% of employees experience Dutch employers as a negative factor. They view their priorities as often being at odds with those of the employees, there is hardly any trust in them, and management is often not liked by the employees (Stoker & de Korte, 2000).

people management

Research also shows that in the view of managers, employees are in general enthusiastic about their work. When good managers are in charge, the employees will be enthusiastic about their job, the job will be challenging and varied and offer promotional opportunities and educational programs to attend. There will be an open, informal culture, more than enough opportunities for initiative and the organization will be flat and only slightly hierarchical. The managers will be aware of the fact that changes in strategy will make other and greater demands on the employees. In recruiting new employees a new employee profile will be sought: young, ambitious, well-educated, self-confident and full of initiative. Older employees will also have to start to show this kind of behavior. There will only be limited room for people of the old school. There is a choice: adapt to the new demands or search for something else.
A survey of the 'new' employee concluded: 'the new employees are an obvious consequence of new recruiting and selection policies on the part of the organization, and partly a response to pressure exerted by the employer. Existing social cultures have been dismantled and in reaction the employees may even start to act like the new employees, not spontaneously, but more or less under the stress of managerial pressure. You could hardly describe this as the older employees adapting naturally to change. The newcomers spark it off, and management plays along with it.'

7.1.3 Beyond employee loyalty?

loyalty In recent years, it has frequently been reported that employee and manager loyalty to their companies is in a process of rapidly decline. However, while employers still have idealized notions of the loyalty of 'their' employees, they themselves are not setting much of an example, as witnessed by ABN Amro and KPN Telecom. Those who have complained loudest about the 'changing labor ethos' were mostly to blame themselves. These companies have been *lifetime employment* taking a harder personnel policy line. As a concept, 'lifetime employment' seems to be a thing of the past. In branches of industry such as IT and telecommunications, this became evident *up or out* (and rapidly so) when things were at their blackest. It is often 'up or out' for both parties – employer and employee alike. Consequently, for many people, future prospects have become less important. They are not even setting their sights on the next three or four years. While this *self-development* is attributed to 'self-development' (and thus to the detriment of good, old fashioned loyalty), in retrospect, this perception mainly applies to the better economic years. The turnover rates of ICT service providers (such as CMG, Cap Gemini and Oracle) went up to 14-20% or even higher in the heydays of 1996-2000, and it was more a matter of salary, bonuses, options and other work conditions than the type of work or how challenging it was.
Where there are poor relationships, whether between employer and employees, between colleagues or between employees and customers, a so-called Loyalty Awareness Program (LAP) can help by raising mutual awareness. Hopefully there will be a turn for the better.

7.2 Groups and the organization

Organizations consist of individuals who have tasks of their own which they perform within departments of their own, but also who form collaborative units. The group phenomenon has a distinctive form within organizations. In the psychological sense, a group is a number of people who are in contact with each other and who regard themselves as a group. The size of a group is a factor of the extent of mutual contact and the degree of mutual awareness. As such, an arbitrary number of people is not by definition necessarily a group. There has to be interaction and awareness of each other for the concept to apply. A work group, a committee, a sub-department and other informal relationships within an organization all satisfy the terms of the concept.
An organization is made up of various different groups:

formal groups
- Formal groups:
  - permanent: board of management, work group, committee
  - temporary: 'task force' for problem-solving, a project group, a committee

informal groups
- Informal groups: come into being at the place of employment and in response to the demands of the job in combination with the needs of people for social contact, companionship and acknowledgment. Such informal group creation can complement the formal organization.

Informal groups can take various forms:

horizontal group
- The horizontal group: informal interaction between operational employees, between managerial employees or between other organization members who have more or less the same rank and are employed in more or less the same field.

vertical group
- The vertical group: a group which is composed of various levels of members in one specific department. These groups usually perform a key function in the upward and downward communication. Employees may know each other from previous or current work situations.

mixed group
- Mixed group: a group whose members come from different ranks, different departments and different geographical areas. It may be a group formed to accommodate specific functions not yet included within the organization, such as the maintenance of equipment. It may also be a group that is lobbying for something to which too little attention is paid in the formal organization.

Informal organizations may arise spontaneously and be based on personal relationships and mutual dependency. There is often mutual emotional support and a useful and complementary communication network. A formal group, just like an informal group, can fulfill a number of psychological functions:

psychological functions

- The possibility of satisfying the sense of belonging as a human need, and the need for companionship, affinity and support
- A way to develop, enlarge or confirm identity and entrance self-respect
- A way to confirm or test standard points of view; for example, how others see the boss
- A means to increase security or to exercise power in the face of a common 'enemy' or source of threat
- A means of getting work done which other members of the group should be doing

Most groups obviously have a formal as well as an informal function, therefore. They satisfy the needs of both the organization and individual members. Groups, be they formal or informal, influence the behavior of individuals. Groups put pressure on individuals to act in certain acquired ways, which means that individuals usually conform to group habits and standards. The individual who does not wish to adapt is put under pressure and may be placed outside the group (sometimes using physical violence) or be treated as a deviant and an outcast.

adapt

outcast

From a managerial point of view, in order to deploy groups successfully, their characteristics need to be identified first. These group characteristics can be used to good advantage in the event of the group causing difficulties. One way of going about this is to engage in preliminary consultations with key figures to investigate how proposals are likely to be received, and what adjustment of plans may be necessary. Important group members in committees can stimulate a certain degree of involvement right from a very early stage.

7.2.1 Organization, group and individual: goals and conflicts of interest

Conflicts of interest are actually built into organizations. It is expected of every work group or individual that they perform their job as well as possible and devote themselves to their own departmental interests. There will probably also be a battle over the available built-in resources, with everyone expecting to be rewarded for their efforts. These forms of conflicts of interest, which are built in by way of division of tasks and functions, can be seen as 'functional' conflicts of interest. However, as soon as these conflicts do not make a positive contribution to the functioning of a part of an organization, they become dysfunctional and damaging.

functional conflicts

Functional organizational conflict can actually have the effect of making an organization function more smoothly. Conflicts of interest and disagreement can prompt a search for the right solution or encourage better performance. For this to happen, though, there must be openness, frank exchange of information and opinions and mutual trust in the case of problem-solving. Contradictions become damaging as soon as they become a goal in themselves. The conflict will escalate, since information will be held back, and there will be mutual distrust.

functional organizational conflict

BETTER TOGETHER THAN ON YOUR OWN

Recently published research shows that companies attach greater value to good teamwork than to individual achievements.

The more dependent departments are on one another, the more companies apply their standards of achievement in order to get employees and departments to collaborate.

According to Jan Bouwens, professor of accounting at the University of Tilburg and the man responsible for the research, 'Normally, you can get people to work harder by setting concrete goals. But this does not apply in situations where there is a large degree of mutual interdependence'.

Research into 136 departments in nineteen large Dutch companies has shown that when mutual collaboration is highly important, companies will even set relatively low personal achievement standards in order to prevent employees focussing more on their own success than on good teamwork with other departments.

By focussing achievement criteria on good teamwork, the organization is playing into the very reasons for having a variety of activities. 'The aim is to set as many synergy-creating factors in motion as possible.'

The study shows that good collaboration pays. But so does working towards the same targets as the boss's.

Most managers pass the achievement standards that they are expected to conform to on to their own employees, the researchers found. A manager who is primarily judged according to the profits will usually use the same criteria to judge the employees he is in charge of.

Achievement standards can even be passed on down all the way through the organization's hierarchy, it would seem. For example, a divisional head whose performance is assessed according to how much profit has been made will usually urge those he is in charge of to focus on profit making. This can have both advantages and disadvantage, according to Bouwens. 'While the main focus may be on profit making, the employees may be judged according to criteria over which they have little control, while they can have a big effect on such things as customer satisfaction.'

The sum of the parts
Pursuing one's own goals can be to the detriment of the whole.

Adjustment
In situations of mutual dependency, individual goals are given less priority

Synthesis
Combine broad profit-making targets with targets formulated with each department in mind.

The solution lies in combining global targets of profit creation with achievement targets formulated specifically for each department. It may be customer satisfaction or sales figures for a particular product. Companies usually limit themselves to a couple of targets in order to avoid a situation where the boss sets managers masses of job-related targets.

In economically trying times, however, the focus is likely to shift from teamwork to individual achievements. When things are tough, people naturally tend to focus on their own situation first, despite the fact that from a financial perspective, this is probably not the best approach for companies.

Source: *Het Financieele Dagblad*, 14 May 2009

The goals of the organization are, of course, determined by people. Organizations do not have goals by virtue of the fact that they are organizations. Goals are set by individual people or by groups that have the interests of the organization or department at heart. A goal might be a desired result or a situation to be created. An organization usually has more than one goal at any one time. Every organization, every department and every individual employee has specific personal goals and specific results they have to attain. Regardless of how many conflicting interests there are, everyone will have at least one interest in common, namely the preservation and continuation of the organization, for its survival enables all to get at least something back. Something has to be sacrificed, though something will be gained in return. If, for example, there is an imminent reorganization, relocation of a subsidiary or closure of a company department, decisions may be hard to make. Differences in interests, feelings and experiences may play a part in this. A formal voting procedure can be introduced, but this is not always advisable. A common form of solution is the compromise. Agreement is reached because everyone drops some aspect of his demands, wishes or desires. Although this will not resolve the problem and it may reemerge later, it is nevertheless better to strive for a new solution that everyone is satisfied with to some extent and consequently there will be a sense of having dealt with the problem. Often the time is lacking for this, and just as often the will as well, so that the only solution is that reached by domination of a minority over the majority, or by reaching a compromise (see Section 8.6).

7.2.2 *Group behavior and productivity*

Individuals behave differently when they are alone than when they are in groups, and group behavior is governed by rules of its own. We have defined a group as two or more mutually dependent individuals interacting together and consciously considering themselves to be a group. Groups can be formal as well as informal. The most common reasons for participating in a group are the need for security, status, self-actualization, power, and sense of belonging and reaching set goals.

contingency variables

The behavior of a group can be described and predicted with the help of the three so-called contingency variables: individual personality characteristics, group size, and the degree of heterogeneity between the group members. Heterogeneous groups work more efficiently than do homogeneous ones. There is a strong connection between those values that Western culture regards highly and the group's productivity, morale and mutual solidarity. Groups of odd numbers large enough to have a lot of interests at stake yet small enough to control the dominance of individual group members, that resist sub-groups forming and make relatively quick decisions, are those that generally function best.

Group cohesion and productivity

group cohesion

The degree to which group members feel drawn to one another, and subscribe to the goals of the group is called cohesion. Factors such as time spent together, rites of initiation into the group, group size, external threats and previous successes will have an effect on the group's cohesion. Research shows that groups with a higher degree of cohesion are often more effective (see Fig 7.1).

		Cohesion	
		High	*Low*
Coincidence of group goals and the organization's goals	*High*	Large increase in productivity	Slight increase in productivity
	Low	Decrease in productivity	No significant effect on productivity

Figure 7.1
Relationship between cohesion and productivity

This should not be taken at face value, however, since a high degree of productivity may give rise to organizational cohesion rather than be a consequence of it. Moreover, the relationship between cohesion and productivity depends on the degree to which the attitude of the group coincides with the formal goals or with the goals of the organization of which the group is a part.

7.3 The power of teams

Teams can deliver high performance levels for a long time as long as a number of prior conditions have been met. They include structural conditions (clear task and clear assignment of authority), 'human resource' conditions (a quantitatively and qualitatively sufficient staffing and reasonable rewards), the right political conditions (sufficient power and influence) and symbolic conditions. The symbolic conditions, especially with regard to the bringing in and maintaining of a common and binding culture, usually receive scant attention.
One such symbolic condition is the creation of barriers restricting entry to a group whose performance level has to be very high. Preventing the group from becoming too homogenous is another. Other elements which encourage close cohesion are a group language, leadership through 'role model' or exemplary behavior, humor and play for both relaxation and the stimulation of creativity, and the development of a group culture through rituals and ceremonies (see sections 1.8 and 8.7).

7.3.1 Interacting forces

We will now look more closely at the four conditions outlined above:

structural conditions
- The main structural conditions are rationality, efficiency, planning and policy. Structure-directed managers value analysis and data, keep track of end results, give clear instructions and hold people responsible for the results. They try to solve organizational problems by developing other policies and new methods – or by restructuring.

human resource condition
- The 'human resource' condition relates to how well the needs of the individual and those of the organization are in balance with each other. 'Human resource'-directed managers value human relationships and feelings: what they aim to do is manage by making facilities and opportunities available. When problems arise, they prefer to solve these by means of participation and training.

right political conditions
- For the right political conditions, resolution of conflicts relating to the allocation of scarce resources among various parties is necessary. Politically directed managers are advocates and negotiators who spend a large part of their time on the development of networks, the bringing about of coalitions, the building up of a power base and the making of compromises. They consider conflicts a source of energy and not as a cause for concern.

symbolic conditions

- In a chaotic universe in which meaning and predictability are constructed societally and in which facts are not objective but open for interpretation, symbolic conditions take on a particular importance. Symbolically oriented managers pay a lot of attention to myths, rituals, ceremonies, stories and other forms of symbolism. When something goes wrong, they try to formulate a new story or return to cherished values.

LEADERSHIP AS HELPING

Help is not limited to one-on-one situations. Group effort and teamwork often hinge on the degree to which members perform their roles properly in accomplishing the group tasks: 'We do not typically think of an effective team as being a group of people who really know how to help each other ... yet that is precisely what good teamwork is – successful reciprocal help,' management theorist Ed Schein writes in *Helping: how to offer, give and receive help*. Schein also lists 27 synonyms for helping. One way or another, it seems, we are helping or being helped most days of the week.

Schein's main thesis is that all human relationships are a mixture of economics and theater, because they all involve what sociologists call 'status positioning' between the parties involved in any social interaction, whether formal or informal. It is human to want to be granted the status and position that we feel we deserve, no matter how low or high that is, and to want to do what is appropriate to the situation and the occasion. If we get it wrong, the relationship doesn't work.

Source: *Strategy + Business* (2009) 57(winter), p. 85

These conditions are all equally important, since each determines an essential part of the organizational reality. Research has shown that for groups to work effectively, all of these conditions have to be met to at least some degree. In the 1960s and 70s, authors such as Douglas McGregor and Rensis Likert presented a series of recipes for successful teamwork. They claimed that a clear goal, open communication, shared leadership and a pleasant informal atmosphere were conditions for successful teamwork.
In more recent research (Hackman, 1990) into groups and teams in various sorts of organizations, the researchers found both structural and human resource variables which were essential for effective group performance. Groups with a clear structure and clear time limits had much better results than groups that did not. A general recipe for failure was burdening the group with a vague goal, variable time limits and unclear criteria, and then ordering the team to work out the 'details'. Other groups were limited right from the start because they lacked resources. Sometimes the main problem was the lack of necessary expertise among the group members or the lack of essential organizational coherence. In other cases the group had unclear or insufficient authority and an uncertain mandate. Hackman and his colleagues also came to the conclusion that the history of the group was very important. Groups which had started out on the right foot and had early successes often developed a self-maintaining impetus whereby they functioned ever better. In groups which had had an unfavorable start, poor functioning had set its own pattern. Attempts to change it were often unsuccessful.

THE CALCULATED CHAOS OF MANAGING

Management theorist Henri Mintzberg reminds us that most managers are prey to events and demands they do not control, and that a wide range of styles can work well for a boss. Balance is the key: keeping up with the hectic pace of business yet making time for reflection; driving change yet maintaining stability; leading and collaborating; leavening analysis with judgement.

For Mintzberg, management is not confined to the inner workings of an organization, but takes into account the larger landscape in which a business functions. 'Is there an economist prepared to argue that social decisions have no economic consequences?' he asks. 'Not likely: everything costs something. Well, then, can any economist argue that there are economic decisions that have no social consequences? And what happens when managers ignore them, beyond remaining within the limits of the law?'

Mintzberg finds the answer in a quote from Russian author Aleksandr Solzhenitsyn, who, describing his life under a Communist regime, said: 'A society that is based on the letter of the law and never reaches any higher is taking very scarce advantage of the high level of human possibilities. The letter of the law is too cold and formal to have a beneficial effect on society. Whenever the tissue of life is woven of legalistic relations, there is an atmosphere of moral mediocrity, paralyzing man's noblest impulses.'

How do we develop managers who can lead businesses in a more sustainable direction? Mintzberg, a reliable critic of business schools, challenges them to go beyond the usual face of courses organized by business functions – marketing, finance, and accounting. That approach 'amounts to a focus on analysis,' he says. Instead of 'calculating managers,' he wants managers 'who can deal with the calculated chaos of managing – its art and craft – which highlights the importance of reflection, worldliness, collaboration and action.' The bottom line for Mintzberg is instilling a sense of commitment in managers – commitment 'to the job, the people, and the purpose, to be sure, but also to the organization, and beyond that, in a responsible way, to related communities in society.'

Source: *Strategy + Business* (2009) 57(winter), p. 100

7.3.2 The symbolic approach

In all of this important and useful research, all too often little attention is paid to factors such as power and conflict even though they often hinder groups from performing at a high level. Even more striking is that only rarely are symbolic elements – charisma, character, myths – touched upon, and these are also a condition for exceptional performances. Managers who are trying to get their teams to work better but who ignore the political and symbolic conditions often find that their efforts come to nothing. Research suggests that managers in the public as well as in the private sector have a tendency to act too much from the structural and the 'human resources' perspective and make too little use of the political and the symbolic approach. Approaches based on structure and human resources may produce good managers but not necessarily good leaders. Recent research has linked structural approaches in particular to managerial effectiveness, but a symbolic approach is the best predictor of effective leadership. Symbolic thinking is subtle and complex. It is based much more on intuition and sensitivity than on analysis and linear thinking. For that reason, managers often reject it as incomprehensible, elusive or unfathomable. However to do so is to overlook the importance of factors such as meaning and trust, which other approaches do not take into account either.

Symbolic thinking

THE DOGMA OF INTERNAL COLLABORATION

The demise of one of the last dogmas of popular management theory was only to be expected. Collaboration in multidisciplinary teams is not at all good and not profitable. Or at least, not as a matter of course. Morten T. Hansen explains how teamwork can create value ... or destroy it. Any decision to change to an internal collaboration model should only be made after the sums have been done. If the bonus that comes with teamwork is lower than the project's expected profits minus the costs associated with teamwork as well as the costs associated with missing out on other opportunities then there is only one option: just don't do it!

Every self-respecting modern manager does it: urging employees to share information, urging departments, teams and specialists to collaborate. After all, anyone can see the logic in the arguments. In an ideal world, collaboration leads to better product development, better sales (cross-selling) and lower costs as a result of the broad application of best practices. Nevertheless, somewhere along the line, a logical error has crept in. Collaboration does not necessary automatically mean that the more people work together, the better the results. Experience has shown that teamwork is just as likely to undermine the company's results!

It's not about more teamwork, it's still about finding the right type of teamwork

While teamwork is good, it is not good by definition and it is not always the best approach. The potential for teamwork is always present, but you will need a thorough analysis of each and every project to see whether the proposed collaboration is likely to be really effective. Enthusiasm and optimism need to be tempered and to some extent replaced by discipline. It will certainly help if a culture and an organizational structure can be created that will facilitate teamwork. In the long term, this will mean lower collaborative costs and hence the sum referred to above will add up differently.

Problems associated with collaborative ventures

Companies are inclined to overlook potential problems when they initiate multidisciplinary projects. The following problems may occur:

- Conflicts within the group
- Within multidisciplinary teams, problems associated with targets, budgets and work processes (who does what with what money)
- Personal problems associated with working times
- Team members having to achieve their usual goals (and get their bonuses) while not being remunerated in the usual way for the teamwork that they do in addition to their usual tasks
- Organizational problems
- Even if the team does function to a reasonable extent and remuneration has been arranged for the extra teamwork, there may still be logical problems (try getting five people from different departments around the table at the same time).

In turn, these problems may cause the following:

- Delays in production and product supply
- Budgetary excesses (often resulting from delays)
- A loss of quality
- A projected though not yet realized reduction in costs
- (If less than optimal sharing of knowledge) lower sales figures than expected
- Worsening customer relations (as a result of such things as conflicting arrangements with team members from other departments).

Source: *Harvard Business Review*, April 2009/Management Executive, July/August 2009

Basic principles of an effective group

symbolic approach

Research into effective groups has shown that the symbolic approach is based on certain principles. These are as follows:

1 It is important how someone becomes a member of the team.
2 There is a competitive advantage to group diversity.
3 Not orders, but behavioral models keep the team together.
4 A group language stimulates cohesion and involvement.
5 Stories contain history and values and supply the team with an identity.
6 Humor and joviality discharge tension and stimulate creativity.
7 Rituals and ceremonies rejuvenate the spirit and strengthen values.
8 How participants contribute to the informal culture need not bear a relationship to their formal position.
9 Inspiration is the real secret of successful teams.

The hard facts are, of course, that managers and employees have to come up with the goods and do so within a budget. They also have to respond to personal needs, legal requirements and economic pressure. Team forming, however, is the creation of a bond between people connected by trust and the culture they share. When the team gets 'the spirit,' its performance will soar.

7.4 Motivation: a closer view

Better labor force performance cannot be extorted. As such, for an organization to reach its goals, its employees must be willing workers. To find out what makes people willing, we have to find out what motivates people to do (or not to do) certain things.

motivation

motives

By motivation we mean all the reasons and motives which move the human being to do things in one way rather than another. Theoretically, there are both conscious and unconscious motives behind every human action: rational or emotional impulses which work on the will and urge it to activity. Consequently, to motivate someone is to meet the needs of the other person in order to ensure for oneself the willingness necessary to attain the set goals.

The notion of motivation has changed since Maslow demonstrated that people have a diversity of needs. This is just as true, naturally, for people whose job it is to be a 'goal realizing cooperative unit.' In the light of contemporary developments, organizations may need to change their ways of motivating people. The organization which is attuned exclusively to the material needs of the employee is out of touch with the times, as material circumstances are unlikely to be the only ones in which the employees are interested.

7.4.1 Contributions from psychology

To date nobody has succeeded in unraveling the mysteries of the human being in such a way that we understand ourselves and others completely. Within the organization, the human factor is still unique, and is likely to remain so. To date, few theories relating to ways of influencing the behavior of the various personality types have been proposed. Despite this lack, contemporary management does need a theoretical basis for developing management approaches and organizational methods and techniques which can lead to optimization of results.

In this section we will look at the ideas of a number of psychologists. Despite the seeming disparity between them, there is generally a fair amount of overlap. They tend to complement rather than contradict one another.

Sigmund Freud (1856-1939)

Freud

One of the best known psychologists and the creator of many important theories in psychology is Sigmund Freud. He is praised by many, reviled by others. He claimed that most of our actions derive from unconscious motives. According to Freud, consciousness can be

compared to the tip of the iceberg: the human being hardly knows what motivates him and what makes him do the things he does.
Freud's theories are particularly persuasive because they trace behavioral patterns back to experiences during childhood. According to Freud, human behavioral patterns have largely been set by the fifth year of life, and after that, only minor changes will occur. Instincts and reactions to stimuli from the environment are the main triggers. These instincts Freud described as holding a kind of primitive power, continuously requiring satisfaction as if survival is at stake.
The child who from youngest childhood is used to others satisfying its instinctive needs has to learn that the environment is no longer at its service, and that in time the environment will make demands on it. The degree to which the child develops to become independent and mature depends on how well he meets these demands. All these matters, as well as the child's experiences of praise and punishment, will affect later work attitudes. Not least is the modeling of one's behavior on that of others.

CARROTS DRESSED AS STICKS

People are contrary creatures. A man may say he would not pay more than $5 for a coffee mug. But if he is told that the mug is his, and is asked immediately afterwards how much he would be willing to sell it for, he typically holds out for more. Possession, it appears, lends things an added allure.

This makes little sense in the world of standard economic theory, where the value of something depends on what it is. But it can be explained by behavioral models in which the value people attach to objects is affected by what they already have, and people abhor losses more than they like equivalent gains.

In a new paper, Tanjim Hossain of the University of Toronto and John List of the University of Chicago explore a real-world use of these insights. The economists worked with the managers of a Chinese electronics factory, who were interested in exploring ways to make their employee-bonus scheme more effective. Most might have recommended changes to the amounts of money on offer. But Mr Hossain and Mr List chose instead to concentrate on the wording of the letter informing workers of the details of the bonus scheme.

At the beginning of the week, some groups of workers were told that they would receive a bonus of 80 yuan ($12) at the end of the week if they met a given production target. Other groups were told that they had 'provisionally' been awarded the same bonus, also due at the end of the week, but that they would 'lose' it if their productivity fell short of the same threshold.

Objectively these are two ways of describing the same scheme. But under a theory of loss aversion, the second way of presenting the bonus should work better. Workers would think of the provisional bonus as theirs, and work harder to prevent it from being taken away.

This is just what the economists found. The fear of loss was a better motivator than the prospect of gain (which worked too, but less well). And the difference persisted over time: the results were not simply a consequence of workers' misunderstanding of the system. Economists have emphasized appearances enough. Carrots, this research suggests, may work better if they can somehow be made to look like sticks.

Source: *The Economist*, January 16, 2010, p. 68

Abraham Maslow

Maslow is the most quoted expert. His theories have been put into practice most often. In *Motivation and Personality* (1954), Maslow describes a hierarchy of human needs. He identified five and arranged them in the form of a pyramid, the most basic at the bottom (Fig 7.2).

Maslow

- Needs of a physiological nature (food, drink, clothing, shelter and so on) fulfilled by wage, salary or government payments.
- Need for safety and security (protection against threats of an economical and physical nature) fulfilled by pay, retirement plans or social security/insurance policies.
- Need for love and social acceptance (affection, companionship, belonging, acknowledgment by family, friends, neighbors, and colleagues) fulfilled by work which offers people a possibility to obtain and maintain acknowledgment and acceptance.
- Need for esteem and appreciation (esteem, respect and status) fulfilled by job importance, title, promotion and so on.
- Need for self-actualization (the need to fulfill one's own potential) fulfilled by growth and development possibilities in the job, being able to deliver creative performances and the bearing of responsibility.

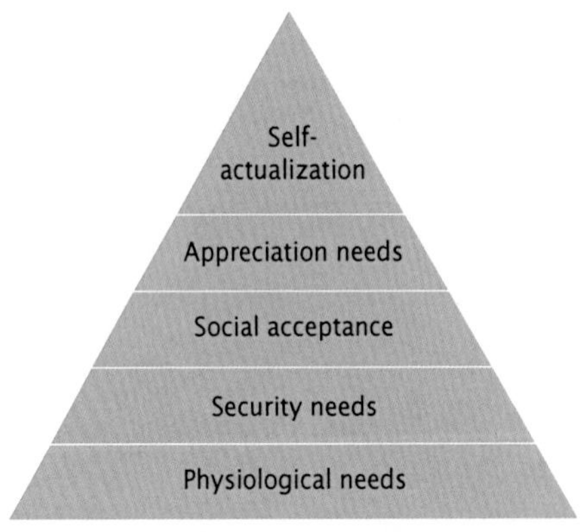

Figure 7.2 *Pyramid of psychological needs*

Source: *After Maslow*, 1954

This pyramid of needs is based on two assumptions:
- The human being is a 'wanting animal' and regardless of position or rank he always wants more and/or something different.
- Satisfied needs no longer form effective stimuli and do not or hardly ever encourage any further change in behavior.

To understand this hierarchy of needs, it is important to know that all the needs are latent in the human being: as soon as one is satisfied, another will take its place. All of the needs will require some satisfaction, and they may all act as a motivating force at any one time. The degree to which they will have to be fulfilled will depend on the person. In practice, the need to satisfy a higher need completely will only arise when the lower need has been satisfied substantially.

7.4.2 *Management by motivation*

What do these theoretical insights mean for managing and for motivating people within the organization? For 'management by motivation' to occur, managers need to know what need is likely to be driving the employee as well as what stimuli are likely to be effective.
The needs described by Maslow can be satisfied by:
- Money (material needs: levels 1 and 2)
- A say in things and involvement (levels 3 and 4)
- A certain degree of autonomy or independence (level 5)

As a human being grows to maturity, the need for respect (both respect for others and self-respect) increases. The same is true for the need for self-fulfillment. Both needs function as a motivator. The following conclusions can thus be drawn:

- People need different things from their jobs and thus display different motivational patterns. A central need, however, is the desire to be able to deploy one's own capabilities.
- This urge, though present in everyone, requires fulfillment in different ways, depending on the relationship between this desire and other personal needs such as safety, independence, power, and affection.
- The need to make best use of one's own capabilities is best fulfilled by creating coherence between people, work and organization.
- The need to make best use of one's own capabilities remains even after a certain level has been reached. After reaching this level, new (possibly higher) goals must be set.

What this means in practice is that it is wise for the manager to start from the principle that every human being has different needs, but in fulfilling any of them the emphasis must be placed on the potential for growth and the development of the human being.

WORKING WITH DR. HAPPY

Amid the financial crisis, human resources departments across Wall Street have been grappling with how to handle dark and brooding employees. Three firms – UBS, Credit Suisse, and American Express – hired Shawn Achor – who for the past decade has co-taught one of the most popular classes at Harvard, 'Positive Psychology' – to help. The first day Achor walked into UBS's offices, employees were ashen faced, he says. They didn't show the slightest interest in anything, even their BlackBerrys. 'All these banks were in such dire straits,' says Achor, aka Dr. Happy. 'Employees had just stopped working.'

To get them moving again, Achor held happiness seminars, which explained how contagious upbeat emotions can be in the workplace and stressed the value of psychological vs. financial wealth. Achor also put employees and their managers under a microscope. His findings: teams whose managers had a positive attitude have fewer sick days and higher productivity.

Source: *BusinessWeek*, December 7, 2009, p. 57

7.4.3 *Vroom's motivation theory: path-goal model*

Vroom

Vroom's theory assumes that behavior is instrumental in attaining something. In other words, the human being acts to attain a certain goal. Vroom does not go into what motivates a human being internally or what a human being strives for; the accent is not on the process but the enactment of events.

motivation, productivity and satisfaction

Vroom's motivation theory clearly connects motivation, productivity and satisfaction. Productivity is not a goal in itself, although a person may see it as a way of increasing his income, which is instrumental in attaining a higher status by, for example, buying a certain type of car. As such his efforts can be seen as instrumental for that enhancement of status. 'Instrumental' in this sense is the perceived link between a need and a reward. If an employee sees higher productivity as a way to attain one or more of his personal goals, then he will be inclined to higher production. If he sees lower productivity as a mean for reaching his goal, he will produce less. Consequently people will be motivated to higher productivity if they:

- feel that they can be highly productive and so can influence the speed and the quality themselves;
- are aware of a number of positive outcomes linked to high production and know that higher and lower productivity are not equally rewarded.

7.4.4 *Practical implications*

Vroom's motivation theory attempts to describe what moves people to do or not to do something, both with regard to paid labor as well as in other areas. We will now look at how Vroom's theories can be applied. The fact that they can be applied is important: managers need to know what drives people and put this knowledge to work in order to increase productivity. The following recommendations can be derived from Vroom's theory.

- Recognize the needs of employees and use this knowledge to encourage employees to work better in areas where better results really can be achieved. Managers must see to it that employees really do affect the outcomes and are involved in the formulation of these outcomes.
- Try to actively link the desired outcomes to the work involved. There are two sides to this: in the first place, make clear that there is a link between the income of the employee and the results achieved, the 'weight' of the function and so on; in the second place, make clear that the non-material outcomes also depend on results. The image of the department, the image of the profession within which one works, and so on, will also depend on the work results.
- Make a detailed and careful analysis of how results are best attained. Make this easier by supervising and giving direction to the employees. Not only does the goal have to be clear, but also how the goal is attained. Involve the employees in analyzing this too, so that the relationship between outcome and effort is reinforced.
- Consult employees to ascertain their expectations. This will help them get a better grip on their own affairs. They too will realize that they can make a contribution to a common goal.
- Eliminate impediments to achieving goals. Provide an effective system for the supply and conveyance of resources and raw materials. Prevent or eliminate frustration by preparing people for changes in time. This will also help make the link between product and effort clear.
- Create the potential for job satisfaction. Do this by, for example, building the following elements into the job and linking them to agreed performances:
  - Variation
  - Autonomy
  - Identification
  - Feedback and information

These recommendations are likely to produce a better match between the human being and the organization because mutual needs and expectations will have been clarified.

7.4.5 *Meaningful work and work engagement: creating satisfying work*

Clearly, there is much room for improvement on the work floor.

Employees are quick to judge their colleagues as being lazy

An overwhelming majority of British bossess and their employees are of the opinion that their immediate colleagues underachieve. Recent research by the British research bureau Investors in People has shown that the main reason for this negative opinion of their colleagues is that employees and managers believe that everybody other than themselves is lazy. 75% of bosses are of the opinion that some of their employees are actually not needed. while 80% of employees are of the opinion that some of their colleagues could go without this having any effect on business. Nearly half of the employees work in close association with a colleague whom they believe is lazy and unsuitable for the job.

The employees are also critical of their bosses. Four out of ten employees believe that their bosses do nothing to get lazy colleagues working.

According to the researchers, these problems are particularly prevalent in large organizations. In organizations with more than one thousand employees, 84% of those surveyed were of the opinion that some of their colleagues were underperforming, as against 50% in companies with fewer than fifty employees.

The main signs of a colleague being lazy were, according to those surveyed, putting personal life above business life, refusing to to take on additional responsibilities and making out that work done by other colleagues was their own work.

Many of those surveyed indicated that laziness on the part of colleagues meant that they themselves had to work longer hours. Moreover, they felt undervalued. Being obliged to work for long periods and intensively with a collegue who just will not put in any effort can even lead to burnout. People who have to work for long periods with a colleague whom they label as lazy are also more likely to go looking for another job.

In addition, the research indicated that one in seven people with an office job are bored, perhaps even chronically so (so-called bore-out). Two thirds of them have a high educational level. 'Bore-out' is not caused by laziness but by a combination of boredom, too little to do and lack of interest.

Bullying at work

bullying

Research shows that in 80% of cases involving bullying, the manager is mentioned as being the bully. 'The sort of manager that we are talking about is the manger that is unable to empathize with others. They are much better at directing mergers and the like than the empathetic manager that sheds a tear whenever he has to sack somebody.' However, it is not only being able to identify with others that causes *bullying behavior*. Jealousy and an unhealthy self-obsession are also mentioned as factors. 'The ones that are bullied are often not the sad cases but quite the opposite: forceful people who are good at their jobs. Managers who are jealous or who have little self-esteem and are addicted to putting others down see this sort of employee as a threat to their own position. In other words, they see them as people who have to be bullied into leaving.'

For example ...

Bullying to get rid of a colleague.
The most frequently used methods are:

- Making false acccusations about a person
- Glaring at a person as a form of non-verbal intimidation
- Publically putting a person down
- Abrupt mood changes: sudden anger
- Not sticking to one's own rules
- Ignoring praiseworthy achievements
- Constant criticism
- Initiating malicious gossip

Following the lead of the US and England, Holland has also adopted November the 7th as the 'Ban bullying at work' day. While workfloor bullying (or 'mobbing') is an international problem, according to research done by the TNO, more work-related bullying goes on in the Netherland than in other European countries. With 650,000 people indicating that they are regularly the victims of bullying, it would seem that Holland is a nation of bullies. The manager is involved in half of all the cases.

Bullies have the following profile: they often have narcissistic traits, they seek power and they are not good at putting themselves in the place of those whom they bully.

Reorganizations make people sick

reorganization stress

A great many employees are suffering from *reorganization stress* as a result of reorganizations and workplace changes. It leads to health complaints such as stress and insomnia. Employees have to be more flexible than ever in order to adapt to changing situations – not only having to change jobs as a result of reorganizations, but also having to change their work methods and work at less regular times. Moreover, employees are increasingly having to meet achievement standards.

As the research shows, health-related complaints can be reduced by involving employees more in the processes of change. As soon as employees are given more say in how they do their work in the new situation the health complaints start to reduce. 'It goes further than that, even: employees are more motivated, happier and more productive the more they are involved in the company changes and changes to their work.' This even applies to company reorganizations and restructurings. If employees are involved at a early stage in how to spread the burden, they will cooperate instead of digging in their heels.

The role of the manager

Research shows that 69% of employee work satisfaction is related to the actions of their boss. Research also shows that the average employee complains about his or her boss an average of four hours per week. Nothing is more lethal for *pleasure in one's work* as an uninspiring manager who sets meaningless or contradictory assignments. In short, it is one of the tasks of management to put meaning into the work that others do. It is not about thinking up meaningful tasks but about removing the barriers that prevent work from being found meaningful.

What changes have you experienced in the past two years?

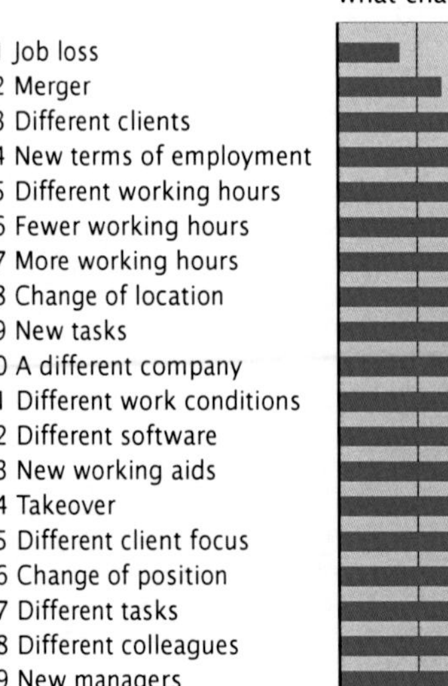

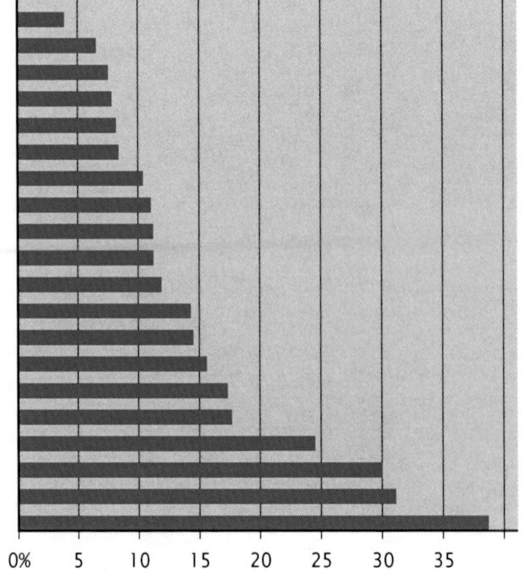

Pressure to achieve is main result of reorganizations

Source: *NRC Handelsblad*, 11 february, 2009

In concrete terms, this may mean, for example, that managers link remuneration to achievement. An employee could be singled out for praise and recognition and be assigned certain duties. Managers could also hand out bonuses, thereby making a distinction between those who have performed best and those who have performed worst. Another option is acting to promote teamwork, thereby making jobs more pertinent and interesting.

Those in middle magement positions tend to forget what the individual employee is capable of and finds interesting and motivating since they in turn are put under pressure by their own bosses to achieve tangible results. As a result, they tend to direct their employees instead of motivating them, which is more important. The crucial thing is learning to show their appreciation.

7.4.6 Design of functions, productivity and motivation

The content and structure of managerial and operational functions can influence the efforts of employees. Function design includes the design of tasks. Functions may differ in the degree of routine, the skills involved, the procedures to be followed, how much freedom there is to deviate from set ways of working, the degree of independence and so on. In the past, function designers have assumed that a high degree of task specialization offered many economical advantages. However, too great a degree of task specialization has led to many functions being experienced by employees as dull, stressful and relatively meaningless. New methods of assigning tasks and design of functions enhance the quality of the work as well as the productivity of employees.
Individual functions may be designed with the following possibilities in mind:

- Job rotation: task switching horizontally or vertically. In consultation, tasks may be switched as rapidly as a couple of times an hour
- Job enlargement: the horizontal enlargement of functions; enlargement of task span and lengthening of task cycle
- Job enrichment: the vertical enlargement of functions; enlargement of depth of tasks

For groups, the following design possibilities are available:

- Integrated teams: task enlargement at the group level
- Semi-autonomous groups: task enrichment at the group level
- Quality circles: a group of employees with shared responsibility in a certain area to solve the quality problems there.

task-characteristic model

The so-called task-characteristic model provides five characteristics of functions by which the design of a function can be analyzed (see Fig 7.3). The model also provides insight into the mutual interrelationships of the five characteristics and predicts their influence on productivity, motivation and satisfaction.

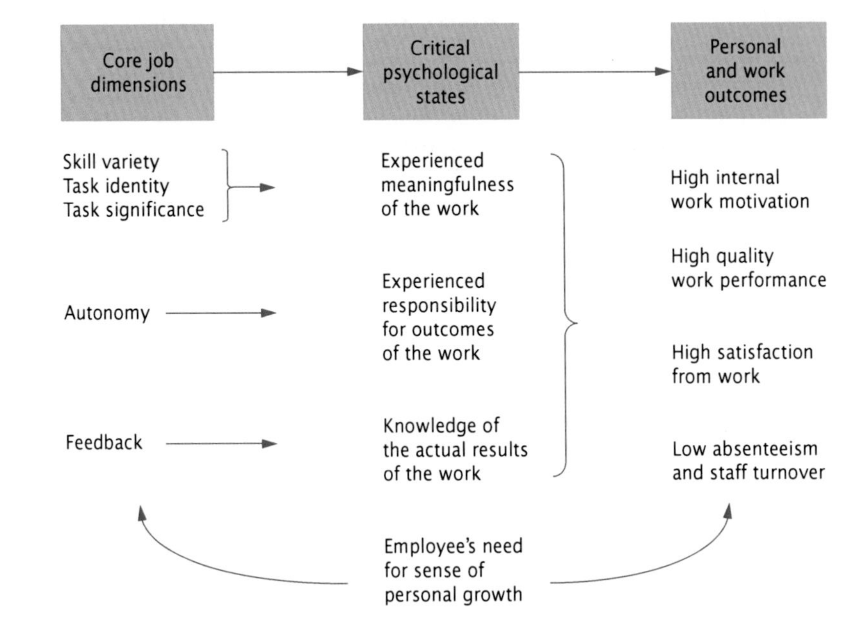

Figure 7.3 *The task-characteristic model*

Source: *Hackman*, 1977

Main task characteristics

Five task characteristics that should be taken into consideration:

- Variation in skills: the degree to which a function involves activities for which various skills and talents are necessary
- Task identity: the degree to which a job requires an identifiable piece of work to be completed
- Task importance: the degree to which a function influences the life and work of others
- Autonomy: the degree to which a function involves discretion/freedom, independence and the right to influence the planning of work and operational procedures
- Feedback: the degree to which performance can be directly and clearly assessed

broad task groups

Broad task groups may increase employee satisfaction. Changes on the work floor may be accompanied by delayering of the organization. The number of hierarchical layers could be reduced and the lines shortened, and the tasks and functions designed to replace the hierarchy (Section 6.6).

7.5 Empowerment

empowerment

When organizations realize that they have to revitalize their operations, the result may be delayering, cost cutting, reduction of overheads, recession and layoffs. In such a situation, the concept of empowerment is likely to gain popularity. Empowerment may have energy and opportunity enhancing effects because it focuses on the following:

- Influencing employee behavior, motivation and efforts positively
- Enlarging effectiveness and flexibility

Though organization theorists, practicing managers and management consultants rarely agree, on this point they do: empowerment can help organizations compete for the favor of the client, be flexible, and, of course, work more efficiently.

Empowerment is a form of self-management and involves the following:

- Independently set goals and decisions made within given constraints

- Responsibility for one's own performance in terms of quantity as well as quality
- Working with others in a way that is flexible, efficient, customer oriented and creative

The notion of empowerment came to Europe from the USA in the late 1980s. The terms 'delegation,' 'semi-autonomy,' 'self-development,' 'self-control,' and 'motivation' have all been bandied about for decades. Is empowerment anything new? However we choose to answer this, we can at the very least say that the notion of empowerment consists of three elements:

1 Two parties are involved.
2 Delegation takes place.
3 There are certain effects, most particularly an increase in effort.

FEMINIST MANAGEMENT THEORISTS ARE FLIRTING WITH SOME DANGEROUS ARGUMENTS

The late Paul Samuelson once equipped that 'women are just men with less money'. As a father of six, he might have added something about women's role in the reproduction of the species. But his aphorism is about as good a one-sentence summary of classical feminism as you can get.

The first generations of successful women insisted on being judged by the same standards as men. They had nothing but contempt for the notion of special treatment for 'the sisters', and instead insisted on getting ahead by dint of working harder and thinking smarter. Margaret Thatcher made no secret of her contempt for the wimpish men around her. (There is a joke about her going out to dinner with her cabinet. 'Steak or fish?' asks the waiter. 'Steak, of course,' she replies. 'And for the vegetables?' 'They'll have steak as well.') During America's most recent presidential election, Hillary Clinton taunted Barack Obama with an advertisement that implied that he, unlike her, was not up to the challenge of answering the red phone at 3am.

Many pioneering businesswomen pride themselves on their toughness. Dong Mingzhu, the boss of Gree Electric Appliances, an air-conditioning giant, says flatly: 'I never miss. I never admit mistakes and I am always correct.' In the past three years her company has boosted shareholder returns by nearly 500%.

But some of today's most influential feminists contend that women will never fulfil their potential if they play by men's rules. According to Avivah Wittenberg-Cox and Alison Maitland, two of the most prominent exponents of this position, it is not enough to smash the glass ceiling. You need to audit the entire building for 'gender asbestos' – in other words, root out the inherent sexism built into corporate structures and processes.

The new feminism contends that women are wired differently from men, and not just in trivial ways. They are less aggressive and more consensus seeking, less competitive and more collaborative, less power-obsessed and more group-oriented. Judy Rosener of the University of California, Irvine, argues that women excel at 'transformational' and 'interactive' management. Peninah Thomson and Jacey Graham, the authors of 'A Woman's Place is in the Boardroom', assert that women are 'better lateral thinkers than men' and 'more idealistic' into the bargain. Feminist texts are suddenly full of references to tribes of monkeys, with their aggressive males and nurturing females.

What is more, the argument runs, these supposedly womanly qualities are becoming ever more valuable in business. The recent financial crisis proved that the sort of qualities that men pride themselves on, such as risk-taking and bare-knuckle competition, can lead to disaster. Lehman Brothers' bankruptcy would never have happened if it had been Lehman Sisters, according to this theory. Even before the financial disaster struck, the new feminists also claim, the best companies had been abandoning 'patriarchal' hierarchies in favor of 'collaboration' and 'networking', skills in which women have an inherent advantage.

This argument may sound a little like the stuff of gender workshops in righteous universities. But it is gaming followers in powerful places. McKinsey, the most venerable of management consultancies, has published research arguing that women apply five of the nine 'leadership behaviors' that lead to corporate success more frequently than men. Niall FitzGerald, the chairman of Reuters and a former boss of Unilever, is as close as you can get to the heart of the corporate establishment. He proclaims, 'Women have different ways of achieving results, and leadership qualities that are becoming more important as our organizations become less hierarchical and more loosely organized around matrix structures.' Many companies are abandoning the old fashioned commitment to treating everybody equally and instead becoming 'gender adapted' and 'gender bilingual' – in touch with the unique management wisdom of their female employees. A host of consultancies has sprung up to teach firms how to listen to women and exploit their special abilities.

The new feminists are right to be frustrated about the pace of women's progress in business. Britain's Equality and Human Rights Commission calculated that, at the current rate of progress, it will take 60 years for women to gain equal representation on the boards of the firm top 100. They are also right that old-fashioned feminism took too little account of women's role in raising children. But their arguments about the innate differences between men and women are sloppy and counterproductive.

People who bang on about innate differences should remember that the variation within subgroups in the population is usually bigger than the variation between subgroups. Even if it can be established that, on average, women have a higher 'emotional-intelligence quotient' than men, that says little about any specific woman. Judging people as individuals rather than as representatives of groups is both morally right and good for business.

Source: *The Economist*, January 2, 2010, p. 48

7.5.1 *Empowerment: a new way to manage people*

It is essential to realize that organizational empowerment is concerned with managing employees in specific ways. The following managerial guidelines may be used to good advantage:

- The classical 'giving of an order' whereby one person tells another what to do is a form of empowerment.
- Conscious delegation is a form of empowerment.
- Empowerment, whether in the form of delegation or not, involves an interaction engaged in for the purposes of improving performance and output.

Seen in Maslow's terms, empowerment is enabling self-fulfillment and the need for recognition. In practical terms, through empowerment, business units, groups and employees are given the means to function independently, with some form of control, though only at a distance. A form of self-control by employees is the desired state. The current interest in empowerment would suggest that past approaches have not worked and something has to be done about this.

Empowerment entails enabling people to do their job more independently than in the past, not because this relieves the pressure on management, but because empowerment unlocks positive forces and energy and may lead to greater efficiency and effectiveness as well as greater innovative and creative abilities. One condition for this is, however, that the potential of the employees needs to be better exploited than in the past.

7.5.2 Empowerment: an attractive concept for young and old

It has been observed that young, highly educated employees are particularly attracted to companies where a climate characterized by decentralization, debureaucratization, downsizing, privatization and customer orientation prevails.
Such a company has the following characteristics:

- It has a flat structure with short lines of communication.
- It allows creativity.
- It delegates responsibility.
- It does not have a strict hierarchical structure but is more inclined to be based on informal collaboration and communication.
- It is more directed at the individual.
- It sees innovation with all the changes it may bring as important.
- It contributes to the development of the employees themselves.

However, it has become absolutely obvious that these kinds of company characteristics are not only attractive to young employees. Older generations often value a similar work climate.
For employees used to other circumstances to do their job more independently and to be empowered to make their own decisions, it is vital that they have the right knowledge and resources at their disposal. In addition to their being involved in the decision-making process, they have to have access to appropriate knowledge and information.
Employees have to (and indeed want to):

- Be informed on all important matters within the organization
- Understand the decisions of management; what is more, they have to be able to participate in, rather than simply affect, the decision-making processes
- Be able to say how they want things to change and be heard
- Participate in policy making
- Use the most modern technologies and methods not only to improve their productivity but for their own development

It is important that the opportunity to change, renew and innovate be guaranteed, and of course, here the structure of the organization plays a part. While the way the organization is structured can facilitate this, it is only one of the tools at the organization's disposal. Having fewer hierarchical levels is certainly advantageous, and project management comes into its own. The crucial thing is that the functional organization be able to adapt quickly to changing circumstances.
In the face of continually changing circumstances, the organization has to be mobile and flexible. It is a good idea to devise various ways of going about important processes, and put these ways to individual groups (perhaps brought together on an ad hoc basis).
The organization's own skills and knowledge should be drawn on wherever possible (see Section 5.6).

CASE

Mini case study 7.2

The older employee: worth his weight in gold

There is much to be said for the older employee. While an employee older than 50 may be more expensive in terms of wage costs, there are benefits in return.

- His knowledge and experience are worth their weight in gold.
- His social skills are often greater.
- He is more stress resistant and has more stomach for the business than younger employees.
- He inspires more trust than younger employees.
- At the age of 55 the employee has the productivity of a 35 year old, and the ability to learn remains the same up to the age of 60.
- Older people are more careful, cause fewer work-related accidents and have low rates of absenteeism.

7.6 The new context for human talent development and human resource management

In the market-oriented organization, new expectations are constantly being aroused and new demands constantly made by both clients and by employees in the industrial as well as in the services sector. Success in the product/market environment is, to a large degree, determined by flexibility, motivation, involvement, creativity and innovative ability. For their part, employees value more interesting work, more consultation and participation and tailor-made rewards. In industry (which is 70 per cent internally provided services) and in the services sector, both predominantly 'people's businesses,' a well-thought-through personnel policy (in terms of marketing, manufacturing and purchase) is necessary. This involves human talent development and human resource management.

7.6.1 New demands and other constraints: the changing organization

Organizations that adapt to changing circumstances are incorporating new human resource management approaches in their policies. They include the following:

1. Pluriformity of work conditions
2. A balance between work and home
3. Better trained employees
4. A flat organizational structure
5. Culture as a binding factor
6. A more interrelated approach and the ability to deal with diversity

Pluriformity of work conditions

The initiative and entrepreneurship that spring from creativity and flexibility need to be stimulated. This requires a rethinking of the existing appraisal and reward system in order to make the necessary adjustments to changing circumstances possible. The present work conditions have many of the characteristics of a welfare structure. They are often the result of negotiations based on satisfaction of needs and the right to fair treatment. Reward systems which provide a uniform package of primary and secondary work conditions in return for a specified performance are characteristic of them. Such structures have a curbing rather than a stimulating influence on entrepreneurship, flexibility and mobility.

Rethinking of the system is absolutely necessary, and there needs to be far more attention paid to individuals' wishes, capabilities and ambitions. Equal treatment and remuneration according to performance should be its basis. One option is a set of employment conditions applicable to both manager and employee which allow both to have a say in what they think can be achieved in terms of quality and increase in production. The package could include the following:

set of employment conditions

- Rewards based on proven capabilities, effort and performance
- The 'cafeteria system,' that is, the employees compose their reward menu themselves: for example, a lower wage, more days off; retirement at a later age (see Section 7.8.5)
- Certain incentives linked to the attained result
- Level of the reward based not only on the job itself, but also how highly the organization values the qualities involved.

Balance between work and home life

Research shows that employees with a family show a higher level of commitment to and satisfaction with the work situation when companies offer flexible employment opportunities and facilities that suit particular work-private life situations. Such arrangements are likely to benefit the single employee of 45+ as well (or in any case, more so than very young employees). These facilities might be flexible working hours, flexible part-time work

work-private life situations

deployment, a four day working week and working from home (teleworking), but also facilities such as healthcare, childcare, training and housekeeping services. At higher levels, job sharing is regarded positively.

job sharing

Facilities of this kind are highly appreciated by employees, certainly where women in managerial positions are concerned, but also in double income family situations or one-parent families. Such facilities improve loyalty to the company and have a positive effect on absenteeism and turnover rates.

Research has shown that about 80% of women with children have the feeling that they have already done a full day's work before they even start work. The average woman has by then already done two hours of housework. Men do housework before they go off to their day job, though it does not amount to more than 49 minutes of work.

Another finding was that women were already busily preparing to get the whole family off to their work, school or daycare safe and sound the evening beforehand. It takes a total of one and a half hours to make sandwiches, pack bags and so on. The evening before, men limit themselves to jobs that take up about 8 minutes.

Better trained employees

The point has already been made that new demands are going to be made on employees: factual knowledge and professional skills are going to be less necessary for positions that do not require them, though they will remain essential for jobs which are specific in nature and have time and place boundaries. In view of the impact of technology on jobs, experience is likely to become less relevant, however.

Information technologies demand knowledge of a different kind and new skills, both of which need to be constantly upgraded. It is thus crucial that employees become familiar with the opportunities offered by information technology, know how to derive information from various fields and on the basis of this information, make considered and independent decisions. This requires the ability to think analytically, a higher general level of education and the ability to react to changes in the immediate environment. Given the changes to be expected in the future, a number of qualitative demands have to be made on employees and management, demands which will make it possible to face an uncertain future optimistically. Characteristics such as entrepreneurial ability, creativity, innovative ability and responsiveness will be increasingly required. This means developing one's learning ability, personal qualities and capabilities further, and a constant willingness to continue to learn.

qualitative demands

internal organization mobility

Once-off professional training for a career is a thing of the past. It will be replaced by internal organization mobility since this widens both knowledge and skills. This requires geographical and functional mobility, even if this does not lead automatically to personal improvement in position within the organization.

Developing one's own talents is an ongoing necessity, even during times of crisis or recession. One way of developing within the same job position is learning on the job: getting work experience within one's own organization, obtaining new work experiences by taking part in challenging projects and seeking mentors who can assist in improving specific areas of functioning. However, this can only be expected of an employee if there is a company culture of trust in objectivity of judgement, and if employees feel safe, are not considered as disposable and know that their interests and those of the organization are synonymous. It also requires management to supervise the employees and put some effort into organizing transfers.

OLD AND YOUNG ON THE WORKFLOOR

The largest cohorts that companies employ are Baby Boomers and Generation Ys. As such, it is handy for employers to be familiar with a number of characteristics of both groups.

Baby Boomers
Working on instead of retiring at 65: 42 percent want to do this.
A lengthy career: 47 percent regard themselves as being mid-career.
Idealism: 55 percent do some form of volunteer work.
Flexibility: 87 percent want flexible work hours.
Voluntary carers: 71 percent look after their parents.

Generation Y
Ambition: 84 percent are highly ambitious.
Loyalty to employer or rather short-term workers: 45 percent expect to spend the rest of their working lives working for the same employer.
Multicultural: 78 percent have no problem with working with people from other cultures.
Enviro-consciousness: 86 percent want to do work that has a positive effect on the planet.
Netwerking: 48 percent think that it is important to have a social network at work.

Source: *Harvard Business Review*, July/August 2009; *Management Trends* October 2009 – www.kluwermanagement.nl

A flat organizational structure

To react effectively to rapid changes will not only make demands on the employee, but also on the organization. Self-aware, entrepreneurial employees who take the initiative readily will not be able to develop within a large-scale, centrally managed organizational structure, and thus the reaction to change will be insufficiently smooth and flexible. What this means is that in the coming years, tight organizational structures are going to have to be replaced by structures where there is only a moderate degree of structuring, leaving room for self-accomplishment of the tasks in response to tangible company goals. It means a network of relatively autonomous units within the organization. Responsibility for quality, vision and goal-directed work, and involvement in the entire process within one's own sub-system from input through to output, are essential characteristics for such structures. A flat, decentralized structure with short decision lines, one that can meet the need for employees to bear responsibility, is an appropriate one (see Fig 7.4).

self-accomplishment

autonomous units

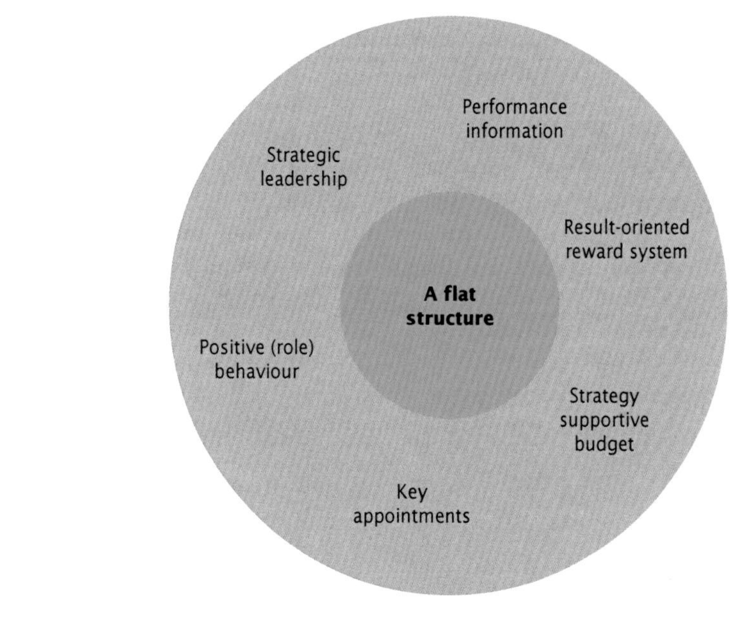

Figure 7.4
Interrelated aspects that contribute to a flat structure

Tasks, authority and responsibilities have to be delineated in such a way that they do not hinder employees' further development, but rather stimulate it. Intimately connected to that is the need for employees to be responsible for their own decisions and to be held to them. Reacting rapidly to changing circumstances, offering new product varieties within existing markets or opening new markets is not possible with slow decision-making processes.

operational freedom

Operational freedom should be as wide as possible within a well considered strategic framework. The new information technologies make it much easier to delayer organizational structures and also make possible other communication patterns.

When the structure is changed by reducing the number of management layers, it does not automatically follow that decision-making is faster, that more energy goes into entrepreneurship or that more attention is paid to the needs of the customers. Use needs to be made, therefore, of several other instruments to increase the effect of the change in structure. Effective delayering involves enhancing or supporting measures.

Culture as a binding factor

The culture within the organization will have to breathe a spirit of openness as well as offer opportunities to anyone suitable who feels called upon to bear more responsibility or take on different responsibilities. The danger of relatively autonomous units is that the link with the rest of the organization can be severed and that employees start losing their psychological and emotional bond with the rest of the organization. If this threatens to happen, the organization's basic philosophy needs to be reviewed and the 'them and us' mentality replaced by a new or renewed sense of unity. That there be a so-called corporate identity is thus vitally important, and it must be more than merely a house-style – the corporate identity is, rather, an organizational culture in which employees can relate to the philosophy of their organization. This demands an organizational climate in which everyone

corporate identity

- is aware of clearly formulated organizational goals,
- trusts in the validity of those goals,
- recognizes his own contribution to the goals, and
- wants to put his effort towards the realization of the end result.

The importance of cross-cultural theories for managers who have to operate in an unfamiliar culture should not be underestimated. Training based on home-country theories is of very limited use and may even do more harm than good. A thorough familiarization with the other culture, for which the organization can use the services of specialized cross-cultural training institutes, is essential – or it can develop its own program by using host-country personnel as teachers.

A more interrelated approach and the ability to deal with diversity

Taking a more interrelated approach is one of the best ways of coping with a rapidly changing world. Involving the environment in one's own activities enables one to react promptly to change. For an organization, this has implications on three levels.

strategic level

On the strategic level, the environment affects the organization and the organization influences the environment through its services and societal added value, hence maintaining a feeling for outside events is essential. Society, industrial life and politics are very much interwoven. Companies consult with political parties, employers discuss employees and their needs and there is consultation about mainstream education by various industrial sectors.

organizational level

At the organizational level, the manager is situated at the crossroads of company activities and needs to involve the environment in his policy intentions and activities. He himself needs to be able to interrelate in order to tackle problems associated with quality of service, customer orientation or willingness to serve. He also has to meet the requirement of being able to think and act in an interdisciplinary and multi-cultural way also where organizational change is concerned.

operational level

On the operational level, the effectiveness of the organization as a whole is to a large degree determined by the extent to which the individual employee is capable of communicating with the environment, whether this be external clients, internal clients or client systems. The shift of responsibility onto operational units to address and resolve problems in direct interaction with one another, or as in service companies, the shift from back office to front office, will supply almost every employee with openings to engage intensively with the environment, and especially with the client.

boundaries within the organization

geographic and cultural borders

Cross-border approaches not only involve breaking down boundaries within the organization and crossing external borders towards stakeholders in the environment, but also crossing geographic and cultural borders such as the borders separating functions, divisions, product groups or units with a focus on the customer. At the same time, the various competencies do have to be maintained. Tasks that fall under Business Process Reengineering (BPR) and team oriented work have to be elaborated in specific proposals and measurements (see sections 6.3 and 10.4).

External borders sometimes become real barriers when identity issues are involved and we-them relationships with external parties block effective relationships with customers, suppliers, governmental agencies or pressure groups. Some of the characteristics of external relationships are frequent withholding of information, slowing down tactics, playing parties off against each other, political games and creating mistrust. Such tactics make it difficult to change the relationship between the organization and its partners along the value-adding chain. If the situation improves, collective use of resources including expert knowledge, collective planning, exchange of information, mutual consultation and development of mutual norms should be aimed at. However, creating a basis for collaboration takes both time and a strong desire to transform existing working cultures in which everybody is on their own.

When organizations work in different international areas or in different national areas or markets, there are likely to be geographic and cultural borders resulting from a sense of national or local prestige, different cultures and geographic and physical distances. Such differences can be bridged with the help of recent information and communication

CUTBACKS: DON'T NEGLECT THE SURVIVORS

By Bill Conaty, former senior vice-president for Human Resources at General Electric

Restructurings, consolidation, salary freezes, a shifting health-care cost burden, furloughs ... this list, as you know, goes on and on. Did your company cancel this year's Christmas party?

These are common responses to our changing corporate landscape. And they can be necessary. Businesses that don't step up and react to reality are unlikely to survive over the long term.

My concern is that, cumulatively, these negative actions are tugging at and fraying the delicate bonds of loyalty that tie employees to their employers. I believe it will be the companies that manage to deftly balance the necessary through competitive actions with genuine compassion for their employees that will win big in the future.

People have long memories. What they don't have right now are a whole lot of career options. And they will judge their employer by how equitably they feel they were treated during the down market. So how exactly do you steer your company through this in a way that won't drive your people into the arms of the first headhunter who calls? (Trust me, they will start dialing again.) Just as vital: how to take the tough steps while energizing your workforce instead of paralyzing them?

As counterintuitive as it may sound, consider going deeper than you might on staff reductions, rather than nibbling around the edges hoping for a quick market turnaround. Some companies believe in 'share the pain' scenarios, where everyone gets to sacrifice equally at the corporate altar. I'm not a fan of such strategies unless they address a short-term crisis in which a company expects to be reducing forces and hiring within the same year. In my view, these practices ensure that 100% of your workforce is demoralized, vs. the 10% to 20% whom you really can't afford in the current climate.

When you're ready to make those cuts, deal compassionately with the casualties, financially and emotionally, to provide them as soft a landing as possible. Career transition centers, training opportunities, and a sincere interest in helping those who are moving on to become more marketable will genuinely help.

Many companies don't need to be told that. Instead, managers often spend a disproportionate amount of time managing the layoff process and do not pay enough attention to the surviving talent. Those survivors need to be recognized and rewarded. Yes, they'll pay close attention to how humanely layoffs are carried out, but they're also aware that their own workload and stress level has just been stepped up. You want this group to play offense, not to fret over when the next shoe will drop or feel that they're being overburdened.

With financial rewards temporarily off the screen, an astonishingly powerful form of recognition is a genuine pat on the back, along with words along these lines: 'I think you're doing a great job under tough circumstances, and you're an essential part of my team.' It doesn't take long to say or cost a penny, but how many of us have ever heard those words?

There's a strong tendency for executives in tight spots to simply clam up, fearing they don't have the answers people want to hear. To avoid appearing inadequate, they'll issue the occasional all-employee e-mail or canned Webcast. But you'll find that you don't need to have all the answers. You'll discover that the rumor mill has painted the most pessimistic picture imaginable, and you will quickly be able to dispel numerous falsehoods and present a clearer and more optimistic view. These times call for a personal touch. Employees who get to see and hear their leaders are far more likely to buy into a future beyond the crisis.

Now back to the subject of holiday parties: it's a mistake to legislate fun out of the workplace. You need to continue to celebrate, especially in tough times. Employees shouldn't feel that it's wrong to appear to be having fun at the risk of their superiors thinking they're not serious enough. We need to dial down how we celebrate, yes, but it's not natural to have to continuously wear a deadly serious game face. Life's too short to have to feel that way, let alone act that way.

As the clouds blow away, I'll be placing my bets on companies that are the most open, ethically compliant, and compassionate with their people. They'll be the ones that succeed in retaining – and therefore attracting – world-class talent.

Source: B. Conaty, *Bloomberg Business Week*, January 11, 2010, p. 68

technology (see Section 3.4), greater employee mobility, cross-border teamwork (Section 7.3) and sometimes product standardization. It is especially important to respect *local interests and preferences* and give them the value they deserve, not only in terms of collaborative relationships, but also as expressed in the product or the way that services are provided. This organizational issue also involves cross-border capacity in the sense of multicultural organizational development and dealing with *diversity* in race, culture, religion, gender, age, sexual orientation and mental/physical abilities and characteristics (see Harvey & Allard, 2002).

In this regard, the career prospects within many companies of employees from an ethnic minority are of particular concern, as are those of groups such as the physically or visually *handicapped*. Blind people can work perfectly well with a Braille screen reader mounted underneath the keyboard and a speech-operated computer. However, doing business with bits of paper is no way to do it. A company with a blind person within its ranks needs to have a modern digital system.

7.6.2 Fostering talent: some practical implications

For talent to be fostered, certain conditions need to be met. In the first place, there needs to be a system of contracting and coaching. Contracting and coaching must provide some insight into the need for development of the employee, both from the point of view of the organization's own demands as well as in the light of his or her own career. Contracting and coaching should result in a program of requirements for talent development and indicate individual and collective learning needs. *Talent development* based on contracting and coaching depends on four conditions:

- The willingness of managers and employees to work with contracting and coaching tactics whereby conditions are created in which the development of talent can be discussed in an open and mutually satisfying.
- Open communication about performance and talent within the organization in the form of discussion about mission, goals, and strategy. The communication must be such that everyone within the organization knows what the expected performances are and how individual talents can be deployed to that end.
- A simple set-up and approach using formal 'instruments': performance judgment, potential prognosis, and discussions about contracts. Keeping the instruments simple will prevent discussion on how to foster and keep track of individual development from being disturbed by more complex issues. The instruments can thus remain a means to an end – fostering development – and not an end in themselves.
- The capacity of managers to work with contracting and coaching tactics. The organization has an obligation to stimulate the development of employee talent. Managers have to be capable of working with the instruments necessary for that purpose, especially contracting and coaching.

After the organization has set the development of individual talent as one of its objectives, it needs to decide how to encourage that development. Coaching and mentoring provide employees with a deeper insight into their functions and encourage learning, and should take priority over other methods. They also make the individual more receptive to other methods, including education, training and instruction.

7.6.3 Coaching and talent development

Developing talent is a high priority with many organizations. Many invest heavily in talented people and aim to make maximum use of their knowledge and skills. One of the main reasons for this investment is that it creates opportunities for further growth and for a competitive advantage. Coaching as a means of encouraging individual growth has becoming very popular in recent years. To be at all successful, *trust* is crucial.

Coaching

Coaching is a form of personal tuition on equal one-to-one terms. The goals are set beforehand. The main objective is enhancing the personal effectiveness of the *coachee*. The coach may be a experienced colleague, an external coach or maybe even somebody from the managerial ranks. The main principles are that the coach is not the one in charge of the process and that there is no shortcoming that must be overcome. However, to develop individual talents, opportunities need to be created.

The coach's role is to encourage the coachee to reflect on things, to enable potential qualities to emerge and to remove the barriers to further development. The coachee decides on the direction and sets the pace and the coach has a facilitating role in the process.

Good coaching is a skill that requires a sound knowledge of behavior and a good deal of practice in encouraging latent talents to emerge. Essentially, it is a process of helping people to make progress by supporting them as they develop self-awareness and learn to take responsibility for their actions.

Although research has shown that coaching within companies is not the most frequently used HR instrument, it is the most effective. American research has shown that training delivers an increase in productivity of 22.4%, while a combination of training and coaching can deliver an increase in productivity of 88% (Oliveiro et al., 1997). 79% of coaching courses have been shown to be effective, as against 69% of training and education courses (TNS NIPO, 2004; NVP-TU-Twente, 2007).

The 2007 survey referred to above showed that managers in particular need greater awareness of how profitable coaching courses can be. *Return on investment* (ROI) is mentioned as the additional denominator to be taken into account in determining the effectiveness of personal development programs. To establish the ROI, the impact on business needs to be made quantifiable, and the Quality Intervention System (QIS) aims to do just that. This *web-based quality testing* instrument measures the results of coaching courses according to four denominators: the coachee's satisfaction with the course, the extent of development, concrete effects, the effect on company results and if desired, the fifth denominator of ROI.

7.6.4 *Developing and managing organizational competencies*

An organization's competencies are the specific resources and capabilities that enable the organization to develop, choose and implement value-enhancing strategies, and include all assets, knowledge, skills and capabilities embedded within the organization's structure, technology, processes and interpersonal relationships.

four types of competencies

Turner and Crawford (1994) describe four types of competencies at the organizational level.

- Personal and intrinsic competencies: the knowledge and skills implicit in systems and processes and intrinsic to people, technologies and structures.
- Management competencies: the ability of management to provide direction, development, motivation, administration and coordination of the organization's performance.
- Operational and renewing competencies: the capability to meet and tackle present and future problems and challenges.
- The fundamentally distinctive competencies: the aspects that give the organization an advantage over their competitors and which are derived from unique combinations of elementary competencies.

performance management

Performance management is management directed at better performance by the organization. Goals are set within a strategic framework, outcomes are constantly measured and used to strengthen or adapt activities, performance is rewarded and management constantly gives feedback through information systems.

Taking a hard look at the organization at the hand of the above four types of competencies might expose both its strengths and weaknesses, especially in terms of how these competencies are combined and how balanced they are. Functional units are likely to possess a lot of the more tangible competencies, whereas the less tangible ones are what tend to hold functional departments together as a whole.

Good coaching by management is an essential factor. Managers and semi-independent employees can make or break one another. Managers have to enlarge the capacity to learn and strengthen the reflective side of their work so that teams are able to look critically at their performance and thus find more effective ways of doing the job.

Development of the knowledge or competence of semi-autonomous teams can be directed effectively by means that may have little to do with further education and training. Learning may arise specifically out of the work that has to be done, and consequently will be initially ad hoc, triggered by deficiencies or challenges which arise from the work itself. While coaching is always important, sometimes the learning that has to take place is only indirectly able to be influenced by coaching.

effective leaders

What makes a manager a good leader? Effective leaders have different styles of leadership, but they are always capable of combining or matching the daily work with the organizational goals. Coaching management matches individual capabilities with the organizational tasks. The manager should nevertheless stand aloof to a certain extent: at crucial moments the results might be dependent on both synergy and on individual 'stars'. Coaching is a skill that takes time to develop and requires a long-term vision, which might be at odds with flexibility and short-term direct results or performance.

It is the same story when it comes to building competencies at the organizational level. The relationship between investment and returns is clearer in the case of material than of intangible competencies. The development and maintenance of these competencies will not pay off in the short term, so the urge to invest in them might be correspondingly hesitant.

It may help to identify the competencies at the various organizational levels to find out which are lacking, or whether they correspond with those required by the customers and the quality standards to be met. Knowledge has to be judged not only on its contents, but also on the applicability and span of application. Learning processes in organizations are both social and collective. Working on projects, rising to challenges and providing for continuous flow might be better and more effective learning strategies than those methods based on a search for deficiencies.

Managing core competencies

competencies

An organization examining its competencies needs to realize that maintaining and improving the capability of an organization to perform is a central strategic activity for the realization of a competitive advantage. The idea of the learning organization and the need for the knowledge of individual employees to be embedded within the organization as a whole is another key consideration to keep in mind.

Hamel and Prahalad (1994) have drawn attention to the tenuous existence of big corporations such as IBM, Philips, Daimler-Benz and Boeing, which for years have held a solid position in their markets, but also seem to have forgotten to keep their eyes on the markets of tomorrow. Innovation and renewal are crucial and require the internal organization to be looked at through fresh eyes, especially where the creation of competitive advantage is concerned.

A prerequisite for this is that organizations learn to bundle their core competencies.

In contrast to traditional concepts, the resource-based perspective on organizations stresses the internal resources of a firm more than the market as such. One key question that is likely to arise is how competitive advantage can be gained, and more particularly, how a sustainable advantage can be created.

competitive advantage

Competitive advantage arises when a firm implements a value-creating strategy that is not simultaneously being implemented by any current or potential competitors. This is only possible if the organizations differ with respect to their available resources (heterogeneity), especially where these resources are not completely mobile. If every organization had similar essential resources (homogeneity) and these resources were so mobile that they could be used freely by everyone, a competitive advantage based on resources could never arise. Any resource that might demonstrate that it had a certain advantage could be used by competitors, imitated or be taken over in one way or another.
To gain a sustainable competitive advantage, resources have to meet certain conditions. Resources need to:

- add value to the organization,
- be unique or scarce,
- be difficult to imitate,
- be hard to substitute by other resources, and
- be applicable in many fields.

Human potential can obviously be a source of sustainable advantage, just as a unique technology or an advanced information system, particularly when human potential is important for the organization's strategies, and where there are unique knowledge systems and skills which cannot be learned simply or substituted by a machine or computer. In such situations, the personnel factor is essential for maintaining a position of strategic advantage. Retaining this advantage via advanced forms of management is crucial. Knowing and exploiting core competencies is an extremely important aspect of organizational strategy formulation. Hamel and Prahalad use the expression 'strategic fit': the fit between changes in strategy and the organization's potential. In their view, core competencies are 'the collective learning within the organization, especially how to coordinate diverse production skills and integrate multiple streams of technologies.'

strategic fit

7.7 Human resource development: an integral concept and a set of instruments

Human resource management within an organization includes the way in which personnel are selected, hired, educated, developed, promoted, salaried, fired and retired. This managerial area covers a whole area of human relations for which both behavioral science and technical administrative institutes have developed systems and methods. Human resource management (HRM) is both a concept and a set of instruments to realize the organization's ultimate goals (see Fig 7.5). HRM is based on the organization's strategies and the structure these give rise to as well as on function demands and on the organization's culture. It needs to be an integral part of the total management process.

human relations

Management has many means of availing itself of human potential at its disposal. The various components of HRM and the relationship between these components, in which the ultimate performance is a dependent variable, are shown in the HRM cycle (Fig 7.6).

HRM cycle

It needs to be clearly realized by HRM managers that employees are the source of all of the prosperity in which the organization wants to invest. It is not so much capital in a financial sense, but rather the quality of the 'human capital' which determines the success of the organization. Quality in a broad sense can be viewed as the level of knowledge and skills, and especially how these are structured into the organizational relationships and put at the disposal of the organization. Rewards, training and non-material rewards are some of management's control instruments.
Harnessing human potential requires the creation of facilities which enable the development of initiative and ideas. What the individual employee wants is a way of being able to both realize the organization's goals as well as a way of furthering his own career.

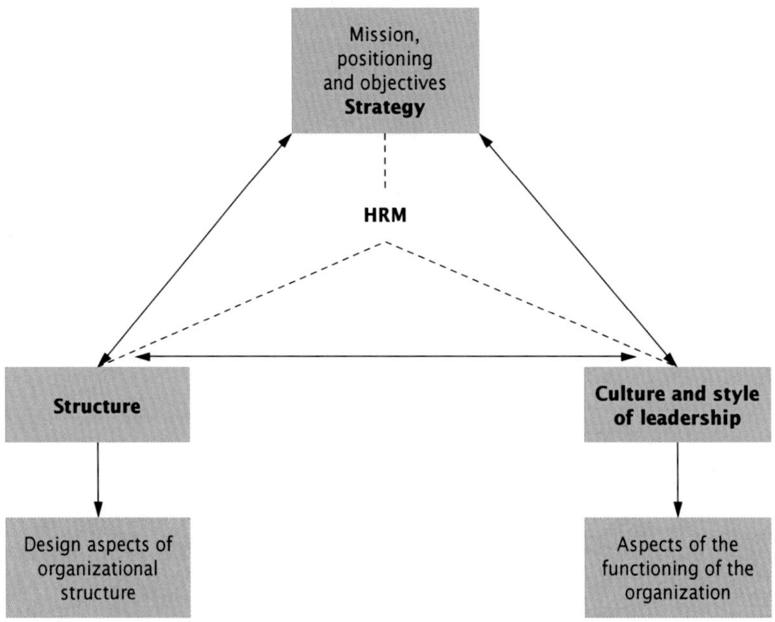

Figure 7.5
HRM in relation to the central problems of the management process

7.7.1 *HRM: characteristics*

HRM

HRM has three main characteristics:

1. It sees work as a source of inspiration, action and result.
2. It values the contribution of the employee.
3. It is social policy integrated into the organization's policies.

Central to HRM is the creation of material and non-material conditions to motivate and stimulate employees to take the initiative themselves, directed by the organization's goals and their own ambitions. The goal is for the employee himself to play an active role in planning his career and assume responsibility for his job. He should expect the organization to help him realize both the organization's goals and his own potential.

Employees who have co-controlling potential can make an essential contribution to the customer-oriented functioning of the organization. They can help the organization to react more quickly to change and attain its goals more effectively. To achieve this, the organizational culture will have to be accepting of small, relatively autonomous operating units and should not stand in the way of internal entrepreneurship. The relationship between social policy and organization policy will demand further integration.

In traditional notions, where social policy was reduced to a package of work conditions, this could easily mean the failure of new organizational policies because of their disregard for human potential: insufficient preparation for changing tasks, little identification with organizational goals and resistance to change. They also carried the potential for developments in areas such as labor morale, social legislation, agreements relating to labor time reductions, employment planning and education to have an increasingly disruptive effect on organizational policy.

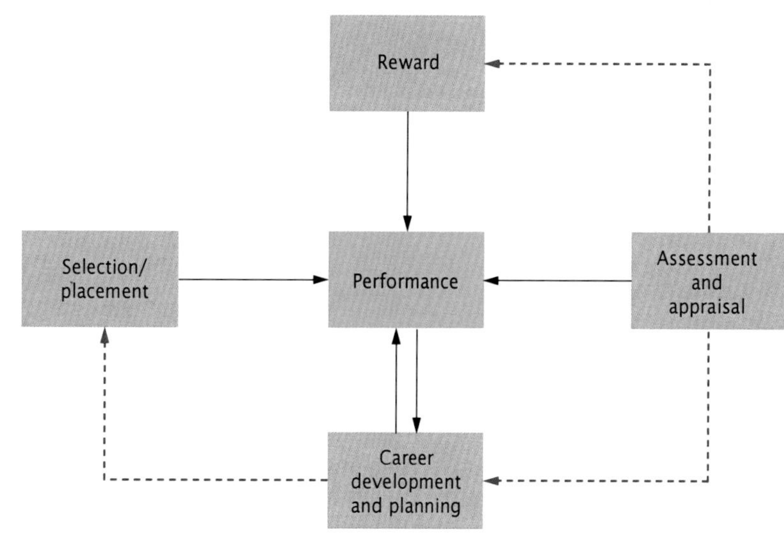

Figure 7.6
The HRM cycle ('Michigan model')

Using HRM, the impact of external influences can be filtered throughout the organization and external developments can be seen in the light of organizational needs. Organizational goals, aspirations and development potential of employees should all have equal standing and organizational relationships wherein aspiration, creativity and operational alertness can be shown to full advantage must be created.

7.7.2 HRM: management of personnel and instruments

The personnel process includes quantitative and qualitative determination of personnel needs, the recruiting, selecting and appointing of personnel as well as the setting of work conditions, the educating, evaluating and promoting of personnel, the co-determining of the working climate, and the transfer, retirement, and firing of individual members of staff. The personnel process is directly related to the other organizational processes, but has an integrating and supporting function.

human resources management

Human resources management assumes the use of an integrated and coherent system of personnel management and personnel development instruments and systems. The managing of intake, flow and departure of employees are central issues. In each of these three phases, management has a number of personnel management instruments at its disposal. To conduct integrated personnel management, the personnel instruments used in the various phases have to be well attuned to each other. Managing the departure of employees is just as important as managing their intake and flow. In the case of flow, there will be both vertical flow to higher functions and horizontal flow to other functions at an equal organizational level.

Strategy, preferred structure and organizational culture will have to inform top management's choices with respect to the various personnel stages. It is assumed that management will obey the rules and laws which protect the employees, leaving sufficient room for their own approaches (see chapters 1 and 6). They will formulate a social policy and implement it. The operational activities which arise from this are known as personnel work.

personnel work

Personnel work is all of the activities performed by personnel managers, including activities which have to do with social insurance legislation, application of the labor laws, handling of legislation in the field of the safety, health and welfare of employees, and application of legislation relating to participation (for example, by works councils).

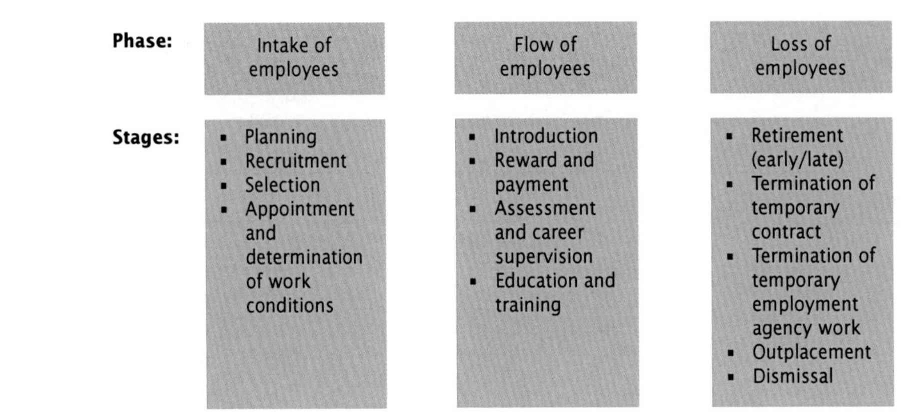

Figure 7.7 *Personnel management and personnel instruments*

HRM: high tech, but first and foremost, people work

Electronic HRM is rapidly finding its way into many an organization. However, it will not replace HRM as we know it. Electronic HRM, or e-HRM for short, can back up HRM and HR processes (recruitment, selection, assessment and so on) via the Internet and intranet, and as such has a facilitating role to play.

e-HRM

Essentially, HRM is simply people work: managers and employees in dialogue with each other as business partners (and where necessary, given support by HRM consultants or specialists (see 6.5.3).

Intake: activities before and on taking up the position

prognosis of personnel needs

The first step is a prognosis of personnel needs and time frames. Department plans and the organization's long-term development plans will show the need for particular kinds of managerial and operational employees over time. The present personnel files and the future personnel needs have to be closely scrutinized. When this scrutiny is offset against future plans, to what extent external recruitment has to take place and when it occurs can be estimated, and then estimates made of the need for internal recruitment and promotion.

personnel planning

Personnel planning requires certain contributing factors to be taken into account: for example, work hours, holidays, work hour reduction, budget available, absenteeism, turnover, absenteeism due to internal or external training and so on. In the short- and middle to long-term, these factors must be incorporated into the figures. Each department's planning is also determined by customer orders, production capacity and any rush orders. If, for example, there is a high level of absenteeism, more people need to appear on the books than the job actually calls for.

Recruitment

Recruitment involves enlisting certain candidates for certain functions. The personnel department will often recruit employees for 'lower' functions via certain standard procedures, preferably in consultation with the department in which the employees will be working. The recruiting of higher managerial staff for key functions within the organization or for top managerial positions does not often take place through the personnel department. External firms or 'head hunters' may be called in to advise management or the board of directors.

job description

An important document in the preparation of a recruitment procedure is the job description. A job description provides possible candidates for the function with information about what has to be done in that function. Advertisements for personnel need to show information in relation to the particular function. This information can be derived from the job description and translated as accurately as possible into function requirements. This means that the job description has to set out how the function has to be fulfilled, and what the individual should know and should be able to do in order to carry out the job successfully.

advertisements for personnel

QUEST FOR TALENT – BUT WHERE IS IT?

Future higher professional education students who have set their sights on a career with Shell or Philips would be well advised to consider chosing a commercial, managerial or specific technical study direction. Philips needs a lot of biochemical, laboratory and biomedical eggheads for its new focus on Life Sciences. Shell has an ongoing need for mechanical engineers.

Source: *Het Financieele Dagblad*, 18 December 2009

In a good personnel ad, in addition to the name and nature of the company or institution, the location and size of the organization, a good personnel ad should also show the name of the function, a job description, the job demands and work conditions. The name and telephone number of a contact person need to be mentioned and it is wise to provide candidates with information about the application procedures and now they should respond (including the closing date). All this provides an applicant with the information to enable him or her to submit a purposeful meaningful application.

electronic recruitment

One of the most frequently used forms of e-HRM is electronic recruitment. In virtually all organizations with an Internet site, that site gives at least some degree of prominence to job vacancies or 'working with us'. Organizations are increasingly trying to make their site as attractive as they can by offering interactive tests of motivation or interest or by providing a virtual tour/stroll through the company. The interested visitor can thus form an impression of the organization as potential employer.

vacancy sites

However, organizations that want to publicize their employment vacancies via the Internet can also make use of a number of general vacancy sites. In the Netherlands, Newmonday (formally known as Intermediair), Monsterboard, JobNews, Banennet and Clickwork are the best known. Job sites tend to focus on the more highly trained workforce.

Selection

Selection is the process by which the most suitable person is chosen from those who are eligible. 'Suitable' in this case does not only refer to professional skills, but also to personality factors. After the first interview, a candidate may be asked to undergo a psychological aptitude test in order to form as complete a picture as possible of his or her capabilities. Such a test is considered only part of the process since it does not provide hard guarantees as such.
The pre-selection tools consist of the following:

- Data relating to the past: education, work experience, reasons for change of job and so on
- Interviews: a good impression of a person can be obtained by engaging him or her in conversation. Information already supplied can be explained in full.
- Tests:
  - intelligence test: aimed at measuring the learning capacities and the general development of the candidate
  - performance test: aimed at testing the professional skill of the applicant and problem-solving and decision-making ability based on simulated or real situations
  - job test: testing someone's familiarity with professional language, ability to handle tools and so on
  - aptitude test: the emphasis is placed on investigating whether the candidate has the capacity to learn the specific requirements of the job
  - personality test: the personal characteristics of the applicant are investigated.

SHELL'S REORGANIZATION IS A RISKY BUSINESS

Immediately after Peter Voser took office as Shell's chairman of the board in July 2009 he announced that there would be staff cutbacks. To that end a central coordinated reorganization process was initiated. All 102,000 employees have had to reapply for their own jobs or those of immediate colleagues via a complex and impersonal process using the intranet. Those found suitable may stay on; the others will be sacked. The bosses will not have the final say on who goes and who stays, warned Ms Lia Belilos, HR director for the Netherlands. Naturally, they are not be allowed to pass on any information about possible competitors for the jobs either.

Source: *Het Financieele Dagblad*, 4 December 2009

digital selection

While recruitment via the Internet is common, the same cannot be said for 'digital' selection. The ICT company CMG provides one example of the selection opportunities available to HRM. Those who wish to put in a job application to CMG can send in their CV online. If CMG is interested in the applicant, he or she can log into a 'job chat' interview site at an arranged time and using a user's name and password. They wait in a virtual waiting room until they are called up, and each candidate then has half an hour to 'speak' to a CMG interlocutor. The final round of the selection process is, however, still just face-to-face, even at CMG.

job chat

The 'job chat' can also be used to acquaint candidates with their future colleagues. By making use of a webcam, they can also actually see each other. In particular, for companies that operate internationally, such virtual job interviews offer savings on travel and accommodation costs and a speeding up of the procedure.

headhunting

With most job sites (both general and specific), the employer can obtain some help in pre-selecting the candidates by making use of pre-screening options, though the process is not very refined. Futurestep(.com), an initiative of the 'headhunting' agency Korn/Ferry is one example of a general job site that does select. The site visitor can register as a candidate free of charge with Futurestep. In addition to filling in his or her personal details, one condition is that he or she perform tests of various kinds.

Not even making use of all of these tools will provide an absolutely sure way of getting the right candidate for the place, although they certainly provide a degree of certainty.

knowledge and skills relevant to the function

It is very important that knowledge and skills relevant to the function be available to the selectors during the selection procedure. This is crucial in determining which of hypothetical candidates A, B or C is most suitable. By this stage it will be more or less known whether a candidate has the qualities to perform well in a function and so will be able to at least perform to meet minimum performance standards. The departmental management will be relying on this. It is also important to test notions to do with task fulfillment. Differences in notions about task fulfillment will, in general, lead to conflict. It is therefore wise to find out in advance whether people can work together well. Candidates have to be compared according to standards that have been set in advance. For a specific function, this means that all candidates should take the professional skill test in the same practice situation, or take a standard psychological test. References may also be required and/or work history checked out. In the case of applications for government positions, in several countries a 'statement of public behavior' is required. A medical test is often a standard element. The personnel selection interview is the final opportunity for obtaining extra information and for making a judgment about more or less equally suitable candidates. This is often done by a recruitment and selection committee that then has to reach a decision as to the most suitable candidate.

Recruitment and selection of employees is not regulated by law, although attempts have been made to develop certain codes of conduct. An organization clearly has a lot of freedom to determine how it goes about recruiting new employees. Paying due consideration to the

interests of the organization and of applicants is, of course, one of the main priorities. Personnel selection methods frequently use the so-called assessment center method. Assessment is evaluation or diagnosis. The assessment center method includes several assessment instruments, including a 'situational test' to gather information about the candidates quickly, with an eye to appointing, promoting or providing employees with further training. Assessment centers are increasingly being used to detect the strengths and weaknesses of current employees. Candidates for a management position may be asked to do a part of the job in set stages during a short period of time (perhaps half a day). A candidate may be asked to engage in serious conversation with an employee (played by a trained professional actor) or deal with mail relating to a fictitious managerial situation as quickly as possible (perhaps as many as twenty letters). The candidate receives a large variety of written documents in the in-basket: telephone notes, scrawls, memos written by top managers, parts of a policy document, personnel documents (letter of application, evaluation and promotion report), letters of complaints from customers, and so on. The candidate has to decide which of these should be dealt with, and how to go about it. The candidate has two or three hours to indicate what he or she would do and why.
The managers/evaluators observe the candidate, consider their decisions and try to reach collective agreement on him or her. This particular test is then combined with others (perhaps a combination of intelligence test + interview + in-basket situational test). The result can be expected to predict at least to a certain extent how the candidate will function as a manager.

Appointment and setting of employment conditions

Suitable employment conditions consisting of rewards and payment for work are of course, one requirement of a good personnel policy. Employment conditions can include holiday arrangements, working times and breaks, retirement regulations and secondary labor conditions such as travel and cost reimbursements and so on. Rewards and payment are important components of work conditions. Special attention is paid to rewards in Section 7.8. Generally speaking, even in these times, higher management functions are rarely filled by women. This is changing, however. More young graduate women are gradually being taken into the trainee programs of large organizations. A number of organizations are taking measures aimed at encouraging young women to embark on careers or at least not abandon them. Pregnancy leave, job sharing, child care, bonuses for re-entering the work force and so on are all measures that improve women's work chances.

part-time work

Part-time work is work carried out for a set number of hours a week/month. In middle and higher functions, little part-time work is available. Job sharing refers to two people sharing one job. It is becoming increasingly widespread.

job sharing

Job sharing in higher functions often requires full time work. Sharing responsibility between employees occupying the same managerial function has, in practice, been a source of disagreement and confusion. This can be prevented, however, by reaching agreement about the approach and style of leadership, by good work planning, by encouraging exchange of employees and so on. There may also be a lingering fear, perhaps reinforced by the prevailing work culture, that you need to work full time to keep your job. For many who have to work full time, it may be difficult to accept that someone who spends less time at work nevertheless has a greater influence on that organization.
Such a practice may be acceptable for directors, consultants in special services and similar, but not for employees in normal line functions, or not yet.

Flow: activities during employment

The introduction of the new employee into the organization is often crucial to the new employee's motivation and view of the organization. The goals of a good introduction procedure are as follows:

- Show the new employee what he or she will mean to the organization
- Meet colleagues and managers with whom he or she will be working

- Make clear what is expected of the new employee's performance within the department and the organization as a whole.

introduction

During the introduction, a new employee will be given the chance to get to know the nature/peculiarities of the organization. This is important, since the new employee will need to adapt his or her behavior to suit the culture of the organization and the department. The new employee has to feel at ease to be able to work productively. Introduction to the organization may be taken care of by someone from the personnel department and could take the form of a general introduction, an introduction to management personnel, an outline of the organizational culture, an outline of house rules and a tour through the organization. The departmental introduction is the responsibility of the departmental heads and is taken care of by them or by one of their immediate colleagues. After the departmental introduction, the employee has to learn the ropes. The process of learning the ropes only gets underway after acquaintance has been made with new colleagues and management and it has been explained how one works in the department and what role has been envisaged for the new employee. Learning the ropes is learning to do the job in the way which is usual in the department. It is an important stage because new employees are often assessed after only a short period of time. New employees have to be able to demonstrate their ability to do the job and do it responsibly. A good training program thus consists of three important components:

- Choosing training tasks
- Spreading these tasks over the training period
- Supervising, controlling and correcting the way the task is performed

An introduction is also referred to as socialization. Socialization can be facilitated by ICT and an intranet application: for example, by providing information about departments, working hours, terms of employment and so on. An e-introduction can additionally take the new employee on a virtual guided tour (a tour via the intranet). The new employee clicks on whatever video images and written texts about the company's organizational components he or she would like to explore. The 'community' (the group that communicates via the intranet) can also make it possible for new employees to meet each other and to exchange experiences.

Assessment and career supervision

career coaching

Career coaching is essential to satisfactory job performance. It should take the form of feedback on whether the employee is meeting the organization's original expectations and listening to what the employee has to say about his or her expectations. Coaching should be directed at the individual employee and provide him or her with information and the ability to develop his or her capabilities further. Assessment of someone's function within the organization should consist of a mutual exchange of thoughts about that function. It should take the form of periodical attention to how a function is being fulfilled, the employee's strong and weak points and what changes are possible and desired. An assessment can lead to a better insight into the employee's own potential and his developmental potential within the organization. To be most effective, assessment needs to be followed by regular work discussions with the manager or with other departmental employees about work, results, progress, problems and such topics. This should ensure that the contents of the function are described precisely and that clear task agreements are made. It is important that what the employee wants to do and the task he or she has been given be attuned to each other. If there is a discrepancy between the job requirements and how these are being fulfilled, the task package and promotional expectations may have to be adjusted, a different position for the employee may have to be found, the employee may have to undertake further training or some other measure.

assessment

It is a good idea to make a distinction between the following three aspects of assessment during the assessment itself:

- Performance assessment: this should be directed at judging recent employee performance.
- Potential assessment: this should be directed at judging the future potential of the employee to develop his or her knowledge and skills.

- Assessment of whether the employee can be shifted around: this is directed at providing insight into the question of whether an employee can function as well in another function at the same level, or perhaps perform even better.

It is important not to confuse performance assessment with career supervision.
Career supervision is not an assessment method as such but rather an assessment based on work-related events. It is primarily directed towards making any necessary changes to the way the job itself is being performed. Problems and bottlenecks are discussed, as well as possible solutions. In such a conversation the following may come under discussion: job conditions, possibilities for task enlargement and career prospects. However, the main emphasis will be on ironing out any problems that have arisen and discussing how to avoid them in the future. Agreement must be reached. A follow-up conversation can ascertain to what extent the agreement has led to improvement in the employee's performance. If it appears that the work cannot be done properly because the right resources are missing, other action will have to be taken. A career supervision discussion is open in character and in view of the fact that it is concerned with exchange of information, improvement in communication, motivating the employee and encouraging positive changes to the job, a lot is required of the manager involved.
Research shows that employees whose performance is assessed regularly are more productive than colleagues who do not receive feedback on their performance. By the end of the 1990s, measurements of productivity were still showing that performance increases as soon as it starts to be measured. Mayo had already observed this in his famous 1930 Hawthorne experiments on organizational change (see Section 1.1.4).

Hawthorne experiments on organizational change

In recent times and in the context of change and coaching in organizations, '360° feedback' has been recommended as an instrument. This is an instrument practiced by Shell, Unilever, Philips, KLM, IBM, Xerox and GE Plastics, amongst others. With 360° feedback, an employee's managers, colleagues, customers and suppliers provide feedback on his or her performance. The employee in question also judges his or her own performance. The name refers to the circle of individuals who make up the group. It is an excellent way of showing someone how he or she is seen by others. Becoming aware of both hidden qualities and blind spots also provides a basis for an improvement in performance. An employee may, for example, rate his or her contact skills much more highly than others in the environment. Realizing this is the first step to improvement. The employee often finds that his or her self-image has to be adjusted.

360° feedback

The 360° feedback process consists of the following steps:

Step 1 Together with the direct manager, the employee chooses seven criteria crucial to successful performance (for example: customer focus, independence, commercial attitude).

Step 2 The manager and the employee draw up a list of people who have insight into the performance of the employee concerned.

Step 3 A questionnaire relating to each criteria is delivered (on disk) to all of the people on the list.

Step 4 The results are processed and the outcomes shown in the form of a histogram. The score given by each person on the list is shown.

Step 5 On the basis of the results there is discussion relating to what the employee should do to improve his or her performance.

E-assessment and e-development

Employee assessment is important. After all, not only do salaries and salary increases depend largely on assessment but assessments also provide a means of gauging the areas in which employees need to develop. The intranet can provide a means of aiding the assessment process in various ways. Here, too, the provision of information is the first step. The intranet can provide managers and employees with information about the procedure, the criteria, ways of preparing for the assessment and so on. The intranet can also be used to view past information about employee assessment, and even to generate state-of-the-art automatic analyses and reports based on the sum total of assessments of any one organizational unit (comparing it with other units or with the previous year).

360° assessment

A digital 360° assessment similar to that described above is another way of facilitating the assessment process. It usually involves an assessment of an employee by colleagues drawn from the hierarchy (superiors, co-workers and those in subordinate positions) though also clients and suppliers if applicable. These colleagues can be selected by, for example, clicking on the 'who's who' column on the intranet, and the program ensures that they receive the questionnaire, and if necessary are reminded to fill it in and then return it. The various assessments are then processed and an aggregate made of the scores, then they are filed in a personnel assessment database, put into diagrammatic form and supplied with a commentary, and then distributed to interested parties.

e-development

E-development refers to the e-HRM applications that assist employees in their development and includes telelearning, virtual learning, online learning, e-ducation, cyber learning and Web-based learning (WBL).

virtual corporate school

Some organizations (mainly the big international ones) expand a virtual learning environment so that it becomes a virtual corporate school or university (a virtual corporate academy). An important part of the education and training can then take the form of telelearning, and include such things as virtual lectures that can be followed online by employees spread over the various locations.

e-coaching

Of the many e-development possibilities, e-coaching deserves a mention. This involves the intranet (or the Internet) being used in coaching situations that take the form of regular conversations about the employee's work situation, personal development or career preferences.

Demotion and function relief

demotion

Demotion is a lowering of rank and involves the removal from a higher to a lower function. Demotion can also be used as a policy instrument to encourage managerial staff (including members of the managerial team or the board of management) who have been employed by the company for many years to take a step back as they approach retirement. As a formal tool, demotion offers managers a way of influencing employee behavior.

The desire to accept a function at a lower level increases as we grow older, as does the desire to work less. The will to work harder in order to be promoted yet again is also less pronounced among older managers.

lower function name

While younger managers are usually prepared to change jobs, this is not the case with older managers. The tendency to accept a demotion will increase under such circumstances. It is a different story if this is accompanied by a 'lower' function name or title. Whatever the age or managerial level, there is likely to be an aggressive reaction.

If someone has to choose between working in another function with a 10 per cent salary cut or early retirement with a 40 per cent salary cut, research has shown that 70 per cent of managers over 55 years of age will opt for another function. Spare time is apparently less attractive than financial rewards.

A straight out demotion is more easily accepted when the employee is older. If not done with care or not chosen voluntarily, demotion is, of course, more than just a step lower on the hierarchical ladder: it is experienced as degradation and is accompanied by negative psychological consequences for the person involved.

The practice is accepted in the Scandinavian countries, however. In these countries, older workers work longer than elsewhere, there is greater mobility, there is more training available and salaries rise less rapidly the older the worker is than in a number of other European countries, including the Netherlands. As part of the policy of *sustainable availability*, demotion is an acceptable principle in the Scandinavian countries.

If demotion is experienced as degradation and this feeling is reinforced, employees will feel

workability euthanasia badly treated: so-called 'workability euthanasia'. They will react bitterly and paint the organization as a risky place to work. However, demotion can be treated openly and information about future possibilities freely given and/or help in finding a new position elsewhere via outplacement together with supervision of the transfer. In a demotion in which degradation is felt to play a part, it is especially important not to increase the pressure by lowering the salary. The salary problem is a crucial issue in demotion. Even if someone can adjust to loss of status and power, a decrease in income remains a bitter pill. There are some ways of lessening the pain, including ensuring that the employee keeps his salary, perhaps at a frozen level, and trying to adjust the salary to the salary scale of a lower level in a creative way. The result may be demotion being accepted as an element of the organization's culture.

relief Demotion can also be experienced as a relief by older employees. Although not yet fully appreciated by Western cultures, careers follow a natural cycle of growth and decline. Demotion offers the opportunity to step aside or step back within the organization, sometimes in a staff function, sometimes via job sharing, thus reducing its negative effects.

flexible retirement Flexible retirement is another possibility. Flexible retirement is a system of retirement in which the retirement date is not set at the year the employee turns 65. Instead, the employee is given the choice of working for a shorter period or for a longer one, which allows for varying rates of diminishing vitality among employees. If the atmosphere surrounding demotion is open and sincere and a respected board or management member asks for demotion for personal reasons or wants to withdraw from an important function at, for example, the age of 55, then the demotional policy is likely to be more easily accepted by the organization. What is important is that there is clarity about the age limit and that no exceptions be made.

Education and training

Education and training are also important aspects of the personnel function. For the individual employee, further educational training is particularly important for his or her promotion prospects. Education and training usually has a professional and an organizational aspect. It may involve learning the ropes, finding out how the organization functions or obtaining an insight into how much potential for growth there is among the employees. Education and training can vary from professional technical education in the classroom of a company school,

training on the job training by actually doing the job ('training on the job'), to the enlargement of general professional skills and general development or preparation for a managerial position within the organization. In the last case, attention will have to be paid to associating with people as individuals and handling of groups, questions of cost control, insight into the workings of the organizational structure and so on. Some frequently used training methods are the holding of lectures and discussions, the giving of instructions, doing case studies and so on.

Management development

Management development is particularly important for future management. Young managers have to be educated by, on the one hand systematic coaching by older managers, and on the other by external education and training. Management development will always be strongly determined by the level of expertise of young managers and by the level they have to attain in time. Systematic management development can take place within a personnel department at the level the highest management level of the organization actually requires. In fact,

management development management development is the responsibility of the highest management levels, because what it is in fact doing is ensuring its own continuity at the various levels.

Young and promising future managers who have been selected to go through a special education program with the prospects of future top functions in mind and who, because of that, may receive preferential treatment, are sometimes referred to as 'crown princes'. In large organizations, a reservoir of potential managers has to be created initially through, for example, the recruiting of trainees. Once they have been selected and are undergoing education and training, there is often the expectation that from this 'nursery' (see Section 7.9) some real 'toppers' will emerge. This expectation can, however, also work to the disadvantage of those involved. The goal of management development is to ensure that managerial positions

within the organization are filled by the right person and that there are enough to choose from. Management development involves doing an estimation of the need for future management (in numbers and quality), noting the interest among present managerial employees, registration of the performance of individual managers (by assessment and career discussions) and drawing up career planning and management education plans.
As such, management development involves taking employee wishes and capabilities into account as well as finding out what the organization needs in order to keep abreast of societal developments.

Departure

Middle to long-term planning of personnel needs must take account not only of what positions need to be filled, but whether the right people in terms of age and education are available to fill the positions. This will have to be reviewed anew every year. Vacancies can arise through retirement, discharge, replacement or death. Vacancies can sometimes be filled by internal promotion, though recruitment of new personnel may be needed.

vacancies

DEPARTING IN STYLE

It happens sometimes: you're sick of your job or the company you work for and a work opportunity beckons elsewhere. Make sure that your exit is a graceful one, advises the British HR bureau The Mind Gymn. *Chat before you scat.* If you want to leave because you feel undervalued or you find your work boring, have a talk with your boss first. It may just do the trick. If you are absolutely sure that you are leaving, don't beat about the bush: just say that you're leaving. Do tell your boss and your colleagues the reasons for your decision: this will make it easier for them to understand and accept it. If you are *fired*, control your emotions and don't explode in anger. You will retain your self-esteem and this will make a better impression on others – and so it will be good for your reputation and the network you are part of. Another tip: whether you go willingly or not, stay *connected*. Maintain contact with the company and with your former fellow colleagues.

Source: *Management Today*, July 2009

If vacancies are likely and new function demands are formulated in time, they can be filled by targeted training of the existing personnel. Sometimes, however, downsizing may be necessary. This can be the consequence of a reduction in demand or have more fundamental causes, perhaps associated with mechanization or automation. Downsizing can be tackled by natural attrition, labor time reduction and early retirement. For such measures, figures relating to employee age and expected age of retirement must be available.

natural attrition
early retirement

Outplacement is a whole series of activities/services, both internal and external to the company, that exist to help someone who has been given notice to find another job outside the organization, but preferably similar to the previous employment. The situation may arise because of the effects of the so-called Peter principle: the experience that an employee promoted to a higher and more demanding position based on good performances in a previous position will not necessarily meet expectations since he may already have reached his natural level of competence in that previous function. Consequently there is a natural tendency within organizations to allow employees to stay in the job until they become incompetent. Outplacement offices then take on the task of finding otherwise respected staff members a new job. Employees from higher and middle management are often the 'victims.' Besides the job itself, their status and esteem among friends and family is under pressure. If everything goes as it should, the outplacement process starts even before the people involved know that discharge hangs over their heads. In the first contacts between an organization and an outplacement office, agreements are reached about the way in which the employee concerned will be supervised, how payment is to be arranged, and so on. Then follows the moment that

outplacement
Peter principle

the discharge is announced, after which the outplacement process proper can commence.

personnel process

Controlling the personnel process is part of a managing process that must be meaningful at both the policy as well as at the operational level. Giving meaning to the personnel function is one of the responsibilities of a company's or institution's top management. Tasks which belong to this can be delegated to the personnel department. The execution of part of the operational work can be delegated to departmental line managers in collaboration with the personnel department. The assessment of an employee, for example, takes place with the department by the department chief, while the assessment system and the accompanying procedure are designed and monitored by the personnel department.

assessment system

Exhibit 7.1

Cultural traditions in management development

There is no best way of tackling management development. If we look at how those with high potential are trained, it will be found that different organizations have different traditions. We have labeled these according to national stereotypes – the Japanese model, the Latin European approach, the Germanic tradition, and the Anglo-Dutch model. There is great diversity in American patterns. Some American firms are 'Latin' in their approach, while other European firms follow the Japanese pattern.

The Japanese Model

The model that emerged in large companies such as Matsushita, Sanyo, and Nissan after the Second World War was based on the recruitment of elite cohorts and a competition (a tournament of elimination), after which the winners are ushered into senior positions. The educational system in Japan fosters the progressive filtering of elite achievers, and it is from the select few at Tokyo and other top universities that high-potential individuals are recruited. Management potential has thus already been identified before the person is employed by a company.

The Japanese system is highly competitive, though widely held beliefs about Japanese lifelong employment and seniority-based promotion are distorted clichés of reality. Most firms apply the system to their foreign subsidiaries, and while the shop-floor climate of Japanese factories abroad has a favorable public image, the managerial development system tends to be viewed as alien. Western managers do not have the same patience or long-term orientation, and Japanese firms have found it difficult to recruit local managerial talent in other countries (this has been described as the Achilles heel of Japanese management practices in an era of globalization).

The Latin Model

It is the structure of management development in Latin Europe that most approximates that in Japan, though without the systematic tracking of cohorts. To take France as an example, selection of potential top managers also takes place at entry, mostly on the basis of elite educational qualifications. Studies have shown that graduates of the three top 'grandes écoles' (the elite engineering schools) who choose an industrial career have a 90 percent probability of ending up as president of a company. The only unknown factor is the size and importance of the company.

The career progression of these individuals is the same 'tournament' as it is in Japan, though one that is more political and without systematic norms. It is a competitive struggle for achievement, selling of oneself, and building alliances, and is encapsulated in the social game theory of the French sociologist Michel Crozier subtly combined with the camaraderie of association of a mafia of fellow peers.

The Germanic Model

The Germanic tradition (embracing to some extent Switzerland and certain Scandinavian and Dutch firms) is characterized by formal apprenticeship and greater attachment to expertise-based functional career paths. For skilled and blue-collar employees, apprenticeship is a well-rooted Germanic tradition: a two- to five-year period of on-the-job training, courses on

company practices and policies, and training in partnership with local technical or trade schools. However, even graduates undergo a two-year apprenticeship – a period of job rotation through the enterprise accompanied by training.
For those with the depth of education that is provided by a doctoral degree in particular, this may ultimately lead into a board-level position where the disadvantages of a functional orientation are balanced by a collegiate sharing of responsibility.
But just as there are two industrial Japans – the former Zaibatsu concerns of international renown and the lesser firms – so there are two Germanies, that of the large established firms and that of the smaller-sized companies; and two Frances, that of the establishment and that of the self-made entrepreneurs. In Germany some are also finding the functional or technical orientations of big business to be unattractive, and leave for positions in smaller companies (the *Mittelstand*) where the responsibilities are likely to be more wide-ranging in nature.

The Anglo-Dutch Model

The wide-ranging model of management development is most strongly rooted in the Anglo-Saxon cultures and in some Dutch firms, joined more recently by the Scandinavians. If there is a model for transnational firms, this approximates it. Entry is less elitist, with most graduates being recruited locally for specific technical or functional jobs. During the early career years (about the first eight years at ICI), these graduates are expected to perform well and climb the ladder of their functional hierarchies.
Around the age of 30, after the testing years, the human resource management problem is to identify those individuals who have potential (a concept that is difficult to operationalize. Since Japanese-style systematic performance appraisal is less traditional, companies resort to a variety of devices for the identification of potential. For some US firms, the MBA diploma has become an entry ticket onto the high-potential development ladder, thus approximating the elitist entry pattern of Japanese and Latin companies. Other firms have invested in assessment centers: two- to three-day simulations of managerial situations where the performance and qualities of aspirants can be observed and evaluated by psychologists and trained managers. Most firms, however, rely to a greater or lesser degree on the collective judgment of top managers in the particular subsidiary.

Source: *Transnational Management*, Bartlett and Ghoshal (1992).

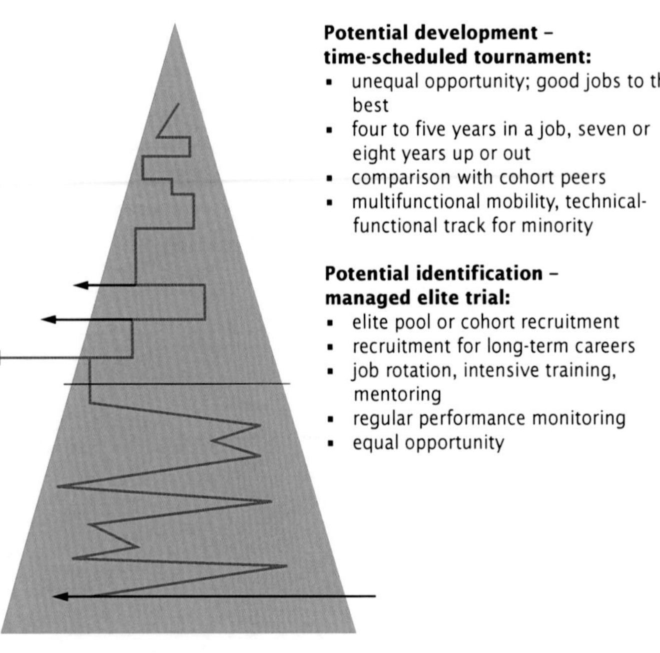

Figure A
Elite cohort approach: the 'Japanese' model

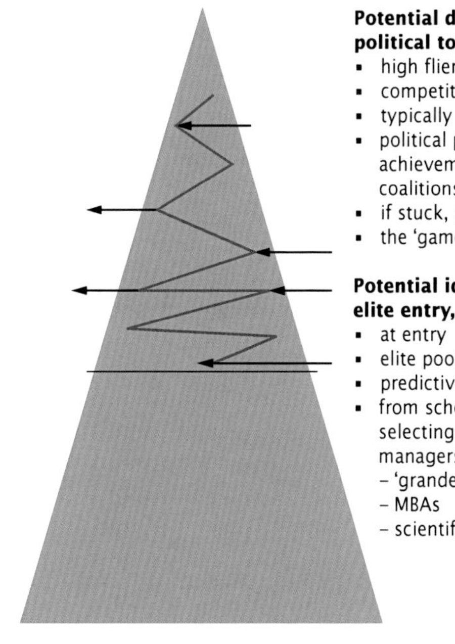

Figure B
Elite political approach: the 'Latin' model

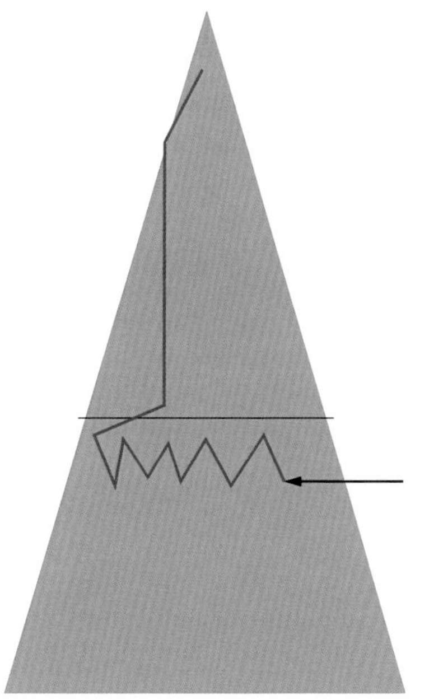

Figure C
Functional approach: the 'Germanic' model

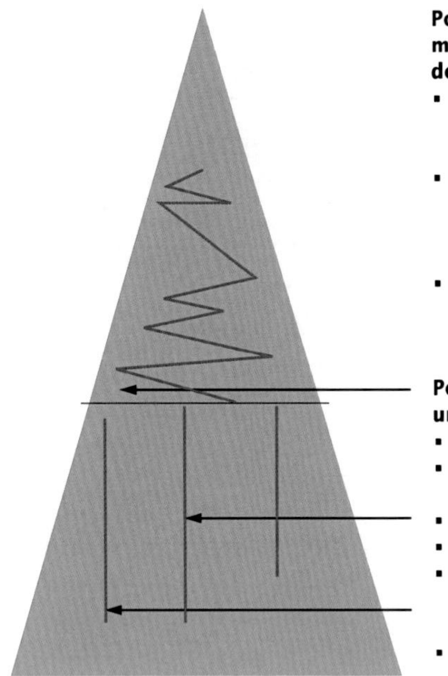

Figure D
Managed development approach: the 'Anglo-Dutch MNC' model

7.8 Payment systems and salary structures

types of rewards

The types of rewards available to managerial and operational employees in organizations are more varied than is generally assumed. The direct rewards are clear-cut. But there are also indirect reimbursements and non-financial rewards. Fig. 7.8 sets out the various types of rewards (Robbins, 1979, p. 365). These may be shared out among individuals, groups or organizations.

intrinsic forms of reward
extrinsic forms of reward

The more intrinsic forms of reward derive from the work itself and the satisfaction it provides. Extrinsic forms of reward may take the form of direct reimbursements, indirect reimbursements and non-financial rewards. An employee expects direct and indirect reimbursements to be in accordance with his contribution to the organization and that they be comparable to the reimbursements paid to other employees with similar qualities and results. The non-financial rewards can readily take the form of anything the organization can possibly grant. They are only limited by the imagination of managers, what employees really want, and the resources managers have at their disposal.

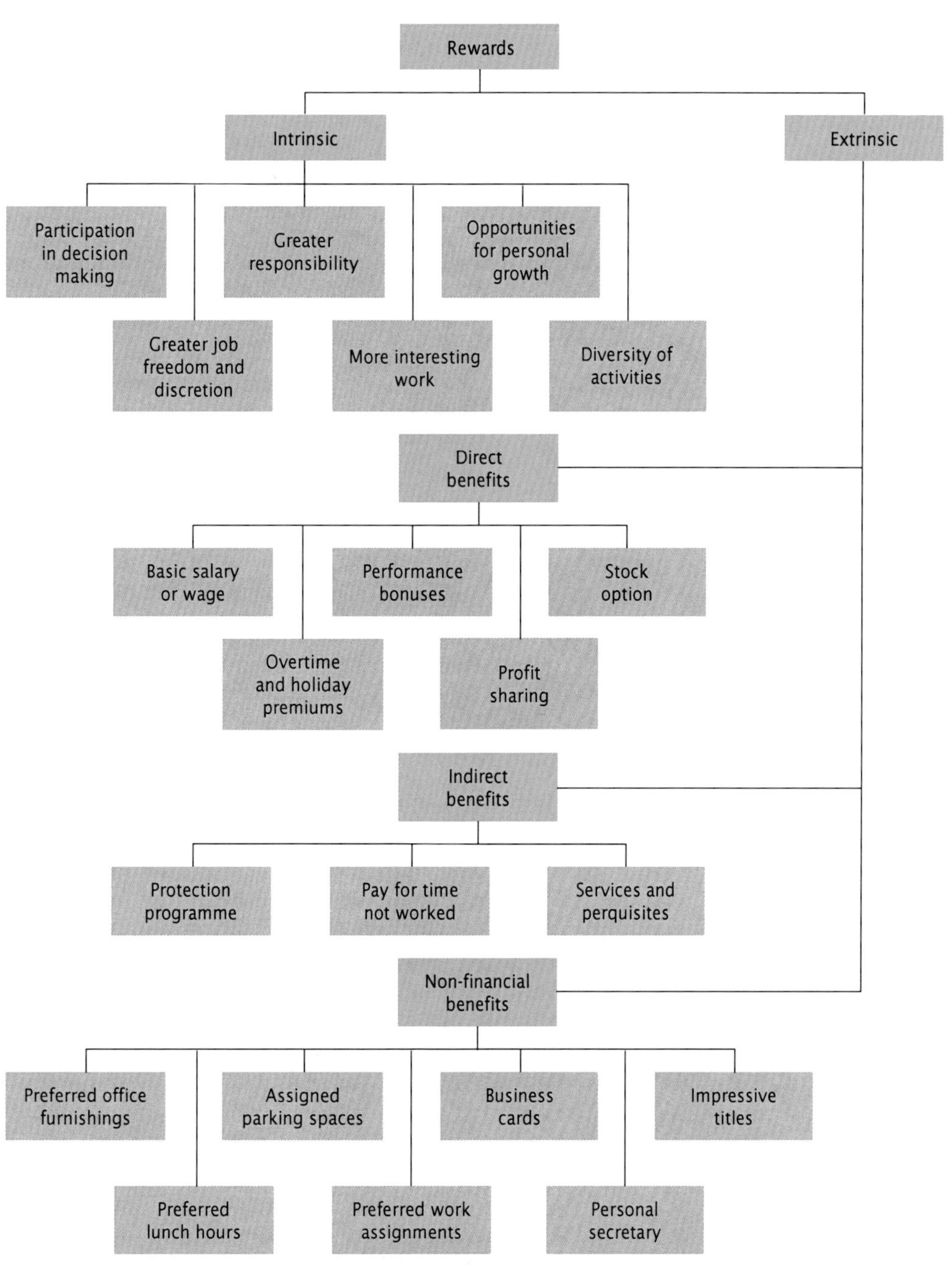

Figure 7.8
Types of reward

Source: *Robbins*, 1979

7.8.1 Payment: performance or merit orientation

Most theorists agree that a reward system has to be based on merit, but what that actually means is debatable. Merit is only one of the many factors which determine the eventual reward. Some of the other factors are the following:

- Performance
- Effort
- Seniority

- Professional expertise
- Degree of difficulty of the work
- Ability to make appropriate decisions

Groups and organizations almost always regard fairness as the main criterion. This demands transparent systems and consultation with employees. Preventing individual and social dissatisfaction is more important than getting a bit of additional performance by gearing rewards to performance (see Section 8.5).
In most countries, employee rewards are based on three or four different criteria. In applying these, however, there may be a great deal of inconsistency, not only between countries but also between sectors of industry, and within a company, between categories of personnel.
One of the main determiners of the reward is the value attached to the position. This may be determined by the qualifications necessary for the job and how much is paid for those on the labor market. Internal considerations can also play a role, although these are usually offset against the guidelines provided by collective labor agreements.

reward according to performance

In cases of reward according to performance, a bonus or premium is paid for performance which exceeds a certain norm or standard. A structural salary increase may be granted: the fixed salary then increases by one or several steps along the salary scale in question.
An EU report has shown that differences in salary between men and women are greatest in the Netherlands. Female workers earn 79% of the salaries of men. The EU average is 84%. Portugal (94%), Belgium (92.7%) and Italy (91.4%) score the best in this respect. Denmark and Sweden have the highest percentages of women in the labor market: 72% and 70.4% respectively.

secondary work conditions

Another factor is secondary work conditions. The issue here is not so much social security provisions, but rather the additional provisions which have been agreed on per company and/ or sector. These provisions may include additional retirement insurance, health insurance or life insurance. Here, too, there may be a good deal of difference between these provisions, even within the same company.

tertiary work conditions

Tertiary work conditions constitute another factor: these apply to several categories of personnel. A wide variety of reimbursements may be available, including car mileage (or a company car), telephone use, and memberships of clubs. Cafeteria subsidies, compensation for mortgage interest, or favorable saving arrangements may also be available, and in some sectors of industry may apply to all employees.

7.8.2 Ad hoc methods or a system?

Many small and middle-sized companies may calculate their salaries on an ad hoc basis. The employer makes an estimate of the amount he would have to pay to the employee in order to prevent him from leaving the company. Age, company loyalty and such aspects all play a part. There is unlikely to be systematic comparison with other salaries, either within or outside the company.
However, if there is a sense that there are great discrepancies between the salaries and some employees feel that they have got the short end of the stick, it is a good idea to try and iron this out by setting salary scales in relation to the function. This of course can only be done for functions whose content and tasks can be reasonably determined, though also for higher company functions, whose content and tasks are designed by the incumbent himself.

7.8.3 *Choice of wage structure*

The wage structure chosen will largely determine how the employees approach their work: their 'work behavior,' so to speak. As such, there needs to be considerable clarity about what the company wants to achieve. In choosing a wage structure, attention will have to be paid to the following factors:

- The amount of precision required by the job
- The extent to which there is control over performance
- The extent to which performance can be measured
- Whether it is individual or group work
- The style of leadership
- The nature of the manufacturing: piece, mass or serial production
- The size of the organization
- The number of performance norms

A functional salary consists of a basic amount to which are added bonuses for seniority, merit and other factors. The legal requirements relating to social security and income tax also need to be taken into account within the wage structure chosen. This will partly determine how much the employee is paid (Fig 7.9).

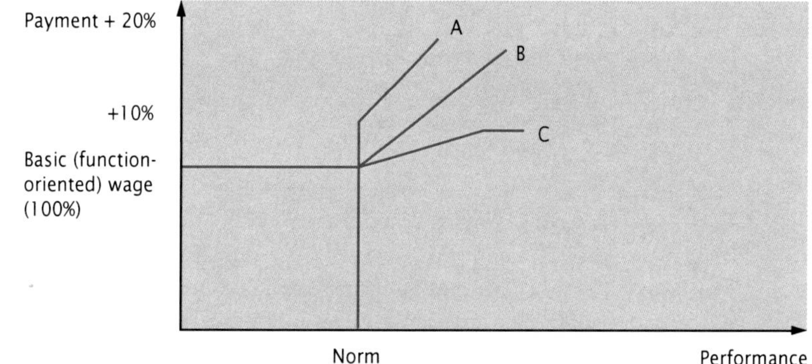

Figure 7.9
The principle of performance-related reward

7.8.4 *Payment on performance*

To be able to pay according to performance, what constitutes a fair performance needs to have been identified. A fair performance can be defined as a performance which, under average circumstances, can be delivered by suitable personnel members (selected, educated, with the necessary experience) and with a normal amount of effort. An increasing amount of research is being carried out in order to try to determine what a fair day's performance actually is. The other issue is that since payment according to performance involves the payment of an amount additional to that which is paid for a 'basic' level of performance, performance needs to be related to relevant core activities which are capable of being performed in a better than average way.
It is important, therefore, that the chosen payment system meet the following demands:

- The employee must be able to have an influence on it via his performance.
- Both employer and employee should have an economic interest in the employee exerting a positive influence on it via his performance.
- The various elements have to be measurable objectively.

In both new technologies and in modern organizational structures, the emphasis is increasingly placed on groups, or even larger units. This means that individual payment based on performance may need to be changed to that of group payment based on performance. When part of the annual profit of the organization is set at the disposal of the employees, this is referred to as profit sharing. Profit sharing is not an independent payment system, but can be regarded as an addition to other systems. One attractive element of profit sharing is that it can create a bond between the employees and the organization in which they are employed. A problem is that the stimulus for delivery of higher performances which radiates from it is not very large.

7.8.5 The 'cafeteria' plan

The cafeteria plan is not a system which determines the level of the payment, but rather a plan which offers employees the opportunity to structure the total payment package in such a way that it best meets personal needs. With this system, personnel members have little or no influence over the secondary and tertiary work conditions which apply to them. It means that almost everyone has some conditions which are not valued, or which one does not even know about (because, the employer for example, pays the premium for it). Certain other conditions may well be attractive, but are not part of the package. To avoid this, personnel members may be given the option of choosing the area in which they want better terms of employment. The areas involved are likely to be the following:

- Duration of working day and/or working week
- Length of holiday
- Level of pension contribution
- Early retirement
- Health insurance package

7.8.6 Perks and incidental rewards

A frequent complaint is that payment systems do not allow managers to show their appreciation by providing incidental rewards for outstanding performance or results delivered by individuals or a group. To meet this need, some organizations offer rewards of an incidental kind. They may include the following:

- Offers of lunch
- Dinner for two
- The opportunity to attend an expensive congress

7.8.7 Bonuses

Many organizations pay bonuses at the end of the year (= 13th month). In many cases this bonus is based on fixed agreements determined in advance and the size of the company profit is not relevant. Bonuses for higher personnel are not usually awarded on this basis but are strongly linked to the degree of economic success. The bonus then becomes a variable component of the income package: it is determined each year anew. The size of bonus usually depends on the level of one's function in the company and on the influence one is believed to exercise on the company result attained.

Awarding bonuses as an additional reward for outstanding achievements has come under heavy fire since the start of the credit crisis (2008/2009), and not only in business contexts but also and most particularly in the finacial sector, and in the Netherlands, for example, in the public sector (such as the energy and care sectors). The culture of bonus-giving in the banking world has come in for heavy criticism world-wide, even in England and the US.

culture of bonus-giving

7.8.8 Top management salaries

In a private or public company, the board of management (respectively, the Remuneration Committee on behalf of the board) has the final responsibility for salary policy within the organization. The income of the members of the board of management is determined by the board of directors or supervisory council. If the directors are at the same time the owners of the organization the board's income will depend on a number of financial and fiscal factors. The managing director's income will be influenced by such factors as company size, company profit and geographical spread. A main consideration is that the managing director be seen to be rewarded for the results that have been obtained. Honoring him or her for the job done is thus an aspect of the salary.

code of good entrepreneurship

According to the code of good entrepreneurship and the rules of corporate governance (the best-earning manager in the US – the CEO of the Blackstone Group – received a salary of \$702 million (± €500 million) in 2008, and in second place with a salary of \$557 million (± €400 million) was the CEO of software giant Oracle; see 2.5.11), transparency is desirable or even essential where top salaries and bonuses are concerned. In the Netherlands, nearly half of its top managers are also in favor of greater openness in respect of high remuneration in the business world. The hospital world and the energy sector also require openness and have sometimes demanded that bonuses that managers have awarded themselves be dropped because of criticism leveled at their organizations and companies.

When it is considered necessary for share values and business returns to simply keep on rising this often leads to short-term thinking, irrational behavior and the taking of irresponsible risks, whether this take the form of presenting prognoses in an unrealistically favorable light or even committing fraud in order to get the extra rewards. Variable remuneration promotes this to a large degree, though governance codes would seem to be keeping its effects at bay.

7.8.9 Stock options: a way of gaining commitment?

option plans

Multinationals such as Shell, Philips, Reed Elsevier and Akzo Nobel have option plans for a select upper managerial level. CapGemini and Ordina and others see option plans as a part of the total reward package for a broad range of employees. The principle is simple: those who work hard and contribute to the market value of the company should also benefit. Staying within the company and working hard is rewarded. Those who leave the company lose their rights. Those who receive options can only cash them after a certain time. Option plans are thought to increase loyalty and gain the commitment of the right people. Not only does the shareholder benefit from an increase in the value of his capital on the stock exchange, but with an option arrangement, personnel and management itself derive some benefit. However if there are eventual stock exchange losses, the story is different. The options may even lose their value entirely.

flexible employment conditions

Of all the European countries, *flexible employment conditions* are most popular in the Netherlands and about a quarter of employers offer their employees options in this regard. One-third of employers is considering following suit. According to the research, 27% of employers in the Netherlands provide at least some employment condition options while 14% make extensive flexible working conditions available.

THE DUTCH EMPLOYER IS THE MOST FLEXIBLE

Research by Mercer into the personnel departments of about 1700 organizations in 47 countries has shown that flexible terms of employment are being offered to employees, whether new or otherwise. Dutch employers are the most flexible in the whole of Europe. About half make flexible terms of employment available. This has been prompted in part by the current crisis. Many employers cannot afford to raise salaries and so they look for other possibilities.

The Mercer research shows that flexible terms of employment include a variety of different possibilities. What sorts of possibilities does the 'flexible employer' offer?

1 Medical insurance (71%)
2 Life insurance (57%)
3 Dental treatment provisions (52%)
4 Accident insurance (47%)
5 Pension plan (46%)
6 Optical insurance (35%)
7 Mobile telephone (29%)
8 Car (29%)
9 Gym membership (28%)
10 Health screening (28%)
11 Childcare (24%)
12 Buy/sell options for holiday pay (24%)
13 Meals (18%)
14 Public transport (15%)
15 Housing (13%)

During job interviews, a lot of applicants express an interest in the salary in particular: the basic salary and the types of extras that they wish to have such as salary increments, performance bonuses, commissions, and perks. However, the real benefits often lie in the minor terms of employment, and many people overlook these. They include reimbursement of means of communication and career-related expenses such as magazines and courses, and reductions in the price of company products. A suitable candidate who lives a long way from the office may be enticed by a good office space that is regularly refurbished in his or her own home.

Source: www.mt.nl/experts/management trends, December 2009

7.9 Careers and management development

career planning

Career development needs to be integrally linked to career planning: a career plan needs to be drawn up in consultation with the employee, these plans implemented and retrospectively evaluated. Career planning is carried out in respect of specific people and specific functions within the organization, as opposed to personnel planning for groups and categories of functions. A dialogue between the organization and its employees is the lynch pin in career planning and the resultant career plan is the tangible outcome of the attuning of the individual's needs to those of the organization. The process of career development has, therefore, both organizational and individual aspects, as is shown in Fig 7.10.
Three models of management development systems more or less meet the objectives of management development, namely effective, current and future management.
The various systems can be graded, ranging from a formal to an ad hoc MD system. Somewhere in between stands the nursery model (otherwise known as the 'fish pond model').

7.9.1 The career path in flat organizations: horizontal promotion

The tall pyramidal structure is increasingly giving way to the flat organization. In a flat organization, every component of the organization is complete and operates as independently as possible.

The motivating idea behind the pyramid is the thought that the human being at the top is better able to cope with complex tasks. The staff think, the top decides and the rest carry out the tasks. The reality may be different.
The manager in a flat organization is to an increasing degree confronted with the question of what his added value actually is. Fortunately for him there is an increasing awareness of the drawbacks of the top positions: too great a focus on vertical steps up the ladder actually hinders one's development. A manager who wants to stay in the race has to be flexible, and be able to, for example, side step or set up a business for him/herself. In the past everyone wanted up within the hierarchy; nowadays more seek a solution in the horizontal direction. Status and salary are no longer decisive; quality and pleasure in the work are.

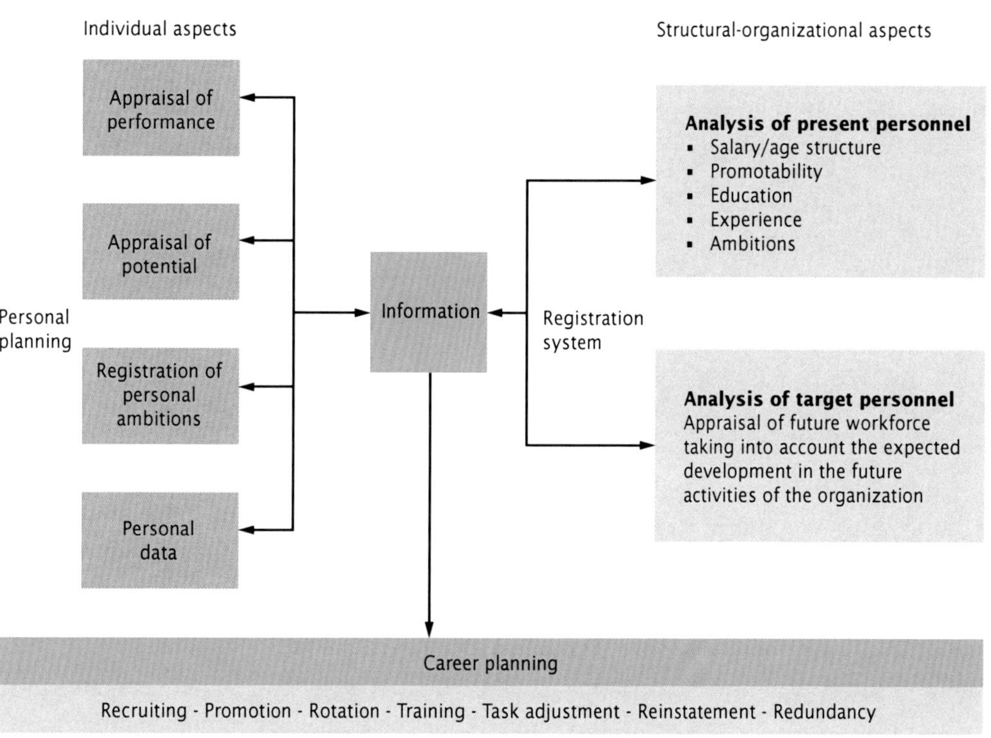

Figure 7.10
Management development (personal planning and career supervision)

When middle management is delayered, internal transfer of employees can constitute a constructive solution. This could be done via mobility offices that are able to keep track of the hidden skills of managers and personnel and offer alternative career possibilities.
For employees in a flatter structure, steps up the career ladder, a traditional part of the concept of hierarchy, no longer exist in the same form. If there is an inherent human need for hierarchical structures, then the flat structure has apparently ignored it. Can employees be motivated without the traditional promotion opportunities? Recent notions on human resources management (HRM) suggest that while promotion is indeed an important factor, acknowledgment of performance, self-motivation, interesting experiences, more challenging assignments and the ability to carry them out are more important. The rise up the ladder, titles, being the boss and the feeling gained from that have taken second place. If vertical promotion has its attractions, so does horizontal promotion, in terms of learning new skills and executing more interesting and challenging assignments: aspects which nowadays are not necessarily linked to the climbing of a vertical ladder.

vertical promotion
horizontal promotion

Flatter organizations demand substantially different HRM concepts. Where this condition is not met and where strongly traditional notions of organization, management and control remain in the forefront, delayering of the organization may well be hindered.

It is a striking fact that despite all the fine words spoken about HRM and all the effort that goes into it, nearly one in five Dutch employees feels no real personal connection with his or her job. 18% say openly that they would never recommend their employer to others. 22% claim that their work does not inspire them to do their best and one in ten could not give a damn about the company's future. Feeling a sense of personal involvement with one's work is consequently an issue. An astonishing 36% of employees plan to leave.

job perks

Dutch employees rate challenging work as the main condition for a sense of personal involvement, with future growth opportunities within the company in second place. Job perks, on the other hand, rate very low.

There is a lot to be done, therefore. However, as long as 'the mood on the factory floor' is that the 'men at the top' are primarily interested in strategy and profit and human relationships are of lesser importance, it is going to be a difficult task to increase productivity within the 'people companies' that advanced economies depend on, and to expand them into the first-rate and highly achieving organizations that are envisaged as the ideal (see 1.5.3).

leadership of a new kind

In other words, leadership of a new kind is desperately needed. In view of this, the next chapter will also deal with leadership, entrepreneurship and inspiration.

Summary

- Organizations are places in which people have to work together. Its members will, to a certain degree, be prepared to make a contribution to the organization in exchange for rewards. Motivation is a crucial aspect of this. Various factors appear to influence individual behavior: the so-called key variables.
- Organizations are places in which groups have to function together. They may be formal or informal in nature. How well they function will depend on a number of factors. These can be classified as structural, human resource, political and symbolic factors.
- Psychology has produced various theories of motivation, including Maslow's hierarchy of needs theory and Vroom's instrumentality theory. The task characteristics model seeks to amalgamate motivation, productivity and function designs.
- Empowerment is a new way of managing employees. As well as an increase in motivation, improvement of effectiveness and flexibility can be expected.
- Within the current framework, the development of employee capabilities and talent is a necessity, and thus there is a need for human resources management (HRM). HRM's basis is the organization's strategies and its structure and culture. HRM thus needs to be an integral part of the managerial process.
- Management of the personnel process encompasses the phases of intake, flow and departure. The personnel instruments that deal with these are recruitment and selection, assessment and career supervision, demotion and dismissal, management development, retirement, discharge and outplacement.
- Valuing the efforts of employees involves rewards and payment. The reimbursement options include functional wage, payment according to performance, multi-factor payment, group payment, profit sharing and the so-called cafeteria plan. The choice of reward system will dictate how the employee approaches his job; his work behavior. A reward system has to be experienced as fair by all those involved. Payment systems can be based on the principles of equal treatment and payment justified by needs, or on equal treatment and payment justified by performance.
- Given developments outside and inside organizations, in the future, career prospects will tend to involve horizontal growth and promotion rather than the traditional vertical career ladder.

Discussion questions

1 With reference to *Management in Action* at the beginning of this chapter: what is your opinion of the motivation practices of Nucor? Do you know other examples of firms practicing this type of motivation management? Describe what they do in this respect.
2 Of the theories on individual motivation covered in this chapter, which appeals to you most? Which of the theories do you think most relevant?
3 What, in your opinion, is the difference (if any) between human resources management and personnel work?
4 **a)** What are the similarities and differences between delegation and empowerment?
b) What is regarded the vital success factor in implementing a diversity program?
5 Give your opinion on the following: 'Management development and horizontal careers are mutually exclusive.'
6 As an employee, how would you prefer to be rewarded: according to position payment for performance, or profit sharing? Does each system still have distinct disadvantages?

Research-based exercise

Perceived investment in employee development, intrinsic motivation and work performance

Introduction
This exercise is based on a research article by Bård Kuvaas and Anders Dysvik, published in *Human Resource Management Journal*. The research question, data collection method, and some of the results of their research project are shown. The exercise, which relates to this research article, consists of two questions. Your answers should be based on the theory in this chapter.

Research question
What is the relationship between perceived investment in employee development and the employee's intrinsic motivation and work performance?

Data collection
A survey of 826 respondents.

Outcomes
When organizations offer organizational inducements in the form of developmental opportunities, employees do not always want to put much effort into activities that are to the benefit of the organization. Employees who are intrinsically motivated are particularly not inclined to do this. They are usually self-motivated and can act independently and competently to help others and to link their actions to outcomes that matter in the lives of other people.

(Based on Kuvaas, B. and Dysvik, A. (2009). 'Perceived investment in employee development, intrinsic motivation and work performance.' *Human Resource Management Journal*, *19*(3), 217-236.)

Questions

1 How can an organization tailor its employee development program to employees with high intrinsic motivation?
2 Does a company that only employs highly intrinsically motivated professionals need an employee development program?

CASE

Management case study

Driven to distraction

This is bonus season in the financial world. That means, of course, that it is bonus-bashing season everywhere else. The righteously outraged have no shortage of arguments on their side, from the mind-boggling size of the bonuses to the fact that the banks were recently rescued with public money. But if they want to mix a bit of theory with their spleen they now have a book to help them: Daniel Pink's *Drive: the Surprising Truth about What Motivates Us*. It seems that bankers are not just slaves to greed. They are also slaves to a discredited management theory: the idea that the best way to motivate people is to use performance-related rewards.

Mr Pink's argument is hardly new. Eminent management theorists have been dismissing payment-by-results as simplistic and mechanical ever since Frederick Taylor tried to turn it into the cornerstone of scientific management in the early 20th century. But Mr Pink's book is nevertheless well timed. The widespread fury about bonuses is sparking a wider debate about the way bankers and other lavishly remunerated people are paid. 'Drive' is a decent summary of the anti-Taylorist school of thinking. And Mr Pink, once Al Gore's chief speechwriter and now a prolific management writer, is a highly motivated self-publicist.

Mr Pink argues that the rich world is in the middle of a management revolution, from 'motivation 2.0' to 'motivation 3.0' (1.0 in this schema was prehistoric times, when people were motivated mainly by the fear of being eaten by wild animals). In the age of routine production it made sense for organizations to rely on sticks and carrots or 'extrinsic motivators', as he calls them. But today, with routine jobs being outsourced or automated, it makes more sense to rely on 'intrinsic rewards', or the pleasure we gain from doing a job well. Look at the success of collaborative marvels such as Wikipedia, Firefox or Linux, which were created by volunteers. Or look at the rise of social entrepreneurs or the movement to promote 'low-profit' limited-liability firms.

Mr Pink argues that carrots and sticks are not only outdated, but can also be counterproductive motivation killers and creativity dampeners. Urging people to give blood actually reduces the number who are willing to do so. Providing managers with financial rewards can encourage them to game the system or, even worse, to engage in reckless behavior.

So how should firms motivate people? Mr Pink argues that the answer is to give them more control over their own lives and thus allow them to draw on their deep inner wells of diligence and drive. Software companies such as Atlassian and Google are giving workers time to pursue their own projects. Even low-tech firms such as Whole Foods and Best Buy are giving people more control over how and with whom they work.

How convincing is all this? Mr Pink insists that all he is doing is bringing the might of science to bear on management: 'There's been a mismatch between what science knows and what business does.' But this argument depends on a highly selective reading of the academic literature. Four reviews of research on the subject from the 1980s onwards have all come to the same conclusion: that pay-for-performance can increase productivity dramatically. A study of an American glass installation company, for example, found that shifting from salaries to individual incentives increased productivity by 44%. More recent research on workers at a Chinese electronics factory also confirms that performance-related pay (especially the threat of losing income) is an excellent motivator.

Linking pay to performance does not just increase motivation. It also helps to recruit and retain the most talented. The world's brightest students are overwhelmingly attracted to organizations that make extensive use of performance-related rewards such as partnerships and share options. Firms are adept at using these rewards to encourage long-term loyalty: people work in the salt mines for years in the hope of becoming partners or top managers. Companies that eschew extrinsic rewards risk lumbering themselves with sluggish dullards.

What about Mr Pink's other worries, about creativity and 'self-determination'? It is certainly true that creative people value the intrinsic things in life. But an enthusiasm for intrinsic rewards can go hand in hand with a taste for extrinsic gain. American universities attract star professors from all around the world by the simple expedient of paying them lots of money. Successful writers employ agents to get the highest possible advances (Mr Pink himself probably hopes to make some money from his book). Creative centers such as Hollywood and Silicon Valley are also hot beds of payment-by-results. It is true that some of the world's best companies are putting more emphasis on 'purpose'. But it is quite possible to mix this with pay-for-performance; indeed, companies that Mr Pink lauds, such as Google and Whole Foods, are highly skilled at using sticks and carrots.

All this suggests that Mr Pink has it backwards: far from abandoning sticks and carrots, organizations are making ever more use of them. Companies are keener than ever on holding bosses' feet to the fire by linking their pay to performance through stock options and the like and on firing them if they fail. But they are also trying to widen pay differentials further down the organization: about 90% of American firms use merit pay, for example.

There is no doubt that sticks and carrots can be badly used. They can encourage risky behavior, as they have in the banking system, or persuade policemen to focus on minor traffic infractions rather than violent criminals, as they have in Britain. But properly managed they can be immensely powerful tools for boosting productivity and attracting the right people. For all the battering he has taken over the past hundred years, Frederick Taylor still has the edge over his critics.

Source: *The Economist*, January 16, 2010, p. 62

Case study questions

1 How should a payment structure combine extrinsic and intrinsic reward?
2 Can you give some examples of firms in which extrinsic rewards should be emphasized?
3 Can you describe some organizations that are more effective when intrinsic rewards are the primary reward mechanism?

CONTENTS

8.1 Leadership, management and entrepreneurship
8.2 Inspiring leadership: the seven habits and the eighth one (from Covey)
8.3 Managers and their motivation
8.4 Leadership and styles of leadership
8.5 Influencing human behavior
8.6 Styles of leadership and conflict resolution
8.7 Organization, styles of leadership and organizational culture

Leadership, motivation and communication

Chapter 8

LEARNING OUTCOMES

After studying this chapter, you should be able to do the following:

- Describe the concepts of leadership, management and entrepreneurship and explain the various factors involved
- Describe the effects of different styles of leadership
- Explain the ways in which situational factors have a bearing on leadership practices
- Identify several sources of influence and explain a number of factors affecting the exercise of power and authority
- Identify and describe diverse modes of communication between people
- Describe and explain different types of conflict resolution
- Describe and explain the typology of organization cultures proposed by Harrison
- Explain the correlation between leadership and influence in an organizational culture
- Apply the terms from this chapter in a practical case setting

CASE

Management-in-action

The Responsible Manager

For the past 33 years, I have ended all my MBA and executive education courses by sharing with participants my perspective on how they can become responsible managers. I acknowledge that they will be successful in terms of income, social status, and influence, but caution that managers must remember that they are the custodians of society's most powerful institutions. They must therefore hold themselves to a higher standard. Managers must strive to achieve success with responsibility. My remarks are intended to serve as a spur for people to reexamine their values before they plunge into their daily work routines. Take a minute to study them:

- Understand the importance of nonconformity. Leadership is about change, hope, and the future. Leaders have to venture into uncharted territory, so they must be able to handle intellectual solitude and ambiguity.

After his lecture at Maastricht School of Management, C.K. Prahalad signs his books.

- Display a commitment to learning and developing yourself. Leaders must invest in themselves. If you aren't educated, you can't help the uneducated; if you are sick, you can't minister to the sick; if you are poor, you can't help the poor.
- Develop the ability to put personal performance in perspective. Over a long career, you will experience both success and failure. Humility in success and courage in failure are hallmarks of a good leader.
- Be ready to invest in developing other people. Be unstinting in helping your colleagues realize their full potential.
- Learn to relate to those who are less fortunate. Good leaders are inclusive, even though that isn't easy. Most societies have dealt with differences by avoiding or eliminating them; few assimilate those who aren't like them.
- Be concerned about due process. People seek fairness – not favors. They want to be heard. They often don't even mind if decisions don't go their way as long as the process is fair and transparent.
- Realize the importance of loyalty to organization, profession, community, society, and, above all, family. Most of our achievements would be impossible without our families' support.
- Assume responsibility for outcomes as well as for the processes and people you work with. How you achieve results will shape the kind of person you become.
- Remember that you are part of a very privileged few. That's your strength, but is also a cross you carry. Balance achievement with compassion and learning with understanding.
- Expect to be judged by what you do and how well you do it – not by what you say you want to do. However, the bias toward action must be balanced by empathy and caring for other people.
- Be conscious of the part you play. Be concerned about the problems of the poor and the disabled, accept human weaknesses, laugh at yourself – and avoid the temptation to play God. Leadership is about self-awareness, recognizing your failings, and developing modesty, humility and humanity.

Every year, I revisit my notes about the responsible manager, which I first jotted down in 1977. The world has changed a lot since then, but I haven't found it necessary to change a word of my lecture. Indeed, the message is more relevant today than ever.

Source: C. K. Prahalad (2010) *Harvard Business Review*, January/February, p. 36

Like all cooperative human ventures, the most important resource of any organization is its people. The art of management requires the proper deployment of this resource. In addition to organizing the workplace, issuing regulations and providing instruction, effective managers must encourage cooperation, supervise task performance and orient work behaviors so that they comply with organizational goals.
The managerial task involves a process of interaction between a leader and his or her subordinates, who are also his or her immediate colleagues. Inspiring leadership encourages people to aim for the best results and it is therefore important for managers to consider the ways in which their tasks affect their co-workers. Each management style is characterized by a certain idea about how a leader should motivate these subordinates and fellow employees. Besides style of leadership and leadership as such, careful consideration should also be given to the problems of conflict resolution and influence exerted over the organizational culture. With regard to the latter, communication and ways of exercising authority and power will be addressed.
Before dealing with these subjects, it is necessary to agree on what is being meant by leadership in the narrow sense of the word. To define leadership, we need to clarify the distinction between an entrepreneur, a manager and a leader.

8.1 Leadership, management and entrepreneurship

Managerial personnel spend a great deal of their time supervising employees and furnishing practical support for employee task performance. This constitutes their leadership function. They also serve managerial functions, by which we mean the processes involved in determining the strategic course of the organization as a whole, along with its overall organizational and communicative structure, both of which must be adapted to the organization's goals.
Managers are, in effect, involved in all activities concerned with an effective and efficient set of goals and with the realization of these goals by means of directed action performed within an

management

organization. Management is, consequently, a more complex notion than leadership in the narrow sense, since leadership is restricted to the realm of personal interaction with employees and the personal influencing of their organizational and work behavior.
Entrepreneurship is another matter altogether. In this concept, the crucial function is how to find and make use of opportunities. By being alert to events in the outside world, the entrepreneur formulates specific goals and strives to attain them (and, naturally, takes risks). In this sense, entrepreneurship involves searching for challenges, finding new combinations, initiating action and taking calculated risks. An entrepreneur sees problems as challenges rather than hindrances. He or she will not just wait for opportunity to knock but go out and create new opportunities. The attributes of such a person are, accordingly, not only applicable in private business but can also bear fruit in the world of such non-profit organizations as hospitals and other governmental agencies, autonomous or otherwise.

8.1.1 Entrepreneurship

Entrepreneurship, then, is the sum of the ideas, mentality and actions needed to avert any risks involved in offering products and services, often with the overt intention of making a profit. It also involves the ability to search for better, different or even potentially new uses of available resources, as well as to utilize ideas already conceived by other people.
In principle, entrepreneurship permeates every level of the organization. The search for new possibilities impacts on external clients as much as on internal employees, as it is the former who have to contend with the results of the latter's actions. In any case, entrepreneurship is an important condition for the future survival of the organization. When board rooms or management teams refrain from taking conscious risks in order to create new services,

products or markets, the first step is made toward the development of an organizational culture in which initiative is no longer appreciated.

entrepreneurship In its most purely theoretical form, entrepreneurship can occur without the entrepreneur interacting with anyone else. Whenever other people are required to undertake such activities as those involved in shaping or realizing ideas, then leadership, organization and management also become necessary.

8.1.2 Leadership

leadership Leadership is needed to create a common sense of direction among employees and includes acts of inspiring and engaging personnel. An accurate definition of leadership is difficult, but good leadership is readily identifiable when experienced. In the first place, it builds a bridge between entrepreneurial plans and their execution. In this respect, leadership is especially directed at employees and at obtaining their commitment.

CASE Mini case study 8.1

Theoretically speaking, it is possible to be an entrepreneur who disregards people. Experience teaches us that some entrepreneurs adopt such an attitude. These isolationists do not consider employees or other parties interested in the organization's activities. They are unwilling and unable to let others participate emotionally in their undertakings. No enthusiasm can be expected from them. In other words, such entrepreneurs lack leadership as they do not have the power to create a common sense of direction for their employees.

8.1.3 Management

management activities In the classical sense, the act of management makes it possible for other people to be able and willing to perform goal-oriented activities. In this classic definition, the important management activities are planning (research, drafting of plans), doing (arranging, coordinating, allocating assignments, creating conditions), checking (testing, measuring, controlling), and acting (reacting, reviewing, adjusting).

Presented in such a list, these activities still say little about what a manager really does, but they do give us glimpses of the ways in which managerial work is generally portrayed. Managers themselves often associate their work with such notions as chaos, communication, employee discipline, and the removal of obstacles to the enterprise's success.

entrepreneurship leadership While entrepreneurship involves the conscious acceptance of risks and the search for new combinations and leadership consists in the goal-oriented motivation of employees, management is occupied with 'how' questions. More specifically, it is concerned with the most effective manner of managing people and other resources to achieve the optimum level of efficiency.

CASE Mini case study 8.2

Yahoo has ambition

Less than three minutes into an interview at Yahoo!'s Sunnyvale (Calif.) headquarters. Chief Executive Carol Bartz is eager to tell reporters how she would grade her first-year performance: She gives herself a B-. Deal-making may help her work up to an A. 'You're going to see more acquisitions this year,' says Bartz, 61, who in January 2009 replaced Jerry Yang as CEO of Yahoo, the Web portal that organizes online information, provides e-mail, and sells Internet advertising. Potential targets include overseas companies and data analytics businesses that help companies assess their advertising results, she says. 'Last year people talked about, "Oh, Yahoo is trying to get smaller",' Bartz says. 'We were never trying to get smaller. We were just trying to get more focused.' Gene Munster, an analyst at Piper Jaffray in Minneapolis, says Bartz may be able to lift annual sales growth to 10%. 'We believe in Carol Bartz and believe that she is going to get the revenue growth to a point that's acceptable,' he says.

Source: *Bloomberg Business Week*, January 25, 2010, p. 55, B. Womack

The manager of the future will have the capacity to get things done for and by people, to provide direction to this end, and to create the internal and external conditions facilitating the activity – conditions that can be adjusted if circumstances change or if plans do not proceed as intended or directed. In the above, we can recognize the traditional management functions of planning, organizing, coordinating, commanding, controlling and adjusting. The more complex notion of management examined in the rest of this chapter will place even stronger emphasis on such elements as leadership, motivation, influence of culture and behavior, communication and conflict resolution.

CASE

Mini case study 8.3

Leading and Managing

Management thinker Henri Mintzberg promotes his belief that management is not merely a science encompassed in a set of analytical skills taught in a classroom, but also an art that depends on imagination and creative insight, and a craft that is learned on the job through apprenticeship, mentorship and direct experience. 'We should be seeing managers as leaders and leadership as management practiced well.' He thinks of both functions in terms of the 'communityship' inherent in them. The effective manager, he says, is one who 'leverages the natural propensity of people to cooperate in communities'.

Source: *Strategy + Business* (2009) 57(winter), p. 100

8.1.4 Towards inspirational leadership: efficiency is not enough

According to Covey, the theoretical and practical aspects of leadership are solely a matter of learning how to manage oneself and then transferring that inspiration to others. Crucially, we have to distance ourselves from the idea that prosperity's driving force is machines and capital. The industrial era revolved around man as a machine (as causa efficiens): people were essential as a means of production but were replaceable. The information age of the future is more likely to revolve around the head and the heart (or in other words, the essence) of man. The main thing will be to inspire and motivate talented employees (as the causa finalis) who want to realize their own potential and as such, want to create their own goals and want to be able to do this within an organization or within a team of people. For the high-performing and first-rate organization of the future (see Section 1.5.3) that recognizes this new reality and wants to make full use of its employees' potential, this means encouraging employee

work engagement

work engagement, thereby creating an immense number of ways of adding value. This is certainly far from being what happens today, and when it does occur it is hardly adequate to the purpose. Not only this, but instead of adding value, a lot of organizations are caught in a downwards spiral, partly because of reorganizations and mergers following the American model (see Section 1.1.3). According to Covey, the associated problems involve the organizational, relational and individual levels.

The qualities of an inspiring leader:

1 Authenticity and transparency
2 The ability to self-reflect
3 The ability and the courage to face up to reality
4 Presence
5 Ability to motivate and inspire
6 Modesty and humbleness
7 Trust, hope and love
8 Clarity
9 The ability to deal with paradoxes

Source: SMO, 2009

LEADERSHIP AND EMOTIONAL INTELLIGENCE

What distinguishes great leaders from merely good ones? It isn't IQ or technical skills, says Daniel Goleman. Its emotional intelligence (EI): a group of five skills that enable the best leaders to maximize their own and their followers' performance. When top managers at one company had a critical mass of EI capabilities, their divisions outperformed yearly earnings goals by 20%. The El skills are:

- Self-awareness: knowing one's strengths, weaknesses, drives, values, and impact on others
- Self-regulation: controlling or redirecting disruptive impulses and moods
- Motivation: relishing achievement for its own sake
- Empathy: understanding other people's emotional makeup
- Social skills: building rapport with others to move them in desired directions

We're each born with certain levels of EI skills. But we can strengthen these abilities through persistence, practice, and feedback from colleagues or coaches.

Source: *Harvard Business Review*, (2009) winter, p. 47

8.2 *Inspiring leadership: the seven habits and the eighth one (from Covey)*

According to Covey (1989 and 2004), the first and foremost condition for effecting change in organizations is for people to learn to see. To be able to see reality through different eyes, people have to learn to put their existing views and assumptions up for discussion. To make crucial breakthroughs requires more than just good intentions or a positive attitude: it requires learning to look at reality 'in the right way', namely, through the paradigm of the complete person. According to this new paradigm the person is no longer an object or a physical body but a completely individual being possessing a soul, a brain and a heart as well as an external body.

paradigm of the complete person

As Covey sees it, the most effective model for leadership towards personal change and for change within organizations is a sort of three-stage one. The first two steps are described in *The Seven Habits of Highly Effective People* (1989).

Three of the habits he mentions are targeted towards laying the basis for independence. People who are independent choose their own goals. Independent people act on their own accord and are not as inclined as others to make their actions dependent on what others do. They take the initiative, set conscious course towards their own targets and draw up priorities.

independence

Independence means letting go of the notion that people's lives are determined by genetic ('it's just in my genes'), psychological ('it's how I was brought up) or social factors ('others come into it'). Achieving independence is described by Covey as 'a personal victory'. Figure 8.1 shows the 7 habits (from 1989) and the 8th one (from 2004).

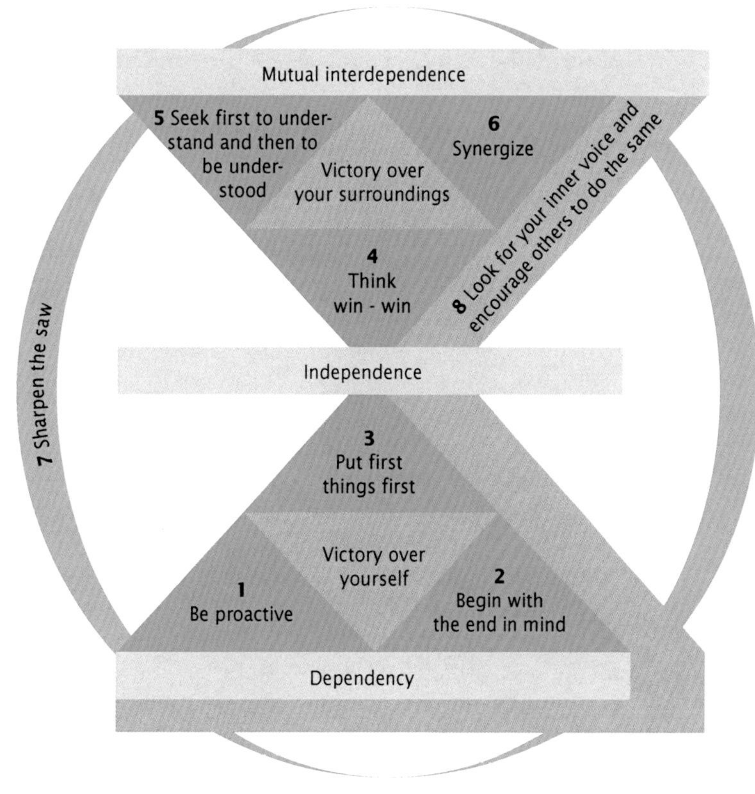

Figure 8.1
The eight habits (after Covey, 1989/2004)

What do you have to do to become independent? Basically, it is a matter of the following: you have to be able to take charge of your own life, you have to have a clear goal and you have to establish priorities by summoning up the discipline to focus on the main things. Once these conditions have been fulfilled, you can focus on more fruitful collaboration with others. Being independent is, after all, not a goal in itself, especially not in a world in which everything is connected. It is at this point that the second step comes into effect: learning to appreciate each others' interdependence. To be able to work meaningfully with others requires another victory, this time not over yourself but over your environment. Such a victory will again be the result of three qualities: thinking in terms of win-win, learning that you must listen to others first before you can expect to be understood yourself, and being resolved to bridge each others' differences by looking for solutions that do justice to everybody's wishes.

independence

Independence and interdependence find their complement in the third step: the ability to inspire people to go about finding their own sources of inspiration. This ability was described by Covey in his book The 8th Habit (2004). Covey explains the importance of the 8th habit as follows. To compete strongly, people and organizations not only have to be effective but also to stick out above others and to extend themselves: they have to demonstrate their own greatness.

passion, satisfaction and relevance
inspiration

The key qualities are passion, satisfaction and relevance. These are on a plane of their own, one that comes close to inspiration. At the personal level, inspiration derives from the deepest convictions, ambitions and motives that people can possibly have (in fact, it is their inner voice) and can of course form an important source of change. At the group level, the main issue is the extent to which and how one can inspire others to discover their own inner voice.

To change successfully, in the first place, people need to be independent (take charge of themselves, formulate goals and then pursue them in a disciplined way). They then need to be able to cooperate effectively with others (win-win, listen well and find the best solution). They will then be capable of inspiring others.
In pursuing such a course, it is very important to realize that real changes come from within.

It is about character, skills, initiative, positive energy and moral activity that can inspire others. The upshot is that people will assume more responsibility and be given greater responsibility, and with the help of others, achieve better results.

Leadership: the person as a whole

inspirational leadership

In fact, leadership is all about the person as a whole. Inspirational leadership assumes that man is a four-dimensional being: one with a body, a head, a heart and a soul. The image of man as an object that must be directed, motivated or controlled leads inevitably to mediocrity, Covey claims. These four dimensions represent man's four basic needs: life (the body), love (the heart), learning (the head), and leaving something of value behind (the soul). If the four dimensions are translated into human capabilities, what we get is a kind of fourfold division: physical or bodily intelligence (PQ), mental intelligence (IQ), emotional intelligence (EQ) and spiritual intelligence (SQ). When we talk about intelligence we often mean mental intelligence: our ability to analyze, rationalize, think abstractly and comprehend abstract things. This is too limited a way of viewing intelligence. Physical intelligence (PQ) has to do with the optimal functioning of our bodily functions: something that we are often hardly conscious of but which is an extremely complex process. Emotional intelligence is our self-knowledge and our social sensitivity. Those with a well developed EQ have a feeling for timing, have empathy with others, can adapt socially and are courageous enough to recognize their weaknesses and to give voice to their differences and respect those of others. Spiritual intelligence (SQ) has to do with our need for meaning, our most basic motivations and passions. According to Covey, SQ is the most important form of intelligence because it serves as a guideline for the other three forms.

fourfold division

Only when the four dimensions of the whole person are given justice will man be able to discover his 'inner voice', which will find expression in a conscience (a spiritual function), vision (a mental intelligence function), passion (an emotional intelligence function) and discipline (a function of physical intelligence).

inner voice

Covey bases his contention that in fact, everything revolves around personal leadership on the following points. Leadership is actually the art of making things possible. It is a matter of voicing the value and the potential of others in such clear and powerful ways that they themselves can see that it is true and can thus initiate their own processes of inner growth. As such, a personal leader conforms to four requirements: he or she will unfold as a reliable role model who will ensure that others receive trust (the soul), he or she will choose the right direction (the head), he or she will ensure the smooth running of the organization because people will be on the same wavelength (the body), and he or she will address the matter of how to empower individuals and teams (the heart). These four requirements or 'roles' give shape to four organizational qualities: its conscience (being a role model), its vision and strategies (choosing a direction), its discipline (streamlined operation) and its enthusiasm (empowerment). According to Covey, all four roles are equally important, but the most important thing is always to start with the building of trust through the right role model. A real leader is a beacon for others and thus inspires trust. Trust is the basis on which the other roles will continue to build.

empowerment

A leader must not only be an example and a lever for change, he must also demonstrate strength of character and capability both as an individual and in dealings with others. As far as capability is concerned, Covey constantly refers to the seven habits of effective leadership (see Figure 8.1), the first three of which are directed towards personal and individual development. They ensure that you learn to take an independent approach. The three following habits are about effective collaboration with others. The seventh habit is about developing and maintaining the other six habits. The eighth habit is about the way in which people use their own leadership to do justice to these habits and is about the path from effectiveness to inspiration.

Exhibit 8.1

Covey's first 7 habits plus the 8th one

1 *Be proactive*
Change the circumstances instead of being changed by them and accept your own responsibility.

2 *Begin with the end in mind*
Begin by creating an image of what you want to achieve. Identify with your goal or goals and remain faithful to what you have chosen (= personal leadership).

3 *Put first things first*
Make sure that you define your priorities and do not let the main things suffer from passing ideas and any urgent but ultimately unimportant business (= personal management and personal effectiveness).

4 *Think win-win*
Use the principle of mutual dependence to collaborate effectively. Do not be afraid to grant others as much as you would grant yourself. Think in terms of surplus: there is always enough of whatever it is for the other as well (= interpersonal leadership).

5 *Seek first to understand and then to be understood*
Listen to the other without first feeling the need to react. Summon up enough courage to remain silent and grant the other the right of first speech. The main thing is to build up the relationship, not to give an answer.

6 *Synergize*
Realize that the whole is greater than the parts. In what others contribute, see the potential above all things. Realize that it is not about 'my' or 'your' way, but about the better one. Respect and value the differences. Think in terms of creative and better solutions.

7 *Sharpen the saw*
Live according to the seven habits but do not let your edge dull over time. Give yourself and others the chance to develop and to grow: physically, mentally, emotionally and spiritually. This requires strength of character and discipline.

8 *From effectiveness to inspiration on the path to greatness*
Live in order to realize your full potential (= discover your inner voice) and in your capacity as a leader, inspire others to do the same and also discover their inner voice. Optimize the hidden potential of others.

Achieve excellence and greatness in the following areas:

- greatness at the personal level. Discover the three gifts you were given at birth: freedom of choice, principles, and the four human dimensions.
- greatness at the relational level. Inspire others to discover their inner voices.
- greatness at the organizational level. Realize this and significantly better returns will follow.

Be an example (= a role model) to others, therefore, and choose the right direction (for the organization or for the team) on the basis of clear vision, mission and strategy, streamline the organization and design structures and systems that strengthen the core values and strategic priorities, and create results by allotting responsibility and handing over authority to others (= empowerment).

(Summarized and freely adapted from Covey 1989 and 2004)

8.2.1 The paradox of management leadership

The traditional manager – the company or department head as a lonely decision maker, untouchable expert or almighty boss – no longer exists. Modern managers are much more concerned with being leaders, coaches or individuals who make it possible for others to do their jobs. Implicitly, they are no longer centers of attention; instead, they are evaluated on their abilities to devise general strategies that they have their employees carry out. In other words, the individual success of the modern manager is inextricably connected with the success of his or her team. This turnaround in the approach to the managerial task is not surprising. For some time, companies have been saying that people were the most important asset, although this valuation of human resources has seldom gone beyond such expressions of appreciation. Present developments are, however, forcing companies to back these words with action.

In this regard, Covey (see 8.2) makes a strict distinction between managers and leaders. *managers* Managers are primarily concerned with controlling things: money, expenses, information, *leaders* structures, systems, equipment and materials. Things require management. Leaders are primarily concerned with optimizing human potential. This is not something that you can control: at the very most, it can only be encouraged. Section 8.2 dealt extensively with the qualities and habits a personal leader must have or must develop. In the various views still to come (views which emphasize different aspects of managing, giving direction and providing leadership), there is one thing that they all agree on: for a long time, companies have been expressing the opinion that 'people are the main resource', but for too long it has merely remained an opinion.
McGregor Not that this is something new. McGregor, for example, had already expressed the opinion in *The Human Side of Enterprise* (1960), in which he advocated a new form of leadership via his Theory X and Y. Present developments – the passing of the industrial age to the age of information and of knowledge-based systems – are more than ever forcing companies to act on their words.

Different types of leadership

Leadership is an essential and integral component of good management. Managers who do not lead will not succeed in fulfilling their managerial functions. Management that lacks the leadership dimension is little more than a merely administrative and supervisory activity. Organizations whose management does not display any leadership qualities generally perform badly; they are bureaucratic, inefficient and unresponsive.
The essential points underlying this observation are shown in Fig 8.2, which divides managerial activities into four distinct categories, including three different types of leadership.
three complementary ways These can be characterized as three complementary ways of conceiving a leader's function: *supervisory leadership* supervisory leadership (the hands), organizational leadership (the head) and inspirational leadership (the heart).
organizational leadership *inspirational leadership* Inspirational leadership is the most universal of the three types. It is unique insofar that it, by definition, precludes the use of authority to coerce behavior. In the case of the other two forms, the contrary applies – it is possible to use coercion in exercising the activities involved in them, and indeed such coercive types of leadership are not at all uncommon.
Certainly, all three types of leadership are essential components of good management. Moreover, organizational leadership constitutes an integral component of management as such, and, accordingly, may not always be identified as a form of leadership. Without this element, management is reduced to the mundane acts of administration, which should only constitute a manager's core concerns when they involve the organizational and supervisory leadership tasks. Inspirational leadership is a class apart, as it is inconsistent with the use of power as means of coercion and authority, and can even be exercised outside an organization. Without this latter form of leadership, the core management activities may still be performed, but only in an autocratic or, at best, bureaucratic manner.
For this reason, the ability to inspire the performance of others is considered an essential feature of good management, even though, strictly speaking, it is perhaps not a necessary

managerial quality. However, the addition of an inspirational capability to a management team's leadership repertoire transforms the supervisory function by endowing it with transformational qualities that may indeed have organization-wide significance.

Management is more than administrative control

Modern organizations have arisen in order to facilitate effective cooperation among large groups of people. In such organizations, people cooperate in various and sometimes complex tasks involving the making of cars, for example, or the provision of banking services, or the production of computer software. The administrative planning, organizational and verification skills needed to provide successful leadership for those undertaking such tasks and involved in the planning, organizing and verifying of organizational activities, are commonly associated with management. Not for nothing is the most widespread Anglo-American management degree known as the Master of Business Administration (MBA).

But, as shown in Fig 8.2, management involves more than administration. When considering the requirements that a successful leader of a large organization must possess, considerations must be given to two sets of factors: one concerning the relationship between the organization and its environment and the other indicating the ways in which a manager motivates other people within the organization to get things done.

Management mix

If we adopt the approach proposed by Nicholls (1993) and apply some of his views to the information presented in Fig 8.2, it becomes clear that the various facets of leadership are integral components of any form of management as well as essential ingredients for good management.

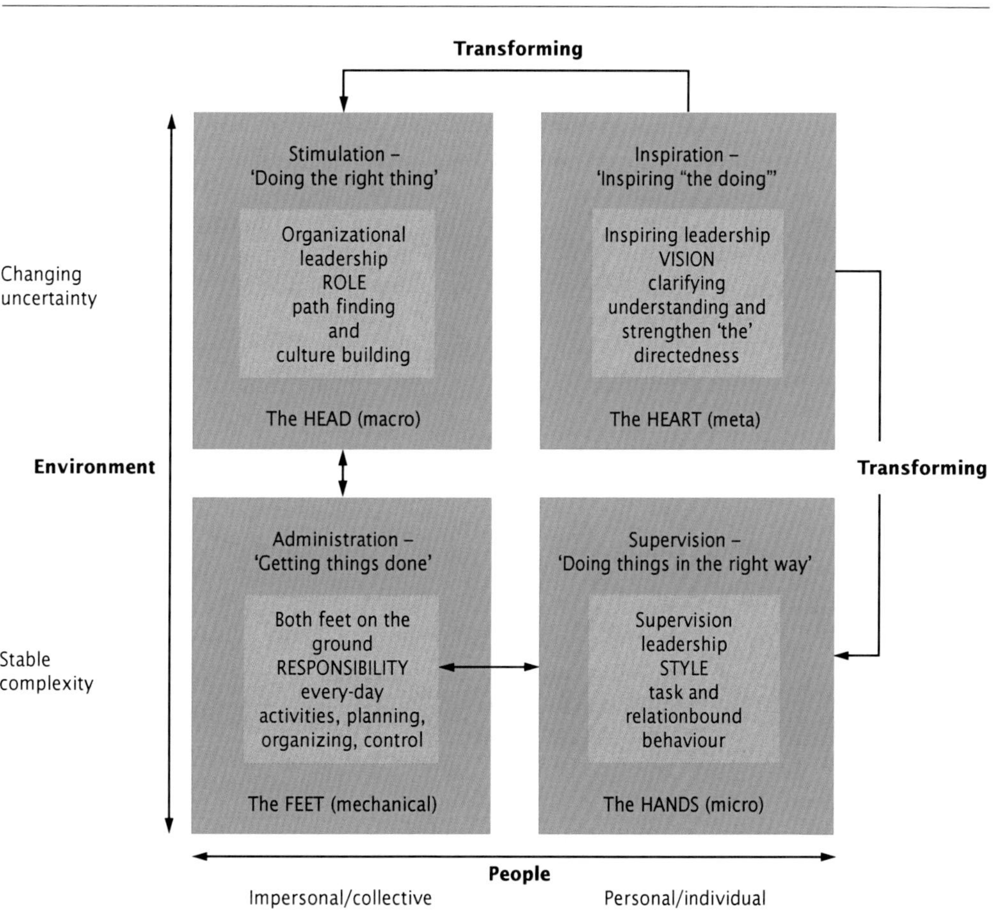

Figure 8.2
Leadership aspects of management

Source: *Nicholls*, 1993

organizational and supervisory leadership

Organizational and supervisory leadership, which can only be exercised within an organization, are features that clearly define the managerial function. Without these leadership tasks, a manager is merely an administrator, a position that can quickly be buried in a bureaucracy unresponsive to changes and insensitive to people.

inspirational leadership

Inspirational leadership can, on the contrary, be exercised outside an organization and, because of this possibility, is not an integral component of management itself. But because it presents an alternative to autocracy, it is essential for good management. Its inclusion in the managerial mix transforms the supervisory task and, consequently, the very nature of management.

Returning to the question initially posed in Section 8.1: do managers differ from leaders? Are organizations managed too much and led too little? The answer is both yes and no: a paradox. Yes, in the sense that inspirational leadership is too infrequently met and that supervisory leadership usually remains untransformed. No, in the sense that some of the leadership qualities said to be lacking are in fact inherent to the managerial task. A lack of inspirational leadership does not result in over-management, but rather bad or incomplete management. Not too much management but too little!

When we consider management more closely, it therefore appears that managers are also necessarily organizational and supervisory leaders and that they inevitably complement administrative activities with these two types of leadership. In addition, the best managers transform the managerial task by inspiring the organizations deeds through inspirational leadership.

In brief

Managers who disregard both the organizational and supervisory leadership requirements of management reduce themselves to administrators, while the ability to inspire has a transformational effect on the managerial function.

Drawing up of weekly or monthly plans or filling in planning schemes in order to ensure that available capacities are used as optimally as possible, although a task of management, does not involve leadership. The deployment of human resources is a totally different matter. The productivity of people is to a high degree constantly affected by their motivation (see Chapter 7).

charisma

In leadership, a certain charisma, the ability to be a source of inspiration for such others as the employees of the company or the institution, is indispensable. It includes an element of charm which offers others the possibility of identifying with the manager in person or with the organization in question.

In addition to a social intelligence and administrative competence, a leader needs to possess the ability to be pleasant while maintaining a professional distance. The capacity to relativize events and to put them in perspective is required of leaders (for example, to put earlier successes in the past), along with a willingness to learn from the past and not to linger on it or to think, complacently, that everything is under control.

8.3 Managers and their motivation

Based on research into actual practice, Maccoby (1988) has identified five types of managers:

- The expert manager
- The helpful manager
- The protective manager
- The enterprising manager
- The development-oriented manager

Fig 8.3 presents a brief outline of these five managerial types.

		Types of manager				
		Expert	Helpful	Protecting	Entrepreneuring	Developing
Characteristics	Positive	▪ delegates ▪ takes risks ▪ decides quickly ▪ is directed towards efficiency	▪ cares for people ▪ has ideals ▪ co-operates well ▪ starts from the positive in people	▪ coaches ▪ protects values ▪ creates loyalty ▪ removes obstacles	▪ thinks holistically ▪ tries and experiments ▪ has vision ▪ is enthusiastic	▪ creates opportunities for others ▪ has sense of humour ▪ is truly interested in others ▪ builds teams
	Negative	▪ takes risks ▪ knows everything better ▪ lusts after power	▪ over-estimates himself ▪ makes others dependent ▪ is idealistic ▪ is a coward ▪ is naive	▪ creates we/they relations ▪ creates followers ▪ avoids conflicts	▪ is utopian ▪ manipulates ▪ is intolerant ▪ forces his own ways and thoughts onto others	▪ is uncertain ▪ is inconsistent ▪ cares too much for himself

Figure 8.3
Types of manager and how they manifest themselves in terms of positive and negative characteristics

expert manager

The expert manager is someone who strives in his own work to obtain professional knowledge and skills as well as technical perfection. An insatiable desire for competence is the most evident characteristic of this managerial type. They are those managers who often emphasize rules and procedures and who, when they become extreme, develop into rigid bureaucrats. Typical examples of this category may be found among the medical staff of hospitals and the managerial teams of other professional service organizations.

helpful manager

Helpful managers are adept at creating team spirit and a sense of unity. They are idealists who are predominantly driven by their need to belong. This type is especially supportive of and occupied with people and can be found in many of the care-giving professions, in education, in R&D organizations and as leading members of policy and planning advisory boards. On the negative side, this type may develop into a naive 'do-gooder'.

protective manager

Protective managers, for whom management predominantly involves the supervision and protection of personnel and the organization as a whole, are primarily motivated by a desire to survive. They demand loyalty and openness from their employees. In extreme cases, they develop into suspicious, self-righteous people. Organizations with a relatively large number of protective managers include many governmental agencies and monopolistic companies.

entrepreneurial manager

Entrepreneurial managers are often good at developing and executing new or renewed ideas. Their strongest motivation is a desire to play. They do not consider an organization as an immutable structure, but rather as a playing field on which, time and again, new and creative things are done. This type is found in all organizations, though any enterprising manager not permitted sufficient 'room to play' does not stay long. Such enterprising spirits become detrimental when they act like blind gamblers who take too many too extreme risks with possible hazards to both themselves and all those who depend on them.

development-oriented manager

Development-oriented managers are facilitators by nature. In general, they consider people to be equal and like to give their employees second and third chances. They are good at building motivated teams. Their most powerful motivation is integrity and the desire to act in a proper manner. They can be found in all kinds of organizations, but especially in organizations that are undergoing growth or change. When there is insufficient development, they will either initiate it or leave. The greatest danger that they present is that they may become narcissists.

8.3.1 *Characteristics of good managers*

Independent from the above catalog of managers and their motivations, we can list the characteristics that managers must possess to be successful (see Table 8.1). Not every arbitrary characteristic mentioned can simply be developed in a human being who wants to become a manager or a leader.

Table 8.1 *Fourteen characteristics of successful managers*

A successful manager		
▪ is loyal	▪ is consequent	▪ is especially trustworthy
▪ likes people	▪ has self-confidence	▪ has ambition
▪ looks across the borders	▪ is optimistic	▪ is modest
▪ is tactful	▪ is courageous	▪ is a teacher
▪ is honest	▪ has managerial power	

(Based on Tracy, 1989)

The following shortcomings – typical of ineffective leaders – also apply to bad managers: they lack energy and enthusiasm, they tolerate their own mediocre performance, they lack a clear vision and sense of direction, they have poor judgment, they avoid collaboration, they fail to provide a suitable example, they resist new ideas, they fail to learn from their mistakes, they have inadequate social skills and fail to develop new ones. It would seem that ineffective leaders are usually not aware of their weaknesses and they overestimate their own qualities, even when they receive 360° *feedback* via their bosses, colleagues and those they are in charge of (Zenger & Folkman, 2009).
Research has also shown that employees often make it hard for their boss to be a good leader. In such situations, managers would be well advised to investigate the forces at work.

Table 8.2 *Interpretations of the boss's behavior depend on how employees regard their boss*

	Employee interpretation	
Managerial behavior	**Good boss**	**Bad boss**
provides critical feedback	honest	hurtful
makes a unilateral decision	decisive	autocratic
indicates that work must be repeated	sets high standards	never satisfied
instigates achievement standards	diciplined	a control freak
works weekends	driven	obsessive
gives unasked-for advice	helpful	interfering
pauses before reacting to proposal	reflective	not helpful
does not reprimand	empathetic	weak
loses self-control in public	passionate	unpredictable
managing by walking around	empathy	no common sense
breaks a promise	seizes opportunities	unreliable
limits interactions with employees	structured	not available

Employees are inclined to be hasty in labeling their boss as a good or a bad one. How they label their boss will determine how they interpret his or her behavior – as well as how they react to that behavior. Behavior can sometimes be determined by earlier impressions, prejudices, rumours, reputations that have preceded them and past experiences with other bosses. According to Manzoni and Barsoux (2009) it is important for managers to have an understanding of the situation that they have inherited as the new boss. They need to make sure that they put a lot of time into their employees right from the start and to act immediately if things threaten to backfire.

We keep hearing that leaders and managers are born and not made, that some managerial qualities are formed in the first years of life and that they are allowed to be expressed and, therefore, strengthened during childhood. There are, however, behavioral characteristics such as optimism, courage and tact that can be developed at any age.
Insofar as leadership qualities important for the management of an organization are concerned, there are a number of resources that can be used with beneficial results, such as training and the extension of practical knowledge. The conscious acquisition, categorization and evaluation of all kinds of experience is a meaningful activity. Becoming conscious of unconscious experiences and situations in management is especially important, as it increases awareness about the consequences arising from action along with their probable causes.

8.3.2 *Managers and styles of leadership*

Modern managers who contribute to the future of many organizations must be able to interact skillfully with other employees. Moreover, they have a good understanding of the primary processes involved in an organization. When managing, a manager – whether director, team leader, department head or foreman – is in direct contact with his employees. It is his or her task to influence employee behavior in such a way that organizational goals are, wherever possible, attained. The manner (or rather the style) of leadership is seen as an important factor, especially insofar as interactions with other people are concerned.

LEADERS' TONE OF VOICE

The finding: It's not what you say; it's how you say it. It's possible to predict which executives will win a business competition solely on the basis of the social signals they send.

The study: Professor Sandy Pentland and colleague Daniel Olguín outfitted executives at a party with devices that recorded data on their social signals: i.e., tone of voice, gesticulation, proximity to others, and more. Five days later the same executives presented business plans to a panel of judges in a contest. Without reading or hearing these pitches, Pentland correctly forecasts the winners, using only data collected at the party.

tone of voice

87%: The accuracy of Pentland's predictions about who would win a business plan competition is 87%.

The challenge: Can we really tell who will succeed in competitive business situations without knowing what they have to offer?

Source: *Harvard Business Review*, January/February 2010, p. 34-35

It involves the knack of getting other people to deliver the performance that the organization requires. It is, of course, important that a manager can and wants to manage, but the social communicative skills involved in observing, listening, having conversations and handling conflicts are also of importance. Managers are required to develop a style that suits them personally and that is suited to their aims, capacities and behaviors, as well as to the demands posed by employees and the organizational context in which they are employed. There is no one single best style of leadership. Rather, different factors are involved in any action enabling other people to do their work in a meaningful way and influencing all this productivity in a manner favorable to the organization.

8.4 Leadership and styles of leadership

The work done in an organization involves people first and foremost. The way a manager acts, or rather his or her style of leadership, has an important influence on this human activity. In this section, we will address the social effects of leadership as seen in interactions with people as well as the attitudes underlying interpersonal communication (see Chapter 7).
The art of management also entails the ability to prevent any tensions between employees that may hinder their functioning. Fear of managers and cringing, docile and nervous behavior are some symptoms of poor management. Insight into one's own way of managing and understanding the way a manager should behave is, consequently, very important. From a managerial perspective, it is extremely beneficial to be alert to factors affecting employee behavior in order to act appropriately whenever this behavior manifests itself.
A leader's role necessarily entails acts of personal contact that influence the behavior of employees. This influence is exercised by means of a combination of direction-giving and task-oriented behaviors as well as supportive or relationship-nurturing activities.
Organizational leadership can be further characterized in terms of the formal basis on which it is established. The organization has given the manager the authority to assign tasks to employees. After all, someone has to be able to take the initiative. Employees are required to perform the activities stemming from that initiative, to let themselves be governed by the manager's directives, model behaviors and tasks, all the while acting with respect for and showing regard to the manager.
Naturally, it is important to give careful thought to the way in which a leader takes up his task and deals with his most immediate colleagues, his subordinates. Resounding through each approach to management and style of leadership is a certain notion of how a leader should motivate employees. Two polarities can be identified: autocratic and participative leadership.

task-oriented behaviors

relationship-nurturing activities

8.4.1 Autocratic leadership

autocratic leaders

Autocratic (auto=self, cratos=governance) leaders manage by instituting stringent directives and assignments, exercising control and threatening sanctions. This last measure is, to a certain degree, meant to propagate fear among employees. When an employee does not act in accordance with a manager's wishes, he or she suffers a form of punishment: reduced compensation, a reprimand, a fine or, perhaps diminished chances of promotion. Autocratic management personnel believe such methods are required to keep employee efforts directed at the organizational goals. Money is seen as an important spur for driving employees to higher levels of performance.

For this type of leader, a straightforward system of rewarding good and punishing poor performance is the best way to ensure that goals are attained. This management method hardly, if at all, includes subordinates in the organizational or departmental decision-making processes. It, of course, reflects the personal characteristics of the leader, who is usually task-oriented and who tends to regard employees as instrumental to the attaining of goals. Besides observations of other people and experiences of their working behavior, the personality of the leader plays an important role in determining his or her adoption of this autocratic approach. It may even be that managers who behave in such heavy-handed ways are themselves insecure about their success and act, consequently, as a result of this insecurity.

task-oriented

instrumental

SUCCESS GETS INTO YOUR HEAD

Neuroscientists have long understood that the brain can rewire itself in response to experience – a phenomenon known as neuroplasticity. But until recently, they didn't know what causes gray matter to become plastic, to begin changing. Breakthrough research by a team at MIT's Picower Institute for Learning and Memory has documented one type of environmental feedback that triggers plasticity: success. Equally important and somewhat surprising: it's opposite, failure, has no impact.

Earl Miller, the lead researcher on the study (published in the journal *Neuron* last summer), says understanding the link to environmental feedback is crucial to improving how people teach and motivate because it's a big part of how we learn. But we absorb more from success than from failure, according to the study.

Miller's researchers gave monkeys a simple learning task: they presented one of two pictures. If it was Picture A, the monkeys were supposed to look to the left; if Picture B, to the right. When the monkeys looked in the correct direction, they were rewarded with a drop of juice. All the while the team recorded brain function.

'Neurons in the prefrontal cortex and striatum, where the brain tracks success and failure, sharpened their tuning after success', says Miller. What's more, those changes lingered for several seconds, making brain activity more efficient the next time the monkey did the task. Thereafter, each success was processed more efficiently. That is, the monkey had learned. 'But after failure,' Miller points out, 'there was little change in brain activity'. In other words, the brain didn't store any information about what went wrong and use it the next time. The monkey just tried again.

Does this research confirm the management tenet of focusing on your and your team's strengths and successes? Miller cautions against making too tidy a connection between his findings and an environment like the workplace, but he offers this suggestion: 'Maybe the lesson is to know that the brain will learn from success, and you don't need to dwell on that. You need to pay more attention to failures and challenge why you fail.'

Source: S. Berinato (2010) *Harvard Business Review* January/February, p. 28

8.4.2 *Participative leadership*

Participative leadership refers to a very different notion about the role of a manager.

participative leader

A participative leader assumes that the goals of the employees and those of the organization are not contradictory. Rather; they can be made to agree with each other.

A participative leader strives to find opportunities to solicit participation from his department. The vertical relationships are then also seen as consultative ones in which contributions may be made from below. Mutual cooperation is promoted by striving to create good team spirit in departments and work groups.

people-oriented

This type of leader is more people-oriented when finding ways to attain goals.

The participative approach to management allows the employees to take part in departmental goings-on. By involving them and by stimulating cooperation, collaboration and coordination, participative leadership aims to have a positive effect on results.

EUROPEAN MANAGERS ARE BETTER THAN AMERICAN MANAGERS

European companies outperform American ones. The reason? European managers are better at managing.

The German consultancy Roland Berger has investigated how well 100 of the world's biggest companies performed during the period 1998 to 2007. It found that on average, European companies outperformed American ones: their contribution to the overall turnover of the companies under investigation was higher, their growth was on average somewhat higher, they were more profitable and their turnover was more stable. The cause lies in the way that companies are managed, and European and American companies diverge considerably in this regard.

The differences
European managers are expected to develop a strong vision and strategy and to continue to build onto the company's existing basis. American managers are primarily expected to be skilful networkers and to act quickly, achieve quick results and make radical changes. European managers are also skilful people managers. American managers are more inclined to follow internal guidelines, have a more direct approach and give employees less room to maneuvre. The fact that the financial focus is greater in the US is partly responsible for this since it allows less room for departure from the norm. Europeans also have more highly developed participatory leadership systems: they encourage debate much more than their American colleagues, are more open to different opinions and expect less obediance and loyalty from their employees. The European business world is more culturally diverse too. Indicative of this is the fact that 42% of young European top managers have worked in other countries as against 25% of young American top managers. Last but not least, Americans have a focus on personal skills (such as knowledge of products) while among European managers, professional competencies such as good business sense and communicative skills are regarded as at least as important.

Source: Trends 9-4-2009/*Management Trends*, July-August 2009

8.4.3 Theory X and Y (McGregor, 1960)

McGregor

McGregor has stated that each form of management can be related to distinct views of what leaders need to do in order to motivate subordinates. He has identified two contradictory notions, both of which are common.

Theory X (McGregor, 1960)

Theory X

The first notion, labeled Theory X, is based on three assumptions:

- The average human being has an adversity to work
- Has to be forced to perform
- Shuns responsibility

autocratic style

Leaders adopting this view will usually display the authoritarian or autocratic style of leadership identified in Section 8.4.1, because, in their opinion, such management methods are necessary in order to attain the desired goals. This form of management will often involve force, control and punishment – types of activities that are normally included under the heading of 'management by direction and control.'
Autocratic managers believe that employees can only be coerced into working towards organizational goals and that any contributions from subordinates will not have such targets in mind. The consequence may be that employees themselves start behaving according to Theory X assumptions, as if this theory were true. This pattern can only be broken by promoting the view that the Theory X image of the human being and human nature is, in fact, not true.

Theory Y (McGregor, 1960)

Theory Y

Theory Y suggests a completely different conception of human nature. It is based on the following assumptions:

- Work is just as natural as rest.
- The human being is prepared to bear responsibility.
- Every human being is a source of creativity.
- Money is not the only impulse to work; the need for self-actualization also plays a role.

On the basis of these assumptions, it can be seen that the goals of the individual and the organization are not contradictory but, indeed, potentially harmonious. Adopting such a position results in managerial practices that may be encapsulated in the notion of 'management by integration and self-control,' a form of managing that can be implemented by applying a system of Management by Objectives (MbO) (see Section 9.3.3).
It will be obvious that any leadership conforming to this notion favors a participative style that essentially implies another role for the leader than the one performed by the autocrat.

integration principle

Participative leaders assume the existence of an integration principle (by means of which the interests of individual employees and organizations are deemed to be compatible), and they can therefore be described as follows:

- Supportive of subordinates
- Trusting the integrity and ability of subordinates
- Having high expectations about performance levels
- Capable of providing good instructions for the tasks to be performed
- Willing to provide assistance to those performing below par

8.4.4 'Linking pin' structure (Likert, 1961)

supportive leadership

linking pin

The qualities mentioned at the end of the previous section can be associated with the notions of supportive leadership and overlapping groups, according to which effective leaders are to strive for the transformation of their departments into groups by finding ways to enable participation. In this vision, managers become group leaders while still remaining members of an overriding group of managers. Between these two levels, the leader fulfills the role of a 'linking pin,' a notion that is diagrammatically depicted in Fig 8.4.

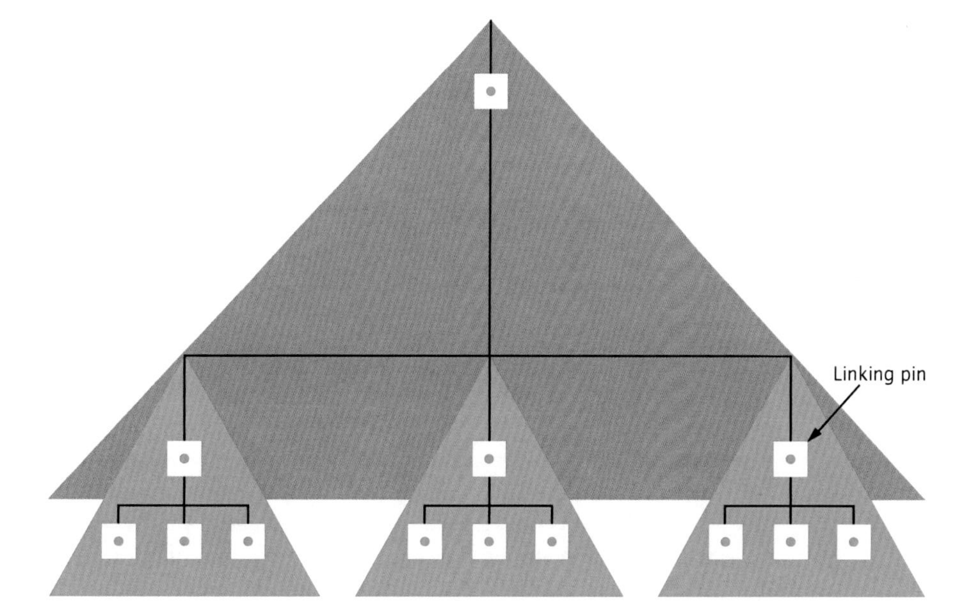

Figure 8.4
Overlapping groups held together by the 'linking pin'

This set-up, though still an organizationally linear structure, can be described as a series of groups that overlap by means of the 'linking pin' function. The structure allows wishes and ideas originating in the lowest levels of an organization to reach the highest level. Though still describable as a linear form of organization, this structure displays a notable variation, insofar as the vertical relationship, instead of being a traditional top-down command relationship, has become consultative. A degree of leveling has been introduced.
According to Likert, leadership in this 'linking pin' structure is based on the positive expectations that the managerial and operational employees have of each other (compare McGregor's 'Theory Y').

8.4.5 *Paths of leadership development*

In order to determine which type of leader one will need in the future, it is important to understand the path along which the organization is developing as well as the ways in which instrumental and social leadership need to evolve. Here, two movements can be detected:

1 The evolution of improvisation into planning
2 The development of a top-down command structure into a consultative form of management

The inclusion of improvisation into planning generally involves three phases. First, one adapts oneself, then one tries to stay ahead of developments, and finally one tries, via planning, to control development to a certain degree.
Any blind acceptance of authority from above is definitely ended. It is obvious that the tendency towards democracy makes totally different demands on social leadership. The way to get people to accept decisions is by consultation in advance and in time, and by asking them to collaborate. These directions are depicted in Fig 8.5, on the basis of which four types of leaders can be identified.

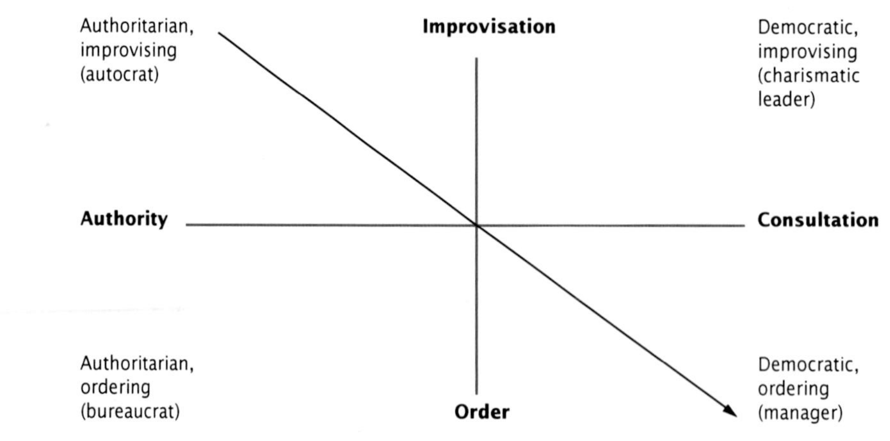

Figure 8.5
Types of leadership and development in characteristics of organization

The authoritarian-improvising type: the autocrat

This type does everything on the basis of personal insight and authority. Intuition also plays a role. In this category, one may encounter brilliant people who, especially in the pioneering phase, can lead any group under their management to great successes. A disadvantage of this type is, however, that too little responsibility is given to other people, as a consequence of which, skilled people leave and lower (or middle) management generally stays weak. Succession presents another problem, as a vacuum develops under the top level of management. The distinctive characteristics of the autocratic style of leadership of the autocrat result in:

- Strict obedience being demanded of employees
- Employee contacts becoming extremely detailed and critical
- Communication being reduced to one-way
- Everything conforming to an essentially 'egotistic' style

The authoritarian-structure type: the bureaucrat

This type arranges everything in accordance to rules and prescriptions. Authority is based on strict ordering. Hardly anything is subject to consultation, often due to the manager's lack of nerve. This style can have a paralyzing effect on employees and the organization. Since contacts with employees are generally avoided, a lack of communication results.

The democratic-improvising type: the charismatic leader

This 'inspired' leader is often depicted as the most ideal type. He inspires his employees by consultation and intellectual improvisation. A frequent negative consequence of this style of leadership is that it develops into a type of father-son relationship. As well as this, the improvisational nature of this style generally precludes the making of definite plans and many decisions are postponed, only being made at the last moment. The result is uncertainty and sometimes even chaos.

The democratic-structure type: the manager of the future

The advantages that this type offers an organization are clear: high-quality instrumental and social leadership, structure and consultation. But the dangers of this type of leadership must not be underestimated. There is a latent but constantly present lack of resolve and decisiveness. Despite such a risk, this type seems to be most strongly in accord with what modern society and the organization of the future require of a leader.

8.4.6 Styles of leadership: different approaches

characteristics

The early, classical approaches to leadership focused special attention on the characteristics of a leader. They were used to determine the characteristics that distinguish a good leader from a bad one. Consideration was given to such issues as:

- Physical characteristics: research has shown that leaders are generally taller than those they manage.
- Personality characteristics: other research shows that good leaders have more self-confidence and are more eager to take the initiative than bad ones are; good leaders also appear to have more understanding for what their employees think and feel than less effective leaders;
- Intellectual characteristics: research shows that good leaders generally appear to be better educated than less capable leaders.

personality of the leader

This approach concentrates exclusively on the personality of the leader and views personality as the sum of a person's qualities, characteristics and traits. Comparing managers with non-managerial employees on this basis, the former would seem to be more socially oriented, self-confident and adaptable, while also displaying more initiative, stronger commitment and greater verbal skills.

One disadvantage of such a personality-based approach lies in its implications for management training. It suggests that management skills cannot really be learned by those who do not possess the required character profile. Unfortunately, few possess it entirely. Another important point to remember is the fact that leadership involves a process of interaction between leader and subordinate and that equal weight must be placed on both sides of that interaction. Recent studies have concentrated on both this relationship and this style of leadership.

Employees, task characteristics, superiors, colleagues and organizational cultures all influence the styles of effective leaders. Employees are frequently able to adapt themselves to a particular leader's approach, an adjustment which is dictated by their experience with other managers (habituation), their own values and norms, and their own ability and willingness to perform a task. It enables the employees to have a direct influence on managerial style.

The nature of the tasks performed by the employees (routine work, amount of uncertainty and so on) also influence the style of leadership. Employees involved in the more prestigious work undertaken in organizations should be increasingly recognized as professionals and allowed to make relatively autonomous decisions, and exercise craftsmanship as well as their own problem-solving capacities in order to realize both organizational and personal goals. If employees capable of performing their work relatively autonomously still have to be managed in a more hands-on manner, good working conditions should be arranged so that a creative contribution, an inspiring working climate and an appropriate work culture is established. Where the work consists of repetitive tasks, a high degree of standardization and clear operational rules, the managerial task is especially concerned with explaining those rules, ensuring that materials and people are in the right place at the right time, and personally recognizing individual contributions.

The behavior of superiors also has an effect. By distributing rewards and granting promotions they influence the behavior of those who are responsible to them. Moreover, they must often function as a role model. The amount of authority that superiors delegate to their managerial employees is an especially significant determining factor, for one of the necessary conditions of management is the ability to wield a certain amount of power.

power

Furthermore, the style of leadership has to accord with the organizational style. The manager has to exercise his influence within the cultural boundaries of the organization. Acting within an organization may be subject to a large number of unwritten notions about what is and what is not done. These may include unexpressed attitudes about professional distance between manager and employee concerning the degrees of familiarity, accessibility and approachability permitted, as well as the amount of necessary consultation between management and employees required. Stated bluntly, the organizational culture determines managerial style (see Section 8.7.1).

WHAT REALLY MOTIVATES PEOPLE

Ask leaders what they think makes employees enthusiastic about work and they'll tell you in no uncertain terms. In a recent survey we invited more than 600 managers from dozens of companies to rank the impact on employee motivation and emotions of five workplace factors commonly considered significant: recognition, incentives, interpersonal support, support for making progress, and clear goals. 'Recognition for good work (either public or private)' came out number one.

Unfortunately, those managers are wrong.

Having just completed a multiyear study tracking the day-to-day activities, emotions, and motivation levels of hundreds of knowledge workers in a wide variety of settings, we now know what the top motivator of performance is – and, amazingly, it's the factor those survey participants ranked dead last. It's progress. On days when workers have the sense they're making headway in their jobs, or when they receive support that helps them overcome obstacles, their emotions are most positive and their drive to succeed is at its peak. On days when they feel they are spinning their wheels or encountering roadblocks to meaningful accomplishment, their moods and motivation are lowest.

Source: T. M. Amabile and S. J. Kramer (2010), *Harvard Business Review* January/February, p. 44

Style of leadership: contingent on the situation and person

effective style of leadership

It is not possible to make absolute statements about the best and most effective style of leadership. Research indicates that there are situations in which employees prefer an autocratic style of leadership. This preference may frequently be held by employees who perform typically individualistic work in which very little contact with colleagues is necessary (truck driving for instance).

There is no one style of leadership that will always lead to the best results in all circumstances. The part played by the personality of the leader in determining the type of leadership displayed by that individual should also not be overlooked. In a nutshell, the most desired style of leadership is one best suited to the individual and the context.

8.4.7 Situational leadership (Hersey & Blanchard, 1986)

situational leadership

task maturity

The idea of situational leadership has been elaborated by, among others, Hersey and Blanchard. In their theory, an appropriate leadership style depends on the degree of task maturity among the employees. Task maturity refers to the willingness to take responsibility for a certain task in a specific situation. The degree of task maturity depends on employee competence and the willingness to work. An employee's capabilities can be measured in terms of his or her knowledge, experience and skill in performing a specific task. Willingness to work depends on the self-confidence, devotion and motivation of the employee in question. Hersey and Blanchard identify four levels of task maturity

- M1: incapable and unwilling or insecure
- M2: incapable but willing or sufficiently confident
- M3: capable and unwilling or insecure
- M4: capable, willing and full of self-confidence

A manager can help to improve an employee's performance by providing guidance and support. This could take the form of the manager determining the results to be attained, organizing the work, setting time limits and verifying the quality of the performance delivered. Such activities are all forms of one-way communication: the manager explains and determines what needs to be done. They are additionally all task-oriented. Conversely, support is first of all concerned with the provision of assistance, maintenance of communication channels, stimulation of cooperation and the giving of feedback. Support is communication in two directions and is relationship-oriented.

guidance and support

Depending on the degree of guidance and support that is provided, four styles of leadership can be identified.

- Style 1: telling (S1). With this style, there is a lot of guidance but little support. The manager prescribes the goals and roles, gives detailed instructions and closely supervises task performance.
- Style 2: selling (S2). With this style, there is a lot of guidance and support. The manager explains the purposes of the instructions and goals, tries to determine what employees think of decisions and listens to their ideas and suggestions.
- Style 3: participating (S3). With this style, there is a lot of support but little guidance. This style of leadership is exemplified by managers who involve their employees in decisions, actively listen to employee comments, support and encourage employees in their work, and make it easier for them to complete their tasks.
- Style 4: delegating (S4). With this style, there is little support and little guidance. Working in this style, managers let their employees take care of the operational and support functions themselves and the responsibility for making and realizing decisions is completely left to the employees.

Hersey and Blanchard state that the leadership style has to accord with the task maturity of the employee. This relationship is depicted in Fig 8.6.

It is the manager's job to increase the task maturity or the capability level of the employees.

Given proper guidance and support as well as appropriate authority and power, employees will become more capable. The manager will, therefore, always need to adapt his style of leadership to match the increasing capability of his employees. This is why the effective manager does not have a uniform style of leadership: instead, he or she adopts a style that is in tune with the employee's abilities.
In the long term, staff development is the key to an effective organization. If the employee task maturity in an organization increases, managers will be able to delegate more responsibilities to employees. For managers, this means that they will have more time for new challenges and tasks.

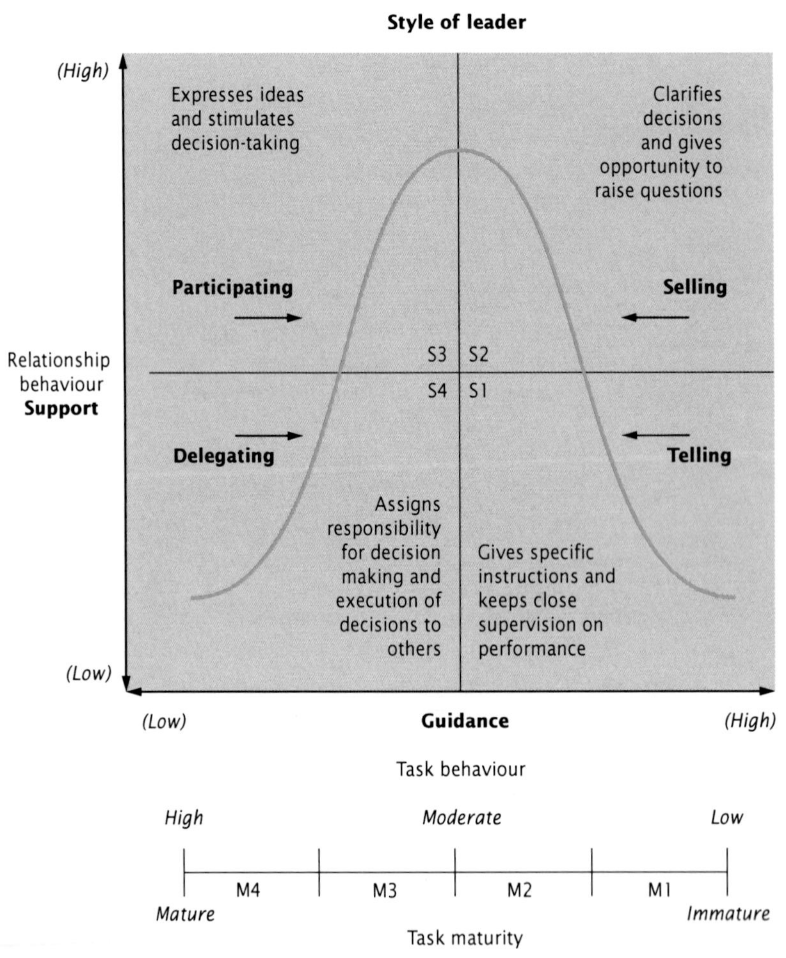

Figure 8.6
Situation-determined styles of leadership

Source: *Hersey and Blanchard*, 1986

CASE

Mini case study 8.4

The power of progress

You can proactively create both the perception and the reality of progress. If you are a high-ranking manager, take great care to clarify overall goals, ensure that people's efforts are properly supported, and refrain from exerting time pressure so intense that minor glitches are perceived as crises rather than learning opportunities. Cultivate a culture of helpfulness. While you're at it, you can facilitate progress in a more direct way: Roll up your sleeves and pitch in. Of course, all these efforts will not only keep people working with gusto but also get the job done faster.

Source: T.M. Amabile and S.J. Kramer (2010), *Harvard Business Review* January/February, p. 45

8.4.8 Transformational leadership

transactional leadership

Transformational leadership is sometimes seen as the antithesis of transactional leadership, a form of leadership which places a strong emphasis on the employee achieving set goals in return for a reward. As such, transactional leadership has a material basis. The task-oriented leadership style discussed previously can be regarded as transactional. The transformational leader, on the other hand, aims to alter (or transform) the goals of the company and change the employees' attitudes. He or she tries to make values concrete and to develop a vision that the employees can relate to and that they find worthwhile striving for. A great deal of attention is paid to drawing the employees into the organization emotionally. Change and inspiration are the key words. Covey's view (1989 and 2004), as described in 8.1.4 and 8.2, has contributed much towards encouraging inspirational leadership 'from within': from one's own inner voice and that of others.

change and inspiration

Exhibit 8.2

Changing from within

The example Covey gives has to do with an alliance between newspapers. He had been asked to intervene and help find solutions to the diminishing returns. A cultural audit that Covey carried out showed that the newspapers were ruled by suspicion, power politics and so on. He took the following approach when he gave feedback relating to the research results. First of all, he posed the question of what newspapers ultimately aimed to do in our present society. The statements that came to his ears as the microphone went the rounds were without exception positive and stressed the vital role of newspapers in serving freedom and democracy. Covey then asked whether they actually believed in this. The answer was a unanimous 'yes'. The following question was more difficult: how do you know for sure that somebody really believes in this. After some hesitation, he was given a couple of examples. Then came the key question: how many of you are in a position to really contribute to society in the way that you would like to (or in other words, to serve the cause of freedom). Only a few people raised their hands. It was at that moment that Covey gave his report on the research results. 'I showed them just how much suspicion, interpersonal conflict, departmental rivalry, misalignment and disempowerment of employees there was. Then the four roles were discussed with them: starting with yourself, involving others by clear discussion about the goals, setting up systems for affirmation and reward in order to create optimal conditions for empowerment.

Source: Covey (1989 and 2004)

8.5 Influencing human behavior

organizational goals

In addition to giving orders, assignments and instructions, managing people involves motivating employees and channeling their actions and working behavior in order to realize organizational goals. Managing people involves a process of interaction between superiors and immediate co-workers. The way this happens depends on the way in which those in charge conceive of the relationship with their fellow workers. Each style of leadership implies certain notions about the methods used to motivate employees.
Peculiar to the work situation is the fact that employees working in organizations are more or less willing to accept an authority relationship as part of the labor exchange process and are prepared to adjust personal goals to a certain degree. As their part of the exchange, organizations offer various material and non-material incentives or rewards to people in order to activate their work behavior. For a given contribution to the effort of attaining organizational goals, employees obtain an incentive. In exchange for this reward, they have to be willing to perform work, maintain loyalty and harmonize their personal desires with the objectives of an organization or perhaps even subordinate their personal ambition in order to accomplish organizational goals. It is essential to remember that through consultation with workers, these goals can be influenced by the employees themselves.

8.5.1 Motivation of others

Managers can contribute to the success of their employees by expecting good performances from them and by making it possible for them to deliver these. One important way of approaching this task is via the notion of co-workership: identifying what actually drives an employee and what an employee does in order to realize his ambitions and intentions.

co-workership

In other words, it involves the state of being motivated and wanting to be motivated. As already discussed in Chapter 7, motivation refers to the totality of motives active in a human being at a certain moment. A motive is a rational and emotional impulse that affects the will and stimulates the human being to act. Having insight into someone's motives consequently provides insight into the factors that generate a certain behavior in him or her. Here, the extent to which various motives are active at any given time and in any particular situation can be coordinated with the various rewards or stimuli available. If we realize that different people are motivated by different factors we will also realize that what is a motivating working environment for one person will not necessarily appeal to another individual in the same way. There will always be people who only view work as a source of income or social contact. Organizational theory is, however, based on the assumption that many people want more from their working time and work situation, and they often seek types of work conforming to their own capacities and development. A certain belief in people underlies such a premise.

It makes a great difference whether motivational practices are based on a pessimistic view of human beings, their inherent laziness, stupidity, disinterest, untrustworthiness, incompetence and unwillingness, or whether there is an opposing, optimistic notion about human behavior. In 'Theory Y,' McGregor confirms his belief that people are creative, sensible, interested, trustworthy and helpful, and certainly willing to work.

Theory X manager

On the other hand, a 'Theory X' manager runs the risk that his or her behavior will actually confirm the basic premises of the theory, inciting the very behavior that they presuppose in a sort of vicious circle. People will tend to behave in accordance with the way in which they are treated. Allowed little freedom and independence while being strictly controlled and subjected to punitive measures, employees will start displaying dependent and childish work conduct instead of developing mature task behaviors.

Theory Y manager

The 'Theory Y' manager, in contrast, creates conditions that allow people to develop within their work situation. Employees treated in such a manner will quickly learn to motivate themselves.

The capable manager can contribute to the successes that employees experience as well as to the factors that motivate them by expecting good performances and by viewing bad experiences as occasions to learn. Managers and employees must consequently agree on definitions of good and bad performances. To detect any timely adjustments that need to be made, employees and managers should, either on a formal or informal basis, regularly review task-fulfillment procedures and efficiency rates. On such occasions, satisfaction with good performance should be indicated, and shortfalls should be used to determine ways of improving situations or learning from them. The manager can ensure that employees act in an appropriately productive manner by playing in on what has motivated them.

task-fulfillment

The managerial task requires both a good understanding of this principle and the ability to put it into action. The issue here is how authority and power are exercised in order to influence work behavior. Whether the influence is felt consciously or not, keeping the employee's performance focused on the organization's goals is the crucial thing.

Exhibit 8.3

Subordinateship for three levels of power distance

Short power distance	Medium power distance (USA)	Long power distance
Subordinates have low dependence needs.	Subordinates have medium dependence needs.	Subordinates have high dependence needs.
Superiors have low dependence needs in relation to superiors.	Superiors have medium dependence needs in relation to superiors.	Superiors have high dependence needs in relation to superiors.
Subordinates expect superiors to consult them and may rebel or strike if superiors are not seen as staying within their legitimate roles.	Subordinates expect superiors to consult them but will accept autocratic behavior as well.	Subordinates expect superiors to act autocratically.
For most, ideal superior is a loyal democrat.	For most, ideal superior is a resource democrat.	For most, ideal superior is a benevolent autocrat or paternalist.
Laws and rules apply to all and privileges for superiors are not considered acceptable.	Laws and rules apply to all, but a certain level of privilege for superiors is considered normal.	Everybody expects superiors to enjoy privileges; laws and rules differ for superiors and subordinates.
Status symbols are frowned upon and will readily come under attack by subordinates.	Status symbols for superiors contribute moderately to their authority and will be accepted by subordinates.	Status symbols are very important and contribute strongly to the superior's authority with subordinates.

Source: *Transnational Management*, Bartlett and Ghoshal (1992)

8.5.2 Influencing behavior: different sources of power and authority

A director who oversees the accomplishment of an organization's goals or a manager in charge of a department who aspires to attain his departmental objectives have to exploit the possibilities presented by employees while working within the intended framework. In other words, managers, whether they are work group leaders, department heads or directors, have to be able to influence employee behavior and channel it in ways so that they achieve the desired ends. To accomplish this bit of managerial coordination, they have five sources of influence at their disposal.

five sources of influence

- Reward or positive sanction. When the actions of an employee are in accord with the assignments or wishes of the superior, a variety of rewards may be granted, including compliments, assignment of new challenging tasks and monetary compensation (as in the case of payment for performance).
- Punishment or negative sanction: influence by instilling fear in the subordinate. When an employee does not act in accordance with the superior's wishes, the result may be a scolding, exclusion of the employee from 'nice jobs,' being banned from work consultation sessions, fewer opportunities to earn extra income and even reduced chances of promotion.
- The position as such: the functional and hierarchical place the manager has within the organization. A president can, based on his professional status, exercise more influence than a division manager or a department head.

- Expertise. Acceptance of directives and assignments by subordinates increases when they are more convinced of the fact that the manager has greater knowledge and experience at his disposal.
- Identification. Influence can also be based on the identification of subordinates with their manager. This often depends on the degree to which the manager possesses a certain charisma.

Power and authority

formal sources of influence

informal sources of influence

The five sources of influence can be divided further into two groups. The first group – reward, punishment and position – stem from the place that the manager occupies in the organizational hierarchy. Managerial authority is substantially based on these formal sources of influence. The second group – expertise and identification – are more informal and emanate from the manager's personality and professional characteristics. These informal sources of influence, in combination with the above-mentioned formal sources, provide the means by which the manager exercises power.

The optimal situation is one in which power and authority coincide. In such cases, the formal authority with which managers are endowed as a result of their positions is experienced by their subordinates as correct and valued positively by them. Authority is entrenched in the formal office and is, consequently, known as positional power. Power, on the other hand, is detached from office and merely involves the ability to promote a particular set of desired values or goals to a dominant position. A situation which deviates from the optimum is one in which an informal leadership exists that does not support the formal authority.

Although forms of informally exercised power may reinforce the formal organization and, therefore, be supportive of an organization's official authority, informal power may also impede productivity (incidental or systematic soldiering), such as in the case of a strike or a work-to-rule campaign. A group can make a stand, exercising its power by undertaking collective action and, resisting such measures as a reorganization. These forms of informal behavior may counteract the will of the organization.

CASE Mini case study 8.5

The actual lines of authority within an organization can deviate from the formal organizational structure and the formal definition of authority. As such an assistant can, in fact, have a greater influence than his or her superior. Such is the case when he or she, without having the authority at his/her disposal, knows how to associate with people in the department in such a way that he or she manages to get things done where the superior cannot.

Handling power and authority (exploiting sources of influence)

In order to function well as a leader in an organization or as participant in processes of decision making and to get the things done for which one can be held responsible, it is important to make wise use of the previously mentioned five sources of influence.

positional power

In the case of positional power (also called formal or legitimate power), the extent of the power entrenched in the office that an employee holds in an organization needs to be properly exercised. People do something for someone else when they think that the act is permitted, and perhaps required. The position held in an organization may entail either a right or an obligation to access various kinds of networks, to attend meetings, to join steering committees and so on. This right of access does not only yield greater information, it also makes people more easily approachable. The position the employee holds may also determine the amount of say that he or she has concerning such resources as personnel, funding, equipment and the like. The most appealing forms of positional power are also likely to involve the authority to inflict punishment and grant rewards. Power can also be based on being allowed to divide or hold back desirable resources such as promotion, time, pleasant work, parking tickets, equipment, trips and congresses. It is obvious that these sources of power only have power when others value them as such. The value of positional power does not only depend on the importance that employees attach to rewards or punishments. Just as important is the degree to which the organization that created the position is flexible with the resources.

personal power

Personal power or personal prestige is granted to people on the basis of their qualities and not just the positions that they happen to occupy. Thus, a person can get others to do things out of a sense of personal respect or out of respect for such attributes as his or her knowledge, personality or experience. Personal power can also be based on the need of employees to follow or to identify with someone and to see that person as an example. The manager/leader of the future will depend predominantly on these person-oriented sources of power, an observation that has been made repeatedly throughout this book.

Even though the everyday notion of power often has a negative connotation, we need to realize that a manager without influence and power cannot fulfill his/her managerial duties. In this sense, power is a resource that allows the organization to attain its goals, a fact that explains why each manager needs to wield power in a conscious and conscientious manner. In order to realize the goals of the organization, managers are, by definition, dependent on others. However, they also have to avoid becoming unnecessarily dependent on them.

According to Kotter (1982), power is obtained and maintained by:

- having control over tangible resources on which others depend; as a result, the manager can, by means of allocating or not allocating such resources, influence the behavior of others
- having control over information and information channels; the power of experts is, to a large extent, based on this ('knowledge is power')
- cultivating positive relationships with others; these can be based on feelings of obligation, professional reputation, a high degree of identification or a sense of interdependence

power of information
personal networks

To the five above-mentioned sources of influence based on someone's position and/or personality should now be added the power of information and personal networks: the power derived from the possession of disposable information and the ability to access other people and/or information. For completeness we can add physical prowess as the archetypal form of power, namely the power of physical strength. In the modern work organization, this form is unlikely to be a source of an individual's organizational power.

Given their personal positions, effective managers need to learn to handle power in a very conscious manner. They should not be careless in their relationships with others and should possess an understanding of how power and authority relationships affect the ways in which organizations function. A sharp eye is needed, especially in relation to how tasks are performed, how obstacles are removed and so on. It is important to know who has influence and who has to be approached to get something done. The sources of power that they need to be able to use and to manipulate are summed up in the following figure (see Fig 8.7).

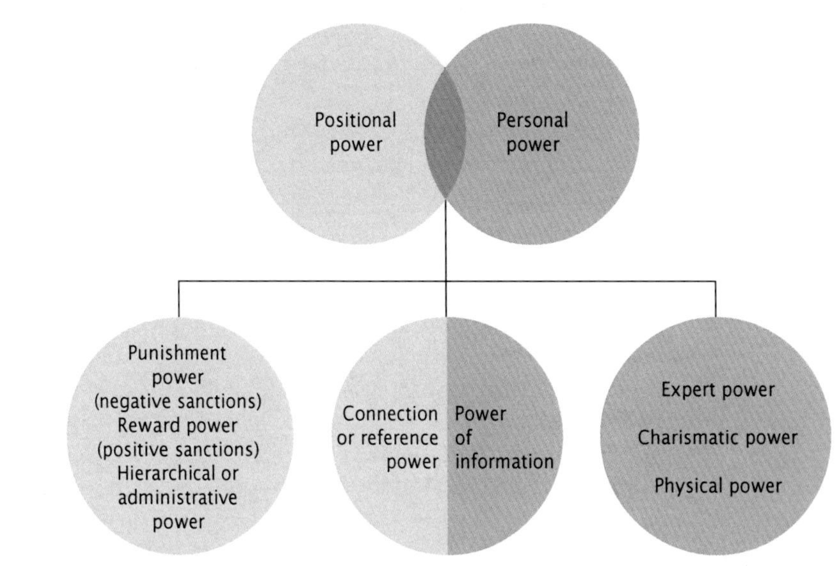

Figure 8.7 *Diagrammatic representation of various sources of power*

Managing with power

Pfeffer

In his book *Managing with Power* (1992), Jeffrey Pfeffer states that the effective handling of political processes in organizations requires a view of management that stresses the development and execution of power. The power perspective offered by Pfeffer consists of seven recommendations addressed to the individual manager.

- Determine what your goals are: what has to be attained.
- Make a diagnosis of patterns of power and interdependence, determine which persons and parties are influential and of importance for the attainment of your own goals. Keep track of what points of view other people and parties express, what opinions they have and how they might react to propositions from your side.
- Determine which sources of power other people and parties have and which of those sources can be activated in relevant situations.
- Determine what sources of power are at your own disposal and how you can develop your sources of power further.
- Determine which power strategies and tactics are most appropriate in which situations and what strategies might follow.
- Choose an appropriate strategy on the basis of the other six steps in order to attain your goals.

power and influence

trust

As Morgan (1986) states in his book on organizational images and metaphors, one can understand an organization well only if one looks at the phenomenon of organization in different ways. The conceptualization of an organization from the perspective of power has many advantages. Power and influence are basic characteristics of organizations. By focusing attention on the power processes, the myth of organizational rationality is broken. One comes to realize that such apparently rational things as goals, structures, technologies, management styles and so on, have a political dimension which co-determines the functioning of the organization and is sometimes even the decisive factor. But there are also disadvantages in using this perspective. Good management also requires trust. When looking at events in and around an organization in terms of power, influence, rivalry and conflict, one runs the risk of developing an extremely suspicious, cynical and paranoid perception of reality. By only looking at hidden agendas, manipulation, intrigues, strategic behavior and political games, suspicion is nurtured and all events in and around the organization are politicized. This could lead to a situation where the power perspective is no longer used as a means of better understanding reality, but only as an instrument to satisfy self-interest. In this respect *Managing with Power* offers enough Machiavellian tips to play the power game in a no-holds-barred manner.

Power: power relationships and power distance

Authority and power have been described as concepts dependent on professional function and personal characteristics. To summarize:

- A certain degree of authority is assigned to a particular position by the organization (= the role to be played within the organization).
- The manager derives authority from his or her function (= formal authority).
- The way in which a manager wields the power of his/her position determines how employees experience (either positively or negatively) the authority being exercised (= power) by the manager as a person.

behavior of others

To a certain degree, power is the ability to determine or to direct the behavior of others. The exercise of power actually determines the behavior of others to a certain degree or channels the behavior of others.

When the exercise of power involves two or more individuals, the more powerful person will determine the behavior of the less powerful person to a greater degree than vice versa. Consequently, the power relationship is one of inequality. The degree of inequality in power between a less powerful person or group (P) and a more powerful person or group (A) is called the power distance (see Fig 8.8).

power distance

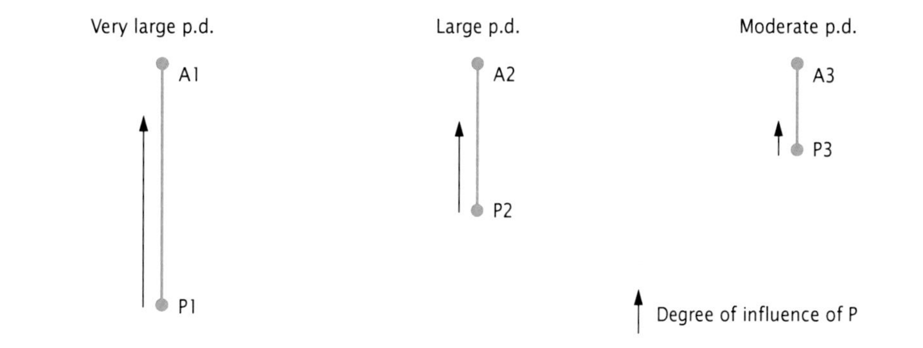

Figure 8.8
Power distance

formal power

In exercising formal power, a subordinate person (P) obeys a superior (A: the leader) because the subordinate feels an obligation to do so on account of the respective positions that A and P hold within the organization.

expertise power

Expertise power is that power attributed to a leader (A) by a person (P) when that person believes that the leader possesses greater ability or more relevant information than P. Another of P's assumptions is that A is prepared to use this larger knowledge honestly.

identification power

Identification power is that power that a person (P) experiences when he/she feels a sense of identity with the leader (A); for this reason, P is more liable to be influenced by A. P may even consciously or unconsciously set A up as an example for him/herself. P identifies with both the thinking and action of A. This relationship occurs frequently, even though it is sometimes considered inappropriate and even denied. A charismatic leader may sometimes deny having such power over his followers and will ignore the negative effects of too little criticism from overly compliant employees.

Non-power

openness to counter arguments

The quality of power is also co-determined by the convincing nature of the leader's commands or directions, as well as his/her openness to counter arguments. This is known as non-power, and can be summed up in the following statements.

- If A and P do not agree on what has to be done, there is an equal chance that the opinion of either will be accepted.

- A lets himself be convinced by P's point of view if P comes up with better arguments than A does.
- A's staff willingly do what A says because A explains why something has to be done.

The contents of an act of communication more often than not determine the outcome of a process in which influence is being exercised. Both A and the P are just as willing to be convinced by the other (non-power relationship). This comes into play in all forms of democratic deliberation that presupposes an underlying equality when certain decisions need to be made.

Influence upward and influence outward

The influence a manager (M) has within the organization and outside his own organizational unit can be summarized in the following statements:
- M has a lot of influence on what happens at higher levels.
- M is listened to by top management.

Expert power and power resulting from identification are, in addition to the power of being convincing, important in this situation, while sanction power and formal power are of limited importance.
Influence outward indicates the influence that someone has outside his own organization, and can be expressed in the following statements.
- X sees to it that certain important things outside the organization can be realized.
- X has a lot of influence in relationships with people outside X's own organization.

Findings from research

In crisis situations, the power distance involved in the leadership situation usually increases, especially in terms of the expert power distance in question, along with the sanction power and the formal power. In non-crisis situations, mild forms of leadership appear to dominate, characterized by a small power distance between leader and employee, ample opportunities to convince superiors, openly argue with them and personally interact with them. The more severe and powerful forms of leadership are likewise more highly valued in crises; in non-crisis situations, the gentle, sympathetic leader who maintains a short power distance is deemed correct.

8.5.3 Interpersonal communication

influencing behavior

Influencing behavior through deliberation, consultation, participation and co-decision making demands intensive and effective communication. Conveying information, receiving signals from and transmitting decisions to the organization take place via communication channels.

forms of communication

These forms of communication are vital. Without efficient means of communication the intended effects of decisions are not achieved or the decisions themselves are not made. Organizations are not only institutions in which exchanges of facts and data occur, they also facilitate the interchange of ideas, feelings and desires. In other words, a lot of communication takes place. Communication involves all activities in which information – that is facts, data, wishes, feelings and thoughts – are transmitted to or are received from other people. Communication can be seen as a process which involves a number of successive steps between a sender and a receiver via a communication channel. Good communication is a two-way activity. After the reception and interpretation of a message, the receiver has to verify that the intention of the sender of the message has been correctly translated by providing feedback. This procedure is illustrated in Fig 8.9.

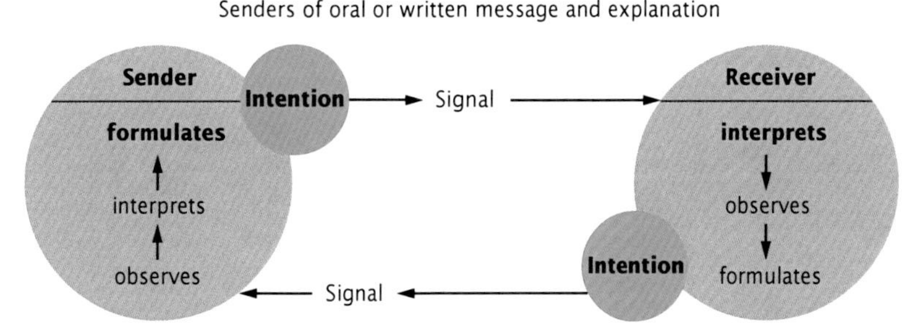

Figure 8.9
Communication as a process

In personal conversations and in meetings, non-verbal communication also plays a part. There is consequently no such thing as non-communication.

Elements of communication

According to Van Thun, the process of communication between a sender and a receiver has four components:

- The sender shares the informational content (the business-like element);
- The sender shows what he thinks to be important or relevant (the expressive element)
- By means of words or especially non-verbal means of communication, the sender makes clear what his or her relationship to the receiver is (the relational element)
- The sender tries to influence the thinking, doing, or feeling of the receiver (the appealing element)

What makes the communication process so fascinating but simultaneously so complicated is that the receiver is free to choose which parts of the transmitted signals will be given responses. For simplicity's sake, it can be assumed that the receiver is able and willing to decode the four elements of the signal (Fig 8.10).
Depending on the situation, the relevant history of the subject matter under discussion, the experiences involved in the receiver's relationship with the sender, the sender's state of mind, character, education and so on, the receiver will tend to observe and interpret one communicational component more closely than another.
In a general sense, the more noticeable and discussable the various elements are, the more effectively the relevant element can be communicated. In the case of the business-like communicative act, such features as stylistic simplicity, short sentences, standard terminology, clear structure and an attractive presentation enhance the chances of being heard or seen and improve the chance of the intended interpretation occurring.

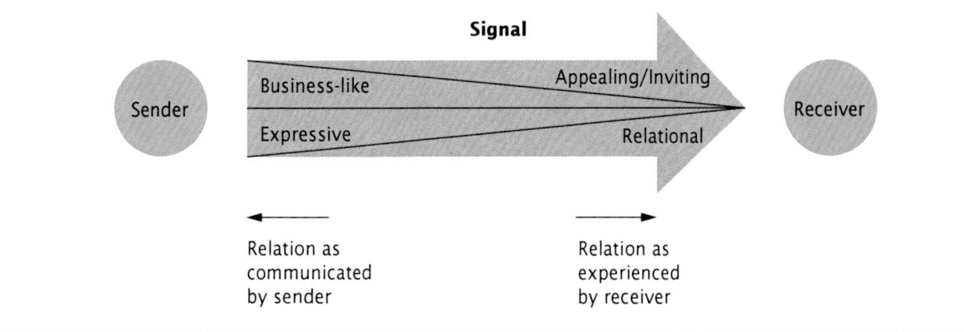

Figure 8.10
Four aspects of communication

expressive component

The importance of the expressive component (whether or not it includes consciously sent information about the sender) is demonstrated by the fact that the less one fears expressing oneself and the greater the need to be honest and open about goals, the smaller the chance that the three other elements will be misread. Any notion that one can communicate with someone else without also giving away something about oneself is an illusion – the possibility that the other person does not always want to or is not able to detect the expressive element is a different matter.

relational component

The relational component (the personal relationship the sender at that moment wishes to have with the receiver) is especially communicated by non-verbal means (intonation, physical distance, posture). In general, a sender's high emotional involvement may make it difficult for the receiver to receive the business-like element in a complete and objective manner.

appealing or inviting element

The appealing or inviting element is primarily communicated via the thoughts, emotions and deeds of those involved. Transmitted signals can contain explicit or hidden invitations to decode the message in a certain manner.

Communication and influential factors

In addition to its importance for the exchange of information resulting from the systematic processing of internal and external organizational data, effective communication is essential for decision making. Unless decisions are communicated, they remain ineffectual. Furthermore, they are subject to mistakes stemming from miscommunication between people within the organization. Communication between organization members may be affected by many shortcomings in human behavior including an inability to listen well or a feeling of frustration. The lack of good open communication channels can also have a negative effect. An organization's communication channels are sometimes blocked because someone does not agree with a message or does not take any notice of it. Censoring and the conscious or unconscious reshaping of messages can also cause problems.

two-way transmissions

Effective communication assumes, as we have already seen, two-way transmissions and demands a willingness to listen as well as to speak. Many organization members, be they high or low within the organization:

- Listen insufficiently
- Pay too little attention to misunderstandings that may occur: formulate sloppy or give ill-considered responses

To prevent such mistakes from disrupting the process of communication, one has to be prepared to step into the shoes of the receiver to understand the perspectives and the language of the receiver of the message and the feelings that may be behind the message. The other's view of a message is of course an important factor determining possible reactions. In other words, the art of communication involves the formulation of a message in such a way that the intention of the message is received and explained in the same manner in which it was originally conceived. Often, however, distortion occurs. This happens for many reasons, including:

- Environmental factors, e.g. noise in a factory hall or geographical distance between subsidiaries and establishments
- Human factors, including intellectual factors (memory, forgetfulness, failure to recognize a line in a story, inability to read between the lines) as well as emotional factors, e.g. fear, frustration, prejudice, and so on.

formal communication

informal organization

In addition to the formal communication that takes place in an organization in any of its prescribed ways, as part of the formal planning system, the budgetary procedure, a job description, or statements of guidelines and procedures, there is also a lot of informal communication. Such unofficial interactions frequently complement the formal organization and provide a means of reacting to unexpected events. Formal organization and formal communication are, of course, necessary. The real power of the organization, however, lies in the effective exploitation of the informal organization and informal channels of communication.

CROSS-CULTURAL ETIQUETTE AND BEHAVIOR: THE BASICS

Books on regional protocol and deportment offer a stew of dos and don'ts that attempt to generalize about the specifics of surface behavior. To quote a handful of rules from Dean Allen Foster's *Bargaining Across Borders*: Never show the sole of your shoe to an Arab, for it is dirty and represents the bottom of the body. Look directly and intently into a French associate's eye when making an important point, but avoid direct eye contact in Southeast Asia until the relationship is firmly established. In Italy, don't touch the side of your nose; it is a sign of distrust. The lists go on and on and can certainly help you avoid mistakes. But the rules are so complex and detailed that it's difficult to keep them straight, and the likelihood of regional variation further complicates matters.

Nonetheless, negotiators would do well to consider a range of questions about these behaviors when preparing for international negotiations, either by consulting the literature or by engaging in conversations with people who have experienced the culture at hand. I've outlined the categories of surface behaviors most likely to affect the tenor of negotiations. While the list that follows is not exhaustive and must be read in the light of obvious caveats about regional, professional, and national variation, seeking answers to these questions will at least provide a degree of familiarity with the basic dos and don'ts in any given culture.

Sensitivity to these basics allows you to avoid giving offense, demonstrate respect, enhance camaraderie, and strengthen communications. But cultural codes of protocol and deportment are not likely to interfere dramatically in your negotiations, apart from blatant disrespect.

Do's and don'ts	
Greetings	How do people greet and address one another? What role do business cards play?
Degree of formality	Will my counterparts expect me to dress and interact formally or informally?
Gift giving	Do business people exchange gifts? What gifts are appropriate? Are there taboos associated with gift giving?
Touching	What forms of body contact are regarded as appropriate?
Eye contact	Is direct eye contact polite? Is it expected?
Deportment	Should I deport myself formally or casually?
Emotions	Is it considered rude, embarrassing, or normal to display emotions?
Silence	Is silence awkward? Expected? Insulting? Respectful?
Eating	What are the approved dining manners? Are certain foods taboo?
Body language	Are certain gestures or other forms of body language rude?
Punctuality	Should I be punctual and expect my counterparts to be as well? Or are timetables flexible?

Source: *Harvard Business Review*, March 2002, p. 80, 'The Hidden Challenges of Cross-Border Negotiations'

Types of communication and choice of communication channel

When transmitting a message and ensuring that it is delivered, it is necessary to be careful about choosing the form in which the communication should occur. This choice will depend on the goal that the sender wants to attain. One can, for example, make use of oral or written communication. Oral communication may take the form of direct conversation between two employees, work-related discussions and oral reporting procedures.

oral communication

written communication

Written communication, including communication in digital form, may take the form of letters, electronic mail, screen messages, newsletters, notice-board announcements, personnel advertisements, written assignments, written reports or even annual reports. One advantage of written communication is that messages can be conveyed in multiple copies. Data can be issued simultaneously to various departments, stored in some form or another, returned, and so on. In oral communication an immediate explanation can be given if required.

vertical communication

Communication occurs at various levels of the organizational structure. Vertical communication involves conveying the wishes of management to lower managerial and operational levels. It generally takes the form of task assignments, instructions, planning directives, or operational plans indicated by departmental budgets. In the opposite direction, vertical channels of communication may be used to report the findings, observations or results of operations to management. The various means that management uses to inform personnel are conveyed via these channels. They may include a speech, a briefing, a lecture or works council discussions. Horizontal communication occurs in the form of consultations among supervisors or executive officers and may involve such issues as order acceptance, delivery times, and so on.

horizontal communication

lateral (or diagonal) communication

Lateral (or diagonal) communication takes place in teams, groups or committees composed of people from different departments or different hierarchical levels (see Section 6.5).

MEETING LOVERS: COLLEAGUES ARE A SOURCE OF IRRITATION

So do you enjoy meetings? In research published in *Workplace Survey*, Robert Half closely surveyed 5000 managers in twenty countries. His findings? Meetings are often a source of major tension.

One in five meetings is unnecessary, or at least in the opinion of 42 percent of Dutch managers. Nearly half of those surveyed (47 percent) were annoyed by colleagues who failed to prepare for a meeting or did not prepare well. Failure to prepare for meetings takes away their clarity, makes them longer than necessary and ultimately pointless.

Discussions that arise during a meeting are experienced by 41 percent as irritating. They claim that discussions detract too much from the main purpose of the meeting. People who have no business being at the meeting are experienced as annoying by about one-third (32 percent).

In the Netherlands, for meetings not to form a natural part of the working day is highly unusual, even though only 24 percent of managers indicated that they took them into account consciously. Managers in other countries are more inclined to plan them into the day. In Austria, 57 percent of managers consciously planned meeting-free days. Of those Dutch managers who planned 'no-meeting' days, 34 percent found these days to be much more productive.

Source: *De Accountant*, November 2009

Communication structures

In addition to the meeting style of a team chairman or the style of leadership of the department head, the structure of the lines of communication influences the way in which people solve problems. The forms that these communication structures take within an organization can be typified (Fig 8.11). In research on communication structures, Leavitt

(1957) has identified the wheel structure, the chain structure, the circle structure and the open network structure as viable organizational structures of communication.

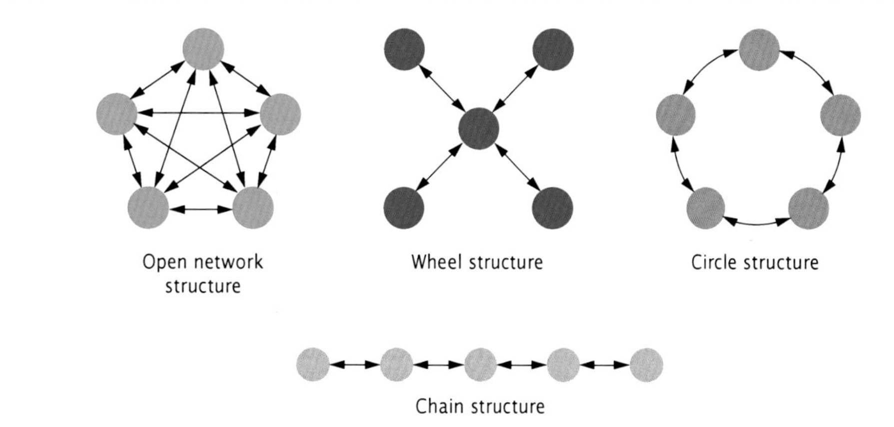

Figure 8.11
Communication structure

An example of a wheel structure is when a superior has four subordinates who report only to him. The chain structure is a hierarchical variant of this, while the circle and open network structures resemble horizontal and lateral forms of consultation.

wheel structure
circle structure
chain structure
open network structure

The effectiveness of the various forms can be evaluated in terms of such factors as time required for solution, number of mistakes, number of messages sent and satisfaction of the participants. Research has indicated that the wheel structure results in the shortest solution time and the smallest number of messages, but also in the least satisfaction. Although this form has clear advantages in terms of efficiency, it tends to produce employee dissatisfaction. The circle structure requires the most time, demands a lot of messages and produces the most mistakes, but, in contrast, provides the highest level of work satisfaction. The chain structure lies in between these two extremes. The open network structure has the same effectiveness as the wheel structure, but only after a much longer period. The satisfaction is also higher. During the course of time, the open network structure almost always develops some degree of hierarchy.

8.6 Styles of leadership and conflict resolution

conflict resolution

Since every human being has his or her own individual needs and emotions, any form of collaboration between people will bring these differences to light. Such things as tensions at home can be introduced into the working situation. Earlier research has shown that middle managers spend about 26 per cent of their time on conflict resolution. At the time that the research was done, the expectation was that this function would demand a larger amount of time in the 1990s and in the future.

In situations where the interests and goals of two people or of management and work groups are contradictory, there are various ways of handling the resulting conflict. The approach taken will depend on the amount of personal involvement, the extent of one's power, the degree to which one is a 'doormat' and/or the degree of which one is willing and prepared to allow others some freedom to resolve the problem. Organizations have certain characteristic styles of conflict resolution, as shown in Fig 8.12.

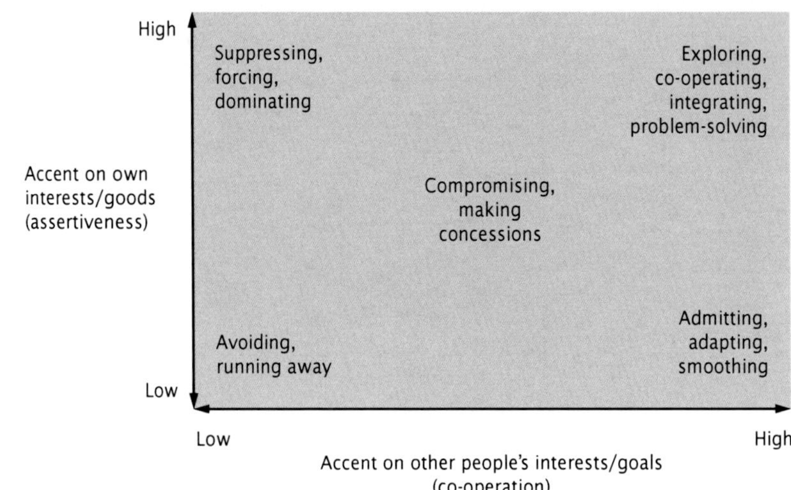

Figure 8.12 *Styles of conflict resolution*

Repression/confrontation

If confrontations are the order of the day, if there is a lot to fight over, if a hard line is taken in conflicts, if an 'all or nothing' attitude exists, then power plays an important role. Anyone who adopts this style will pursue personal interests while neglecting everyone else's concerns. In conflict situations, competing interests are considered contradictory and mutually exclusive, and the matter is only settled by deciding on a winner and a loser. This style is oriented towards power: a personal goal has to be attained, and to do that, one either uses or threatens to use all available power resources.
Organizations in which this style predominates encourage their employees to:

- Be persistent
- Suppress contradictions
- Display threatening behavior, even involving the use of violence
- Follow the hard line
- Overrule the opinions of others

The result is that a conflict is never properly resolved. Open or indirect resistance may arise and the motivation of the person on whom another's will is imposed will diminish perceptibly. This tendency will be extremely noticeable in employee relationships as well as in the lines of communication.
There are, nevertheless, some occasions when this style should be used, including:

- Crisis situations
- Situations involving vital interests and unquestionably justifiable action
- Occasions when unpopular measures have to be taken

Avoidance/flight

Formal, hierarchically oriented conflicts are avoided rather than openly discussed, and potential problems are ignored. Anyone adopting this style strives neither for his or her personal interests nor for the interests of others. Mutual relationships are regarded with indifference. When contradictions arise, he or she retreats (either figuratively or sometimes even literally). One avoids accepting points of view that could lead to controversy.
This style is characterized by a number of behaviors:

- Acting dumb
- Handling delicate subjects as a joke
- Avoiding adversaries
- Postponing a sensitive subject to a more suitable moment

A consequence of such behavior is that the conflict is never really resolved. It also allows conflict to be avoided: everyone goes his or her own way.
There are situations in which this method of handling conflict is appropriate, including:
- Situations when a 'cooling off' period is necessary
- Cases in which more information has to be gathered first
- Occasions when the subject is not important enough to enter into immediate conflict about it

Admission/adaptation
The human-oriented approach, usually displayed in situations involving mainly professional employees (see Section 8.7) enables conflicts to be resolved in a mutually satisfactory manner. In this situation, one's own interests are neglected in order to satisfy those of others. Conflicts are prevented by stimulating a harmonious atmosphere and friendly relationships.
This style is recognizable by a number of practices, including
- The avoidance of painful subjects
- The treatment of controversial subjects in such an abstract and general manner that everyone can agree
- The rapid pacification of parties involved in conflicts
- The raising of subjects on which all can agree

Adopting this approach prevents conflicts of interest from piercing the organizational armor, but does not actually provide a means of resolving conflict.
Such a style is applicable to situations in which:
- Maintaining harmony is important
- Building up 'credit' is important so that important subjects can be broached at a later date
- Fighting would be harmful

A LITTLE ANGER IS A GOOD THING

Gentlemen: don't hold in your anger at work. Let it out, says a new study that originally appeared in the *Journal of Epidemiology & Community Health*. A team of Swedish researchers found that men who suppress their anger in the workplace are two to five times more likely to suffer a heart attack or die from heart disease. A big culprit is 'covert coping,' in which men who feel they have suffered unjust treatment simply walk away or ignore the situation rather than dealing with it. 'You have to act,' says lead researcher Constanze Leineweber of Stockholm University's Stress Research Institute. 'It's better to say that you feel unfairly treated.'

Source: *BusinessWeek*, December 7, 2009, p. 57

Compromise/concession
This approach is a highly democratic one. Compromise takes precedence over being innovative. There is an emphasis on sharing and cooperation. In this approach, an interim solution is sought in which each party can find some feature that responds to its point of view. The process does not necessarily result in the qualitatively best solution, but rather the fairest, most acceptable, and realistically attainable solution for both parties. Looking for compromises means making concessions and accepting differences.
This approach is often taken in negotiations in which it is important to undergo a process of give and take in order to find a common denominator among diverse points of view.
This manner of dealing with conflict can be used when:
- A rupture cannot be risked because goals are important for both parties
- Temporary measures have to be taken on account of time pressures
- Force is not an option

Exploration/cooperation

New ideas are shared so that there is an opportunity to experiment while other possible solutions are investigated and tested. There is a large measure of freedom and creativity in the process. The following are now vitally important:

- Direct and open communication in which the business and emotional components of the contradiction are openly discussed
- Mutual analysis of underlying causes
- Expression of emotions and sharing of the images that one party has of the other
- Resolution of misunderstandings

negotiation Problem-solving by negotiation is potentially able to find a real solution to the problem, one that is acceptable to both parties. Contradictions are now permanently resolved and all parties feel involved in the result.

This style of conflict resolution necessarily takes time and energy. In situations in which increased involvement is desirable, learning is important or disturbed relationships have to be restored, this style will – given time and energy – arrive at a solution in a manner that is more generally beneficial to the organization and that promotes creativity.

8.6.1 Conflict as a process

Where there is less authoritarian leadership and greater participation in decision making, other types of conflict will nevertheless still arise. The organizational culture determines to a large degree how these events are handled.

conflict A conflict is a process in which A consciously attempts to frustrate B by means obstructing B's effort to attain goals or to safeguard interests. The process can be modelled in four phases (Fig 8.13):

1 Potential resistance
2 Awareness and personification
3 Behavior
4 Consequences

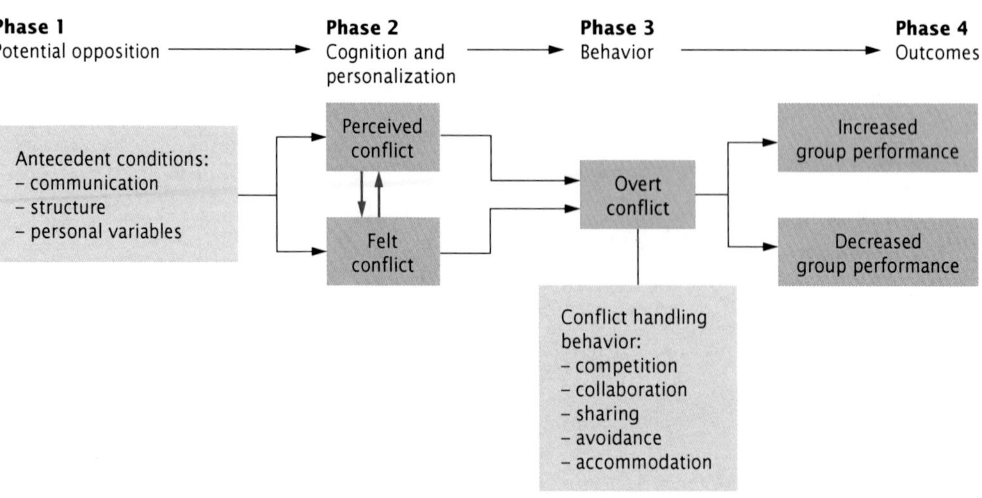

Figure 8.13
Conflict as a process

Source: *Robbins*, 1979

The first phase in the process involves the act of becoming aware of the circumstances in which conflicts can arise. These conditions are comprised of communicative, structural or personal variables. When the circumstances in phase 1 produce frustration, potential contradictions become real contradictions in the second phase. The existing conditions only lead to conflicts when one or more of the involved parties are affected by them and become conscious of the resulting conflict. In phase 3, there is open conflict. Involved parties have to start negotiating in order to contend with the conflictual situation.

cooperation
self-assertion

If we assume that there are two fundamental approaches – cooperation (the degree to which someone tries to meet the needs of the other) and self-assertion (the degree to which a party tries to fulfill his own needs) – there are, as we have seen, five possible forms of conflict resolution: confrontation (or competition), cooperation (or collaboration), avoidance, adjustment (or accommodation) and compromise (or sharing).

open-conflict behavior

Where there is alternating open-conflict behavior and a conflict-handling behavior (with the one provoking the other), there will be consequences, including ones that affect a person's work performance. In other words the conflict may lead to improved group work but also, conversely, to dysfunctional performance, if no adequate resolution is reached.

8.6.2 The best style is the one suited to the situation

No one best style for handling conflicts exists. Approaches all depend on, among other things, the position one occupies in one's professional life. Project leaders (people who have to act as innovators) will in general be best served by an exploratory style, and people who handle the chairman's hammer will be better off adopting a more compromise-seeking attitude. Most people will have a mixture of methods, a much more eclectic manner of dealing with conflict than any of those that have been described above.

Exhibit 8.4

Organizational conflict and national cultures

On a research project (at INSEAD) MBA students from Germany, Great Britain, and France were asked to write their own diagnosis and solution for a small case study of an organizational problem – a conflict in one company between the sales and product development departments. The majority of the French referred the problem to the next higher authority (the president of the company); the Germans attributed it to the lack of a written policy, and proposed establishing one; the British attributed it to a lack of interpersonal communication, to be cure by some kind of group training.
The conclusion was that the 'implicit model' of the organization for most French was a pyramid (both centralized and formal); for most Germans, a well-oiled machine (formalized but not centralized); and for most British, a village market (neither formalized nor centralized). What is missing is an 'implicit model' for four Asian countries, including India. The family (centralized, but not formalized) is placed in this quadrant as the 'implicit model' of the organization. Indian organizations tend to be formalized as far as relationships between people go (this is related to Power Distance), but not as far as workflow goes (this is Uncertainty Avoidance).

(Adapted from *Transnational Management*, Bartlett and Ghoshal, 1992)

The same holds true for organizations: not all organizations have one clear style of conflict resolution. Most organizations use a variety of these styles. An organization should, however, settle on a single style of conflict resolution because it can then exploit all the possibilities involved in the chosen method. Ways of expanding the flexibility of the style will quickly become apparent, and they will help stimulate further organizational operations.

8.7 Organization, styles of leadership and organizational culture

organizational culture

Organizational culture can be defined as the common understanding of the members of an organization and the ways in which things are done in that organization on a daily basis. It includes all the written and unwritten rules which channel and shape the social intercourse of the employees of the organization, as well as dealings with customers, suppliers and other parties in the external environment. The organization expresses itself by means of a house style – logos, company cars, uniforms, buildings, portraits, myths and stories, jubilee celebrations, use of language, meeting style, and so on. These are all forms of cultural expression. In essence, however, it is not the expressions themselves that are important, but rather the meaning that the organization attaches to them. Such cultural expressions as symbols, heroes and rituals are indications of the deeper values and norms in which the cultural manifestations are rooted and which constitute the heart of an organization's culture. Cultural phenomena may have a strong presence, and if so, all organizational members will be aware of them. There are also likely to be inconsistent and even conflicting value patterns, which are then said to constitute a weak culture. A weak culture can be said to exist when there is a clash between the various inter- and intradepartmental subcultures.

symbols, heroes and rituals

values and norms

Values unconsciously determine human behavior. This tendency can cause a corporate community to think of what suits or does not suit the organization in moral terms (good or bad) and to develop 'we do it this way' and 'we think it important' attitudes. Basic principles and values obviously form the 'inside' of the culture, while the symbols lie mostly on the 'outside'. Consequently, symbols are the things which are most easy to change: a new logo, a new house style, new slogans. A 'hero mentality' will change when new staff are appointed to key positions and allowed to play important roles within the organization. When current staff are engaged in new situations and new meaning is given to their new roles, the rituals are also likely to change.

CASE

Mini case study 8.6

Now for sale, the Zappos culture

Visitors touring Zappos.com's suburban Las Vegas headquarters can see Chief Executive Anthony C. 'Tony' Hsieh waving from his cubicle or get their photos taken in goofy, mullet-shaped wigs. On the tour, which the online shoe retailer offers 16 times a week, staffers blow horns and ring cowbells to greet the guests, who move among the aisles in groups of 20, trying to get a handle on the company's unique culture. 'The original idea was to add a little fun,' Hsieh explains. Then it all escalated 'as the next aisle said "we can do it better."'

Zappos already knows how to sell shoes. Now it's hoping to profit from people's fascination with its friendly, antics-filled business model. Last summer, the company began holding two-day, $4,000 seminars on how to recreate the essence of its corporate culture. At the third such session, the 25 attendees included an executive from the Girl Scouts, some competing e-tailers, and an entrepreneur from Scotland – a market Zappos doesn't even serve. In coming weeks the company will also relaunch Zappos Insights, a Web site offering management videos and tips from staffers at a cost of $39.95 a month.

The goal behind these activities is to build more buzz around the Zappos brand and its extreme customer service. Hsieh, 36, is an avid consumer of management tomes. He has 1.6 million followers on Twitter – more than either CBS News or the NFL – and he regales these fans with inspirational quotes, riffs on the news, and whatever else is on his mind. In the October seminar, which will be repeated once every quarter, Hsieh, the chief financial officer, and two dozen other staffers shared tips on hiring, compensation, customer care, and creating the right work environment.

There's certainly much for students of management theory to try on at Zappos. For example, pay for call-center operators starts at a modest $11 an hour and there are no bonuses because Hsieh believes the most productive employees work for the psychic gratification of helping others. Customer service reps are given plenty of freedom.

They may chat for hours with customers, write thank-you notes, send flowers, and even direct shoppers to rival Web sites if an item is out of stock. In a tough year for retail, sales are up by double digits.

Zappos rep Michele Robles recently showed a reporter how the approach works. She offers coupons and free shipping to one unhappy customer while grabbing a returned pair of shearling boots for another. Robles knows her top priority is to establish an emotional connection. More than 95% of Zappos' transactions take place over the Web, so each actual phone call is a special opportunity. 'They may only call once in their life, but that is our chance to wow them,' Hsieh says.

A Zappos seminar last July impressed David Brautigan, who runs a family heating and air-conditioning repair business. It prompted him to fire 12 employees who were 'just not being nice,' while rewarding those who remain with such perks as sky diving trips. 'The nicer we are to people,' he says, 'better things are happening.' Hsieh appears pleased to spread that message: 'Sharing is how we build our brand.'

Source: *Bloomberg Business Week*, January 11, 2010, p. 57

8.7.1 *Influencing organizational culture and leadership*

Often a crisis caused by external influences is necessary in order to effect a change within the organizational culture. A crisis throws an organization off balance, and this forces management – perhaps by appointing a new leader – to revamp the common values underlying the organization by developing a new culture. Management can also consciously choose to instigate a crisis. Leadership is necessary to shape and influence the organizational culture. At the same time we need to realize that management can become a prisoner of the prevailing culture. Leaders also have to be replaced during the course of time, and this often provides an opportunity to change the prevailing culture and thus the organization's style. To accomplish such a transformation, the organization needs to answer two important questions.

- How do we view ourselves and associate with each other within the organization?
- What do we want to become and how do we want to associate with each other?

Diagnosing culture

Harrison

To diagnose the organizational culture, one can make use of the culture types identified by Harrison (1986; see Fig 8.14). This classification also identifies two key factors: the degree of cooperation and the distribution of power. The former represents the degree to which an organization's members cooperate with each other during the daily performance of duties. On rare occasions, virtually no employee consultation occurs (everyone works alone). The other extreme – continuous consultation and stable team relationships – may also occur. The second factor is the degree to which power is spread throughout an organization. When it is widely spread, there is no clear power center and a state of decentralization will often exist. Where there is little distribution of power, most decisions will be taken at the top of the organization.

Role culture

role culture

In a role culture, there is little distribution of power (centralization) and a low degree of cooperation. Employees expect each other to follow the rules and procedures established by higher management. New problems are solved with great difficulty because they fall outside the framework of existing procedures.
In a role culture, new problems demand the development of new procedures. When this happens the learning of new routines takes precedence over conceptual learning (see Section 3.5).

Person culture

person culture

In a person culture, power is widely distributed (decentralization). Organization members in all sorts of positions within the organization are free to make a variety of decisions. However, there is only a small amount of mutual collaboration – in general, the organization's members work individually.

CASE

Mini case study 8.7

Examples of organizations in which there are person cultures: Hospitals where doctors receive patients individually during consulting hours, schools where teachers are responsible for their own classes, and legal firms where each lawyer serves clients individually.

Power culture

power culture

Power cultures are characterized by a limited distribution of power (centralization) and a high degree of cooperation. This type of culture frequently occurs in small pioneering companies, where a group of experts cooperate intensively, work in an informal atmosphere and call everyone by their first name except the pioneers or founders of the company.

Task culture

task culture

The task culture is characterized by a wide distribution of power (decentralization) and a high degree of cooperation among the organization's members.
There are various ways of influencing the culture of an organization. Changing personnel in key positions is a direct way of doing this. Recruiting new people with other backgrounds and experiences can have an important influence on an organization's culture (Fig 8.14).

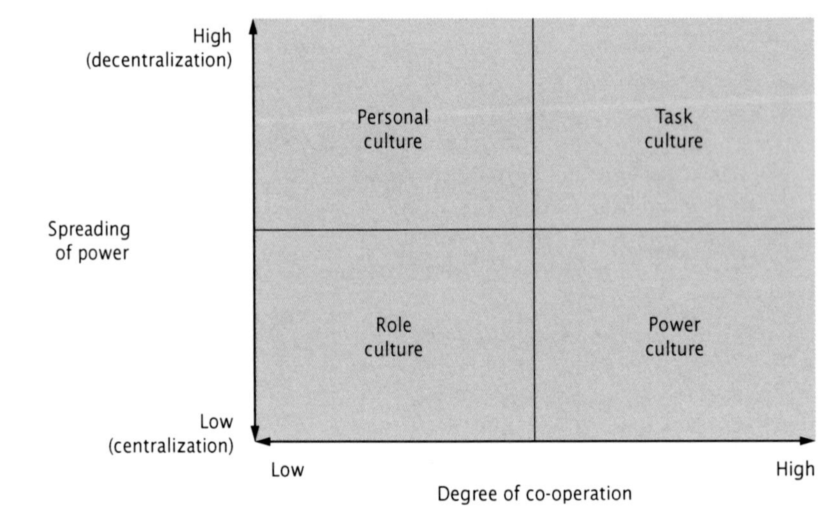

Figure 8.14
Typology of organizational cultures (derived from Harrison)

A slower method involves team discussions relating to the present and the desired styles, perhaps with the aid of an external trainer. Team training and work conferences can be an important instrument for instigating these discussions or for initiating other forms of intervention. Whenever such proceedings are undertaken, several departments and professional levels must be represented. Some examples of cultural interventions include the following:

cultural interventions

- Adapting the style of leadership
- Changing key personnel
- Team training or conferences involving as many departments and professional levels as possible

Sometimes these changes in culture are only really meaningful when a change in organizational structure also occurs. In organizations with no or only poor task definitions and a large overlapping of responsibilities and authorities, greater clarity has to be introduced into the structure. Only after such clarification is it possible to try to change the style of leadership and conflict resolution via cultural interventions.

CASE

Mini case study 8.8

A task culture is typical of organizations that work with temporary project groups composed of employees originating from different departments and several specialized areas. They are described as project or matrix organizations (see sections 5.3.7 - 5.3.9).

CHIEF CULTURE OFFICER

Is it possible to clone Steve Jobs or Martha Stewart? That's the question at the heart of *Chief Culture Officer: How to Create a Living, Breathing Corporation*, by Grant McCracken, an anthropologist at the Massachusetts Institute of Technology and a business consultant. McCracken argues that corporations need to focus on 'reading' what's happening in the culture around them – a task at which Jobs and Stewart excel. Otherwise, companies will suffer the consequences, as Levi Strauss did when it missed out on the rise of hip-hop (and the baggy pants that are part of that lifestyle).

McCracken doesn't advocate that companies launch an extensive search for an all-knowing guru or rely on so-called cool hunters or design agencies. Instead, he believes the skills of a Steve Jobs, often viewed as exceedingly rare, are in fact reproducible: they can be learned by managers and made a part of doing business. Offering examples of failures and successes in culture reading, McCracken dishes up good helpings of practical advice.

At present, says McCracken, most companies do a lousy job of sensing cultural currents. That's because they tend to concentrate on what he calls 'fast culture,' the kind tracked by cool-hunting, whether it's the latest Italian furniture design or tins week's hottest iPhone app. Too often that means companies miss slow culture, the kind that makes up the fabric of people's lives. Homeyness, or how we turn our houses into a home, is an example of slow culture. Former Procter & Gamble Chairman A.G. Lafley understands slow culture, McCracken says, and because Lafley gets it, he changed the way P&G studies people. Instead of using narrow focus groups to examine why a consumer prefers one toothpaste over another, Lafley got company researchers to look at how people generally lived their lives and how the choice of toothpaste fitted in.

Some of the changes McCracken discusses will sound familiar to most readers. For instance, it's a cliché that consumers are producers of culture these days and that companies must embrace this shift. The book's most helpful chapters offer how-tos and profile executives who've become culture officers within their companies.

For example, there's Silvia Lagnado, global brand director for Unilever's Dove products. Lagnado's fresh take on consumer research data led her to trend beauty marketing. When she looked at global ads, the models were mostly 'young, white, blond, and slim'. That comes as no surprise, but the impact of such homogeneity is enormous. According to a survey of women worldwide, only 2% consider themselves beautiful. Rather than accepting the marketing status quo and emphasizing other aspects of Dove products, such as healthiness, Lagnado embraced inclusiveness, creating the 'Campaign for Real Beauty' that starred ordinary women.

McCracken's how-tos include the development of soft skills people often don't appreciate, such as the skill of noticing. Advertising firm Crispin Porter Bogusky remarked that, though Apple's funny 'Mac vs. PC' ads seemed to put people in either the avant-garde camp or the square mainstream, a growing group of people didn't want to be labeled at all. So the firm dreamed up the 'I'm a PC' campaign that made it seem cool not to be hip. McCracken also purveys more specific advice, including a list of deep thinkers to lunch with, such as new-media whiz Jerry Michalski.

While McCracken's book is full of managers who read culture well, it's obviously not easy to develop the keen receptors of a Jobs or a Martha Stewart. But maybe that's asking too much. The book makes a compelling case that companies will reap rewards just by working toward more cultural sensitivity.

Source: *Bloomberg Business Week*, January 11, 2010, p. 66, H. Green

8.7.2 Functions of an organizational culture

Organizational culture involves the way in which members perceive the organization, its nature and ways of working, and their contribution to it. It is the result of a mutual understanding and is influenced by the organization's past just as the structure and strategy of the organization reflect the mutual understanding and the experiences of those in authority with regard to the execution of power, the allocation of responsibility and the reaction of the organization to events in its external environment. Organizational culture is considered to have two important functions:

1 *To provide relatively fixed patterns for handling and resolving problems* – relating to the organization's ability to cope with changing external and internal factors. Reactions which proved to be an effective way of solving problems in the past are used again. Mutual understanding takes the form of a 'recipe book' for the solution of external and internal adjustment problems.
2 *To reduce uncertainty for the members of the organization when confronted with new situations.*

standardization of problem solution
reduction of uncertainty

The two functions of organizational culture – the standardization of problem solution and the reduction of uncertainty – will crystallize over time. The form the culture takes will depend on the way in which the 'leaders' find solutions for problems and how they interpret the events and activities that go on around them. The reduction of uncertainty and the giving of meaning to daily actions can only take place when there is a connection between the individual values of the members of the organization and the core of the organizational culture. A company in western Europe, for example, will need to give employees the opportunity for relatively individualistic value patterns compared with the more collective value patterns of employees working in other economies.

The values of the organization's employees will be especially determined by the kind of people that the organization recruits – their nationality, education and age. The company can only influence the values of its employees to a limited extent after they have been appointed; a company is rarely able to re-educate its members where values are concerned. For most people values are developed in the first ten years of life. A company can only inform new employees of existing rituals, heroes and symbols and ask that they adopt these so as to comply with existing patterns of work behavior.

8.7.3 Professional cultures

In addition to national and company cultures, there are also the so-called professional or job cultures, whose values are usually picked up and developed by professional staff during their training for the job they perform – for example, certified accountants or medical specialists. Of course, this is particularly apparent in the professional organization – one in which most people are employed with the same professional training, such as an accountancy practice, a hospital, a faculty within a university, a consultancy or an engineering firm.

8.7.4 Culture preservation versus cultural change

The organizational culture is important to the survival of the organization. It is important to constantly question the degree to which the existing culture is still appropriate, given the goals to be attained.

For those placed and working at the center of the organization, it is not easy to answer this question: the company culture determines to a high degree the things they see and the way they react. The culture can become a self-preserving cycle of values and norms. For example, the instruments used in the personnel function are largely directed at maintaining the existing organizational culture: recruitment and selection, induction, assessment, succession in management positions and management development. These processes guarantee that the values of future employees and those of the company as a whole rarely conflict. In selection, for example, this is expressed in the question of whether the candidate will 'fit in with the organization.' In assessment, this is also addressed, either implicitly or explicitly, when the question is asked of whether the person 'behaves in accordance with the values, norms and beliefs' of the unit or department of the company.

In the long term, all this can also mean that an existing organizational culture is no longer in line with the desired strategy, goals and demands of the organization with regard to primary processes crucial to the company's survival. Change is then imperative. Adjustments to strategy and to the design of the organizational structure will not be enough. Sometimes cultural change will be necessary and may even be a condition for enabling strategic renewal to take place and allowing the organizational structure to function in quite a different way.

cultural change

8.7.5 Influencing organizational culture: instruments

It is usually not very easy to consciously change an organization's culture. People have the tendency to maintain safe behaviors and they frequently resist change. To be effective, the measures taken to change the culture have to be internally coherent. If not, the employees will become confused and important stakeholders such as customers will reject the new culture. The main instruments for influencing organizational culture can be divided into two groups.

influencing organizational culture

direct instruments

Direct working instruments:

- Making new appointments in key positions
- Modifying criteria governing recruitment, selection, promotion, retirement and exclusion
- Introducing and training new employees, e.g. through in-company training
- Bringing important matters to the attention of top management
- Having top management react to crucial events
- Modeling behavior
- Altering criteria for assigning rewards and status

UNILEVER REPLACES A MAJOR PART OF ITS TOP MANAGEMENT

Under the leadership of Paul Polman, Unilever, the Dutch-British producer of consumer goods, is rapidly replacing its 100 most top managers. Since the chairman of the board took office in January of this year, forty managers have been replaced. More replacements will follow.

Management changes are the order of the day in large companies, and Unilever is no exception. It is replacing a lot of dead wood with a mix of people from outside and new blood from inside Unilever. According those who know the market, the chairman, who came from Nestlé and Procter & Gamble, wants to speed things up within the company in order to increase autonomous sales growth.

Source: *Het Financieele Dagblad*, 30 October 2009

indirect instruments

Indirect working instruments:
- Designing and structuring the organization
- Updating systems and procedures
- Redesigning buildings and/or their interiors
- Disseminating stories and myths
- Formally declaring new policies

Exhibit 8.5

Organizational change and national cultures

It is tempting to view the task of managing change as one of sketching alternative chart structures by moving boxes and redrawing lines. Such a view loses sight of the real organization behind those structural representations. The boxes that are casually shifted around represent people with abilities, motivations, and interests, not just formal positions with specified roles. The lines that are redrawn are not just formal reporting channels, but interpersonal relationships that may have taken years to develop. As a result, forcing changes in organizational process and management mentality by altering the formal structure can have a high cost. The new relationships defined in the reorganized structure will often take months to establish at the most basic level, and a year or more to become truly effective. Developing new individual attitudes and behaviors will take even longer, since many employees will be frustrated, alienated, or simply unequal to the new job requirements.

Most European and Japanese companies tend to adopt a very different approach in managing organizational change. Top management in these companies consciously uses personnel assignments as an important mechanism of organizational change. Building on the informal relationships that dominated their earlier management processes, European companies use assignments and transfers to forge interpersonal links, build organizational cohesion, and develop policy consistency. Such mechanisms are at least as important as structural change for developing their desired international processes.

Japanese companies place enormous emphasis on socializing the individual into the organization and shaping his or her attitudes to conform with overall corporate values. Organizational change in these companies is often driven more by intensive education programs than by reconfigurations of structure or systems.

Source: *Transnational Management*, Bartlett and Ghoshal (1992)

Summary

- Good leadership is making optimal use of staff capabilities, listening to people and observing the way they act.
- The concepts of leadership, managing and enterprising have been discussed. Inspiration, vision, creating the right conditions and daring to take risks are essential elements of modern management. The motives and characteristics of managers have been examined with special attention paid to styles of leadership and the need for situation-specific leadership.
- Ways of influencing human behavior and the resources used to do so have been thoroughly investigated. The handling of power and authority are central issues here. Any attempt to influence human behavior is doomed to failure if there is poor communication.
- Whenever people work together there is likely to be a clash of ideas, goals and interests. Conflict resolution procedures may be required.
- To realize changes in an organization and to activate human potential, an understanding of an organization's culture is essential. The prevailing culture can be influenced by using direct or indirect measures. The same measures may also be employed to channel inculcated behaviors in desired ways.

Discussion questions

1. Do you agree that a wellbeing program is a business responsibility and that companies should provide fitness centers, running programs, etc?
2. Which of McGregor's theories – Theory X or Theory Y – would you use if you had to manage?
3. How do Hersey and Blanchard describe task maturity?
4. Give your opinion of the following statement: 'Informal groups always work within a circle communication structure.'
5. Comment on the following contention: 'Labor divisions build conflict automatically into organizations. The best conflict handling method is to discontinue the organization.'
6. **a)** What are the main factors causing high stress levels?
   b) What can companies do to prevent stress caused by these factors?
7. If the external and/or internal stakeholders believe that the organization's management has failed, heads may have to roll. Can this be described as a direct or an indirect measure undertaken to influence organizational culture?

Research-based exercise

Leading people in times of chaotic change

Introduction
This exercise is based on a conceptual article by Tom Karp and Thomas Tveteraas Helgo, published in *Journal of Management Development*. The research question and some of the results of their research project are shown. The exercise, which is related to this research article, consists of three questions. Your answers should be based on the theory in this chapter.

Research question
How do leaders manage chaotic change: i.e. changes in an organization when the external and internal complexity and uncertainty are high?

Methodology
A conceptual discussion based on a review of the literature.

Outcomes
Successful change management practices must take better account of unpredictability, uncertainty, self-governance, emergence and other premises describing chaotic circumstances. For a leader, this necessitates paying attention to how people form identities in organizations and means avoiding design-oriented command-and-control managerial interventions as well as keeping at bay the anxiety caused by not being in managerial control.

(Based on Karp, T., and Tveteraas Helgo, T.I. (2009). 'Reality revisited: leading people in chaotic change,' *Journal of Management Development*, *28*(2), 81-93.)

Questions

1 Which leadership styles in this chapter could be exercised by a leader in times of chaotic change?
2 Should a leader use power in times of chaotic change?
3 What might be the effect of an absence of leadership in times of chaotic change?

CASE

Management Case Study

Leadership for growth

Irene Rosenfeld hasn't been around Kraft Foods' suburban Chicago headquarters much lately. The door to her wood-paneled office is kept closed. Her desk is bare. Rosenfeld has grabbed her leather folders of meticulously compiled research and is traveling to London and around the U.S. in Kraft's Gulfstream jet. These trips weren't supposed to be urgent or secretive, but they've become both as Rosenfeld scrambles to reassure shareholders that her surprising $17 billion hostile bid to buy British candy maker Cadbury will be good for them.

Rosenfeld, 56, has led Kraft since 2006 and has worked there for almost her entire professional life. She can be pretty persuasive. Early on she told her bosses that commercials for Kool-Aid should be aimed at kids (not mothers), and that Jell-O could be made modern with new flavors. In the late 1990s, she turned around Kraft's business in Canada; troubled as it was when she arrived, the first thing she had to do was show skeptical colleagues that an American could understand Canadian consumers. As chief executive, she has won most employees' co-operation for a wrenching reorganization. 'When she is trying to persuade you of something, she will be relentless in coming back with facts and showing you she has the support of other people,' says John Bowlin, who ran Kraft North America in the mid-1990s. 'She will be totally emotionally and intellectually committed to her idea.'

Now Rosenfeld must summon all of her powers as she takes on her biggest marketing challenge yet: selling the Cadbury deal to shareholders. Her task is all the more difficult because she has alienated her biggest shareholder and one of the world's most influential investors, Warren Buffett.

So confident was Rosenfeld of the deal's potential to transform Kraft into a global juggernaut that she told investors she planned to issue new stock to help pay for the purchase. The subtext: she might be willing to raise her original $17 billion bid, which Cadbury management had complained was too low. But Buffett didn't like the idea of paying more. He issued a press release warning Rosenfeld not to sell more stock or increase her price, even if other bidders emerge. It was an unusually public smackdown for an investor used to operating behind closed doors. Rosenfeld and Buffett declined to comment.

Now, to save the deal, Rosenfeld is traveling the world to placate two groups of shareholders: Kraft's, who are increasingly worried that she'll pay too much, and Cadbury's, who are being told she's offering too little. Win or lose, says former Kraft CEO Robert S. Morrison, the Cadbury affair 'will be defining for her career'.

Kraft is the world's No. 2 food company after Nestlé, selling $42 billion worth of Kraft Macaroni & Cheese, Oreos, Oscar Mayer cold cuts, and hundreds of other brands each year. It is the product of two decades of deal making. Philip Morris International, seeking to broaden its reach beyond cigarettes, bought General Foods (which had among its brands Jell-O, Minute Rice, and Kool-Aid) in 1985, succeeded in a hostile takeover of Kraft in 1988, merged the two companies by 1995, and five years later bought Nabisco.

Midnight brainstorming

During the 1980s, General Foods, which was based in Westchester County, N.Y., had a reputation as an intellectually challenging workplace where debate was encouraged. It was here, in 1981, that Rosenfeld got her start in market research. She had spent most of the previous decade at Cornell University completing an undergraduate degree in psychology, an MBA, and a PhD in marketing and statistics. Her thesis adviser, Vithala R. Rao, recalls that even though she was working and pregnant she was determined to finish her dissertation on how consumers make decisions about purchases. 'She knew a PhD would give her an edge in the business world,' says Rao. 'And her husband was getting one. They were a little competitive.'

When Rosenfeld presented her bosses at General Foods with research showing that Kool-Aid should be marketed directly to kids, the pitch won her a job working on the brand full-time. It was an unexpected turn for a researcher. After a presentation at one of her first meetings with Grey Advertising, Rosenfeld was so excited that she applauded. Back then, junior employees were expected to stay silent. 'We were all so shocked and amused by her reaction,' says Carol Herman, who worked at Grey and remains a close friend of Rosenfeld's. As Rosenfeld came up through the ranks at General foods and Kraft – eventually overseeing the Nabisco integration and serving as president of Kraft North America – she developed a reputation as a tough and insistent boss. She would call people with ideas, however big or small, late into the night. Conversations about kids turned into discussions about Kraft products. I can't tell you how many midnight talks we had about Minute Rice and Stove Top stuffing,' says Herman, who worked on various accounts for Kraft through the 1990s. Says James M. Kilts, a former Kraft president who later ran Gillette: 'Irene didn't need a lot of advice. That's why I liked her. She was giving me the right answers.' Yet her intensity and self-confidence didn't always endear her to colleagues. One former executive recalls a time when Rosenfeld provided helpful insight into a business she had once managed. When the executive offered to return the favor, Rosenfeld took a pass.

In 2001, Rosenfeld suffered her first big professional setback when a contemporary, Betsy D. Holden, was appointed co-chief executive alongside Roger Deromedi. Rosenfeld stayed on almost two more years, then left to join Frito-Lay, a Kraft rival more global in its outlook and more local in its decision-making. 'Irene thought about the marketing agenda and innovation much more aggressively than the company was used to,' says India Nooyi, the CEO of PepsiCo, which owns Frito-Lay. 'She was fearless in what she did.'

Rewire for growth

Rosenfeld gave every impression that she was committed to Frito-Lay for the long term. But when Kraft asked her to return as CEO in June 2006, she jumped. The dual leader experiment had failed; Kraft was faltering amid high commodity prices, increasing competition from private labels and a misplaced focus on cost cutting. She told Kraft's nearly 100,000 employees that the company had lost its heart and soul and needed to 'rewire for growth'. In a speech at Cornell in 2007, Rosenfeld described her return to Kraft. 'The staff was tired, raw, disillusioned,' she told the audience. 'My slogan was, "let's get growing." It's not a warm and fuzzy strategy.' She replaced half of her executive team and half of those in the next two levels down. She reorganized the structure of the company, changed how people receive their bonuses, and told everyone 'to stop apologizing for our categories and make them more relevant'. She concluded her talk: 'Sometimes I lie awake thinking, "Should we?" And then I think, "How can we not?"'

Rosenfeld wasn't alone in wanting change – activist investor Nelson Peltz was demanding it. She learned that engagement and conciliation were the best ways to handle powerful dissenters. 'When Peltz pushed her to sell some brands, she did; unloading Veryfine fruit juice and Post cereals. And when she asked him not to purchase more than 10% of the company,' he agreed.

Peltz was also a big investor in Cadbury Schweppes, and he persuaded the British food giant to sell its soft drink division in 2008 and become purely a candy company. That would set the stage for Rosenfeld's eventual hostile takeover bid and provide Cadbury its philosophical defense: It didn't want to lose focus on its core business by becoming part of a conglomerate.

As the Great Recession took hold, Kraft should have thrived. But even though consumers ate at home more often and ingredient prices fell, the company was forced to cut prices to compete with private label products. For 2009, Rosenfeld's goal was sales growth of 4% and profit growth of at least 7%. Instead, revenue fell 6% through the first three quarters of 2009, with net income down 14.6% over the same period. Kraft stock, which went public at $31 a share in 2001, fell as low as $21. The company introduced items such as Bagel-fuls, bagels stuffed with Philadelphia cream cheese. The products did well, but not well enough to have a major impact. Rosenfeld also devoted considerable resources to creating premium toppings for Kraft's DiGiorno frozen pizza, and frequently pointed to the brand's success.

With the recession abating, Rosenfeld started thinking of ways to transform the company. 'She wanted to capture the imagination of the world about what Kraft could be,' says Shelly Lazarus, chairman of ad agency Ogilvy & Mather Worldwide, which works with Kraft. Rosenfeld began studying the possibility of buying Cadbury, which sells Trident gum and chocolate in 60 countries and has sales of about $8 billion. It's a fast growing global business with high profit margins.

Eventually she fixed on a price, and decided to approach Cadbury Chairman Roger Carr with an offer. She met with Carr in London to lay out her plan. 'She was brisk, efficient, delivered her proposal and left quite quickly,' says Carr. The two haven't spoken since, he says.

They have, however, exchanged a few letters. In the first, which Carr sent to Rosenfeld the next week, he called the offer 'derisory'. Then on Labor Day, Rosenfeld announced Kraft's bid in a news release on the corporate Web site, hoping to win over shareholders directly. She spoke to several British newspapers about her admiration for Cadbury and the great promise of a merger. In a video interview posted on the Kraft site, she expressed her enthusiasm for Cadbury's products in a way only a marketer could appreciate: 'I am a heavy, heavy user of Trident gum and, on a seasonal basis, I love those Cadbury eggs.' But after receiving no encouragement from the candy maker, Rosenfeld launched a hostile bid. 'We believe that our proposal offers the best immediate and long-term value for Cadbury's shareholders and for the company itself compared with any other option currently available, including Cadbury remaining independent,' she wrote in the formal offer.

Meanwhile, Rosenfeld was juggling another deal that would determine how much Kraft could spend for Cadbury. In early 2009, Nestlé made a surprise offer to buy DiGiorno and the rest of Kraft's pizza business. Rosenfeld concluded that selling the unit made sense: Frozen pizza wouldn't do well outside of North America, and within the company it was an isolated brand. Next she had to persuade the board. 'It was a difficult decision. But once we got our heads around the strategic and financial rationale for the deal, it became clear,' says Perry Yeatman, a Kraft spokeswoman. Closing the sale proved difficult; but Kraft announced it would sell the pizza business to Nestlé for $3.7 billion. Some investors thought the price was too low. But the deal would give Rosenfeld the cash she'd need to pursue Cadbury. And there was another benefit: Nestlé, Kraft's main rival for Cadbury, said it wouldn't bid.

Whatever sense of relief Rosenfeld might have felt didn't last long. On the same day, Buffett went public with his concerns, calling Rosenfeld's proposal to issue more shares a 'blank check'. He noted that while the company had bought back shares at a price of $33 a piece in 2007, it would be selling the new shares for the Cadbury transaction for far less. He did say, though, that he would support an offer that 'does not destroy value for Kraft shareholders'. Other investors share Buffett's skepticism. 'What is she wasting our money for?' asks John Kornitzer, founder of Kornitzer Capital Management. 'To chase after these guys is ridiculous.' Alice Schroeder, a former Wall Street analyst and author of a biography of Buffett who also writes a column for Bloomberg News, says even if Rosenfeld had consulted with Buffett it might serve his purposes to take a public stand. He can take credit for reining her in and defending shareholders. 'No matter how this turns out, Warren looks great,' she says.

Rosenfeld, however, is under attack from all sides. Carr released a stinging 'defense document' on Cadbury's Website, saying: 'The bid is even more unattractive today than it was when Kraft made its formal offer.' Kraft called the argument 'underwhelming'. Carr responds: 'I think the clarity with which we reviewed Kraft's own record must have been disturbing for them and illuminating for our shareholders.' While Rosenfeld remains determined to make Kraft bigger and more global, finding a price for Cadbury that works for everyone might be impossible. 'Rosenfeld has made it clear that she's disciplined, that she won't overpay,' says Donald Yacktman, president of Yacktman Asset Management, a longtime investor. 'I guess we'll find out how much she really means what she says.'

Source: S. Berfield and M. Arndt (2010), *Bloomberg Business Week*, January 25, p. 37-39

Case study questions

1 Would you categorize Irene Rosenfeld as an entrepreneur, a leader, a manager, or a combination of these three?
2 Is Irene Rosenfeld an inspiring leader as described in Covey's model?
3 How would you characterize Irene Rosenfeld's leadership style in terms of the fourteen characteristics of successful managers?
4 How would you characterize Irene Rosenfeld's leadership style in terms of Hersey and Blanchard's model of situation-determined styles of leadership?

Principles of management

Motivating people

Part One Management and society

Chapter 1
Manager and management

Chapter 2
Organizations and environment

Part Two Strategic management and the learning organization

Chapter 3
Decision making and creativity

Chapter 4
Strategy formulation and strategic management

Part Three Organizational structure and design

Chapter 5
Designing the organization

Chapter 6
Structuring tasks for groups and individuals

Part Four Organizational behavior and people at work

Chapter 7
Motivation, work and career

Chapter 8
Leadership, motivation and communication

Part Five Operational planning, control and information management

Chapter 9
Operational planning and control

Chapter 10
Managerial process control: functional processes and process redesign

Part 5

Operational planning, control and information management

CHAPTER 9 Operational planning and control

CHAPTER 10 Managerial process control: functional processes and process redesign

After a long-term course of action has been determined (Part Two), a fitting organizational structure developed (Part Three) and the employees as well as the managers motivated to work (Part Four), the extent to which the daily work contributes to long-term objectives still has to be verified.

Part Five will be devoted to managerial practices, control procedures and dissemination of information relating to organizational processes when a long-term plan is implemented as a guiding strategy. To determine if an organization is indeed on course, instruments and techniques have to be developed to evaluate the work being done daily. Techniques to be discussed in this section include budgeting, management by objectives, network planning and the use of such instruments as ratios (Chapter 9).

Because of the considerable influence that information management has on an organization and the rapid developments in automation and information technology (IT), it is given separate consideration in Chapter 10.

Automation projects have to suit the strategies of information planning, which must, in turn, conform to an organization's information policy. Some attention will be focused on the factors causing automation projects to fail, since applications of advanced information technologies have strategic and organizational consequences. In Chapter 10 we will deal with the process approach to organizational activities and the methods of exercising control over such processes. Such issues as quality control, care for the environment and logistics management will be discussed.

The act of organizing involves the ordering of processes in accordance with a given structure. This structure is a tool or an instrument to facilitate the activities in question. If the structure no longer aids or is even impeding the course of events, then it may be necessary to redesign the processes and, as a consequence, to modify or to adapt organizational structures. Processes are primary; structures have to be facilitative: this is the principle underlying business process re-engineering (BPR).

CONTENTS

9.1 Planning
9.2 From planning to budgeting
9.3 Management of operations
9.4 Production planning: methods and techniques
9.5 Time management: project and network planning
9.6 Improving quality: quality management
9.7 Benchmarking: learning through comparison
9.8 Ratios: a method of self-regulation
9.9 Performance measurement: financial and non-financial indicators
9.10 Operational control: adaptation and corrective actions

Operational planning and control

Chapter 9

LEARNING OUTCOMES

After studying this chapter, you should be able to do the following:

- **Give a definition of planning**
- **Explain the relationship between planning and budgeting**
- **State the relationship between management, budgeting and management by objectives**
- **Explain the goal, structure and procedures involved in network planning**
- **State the differences between financial and non-financial ratios**
- **Explain and exemplify the concepts of integral quality management and benchmarking**
- **Characterize managerial practices specific to non-profit organizations**

CASE

Management-in-action

Make or buy

Samsung Electronics and Sony both are set to unveil new 3D TVs at the annual Consumer Electronics Show in Las Vegas. The products are similar. The strategy behind them is not. The difference, simply put, is about making stuff. Sony increasingly believes hiring others to build its TVs will cut costs and help it regain financial health, while Samsung continues to make its own sets. 'Giving up manufacturing is tantamount to abandoning your brand,' says Yoon Boo Keun, president of Samsung's TV business.

Sony co-founder Akio Morita once held manufacturing sacred, too, so why the switch? The Japanese giant is headed for its first back-to-back annual losses since its 1958 listing – a total of some $1.9 billion over two years. Morita's successors believe their advantage is in games, movies, and music. 'We would like to concentrate our resources on Sony-unique applications,' says spokeswoman Sue Tanaka. This year Sony hopes to boost sales of its Bravia TVs by giving buyers content via the Internet, including streaming Sony films before their DVD or Blue-ray releases.

Now, Sony aims to outsource production of 40% of all TVs. It sold its biggest North American TV plant, in Tijuana, Mexico, to Taiwan's Hon Hai Precision Industry. Citigroup notes the fastest growth in TVs is in low-end sets sold in China and other developing countries – production that can more easily be outsourced than sophisticated models. Another argument for outsourcing is that even when Sony builds its own liquid-crystal-display TVs, it relies on Samsung and Sharp for LCD panels, a key component.

In contrast, Samsung is becoming more like the old Sony. It's now the only major TV maker that also produces the computer chips at the heart of new digital TVs. Samsung says that helps it more quickly introduce newfangled services such as Internet access, turning TVs into the centerpiece of home entertainment. Owning its factories, Samsung says, also lets it reap all the benefits from new efficiencies. 'You need a harmonious chorus of manufacturing, design, and marketing for a TV business,' says TV chief Yoon. 'But manufacturing remains the key.'

Source: *Bloomberg Business Week*, January 18, 2010, p. 52, M. Ihlwan

When the various strategic possibilities in an organization have been weighed up and a choice has been made, this choice will have to be further elaborated into various operational plans for marketing and sales, manufacturing, servicing, personnel, finance and so on. The establishment of a strategic model (see Fig 3.3) has a substantial effect on the processes of decision making, operational planning and the implementation of functional plans, as these procedures will be altered in such a manner that they will resemble the scheme depicted in Fig 9.1.

Whether a responsible manager in an existing company or a beginner in a new company, it is necessary to think ahead and to consider what needs to be done, how it will be undertaken, where problems will occur, and so on. In other words, courses of action for upcoming periods must be decided and signposts provided marking the routes to be taken. People and resources can then be steered in the appropriate direction and a necessary structure given to managerial activities. Not just goals are determined but also the ways in which they are to be attained and the resources with which the procedures are to be undertaken.

Furthermore, such policy intentions and statements must be transformed into specific actions, after which the actual outcomes and methods of execution must be checked to ensure that they conform in fact to the goals and methods prescribed in the original action plan.
As one might expect, elaboration of strategic plans helps to enhance the effectiveness of short-term performance by providing a means to evaluate organizational activities in terms of the policies established in the operational plans. There are, as they say, several ways to skin a cat. An organization should, however, determine its operational orientation in advance, select a preliminary manner of proceeding and specify the proposed organizational category in terms of specific actions leading to realizable short-term goals. The longer the time frame for this plan, the fewer the details it is likely to contain and the greater the chance that circumstances will change. If such changes should, in fact, occur, adjusting the plans remains a viable option.

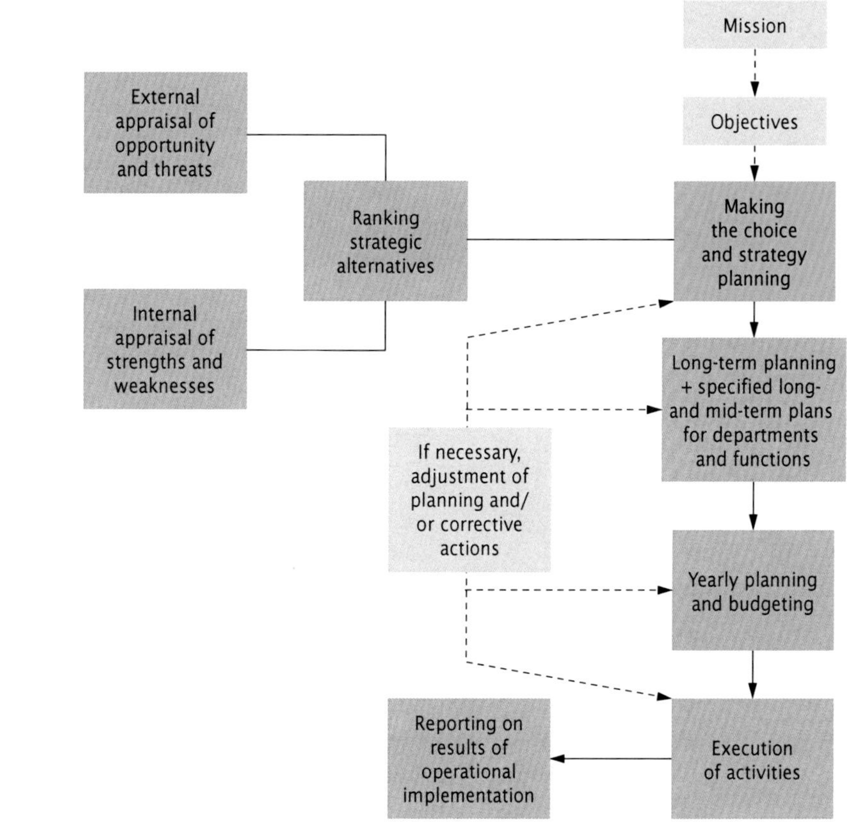

Figure 9.1
From strategic plan to operational planning and execution (and adjustment)

9.1 Planning

Planning is the systematic preparation and fine-tuning of decisions meant to realize future goals. It precedes action, as the making of plans requires management to look forward and to devise task-performance strategies based on their projections. The formulation of operational plans requires planners to determine what will be manufactured and sold, where this will take place, how this will happen, when this will occur, how much/many will be manufactured and, finally, who will undertake the task and with which resources. Good operational planning allows control to be maintained over organizational activities. A grip is kept on things. Expected developments are considered in advance in the plans, and how they will be dealt with is thoroughly plotted, regulated in advance and harmonized. This enables planning to guide the process. Should new and unexpected developments occur during execution, the plans will, of course, have to be adjusted, although well-conceived plans are always based on

operational planning

adequate and reliable data about the future. They provide a basis for decisions. During the operational phase, planning must be continued, as adjustments may indeed have to be made. Only if there are unexpected developments, *force majeur* and sudden new possibilities is there cause to review the plans entirely.
All plans are concerned with future activities over the long, middle-long, or short terms and must, therefore, precede the actual event. Regulation of required actions and coordination of the activities involved is therefore essential. Work must proceed in an orchestrated manner, which means that all levels of execution are synchronized and directed towards the same end. Planning constitutes the principal tool for structuring tasks in this way.
Besides regulating future actions and coordinating performance, plans provide a means of supervising the progress of the activities in question. Comparison of projected and actual outcomes can lead to additional and perhaps corrective decisions, and/or adjustments to the operational norms.

Types of planning

strategic plan

In addition to formulating the future corporate or strategic plan of an entire company or institution, the various departments of an organization may also engage in planning activities.

overall plan

The scope of an organization's overall plan is relatively broad. It is directed at the longer term and, more particularly, provides a basis for the necessary acquisitions of and investments in buildings, machines, equipment and people.
Planning for the various areas within an organization, often in the form of operational plans drafted at the departmental level, is primarily concerned with shorter-term activities. This planning specifies the guidelines provided by the more general strategic plan in ways relevant to an organization's various functions and/or divisions. Sample outcomes of such procedures include a marketing and sales plan, a manufacturing plan, and a research and product development plan (see sections 9.1.2 - 9.1.7).

Controlling processes by planning

All forms of planning consist of the following three basic elements:
- Information
- Norms
- Plans

Information

Planning involves the systematic processing of external and internal data, without which there is nothing to plan. Formulating policy and long-term plans requires financial information, as well as facts about developments and trends occurring in the social environment. Moreover, an awareness of an organization's self-image, based on some type of internal appraisal, will also affect plans. The more planning is concerned with the specifics and details of an organization's daily activities, the more internal information becomes important. The quality of such a detailed planning procedure therefore depends on the quality, reliability and general applicability of information from within the company itself, as well as on the speed in which such information can be supplied. The quality of information processing in general and the ability to provide valid internal information constitutes a decisive ingredient for the formulation of plans.

Norms

Norms are guidelines, prescriptions and so on that indicate the constraints within which an activity may occur. Norms specify the way of acting, the methods or procedures relating to the performance of each task. These norms can apply to the organization as a whole, but can also be applicable to certain departments or functional areas, or even be specific to a given task.

Plans

Plans describe organizational or departmental goals, determine the measures necessary to attain these goals, identify the required personnel and financial resources, and indicate the period or the time frame within which the stated goals have to be attained. A plan can be seen as the product of a planning activity.

Planning for functional areas and departments

Plans may be formulated for a variety of functional areas or departments, including:

- Marketing and sales
- Manufacturing/servicing
- Product development
- Finance
- Personnel
- Purchasing

In other words, there is no function or department in an organization for which planning is inappropriate. The goals and means of attaining them can be specified for all primary processes or supporting activities. The final step always involves short-term operational planning and budgeting, which translate more general strategic plans into viable and affordable operations.

9.1.1 Marketing and sales planning

marketing mix

The act of formulating marketing and sales plans requires an organization to determine its markets and to identify the ways in which these markets may be approached. This procedure should be applied to the so-called marketing mix or 4 Ps: the Products which one wants to introduce, the Placement of these products in selected locations, the Promotion of the items by means of advertising and sales campaigns and the Price of the product(s) in question. The marketing and sales plan must contain statements about:

- Sales and sales growth
- Market share
- Profitability
- The product and its development
- Distribution channels
- Price
- Promotion of the product

In considering all these factors, a long-term vision as well as a short-term plan for the first and even the second year will have to be developed.

ENERGIZED DIFFERENTIATION

Why do certain brands continue to resonate with consumers? What is it about Apple, Nike, Virgin, Whole Foods, and Google? They've all achieved 'energized differentiation'. These brands don't rest on their laurels, they are continually looking forward and staying in motion. We used to think of positioning as a hole in the ground in which to plant a brand. Water it with repetitive messages and GRPs (gross rating points) until it bears the fruit of brand equity. But the marketplace is in constant motion. Competitors, consumers and culture are constantly reordering brand meaning ... It's no longer effective to stake a claim to a perpetual territory and defend it through repetition. Instead, the best way for a brand to own a position is to be constantly dynamic with it. The power of Apple's iPod isn't in the core invention, but in how the brand is constantly evolving. And the decades-old skin-care brand Dove is still relevant because it 'elevated itself from a memorable product attribute focus ("one-quarter cleansing cream") to engaging in a cultural conversation with consumers (reframing social perceptions of beauty)'.

Source: *Strategy + Business* (2009) 57(winter), p. 106

9.1.2 Production planning/planning of services

Based on an organization's strategic plan, steps can be taken to detail manufacturing or production plans.

Capacity planning

The first step is to determine the required amounts of capacity based on the sales expectations for the new product(s). Consideration should not only be given to needed buildings and machines, but also to the personnel requirements. This latter matter is especially important when further education or supplementary training has to be made available to new recruits or existing personnel before they are competent to perform the new tasks. If sales expectations are not easily ascertained, a degree of flexibility should be taken into account by, for example, setting up a relatively small but potentially expandable initial capacity. Such planning will be relatively lacking in detail.

Manufacturing planning

As soon as capacity has been determined, it is necessary to examine how the order flow fits into the capacity or, in other words, the extent to which the capacity will be occupied. If adjustments need to be made, the possibility exists to adopt such measures as the recruiting of temporary employees or the use of overtime to deal with overutilization on the one hand, or increased sales efforts (possibly enhanced by the implementation of temporary discounts) to offset underutilization on the other.

overutilization

underutilization

Production level planning also provides useful information for purchasing. Such is certainly the case in companies that make one product or only a small variety of products. Producers who manufacture a large number of items are better off basing their purchasing requirements on the rates of incoming orders for individual product types.

Delivery planning

Although it is primarily production planning that is concerned with the utilization of capacity, delivery planning helps to optimize production by determining when raw materials and tools are available to certain departments or machine groups.
In this form of planning, concerns focus on the most effective way the manufacturing department can process the order and the appropriate allocation of production times. For this reason, delivery planning is also known as work planning.

Detailed order and machine planning

At this stage – the last phase before the actual manufacturing begins – work is assigned to various machines and/or employees. The procedure is frequently labeled as work distribution or dispatching. Depending on the kind of manufacturing involved, this form of planning will be done by the planning office or its director. In capital-intensive companies engaged in series or mass production, the planning office will play an especially important role.

work distribution

planning office

monitoring procedure

The last two above-mentioned planning phases must be supplemented by a monitoring procedure, the goal of which is to determine whether the activities are being performed according to plan. It may disclose an actual situation which, if it deviates too much from the planned projections, may require corrective action. Such adjustments can, of course, only occur when information is quickly gathered and processed. Comparison of planned and actual operations also requires instruments such as planning charts. Planning and implementation control are important in every organization. An effective system for making short-term plans, an operation assigned in industrial organizations to the planning office, does not only result in a higher degree of efficiency but also better provision of services to customers, especially insofar as delivery times are concerned.

9.1.3 Product development planning

It should be noted that the notion of product used here is a broad one and includes services. Any activity involving product development must initially be regarded as an unfettered *exploration* exploration of new possibilities. All or a selected number of these possibilities are subsequently elaborated and evaluated on the merits of their potential benefits for the *economic analysis* organization. Next, an economic analysis of the product idea is undertaken, after which the chosen idea is developed into a complete product ready for manufacture. This product has then to be tested and, finally, brought on the market. Even though these steps seem obvious, a lot can go wrong during the process of developing new products and introducing them to the market. Only a fraction of all new product ideas (about one in forty) end up as successful products.
Of course, the first requirement for any possible success in this developmental process is good coordination of both new and existing marketing practices.

9.1.4 Financial planning

When it comes to financial planning, a number of factors need to be closely examined. They include the debt and equity structure, the allocation of financial resources to various investment projects and the control maintained over working capital. Financial needs represent a long-term concern for most organizations, particularly in times of high inflation and high interest rates. Where there is moderate or slight profitability, equity capital grows insufficiently to finance all the needs that arise from the growth of inventories and accounts receivable. Sometimes this can even result in the development of a negative leverage effect, which only serves to intensify the problems further.
Furthermore, the answers to questions concerning the financing or leasing of assets (buildings, machinery) or the dividend policy to be followed are provided by financial planning. In such cases, references can be made to investment selection methods, techniques for the control of working capital, optimization of funding, and so on.

9.1.5 Personnel planning

By means of its personnel planning an organization tries to obtain insight into the question: 'What quantitative and qualitative consequences does the chosen strategy have for the personnel structure?' When activities are expanded, a lack of sufficient and appropriately trained personnel can severely hinder the execution of a strategy. In the case of a planned phasing out of activities, the social consequences of any work-force reductions must be given close examination at an early stage.
Personnel planning primarily focuses on the short term (perhaps only weeks or months), and the outcome of the plans will have consequences especially for the recruitment or dismissal of personnel, both of which may occur on a temporary basis.
The longer the term encompassed by personnel planning (a year or longer), the more complex the task becomes. An increasing number of factors must be taken into account: intake, flow of personnel, career development, management development, training and further education, promotions, work structuring, organizational change, and so on.
In personnel planning, specific attention must be given to both social policy and the goals formulated to that end. (See human resources management in Chapter 7.)

9.1.6 Purchasing and material resources planning

The purpose of material resources planning, a field generally given little attention, is to indicate when necessary materials should be purchased, to assure the quality of the materials to be acquired, to ascertain the quantities required, to determine the appropriate prices, to designate the supplier(s) to be used, and to establish the places to which the goods should be delivered.

Given the scarcity and therefore the increasing costs of a number of raw materials, along with the resulting diminished competitive and profit positions, the purchasing function is becoming progressively more important. Such circumstances frequently prompt a search for alternative suppliers and substitutes for certain material requirements. The concerns of material resources planning also include such problems as those involved in the outsourcing of work.

Large multidivisional companies, in which cross-deliveries are likely to take place, often have guidelines limiting the autonomy of their divisions. They are, for example, not allowed to purchase materials from third parties when such materials are produced elsewhere in the company. The resulting determination of transfer prices and internal pricing systems also falls under material resources planning.

9.2 From planning to budgeting

Once policy has been set and plans formulated, the framework and the conditions are created within which actions will be performed. The best way to use current facilities and available resources must be decided on a month-to-month, week-to-week and even day-to-day basis (via short-term planning procedures). Once important long-term planning decisions have been made and profit levels determined, such considerations as market share, product assortment, production resources and so on, have to be translated into task assignments by means of short-term planning procedures. One has to make the best use of the existing possibilities, people and resources available to realize the planned objectives. Long-term plans establish the framework within which short-term operational plans, such as those relating to the coming year have to be formulated. Conversely, short-term planning is task specific, prescriptive and concerned with the immediate future.

short-term planning
long-term planning
operational plans

Short-term planning is operational planning and specifically indicates by means of task assignments what has to be done by whom, when, with the aid of which resources, and in what quantities. When these task assignments are translated into financial terms, we speak of budgets (see Section 9.2.1). Short-term planning usually takes place at the departmental level. The department head, the supervisor of a sub-department or a group leader is often charged with this task. It is consequently at this level that both work and resources are allocated.

budgets

One of the goals of a commercial organization is to make a profit. The goals of non-profit organizations, such as public utilities involve such things as the delivery of services for a certain fee, or perhaps at the lowest possible cost. Consequently, management in both types of organization always needs to monitor costs and revenues. Such auditing can only occur if, prior to the operational phase of the activities in question, effective plans have been formulated according to which operations can be monitored as a matter of course.

With the help of budgeting and planning, attempts can be made to maintain as much control over activities as possible. The broader context (the organizational strategy) outlined in the strategic plan, is given more detailed elaboration in the form of short-term operational plans. For this purpose, departments and responsible employees must be made aware of the performances expected of them in the organizational plan.

The task of determining the financial consequences of such plans belongs to budgeting, the process of translating plans into monetary terms. By budgeting costs, expenses, revenues and income, the organizational results for a period can be expressed as sums of money. If a plan is task specific, its budget (i.e. a formal plan expressed in terms of money) also has a task specific function. With it in hand, management distributes task assignments, expressed in terms of allocated funds, to sales, manufacturing, purchasing and so on, which together have to realize the organizational goals detailed in the budget.

9.2.1 Budgeting and the setting of norms and targets

Budgeting is nothing more than a planning procedure involving sums of money, the only common denominator of the various organizational activities. Since all planning must have a financial element, budgeting is the logical consequence of planning. Just like planning, budgeting has an active character.

task assignments

To a certain degree, budgeting always involves task assignments, since budgets are nothing more than sets of performance norms expressed in monetary terms. When everything is right, these norms meet several requirements. Just like plans, they have to be based on adequate future projections. A plan based on inaccurate and insufficient information can never produce good results. A good plan also needs to be quantified, and budgets frequently indicate data relating to such things as required machine time, man-hours and associated costs. Moreover, budgets must also formulate attainable norms, as it makes no sense to create an unrealistic and therefore disheartening assignment. The best norms represent accomplishable challenges that stimulate the work effort without creating the feeling that employees really need to strain themselves and to perform at their maximum levels. Conversely, norms set at too low a level are not challenging and will in time also have a demoralizing effect.

A last but still important requirement is that norms be measurable. If not it will become hard, if not impossible, to monitor task performance. This requirement is, however, related to the condition that a plan has to be quantifiable. Budgeting is the principal means of satisfying these requirements. Consequently, there is a close relationship between the planning process and the budgetary procedure.

budgetary procedure

fixed or variable

Budgets can either be fixed or variable. Fixed budgets are formulated whenever it is possible to determine the utilization of capacity in a stable manner. In contrast, a variable budget is preferable when the deployment of capacity fluctuates a great deal. In either case, the company results depend on the use made of capacity. In an organization, operational employees are frequently involved in the formulation of departmental plans and budgets. Their involvement in budgeting and planning motivates their work effort and stimulates their participation in activities meant to realize budgets and plans. The consequences may well involve cost reductions.

analysis

budget result

Differences between actual and budgeted outcomes always have to be subject to careful analysis. Measuring and monitoring must precede such budget-based analyses (of either the discrepancies or results). In business terms, the periodical comparison of projected costs to actual costs is labeled 'post-calculation'. As soon as the deviation (i.e. the budget result) exceeds tolerance levels, it needs to be examined with the intent of making possible planning or budgeting adjustments. To verify budgeted forecasts, the information book-keeping system needs to be capable of furnishing the required data.

The causes of deviation can be very varied, and before adjustments are made, the actual cause should be determined. When the reasons for such deviations lie outside the organization, for example in stagnating sales or increased prices of raw materials, the supervisor in charge of the final assembly department cannot be held responsible for an increased inventory of the final product.

9.2.2 Budgeting as a management tool

Seen in this way, budgeting is first and foremost an important tool for management. By composing budgets, planning is translated into the monetary terms involved in the daily task assignments given employees in various departments.

marketing and sales Marketing and sales: The sales plan is translated into the general results which have to be realized and into more specific sales data (projected and actual results and costs) involving particular product groups. In this relationship, direct cost budgets can be drawn up for such items as advertising, sales promotion and the activities of representatives. In the marketing and sales domain, indexed figures for sales per client, per representative and per area, average order size, and sales costs per order can be used to monitor activities and results.

manufacturing Manufacturing: By means of a budget, the manufacturing plan is translated into the different cost components of the manufacturing process (e.g. raw material, labor and machines), as well as into total production costs and the cost of manufacturing particular products, product series, and so on. Such measures as quality norms and productivity norms are invoked to monitor production activity per unit, machine, man hour, and so on.

purchasing Purchasing: To facilitate company activities, supplies of raw materials and components usually have to be purchased in advance. Sufficient supplies have to be present to process orders, and to maintain these levels, delivery times must be taken into account. Further consideration of seasonal fluctuations will often be required. The nature and duration of the manufacturing process is closely aligned with the purchase of materials, components, installations and other durable production resources, all of which have to be assigned monetary values in budgets involving purchasing and/or capital investments.

research and development Research and development: In this type of budget, statements are made about the sums of money allocated to the improvement of existing products and the development of new ones, or to the development of new production methods. Such activities can be monitored in terms of costs per development hour, investments and other costs per development activity.

financing Financing: This activity involves the drafting of a statement of projected results for the coming years, along with statements of projected profits and losses as well as cash flows projections. Cash or liquidity planning helps to identify financial needs or surpluses that may arise in the coming period and, therefore, to indicate the additional financial resources that have to be found or the surplus resources that can be invested (either in the short or the long term).

personnel Personnel: The personnel budget establishes the monetary amounts expended in the form of wages, salaries, social security payments, and so on. It also indicates the sums of money made available for such items as education and training, company social care and other personnel policy costs. In this area, it is important not only to work with ratios involving wages and other personnel costs, but also with ratios relating to absenteeism, turnover and so on. An increasing amount of information about such issues is now required for publication in annual reports.

Specifications of the tasks performed in various departments need to be coordinated with each other and, accordingly, expressed in terms of the financial consequences of the performances delivered by each department. Budgeting, in other words, is also a tool for coordinating the efforts of departments and employees so that they remain geared towards the accomplishment of organizational goals. The unity of an organization is thus strengthened.

budgets Formulating budgets requires the functions and tasks of departments and employees to be clearly defined. At the same time, assignments of authority need to be clarified, so that the responsibilities in a department are apparent and the lines of accountability easily drawn. Budgets empower authorized personnel to make decisions and to incur expenses.

Budgetary coherence

The departmental budgets can be divided further into operational and capital budgets.

operational budget *capital budget* Operational budgets are concerned with daily activities, expressed in terms of costs and revenues. Capital budgets reflect decisive changes to overall account entries and deal with items such as inventories, accounts receivable, accounts payable and investments in land or buildings.

liquidity budget Both kinds of budgets are components of a liquidity budget, in which the financial consequences of all plans are brought together. Based on a provisional liquidity budget, it can, for example, be determined if a planned investment should be financed out of the normal cash flows. If this is not possible, other sources of financing will have to be found, and when

these cannot be found, the intended investment will possibly have to be dropped.
The interrelationship of the various departmental budgets is depicted diagrammatically in Fig 9.2. The department-level budgets can be summarized and combined into a so-called general or master budget, which will be discussed further in the following section.

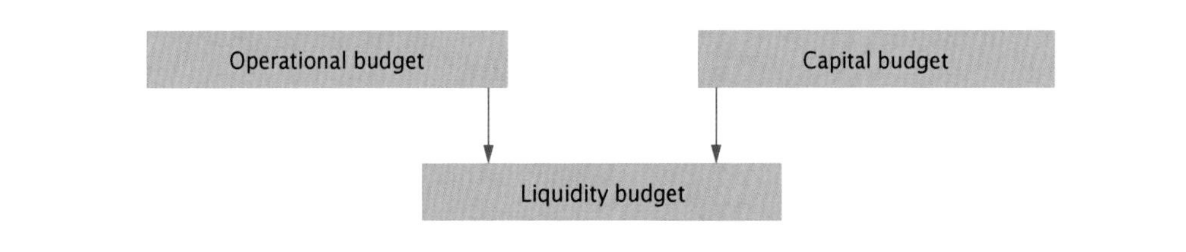

Figure 9.2
The coherence between types of budgets

9.2.3 Budgeting and the general (or master) budget

We have seen that budgeting is a technique used to specify the tasks constituting the total activities of an organization. The process provides a basis from which the various departmental annual budgets are derived. These operational budgets constitute a financial translation of intended programs into the actual activities involved in various functional areas. Together, they need to be examined in a coordinated manner in order to synchronize them with each other and to facilitate the ensuing task specifications.

revolving budget

A year is the usual time frame covered by any budget, although rolling or shifting periods may also be involved (resulting in a so-called revolving budget). In such cases, the budget has a task-specific character for the initial period, and an orienting function for the subsequent one (for example, a quarter of a year). Using the revolving-budget method allows for flexibility and, at the same time, continuity, as costs and revenues for the following period are already estimated, along with the sums of money for which employees will be given responsibility.
As such, budgeting functions is a tool that management can use to control various organizational processes, both in advance of and after the fact. Budgeting is the main tool for determining the results to be attained and for enabling, in response, opportunities to monitor, adjust and correct operations.
Budgets drawn up for various departments can be summarized in a so-called general or master budget, on the basis of which the profit and loss statement for the coming budget year can be derived. The general or master budget gives an overall account of the task-specific income, cost and/or expenditure budgets of the departments, including expenditures requiring liquidity or cash resources such as the payment of wages and salary.

general budget

In the general budget, costs are also included which do not require immediate expenditure, but for which cash resources will have to be allocated in the future. Included in this category are such items as depreciation, provision for maintenance and so on. Interest costs associated with credits/accounts receivable, inventories and other company resources are also part of the summarizing company budget. These factors must be taken into account in order to determine a fair business result from an economic point of view.
Consequently, the general or master budget of an industrial company can, for example, be composed of the sales budget, the manufacturing budget, the purchase budget, the personnel budget and the capital investment budget. A cash forecast and a forecast of cash needs is one result of such a compilation. They subsequently provide a basis for a projected balance and profit/loss statement covering the ensuing period.
The relationship between the various departmental budgets, the general budget, and the forecast balances and profit/loss statements has been depicted diagrammatically in Fig 9.3.
The relationships between the various departments in an organization and the degree to which they can make use of each others' services are important factors in determining the nature of such a structure. If these relationships are known, it becomes possible to estimate costs for a given budget year.

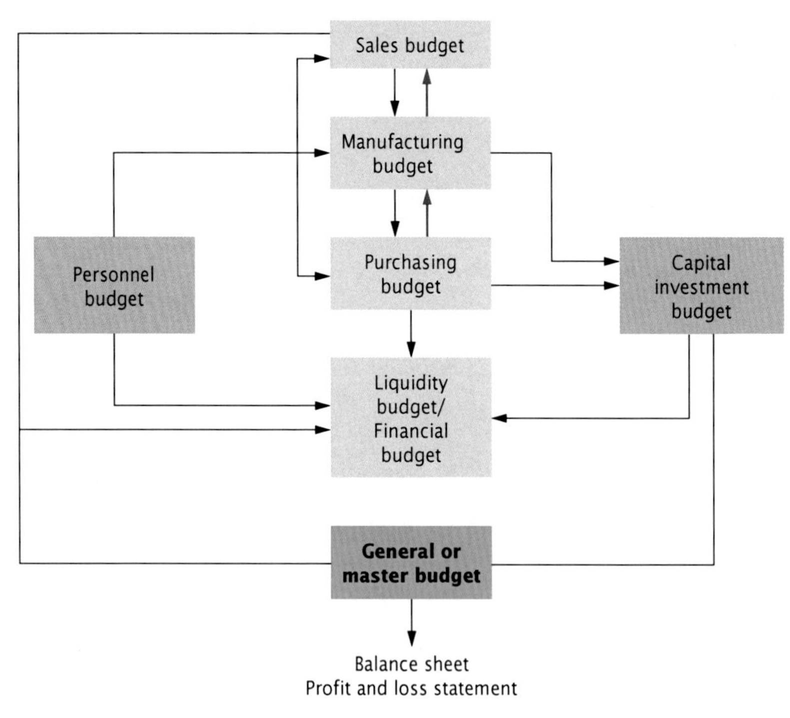

Figure 9.3
From functional budgets to 'master budget'

9.2.4 Functions of budgeting

As previously mentioned, a budget is a summary of a plan translated into monetary terms and may, indeed, be the product of one particular employee. Although sometimes labeled an *estimation* rather than a budget, the former term has, strictly speaking, a different meaning: it identifies an estimate of costs and revenues that, seen in itself, does not have a budget's task specific character of fulfilling four functions.

First of all, budgeting makes projections about the future, the policy to be adopted and the actions to be undertaken to implement the policy. This function of the budget underlines its importance in an organization's total planning process. By means of budgeting, organizational activities are coordinated with each other and cohesiveness of activities is brought about.

organizational policies Secondly, a budget is a tool for transmitting broad organizational policies to lower organizational levels. Based on the budgets, task assignments are given to the various employees. Higher management then grants them the authority to make independent decisions, to perform the actions necessary to perform the tasks, but to do so within the constraints of the approved budget. In other words, a budget is an instrument of communication. Management will, however, frequently involve lower-level personnel in the preparation of plans, so that the communication function is two way. Communicating policy in this manner means that it is possible to use budgets to assign tasks to any number of employers, all of whom will have the competence and the authority to carry them out.

Besides being a means of transmitting strategy and policy to responsible employees, in the third place, budgeting is an instrument to motivate these employees to perform tasks as well as they possibly can. When higher management involves lower-level personnel in the preparation of the budgets the participants in the budgetary process can, based on the budget, *task performance* be held accountable for task performance. A budget states what is expected. A responsible employee will thus try to attain the goals budgeted for the task. If they succeed there is plenty of reason for satisfaction; if they do not, then the shortcomings have to be justified.

The fourth function of budgeting is applicable to both higher management and the operational employers themselves. A budget is a tool to test whether the plans have been successfully implemented. Budgeting allows for the retrospective appraisal of departmental performance, an important method of gaining insight into the reasons the plans were not successfully implemented. Failure can sometimes be the result of external factors such as the decreasing demand for a certain product. Sometimes it is a consequence of internal causes such as inefficient work practices or low-quality raw materials. Based on such conclusions, possible improvements can be made to the organization or better raw materials acquired. Comparison of a financial plan and actual outcomes leads, generally speaking, to corrective actions and measures (see Fig 9.4). Sometimes improvement of performance will be recommended. On other occasions the norms may have to be adapted, although such adaptations must be carefully aligned with the budgets formulated by other departments. These four functions make the organization's budgeting process able to control business processes both in advance and after the fact. Budgeting is one of the main ways an organization can determine attainable results and establish a means to supervise, adjust and/or correct its business activities.

9.2.5 *Conditions for effective budgeting*

Even though budgeting clearly has financial and technical characteristics, effective budgeting can only occur if a number of conditions are met.

Support from upper management
Support from the top is a must. Besides being a technique, budgeting constitutes a management philosophy. No single technique can be successfully applied without acceptance of the notions or thoughts which form its basis. Budgeting demands that upper management be prepared and willing to delegate and hence relinquish a part of its decision-making authority to a lower organizational level.

There has to be a clear organizational structure
By means of budgeting, every employee is given the responsibility for performing certain tasks or for attaining certain results. These have to be clearly indicated in the organizational structure, even when the responsibilities are those of upper management. Supervisory procedures are not otherwise possible.

The budget system has to be a part of the total planning system
Budgets detail which activities have to be undertaken in the coming year and which sums of money are allocated to them. Budgets must, therefore, be clearly connected to company strategy and policy. The budget system provides the possibility of coordinating the diverse short-term activities.

Responsibility for the budget system has to be assigned
Even though budgeting is, ultimately, the responsibility of upper management, supervision of the budgeting process in larger organizations will often be delegated to the head of the administration and finance department or to the controller. This individual oversees the collecting and transmitting of the information needed by the various employees.

The use of business or economic jargon has to be limited
Despite the fact that budgets are drawn up in financial terms, they still have to be understandable to all employees involved. An average person should be able to comprehend the language in which they are couched. If they become obscure documents, budgeting loses its usefulness as managerial tool. In other words, budgeting has to remain an understandable technique in order to be useful to management.

Clear goals and norms have to be determined

Goals provide the basis for the budget. If goals and norms are not clear, it will not be possible to translate them properly into sums of money. Retrospective comparison of the actual production practices to poorly defined norms would not be a meaningful exercise either.

Need for participation in the development, formulation and implementation of budgets

Few people like to be watched, and budgeting is a technique and tool which does involve this function. To prevent sabotage of the system, it is necessary to involve organizational members in the drafting of budgets. Through such involvement the information on which the budgets are based is validated and made as complete as possible. In addition, the organization members will be better motivated because they are themselves involved in determining the goals. They will then also start to see the budget more as a challenge than as a threat.
When all these conditions are met, an organization not only possesses a management tool that can track and monitor the execution of plans, but also one that provides a good basis for managerial activities at all organizational levels.

9.3 Management of operations

It is important to ensure that all organizational activities and operations are directed towards the same goals. For this reason, it is necessary to convert strategic plans into action plans that relate to specific functional areas. Departmental goals can be set which, if the organization is a large one, need to be broken down into sub-goals. Certain employees are made responsible and accountable for the attainment of these goals.
To oversee the process of goal attainment, the successful implementation of plans must be verified both during and after their execution. When deviations become apparent, adjustments may have to be made to the process or the established norms modified. The control process or control cycle is diagrammatically depicted in Fig 9.4.

control process

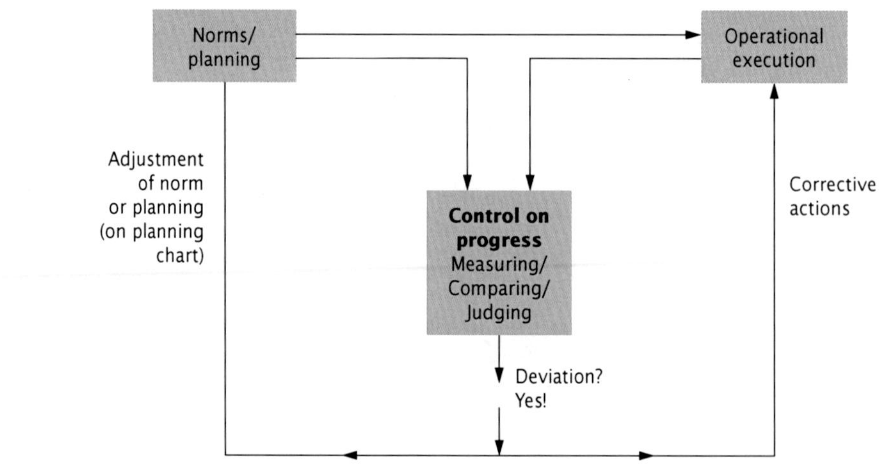

Figure 9.4
The control process (control cycle)

In management, cycles of execution, verification and correction or adjustment are required by such budgeting procedures as the one discussed in Section 9.2. Differences between projected and actual costs are pinpointed, and potential corrections or adjustments examined. When discrepancies exceed a certain level of tolerance one has to intervene and either revise practices or adjust norms. Deviations within tolerance levels do not require any further intervention.

Employees often participate in procedures for developing departmental plans and determining operational norms. This practice can motivate and stimulate productivity and encourage employee acceptance of management plans.

9.3.1 Operational control: keeping a systematic grip on activities

To maintain control of activities and operations they have to be well planned prior to and carefully monitored during the process of execution. Planning, execution and verification procedures all have a role to play in regulating the organizational processes. When systematically done, this involves five procedures:

five procedures

1 Setting operational norms (via planning)
2 Assigning tasks and issuing instructions
3 Supervising and measuring task performance (i.e. collecting data relating to actual performance during execution)
4 Comparing execution with projections (according to a budget or planning chart), along with planned and accurately issued assignments and instructions, as well as stating and analyzing possible differences
5 Adjusting plans and/or how they are to be performed (for example, implementing longer working hours or redistributing workloads may result in changes to norms, plans and/or task assignments)

Monitoring and revising plan implementation is a way of detecting possible deviations, enabling timely notification of potential budgetary deficits or overruns, and indicating projected standstills and disadvantageous uses of machine time (according to the planning chart). There may be deviations from the projected costs, revenue or production times caused by the following:

- Late replenishing of materials, components, etc.
- Bad materials
- Absenteeism
- Machine standstills because of defects
- Low levels of motivation
- Falling demand

The quality of the products or services will also have to be ascertained. Sometimes quality control is done by the production department. In other cases, it is a task performed by a separate department in an organization so that it can be carried out independent of the production department.

quality control

Quality control may be carried out by conducting random tests of products according to pre-determined quality requirements. Adjustments can then be made either to the product design or to actual production practices and thus ensure that better products are manufactured in the future.

Administrative procedures must ensure adequate supervision of the manufacturing processes. Data relating to materials used, hours worked, disruptions and other factors needs to be collected and presented in an orderly manner to monitor production operations. The person or department responsible for the organization's financial administration has to supply employees with information on which departmental decisions can be based. In a certain sense, this information supply is the nervous system linking all company functions. It sends signals to indicate when sales per client are lagging behind expectations, when suppliers should be paid and letters of demand be sent to debtors, when cost budgets have been exceeded or when calculations need to be adjusted. Timely information processing is therefore crucial (see Chapter 10).

information processing

Various methods can be employed to remain informed about production practices. Sometimes deviations are detected by means of personal observation. More often, controls occur in an indirect manner and deviations are only retrospectively discernible. As long as deviations do not transgress set tolerance levels, the authority to implement adjustments can be delegated to operational employees. When these limits are exceeded, a more senior level may have to be involved.

management by exception

Conscious and systematic delegation of the authority to make independent adjustments is termed 'management by exception'. Under such a system, a manager only deals with exceptional cases. This way of working relieves the manager of a large amount of routine decision making, so that he or she can pay more attention to more important tasks and problems. Good employees can very often solve their problems themselves if they are given the responsibility and freedom to do so.

Adjusting the operational norms or departmental plans is never an isolated event. It almost always has consequences for other departments or production stages and must therefore involve consultation with others. Adjustments have to be carefully aligned with operational norms or plans drawn up for other processes, which is why they should always be authorized by management. The granting of such authorization should occur in consultation with the employee involved in the production process. Such subjects as valid procedures, existing plans, accepted standard methods and relevant policy guidelines (see Section 6.7) should be discussed.

9.3.2 Issuing assignments

A plan can only be implemented when management actualizes its implementation plan by assigning tasks, providing instructions or issuing directives. A task assignment is the act of appointing someone to undertake certain activities or to attain certain results. In the latter, the appointee has greater freedom of action than in the former. There are two important factors to be considered when assigning tasks:

- The manner in which the task assignment is made
- The type of task assignment

Task assignment: oral or written

oral tasks assignment

Oral tasks assignments differ from written ones. Since both have certain advantages and disadvantages, a careful choice should be made. The advantages of the oral task assignment are speed, simplicity and reduced paper work. The main disadvantage is the danger of misinterpretation. In cases involving tasks performed over long periods of time, the precise nature of the original assignment may no longer be apparent when the results are assessed. This danger is greatest when performance has not been up to scratch.

written task assignment

The written task assignment has the advantage that it facilitates later verification. In addition, it can be issued in multiple copies and given to more than one employee or group at the same time. A written task assignment needs to be carefully formulated. Its disadvantages are the increased paper work that it generates and its explanatory limitations. A face-to-face encounter allows greater opportunity for clarification.

The form chosen will depend on the specific situation. A regular assignment will usually be given orally and a complex task assignment preferably in written form.

Task assignment: simple or multiple

simple task assignment

Tasks may be either simple or multiple. A simple task assignment is one intended to produce a certain result. The employee is free to determine how to perform the task and can use his or her own initiative since it is only the result that counts.

multiple task assignment

In the case of a multiple task assignment, how the task is to be performed is stipulated. For example, necessary procedures or steps are identified, as well as a person to whom feedback must be provided. The initiative of the operational employee is curtailed. The more detailed the procedure, the more limited are the opportunities for acting on one's own initiative.

Instructions

Instructions may replace the task assignment. Instructions are sets of general guidelines that have to be considered when specific tasks are performed.
Instructions can complement a task assignment by limiting the possibilities for self-initiated action. They are particularly valuable if they succeed in this regard. To keep instructions up to date, it is necessary to examine whether they are actually being followed.
Depending on the circumstances, instructions may have to be reviewed on an ongoing basis. When they appear to be partially superseded, it is better to delete the irrelevant part than to allow it to be ignored. Once even one element of an instruction becomes irrelevant, the danger exists that employees will start neglecting the relevant parts of it as well.

9.3.3 Management by objectives

'Management by objectives' is a method of formulating orders in relation to key issues. Managing in this way involves more than giving orders. Instead, this management technique is especially concerned with the improvement of an organization's total performance. The philosophy underlying this approach along with the techniques it employs will now be briefly examined.

consultation

The key element underlying the practice of management by objectives is consultation between the manager and the employee. They jointly formulate a description of the employee's function and the main results to be attained by them, both jointly and individually, in the coming period. These agreed targets are called the key results and are preferably defined in such a way that they constitute measurable goals. Dates are set at which time progress is to be assessed. The method is based on the basic notions expressed in McGregor's 'Theory Y' (see Section 8.4.3).

Theory Y

Since employees are able to bring their own ideas and desires to the consultation, the goals of the individual and the organization are likely to become better coordinated. This state of affairs is a favorable one for improving the motivation and collective efforts of all of the organizational members.

PLANNING FOR ACTION

Consider the experience of a newly appointed hospital administrator. The hospital was big and prestigious, but it had been coasting on its reputation for 30 years. The new administrator decided that his contribution should be to establish a standard of excellence in one important area within two years. He chose to focus on the emergency room, which was big, visible, and sloppy. He decided that every patient who came into the ER had to be seen by a qualified nurse within 60 seconds. Within 12 months, the hospital's emergency room had become a model for all hospitals in the United States, and within another two years, the whole hospital had been transformed.

As this example suggests, it is rarely possible – or even particularly fruitful – to look too far ahead. A plan can usually cover no more than 18 months and still be reasonably clear and specific. So the question in most cases should be. Where and how can I achieve results that will make a difference within the next year and a half? 'The answer must balance several things. First, the results should be hard to achieve – they should require "stretching", to use the current buzzword. But also, they should be within reach. To aim at results that cannot be achieved – or that can be only under the most unlikely circumstances – is not being ambitious; it is being foolish. Second, the results should be meaningful. They should make a difference. Finally, results should be visible and, if at all possible, measurable. From this will come a course of action: what to do, where and how to start, and what goals and deadlines to set.'

Source: P. F. Drucker (2009), *Harvard Business Review* (Winter), p. 39

'Management by objectives' in steps

Fig 9.5 summarizes the steps involved in this managerial approach. The diagram clearly shows that both the individual employee and management have a role to play. The manager has to furnish the conditions under which the individual can achieve his or her personal goals. Determining key results and performance norms is one way of doing this.
Firstly, what constitutes employee effectiveness is ascertained and required levels of performance established. This analysis results in a description of expected performance.
The relevant performance norms are then divided into quantitative and qualitative types. It is highly desirable to set as many quantitative norms as possible, as this facilitates the comparing of norms and results. It also becomes easier to discuss deviations in objective terms, and virtually excludes the possibility of misinterpreting the results.

Although it is not always possible to set purely quantitative norms, quantitatively measurable indicators can be used to review certain results. For example, turnover and absenteeism in a department are objectively measurable, and they give at least an impression of the morale, working climate or work satisfaction within that department.

Drawing up plans of actions

personal plan
management plan

This procedure consists of two complementary steps: the drawing up of an employee personal plan of action for attaining desired results and a management plan of action intended to eliminate any environmental factors impeding the employee's ability to attain his or her goals.

CASE Mini case study 9.1

In an American investigation into the degree of agreement between managers and subordinates about results to be attained by the latter, it appeared that agreement existed in only 10% of researched cases. In 40%, there was what amounted to total disagreement.

In a personal plan of action, measures can be included to eliminate such bottlenecks as those resulting from the organizational structure, division of labor or coordination. If the employee does not have sufficient authority to be able to maintain a norm, management will have to increase the employee's authority or adjust the norm. Management needs to ensure that the employee will be working under optimal conditions.

Execution of the personal plan of action

After the personal plan of action has been formulated, the employee must implement it. Management's task is setting goals on an ongoing basis, whether they be short, middle or long-term.

Performance appraisal

After a pre-determined period, the results are compared to the norms. Questions concerning the reasons for possible deviations may be asked, or the employee may request further education and training. New performance norms for the following period will have to be established according to the procedures described above. Action plans may also have to be adjusted. These steps are then repeated.

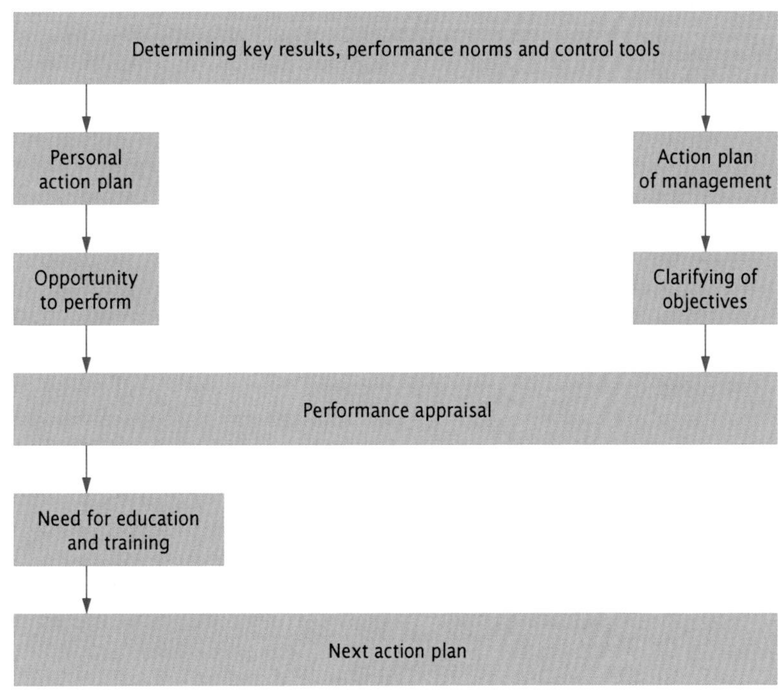

Figure 9.5
Management by objectives

The advantages of Management by Objectives

For both manager and the employee involved, management by objectives has a number of obvious advantages. For the manager, MbO has the obvious advantage that it motivates subordinates to work toward attaining core results. The formulating of these goals and the associated plan of action creates favorable conditions for delegation, management by exception and performance appraisal. Furthermore, MbO supplies a framework for supervision, coaching and the establishment of good personal relationships between managers and subordinates.

MbO

performance appraisal

Since employees participate in the determination of key results, they know what is expected of them and are more accepting of the agreed norms to which the results can always be compared. Conditions existing at any one time can influence future performance, since existing hindrances can be discussed and remedies found.

Management by objectives is likely to lead to improved morale and increased productivity.

9.4 Production planning: methods and techniques

Planning and supervision can involve a variety of methods and techniques, including planning charts, Gantt charts and optimization techniques. Moreover, application of priority rules can contribute to shorter waiting periods, and consequently improved delivery times.

9.4.1 Planning charts

To attain a high degree of efficiency and to provide good customer service, easily accessible and well-ordered information has to be readily available. It will provide a basis for decisions about the deployment of people and machines; the sequencing of processes, orders, rush orders, and so on. Planning charts are particularly suited for this purpose.
A good planning system highlights promises and agreements sequences activities and allocates

people and resources and any remaining capacity still available. The use of such devices as order plans, machine schedules and planning relating to people, groups or shifts prevents late delivery of orders or periods of machine standstill due to late delivery of materials. The state of the flow of orders becomes visible at a glance.
The use of color-coded slips, ordered according to order number and working week, provides an easy means of recording production times, processes involved, and the planned production time that can, each day (via the date line), be correlated with the actual process that an order makes through the system. Deviations are marked with a progress symbol, such as 'delay' with a red triangle, 'on schedule' no indication and 'ahead of schedule' with a blue triangle. This can be indicated on an old fashioned wall-mounted planning chart with attachable symbols, or on the screen of an automated system. There are various electronic planning charts: Optimal Plan, Timeline and Plantrac, to name just a few.

Gantt chart

An early version of the planning chart is the so-called Gantt chart. On a Gantt chart, information is registered permanently, with the consequence that replanning is easier on a planning chart than a Gantt chart. The Gantt chart is, however, cheaper. With the decreasing costs of computers and better software, replanning and optimization problems are rapidly being resolved.
In small organizations, such methods are often used by the production manager himself. As soon as the organization expands, a planning office which undertakes the work involved in preparation, dispatching, routing, and so on, as well as planning and supervising production may be necessary.

CASE

Mini case study 9.2

Machine planning makes the utilization rates of machines readily apparent. Usage is recorded according to type of machine and period of the day. The use times of each machine are indicated by color strips. Date-line deviations can be marked by progress symbols.
With the aid of such planning charts, a hospital can keep a record of the patients in its beds, and a company that rents villas can schedule occupants for its accommodation.

9.4.2 Inventory control

Manufacturing companies usually maintain inventories of raw materials, components and final products for various purposes. They enable fluctuations in demand to be accommodated as well as the advantages of scale in production and purchasing to be exploited. Some estimates indicate that 25 per cent of the total balance exists in inventory. Costs linked to the storage of inventory can thus be considerable and include such items as rent for the required space, lost interest, depreciation due to age, loss due to decay or theft, administrative charges, and so on. Total inventory costs usually consume about 15 per cent of an organization's budget, though most organizations will try to reduce this financial burden as much as possible.

9.4.3 Optimal ordering

Inventory costs can be reduced by optimizing ordering practices so that goods are ordered in such a way that the ordering costs and the costs of keeping the inventory are as low as possible. Larger orders lower the cost per unit product, as the cost of placing an order is generally independent of the quantities ordered. Conversely, increased order sizes will obviously also increase the costs of storing inventory.
When the demand curve, the period between ordering and delivering, the ordering costs and the inventory costs are all known, one can with the help of a formula (the so-called Camp formula) calculate the optimal order size. Since the demand curve and the ordering term can

safety inventory

never be predicted with absolute certainty, there is still a need to maintain a 'safety' inventory.

9.4.4 MRP (Materials Requirement Planning)

MRP is not only a procedure that reduces inventory but also a method of formulating production plans. The MRP approach starts by predicting demand for the product. Based on this prediction, a so-called master production schedule is drawn up in which the quantity of goods to be produced is indicated. A list of necessary components for every product (the 'bill of materials') allows management to determine the amounts and types of components needed for production at any given time. After comparing this need with the inventory status record indicating the present inventory of each component, the reserved amounts required for the production of other orders, ordering times and ordered amounts, it is possible to calculate the quantities of the various components that need to be reordered.

push system Based on this predicted need, the materials are, as it were, pushed into the production departments. This is, in fact, known as the 'push' system.

9.4.5 'Just in time'

'Just in time' (JIT), a system first implemented in Japan by Toyota at the beginning of the 1970s, has since become well known. This approach begins with the reception of orders. Based on them, a production scheme is devised encompassing all assignments allocated to every department involved in the production process and arranged as a series of orders placed with internal customers. Structured as a 'pull' system, orders are placed by the internal customer (client or next department) at the output side of a production unit. By shortening production and changeover times the work process can function with extremely low inventories. Such a system is also called a kanban system.

pull system

kanban system

A JIT system poses heavy demands on the organization and its suppliers. Supplied components have to meet established quality demands without exception. Any mistake can lead to stagnation of production. Suppliers need to be located in the organization's immediate vicinity ('Toyota City,' a complex comprising the factory and its suppliers, provides such a centralized location). A trustworthy group of suppliers must also be maintained: disruptions in supply result in production disruptions in the main factory. Moreover, the system requires a disciplined work force, as any coordination error can cause production disruptions. The system has hardly any leeway or margin of error to absorb mistakes.

9.4.6 Eliminating delays

One of the causes of inefficient machine usage or low labor productivity is a lack of orders (the machine or worker stands still). To overcome this and to prevent any standstill of production resources, plans should be constructed in such a way that capacity never remains unused. The elimination of standstills resulting from lack of orders can, in practice, only occur when sufficient orders are always ready to be processed. Such planning must take several things into account, including the sudden cancellation of an order during production. To prevent machine standstill in such circumstances, another order has to be awaiting processing at all times.

These idle periods can, however, be reduced by means of the following measures.

- Increase of capacity. Although this measure would decrease the degree of utilization or occupation of the capacity, idle periods would be shortened. By reducing inactivity in the manufacturing process and decreasing the amount of work in progress, the production flow time will also be shortened. The costs of increasing capacity may be offset by savings in work in progress.
- Concentrating similar processes. In the language of efficiency, this procedure involves having several 'counters' or 'stations' do the same work. In a post office, for example, the result is shorter line-ups.

- Favoring a more gradual approach to the issuing of work orders in the manufacturing process. This alone will shorten periods of idleness.
- Application of priority rules: giving out orders according to predetermined priorities and capacities to be used. Examples of such priority rules are:
  - Small jobs first
  - First in, first out (FIFO): round off the 'oldest' orders first

priority rules

9.5 Time management: project and network planning

period planning

The types of planning described above can be grouped under the heading of 'period planning'. In fact, they are methods of planning one department's activity over a given period and are not primarily concerned with the functional integration of various departments.
A form of planning which does pay attention to this aspect is project or network planning. Project and network planning is especially applicable to large, one-off activities, such as large construction projects or joint ventures.
Network planning determines the total necessary flow time needed for completion of a project and identifies possible ways to shorten this flow time. Examining the relevant network provides an overview of an entire project as well as insight into the complex interrelationships between the project's various activities.
Network planning involves a number of steps. First of all it is necessary to determine what actions or activities have to be undertaken. Next the interrelationships and the necessary sequencing of the activities have to be determined. These can then be incorporated into a relationship or network diagram (Fig 9.6).

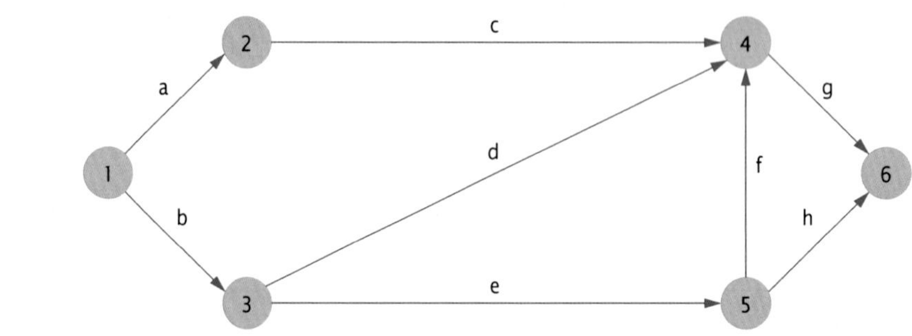

Figure 9.6
Relationship diagram or network

In Fig 9.6, only the logical connections among the successive activities are shown, and not the time element. To include this factor, an estimation of the time necessary per activity needs to be made. Once the time needed for each activity has been determined, the diagram resembles Fig 9.7.
Fig 9.7 provides a basis for calculating the flow and completion times, as well as the project's earliest possible completion time. The case represented in Fig 9.7 appears to require fifteen time units for the completion (i.e. 8+5+2=15) of activities identified as b, d and g. Since every other sequence requires less time, the b, d, g series of activities is called the critical path and represents the shortest time in which the project can be completed.

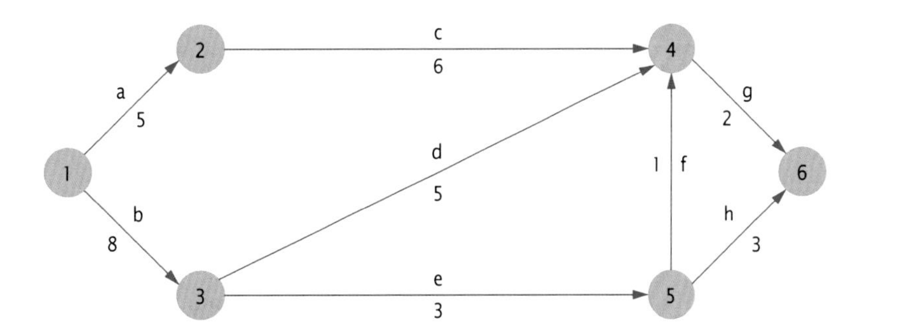

Figure 9.7
Relationship diagram or network with time estimates

Network, critical path and slack time

In plotting the network of a project, the following two symbols are generally employed:

1 An arrow to represent an activity; the length of the arrow and the angle at which this is drawn are not significant. Only the relationships among the arrows is important
2 A circle placed at the beginning and end of every arrow representing a junction or milestone; a junction or milestone is only reached when the activities represented by all the arrows leading to the junction/milestone are completed. An activity can only start once the junction or milestone from where the arrow starts has been reached. In other words, the next activity can only start when all preceding activities have been completed

critical path

Once the network has been plotted, the time required for each activity must be determined in order to ascertain the total duration of the project. As mentioned, the series of activities that is determinative of project duration is called the critical path, as it identifies the sequence of processes requiring the most time. An acceleration or delay of any activity on this path immediately and directly affects the completion time of the project.
Activities not part of the critical path have a certain latitude or slack. In order to determine the extent of this slack, it is necessary to establish:

- The earliest possible start time for the activity (earliest moment)
- The latest time that the activity can be begun without affecting total project duration (latest moment)

slack

Slack is indicated in the circles designating junctions or milestones. They are divided into three parts, as shown in Fig 9.8. The earliest start time is indicated at the top left, the latest at the top right, and the junction/milestone number in the bottom half.

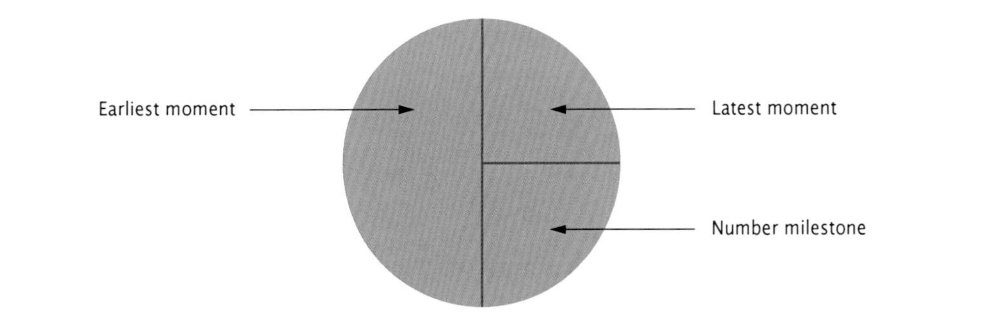

Figure 9.8
Determination of slack time

The slack time per junction is determined by comparing the figure at the top left with that at the top right: the difference is the slack time at that junction. To calculate the latest moment that a milestone needs to have been reached without affecting total project duration, one always starts from the end of the project and works back to the beginning. The latest allowable completion times for each activity can then be identified by subtracting the time(s) required for any subsequent activities from the time required to complete the critical path.

Network analysis: PERT and CPM

Network analysis is a technique for planning the execution of usually large and complex works in order to control time (and costs). The technique was applied in the 1950s to the development of weapon systems under the label of PERT (Program Evaluation and Review Technique). At the same time, the chemical industry was developing the so-called critical path, also known as CPM (Critical Path Method). In PERT one plots milestones to be attained, taking some account of the uncertainties implicated in the time estimates. The development of PERT-cost established the relationship between durations and costs so that any effort to regulate time could also be seen to have the effect of controlling costs. Cost-price/time relationships also came to be included in planning.

PERT

CPM

However, while expensive techniques are no guarantee that projects will be successfully completed (will be on time and for an agreed price), applying project management techniques (see 5.3.7) will not automatically resolve mismanagement problems either.

Network diagrams can be used to make decisions during production affecting the further sequencing of activities. Take, for example, the case that arises when, upon execution of activities a, b and c, it becomes apparent that activities d and e will, for several reasons, experience delays. The network can then be used to make a number of analyses and to come to a decision about subsequent production scheduling. By revising time estimates and designating an earlier completion time for activities a and b, the critical path may be plotted differently: the minimum completion time becomes, for example, 17 months. The additional time requirement may cause problems if the contract involved specifies both a delivery date and a fine to be paid should the date be exceeded. It then becomes necessary to identify the actions to be undertaken in order to meet contractual obligations as well as the costs of these extra efforts, which must then be weighed against the costs of the imposed fine. In the above example, the possibilities of shortening the critical path by 2 months need to be examined. When no other considerations come into play, the combination of measures resulting in the lowest cost of shortening the critical path will be adopted.

completion time

9.6 *Improving quality: quality management*

Quality management has a positive effect on a company's market share. As such, quality is its own distinctive weapon in the battle to compete for the company's external market position. After all, the consumer will always compare a product or a service to others it is in competition with. Quality of a high degree can provide such advantages as the following:

distinctive weapon

- stronger customer loyalty
- more repeat purchases
- a stronger position in the event of a price war
- more possibilities in relation to price setting: for example, the opportunity to raise the price while retaining market share
- greater market share as a result of an improved quality image

A focus on quality can thus lead to better business returns. Among other things, a better price or greater market share also has a favorable effect on profitability and company growth. In other words, there are definitely good economic reasons for a company to pursue a strategic quality policy. Japanese company returns confirm the fact that increases in productivity and greater market share can be achieved by amongst other things, a strategy focusing on quality. Toyota, Honda, Nissan and Hitachi come to mind as pioneers in this area. In recent research done in the Netherlands, raising the quality of services and products has emerged as the most frequently mentioned growth target amongst entrepreneurs. Virtually everybody has mentioned this as a growth target for the coming years. There is thus every reason for dealing with it here.

9.6.1 Quality-related costs and the value chain

strategic quality management

There is a proven connection between strategic quality management in which quality creates a competitive advantage and striving for a low cost price. An analysis of quality-related costs and the value chain will clearly show how to avoid costs associated with such things as technical and organizational mistakes. Quality management will make an overall drop in costs possible, though when viewed on an item-by-item basis there will usually be a proportional rise in costs associated with prevention. Imai has given (as far back as 1986) an extensive treatment of the Japanese kaizen system, a system which seeks to implement a large number of small changes on an ongoing basis. Organizations that use this system believe in the necessity to constantly strive for such improvements. The contribution made by personnel on the factory floor is highly valued: after all, most of the understanding relating to processes resides there and realistic proposals for improvement originate from there. The origins of much of the work being done in this field and others that fall within the same category can be traced back to Deming and Juran. They can be seen as the pioneers of the 'total quality' concept.

kaizen system

9.6.2 'Lean' Six Sigma: looking for the best of both worlds

lean manufacturing

'Lean manufacturing' ('Lean' for short) is the most advanced version of the production system that Toyota has had a lot of success with (success which it continues to enjoy). Lean provides a framework for analyzing processes within an organization. Its main features are as follows: eliminating waste, synchronization of production flows and management of variability. Furthermore, a clear distinction is made between value-adding and non-value-adding activities.

quality control

Six Sigma places prime importance on quality control, which it approaches in the form of improvement projects that offer made-to-measure solutions to complex problems based on thorough analyses. The two systems combine well to form a single integrated approach that eliminates the disadvantages and showcases the strong points. This will result in the following:

- a programmatic approach according to the Six Sigma principles
- project-based implementation along 'quick win' (Lean) and advanced (Six Sigma) lines
- a training program largely derived from Six Sigma
- a strong focus on imbedding solutions at the organizational level
- a built-in link between strategy and project selection

improve quality
reduce production costs

By combining the strong points of both systems, companies can help improve quality and can simultaneously reduce production costs.

As such, 'Six Sigma' also has a role to play in the various service sectors, not only by lowering costs but also by raising profits via 'Six Sigma Pricing'. Meanwhile, managing one's own 'human sigma' in order to gauge and improve effectiveness in the employee-customer relationship is under discussion. Such a gauge has been demonstrated to have a strong positive correlation to the organization's ability to achieve financially.

TQM

Six Sigma processes are data-driven, logical and highly analytical. First used (as a combination of Six Sigma and Total Quality Management, or TQM) in the area of physical production in order to find qualitatively better production methods and encouraged by the successes achieved, Six Sigma principles are now being applied to such areas as sales and service provision processes that aim to achieve a 'four-star' rating within high-performing organizations (see 1.5.3, 8.1.4 and 8.2). This constitutes a more than adequate reason for looking further into Six Sigma as a quality program.

9.6.3 Six Sigma: a 'new' strategy for achieving better returns

Six Sigma is a quality management method that aims to improve business operational returns by identifying where the business processes are falling down and improving them.

Six Sigma is viewed by many as an extension of existing management methods and is partly based on statistical process control (SPC) as the underlying approach. In actual fact Sigma Six is described as being a way of measuring mistakes. As such Six Sigma stands for striving towards virtual perfection: being fault-free.

SPC

Processes can only be controlled and improved if one has an insight into these processes. This requires measurements: 'measure and know'. Six Sigma is statistics-based (see below). In addition, there is a set methodology for resolving problems, namely, DMAIC methodology. DMAIC stands for Define-Measure-Analyze-Improve-Control. DMAIC can be applied to every business process. Six Sigma has a decided customer focus (the 'voice of the customer'): knowing what the client wants is crucial. The client, not the company, determines whether a product or service has conformed to what is required. This principle applies just as equally to the long term, regardless of whether the company is a manufacturing one or a service provider.

DMAIC

How Six Sigma came into existence

Six Sigma owes its existence to Motorola, where it was developed (in about 1980) as a solution for problems associated with product quality and client satisfaction. In fact, quality improvement had become crucial. Goals were not being achieved by working just a bit harder or polishing up the results a bit. The results of the first efforts to improve things were so encouraging that by 1985 or thereabouts, targets for the next seven years could be formulated: so-called Sigma Six program 'stretched goals' which were to be responsible for each project's high achievements. Later on, one of the architects of the program started a consultancy agency and, together with his business partner, published the book from which Six Sigma has become known. Its fame grew when General Electric applied it on a big scale. It was responsible for saving billions over a period of only a few years. Other big businesses such as Xerox, Siemens, Microsoft and many others then saw the potential of Six Sigma. At the moment, Six Sigma is attracting a lot of interest in Dutch organizations, partly because of a recent publication by Ford Europe, which has carried out 622 projects in the last 18 months, with an average saving of $350,000. This has certainly recommended it to a lot of other organizations and managers.

Exhibit 9.1

Six Sigma and statistics

In the field of statistics, sigma (σ) is used as a measure of metric distribution. Within Six Sigma, metric distribution gives an indication of the extent to which the process is under control. The metric distribution is tied in to the client's requirements (see Fig. A).

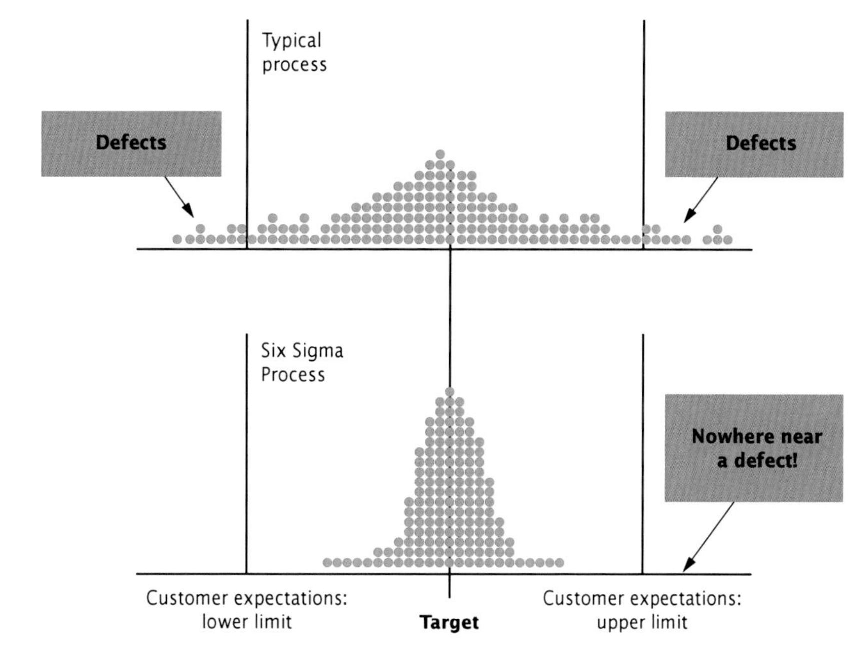

Figure A
Deviation in process outcome

Everything that fails to meet the client's requirements is regarded as a 'defect'. If the processes are such that there is a lot of deviation and consequently show a lot of flaws, customers will consider the supplier in question as being unreliable. Sometimes the client will get what he wants, but often not (see the previous figure) In the graph below, all the points are clustered close to the center. Such a situation will be regarded by the client as reliable. The point is to obtain results that show as little deviation as possible, and eventually to eliminate all deviation.
The next table shows the connection between the returns obtained as a result of a particular process (the number of items or those services deemed good enough for sale) and the Sigma figures.

Sigma figures and returns

Return	Sigma level
30.85%	1
69.15%	2
93.32%	3
99.38%	4
99.977%	5
99.99966%	6

Low Sigma figures indicate low returns, and high figures high returns. The higher the Sigma level, the smaller the increase in returns. A leap of more than 30% in the returns is needed to go from Sigma 2 (= about 69%) to Sigma 3 (= about 93%). But for all Sigma levels higher than 4, the returns are within the area of 99%. Why this difference? It is because the better the process, the more difficult it is to add anything more to the returns. In other words, it is relatively easy to improve a process that is functioning poorly – a process with a Sigma level of 1 or 2 – but it is difficult to improve a process that is already functioning well.
In general, companies that are not consciously pursuing quality improvement operate within a process quality range roughly between Sigma 2 and 3. A level even higher than Sigma 6 is not unheard of: the aviation industry, for example, achieves it. To ensure that there are not too many dissatisfied clients, when the processes are on a big scale or are complex ones with a lot of repetitive or consecutive steps, quality improvement is very important, therefore.

The DMAIC cycle: Sigma Six methodology for process improvement

five steps

The structural way of carrying out Sigma Six projects is known as DMAIC, which stands for the five steps of Define-Measure-Analyze-Improve-Control:

- *Define* Definition of the problem and adapting the way the project is organized.
- *Measure* Making how well the process is doing tangible (i.e., determine the zero point)
- *Analyze* Substantiation of the causes of the problem: what exactly are they?
- *Improve* Designing and selecting solutions (i.e., determine how the process can be optimized)
- *Control* Implementing the improvements and make sure they stay that way

---

- Develop a charter for the product
- Identify internal and external clients
- Identify client needs
- Formulate the problem
- Establish the scope of the project
- Define Critical to Quality (CTQ)
- Create process maps

- Identify possible solutions via DOE
- Verify the solutions
- Make the process mistake-proof

- Develop a control system
- Implement solutions
- Request correct installation of control charts
- Report on the project
- Measure progress
- Make sure that the gains are maintained

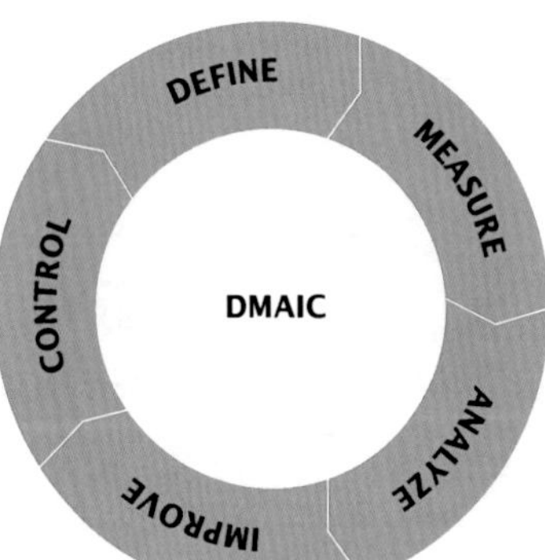

- Ensure that the process is understood
- Identify common and specific causes of deviation
- Test hypothesis

- Identify those process parameters that can affect the CTO variables
- Analyse the present measurement system
- Define the basic process

Figure B
The DMAIC cycle: the 5-step plan

---

justified
statistics

Within the DMAIC cycle, decisions have to be justified by factual information, and consequently, statistics play an important role. However there is more to Sigma Six than this. Its essence is working structurally and in stages on matters that will have a big impact on the main business issues.

DMAIC is the Sigma Six way of improving processes. For the design of new products and redesign of existing ones, the recommended method is Design for Six Sigma, or DfSS.

Six Sigma organization

task forces

Six Sigma's internal structure is laid down in terms of 'task forces'. The roles are defined by analogy with that decisive and disciplined sport, karate: there are Champions, Master Black Belts, Black Belts, Green Belts and Yellow Belts. Ideally, process improvements are a top-down process (starting at the top and working down) in which the top management directs the entire process and carries it out.

Champions

There are the Champions (the owners of the process) and the Sponsors (those who take care of the budget) and those who are responsible for the active support and promotion of the Sigma Six program and the proceeds that are derived from it. They are the managers who report directly to the board (or are even part of it). The Master Black Belts are the specialists – often external consultants – who train the Black Belts and supervise the project and give coaching. The Black Belts are often middle managers who carry out the projects (project

Master Black Belts
Black Belts

Green Belts leaders, in fact). The Green Belts, trained by the experienced Black Belts, help them to carry out the projects successfully. The term 'Black Belts' for the project leaders was chosen because 'to fight the good fight' as far as the process is concerned, the leader also has to possess some of the characteristics of a sports player of this type, such as patience and respect. The project leaders are selected from amongst the most capable of the organization's employees and receive four weeks of training. During the training period they already start working on projects that have to be brought to completion within four to six months and show the agreed-on results. Such an approach increases the effectiveness of the course.
Various departments are represented within the project group, including the financial department, the ICT department and the personnel department. The owner of the process is ex officio a member of the project team. In addition to the roles mentioned the filler of a Green Belt role also does an appropriate course, though this one lasts three to five days. The Green Belt supports the Black Belt in carrying out the projects or even carries out small projects independently.

9.6.4 Six Sigma: combining old and new methods

As a program, Six Sigma combines various managerial and organizational elements that can be used to obtain new results. In particular, it is the combination of the various elements that makes this concept such an appealing one. These elements are as follows:
- its highly structured approach via the DMAIC cycle
- taut project management
- the use of methods and techniques such as those of Deming
- results expressed in financial terms
- set roles for those who have positions within the organization, and thus maximum involvement on the part of top management
- the use of a standard metric distribution for determining process quality
- projects of short duration
- a good project selection procedure on the basis of important strategic subjects
- training both for those who will direct the process and for employees who will make the improvements themselves and implement them

Porsche's experience provides a good example. A situation can sometimes be so serious that shock therapy is justified. The following example is taken from the book by Womack and Jones, *Lean Thinking*. They describe how the *sensei* Chirhiro Nakao entered the Porsche assembly factory in the autumn of 1992.

CASE Mini case study 9.3

Six Sigma makes use of a systematic method for making improvements called DMAIC

In a loud voice he asked Wiedekind, the general director, where the factory was, since this was obviously the storeroom: the large amount of stock piled up here and there made that clear. When he was told that this *was* the factory, he said that if that was the case, it would be impossible for Porsche to make any profit. And when Wiedekind told him audibly in front of everybody that Porsche's losses were increasing by the day, Nakao answered that drastic measures needed to be taken, starting from that very day. This was unheard of in German industry, where every change had to be planned months beforehand and negotiated with the trade unions. This applied to every change of work method or shifting of machines. The *kaizen* method that Nakao proposed for improving things was not legal in Germany. Nor was it normal for a foreigner who spoke no German and who communicated via an interpreter to speak to a Doctor of Engineering who was the head of the production department in such an impertinent way and in the presence of all of his staff. The shock on the factory floor (where it was thought that the problem could not possibly have anything to do with Porsche but must be related to the poor market situation outside the company) increased a few days later, when Nakao and his team made the observation that the first step towards improving things was to dramatically reduce stock. Something of crucial importance happened the day that this was planned to get underway. Nakao handed a circular saw to Wiedekind (who was now dressed in the same blue overalls that all the factory workers wore) and instructed him to walk through the gangway and cut every rack off at a height of 1.3 meters. This moment set the scene for all the changes to follow. Before this moment, nobody had ever seen anyone from top management dirty his hands in the factory and nobody had ever seen such dramatic measures being taken so directly and so swiftly. It initiated improvements the like of which has never been seen in the German car industry. The figures are proof of what happened. Over a period of five years, Porsche:

- reduced the time needed to go from product conception to lancing the product from seven to three years
- reduced the time needed to produce a car from six weeks to three days
- reduced the period of current stock storage from seventeen days to three.
- reduced the time needed to produce a car from 120 to 45 hours
- reduced the number of faults in spare parts from 1% to 0.01%
- reduced the number of residual faults at the end of the production line to a quarter of the original number.

Source: *Business Process Magazine*, no. 8, December 2005

9.6.5 *The introduction of Total Quality Management (TQM)*

quality care programs *work attitude*

To introduce quality care programs – Six Sigma, MANS, TQM based on using 'measure and know' (Juran, Deming, Six Sigma or Kaizen) requires first of all an understanding of quality assurance and the conditions necessary to foster a new work attitude. Only after these factors have been addressed can work behavior really change and the new work behavior be adopted on a permanent basis.

Gaining integral quality assurance results in better process control, signaling of mistakes and surmounting of structural inadequacies. The people at the machines are closest to the production process and thus fulfill a central role in the monitoring of that process. Quality assurance leads almost certainly to the delegation of more tasks and greater responsibilities to operational personnel. Their capabilities and skills are also more effectively used. Management has to make sure that people on the work floor have the tools needed to perform the new, more responsible tasks properly. Departments should have the power to make demands on their internal suppliers, the other departments and employees within the organization. Both of these groups need, in their turn, to satisfy the requirements of the departments they supply and who constitute their internal customers. The same holds true for similar relationships with external business partners such as independent suppliers and customers. In this respect, the involvement of employees is decisive.

quality control program

Once a quality control program has been instituted, a decision needs to be made (either in regular work consultations or in new consultative structures) about how tasks and authority should be delegated and how the interrelationships among departments should be modified in response to the increased responsibility. A flatter organizational structure, increased employee flexibility and multi-functionality, changes in rewards and payment systems, restructured work assignments and manners of working are all matters to be given close attention.

Quality assurance demands cultural change

Quality assurance has in many organizations had only limited success because insufficient attention is given to organizational structure. According to quality gurus, people must become more involved in the organization. Working without mistakes (zero faults) must be seen as a new personal challenge. Motivation must increase and absenteeism has to be reduced. Employees have to be creative and flexible, always prepared to think about possible improvements, often without being rewarded with any extra money. People may be asked to participate in quality control committees or other innovative forms of consultation, and to do so in their leisure time.

participative management

Participative management – a leadership style which helps to increase quality – is hard to implement overnight. Few managers have the courage to be self-critical; in many company cultures, managers who ask employees questions are considered to be incompetent, and people used to authoritarian leadership mistrust a managing director who, having never been visible previously, now spends half his day on the shop floor.

9.6.6 Problems in introducing integral or total quality management (TQM)

Research has identified a number of bottlenecks that obstruct the introduction of TQM integral quality assurance programs and that involve:

- Upper management
- Middle management
- Employees
- Organizational structure
- Information systems
- Goals and plans

HYUNDAI'S INCREASING QUALITY SCORES

Chung, who rarely gives interviews to English-language publications, spoke with a journalist through an interpreter from his penthouse office in the Hyundai tower. Chung attributes his company's success to the investment it has made in improving its products. He believes that Hyundai's quality, as well as its technology, 'are head to head with Toyota at this moment,' a statement he makes with some confidence since 'we are monitoring what is going on with Toyota all the time'. Asked what scares Hyundai the most, he replied: 'The thing we fear is uncertainty. There are many announcements about demands shrinking and all the numbers are different.'

Hyundai's quality success is a testament to the power of focused management and aggressive goals. In 2001 Hyundai ranked 32nd out of 37 brands in J.D. Power's study of new vehicle quality after 90 days of ownership – close to the bottom. As its quality efforts took hold, it began moving up the list, and it achieved a breakthrough in 2004 when it reached seventh place. Since then, Hyundai has placed third in 2006 and then fourth in 2009, displacing Toyota as the highest-ranked mass-market brand in the world. (Three luxury brands – Lexus, Porsche and Cadillac – finished ahead of it.)

Source: *Fortune*, January 18, 2010, p. 42-43

Upper management

Upper management has not been successful enough in translating the notion of quality into specific action plans. For the employees, it remains a concept with many slogans but little reality. There is also often a lack of unity within the managerial team when addressing the quality problem. Not everyone can or wants to be identified with such a program, although they may actually give quality assurance the highest priority. There is also uncertainty about the personal consequences of such programs. Authoritarian management frequently finds the new style to be threatening and reacts by allotting insufficient time to quality assurance issues.

Middle management

When an organization has to contend with a 'no change' middle management insufficiently convinced of the importance of quality assurance, the introduction of the process can stagnate and even stall. Confronting middle management with top-down imposed goals in which there is no room for individual translations and interpretations will certainly not enhance the chances of successful implementation.

Employees

If quality has inadequate operational definitions, it remains insufficiently recognizable and therefore difficult for employees to perceive. Consequently, they provide insufficient feedback about their task performances. Within many companies, there is also a traditional relationship between superior and subordinate deterring employees from becoming more involved in their work and from developing the necessary motivation for a successful quality assurance program.

Organizational structure

Maintaining existing, often functionally hierarchical, organizational structures clashes with any notion of integral quality assurance. Existing organizational structures are characterized by a far-reaching and deeply significant segregation of regulatory and operational tasks.

Information systems

Information systems are often only able to supply financial information such as sales data, expenses, profit figures and so on, and not the information required to improve quality.

Goals and plans

Quality goals and plans are often discussed with an organization's lower-level employees to an insufficient degree. Quality management can be a strategically important response to managerial and organizational problems, one that aims simultaneously at three goals: higher quality, higher productivity and optimal involvement of employees.

9.6.7 Deming: measurement and control

In the approach to quality control proposed by the American statistician William Edward Deming (1982 & 1986), the effectiveness of a simple set of statistical tools is highlighted. They are even claimed to be generally applicable. However, an overly dogmatic use of these simple instruments can cause a lot of damage, especially if applied in the wrong circumstances.

They should not be employed unthinkingly but only used as methods to analyze appropriate processes. Furthermore, statistical analysis of various issues can become difficult when certain factors interfere with each other and wrong conclusions are drawn. An even more important question involves the fundamental application of the technique. How does one calibrate measurements so that one receives meaningful information?

CASE

Mini case study 9.4

The seven ingredients of Deming's 'statistical recipe'

1 Diagram of cause and effect, also called fish bone or Ishikawa diagram. All of the factors crucial to a particular manufacturing process and any mutual relationships are shown on the 'fish bone' axis.

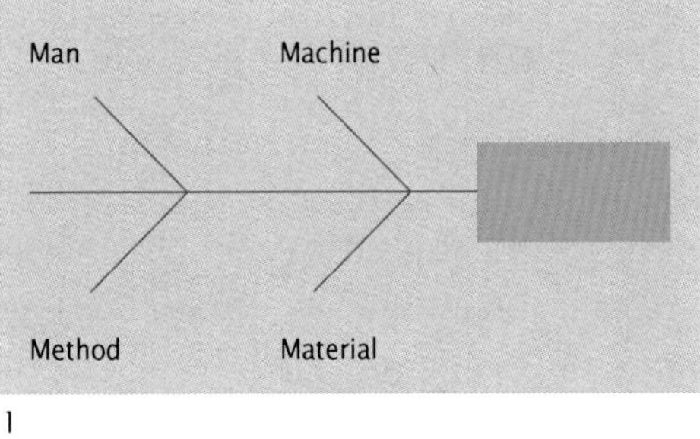

1

2 Line diagram: the most simple and the most used graphical representation of a development in time. The X-axis is the time axis and the Y-axis is quantity to be measured.

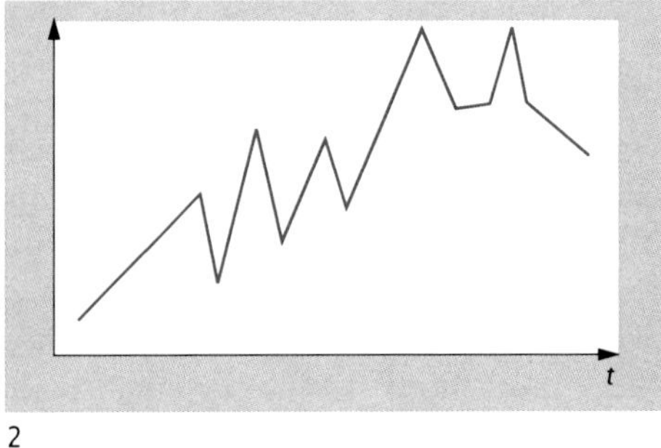

2

3 Control chart: in principle, this is also a line diagram but it also contains an indication of the top and bottom limit and the median. This is more for the short term, and the production employee can see at a glance whether production meets demands.

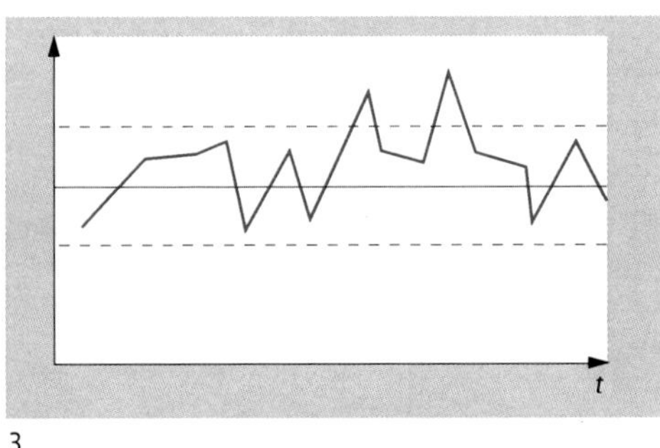

3

4 Histogram: a simple form of a bar chart, in which the frequency of a certain phenomenon is set forth along the horizontal axis and along the vertical axis the size of those same phenomena.

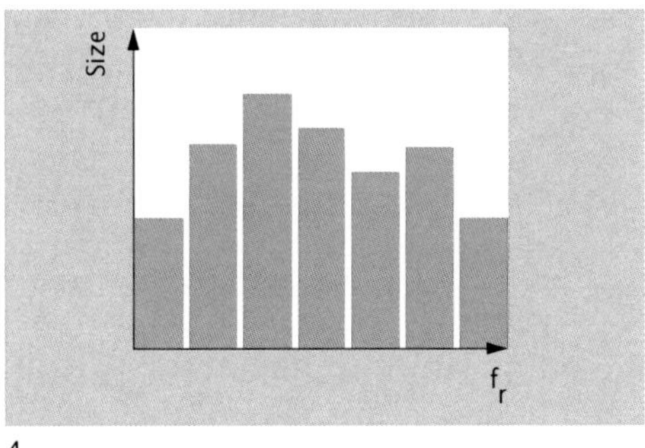

4

5 Paretogram: in fact, this is a block diagram in which the cubes are placed in sequence of size. In this example, 'type of mistake' (as shown on the horizontal axis) is related to causes.

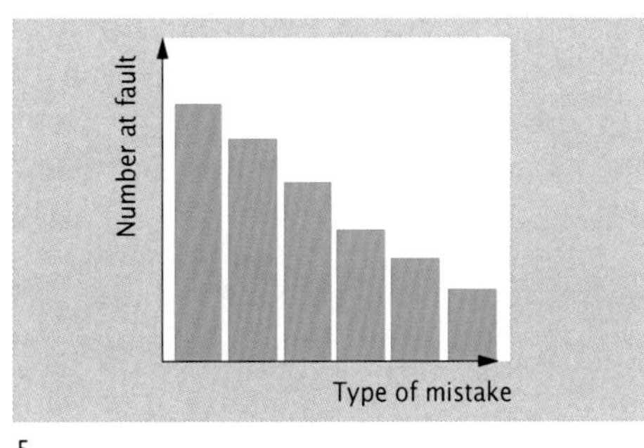

5

6 Flow diagram: a kind of graphical map in which the course and the size of each separate production flow in the total company process is made visible.

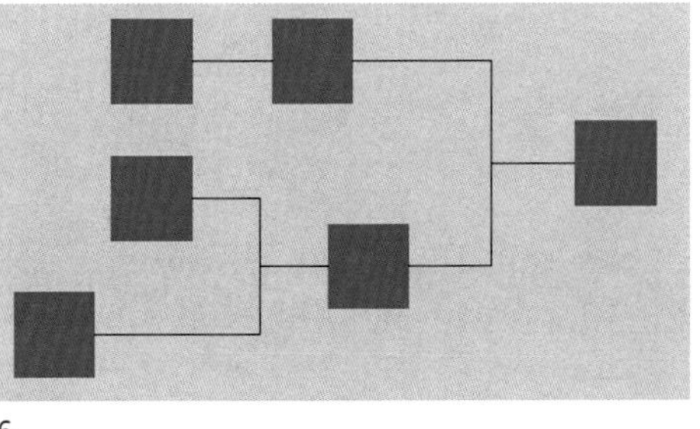

6

7 Spread diagram, also called scatter diagram. Along the vertical axis, such data as the exact size of products made on the line, including any deviations from the specification are indicated. For every unit produced a point is placed at the point which corresponds to the produced size and the operational speed at that moment, and after placing fifty or a hundred points, the relationship between the speed and the correct dimensioning can be read on the basis of the form and density of the scattered points in the diagram.

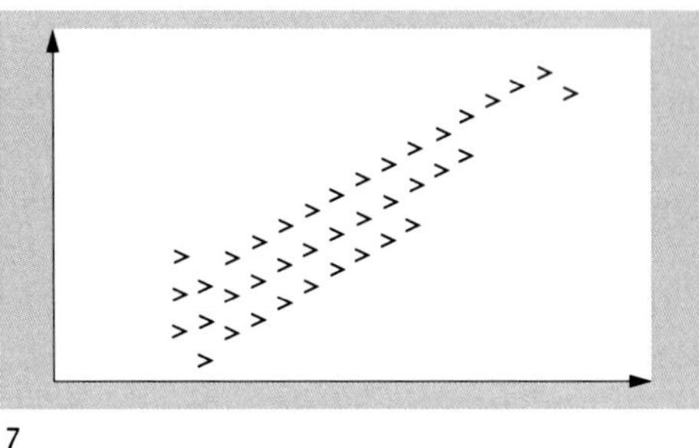
7

9.6.8 *International quality norms*

ISO 9000

The ISO 9000 quality assurance standards include the ISO 9000, 9001, 9002, 9003 and 9004 norms.

- ISO-9000. Quality management and quality assurance standards: guidelines for selection and use. The norm can be used to select a quality norm for a specific organization and purpose.
- ISO-9001. Quality systems: model for quality assurance in design/development, production, installation, and servicing. The norm contains requirements for a quality management system in organizations with primary processes that consist of design and development, production, installation and after sales service.
- ISO-9002. Quality systems: model for quality assurance in production and installation. The norm contains the requirements for a quality management system in organizations that produce and/or install products.
- ISO-9003. Quality systems: model for quality assurance in final inspection and test. The norm is suitable for usage in the final inspection phase of production processes and in testing processes.
- ISO-9004. Quality management and quality system elements: guidelines. The norm contains definitions, concepts and guidelines that are used in a quality management system. The norm can be used to gain insight into the essentials of a quality management system.

The norms are published by the International Organization for Standardization (ISO). The purpose of the standards is to provide norms for an effective management system for quality assurance in an organization. The underlying philosophy is that when an organization can control its processes and can assure a certain product quality, both producer and customer will benefit. The producers control their processes and the customer is provided with quality assured products. The basic principles of a quality management system are as follows:

- Conformance: products and processes have to conform to specified requirements.
- Documentation: the requirements of products and processes, the organizational rules and procedures to assure that products and processes conform to these requirements, and the actual results of the quality management system have to be documented.
- Design quality and prevention: the organizational rules, procedures and processes aim at the design and development of goods and services that customers want and prevent goods and services from failure.
- Inspection and testing: goods and services are inspected, tested and evaluated to ensure that they conform to the documented requirements and specifications.

When the quality management system of an organization meets the standards of one or more of the ISO norms, an external authority can award the organization an ISO-9000 quality certificate. Organizations use these certificates to show their trustworthiness to customers and to motivate their employees to further improve the quality of products and processes.

9.6.9 The European quality award

EFQM

The European Foundation for Quality Management (EFQM) established the European Quality Award (EQA) in 1992 to support quality management practices in Europe. Organizations can use the nine criteria defined and described by the award committee to assess and improve their performance from the viewpoint of quality management. The EQA is also supported by the European Organization for Quality (EOQ). The quality assessment of the EQA is based on nine criteria for evaluation. An organization's quality management performance is measured and evaluated on the basis of the following criteria:

quality management performance

1 Leadership: individual and organizational leadership
2 Policy and strategy: the overall strategy of the organization and the integration of quality in the organization's strategy
3 People management: HR management initiatives and satisfaction of employees
4 Resources: the physical and intellectual resources of the company
5 Processes: the management of primary and supporting processes within the organization
6 Customer satisfaction: satisfaction of customers
7 People satisfaction: satisfaction of employees and stakeholders
8 Impact on society: the contribution of the organization to societal development and improvement
9 Business results: the financial results of the organization

Top class organizations join the contest and strive to win the award. Organizations that do not qualify for the contest use the criteria to improve their integral quality management practices. The American equivalent of the EQA is the Malcolm Baldridge National Quality Award (MBNQA).

9.7 Benchmarking: learning through comparison

In response to problems arising from the increasingly intense competition on national and international markets, prominent American companies have taken a series of initiatives to improve their strategic and operational performances and results. One of those strategic management techniques is called 'benchmarking': the systematic comparison of company performances. In America, Xerox, Ford, Eastman Kodak, General Motors, Motorola, AT&T and Du Pont are a few of the notable corporations that have adopted this methodology. It is said that Xerox was the first American company to introduce a systematic benchmarking procedure for the company as a whole. Japanese companies are already well known for the use that they make of competitor products. They are thereby able to exploit the weaknesses in American companies and even win strong positions in sectors or businesses such as steel production, automobile manufacturing, microchip technology and the manufacturing of consumer electronics.
Benchmarking is the ongoing process of measuring the products, services, methods and procedures used by an organization's toughest competitors, or of companies acknowledged as sector leaders, to compare them with those employed by the organization itself.
The process of measuring and comparing has to be ongoing and systematic in order to identify best practices and methods in the sector or line of business and to discover how these performance levels can be emulated or even improved. Information obtained in such a way is used to establish goals and strategies. Benchmarking can be applied to almost all the functional areas of an organization, including manufacturing and marketing, but also supporting functions such as human resources management, accounting and management information systems.
Successful companies use company comparisons to strengthen their own creativity. They learn what their competitors do, but also develop a vision of what customers want, a crucial factor for formulating a competitive strategy. Both points of view are obviously necessary.
Information about customer needs connected to the best practices in a particular line of business improves the ability of the company to adapt to market circumstances.

best practices

9.7.1 Types of benchmarking

There are three main types of benchmarking:
1 Strategic
2 Operational
3 Management

strategic benchmarking

Strategic benchmarking compares various company strategies in order to identify the elements of a successful strategy.

operational benchmarking

Operational benchmarking concentrates on the relative costs, product characteristics and product positioning in order to find ways to improve cost position and/or to increase the product differentiation. Company components to be compared depend on the function to be analyzed. For example, if technical development and process functions are being considered, then analysis should be directed at the efficiency of the design process. Cost effectiveness can be the central issue when considering manufacturing, distribution and sales activities.

benchmarking of management

Benchmarking of management involves the analysis of supporting services. Every type of supporting service can be subject to external comparison, including P&O and HRM functions, marketing planning, management information systems, logistics and order processing.

9.7.2 Benchmarking as a process

The benchmarking procedure comprises five steps:
1 Identifying functions to be compared
2 Selecting companies with superior performances and/or results
3 Collecting and analyzing data
4 Determining performance or result goals
5 Implementing plans and monitoring results

Identifying functions to be compared

value chain analysis

Elements subject to possible benchmarking include: costs per unit, sales turnover, number of times the service is requested, and customer satisfaction. Every function within the organization provides or produces a certain product, which can be physical goods, an order or a service. Benchmarking can be focused on, for example, the outcomes of activities as well as on procedures, processes and methods. In other words, it is concerned with the factors determining cost levels, service levels, etc. In general, activities will be benchmarked when they are essential for the development of a competitive advantage. A company like Xerox, which is interested in production costs, will therefore compare activities whose costs are increasing or were already significantly high. Methods such as the value chain analysis (Porter, 1985; see Section 1.7.2) can be used to identify such key activities.

Selecting companies with superior performances and/or results

The competitor or the leading company in the sector or line of business (business-to-business or direct competitors for products or services) is the first candidate for comparison. But benchmarking may also involve companies or organizations in general, regardless of the specific areas in which they are active.

For example ...

... When the Business Systems Logistic and Distribution unit at Xerox was looking for ways to improve productivity, it examined as its benchmarking standard the practices of L. L. Bean, a mail order company known for its effective and efficient storage and distribution activities. This Xerox department also selected other non-competitors and subjected them to a systematic comparison of order collection procedures and automated inventory control.

Collecting and analyzing data

Data relating to competitors can be collected in many ways. The analysis should, however, be based on a clear insight into and thorough knowledge of the existing practices of one's own organization and of the organization chosen as the benchmark. The collected data has relate to all part of the processes, procedures or practices in question and should not focus exclusively on results.
Comparison of one's own operations with best practices existing somewhere else is likely to expose potential performance gaps.
When the analysis indicates that the organization already performs better than the organization to which it is being compared, then emphasis shifts to the task of identifying the ways of maintaining the advantage.

For example ...

... In the above-mentioned benchmarking activity, Xerox used public sources, consultants, personal contacts with leading companies, the knowledge and insights of their own employees and questionnaires filled in by students of business schools. Xerox also sent a team to examine L. L. Bean's operations.

Determining performance or result goals

The results of the analysis have to be communicated in a clear way to all organizational levels. Employees must have sufficient time to evaluate the outcomes of the benchmarking process. They will agree more readily with performance levels and the procedures, practices or processes to be introduced if they are provided with the information justifying the changes.
performance goals Performance goals and the selected best practices have to be worked into the functional, operational and strategic plans.

CASE

Mini case study 9.5

Hyundai benchmarking Toyota

How do the Koreans do it? In addition to getting big, Hyundai has gotten good. Once known as a cheap and cheerful brand that offered a comprehensive warranty to make up for mechanical shortcomings, Hyundai has become a respected name and a smart buy. 'Hyundai is a brand that is on the verge of being aspirational,' says New York-based consultant and investor John Casesa. 'People are saying they are proud to own it, not just to settle for it.' The evidence can be seen in the strengthening demographics of Hyundai owners. Last year some 49% were college graduates, compared with just 36% in 1999. By comparison, Toyota has a higher percentage of college grads – 57% – but the number hasn't grown much, up only two percentage points in 10 years.

Hyundai's success reflects a shift in attitude that occurred nearly a decade ago. In the 1990s the company was more interested in how many cars it could build than in how good it could make them. That changed in 1999 when founder Ju-Yung Chung passed corporate leadership to his son, Mong-Koo Chung. According to company lore, the younger Chung decreed that Hyundai would henceforth concentrate on quality, not volume. With the chairman behind the push, and with its characteristic intensity, Hyundai went after quality improvements with a vengeance.

Hyundai benchmarked Toyota, then the industry's quality leader, to understand its processes. It installed Six Sigma at its engineering center to measure its improvement. It made quality a cross-functional responsibility, with involvement from procurement, finance, and sales and marketing. It enlisted outside suppliers and put them together with designers and engineers to work out problems before they occurred. Quality oversight meetings, which had been poorly attended, became must-go-to events after chairman Chung began to show up for twice-monthly gatherings.

Source: *Fortune*, January 18, 2010, p. 40-42

Implementing plans and monitoring results

The benchmark method makes it necessary to periodically measure and evaluate the degree to which the selected goals have been attained. Corrective measures have to be taken if performances remain sub-par. To account for changes in the competitive environment, provisions also have to be made for the calibration of measurements, variations in the measuring technique and the altering of customer perceptions. Such an approach makes it possible to balance the attention paid to competitors with that required by customers and reduces the danger of selective attention and over-simplification. Progress has to be reported so that there is an opportunity to stimulate the feedback necessary for the implementation of any plan. This feedback can also be helpful when the time comes to set new performance goals.

9.7.3 Benchmarking: advantages and limitations

The process of benchmarking is a method of promoting change. This method ascertains the standards that customers may come to require and to expect, and consequently compels employees to think in terms of the competitive consequence of their activities. It often makes the employees more conscious of the costs and results of the products and services furnished by the organization. The process also inspires personnel to look beyond the borders of their own organization for solutions to problems, as well as for models with which to compare company results and to put them into perspective.

If company comparisons are only used to match or to imitate a competitor's performances, a superior market position can never be attained. The resulting success is, at best, short-term, and the actions of innovative employees are frequently restrained.

Benchmarking certainly goes further than the standard analysis of 'strengths and weaknesses' in the strategy formulation process (see Section 3.2.3). In a strategic partnership and co-makership, the Strengths, Weaknesses, Opportunities and Threats (SWOT) analysis is insufficient. In the case of a strategic partnership, the best practices in one's own organization have to be used and constantly promoted. If performance lags, the basis of the cooperative relationship is shaken and new partners will be sought who do indeed know how to maintain the highest standards.

SWOT

Benchmarking is, consequently, a method used to compare an activity, function or process in an organization with the 'best practices' of other organizations, such that the ways in which the activity can be improved are revealed. Benchmarking assumes that organizations and the people they employ are eager to learn and are willing to follow the examples of others.

9.7.4 In search for operational excellence

GEO

The Global Excellence in Operations (GEO) program was developed (by A.T. Kearney) to evaluate the ways in which industrial organizations operationalize strategies involving research and development, purchasing, production, distribution and sales. GEO's purpose is to judge the performance of companies belonging to various crucial 'territories' in the international manufacturing industry: aircraft manufacturing (Rolls Royce, EADS, Airbus), electronics (Philips, Siemens, Sony, Whirlpool, Thomson, Schneider), automobile production (BMW, Peugeot, Citroën), glass production (Saint-Gobain), computers and software (Gateway, Atos Origin) and pharmacy and chemistry (DSM, DuPont). Judgment involves four factors. The most general area of concern is the operational strategy: a company's general marching direction. There are six intermediate areas between this strategic level and the resources actually engaged in the production process, but they all have to do with integration. The goal of increased integration (of suppliers, customers, research and development programs, etc) is a key notion, because only thus can there be rapid and flexible reactions to changing market conditions. The GEO analysis reveals that many leading industrial companies share several

operational strategy

features: an active director in the distribution and supply chain, a team-based organizational structure, a sensitive use of human resources exemplified by an ability to adapt to local cultures, and GEOs who are passionately committed to their own products.

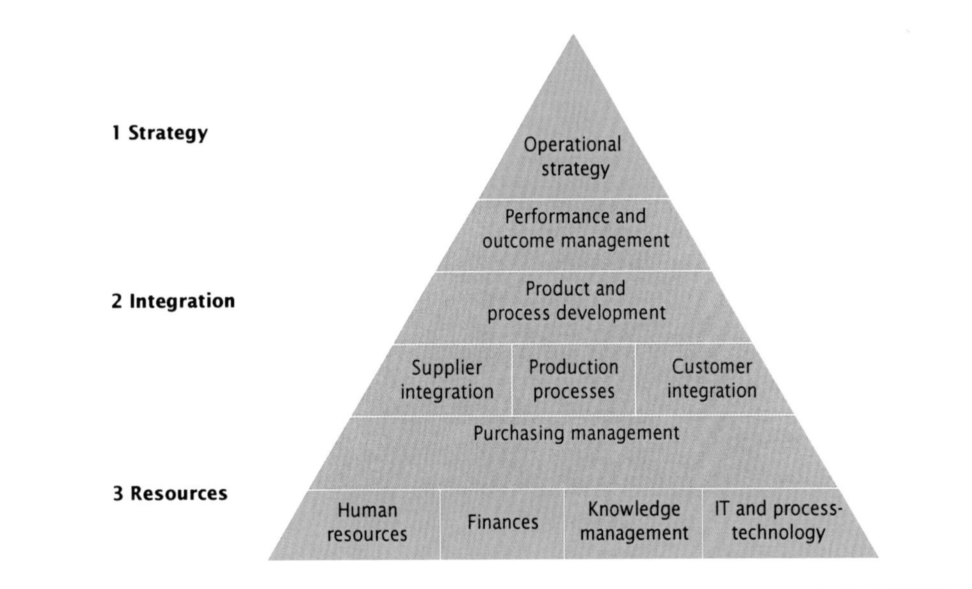

Figure 9.9 *GEO-calibration: a framework*

9.8 *Ratios: a method of self-regulation*

'Ratios' are used as a method of regulating processes ratios. Ratios serve to obtain insight into complex situations and not to control and to direct processes as such.

Management must be able to have at its disposal as much reliable hard data as possible so that it is not acting the basis of unfounded stories. The method based on ratios makes it necessary to analyze situations as precisely as possible and to introduce the greatest possible degree of systematization, both of which contribute significantly to the detection of problems.

The size and complexity of the information on which a manager has to base the task of managing an organization makes it inevitable that some quantification in the form of ratios, statistics and so on must occur.

Ratios involve two (in our case business-economic) phenomena, on the basis of which some element of a company or institution can be represented. The goal of such ratios is to describe a certain portion of an organization's performance. A partial impression of the returns or risks involved is gained, but often activities themselves are measured in order to determine whether the organization makes efficient use of available resources and whether it is effective in attaining set goals.

organization's performance

9.8.1 *Types of ratios*

In addition to their application to a single company or institution, ratios can also be used to investigate a total business line or business group. While some combinations of ratios are relatively standard, every organization needs to develop its own types, since circumstances are frequently specific to a particular operation. Fig 9.10 provides an overview of a number of frequently used ratios.

Financial management	Commercial	Manufacturing	Personnel
Debt to assets (leverage)	Market share	Inventory turnover	Composition of personnel
Liquidity	Turnover utilization	Production costs	Productivity
Return on net worth	Customers		Turnover
Gross operating margin	Stock turnover	**Efficiency**	Wages and salaries
Productivity of assets	Collecting	Productivity	
	Debtors	Cost per product group	
Investment ratios	Purchasing	Cost turnover	
Earnings per share	Product mix	Added value	
Price/earnings	Sales representatives	Cost control	
Dividend yield			

Figure 9.10
'Standard' ratios categorized by subject

Based on its own peculiar set of circumstances, every organization will have to determine the content of the ratios that it uses. Once this is decided, the extent to which the ratios apply to a general or a partial situation also has to be determined. Ratios may be applied to costs, manufacturing and personnel in general, but also to distinct cost categories, product groups or personnel categories. Fig 9.11 displays a selection of important ratios selected from a series of frequently used ones. These are grouped according to various important managerial responsibilities (taken from the subjects mentioned in Fig 9.10). Every individual organization must choose its own ratios.
This series of ratios represents a selection of those available (or to be developed), of which surveys have now identified more than 120.

Exhibit 9.2

Which tools and techniques will be the most important?

Tools and techniques	No of mentions	Independent company %	No of mentions	Subsidiary firm %
Budgets	78	73	104	68
Strategic management accounting	65	61	91	59
Variance analysis	64	60	87	56
Rolling forecasts	57	53	86	56
Value added accounting	41	38	53	34
Total quality management	40	37	39	25
Activity-based costing	31	29	61	40
Balanced scorecards	27	25	47	31
Standard costing	23	21	42	27
Economic value added	18	17	39	25
Just-in-time	10	9	14	9
Target costing	10	9	17	11
Driver analysis tables	7	7	15	10

Source: Hassan Yazdifar, 'The future of the profession,' *Financial Management*, November 2005

Liquidity	Current ratio (CR)	$\frac{\text{Current assets (CA)}}{\text{Current liabilities (CL)}}$
	Acid test	$\frac{\text{Liquid assets (LA)}}{\text{Current liabilities (CL)}}$
	Working capital (WC)	Current assets – current liabilities
Solvency/leverage	Debt to total assets	$\frac{\text{Total debt}}{\text{Total assets}}$
	Interest cover	$\frac{\text{Profit before taxes + interest + charges}}{\text{Interest charges}}$
Profitability	Return on Equity (RoE)	$\frac{\text{Profit after tax}}{\text{Equity}}$
	Return on Net Assets (RoNA)	$\frac{\text{Profits before interest and tax}}{\text{Net assets}}$
	Gross operating margin	$\frac{\text{Gross operating profit}}{\text{Sales}}$
	Net operating margin	$\frac{\text{Net operating profit}}{\text{Sales}}$
Activity (financial/ non-financial)	Net assets turnover	$\frac{\text{Sales}}{\text{Net assets}}$
	Stock or inventory turnover	$\frac{\text{Sales}}{\text{Inventory or stock}}$
	Average collection period	$\frac{\text{Receivables}}{\text{Sales per day}}$
	Market share	$\frac{\text{Sales own company}}{\text{Total sales in the industry}}$
	Sales ▪ development	$\frac{\text{Sales this period}}{\text{Sales basis period}}$
	▪ per customer	$\frac{\text{Sales}}{\text{Number of customers}}$
	Product mix ▪ innovation	$\frac{\text{Sales new products}}{\text{Sales}}$ $\frac{\text{Number of new products}}{\text{Number of elimated products}}$
	▪ results	$\frac{\text{Sales per product group}}{\text{Total sales}}$ $\frac{\text{Sales}}{\text{Number of sales representatives}}$
	Product costs	$\frac{\text{Total production costs}}{\text{Number of products}}$ $\frac{\text{Production costs product group}}{\text{Total production costs}}$
	Productivity of personnel	$\frac{\text{Gross profit}}{\text{Number of employees (per category)}}$ $\frac{\text{Absenteeism days}}{\text{Total productive days}}$
		$\frac{\text{Number of employees resigned}}{\text{Average number of employees}}$
Investment	Earnings per share	$\frac{\text{Profit after tax}}{\text{Number of ordinary shares}}$
	Price/earnings ratio	$\frac{\text{Share price}}{\text{Earnings per share}}$
	Dividend ▪ yield	$\frac{\text{Dividend per share for one year}}{\text{Share price (at start of year)}}$
	▪ cover	$\frac{\text{Earnings per share}}{\text{Dividend per share for one year}}$

Figure 9.11
A selection of financial status, performance, activity and investment ratios

9.8.2 *Ratios and periodic record keeping*

In the set-up illustrated in Fig 9.12, spaces are left in which to record the periodic outcomes of a ratio. By means of these the changes in the ratios can be followed over time. Two columns have been reserved for the recording of certain standard values enabling actual and standard calculations to be compared. These two columns can also be used to register ratio values from comparable organizations, so that to the extent that an external comparison of the ratios is possible, notions underlying the ratios can be compared. If such an external comparison is possible, the use of ratios will be more productive and meaningful.

use of ratios

	Development of ratio in time					Normal level	
	Basis situation per:	*Situation per:*	*Situation per:*	*Situation per:*	*Situation per:*	*Normal level*	*Standardized level*
Current ratio (CR) Acid test Working capital (WC) Debt to total assets Interest cover Return on equity (RoE) Return on Net Assets (RoNA) Gross operating margin Net operating margin Net assets turnover Stock or inventory turnover Average collection period Market share Sales ▪ development ▪ per customer Product mix ▪ innovation ▪ results Product costs Productivity and personnel Earnings per share Price/earnings ratio Dividend ▪ yield ▪ cover							

Figure 9.12
Ratios: periodic registration and trends

A NEW MANAGEMENT RATIO?

In business as in life, be careful what you wish for. I know a company that wished for a better return on equity (ROE). What could be wrong with that? It paid its executives according to that measure, and man, did they deliver. In some years the firm had the best ROE in its industry. It was winning big time.

The firm was Lehman Brothers, now dead because managing for ROE caused executives to overborrow; after all, debt is capital that earns a return (in good times). Yet it isn't equity, so extreme leverage simply juices ROE until bad times arrive. Wishing for the wrong thing – managing for the wrong ratio – killed the company.

The larger, chilling reality is that every other ratio out there can lead to the same disaster. Gross margin? Earnings per share? It's easy to make any of them look better while damaging the business. Which is why a new ratio that you've never heard of, EVA momentum, is so intriguing. It has been developed by consultant Bennett Stewart, one of the creators (with Joel Stern) of the measure called economic-value added, or EVA. Now used by myriad firms, including Siemens, Best Buy, and Herman Miller, EVA is essentially profit after deducting an appropriate charge for all the capital in the business. Because it accounts for all capital costs, its proponents say, EVA is the best measure of value creation. Now Stewart is making a bold claim about his latest idea: EVA momentum, he says, is the one ratio that can't be manipulated. 'It's the only percent metric where more is always better than less,' he says. 'It always increases when managers do things that make economic sense.' If he's right, it is worth knowing about – for managers at every level and for investors.

EVA momentum is a simple concept. It's the change in a business's EVA divided by the prior period's sales. So if a company increases its EVA by $10 million and the prior period's sales were $1 billion, then its EVA momentum is 1%. That's not bad, considering that for most companies this figure is zero or negative, and the average for many companies is generally around zero. Stewart's firm, EVA Dimensions, has crunched the five-year data for firms with revenues of at least $1 billion. The three top performers by EVA momentum: Gilead Sciences (with an average annual EVA momentum of 24.3%), Google (22.7%), and Apple (12.1%).

It's no surprise to see those names identified as excellent performers; what's interesting is the way they did it. The key insight is that achieving high EVA momentum requires a business to do two difficult things at once. It must grow while at the same time maintaining healthy EVA profit margins or improving poor ones. Apple and Gilead, a biopharmaceutical company, grew spectacularly while also increasing their EVA profit margins impressively; Google simply maintained an excellent EVA profit margin while growing sales 760% during the five years. That combination of increasing sales and an excellent or improving EVA is the extremely rare basis of great financial performance.

Can this ratio be gamed? It's hard to see how. A popular gambit of conniving managers is to shrink a ratio's denominator recklessly, which is what Lehman executives did when they cut the E in ROE dangerously low. But the denominator in EVA momentum is the last period's sales, so it's fixed going in. Relentlessly jacking up EVA – the numerator – is difficult; a proper calculation of EVA values spending on R&D and employee training, the kinds of long-term investments that help companies over time.

Source: *Fortune*, January 18, 2010, p. 11, G. Colvin

9.8.3 *Industry-wide ratios*

interpretation of ratios

The interpretation of ratios demands a certain amount of care, as there is no one universal set of standard values valid for all organizations. The circumstances peculiar to a sector or line of business have to be understood before meaning can be attached to a ratio. In many countries, periodic research results appear containing the outcomes of ratio calculations involving a large number of companies in various lines of business or industries. This published data provides a basis for comparison by which the outcomes of one organization can be related to the averages in that sector or line of business.

9.9 *Performance measurement: financial and non-financial indicators*

checking

The measuring of performance, or review and comparison of outcomes with established norms, is called checking. This notion should not be confused with the broader notion of 'operational control,' which is comprised of checking, adjustment and corrective actions. This

section is concerned with the activities of checking, reviewing, revising and inspecting.
The first question involved in monitoring and checking is who carries it out. This may be the task of the manager of the department concerned. But the person giving the order is not always the right person to examine the outcomes. Sometimes checking and inspecting is such a specialist matter that it has to be undertaken by a separate department (e.g. in the case of chemical or pharmaceutical products). To determine whether such potentially dangerous products meet the required specifications, extensive lab tests must first be conducted. Moreover, because of lack of time, a manager may have to delegate the inspection task to an assistant or a special supervisory office attached the manager's own department. In many manufacturing companies the planning office is charged with the task of ensuring work efficiency. Because adjustment is, in principle, a responsibility implicated in a department manager's working relationship with an operational unit, monitoring, inspecting and checking should as far as possible involve both the manager and the unit in question.

9.9.1 'Traditional' performance measurement

What needs to be monitored and supervised and how this is to be done depend strongly on the type of department involved. The degree to which an organization's input can be related to its output will depend on the type of cost center. They may take various forms:

- Standard cost centers
- Revenue centers
- Discretionary/expense centers
- Profit centers
- Investment centers

standard cost centers

Relating input and output is easiest with standard cost centers and most difficult with investment centers. For such standard cost centers as manufacturing departments, this relationship is quite straightforward, and the goal of monitoring them is to control costs. The number of units of product is multiplied by standard costs per product unit and then compared with actual expenses.

revenue centers

With revenue centers such as sales departments, the relationship between revenues and costs is rather more complicated. An important factor to be considered is the manner in which prices are set. When prices are fixed, the actual costs and revenues in these departments can be directly compared with budgeted costs and revenues. In the case of a variable pricing policy, the relationship is much more difficult to determine.

expense centers

It is even more difficult to determine the relationship in expense centers (e.g. staff and research departments) whose output is difficult to discern. The orientation of their activities must be clearly indicated and their actual expenses must be itemized in budgets. Strict cost control is, however, not always the best way of supervising their results, as purely quantitative data only presents one of the factors involved in such centers. A certain extra expense might increase the effectiveness of a research department, for example, and a too stringent effort to keep costs low could be counterproductive.

profit centers

Profit centers – the parts of an organization generating profit – present additional problems. In companies with various divisions, the following represent areas of difficulty: inter-company transactions, intra-company transactions and transfer prices between divisions, as well as the pricing of and payment for services delivered to divisions by central staff or service departments.

investment centers

Investment centers are cases where not only the profit per center is measured, but also the size of investments per center. In such cases, the system of measuring will clearly be even more complex than it is for profit centers.

Limitations of traditional performance measures and resulting new developments

In recent times, the nature of business and competition has undergone change. Quality, innovation, speed and service have become just as essential as costs. These factors are, however, rarely expressed in existing internal and external reports and performance measurements, and their importance is often undervalued. It is also becoming increasingly apparent that the organizational measurement system has a strong influence on the behavior of managers and employees. Moreover, the notion is growing that traditional financial measurements such as the Return On Investments (ROI) and profit per share can give misleading signals in relation to ongoing progress and innovation, qualities that are being hotly demanded in the current competitive environment. Traditional indicators may disclose apparent short-term improvements in these areas when there is, in fact, a long-term negative effect. Such is the case, for example, with quarterly reports: managers tend to postpone necessary actions that might have a negative effect on the quarterly figures, and the long-term effects of actions are not expressed in the report. It is also the case that traditional financial measurements are mostly meant to satisfy the obligations of external reporting. Even though such types of reporting are very important, they do not help management improve the effectiveness and efficiency of the organization as a whole. They tend to analyze past results rather than the factors that will determine future performance and effectiveness.

ROI

traditional indicators

The limitations of the traditional indicators can be stated as follows:

- They are primarily financially oriented and therefore provide an indirect indication of operational efficacy.
- They are mostly reactive, not proactive; 'backward looking' instead of 'forward looking'.
- They insufficiently reflect the relationship between the strategy implemented by an organization and the operational execution of activities. The consequence is a gap between what is being measured and the tasks that an organization must perform well in order to be competitive.
- When they are not specifically coordinated with strategy, they can supply irrelevant or misleading information, or worse, encourage behavior which undermines the 'result' targeted by strategic goals.
- They are often components of external financial reporting, in which principles of precaution are most frequently preferred. Additionally, performances are influenced too strongly by principles concerned with the value of assets and liabilities.
- 'Bottom line' measurements (such as profitability) come too late for mid-course corrections and recovery/reparative actions.
- They are often concerned solely with maximizing profit.
- They are mostly directed at short-term results.
- Mostly they do not work in a motivating way, nor do they stimulate learning from past actions; on the contrary they are often seen as a justification for punishment.
- They often do not distinguish between value adding and non-value adding activities. Often too many measurements are used as a result of which the scope of each diminishes.

The idea that traditional performance measurements have limitations is reinforced by the fact that performance is perceived as having various dimensions.

- On the workfloor, performances are measured in numbers, costs, delivery and completion times and so on.
- Some performances are evaluated with the aid of a management information system (emphasizing consolidation and financial quantities).
- Other performances are judged on an experiential basis (according to intuitive but important features of company well-being, such as culture, climate of cooperation, creativity and learning environment).
- Some performances are valued in terms of their contribution to the realization of a vision or organizational strategy.

In many organizations, these various dimensions are insufficiently related or compared to one another. Modern organizations demand better communication, greater speed and, particularly, more flexibility. Markets are more turbulent and competition is more intense (see Fig 9.13). When all types of performance are well integrated, organizations function better in rapidly changing market conditions.

Changes	1960s	1990s
Entrepreneurial climate	Product driven 'sellers' market'	Market driven 'buyers' market'
Processes	Simple	Complex
'Product range'	Limited	Wide and varied
Production size	Mass production with high conversion costs	Series/piece production with low conversion costs
Costs	Low fixed costs, high labour costs	High fixed costs, low labour costs
Lifecycle	Long	Short
Competition	Regional	Worldwide, global
Clients	Quickly satisfied	Very demanding

Figure 9.13
Internal and external developments

Managers need to realize that one single measurement cannot supply a clear idea about a performance goal or the crucial areas of an organization.
It is vitally important to measure the factors that determine future organizational effectiveness as such measurements will diagnose the underlying health of the organization. To measure this state of health from more than one point of view, it is also necessary to evaluate both financial and non-financial indicators in an integrated manner, so that a more balanced picture of actual performance is obtained. To enable managers to direct their attention to the right areas, non-financial indicators must have the same status as the financial indicators. If not, managers will tend to undervalue quality, client satisfaction and innovation.

CASE *Mini case study 9.6*

Modern performance control procedures can be compared to the monitoring of the meters and lights on the dashboard of a racing car. To perform the task of driving at high speed without damaging the automobile, the driver must have access to detailed information about many different factors involving vehicle performance and race conditions. Such data includes speed, fuel level, oil pressure, engine temperature, tire conditions, race position and other indicators summarizing the present and future race environment. Focusing on one instrument may prove fatal. The same can be said of the task complexity involved in modern management of organizations: managers must be able to examine performance simultaneously from multiple points of view.

9.9.2 *Non-financial indicators*

Non-financial measurements have to be based on the organizational strategy. Furthermore, one has to make key measurements of manufacturing, marketing, customer satisfaction and R&D results. The organization, divisions and units will be required to attain a certain number of long-term results. This means that managers have to put less emphasis on short-term measurements such as return on investment and net profit, which will have to be replaced or

complemented by a number of non-financial indicators to provide better targets and predictions of the organization's long-term performance.
Measurements have to be developed to help management (and not exclusively as an aid to financial reporting). Simply put, non-financial measurements or operational indicators focusing on internal processes, customer satisfaction, improvement and innovative activities within the organization, need to form the basis for future financial performances. A forward-looking strategy is very important when market conditions change.

Requirements of renewed performance measurement

four main rules performance indicators

Four main rules guide individuals who undertake the task of revising performance indicators:

1. Understand and know the critical success factors of the organization.
2. Relate performance measurements to the objectives and goals of the organization.
3. Only measure factors which can be influenced or regulated.
4. Set goals ('targets') which are attainable.

Critical success factors (CSFs)

Critical success factors are factors that are decisively important for the success of an organization. Critical success factors can be drawn up to assess company functions that deserve management's constant attention. Experience teaches that there are between three to eight factors likely to determine an organization's success or failure.
Based on an inventory of an organization's internal and external strengths and weaknesses, as well as of the opportunities and threats stemming from its relationship with the environment (competition), the organization determines its goals, develops a strategy and, on that basis, determines its critical success factors. CSFs are established by management. In identifying them the types of information that management deems necessary will also be identified.

MEASURING ACHIEVEMENT: FIVE PITFALLS TO AVOID

A lot of executives find doing performance evaluations difficult to do and boring. This is not acceptable.
Everyone agrees that organizations have to evaluate their achievements. However, not many executives like doing this much. They would prefer to pass the task on to employees who are good at figures and spreadsheets. This produces a mountain of figures and comparisons that say little about the performance of the organization and may even lead to the wrong decisions being made. This is just not acceptable: executives must take full responsibility for performance evaluations themselves and ensure that they are performed correctly. The five main performance evaluation pitfalls to avoid are as follows:

- **Evaluating according to your own terms.** It doesn't matter if you've done better than the plan set out or have stayed within the budget. What matters is doing it better than your competitors. Always measure your performance according to benchmarks external to the organization.
- **Looking backwards.** It doesn't matter whether this year's figures are better than last year's. A performance eveluation must be able to tell you whether your decisions will help you in the near future. Look for standards that will determine tomorrow's profits instead of those of yesterday and today.
- **Blind reliance on figures.** The problem is that figures-lead managers often produce figures that don't say much. Figures never tell the whole story and often produce a distorted picture of the situation. Moreover, they are susceptable to influences of a conscious or unconscious nature (the collection method may not have been reliable).
- **Manipulating the figures or using manipulated figures.** Within business life, it's almost the order of the day and it is also virtually unavoidable: chosing a certain metric is almost an open invitation to others to manipulate it. It's better to accept this as a fact than to pretend that it is not so. It is useful to use a variety of metrics. It is also useful to link bonusses less strongly to staying within budget and to achievements: managers are highly skilled at presenting the figures in such a way as to make them stand up well.
- **Sticking to metrics for too long.** The stage of development that the company is at and its circumstances change, and so too should the standards – the metrics. Be very precise about what it is that you are measuring, be explicit about the metrics that you are using and ensure that everyone is clear about this. If the indicators are explicit, everyone will be able to judge whether they are suitable for the objectives in question.

Source: *Harvard Business Review*, October 2009; kluwermanagement.nl/managementtrends, November 2009, p. 5

CASE

Mini case study 9.7

Managing operations strategically

The operations strategist should identify the key operations processes for the specific industry in which the company competes. To illustrate the concept, we will look at five general processes that provide a reasonably comprehensive coverage of operational contexts.

1. **Innovation and product development**. To generate a competitive advantage, an operation's capability must support the firm's competitive position. Consider Inditex/Zara, which competes by quickly copying ideas from the Paris and Milan catwalks as well as the nightclubs of New York and Tokyo. Unlike the fashion leaders, Inditex has not built an innovation and product development capability around big-name designers who create the next fashion trend. Its approach of using teams of designers does not represent a general 'best practice', but it provides a competitive advantage given the positioning of the Zara brand. These teams work collaboratively, gathering insight from more than 500 Zara store managers who report daily on what is selling.

2. **Customer service management**. The auto insurer Progressive Corporation has built its reputation on the way it manages claims processing. The company has developed a competitive advantage through on-the-spot claims settlement with its ubiquitous fleet of white SUVs. More recently, in selected markets, Progressive has taken its customer service a step further. Rather than issuing a claim check quickly, it now offers to take care of the repair. Customers drop their vehicle off at a Progressive customer service center and the company returns it with repairs guaranteed for as long as the customer owns the car. Progressive didn't raise its prices to cover these increased service levels. Instead, it self-funded those capabilities through savings in managing the repair process more effectively than the customer would.

3. **Operations planning and control**. Amazon made a strategic decision to vertically integrate into fulfillment. To leverage that structural investment, Amazon has built a competitively advantaged capability under the generic banner of operations planning and control. For example, Amazon informs the customer of the precise cutoff time for ordering to receive a delivery the next day. No competitor manages such a broad product range with such precision. To leverage its scale and strengthen its operational competitive advantage, Amazon continues to pursue some of the most daunting Internet retailing challenges, such as selling groceries and shoes.

4. **Purchasing and supplier development**. Over the past 20 years, Honda of America Manufacturing Inc. has invested heavily to develop its local supply base, leveraging a capability in purchasing and supplier development inherited from its parent in Japan. Given a strategic need to localize and a domestic supply base incapable of meeting its quality standards, Honda had little choice but to invest in supplier development initially, but over time it reaped huge rewards; the suppliers now play a key role in its continual pursuit of affordable, mass-produced cars such as the Accord.

5. **Quality management**. A company's approach to quality management also represents an opportunity to build a capability to support a differentiated competitive position. For example, the Palm Restaurant and McDonalds Corporation both have strong quality management capabilities, but they focus on different quality positioning. The Palm Restaurant chain, with nearly 30 locations from London to Los Angeles, has built its reputation on ample servings of hand-cut, aged steaks cooked to the individual tastes of the customer. McDonalds' quality management process focuses on delivering consistent meals in 31,000 restaurants in more than 100 countries worldwide. In quality management parlance, the Palm competes on 'quality of spec' (short for 'specification') and McDonalds competes on 'quality to spec'. Each has tailored its quality management capability to support its quality positioning.

Source: T. Laseter (2009) *Strategy + Business* (Winter), p. 30-31

CSFs are related to the type of environment:
1 The structure of the relevant line of business
2 The position of the organization in the line of business
3 Socio-economic relationships
4 Specific circumstances

CSFs also affect an organization's overall strategic plans. Since internal reports are not only concerned with this strategic level but other more specific management levels as well, a number of so-called critical factors (Cfs) affecting these other managerial levels can also be identified. Cfs do not apply to the organization as a whole, but to specific business units, departments and so on. They can, however, often be derived from the CSFs.

critical factors

Anthony et al. (1992) state that financial performance is the final result of management decisions and actions. Effective management control should therefore not only be occupied with final results but also with the processes and the resources themselves. For this purpose, non-financial information (critical success factors, which Anthony et al. label as the 'key variables') must be included in the picture. Such a key variable can be described in terms of the following statements:

key variables

- It is important for explaining the success or failure of a company
- It is mobile and can change quickly
- Such changes are unpredictable
- In the event of an essential change, quick action must be possible
- It can be measured directly or indirectly

exception variables

Other variables include the so-called exception variables. Unlike the key variables, they are not regularly reported, but only when their behavior exceeds certain limits. (They can be compared to the alarm lights on the instrument panel of a plane, which only light up when something goes wrong. This is in contrast to instruments which have to be read continuously). The key variables differ per sector or line of business, varying from productive or available hours in an accounting firm to 'the sold kw' in a power plant.

9.9.3 The Balanced Business Scorecard: a new way of internal reporting

The Balanced Business Scorecard has been developed to help management map performances. It permits companies and institutions to adapt better to the quickly changing circumstances in which they have to compete. Better products have to be brought onto the market more quickly and they must satisfy the individual wishes of the customer. The structure and functioning of organizations may completely change as a result. Since the traditional performance indicator is still geared to the old organizational structures, it must, consequently, also be changed.

The basic motivation for the Balanced Business Scorecard is the need to examine performances in four important ways:

1. From the customer's perspective
2. In terms of company processes
3. In consideration of organizational learning processes and innovation
4. From the financial perspective

In other words: the Balanced Business Scorecard looks at the organization by posing four questions:

1. How do customers view us?
2. What do we have to excel at?
3. How can we continue to improve and create added value?
4. How are we perceived by shareholders?

Goals are determined in response to each of these questions. These goals then have to be translated into CSFs appropriate for each of the above-mentioned points of view. To prevent an overabundance of information for any individual point of view, only a few measurements should be used. Management is thus forced to address the most critical factors.

scorecard

The 'scorecard' protects the organization from sub-optimization; by presenting everything in one report, management is prevented from stressing one element at the expense of all the others.

THE BALANCED SCORECARD AT A GLANCE

Linking measurements to strategy is the heart of a successful scorecard development process. The three key questions to ask here:

1 If we succeed with our vision and strategy, how will we look different:
   - to our shareholders and customers?
   - in terms of our internal processes?
   - in terms of our ability to innovate and grow?

2 What are the critical success factors in each of the four scorecard perspectives?

3 What are the key measurements that will tell us whether we're addressing those success factors as planned?

The balanced scorecard also brings an organizational focus to the variety of local change programs underway in a company at any given time. As the benchmark against which all new projects are evaluated, the scorecard functions as more than just a measurement system. In the words of FMC Corporation executive Larry D. Brady, it becomes 'the cornerstone of the way you run the business,' that is, 'the core of the management system' itself.

Example: Rockwater, an underwater engineering and construction firm. It crafted a five-pronged strategy: to provide services that surpassed customers' expectations and needs; to achieve high levels of customer satisfaction; to make continuous improvements in safety, equipment reliability, responsiveness, and cost-effectiveness; to recruit and retain high-quality employees; and to realize shareholder expectations. Using the balanced scorecard, Rockwater's top management translated this strategy into tangible goals and actions.

- The financial measures they chose included return-on-capital employed and cash flow, because shareholders had indicated a preference for short-term results.
- Customer measures focused on those clients most interested in a high value-added relationship.
- The company introduced new benchmarks that emphasized the integration of key internal processes. It also added a safety index as a means of controlling indirect costs associated with accidents.
- Learning and growth targets emphasized the percentage of revenue coming from new services and the rate of improvement of safety and rework measures.

Source: *Harvard Business Review* (2009) Winter, p. 57

The points of view included in the Balanced Business Scorecard

The point of view of the customer: how do customers view us?
The interests of the customer can usually be broken down into four categories: time and being on time, quality, performance and service, and price. Indicators can be formulated for each of these categories. Time, for example, can be represented by lead time: the interval between the reception of an order and the delivery of it. On the other hand, to measure performance in the area of price, one needs to conduct periodical investigations into competitor prices for similar products. The concordance between the measurements used and actual customer wishes must also be verified: what a customer considers a good delivery time must comply with the measurement that an organization uses.

The internal point of view: at what do we have to excel?
An internal translation of the customer perspective must decide what the organization has to do to satisfy customer expectations. Inevitably, good sales performances are derived from the processes and decisions of the organization itself. An example of this is the employment of account managers so that every client has a permanent contact within the organization.

The point of view focusing on innovation and knowledge gathering: how can we continue to improve and create added value?
In the preceding points of view, parameters are set which are considered to be the most important for the success of the organization. But goals keep changing: fierce competition means that companies have to be constantly improving their existing products and be capable of introducing new products. It is only if such innovation is possible that customers can be provided with added value, the internal efficiency can be improved, and accordingly, the value of the organization for the shareholders be increased. The percentage of total sales represented by new products is one indicator that relates to this perspective.

The financial point of view: how are we perceived by shareholders?
This perspective is concerned with the degree to which the organizational strategy contributes to the improvement of the bottom line: the net profit after taxes. Typical goals are profitability, growth and shareholders' value. In terms of the scorecard, the financial point of view is, however, considered to be the least interesting: too strongly focused on the short term, overly preoccupied with the past, and unable to estimate the future value of present investments. It can even be assumed that when operational indicators are all on green (i.e., they indicate goal attainment) that financial markers will also indicate good values. Although there is a danger of overstating this point, a correspondence between financial and operational gauges remains important for the composition of a representative scorecard.

Several different types of measurement for all of the above points of view are presented in Fig 9.14.

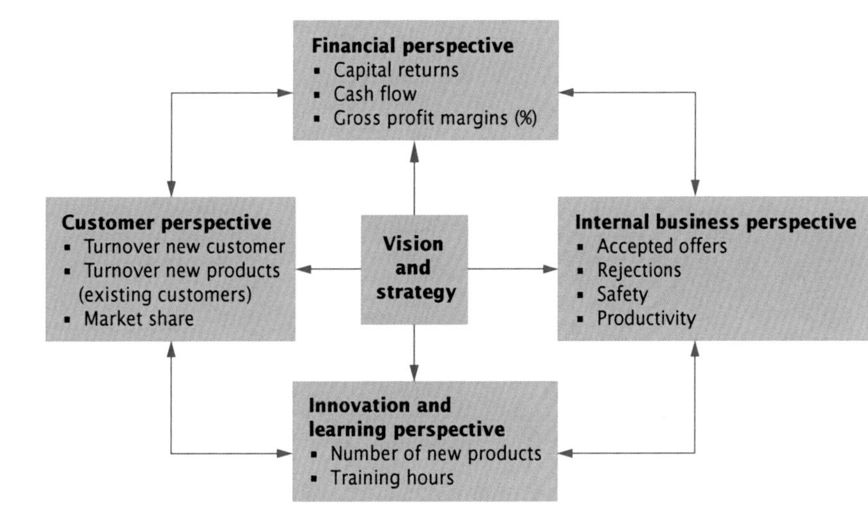

Figure 9.14
The Balanced Scorecard

Internal reporting

The introduction of the scorecard implies a change in the thinking about internal reporting. Not only does the financial controller formulate ratios, but the whole management team is involved.

traditional performance measurement
strategy and vision

In traditional internal reporting and performance measurement, verification is the central issue. Employees were investigated to determine whether they had actually completed the actions they were supposed to have undertaken. In the scorecard, however, strategy and vision are the central issues rather than verification. The scorecard presents goals and makes the employee responsible for attaining them. This new approach fits into the current nature of business and commerce, which is characterized by scale enlargement, speed and services, cooperation, constant innovation, and teamwork. By integrating the four areas of attention, many interrelationships may be better understood by management, which is forced to maintain at least four different points of view and to look beyond the boundaries of their own department. The main contribution of the scorecard is perhaps the fact that it requires individuals to focus on the future instead of the past.

The Balanced Scorecard: a greater focus on strategy

The goal of the insights derived from the four areas of attention (Fig. 9.15) is a well-considered and hopefully stable view of where the organization stands and what needs to happen. However, Kaplan – one of the architects of the Balanced Scorecard – believes that to date, the scorecard has made too many inroads into the managerial field and too little into the leadership field. This fits in with recent opinions as described more or less extensively in 1.4.3, 8.1.4 and 8.2. As Kaplan (2005) has put it, managers are not unimportant. Quite the contrary, but they are not hired in to make strategic decisions for the high performing organization.

The strategy map: the five steps of strategy development

five-step plan
strategic organizations

Kaplan (2004/5) developed a five-step plan to enable companies to transform themselves into strategic organizations (see Exhibit 9.8). It gave both leaders and managers an important role. Leadership on its own is not enough, according to Kaplan, who observed that the obsession with leadership that was characteristic of lot of organizations during the late 1990s did not do these organizations much good.

strategy map

The strategy map is a tool for applying the balanced scorecard method to strategy. The map aims to give organizations an insight into the way in which they create value or have the potential to do so. Just as with the balanced scorecard, the description begins on the factory floor: with human resources and the organization's information bank. It is from here that insight into the organization's operational possibilities can be derived, from which the best way to serve the client can be deduced. Such an insight will produce an indication of the strategy that will serve the organization's purposes best as well as the accompanying financial picture. The ultimate goal is to preserve long-term share value. What this requires is leaders who can use their own personal vision to inspire their personnel and thereby satisfy both customers and shareholders.

vision

In this new version, Kaplan places a lot of emphasis on measurability. After formulation of the strategic goals come the following steps: ascertaining how to gauge things, formulation of concrete operational goals and documenting what has to be done to achieve these goals.

THE BALANCED SCORECARD IN BRIEF

What makes a balanced scorecard special? Four characteristics stand out:

1 It is a top-down reflection of the company's mission and strategy. By contrast, the measures most companies track are bottom-up: deriving from local activities or ad hoc processes, they are often irrelevant to the overall strategy.
2 It is forward-looking. It addresses current and future success. Traditional financial measures describe how the company performed during the last reporting period – without indicating how managers can improve performance during the next.
3 It integrates external and internal measures. This helps managers see where they have made trade-offs between performance measures in the past, and helps ensure that future success on one measure does not come at the expense of another.
4 It helps you focus. Many companies track more measures than they can possibly use. But a balanced scorecard requires managers to reach agreement on only those measures that are most critical to the success of the company's strategy. Fifteen to twenty distinct measures are usually enough, each measure custom-designed for the unit to which it applies.

Source: *Harvard Business Review* (2009) winter, p. 57

An ongoing process

strategy map

After the strategy map has been formulated for the organization in its entirety and according to the terms of the main strategy, it is important to draw up strategy maps for the individual company department or business unit. There are three ways this can be done.
The first approach assumes complete homogeneity: the strategy that applies to the organization as a whole applies in its entirety to all of its branches. As such, the strategy map of a company department will be virtually identical to the corporate strategy map. This approach cannot help but provide benefits to strong and homogenous organizations that supply a similar product (McDonald's, for example).
The other extreme is to leave every part of the company free to choose its own organizational goals. They will produce a completely individual strategy map. Such an approach lends itself best to heterogeneous organizations whose company branches have no clients or processes in common.
A third variant assumes that the main strategy will be adopted largely at the departmental or branch level. The various parts of the company will then have the freedom to deviate from the main approach and in doing so, to create strategy maps of their own.

9.9.4 The operations measurement dilemma

performance measurement

Performance measurement and the apparent contradiction between timeliness and accuracy can create a dilemma. When signals indicate that performance is deviating from a norm, it is important that these discrepancies be revealed in order to limit any negative effects. However, the speed with which deviations are reported can in itself have a number of negative effects on the accuracy of the measurement, making the reliability of the analysis somewhat less likely. The decision to emphasize either speed or accuracy in reporting will depend on the goals which have been established. For an overall assessment of a situation, an accurate report is required. For activities requiring immediate adjustment, more value needs to be placed on the rapidity of the process. The manager will have to make his or her own choice.
The fact that all results of strategic decisions can be measured quite easily (and according to Kaplan and others, this is crucial: see the strategy map in 9.9.3) creates another dilemma. Such a strong emphasis on measurability means that activities whose effects are not yet measurable automatically run the risk of being underestimated.

9.9.5 Management of non-profit organizations

The management problem in non-profit organizations operating in the areas of welfare, health, education and culture can be compared to that experienced by discretionary or expense centers in commercial organizations. They both require a non-monetary method of evaluating output and of relating costs to results. Non-profit organizations additionally have characteristics which make management even more difficult. They frequently enjoy a monopoly position for their client services (for example, those provided to patients in a hospital), and consequently no market price against which one can offset costs. Additionally, non-profit organizations predominantly employ professionals with their own sometimes divergent value patterns and specific know-how in areas about which management sometimes has little understanding. Finally, the management of such organizations often includes several societal interest groups, all of which wish to implement their own goals.
To manage non-profit organizations, an agreement on goals must be reached: not only on abstract guidelines but on the concrete objectives for the service being rendered, precise identification of target groups for these service and the extent to which services will be provided. Moreover, clear and preferably quantifiable norms for the 'production process' (the delivered performance and its quality) have to be established. If such specifics are defined, the social services of a village or town will be able to indicate how many requests an employee

has to handle per day or per week. One condition is that the effect of this specification process on quality and customer relations must be known. This is difficult to measure. In non-profit organizations those involved (politicians, customers and professional service providers) will have to try to determine generally accepted norms making it possible to solve the quality problem.

9.9.6 *Evaluating the entire organization: the EFQM-model*

EFQM-model
management improvement model

A recent model frequently used by organizations to monitor their own performance is the so-called EFQM-model (see Fig. 9.15), a model developed by the European Foundation for Quality Management. This model was originally intended as a means of improving quality. It can, however, also be used as a general management improvement model that enhances the performance of an entire organization and improves organizational relationships with external actors.

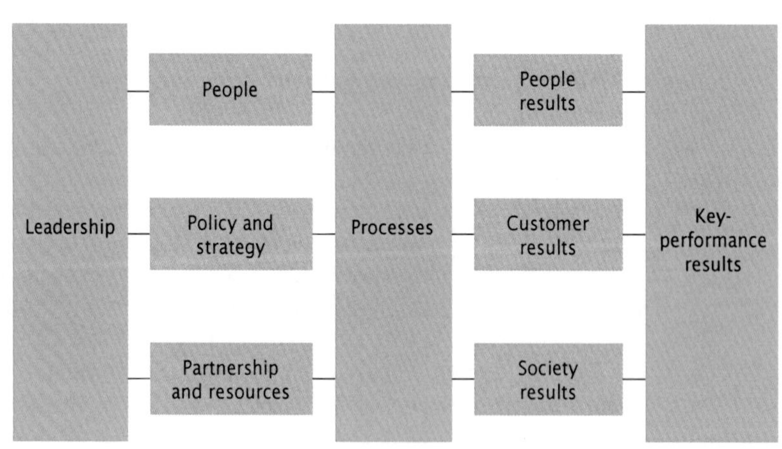

Figure 9.15
EFQM model

result areas
organizational areas

The model focuses on nine areas that are important for improving an organization's performance. Four of these areas are result areas. These are the key performance results, the people results, the customer results and the society results. Five areas are organizational areas: leadership, personnel management, policy and strategy, management of resources, and management of the relevant processes. These areas have an influence on the scores in the result areas. In this model strategic management (see Chapter 4) and operational management (see chapters 9 and 4) are closely connected. Although the result areas resemble the categories on the 'balanced scorecard' (see Section 9.9.3), the balanced scorecard does not give any account of causal organizational factors or areas.

The EFQM-model can not only be used for guiding and judging performance, it can also be used as a diagnostic tool. There are several books on this subject, some of which are published in the Netherlands by the Dutch Quality Institute. The model (adapted to suit particular circumstances) also provides the basis for the managerial systems of a number of Dutch organizations.

9.10 Operational control: adaptation and corrective actions

When review and monitoring of performances reveals that actual performances deviate from norms, the manager is faced with the choice of adjusting either the norm or the practice. In essence, the decision cycle discussed in Chapter 4 is initiated. Once the discrepancy has been detected, the manager needs to decide how to eliminate it. For this purpose, the cause of the deviation must first be determined. Proper diagnosis is the key to effective problem-solving. Treating the symptoms will not bring about a cure.

As a rule, the norm should be adjusted when the deviation is caused by structural deviations in circumstances. When, for example, it appears that exports to a certain country have decreased because of extra heavy import tariffs, it makes little sense to increase export activities. The sales department will have to formulate a new norm for that country. Furthermore, possible ways to compensate for lost sales need to be explored.

adjustment of operations

Correction or adjustment of operations is recommended when deviations are caused by accidental circumstances. If sales have decreased because of a competitor's temporary advertising campaign, this deviation can be redressed by making an extra effort in the sales area by for example, a temporary price cut or additional advertising. In such a case, it would be inappropriate to use the lower sales as a norm for the future.

A corrective system is often seen as a cybernetic system. Some everyday examples of this are thermostats and self-adjusting brakes. In designing an organizational system of adjustment, it is important to be aware that such a system differs from a cybernetic system and not simply apply the design rules of a thermostat to an organization. An essential distinction is that an organization deals with people, with all their needs, wishes and characteristics. In the structure of a management system, one certainly needs to render account to this human variable. Nobody reacts like a machine. The person who turns the thermostat to another temperature does not meet any resistance from this piece of equipment. Changing a reward or performance measurement system can, however, never be so simply done. A great deal more is involved. To start with, the change in the system will have to be justified to the people involved (see Part Four). In addition, they must be convinced that the changes are desirable and meaningful. The effectiveness of change increases even more when they get the chance to participate in the design of the new system.

One always has to conceive of a deviation from the norm as an impulse to instigate a decision-making process. The manager then has to examine the decisions to be made and make them.

adjustment

Any adjustment can affect policy (see Part Two), as well as operational procedure (see Part Five) and structure (see Part Three). Multiple adjustment measurements must therefore always be taken and correlated in ways that have already been discussed in this book.

Summary

- Planning is the activity of correlating decisions to achieve formulated goals. In this chapter, several types of plans have been discussed and the relationship between planning and budgeting indicated. To clarify the processes involved, various planning techniques and methods have been explained. Close attention was paid to the budgeting features that enhance its function as a managerial tool.
- In an organization, budgets express performance norms in terms of money. In addition to using budgets to gain insight into complex situations and to monitor and direct processes, one can use appraisals of company performances and ratios. In 'one-off' activities, project and network planning can be used. Control of the flow of goods may be based on either a 'push' or a 'pull' system.
- It is important to monitor the execution of actions and to determine whether the desired outcome has occurred. If necessary, adjustments and corrective actions can be undertaken. In measuring performance, some new non-financial indicators have taken their place alongside the traditional ones. The traditional financial indicators are past-oriented; the non-financial indicators are more strongly concerned with the future effectiveness of the organization.
- The use of non-financial indicators takes place when statistical techniques are employed in the framework of total quality management. Moreover, non-financial variables are important in benchmarking practices, as this procedure traces the factors that influence an organization's present and future effectiveness. Adjustments can be made once results have been measured, evaluated and analyzed. Managers can then adjust organizational performance by deciding via a creative search and design process to change an organization's course (see Part Two), change the organizational structure (see Part Three) or conduct operations differently (see Part Five). Considering that an organization is a cooperative human venture, a manager will always have to be able to explain a corrective decision to others. Such communication is necessary to convince the external (see Part One) as well as the internal (see Part Four) stakeholders to continue making their contributions to the organization.

Discussion questions

1. With reference to *Management in action* at the beginning of this chapter, why do you think the basic elements of Prahalad's responsible management have not changed over time? Are all his rules of thumb practicable? Do any of them come at a cost? If so, what cost?
2. Suppose you have to formulate a strategic plan for an organization. How would you make use of project planning in undertaking this task?
3. Why should a clear organizational structure be a condition for budgeting?
4. Can you explain the research findings indicating that autocratically oriented managers experience integral quality management as a threat?
5. Give your opinion on the following statement: 'Benchmarking means analyzing your competitor.'
6. Give your opinion on the following statement: 'Management by objectives is only suitable for formulating the departmental and personal goals for a certain period but is not the right instrument for the evaluation and possible adjustment of activities.'
7. With reference to exhibit 7.4
   a) In what way does Hyundai benefit from increasing its quality scores?
   b) How can Toyota protect itself against Hyundai's benchmarking practices?

Research-based exercise

Total Quality Management and changing organizations

Introduction
This exercise is based on a research article by Man Hyung Hur published in *Total Quality Management & Business Excellence.* The research question, research method, and some of the results of his research project are shown. The exercise, which is related to this research article, consists of two questions. Your answers should be based on the theory in this chapter.

Research question
How do total quality management practices influence and transform how organizations work?

Method
A quantitative analysis with data collected from a survey of government employees and a content analysis with data collected from the same source using open-ended questions.

Outcomes
Total quality management practices have let government employees change their attitudes at work from a rule-of-thumb estimate to a rational judgment style on the basis of analysis. Their learning mechanisms have changed from individual to collective learning and their decision-making style from individual-based to a team-based type.

(Based on Hur, M.H. (2009). 'The influence of total quality management practices on the transformation of how organizations work.' *Total Quality Management & Business Excellence,* 20(8), 847-861.)

Questions

1 Do the changes that Hur identifies fit with the description of the essentials of quality management in this chapter or are these changes contradictory?
2 Can you give an example of a firm that could benefit from the organizational changes that Total Quality Management entails?

CASE Management case study

The operations footprint decision

An operations strategy should guide the structural decisions and the evolution of operational capabilities needed to achieve the desired competitive position of the company as a whole.

To be sure, the operations strategy of most companies has been determined on an ad hoc basis by the accumulated effect of many small and large operational decisions. Rarely does a company formally design and document its operations strategy in a deliberate fashion. At best, guidance on a few key operational choices might be found in an overall corporate strategy. Looking at a few cases of past decisions at leading companies, however, can highlight the importance of well-designed operations strategies.

Structural decisions define the what, when, where, and how of investing in operations bricks and mortar. The original logic of operations strategy focused on manufacturing plants, but the same issues need to be addressed for distribution plants or call centers. Four interrelated decision areas ultimately influence the size and scope of a company's operational footprint, and they should be addressed explicitly and collectively in light of the company's competitive positioning.

1. Vertical integration
The logical starting point is to consider, with competitive advantage in mind, which activities should be conducted in-house versus outsourced. Henry Ford's original River Rouge complex in Detroit was the epitome of vertical integration in the days when Ford revolutionized the automobile business with the Model T and Model A. Barge loads of raw iron ore fed the plant's steel mills, which supplied virtually all of the individual parts for the assembly plants. Ford's system used the new paradigm of mass production and scale economies to dominate the company's dozens of smaller rivals.

More recently, at its formation in the mid-1990s, Amazon.com Inc. went against the general trend of outsourcing and the dominant pattern among Internet retailing startups by building a vertically integrated network of fulfillment centers that would assemble and ship the orders customers submitted over the Web. Amazon invented and continues to perfect the operating model for Internet fulfillment, and it knew that outsourcing would put its competitive advantage at risk. 'We would be the teacher and then they would offer those services to our competitors,' explained a senior operations executive in the early days.

2. Facility capacity
Assuming a company envisions a sufficiently competitive advantage from some degree of vertical integration, the specifications for the facility come to the forefront. Should a company aggressively build capacity ahead of demand or take a more conservative path of adding capacity only in smaller increments and only when market uncertainty subsides? Consider the example of Copeland in 1987. Then a division of Emerson Electric Company, Copeland introduced the scroll compressor, a fundamentally new design concept for initial application in residential air conditioning. The company built capacity ahead of demand and even continued with a capacity expansion in 1989 despite initial demand that fell short of forecasts. Management was convinced – correctly, as history showed – that new regulatory efficiency standards would favor the new technology, and it created a competitive advantage that it retains today. Today, the scroll technology dominates the market; Copeland's design leads the industry, and Copeland maintains unmatched scale economies.

3. Facility location
Choosing where to site facilities also requires trade-offs in designing the operations footprint, regardless of whether the facility is in-house or outsourced. Inditex (the Spanish clothing company better known by its leading brand, Zara) maintains scale-intensive pattern-cutting operations in-house and subcontracts the labor-intensive sewing to small mom-and-pop facilities in the surrounding region. Most fashion retailers outsource cut-and-sew operations to Asia to tap into law labor costs, but they face long supply chains requiring early design decisions and advanced volume commitments. Inditex's more responsive supply chain fits its strategy: in-house cutting offers enhanced control and helps offset some of the labor-cost disadvantages of the geo-graphic location of its sewing plants.

Plant location decisions must also balance intellectual property risk and the cost of transportation. Accordingly, the Intel Corporation builds most of its high-tech wafer fabrication facilities in the developed world to protect its intellectual property, and Chinese appliance maker Haier Group built a refrigerator plant in South Carolina to avoid the prohibitive cost of shipping big refrigerators across the Pacific to the U.S. market.

4. Process technology

Finally, the structural footprint decision should address the process technology used in the facility. Again, consider the case of Copeland's scroll compressors. A dozen years after the introduction of its new design, Copeland felt compelled to add a Chinese plant to its operations footprint: many competitors were producing in China by then, and the labor-cost advantage of the region could onset some of Copeland's scale advantage. Accordingly, Emerson opened a new scroll compressor plant in Suzhou in 2000. But Copeland made distinctly different decisions regarding process technology at this new plant. Concerns over intellectual property protection, for example, led the company to exclude proprietary process technology and import the critical scroll plates from its U.S. plants.

Source: T. Laseter (2009), *Strategy + Business* 57(Winter), p. 26-27

Case study questions

1 What types of budgets would you propose for the financial control of a firm's vertical integration, facility capacity, facility location, and process technology?
2 Can the four elements of the operations footprint be integrated in the 'Management by objectives' approach?
3 Can you think of and describe a fifth important element of an operations footprint?

CONTENTS

10.1 Information and control
10.2 Management and operational information systems
10.3 Information planning and planning of automation
10.4 Information and communication technology (ICT)
10.5 Functional processes and process control
10.6 Process redesign
10.7 ICT entrepreneurship

Chapter 10

Managerial process control: functional processes and process redesign

LEARNING OUTCOMES

After studying this chapter, you should be able to do the following:

- Describe the essence of control in the process model of an organization
- Identify the various kinds of processes involved in the full range of company activities
- Clarify the notion of the 'value chain'
- Describe the various functional components of the manufacturing and service-provision processes
- Describe what is meant by process redesign
- Describe how the characteristics and goals of redesign/re-engineering have been influenced by information technology

CASE

Management-in-action

Big SIS is watching you

Remember 'The Matrix', the 1999 film in which human beings are plugged into machines? These simulate reality to control humankind and harvest their bodies' heat and electrical activity.

Such a parallel universe is indeed emerging. Fortunately, it is not intended to subdue humans, but to allow them to control their environments better. Some computer scientists already talk of the birth of 'societal information-technology systems', or SIS. In 2010 such systems will start to make their presence felt.

To grasp this trend, one has first to recognize that the world is exceedingly wasteful. Utilities lose more than 50% of water supplies around the world because of leaky infrastructure. In America alone, congested roads cost billions of dollars a year in lost work hours and wasted fuel. And if the country's power grid were only 5% more efficient, this would eliminate greenhouse-gas emissions equivalent to those of 53m cars.

The reason for such inefficiencies? The infrastructure is not intelligent: roads, power grids and water-distribution systems are all essentially networks of dumb pipes. Over the past few years, momentum has been building to make them smarter. More recently, in attempting to overcome the economic crisis, the pace has picked up. Many countries have earmarked a big chunk of their stimulus packages for infrastructure projects.

The other main driver is technology. Until now, the Internet has mainly been about connecting people. Today it is more and more about connecting things – wirelessly. Thanks to Moore's law (a doubling of capacity every 18 months or so), chips, sensors and radio devices have become so small and cheap that they can be embedded virtually anywhere. Today, two-thirds of new products already come with some electronics built in. By 2017 there could be 7 trillion wirelessly connected devices and objects – about 1,000 per person.

Sensors and chips will produce huge amounts of data. And IT systems are becoming powerful enough to analyze them in real time and predict how things will evolve. IBM has developed a technology it calls 'stream computing'. Machines using it can analyze data streams from hundreds of sources, such as surveillance cameras and Wall Street trading desks, summarize the results and take decisions.

Transport is perhaps the industry in which the trend has gone furthest. Several cities have installed dynamic toll systems whose charges vary according to traffic flow. Drivers in Stockholm pay between $1.50 and $3 per entry into the downtown area. After the system – which uses a combination of smart tags, cameras and roadside sensors – was launched, traffic in the Swedish capital decreased by nearly 20%.

More importantly, 2010 will see a boom in 'smart grids'. This is tech-speak for an intelligent network paralleling the power grid, and for applications that then manage energy use in real time. Pacific Gas & Electric, one of California's main utilities, plans to install 10m 'smart meters' to tell consumers how much they have to pay and, eventually, to switch off appliances during peak hours.

Smart technology is also likely to penetrate the natural environment. One example is the SmartBay project at Galway Bay in Ireland. The system there draws information from sensors attached to buoys and weather gauges and from text messages from boaters about potentially dangerous floating objects. Uses range from automatic alerts being sent to the harbor master when water levels rise above normal to fishermen selling their catch directly to restaurants, thus pocketing a better profit.

Yet it is in big cities that 'smartification' will have the most impact. A plethora of systems can be made more intelligent and then combined into a 'system of systems': not just transport and the power grid, but public safety, water supply and even health care (think remote monitoring of patients). With the help of Cisco, another big IT firm, the South Korean city of Incheon aims to become a 'Smart+Connected' community, with virtual government services, green energy services and intelligent buildings.

What could stop the world from becoming smart? Surprisingly, the main barriers are not technological. One is security: such systems will be vulnerable to all sorts of hacker attacks. Another is privacy. Many people will feel uncomfortable having their energy use and driving constantly tracked. Bureaucracy will also slow things down.
For SIS to work, in many cases several administrations and departments have to collaborate. And then there is the worry that all these systems will one day gang up on their creators, as in 'The Matrix'. July 2009 computer scientists, artificial-intelligence researchers and roboticists met in California to discuss the risk. But the vendors of smart systems insist that the idea will remain just science fiction. 'These systems are designed to operate only within certain boundaries,' says Bernie Meyerson, of IBM's systems and technology group. 'They don't go off into the "weeds".'

Source: L. Siegele (2010), 'The World in 2010,' *The Economist*, p. 118

process control The central issue of this chapter is managerial process control. Structures need to stimulate the flow and progress of processes. When the 'natural' course of functional processes in an organization breaks down and the processes do not flow fluently into each other, those processes need to be remapped.
Problems of all kinds arise in companies and institutions and decisions have to be made based on available internal and external information. The decisions are usually about:

- The positioning of an organization (= external tuning, positioning and adaptation)
- The organizational structure (= structuring/design)
- The daily operational process arrangements (= internal tuning and adaptation)

The first point was extensively studied in Chapter 3. Chapters 5 and 6 were concerned with the organizational structure of companies and institutions. The daily operational processes were discussed in chapters 7, 8 and 9, but we are now going to conclude the discussion by providing a more detailed examination of various company processes, an area in which process control is always the most important matter. Firstly, we will investigate the essence of managerial process control, after which various business processes will be mapped out. Introductory material for this discussion can be found in Chapter 9, which focuses on the methods and techniques for planning, management of organizational activities and control of the information supply. All three of these perspectives offer excellent starting-points for a discussion relating to redesigning business processes. The principle of process control and the importance of processes in organizational design have long been recognized. The notion of redesign can, however, be regarded as new.

10.1 Information and control

The notions of 'data' and 'information' are distinct from that of 'content,' and these three terms must be distinguished from each other in order to have a good understanding of information technology and management.

information *data* Information is ordered data based on certain criteria or points of view. Consequently, information consists of meaningful combinations of data. Data is, in contrast, any term having meaningful content, such as a figure, a letter or a word. When information is needed, the available data must first undergo processing.
Defined in this way, data only becomes information when it conveys relevant meaning for people. Employees often receive thick computer printouts with an enormous amount of figures and other data not clarified in any way, and consequently not presented in such a manner that they may be understood. As a result, such data provides little or no information.

Formal and informal information

Information is made available to management in various forms, such as texts, images, and/or spoken words. It may also come from formal or informal sources, and be concerned with the strategy, tactics or operations of an organization.

The performance of all kinds of tasks requires employees to make decisions. To provide help in the decision-making process, formal information is provided according to certain rules concerning content, presentation, frequency and the times when information is supplied (for example, a balance of assets and liabilities, profit and loss statement, surveys of debtors and receivables or inventory lists). In addition to such formal information, employees also make use of informal information such as scribbled lists and notes in their notebooks. To a certain extent, the existence of these supplementary records suggests that personnel often consider the formal information to be inadequate, and demonstrates the impossibility of devising general procedures for saving and processing all necessary information. If, however, an organization relies more heavily on the informal information resources of its individual employees than on formal information channels, something is wrong with the information provision in that organization.

information provision

Formal information (structured information) such as balance sheets, reports on employee evaluations, and so on, and informal information (unstructured information) involving intuition, rumors in the lobby, emotions and experiences, all contribute to decision making. Although formal information is primarily provided via information systems and administrative processes, both formal and informal information may also come from other employees and/or sources outside the organization.

Strategic, tactical and operational information

strategic information

Strategic information provides long-term support for an organization's policy-making processes. This information comes from external and internal sources, but is hard to predict. For this reason, it is important to keep strategic possibilities open and to take advantage of opportunities of gathering ad hoc information.

tactical information

The goal of tactical information is to compare planning data to actual attained results. When deviations occur, corrective actions need to be taken. Tactical information is especially intended to help middle management supervise operational employees, and is based on such sources as weekly surveys of receivables and/or debtors, cost surveys, sales figures, production lists, recruitment data, surveys of utilization of machinery and so on.

operational information

Operational information deals with the daily performance of tasks, and as such is concerned with the details of the organization's operational procedures. Characteristic of this type of information are the established rules and procedures whose purpose is to regulate routines. This information goes to various departments at different levels of the organization and often to persons or institutions outside the organization proper.

For a management team to make decisions, it must be supplied with all types of information, including insights into the past year's results (to be compared to the budget), along with facts about the order portfolio, the work, the cash flow and inventory. A board about to make an investment decision concerning the purchase of a new machine will want to be informed about the cost price, the expected sales increase and so on.

When accepting new orders, it is important that the sales and production departments have access to information about delivery times, accounts receivable, inventories of raw materials and final products, quality and quantity of the production, and utilization of the manufacturing resources.

information needs

To determine an organization's information needs, the form and the frequency of the required information and the manner in which it should be made available, it is necessary to know who is allowed to make various decisions and at which organizational level.

information triangle

A representation of organizational levels, their information needs, and the manner of providing information to satisfy these requirements is furnished by the so-called information triangle. Strategic information, for example, involves aggregation or distribution of information originating at the operational and tactical levels. More detailed views of short-

and middle-term activities are incorporated in summarizing surveys so that long-term conditions and consequences (see Fig 10.1) can be considered.

Figure 10.1
Information supply and level in the organization

10.1.1 Supervision, information and control

To ensure proper implementation and to verify the results of plans, the progress as well as the actual outcomes of the instituted processes must be constantly monitored. The plan is then confronted by reality. If there are any discrepancies, corrective actions can be undertaken, but only if there is a responsive system of information processing to provide management with feedback. In Section 10.1.2, we will pay special attention to the procedures involved in signaling and monitoring.

Some reasons for internal supervision

Supervision is necessary because people and systems are liable to error. Often things can be carried out better or differently than at first seemed possible. A judgment may turn out to be partly flawed. Consequently, it is always important to remain informed about the actual course of affairs.

delegated tasks

If tasks are delegated (see Chapter 6) the delegated task also needs to be monitored in order to determine whether it is being performed properly. Only when there is a procedure for verifying performance should tasks be delegated to others. For this reason, a company's or institution's management must employ appropriate means of internal supervision and be equipped with the right sorts of measurements and effective performance norms by which to gauge activities. Only then will comparison between norm and reality provide management with meaningful administrative information. Internal supervision monitors the processes in which an organization is engaged. Without purposeful supervision, management cannot exist.

internal supervision

Managerial or operational employees can use several methods to remain informed about the progress of an activity. Sometimes deviation can be determined by direct examination or observation. Often, however, there is indirect monitoring whereby deviations are detected afterwards by means of a report on existing practices.

Supervision may involve the task of verifying whether actions were appropriately authorized, whether duties were performed correctly and efficiently, whether the work progressed as required, or whether the appropriate times, quantities and qualities were maintained. While the main focus of supervision will, of course, be on the current company activities, feedback in relation to decisions made, the material values present in the company (in money and/or in goods) and the accuracy of records may also be given.

From supervision to control

Supervision should be limited to the act of monitoring present practices and comparing them to the established norms. Besides setting norms and making plans for the execution of activities, supervision also involves the adjustment and/or correction of plans to be implemented and possibly revised. As such, it comprises more than merely checking, reviewing, monitoring or supervising – it is the act of successfully managing affairs: keeping everything in hand.

The authority to make decisions and adjust practices can often be granted to operational employees, but only as long as the deviations are within certain limits or zones of tolerance (see Section 9.3). Such authorization can certainly be given where simple task assignments are involved: undertakings for which there is only one expected result indicated in the budget, for example. As soon as tolerances are exceeded, however, it will become necessary for deviations from norms to be addressed by management in consultation with operational employees. Problems involving plans or operational norms can only be resolved by a manager with the relevant authority, or in the last resort, by the managerial team or board.

authorization

Supervisory responsibilities of the controller and technical planner

In middle-sized and large companies, the board receives advice from an official called the controller, a person in charge of the business finances. In small organizations, this staff member may be called the head of administration and book-keeping. As an advisor to the managerial team and to the company directors, a controller is concerned with plans and budgets, audits and reviews, interpretations and analyses of deviations of the actual results from projected norms, making recommendations to management and providing it with advice. In addition, the controller often manages the organization's department of financial administration. The controller becomes, as it were, the business and financial conscience of the organization.

business finances

The business and technical conscience is the head of the planning staff of the manufacturing or production department. This official is also occupied with planning, reviewing, monitoring, interpreting and analyzing deviations and making recommendations. Within the organizational hierarchy, the person in charge of planning is the chief advisor to the head of the manufacturing department. A great deal of very important data is made available by means of the signaling systems (see Section 10.1.2) installed by the technical planning department. The managerial team is usually directly advised by the heads of the production and technical planning departments. However, the managerial team may get information about the quality or quantity of products and services by other means: for example, via a periodical report. Managers can thus form their own opinions about the performance of the manufacturing department based on quality, quantities and time requirements.

production department

technical planning department

Information management and the information manager

The old book-keeping and accounting functions have evolved to such an extent (especially in large organizations) that their tasks have now become divided into four specialist functions: the controller function, the treasury function, the tax planning function and the information management function.

The importance of information and communication technology (ICT) has grown to the degree that the effective managing of information now has consequences not only for processes and organizational forms, but also for products and competitive position. The hiring of personnel to fulfill this function usually occurs at the highest level, the information manager reporting to the financial director, or sometimes the CIO (Chief Information Officer). The latter is especially to be found in large and/or information intensive organizations such as banks, insurance companies, and government ministries and services. In such cases, the possibilities offered by information technology frequently have great strategic importance, since there is a pressing need for information, and consequently, information systems and the necessary applications of information technology that they require.

ICT

CIO

In many companies and institutions, an information manager is responsible for providing the information in the various functional areas. Sometimes the information manager is answerable to the EDP manager (electronic data processing manager) who, as a technical expert, is in charge of equipment and program acquisitions, the design of systems and the control of the computer center. The functions of the information manager and EDP manager overlap insofar as they contribute to the technical development of information products and services better adapted to the information needs in the functional areas of various company departments.

EDP manager

Food for thought: according to futurologist Paul Ostendorf, 'The speed with which information is processed will increase a thousand times in the coming years.' (SAP World & Tech Tour 2009 on 14 October 2009 in Rotterdam)

10.1.2 Internal reporting

Internal reporting is that part of an organization's information system by means of which the various levels of management in all departments receive prompt and pertinent information allowing proper supervision and appropriate adjustments to the planning and practice of business activities. Budgeting and budgetary controls, as well as planning with either planning charts or software constitute at least some of the elements on which internal reporting is based. Data can also become available in other ways. In addition to bookkeeping, for example, data can be supplied about material use, quality, personnel utilization, order processing and the order portfolio. Besides data expressed in terms of money, data about quality or quantity will provide clearer views of an organization's or a department's state of affairs. This data needs to be regularly (daily/weekly/monthly) available in a summarized form to enable any corrective action to be promptly taken. If, for example, signals indicate that the sales per client are falling or cost budgets are exceeded, or that calculations do not appear to be attainable, adjustments to the planning and/or implementation of corrective actions to production practices will become necessary. Internal reporting thus forms an important tool for the systematic control of planned activities.

data about quality or quantity

10.1.3 Information and book-keeping

Information provision is consequently certainly more than bookkeeping. Bookkeeping is static in nature. It is, however, an essential element and has to be used to provide signals for management in the areas of, for example, adjustment of sales, production, or purchase activities. A contribution also has to be made to the setting up of the schedules and the company and departmental budgets.

future activities

Information provision is especially required for determining possible future activities: investments, recruitment of personnel, development of new products, restriction of financial resources. Information provision is also required in order to be able to chart and adjust present company activities: exceeding of costs, absenteeism, numbers of produced and sold products, machine return, and so on.

present company activities

Finally, information has to be supplied to external stakeholders, such as shareholders and the bank, and to the internal stakeholders. Information of this kind will relate to profitability (return), solvability, liquidity and the important developments in the sector or line of business and so on. It is provided via the published profit and loss statement, balance sheets and the report of the board, via the annual report, via announcements to the works council and via periodical external financial messages in, for example, quarterly reports.

If this is depicted diagrammatically, it will take the form of a pyramid linking the managerial level, decision areas and aspects of management (see Fig 10.2).

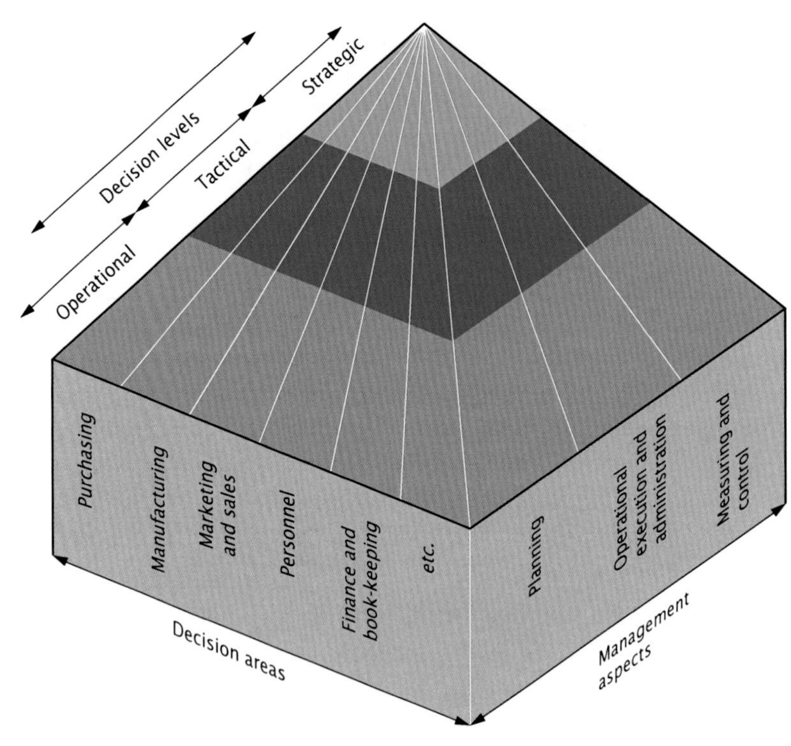

Figure 10.2
Management information in decision-making areas: the 'information pyramid'

handling of data

Handling of data takes place within each of the information systems that have been set up. The data handling process will include the following activities:

- Collecting
- Transforming
- Communicating
- Changing
- Analyzing
- Organizing
- Storing
- Searching

The goal of these activities is threefold.

1 The bridging of time. When an invoice is sent to a client on a certain date, and a statement a month later, the data on the original invoice has to be mentioned in the statement.
2 The bridging of distance. All departments within a company have to have the inventory data at their disposal if an article is not in stock at that department.
3 The bridging of access to information. More or less complex information must be made available in order to draw conclusions from it. Reports can be drawn up on the basis of inventory registration. They can then be used to plan future inventory levels. Too large an inventory means greater use of working capital. Too small an inventory means, however, that one cannot deliver in time.

decision making

Timely decision making requires reliable information to be readily at hand and in a surveyable form. It also has to be complete, correct and in continual supply.
The loci or points of decision within the organization should be included in the information, along with how it is to be made available to the organization: the lines of communication.
If information has to fulfill a need, it should be:

- Problem oriented: that is, connected to the problems to be handled at the point of decision
- Current

- Simple and not needing complex explanations
- Easy to obtain

Tools for this include pre-printed forms and readable and surveyable statistical surveys. Data can be processed and presented by computer or on screen or in another way but still available for presentation by hand. It is wise, however, to bear in mind that there is a distinction between essential information (information which is vital for the work – 'need to know' information) and information in the 'rather interesting but not really important' category ('good to know' information).

10.2 Management and operational information systems

management information systems

In addition to information relating to the administration of company resources, management information systems also have to furnish input for organizational plans such as those affected by the long-term prognosis of return on investments, or developments in a certain sector of the labor market. Short-term oriented information might include a survey of personnel costs and data about quality control, while department-specific information will be concerned with such items as prediction of sales per product, per country or per market segment; production planning for the following month and inventory control; credit control of clients and surveys of employee training programs.
Tasks assigned to staff at each of the various levels and departments in a company or institution share three recognizable features. In accordance with their individual levels of authority and within the scope of their decision-making capacity, personnel are responsible for planning, performing tasks and administrating company resources (including reviewing

control cycle

and verifying their uses). These elements together form the control cycle.

10.2.1 External reports and information

The external information supplied by an organization either takes the form of reports written for groups or agencies outside the organization or direct communications addressed to such parties. Included in this category are annual reports and quarterly reports to shareholders, both of which provide an overview of the company's financial position (balance sheet and profit and loss statement) to facilitate credit negotiations. Other examples of external communications are the provision of data on sales, cost development, and so on to labor or trade organizations, or the provisions of data on wages, sales, profits and so on to the taxation authorities to help determine social security and tax payments.

10.2.2 Information supply and information needs

Designing an organization's management information system involves two important steps:

1. Determination of the information need. To determine what function the information has to fulfill it is important to set clear information goals. For more information on this procedure, see the functional processes which are described in Chapter 9.
2. Provision of the needed information. For the healthy functioning of an organization, it is important to know the kind of information needed, the frequency of this need and the format in which managers need to have the information.

decisions

Both steps require knowledge about where decisions are actually made within the organization and the issues the decisions relate to.

10.2.3 Functional information systems (FIS)

Figure 10.2 illustrates how the functional information systems within an organization are arranged. It shows the type of relationship between the various parts and the corresponding relative independence of the various functional company divisions.

CASE Mini case study 10.1

For the supply of information, it makes quite a difference whether decisions (e.g. about an investment in a foreign company) are made at a certain point in the organization's policy development procedure, whether operational decisions (e.g. assigning machine 90 to product 12A or 15C), are made at regular intervals, or whether certain information is used to control the manufacturing process, task performance, and reporting on activities (to take some examples). In the first situation, information is needed about economic and societal developments in the company's home country. In the second, facts about the utilization of machines and personnel, the processing of orders, stocks of final products, inventories of raw materials, and so on. The final situation requires an overview of such items as each product's production time, required materials and quality control.

FIS purchase

Dealt with also in chapters 4 and 9, this system involves the following:

Strategic planning:
- Policy choices with regard to purchasing markets
- Policy choices with regard to maintaining inventories
- Policy choices with regard to distribution methods

Tactical planning:
- Determining purchase conditions
- Quota reservations with suppliers
- Determination of inventory control variables
- Determination of degree of service (total percentage of non/negative sales)

Operational management:
- Inventory control of raw materials, components or parts, semi-manufactured products (including packaging), final product (both in total and per location)
- Analysis of turnover, age, decayed and dead stock, corrective measures taken
- Administration of accounts payable, monitoring of prompt payments and allowing discounts
- Administration of accounts receivable, monitoring of credit level, initiation of special collection procedures
- Monitoring of delivery times of purchases and sales

Transactions:
- Purchasing orders and requests
- Purchasing invoices
- Reports
- Receiving and issuing of goods
- Payment to suppliers
- Transactions on futures markets
- Sales orders and calls
- Sending messages and documents
- Final product storage and shipment
- Sales invoices
- Collection of amounts owing from customers

Definition problems may arise in relation to the above contents. For example, FIS production includes calls and production announcements. These are related to several elements in the purchase (or logistic) function, including final product storage and the shipment of goods. In FIS finance and administration, a record of cash/liquidity levels is kept. These levels are related to logistical transactions directly influencing the cash position, namely those involving payments to suppliers and collections from clients.

FIS production

Dealt with also in chapters 4 and 9, this system involves the following:

Strategic planning:

- Long-term capacity prognosis/planning
- Policy choices concerning new production technologies
- New production organizations and product innovation

Tactical planning:

- Utilization planning per production phase
- Choice of suppliers
- Documentation of production process: routing, norms used, tools and machinery employed (recorded according to type, time requirement and standard times in worker hours)
- Determination of production series sizes, completion times, waiting times and levels of intermediate inventories
- Assessment of the effectiveness of manufacturing processes based on analysis of production reports
- Determination of investments required to expand or replace machinery

Operational management:

- Detail planning, work scheduling and dispatching
- Efficiency control: issuing of production reports, analysis of actual uses and involvement of tools and machinery based on norms and budgets

Transactions:

- Production assignments, assembly assignments
- Production reports
- Material requests
- Material consumption reports
- Man and machine hour records
- Waste material reports
- Work-in-progress reports

Manufacturing involves the processing of raw materials, components, materials or semi-manufactured articles in order to produce products or services. When companies have diversified and/or geographically dispersed manufacturing activities, it is also important to include the intercompany traffic in the system. The final product of one production unit then serves as raw material or as semi-manufactured products for another unit within the larger corporate structure.

FIS Marketing and sales

Dealt with also in chapters 4 and 9, this system involves the following:

Strategic planning:

- Sales market developments: geographical dispersal fashion/taste/need/trends
- Price developments
- Company accounts and potential client/customer accounts: composition, purchasing power
- Technology, innovations instigated by competitors

Tactical planning:
- Middle-, long- and short-term market analysis or demand analysis
- Acquisition, sales promotion/stimulation
- Sales and comparable activities: absolute data, comparable figures, ratios, analysis
- Commercial results, market share

Operational management:
- (Categories of) potential clients
- Terms of credit
- Payment and delivery terms
- Price determination or pricing criteria
- Permissible discounts
- Availability or deliverability of products and services: delivery or production terms, reservations, order levels
- Possibilities/norms for maintaining maximum inventory/capacity

Transactions:
- Delivery contracts, production orders or servicing requests
- Standing customer, product and service data
- Data relating to available credit, short-term inventory levels, available storage space, or scheduling time

CASE

Mini case study 10.2

Virtualization versus the cloud

It used to be that something virtual wasn't real. And that clouds were just that – those puffy things in the sky. Today we have the tech industry terms 'virtual computing' and 'cloud computing', which often get mixed up. Fortunately, there's an easy way to tell them apart, and it involves hearkening back to the age-old distinction between hardware and software. When you're talking about virtual computing, you're invariably talking about hardware; specifically, making PC-style hardware available to users in a new way. A new layer of software, typically running in a far-off data center, tricks users into thinking they are using a desktop PC like before.

Cloud computing, by contrast, usually refers to the sorts of software that run once a computer gets turned on. The 'cloud' indicates that the software is hosted in a data center, not sitting on your desktop. If you use Google Docs instead of Microsoft Officer for your word processing or spreadsheets, that's cloud computing. You can mix and match these two approaches, undertaking cloud computing on a non-virtual, traditional PC. And the opposite: you can use traditional, Office-style programs on a virtual PC.

Source: *Forbes*, December 28, 2009, p. 53

FIS Personnel

Dealt with also in chapters 4 and 9, this involves the following:

Strategic planning:
- Information recruiting policy
- Information reward policy
- Information education and training policy (including management development)
- Analysis of developments in employment
- Analysis of the labor market: regional, national and international
- Analysis of external educational and training possibilities
- Analysis of national income policy (including secondary and tertiary work conditions)
- Analysis of personnel file changes
- Assessment of present versus potential personnel file (sorted into capabilities, functions)

Tactical planning:
- Analysis of differences in present planning processes versus budgeted personnel numbers

- Analysis of actual versus budgeted personnel costs
- Analysis of recruitment, education and training costs
- Structure of personnel data files (career planning, capabilities, history of employment, performance appraisal, function description, educational data, personal data)
- Administration of reward systems
- Collective labor contracts
- Administration of education and training programs

Operational management:
- Appointments, discharges, discharge requests, suspensions, change of fees, acknowledgement of special rewards, special relief and advances
- Suitable media for recruiting (print number, reader cycle, kind of advertisement, response to advertisements)
- Recruitment actions
- Personnel costs to be allocated to cost centers, projects, and so on
- Directives to be given for payment of salaries, other personnel payments as well as miscellaneous personnel costs

Transactions:
- Work assignments
- Standing personnel data
- Norms, tables, calculation rules and legal prescriptions
- Decisions relating to appointments, discharges, suspensions and changes
- Absenteeism reports

FIS Finance and Administration
Combined with information given in chapters 4 and 9, this system involves the following:
Strategic planning:
- Long-term prognosis in respect of investment plans, property needs and flows of money (liquidity)
- Long-term indications in respect of tax developments and stimulative, constraining, and subsidizing measures by various governments
- Prognoses in respect of capital and money markets (loan and investment possibilities, interest levels)
- The annual report, i.e. balance sheet, profit and loss statement along with an enclosed explanation of these documents

Tactical planning:
- Financial long-, middle and short-term planning projections and budgets, for the whole as well as parts of the organization
- Norms for evaluating activity levels
- Actually realized activities, performance levels, production figures, and so on
- Fees, cost prices, reserves, distribution rates, taxes, and so on
- Calculation of rates of return, cost/revenue analysis; analysis of differences between estimates, norms and real situations, sorted into periods, causes, and types of difference
- Short-term developments in relation to liquidity, credit arrangements, market interest rates and foreign currency exchange rates

Operational management:
- Short-term planning of financial administrative activities (including closing dates, dates for delivering data to computer centers, holiday schedule)
- Reporting activities in relation to the remaining company functions (utilization reports, core figures)
- Changes in liquidity, foreign currency transactions/ positions
- Age of accounts receivable, formal notices
- Notices of error, delay, disruption and other exceptional financial and administrative circumstances

Transactions:
- Work assignment for execution of non-recurrent activities (e.g. drawing up inventories)
- Coding instructions for financial and administrative transactions involving money
- Work procedures and technical/operating manuals for routine activities and the equipment/software used in them

10.3 Information planning and planning of automation

The introduction of information systems must be accompanied by considerable supervision by management and administration. Despite the large amounts of money which often accompany the development of information systems and information supply, organizations do not always plan the process. Planning is vital since it offers possibilities at an early stage to:
- Signal information needs
- Define projects
- Set priorities
- Determine personnel and organizational consequences

Organizations consist of systems. Computerization can thus be considered a more or less intrusive change in that organization. The greater the extent of the computerization occurring within an organization, the larger the influence on the organization and the people employed there.
Computerization is never an independent process, nor do systems operate in isolation from one another. In view of the interrelatedness of the various systems, computerization must obviously be well planned.

10.3.1 Information planning: objectives and reasons for having them

long-term vision

Information management has to be embedded in an organization's total policy. The technological possibilities on the one hand and the organizational needs and demands on the other have to be finely tuned. This requires organizations to formulate a long-term vision in which clear goals and constraints are taken into account. This activity is called information planning, and has two goals.
1. Adjusting the information supply so that it conforms to organizational needs
2. Establishing consistency in information management practices

In effect, information strategy has to be correlated with reorganization policy and developments in information technology (IT). The resulting information structure forms a stable basis for future developments and serves as a starting-point for planning an information system and the effective use of technology.

information plan

An information plan is derived from the information policy (which constitutes the part of the total organization policy concerned with IT supply). From the information plan the separate automation plans are formulated, that, in turn, consist of different system development projects. In this, planning is the activity and the plan is the product or result.
As such, there is a progression from the general to the specific: from information policy, via information planning, to computer system planning. In establishing a process of information planning and an information plan, it is important to consider the time frame and in any case, to plan for the longer term – perhaps three years. Some issues should also be considered in advance. These include:
- Applications and priorities (based on costs, necessity and logic)
- Involvement of general and functional management
- Organizational changes resulting from execution of the information plan
- Technical relationships (as desired business relationships) with the outside world

10.3.2 The pitfalls of ICT projects

Organizations sometimes find their computer system disappointing. After a considerable outlay of capital the outcomes are not in accordance with original expectations.
The pitfalls of ICT projects are indicated in Fig 10.3. and can be grouped into three categories:

- Those belonging to the managerial structure of projects
- Those occurring in the start-up and planning phases
- Those arising during the execution of projects

In theory, all pitfalls are avoidable. Management, programmers and users can all recommend ways of avoiding them or rectifying the faults.

Figure 10.3
Pitfalls and failures in automation at the fault line of expectations and outcomes

Expectations	Outcomes
Working more efficiently	Exceeding of planning and budget
Operating more flexibly	Unsatisfied users
Quality improvement	Bad acceptance
Better management information	Unintended side-effects
Better work circumstances	Premature termination
Faster communication	Worsened working climate
Competitive advantage	

The pitfalls that management should avoid

Even though every organization that is computerized claims to have a team in charge of the project, it is often unclear who is responsible and accountable. One consequence of this lack of clarity is a conflicting project management structure with no definite lines of authority. Procedural disagreements may arise and the quality of the intended final product is placed in jeopardy.
Often the programmer is more familiar with his own specialization than with the organization and often strives for the perfect system rather than one that best serves the goals of the user. The technical orientation of system developers can hinder effective communication with users and management, with the limited insight of users into the possibilities and especially the limitations of the computer contributing to an ever expanding communication gap between the parties. Because many managers follow projects at a distance, technical arguments are convincing and if organizational and company aspects remain underexposed, the rest of the organization will not understand the outcome or not see where it fits into the picture. If management takes such a high-handed attitude, the result may well be that the system's users are discouraged. Skimping on the composition of project teams may mean that the computerization, the goal of which is to design a new way of working, will be implemented by programmers, a state of affairs guaranteed to lead to problems.

limited insight of users

resistance

There is always some resistance to any change being made to tried and true working routines. When there is insufficient information about the goals and consequences of the project, such resistance increases. Ineffective use and lack of motivation in learning to handle and use a new system can be the result. Consequently, the success of a project depends on:

- A clear task definition and definition of responsibility
- The involvement of management in drawing up the plan
- Employee representation and clear goal formulation by management

Pitfalls and failures in the start-up and planning phase of projects

First of all one has to accept the fact that total commitment of all involved is probably a utopian dream. Not everyone has the same interests. Furthermore, many projects are initiated from a technological or telematic point of view without a thorough analysis having previously taken place. Automation processes are complex and frequently confused by a tendency to run blindly after the newest technological developments.

The pitfalls to avoid

An unsatisfactory result can also be related to an incorrect working procedure, development philosophy or project method (see also 5.3.8 and 9.5).

- Computerization may be seen as a technological solution to a business problem. *insufficient input* Insufficient input by managers and employees to the system development project will result in insufficient or unsuitable functionality: 'the computer does not do what we say.'
- *striving for complete computerization* Striving for complete computerization without a correct cost/revenue assessment will lead to a situation in which every exceptional situation has to be included, as a result of which the system will become untenable.
- *particular situation* The organization has not consciously chosen a system to suit its particular situation. Instead, methods recommended by external consulting firms have been adopted without any questions being asked. Because of this, the information supply within the organization is never specific to any of its individual processed. It only represents a pre-determined standard as dictated by the system.
- In the development of an automated information system, emphasis has been placed on the *functionality of the system* functionality of the system with little attention paid to its consequences for the quality of work done by employees, the definition of tasks and duties or the structure of organizational units and departments.

CASE

Mini case study 10.3

In the 1970s and 80s, the goal of insurer computerization was modification of existing ways of work. They remained unchanged. Transformation and BPR became magic words. A large number of insurance companies have restructured their primary processes with the help of BPR (= Business Process Redesign).

10.4 Information and communication technology (ICT)

ICT The main benefit of ICT lies in its ability to link the various activities of an organization. ICT greatly influences information planning and other activities in such companies and institutions as banks and insurance firms. Applications are especially prevalent in the financial services sector for the following reasons:

- Many activities in the financial services lend themselves very well to computerization because many processes are routine and standardized.
- A considerable amount of the traditional paper work can be replaced by automated input and electronically stored data.
- Many processes are comprised of a large number of sequential activities that are sufficiently complex to justify the help of computers (e.g. credit granting process, risk assessment process, etc.).
- Compared to past manual or even mechanical procedures, the use of computers makes a difference in terms of time and energy.
- Because of the positive 'time effect' and the reduction in the number of mistakes, ICT meets the standards and criteria of cost/revenue analysis. Such is especially the case for the youngest generation of computers and information systems. They can be brought into action swiftly and are more decentralized and flexible than their predecessors.

MAKING MONEY WITH SMARTPHONES

Apple has ridden the iPhone to 14% of the smartphone market in three years. The 125,000 apps iPhone users can download bolster the popularity of Apple devices and give it influence over how people use their phones. iPhone users can fire up the *New York Times* app for news or Yelp for local restaurants. Apple aims to break into the mobile advertising business Google has been eyeing by creating new ways to advertise within apps on the iPhone and other Apple devices.

Source: *Bloomberg Business Week*, January 25, 2010, p. 30

10.4.1 The strategic importance of ICT

ICT strategy

By ICT strategy we mean strategic/tactical decisions relating to all ICT applications in either an office or factory and relating to the final product as well as the provision of external services. Information technology provides three main types of strategic benefits:

- Cost control
- Service improvement
- Product innovation

All in all, the result is higher productivity. A low cost price is an important factor in establishing, maintaining or improving a competitive position. It can improve work efficiency so that processes move faster and fewer mistakes are made. This in turn results in lower costs, and consequently, a greater market share. Improved quality of products and services along with increased productivity contribute added value, enhance organizational achievements and allow employees to remain in contact with the outside world.
ICT helps organizations to develop progressive products and distribution methods. Customers have specific needs, and these may not always be met by the existing products or service due to cost considerations. Use of ICT can effect a change in the situation by facilitating the development of more suitable articles and services.

Influence of computerization on competitive relationships
Computerization will affect commercial relationships and the organization's competitive position on three different levels: the sector level, the organizational level and the strategic level. Research has indicated that changes at the sector level are crucial: computerization changes the rules relating to economies of scale, entrance barriers, competition and competitive relationships. It makes it possible for larger organizations to do such things as shifting their distribution from regional to national and even international levels.

economies of scale

CASE

Mini case study 10.4

Leadership in the information age

Information will be the greatest opportunity for business leaders in the coming years – and perhaps our biggest headache. Since the dawn of the Internet, all of us in business have been swept up by the Niagara of information that fills our daily life. Real-time updates from the Hang Seng index, online earnings calls, photos shared around the world seconds after they've been taken, customized maps and directions delivered to you even as you drive. It's all breathtaking.

But for leaders in business, the information surge has triggered its own unintended consequences, especially for those of us over 40. Today, new employees arrive on their first day with an alarming amount of know-it-all.

They have already read about you, and the online critiques of your plans, strategies and management style. The bloggers and the tweeters – all receiving steady streams of in-house gossip – analyze, assess and ridicule every business moment. At some companies, insider information can barely be said to exist.

In this environment, traditional management is impossible, or at least ill-advised. The hierarchical, layered corporate structures in which company information was carefully managed and then selectively passed down the line have crumbled. The online era has made command-and-control management as dead as dial-up Internet.

As someone who came up through the ranks of the often hidebound and highly deferential corporate world, I am glad to say good riddance to much of the old office culture. But as chief executive of a dynamic information business, I also see how debilitating the stream of news and reaction can be for an organization if mishandled. Public companies in particular are so besieged by 24-hour commentary and instant opinion that many managers find themselves paralyzed.

That's why the greatest mandate for leadership in business is the ability to cut through the information clutter and make clear decisions without apology. More than at any time, employees need – in fact, desperately want – unequivocal direction.

Although decision-making has always been the task of a leader, it has become harder. The online world has guaranteed that every remark about your business and every change you implement will trigger a viral frenzy of second-guessing. Borrowing from the black bag of politics, your competitors will also be spreading their own version of 'opposition research', feeding the blogosphere with critiques of your leadership.

Learn to live with it. Leaders should not only grow a thicker skin but also understand how important they can be to their own team by interpreting both the news and the disinformation that swirls around them.

Whenever I speak to an audience, internal or external, I am struck by how many people want to know my reaction to some recent press story or the latest legislative debate. They want someone to tell them what it all means. These are wonderful opportunities for leadership. Employees, investors, customers and business partners are heartened by executives who can sift through the avalanche of opinion and clearly communicate what matters – and what doesn't – to the enterprise.

Of course, communication cannot be a one-way street. The central role of information in business life has made two other much neglected leadership tasks more urgent.

The first is listening. It is a hoary cliché of management schools that a good boss knows how to listen. But this shouldn't be merely an exercise in empathy. Listening to your employees at every level is one of the best paths to new insights. Precisely because the Internet has made information so plentiful, your own team is likely to be full of ideas that should be tapped into. A leader who is sequestered in a corner office is missing out on the rich discussions babbling a few floors below.

The second obligation that information creates for executives is to identify and mentor thought leaders. In the past, seeking out 'high potential' employees typically meant looking for those who could climb the next rung of the management ladder. That remains important. But equally pressing is finding those employees who, though perhaps not the best managers, have the ability to digest and interpret information for others. Grooming these in-house ideas people helps foster a culture of openness to fresh thinking – the greatest energy an organization can have.

The deluge of information is only going to rise. Leadership will increasingly mean leveraging that information, clarifying it, and using it to advance your strategy, engage customers and motivate employees. Business stakeholders are interested not only in your products and services, but also in your ideas.

So, welcome the information flood. Those who learn how to keep their head above it will be the most effective leaders.

Source: C. Bartz (2010), 'The world in 2010', *The Economist*, p. 119

At the organizational level, there are many examples of the benefits provided by information technology: automated strategic purchase and supplier information offers numerous advantages, as do computer aided manufacturing and robot techniques. Insurance firms are particularly dependent on their degree of computerization.
At the strategic level, it can be shown that the most successful organizations have information systems which strongly support the strategy of the organization.

A frequently repeated opinion is, however, that the influences of automation and of new technologies have up to now been relatively slight because top management has not really embraced these new techniques. Reasons for this reticence vary: from lack of understanding to fear of the implications and the subsequent risks which may emerge.

WHAT PREVENTS IT FROM BEING SUCCESSFUL?

1 *Too many priorities*
There are too many items on the 'must have' list and there are inadequate arrangements relating to what takes priority, giving rise to conflict.

2 *Not enough coordination between departments*
An age-old problem. New technologies require optimal coordination between the IT department and the business. There is always room for improvement.

3 *The business has an inadequate overview of the consequences of the choices that it makes*
Strategic IT choices may have far-reaching effects. According to many CEOs, managers rarely realize the negative effects that decisions that are made now can have in the long term.

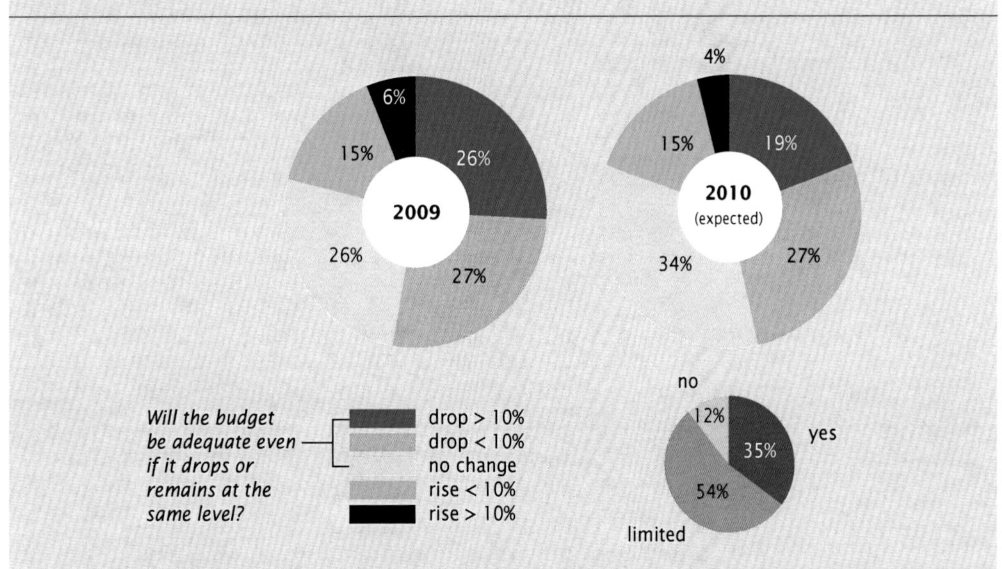

The changing IT budget

Source: *Scope*, no. 12/2009

ERP An increasing number of software manufacturers are now focussing on producing smaller ERP packages for small businesses. For many small businesses, the transition from separate software for individual business processes (administration, production, stock management, customer relations mangement and HRM) to an ERP system that integrates all these systems is a major step.

SaaS SaaS – software as a service – is another development that makes complex software accessible for small businesses or new entrepreneurs. SaaS ('computing in the cloud') is accessed via the Internet and the user pays in the form of a subscription. Cloud computing however requires extra measurements concerning safety of data, privacy aspects and availability of data.

In 2003, Nicholas Carr stirred things up in the ICT world with his controversial article 'IT doesn't matter'. Just like earlier technological innovations (electricity, railways and so on), information technology is rapidly becoming a mass commodity. It is becoming an infrastructural technology that is hardly producing any competitive advantage. It is more a necessity than an advantage and as such, has to be managed primarily in terms of costs and risks. It is better to be a follower than a leader. The tide seemed to turn (again) in 2005. It is not as if ICT is no longer relevant, though. Seen from a strategic and organizational point of view, ICT's consequences for companies are far reaching: to mention just some of them, offshoring and contracting out of ICT to low-wage countries along with the effect that this has on labor organizations both in the home country and in the country to which operational and developmental activities have been transferred (ABN Amro, IBM, Siemens and ING in India). Whether offshoring of IT will end up cheaper in the long run and will remain that way is something only the future will tell. For the moment, considerable savings are being reported.

offshoring

contracting out of ICT

In addition, the necessity of designing better ICT systems is becoming even more pressing. The current (2005) complexity of many ICT systems makes organizations highly vulnerable (take the Dutch railway breakdowns, for example). ICT systems are being linked within business sectors of all types without any definite arrangements to this effect having been made. This is having quite an impact on virtually every aspect of our day-to-day lives: on production, logistics, the retail industry, money, entertainment, health care, education, transport, and the supply of gas, water, electricity and culture.

Despite this, only 30% of CIOs (Chief Information Officers) in the field of business are of the opinion that ITC will have much effect on the organization.

WHAT DEVELOPMENTS ARE ATTRACTING ATTENTION?

1 *New ways of working*

Working from home, making use of new forms of software to communicate with each other and supporting mobile devices are high on the agenda. The emphasis lies on increasing worker productivity.

2 *Client interaction*

In the current economic climate, clients need as much help as they can get. The Internet can provide a lot of assistance. Interactive client systems used in conjunction with systems such as customer relations management are still in their infancy and have to be made more effective in the years to come.

3 *New forms of infrastructure*

Current internal IT infrastructure systems are often very costly. IT organizations are investigating technologies such as virtualization and *cloud computing* with a view to reducing the cost and at the same time enhancing the efficiency of their own IT environments.

Source: *Scope*, no. 12/2009

10.4.2 *ICT, business processes and redesign*

process design

To an ever increasing degree, companies and institutions are trying to structure their work processes as efficiently as possible. The resulting advantages can only be realized when new processes, organizational forms and ICT are combined. Process design is specifically concerned with quality, flexibility and cost level. Organizational concerns are focused on efforts to balance the control structure, culture and expertise. The introduction of information technology affects all other technologies used within the organization, and raises issues concerning applications, user level and ICT management.

CASE

Mini case study 10.5

The credit granting process demonstrates what process redesign can do.
Credit granting involves many degrees of risk, ranging from those incurred when making small private loans to those incurred when the debtor is a large corporation. Often the structure of the system for processing the various credit forms is the same. Making distinctions could, however, yield substantial savings, as simple credit should be structured in a simple manner. Banks consistently able to make this distinction and simplify relevant procedures reduce the costs and time required for processing by 50%. IT makes such reductions possible.
Insurance companies constitute another good example. Traditionally, policies were processed according to sequentially-linked company procedures undertaken in functionally separate departments. The policies were sold by agents, and then processed by using technically and functionally antiquated systems. The consequences were:

- Higher costs passed on to customers as higher premiums
- Longer completion times experienced as poor service
- More mistakes, also experienced as poor service

After computerization, 90% of customer contacts are handled directly by one person, As a result, the number of mistakes is reduced and completion time shortened. Routine tasks are completely computerized. The result is fewer mistakes and higher volumes of work.
The information technology that makes the above improvements possible consists of a system for reading policy and damage claim data and making this data available to employees on demand. Employees participate in teams that perform all the tasks that involve particular clients. The better the automated support, the greater the variety of the tasks performed by employees.

10.4.3 The organizational consequences of ICT

IT has various consequences for organizations. In the strategic planning and personnel management, rapid development of ICT processes is especially noteworthy. Insofar as these activities are concerned, there are three major consequences involving:

1 Further customer orientation and direction
2 De-layering
3 Decentralization

customer in mind

More sophisticated consumers, tougher competition and technological advancements mean that companies and institutions are having to provide external access to their information systems. The internal systems must increasingly be structured with the customer in mind and the network geared primarily to the provision of improved communication with the outside world. The direct customer-oriented function is becoming increasingly more important.

organizational level to disappear

Computer networks have an intrinsic influence on employee relationships and the assignment of work and tasks within an organization. Practical experience has revealed that the introduction of automated networks causes an organizational level to disappear. The disappearing level can be one involving inventories, warehouses, middle management or a link in the distribution chain. Through the network, an intermediary can have direct access to customers and products and, with the help of a network, customers can be directly contacted and the old intervening links made superfluous.
There is a noticeable influence of highly developed ICT on the degree of decentralization. On the one hand, ICT enables the organization to make good, current information available to the employees at lower levels. Accordingly, those employees are better able to make decisions, as a result of which their relative autonomy is enlarged.
It is now possible to disperse employees geographically by supplying them with terminals in branch offices and allowing them to make all necessary computations at such locations. This is in line with the 'profit center' approach. Decentralization within the main office is also possible. Computers in departments are connected to a central network, so that users have a high degree of autonomy provided they adhere to the centrally established procedures.
On the other hand, ICT also enables the organization to report back to higher levels,

sometimes almost in 'real time,' on what is happening at lower levels and to inform upper management of current developments. As a consequence, the decentralized authorities are theoretically able to protect their interests and maintain control.

10.4.4 Value chain mapping and supply chain management

Under the influence of technological developments in the information and communication technology (ICT) and as demonstrated by several trends in the competitive environment, international and otherwise a new light is cast on the classic concepts of managing a stream of resources by means of the links in an industrial column. Globalization and the new ICT capabilities are resulting in a world-wide reallocation of commercial interest and opening, as one of their consequences, new purchasing markets. New entrepreneurial concepts (see sections 2.4.7 and 5.7) are allowing competitive partnership relationships with suppliers and the formation of integrated supply networks in the industrial and retail sectors. Transactions are increasingly being processed through EDI (Electronic Data Interchange) and/or via the Internet, so that companies which do not engage in such activities are being left behind. Coupled with developments in the marketing function involving databases and other new media or techniques aimed at customers, these market innovations are providing alternatives to traditional management practices and enabling a focus on added value. Suppliers are increasingly involved with customer-focused product innovations. Active supplier management is essential. Some notions of integrated service, including 'servicing the products,' have become essential.

partnership relationships
supply networks
EDI
supplier management
servicing the products

In the modern (and recent) way of doing business, customer-focused or demand-directed working procedures are increasing in importance. The new ICT capabilities allow a pull model to be instituted (for further information, see Section 10.5.6). This approach involves a form of chain turnover by which the customer effectively co-produces the desired product, with input that penetrates – sometimes deeply – into the organizational processes of the supplier. Purchasers and purchasing departments have an increasing interest in outsourcing and chain management (or supply chain management) and, concurrently, in value chain mapping. By undertaking such these activities, purchasing acquires a strategic perspective in relation to business resource management – functional changes that are especially prevalent in the fast-food and the automobile industries. The consequences of this innovation affect the ways in which suppliers administer their sales and introduce marketing methods, direct or otherwise. Tailor-made work and customer focus play a central role. The requirement that the complex flow of goods and the relevant organizational functions add value to the chain is stronger than ever.

pull model
chain turnover

Popular software (in chain management) is Customer Relations Management (CRM), Supply Chain Management (SCM) and especially e-commerce. This new software is provided by traditional ERP-suppliers, such as My SAP.com. My SAP.com is a virtual marketplace to which different companies active in the same field can log on and gain direct access to potential customers and potential suppliers. CRM only provides information about customers.

CRM

E-commerce, especially B2B (business-to-business), makes it possible to place orders via the web, maintain inventories and production capacity, and fill the order. Philips has its Philips Purchasing Excellence (PPE) Framework web site, which provides an integrated system of purchasing and supply market management.

E-commerce
B2B

10.4.5 RFID standards and tags

RFID (Radio Frequency Identification) is a technology that allows people and goods to be tracked and recognized (identified) without there being a need for physical or direct contact (as there still is with a magnetic strip or a barcode). It is an automatic recognition process that will be able to be applied in many areas, from the simple registration of the presence (or

RFID
automatic recognition process

passage) of a coded item or person to the registration of the presence of a certain sea container or a valuable work of art among many hundreds of other ones. In addition it will be able to register the temperature in that particular container or area as well as its relative humidity.
This can be expected to not only have a considerable effect in the area of logistical services, but also in transport or people tracking systems such as libraries, hospitals, packaging and transport, animal recognition, entry checks and so on.

RFID can provide the following:
- time savings in the handling of materials (faster, fewer mistakes)
- the ability to identify a variety of data at a distance (up to 350 meters), including uniquely coded items, temperature and movement
- the ability to identify items that are in a rapidly moving state (speeds of between 10 km/hour or more, up to about 200 km/hour)
- the absence of label and other press coding systems (and of labels, printer carbon and so on)
- increased efficiency in registration and consequently of processing.

RFID chips
tracking and tracing

In the meantime, RFID is booming. Chains such as Wal-Mart, Tesco but also Albert Heijn have lately been encouraging their suppliers to make more use of tags (instead of bar codes). Data can be sent to a sender via RFID chips. The chip may be on a pallet or a transport box, but also in a book, on a work of art, in a telephone or on a person or an animal, and so on. 'Tracking and tracing' may also mean that with a chain-based approach, an increasing number of marketing and sales processes will be organized on the basis of specific client needs and preferences.

To take an example: the bookselling group Selexyz provides every book with a RFID tag. This streamlines the purchasing process and makes it more controllable, and enables it to tell shop customers exactly where they can find the book they want or what the alternatives are.

shift in power
infrastructure reviewed

A reverse supply chain approach which shifts the focus to the end user (as the final link in the chain) will exert a pull on the supply chain and put an end to bottlenecking. The pull will come from the final link. The client will stipulate what product information he/she wants and when and how goods will be delivered. Wal-Mart, to take an example, is stipulating how it wants its deliveries to be made: containers, pallets and boxes must be supplied with a chip. This shift in power from the manufacturer to the retailer and consumer means that the role played by the various links and their relative importance has to be reassessed, the infrastructure reviewed and the technological possibilities redefined. Consequently, supply chain management must also start with the final link. Technology is causing a change in how things are directed and what skills are involved. RFID provides many opportunities and generates a lot of data. But to really make full use of what it has to provide requires an integrated approach.

CRM

This also applies to CRM (Customer Relationship Management) systems. These can also enhance an organization's external orientation. To optimize added value requires adaptation on the part of the organization, different work methods and in particular, the imbedding of new technology within a new culture of organization and collaboration. The leaders of the 'high performance' organizations of the future will realize that the initiative lies with the customer: they will instigate business activities rather than merely be there at the end (see 1.5.3). The processes and structures will have to take their cue from them as they take shape, and the other functions and activities along the value chain will have to adapt to them.

10.4.6 The Internet and sourcing

It is expected that the Internet will play a particularly prominent role in sourcing. Recently Unilever announced that it would work with software producer Ariba to organize its purchases via the Internet. The new system is supposed to result in a cost reduction of several hundreds of millions of dollars in the United States alone.
The system will resemble similar ones announced by other large multinationals and consist of a central point where thousands of suppliers can provide their merchandise.
Shell has teamed up with the software producer Commerce One to provide a platform which Shell has invited other energy companies to join. The joint purchase platform for such automobile producers as General Motors, Ford and Daimler Chrysler has attracted the most attention. Early in 2002, Ford, Daimler Chrysler and General Motors introduced their joint e-marketplace initiative through which they intend to shorten the development time for new cars from 24 to 17 months. E-procurement, which is sourcing through the Internet, requires the streamlining of operational processes within the organization, a procedure facilitated by ERP software from SAP, Baan and Oracle. Given a product specification, the cheapest or fastest deliveries will automatically be chosen. Dynamic pricing and collaboration in, for example, the development of a new car is then made possible. These innovations have taken place in the years since 2004.

10.4.7 The Internet and marketing and sales

The early years of e-commerce were not characterized by en-masse purchasing via the Internet. The local shop was too much of an institution for that, and moreover, there was uncertainty about how those unknown Internet suppliers were going to supply the goods and how you would pay for them. Then you had to wait for them to be supplied. Nevertheless, Internet-based sales have grown steadily.

Web-based shops

Despite the economic recession, the big Web-based shops had their biggest turnover ever in 2009. Not even including the Christmas period, Amazon.com sold 6.3 million articles, more than it had ever sold. For Bol.com, 2009 was a record year. Coolblue, the owner of laptopshop.nl and smartphoneshop.nl had by Christmas 2009 recorded a 48% increase in sales, with a peak of 50% being recorded in early December. An increasing number of online shops are, however, finding it profitable to have a physical sales channel in addition to their Internet channels.

WEB SHOPS: OFFLINE IS BACK

- In addition to its shops in the US, England and Japan, Dell will open 50 shops in China this year.
- Coolblue (of pdashop.nl fame) will open 7 flesh-and-blood shops

Source: *Het Financieele Dagblad*, 7 August 2008

Web 2.0 technology

Dutch consumers are also making increasing use of the Internet. Research has shown that they are not the only early adopters. In the years from 2010, Internet shopping will increasingly become common in the household area, partly because fast broadband connections (via the cable or ADSL) and Web 2.0 technology (see also 10.7.1) are making Internet shopping easier. Ford has started to sell its cars via e-mail and text messaging, and is using them to get its large-scale marketing campaigns underway. The target group is people in the 25 to 39 age bracket.
Nowadays, according to Thuiswinkel Markt Monitor (a home shopping market monitor) in an average week, a quarter of those in the 65 plus age bracket are online.

Technology has already determined the behavioral patterns of the young. In ten years time they will form the main social group in terms of purchasing power and in all likelihood they will still be exhibiting technology-driven behavioral patterns.
We have come to expect the information we want to be available to us when and where we want it. Not only this, but we expect nowadays to be able to track things down and to be tracked down. RFID, smart postering and smart messaging are only some of the tools used.

RFID

HOW AMAZON KEEPS THE GOODS FLOWING FOR CHRISTMAS

There is order in the chaos at the online retailer's warehouses.

Amazon, the leading online retailer, faces a dilemma of how to arrange the stock in its giant warehouses. The company, which started out as an online retailer of books and then CDs, now provides products as diverse as shoes, cosmetics and vacuum cleaners.

Amazon's arrangement of its goods – which must be hand-picked ahead of sorting for particular orders and dispatch – looks so random as to border on chaos.

At one of the company's UK distribution centres, north of London near Milton Keynes, millions of goods are stored on shelving systems that dominate a site the size of eight football pitches.

Allan Lyall, Amazon's vice-president of European operations, insists there is cold commercial logic lurking in this apparent chaos.

Hand-held computers help guide hundreds of picking-staff along kilometres of shelving to the location of ordered goods. Popular-selling items are strategically placed in several locations rather than at just one point. This geographical spreading of hit items such as Dan Brown's *The Lost Symbol*, DVDs of the film 'Mamma Mia' and CDs by Canadian crooner Michael Bublé across the 550,000 sq ft, multi-storey site helps picking-staff to minimise the distance and time spent walking to fulfil several orders simultaneously.

This structure is crucial to enabling Amazon to deliver goods, sometimes on the same day that they are ordered, for some UK postcodes.

While this stage of Amazon's order fulfilment is labour-intensive, once goods are sorted for parcelling, automation and scanning technology largely take over from the human hand.

At its peak last year, Amazon's UK operations dispatched 1m items on one day. Orders peaked at 1.4m items on Monday, December 8. Amazon expects another 'cyber Monday' peak this December.

Amazon is working to solve a perennial stumbling block for some potential customers who cannot be at home or work to receive large items that cannot be delivered through a letterbox.

In France, for example, it has teamed up with Kiala, which operates 'Point Relais' or collection points at a network of grocers, dry-cleaners and newsagents, which are open most hours.

In Germany, customers can use Packstation, a service run by DHL, which operates automated booths for letter and package collection at busy locations such as railway stations.

The expanding service is particularly popular with busy professionals for whom time is as valuable as it is to Amazon.

Source: *Financial Times*, December 2009; *Het Financieele Dagblad*, 23 December 2009

10.4.8 ICT and changes in industries: intermediation and disintermediation

new intermediaries

ICT applications via the Internet and call centers allow suppliers to conduct business directly with the consumers and to bypass the existing intermediaries such as Internet travel agencies, Internet stock equity trade, an Internet toy shop (e Toys) and new Internet insurers. New intermediaries are arising and at least partly eliminating the 'old' parties. This means the disappearance of the information-providing function of such organizations as travel agencies or insurance agents as we knew them.
To overcome this gap, new parties are introducing themselves via the Internet. The process of intermediation and disintermediation involves situations in which the intermediaries – as a link in the value chain – are cast in a new role, bypassed or even eliminated. With the Internet, intermediaries must transform or disappear (think of insurance brokers).

infomediary
aggregator

New parties then move in to occupy the new position of infomediary (or navigator) and/ or the role of aggregator (compare the role of the wholesale trader and the retailer in terms of collecting and distributing in the traditional vertical industrial columns). Infomediaries are new intervening parties who serve a purely information-providing or advice-giving function. They inform, make the market transparent and provide help with searching and selecting. They are in a way sign posts (or navigators), and include Internet search engines such as Yahoo! and theme focused portals such as Web MD (for doctors, consumers and care insurers in the US). Besides information and advice, aggregators can also take care of matching. They aggregate parties on the demand and/or supply side and thereby bring together demand and supply. This can occur by linking parties with a similar purchase or sale request for a joint action in the market. It can imply agreements between contractors and/or negotiations with contracting parties on behalf of a group or an individual. In the B2B (business-to-business) market the appearance of vertical purchase portals is a good example. On such sites we find competitors cooperating to develop market power. Well-known examples of aggregators in the B2C (business-to-consumer) market are 'communities' like Garden (for the flower and garden lovers), Seniornet (for those above 50) and Home Warehouse (for the do-it-yourself market).

market power
communities

10.5 Functional processes and process control

The basic principles and elements of process control described earlier are also applicable to each of the mutually interrelating functional organizational processes identified in Fig 1.10. We will now discuss these processes briefly.

10.5.1 Manufacturing and production

Technical production and knowledge-intensive transformative processes are involved in the manufacture of products or the provision of services of a specified nature and quantity and within the time available. A manufacturing process is a composite set of procedures that is dependent on the kind of product or service provideed. In this regard, it makes sense to identify a manufacturing process by relating it to its product. Accordingly, manufacturing processes and their resulting products and services can be identified in the following ways:

manufacturing processes

- Raw materials and semi-fabricated products are the products of continuous mass production processes (e.g. petroleum, paper, steel, gas, water, electricity)
- Simple products or services are produced in series mass or series piece production (e.g. bottles, plastics, nails)
- Composed/complex products result from processes varying from simple to complex series piece or series mass production (e.g. bicycles, dresses, cassette players, cars, locomotives, computers)
- One-off (large) items are manufactured in a piece production process on a project-by-project basis (e.g. an office building, city expansion plan, oil tanker)

Technical transformation in development and manufacturing processes

The activities involved in the manufacturing process include work scheduling, production planning, the actual manufacturing and the maintenance of machines. The design and development of new products are also a part of the organization's technical function. Manufacturing cannot, of course, be seen in isolation from other functions. Good coordination of all processes is required to achieve the desired end results. Market research (a task of the commercial department) detects, for example, how many units of a product can be sold, and stipulates the characteristics that the product should have. These features include the function of a product, the design, the packaging and so on. They all have to be built into the product by the design and the development department. The task requires the formulation of a certain product design which, via a production development plan, is then translated into a series of assembly instructions, work drawings, manufacturing and assembly manuals and other elements required for production.

new products

In large, middle-sized and small companies, the design and development phase of a product often involves the use of Computer Aided Design (CAD) to assist design activities in such fields as mechanical engineering, architecture, aircraft design, shipbuilding, electrotechnology, electronics, road construction, hydraulic engineering, and even in the designing of new crates and bottles.

CAD

A CAD-related application is Computer Aided Manufacturing (CAM), which uses data about an item to be manufactured already generated with the help of CAD technologies in order to manufacture programs for the machine tools required in the production of the item. The automated system both saves time and, theoretically, at least, (if the assumption that 'the computer never makes mistakes' can be maintained), ensures an accurate execution of the processing instructions.

CAM

Another phase of product development might involve the construction of a pilot model and prototypes to examine the best ways in which the products can be mass produced over time. In addition to product design, attention will also have to be paid to product monitoring. Signals from clients about possible uses for the products, shortcomings, complaints and so on will have to be analyzed and converted into proposals for product improvement.

To control costs and time factors, progress control and cost reviewing have to be conducted during the product development phase. Based on intermediate reports, adjustments can be made and a decision made about the continuation of a project. Additional finances may need to be made available.

The financial consequences that a new product will have on the profitability of the organization will also need to be examined. What investments should be made for production on a large scale? How will the profit potential develop over time? What price can be asked for the new product? As soon as the product appears to be commercially viable, it will be made part of the regular assortment. Once the composition of the product has been finalized, the components and materials can be acquired by the purchasing department. The manufacturing department will then have to determine the production method and the layout of the machinery.

It will also have to plan and manage the production process in such a way that the various products can be delivered in the desired composition and variety. In consultation with the sales department, estimates of the amounts and delivery times for the products to be manufactured have to be made. During the actual production, various forms of process control can be implemented.

CASE Mini case study 10.6

An example of a partial system is a pair of electronic scales, linked to a micro- or minicomputer. With the help of the computer, the weighing of goods is controlled and checked, weight lists are printed, the weights are stored in a file for further processing, etc. A numerically controlled lathe or milling machine is another example, the so-called NC equipment.
The management of a complete animal feed factory, staffed by four or five people and a computer, is an example of an integrated system. The computer sees to packaging, unit weight, failure signaling, and so on, and is integrated into the administrative data processing system.
In the process, system orders are received from the registration system. There orders form the basis for manufacturing. After shipment or the final product in bulk wagons, the actual delivery data (especially the weights) are sent to the 'financial computer,' where the invoicing occurs.

---

process control

Process control is essential within not only the system as a whole, but also within each individual system. If performed properly, this can enable the manufacturing process to be related to the:
- Purchasing process and inventory process
- Sales process and inventory process
- Product design and development process
- Financial process, especially in relation to costs and investment planning

It goes without saying that the manufacturing process is a composite one. A detailed examination will show that it consists of a number of partial processes involving such activities as work scheduling and quality control.

The components of the manufacturing process

During the manufacturing process, the organizational goal formulated in response to the question of what products the organization wants to make is translated into a production method. The production method determines the manner in which production can take place. During the actual production, it is important to monitor the costs of the production activities. It is also necessary to verify the planning projections for the quantities to be delivered, the quality standards obtained, along with the cost and time requirements. As soon as a deviation is detected, action has to be taken to adjust the process or rectify it.

Decisions in the production department

The manager of a production department will be responsible for:
- Effective technical structuring and staffing of work stations
- Efficient production, which consists of proper and accurate execution of orders in compliance with quality, time and cost requirements

Decisions which have to be taken concern:
- Acceptance of production orders and setting of delivery times
- Work scheduling and distribution of work to people and machines
- Ordering, storage, transportation of raw materials, secondary materials and final products and the control of intermediate and final inventories
- Determination of the most effective way of handling the product
- Calculation (before and afterwards) of costs and time
- Quality control
- Maintenance of machines

Determining the optimal production program

optimal production

Determining the optimal production and sales program not only depends on available capacity, but also on the possibilities for and the costs of modifying such production resources as machinery, work-station lines, or operational employees. In a changeover from one product to another, certain modifications are always necessary, and this usually takes time. Machines

not only have to be cleaned, but also reprogrammed or adjusted, and production lines may even have to be rebuilt.
At the beginning of a new production series, switching over, adjusting things and so on can cause considerable loss of material and time. The ensuing costs must be included in the calculations required to establish the best production program. If resources have to be reassigned to the temporary production of a different product, sales of the product for which production has been halted must nevertheless continue. To this end, a certain amount of inventory must be accumulated. Inventory overheads (warehouse space, interest on the inventory and so on) have to be included in any calculation of production costs, and they must also include the costs of holding an extra inventory (as safety stock) in order to prevent 'negative sales' or to prevent the need for a small production series. Sales should always be able to continue.

optimal production program

In determining the optimal production program, consideration must be given to the relationships between series size, adjustment and switching costs, and inventory costs. In a manufacturing company, it is the task of the production manager to monitor these relationships. The requirements for efficient production and prevention of negative sales govern this monitoring activity. In striving for the lowest possible costs, sales of products (from inventory) should be able to continue even when production has been interrupted. Sales, production and inventory should therefore all be planned in a coordinated manner.

The steps involved in process activities

process activities

The mapping out of process activities comprises a number of steps.

- Process analysis: the production process is divided into a number of basic elements. In a manufacturing context, these include:
  - Components, raw materials and materials from which a product is manufactured
  - The necessary operations
  - The final product
- Analysis of operations: operations are broken down into components of the process: for example, sawing, painting, storing
- Analysis of actions: actions are further subdivided into elementary movements: for example 'Pick up component 3 with the right hand.' 'Place the component in the machine'

control of the production process

In the management and control of the production process, various management techniques are employed to prepare, plan and adjust these activities in a systematic and effective manner. These include:

- Labor studies: time and motion studies, method and action studies
- Planning techniques
- Quality control
- Internal reports, monitoring and signaling. Determination of production methods

Lay-out and routing: mapping out the production process

In order to find the most favorable method of production, it is advisable that the entire production process be first mapped out (See sections 6.2 and 6.3 for the so-called linear, functional, and group-like structures). The purpose of this exercise is to give a handy overview of the structures involved in the process.

lay-out
routing

The lay-out (= spatial planning) and routing (= pathway or route determination) are meant to arrange productive resources and inventory (including components and semi-fabricated products) in such a way that:

- Production resources are easy to use in executing processes
- Cleaning, repair and maintenance can take place
- Arrival and conveyance routes are short, wide and straight, so that internal transportation is facilitated
- No unnecessary walking back and forth is required, and no unnecessary transporting is involved
- Inventories are within reach of processing locations
- As short a waiting time as possible occurs

Similar strategies are used in trading companies, but they are especially concerned with warehouse lay-out. Furthermore, these basic principles can also be adapted to the lay-out of offices, repair work stations, etc.
To determine lay-out and routing, a map should be drawn of the room on which the following items should be indicated: the position of machinery, means of transportation, intermediate storage and warehousing areas. In this fashion, one can examine whether the chosen lay-out allows for the most efficient production route. If such proves not to be the case, a more favorable lay-out must be chosen.

Work scheduling, progress and quality control

To allow actual production to run in an efficient and timely manner, a system of work scheduling will have to be implemented. In large industrial companies, this task is performed by the planning office and is based on data and standards derived from experience.

work scheduling

By means of work scheduling, potential or existing orders for a certain product are transformed into a set of instructions for actual production. Work scheduling establishes guidelines and task assignments for various departments and operational employees.

work dispatching

Subsequently, work dispatching, the act of distributing task assignments, instructions, primary and secondary materials, actually sets the work in motion.
Work scheduling, which occurs after a product has been designed but precedes the actual assignment of work, determines the production methods, material preparation and supply, and can even involve the ordering of raw materials, preparation of components or semi-fabricated items and so on. In this way, the on-time delivery of materials from main warehouses to the appropriate intermediate storage areas, machines or production stations is ensured. To deliver the required products at the designated time, the production times, including the staffing and machine time requirements, must be carefully calculated.
The act requires standard performance times to be set for all operations involved, the cost price to be determined (for the sake of the pre- and post-calculation of material and machinery costs) and required machine time designated. This latter task means that the available capacities must be evaluated and coordinated. The challenge is to avoid peaks in utilization (under- or over-capacity) and bottlenecks at points in the production process where waiting time is required. Losses of material caused by waste or refuse need also to be minimized, while the processing stations should be chosen so that efficiency is maximized. In this respect, walking back and forth, along with internal transport requirements, should be, wherever possible, avoided.

safety regulations

Legally prescribed safety regulations for production personnel also have to be respected.
In regulating the course of the manufacturing process, the standard performance and processing times need to be based on time and method studies. These can serve as a basis for calculating the standard cost price, which is itself used as standard by which deviations in production costs are evaluated.

assigning tasks

In the production plan, assigning tasks to the various departments and work stations can now be indicated in terms of a product's:
- Quantity
- Variety
- Delivery times
- Quality

This plan, frequently drawn up by the planning office, enables the dispatching or assignment of work to take place.

progress control

Progress control serves to determine possible deviations, and promptly detects any problem areas where budgetary or machine-based insufficiencies, standstills or excesses (according to planning charts or screens) are occurring. Deviations of actual costs or performance time from the projected costs and time may arise due to:
- Complementary materials, components and so on, arriving too late
- Bad materials

- Absenteeism among the personnel
- Machine standstill because of defects
- Lack of motivation

The quality of products or services will also have to be monitored. Sometimes quality control is made the responsibility of the production department. In other cases, the quality control department is kept separate so it can operate independent of the manufacturing department. Quality control can take place by conducting random samples and testing the product according to quality standards. These tests will show whether the process needs to be adjusted (either in the production design or in the actual production activity).
Controlling production activities is made possible by keeping good measurement records. Readily understandable data on materials used, hours worked, disruptions and so on must be available in order to form a clear view of the progress and state of affairs of production processes.

Mass customization as a recent development

production techniques Recent production techniques made possible by robotics has made it possible to make customer specific products under conditions of serial mass production. In terms of availability, delivery time and price setting, this type of product has almost the same advantages as serial mass products. The products can be made to the requirements of the individual customer.
A frequently cited example is that of National Bicycle in Japan, where a production system has been developed that enables bicycles to be built in accordance with individual customer demands. The price of this tailor-made product is only 15% above that of the top model manufactured by serial mass production. Customer measurements are taken in the shop on a specially designed frame and the customer can choose style, color, brakes, tires, pedals and so on. The unique bicycle will then be delivered within two weeks. The practice emulates the Toyota principle in the automobile world and is popularly termed mass customization. The key factor is the link provided by information technology with production technology or computer aided manufacturing (CAM). Levi Strauss does a similar thing with such products as jeans, shoes, T-shirts and golf clubs.

tailor-made product

mass customization

CAM

10.5.2 Services: transformation of intangible products

tertiary sector In the personnel and business services provideed by the so-called tertiary sector, the central issue is the provision of service-related activities in such areas as real estate, banking and insurance, retailing and so on. Organizations can display marked differences in the ways that they conduct their activities. The differences in primary, secondary or tertiary sector companies codetermine the structure or form of company activities, including type of computer system and mechanization. Some activities will be capital intensive, while others remain labor intensive. The unique thing about the banking and insurance industry is that enormous sums of money have been and are still being invested in information technology, even though the services provided are very labor intensive and person oriented.

service A service is an activity or a series of activities of a more or less intangible nature that usually, but not necessarily, involves a direct interaction between the customer and the employee and/or the physical resources and/or the systems of the service provider. While a product is an object or a thing, a service can be described as an experience, act or performance. Thus, by its very nature, a service is intangible. Services often have tangible components. For example, travel insurance is intangible, since security has no physical qualities. The service itself, however, is delivered in such a way that the customer receives something tangible as proof: a policy, a folder, or luggage labels. Because a service is an experience or a process rather than a tangible good which one can hold or store, it cannot be kept in stock. The necessary equipment, facilities and labor can, of course, be available to create the service, but these form only the production capacity, not the service itself. Providing a service requires a combination of physical facilities and mental or physical labor. Customers are often personally involved in the provision of the service, especially where this involves self-serve interfaces (for example, ATMs) or cooperation with the personnel of the service provider (e.g. with a mortgage agent in determining a mortgage payment scheme). This practice contrasts with the production activities for most goods, in which collaboration with the customer is minimal. A service can sometimes only be provided when the customer is present and engaging in what is described as interactive consumption. In such circumstances, production and consumption occur together and the quality of the personal contact with the customer is what distinguishes two otherwise identical services.

Since customers frequently participate in service-provision processes, they are often very difficult to standardize. Any assessment of the quality of the service will, therefore, require subjective as well as objective standards. Assessment of technical performance will not suffice.

service-provision process

From the operational perspective, we can identify three kinds of input for the service-provision process: the customers themselves, goods (often the property of the customers) and information. The first kind of input is required for transportation, hotel, catering, entertainment and hairdressing services. To receive the service, the customer has to enter into the servicing system, either in person or via telecommunication. The 'output' is represented by the same customer, who later finds himself in a different place or state (of being entertained, well-fed or well-groomed). The input can, however, also consist of goods provided by customers who desire some sort of property handling. Examples of a servicing process in which property is the input include house cleaning, pest control, computer maintenance, car repair, and building demolition. In each individual situation, the output will be some form of improvement to the experience or to the use of the property.

information

Information is the most intangible form of input for service provision. In the banking and insurance industry, information is the most important production factor. Other service providers that depend to a large degree on information are accountants, lawyers, teachers, market researchers, consultants and physicians. The processing of information has been given quite a boost by the computer revolution. The output can be intangible (information) as well as physical (information media: reports, books, tapes).

Service and production: the so-called servuction system

service organization

A service organization in the banking and insurance industry can be seen as a system which consists of two partially overlapping sub-systems:

- A production sub-system in which information is processed as input and the various elements of the services are created. One part of this sub-system is visible to the customer; the other is not.
- A delivery sub-system, by means of which the desired services composed of the various elements and component services are delivered to customers who have mutual contact with each other. This is the so-called servuction system.

The servuction system consists of all the elements contained in a service organization that are visible to the client and that influence the customer's image of the service provider in question: his or her evaluation and buying behavior. This includes desk personnel, any available physical aids and general psychological impressions. All these factors have an effect on customers.

Every service organization must be conscious of these system elements and the mutual relationships between them. Improving operational efficiency and ease of use for the customer sometimes even eliminates the need for direct contact between service provider and customer, as there are several types of operation where customers do not have to be physically present during the servicing process. A modern example is teleshopping.

Front office and back office

In the service-provision process, the terms front office and back office are used to distinguish between the visible and the invisible parts of the operation. Individual back office activities in the banking and insurance industry are becoming increasingly standardized, so that front office quality is often decisive for the customer's assessment.

Productivity and quality

back office *front office*

The distinction between the front and back office is important particularly where the issue of productivity is concerned. The back office includes those activities the customer does not have much insight into and particularly the record-keeping work usually done by computer and productivity improvements. The front office is where direct interaction with the customer takes place. The principles of efficiency cannot be applied to these activities in such a straightforward manner because both the participation of the customer has to be taken into account and the forms of interaction which yield the best results. For this reason, the notion of quality used in the service sector is marketing based.

quality

Quality of service is sometimes described as the degree to which the customer's expectations about the service are actually met. Research has shown that there are five factors on the basis of which the user usually assesses quality. These five factors are found in tailor-made as well as standard services, and are furthermore involved in either core or supplementary activities. In general, they reflect the advantages that a service provides a customer and concern:

- Tangible matters: technical facilities, skilled personnel, and so on
- Reliability: ability to perform a promised service reliably and accurately
- Responsiveness: willingness to help clients and to deliver the service quickly
- Care: knowledge and courtesy of personnel and the degree to which they are capable of transmitting confidence
- Identification with the client: the care of and individual attention paid to the customer by the organization's personnel

10.5.3 Research and development: aiming for innovation

Until recently, it was held that not much in this area could or indeed had to be organized. Development of new products or servicing ideas and applications of them demands, it was argued, a climate of freedom and few rules and procedures. In response to changing patterns of need and evolving environmental demands, organizations must increasingly renew products and processes or come up with innovations. This continuous process of renewal and innovation requires the improved effectiveness that the implementation of research and development controls can bring to an organization.

innovation

Subsidization by the government or the EU has certainly stimulated the innovation activities of many companies; however, it also compels management to take the initiative in this arena and to bear the responsibility for effective use of subsidies.

Although a systematic approach to product and process development is often already employed in large companies, it needs also to be adopted in middle-sized and small organizations in both the commercial and non-profit domains. Such practices involve the implementation of project management as well as other control procedures.

research and development

Research and development should certainly be conducted by both producers and service providers, but it is, in fact, also beneficial to governmental and other non-profit organizations. Besides the systematic approach to research into new possibilities, the further development and improvement of existing products, processes and ways of working also belongs to this activity. In large organizations, there are special departments and/or employees which are charged with the research and development task. In small organizations, production managers and other production-line personnel carry it out. In those cases, research and development is actually a side activity, and is often therefore somewhat neglected when current production work must take precedence. Chances for development often go unrecognized, with the accompanying danger that production practices become dated and new opportunities are missed. Some organizations are too small to bear the costs of fundamental research. In certain industrial sectors and lines of business, there are consequently external research laboratories that are collectively financed.

In service-intensive organizations, various levels of service innovation and improved service-provision processes can be identified.

- Services which are totally new to the organization and the market
- New service classes or additions to the existing service class
- Important changes in service forms, types of services, new brands and service varieties that a company has developed
- Repositioning of certain services
- Existing products adapted for new market segments
- New services which yield the same result at lower costs for the company

product – market matrix

The relationships between these and the available options can be identified by referring to Ansoff's product – market matrix (Chapter 4).

Innovations yielding competitive advantage must anticipate both domestic and foreign needs. For example, as international concern for product safety has grown, Swedish companies like Volvo, Atlas Cop co, and AGA have succeeded by anticipating the market opportunity in this area. On the other hand, innovations that respond to concerns or circumstances that are peculiar to the home market can actually retard international competitive success. The lure of the huge US defense market, for instance, has diverted the attention of US materials and machine-tool companies from attractive, global commercial markets.

Source: Transnational Management, Bartlett and Ghoshal (1992). Reproduced by permission of McGraw Hill

THE PATENT RACE

Has the U.S. lost its Yankee ingenuity? For the first time in 2009, non-Americans were granted more U.S. patents than resident inventors, accounting for 50.7% of new grants, according to recent data from the Patent & Trademark Office. Moreover, for only the second time in the last 25 years, patent applications fell overall in the year ended Sept. 30.

The role reversal had been only a matter of time. Led by Japan and the likes of South Korea and China, other countries have been zigzagging their way higher in patent awards for decades, while the number granted to U.S. residents peaked in 2001. Still, the inflection point troubles American tech industry advocates and other analysts. 'The U.S. is losing its innovation base,' says Robert D. Atkinson, founder and president of the Information Technology & Innovation Foundation (ITIF), a Washington think tank.

The shift reflects in part moves by U.S.-based companies to offshore research and development. Take IBM, a company that for 16 years running has ranked No. 1 in patent volume. Big Blue still owns the rights to an invention that originated in one of its Indian labs, but the Patent Office would include it in its foreign resident tally. Taxes are one reason more innovation is going abroad. The U.S. once boasted the most generous research and development tax credits among the 30 countries in the Organization for Economic Cooperation & Development. Now, according to the ITIF, it ranks 17th, as other nations have cut taxes to spur investments in labs and equipment.

U.S. education gets rapped, too. India and China produce more scientists and engineers than the U.S., and international students who attend American Universities generally must return home as soon as they've graduated. 'We're forcing these people to do their productive work elsewhere,' says Mark Chandler, general counsel of Cisco Systems. 'They should have a green card stapled to their admittance letter.'

The 2.3% drop in overall patent applications is likely a byproduct of the Great Recession, as companies slash R&D budgets to help maintain profits. The last decline was in 1996, when new global rules on the duration of patent protection went into effect, prompting applicants to hustle and file in 1995. The only other time over the past three decades that the number of patent seekers fell was in 1983, when the U.S. was emerging from a deep recession.
As before, the slide in applications will likely last just a year. But 2008 could turn out to be the last time the U.S. won the patent race.

Source: *Bloomberg Business Week*, December 28, 2009 and January 4, 2010, M. Arndt

Innovation complexity

four forms

In general, innovation may take one of four forms: incremental innovation, radical innovation, the alteration of a technological system, and the alteration of an entire techno-economic paradigm.

incremental innovation

radical innovation

The least complex form of innovation is incremental innovation. Incremental innovation can be defined as small improvements or changes to already existing products, services or processes. Radical innovation is more complex: a sudden improvement or change to new products, services or processes. A radical innovation can initiate the development of new markets and new competitive games between organizations within the marketplace. Take the introduction of the digital compact disc player in the 1980s: this initiated the development of a market for compact discs.

altering a technological system

The third type of innovation, one which is more complex than incremental and radical innovations, is altering a technological system. Altering a technological system entails a considerable degree of incremental and radical innovation. Altering a technological system can initiate the development of completely new branches of industry, as demonstrated by the large number of incremental and radical innovations in the information processing industry. They gave rise to the development of the computer industry, the software industry, and consulting businesses concerned with the installation, implementation and maintenance of hardware and software.

alteration of an entire techno-economic paradigm

The fourth and most complex type of innovation, the one with the highest impact on society, is alteration of an entire techno-economic paradigm. Altering an entire techno-economic paradigm involves a number of innovations of the third type – modification of technological systems – and causes a drastic change in the functioning of entire economies. An example of a modification of an entire techno-economic paradigm is the integration of the concept of 'sustainability' or 'environmentally friendliness' into the functioning of civil services, trade and industry. A sustainable society needs to constantly work towards such changes as improving the biodegradability of plastics. Such a society must also be able to absorb any costs associated with finding alternatives for scarce natural resources within the sales costs of the products. Various alterations to technological systems also have to be made to create a cyclical economy. For example: in a cyclical and sustainable economy, production processes do not have a starting point or an end. Production processes give rise to new processes, one of whose objectives may be to complete a cycle. In a sustainable economy, industry becomes capable of using and re-using its own waste in such a way that there is no more waste.

Technological innovation: product innovation and/or process innovation

New technological findings are being transformed into new product applications at an increasing rate often by specifically-constituted project organizations. In this way of organizing the research and development function, the application of knowledge is accelerated, and can facilitate the passage from research through product development, pilot production, manufacturing and sales to the market.

Technological innovation is the successful bringing to market of new or modified products in which new technological findings or combinations of findings are applied. The successful introduction to the market of soap with a new color, smell, shape or packaging does not represent a technological advance as it is not a product innovation with any technological content.

A distinction can be made between innovations based on a 'technological push' and a 'market or application pull'. The push originates from new technological developments. The pull arises from the market or the application and is caused by the needs that exist there.

In theory, a business firm can acquire technological know-how in four ways:

- By buying machinery including operating instructions and the know-how for maintenance
- By acquiring technologically advanced companies
- By know-how contracts or license agreements
- By its own research and technological development

In most cases companies acquire new technological knowledge by buying it or taking it over from others. This applies particularly to small and medium-sized companies that are not financially strong, though larger firms also find it cheaper and easier to buy technological solutions from others.
The development of many successful products follows a recognizable pattern. After an introductory phase, there is a period of rapid growth in demand, after which a period of stabilization follows due to saturation of the market (see Fig 10.4). Through product or process innovations, a firm can try to stimulate sales and volume of business. In the end, there is bound to be a drop in sales, which may be caused by the introduction of a better or cheaper substitute product. The product lifecycle ends with a phasing out, which often provokes resistance both inside and outside the organization.

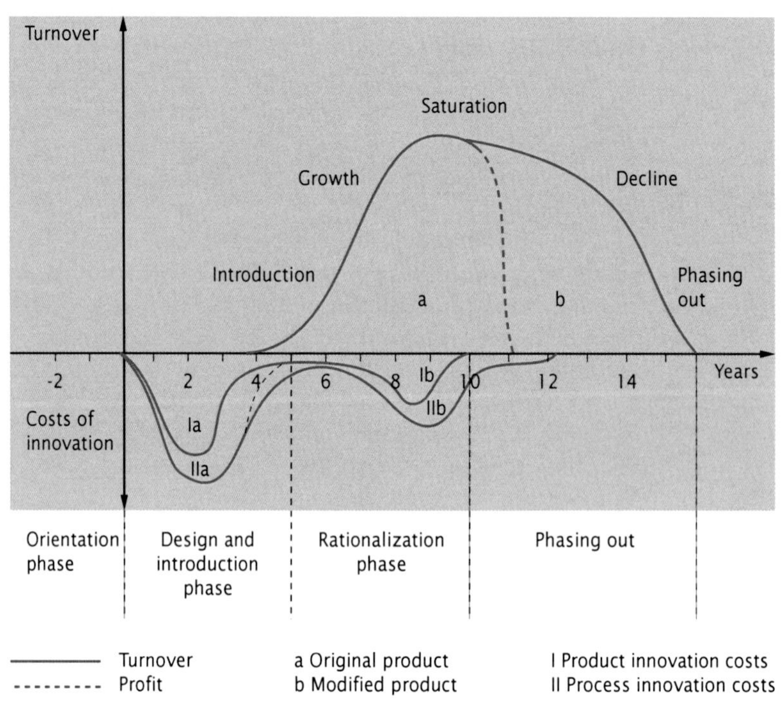

Figure 10.4
Model of innovation phases and product lifecycle for simple and complex products

Source: *After Botter*, 1980

Figure 10.4 shows this development in terms of volume of business. In the design phase, the original product (a) is designed. During the later rationalization phase, the improved product (b) is prepared and modifications are included in the product design (this is product innovation) or are introduced into the manufacturing process (this is process innovation).

process innovation

In a normal pattern of increasing competition, quality improvements have to be made on an ongoing basis. At the same time, the cost price has to be brought down.

product innovation

In Figure 10.4, the basis is the costing of product innovation. These costs are included at phase Ia. The incurring of process innovation costs begins almost one year later. These are represented in IIa. These costs are incurred in acquiring machinery and other equipment for the manufacture of prototypes during the pilot production phase or in making the so-called pilot series.
During the rationalization phase of (a), an effort is made to introduce an up-graded product to the market. The resulting incurred costs are depicted in Ib and IIb. In this figure the sales volume of the improved product is depicted in (b). When the market situation allows it, a second and possibly even a third and fourth improvement phase may be included in the rationalization phase.

Type of business and type of innovation

innovation

Innovation can be typified as follows:

- The upper levels of the industrial sector normally emphasize process innovation
- In the middle of the industry sector, the same attention has to be given to product as to process innovation
- On the lower levels of the industrial sector, product innovation only occurs

For companies that design industrial installations, the construction of an installation constitutes its product, whereas it represents a process both for the construction company and the industry in which the equipment will be used.
Companies that wish to develop their products successfully need to know the difference between the various types of R&D. Among the many different factors that play a role in product innovation, time, capital and quantity are of particular importance. As such, three basic categories of innovation can be identified. These are urgent, capital intensive and quantitative innovation.

Urgent innovation

These are usually rather uncomplicated products that cost less than 15.000 euros: PCs, audio, video and communication equipment, cameras and household equipment. These products have a short lifecycle and are used only for short periods of time. Users soon want something new.

Capital intensive innovation

Included in this category are capital goods with a value of more than 3 million euros used in public or private infrastructure, for example railway systems, aircraft, weapon systems, satellites, process control equipment, energy works, chemical facilities, telephone systems or databank systems. These products have a longer lifecycle (more than five years) and frequently remain in use even longer. There may be high costs associated with user logistics. They may cause the starting and switching costs to be quite considerable.

Quantitative innovation

These involve mass products (low costs/large volume utility) manufactured in locations far away from the end users and for which older technologies are employed. They involve the use of raw materials (such as glass, plastics, resins and mineral oils) semifabricated items, and basic materials (such as paper, cardboard, fibers, etc.). The lifecycle for these products is normally longer than ten years. Unless the market intervenes, these products go through several stages during the manufacturing and the distribution process, each of which usually involves a lot of time.

Innovation and project management and control

innovation project

An innovation project starts formally after a strategic reorientation has been decided and ends at the phase of operational maintenance. Every phase has to be a surveyable and clearly defined part of the total project. The activities to be completed in each phase have to be clearly identified, as does the individual who has to be informed about the various activities, the people who have been authorized to make certain decisions, and other such matters.
In real life, however, the phases through which projects move are frequently poorly defined (see also Section 5.3.7). Although the activities to be completed during a given phase may indeed be stipulated, the time of completing a phase and the manner of progressing to the next one often remains unclear. The only way to clarify these issues is to define the specific results – in terms of documents and products – that have to be ready by the end of each phase and the individual responsible for releasing these intermediate results or products.

10.5.4 Quality control

Quality control requires first of all that the notion of quality be specified by, for example, an indication of the performance (primary characteristics), reliability, specifications, durability, maintenance friendliness, aesthetic quality and subjective (perceived) quality that a product should have. For specific products and situations (for example in the car industry or in aviation) these qualities need to be very precisely specified. Quality can be approached in various ways, but management must coordinate the methods used by implementing quality standards and employing control procedures. Differences in interpretation can arise within an organization in relation to the quality of products because each department may have a different point of view. For example, the marketing department usually uses a user-oriented approach, while the factory usually takes a production-oriented approach. The financial department will look particularly at costs and revenues, thereby displaying a 'value-oriented approach'.

product-oriented approach

The typical product-oriented approach assumes quality to be an objectively measurable feature. As such product quality will be seen as being based on specific characteristics which may be present to a certain degree. Improving the quality entails adding more of a certain characteristic to the product. With this approach, quality improvement will lead to more expensive products.

user-oriented approach

In a user-oriented approach, quality is determined by the eventual user in relation to the purpose for which the product is used. Consequently, the same product can be deemed a good product by a user in one situation, while in another situation that same product will be viewed as a bad one. The user is the central factor in this approach: quality is suitability for use.

production-oriented approach

The production-oriented approach presupposes quality to be translatable into a set of specifications that products need to satisfy. The production process needs to be structured in such a way that those specifications are met in the best possible way. Deviation from the specifications will lead to an increased number of rejects, quantify of waste, need for reprocessing, and so on. The result will be higher-than-necessary costs. Improvements to the production process will therefore lower costs. With this approach, 'right first time,' and 'zero defects' are appropriate.

value-oriented approach

The value-oriented approach is concerned with the value that a product or service represents for the user. Costs, revenues and prices are the central issues here.

Quality costs

Quality costs can be grouped into four categories: external costs (e.g. guarantee and repair costs); internal costs (e.g. those incurred as a result of reprocessing), assessment costs (e.g. inspection costs) and prevention costs. Through quality management, the total costs of quality will decrease and the share of the prevention costs will usually increase (in proportion to total quality costs). Quality costs are a good starting-point for any campaign to implement a quality policy in organizations, for the following reasons:

- The size of quality problems can be made visible (increased awareness)
- Priorities for improvement can be set
- Quality goals can be expressed in cost terms (improvement projects)
- Cost indicators can be used to control the progress of a quality policy (feedback)

A strategic approach to quality means that even in the product design stage, consideration must be given not just to the actual production (design for manufacturing) and the product reliability (design for reliability), but also to the requirements of user-friendliness (design for usability) and ease of service (design for serviceability). Suppliers are also included in the quality improvement programs (in the form of co-producers).

quality control

As such, quality control goes further than just meeting a priori set standards or specifications. It also reacts to the latent expectations, needs or requirements of the customer, as they are revealed by market research. A shift in the emphasis on quality can be seen to have occurred in recent years: from inspecting for quality (first phase), via controlling quality (second phase) and building-in quality (third phase) to managing quality. This shift has been accompanied by changing responsibilities in relation to quality. In the first phase, the responsibility for quality lies with the department for quality inspection, then with the manufacturing department, after that with all departments in respect of their own activities, and finally with everyone within the organization, including with upper management, which is responsible for the formulation of a quality policy and for the active administration of that policy.

Certification of quality systems

quality system

When the quality system of an organization meets certain standards and requirements as determined by an external authority, it may be awarded a certificate. 'Quality system' includes all the organizational structures, responsibilities, procedures and provisions concerned with quality.

certification

The standards and requirements represent a description of the conditions that a quality system has to satisfy. Certification of quality systems is becoming increasingly important to companies for several reasons, including the following:

- The ever increasing quality demands from the client/consumer. When a company is in possession of a quality certificate, it can be shown to the client as evidence of the company's dependability and reliability.
- European integration and the subsequent increase in competition in various market segments. A company that possesses an internationally recognized quality certificate can improve its market position considerably.
- New international and national legislation regarding product liability. Such laws are making the producers responsible for damage resulting from the products that they manufacture. Having a quality certificate could limit the amount of the claim. Insurance companies are likely to impose demands in this area. They could require a company to obtain such a certificate.

CASE

Mini case study 10.7

Customer value instead of shareholder value

The big idea: it's time to discard the popular belief that corporations must focus first and foremost on maximizing value for shareholders. That idea is inherently, and tragically, flawed.

The argument: it's impossible to continually increase shareholder value, because stock prices are driven by shareholders' expectations about the future, which cannot be raised indefinitely.

What the data show: the focus on shareholder value hasn't done shareholders any favors. They have actually earned lower returns since corporations adopted it as their guiding principle.

A better approach: make customer value the top priority, as Johnson & Johnson and Procter & Gamble have done. These two companies have generated shareholder returns that are at least as high as, if not higher than, those of leading shareholder-focused companies.

Source: R. Martin (2010), *Harvard Business Review* January-February, p. 61

International quality standards

ISO

Many of the standards that quality systems have to meet originate with the International Organization for Standardization (ISO). The standards can be applied to the contractual relationships between suppliers and customers.

10.5.5 Environmental control

A company's internal environmental care and control measures are intended to counteract any environmental damage caused by the company's activities. Environmental concern in companies and institutions is, in the first instance, usually motivated by the need to respect laws, rules and regulations relating to environmental care. Some laws are linked to a system of permits. These laws, permits and regulations often have a direct influence on the functioning of a company. Environmental concern motivated by a generally increasing awareness of environmental problems among customers can be expressed in an organization's own environmental policy.

environmental concern

environmental policy

The ramifications of the policy should eventually extend to all areas of the organization. This total commitment should lead to the development of a form of built-in supervision for the internal environmental care system.

In companies where doing sustainable business has a high priority, environmental care in the sense of ecological sustainability of all business processes is, so to speak, the 'natural way'.

Goals for internal environmental care and control

environmental care system

The environmental care system is a tool for the building environmental care into an organization. An environmental care system is an instrument enabling management to observe government rules in an efficient and effective way. Such a system can also enhance an organization's ability to respond to future environmental developments.

The introduction of internal environmental practices as one of the tasks of management allows a variety of goals to be targeted.

- Environmental goals. Observation of government rules in the field of environmental care, observation of internal company guidelines and instructions, control and/or prevention of environmental damage as a consequence of company activities, limitation of environmental risks, and timely anticipation of environmental developments
- Economic goals. Setting up an efficient environmental policy, cost savings in the long term
- Other goals. Less government regulation, more effective government regulation, good relationship with governments and stakeholders, better company image, anticipation of future developments in the technical and social fields, appropriate handling of complaints about the environment

Design of environmental care system and management tasks

In theory, environmental concerns affect all company activities: research and development, product design, the purchase of raw materials and components, as well as the actual manufacturing process. Moreover, environmental awareness requires vigilance. The organization should not merely be occupied with respecting government rules, but also systematically seeking to reduce environmental damage at all times. If feedback reveals any significant deviations corrective measures should be taken. Feedforward measures directed not only at the correction of existing problems but also at the prevention of future ones should be taken.

feedback

feedforward

In an environmental care system, management is responsible for:

- Formulation of an environmental policy statement in which management indicates what this environmental policy entails for each particular section of the organization
- Development of an environmental program in which management may include environmental measures to be undertaken. This could entail investments and overhaul of equipment, implementation and revision of permit conditions, proposals for studies and research projects, structuring of a monitoring and regulatory program and specification of special points of attention.
- The institution of a measurement and registration program designed to quantify an organization's environmental effects. Check points should be identified and information obtained to guide readjustment.
- The installation of an internal monitoring and inspection system which also includes inspections, functional checks of the system and screening of data to facilitate inspections

- The provision of internal information, education and training to stimulate involvement of personnel and the establishment of a system of internal reporting on the general state of affairs within the environment
- External reporting on the functioning and the development of the system, implementation of the environmental program, and the results of inspections, audits and required reports

environmental care system

Besides drawing up an environmental policy, these managerial tasks embed environmental care into the organizational structure and supply the content required to perform, supervise and ensure environmental care. To function well, the environmental care system has to be clear and simple to implement. The system should be able to cope with virtually any situation within the organization, which means that the size and complexity of the system will depend on the degree (that is, nature and intensity) of the potential environmental damage.
Factors influencing the organizational measures to be taken are as follows:
- Scale and complexity
- Degree of environmental damage
- Number of relevant environmental laws and rules

If the measures to be taken are considerable, the environmental damage is increasing and there are a growing number of environmental regulations and laws, a separate environmental department should be set up to provide environmental guidelines for organizational activities. For good integration of environmental care, it is important, however, that responsibility for the execution of environmental measures remains at the work-stations and is stressed in the task and job descriptions of the individual company employees.

10.5.6 Business logistics: control of physical resources and information

logistics management

physical distribution

business logistics

Logistics management is comprised of all activities involved in planning, organizational structuring and operational management of the flow of goods, including the information supply necessary for this flow. Within the total flow of goods from supplier to consumer, a division should be made between material management and physical distribution. Material management encompasses all activities conducted to ensure that the flow of raw materials and semifabricated articles to and through the production process, along with the accompanying flows of data, occur as efficiently as possible. Included in this undertaking are activities conducted to facilitate efficient use of production resources. Physical distribution is concerned with the goods and flows of data associated with the above flow of materials but which start at the end of the production process and finish with the consumer. Business logistics, or rather logistics management, is the collective name for all activities performed to control the in and outgoing flow of goods (see Fig 10.5).

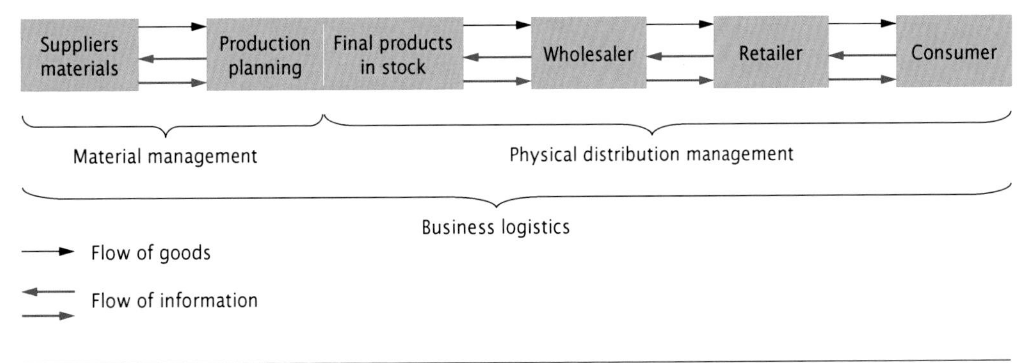

Figure 10.5
Elements of management in the flow of goods

Improvement in the flow of goods via logistical management

Control of logistical activities can occur by means of improvements in inventory positions and cost control, by enlargement of flexibility and service, or by strengthening the competitive position of an organization. Logistical management is an integrated approach for controlling all the factors involved in the flow of goods. Thus, logistics is implicated in all functions such as product development, marketing and sales, purchasing, manufacturing (as well as inventory control and work scheduling), transportation and distribution and financial administration.

MRP II *DRP* *JIT*

In this framework and with the help of computer systems, new organizational methods can be implemented including MRP II (Manufacturing Resources Planning), DRP (Distribution Requirements Planning) and JIT (Just In Time). MRP II is especially concerned with management of the flow of goods for long-running production processes involving the transformation of simple into complex product compositions. JIT is most suitable for organizations with short completion times, small series sizes, few materials per production step, a total production scheme and products with a relatively long lifecycle. JIT has been imported from Japan (see Section 10.4.4) and is intended to reduce inventories. JIT stresses the importance of making problems visible, synchronization of products and sales, and simplification of the processes involved. Inventory is often a bad thing and usually hides underlying problems, including machine breakdown, incorrect inventory data, quality problems and inflexibility in the production resources.

The location of inventory points within the goods flow and the resulting formation of disengagement points between customer-oriented external activities and planning-oriented internal activities can be problematic for management. By identifying potential disengagement points in the logistical chain, orders can be disengaged from completion times of the logistical production chain. The maintenance of optimal inventories at the disengagement points will to a certain extent resolve the constant tension between production and sales by providing both stability and flexibility.

A DEMAND FOR STEADY SUPPLY

Managers can minimise the forecasting risks that leave stores empty – or overstocked – at crucial times.

Key steps on the road to a demand-responsive supply chain. Responsiveness in the supply chain can be achieved in a number of ways.

- Range forecasting – such as forecasting over a month, quarter and year – helps companies gauge demand.
- Demand predictions for common components used in many different products can be aggregated.
- Shortening the time from concept to market makes for more accurate predictions.
- Where there is no history of demand for a product, makers can test the market with small batches.
- Closer collaboration with suppliers and customers can help improve forecast accuracy.

Source: *Financial Times*, August 22, 2005

In service-provision processes, the logistics involved in the flow of either physical goods (of restaurant supplies at a congress center, for example) or information (in banking or insurance companies) should be treated independently.

Enterprise Resource Planning (ERP)

ERP systems

ERP systems are used to link all of an organization's resources. This software usually includes the following modules: order administration, purchasing, inventory control, storage, project management and production. Upon receipt of an order, the software will help management to determine if a delivery can be made from inventory and which actions have to be undertaken when such is not the case (what has to be ordered, how the production has to be planned, and so on). If desired, the ERP package can be linked to a software package enabling integration with the accounting and budgetary process, as well as to the financial administration and HRM. Such interlinking facilitates measurement and evaluation of performance as well as planning. It is also possible to integrate the ERP systems with a so-called front office application, so that a link is established with marketing and sales, and possibly also with a sales department call center. Such software removes the differences between front office (where customer contact takes place) and the back office (where customer transactions are undertaken). This obviously has efficiency benefits, but the disappearance of this distinction also eliminates the possibility of internal control. Another way has to be found to compensate for this deficiency.

supply chain

Management systems for the so-called supply chain also exist. They are especially important in industrial operations in which component operations have to be precisely synchronized, such as the aircraft industry, automobile production, nutrition, and so on. SAP and Baan are examples of packages that provide the possibility of planning to meet demand and to pass 'charges' on from one stage to the next until the end product is completed. By so coordinating the links of the chain and by using both Internet and intranet technologies, inventories can be reduced and greater adherence to delivery times can be achieved. These features sometimes lead to a substantial decrease in costs incurred throughout the entire chain.

Based on the experiences of companies using this kind of software, it appears that the time, impact and cost benefits resulting from the implementation of ERP systems are often underestimated.

HOW IS ERP USED?

A recent Accenture survey of senior IT professionals found that companies in the UK lag behind their North American counterparts in terms of adoption and usage of enterprise systems.

It found that:

- Three-quarters (76 per cent) of respondents say enterprise systems contribute substantially to their organisation's competitive advantage and strategic value.
- Enterprise systems are under-utilised in a third of organisations.
- Forty-seven per cent of companies that are not using their systems' full capability could increase enterprise systems utilisation if they had more time, training and/or budget.
- About half of respondents not using full system capability say this is because they 'don't need all the capabilities'.
- Only 19 per cent overall have fully integrated their enterprise system with customers' systems.
- The UK is more sceptical about the impact of emerging technologies than North American respondents.

Source: *Financial Times*, Special Report, May 14, 2009

ERP systems

When the systems work properly, the advantages are substantial. At present, there is a shift in the application of ERP systems from large and general systems to scalable and customer specific solutions. A lot of money has been wasted, as clearly demonstrated by several CRM projects: 55% of the projects do not deliver the results that were expected and existing long-term customer relations can even be damaged. 'Think before you start' is a sound piece of advice.

Things are changing, however. Smaller ERP providers are expanding and starting to challenge the established vendors. Conversely, the larger ERP vendors now provide functionality in manageable modules with service-oriented and hosted solutions.

These two approaches are meeting in the middle, where falling ERP costs, increased competition from suppliers, modern agile architectures and a more mature delivery capability are resulting in fewer project failures.

10.5.7 Marketing and sales

Marketing is the practice of approaching sales and production from the market (i.e. client) point of view. The needs and wishes of the clients are adopted as the actual starting-points for all company activities.

marketing

Marketing comprises:
- The recognition of needs in the market
- The identification of user requirements relating to goods and services aimed at satisfying these needs
- The instigation and stimulation of demand for these goods and services
- The satisfaction of that demand by selling the goods and services, and in so doing, realizing a profit

Marketing and sales are actually both the starting-points and the finishing-points of all organizational activities. Market research will usually initiate the planning that an organization undertakes. The marketing plan will generally provide the basis for next year's sales plan, from which the inventory plan is derived, and in turn, the production plan, purchasing plan, and so on.

planning and control processes

The planning and control processes involved in the commercial activities of an organization can be specified as follows:
- *The determination of marketing and sales goals.* In the sales policy, general organizational goals have to be specified as market goals. In other words, the target client groups must be identified in order to conduct sales for their benefit. These may be specified directly (industrial clients or consumers) or in terms of a product type (ladies', men's or children's wear), or by geographical regions (in France, all cities with more than 25,000 inhabitants, or maybe other countries).
- *Planning in the long and the short term.* For the benefit of the commercial function, the result should be a sales plan comprising market goals as well as the instruments by means of which they will be achieved. Both these items should be expressed in terms of costs and anticipated revenues.
- *The organization of the marketing department.* This involves both sales and other departmental operations, particularly the way in which this department maintains external relationships with clients. Marketing policy should be implemented by this department.
- *The execution.* Plans have to be converted into action. Everyone should know what is expected of him or her. This means, for example, that tasks must be assigned to sales representatives on a regional, client-group, or even client-by-client basis. Advertising campaigns also have to be carried out according to clearly stated guidelines, instructions and task assignments.
- *Monitoring and adjustment.* These activities rarely go completely according to plan. The market place can be unpredictable. Developments have to be promptly signaled, so that corrective measures can be taken.

Experiences with e-commerce and e-tailing

Internet

Research into surfing behavior on the Internet shows that 80% of Internet users buy from local rather than international companies. Surfers tend to use the web to obtain information, to find out about various product areas and to communicate with manufacturers and retailers, but after that go – admittedly well informed – to the store and make their purchases over the counter. The effect is a decrease in sales time. Men surf differently to women and there are differences according to age, country of origin and product area. The particular medium that a user employs remains uncertain. In the mobile phone sector (the so-called M-business), WAP (Wireless Allocation Protocol) has been used to access the Internet via the mobile telephone. The service has also been included in I-mode, which works on the basis of GPRS (General Packet Radio Service) and 'M-mode' (under the GGTP – General Global Transfer Protocol – and Ipv6) with its interactive access to the virtual world (with or without cable) and so virtually unlimited possibilities (via broadband, Digital ME and so on). Banks, for example, provide I-mode services enabling customers to inquire about their bank accounts or to arrange transactions. However, in the short term, the Internet is unlikely to be important as a new sales channel. Research shows that 70% of all surfers initiating a sales process do not complete it. Most of the time it is press the button, but do not buy, because people prefer to go to shops, either because they are still unconvinced about the trustworthiness of paying by web or because they are not sure whether they will be home when the goods are delivered. American statistics suggest that about 70% of all new Internet companies will be bankrupt within a short period of time.

A couple of comments:

- *ease and service.* Should they want to, customers can easily exchange articles that they have bought via the Internet: articles can be ordered and even returned without difficulty and without sales pressure. It makes no sense to have to pay a higher price just to get a recommendation from a salesperson. After all, thanks to the Internet, customers often know more about the product or what the product can do than shop assistents.
- *knowledge and service.* Customers are becoming aware of products through Weblogs or even Google. They can also have some idea of prices by looking at Web-based shops. Clients are unlikely to accept shop prices that differ from those on the Internet. Even now, 10% of clients are indicating that they see no point in bargaining to reduce the price of more expensive articles.
- *communication.* Shopkeepers rarely know their customers personally or know much about their needs. Web-based shops do have to have some knowledge about their clients, even if only to be able to send the purchases to their addresses or to arrange payment with them. This knowledge makes direct contact possible – via e-mail – and enables Web-based shops to react to purchasing behavior, thereby creating a sense of a personal relationship with the customer.
- *mobility.* Shopping has become a leisure activity for Dutch people. However, this has not been to the advantage of the shopkeeper. Parking problems, parking costs and local government policies have, in general, not favoured the retail trade. Customers are looking for other ways of shopping as a form of recreation. Ikea and Mediamarkt have played in on this with extended shopping hours, adequate parking facilities and lots of fun activities.

Source: Cor Molenaar, 2009

Amazon

The results for Amazon, which started as a bookstore but has grown into a kind of Internet department store selling everything from music and video to garden products, are seen as an important indicator of the potential success that Internet companies might enjoy.

Internet customers

However, the loyalty of Internet customers is generally not great. Amazon needs an average annual turnover of $207 for each active customer. McKinsey reported that to that end, Amazon had to handle more packages per day than Federal Express does. To maintain the required sales level, a fourfold increase in storage place was required, and to remain viable, Amazon had to realize a cost reduction of 25% on its order processing activities.

The turning point may have been the January 2002 announcement of Amazon's first quarterly profit – net income of $5 million during the final quarter of 2001, after cumulative losses of $2.86 million since 1995. But Amazon still had a mountain to climb in order to overcome its $2.8 million debt. There are all sorts of hazards along the way. The shares have weakened since rival e-tailer Buy.com announced it would beat Amazon's prices on books. It is still not sure how Amazon will generate enough profit and cash flow to service its debt. Amazon.com first started to make a profit (with a net profit of $35 million on a turnover of $5.3 billion) in 2003. It counted on better results in 2004 but in 2005 (October) found itself forced to issue a profit warning. Its margins and its operational income dropped sharply. Expenditure shot up further than sales. Amazon was thus forced to sell more and more.

AMAZON SHOPPING

Gijs van Wulfen, who initiated the website 'Imagining new products':
'Why is one of the icons of the dot.com world going back to the prehistoric period? Well, as it it turns out, that flesh-and-blood world is not as passed its used-by date as it seems. Sure, books and cds fit into the mailbox. But what about Amazon's other online products: laptops, children's bikes and lawn mowers? Some clients would prefer to pick these big purchases up in person and when it suits them. It makes sense to experiment with actual shops or collection spots for these items.'

Amazon, the biggest Internet-based shop for books and CDs, is looking for **suitable shop premises** from which customers can pick up their purchases. Neither Bol.com nor Wehkamp have announced similar plans.

Alwine de Jong, Y&R Not Just Film's artistic director:
'The mother of all Webshops is going to open an ordinary shop. This isn't as odd as it sounds: of all the successful Webshops, Amazon is most in need of a new idea. Amazon is suffering from having a shackling advantage: its recipe for success is being copied left and right. As long as it keeps abreast of the times, a flesh-and-bones flagship may be able to inject new life into the brand. In any case, Amazon owes it to itself to turn an ordinary bookshop in a London shopping street into something that nobody has thought of yet.

Source: *Het Financieele Dagblad*, 23 December 2009

In Europe, the German media giant Bertelsmann had, in the meantime (August 2002), announced the discontinuation of its Bol.com activities (books, CDs and films sold over the Internet) in the Netherlands, Germany, Sweden and Switzerland, but has become active again since then.

New media and marketing

approaching the customer

Marketing is about approaching the customer. The new media are highly suitable for this. Clients just log in and then find their own way into a site, a community, a portal or a search machine. Marketing specialists deliberate about the support they should provide customers and what stage of the purchasing process is most suitable for providing them with information of various types. The Internet site must tie in with this. An effective demand-directed site has a search function, can answer questions, has an easy e-mail function at its disposal (for ease of contact), possibly has a 'call me now' button and has a weblog for information and mutual distribution of information amongst customers. Demand-directed sites have a clear navigation system and provide easy access. Molenaar (2006) points out that in the switchover from supply-driven to demand-driven approaches, the old media are inadequate in every way. Table 10.1 shows why.

Table 10.1
The differences between the old and the new media

The old media	The new media
Broadcasting, mass communication	Narrowcasting, small-scale communication directed at the individual
Supply based, supplier plays the main role in communication and information provision	Demand-driven, the customer plays the main role in communication and information provision
Communication directed at the target group (about whose individual members nothing is known)	Communication based on what is known about the individual
A multi-channel approach whereby the supplier chooses the channel and the goods to match	The customer determines the channel and what he/she wants to do or know
Rating on the basis of viewing time or attention attracted (readership, subscriptions, viewers)	Rating on the basis of visits and direct response
Suitable for general messages	Suitable for individual messages

Source: Molenaar, 2006

The new media (including those that are Internet-based) are producing new and different purchasing behavior. Customers are well informed and have a lot of choice. If they want to they can even have their goods home delivered.

AMAZON TO EXPAND ONLINE TRADE-IN RANGE

Amazon, the world's largest online retailer, is planning to start buying more goods back, as well as selling them, by setting up its own online trade-in platform for used consumer electronics.

The retailer is recruiting software engineers to work on a service to allow consumers to trade in used consumer electronics gadgets in exchange for Amazon gift cards.

The move highlights the surge in interest in trade-in services, spurred in part by the newly frugal mood of US consumers, with leading retailers including Wal-Mart, Target and Costco starting partnerships last year with a variety of online services.

This month Amazon also launched an initial trade-in and recycling partnership for consumer electronics with CExchange, one of a number of US web-based services that buy back used electronics in partnership with retailers, which have grown up in recent years.

Best Buy, the largest US consumer electronics retailer, was one of the first national retailers to set up a trade-in service for laptops, mobile phones and other devices through its Dealtree subsidiary, a web-based service it acquired in 2008.

Amazon entered the trade-in market in March last year, with the launch of its own online trade-in service for used video games.

Similar video-game buy-back ventures had previously been launched by Best Buy and Wal-Mart, which were in turn following the early success in the second-hand business of GameStop, the computer video game store chain.

Amazon subsequently extended the service to include DVDs, and in December started buying back and reselling college text books.

Source: *Financial Times*, January 25, 2010

CASE

Mini case study 10.8

Building long-term customer relationships

Companies have powerful technologies for understanding and interacting with customers, yet most still depend on mass media marketing to drive impersonal transactions. To compete, companies must shift from pushing individual products to building long-term customer relationships. The marketing department must be reinvented as a 'customer department' that replaces the CMO with a chief customer officer, makes product and brand managers subservient to customer managers, and oversees customer-focused functions including R&D, customer service, market research, and CRM. These changes shift the firm's focus from product profitability to customer profitability, as measured by metrics such as customer lifetime value and customer equity. This organizational transformation will uproot entrenched interests and so must be driven from the top.

Source: R.T. Rust, (2010), *Harvard Business Review* January–February, p. 97

Twitter: is this the future?

Twitter Twitter is a microblog to which users send so-called tweets – short messages consisting of no more than 140 signs – via SMS, e-mail, IM, the Twitter website or an application.

These messages then appear on Twitter and may be read by anyone if you have given permission to do so. The twitterers who have indicated that they want to read your tweets are sent the tweets straightaway. As such, Twitter is a medium for corresponding with or exchanging experiences with people within a particular community. It has the potential to become a powerful communication plaform, as the following two examples show.

During the terrorist attacks on hotels and a train station in Mumbai, the world was an almost real-time witness to the events as they unfolded via the ongoing stream of Twitter messages that were made public. A photo on Twitter of an American aircraft that was forced to make an emergency landing in the Hudson River produced a quick reaction from emergency services, who were able to rescue all of the plane's occupants.

Companies have also become aware of the opportunities that Twitter provides and are opening their own Twitter channels in order to promote their own products (go to sites asuch as http://twitter.com, http://www.dell.com/twitter, http://twitter.com/ahbonus). Dell, the American computer manufacturer has various Twitter sites that announce news about their products.

Yammer Very much like Twitter, Yammer (www.yammer.com) is another tool for communicating in short messages. The difference lies in the fact that Yammer focuses on communication within a particular company.
How and whether Twitter and other similar communication systems develop is anyone's guess. As a company, Twitter has in mind a great future for itself. In November 2008 it even rejected a takeover bid of 500 million dollars from Facebook.

Up to now, Twitter has not generated any revenue worth mentioning. Twitter is free to use and up to now has not including any advertising material on its site.
However, its founder, Biz Stone, has since indicated that any extra services may have to be paid for.

MEDIA-COMMERCE WILL FLOURISH

Through good times and bad, the world's love affair with the mobile phone remains undimmed. There will be 80 mobile-phone subscriptions for every 100 people in the world in 2010. Penetration will be highest in Europe (132%), where competition among operators is intense.

Smartphones will be the fastest-growing category of handsets, even in poorer countries, where they often serve as a substitute for PCs. India and China, where more advanced third-generation (3G) mobile-phone networks are being rolled out, will see strong growth, given their lack of fixed-line infrastructure. According to Pyramid Research, 17% of Indian mobile-phone customers will be using 3G technology by 2013.

After fits and starts, m-commerce will flourish in 2010. Nokia, the world's largest handset-maker, will roll out an m-payment system that will allow users to transfer money, buy train tickets, pay bills or top-up their phone. Mobile banking, primarily an emerging-market trend, will move into the developed world. Music fans in South-East Asia will help the region account for more than a third of global spending on entertainment bought over the phone. Globally, this business will grow by 28% in 2010 to more than $40bn, according to the Mobile Entertainment Forum.

Source: 'The world in 2010', *The Economist* (2010), p. 110

10.5.8 *Purchasing*

The purchasing process consists of activities involving purchasing contracts, purchasing price determinations, specifications of order size and sales conditions, and the distribution of purchases over several suppliers. These process activities must, of course, tie in with the primary processes of manufacturing and sales. The nature of the mutual interrelationships can differ, however. In a trading company, the role of purchasing is different from that in an industrial company, where sales and manufacturing are important considerations.
The purchasing procedures selected must conform to the nature of the purchasing process.

purchases

Purchases can be categorized in several ways, including the following:

- Technical-oriented purchases; technical specifications are of great importance in this category. The ability to meet specifications is decisive and is even more important than price level as such
- Commercial-oriented purchases; this class is predominant in trading companies, which tend to be price sensitive
- Administrative-oriented purchases. In this group, purchases are made according to pre-set guidelines

In a trading company, the relationship between purchases and sales is decisive for business success. In purchasing, all factors affecting the sale of a product must be given consideration, including the price level at which sale is possible. The commercial policy should thus be concerned with both the purchasing and sales functions. There will then be integrated policy of purchasing and sales.

process of purchasing

In an industrial company, the process of purchasing takes another form, allowing for the following distinctions to be made:

- Purchases of primary materials for the manufacturing process. These are negotiated by the purchasing department and must be synchronized with production

- Purchases of installations/plants and other long-lasting production resources. These are often handled by the managing director of a company in consultation with the technical service and the purchasing department
- Purchases of secondary materials for the manufacturing process and materials for the support services. These can be handled according to administratively standard procedures, sometimes by the departments themselves, sometimes by the purchasing department

Sourcing portfolio: financial result and supply risk

Some suppliers are more important to buyers than others. The well-known 20-80 principle will hold, and many companies and institutions benefit from a differentiated sourcing strategy (van Weele, 1997). The development of such a policy starts with an analysis of the present situation with the help of a so-called sourcing portfolio. Products and services to be purchased are positioned on the basis of two criteria: influence on the financial result and supply risk. On the basis of these two criteria, supplies can be differentiated into the following four product groups:

influence on the financial result and supply risk

- Strategic products
- Leverage products
- Bottleneck products
- Routine products

These product groups are described in Figure 10.6. With the help of this portfolio, the relative importance of the products and services provided by suppliers and buyers can be estimated. It is also important to take into account the relative power position of suppliers and buyers.

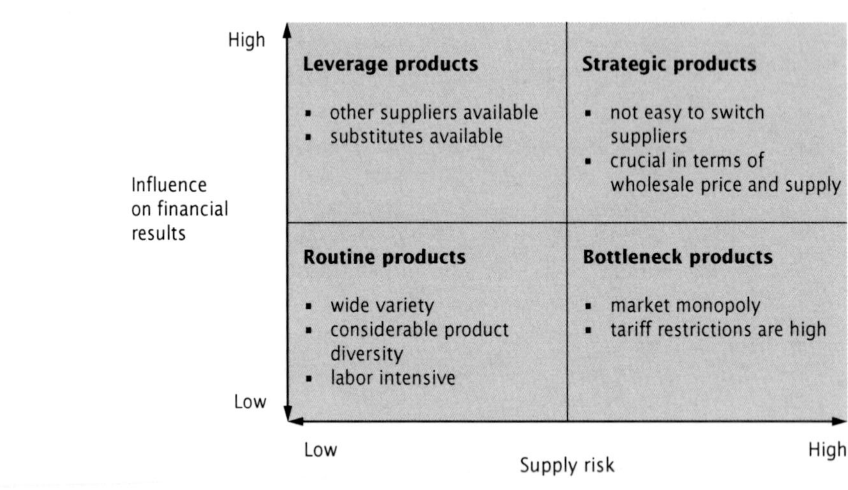

Figure 10.6
Portfolio of purchase products

In this regard, it would make a difference if, for example, buyers dominate a particular sector (e.g. the automobile industry), suppliers dominate (e.g. information technology) or whether there is a balanced relationship. In each case, there are consequences for corresponding policy issues governing sourcing operations. The development of partnership relationships in a supply network is also significant. When, for example, a commitment to product innovation is expected of a supplier, there will be a noticeable effect on pricing, quality (control), product specification and so on.

10.5.9 Human resources: the personnel process

management of human resources

Management of human resources affects the way in which personnel is selected, hired, educated, promoted, compensated, fired and retired. This decision-making category covers the wide area of human relations for which methods and procedures have been developed based on systems elaborated in the behavioral sciences and studies into administrative techniques (see chapters 6, 7 and 8).

Control of the personnel process demands that management assigns it some strategic and operational content. This content-giving task is one of the responsibilities of a company's or institution's board of directors. The resulting duties can be assigned to an official personnel department, which can then delegate part of the operational activities to the managers of the various departments, who perform them under its supervision. For example, the assessment of an employee takes place in the department by the departmental head, while the assessment system and the accompanying procedures are designed and monitored by the personnel department itself.

personnel policy

In personnel policy, a directorate or board expresses how the company or institution wants to handle matters which affect the people who work there. Since the personnel policy is a company affair, it is important that the directorate or board, acting as the responsible authority for the content of the personnel policy, expressly considers all proposals offered by the works council.

Besides input from the works council, the workstation line needs to contribute to any formulation of personnel policy. The directorate or board will itself have been advised about any workfloor suggestions by the personnel officers that it has appointed and who have the professional training and required expertise to handle such matters. If an organization is too small to be able to hire its own full-time personnel staff, the managerial team can seek advice from external experts from, for example, other organizations in the same sector or from management consulting firms for small businesses.

HRM outsourcing

A recent development in the human resources management of large companies is HRM outsourcing to a third party (i.e. by BP). BP determines its own HRM policy and makes decisions related to future personnel policy, but the actual human resource work, which is to say, all the administrative and operational duties (administration of salary and payments, training, recruitment, selection, transfers and maintenance of personnel data), is outsourced to a specialized service provider on the basis of a five-year contract.

In formulating personnel policy, labor legislation needs to be respected, as well as a number of elementary and employee-related obligations.

job description

The elementary matters include the keeping of personnel records containing personal data, job title and job description. In addition, the performance of personnel must be monitored and compensated, which involves salary administration and social provisions such as employment insurance, pensions and so on. In the same area, there are related duties involving the registration of reimbursements, special bonuses and so on.

education, training and personal development

Education, training and personal development of organizational members are also included among the tasks assigned to employees responsible for the management of personnel. Any organization that wants to keep up-to-date with the latest developments will have to undertake the training and education of its own workers. Some organizations pay a lot of attention to this activity and have a department for training and development. Although the wishes and abilities of existing staff have to be taken into account in the plans, it is nevertheless important to know what the organization needs in order to keep up with recent social developments (see sections 7.6-7.9).

JAPAN: BOOSTING GROWTH WITH DAYCARE

Nana Nakagawa would love to have another baby, but given the problems she has finding daycare for her two-year-old daughter, she's not sure she could manage. Although her apartment complex in the port city of Yokohama has a nursery, more than 50 children applied for fewer than 10 spots. So Nakagawa's morning commute involves a train ride and a walk to a different daycare center, then another hour on the train to her job at Daiwa Securities in Tokyo's Marunouchi business district. 'I realize that the clock is ticking,' says the 33-year-old, 'but unless I get more backup from the government, it's difficult to imagine bearing a second child.'

As Prime Minister Yukio Hatoyama sets about getting Japan's economy back on its feet, he understands he needs to help women like Nakagawa. Hatoyama's government said it would spend $225 million to expand daycare facilities. The effort is part of an $81 billion economic stimulus package, a sweeping measure that includes everything from subsidized loans for small businesses to incentives for eco-friendly cars and appliances. The government 'aims to create a society in which everyone can play a role,' Hatoyama said in a speech to Parliament. 'This will mean promoting gender equality in all aspects of life, including employment and child-rearing.'

With the lowest birth rate of any industrialized country – 1.34 children per woman – Japan has a dramatically shrinking population, so there are fewer workers to support growing numbers of pensioners. Providing easy access to child care would make women more willing to have babies, says Social Affairs Minister Mizuho Fukushima, who has been instrumental in the push to improve daycare. 'Women working for companies have long hours, and that's a struggle,' Fukushima says. She knows how hard it is: when her daughter was young, she had to move to a new neighborhood to get after-school care that would allow Fukushima to continue her work as a lawyer.

Just as important, better daycare could bring more women back into the workforce, boosting economic growth. Last year, just 67.5% of Japanese women worked, vs. more than 80% in Scandinavian countries and 72.3% in the U.S. Increasing that rate would give a big boost to consumer spending, according to Dai-ichi Life Research Institute, and it could send the Nikkei 225 Stock Average up by more than 3% – creating $70 billion in wealth. 'Given how acute the demographic pressures are, Japan can't afford not to make better use of its women,' says Kathy Matsui, the chief strategist at Goldman Sachs Japan and a mother of two.

So far, details of Tokyo's plans for improving daycare are vague. Early next year the government aims to ease rules restricting the maximum number of children at Japan's nearly 23,000 daycare centers, and Hatoyama plans to offer families a monthly allowance of $145 per child under 15. Some skeptics, though, say many Japanese women are far more interested in careers and travel than in having children, so the government's efforts may have little effect. 'I just don't believe it's a matter of child support,' says Nicholas Smith, strategist at MF Global FXA Securities. 'It's a matter of changing the mindset.'

Hatoyama can look to France as a model. Since expanding child support programs in 2004, Paris has provided as much as $660 a month to subsidize daycare, hands out $1,300 for each newborn, and offers families some $260 monthly for each child under three. French women now give birth to an average of 1.96 children each, the most in Europe and up from 1.78 a decade ago.

The emphasis on getting women back to work represents a significant change in Japan. Under the previous liberal Democratic Party government, which Hatoyama's Democrat unseated in August elections, the issue received little attention. Just three years ago, then-Health & Welfare Minister Hakuo Yanagisawa said Japanese women – whom he called 'baby-making machines' – simply needed to get busy (though he later apologized for the remark). 'Until now, efforts to improve child-care facilities were shoved aside because they didn't win votes,' says Yutaka Sanada, a manager at a trade group representing after-school care centers.

Many experts believe Hatoyama must move quickly. Japan has already returned to deflation, the downward spiral of prices that plagued the country for a decade until 2006. And economic growth was an anemic 1.3% in the third quarter, while the yen's rise to a 14-year high against the dollar is threatening corporate profits.

Any change will be welcomed by Yoko Furukawa. The 28-year-old public relations executive loves her job at shipping line Nippon Yusen, but she's worried about keeping it. When her son turns three next November, he'll no longer be eligible for the company nursery, and Furukawa fears she won't find an alternative: 'It would almost be a miracle for my child to get into any of the government-run centers.'

Source: *Bloomberg Business Week*, December 28, 2009 and January 4, 2010, p. 96-97

ATTRACTION AND DEVELOPMENT OF PEOPLE

Many companies proclaim that people are their most important asset (though few behave as though they believe it). All operations capabilities depend on people, and, accordingly, a comprehensive operations strategy must explicitly address how the company will attract, develop, and retain the right people. Management gurus laud General Electric Company's Crotonville learning center and its succession planning process for developing executives. GE's scale and diverse businesses justify its investment in managers who can move around the company to provide fresh energy and perspective. Few competitors can match its ability to develop great executives.

Source: T. Laseter (2009) *Strategy + Business* 57(winter), p. 31

10.5.10 *Financial process and information supply*

Financial and administrative processes are necessary in every organization in order to control the incoming and outgoing flows of money, as well as to report on and supply information about the extent to which value is being added to the primary processes (manufacturing, servicing and sales). The course and the character of these financial and information flows do, of course, strongly depend on these primary processes.
In a financial institution such as a bank, the incoming flow of money undergoes a process completely different from that of the incoming flow of materials in an industrial company. In all cases, monitoring of the flows of money, properties or goods is essential.
In a financial institution, the incoming flow of money entrusted to the bank by its clients or created by the banking institution itself is made available to clients in the form of credit or loans. The obligations of maintaining a sound liquidity position requires the institution to strive for a balance between the amounts and times of incoming and outgoing flows of money.
In an industrial company, the incoming and outgoing flow of money can be derived from marketing and sales plans as well as from the production and inventory plans. The financial process consists therefore of the determination of long and short-term investment strategies, the related task of indicating financial needs, the monitoring of liquidity and solvability positions, and the formulation of a well-conceived reservation policy. In this process, the laws and practices of economics will play a substantial role.

Financial planning and budgets

planning procedure

For the control of the financial process, a planning procedure involving the formulation of projections and budgets is essential. It will be used to create the:

- Sales budget
- Manufacturing budget
- Purchase budget
- Inventory budget
- Investment budget for fixed assets and machinery
- Cost budget
- Liquidity budget

process control

In all such documents, the desired level of return, profitability and solvability has to be taken into account. This requirement involves not so much the drawing up of budgets as the monitoring of them. Changes to them, which are made by calling in managerial or responsible departmental employees in combination with other departments, have to fall within tolerable limits. Process control is only effectively possible when prompt and readily understandable information is available at the time of an event and/or when deviations are reported as a part of the routine monitoring of activities (see sections 10.1 and 10.2).

10.6 Process redesign

The application of old organization principles often leads to work processes being analyzed and segregated into separate activities. Processes such as product development, execution of an order and supplying information to a client can be divided into smaller operations and distributed to several sub-units within the organization. Slowness, rigidity and a high level of supervision are unavoidable in such situations.

cross-functioning of company processes

Often the 'ownership' of a company process cannot be simply assigned according to the traditional, functional-hierarchical structure of organizations and systems. Such a company process as product development (Fig 10.7) is often carried out and directed by various departments (R&D, marketing and manufacturing). Such cross-functioning of company processes is frequently hindered by laborious coordination problems inflicting both management and the execution of the functions in question. They can also be additionally plagued by a lack of clarity concerning the ways in which goals and responsibilities are shared.

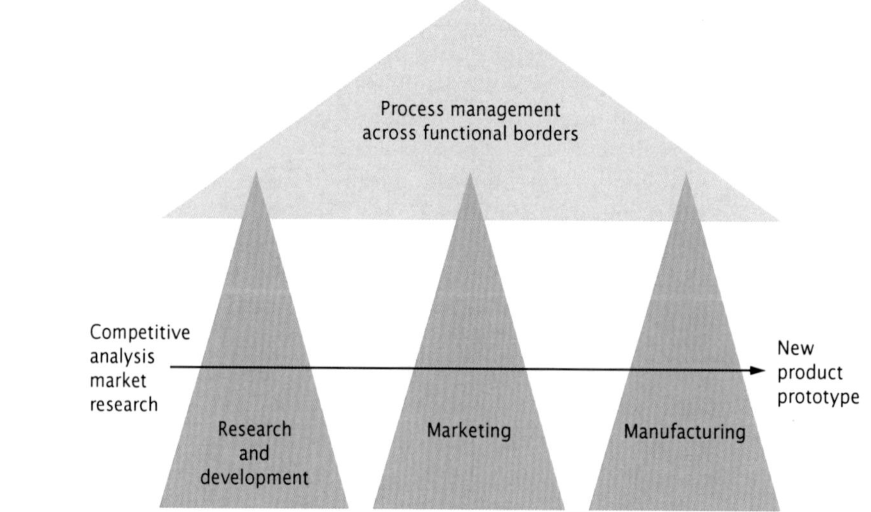

Figure 10.7
Product development as a company process

Despite the emphasis placed on processes by the older and even classic organizational models, modern practice has revealed that this process-oriented point of view is insufficient for many functionally structured organizations, especially when company processes involve data processing. In fact, these types of processes play a central role in many administrative environments.
In such organizations as financial institutions and many governmental agencies, the primary processes are of a data-processing nature. In Michael Hammer's well-known sketch (1991) simple company processes are transformed via computerization into many separate company functions and information systems. They take much longer to complete than previously, and as a result, customer service falls below acceptable levels. Although information technology (IT) appears to have contributed to the efficiency of certain parts of some company processes, the overall efficiency and effectiveness of the chain of activities that constitutes a company's primary processes are not necessarily improved. On the contrary: functionally-oriented departments often maximize their interests at the expense of the effectiveness of the wider organization. In short, sub-optimization occurs. Inefficiency is embedded in the boundaries between functional departments. These dividing lines require coordination mechanisms that do not necessarily add any value at all, but may, indeed, work as a restraint. For this reason, these divisions and the intermediate links needed to overcome them must be eliminated by redesign or re-engineering as far as possible.

sub-optimization

10.6.1 Process orientation: a must in the IT era

chain of activities

A company process consists of a chain of activities with a beginning, an end, input and output. The activities in a chain are performed at different locations and points in time. They can therefore be temporarily organized in different ways and designed into an organizational structure (see Chapter 6). An integral company process (e.g. costs, time, amount of input, quality of output and customer satisfaction) can be measured much more easily than a departmental function operating as a small detached part of the total operation.

integral company process

Decades ago, Japanese business life became aware of the fact that a process orientation has definite advantages. Just In Time and Total Quality Management are, in effect, examples of such process-oriented approaches. But where these approaches are concerned with continuous improvement, BPR (Business Process Redesign), with the use of IT, concentrates on the need to make radical changes: the complete redesign of all processes. Where the Japanese applications originated in industry and were later also applied to non-manufacturing processes, BPR can be found especially in the more administrative, service-oriented organizations such as banks and insurance companies, or in similar parts of industrial organizations (marketing, sales and order administration).

radical changes

re-engineering

By definition, re-engineering is radical. The primary question is not how to improve the existing situation, but why do we actually do what we do? With BPR, an organization can improve its performance radically. The company process is seen not as the sum of the organized functions, but as a collection of related, customer-oriented core processes: the processes which add value for the customer. Consequently, it is expressly seen as involving a series of mutually connected activities that crisscross through possible functional dividing lines and are intended to generate customer-oriented output.

In most applications of re-engineering, tasks that have been separated from main functions are bundled together and organized into a single coherent process and performed by one person or by a team acting as the process owner. It has been wrongly assumed that the complexity of labor processes is a function of the intricate nature of individual tasks. Current views now locate the greatest source of complexity in the many coordinating activities required by excessive division of labor.

CASE

Mini case study 10.9

Some examples of BPR

By means of re-engineering, the time IBM Credit needed to make a business transaction (the IBM daughter company which finances purchase of computers and software for IBM clients) was reduced from six days to four hours. Instead of feeding a financing problem through four specialists all burdened with a single component of the assessment, the request is now handled by one generalist who has on-line access to data files and who only consults a specialist in particular cases (10 per cent of all cases). Because Ore forms no longer have to travel from one department to the other, the service is now much faster.

An insurance firm switched from an insurance request procedure consisting of thirty steps in which twenty people and five departments were involved, and with a total completion time of five to ten days, to a system with case managers who handled all but the most complicated cases and with a completion time of two to five days. The processing capacity was doubled and hundreds of functions were eliminated. Information technology played a crucial role in this.

Exhibit 10.1 *Is your company ripe for re-engineering?*

The following self-assessment questions have been devised by consultants Coopers & Lybrand to determine whether a company is ready to make a success of business process re-engineering. Circle either yes (Y) or no (N).

1 Do you review customer perception of your products and services more than once a year? Y/N
2 Does your company have anyone whose pay depends specifically on achieving some measure of customer satisfaction? Y/N
3 Can you define your company's basis of competition as one of cost, service, flexibility or quality? Y/N
4 Have you benchmarked your company's core business processes against those of your competitors? Y/N
5 Does your business use activity-based costing? Y/N
6 Could you write down more than three non-financial quantified targets for your company? Y/N
7 Has a new technology caused a major shift in your company's activity during the past three years? Y/N
8 Do you have a unique technical competitive advantage in any of your business processes? Y/N
9 Is your company vulnerable to a takeover? Y/N
10 For new investments, do you have a return-on-capital-expenditure hurdle of at least 25%? Y/N
11 Does the head of your company pursue personal recognition ahead of recognition of your business? Y/N
12 Does the head of your company communicate personally with every employee at least once a year? Y/N
13 Does the head of your company emphasize how people are expected to act? Y/N
14 Is there a commonly held view of the likely market share which will be held by your company in five years' time? Y/N
15 Have you any business process or cross-functionally orientated teams? Y/N
16 Do you consider that teams are less successful at achieving their goals than individuals? Y/N
17 Was the last major re-organization in your company more than three years ago? Y/N
18 Has your company ever launched a new product or service which, if it failed, would destroy the business? Y/N
19 Is it difficult for individuals to make career moves between different positions within the company? Y/N
20 Is everyone in the company encouraged to undertake more than five days' training each year? Y/N

Assessment

Score 1 for each answer that tallies with the following:
1 Y; 2 Y; 3 Y; 4 Y; 5 Y; 6 Y; 7 Y; 8 Y; 9 N; 10 N; 11 Y; 12 Y; 13 Y; 14 Y; 15 Y; 16 N; 17 N; 18 Y, 19N; 20Y.

Interpretation
Score 0-7

You have a long way to go. So many of the conditions for success are absent that the scale of the change needed will be beyond your current capability. Instead you should undertake targeted improvement programs in a few areas such as customer research, market share projections and cross-function teams.

Score 8-14
You have got some of the conditions – begin to think about how a re-engineering program could make a significant difference.

Score 15-20
You have great potential for re-engineering but probably need to get senior people together to find your 'breakpoints' – those aspects of your product or service which have achieved excellence and bring a sustained leap in market share.

10.6.2 Objectives and business process redesign

The goals formulated before a BPR project gets underway are often highly ambitious. The nature of these goals may be quite diverse:

- Reduction of time, often shortening of completion time
- Reduction of costs, often those resulting from manpower and resources
- Improvement in quality, often intended to enhance customer satisfaction by increasing the speed or reliability of deliveries
- Another way of managing the organization, especially by viewing company processes in a trans-functional manner

active participation

To achieve such ambitious goals, the active participation of a company's highest management level is absolutely necessary. Without such commitment, 'bottom up' changes to the many company processes will fail as a result of conflicts between organizational units. These conflicts will probably have to do with competency. Formulating and realizing such goals as those mentioned above is sometimes easier if it occurs incidentally. Mergers or acquisitions, privatizations, or outsourcing of certain tasks may facilitate bottom-up restructuring of company processes.

10.6.3 Business process redesign: the combination of 'old' concepts with ICT

Briefly summarized, the methods and techniques of BPR are:

- A view of operations in terms of customer-to-customer contact
- Critical choice of company processes to be restructured
- Measurement of process performance (benchmarking) in terms of completion time, costs and quality
- Structuring of activities and flows of information so that they contribute to the realization of process goals: for example, from the point of view of logistics when the completion time is important
- Cultivation of a willingness to restructure the present organization in a radically different manner
- Screening of resource possibilities (e.g. ICT) before or at the same time as determining goals

information technology

Information technology is a powerful tool with which to initiate process changes in organizations. Organizational and personnel concerns virtually always acquire an important place in any BPR project.
BPR comprises more than just computerization. Older and more recently developed methods and techniques come under the same heading, and here the interface between BPR and computerization is considerable.
When company processes are redesigned, traditional control resources are still valued in any description, analysis, redesigning practice or revised policy document. In applying BPR, it is

necessary to devise methods and techniques that can appropriately map out the various BPR procedures. These can include information about workplace research, data logistics, administrative structure, and so on. In addition, use should be made of organizational concepts such as horizontal structure, teamwork and socio-technical system design. Nevertheless, the old issue of lack of a well-thought-out and formulated strategy may still mean that specific goals for redesign (in terms of time, money and quality) are not achieved. Fundamental to the notion is that BPR redesigns primary processes in ways that break down functional boundaries and link together functionally specific partial processes so that they are fully geared towards realizing company goals.

organizational concepts

Even though BPR is promising, any organizational change remains a difficult prospect, and possessing a new integrated view of company processes via BPR does not necessarily make it any easier.

From process redesign to business redesign

The most advanced ICT is likely to prompt an increasing number of companies to completely reorganize or establish new companies that exploit the new technologies and what they offer right from the start. This is particularly likely in the areas of marketing, logistic control and networking, all of which are strongly driven by new ICT applications. The home service system is a good example of business redesign. It is electronic shopping service offered via the Internet by Ahold and coupled with home delivery. Coupled with logistics as part of the partnership and a new national delivery system, this new shopping concept is a good example of business network redesign.

10.7 ICT entrepreneurship

The most suitable type of marketing will depend on a company's specific orientation. Organizations with an internal orientation operate in reasonably homogeneous and stable markets such as the petroleum market. They are concerned with the minimization of costs, optimization of distribution processes and enhancement of contacts with suppliers. Customer relationships mean product sales. These relationships are facilitated by the distribution channels and the types of advertising permitted by various forms of mass media. Brands play a major role. The role of the Internet will be restricted and will be primarily used to provide information to customers (potential and existing) and to facilitate organizational processes.

internal orientation

brands

Organizations that focus on specific target groups operate in markets that are extremely dynamic, and they therefore offer more products and services with the intention of becoming market leaders. The various types of customers are categorized so that each group can be easily qualified and quantified (Nike is an example of this type of company). Various marketing communication channels are used for various products targeting various groups of customers. The heterogeneity of demand is relatively high. A more immediate contact with the target group is required, and it is the Internet that is used for this purpose. Selling over the Internet is not a particularly effective practice as it could give rise to conflicts between the producer and licensed retailers.

The benefits and uses of the Internet are different for companies with a customer- or network-orientation. Such companies are primarily concerned with the development of direct relationships with and commitments from various individuals. The product is made customer-specific by adding certain services or features in a way that resembles tailor-made working practices. The process is especially applicable to financial products or modular built products, such as cars. The organization also establishes databases that record the purchase data and consumer behavior of individual customers. This can result in the customer developing a preference for certain products or for certain distributors. The differences between individual customers (groups) mean that there has to be a multi channel strategy which allows the customer to decide which medium he or she wants to use for communications and/or purchases. In a customer-focused orientation, management would be involved in relationships,

customer- or network-orientation

multi channel strategy

as the cultivation of a good customer relationship is worth far more than a one-off transaction. A network orientation promotes an even closer relationship between customers and sellers. A relatively heterogeneous demand and a largely dynamic market are assumed. Where the market is strong and rapidly changing, and there is close cooperation between several parties (for example collective purchasing by a chain of supermarkets), a network orientation is ideal. It not only requires suppliers to focus on relationships, but also to consider the interests that it actually shares with its business partners and, therefore, to participate in each other's organizational processes (for example in the form of a just-in-time delivery process). The use of ICT becomes even more necessary when the customer plays a central role and has a greater influence on the commercial process (for example, via the Internet).

network orientation

10.7.1 Web 2.0: business advantages

Web 2.0

In general, Web 2.0 refers to all Internet technologies that make Web experiences more interactive and give them a social content: Weblogs, Twitter, websites with product reviews, social networking sites such as Hyves, LinkedIn and Facebook, and websites such as YouTube which allow users to share their videos and discuss them.
Research involving nearly 1,700 top managers carried out by McKinsey has confirmed that managers are unequivocably positive about Web 2.0, with 69 procent of those surveyed indicating that there are tangible business advantages to be gained from it, including more innovative products, more effective marketing, quicker access to information, greater customer satisfaction and lower marketing and transaction costs. Companies that use these technologies obtain better results.
The research also showed that successful companies do not only integrate Web 2.0 tools within their internal business processes: they also put them to the use of customers, suppliers and partners, thereby creating a networked company. These new applications rate highly, particularly in the high tech, telecom and business services sectors.

networked company

THIS IS HOW WEB 2.0 CAN WORK FOR YOU

- Let your employees communicate freely throughout the organization and collaborate in systematizing managerial information, exchanging best practices and coordinating activities.
- Make it possible for external parties to also provide feedback and to contribute to such things as product development.
- Allow the formation of a large-scale and intricate network that invites experts (both internal and external) to participate. Enlist their help in finding solutions to problems. Hold competitions.
- Take part in intercative marketing. Build brand communities.
- When decisions are being made and new ideas thought up, drawn on the ideas of a lot of different people.

Source: *McKinsey Quarterly*, no. 2, 2009

The respondents mention that the main advantage to the company's internal organization is that it is easier for employees to get in touch with each other, and as a consequence, employees are more inclined to participate in projects and to exchange ideas, which in turn may mean a shorter time to market of new products. Operational costs will drop too since there is less need to travel: the employees can make their contribution via internal blogs or Wiki pages.

time to market

THE CUSTOMER IS NOW PART OF THE DESIGN PROCESS

Second on the list of the top three ways that companies like to employ in order to obtain a competitive advantage is a good customer relationship. Despite this, customers are rarely involved in value creation. It would seem that the fact that a product's added value lies in the experience of the customer has not yet got through to most companies. However, Nokia has realized this. It is letting its customers into its business secrets (well, to a certain extent) and thus directly including the customer in its value creation. From September onwards, anyone can take part in the co-creation project *Nokia Pilots*. Those who are computer-selected to take part may share their reactions, wishes and annoyances with the mobile phone manufacturers. This will happen early in the design process, and as such, the chosen *bèta testers* will have to sign a confidentiality agreement. But Nokia isn't the only company that is letting its customers take a look behind the scene: Google lets so-called trusted testers try out products that have not yet been launched.

Source: www.emerce.nl/2008

co-creation
crowd sourcing

Web 2.0 can also benefit customers, the most frequently mentioned benefits being lower marketing costs and greater customer satisfaction. *Co-creation* (also known as 'crowd sourcing') would have been impossible without Web 2.0. Co-creation involves companies working alongside their customers to create new products. One company that comes readily to mind is Lego. Lego invited children to upload photos of their best creations and then got site visitors to vote for their favorite design. The one that attracted the most votes then went into actual production. This sort of model can also be applied to the business market: customers have a say in product innovations and the virtual community chooses the improvements that they think are most desirable. Cisco has done this with quite some success: one invitation resulted in 2,500 contributions from 104 countries.

Companies have the benefit of free mental energy and enhanced customer loyalty.

CROWD SOURCING BY CISCO

'Inside Cisco's search for the Next Big Idea' describes how Cisco used Web 2.0 to involve the public in thinking up innovative new products. The company received 2,500 contributions from 104 countries. This article described the operational process and showed that competitions of this sort are much more than merely promotion of a website.

Source: *Harvard Business Review*, September 2009

main communication channel

The Internet is now predicted to become the main communication channel of the future, with other channels playing a supporting role. While it would once take five days before a complaint was dealt with, clients now expect to be helped immediately. Video chatting is now possible, with customers using their webcam to speak directly to helpdesk workers. To take the customer seriously now means keeping track of them as users of the new technologies, or so it is claimed: maintaining personal contact with the customer and listening to what he or she wants, co-creation being the ultimate ideal. All Web 2.0 applications tie in with the human need for contact, as the popularity of weblogs., video sharing and on-line chatting demonstrates.

McKinsey indicates that use of Web 2.0 is starting to take on within companies. A large number of those surveyed (50%) thought that new technologies needed to be invested in as against one-quarter who were happy for things to remain as they are. According to McKinsey, the research results indicate that a new type of organization is coming into existence – a *networked organization* that makes very intensive use of interactive technology, both internally and in relation to customers and partners. Those respondents who said that they had achieved tangible results already maintain Web 2.0 contact with 35 percent of their customers and 50 percent of their partners. According to the researchers, such organizations promise to be more resilient and flexible because they have quicker access to information and consequently can be more innovative.

networked organization

However, it is worth mentioning that one third of respondents indicated that they were experiencing no business advantages at all, mainly because they had not yet found a suitable way of applying the technology.

From Web 2.0 to Web 3.0

semantic web

Technology never remains still, and we are now being told that the next development will be Web 3.0, also known as the 'semantic web', and computers that are able to understand information without human intervention. Web 3.0 robots will read and understand Web pages. Consumers will soon have their own online agents – robot 'butlers' who will go searching for information on behalf of their 'masters' and interpreting it, making the required decisions and providing protection from (or rather, screening out) unwanted marketing advertizing.

Type of orientation decisive for Internet use and marketing approach

traditional marketing principles

It is important to decide which orientation is suitable for a given organization because such a decision will determine the role of the Internet. In theory, the Internet can supplement regular organizational processes by giving them either an internal or target-group orientation. In either case, the traditional marketing principles and approaches involving segmentation and target groups remain applicable. When one chooses a customer or network orientation, the Internet becomes an integral part of the organizational concept. It affects what the customer wants, how the customer relationship develops and with whom he or she communicates. Adapted approaches and websites that take into account the different orientations are consequently to be recommended. Organizations thus have to decide on their portal strategy. From the marketing point of view, taking a pot shot at everything is too unfocussed an approach. A recent McKinsey study recommended that organizations think about their vertical (industrial sector focused) portals and their segment portals.

vertical portals

Vertical portals are dedicated to the function or link which one wants to fulfill within an organizational sector, whether this be offering types of car insurance, financial services, or some such activity.

segment portals

Segment portals are, in fact, sub-sites inside general portals focusing on mass markets, but the segments serve specific target groups (think for example of Yahoo! Finance) who are only interested in a few of the offered products or services. The difference between B2B (business-to-business) forms of e-commerce and B2C (business-to-consumer) sales should also be kept in mind. Choosing an effective organizational strategy for the Internet is therefore not a computer system issue, but requires a tailor-made approach. Conflicts between channel interests and the parties belonging to a given industrial sector are always a possibility. And with a multi-channel approach, further caution should be taken to avoid cannibalization effects, in which the possibility for returns are undermined by practices that engage contradictory activities on different channels, for example in price setting, service providing, and so on.

multi-channel approach

10.7.2 E-business: integrated management approach demanded

Internet strategy

Just announcing the fact that a company is adopting an Internet strategy is not enough. Internet and e-commerce are not magical formulas, but demand a clearly laid down approach and especially an integrated management strategy. From the technological point of view, system integration, security and user friendliness must be taken into account. If changes to the organizational structure are also involved, attention must also be paid to the integration of departments, process design or redesign, reduction of material facilities and possibilities of outsourcing. Insofar as power and cultural factors are involved, a restructuring of the value chain and a renewed readiness to co-operate with suppliers and customers is essential. Focusing on such concerns will reduce though not eliminate the possibility of channel and structural conflicts.

An implementation strategy also has to take account of the organizational vision and degree of uncertainty. The organizational goals may vary from highly target-focused and clearly defined to relatively unspecified, longer-term and incorporating room for experimentation. The chosen approach will also depend on what competitor or market newcomers are doing. As such, E-commerce is more than just doing business electronically or via the Internet: it has a number of organizational consequences. The major change that the Internet and the arrival of e-commerce have brought to the business world is the opportunity to make transactions in different ways via the Internet and over the mobile phone via I-mode, so that the physical location of a company is often no longer important.

E-commerce

Since traditional or 'old economy' companies are increasingly viewing the Internet as an integral component of their overall business, these old economy companies are starting to evolve into so-called dot-corps. The distinction between established companies and dot-coms has in the meantime become more blurred, particularly since the roller-coaster days of the dot-com boom.

dot-corps

CORPORATE BLOGS

Used properly, web-based tools can be an effective way to get your message across.

Once dismissed as mere online diaries, weblogs – or blogs for short – have become corporate tools. Today they go beyond sharing product information and have the potential to communicate with a wide range of stakeholders, including prospective employees, investors, suppliers – even consumers or non-profit organizations.

Online communication can be used to serve a brand's clientele while building reputation. Henkel demonstrates this with its Persil blog (www.persilblog.de).

It has a clear focus: informing readers about what is happening with the product, including the brand's history. The content is varied: sometimes blog posts provide information on getting clothes cleaner, sometimes they cover new developments.

Procter & Gamble is less direct, supporting blogging activities that focus on social responsibility issues and safer drinking water. But again it illustrates how blogs can support corporate efforts to resonate with consumers.

Some reputation-focused blogs are linked to a particular product, such as the Royal Bank of Canada, which focuses on issues of interest to school leavers going on to further education. Volvo has numerous blogs, one related to its sponsorship of sailing activities.

GE became one of the first companies to use a specific domain for a blog targeted at investors, shareholders and analysts (see www.gereports.com). The blog is the only source of information about cost-cutting efforts (for example at GE Capital). Similarly, Daimler has used its blogs to inform employees and suppliers about its strategy to weather the current economic storm.

Other companies use their blogs to make students aware of career opportunities. One of the more successful examples is Oracle's oraclerecruiter.blogspot.com.

The impact of a takeover can also be explained in a blog. US bank Wells Fargo, for example, launched a corporate blog on its takeover of Wachovia. The blog addressed issues such as how the takeover and revamp of operations would pay off for the company, for employees and for shareholders.

Companies included in the FT ComMetrics Blog Index have effectively leveraged their brand by using social media to reach a larger audience. There is a strong case for saying that, while Twitter or Facebook may be all the rage, when used well, blogs work better to raise brand awareness, as well as to initiate and maintain a long-term conversation to foster better relationships with a company's stakeholder groups.

To view the FT ComMetrics Blog Index, go to: FTindex.ComMetrics.com

Source: *Financial Times*, May 14, 2009

Recent developments

Latest developments show that after the dot.com carnage, Europe like America is seeing increasing consolidation (and domination) by a small number of Web survivors such as Amazon.com and Dell.
Europe's Internet service providers are also seeming to get a boost from the 'new': think of T-online (Deutsche Telecom), Wanadoo (France Télécom) and Google.
While the perception is still that B2B e-commerce never really happened widely and on a large scale, the reality is that while hundreds of B2B exchanges did indeed fail, at the same time recent surveys show that e-businesses are plunging ahead. Online advertising is currently experiencing a surge in growth prompted by the popularity of banner ads, Twitter and other Web 2.0 technologies.
Productivity has accelerated in industries that make a lot of use of modern technologies. These industries include the automobile industry. Broadband subscription is growing. Only the future will show whether the firms of both the 'old' and the 'new' economies can stimulate new growth and profitability in the new e-business era.

CASE

Mini case study 10.10

The return of the mainframe

Geeks may roll their eyes at the news that Namibia is only now getting its first mainframe – a technology that most consider obsolete. Yet the First National Bank of Namibia, which bought the computer, is at the leading edge of a trend. Comeback is too strong a word, but mainframes no longer look that outdated.

Until the 1980s mainframes, so called because the processing unit was originally housed in a huge metal frame, ruled supreme in corporate data centers. Since then, these big, tightly laced bundles of software and hardware have been dethroned by 'distributed systems', meaning networks of smaller and cheaper machines, usually not based on proprietary technology. But many large companies still run crucial applications on the 'big iron': there are still about 10,000 in use world-wide. Withdraw money or buy insurance, and in most cases mainframes are handling the transaction.

Some companies like mainframes because they are reliable, secure and easy to maintain. But others have no choice. Banks, for instance, use decades-old applications to manage customer accounts. Moving these programs to other computers would be expensive and sometimes impossible. Most firms that can move off the mainframe have already done so, explains Rakesh Kumar of Gartner, a market-research firm.

High 'switching costs' explain in large part why mainframes are still a good business for IBM. It is the only big firm left selling them, at prices that start at $100,000 but often reach the millions. Sales of mainframes are said to have brought in about $3.5 billion a year, on average, in the past decade. Although this is only about 3.5% of the firm's overall revenue, each dollar spent on hardware pulls in at least as much from sales of software and maintenance contracts. Tony Sacconaghi of Bernstein Research estimates that 40% of IBM's profits are mainframe-related.

To preserve its mainframe business, IBM has regularly modernized its line-up of machines, lowering prices and improving performance. It has also given cash and computers to hundreds of universities and schools to get them to train replacements for retiring mainframe administrators.

In addition, IBM is trying to get customers to use mainframes for more functions. For some years it has offered specialized add-on processors at considerably lower prices, to run a greater variety of programs, mostly based on Linux, an open-source operating system. And last year IBM started bundling mainframes with applications at a discount.

IBM is also trying to attract new customers, particularly in fast-growing emerging markets. Without mainframes, India's Housing Development Finance Corporation and the Bank of China in Hong Kong would have a hard time dealing with their explosive growth, says Tom Rosamilia, who heads IBM's mainframe business.

All these efforts have had a degree of success, although mainframe revenues have been badly hurt by the recession. About 2,300 firms, a third of IBM's mainframe customers, have bought add-ons enabling them to use Linux. But IBM is in legal trouble again, as it was in the 1970s. It is accused of abusing its mainframe monopoly by refusing to license software that allows other firms to build cheaper clones of its machines. Regulators in Washington and Brussels are looking into the case.

More worrying to IBM is a run-in with Neon, a software company. It sells a program that allows computing tasks that usually run on a mainframe's regular processors to be shifted to the discounted ones meant to run things like Linux. Predictably, IBM is not happy and is said to have threatened to charge higher licensing fees to customers using Neon's software. This, in turn, has led Neon to file a lawsuit against IBM. Defeat would make a big dent in IBM's mainframe revenues.

Still, the computer industry seems to be moving IBM's way. The mainframe may well find a new home in corporate computing clouds, the pools of data-processing capacity many firms are building. Many companies are also increasingly interested in buying simpler, more integrated computer systems, even if this means a higher price. Reacting to this, IBM's rivals are making bets on mainframe-like products. On January 13th, HP and Microsoft announced a pact to come up with tight packages of hardware and software. Brad Day of Forrester Research, another market-research group, puts it thus: 'We are on the way back to the future.'

Source: www.economist.com

Summary

- We have to be completely familiar with the company processes before we can redesign them. How they and the company's activities are synchronized will determine their functionality. If well synchronized, the processes can continue. Goals are attained on time, at low cost, within contracted delivery times, and at the required service and quality levels.
- To ensure that good business practices as outlined in this chapter occur, the processes need to be precisely mapped and controlled.
- This chapter has dealt with both industrial and service organization processes. Process control has been defined and the elements that play a part in it identified.
- Under the influence of modern forms of information technology, organizational processes can sometimes be considerably accelerated. For this to occur, the existing structures involved in the processes need to be modified. The transformation frequently requires business process redesign (BPR) or re-engineering. The advantages speak for themselves.
- E-business is plunging ahead. A company-wide integrated approach is required with the Internet and available Web 2.0 technologies as an important component of their business.
- The old notion that processes constitute the basic elements of organizations and that one has to know the processes well before restructuring them is as valid now as it used to be. Where established structures hinder process performance, they must be modified.

Discussion and review questions

1 With reference to *Management in action* at the beginning of the chapter
  a) What is the role of information in the smart city of the future?
  b) Which elements of the smart city of the future do you think are sure to become reality?
  c) What is the role of commercial firms in 'smartification'? Do they follow or drive the changes?

2 What different approaches to the concept of quality can you identify?

3 With service industries, why does the back office lends itself particularly to automation?

4 Describe the relationship between 'routing' and the 'lay-out' of departments? How do both of these affect the structure of the work-station line, the distribution of tasks, and the grouping of machinery and people?

5 How would you explain the following concepts?
  a) process redesign or re-engineering
  b) business redesign
  c) business network redesign
  You should refer to the increasing degree of complexity in the redesigning of activities (at three levels) and you should focus on a customer-focused retailing model.

6 What would be your comments on the introduction of new APD products from the viewpoint of implementing marketing strategy?

7 What differences (if any) can you identify between the Japanese notion of continuous improvement and BPR?

8 Now that you have read this book on management, how would you answer the following question: what is the added value that management contributes to an organization?

Research-based exercise

Assessing readiness for business process re-engineering

Introduction
This exercise is based on a research article by Neda Abdolvand, Amir Albadvi and Zahra Ferdowsi, published in *Business Process Management Journal.* The research question, research method, and some of the results of their research project are shown. The exercise, which is related to this research article, consists of two questions. Your answers should be based on the theory in this chapter.

Research question
How can the risks of implementing business process reengineering be minimized?

Method
A survey in two companies measuring their readiness for business process reengineering

Outcomes
The indicators of a firm's readiness for business process reengineering are as follows: egalitarian leadership, a collaborative working environment, commitment on the part of top management, supportive management, and the use of information technology.

(Based on Abdolvand, N., Albadvi, A., Ferdowsi, Z. (2008). 'Assessing readiness for business process reengineering,' *Business Process Management Journal, 14*(4), 497-511.)

Questions

1 Can you explain the five indicators for BPR readiness on the basis of the theory in this chapter?
2 For each of the five indicators, can you give a reason for why these indicate a firm's readiness for BPR?

CASE

Management case study

VW is a car giant to watch

When Volkswagen CEO Martin Winterkorn said two years ago that he was determined to zoom past Toyota to become the world's biggest automaker, the notion seemed laughable. At the time, the German automaker sold 3 million fewer vehicles than Toyota, was losing ground in the U.S., and had a reputation for iffy quality. Toyota, then set to pass General Motors as the best-selling carmaker on the planet, seemed unassailable.

Today Toyota is vulnerable, and Winterkorn's ambitions seem a lot less outlandish. In November, for the first time, VW built more cars than its Japanese rival. Toyota still sells more each year, but VW has closed the gap to less than 1.5 million cars. Quality continues to be an issue for VW in the U.S., but Toyota is the one suffering negative headlines after a series of embarrassing recalls. Toyota's CEO – in an act of extreme self-flagellation – has even said his company's best days may be behind it.

By the end of 2006 it was clear that VW's move upmarket wasn't working, and in January 2007 Piëch installed Winterkorn as CEO. Before his elevation, Winterkorn ran Audi, where he boosted quality and supercharged growth with new models that rivaled BMWs cars. Winterkorn rewarded employees for speaking their minds and bringing ideas to his attention.

In the summer of 2007, Winterkorn and the board met to brainstorm ways to become the world's biggest automaker, says VW's U.S. chief, Stefan Jacoby. High on the agenda was fixing VW's America problem. That year, VW expected to sell 200,000 cars in the U.S., a 40% drop from 2000 and a third of what VW sold in 1970 when the Bug and Bus were Hippie icons. Jacoby says executives at the meeting saw three choices: they could continue to lose buckets of money selling cars that were too small and too expensive; they could wave the white flag; or they could go on the offensive. They chose Door No. 3.

Jacoby says he persuaded the board to build VW's first U.S. plant. He recalls arguing that doing so would help VW overcome resistance in the American heartland to imported vehicles. If VW built the plant, Jacoby recalls saying, he would sell 150,000 cars from that factory alone each year. The board approved the plan and allocated $1 billion for the facility, which is scheduled to open next year in Chattanooga, Tenn. VWs decision to build cars in the U.S. has not gone unnoticed by its main rival. 'The fact that they are producing in the U.S. gives them a leg up,' says Donald V. Esmond, senior vice-president for automotive operations at Toyota Motor Sales USA. 'But we'll just keep focusing on our customers.'

Winterkorn and Piëch have put in place the pieces of their global strategy. Now that VWs two main rivals, Toyota and GM are retrenching, they're speeding up their plans. The big question is whether size for size's sake generates real benefits for a car company. Automakers like to be big so they can spread the huge costs of developing new models over mass volumes. Of course, car companies have a tendency to get so big that they become unmanageable. That's what happened to GM. Bolting together various acquisitions also can be problematic. Exhibit: the unhappy Daimler-Chrysler marriage. Winterkorn and his executives argue that they can retain management control of their sprawling enterprise because VW is more decentralized than many automakers. Winterkorn: 'The critical factor is that each brand has its independence, a clear positioning, and autonomous management.'

Source: D. Welch (2010), *Bloomberg Business Week* January 25, p. 44-48

Case study questions

1 What are the pros and cons of building a VW plant in the US in terms of process and information control?
2 What are the logistical consequences of a VW plant operating in the US?
3 Should VW copy its production and service processes from existing plants to the US plant?

Bibliography

Selected references

- Abell, D. F., Defining the Business: the Starting Point of Strategic Planning, Prentice Hall, 1980
- Algera, J. A. et al., 'Prestatiesturing en teamvorming,' *Gids voor Personeelsmanagement* 6, 1994
- Amabile, T. et al., 'Creativity under the Gun,'*Harvard Business Review*, August 2002, pp. 52–61
- Ansoff, H. I, *Corporate Strategy*, revised edition, McGraw Hill, 1987
- Anthony, R. N., Dearden, J. and Govindarajan, V., *Management Control Systems*, 7th edition, Irwin, 1992
- Arendsen, L, 'Valkuilen van de Balanced Scorecard,' *Elan*, December 1995, pp. 57–59
- Argyris, C., 'Double loop learning in Organizations,' *Harvard Business Review*, 55, 5, 1977
- Argyris, C. & Schön, D., *Organizational Learning: A Theory of Action Perspective*. Reading (Mass.), Addison-Wesley, 1978
- Argyris, C., Integrating the Individual and the Organization, Wiley, 1964
- Bartlett, C. A. and Ghoshal, S., *Transnational Management*, Irwin, 1992
- Bennis, W. G., 'Revisionist theory of leadership,' *Harvard Business Review*, January–February 1961
- Berge, D. ten, De eerste 24 uur, Handboek voor crisismanagement, Tirion, 1989
- Bohn, R, 'Stop fighting firs,'*Harvard Business Review*, July–August 2000, pp. 83–91
- Bolman, L. G. and Deal, I. E., 'What makes a team work?,' *Organizational Dynamics*, Fall 1992
- Bono, E. de, Lateral Thinking for Management, Penguin Books, 1971
- Bosma, T. & Wijland, M. van, *Een Hel(s)e onderneming, bepaal zelf de toekomst*, Heerhugowaard, F en G Publishing, 2006
- Botter, C. H., *Industrie en Organisatie*, Kluwer/Nive, 1980
- Bové, J and Dufour, F., *Le monde n'est pas une marchandise*, Paris, 2000
- Bowen, D. E. & Ostroff, C., 'Understanding HRM firm performance linkages: the role of the 'strength' of the HRM system,' *Academy of Management Review*, 29 (2), 2004, pp. 203–221
- Brown, G. & Chew, D. (eds.), *Corporate Risk Strategies and Management*, Risk Books, London, 1999
- BusinessWeek, *The Kings of Quality*, August 30, 2004
- Chowdhury, S. *The power of Six Sigma*, Dearborn, 2001
- Churchill, N. C. and Lewis, V. L., 'The five stages of small business growth,' *Harvard Business Review*, May–June 1983
- Collins, J., 'Level 5 leadership: the triumph of humility and fierce resolve,' *Harvard Business Review*, January 2001, pp. 67–76
- Conger, Jay A., Lawler III, Edward E. et al., *Corporate Boards, new strategies for adding value at the top*, Jossey-Bass, San Francisco, 2001
- Covey, Stephen R., The 7 habits of highly effective people, powerful lessons in personal change, New York, Free Press, 1989
- Covey, Stephen R., *The 8th habit from effectiveness to greatness*, New York, Free Press, 2004
- Cramer, Jacqueline, *Op weg naar duurzaam ondernemen*, The Hague, SMO-99-4
- Christensen, Clayton M. et al., 'Marketing malpractice: the cause and the cure,' *Harvard Business Review*, December 2005, pp. 74–83
- Crouch, C. and Heller, F. A. (eds), Organizational Democracy and Political Procession, Wiley, 1983
- Dale, E., Management: Theory and Practice, McGraw Hill, 1973
- Daniell, M., 'Webs we weave,' *Management Today*, February 1990
- D'Aveni, Richard, 'Strike-back counterrevolutionary strategies for industry leaders,'*Harvard Business Review*, November 2002, pp. 67–74
- Davenport, Thomas H., 'The coming commoditization of processes,' *Harvard Business Review*, June 2005, pp. 101–108
- Davis, S. M. and Lawrence, P. R., *Matrix*, Addison Wesley, 1977
- Davis S. M. and Lawrence, P.R., 'Problems of matrix organizations.' *Harvard Business Review*, May-June 1978.
- Deming, W. E., Quality, Productivity and Competitive Portion, MIT, 1982
- Deming, W. E., *Out of the Crisis*, MIT, 1986
- Does, Ronald et al., *Zes Sigma zakelijk verbeterd*, Kluwer, 2001
- Donaldson, G. and Lorsch, J.W., Decision Making at the Top: the Shaping of Strategic Decisions, Basic Books, 1983
- Duyser, J. and Keuning, D., 'Verplatting als vehikel voor effectiviteitsverhoging; actualiteit, mogelijkheden en voorwaarden,' *Bedrijfskunde*, Vol. 66, 1994, No. 2
- Eckes, George, *The Six Sigma Revolution*, John Wiley, 2001
- Eckes, George, *Making Six Sigma last*, John Wiley, 2001
- Ernst, David & Bamford, James, Your alliances are too stable, in: *Harvard Business Review*, June 2005, pp. 133–141
- Exley, M., 'Building the Empowered Organization,' *Empowerment in Organizations*, 1993, Vol. 1, No. 2
- Fayol, Henri F., Administration Industrielle et Générale, Dunod, 1916/1950
- Fleming, John et al., Manage your human Sigma, in: *Harvard Business Review*, July-August 2005, pp. 107–114
- Forrester, Viviane, *De terreur van de globalisering* (orig. title *Une étrange dictature*, 2000), Dutch translation Byblos, Amsterdam, 2001
- Galbraith, J. R., Lawler III, E. E. et al., *Organizing for the Future*, Jossey-Bass, 1993
- Gelder, T. J. & Ridder, W. J. de, *Mondiale Revoluties*, The Hague, SMO, 2003-3
- George, Mike et al., *What is Lean Six Sigma?*, New York, McGraw Hill, 2004
- George, Mike et al., Wat is Lean Six Sigma? Sneller en slimmer werken met beter resultaat, Thema, 2005
- Ghemawat, Pankaj, 'Regional strategies for global leadership,'*Harvard Business Review*, December 2005, pp. 98–108
- Goffee, Rob & Jones, Gareth, 'Managing authenticity, the paradox of great leadership,'*Harvard Business Review*, December 2005, pp. 87–94
- Goleman, Daniel, 'Leadership that gets results,'*Harvard Business Review*, March/April 2000, pp. 78–90
- Goold, Michael & Campbell, Andrew, 'Structured networks: towards the well-designed matrix,' *Long Range Planning*, 36, 2003, pp. 427–439
- Graves, C. W., 'Levels of Existence: an open systems theory of values,' *Journal of Humanistic Psychology*, Fall 1970
- Greenwold, Bruce & Kahn, Judd, 'All strategy is local,'*Harvard Business Review*, September 2005, pp. 95–104
- Greiner, Larry E., 'Evolution and revolution as organizations grow,' *Harvard Business Review*, July–August 1972, pp. 37–46
- Hackman, J. R., 'Work design,' Hackman, J. R. and Suttle, J. L. (eds) *Improving Life at Work*, Scott Foresman and Company, 1977
- Hackman, J. R. (ed), Groups That Work: Creating Conditions for Effective Teamwork, Jossey-Bass, 1990
- Hagel III, J., 'Spider versus Spider,' *McKinsey Quarterly*, 1996, No. 1
- Handy, Charles, 'What's a business for?,' *Harvard Business Review*, December 2002, pp. 49–55
- Harry, Mikel & Schroeder, R, *Six Sigma*, Random House Audio, 2001.
- Harvard Business Review Special: The High-performance Organization: July–August, 2005
- Heijmann, P. M. G., Gids Europese medezeggenschap vergelijking wetten en regels, FNV, Amsterdam, 1995

- Heller, R. A., *Managerial Decision Making*, Van Gorcum/Tavistock, 1971
- Hersey, P. and Blanchard, K. H., *Management of Organizational Behavior*, Prentice Hall, 1986
- Herzberg, F., 'One more time: how do you motivate employees?,' *Harvard Business Review*, January–February 1968
- Herzberg, F., 'The wise old Turk,' *Harvard Business Review*, September–October 1974
- Hofstede, G. H., *The Game of Budget Control*, Van Gorcum, 1967
- Hofstede, G., Culture's Consequences, International Differences in Work-related Values, Sage Publications, 1980
- Husted, Kenneth and Michailova, Snejina, 'Diagnosing and fighting knowledge-sharing hostility,' *Organizational Dynamics*, August 2002, pp. 60–72
- Huyzer, S. E. et al., *Strategische samenwerking*, Samsom, 1990
- Imai, Masaaki, Kaizen, *The key to Japan's competitive success*, New York, McGraw Hill, 1986
- Jansen, P. G. W., *Het beoordelen van managers*, Nelissen, 1991
- Jaspersz, Jeff et al., *Tijd van leven*, The Hague, SMO, 2002-1
- Johnson, H. T. and Kaplan, R. S., *Relevance lost: the rise and fall of Management Accounting*, Harvard Business School Press, 1991
- Jones, M. and Sutherland, G., Implementing Turnbull: a Board Room Briefing, ICAEW, 1999
- Kalff, Donald, Onafhankelijkheid voor Europa. Het einde van het Amerikaanse ondernemingsmodel, Amsterdam, Business Contact, 2004
- Katzenbach, Jon R. & Smith, Douglas K., 'The Discipline of Teams,' *Harvard Business Review*, 1993
- Kaplan, R. S. and Norton, D. P., 'The Balanced Scorecard – measures that drive performance,' *Harvard Business Review*, January–February 1992, pp. 71–9
- Kaplan, R.S. and Norton, D.P., 'Putting the Balanced Scorecard to Work,' *Harvard Business Review*, September-October 1993, pp. 134–46.
- Kaplan, Robert S. & Norton, David P., *Strategy maps*, Boston, Harvard Business School Press, 2004.
- Kaplan, Robert S., & Norton, David P., The office of strategy management, in: *Harvard Business Review*, October 2005, pp. 72-80.
- Kennedy, Allan, *The end of shareholder value*, Orion Business Books, Londen, 2000.
- Keuning, D., *Bedrijfskunde*, Stenfert Kroese, 1988.
- Keuning, Doede, *Groei en ontwikkeling van een bedrijf*, Groningen, Wolters-Noordhoff, 2006.
- Keuning, Doede, De val van de euro is nabij, *Het Financieele Dagblad*, 24-4-2010, p. 19
- Keuning, D. and Eppink, D. J., *Management en Organisatie: Theorie en toepassing*, Stenfert Kroese, 6th edn, 1996
- Keuning, D. and Opheij, W., *Delayering Organizations*, Pitman Publishing, 1994
- Keuning, D., Opheij, W. and Duyser, J., 'Herstructureren door verplatten,' *Holland Management Review*, 1993, No. 35
- Kim, D. H., 'The link between Individual and Organizational Learning,' *Sloan Management Review*, Autumn 1993
- Kimberley, J. R. and Quinn, R. E., New futures: The Challenge of Managing Corporate Transitions, Dow Jones Irwin, 1986
- Kimman, E. J. J. M., *Organisatie-ethiek*, Van Gorcum, 1991
- Kirby, Julia, 'Toward a theory of high performance,' *Harvard Business Review*, July–August, 2005, pp. 30–39
- Klein, Naomi, *No Logo*, Knopf Canada, 2000
- Koene, A. M., Slomp, H., *Medezeggenschap van werknemers op ondernemingsniveau*, No. 29, 1991. Ministerie van SZW
- Kolb, D. A. Experiential Learning: Experience as the Source of Learning and Development. Englewood Cliffs, Prentice Hall, 1984
- Kolb, D. A., Experiential Learning: Experience as the Source of Learning and Development, Prentice Hall, 1984
- Koopman, P. L. et al., *Complexe besluitvorming in organisaties*, A&O Psychologie, 1988
- Kor, R., Wijnen, G. and Weggeman, M., *Management in motiveren: inhoud geven aan leiderschap*, Kluwer Bedrijfswetenschappen, 1991
- Kotter, John P., *The General Managers*, The Free Press, 1982
- Kotter, John P., 'What effective general managers really do,' *Harvard Business Review*, November-December 1982.
- Kotter, John P., *The Leadership Factor*, The Free Press, 1988
- Lammers, C. J., 'Organizationele democratie,' *Men O*, 1985/6
- Lash, Kalle, *Culture Jam*, Londen, Harper Collings, 1999
- Lawler III, E. E., 'Substitutes for Hierarchy,' *Organizational Dynamics*, 17, 1988, pp. 4–15
- Leavitt, H. J., 'Some effects of certain communication patterns on group performance,' *Journal of Abnormal and Social Psychology*, Vol. 46, January 1957
- Levinson, Harry, 'Management by whose objectives?', *Harvard Business Review*, January 2003/1970, pp. 107–116
- Levitt, Theodore, 'Creativity is not enough,' *Harvard Business Review*, August 2002 (1963), pp. 137–144
- Lewin, K., 'Frontiers in group dynamics: Concept, method and reality in social science,' *Human Relations*, Vol. 1, 1984, pp. 5–42
- Lievegoed, B. C. J., *Organisaties in ontwikkeling*, Lemniscaat, 1969
- Likert, R., *New Patterns of Management*, McGraw Hill, 1961
- Lindberg, R. & Berger, A., 'Continuous improvement: design, organization and management,' *International Journal of Technology Management*, 14, 1, 1997, pp. 86–101
- Lobry, Randy, *Shared Services: Kiezen én delen*, Soesterberg, Magnitude Consulting, 2002
- Lubbers, E. et al., Battling Big Business, Countering greenwash, front groups and other forms of corporate deception, Green Books, UK, 2002
- Luijk, H., Waar blijft de tijd van de directeur, Samsom, 1984
- Lumpkin G. T. et al., E-commerce strategies: Achieving Sustainable Competitive Advantage and Avoiding Pitfalls, in: *Organizational Dynamics*, Spring 2002, pp. 325–339
- Luyten, Hans & Tuitjer, Kees, 'INK-managementmodel vernieuwd,' *Management Tools*, no. 1, 2004, pp. 12–21
- Maccoby, M., Why work: leading the new generation, Simon & Schuster, 1988
- Mace, M., *Directors: Myth and Reality*, Harvard Business School Press, 1986
- Mack, David A. and Quick, James C., (eds), 'An inside view of a corporate life cycle transition,' *Organizational Dynamics*, Spring, 2002, pp. 282–293
- Mahangi, M., *De overtreffende trap van ondernemen*, The Hague, SMO, 2002-10
- Mankins, Michael C. & Steele, Richard, 'Turning great strategy into great performance,' *Harvard Business Review*, July–August, pp. 65–72
- Maslow, A. H., *Motivation and Personality*, Harper & Row, 1954
- Mastenbroek, W. F. G., *Onderhandelen*, Het Spectrum, 1984
- Mayo, Anthony J. & Nohria, Nitin, 'Zeitgeist leadership,' *Harvard Business Review*, October 2005, pp. 45–60
- McGregor, D., *The Human Side of Enterprise*, McGraw Hill, 1960.
- Meijers, Loek, 'Wat kosten SOX en Tabaksblat u?,' *ControllersMagazine*, May 2004
- Miles, R. E., 'Adapting to technology and competition: a new industrial relations system for the 21st century.' *California Management Review*, Winter 1989
- Mintzberg, H., *The Nature of Managerial Work*, Harper & Row, 1973
- Mintzberg, H., 'Crafting Strategy,' *Harvard Business Review*, July–August 1987
- Mintzberg, Henry, 'Covert leadership: notes on managing professionals,' *Harvard Business Review*, November–December 1998, pp. 140–147
- Mintzberg, Henry et al., *Strategy safari*, New York, Prentice Hall, 1998
- Moerland, P. W., 'Corporate governance in Marktwerking,' *De Naamlose Vennootschap* 73, December 1995
- Molenaar, Cor, *Wisseling van de macht*, Amsterdam, Pearson, 2006

- Mosby, David & Weisman, Michael, *The Paradox of Excellence*, San Francisco, Jossey-Bass, 2005
- Mulder, M., Conflicthantering: theorie en praktijk in organisaties, Stenfert Kroese, 1980
- Neilson, Gary L. et al., 'The passive – aggressive organization,'*Harvard Business Review*, October 2005, pp. 83–92
- Nicholls, J., 'The paradox of managerial leadership,' *Journal of General Management*, Summer 1993
- Noordam, Peter et al., *Trends in IT 2004/2005*, The Hague, Ten Hagen Stam, 2004
- Ofman, D. D., Bezieling en kwaliteit in organisaties, Cothen: Servire, 1992
- Oosterhaven, J. A., 'Hebben IT-innovaties nog wel zin? Nicholas Carr heeft eigenlijk toch wel gelijk,'Tiem-1, March/April 2004
- Paine, Lynn et al., 'Up to Code,'*Harvard Business Review*, December 2005, pp. 122–133
- Peiperl, Maury A., 'Getting 360° feedback right,' *Harvard Business Review*, January 2001, pp. 142–147
- Peter, Thomas J. and Waterman, jr., Robert H., *In Search of Excellence, Lessons from America's Best-Run Companies*, Harper & Row, 1982. (Also book review: Carroll, Daniel T., 'A disappointing search for excellence,' *Harvard Business Review*, November–December 1983)
- Pettigrew, A. M., The Politics of Organizational Decision Making, Tavistock/Van Gorcum, 1973
- Pfeffer, J., *Managing with Power*, Harvard Business School Press, 1992. (Also book review in: *Men O*, 1994/5.)
- Porter, M. E., Competitive Strategy: Techniques for Analysing Industries and Competitors, The Free Press, 1980
- Porter, M. E., Competitive Advantage: Creating and Sustaining Superior Performance, The Free Press, 1985
- Porter, Michael E. & Kramer, Mark, R., 'The Competitive Advantages of Corporate Philanthropy,' *Harvard Business Review*, December 2002, pp. 57–68
- Prahalad, C. K., The Fortune at the bottom of the Pyramid. Eradicating Poverty through Profits, Wharton School Publishing, 2004
- Prahalad, C. K., Lierberthal, K., 'The end of corporate imperialism,' *Harvard Business Review*, July–August 1998, pp. 69–79
- Reinartz, Werner & Kumar, V., 'The mismanagement of customer loyalty,'*Harvard Business Review*, July 2002, pp. 86–94
- Ridder, W. J. de, *Koers 2020, nieuwe toekomst, nieuwe leiders*, The Hague, SMO, 2005
- Robbins, S.P., Organizational Behavior: Concepts and Controversies, Prentice Hall, 1979
- Ross, Jeanne W. & Weill, Peter, 'Six IT Decisions your IT people shouldn't make,' *Harvard Business Review*, November 2002, pp. 85–91
- Rothuizen, W., 2005, 'Tabaksblat "in control"?,' *De Accountant*, 7 March 2005, p. 42–44
- Schein, E.H., Organizational Culture and Leadership: A Dynamic View, Jossey-Bass, 1985
- Schoenmaker, M. J. R., Managen van mensen en prestaties: personeelsmanagement in moderne organisaties, Kluwer Bedrijfswetenschappen, 1994
- Schroeder, D. M. & Robinson, A. G., 'America's most successful export to Japan: continuous improvement programs,' *Sloan Management Review*, 32, 3, 1991, pp. 67–81
- Semler, R., *Semco-stijl*, Forum, 1993
- Senge, P. M., 'The leaders' new work: building learning organizations.' *Sloan Management Review*, 32, 1, 1990, pp. 7–23
- Shetty, Y. K., 'Aiming High: Competitive Benchmarking for Superior Performance,' *Long Range Planning*, No. 1, 1993
- Simms, Robert, 'Designing high-performance jobs,' *Harvard Business Review*, July 2006, pp. 54 ff
- Simon, H. A., *Administrative Behavior*, Macmillan, 1947
- Simon, H. A., The Shape of Automation for Man and Management, Harper & Row, 1965
- Smit, Jeroen, *Het drama Ahold*, Uitgeverij Balans, 2004
- Snow, C., Davison, S. C., Snell, S. A. and Hambrick, D. C., 'Use Transnational Teams to Globalize your Company,' *Organizational Dynamics*, Spring 1996
- Sobek II, Durward K. et al., 'Another look at how Toyota integrates product development,' *Harvard Business Review*, July/August 1990, pp. 36–49
- Socrates, noted in Xenophon, *Memorabilia* (III. IV. 6–12) and *Oeconomicus*, Loeb Classical Library, William Heineman Ltd
- Sodhi, S. & Sodhi, N, 'Six Sigma Pricing,' *Harvard Business Review*, May 2005, pp. 135–142
- Spear, Steven J., Learning to lead at Toyota, in: *Harvard Business Review*, May 2004, pp. 78–86
- Staerkle, R., 'Der Entscheidungsprozess in der Unternehmungsorganization,' *Die Unternehmung*, March 1963.
- Stewart, Rosemary, *Managers and their Jobs*, Macmillan, 1967
- Stoner, J. A. E and Freeman, R. E., *Management*, Prentice Hall, Dutch edition, 1993
- Strikwerda, J., *Shared Service Centers*, Assen, Van Gorcum/SMS, 2003
- Stulz, R. 'Rethinking Risk Management,' *Journals of Applied Corporate Finance* 9 (3), pp. 8–24, 1996
- Swieringa, J. & Wierdsma, A. F. M., *Op weg naar een lerende organisatie*, Groningen, Wolters-Noordhoff, 1990
- Thompson, J. D., *Organizations in Action*, McGraw Hill, 1967
- Tillema, Kees & Markerink, Frank, *Gericht presteren met het INK-managementmodel*, Deventer, Kluwer, 2004
- Tracy, D., The First Book of Common Sense Management, William Morrow Company, 1989
- Trompenaars, E, Riding the Waves of Culture: Understanding Cultural Diversity in Business, Economist Books, 1993
- Turnbull Workgroup, Internal Control; Guidance for Directors on the Combined Code, Londen ICAEW, 1999
- Turner, D. and Crawford, M., 'Managing current and future competitive performance: the role of competence,' in: Hamal and Heene (eds), *Competence-based Competition*, John Wiley, 1994
- Twijnstra A. and Keuning D., *Organisatie-advieswerk*, Stenfert Kroese, 2nd edn, 1995
- Vogt, G. G., *De virtuele onderneming*, originally appeared in *Der Organisator*, March 1994
- Wildeman, B. & Betrand B., 'Van comfortabel naar compliant, effecten van de Sorbanes-Oxley Act,' *ControllersMagazine*, March 2005
- Wempe, J. & Kaptein, M., *Ondernemen met het oog op de toekomst*, The Hague, SMO-2000-3
- Wijnen, G., Renes, W. and Storm P., *Projectmatig werken*, Het Spectrum, 1984
- Wijnen, G., Weggeman, M. and Kor, R., *Verbeteren en vernieuwen van organisaties*, Kluwer Bedrijfswetenschappen, 1988.
- Wilpert, B. and Sorge, A. (eds), International Perspectives on Organizational Democracy, Wiley, 1988
- Wortel, Eva, *Business ethics in conflict areas*, The Hague, SMO, 2004–1
- Zaleznik, Abraham, 'Managers and leaders, are they different?,' *Harvard Business Review*, January 2004/1977, pp. 74–91.
- Zuyderhoudt, R., 'Principes van synergie en zelfordening: Introductie in de chaos theorie binnen de organisaties,' M & O, No. l, 1992

Further reading

General

- Amabile, Teresa M., Hadley, C. N. and Kramer, S. J., 'Creativity under the Gun,' *Harvard Business Review*, August 2002, pp. 52–61.
- Athos, A. G. and Pascale, R. T., *The Art of Japanese Management*, Penguin Books, 1982
- Battes, Prisco and Elshout, Pieter, 'De val van ABN Amro,' Amsterdam, Business Contact, 2008.

- Berrone, P., et al., 'The impact of symbolic and substantive actions on environmental legitimacy,' Academy of Management, 2009
- Bibeault, D. R., Corporate Turnaround, How Managers Turn Losers into Winners, McGraw Hill, 1982
- Bonini, Sheila et al., 'Rebuilding Corporate Reputations,' *McKinsey Quarterly*, 2009, No. 3, pp. 75–83
- Burrell, Gibson and Morgan, Gareth, *Sociological Paradigms and Organizational Analysis*, Brookfield, Ashgate Publishing, 1979/1994
- Carey, Dennis et al., 'Leadership lessons for hard times,'McKinsey Quarterly, 2009, No. 4, pp. 51–61
- Casey, Catherine, *Critical Analysis of Organizations*, Londen, Sage Publications, 2002
- Collins, J. C. Good to Great: why some companies make the leap ... and others don't.' New York: Harper Collins, 2001
- Collins, J. C., and J. I. Porras (2002), 'Built to Last: Succesful Habits of Visionary Companies,' New York: Harper Business
- Collins, Jim, 'How the mighty fall, and why some companies never give in,' Harper Collins New York, 2009
- Drucker, Peter F., 'The discipline of innovation,' *Harvard Business Review*, August 2002, pp. 95–102
- Financial Times http://news.ft.com/ft.reports
- Ghoshal, S., C. Bartlett (1996), 'Rebuilding behavioral context a blueprint for corporate renewal,' *Sloan Management Review*, winter 1996
- Guild, Todd, 'Competing for Asia's consumers,' *McKinsey Quarterly*, 2009, No. 4, pp. 25–35
- Handy, C., *The Age of Unreason*, Arrow Books, 1989
- Keuning, D. and Eppink D.J., *Management en Organisatie: theorie en toepassing*, Stenfert Kroese, 6th edn, 1996.
- Koning, C. de, Goed bestuur: de regels en de kunst, Kluwer, 1987
- Kotter, John P., 'What effective general managers really do,' *Harvard Business Review*, November–December 1982
- Lammers, C. J., Organizeren van bovenaf en onderop. Spectrum, 1993
- Lawler III, Edward E. et al., 'Corporate Boards: Keys to effectiveness,' *Organizational Dynamics*, Spring 2002, pp. 310–324
- Lawrence, P.R., Lorsch, J.W., *Organization and Environment*, Harvard Business School Press, 1986
- Levitt, Theodore, 'Creativity is not enough,' *Harvard Business Review*, August 2002, pp. 137–144
- Lindgreen, E. Roos et al., Het nieuwe ondernemen, The Hague, SMO, 2009-2.
- McDonough, William and Braungart, Michael, *Cradle to cradle: remaking the way we make things*, North Point Press, 2002
- Mintzberg, H., 'Rounding out the Manager's Job,' *Sloan Management Review*, Fall 1994
- Mintzberg, H., 'The Manager's Job: Folklore and Fact,' *Harvard Business Review*, July–August 1975
- Morgan, G., *Images of Organization*, Sage Publications, 1986
- Mueller, R.K., *Corporate Networking*, The Free Press, 1986
- Niendorf, Bruce and Beck, Kristine, 'Good to Great, or Just Good?,' *Academy of Management Perspectives*, 2008, pp. 13–20
- Pascale, R., *Managing on the Edge*, Penguin Books, 1990
- Peters, T., *Liberation Management*, Macmillan, 1992
- Porter, M. E. and Kramer, M. R., 'Strategy and society, the link between competitive advantage and corporate social responsibility,' *Harvard Business Review*, December 2006
- Prahalad, C. K. et al., 'How to Thrive in Turbulent Markets,' *Harvard Business Review*, February 2009, pp/ 79–88 (hbr.org)
- Prahalad, C. K. et al., 'Why sustainability is now the key driver of innovation,' *Harvard Business Review*, September 2009, pp. 57–64
- Quinn, J. B., *Intelligent Enterprise*, The Free Press, 1992
- Resnick, Bruce G and Smunt, Timothy L., From Good to Great to ... , in: Academy of Management Perspectives, 2008, pp. 6–12
- Senge, P. M., *The Fifth Discipline*, Doubleday/Random House, 1990
- Slocum, John W. et al., 'On death and dying: the corporate leadership capacity of CEOs,' *Organizational Dynamics*, Spring 2002, pp. 269–281
- Smit, Jeroen, De Prooi, 'Blinde trots breekt ABN Amro,' Amsterdam, Prometheus, 2008
- Vanosmael, P. and Bruyn, R. de, *Handboek voor creatief denken*, DNB/Pelckmans, 1991

Strategy

- Ansoff, I., Implanting Strategic Management, Prentice Hall, 1990.
- Aron, Ravi and Singh, Jitendra V., 'Getting Offshoring Right,' *Harvard Business Review*, December 2005, pp. 135–143
- Buzzell, R.D. and Gale, B.T., *The PIMS Principles*, The Free Press, 1987
- Daems, H. and Douma, S., Concurrentiestrategie en concernstrategie, Kluwer, 1989
- Doz, Y., Strategic Management in Multinational Companies, Pergamon Press, 1986
- Galbraith, J.R. and Kazenjiam, P.K., *Strategy Implementation: Structure, Systems and Processes*, 2nd edition, West Publishing, 1986
- Goold, M., Campbell, A. et al., Corporate-level Strategy; Creating Volume in the Multibusiness Company, Wiley, 1994
- Hamel, G. and Prahalad, C. K., *Competing for the Future*, Harvard Business School Press, 1994
- Haspeslagh, P. C. and Jamison, D. B., *Managing Acquistions*, The Free Press, 1991
- Johnson, Gerry and Scholes, Kevan, *Exploring Corporate Strategy*, Londen, Prentice Hall, 2002
- Kale, Prashant, and Singh, Harbir, 'Managing Strategic Alliances: What Do we Know Now,' *Academy of Management Perspectives*, 2009, pp. 45–62
- Lynn, A. Isabella, 'Managing an alliance is nothing like business as usual,' *Organizational Dynamics*, August 2002, pp. 47–58
- Mintzberg, H., Ahlstrand, B., Lampel, J., Strategy Safari: *A guided tour through the fields of strategic management*, Prentice Hall, 1998
- Mintzberg, H., The Rise and Fall of Strategic Planning, Prentice Hall, 1994
- Pfeffer and Salancik, The External Control of Organizations: A Resource Dependence Perspective, Harper & Row, 1978
- Porter, M. E., *Competitive Strategy: Techniques for Analysing Industries and Competitors*, The Free Press, 1980
- Porter, M. E., *Competive Advantage: Creating and Sustaining Superior Performance*, The Free Press, 1985
- Porter, M. E., *The Competitive Advantage of Nations*, Macmillan, 1990
- Porter, Michael E., 'The Five Competitive Forces that Shape Strategy,' *Harvard Business Review*, January 2008, pp. 79–93
- Trautwein, F. (1990), 'Merger motives and merger prescriptions, Friedrich Trautwein,' *Strategic Management Journal*, May/June 1990, Vol. 11, Iss. 4
- Yoshino, Michael Y. and Rangan, U.S., *Strategic Alliances*, Boston, HBR Press, 1995

Structure-organizational design

- Aiken, Carolyn and Keller Scott, 'The irrational side of change management,' *McKinsey Quarterly*, 2009, No. 2, pp. 101–109
- Armenakis, A. A., Harris, S. G. & Mossholder, K. W.: *Creating readiness for organizational change*, Human Relations, 46(6), pp 681–703
- Ashkenas, Ron et al., *The Boundaryless Organization*, Jossey Bass, San Francisco, 1995
- Birchell, David and Lyons, Lawrence, *Creating Tomorrow's Organization*, Pitman Publications., London, 1995
- Brooke, M. Z., *Centralization and Autonomy*, Holt, Rinehart & Winston, 1984
- Campbell, Andrew and Gould, Michael, *The collaborative enterprise*, Cambridge (Mass.), Persons Publishing, 2000
- Daft, R. L., *Organization Theory and Design*, South Western, 2001

- Galbraith, J.R., *Designing Complex Organizations*, Addison Wesley, 1973
- Galbraith, Jay R., *Designing organizations*, Jossey Bass, San Francisco, 1995.
- Galbraith, Jay R., Lawler III, Edward E. et al., *Organizing for the Future*, Jossey Bass, 1993
- Goold, Michael and Campbell, Andrew, 'Do you have a well-designed organization?' *Harvard Business Review*, March 2002, pp.117–124
- Handy, C. and Tank, A. (eds), *From Hierarchy to Network*, The Conference Board Europe, Research Monograph No. 2, 1989
- Keuning, D. and Eppink, D. J., *Management en Organisatie: theorie en toepassing*, Stenfert Kroese, 6th edn, 1996
- Keuning, D. and Opheij, W., *Delayering Organizations*, Pitman Publishing, 1994
- Keuning, Doede and Wolters, Matthijs, *Structuur doorzien, over ontwerp van organisatiestructuren*, Amsterdam, Pearson Educatie/FT Prentice Hall, 2007
- Keuning, Doede, *Structuurhygiëne geboden!*, Amsterdam, FT Prentice Hall/Pearson Education, 2008
- Lei, David and Slocum jr., John W., 'Organization designs to renew competive advantages,' *Organizational Dynamics*, August 2002, pp.1–18
- Lorsch, J. W. and Allen III, S., *Managing Diversity and Interdependence*, Harvard University Press, 1973
- March, J. G. and Simon, H. A., *Organizations*, Wiley, 1958
- McKinsey: 'Creating Organizational transformations,' *The McKinsey Quarterly*, July 2008, pp 1–7
- Mehri, Darius, 'The Darker Side of Lean. An Insider's Perspective on the Realities of the Toyota Production System,' *Academy of Management Perspectives*, 2006, pp. 21–42
- Miles, Raymond E. and Snow, Charles C., *Fit, Failure and the Hall of Fame*, Free Press, New York, 1994
- Mintzberg, H., 'Organization design: fashion or fit?,' *Harvard Business Review*, January–February 1981, pp. 103–16
- Mintzberg, H., The effective organization: forces and forms,' *Sloan Management Review*, Winter 1991, pp. 54–66
- Mintzberg, H., *The Structuring of Organizations*, Prentice Hall, 1979
- Mohrman, Susan A. et al., *Designing team-based organizations*, Jossey Bass, San Francisco, 1995
- Simons, R., 'Designing high-performance jobs,' *Harvard Business Review*, July/Aug., 2005, pp. 54 ff
- Smythe, J., 'Employee engagement–its real essence,' *Human Resource Management International Digest*, Vol. 15. No. 7, 2007 pp 11–13
- Stoker, Janka and Korte, Ton de, *Het onmisbare middenkader*, Van Gorcum/SMS, Assen, 2000
- Tank, A., *The Role of the Center: New Linkages in Fast Changing Companies*, The Conference Board Europe, Research Monograph, No. 6, 1991
- Wissema, J. G., *Unit Management: het decentraliseren van ondernemerschap*, Van Gorcum, 1987

People, organizations and culture: Human resources management and organizational change

- Bolwijn, P.T. and Kumpe T., *Marktgericht ondernemen, management van continuïteit en vernieuwing*, Van Gorcum, 1992
- Boxall, P. & Purcell, J.: *Strategy and Human Resource Management*; 2008 (2nd edition) Palgrave MacMillan, New York
- Brett, Jeanne M., *Negotiating Globally*, Jossey Bass, 2001
- Coleman, D., 'What makes a leader,' *Harvard Business Review*, November–December 1998, pp. 93–102
- Conaway, Wayne A. and Borden, George A., *Kiss, Bow, or Shake Hands?*, Adams Media Corporation, 1994
- Covey, S. R., *The 8th Habit: From effectiveness to greatness*. New York: Franklin Covey Company, 2004
- Covey, S. R., *The seven habits of highly effective people. Restoring the character ethic*. New York: Simon & Schuster, 1989
- Dass, P. and Parker, B., 'Strategies for managing human resource diversity' *Academy of Management Executive*, May 1999, pp. 68–80
- Eecen, A. (2004). *Coaching meest effectief qua resultaat*. Amsterdam: TNS Nipo
- Evans, P., Doz, Y. and Laurent A. (eds), *Human Resource Management in International Firms*, St. Martin's Press, 1990
- Fieldman, D. F. and Lankau, M. J., 'Executive Coaching: A Review and Agenda for Future Research.' *Journal of management*, No. 6, 829–848
- Foster, Dean Allen, *Bargaining across borders*, McGraw Hill, 1992
- French, W. L., Bell, C. H. et al., *Organizational Development*, B.P.I/Irwin, 1989
- Gesteland, Richard R., *Cross-cultural Business Behavior*, Handelshøjskolens Forlag, 1996
- Haan, E. de and Burger, Y. (2009). *Coaching met collega's*. Assen: Koninklijke van Gorcum
- Hampden-Turner, Charles and Trompenaars, Fons, *Mastering the infinite game*, Capslone, Oxford, 1997
- Harrison, R., *Leiderschap en strategische planning in een nieuwe tijd*, Lemniscaat, 1986
- Harvey, Carol and Allard, June M., *Understanding and managing diversity*, 2nd edition., Upper Saddle River, Prentice Hall, 2002
- Hofstede, G., *Allemaal andersdenkenden, omgaan met cultuurverschillen*, Contact, 1991
- Jong, G. R. A. de, *Personeelsmanagement: zorg voor maatwerk in de praktijk*, Kluwer Bedrijfswetenschappen, 1992
- Korte, A. W. de and Bolweg, J. F., *De nieuwe werknemer*, Van Gorcum, 1994
- Lawler III, E. E., *Motivation in Work Organizations*, Jossey Bass, 1994
- Leaptrott, Nan and Morrison, Terri, *Rules of the Game: Global Business Protocol*, Thomson Executive Press, 1996
- Lee, R. and Lawrence, P., *Organizational Behavior, Politics at Work*, Hutchinson Management Studies, 1985
- Lorsch, J. W. and Morse, J. J., *Organizations and Their Members: a Contingency Approach*, Harper & Row, 1974
- Manzoni, Jean-Francois en Barsoux, Jean-Louis. Are your subordinates setting you up to fail? in: MIT Sloan Management Review, Summer 2009
- Mintzberg, H., 'Planning on the left side and managing on the right,' *Harvard Business Review*, July–August 1976, pp. 58–9
- Mintzberg, H., *Power in and around Organizations*, Prentice Hall, 1983
- Nord, Walter et al., 'Real-world reacting to work-life balance programs: lessons for effective implementation,' *Organizational Dynamics*
- Oliveiro, G., Bane, D., & Kopelman, R. (1997). Executive coaching as a transfer of training tool: effects on productivity in a public agency. *Public Personnel Management*, winter
- Quinn Mills, D., 'The Truth About Empowerment,' *Training & Development*, 1992, pp. 31–2
- Quinn Mills, D., *Rebirth of the Corporation*, Wiley, 1991
- Salacuse, Jeswald W., 'Making Global Deals,' *Times Business*, 1991
- Sanders, G. and Nuijen, B., *Bedrijfscultuur: diagnose en beïnvloeding*, Van Gorcum, 1987
- Schein, E. H., *Organizational Culture and Leadership*, Jossey Bass, 1985
- Schoenmaker, M. J. R. and Geerdink, T, *Human talentmanagement, een visie op besturen, faciliteren en ontwikkelen van personeel*, Kluwer Bedrijfswetenschappen, 1991
- Scott, D. S. and Jaffe, D. T., *Empowerment: Building a Committed Workforce*, Kogan Page, 1991
- Trompenaars, Fons and Hampden-Turner, Charles, *Riding the Waves of Culture*, McGraw Hill, 1998
- Vroom, V. H., *Work and Motivation*, Jossey Bass, 1995
- Wissema, J. G., Messer, H. M. and Wijers, G. J., *Angst voor veranderen? Een mythe?*, Van Gorcum, 1986
- Woodcock, M. and Francis, P., *Clarifying Organizational Values*, Gower, 1989
- Zenger, J. & Folkman, J., 'Ten Fatal Flaws That Derail Leaders,' Harvard Business Review, June 2009

Quality Management

- Crosby, P. B., *Quality is Free*, McGraw Hill, 1979
- Feigenbaum, A. V., *Total Quality Control*, McGraw Hill, 1983
- Garvin, D. A. *Managing Quality, The Strategic and Competitive Edge*, The Free Press, 1988
- Garvin, D. A., 'Competing on the eight dimensions of quality,' *Harvard Business Review*, 1987
- Ishikawa, K., *Guide to Quality Control*, Asian Productivity Organization, 1998
- Juran, J. M., *Managerial Breakthrough*, McGraw Hill, 1964
- Juran, J. M., *Juran on Leadership for Quality*, The Free Press, 1989
- Juran, J. M., Blanton Godfrey, A., Hoogstoel, R. E., Shilling, E. G., *Juran's Quality Control Handbook*, McGraw Hill, 2001
- Tummela, V. M. R., Tang, C. L., 'Strategic quality management, Malcolm Baldridge and European Quality Awards and ISO 9000 certification; core concepts and comparative analysis,' *International Journal of Quality and Reliability Management*, no. 3, 1996

Technology, information and organizations

- Acohen, J. and Florijn, R., 'Besturen en beheersen van de kosten van automatiseringsprojecten,' *Holland Management Review*, No. 35, 1993
- Akten, Mahmet et al., 'Just-in-time budgeting for a volatile economy,' *McKinsey Quarterly*, 2009, No. 3, pp. 115–121
- Batelaan, M. V. and Doorn, P. van, 'De strategische betekenis van informatietechnologie,' *Harvard Holland Review*, No. 27, Summer 1991
- Beenker, Nico, *Handboek CRM*, F en G Publishing, Utrecht, 2002
- Bemelmans, T. M. A., *Bestuurlijke informatiesystemen en automatisering*, Stenfert Kroese, 4th edition, 1991
- Benson, R., 'Preparing IS for the 1990s: improving enterprise performance with information technology,' *BIKMag, Bestuurlijk informatiedeskundig Magazine*, August 1991
- Buitelaar, M. and Groen, U., 'Business process redesign: Een nieuwe kijk op informatisering?,' *Informatie*, 1994, 36, No. 6, pp. 388–97
- Burgelman, R.A., Maidique, M.A., Weelwright, S.C., *Strategic Management of Technology and Innovation*, McGraw Hill, 2001.
- Burns, T. and Stalker, G.M., *The Management of Innovation*, Tavistock Publications, 1971
- Chui, Michael et al., 'Six ways to make Web 2.0 work,' *McKinsey Quarterly*, 2009, No. 2, pp. 65–73
- Court, David, et al., 'The Consumer Decision Journey,' *McKinsey Quarterly*, 2009, No. 3, pp. 97–107
- Davenport, T. H. and Short, J. E., 'The New Industrial Engineering: Information Technology and Business Process Redesign,' *Sloan Management Review*, 1990, vol. 31, no. 4
- Davenport, Thomas H. and Glaser, John, 'Just-in-time delivery comes to knowledge management,' *Harvard Business Review*, July 2002, pp. 107–111
- Fisher, Kimball and Fisher, Mareen Duncan, *The Distributed Mind*, AMACOM, New York, 1998
- Hammer, M., 'Bedrijfsprocessen herstructureren: zet het mes erin,' *Harvard Holland Review*, no. 27, Summer 1991
- Hopper, M., 'Concurreren met IT: een nieuwe benadering,' *Harvard Holland Review*, no. 26, Spring 1991
- LePine, J & Van Dyne, L., 'Predicting voice behaviour in workgroups,' *Journal of Applied Psychology*, 1998, Vol 83, No. 6, pp. 853–868
- LePine, J & Van Dyne, L. 'Voice and Cooperative Behaviour as Contrasting Forms of Contextual Performance: Evidence of Differential Relationships with Big Five Personality Characteristics and Cognitive Ability,' *Journal of Applied Psychology*, 2001, Vol 86, No. 2, pp. 326–336
- Lumpkin, G. T. et al., 'E-commerce strategics: achieving sustainable competitive advantage and avoiding pitfalls,' *Organizational Dynamics*, Spring 2002, pp. 325–340
- Malone, T. W., *Organizational Structure and Information Technology: Elements of Formal Theory*, Sloan School of Management, MIT, 1985
- Molenaar, Cor, *E-strategie*, Financial Times/Prentice Hall, Amsterdam, 2001
- Morris, D. and Brandon, J., *Re-engineering your business*, McGraw Hill, 1993
- Noordam, Peter, Vlist, Aart van der, Derksen, Barry, *Trends in IT*, ten Hagen Stam, The Hague, 2001
- Oosterhaven, J. Arno, *E-business voor gevestigde ondernemingen*, Van Gorcum/SMS, Assen, 2000
- Roussel, A. et al., *Management of Research and Development*, Harvard Business School Press, 1991
- Sitter, L. U. de, *Op weg naar nieuwe fabrieken en kantoren*, Kluwer, 1987
- Smit, William & Bruin, Wieger de, BloteBits, *De naakte waarheid over E-business*, BZZToH, The Hague, 2001
- Tapscott, D. and Gaston, A., *Paradigm Shift: the new promise of Information Technology*, McGrawHill, 1993
- Tobin, Daniel R., *The Knowledge Enabled Organization*, AMACOM, New York, 1998

Management consultancy and change

- Bennis, W. G., Benne, K. D. and Chin, R., *The Planning of Change*, Holt, Rinehart & Winston, 1985
- Block, P., 'Dealing with Resistance,' *Flawless Consulting*, U.A.C., 1981
- Caluwé, L. I. A. de, 'Denken over veranderen in vijf kleuren,' *M&O*, no. 4, August 1998
- Clark, Timothy and Fincham, Robin, *Critical Consulting*, Oxford, Blackwell, 2002
- Feitman, C. E., *Adviseren bij organizeren*, Kreits, 1984
- Greiner, L. E. and Metzger, R. O., *Consulting to Management*, Prentice Hall, 1983
- Kubr, M. (ed.), *Management Consulting*, ILO, 1986
- Levy, A. and Merry, U., *Organizational Transformation Approaches, Strategies, Theories*, Preager Publishers, 1986
- Maister, D.: *Managing the professional service firm*, 4th Dutch edition, 2007, Academic Service
- Maister, D. H., 'Balancing the professional service firm,' *CPA Journal*, November 1986, pp. 126–34
- Maister, D. H., *Managing the Professional Service Firm*, The Free Press, 1993
- Maister, D. H., *True Professionalism*, The Free Press, New York, 1997
- Mangham, I., *The Politics of Organizational Change*, Associated Business Press, 1979
- Margerison, C. J., 'How to Raise Energy Levels,' *Managerial Consulting Skills*, Gower, 1988
- Otto, M. M. and Leeuw, A. C. J. de, *Kijken, denken, doen. Organisatieverandering: manoeuvreren met weerbarstigheid*, Van Gorcum, 1994
- Schein, E. H., *Helping: how to offer, give and receive help*. San Francisco: Berrett-Koehler Publishers, 2009
- Schein, Edgar H., *Process Consultation Revisited*, Reading Mass., Addison Wesley, 1999
- Twijnstra, A., Keuning, D., Caluwé, L. I. A. de, *Organisatie-advieswerk* (3rd edition), Kluwer, Deventer, 2002

Websites

http://www.globalreporting.org
http://corporate.klm.com/nl
http://www.sustainability-index.com
http://www.ft.com/china
http://www.ft.com/bric
http://www.millwardbrown.com/brandz
http://www.brandz.com

Illustratieverantwoording

Tom Brakefield/Getty Images, p. 256
Corbis, p. 6, 62, 150, 192, 370, 490, 550
Flicker RM/Getty Images, p. 4
Robert Hallam/Rex features, p. 318
Hollandse hoogte, p. 258
Chris Keulen/Hollandse hoogte, p. 434
Harry Meijer/Hollandse hoogte, p. 548
Nancy Nehring/Getty Images, p. 60
Hans Neleman/Getty Images, p. 316, 488
Franco Origlia/Getty Images, p. 432
Klaas Jan van der Weij/Hollandse hoogte, p. 368
Gordon Wiltsie/Getty Images, p. 190

Glossary

360° Feedback
Information/feedback on an employee's performance provided by colleagues, customers, suppliers and managers directed at enabling the employee to evaluate his or her own performance

Account manager
An employee responsible for planning and policy as well as the sales of all products of an organization, directed at larger clients

Aggregator
A market agent who collects demand in order to arrange discounts (or other benefits) on the supply side

Agility
Having flexible production capacity and/or flexibly deployable personnel

Annual report (fiscal)
Report on behalf of the fiscal authorities, drawn up according to legal guidelines in determination of fiscal profits, including the balance sheet and the profit and loss statement of the company

Annual report
Written report of the board to shareholders, in which a description of the events of the past year and prospects for the coming year have been included

Artificial Intelligence (AI)
That part of information sciences occupied with processes which produce intelligent actions

Attitude
A tendency, formed by information and experience from the past, to react consistently to an idea, event, company or person. An attitude creates a link between the feelings and ideas a person has and his/her behavior. For an organization, labor satisfaction, involvement and loyalty are important people attitudes.

Autocratic leadership
A style of leadership accompanied by rigorous directives, strict supervision and threats of sanctions

Backsourcing
Bringing outsourced activities back into the company

Balanced Business Scorecard
A method to help management map out performances. It takes in four points of view: the customer perspective, the company processes, the organizational learning processes and the financial perspective.

Basic organization
The permanent organization for the control of the company processes. It forms a reservoir for the creation of a project organization.

BCI technology
(Brain-Computer Interfaces) Operating systems by means of applying electrodes to the brain

Benchmarking
The ongoing process of measuring of products, services and practices in which the results are compared against those of the toughest competitor or of organizations which are acknowledged as business sector leaders

Bill of material
A diagrammatic representation of the interrelationships between components and structure of a product

BOP
Bottom of the Pyramid (Prahalad)

Boston Consulting Group approach
Approach of portfolio management with position determining factors being market growth and relative market share

Bottom up approach
An approach of the planning cycle in which the initiative lies especially with the divisions and/or business units or departments

Brainstorming
A technique to stimulate creativity in the development of new ideas

Branding
Making a brand/brand name stand out against others in the experience of customers and clients

Budget
A plan translated into sums of money which also constitutes a task-setting exercise

Budget result
The difference between allowed and actual costs post-calculation

Budgeting
A delegation instrument in management. Translating plans into sums of money makes it possible to delegate tasks and authority and maintain control.

Business ethics
Systematic analysis and coverage of moral problems which occur in the course of business and organizational affairs

Business or activity
A description of that domain of an organization that the client group indicates as being worthy of attention in order to provide for his/her needs, and the technology through which that happens

Business policy
A statement of the means and resources through which management wants to achieve a set of defined goals and objectives

Business Process Redesign (BPR)
An integral approach towards functional partial processes whereby the existing course of the process is radically redesigned by means of intervention within the organizational structure with the help of new information technology

Business unit
An organizational unit within which business activities are grouped

Cafeteria plan
A payment system according to which employees compose their own payment package ('menu') so as to best suit personal needs

Capacity planning
The component of production planning in which the planning and size of the necessary capacities (factories, machines, employees) is roughly determined

Cash cow
A business with low market growth and a high relative market share

Cash flow
Change in liquid cash resources. Net profit + depreciation

Cash flow control
Guarding of liquidities and of incoming and outgoing cash flows

Centralized functional structure
An organizational structure which arises from the combination of internal differentiation in departmentalization and centralization in decision making

Chain of business activities
A series of organizations involved in the bringing about of goods and services (for example, from forestry to the furniture store)

Charisma
A natural quality exuded by those leaders whom others trust

Cloud computing (SaaS)
The phenomenon of offering software applications (ERP, CRM, G-HRM etc.) via the Web on the basis of a subscription

Cluster(ing)
Collaborative connections, often at the regional level, between independent companies operating within the same sector

Coach
A person who provides personal guidence to another person

Coachee
A person who is coached

Coaching
A form of personal guidence on the basis of a one-to-one relationship (between the coach and the coachee)

Cognitive dissonance
Doubt and feelings of discomfort experienced by an individual in relation to the correctness of that individual's sense of reality as a result of certain cognitions not being in agreement with each other: for example, 'holiday' and 'bad weather'

Color (change) thinking
A way of thinking about organizational change in five different ways (an image of man, degree of planning and role of agent of change)

Co-maker
A supplier who receives and accepts co-responsibility for his client's final product

Commitment
An employee's desire to remain in an organization and the willingness to exert effort on its behalf and acceptance of the values and goods of the organization

Company
An independent unit operating in society as an organizational unity and in which work is conducted on the basis of a labor agreement

Competitive advantage
Relative advantage; the advantage an organization possesses over its competitors in relation to an aspect which is considered relevant by clients

Compliance
Behavior that conforms to accepted rules

Composed task assignment
An order to achieve a certain result with compulsory directives in relation to the way the results have to be attained

Conflict handling
A two-dimensional approach to resolving a problem: an emphasis on one's own interests/goals (assertive) and an emphasis on someone else's interests/goals (cooperative)

Consistency criteria
Criteria governing the choice of a strategy which take into account whether the organization can meet the demands the strategy requires and whether the strategy accords with external developments and goals

Constituting
Creating a regulatory framework within which actions can be performed

Consultation group
Within a labor organization, a decision-making temporary or permanent group that is composed of representatives from more than one department

Contract wage
A way of determining wages based on an agreement between employer and employee in relation to the extent of the activities to be performed

Control
Drawing up of norms and plans relating to the performance of activities, including the authority to adjust/correct them

Control cycle
Supervising, monitoring, checking, and if necessary, adjusting and/or correcting

Corporatism
A societal and political system in which government, business organizations and labor organizations are strongly interwoven in the governing of society

Costs
The value expressed in terms of money of all means of production used in the production of goods and/or services

Creativity
The ability to link elements and matters which are experienced as new or unusual in terms of existing perspectives or ideas

Crisis management
The active handling of sudden disruptions in the desired relationship between the internal and external environment of the organization

Critical Success Factors (CSFs)
Factors of decisive importance for the success of an organization

Crowdsourcing/Co-creation
Involving the public or customers via Web 2.0 technologies in thinking up ways of making innovative changes

Cybernetic cycle
See Control cycle

Cyberspace
Another term for the Internet

Cycle lengthening, horizontal task enlargement or job enlargement
The expansion of the task cycle by preceding or subsequent activities on the same level

Day extension
Sending work at the end of the working day to another work location in a different time zone with the purpose of extending the working day

Decentralization
The spreading of decision-making authority over a number of staff and hierarchical levels within the organization

Decentralized division structure
An organizational structure which arises from a combination of internal specialization at the departmental level and decentralization in decision making

Decision making
A process which unrolls in sequential phases from the moment information identifying a problem becomes available, until the moment at which a solution is found

Decision Support System
(DSS)A decision-supporting information system (for such purposes as the making of order advice lists)

Delivery planning or work preparation
The process that takes place after planning utilization/occupation of machinery and people, the outcome being decisions relating to when raw materials and tools have to be at manufacturing departments or machine groups

Demotion
Voluntarily relinquishing a higher position within an organization for a lower or different position

Departmentalization
The combining of work units and sub-departments into main departments and services based on managerial considerations

Depth of control
The number of levels which one can manage directly or indirectly

Detaching
The temporary or permanent assigning of organizational capacity (employees) to another organizational unit or department

Detail planning or work dispatch
Division of production order work over various people and/or machines

Differential piece wage
A way of paying employees in which a direct relationship exists between manufacturing units and wage

Differentiation strategy
A strategy of equipping a product with unique characteristics

Disengagement point
An inventory whose function it is to make two partial processes within a production process less dependent on one another. By less interruption sensitivity the need for planning and coordination is reduced.

Disintermediation
A situation whereby an intermediary or a link in the value chain is removed or bypassed

Diversification
A strategic choice alternative in which the organization enters new markets with new products

Division manager
A person responsible for strategy, structure and processes within a division

DMAIC cycle
Define, Measure, Analyze, Improve and Control as a 5-step structured way of instigating Six Sigma projects

Dog
A business with low market growth and a low relative market share

Double loop learning
Double loop learning assumes the human capacity to be able to take a double look at situations: not only to detect and correct errors in relation to a given set of norms, but also the capability to question the relevance of operating norms

E-commerce
Marketing and selling/buying products and services via the Internet

E-HRM
The application of digital HRM instruments such as e-assessment, digital selection, job chat and e-coaching

E-mail
Electronic mail

E-market
An auction style of market where supply and demand meet in virtual reality

E-(re)tailer
Retailing goods and services through the web

Earning capacity/rate of return
Revenue in relation to the invested equity capital

Effectiveness
The degree of goal realization

Efficiency
The relationship between the planned and the actual use of resources

Entrepreneurship
The sum of the thoughts, mentality and actions directed at the conscious acceptance of risks in the supply of products or services, often with the intention to make a profit

Environmental care
The sum of those provisions in a company that are directed at the control and, where possible, reduction of the burden on the environment exerted by company activities

ERP-systems
Information (and planning) systems designed to link and optimize internal business processes (coupled to external demand and supply/sourcing)

Escrow agreement
An agreement between clients and suppliers of software in which the supplier deposits the source codes of the software produced by him with a third, independent party so that, in the event of a calamity (for example fire, bankruptcy of the supplier) the software remains available to the client

Ethics
Systematic analysis and handling of moral problems

Exercise of power or realized power
The actual determining of behavior to a certain degree or giving direction to the behavior of another

Experience effect (learning curve)
The effect that in the event of an increase in production volume, the cost price per unit product, corrected for inflation, decreases

Expert power
The power someone has based on knowledge and expertise

Expressive Organizations
Organizations that consciously and actively communicate the desired self-image to internal and external stakeholders

External adaptation
The tuning of the organization into the environment which surrounds it

External appraisal
An investigation directed at the external societal environment and markets in order to signal opportunities and/or threats

Extrinsic form of payment
Payments/rewards which lie outside the activities themselves, such as direct reimbursements, indirect reimbursements and non-financial reimbursements

Facilitator
A market agent who fulfills the role – through the transparency given by the Internet – to compare prices (and other conditions) of products and services

Flat organizational structure
The organizational form in which managers are in charge of a relatively large number of subordinates (i.e. there is a large span of control)

Flexible retirement
A system in which the retirement data is not fixed at the year that the employee turns 65 years of age, but in which the choice is left to the employee to work less or for longer

Flexibility
Having operational control over flexible production capacity and flexibly deployable personnel

Formal organization
The established assignment of tasks by means of the management of complemented tasks and function descriptions, guidelines and procedures

Formalism
Maintenance of rigidity when rules are broken in order to maintain the structure of the organization as it was

Franchise
A form of cooperation between a franchise giver and a franchise taker. In exchange for payment, the franchise taker receives the right to make use of certain sales and distribution systems (for example, shop formulas and logos).

Front-line managers
All managerial employees who are in direct contact with operational employees

Function
General: a contribution to the realization of goals and values. *Sociological:* the contribution of a component to the whole and to the maintenance of that whole. *Organizational:* the common purpose of a number of coherent tasks.

Function appraisal and evaluation
A system in which the relative weight of a function is determined by means of the assigning of points and according to which a wage can be assigned

Function description
A written form in which the tasks, authorities, obligations, responsibilities and interrelationships that fall under a particular job function are described

Function-forming process
The division of tasks between people and groups and the formation of cohering tasks into functions

Functional area
An area within the organization which is oriented towards a specialized field or technical aspect of functioning (for example, the Personnel Department, Finance Department)

Functional authority
The authority to give compulsory directives/indications in relation to how something needs to be done from a certain specialist point of view and/or to perform certain tasks in this specialist area independently

Functional Information System (FIS)
An information system for a functional area within an organization (for example, purchase or manufacturing)

Functional management
Managing a single specialized task as a component of a complex combined action

Functional wage
The salary which belongs to a certain function based on function appraisal and evaluation, without considering actual performance

Geo-engineering
Advanced technologies aimed at manipulating the earth's climate

Globalization
Making products available on markets worldwide

Goodwill
An extra amount of money paid for the organization's good name in the case of a takeover or acquisition by another organization

Gross profit
The difference between the sale prices and the purchase price of the goods sold

Group ethics
The sum of the unwritten notions of the members of a society or group with regard to proper/improper behavior

Groupware
A collective name for methods and systems (software) to support and/or facilitate the cooperation (and/or decision making) between employees, irrespective of time and place

Hierarchy of needs
Motivation theory from Maslow which states that most people have five types of needs which can be ranked in terms of their importance to the individual in question: physical needs, security, belonging and social contacts, respect and self-development/actualization

High-performance organizations
Organizations that achieve first-rate results

Holding
A variant on the decentralized divisional structure in which there is no relationship between the activities of the various divisions other than a financial relationship and so the tasks of the parent company's top management are mainly to maintain financial and administrative strategic control over the concern

Horizontal organization
Dividing activities and assigning authority at the same level of management and execution

Horizontal relationship
The consultative relationship between employees at the same level with the goal of achieving coordinated action by direct contact

Human relations theory
Management theory based on the knowledge that there is an indirect relationship between the attention which is paid to the worker and his/her performance

Human Resources Management (HRM)
The coordinated steering and development of supply and demand of human potential and skills within the organization by integration of the personnel policy in the strategy to be followed, the structure to be designed and the desired organizational culture

Identification power
Power which arises because others can identify themselves with someone or like to feel they belong to someone

IFRS
International Financial Reporting Standards

Infobesitas
Suffering from an overabundance of facts, information sources etc. and being unable to work or study in a structured way

Infomediaries
Agents who fulfill the role of a broker of information (collective term for aggregators and facilitators)

Information management
The directing and managing of information activities (in the first place, those that have to do with management of the flow of information on behalf of the productive, primary and supporting processes, and in the second place, those that have to do with information supply on behalf of the management process)

Information plan
A statement of the projects and the actions necessary in order to implement an information policy in order of time and priority

Information supply
Providing for the information needs of the members of an organization with regard to the functioning of the organization in general, and external stakeholders with regard to the organization

Information system
The sum of the people, machines and activities directed at the collecting and processing of data in such a way that the information needs of external and internal stakeholders are satisfied

Information technology (IT)
A collective term for all knowledge and skills relating to digital and analog transmission, storage, processing, and representation techniques that are needed to manipulate data which, for the human perception, is of a visual/sensual/auditory nature (from scribbling block to multimedia/virtual reality)

INK management model
A model developed by the Instituut Nederlandse Kwaliteit aimed at assessing an organization for the purposes of diagnosis and for devising proposals that target better performance

Inshoring
Working with shared services

Inspiring leadership
Leadership that comes from the heart and which inspires and energizes co-workers

Instrumentality theory
Vroom's motivation theory: work motivation is a function of the strength of someone's preference for a certain outcome and the expectation that the work goal can be attained by their own knowledge, in return for the receipt of a reward

Integrity
Acting in an honest and trustworthy way

Interactive consumption
The production of those services in which the consumer is present

Interim manager
A temporarily appointed manager from outside the organization with the authority to provide specific management expertise which is not available within the organization itself

Intermediation
The performing of a new role by an intermediary or a link in the value chain

Internal adaptation
The mutual attunement of the available capacity within an organization in terms of people and other resources (machines, money, information, buildings)

Internal appraisal
A systematic analysis of the characteristics and functioning of an organization at a given point in time, in relation to a situation in either the past or the future of that organization, or in relation to another comparable organization

Internal communication
Communication in which the target group is situated within the organization

Internal differentiation
Grouping actions or processes by similarity in terms of expertise, knowledge, skills and attitude

Internal environmental care
The provisions in an organization directed at obtaining an insight into the control of, and where possible the reduction of, the burden placed on the environment by company activities

Internal operational signaling
The system of internal information supply in a company or institution which provides management at different levels and in different departments, with specific and timely information for the supervision of and adjustment to planning and the performing of current company activities

Internal or horizontal differentiation
Division of labor into phases of the operational processes (functional or F-grouping)

Internal or horizontal specialization
Division of labor based on the interrelated actions to product, geographic location or market segment (P, G, M grouping)

Intrinsic form of reward/payment
Form of payment which derives from the work itself, especially job satisfaction

Intuitive approach to strategy
Strategy formulation in which the steps to be taken are not based on explicit decisions

Islamic banking
Banking that takes account of sharia rules (that is, rules deriving from the Islamic religion that forbid both the paying and the receiving of interest – *riba* – and speculation and gambling – *gharar* – as well as investment in companies whose activities include gambling, alcohol or pornography)

Islamic banking/Islamic insurance
See Sharia-compliant financing and insurance

Islamic insurance
Insurance that takes the form of mutual assistance and sharing of risks (*takaful*)

IT strategy
Strategic and tactical decisions with regard to all applications of information technology

Job rotation
Frequent exchanging of tasks with other members of the organization

Job share
A job that is performed by employees who each work for a set percentage of time

Joint venture
Two companies which jointly found a single new organization

Just-in-time
A way of approaching inventory control (originating in Japan), in which the necessity for inventory is eliminated by delivering 'just-in-time'. The ideal inventory size is zero, because all goods are in the process of being processed.

Kanban
Literally 'small card.' A manufacturing management method introduced by Toyota, in which in the manufacturing department components go from phase to phase in trays with a small card attached to them. When the materials are used, the card goes back. This is the signal that a new tray of components needs to be prepared. The size of the series is standard. The consequence is minimum supply of departments.

Key factors (KFs)
The key factors at tactical and operational level which can be derived from the Critical Success Factors (CSFs)

Key variables of individual behavior
The variables which play a part in invoking the behavior of an individual, namely values, attitudes, personality, motivation, perception, and learning.

Knowledge management
The methods used to gather knowledge/information and to apply and spread that knowledge/information

Labor division
The grouping of activities according to tasks and functions assigned to employees, work groups, departments, divisions and the organization as a whole

Lateral thinking
A method of developing new ideas by taking an indirect and/or creative approach

Lay-out
The spatial mapping-out of the method of production to be followed

Leading
The influencing of organizational and working behavior of employees based on personal contact

Learning
Behavioral changes of a longer lasting nature, as a consequence of processing and interpretation of information and experiences via the learning cycle. Innate reactions and temporary behavioral changes are not part of this process.

Learning organization
The enlarging of the capacity of an organization to achieve effective action as well as an organization that systematically bundles the experiences of its individual members and develops new common ways of behavior

Line organization
An organizational form which reflects the managerial and operational functions of employees at different hierarchical levels

Line relations
An authority relationship between a superior and a subordinate whereby the superior gives orders, bears responsibility and exercises supervision, and the subordinate has to execute those orders and render account

Line staff organization
An organizational form in which specialists in policy formulation have been added to the line organization at one or more levels of management

Linking pin
A way of organizing and managing in which the manager consults his employees and in which the manager, as the linking pin, represents the team or the department in a higher consultation group. The use of this type of consultation implies horizontalization of the line relationship

Logistics management
All activities which have to do with planning, organizing and managing of the flow of materials, including the flow of information necessary for this. Logistics management is comprised of two aspects: materials management and physical distribution.

Long-term planning
An approach to strategy formulation based on the assumption that the future developments are determined by the same forces as in the past

Management
(a) A collection of people who perform a managerial function within an organization; (b) the processes which a managerial person performs: goal and policy determination, planning, organizing, giving of orders and support, coordinating, monitoring and checking and when necessary, adjusting; and (c) a scientific/specialist field: all of the scientific and applied knowledge and methods and techniques relating to managing people

Management by exception
An organizational model in which higher management only intervenes when it deems that tolerance zones have been exceeded

Management by objectives
A way of managing and delegation in which the manager and the employee reach agreement about goals and core results to be attained during a certain period

Management consultancy
Supply of independent and expert advice directed at identifying and resolving organizational problems

Management development
The systematic supply and development of managers, taking into account the individual wishes and interests of those involved

Management leadership
A notion which indicates that leadership is always an integral component of management in the sense that it always involves aspects of administration, stimulation, supervision and inspiration

Management of change
A directed effort that aims to bring an organization from an unconscious experience of a situation to the conscious experience of a new situation

Management process theory
Goal-oriented activities which give direction to the primary and supporting secondary processes within an organization

Manager
Anyone in an organization who sets in motion and directs the actions of other people

Managing
In the widest sense: the determining of the goals of the entire organization, the designing of organizational structure and the recruiting and developing of the necessary capacities in order to be able to achieve the goals

Manufacturing Resources Planning (MRP II)
As an extension of MRP I, MRP II maps out capacities (resources) by means of task-setting agreements between the various functional areas with regard to the availability of their capacities. The main production plan is derived from these agreements. The need for materials is derived from the main production plan and is calculated via MRP I.

Market development
A strategic alternative in which the organization approaches new markets with existing products

Market penetration
A strategic alternative in which the organization, within the framework of the present activities, strives for an improvement of the results/market share. These can be attained by reduction of competition and/or improving the organization's own position.

Master budget
Income, cost, and expenditure budgets from the various departments processed to form one set and including expenditure that will require liquidity resources

Materials management
Control of the flow of goods and the accompanying flows of information from the obtaining of raw materials up to the production phases (half fabrics/inventory goods in process). The finished product inventory falls under physical distribution (see also Logistics Management).

Materials Requirements Planning (MRP I/II)
A production management method which has been developed for composite products. Taking the finished product as the basis, the number of components to be ordered or produced is calculated. MRP I is materials-directed and takes no account of the available capacities, unlike MRP II, which does do so.

Matrix organization
A form of organization characterized by dual authority and balance. Matrix organization is an extreme way of attaining coordination between two important goal orientations or aspects entrenched in an organization.

Mental model
A 'world picture' deeply anchored in the individual personality which provides a basis for interpretation of reality and because of that, has a considerable effect on how the individual acts

Mission
The role and the ambitions of the organization in the defined domain(s)

Mission statement
Giving form to an organization's vision in a direction-providing short document

Mobbing
Workfloor bullying

Multi-factor reward
A way of rewarding/payment in which one not only considers the quantity of delivered performances but also the quality (for example, careful use of materials, loyalty, relationship skills)

Multitasking
Being able to process more than one flow of information at the same time

Nearshoring
Transferring activities to nearby low-wage countries

Net sales
The sales after deduction of sales tax and issued discounts

Network organization
An organizational form in which the various functions (product design, manufacturing, distribution and sales, and so on), are not performed by or within an organization but by different organizations, which may only be linked to each other for a single 'product event'

Network planning
See Project planning

Noise
Interruption of the communication process

Non-power
The willingness to let oneself be convinced by others

Nordic model
Model of social capitalism practised in Norway, Sweden, Denmark and Finland

Office automation
The computerization and integration of text processing and data processing processes

Offshoring
Transferring work to supplying companies or to the company's own departments in a low-wage country

Open system
The sum of the flow of material, information and energy which can be described in terms of input, transformation (throughput) and output and which is directed at the performing of functions within the business environment

Operational employees
Those employees in a labor organization who do not have managerial tasks

Operational learning
Learning of new routines within previously learned frameworks or concepts

Opportunity
A development which provides the organization with the possibility of improving its own functioning/basis of existence

Optimal delegation
An application of the delegation principle such that at the various levels of management, sufficient authority is given to take make well-considered decisions

Optimal order size/series
A series size in which the sum of the ordering costs and the inventory costs are as low as possible

Organic structure
Coherence of organs within a labor organization. In this sense, organs are the main departments and functions.

Organization
Every goal-realizing cooperative unit in which participants consistently enter into a mutual relationship and work together in order to reach common goals

Organization chart or organogram
Diagrammatic representation of the main characteristics of the formal division of tasks and of the formal division of authority in an organization. In short: an overview of the organic and/or personnel structure

Organization culture
The common expectations of the members of an organization with regard to the behavior (work and otherwise) of others

Organizational equilibrium
A state in which when the organization rewards its internal and external participants in such a way that they remain motivated to continue contributing to the organization

Organizational structure
(a)The division of activities into tasks, functions, working groups and departments; (b) the assignment of authority and the relationships linking employees, working groups and departments in the execution of their tasks; (c) the built-in communication mechanisms through which employees, working groups and departments are connected

Organizing
The creating of effective relationships between people, resources and actions in order to attain certain goals (organization in the functional sense)

Outplacement
(a) Activities performed to assist someone outside the organizational unit; (b) a term used to describe the efforts made by a downsizing company to help its redundant employees through the redundancy transition and help them find new positions on the job market

Participation
A mutual consultation or deliberation which is experienced as legitimate and in which a conscious influencing of the decision making of those involved takes place

Participative leadership/management
A style of leadership in which the employee is given an opportunity to participate in decision making

Perception
The process of interpreting and processing of sensory impressions so that meaning can be given to the environment

Performance payment
Payment that varies with the performance delivered. *See also* Differential piece wage and Multi-factor reward

Personal culture
An organizational culture which is characterized by a low degree of cooperation and a high degree of spreading of power (decentralization)

Personal ethics
All those notions which constitute an individual's idea of what is right and proper

Personal power or prestige
Power assigned to someone based on who he/she is (personality and experience) and not based on the function he or she performs

Personnel management
A component of HRM, namely the management of the inflow, throughflow and outflow of personnel

Personnel structure
The occupation of functions in departments by individuals

Physical distribution
Control over the materials and accompanying flow of information from inventory of finished products up to the phase of delivering the products to the final consumer (see Logistics Management)

Planning
The process of information processing which leads to decisions in the present that affect future actions and takes into account the coordination and controlling of those actions

Planning cycle
The sequential steps between analysis and budgeting (often parallel to the book year)

Policy guidelines
An indication of how an individual has to act in any given situation

Policy intensive
The kind of work which is especially characterized by policy-developing activities

Policy matrix (from Shell)
Portfolio management approach with the attractiveness of the sector and competitive position as policy-determining factors

Policy plan
A plan which states in which way, in what period of time and with which resources goals are to be attained

Pooled dependence
The mutual dependency or relatedness of parts of an organization which is limited to indirect dependency (via the hierarchy)

Post-calculation
Periodical comparison of the budgeted costs with the actual costs. Any difference is known as the budget result.

Power culture
An organizational culture characterized by a high degree of cooperation and a low degree of spreading of power (centralization)

Power distance
(a) As a dimension of national culture: the degree to which the less powerful members of organizations in a country expect and accept that the power is unequally distributed; (b) without taking into consideration or not accepting the power distance of those involved: the degree of inequality in power between a less powerful person or group and a more powerful person or group

Power or potential power
The capacity to influence the behavior of others and to cause others to act in a certain manner, possibly even forcibly

Pragmatic aspect of information
Regards the use of data by a sender of information and the intended effects by the sender in a certain context

Preparedness or willingness to change
The degree to which the members of an organization are willing to accept the changes within an organization

Present picture of the portfolio
A survey of present businesses in relation to market growth and relative market share

Present strategic profile
A characterization of the organization in which the goals, the work domains, the competitive advantage and the synergy are laid out and which forms the basis of any new strategy that the organization implements

Primary labor conditions
A combination of wage, salary and vacation pay

Primary process
That process by which an organization derives its existence: its *raison d'être*

Procedure
A series of connected tasks which form a whole

Process
A number of sequential activities or events

Product development
A strategic option in which the organization starts developing new products for existing markets

Product lifecycle
The period between the introduction of a product and taking that product off the market

Product/market combination
Products or services for which sales is sought in a certain market or market segment and for which a separate strategy is developed

Productivity
The relationship between results and resources used

Project
A series of activities to be performed by more than one specialist group acting in a temporary cooperative relationship directed at a specified result to be attained within a certain time and with defined resources

Project management
The managing of a set of activities, directed at a specific goal, which are performed once only within a limited time and within a certain budget

Project planning or network planning
A method of planning once-off activities. The goal is determination of the total completion time needed. The critical path indicates which activities cannot be delayed since doing so will affect the completion date.

Pull system
A way of approaching the managing of production processes in which the production is regulated by client order. The goods and the orders are, as it were, 'pulled' out of the organization by the client. The alternative is the push system (see below).

Push system
A way of approaching the management of production processes in which the flow of goods/production is controlled on the basis of prognoses or marketing research. The goods and orders are 'pushed into' the organization, based on planning. The alternative is the pull system (see above).

Quality
A general evaluative notion which always has to be viewed in terms of the context within which the notion is used (for example, in terms of technical performance, extra possibilities, user friendliness, reliability, the meeting of specifications, durability, maintenance friendliness, aesthetic value)

Quality care
The attuning of product or service characteristics as well as the organization which produces them to the demands of the client in such a way that the demands can be met on an ongoing basis and at an acceptable cost

Quality circles
Groups within departments which are directed towards studying and combating quality-related problems, production problems and other problems within that department

Quality system
All those quality-directed organizational structures, responsibilities, procedures and provisions

Quantitative overutilization/occupation
A workload which is clearly above a reasonable minimum performance level

Quantitative underutilization/occupation
A workload which is clearly below a reasonable minimum performance level

Question mark
A business with a high market growth and a low relative market share

Rate of return on equity
Net profit in relation to equity

Rate of return on total capital
Profit before tax, increased by interest to be paid over the loans, in relation to the total capital

Ratio
A figure which relates two organizational phenomena in a certain way

Realized power
See Exercise of power

Rebundling
Integration within the integrated company of those processes that were previously performed by autonomous/separate organizations

Reciprocal interdependence
Mutual dependency or interrelatedness between parts of an organization in which, besides pooled interdependence, there is a direct mutual interdependency. Each part supplies outputs which form inputs for the other parts and every part receives output from the other parts which form inputs for one's own unit.

Relative market share
One's own market share divided by that of the largest competitor

Responsibility
The moral duty to perform a task to the best of one's ability and to report on how that task was performed

Return on invested capital
Sales in relation to capital. This ratio gives the relationship between the size of activity and the investment made for the purpose

Return on investments (ROI)
The degree of profitability expressed in terms of the profit margin (profit/sales) multiplied by the rotation time (sales/invested capital) of the invested capital

Revolving budget
A budgeting system in which a budget for the initial period has a task-setting character while the figures for subsequent periods have an orientating character

RFID
Radio Frequency Identification

Role culture
An organizational culture characterized by a low degree of cooperation and a low degree of spreading of power (centralization)

Routing
The way or route between and within phases of manufacturing, with optimal deployment of people and machines as the goal

Safety inventory or stock
The extra inventory of an article held in order to avoid running out of stock during the ordering period if demand increases

Secondary labor conditions
Complementary payment provisions which can differ per organization, such as complementary retirement insurance, life and health insurance

Self-control
The exercising of the authority to regulate and to steer production in a unit within previously set frameworks without direct intervention from outside during that process

Self-regulating/controlling teams
Teams with operational and possibly also organizational authority to decide on planning and the way the work is to be performed in order to attain the goals

Semantics
The meaning which is given to sender-receiver

Semi-autonomous working group
A working group which has the authority to organize its own work

Serial or sequential interdependence
Mutual dependency or interrelation between parts of an organization in which, besides the pooled interdependence, there is direct, unilateral dependency in the sense that the activities have a coercive, fixed order. The output of one part is the input of the next part.

Service/servicing
An activity or a series of activities of a more or less tangible nature, which usually take place in direct interaction between the client and the employees and/or physical resources and/or systems of the supplier

Servuction system
The part of a servicing organization which is visible from the point of view of the client, and exerts an influence on the forming of his/her image of the supplier as well as on his/her evaluative and purchasing behavior

Shared services
Support services accommodated in central units and that provide customer-supplier services to client units (departments, business units, divisions)

Sharia compliance
Respecting and following Islamic religious rules in the financial aspects of business practice

Sharia-compliant financing
Financing which avoids the use of interest (or *riba*) and/or gambling (*gharar*) and forbids/avoids investments in gambling, alcohol and pornography

Sharia-compliant insurance
A form of mutual assistance and risk-sharing (*takaful*)

Situational leadership
The notion that there is no one specific style of leadership which will produce the best results in every case. The best style depends on the situation.

Six Sigma
A strategy for improving results. Six Sigma stands for near (99.999967%) perfection and faultlessness.

Slip chart planning board
An order planning instrument in which the order is indicated through colored slips, set off against the time (week/day) within which the order has to be completed. Deviations from the schedules can be indicated by signaling signs, such as colored triangles and green dots.

Social annual report
A summary of the general annual report rewritten in understandable language for the company's own personnel, with an emphasis on the social aspects of business policy

Social networking ('communities')
Using interactive technologies to communicate between clients and partners and exchange information relating to a certain theme

Socio-psychological factors
In addition to physical factors, the co-determining elements of human behavior, based on a philosophy of human beings as social beings

Solvency
The degree to which an organization can meet its financial obligations in the event of liquidation

Span of control
The number of employees a manager can manage directly and effectively

Span of support
The extent to which a manager receives the support of other members of the organization in acquiring the staff, means and/or information necessary for effective job performance

Standard cost price
The estimated cost price for a certain period, based on allowed costs per unit of product

Star
A business with a high market growth and a high relative market share

Strategic alliance
A form of agreed cooperation which does entail any loss of identity or autonomy

Strategic business unit (SBU)
An organizational unit in which different business activities are accommodated via an interrelated or mutual strategic relationship

Strategic goals
Goals that the organization has to strive for, the methods of attaining these and the resources which are necessary to achieve them

Strategic management
An approach to strategic problems in which attention is paid to the choice of the product/market combinations, the development of and the maintenance of necessary skills as well as the implementation of a chosen strategy and any adjustment of the strategy that may be needed

Strategic planning
An approach to strategy formulation which highlights the choice of product/market combinations

Stress
A psychological and physical situation which arises when demands are made on a person which he or she cannot meet

Sukuk
An Islamic bond or loan without a fixed interest rate (*riba*), and instead, temporary co-ownership of the business or project

Supervision/control
The testing/checking of the reality against the norms which were set

Support department
A department which is added to the line organization in order to render certain internal services (to the organization as a whole or to parts of it)

Sustainability
Managing business affairs in a consistent way with future ecological and societal solutions to business problems in mind

Synergy
An advantage that may arise when the organization starts developing new activities that can utilize existing facilities

Tall or deep organizational structure
An organizational form in which leaders manage relatively few subordinates directly (i.e. a narrow span of control)

Task culture
An organizational culture which is characterized by a high degree of cooperation and a high degree of spreading of power (decentralization)

Task enlargement
See Cycle lengthening

Task enrichment
See Vertical enlargement

Task maturity
The degree to which an employee is capable and willing to take responsibility for a certain task

Technical aspect of information
Relates to the way in which the data/information is transported to the 'receiver.' This aspect relates to the so-called information carrier (for example, CD-ROM, slide, book, X-ray)

Tertiary labor conditions
A company car, free telephone or reimbursement of expenses such as car costs, mortgage interest

Time study
A method for determining standard performance times for the activities to be performed

Time shifting
Passing on work to employees in different time zones in order to take advantage of the difference between working hours between these zones

Timing
Criteria in the choice of a strategy in which, on the one hand, the speed of execution of the alternative is important and which, on the other, regards the question whether the organizational structure is ready for introduction of the alternative.

Tolerance zone
The zones above and under the set norm within which there should be no intervention

Top management
The highest management level within a labor organization. This level bears ultimate responsibility for management of the business and the organization.

Top-down approach
A planning cycle approach in which top management plays a major role in determining the direction taken

Twitter
A microblog application whereby users 'tweet': send short messages via sms, e-mail etc

Unbundling
The splitting off of processes from core processes within an integrated chain in order to separate organizations

Uncertainty avoidance
The degree to which the members of a culture feel threatened by uncertain or foreign situations

Unit management
A management style and an organizational form which, in combination, are directed towards decentralization of entrepreneurship within the organization as a whole

Unity of direction
An organizational principle whereby every employee has to accept binding orders issued by one superior (or another employee) only

Utilization or occupation planning
That part of the production planning which takes place after capacity planning. When the capacities are known, it will be evident whether the flow of production will match those capacities.

Value
A state of affairs that an individual, group or society wishes to strive for

Value chain
A notion originating from Porter which considers activities in the primary and secondary processes as a chain of value additions

Value system
The sum of the values, ranked in order of priority, held by an individual, group or society

Vertical differentiation
The extension of activities to a lower level of execution

Vertical integration
Expansion of an organization's activities within a particular business sector by taking over the activities of supplier organizations (backward integration) or buyer organizations (forward integration)

Vertical organization
Dividing activities among various levels

Vertical task enlargement or job enrichment
Expansion of the task to include activities of a higher level (work preparation, supervision, administration)

Virtual teams
Teams that collaborate with each other from various parts of the world and as such, do not meet in real life

Vision
Being able to envisage the organization's future

Voice (systems)
The process in which individual employees challenge the status quo of an organization in a constructive way with the purpose of improving the situation

Web 2.0
A collective terms for interactive/social Internet technologies (such as social networking via weblogs, Twitter, Yammer etc.)

Web 3.0
Semantic Web-based technologies whereby computers can understand information without the need for human intervention and make appropriate decisions

Webshop
A virtual or Internet-based shop

Whistleblower
A member of the organization who reports irregularities and/or breaches of rules or standards and/or makes them public

Work consultation
The institutionalized, periodical consultation within an organizational unit (department/team) between a manager and employees in relation to the work situation and the work itself and how it is to be performed

Work distribution
See Detail planning

Work engagement
The positive and fulfilling work-related state of mind that is characterized by vigor, dedication and absorption

Work extrinsic
Those things that form part of the work environment

Work intrinsic
Those things that form part of the work itself

Work preparation
See Delivery planning

Work science
The systematic study of how labor is organized and of work methods

Work structuring
A way of assigning or grouping of tasks in such a way as to utilize the capacities of the members of the organization as fully as possible

Work study
The study of human action, individually or collectively, in combination with machinery or tools, with special attention to improving work methods

Works council
A company or institution organ in which employees participate formally via their representatives

Yammer
A means of communication within a company via short messages

Index

360° assessment 412
360° feedback 411, 623

A

ability 16
ability and the willingness to change 350
ability to delegate 298
ability to motivate 438
absenteeism 395, 406, 518, 579
acceptance 372
acceptance of authority 15, 452
accepted leadership 341
accordion effect 343
account manager 273, 623
accountants 219
accounting functions 554
accounting rules 110
achievement 389
acquisitions 13, 88, 96, 236
action groups 38, 70, 75, 130
action plans 344
actions 491
activities 260, 500
ad hoc learning 178
adaptation 471, 551
added value 202
adhocracy 287
adjusting plans 503
adjustment 473
adjustment of operations 543
administration 7
administrative and tactical decisions 36
administrative boss 281
administrative boss relationship 282
administrative competence 444
administrative-oriented purchases 597
admission 471
advantage of the divisional structure 275
advantages of the business unit structure 277
advantages of the divisional structure 276
advantages of the functional structure 275
aggregator 574, 623
agility 53, 623
agriceutica 76
agronomics 17
aktiengesellschaft (AG) 32
alliances 84, 85, 96, 226
allocating assignments 436
alternatives 156, 157, 201, 227
alternative solutions 158
Amazon 593, 595
amount of authority 329
amount of change 272
analysis of actions 577
analysis of competitors 204
analysis of operations 577
analysis of problems 152
analysis of profitability, product-customer groups and distribution channels 244
analysis of sales patterns 244
analysis of the forces 204
analysis of the marketing mix 244
Anglo-Dutch Model 416
Anglo-Saxon 117
Anglo-Saxon model 115, 116
annual budgets 499
annual plans 242
annual report 623
annual report (fiscal) 623
Ansoff 199
anticipated changes 157
anti-globalists 70
application 177
application pull 583
appraisal of a company's performance 211
appraisal of internal strengths and weaknesses 219
appraisal of strengths and weaknesses 219
appraisal of the environment 220
appropriate employment 13
appropriate training 341
aptitude test 407
arbeitsdirektor 126
arbitrary management 21
areas of knowledge 41
arena model 161
Argyris 23
art of management 448
Artificial Intelligence (AI) 169, 623
aspects of leadership 437
assertiveness 41
assessment 410
assessment center method 409
assessment instruments 409
assessment of the strengths and weaknesses 218
assigning tasks 504, 578
assignment of authority 273
assignment of tasks 264
assignments 344, 503
attitudes 176, 247, 623
audit committee 117
aufsichtsrat 125
autarchy 343
authentic leadership 36
authenticity 44, 438
authoritarian leadership 472
authoritarian-improvising type 452
authoritarian-structure type 453
authorities 476
authority 15, 261, 263, 267, 281, 319, 329, 331, 397, 460, 463, 504, 554
authorization 158, 504, 554
autocratic 448
autocratic leadership 623
autocratic style of leadership 452, 455
automated knowledge 180
automation processes 563
autonomous process-oriented teams 34
autonomy 51, 323, 386, 390
avoid uncertainty 100
avoidance 470, 473

B

B2B (business-to-business) 17, 570, 574, 609
B2C (business-to-consumer) 17, 107, 574, 609
back office 580
backsourcing 85, 93, 623
backward integration 223
backward looking 533
balance 394
Balanced Business Scorecard 537, 538, 539, 540, 623
balance sheets 110
ban bullying at work 387
banks 65, 70
bargaining power 207
bargaining power of buyers/clients 80
bargaining power of the supplier 80
basic organization 623
BCI technology 623
behavior 371, 373, 382, 446, 458, 459, 463
behavior of groups 371
behavior of superiors 454
behavioral change 356
behavioral factors 160
benchmark method 526
benchmarking 303, 523, 623
benchmarking of management 524
benchmarking procedure 524
benchmarking process 525
Bennis 23
best practices 523
bilateral information and reporting system 286
bill of materials 509, 623
bio-economy 84
bio-related sciences 16
biogenetics 17, 76
Black Belts 516
blue print thinking 359, 360
board of directors 26, 27, 28, 31, 32, 121, 122, 125, 232, 294
– functions 28
board of management 26, 31, 121, 125, 126, 423
bonus 420, 422
bookkeeping 110, 554, 555
book-keeping system 497
BOP 623
bore-out 387
boss 388, 446
Boston Consulting Group 199, 215, 623
bottleneck products 598
Bottom of the Pyramid (BOP) 90
bottom-up 233
bottom-up approach 233, 234, 623
bottom-up development 328
bottom up principle 343
boundaries 398
bounded rationality 24
BPR (Business Process Redesign) 603, 605, 606
brainpower 178
brainstorming 156, 164, 623
brainwork 179
brand 17, 18
brand loyalty 91
brand values 17
branding 19, 623
breaking the quasi-equilibrium 351
bribes 131
BRIC countries 80
bridging of access to information 556
bridging of distance 556
bridging of time 556
broad task groups 328, 390
budget 245, 496, 502, 623
budget controls 300
budget result 623
budgetary controls 555
budgetary excesses 283
budgeting 245, 496, 497, 500, 555, 623
budgeting as a management tool 497
budgeting procedures 502
budgeting system 246
budgets 234, 242, 273, 496, 497, 498, 499
build up 291
bullying behavior 387
business chain 91
business environment 64, 65
business ethics 623
business growth and internationalization: globalization 13
business logistics 589
business network redesign 24, 606
business or activity 624
business plan 39, 45
business policy 624
Business Process Redesign (BPR) 24, 624
Business redesign 606
business start-up 293
business unit 276, 307, 624
business unit level 277
business unit management 344
business unit structure 277
business-to-business (B2B) 107
BU structure 277

Cadbury Report 129
cafeteria plan 394, 422, 624
calculation of material and machinery costs 578

call centers 574
Camp formula 508
cannibalism 19
cannibalization 609
capabilities 228
capabilities of employees 7
capability and ability to change 349
capacity planning 494, 624
capital budgets 498
capital intensive innovation 585
care 581
career 395
career development 424
career improvement 372
career planning 424
career prospects 400
career supervision 411
cash 298
cash cow 214, 215, 624
cash flow 216, 624
cash flow control 624
cash flow forecast 300
causa efficiens 437
causa finalis 437
cause and effect 521
causes 155
causes of deviation 497
centralization 160, 343
centralization/decentralization 12
centralize 343
centralized functional structure 272, 274, 275, 294, 624
CEO 26, 27, 131
certification of quality systems 587
chain-focused approach 94
chain of business activities 624
chain of business clusters 91
chain of command 12
chain producers 106
chain structure 469
champions 516
change 349
change management 351, 354
changes in culture 476
changes to organizational structures 350
changing (moving) 354
channels of communication 261
characteristics 137, 453
characteristics of good managers 42
characteristics of managers 10
characteristics of succesful managers 446
charisma 380, 444, 624
charismatic leader 41
chief executive 27
Chief Executive Officer 26
chief financial officers (CFOs) 110
choice criteria 157
choice of one form of strategic collaboration 235
– market 235
– need for confidentiality 235
– position product-market 235
– strategic goals 235
choice options 166
choice rules 162
Churchill & Lewis 299
CIO (Chief Information Officer) 554, 568
circle structure 469
classical chain of command 266
clear vision 341
client-oriented execution 324
climate 157
climate control 78
cloud computing (SaaS) 567, 624
cluster(ing) 91, 624
co-creation 608
co-option system 119
co-sourcing 106
co-workership 458
coach 401, 624
coachee 401, 624
coaching 400, 401, 402, 410, 624
coalition 162
code 121, 130
code of ethics 131
cognitive dissonance 624
cognitive school 200
coherence between activities 320
cohesion 378
cohesiveness of activities 500
collaboration 235, 381, 398
collaborative model 241
Collins 44, 51
color (change) thinking 624
color thinking 360
co-maker 624
co-makership 69, 241
command and control authority 331
commander 22, 44
commercial life cycle of a product 212
commercial-oriented purchases 597
commitment 159, 355
commitment of the partners 98
committee form of strategic planning 232
committee system 339
committees 152, 181
commitment 624
communication 41, 45, 260, 435, 464, 466, 468
communication and information theory 24
communication channels 260, 466
communication processes 152, 465
communication structures 24, 152, 264, 468, 469
companies 7, 64
company 26, 624
company culture 51
company espionage 35
company loyalty 420
company scandals 131
company succession 288, 290
company takeover 288, 290
company's reputation 134
competence 16
competencies 402
competition 80
competitive advantage 201, 226, 403, 513, 624
competitive environment 272
competitive position 72, 215, 216
competitive profile 205
competitive strategies 221
competitor portfolio analysis 212
competitors 70
compliance 624
compliance officers 121
composed task assignment 624
composition of the market 80
compromise 171, 471, 473
compromise strategy 171
computational strategy 171
Computer Aided Design (CAD) 575
Computer Aided Manufacturing (CAM) 575, 579
computer networks 569
computer technologies 168
concentration of decision-making authority 343
concept of hierarchy 425
concession 471
conditions for effective budgeting 501
configuration school 200
conflict as a process 472
conflict handling 624
conflict resolution 35, 437, 476
conflicts 381, 462, 470, 472
conflicts of interest 159, 375, 471
confrontation 470, 473
conglomerates 197
consciousness 382
consistency 227
– capabilities 228
– goals 228
– personal values 228
consistency criteria 625
consistent behavior 44
consistent information 133
consolidation phase 352
constituting 625
constituting tasks 267
constraints 65
consultation 152, 153, 181, 505
consultation and participation 339
consultation groups 181, 182, 625
consultative groups 152, 339
consultative relationship 338
consultative structure 260, 261
consumer associations 13
consumer behavior 90
consumerism 75
content of a task 329
continental model 115
contingency theory 25
continuity 7, 39
contract wage 625
contracting 97
contribution 68, 70
control 7, 22, 41, 491, 494, 501, 520, 601, 625
control chart 521
control cycle 45, 502, 625
control of activities 503
control of the production process 577
control of working capital 495
control over information 461
control over tangible resources 461
control process 502
control system 293, 295
control the actions of other people and resources 9
contrôler 22, 44
controlled organizational network 241
controller 554
controller function 554
controlling 436
convictions 53
cooperation 8, 263, 435, 472, 473
cooperative relationship 235
– costs 235
– risks 235
– timing 235
coordinating 22, 44, 45, 344, 436
coordinating mechanisms 261
coordinating role 232
coordination 105, 196, 261, 285, 344, 345
coordination mechanism 260, 271, 272, 279, 280, 281, 338, 339
coordination of the activities 492
coordination problems 602
coordination roles 340
coordonner 22, 44
coping with resistance to change 353
core activities 91
core competencies 304, 402
core ideology 51
corporate culture 131
corporate ethics 131
corporate governance 16, 114, 423
corporate identity 397
corporate intelligence 130
corporate interests 115
corporate philanthropy 133
corporate responsibility 133
corporate values 130
corporation 26
corporatism 115, 625
corrective actions 501, 531, 553, 555
corrective system 543
COSO Report 128
cost analyses 21
costs 235, 625
counterattack 231
countervailing power 71
Covey 44, 437, 438, 440
CPM (Critical Path Method) 512
cradle-to-cradle (C2C) 95
creative abilities 156, 392
creative employees 175
creative organization 173
creative thinking 173
creativity 35, 156, 173, 175, 176, 303, 472, 625
creditors 111
crime prevention 129
criminality 82
crises
– characteristics 137, 138, 475
crisis management 138, 139, 625
crisis plan 138
crisis situations 343, 464
critical approach 157
critical factors (Cfs) 537
critical mass 353
critical path 510, 511, 512
critical success factors 298, 535

Critical Success Factors (CSFs) 625
CRM (Customer Relationship Management) 571
CRO (Chief Risk Officer) 121
cross-border takeovers 14
cross-border teamwork 400
cross-cultural theories 397
cross-cultural training 398
crowdsourcing/co-creation 608, 625
CSFs 535, 536, 537
cultural borders 398
cultural change 357, 358, 479
cultural differences 98, 102
cultural school 200
cultural/societal influences 66
culture 378, 394, 397, 403, 478
culture jammers 18, 70
culture of the organization 34, 410
current activities 202
customer orientation 43, 393
customer relations management 16
Customer Relations Management (CRM), Supply Chain Management (SCM) 570
customer value 69
customer-directed attitude 51
customer-focused marketing 17
customer-focused orientation 606
customer-supplier relationship 94
customers 69, 370
cutting jobs 14
cutting of costs 35
cybernetic cycle 50, 625
cybernetic system 543
cybernetics 16
cyberspace 625
cycle lengthening, horizontal task enlargement or job enlargement 625
cycle of activities 67

D

daily execution of tasks 33
data 551, 555, 556
detailed process model of an organization 47
day extension 169, 625
De Caluwé 359
debureaucratization 393
decentralization 84, 160, 276, 343, 393, 569, 625
decentralized business unit structure 274
decentralized decision making 124
decentralized divisional or business unit structure 272
decentralized divisional structure 274, 275
decentralized division structure 625
decentralized multidivisional organization 296
decentralized multi-divisional structure 296
decision 334
decision maker 24, 157, 158
decision making 10, 23, 36, 45, 123, 151, 152, 153, 158, 160, 161, 163, 267, 466, 472, 490, 552, 556, 625
decision making processes:
– motivation 160
– quality of communication 160
– structure of the organization 160
decision matrix 166, 167
decision support systems 169, 625
decision tree 165
decision-making activities 34, 35
decision-making authority 260, 296, 342, 343
decision-making methods 165
decision-making process 151, 156, 159, 160, 163, 194, 393, 543, 552
decision-making theory 23
decisions 9, 46, 151, 152, 167, 503
decline 212
deep change 351
degree of authority 463
degree of autonomy 320
degree of centralization/decentralization 232, 271
degree of competition 206
degree of concentration 206, 342
degree of decentralization 272, 273, 569
degree of flexibility 230
degree of its acceptance 37
degree of reorganization 295
degree of risk and uncertainty 230
degree of self-confidence 43
degree of task maturity 455
degree of their influence 66
degree of uncertainty 158
delayering 300, 303, 397
delayering of middle management 301
delayering of the organization 425
delayering of top management 301, 302
delegated tasks 329, 553
delegating 299, 456
delegating decision-making authority 260
delegating (S4) 455
delegation 31, 329, 342, 391, 504
delegation of authority 343
delegation of tasks 329, 347
deliberation 153
delivery planning or work preparation 494, 625
delivery sub-system 580
delivery times 69, 507, 576
demand side 106
Deming 325, 513, 520
democratic-improvising type 453
democratic-structure type 453
demographic changes 89
demographic factors 71, 203
demotion 101, 412, 413, 625
departmental 502
departmental budget 498
departmental introduction 410
departmental plans 33, 504
departmental policies 33
departmentalization 264, 625
departmentalized organization 294
departments 260, 268, 269, 319
dependency on others 10
depth of control 321, 346, 625
deroutinizing 352
descriptive schools 200
design 177
design and development of new products 575
design of functions 371
design of operational tasks: criteria 320
design of the organizational structure 479
design process of an organizational structure 319
design rules 272
design school 199
designing 260
designing organizational structure 44, 342
desired solution 157
DESTEMP forces 71
detaching 625
detail planning or work dispatch 626
detailed order and machine planning 494
develop a vision 43
developing ability 356
developing alternatives 156
development 157
development-oriented 445
development-oriented manager 444
deviant 375
deviations 502, 503, 504
diagnose the organizational culture 475
diagnosis 155
differences 35
differences in salary 420
differential piece wage 626
differential piecework plan 21
differentiation 107
differentiation strategy 222, 626
differentiation tactic 91
digital technology 16
direct communication 281, 324
direct contact 273
direct rewards 418
direct task feedback 324
direct voice systems 355
directing 41
directing actions 9
directing tasks 267
direction 7
directives 114
– international 113
– national 113
directors 26
directors' responsibilities 117
disadvantages of the business unit structure 277
disadvantages of the divisional structure 276
disadvantages of the functional structure 275
discharge 414, 415
discipline 7, 9
discretionary decision-making authority 342
discretionary/expense centers 532
discretionary power 33
disengagement point 626
disengaging (unfreezing) 354
disintermediation 106, 626
disposable income 72
dissipated learning 178
distinctive competencies 401
distribution channels 16, 106, 224
diversification 221, 224, 226, 296, 343, 626
diversified enterprise 198
diversity 394, 400
diversity of interests 112, 162
diversity of its activities 273
diversity of needs 382
division 268, 343, 344
division manager 626
division of labor 232, 261
division of tasks 262, 264
division of work 21, 260, 272, 319
– functions 271
– geography 271
– markets 271
– products 271
divisional level 276
divisional managers 33, 257
divisional structure 275
divisionalization 343
divisionalized organization 344
divisions 269, 344
DMAIC cycle 516, 517, 626
DMAIC methodology 514
documented knowledge 180
dog(s) 214, 215, 626
dot-com boom 610
dot-corps 610
double loop learning 626
Douglas McGregor 379
downcycling 95
downsizing 393, 414
downstream 106
dual information and reporting function 286
dual lines of authority 286
dualistic or two-tier system 114
dualistic system 114
duties 260, 261
dynamic equilibrium 68
dynamic network(model) 104, 105
dynamic networks and webs 305
dynamic network structure 305
dynamics of organizations 349
dynamics of the portfolio 217

E

E-coaching 412
E-commerce 570, 592, 610, 626
E-development 412
E-HRM 406, 407, 412, 626
E-introduction 410
E-mail 626
E-market 626
E-(re)tailer 626
early adopters 353

early retirement 414
earning capacity/rate of return 626
ECB (European Central Bank) 73
eco-effectiveness 95
eco-efficiency 94, 95
ecological factors 71, 204
ecological sustainability 95
Economic and Monetary Union (EMU) 73
economic efficiency 53
economic factors 71, 72, 203
economic goals 588
economic influences 66
economic objectives 202
economic situation 343
economical sustainability 94
economies of scale 213
EDI (Electronic Data Interchange) 570
EDP manager (electronic data processing manager) 555
education 413, 599
effective budgeting
– conditions 501
effective communication 466
effective cooperation 263
effective design of functions 319
effective groups 382
effective leaders 402
effective model for leadership 438
effective performance 45
effective style of leadership 455
effectively 7, 11
effectiveness 392, 440, 626
effectiveness of communication 24
effectiveness of the organization 398
efficiency 21, 53, 392, 507, 509, 581, 626
efficient 7, 11
EFQM-model 542
egalitarianism 101
eight habits 439
Electronic HRM 406
elementary coordination mechanisms 273
elements of communication 465
elements of management 22
eliminating delays 509
emerging strategy 247
emotional intelligence (EQ) 440
emotional intelligence function 440
emotional involvement 466
employee acceptance 503
employee assessment 411
employee mobility 89, 400
employee participation 125
employee satisfaction 390
employee voice 355
employee work satisfaction 388
employee's performance 458
employees 26, 69, 111, 370, 388, 393, 394, 395, 398, 404, 422, 446, 447, 454, 457, 458, 459, 500, 518, 525, 569
employees potential 437
employment conditions 409, 423
empowerment 303, 390, 391, 392, 440
enterprise as structured network 287
Enterprise Resource Planning (ERP) 590
entrepreneur 196, 289, 300, 435
entrepreneurial ability 395
entrepreneurial concepts 570
entrepreneurial managers 445
entrepreneurial school 200
entrepreneurial skills 43
entrepreneurs 289
entrepreneurship 51, 289, 371, 394, 423, 426, 435, 436, 626
environment 24, 46, 65, 66, 95
environment theory 24
environmental care 589, 626
environmental care system 588, 589
environmental concern 588
environmental consequences 227
environmental factors 64, 71, 193, 466
environmental forces 66
environmental goals 588
environmental influences 65, 215
environmental issues 65
environmental policy 78, 588, 589
environmental problems 131
environmental protection 78
environmental responsibility 84
environmental school 200
environmental technology 78
equity 70
ERP 567, 570, 572
ERP systems 590, 591, 626
escrow agreement 626
ethical dimension 130
ethical programs 130
ethics 121, 130, 626
EU 81, 118, 125
EU countries 115
EU directive 14, 113
EU legislation 122
Euro 73, 74
Euro skepticism 73
Euro Works Council 124
Euro-cynics 73
European Foundation for Quality Management (EFQM) 523, 542
European population 71
European Union 13, 70, 113, 126
European Works Council (EWC) 123, 124
Eurozone 74, 75
events 64, 65
excellent organizations 51
exception variables 537
execution of duties 260
executive 9
executive board 125
executive committee 26, 117
executive directors 28, 114
executive managers 26
exercise of power 463
exercise of power or realized power 626
exercised power 460
exercising authority 435
existing organizational 479
expense centers 532
experience curve 212, 213
experience effect (learning curve) 626
experimental learning model 177
expertise 460
expertise power 463
expert manager 444, 445
expert power 464, 626
explicit strategy formulation 196
exploration 472
export of products/services 96
export of technology, patents and licenses 96
expressive component 465, 466
expressive organization 133, 627
extent of the power 460
external adaptation 67, 627
external adaption 49
external and internal customer contact 341
external and internal stakeholders 68
external appraisal 39, 201, 208, 627
external borders 398
external communications 557
external consultant 183
external dependency 303
external environment 31, 38, 67, 133, 193, 203
external groups 64
external information 557
external regulators 121
external reporting 113
external stakeholders 68, 555
external suppliers 69
extra horizontal and/or lateral coordination mechanisms 273
extrinsic form of payment 627
extrinsic forms of reward 418

F

F grouping 274, 326
F grouping system 268
F-decentralization 343
F-group 321
F-grouping advantages 322
F-grouping disadvantages 322
F-structure 279, 296
F-to P-grouping 347
facilitator 627
factors and their relative importance at various stages of growth an development 298
fair day's work 21, 320
fair performance needs 421
fair trade 19
family-owned companies 29
father of scientific management 21
favoritism 131
Fayol 40, 44, 49
feedback 50, 154, 234, 242, 323, 328, 390, 411, 464, 526, 553, 588
feedback and information 386
feedback information 341
feedback mechanisms 50
feedback principle 24
feedforward 50, 588
Female Board Index 119
field in which they work 41
field of knowledge 9, 10
fields of expertise (F) 287
fighter brands 19
finance 210, 228, 493
financial conglomerate 297
financial crisis 14, 74
financial holding 116
financial information 112
financial performance 211, 537
financial planning 495
financial planning and budgets 601
financial point of view 539
financial risk 119, 120
fine tuning 49
first in, first out (FIFO) 510
first-class worker 21
FIS Finance and Administration 561
FIS Marketing and sales 559
FIS Personnel 560
FIS production 559
FIS purchase 558
five different ways of viewing organizational change 359
five sources of influence 459, 460
five types of managers 444
fixed budgets 497
flat organization 31, 346, 424, 425
flat organizational structure 276, 394, 627
flat structure 393
flat structure (wide 'span of control') 346
flatter organizations 122
flatter structure 425
flexibility 53, 69, 231, 274, 299, 394, 590, 627
flexible employment 394
flexible employment conditions 423
flexible retirement 413, 627
flexible structures 305
flow approach 180
flow diagram 521
focus on results 10
food engineering 76
formal authority 15, 460, 463
formal communication 466
formal competence 15
formal division of tasks 261
formal group 374, 375
formal information 552
formal lines of authority 261
formal organization 262, 460, 627
formal organizational structure 262
formal power 463, 464
formal rules 264
formal sources of influence 460
formal strategy formulation processes 248
formalism 627
formalized communication 264
forms of communication 464
forms strategic collaboration 236
formulation of a strategy 196
formulation of norms 245
forward integration 223
forward looking 533
four aspects of communication 465
four phases of the decision-making process 153
four types of competencies 401

four types of decision strategy 171
franchise 627
franchising 96, 238
fraud 129
freedom 324
frequent problems of a project-based approach 284
Freud 382
front-line management 31, 34, 264
front-line managers 26, 33, 34, 266, 627
front office 580
full bureaucracy 99
function 627
function appraisal and evaluation 627
function description 627
function design 389
function-forming process 627
functional 602
functional area 242, 243, 493, 627
functional areas approach 209
functional authority 336, 627
functional boss 286
functional conflicts 375
functional democracy 124
functional fields 201, 242
functional foremanship 21
f(unctional) form 273
f(unctional) grouping 295
Functional Information System (FIS) 627
functional level 197
functional management 627
functional organizational conflict 375
functional relationships 336
functional salary 421
functional sense 12
functional services 91
functional specifications 242
functional structure 274, 275
functional wage 627
functional way 281
functionalization 264
functions 260, 389, 478
functions of a board of directors 28
functions of budgeting 500
funding 495
F.W. Taylor 21

G

G-grouping 269, 270
Galbraith 273, 286
Gantt chart 508
garbage can model of decision making 162
gender 400
general budget 499
general management activities 48
Generation Y 371
generic brands 19
genetic technology 76
GEO analysis 526
Geo-engineering 79, 627
G(eographical) 295
G(eographical) grouping 274, 343
G(eographical) structure 296
Geography (G) 287
Germanic Model 415
gharar 103
giving instructions 22, 44
global company 96
Global Excellence in Operations (GEO) 526
global geo-political relationships 83
global matrix structure 287
globalization 14, 18, 19, 76, 91, 570, 627
globalization strategy 226
goal attainment 50, 502
goal setting 328
goal-realizing unit 11, 67, 110
goals 38, 39, 202, 228, 402, 462, 502, 588
goals of a company 13
goals of the organization 377
good communication 464
good governance 133
good management 373, 442, 443, 462
goodwill 110, 627
Goold and Campbell 287
governance structure 26
governance systems 115
governing 41
government 65, 70, 81
governmental agencies 111
greed at the top 16
Green Belts 517
green print thinking 360
greenhouse effects 79
Greenpeace 70
Gross National Product 73
gross profit 628
group 374, 375, 379, 460
– heterogeneous 377
– homogeneous 377
group behavior 377
group characteristics 375
group cohesion 377
group control 27
group culture 378
group decision making 27
group ethics 628
group payment 422
group performance 379
group resistance 246
group set-up 326
group structure 28
grouping of tasks 319, 341
groupware 169, 628
growth 39, 212
growth and development of organizations 319
growth rate of the population 71
guidelines 39, 260, 261, 262

H

Hackman 379
Hamel and Prahalad 402
Harrison 475
Hawthorne factories 22
head hunters 406
hedge funds 16
helpful managers 444, 445
Henri Fayol 22
hero mentality 474
Herzberg 323
heterogeneity 272, 403
heterogeneous groups 377
heterogeneous product-market combinations 275
heterogeneous products 274
heuristic methods 168
hierarchical ladder 33
hierarchical order 266
hierarchical structure 393
hierarchical way 281
hierarchy 12, 98, 122, 264, 344, 390
hierarchy of a company 31
hierarchy of human needs 383
hierarchy of needs 384, 628
hierarchy of preferences 162
hierarchy of the organization 99
high performance 43
high performance jobs 44
high performance organization 44, 52, 628
higher consultation groups 182
higher middle management 33
histogram 521
Hofstede 98
holding 628
holding company 297
homeshoring 85
homo economicus 24
homogeneity 403
homogeneous 377
horizontal communication 468
horizontal decentralization 342
horizontal differentiation 320
horizontal differentiation: advantages and disadvantages 321
horizontal differentiation (F-grouping) 372
horizontal direction 346
horizontal group 374
horizontal job enlargement 320
horizontal organization 628
horizontal relationship 338, 628
horizontal structure 606
hostile takeovers 14, 35
hour-glass model 26
house style 474
HRM 404, 405, 425, 426
HRM managers 403
HRM outsourcing 599
human being 384, 385
human capital 403
human factors 382, 466
human habits 44
human knowledge 180
human motivation 356
human potential 403
human relations theory 20, 22, 628
human resource condition 378
human resources management (HRM) 370, 403, 405, 628
human sigma 44, 52
humanization of work 23
hybrid car technology 76, 78
hydrogen technology 80

I

IASC 114
ICT 78, 106, 241, 327, 564, 568, 569, 570, 607
ICT applications 565, 574
ICT projects 563
ICT strategy 565
ICT systems 568
ideal portfolio 214
identical products 223
identification 323, 386, 460, 464, 581
identification phase 155
identification power 463, 628
identity 26, 110, 133, 134, 375
IFRS 110, 628
image 133, 134
image improvement 227
implementation 242
implementation of plans 502
implementation of strategic plans 193, 242
implementation of the strategy 246
implement the new strategy 231
improvement in quality 605
improvement of performance 501
incidents 133
income 39
incomplete diagnosis 155
increasing competition 82, 91
increasing degree of decentralization 273
incremental innovation 583
independence 438, 439
indirect reimbursements 418
individual employees 260
individual functions 389
individual learning 178
individual performance planning 372
individual resistance 246
individual work groups 319
individualization 372
inducement 68
inducement/reward 68
industrial democracy 116, 122, 125
industrial democracy in EU countries 128
industrial democracy in Europe 126
industrial groups 116
Industrial Revolution 7, 21
industrial sector 80
industrial transformation 17, 91
ineffective 11
ineffective leaders 446
inefficient 11
inequality in power 463
influence 16, 41, 65, 459, 460, 462, 464
influence on the financial result 598
influence strategies 355
influencing behavior 464
influencing organizational culture 479
infobesitas 628
infomediaries 574, 628
informal channels of communication 466
informal communication 263, 293, 294

informal culture 373
informal function 375
informal groups 374
informal information 552
informal leader 263
informal leadership 460
informal organization 262, 263, 375, 466
informal power 460
informal social group 22
informal sources of influence 460
information 50, 110, 152, 154, 219, 492, 503, 551, 552, 556
information and communication technology (ICT) 554
information management 562, 628
information management function 554
information manager 554
information need 557
information plan 562, 628
information processing 553
information provision 555
information pyramid 556
information sharing 160
information supply 628
information systems 300, 562, 628
information technology 16, 24, 88, 179, 551, 605
information technology (iT) 562, 602, 628
information triangle 552
information-related activities 34
ingredients of an effective grouping of tasks and design of functions 323
INK management model 628
inner voice 440, 457
innovation 19, 43, 539, 581, 583, 585
innovation project 585
innovative ability 395
innovative capabilities 274
inshoring 85, 628
inspiration 43, 171, 426, 439, 440, 444
inspirational leadership 43, 44, 440, 442, 444, 457
inspirational strategy 171
inspiring leader 438
inspiring leadership 36, 435, 628
institutional sense 12
institutions 7, 64
instructing 33
instructions 344, 503, 504, 344
instrumental 448
instrumental meaning 12
instrumentality theory 628
intake 406
integrated risk management 119
integrated teams 389
integrity 44, 134, 629
integrity of directors and managers 121
intellectual characteristics 453
intelligence test 407
intelligent 303
intelligent organization 303
intensity of competition 80
intensity of rivalry 205
intensive competition 205
interactive consumption 629
interdependence 269, 281, 439
interdependencies 161, 278
interdisciplinary 25, 398
interest groups 64, 65, 69, 70
interests 246
interim manager 629
interlocking directorships 116
intermediaries 106
intermediation 629
internal adaptation 49, 67, 629
internal and external collaboration 44
internal appraisal 39, 201, 208, 220, 629
internal capabilities 193
internal collaboration 381
internal communication 629
internal democracy 23
internal differentiation 268, 269, 279, 629
internal environment 193
internal environmental care 629
internal operational signaling 629
internal organization 31
internal or horizontal differentiation 629
internal or horizontal specialization 629
internal orientation 606
internal point of view 538
internal product specialization 269
internal promotion 414
internal reporting 539, 555
internal reports 577
internal specialization 269, 272, 273
internal stakeholders 111
internal supervision 553
international developments 73
International Organization for Standardization (ISO) 522, 587
internationalization 224, 225
internationalization of company 96
internationalization strategy 226
internet 106, 406, 407, 408, 574, 592, 594, 606, 608
internet companies 593
internet customers 593
internet strategy 610
inter-organizational cooperation 24
inter-organizational networks 104
interpersonal activities 34
interpersonal effectiveness 41
interpretation of ratios 531
interrelationship between business and society 13
interrelationships 261
interviews 407
intranet 406, 410, 412
intrapreneurship 290
intrinsic competencies 401
intrinsic form of reward/ payment 629
intrinsic satisfaction 11
introduction 212
introduction procedure 409
intuition 196
intuitive approach 193, 196, 248
intuitive approach to strategy 629
inventory control 508
inventory costs 508
inventory points 590
investment 228
investment centers 532
investment climate 72
investment companies 87
investment opportunities 97
investments in foreign subsidiaries 96
IPod Generation 371
irrational aspects of organizational behavior 160
irrational influences 24
irrational side of change management 356
Islamic finance 103
Islamic insurance 629
ISO norms 522
ISO-9000 522
ISO-9002 522
ISO-9003 522
ISO-9004 522
issuing directives 504
issuing instructions 503
IT 179, 180
IT strategy 629

J

Japanese Model 415
job 9, 262
job chat 408
job description 406, 599
job enlargement 324, 326, 389
job enrichment 324, 389
job rotation 325, 326, 389, 629
job share 629
job sharing 409
job sites 407, 408
job specification 31
job test 407
joint decision making 122, 126
joint decisions 182
joint manufacturing agreements 239
joint venture 85, 96, 237, 241, 629
judgement 177
judgmental strategy 171
Juran 325, 513
justice 130
just-in-time 509, 607, 629
Just In Time 603

Kaizen system 513
Kanban 629
Kanban system 509
Kaplan 540
Keiretsu 116
Keuning and Eppink 53
key factors (KFs) 630
key performance results 542
key variables of individual behavior 630
knowledge 41
knowledge economy 178
knowledge management 178, 179, 180, 630
knowledge of planning, organizing 41
knowledge of technology 41
knowledge of the organization 41
knowledge transfer methods 180
knowledge-creating organizations 180
Kolb 176, 177
Kotter 41, 461

L

labor division 630
labor productivity 73, 509
labor studies: time and motion studies 577
labor time reduction 414
lack of acceptance 334
lack of attunement 163
lack of consensus 163
lack of consistency 248
lack of courage 163
lack of guidance and control 163
lack of information 163
lack of interest 387
lack of policy 163
large company 274
lateral (or diagonal) communication 468
lateral (or diagonal) relationship 338
lateral thinking 164, 165, 630
Latin Model 415
Latin Monetary Union 73
Latin-European model 116
lay-out 577, 578, 630
layers 31, 264
layers in the governance structure 30
layers of authority 264
layers within the organization 100
laziness 387
leader 40, 435, 440
leaders 39, 442, 447, 448
leadership 39, 41, 247, 379, 426, 436, 440, 442, 443, 447, 448, 451, 464, 475
– characteristics 453
leadership styles 371, 455, 519
leading 630
leading and controlling activities 36
lean manufacturing 513
learning 177, 178, 179, 630
learning curve 213
learning cycle 177
learning organization 176, 178, 179, 303, 630
learning process 353
learning school 200
Leavitt 468
legislation 405
legislative processes 81
legitimate power 460
level 5 leadership 44
level of acceptance of the strategy 246
level of commitment 394
level of performance 421
levels of authority 557
levels of management 9, 30
leverage products 598

Lewin 176
life cycle 218
life science industry 16
life sciences 76
life-science economies 84
lifetime employment 374
Likert 451, 452
limitations 65
limiting factors 163
line activity 232
line authority 331, 336
line diagram 521
line managers 152, 334
line organization 329, 338, 630
 – advantages 330
 – disadvantages 330
line organization: advantages v. disadvantages 332
line organization: functioning 332
line relations 630
line relationships 12, 331, 332
line staff organization 329, 333, 630
 – advantages 334
 – disadvantages 334
lines of communication 556
linking pin 451, 630
linking pin function 452
linking pin structure 452
liquidity budget 498
list of priorities 158
lobbying 136
local brands 19
local managers 307
local subsidiary 97
logistical activities 590
logistics management 589, 630
logo 474
long-term consequences 227
long-term planning 496, 630
loss of reputation 119
low-wage countries 14
lower middle management 33
lower working groups 182
lowest cost price 222
lowest cost strategy 222
loyalty 22, 132, 374
Loyalty Awareness Program 374

M

M-grouping 269, 270
machine time 578
macho-acquisitions 88
maintenance of machines 575
majority 377
making a choice 231
making of decisions 7, 342
management 7, 8, 9, 12, 202, 228, 261, 300, 435, 436, 442, 630
 – as a job 9
 – discipline 7, 9
 – field of knowledge 9
 – group of managers 34
 – process 9
 – profession 7
 – three meanings 9
management activities 436
management and organizational processes 46
management as a group of managers 34
management as a process 20, 44, 45
management audit 129
management buyouts 226, 288, 290
management by direction and control 450
management by exception 329, 504, 630
management by integration and self-control 451
management by motivation 384
management by objectives (MbO) 451, 505, 506, 507, 630
management capability 40
management charisma 171
management competencies 401
management consultancy 630
management consultants 219
management cycle 45
management development 413, 415, 630
management effectiveness 39
management functions 437
management information 46
management information systems 557
management layers 31, 275, 303
management leadership 442, 630
management levels 34
 – differences 35
management of change 631
management of human resources 599
management of infrastructure 16
management of the resistance 247
management plan 506
management processes 47
management-process theory 44, 631
management science 16
management skills 22
management structure 303
management tasks 41, 45, 371
management theories 20, 22
 – characteristics 22
management tools 16
manager 8, 9, 40, 152, 435, 443, 631
manager of the future 437
manager's authority 281
managerial 458
managerial activities 33
managerial authority 460
managerial efficiency 53
managerial functions 435
managerial layers 348
managerial or regulatory and condition-setting processes 48
managerial process 46
managerial style 454
managerial task 435
managers 7, 41, 435, 436, 442, 447, 453
 – areas of knowledge 41
 – characteristics 10, 42
managers per level 100
managing in the 'broad' sense 44
managing in the 'narrow' sense 44
managing methods 340
man as a machine 437
maneuverability 231
manipulating figures 131
MANS 518
manufacturing 498, 575
manufacturing or production plans 494
manufacturing planning 494
manufacturing processes 46, 574, 575, 576
Manufacturing Resources Planning 590
Manufacturing Resources Planning (MRP II) 631
manufacturing/servicing 493
map out a strategy 43
mapping 49
mapping out of process activities 577
margin of tolerance 50
market 583
market (m) 287
market and industry factors 71
market development 66, 221, 224, 225, 631
market environment 64
market factors 80
market growth 215
market integration 74
market penetration 221, 631
market position 39
market quality 215
market segmentation 223
M(arket segment) grouping 273, 295
market share 85
market-oriented organization 394
marketing 210, 244, 592, 594
marketing and sales 243, 493, 498, 592
marketing and sales goals 592
marketing and sales plans 493
marketing department 244, 592
marketing philosophy 17
markets 64, 66
Maslow 382, 383, 384, 392
mass customization 579
Master Black Belts 516
master budget 499, 631
matching business goals and the personal goals 299
matching of components 67
material management 589
material resources planning 496
materials management 631
Materials Requirements Planning (MRP I/II) 631
matrix 215
matrix organization 274, 281, 284, 286, 631
matrix organizational structure 287
matrix structure 285, 287, 288
matrix-like structure 287
maturity 212, 385
maximizing 162
maximizing behavior 162
Mayo 22, 411
McGregor 442, 450, 451
measurement 520
measuring of effectiveness 53
measuring of performance 531
measuring task performance 503
mechanical engineering 91
mechanism of coordination 344
mechanized knowledge 180
mechatronics 91
medium-sized companies 29
mega-mergers 13, 88
mental intelligence function 440
mental intelligence (IQ) 440
mental model 631
mentoring 400
merger 88, 102, 236
merger mania 88
merger-euphoria 88
mergers 13, 87, 226, 229
mergers and acquisitions 88
merger / takeover 241
merit 419
metaphors 462
method studies 21
middle management 31, 32, 33, 36, 264, 265, 425
middle management level 265
middle management positions 389
middle management tasks 32, 265
middle managers 26, 305
middle-long 492
milestones 511
millennials 371
millennium problem 16
minority 377
Mintzberg 199, 247
miscommunication 466
mismanagement 131
mission 194, 226, 227, 631
mission statement 227, 631
mixed group 374
mobbing 387, 631
model of strategy formulation 234
model of the control process the cybernetic cycle 50
modern management
 – elements 12
modern management theory 49
modern manager 442, 447
modern schools of management 23
money stimulus 21
monistic or one-tier system 114
monitoring 503, 532, 553
moral activity 440
moral behavior 134
moral development 130
moral leadership 36
morale of the workers 22
morality 130, 131
Morgan 462
Most Competitive Countries in 2009 82
motion studies 21
motivating employees 36, 457
motivating working environment 458
motivation 33, 43, 371, 382, 385, 389, 391, 458, 518
motivation of the members of the organization 160
motivation theory 385, 386
motivational effect 328, 341

motivational theory 21
motivator 385
MRP (Materials Requirement Planning) 509
multi-channel approach 609
multi channel distribution 106
multi-cultural 398
multi-divisional organization 296
multi-factor reward 631
multidisciplinary projects 381
multidisciplinary teams 381
multinational company 97
multinational strategy 226
multinationals 14, 83, 95
multiple task assignment 504
multitasking 631
mutual adjustment 328, 345
mutual agreement 155
mutual consultation 398
mutual cooperation 261
mutual distrust 375
mutual trust 375
myths 380

N

Naamloze Vennootschap (NV) 32
nanotechnology 17, 76
narrow task specialization 21
national and international directives 113
national income 72
natural attrition 414
natural coherence 269
nature of its primary activities 273
nature of the environment 272
nature of the mutual interdependence 279
navigator 574
nearshoring 85, 92, 631
need for a hierarchy 340
need for change 351
need for confidentiality 235
need for coordination 341
need for esteem and appreciation 384
need for external adaptation 259
need for internal adaptation 260
need for love and social acceptance 384
need for recognition 392
need for respect 385
need for safety and security 384
need for self-actualization 384
need for self-fulfillment 385
needs of a physiological nature 384
negative sanction 160, 459
negotiating 473
negotiation 472
negotiations 158, 471
net sales 631
network 105, 304, 396, 511
network analysis 512
network contacts 33
network diagram 510
network of organizations 24
network organizations 105, 306, 631
network orientation 607
network planning 510, 631
network structure 307
networked company 607
networked organization 609
networking 105
networks 304
neuro-sciences 16
new activities 224
new culture 479
new employee 410
new entrepreneurial model 241
new forms of growth 291
new product applications 583
new products 223
new technologies 84
NGOs 130
noise 632
nomination committee 117
Nonaka 180
non-crisis situations 464
non-executive directors 27, 28, 29, 114, 219
non-executives 26
non-financial measurements 534
non-financial rewards 418
non-governmental organizations 130
non-material incentives 457
non-power 463, 632
non-power relationship 464
non-profit organizations 12, 541
non-programmed decisions 168
non-verbal communication 41, 465
Nordic model 100, 632
norm 543
normal pattern of a product-market combination 214
norms 130, 474, 492, 497, 501, 502, 503, 531, 543, 554

O

objective rationality 24
objectives 7, 13, 39, 194, 201, 202, 220, 226
 – economic 202
 – non-economic 202
observation 177
OECD 81, 82
office automation 169, 632
offshore activities 84
offshoring 14, 69, 92, 568, 632
OJDA cycle 177
old economy companies 610
one-parent families 395
one-tier 26
one-tier system 28, 117, 118, 119
OPEC 81
open atmosphere 175
open communication 379
open network structure 469
open system 632
open-conflict behavior 473
operational 119, 498, 607
operational and conceptual learning 177
operational and renewing competencies 401
operational benchmarking 524
operational boss 286
operational boss relationship 282
operational budget 498
operational control 33, 531
operational core 26
operational decisions 36, 37, 152, 153, 167, 296
operational employees 31, 264, 266, 553, 554, 632
operational freedom 397
operational functions 46
operational information 552
operational learning 632
operational level 398
operational management 558, 559, 560, 561
operational norms 503, 504
operational planning 490, 491
operational plans 197, 490, 491
operational processes 47
operational responsibility 282
operational risk 120
operational staff 34
operational standards 50
operational strategy 526
operational way 281
operations research 16
opportunistic learning 178
opportunities and threats 201, 208, 219
opportunity 632
optimal degree of delegation 321
optimal delegation 632
optimal order size/series 632
optimal production 576
optimal production program 577
optimal satisfaction 13
optimizing 162
option plans 423
oral communication 468
oral tasks assignment 504
ordering costs 508
organic structure 262, 632
organiser 22, 44
organization 7, 9, 11, 65, 67, 231, 632
 – functional 12
 – institutional 12
 – instrumental 12
organization and its environment 64, 265
organization as a network 24
organization chart 261
organization chart or organogram 632
organization culture 632
organization members 371
organization of the strategic planning process 232
organization principles 602
organizational 36, 119, 167, 296, 397, 404, 478, 500
organizational activities 491
organizational and supervisory leadership 444
organizational behavior 41
organizational change 319, 350
organizational cohesion 378
organizational conflicts 162
organizational culture 53, 54, 102, 339, 350, 454, 472, 474, 475, 478
 – direct instruments 479
 – functions 478
 – indirect instruments 480
organizational decisions 37, 153, 342
organizational democracy 123, 124
organizational development 353, 400
organizational effectiveness 53
organizational empowerment 392
organizational environment 160
organizational equilibrium 68, 632
organizational goals 40, 371, 457
organizational hierarchy 460
organizational instruments 340
organizational leadership 442
organizational levels 100, 502, 566
organizational network 241
organizational or administrative decisions 152
organizational policies 500
organizational processes 47, 503
organizational risk 119, 120
organizational slack 343
organizational strategy 403
organizational structure 23, 26, 232, 242, 260, 261, 262, 271, 272, 273, 281, 283, 396, 476, 551, 632
organizational structure in the early stages of the growth phase 294
organizational structure in the growth phase 293
organizational structure in the start-up phase 293
organizational style 454
organizational sustainability 94
organizational theory 458
organizational webs 24, 104, 307
organization's competencies 401
organization's environment 64
organization's information needs 552
organization's performance 527
organization's strengths and weaknesses 218
organizations 7, 8, 12, 13, 64, 110, 153, 231, 370, 374, 377, 387, 442, 464, 581
 – common features 12
organizations as 'open' systems 24
organizations without people 23
organized anarchies 162
organizing 11, 22, 44, 632
organizing brainpower 179
organizing the work around processes 327
ossification and rigidity 291
outcast 375
outplacement 414, 415, 632
output of the products or services 67
output side 66
outside directors 114
outsource business activities 84
outsourcing 14, 69, 78, 85, 91, 92, 106, 241
outsourcing company 240
overall coordination 27
overcoming resistance 247
overcoming resistance to change 354
overlapping groups 451
overutilization 320

own businesses 289
owner of the process 517
owner-entrepreneur-manager 38
owner-leader-manager 31
owner-manager 29, 293, 294
owner-manager of a small company 38
owner-shareholders 70
owner's ability 298
owner's ability to delegate 298
owners 26
ownership 29

P

paradox 438, 442, 444
paretogram 521
part-time work 394, 409
participants 111
participating 456
participating (S3) 455
participation 124, 153, 181, 472, 632
participative decision making 122
participative leader 449
participative leadership 449
participative leadership/ management 632
participative management 519
partnership relationships 570
partnerships 14
passion 43, 439
patterns for handling and resolving problems 478
patterns of power and interdependence 462
payment 409, 419
payment systems 21, 421, 422
people 298, 299, 435
people and the organization 23
people without organization 23
people-oriented 449
people-oriented activity 7
perception 632
performance 211, 391, 394, 411, 420, 421, 422, 425
performance assessment 410, 411
performance goals 525, 526
performance indicators 329, 535
performance levels 21
performance management 328, 402
performance measurement 293, 295, 297, 539, 541
performance measurement system 543
performance payment 632
performance test 407
period planning 510
permanent committees 339
person culture 475
personal accountability 324
personal bureaucracy 99
personal change 438
personal culture 633
personal development 599
personal ethics 633
personal freedom 22
personal goals 298
personal observation 503
personal plan 506
personal power 461
personal power or prestige 633
personal prestige 15, 461
personal recognition 22
personal responsibility 371
personal staff 348
personal values 228
personalities 28
personality 26
personality characteristics 453
personality of the leader 453, 455
personality of the manager 7, 347
personality test 407
personality types 382
personality-based approach 453
personnel 210, 493, 498
personnel management 633
personnel managers 405
personnel planning 406, 495
personnel policy 599
personnel process 405
personnel selection 409
personnel structure 262, 633
personnel work 405
perspective of power 462
persuasive communication 355
persuasive power 41
PERT 512
PERT-cost 512
Peter principle 414
Peters and Waterman 51
Pfeffer 462
P-, G- or M-structure 296
P-group 322
P-grouping 269, 274, 325, 326, 341
P-grouping advantages 323
P-grouping and F-grouping: advantages and disadvantages 321
P-grouping disadvantages 323
phase model of decision making 151
phase model of the decision-making process 154, 159
physical characteristics 453
physical distribution management 589, 633
physical intelligence 440
physical or bodily intelligence (PQ) 440
piecework wage 21
pitfalls of ICT projects 563
plan 38, 497, 553
planning 21, 22, 36, 39, 44, 152, 196, 199, 280, 436, 491, 492, 497, 507, 633
planning and systems 299
planning charts 507
planning cycle 233, 633
planning cycle with a top-down approach 233
planning procedure 601
planning process 233
planning school 199
planning specialists 232
planning system 507
planning techniques 232, 577
plans 39, 201, 491, 492, 496
plans for the functional fields 234
point of view 539
policy 496
policy decisions 38
policy formulation 267
policy guidelines 344, 345, 504, 633
policy intensive 633
policy making 22, 44
policy matrix 212, 215
policy matrix (from Shell) 633
policy plan 633
political acceptance 357, 358
political factors 71, 81, 204
political influences 66
political integration 74
political processes 462
pollution 79, 80
pooled interdependence 279, 280, 344
portals 574
Porter 48, 199
portfolio 226
portfolio analysis 197, 212, 217
portfolio approaches 199
portfolio of a company 198
portfolio of purchase products 598
position 459
position improvement 221
position in the product-market 235
positional authority 15
positional power 460, 461
positioning school 199
positive energy 440
positive sanction 160, 459
possible consequences 157
post-calculation 633
potential assessment 410
potential or new entrants 208
power 7, 15, 435, 460, 461, 462, 463, 470, 475, 476
power and conflict 161
power culture 476, 633
power differences 124
power distance 98, 100, 463, 633
power game 462
power of information 461
power or potential power 633
power perspective 462
power position 206
power school 200
power strategies 462
power structures 7
power to control 26
powers of control 29
Prahalad 53, 90, 94
pre-selection 407
preparedness or willingness to change 633
prescriptive schools 199
present picture of the portfolio 633
present strategic profile 200, 201, 633
prestige 15
prévoir 22, 44
price-setting 69
primary activities 48
primary labor conditions 633
primary or main processes 48
primary process 601, 633
primus inter pares 27
private equity 16
private labels 19
proactive guidelines 120
problem 154
problem management 136
problem-solving 472
procedures 158, 260, 261, 262, 264, 273, 344, 345, 633
process 9, 633
process analysis 577
process control 551, 574, 575, 576, 601
process design 568
process innovation 583, 584
process model of an organization
– more detailed 47
– simple 47
process of benchmarking 526
process of communication 466
process of decentralization 302
process of decision making 24
process of management 7, 22
process of strategy formulation 219
process orientation 327, 603
process re-engineering 24
process-oriented 602
process-oriented structures 327
processes 49, 601
producer-to-consumer chain 78
P(roduct)-decentralization, M(arket)-, or G(eographical)-decentralization 343
product development 209, 221, 224, 225, 243, 493, 633
product development planning 495
product group 275, 296
P(roduct) grouping 273, 295
product innovation 16, 223, 583, 584
product life cycle 84, 212, 634
product managers 273
product or process innovations 584
product portfolio matrix 212, 213
product recall 120, 137
product/market combination 634
product-market grouping 343
product-market matrix 220, 582
production 21, 210, 228, 243, 244
production department 244, 554, 576
production groups 22
production level planning 494
production management 21
production methods 577
production networks 90
production planning 575
production sub-system 580
production techniques 579
production-oriented approach 586
productivity 21, 22, 39, 51, 213, 371, 378, 385, 389, 444, 503, 507, 565, 581, 611, 634
productivity levels 21
products and services 7, 574
profession of management 7
professional 478
professional management 38
professional skills 395
profit 12
profit center approach 569
profit centers 532

profit decentralization 343
profit sharing 422
profitability 39
profound change 351
Program Evaluation and Review Technique 512
programmed and non-programmed decisions 167
progress control 578
project 282, 634
project group 281
project groups 152, 181, 273, 282
project leaders 517
project management 634
project manager 282
project organization 274, 281, 282, 583
project planning or network planning 634
project-based approach 283
projections 503
protective managers 444, 445
psychological test 408
psychosocial efficiency 53
Public Limited Company (PLC) 32
pull model 106
pull system 509, 634
punishment 459
purchasing 209, 243, 493, 496, 498
purchasing department 243
purchasing procedures 597
purchasing process 594, 597
pure project structure 284
push driven 106
push system 509, 634
pyramid of psychological needs 384

Q

quality 69, 581, 634
quality assurance 518
quality care 634
quality circles 325, 389, 634
quality control 503, 520, 576, 577, 579, 586
quality control program 518
quality control system 240
quality costs 586
quality management 512, 513
quality management method 514
quality management performance 523
quality of communication 160
quality of coordination 286
quality of the decision 37
Quality of Working Life (QWL) programs 124
quality system 587, 634
quantitative innovation 585
quantitative overutilization/ occupation 634
quantitative underutilization/ occupation 634
quasi-equilibrium 351, 352
question mark 214, 215, 634

R

Raad van Bestuur 125
Raad van Commissarissen 125
radical innovation 583
raison d'être 67, 110
range of alternatives 246
rate of return on equity 634
rate of return on total capital 634
ratio 529, 634
rational 7
rational decision making
– limiting factors 163
rationalization phase 584
ratios 527, 528
raw materials 207
re-engineering 602, 603
realized power 634
real time 570
reasonable compensation 13
rebundling 16, 106, 634
reciprocal interdependence 279, 280, 634
recognition 155, 389
recognition and diagnosis 154
recruitment 406, 408
recruitment procedure 406
recycling 95
red print thinking 360
redesign 551, 602
redistribution of tasks 347
reduce uncertainty 478
reduction of competition 221
reduction of costs 605
reduction of time 605
reduction of uncertainty 168, 478
refreezing 352
reintermediation 106
relational component 466
relationships 461
relative market share 216, 634
relevance 439
reliability 219, 581
remuneration 16, 389
remuneration committee 117, 423
Rensis Likert 379
reorganization stress 388
reorganizations 14, 16, 88, 388
reporting system 234
repression 470
reputations 446
research and development 293, 295, 296, 498, 581
resistance 246, 247, 372
resistance to change 350, 352, 354, 404
resource maturity and optimal position 291
resource-based perspective 402
resources 11, 38, 66
responsibilities 31, 65, 264, 397, 476
responsibilities of middle management 33
responsibility 10, 159, 321, 324, 329, 373, 391, 393, 396, 634
responsiveness 53, 395, 581
results approach 211
retirement 414
return on invested capital 635
Return On Investments (ROI) 533, 635
return to centralization 343
revenue centers 532
Revisionism 23
revolving budget 499, 635
reward 420, 459
reward/payment 293, 295, 297
rewards 357
reward systems 341, 419
RFID (Radio Frequency Identification) 570, 571, 573, 635
Rhineland model 14, 115, 117, 118
right political conditions 378
rise of nationalism 75
risk management 112, 121
risk managers 121
risks 235
rites of initiation 377
rituals 474
rivalry 80, 462
role 463
role culture 475, 635
role model 378
Role of ICT 16
roles of middle management 340
root cause 155
routine products 598
routing 577, 578, 635
rules 130, 273

S

SaaS – software as a service 567
safety inventory or stock 635
safety regulations 578
salaries 420
salary policy 423
sales 210, 228, 245
sales department 245
Sarbanes-Oxley 131
Sarbanes-Oxley Act (SOX) 121
satisfaction 22, 53, 385, 389, 394, 439, 469, 500
Scanlon plan 124
scarce metals 78
scarcity of resources 161
scientific development 7
Scientific management 20, 21
scope of 267
scope of control 31, 346, 347
scope of control is exceeded 346
scope of managerial control 347
scope of their decision-making capacity 557
scorecard 537
screening 157
secondary labor conditions 635
secondary or supporting processes 48
secondary work conditions 420
segment portals 609
segmentation of business functions 106
selection 407, 408
selection committee 408
selection opportunities 162
self-accomplishment 396
self-control 324, 391, 635
self-development 374, 391
self-fulfillment 392
self-knowledge 42
self-management 390
self-motivation 425
self-preservation 53
self-reflect 438
self-regulating/controlling teams 635
self-regulating teams 341
self-respect 375
self-steering 34
self-sufficiency 343
selling (S2) 455, 456
semantic web 609
semantics 635
semi-autonomous 341
semi-autonomous groups 389
semi-autonomous operations 296
semi-autonomous (P-) work group 325
semi-autonomous units 282, 302
semi-autonomous work groups 325
semi-autonomous working group 635
semi-autonomy 391
sense of belonging 375
serial interdependence 279, 280
serial or sequential interdependence 279, 280, 635
service innovation 581
service organization 580
service-provision process 580
service-related activities 579
services 46, 207, 582
service/servicing 635
servicing process 580
servicization of industry 91
servuction system 580, 635
set of goals 194
setting up a new firm 288
share participation 241
shared services 94, 337, 635
shareholder 13, 35, 69, 115
shareholder value 13, 16
shareholders 26, 27, 29, 32, 65, 111, 557
sharia 103
sharia compliance 635
sharia screening 103
sharia-compliant 103
sharia-compliant financing 635
sharia-compliant insurance 103, 635
short power distance 464
short product cycles 90
short terms 492
short-term 227
short-term goals 491
short-term operational plans 496
short-term planning 496
short-term plans 494
signal for execution 50
signals 466
Simon 24, 167
simple organization 293
simple process model of an organization 47
simple task assignment 504
sincerity 42
situation-determined styles of leadership 456
situational test 409
situational leadership 455, 635

situationally dependent 25
situations 64, 65
Six Sigma 513, 514, 517, 518, 635
size of a group 374
skills 22
slack 511
slack time 511
SLAs (service level agreements) 337
slip chart planning board 635
small and medium-sized organizations 273
small company owner-managers 29
social abilities of a manager 42
social annual report 636
social change 7
social intelligence 444
social networking 89
social networking ('communities') 636
social security 13
social skills 43
social sustainability 95
socialization 410
socially oriented style of leadership 22
societal demands 64, 65
societal efficiency 53
societal entrepreneurship 13
societal factors 71, 204
societal forces 66
societal interest 7
societal macrocycle of events 65
societal responsibilities 117
societal responsibility 39
societal sustainability 95
Societé Anonyme (SA) 32
society of organizations 7, 64, 66
socio-psychological factors 22, 636
socio-technical reorganization 124
socio-technical system design 606
software 567
software engineering 91
solvency 636
sources of power 461, 462
sources of profits 212
sourcing 572
sourcing portfolio 598
sourcing strategy 598
Sox 122
span of control 265, 321, 330, 346, 636
span of influence 347
span of support 347, 636
spatial planning 577
specialist advice 268
specialist boss 281
specialist boss relationship 282
specialists 152, 267, 333
specialized knowledge 267
specialized staff 267
specialized staff functions 267
specialized staff services 348
specialized staff worker 334
specialized support 335
specialized support services 348
specialized support staff: functioning 336
specialized support staff services 329
specific goals 263
specified goals 11
speed of change 349, 353
speed of decision making 274
spiritual function 440
spiritual intelligence (SQ) 440
splitting up 88
spread diagram 522
Stability and Growth Pact 73
stabilizing (freezing) 354
staff 267
staff and support services 267, 296
staff departments 152
staff functions 267
staff meetings 152
staff organ 333, 334
staff relationship 333
staff relationships 12
stage of development 298
stages of development in the internationalization 96
stages of the product life cycle 212
stakeholders 13, 64, 65, 67, 68, 69, 111, 116, 162
standard cost centers 532
standard cost price 636
standard methods 344, 345
standard procedures 345
standardization of output 279
standardization of problem solution 478
standards 50
standing plans 344, 345
stars 214, 215, 636
starting a business 300
starting up 289
statistical process control (SPC) 514
steep organization 31
steep structure (narrow 'span of control') 346
stimuli 384
stimulus 21
stock 26
stock approach 180
stock exchange 69
storytelling 356
strategic 119, 167, 403
strategic alliance 109, 239, 241, 636
strategic alternatives 220, 227
strategic benchmarking 524
strategic business units 343
strategic business unit (SBU) 636
strategic center 304
strategic choices 193, 293, 295, 297
strategic collaboration 109, 226
strategic control 196
strategic decision making 39
strategic decisions 31, 36, 152, 153, 265, 296
strategic formulation 193
strategic formulation process 200
strategic gap 201, 219
strategic goals 636
strategic goals of the organization 235
strategic information 552
strategic level 398, 566
strategic management 193, 636
strategic management capacity 277
strategic outsourcing 304
strategic partnering 109
strategic partnerships 108
strategic plan 196
strategic planning 196, 231, 232, 298, 558, 559, 560, 561, 636
strategic planning process 246
strategic problem 200
strategic products 598
strategic profile 219
strategic quality management 513
strategic reorientation 357
strategies directed at customers 223
strategies directed at new market entrants 224
strategies directed at suppliers 223
strategies for current product-market activities 221
strategies for new product-market activities 221
strategies for phasing out activities 226
strategies for phasing out of product-market activities 221
strategy 39, 151, 193, 196
strategy at a business level 197
strategy at a corporate level 197
strategy determination 194
strategy formulation 194, 195, 199
strategy formulation process 219
strategy map 540, 541
strategy theory 24, 198, 199
strengths and weaknesses 201, 205, 208, 209, 211, 219
stress 636
structural adjustment 357, 358
structural conditions 378
structural deviations 543
structure 260, 319, 396, 602
structure of the organization 160, 176, 293, 295, 296
structure theory 23
structured information 552
structuring 49, 551
structuring of organizations 260
style of conflict resolution 472, 473
style of leadership 23, 34, 101, 339, 409, 447, 454, 468, 476
style of management 22
styles of conflict resolution 469, 470
styles of effective leaders 454
sub-departments 268, 269
sub-goals 502
sub-groups 377
subordinate 331, 460
subsidiaries 101
substitute products 207
substitutes 76
success 291
successful teamwork 379
sukuk 103, 636
superficial change 351
supervision 507, 553, 554
supervision/control 636
supervisors 26
supervisory boards 124, 125
supervisory council 119
supervisory leadership 442
supplier power 207
suppliers 207
supply chain 591
supply chain management 570
supply of information 112
supply of resources 215
supply risk 598
supply side 106
support department 636
support mechanisms 356
support services 267, 268, 296
support staff 268
supporting role 232
survival 291
survival of the organization 67, 68, 265
survival options 220
survival stage 299
sustainability 94, 95, 583, 636
sustainability strategy 95
sustainable 95
sustainable advantage 403
sustainable business 17
sustainable business practices 112, 113
sustainable energy 80
sustainable entrepreneurship 69
sustainable growth 84
sustainable production 84
sustainable society 13
SWOT analysis 201, 217, 231
symbolic approach 380
symbolic conditions 378, 379
symbolic elements 380
symbolic gestures 357
symptoms 155
synergy 201, 202, 227, 228, 274, 278, 636
– finance 228
– investment 228
– management 228
– production 228
– sales 228
synergy effects 226, 228, 229
system integration 610
system of coordination mechanisms 271
systematic 193
systematic analysis 22
systematic approach to management 294
systematic control 555
systematic feedback 329
systematic soldiering 21, 460
systems controls 298
systems theory 24

T

Tabaksblat Code 131
tacit knowledge 180
tactical decisions 37
tactical information 552
tactical planning 558, 559, 560, 561
tailor-made product 579
takaful 103
take-off and expansion 291
takeover 236
takeover fever 87
takeovers 87, 226

talent development 400
talents 395, 400
talents of the owners 298
tall or deep organizational structure 636
tall or steep organizational structure 346
task 329
task assignment 273, 504
task assignments 245, 500
task culture 476, 636
task descriptions 262
task enlargement 636
task enrichment 326, 636
task environment 272
task forces 152, 181, 273
task fulfillment 408, 458
task identity 390
task importance 390
task maturity 455, 636
task of management 38
task of top management 31
task performance 500
task-characteristic model 389, 390
task-oriented 448
task-oriented leadership style 457
tasks 260, 261, 397, 504, 553
tax planning function 554
teams 273, 378
teamwork 381, 606
technical aspect of information 636
technical capability 40
technical skills 22
technical transformation 46
technical-oriented purchases 597
techniques 163, 340
technological developments 76
technological factors 71, 76, 204
technological influences 66
technological innovation 78, 583
technological push 583
telecommunication revolution 78
teleworking 395
telling (S1) 455
temporary project groups 339
terror of globalization 14
terrorism 75
tertiary labor conditions 637
tertiary sector 579
tertiary work conditions 420
testing of alternatives 157
tests 407
The International Monetary Fund (IMF) 81
theory of organization and management 25
theory of the growth and development 25
Theory X 450
Theory X manager 458
Theory Y 451, 452, 458, 505
The Scandinavian Monetary Union 73
Thompson 171, 279
threat of new entrants 80
threat of substitute products 80
three basic elements 492
three types of decisions 152
time management 10
time scale 38
time-shifting 169, 637
time studies 21
time study 637
time to market 607
timely information processing 503
timing 230, 235, 637
timing of decisions 16
tolerance levels 50, 497
tolerance zone 637
tone of voice 447
tool for management 497
top 302
top-down 233
top-down approach 233, 234, 343, 637
top management 26, 31, 264, 275, 277, 637
top management tasks 265
top managers 35
to take on responsibility 347
total quality concept 513
Total Quality Management (TQM) 513, 518, 519
TQM 518, 519
trade unions 13
traditional indicators 533
traditional marketing 609
traditional performance measurements 533
trained labor 263
training 413, 599
training on the job 413
training program 410
transactional leadership 457
transactions 558, 559, 560, 561, 562
transformation 350, 351
transformation process 66
transformational leadership 457
transforms resources 66
translation of strategic plans 242
transmitting information 10, 152
transparency 438
treads and developments in an organization's environment 83
treasury function 554
trends in the environment 64
trends in the results 211
Trompenaars 98
trust 132, 438, 462
turnaround management 184
turnover 406
turnover rates 374, 395
twitter 596, 607, 637
two functions of organizational culture 478
two-tier system 26, 118, 119
two-way traffic 24
type of cost center 532
type of interdependence 279
types of conflict 472
types of decision 154, 167
types of executive authority 281
types of information 552
types of leadership 452
types of planning 492, 510
types of ratios 527
types of rewards 418
typical product-oriented approach 586
typology of organizational cultures 476

U

unbundling 16, 106, 107, 637
uncertainty 162, 168, 246
uncertainty avoidance 637
underachieve 386
underutilization 320
undesired consequences 157, 227
unemployment 21
unfreezing 352
uninspiring manager 388
unions 38
unit management 637
unity of command 12, 281, 284, 286, 332
unity of direction 12, 281, 332, 637
unity of direction and control 264
unlearning 352
unstructured information 552
upcycling 95
upstream 106
urban concentration 89
urgent innovation 585
use of ratios 530
user-oriented approach 586
utilization or occupation planning 637

V

vacancies 407, 414
value 46, 637
value chain 48, 199, 304, 637
value chain mapping 570
value chain Porter 48
value system 637
value-oriented approach 586
values 53, 474
variable 497
variable budget 497
variation 321, 386
variation in skills 390
variety 323
variety of activities 271
vertical communication 468
vertical decentralization 342
vertical differentiation 637
vertical direction 346
vertical group 374
vertical integration 106, 637
vertical line relationships 332
vertical organization 637
vertical portals 609
vertical task enlargement or job enrichment 637
vertical thinking 165
view of the customer 538
village model 99
virtual teams 181, 637
vision 194, 226, 540, 637
voice 355
voice systems 355, 637
Vorstand 125, 126
voting procedure 377
Vroom 385

W

wage differential 100
wage structure 421
Wal-Mart 134, 135
water and waste management 78
weak culture 474
Web 2.0 80, 607, 608, 609, 637
Web 2.0 applications 608
Web 2.0-technology 90, 572, 611
Web 2.0 tools 607
Web 3.0 609, 637
web-based quality testing 401
web-based shops 572
webshop 638
well oiled machine 100
well-being 13
wheel structure 469
whistleblower 131, 638
white print thinking 360
willingness 159, 347
willingness/preparedness to change 349
willingness to delegate 347
withdrawal 205
withdrawal threshold 205
withholding information 137
women 395, 409, 420
workability euthanasia 413
work and home 394
work behavior 421, 435
work boss 281
work conditions 394
work consultation 123, 339, 340, 638
work dispatching 578
work distribution 638
work efficiency 565
work engagement 355, 638
work extrinsic 638
work group 374
work groups 181, 260, 469
work intrinsic 638
work preparation 638
work prescriptions 262
work processes 602
work satisfaction 321
work scheduling 575
work science 638
work situation 394
work structuring 638
work study 638
worker representatives 122
workflow bureaucracy 99
workforce 407
working behavior 457
working climate of the organization 124
working conditions 22, 39
working environment 13, 321
working methods 21
working relationships 319
works council 38, 125, 126, 152, 638
works councils 125
World Bank 81
world's population 71

world-wide brands 19
worldwide operations 96
worthwhile work package 320
written and unwritten rules 474
written communication 468
written task assignment 504

yammer 596, 638
yellow print thinking 359, 360

zero faults 518
zones of tolerance 554

An environmentally friendly book printed and bound in England by www.printondemand-worldwide.com

This book is made of chain-of-custody materials; FSC materials for the cover and PEFC materials for the text pages.

#0698 - 150715 - C664 - 270/210/35 - PB - 9789001703820